ALSO BY THE EDITORS OF COOK'S ILLUSTRATED
HOME OF AMERICA'S TEST KITCHEN

To order any of our books, visit us at
http://www.cooksillustrated.com
http://www.americastestkitchen.com
or call 800-611-0759

THE NEW BEST RECIPE

The New Best Recipe

BY THE EDITORS OF

COOK'S ILLUSTRATED

PHOTOGRAPHY

CARL TREMBLAY

DANIEL J. VAN ACKERE

ILLUSTRATIONS

JOHN BURGOYNE

AMERICA'S TEST KITCHEN

BROOKLINE, MASSACHUSETTS

America's Test Kitchen
17 Station Street
Brookline, MA 02445

0-936184-74-4
Library of Congress Cataloging-in-Publication Data
The Editors of *Cook's Illustrated*

The New Best Recipe: All-New Edition
2nd Edition

ISBN 0-936184-74-4 (hardcover): $35.00
I. Cooking. I. Title
2004

Manufactured in the United States of America

10 9 8 7 6 5 4 3

Distributed by America's Test Kitchen, 17 Station Street, Brookline, MA 02445.

Senior Editor: Lori Galvin
Series Designer: Amy Klee
Jacket Designer: Amy Klee
Photographers: Carl Tremblay; Daniel J. Van Ackere
Illustrator: John Burgoyne
Senior Production Manager: Jessica Lindheimer Quirk
Book Production Specialist: Ronald Bilodeau
Copyeditor: Evie Righter
Proofreader: Barbara Jatkola
Indexer: Cathy Dorsey

Pictured on front of jacket: Crème Caramel (page 958)
Pictured on back of jacket: Pasta with Bolognese Sauce (page 254), Oven Fries (page 197), Broiled Salmon with Mustard and Crisp Potato Crust (page 509),
Summer Berry Pie (page 900)

CONTENTS

WELCOME TO
AMERICA'S TEST KITCHEN

THIS BOOK HAS BEEN TESTED, WRITTEN, AND edited by the folks at America's Test Kitchen, a very real 2,500-square-foot kitchen located just outside of Boston. It is the home of *Cook's Illustrated* magazine and is the Monday through Friday destination for close to two dozen test cooks, editors, food scientists, tasters, and cookware specialists. Our mission is to test recipes over and over again until we understand how and why they work and until we arrive at the "best" version.

We start the process of testing a recipe with a complete lack of conviction, which means that we accept no claim, no theory, no technique, and no recipe at face value. We simply assemble as many variations as possible, test a half dozen of the most promising, and taste the results blind. We then construct our own hybrid recipe and continue to test it, varying ingredients, techniques, and cooking times until we reach a consensus. The result, we hope, is the "best" version of a particular recipe, but we realize that only you can be the final judge of our success

(or failure). As we like to say in the test kitchen, "We make the mistakes, so you don't have to."

All of this would not be possible without a belief that good cooking, much like good music, is indeed based on a foundation of objective technique. Some people like spicy foods and others don't, but there is a right way to sauté, there is a "best" way to cook a pot roast, and there are measurable scientific principles involved in producing perfectly beaten, stable egg whites. This is our ultimate goal: to investigate the fundamental principles of cooking so that you become a better cook. It is as simple as that.

You can watch us work (in our actual test kitchen) by tuning in to America's Test Kitchen (www.americastestkitchen.com) on public television or by subscribing to *Cook's Illustrated* magazine (www.cooksillustrated.com), which is published every other month. We welcome you into our kitchen, where you can stand by our side as we test our way to the "best" recipes in America.

INTRODUCTION

I STARTED COOKING WHEN I WAS 8 YEARS OLD. My first project was a basic chocolate layer cake with boiled icing, a recipe I had found in the old *Fannie Farmer Cookbook*. The cake wasn't bad, but the icing turned out like gruel—so thin that it dribbled down the sides of the cake, pooling onto the platter underneath. Given my complete lack of cooking experience, this may indeed have been my fault, not the recipe's, but it was the first of hundreds, if not thousands, of cooking disasters that I have suffered over a lifetime of cooking. I bet that you have had your share of them, too.

Eventually, most of us start perusing cookbooks defensively. Does that recipe look like it might work? Does that combination of ingredients sound odd? Could the oven temperature for that roast be too high? How does that ratio of fat to flour compare with the ratio for pie crusts I've made in the past? Cooking soon becomes a risky business, a process by which eliminating bad recipes is as important as identifying good ones.

Many cooks would argue that recipes are completely subjective, that there are no hard and fast culinary rules. I once held that same opinion about horses. A Vermont neighbor of ours, Nancy, was always full of do's and don'ts when it came to training and riding. Being cavalier about these things, I ignored most of her words to the wise until one day when, totally against her advice, I carried a bucketful of grain into a paddock with six new horses. In the food riot that immediately followed, I got kicked so badly that I limped for a month. That's when I started to get the idea that riding and training horses, just like cooking, has a science to it. It's not just mind over matter.

So here is where *The New Best Recipe* comes in. The original *Best Recipe* was published in 1999 and was an instant success. (We have sold almost 400,000 copies since then.) Based on the recipes in *Cook's Illustrated* magazine, it was the first cookbook to treat cooking like a science and to discuss openly the process by which our test cooks take a mediocre recipe and turn it into a "best" recipe. Now, before we are accused of culinary exaggeration, I want to define what we mean by "best." We mean simply the best version of a particular recipe (in a particular style) that we can develop in our kitchen through our testing process. But, on the whole, our guarantee is that these recipes (as long as you follow our directions) will work in your home kitchen. If you think this is yet more publishing hyperbole—and I wouldn't blame you—try a few of the recipes in this volume and compare them head-to-head with recipes for the same dishes published in other books or magazines. Ours ought to compare favorably.

So what's really new here? Well, we have almost doubled the size of *Best Recipe* by adding close to 500 new recipes, bringing the total to 1,000. This volume also includes 800 hand-drawn illustrations. Now it is truly comprehensive and should offer the same culinary range as other major American cookbooks.

These days, my culinary skills are much improved because I take cooking seriously—I truly believe that there are right and wrong ways to cook any food. OK, maybe the odd baking project still turns out badly, but at least I have a clue as to what went wrong. If you are like me, and you really want to understand the whys of cooking, or if you just want a cookbook with recipes that really work, then this book is for you. As we often say around the test kitchen, "We do the testing, so you don't have to." Either way, our guarantee is that you will start having a lot more success in the kitchen.

As far as horses go, I have started listening to Nancy more often and seem to be spending more time in the saddle than on the ground. Given the fact that I recently attended my 35th high school reunion, that is a very good thing indeed.

Christopher Kimball
Founder and Editor
Cook's Illustrated Magazine

1

APPETIZERS

THE NEW BEST RECIPE

WHEN WE'RE PREPARING AND SERVING appetizers, that's usually not all we're doing. We're also answering the front door, pouring drinks, and catching up with old friends who know their way to our kitchen. Appetizers are, after all, party food. If we're the hosts, we can bet that having lots of time alone in the kitchen is an unlikely proposition.

The first challenge, then, when choosing recipes for this chapter was to find those dishes that won't keep us away from our guests for very long. Most of the recipes in this chapter require 20 minutes or less of hands-on preparation time, and we offer ideas for doing as much ahead as possible.

The question we hear most often about appetizers concerns quantity. How many types of hors d'oeuvres and how many pieces are required? The answer depends on how long you plan to be serving the appetizers and what follows. Some examples:

If you plan a short cocktail hour (let's say 45 minutes to one hour, while you wait for all of your guests to arrive) followed by a multicourse meal, you may want to serve just one or two appetizers. (If you are expecting a larger crowd, you might consider making three.) Plan on three or four pieces per person if you plan on one hour or less for cocktails. For more than one hour, make at least two appetizers and plan on four to six pieces per person.

Take into account how rich and filling the appetizers you have chosen are. Guests are likely to be satisfied by one or two slices of topped bruschetta, but might want a half dozen marinated olives or a handful of spiced nuts.

The other area that perplexes many cooks is choosing particular appetizers. There are no hard-and-fast rules, but these guidelines should help. Keep the season in mind, serving lighter foods in summer and heavier fare in winter. Figure out where you plan to serve the hors d'oeuvres. If guests will be seated on sofas and can hold forks and plates on their laps, then almost anything will work. If guests will be standing or are outside, on a patio, for example, limit your selection to true finger foods and dips.

Plan the meal first and then, for the appetizers, use foods not already on the menu. If your main course includes beef, mushrooms, and asparagus, you would not want to serve any of these as appetizers.

If making more than one or two hors d'oeuvres, choose ones that go well together. It's fine to have one rich hors d'oeuvre made with cheese, but don't serve a multitude of cheese hors d'oeuvres.

For a shorter cocktail hour before dinner, you may want to stick with cold appetizers, which don't require any last-minute preparation. If you want to serve a hot appetizer, consider serving it in the kitchen so you don't have to excuse yourself from your own party.

SPICED NUTS

AT PARTIES, SPICED NUTS USUALLY DISAPpear faster than the host can replenish the bowl. But most spiced nuts are made with a heavy sugar syrup, which can leave your hands sticky and cause the nuts to clump together in unappealing, indelicate clusters.

Finding the right coating method required a good deal of testing on our part. The most common technique, boiling the nuts in a thick, sweetened, seasoned syrup, was not even an option because it made the nuts sticky. Another popular method, toasting or sautéing the nuts in butter or oil before tossing them with spices, dulled the finish of the nuts and made them taste bland or oily. A third possibility, coating the nuts with a spiced egg white mixture, created such a chunky, candy-like coating that the nuts themselves were barely visible.

Our answer came when we made a light glaze for the nuts from very small amounts of liquid, sugar, and butter. It worked like a charm. This treatment left the nuts shiny and just tacky enough for a dry spice coating to stick perfectly, giving the nuts both a consistent, beautiful appearance and plenty of flavor.

Kosher salt is important here because it adds crunch and has a clean flavor. If you can, make the nuts ahead of time; as they sit they will better absorb the flavorings.

Spiced Pecans with Rum Glaze

MAKES ABOUT 2 CUPS

We like the crunch and clean flavor of kosher salt in our spiced nut recipes, but table salt can be substituted—just reduce the amount used by half.

2 cups (8 ounces) raw pecan halves

SPICE MIX

2 tablespoons sugar
3/4 teaspoon kosher salt
1/2 teaspoon ground cinnamon
1/8 teaspoon ground cloves
1/8 teaspoon ground allspice

RUM GLAZE

1 tablespoon rum, preferably dark
2 teaspoons vanilla extract
1 teaspoon light or dark brown sugar
1 tablespoon unsalted butter

1. Adjust an oven rack to the middle position and heat the oven to 350 degrees. Line a rimmed baking sheet with parchment paper and spread the pecans on it in an even layer. Toast for 4 minutes, rotate the pan, and continue to toast until fragrant and the color deepens slightly, about 4 minutes longer. Transfer the baking sheet with the nuts to a wire rack.

2. FOR THE SPICE MIX: While the nuts are toasting, stir the sugar, salt, cinnamon, cloves, and allspice together in a medium bowl; set aside.

3. FOR THE GLAZE: Bring the rum, vanilla, brown sugar, and butter to a boil in a medium saucepan over medium-high heat, whisking constantly. Stir in the toasted pecans and cook, stirring constantly with a wooden spoon, until the nuts are shiny and almost all the liquid has evaporated, about 1½ minutes.

4. Transfer the glazed pecans to the bowl with the spice mix; toss well to coat. Return the glazed and spiced pecans to the parchment-lined baking sheet to cool. (The nuts can be stored in an airtight container for up to 5 days.)

Mexican-Spiced Almonds, Peanuts, and Pumpkin Seeds

MAKES ABOUT 2 CUPS

1¼ cups (4 ½ ounces) sliced almonds
2/3 cup (3 ounces) unsalted roasted peanuts
1/4 cup (1 ounce) raw pumpkin seeds

MEXICAN SPICE MIX

1 tablespoon sugar
1 teaspoon kosher salt
1/4 teaspoon ground cinnamon
1/4 teaspoon ground cumin
1/4 teaspoon ground coriander
1/8 teaspoon cayenne pepper
1/8 teaspoon garlic powder

SIMPLE GLAZE

2 tablespoons water
1 teaspoon light or dark brown sugar
1 tablespoon unsalted butter

1. Adjust an oven rack to the middle position and heat the oven to 350 degrees. Line a rimmed baking sheet with parchment paper and spread the almonds on it in an even layer. Toast for 4 minutes and rotate the pan; add the peanuts and pumpkin seeds. Continue to toast until fragrant and the color deepens slightly, about 4 minutes longer. Transfer the baking sheet with the nuts to a wire rack.

2. FOR THE SPICE MIX: While the nuts and seeds are toasting, stir the sugar, salt, cinnamon, cumin, coriander, cayenne, and garlic powder together in a medium bowl; set aside.

3. FOR THE GLAZE: Bring the water, brown sugar, and butter to a boil in a medium saucepan over medium-high heat, whisking constantly. Stir in the toasted nuts and seeds and cook, stirring constantly with a wooden spoon, until the nuts are shiny and almost all the liquid has evaporated, about 1½ minutes.

4. Transfer the glazed mixture to the bowl with the spice mix; toss well to coat. Return the glazed and spiced nuts to the parchment-lined baking sheet to cool. (The nuts can be stored in an airtight container for up to 5 days.)

Indian-Spiced Cashews and Pistachios with Currants

MAKES ABOUT 2 CUPS

If substituting table salt for kosher, reduce the amount specified by half.

1¼	cups (6 ounces) raw cashews
½	cup (2 ounces) raw unsalted shelled pistachios
2	tablespoons currants

INDIAN SPICE MIX

1	tablespoon sugar
1	teaspoon kosher salt
1	teaspoon curry powder
¼	teaspoon ground cumin
¼	teaspoon ground coriander

SIMPLE GLAZE

2	tablespoons water
1	teaspoon light or dark brown sugar
1	tablespoon unsalted butter

1. Adjust an oven rack to the middle position and heat the oven to 350 degrees. Line a rimmed baking sheet with parchment paper and spread the cashews on it in an even layer. Toast for 4 minutes, rotate the pan, and toast for 4 minutes more. Add the pistachios, spreading them in an even layer; continue to toast until fragrant and the color deepens slightly, about 2 minutes. Transfer the baking sheet with the nuts to a wire rack; add the currants.

2. FOR THE SPICE MIX: While the nuts are toasting, stir the sugar, salt, curry powder, cumin, and coriander together in a medium bowl; set aside.

3. FOR THE GLAZE: Bring the water, brown sugar, and butter to a boil in a medium saucepan over medium-high heat, whisking constantly. Stir in the nut mix and cook, stirring constantly with a wooden spoon, until the nuts are shiny and almost all the liquid has evaporated, about 1½ minutes.

4. Transfer the glazed nuts and currants to the bowl with the spice mix; toss well to coat. Return the glazed and spiced nuts and currants to the parchment-lined baking sheet to cool. (The nuts can be stored in an airtight container for up to 5 days.)

MARINATED OLIVES

IF YOU START WITH GOOD OLIVES (AND THAT can be a big if) and good olive oil, it's pretty hard to make bad marinated olives. That said, some olive mixes are better than others, with more complex flavors. We wanted to make a mixture of marinated olives that would be easy to put together and worth the wait.

Good olives are the right place to begin, and that means olives with their pits and packed in brine. (Oil-cured olives can be added in small quantities, but in large quantities we find their flavors too potent for this dish.) Pitted olives generally have little flavor, and you can't expect marinating to make them taste better. Our tasters liked a mix of black and green olives. We tested half a dozen varieties of each color and didn't find a bad olive.

In addition to the olive oil, the marinade typically includes garlic, herbs (our tasters liked thyme best), and red pepper flakes (we found that more heat was better than less and opted for a full teaspoon). We liked thinly sliced shallots as well; they softened in the marinade and added their gentle allium flavor to the mix. Grated orange zest (rather than the more traditional lemon zest) won the day in the test kitchen for its fresh, lively citrus kick.

The real surprise was the addition of sambuca, an Italian after-dinner liqueur that tastes like licorice. The heady anise flavor worked wonders on the olives and made the mix much more interesting.

The final issue to resolve was how long to marinate the olives. Tasters found that the olives required 12 hours to pick up sufficient flavor and were even better after a day or two. In fact, we held marinated olives in the refrigerator for several weeks and concluded that time only served to improve the flavor.

Marinated Black and Green Olives

MAKES ABOUT 3 CUPS

These olives will keep in the refrigerator for at least a month and are perfect to have on hand for impromptu entertaining. (Be sure to remember to put out a small bowl for the pits.) Sambuca is a sweet, licorice-flavored Italian spirit. You can substitute ouzo.

8	ounces large, brine-cured green olives with pits
8	ounces large, brine-cured black olives with pits
5	large garlic cloves, crushed
3	large shallots, sliced thin
1	teaspoon grated zest from 1 orange
1	teaspoon minced fresh thyme leaves
1	teaspoon red pepper flakes
$1/2$	cup sambuca (see note)
$1/4$	cup extra-virgin olive oil
$3/4$	teaspoon salt
	Pinch cayenne pepper

1. Drain the olives in a colander and rinse them well under cold running water. Drain the olives of excess water.

2. Combine the remaining ingredients in a glass or plastic bowl. Add the olives and toss to combine. Cover and refrigerate for at least 12 hours. Remove from the refrigerator at least 30 minutes before serving.

INGREDIENTS: Olives

There are literally hundreds of varieties of olives, but all can be categorized by two factors: their ripeness when picked and the manner in which they are cured. Green olives, picked before they are fully ripe, tend to have fruitier and somewhat lighter flavors, while ripe olives—which range in color from dark brown to purple or deep black—have deeper, more fully developed flavors.

Most olives are brine-cured by a process that involves fermenting them in a strong salt solution. Others are oil-cured by a process that gives them a wrinkled appearance and sharper flavor. These olives are sold loose and kept refrigerated. It almost goes with saying that canned (or jarred) pitted olives (which are not refrigerated and reside in the condiments aisles of supermarkets) are to be avoided. We find they are devoid of flavor.

As for particular names, olives may be named after their type of cure, their place of origin, or their actual varietal name. The most important thing to remember about these little fruits (yes, olives are technically a fruit) is that they vary widely from batch to batch and year to year. Tasting is the only way to judge the quality of any particular batch.

CHEESE TRAYS

LONG HAILED AS A COCKTAIL PARTY centerpiece, cheese trays are easily assembled well ahead of serving time, yielding maximum impact with minimal effort. Two or three different cheeses, crackers or bread, and crisp apples or pears take minutes to plate, yet look elegant and offer a little something for everyone.

A cheese's flavor is dependent upon a long list of factors, including the type of milk, the fodder the animals were fed that produced that milk, the age and salt content of the cheese, the mold strain (for blue cheeses), and the region of the world where the cheese originated. A Danish-made fontina shares little in common with an Italian-made fontina (save its name); the same can be said for American and Alsatian Muenster as well as many other cheeses.

All cheeses, however, start with just three components: milk, a starter culture, and rennet. The milk, unpasteurized (rare in the United States because of U.S. Department of Agriculture regulations) or pasteurized, is combined with a culture that converts the milk sugars into lactic acid, which, in turn, prompts the proteins in the milk to convert to curds. Rennet, an enzyme extracted from either animal (the stomachs of calves, kids, and lambs) or plant sources, causes the curds to clump together. From here on, processing depends upon the style of cheese being made. Fresh, soft cheeses have little further processing; hard, aged cheeses may be years away from readiness.

Like fruits and vegetables, cheeses have a period of peak "ripeness," at which time their flavor and texture are at their very best. Creamy cheeses, like Brie, become runny and more distinct in flavor as they age; blue cheeses grow earthier and more pungent. For very commercial cheeses, like the shrink-wrapped pieces of cheddar in the dairy case, ripeness is less of a concern, though mold and age are. Small patches of mold can be trimmed away, and the cheese is still perfectly edible. Large patches of mold (especially new mold on blue cheeses) or dried, cracked patches suggest the cheese is well past its prime.

When storing cheese, it is crucial to keep it tightly wrapped. Air will dry it out and prompt the development of molds. In a perfect world, cheese should first be wrapped tightly in parchment or waxed paper and then sealed in plastic wrap, aluminum foil, or a zipper-lock bag. Cheese can absorb off flavors and odors from plastic wrap or plastic containers. If the cheese has a rind, like Parmesan, Brie, or Gouda, make sure to leave it on the cheese until serving time as the rind provides an extra layer of protection. And buy cheese in reasonable amounts that can be consumed within a couple of weeks.

When preparing a cheese tray, think about pairing different flavors, textures, and types to provide interest. If all the cheeses are similar, your tray will quickly become boring. For example, match a creamy Brie with a sharp cheddar and a rich blue, or a pungent goat cheese with a dry, aged Parmesan and a nutty, firm Gruyère. Feel free to experiment with different varieties and styles. As for the amount to serve, figure on just two to three ounces per person.

As for the accompaniments to your cheese plate, choose simple crackers and breads (toasted or not, that will allow the cheese to take center stage). Other sweet and savory additions might include toasted almonds, walnuts, or hazelnuts; a mixture of black and green olives; or dried fruits, such as apricots and figs. Fresh fruit is also welcome on a cheese platter and cuts the richness of some cheeses as it softens the pungency of strong blue-veined Stiltons and Gorgonzolas. Grapes and thinly sliced sweet apples and pears are especially attractive. Parmesan pairs well with vegetables, such as slices of crisp fennel or crunchy celery. And paper-thin slices of Italian-style sausage like sopressata or pungent, salt-cured prosciutto go well with Italian fresh mozzarella, creamy fontina, or the more pronounced taste of Pecorino.

Finally, make sure to allow time for your cheeses to come to room temperature before serving them as the cold mutes both their flavor and aroma. Keep cheeses wrapped until serving to prevent them from drying out. In lieu of, or in addition to, a cheese tray, consider the following recipes, which highlight some of our favorite cheeses in basic appetizers.

Marinated Goat Cheese
SERVES 4

The garlic should be broken down into a fine puree for this recipe. After you mince it, sprinkle the garlic with the salt, mash the garlic-salt mixture with the side of a chef's knife, and then continue to mince until the garlic forms a smooth puree (see the illustrations on page 626). Serve this marinated goat cheese with bread or crackers.

1	(8-ounce) log goat cheese, chilled
1/4	cup extra-virgin olive oil
3/4	teaspoon chopped fresh thyme leaves
3/4	teaspoon minced fresh chives
1/4	teaspoon minced fresh rosemary leaves
1	small garlic clove, minced to a puree with
	1/8 teaspoon salt
	Ground black pepper

1. Following the illustration below, use a piece of dental floss to cut the cheese crosswise into slices 1/3 inch thick.

2. Whisk the oil, thyme, chives, rosemary, garlic-salt puree, and pepper to taste together in a small bowl.

3. Pour the oil mixture over the cheese. Serve immediately or cover and refrigerate for up to 1 day.

SLICING GOAT CHEESE

A knife quickly becomes covered with goat cheese, making it difficult to cut clean, neat slices. A piece of dental floss makes much neater cuts. Just slide an 18-inch length of floss under the log of goat cheese, cross the ends of the floss above the cheese, and pull the floss through the cheese to make slices at 1/3-inch intervals.

Dates Stuffed with Parmesan

MAKES 16 PIECES,

SERVING 4 TO 6

Use high-quality dates (such as Medjools) and only the finest Parmigiano-Reggiano in this exotic pairing. For information on Parmesan, see below.

16   large dates

1   piece (3 ounces) Parmesan cheese

16   walnut halves, toasted in a dry skillet over medium heat until fragrant, about 5 minutes

1. Slit the dates lengthwise with a paring knife and remove the pits.

2. Following the illustrations to the right, cut the cheese into thin shards about 1 inch long. Place a piece of cheese and 1 walnut half in each date and close the date around the cheese to seal. Place the dates on a platter and serve. (The stuffed dates can be wrapped in plastic and kept at room temperature for several hours.)

CUTTING PARMESAN INTO SHARDS

1. Use a chef's knife to remove the rind from a square block of Parmesan cheese. Cut the trimmed block in half on the diagonal.

2. Lay each half on its cut side and slice the cheese into thin triangles about 1/16 inch thick. These thin shards should be about the size of a date.

INGREDIENTS: Parmesan Cheese

Authentic Parmesan can cost a great deal and be tricky to find. There are less expensive options out there, like the "green can" we all grew up with and domestically produced Parmesan, but how do they compete? We decided to test a variety of whole and pregrated Parmesan to see how they taste compared to the "good stuff." Parmesan is a grana—a hard, grainy cheese. The grana cheese category is composed mostly of Italian grating cheeses. Parmigiano-Reggiano is the most famous (and expensive) of the granas, and its manufacture dates back 800 years. Parmigiano-Reggiano has become an increasingly regulated product, and in 1955 it became what is known as a certified name (not a brand name). The name indicates that the cheese was made within a specific region of northern Italy and approved by a certifying consortium.

American cheese makers need not abide by regulations any more stringent than basic U.S. Department of Agriculture standards. There is no lack of pregrated products, but only a handful of domestic Parmesans come in wedges. Other granas considered Parmesan types are Grana Padano (from Italy) and Reggianito (from Argentina).

In our tasting, nothing came close to the flavor of the real Parmesan. We tasted two different authentic Parmesans (one from a specialty store, the other from the supermarket) and found the flavor without equal among the other cheeses we chose. If you can find it, authentic Parmesan is well worth the price, which is generally between $12 and $14. For the best flavor, try to buy a wedge that you will use within a few weeks; otherwise, it can dry out and develop off flavors.

As for the other Parmesans we tried, the only one our tasters gave the nod to was DiGiorno Parmesan, a domestic version made in Wisconsin. Priced around eight dollars a pound, DiGiorno Parmesan doesn't pack the complex punch of the real deal, but tasters agreed that its flavor was thoroughly acceptable.

Always buy Parmesan in chunks, preferably cut fresh from the wheel and with the rind still attached. The rind helps protect the cheese from drying out. Watch out for cheese pockmarked with white splotches, which signals oxidation. Parmesan is best stored wrapped in parchment paper or waxed paper and then again in aluminum foil, though a zipper-lock bag works as well, in the cheese drawer of the refrigerator. Do not freeze cheese, as its texture will be grainy and unpalatable.

Cheese Straws
MAKES 14 STRAWS

Cheese straws harken back to another time. Old-fashioned or not, they never fail to impress. Stand the baked cheese straws straight up in a tall glass and serve with drinks and olives.

Thaw the puff pastry on the counter as you preheat the oven and grate the cheese. See the illustrations below for tips on shaping cheese straws. Note that this recipe requires parchment paper.

1/2	box (1 sheet) frozen puff pastry (Pepperidge Farm), thawed on the counter for 10 minutes
2	ounces Parmesan or Asiago cheese, freshly grated (1 cup)
1/4	teaspoon salt
1/4	teaspoon ground black pepper

MAKING CHEESE STRAWS

1. Using a sharp knife or pizza cutter, cut the dough into fourteen ¾-inch-wide strips.

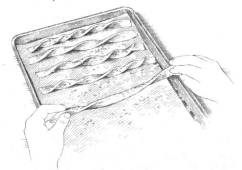

2. Holding 1 strip of dough at each end, gently twist the dough in opposite directions and transfer it to a parchment-lined baking sheet. Repeat with the remaining pieces of dough, spacing the dough strips about 1 inch apart.

1. Adjust the oven racks to the upper-middle and lower-middle positions and heat the oven to 425 degrees. Line 2 baking sheets with parchment paper and set them aside. Lay the puff pastry on a sheet of parchment and sprinkle with ½ cup of the cheese and ⅛ teaspoon each of salt and pepper. Place a sheet of parchment over the cheese and, using a rolling pin, press the cheese into the dough by gently rolling the pin back and forth. Without removing the parchment, carefully flip the dough over, cheese-side down. Remove the top layer of parchment and sprinkle with the remaining cheese, salt, and pepper. Cover the pastry with the parchment. Measure the piece of dough and continue to roll it out, if necessary, to form a 10½-inch square.

2. Remove the top sheet of parchment and, using a sharp knife or pizza cutter, cut the dough into fourteen ¾-inch-wide strips. Gently twist each strip of dough and transfer it to a parchment-lined baking sheet, spacing the strips about 1 inch apart.

3. Bake immediately until fully puffed and golden brown, about 10 minutes, reversing the positions of the baking sheets from top to bottom

SCIENCE: Can You Freeze Cheese?

To find out if cheese could withstand the rigors of freezing, we bought two blocks each of cheddar, Parmesan, and shrink-wrapped mozzarella and placed one of each in the freezer and one in the refrigerator. Two days later, we thawed them out, brought all samples to room temperature, and held a blind tasting. We tasted the cheeses raw and melted on toast to see if the texture or melting ability was affected.

Frozen cheddar and Parmesan were easily identifiable for their off flavors and disagreeable textures. The Parmesan was very dry, with a muted flavor. The cheddar was mealy and grainy, with a flavor that several tasters described as "flat." Once the cheeses were melted, the textural differences disappeared, but the flavor of the frozen cheeses remained duller than that of their fresh counterparts. The cheese that froze the best was the mozzarella. Tasters found both the frozen and refrigerated samples to be virtually identical, in both texture and flavor, when tasted raw and when tasted melted.

So what to do with your leftover cheese? For mozzarella, go ahead and throw it in the freezer (wrapped tightly in plastic wrap, of course). But for hard cheeses like Parmesan and cheddar, skip the freezer and keep them in the refrigerator.

halfway through the baking time. Remove the straws from the oven and cool on a wire rack for 5 minutes before serving. (The cheese straws, completely cooled, can be stored in an airtight container at room temperature for up to 3 days.)

CRUDITÉS

WITH AN EXTENSIVE SELECTION OF vegetables now available year-round in most markets, a platter of crudités should be downright tempting, if not exotic, and offer a colorful variety of flavors and textures. But the key to good crudités doesn't lie only in the selection and arrangement of good-looking vegetables. If you want vegetables that actually taste good, we have found that some of them must first be prepared—beyond rinsing and being cut, that is.

Not all vegetables are meant to be eaten raw (unless you're a rabbit), and after extensive kitchen tests we concluded that many require a quick dunk in boiling, salted water (blanching) before being added to the platter. This crucial step is often overlooked for the sake of convenience, but we

found it makes all the difference between medio-cre and great crudités. Not only does blanching render tough vegetables toothsome, but the salty water also seasons the vegetables as they cook, enhancing their natural flavors.

Here are three keys to successfully blanched vegetables:

First, to prevent carrots from tasting like asparagus or cauliflower from turning green, blanch each vegetable separately. Being mindful of the order in which you blanch them, begin with the bland and pale ones and finish with the bold-flavored and dark. The vegetables listed in the cooking chart on pages 10–11 are organized in the order in which they should be blanched.

Second, use a large pot that allows the vegetables to cook in ample water and become seasoned. A large volume of water—we use 6 quarts—ensures quick cooking times and brightly colored vegetables.

Third, once the vegetables are crisp-tender, transfer them from the boiling water to an ice-water bath immediately. This process, called shocking, prevents residual heat in the vegetables from cooking them further, which compromises their final color, texture, and flavor.

Blanched Vegetables for Crudités

Celery, bell peppers, endive, jícama, tomatoes, and radishes taste best raw, but the vegetables listed below are best served by a quick blanch-and-shock before joining the rest on the platter. Blanch the vegetables in the order given, which starts with the mildest in flavor and ends with the strongest. See the illustrations on pages 10–11 for tips on preparing some of these vegetables. We found that 2 pounds of prepared vegetables and 1½ cups of dip are sufficient for a group of 8 to 10 people.

CARROTS	15 seconds
SNOW/SNAP PEAS	15 seconds
CAULIFLOWER	1 to 1½ minutes
GREEN BEANS	1 minute
FENNEL	1 minute
BROCCOLI	1 to 1½ minutes
ASPARAGUS	30 to 60 seconds

KEY STEPS FOR BLANCHING VEGETABLES

1. Bring 6 quarts water to a boil in a large pot over high heat and season with 5 teaspoons salt. Cook the vegetables, one variety at a time, until slightly softened but still crunchy (crisp-tender), following the times recommended in the chart at left.

2. Using tongs or a strainer transfer the blanched vegetables to a bowl of ice water and allow to soak until completely cool, about 1 minute. Place on several layers of paper towels and pat dry. Blanch and shock the next vegetable on your list.

Preparing Vegetables for Crudités

To make vegetables more palatable and a lot easier to swipe through a dip, prepare them according to the following tips:

ASPARAGUS

1. To trim a bunch of asparagus efficiently, gently bend one stalk until the tough portion of the stem breaks off.

2. Place this broken asparagus alongside the still untrimmed ones. Using the shorter stalk as a guide, cut the tough ends off the remaining asparagus.

BROCCOLI AND CAULIFLOWER

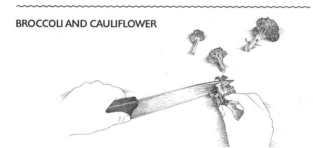

To cut attractive, bite-size florets, slice down through the main stem and out through the buds to produce 1-inch florets with 2-inch stems.

CARROTS

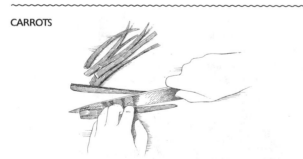

Although it is tempting to use bagged, prewashed baby carrots, their stubby stature makes it all too easy for dippers' fingers or knuckles to graze the surface of the dip when swiping. For long, elegant lengths of carrot, slice peeled carrots in half lengthwise. Then, with the cut side flat to the board, slice each half into 3 long pieces.

CELERY

Celery often tastes harsh and vegetal, but its flavors can quickly turn sweet and mellow after its bitter skin and stringy fibers are removed with a vegetable peeler.

GREEN BEANS

Instead of trimming the stem from one green bean at a time, line the beans up on the counter and trim off all the ends at one time with just one slice.

SNOW AND SNAP PEAS

Delicate snow and snap peas taste best when the fibrous string that runs along the straight edge of the pod has been removed. Using a paring knife, remove this string.

ENDIVE

Pull the leaves off gently, one at a time, continuing to trim the root end as you work your way toward the center.

BELL PEPPERS

1. To turn this unusually shaped vegetable into uniform pieces, first slice a ½-inch section off both the tip and stem ends. Make one slit in the trimmed shell, place it skin-side down, and press the flesh flat against the cutting board.

2. After removing the seeds and core, use a sharp knife to remove a ⅛-inch-thick piece of the tasteless inner membrane, then cut the pepper into ½-inch-wide lengths.

ZUCCHINI, SUMMER SQUASH, AND DAIKON RADISH

1. Though somewhat unusual for crudités, these vegetables can easily be added to the platter. Using a mandoline, cut them into ⅛-inch-thick slices.

2. To make the thin slices easy to dip and eat, roll them into tidy cylinders and secure with a toothpick.

JÍCAMA

1. After peeling the jicama, slice it into ½-inch-thick disks.

2. Cut each disk into ½-inch-thick strips.

FENNEL

1. After trimming the base and removing the upper stalks and fronds, slice the oval bulb in half lengthwise.

2. Remove the layers of fennel from each half, then cut them into ½-inch-thick strips.

RADISHES

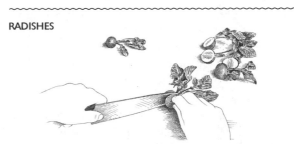

Choose radishes with their green tops still attached so each half has a leafy handle for grasping and dipping. Slice each radish in half through the stem.

SPINACH DIP

SPINACH DIP—A SIMPLE CONCOCTION OF vegetable soup mix, sour cream, and frozen spinach—often tastes flat, exorbitantly salty, and nowhere near fresh. We wanted a rich, thick, and creamy spinach dip brimming with big, bold flavors, especially of spinach.

To begin, we gathered five varieties of spinach: curly (or crinkly), flat (or smooth), semi-savoy (a hybrid of the two), baby, and, for the sake of comparison, frozen spinach. We then trimmed, washed, chopped, and wilted the fresh spinaches in hot pots (we simply thawed the frozen spinach), made the dips, chilled them to set (cool and thicken), and let tasters dig in. The results were so surprising we had to tally them twice. Frozen spinach was the victor. Tasters liked its "familiar," "intense" flavor and even used the word "fresh" to describe it. The fresh varieties were too "meek," their flavor lost among the other ingredients. After a few more tests to determine consistency, we found that 20 to 30 seconds in the food processor chopped the thawed frozen spinach into small, manageable bits and made the dip smooth and creamy.

Armed with a host of fresh herbs and other pungent ingredients, we began developing the flavor components for the dip sans soup mix. Among the herbs, parsley and dill were by and large the standards, and they worked appealingly well when combined. Onions and shallots were problematic, however, as they required cooking to mellow their astringency and soften their crunch. We weren't cooking the spinach and thought it would be a waste of time and effort to start pulling out pots and pans now. In the end, a combination of raw scallion whites and a single small clove of garlic added the perfect amount of bite and pungency. With a dash of hot pepper sauce for a kick of heat and some salt and pepper, the dip came out of the processor light, fresh, and full of bold flavors—far better than the soup mix recipe and not much more work.

The only problem remaining was that the dip, which took only about 15 minutes to make, took almost two hours to chill. Wanting to save time, we found the solution was simple. Instead of thawing the spinach completely, we thawed it only partially. Before processing, we microwaved the frozen block for three minutes on low, broke it into icy chunks, and squeezed each to extract a surprising amount of liquid. The chunks were still ice-cold and thoroughly cooled the dip as they broke down in the processor. Although our hands were slightly numb, the dip was quick to make, thick, creamy, and cool enough for immediate service.

❧

Herbed Spinach Dip

MAKES ABOUT 1½ CUPS,
SERVING 8 TO 10

Partial thawing of the spinach produces a cold dip that can be served without further chilling. If you don't own a microwave, the frozen spinach can be thawed at room temperature for 1½ hours, then squeezed of excess liquid. The garlic must be minced or pressed before going into the food processor; otherwise, the dip will contain large chunks of garlic. See pages 10–11 for information about preparing vegetables to accompany this dip.

1	(10-ounce) box frozen chopped spinach
½	cup sour cream
½	cup mayonnaise
3	medium scallions, white parts only, sliced thin
1	tablespoon chopped fresh dill leaves
½	cup packed fresh parsley leaves
1	small garlic clove, minced or pressed through a garlic press
¼	teaspoon hot pepper sauce
½	teaspoon salt
¼	teaspoon ground black pepper
½	medium red bell pepper, cored, seeded, and diced fine

1. Thaw the spinach in a microwave for 3 minutes at 40 percent power. (The edges should be thawed but not warm; the center should be soft enough to be broken into icy chunks.) Squeeze the partially frozen spinach of excess water.

2. In a food processor, process the spinach, sour cream, mayonnaise, scallions, dill, parsley, garlic, hot pepper sauce, salt, and pepper until smooth and creamy, about 30 seconds. Transfer the mixture to a serving bowl and stir in the bell pepper; serve. (The dip can be covered with plastic wrap and refrigerated for up to 2 days.)

HUMMUS

THIS SIMPLE CHICKPEA PUREE, ALTHOUGH relatively new to the American diet, has been eaten since the time of Socrates and Plato—and with good reason. Unfortunately, however, many of us are more familiar with the packaged tubs of prepared hummus sold in supermarkets across the United States, which don't taste very good. We wanted to make a great homemade hummus, similar to versions we'd tasted in Middle Eastern restaurants.

We did some research and found that hummus actually has multiple interpretations. Across the Middle East and throughout the Mediterranean region, individual families each have their own recipe; these vary by texture and flavor. What they have in common is only the combination of chickpeas and tahini (sesame paste). Tasting several hummus interpretations side by side, tasters homed in on a hummus seasoned with lemon and garlic, with a smooth, stiff, dip-like texture that was far less oily than that of the other contenders.

We were impressed by the results obtained with canned chickpeas. Typically, the beans are packed in a slippery, water-based liquid, and we found that the hummus tasted cleaner when we rinsed the chickpeas before pureeing them. We also noted that some of the thin skins would come off the beans if they were then quickly towel-dried, ensuring a smoother puree.

A 15-ounce can of chickpeas made a good-size batch of hummus, so we then moved our attention to the seasonings. We tried various amounts of tahini and found that ¼ cup yielded a good balance of flavors. One clove of garlic along with a pinch of cayenne added just the right bite. Three tablespoons of lemon juice contributed just enough brightness.

Last but not least, we needed to address the texture. Extra-virgin olive oil was the obvious choice, but we soon discovered that the amount of oil needed to achieve a smooth yet sturdy consistency was overpowering in flavor. We corrected this by replacing half the oil with water, which brought all the flavors into line. We also refrigerated the hummus for 30 minutes or so to mellow the flavors. At last, we had realized our goal: hummus that tasted far better than anything one could buy at the store.

Hummus

MAKES ABOUT 2 CUPS, SERVING 8 TO 10
Serve hummus with Pita Chips (page 16) or fresh pita breads cut into wedges, or with crudités (pages 10–11). Tahini can be found in Middle Eastern markets as well as in the international foods aisles of many supermarkets.

1	(15-ounce) can chickpeas, drained and rinsed
1	medium garlic clove, minced or pressed through a garlic press
¾	teaspoon salt
	Pinch cayenne pepper
3	tablespoons juice from 1 large lemon
¼	cup tahini
¼	cup extra-virgin olive oil
¼	cup water

Process all of the ingredients in a food processor until smooth, about 40 seconds. Transfer the hummus to a serving bowl, cover with plastic wrap, and chill until the flavors meld, at least 30 minutes; serve cold. (The hummus can be refrigerated for up to 2 days.)

BABA GHANOUSH

IN MIDDLE EASTERN COUNTRIES, BABA GHANOUSH is served as part of a meze platter—not unlike an antipasto in Italy—which might feature salads, various dips, small pastries, meats, olives, other condiments, and, of course, bread. The driving force behind baba ghanoush is grill-roasted eggplant, sultry and rich. The dip's beguiling creaminess and haunting flavor come from tahini (sesame paste) enhanced with a bit of garlic and brightened with both fresh lemon juice and parsley.

The traditional method for cooking the eggplant for baba ghanoush is to scorch it over a hot, smoky grill. There the purple fruit grows bruised and then it blackens, until its insides fairly slosh within their charred carapace. The hot, soft interior is scooped out with a spoon and the outer ruins discarded.

While eggplant cooked to the sloshy, soft stage may sound woefully overcooked to some, we realized that undercooked eggplant would taste spongy-green and remain unmoved by seasonings. This finding elicited an important question: Can a decent baba ghanoush be made without a grill? Taking instruction from the hot grill fire we had used, we roasted a few large eggplants in a 500-degree oven. It took about 45 minutes to collapse the fruit and transform the insides to pulp. Though the baba ghanoushes we made with grill-roasted eggplants were substantially superior to those made with the oven-roasted eggplants, the latter were perfectly acceptable.

Eggplant suffers from persistent rumors that it is bitter. Most baba ghanoush recipes call for discarding the seedbed. But the insides of the eggplants we were roasting were veritably paved with seeds. We thought it impractical and wasteful to jettison that amount of produce, so we performed side-by-side tests comparing versions of the dip with and without seeds. We found no tangible grounds for seed dismissal. The dip was not bitter. The seeds stayed.

Our research on this recipe disclosed that one variety of eggplant was sometimes favored over another. That prompted us to make baba ghanoush with standard large globe eggplants, with compact Italian eggplants, and with long, slender Japanese eggplants. All were surprisingly good. The globe eggplants resulted in a baba ghanoush that was slightly more moist. The Italian eggplants were drier and contained fewer seeds. The Japanese eggplants were also quite dry. Their very slenderness allowed the smoke of the open flame to permeate the flesh completely, and the resulting dip was meaty and delicious.

The eggplant can be mashed with a fork, but we preferred to use the food processor, which makes it a cinch to incorporate the other ingredients and to pulse the eggplant, leaving the texture slightly coarse.

As for the proportions of said ingredients, tests indicated that less was always more. Minced garlic gathers strength and can become aggressive when added in substantial amounts. Many recipes we reviewed also called for tahini in amounts that overwhelmed the eggplant. The same can be said for the amount of lemon juice: Too much will dash the smoky richness of the eggplant with astringent tartness.

If you're serving a crowd, the recipe can easily be doubled or tripled. Time does nothing to improve the flavor of baba ghanoush. An hour-long stay in the refrigerator for a light chilling is all that's needed.

Baba Ghanoush
MAKES ABOUT 2 CUPS

When buying eggplants, select ones with shiny, taut, and unbruised skin and an even shape (eggplants with a bulbous shape won't cook evenly). We prefer to serve baba ghanoush only lightly chilled. If yours is cold, let it stand at room temperature for about 20 minutes before serving. Baba ghanoush does not keep well, so make it the same day you plan to serve it. Pita bread, black olives, tomato wedges, and cucumber slices are nice accompaniments.

2 pounds eggplants (about 2 large globe eggplants, 5 medium Italian eggplants, or 8 small Japanese eggplants), each eggplant poked uniformly over its entire surface with a fork to prevent it from bursting
I tablespoon juice from I lemon
I small garlic clove, minced or pressed through a garlic press
2 tablespoons tahini
   Salt and ground black pepper
I tablespoon extra-virgin olive oil, plus more for serving
2 teaspoons chopped fresh parsley leaves

1. Grill the eggplants over a hot fire (you should be able to hold your hand 5 inches above the grill grate for only 2 seconds) until the skins darken and wrinkle on all sides and the eggplants are uniformly soft when pressed with tongs, about 25 minutes for large globe eggplants, 20 minutes for Italian eggplants, and 15 minutes for Japanese eggplants, turning the eggplants every 5 minutes.

Transfer the eggplants to a rimmed baking sheet and cool 5 minutes.

2. Set a small colander over a bowl or in the sink. Trim the top and bottom off each eggplant. Slit the eggplants lengthwise. Use a spoon to scoop the hot pulp from the skins and place the pulp in the colander (you should have about 2 cups packed pulp); discard the skins. Let the pulp drain for 3 minutes.

3. Transfer the pulp to a food processor. Add the lemon juice, garlic, tahini, ¼ teaspoon salt, and ¼ teaspoon pepper and process until the mixture has a coarse, choppy texture, about eight 1-second pulses. Adjust the seasonings with salt and pepper to taste. Transfer to a serving bowl, cover with plastic wrap flush with the surface of the dip, and refrigerate until lightly chilled, 45 to 60 minutes. To serve, use a spoon to make a trough in the center of the dip and spoon the olive oil into it. Sprinkle with the parsley and serve.

➤ VARIATIONS

Baba Ghanoush, Oven Method
Adjust an oven rack to the middle position and heat the oven to 500 degrees. Line a rimmed baking sheet with foil, set the eggplants on the baking sheet, and roast, turning every 15 minutes, until the eggplants are uniformly soft when pressed with tongs, about 60 minutes for large globe eggplants, 50 minutes for Italian eggplants, and 40 minutes for Japanese eggplants. Cool the eggplants on the baking sheet 5 minutes, then proceed with the master recipe from step 2.

Baba Ghanoush with Sautéed Onion
Sautéed onion gives the baba ghanoush a sweet, rich flavor.

Heat 1 tablespoon extra-virgin olive oil in a small skillet over low heat until shimmering. Add 1 small onion, chopped fine, and cook, stirring occasionally, until the edges are golden brown, about 10 minutes. Follow the recipe for Baba Ghanoush, stirring the onion into the dip after processing.

Israeli-Style Baba Ghanoush
Replacing the tahini with mayonnaise makes this baba ghanoush pleasantly light and brings out the smoky flavor of charcoal-grilled eggplant.

Follow the recipe for Baba Ghanoush, substituting an equal amount of mayonnaise for the tahini.

ROASTED RED PEPPER SPREAD

MUHAMMARA, MADE FROM ROASTED RED peppers, walnuts, and pomegranate molasses, is a popular spread made throughout the eastern Mediterranean. We wanted to develop a quicker version, based on pantry staples, without losing the sweet, smoky, savory flavors that make this spread so popular.

The first hurdle was the roasted peppers. Although roasting red peppers is fairly easy, we found that good-quality jarred peppers could be used (see page 16 for more information). The trick is to rinse them of their brine before using them. Our next challenge was to find a replacement for the pomegranate molasses, which is difficult to locate in typical American supermarkets. Seeking its thick, syrupy texture and sweet-sour flavor, we tested a variety of pantry ingredients to come up with a substitute. In the end, we found that a combination of lemon juice, honey, and mild molasses worked well. Seasoned with cayenne, ground cumin, and salt, the spread required only a small amount of olive oil to help loosen its consistency and toasted walnuts to enrich it.

At this point, our dip tasted good, but it was still missing something. Taking a look at Paula Wolfert's recipe for muhammara, we quickly realized what it was—crumbled wheat crackers. We added a generic brand of plain wheat crackers from the supermarket and found they contributed both flavor and substance to the mix, turning our roasted red pepper spread into a fair replication of authentic muhammara. Last, we noted that the flavors needed time to meld—at least 30 minutes—before serving.

Roasted Red Pepper Spread

MAKES ABOUT 2 CUPS,
SERVING 8 TO 10

Serve this dip with Pita Chips (below), fresh pitas cut into wedges, or baguette slices. See right for information on our testing of jarred roasted red peppers.

1	cup walnuts
12	ounces jarred roasted red peppers, drained, rinsed, and patted dry with paper towels
1/8	teaspoon cayenne pepper
1/4	cup coarsely ground plain wheat crackers
3	tablespoons juice from 1 large lemon
1	tablespoon mild molasses
1	teaspoon honey
1/2	teaspoon ground cumin
3/4	teaspoon salt
2	tablespoons extra-virgin olive oil

1. Place the walnuts in a medium skillet over medium heat and toast, shaking the pan occasionally to turn the nuts, until they are fragrant, about 5 minutes. Cool the nuts on a plate.

2. Process the toasted walnuts with the remaining ingredients in a food processor until smooth, about ten 1-second pulses. Transfer the mixture to a serving bowl, cover with plastic wrap, and chill until the flavors meld, at least 30 minutes; serve cold. (The spread can be refrigerated for up to 2 days.)

INGREDIENTS:
Jarred Roasted Red Peppers

Jarred peppers are convenient, but are all brands created equal? To find out, we collected six brands from local supermarkets. The top two brands, Divina and Greek Gourmet, were preferred for their "soft and tender texture" (the Divina) and "refreshing," "piquant," "smoky" flavor (the Greek Gourmet). The other brands were marked down for their lack of "roasty flavor" and for the unpleasantly overpowering flavor of the brines. These peppers tasted as if they'd been "buried under brine and acid," or they had a "pepperoncini-like sourness" or a "sweet and acidic aftertaste." The conclusion? Tasters preferred peppers with a full, smoky, roasted flavor, a brine that was spicy but not too sweet, and a tender texture.

**THE BEST JARRED
ROASTED RED PEPPERS**
Divina peppers (left) were the top choice of tasters. Greek Gourmet peppers (right) came in a close second.

Pita Chips

MAKES 48 CHIPS, ENOUGH TO ACCOMPANY 2 CUPS DIP

Pita chips are a natural accompaniment to spreads and dips, and when made at home, they taste far better than the expensive bags of broken chips available at the grocery store.

4	(8-inch-diameter) pita breads
1/4	cup olive oil
1	teaspoon salt

1. Adjust the oven racks to the upper-middle and lower-middle positions and heat the oven to 350 degrees.

2. Using kitchen shears, cut around the perimeter of each pita bread to yield 2 thin rounds. Stack the pita rounds and, using a chef's knife, cut them into 6 wedges each. Spread the pita triangles, smooth-side down, over 2 rimmed baking sheets. Brush the top of each chip lightly with oil and sprinkle with salt.

3. Bake the chips until they begin to crisp and brown lightly, about 6 minutes. Remove the baking sheets from the oven and flip the chips so their smooth side is up. Return the baking sheets to the oven, reversing their positions from top to bottom, and continue to bake until the chips are fully toasted, about 6 minutes longer. Remove the baking sheets from the oven and cool the chips before serving. (Store the completely cooled pita chips in a resealable bag at room temperature for up to 2 days.)

BRUSCHETTA

AUTHENTIC ITALIAN GARLIC BREAD, CALLED bruschetta, is never soggy or soft. Slices of country bread are first toasted, then rubbed with raw garlic, brushed with extra-virgin olive oil (never butter), and topped with various ingredients. These combinations can be as simple as salt and pepper or fresh herbs. Ripe tomatoes, sautéed peppers, and pureed white beans make more substantial offerings.

We found that narrow loaves of Italian bread are not suitable for bruschetta. Crusty country loaves that yield larger slices are preferable. Oblong loaves that measure about five inches across are best, but round loaves will work, too. As for the actual thickness of each bruschetta, slices cut about 1 inch thick provide enough heft to support weighty toppings and provide good chew.

Toasting the bread, which can be done over a grill fire or under the broiler, makes little jagged edges in the crumb of the bread that hook tiny bits of garlic when the raw clove is rubbed over the surface. For more garlic flavor, rub the toast vigorously. Oil can be drizzled over the garlicky toast or brushed on for more even coverage.

One piece of toast is enough for a single serving, and a few slices make a light lunch.

Toasted Bread for Bruschetta
MAKES 8 TO 10 SLICES
Toast the bread as close as possible to the time you plan to assemble the bruschetta. If you prefer, grill the bread.

- 1 loaf country bread (about 12 by 5 inches), cut crosswise into 1-inch-thick slices, ends discarded
- 3 tablespoons olive oil, preferably extra-virgin
- 1 large garlic clove, peeled and halved

Adjust an oven rack to about 4 inches from the heating element and heat the broiler; broil the bread slices until golden brown on both sides. Brush both sides of each slice with the oil and rub with the garlic clove.

Bruschetta with Tomatoes and Basil
SERVES 8 TO 10
This is the classic bruschetta, although you can substitute other herbs. If using more boldly flavored herbs, such as thyme or oregano, decrease the amount called for below.

- 4 medium, ripe tomatoes (about 1²/₃ pounds), cored and cut into ¹/₂-inch dice
- ¹/₃ cup shredded fresh basil leaves
  Salt and ground black pepper
- 1 recipe Toasted Bread for Bruschetta (at left)

1. Mix the tomatoes, basil, and salt and pepper to taste in a medium bowl. Set aside.
2. Use a slotted spoon to divide the mixture evenly among the toasted bread slices. Serve immediately.

Bruschetta with Sautéed Sweet Peppers
SERVES 8 TO 10

- 3 tablespoons plus 1 teaspoon extra-virgin olive oil
- 4 large red bell peppers (about 2 pounds), cored, seeded, and cut into ¹/₄ by 3-inch strips
- 2 medium onions, halved and thinly sliced
- ³/₄ teaspoon salt
- 3 medium garlic cloves, minced or pressed through a garlic press
- ¹/₄ teaspoon red pepper flakes
- 1 (14.5-ounce) can diced tomatoes, drained, ¹/₄ cup juice reserved
- 1¹/₂ teaspoons chopped fresh thyme leaves
- 4 teaspoons sherry vinegar
- 1 recipe Toasted Bread for Bruschetta (at left)
- 2 ounces Parmesan cheese, shaved with a vegetable peeler (see the illustration on page 134)

1. Heat the 3 tablespoons oil, the bell peppers, onions, and ¹/₂ teaspoon of the salt in a 12-inch

17

skillet over medium-high heat; cook, stirring occasionally, until the vegetables are softened and browned about the edges, 10 to 12 minutes. Reduce the heat to medium, push the vegetables to the side of the skillet, making a clearing in the center, and add the remaining 1 teaspoon oil, the garlic, and red pepper flakes to the clearing; cook, mashing the garlic with a wooden spoon, until fragrant, about 30 seconds, then stir into the vegetables. Reduce the heat to low and stir in the tomatoes, reserved juice, and thyme. Cover and cook, stirring occasionally, until the moisture has evaporated, 15 to 18 minutes. Off the heat, stir in the vinegar and remaining ¼ teaspoon salt.

2. Divide the pepper mixture evenly among the toasted bread slices, top with the shaved Parmesan, and serve.

Bruschetta with Arugula, Red Onion, and Rosemary–White Bean Spread

SERVES 8 TO 10

In a recent tasting, we preferred Progresso cannellini beans—by far—to the other brands sampled.

1	(19-ounce) can cannellini beans, drained and rinsed
3	tablespoons extra-virgin olive oil
2	tablespoons water
1	tablespoon juice from 1 lemon
1	small garlic clove, crushed
¾	teaspoon salt
¼	teaspoon ground black pepper
¼	teaspoon chopped fresh rosemary leaves
1	tablespoon balsamic vinegar
¼	medium red onion, sliced thin (about ¼ cup)
1	recipe Toasted Bread for Bruschetta (page 17)
1	small bunch arugula (about 2 ounces), washed, dried, and cut into ½-inch strips (about 4 cups)

1. In a food processor, process two thirds of the beans, 2 tablespoons of the oil, the water, lemon juice, garlic, ½ teaspoon of the salt, and ⅛ teaspoon pepper until smooth, about 10 seconds.

Add the remaining beans and the rosemary; pulse until incorporated but not smooth, about five 1-second pulses.

2. Whisk the remaining 1 tablespoon oil, the vinegar, the remaining ¼ teaspoon salt, and the remaining ⅛ teaspoon pepper together in a medium bowl; add the onion and toss.

3. Divide the bean spread evenly among the toasted bread slices. Add the arugula to the onions and toss until coated. Top each bread slice with a portion of the arugula mixture. Serve immediately.

MELON AND PROSCIUTTO

THE PAIRING OF JUICY, SWEET MELON and salty, toothsome prosciutto is classic—the quintessentially elegant hors d'oeuvre from Italy.

Prosciutto refers to a ham that has been salted and air-dried in the Italian fashion. Unlike many other hams produced elsewhere, prosciutto is not smoked, and it is usually not cooked (because it is cured). As an antipasto, it is served in paper-thin slices. Although prosciutto can be served on its own, the addition of melon (or figs) is customary and delicious. While prosciutto is now produced in various parts of the world and can be quite good, the best comes from two regions of Italy: Parma and San Daniele. Italian prosciutto has been available in the United States for more than a decade, and our testers found it is the best choice for this combination.

There are no secrets to assembling this hors d'oeuvre. There is one caveat: Each ingredient must be prime quality. The prosciutto should be supple and perfumed, and the melon must be sweet and ripe. It is best not to let the melon and prosciutto stand for too long, or the salt from the meat will draw moisture out of the melon, turning the fruit wet and the meat soggy.

Melon and Prosciutto

MAKES 16 PIECES, SERVING 6 TO 8

Cantaloupe is the classic choice, but any ripe melon, including honeydew, can be used in this pairing.

1   medium, ripe cantaloupe

½   pound thinly sliced imported prosciutto

1. Peel the melon and discard the rind. Cut the melon in half and scoop out the seeds with a spoon; discard the seeds. Cut each half into eight ½-inch-wide crescents.

2. If the prosciutto slices are long (over 6 inches in length), wrap one piece of prosciutto around the middle of each melon slice. If the prosciutto slices are short (under 6 inches in length), wrap two around the middle each melon slice. Arrange the melon on a platter and serve immediately.

➤ VARIATION

Asparagus Wrapped with Prosciutto
MAKES ABOUT 20 PIECES,
SERVING 4 TO 6
Let the asparagus spears cool slightly before wrapping them in the prosciutto, but don't let the asparagus cool completely. Part of the charm of this dish comes from the contrasting temperatures (and textures). Make sure you have the same number of asparagus spears (no thicker than your pinkie) and pieces of prosciutto once it has been cut. You need 20 of each.

1   pound thin asparagus spears, tough ends
     snapped off (see the illustration on page 10)
1   teaspoon extra-virgin olive oil
     Salt and ground black pepper
1   teaspoon balsamic vinegar
3   tablespoons grated Parmesan cheese
3   ounces thinly sliced imported prosciutto, cut
     crosswise into 3-inch-long pieces

1. Adjust an oven rack to the highest position and heat the broiler. Toss the asparagus with the oil on a rimmed baking sheet. Sprinkle with salt and pepper to taste. Broil, shaking the pan halfway through to turn the asparagus, until lightly browned, about 5 minutes.

2. Sprinkle the asparagus with the vinegar and Parmesan cheese. Cool slightly. Wrap a piece of prosciutto around the bottom half of each asparagus spear, making sure to leave the tip of the asparagus exposed. Arrange the asparagus on a platter and serve immediately.

CLASSIC SHRIMP COCKTAIL

NOTHING IS MORE BASIC THAN SHRIMP COCK-tail: "boiled" shrimp served cold with "cocktail" sauce, typically a blend of bottled ketchup or chili sauce spiked with horseradish. Can something so simple and good be improved upon? We thought so and set out to do just that.

If you start with good shrimp and follow a typical shrimp cocktail recipe—that is, simmer the shrimp in salted water until pink—the shrimp will have decent but rarely intense flavor. The easiest way to intensify the flavor of shrimp is to cook them in their shells. But, as we found out, this method has its drawbacks. First of all, it's far easier to peel shrimp when they are raw than when they have been cooked in liquid. More important, however, the full flavor of the shells is not extracted during the relatively short time required for the shrimp to cook through. It takes a good 20 minutes for the shells to impart their flavor to the cooking water, and this is far too long to keep shrimp in a pot.

It's better, then, to make shrimp stock, a simple enough process that takes only 20 minutes using just the shrimp shells. Simply place the shells in

PEELING SHRIMP

1. Hold the tail end of the shrimp with one hand and the opposite end of the shrimp with the other, then bend the shrimp back and forth and side to side to split the shell.

2. Lift off the tail portion of the shell, then slide your thumb under the legs of the remaining portion and lift it off as well.

a pot with water to cover, then simmer them for 20 minutes.

Next, we thought, it would be best to see what other flavors would complement the shrimp without overpowering it. Our first attempt was to use beer and a spicy commercial seasoning, but this was a near disaster; the shrimp for shrimp cocktail should not taste like a New Orleans crab boil.

After trying about 20 different combinations, involving wine, vinegar, lemon juice, and a near-ludicrous number of herbs and spices, we settled on the mixture given in the recipe on page 21. It contains about 25 percent white wine, a dash of lemon juice, and a more-or-less traditional combination of herbs. Variations are certainly possible, but we caution against adding more wine or lemon juice; both were good up to a point, but after that their pungency became overwhelming.

Although we were pleased at this point with the quality of the shrimp's flavor, we thought it could be still more intense. We decided to try to keep the shrimp in contact with the flavorings for a longer period of time.

We tried several methods to achieve this, including starting the shrimp in cold water with the seasonings and using a longer cooking time at a lower temperature. But shrimp cook so quickly—this is part of their appeal, of course—that these methods served only to toughen the meat. What worked best, we found, was to bring the cooking liquid to a boil, turn off the heat, and add the shrimp. Depending on their size, we could leave them in the liquid for up to 10 minutes, during which time they would cook through without toughening, all the while taking on near-perfect flavor.

Improving traditional cocktail sauce proved to be a tricky business. We wanted to make a better sauce, but we still wanted it to be recognizable as cocktail sauce. Starting with fresh or canned tomatoes, we discovered, just didn't work. The result was often terrific (some might say preferable), but it was not cocktail sauce. It was as if we had decided to make a better version of liver and onions by substituting foie gras for the calves liver. Undoubtedly, it would be "better," but it would no longer be liver and onions.

We decided to find the bottled ketchup or chili

DEVEINING SHRIMP

1. With a paring knife, make a shallow slit along the back of each shrimp. With the tip of the blade, lift up and loosen the vein.

2. Because the vein is quite sticky, we like to touch the knife blade to a paper towel on the counter. The vein will stick to the towel, and you can devein the next shrimp with a clean knife.

sauce we liked best and season it ourselves. First we had to determine which made the better base, ketchup or chili sauce. The answer to this question was surprising but straightforward: ketchup. Bottled chili sauce is little more than vinegary ketchup with a host of seasonings added. In addition, chili sauce can be four to eight times as expensive as ketchup.

Our preference in cocktail sauce has always been to emphasize the horseradish. But ketchup and horseradish, we knew, were not enough. Cocktail sauce benefits from a variety of heat sources, none of which should overpower the other, and the sum of which should allow the flavor of the shrimp to come through. We liked the addition of chili powder. We also liked a bit of bite from cayenne. Black pepper plays a favorable role as well (as does salt, even though ketchup is already salty). Finally, after trying a variety of vinegars, we went back to lemon, which is the gentlest and most fragrant acidic seasoning.

Now that we had our classic cocktail sauce, we set our sights on developing a more exotically flavored cocktail sauce for our shrimp. One member of our test kitchen staff recalled having enjoyed a spicy-sweet dipping sauce served with shrimp while vacationing in the Caribbean. Making a sauce with lime juice, hot chiles, and brown sugar, we noted this combination had sweet and spicy components similar to those of the classic ketchup-horseradish mixture, yet it was livelier. After a little retooling, we found an equal ratio of sugar to lime juice was necessary to balance the spicy nature of the hot chile. Supplemented with garlic, ginger, and scallions, this sauce was a welcome (and potent) change from classic tomato-based cocktail sauce.

Herb-Poached Shrimp
SERVES 4

When using larger or smaller shrimp, increase or decrease the cooking time by 1 to 2 minutes. For jumbo shrimp, deveining is essential.

1	pound jumbo (16 to 20 per pound) shrimp, peeled, deveined, and rinsed, shells reserved
1	teaspoon salt
1	cup dry white wine
4	whole black peppercorns
5	coriander seeds
$1/2$	bay leaf
5	sprigs fresh parsley
1	sprig fresh tarragon
1	teaspoon juice from 1 small lemon

1. Bring the reserved shells, 3 cups water, and the salt to a boil in a medium saucepan over medium-high heat; reduce the heat to low, cover, and simmer until fragrant, about 20 minutes. Strain the stock through a sieve, pressing on the shells to extract all the liquid, into a bowl.

2. Bring the stock and remaining ingredients except the shrimp to a boil in a 3- or 4-quart saucepan over high heat; boil 2 minutes. Turn off the heat and stir in the shrimp; cover and let stand until the shrimp are firm and pink, 8 to 10 minutes. Drain the shrimp, reserving the stock for another use. Plunge the shrimp into ice water to stop the cooking, then drain again. Serve the shrimp chilled with cocktail sauce (recipes follow).

Classic Cocktail Sauce
MAKES ABOUT 1 CUP, ENOUGH FOR 1 POUND JUMBO SHRIMP

For maximum flavor, use horseradish from a newly bought jar and mild chili powder.

1	cup ketchup
$2^1/2$	teaspoons prepared horseradish
$1/4$	teaspoon salt
$1/4$	teaspoon ground black pepper
1	teaspoon ancho or other mild chili powder
	Pinch cayenne pepper
1	tablespoon juice from 1 small lemon

Stir all of the ingredients together in a small serving bowl; adjust the seasonings as necessary.

Spicy Caribbean-Style Cocktail Sauce
MAKES ABOUT $1/2$ CUP, ENOUGH FOR 1 POUND JUMBO SHRIMP

This cocktail sauce is a sweet and spicy alternative to our classic version. Because this sauce is potent, less of it is needed to accompany the same amount of shrimp.

1	medium garlic clove, minced to a paste with $1/8$ teaspoon salt (see the illustrations on page 626)
$1^1/2$	tablespoons minced fresh ginger
2	medium scallions, white and green parts, minced
1	large jalapeño chile, stemmed, seeded, and minced
$1/4$	cup juice from 2 limes
$1/4$	cup packed light brown sugar

Mix the garlic paste, ginger, scallions, chile, lime juice, and brown sugar together in a small serving bowl; adjust the seasonings as necessary.

DEVILED EGGS

DEVILED EGGS SEEM TO BE MAKING A BIT of a comeback of late and with good reason. They are simple to make and tasty, always a crowd-pleaser, and can be quickly put together with ingredients already on hand. When we set out to develop this recipe, we had in mind the deviled eggs of our childhood: perfectly cooked nests of egg whites cradling a creamy filling, balanced with the flavor of mayonnaise and a hint of spiciness, but no dominant egg overtones.

Great deviled eggs begin with perfectly cooked hard-boiled eggs. We used our preferred method for hard-boiling eggs, then moved on to the filling. (See the information about preparing hard-boiled eggs on page 121.)

We started by testing the main ingredient in most deviled egg recipes—mayonnaise. We sampled deviled eggs made with our favorite commercial mayonnaise (Hellmann's), Miracle Whip salad dressing, butter (several recipes called for butter in addition to or instead of mayonnaise), and homemade mayonnaise. The filling made partially or wholly with butter was dry and bland, and the homemade mayonnaise just wasn't worth the trouble. When it came to salad dressing versus commercial mayonnaise, the results were mixed. Talking over the fine points after the tasting, we discovered that tasters had chosen the eggs made with the ingredient they had had when they were growing up, the one they still associated with deviled eggs. But the majority went with mayonnaise.

FILLING DEVILED EGGS

A pastry bag fitted with a star tip makes the most attractive deviled eggs. If you don't own a pastry bag, spoon the yolk mixture into a small zipper-lock plastic bag. Snip a small piece from one bottom corner of the bag and then gently squeeze the filling through the hole into the egg halves.

To be "deviled," the eggs needed some spiciness. Since mustard was the prevalent source of spicy flavor in most recipes, we made that our next test. We tried French's mustard (the hot dog mustard); dry, or powdered, mustard; Dijon mustard; whole-grain mustard; and brown (Gulden's) mustard. The winner was whole-grain mustard.

Next, we turned to vinegar, another ingredient common to many recipes for deviled eggs. After testing six, we chose cider vinegar. In this case, 1½ teaspoons was just right; add more and that's all you'll taste.

Having made the "big" decisions, we moved on to the accent flavors. We tested sour cream, curry, Worcestershire sauce, and cayenne pepper. Sour cream dulled the impact of the accompanying ingredients, and even the smallest amount of curry dominated all the other flavors, so we left both out of our final recipe. Worcestershire sauce added a touch of savory pungency. Cayenne pepper is a good substitute if you like a bit of heat.

While testing the easiest manner in which to fill the egg whites, we found that stuffing them as close to serving time as possible was key to a fresh, bright flavor. If last-minute preparation is not possible, cook the eggs up to one day ahead and store the whites in an airtight container and the filling in a sealed zipper-lock plastic bag.

Classic Deviled Eggs

MAKES I DOZEN FILLED EGG HALVES

If all of your egg white halves are in perfect shape, discard two. During testing, we found it usual for a couple to rip at least slightly, which worked out well because it meant the remaining whites were very well stuffed. If you have a pastry bag, you can use it to fill the eggs with a large open-star tip or a large plain tip. If not, see the illustration at left to improvise with a zipper-lock plastic bag.

7	large eggs
³/₄	teaspoon whole-grain mustard
3	tablespoons mayonnaise
1½	teaspoons cider vinegar (or vinegar of your choice)
¼	teaspoon Worcestershire sauce
	Salt and ground black pepper

1. Place the eggs in a medium saucepan, cover with 1 inch of water, and bring to a boil over high heat. Remove the pan from the heat, cover, and let stand 10 minutes. Meanwhile, fill a medium bowl with 1 quart cold water and 14 ice cubes (one tray). Transfer the eggs to the ice water with a slotted spoon; let sit 5 minutes.

2. Peel the eggs (see the illustrations on page 122) and slice each in half lengthwise with a paring knife. Remove the yolks to a small bowl. Arrange the whites on a serving platter, discarding the two worst-looking halves. Mash the yolks with a fork until no large lumps remain. Add the mustard, mayonnaise, vinegar, Worcestershire, and salt and pepper to taste; mix with a rubber spatula, mashing the mixture against the side of a bowl until smooth.

3. Fit a pastry bag with a large open-star tip. Fill the bag with the yolk mixture, twisting the top of the pastry bag to help push the mixture toward the tip of the bag. Pipe the yolk mixture into the egg white halves, mounding the filling about ½ inch above the flat surface of the whites. Serve immediately.

➤ VARIATIONS

Deviled Eggs with Anchovy and Basil
Rinse, dry, and finely chop 8 anchovy fillets. Mince 4 teaspoons basil leaves. Follow the recipe for Classic Deviled Eggs, mixing the anchovy fillets and 2 teaspoons minced basil into the mashed yolks along with the mustard, mayonnaise, vinegar, Worcestershire, and salt and pepper. Continue with the recipe, sprinkling the filled eggs with the remaining 2 teaspoons basil.

Deviled Eggs with Tuna, Capers, and Chives
Drain and finely chop 2 ounces canned tuna (you should have about ½ cup). Rinse and drain 1 tablespoon capers; chop 1 tablespoon chives. Follow the recipe for Classic Deviled Eggs, mixing the tuna, capers, and 2 teaspoons of the chives into the mashed yolks along with the mustard, mayonnaise, vinegar, and salt and pepper. Omit the Worcestershire. Continue with the recipe, sprinkling the filled eggs with the remaining 1 teaspoon chives.

KEEPING FILLED EGGS STABLE FOR TRANSPORT
Preparing beautiful deviled eggs requires care, so it goes without saying that you want them to arrive at your destination looking as perfect as they did in your kitchen. Here's how to keep the eggs upright if you want to transport them.

1. Cut a clean piece of rubberized shelf or drawer liner (available at hardware stores) to the size of the dish that will hold the eggs. Make sure to choose a dish with relatively high sides—a square plastic storage container with a lid is perfect.

2. Place the fitted liner on the bottom of the container, then stock it with enough eggs to fill it in a single layer. The liner keeps the eggs from sliding when the container is moved.

QUESADILLAS

QUESADILLAS ARE NOT HARD TO PREPARE. Yet, all too often, they taste terrible, with bland, unmelted cheese sandwiched between flabby, floury tortillas. So, although quesadillas appear to be effortless, we realized they need thoughtful attention.

Noting that flour tortillas come in a variety of sizes, we preferred those with an 8-inch diameter because they fit easily into a 10-inch pan. As for the cheese, we tried a few varieties; although many tasted good, we found that Monterey Jack melted well and had an easygoing flavor that paired well with other quesadilla-friendly ingredients. We tried using preshredded cheese but were unimpressed with its artificial flavor and gummy texture. Take a couple of minutes to shred the cheese yourself.

For our quesadillas, we wanted bold flavors, such as roasted red peppers, cilantro, and red onion, along with the spicy, smoky flavor of chipotle chiles in adobo sauce. To help prevent the filling from leaking out of the sides, we found it necessary to leave a 1-inch border around the tortilla edge.

Cooking quesadillas is fairly straightforward, but after making a few batches we discovered a few little tricks. Although both regular and non-stick pans work, we liked the absolutely effortless release guaranteed by using a nonstick.

Wanting to use the least amount of oil possible, we found it easy to brush just the outside of the tortillas with oil rather than adding it to the pan. A hot pan is absolutely necessary to a well-crisped tortilla, but if the pan is too hot, the tortilla will burn in spots. Medium heat, we found, toasted both sides of the quesadilla without burning or requiring an oven finish.

Last, we discovered the benefits of weighting the quesadilla down as it cooked. An empty saucepan, roughly 8 inches across, placed directly on top of the quesadilla in the skillet flattened the nooks and crannies of the sandwich against the hot pan without forcing the filling out of the sides. The result was a crisp, toasty quesadilla with melted cheese throughout and a flavor that left tasters wanting more than just one slice.

Spicy Roasted Red Pepper Quesadillas

MAKES 16 SLICES, SERVING 4 TO 6

For a pleasing contrast of flavors and textures, serve the quesadillas with the salsa (recipe follows) and/or one of the guacamole recipes on page 26. However, if you are pressed for time, the quesadillas are tasty enough to serve as is. See page 16 for information about buying jarred roasted red peppers. Soft taco-size tortillas will work best in this recipe.

8   ounces jarred roasted red peppers, minced (about 1 cup)

1   small canned chipotle chile in adobo sauce, minced

½   small garlic clove, minced or pressed through a garlic press

2   tablespoons minced fresh cilantro leaves Salt and ground black pepper

4   (8-inch-diameter) soft flour tortillas

3   thin slices red onion, rings separated

4   ounces Monterey Jack cheese, shredded (about 1 cup)

2   tablespoons vegetable oil

1. Combine the roasted red peppers, chipotle, garlic, and cilantro in a small bowl and season with salt and pepper to taste. Spread half the mixture evenly over 1 tortilla, leaving a 1-inch border bare. Arrange half the onion slices over the pepper mixture and sprinkle with half the cheese, again leaving a 1-inch border. Place a second tortilla over the cheese and press slightly to position. Repeat with the remaining ingredients to make a second quesadilla.

2. Set a 10-inch nonstick skillet over medium heat for 2 minutes. Brush one side of one of the tortillas with 1½ teaspoons of the oil and place it, greased-side down, in the heated pan. Place a clean saucepan on the quesadilla as a weight and cook until the bottom of the quesadilla is golden brown and crisp, 3 to 4 minutes. Remove the weight and brush the top with 1½ teaspoons oil. Using a wide spatula, flip the quesadilla over in the pan and replace the weight. Cook until the second side is golden brown and crisp, about 3 minutes more.

3. Transfer the quesadilla to a cutting board to cool slightly; return the skillet to medium heat. Cook the second quesadilla in the same manner. Cut each quesadilla into 8 wedges and serve warm with accompaniments (see note).

Classic Red Tomato Salsa

MAKES ABOUT 5 CUPS

Our favorite Mexican-style salsa, which is great with our Spicy Roasted Red Pepper Quesadillas, is also good with Classic Fajitas (page 575), or can be served simply with a bowl of tortilla chips. To reduce the heat in the salsa, seed the chile.

3 large, very ripe tomatoes (about 2 pounds), cored and diced small

¹/₂ cup tomato juice

1 small jalapeño or other fresh hot chile, stemmed, seeded (if desired), and minced

1 medium red onion, diced small

1 medium garlic clove, minced or pressed through a garlic press

¹/₂ cup chopped fresh cilantro leaves

¹/₂ cup juice from 6 large limes

Salt

Mix all of the ingredients, including salt to taste, together in a medium bowl. Refrigerate the salsa in an airtight container to blend the flavors, at least 1 hour and up to 5 days.

GUACAMOLE

GUACAMOLE HAS TRAVELED A LONG ROAD. Once a simple Mexican avocado relish, it has become one of America's favorite party dips. Unfortunately, the journey has not necessarily been kind to this dish. The guacamole we are served in restaurants, and even in the homes of friends, often sacrifices the singular, extraordinary character of the avocado—the culinary equivalent of velvet—by adding too many other flavorings. Even worse, the texture of the dip is usually reduced to an utterly smooth, listless puree.

We wanted our guacamole to be different. First, it should highlight the dense, buttery texture and loamy, nutty flavor of the avocado. Any additions should provide bright counterpoints to the avocado without overwhelming it. Just as important, the consistency of the dip should be chunky rather than perfectly smooth.

Good guacamole starts with good (i.e., ripe) avocados. Assuming you have ripe avocados, how should you handle and mix them with the other ingredients? Most guacamole recipes direct you to mash all the avocados, and some recipes go so far as to puree them in a blender or food processor. After making dozens of batches, we came to believe that neither pureeing nor simple mashing was the way to go. Properly ripened avocados break down very easily when stirred, and we were aiming for a chunky texture. To get it, we ended up mashing only one of the three avocados in our recipe lightly with a fork and mixing it with most of the other ingredients, then dicing the remaining two avocados into substantial ½-inch cubes and mixing them into the base using a very light hand. The mixing action breaks down the cubes somewhat, making for a chunky, cohesive dip.

Other problems we encountered in most recipes were an overabundance of onion and a dearth of acidic seasoning. After extensive testing with various amounts of onion, tasters found that 2 tablespoons of finely minced or grated onion

PITTING AN AVOCADO

Digging out the pit with a spoon can mar the soft flesh and is generally a messy proposition. This method avoids this problem.

1. Start by slicing around the pit and through both end with a chef's knife. With your hands, twist the avocado to separate the two halves.

2. Stick the blade of the chef's knife sharply into the pit. Lift the knife, twisting the blade to loosen and remove the pit.

3. Don't pull the pit off the knife with your hands. Instead, use a large wooden spoon to pry the pit safely off the knife.

gave the guacamole a nice spike without an over-whelming onion flavor. We also tried various amounts of fresh lemon and lime juice. The acid was absolutely necessary, not only for flavor but also to help preserve the mixture's green color. Tasters preferred 2 tablespoons of lime juice in our 3-avocado guacamole.

Chunky Guacamole

MAKES 2 1/2 TO 3 CUPS

Like our Classic Red Tomato Salsa (page 24), our guacamole makes a great accompaniment to Spicy Roasted Red Pepper Quesadillas (page 24) and other Mexican-style dishes, as well as a dip for tortilla chips. To minimize the risk of discoloration, prepare the minced ingredients first so they are ready to mix with the avocados as soon as they are cut. Ripe avocados are essential here. If you like, garnish the guacamole with diced tomatoes and chopped cilantro just before serving.

3	medium, ripe avocados, preferably pebbly-skinned Hass
2	tablespoons minced onion
1	medium garlic clove, minced or pressed through a garlic press
1	small jalapeño chile, stemmed, seeded, and minced
1/4	cup minced fresh cilantro leaves
	Salt
1/2	teaspoon ground cumin (optional)
2	tablespoons juice from 1 lime

1. Halve one of the avocados, remove the pit, and scoop the flesh into a medium bowl. Mash the flesh lightly with the onion, garlic, chile, cilantro, 1/4 teaspoon salt, and cumin (if using) with the tines of a fork until just combined.

2. Halve, pit, and cube the remaining 2 avocados, following the illustrations on page 25 and this page. Add the cubes to the bowl with the mashed avocado mixture.

3. Sprinkle the lime juice over the diced avocado and mix the entire contents of the bowl lightly with a fork until combined but still chunky. Adjust the seasonings with salt, if necessary, and serve. (Guacamole can be covered with

DICING AN AVOCADO

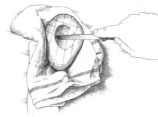

1. Use a dish towel to hold the avocado steady. Make 1/2-inch cross-hatch incisions in the flesh of each avocado half with a dinner knife, cutting down to but not through the skin.

2. Separate the diced flesh from the skin using a spoon inserted between the skin and the flesh and gently scoop out the avocado cubes.

plastic wrap, pressed directly onto the surface of the mixture, and refrigerated up to 1 day. Return the guacamole to room temperature, removing the plastic wrap at the last moment, before serving.)

➤ VARIATION

Guacamole with Bacon, Scallions, and Tomato

Follow the recipe for Chunky Guacamole, substituting 3 large scallions, sliced thin (about 1/3 cup), for the onion and adding 6 slices bacon, cooked, drained, and crumbled, with 1 teaspoon rendered fat and 1/2 medium tomato, seeded and diced small.

BUFFALO WINGS

FIRST CONCEIVED OF AT THE ANCHOR BAR in Buffalo, New York, in the 1960s, Buffalo wings are now found throughout the country at any bar or Super Bowl party worth its salt. The odd combination of chicken wings slathered with hot sauce and dunked in blue cheese dressing may seem like a drunken concoction best forgotten about the next morning, but it is actually a harmonious union. The sauce's bright heat is tamed by the soothing, creamy dip.

For Buffalo wings, the raw chicken wing itself is almost always cut in two segments, and the relatively meatless wingtip is removed. The wings come packaged as whole wings or as already cut into pieces affectionately referred to as drumettes. We found that precut wings were often poorly cut and unevenly sized, so we chose to buy whole wings and butcher them ourselves, which was easy and economical. With kitchen shears or a sharp chef's knife, the wing is halved at the main joint and the skinny tip of the wing is lopped off and discarded (or saved for stock).

While the wings were easy to butcher, cooking them proved a little trickier because of their high fat content. At the Anchor Bar, Buffalo wings are deep-fried, which renders the fat and leaves the skin crisp and golden. But deep-frying can be a daunting project in a home kitchen, with hot fat splattering about, coating the stovetop and stinging uncovered arms. We found that if we used a deep Dutch oven and kept the oil at a constant 360 degrees, splattering oil was minimal (and much safer) and cleanup easy.

We tossed the wings with salt, pepper, and cayenne and then fried them for about 12 minutes, or until golden. While these wings were juicy and crisp, most tasters wanted an even crispier exterior. We did not want to resort to a batter, so we tried dredging the wings, testing one batch dredged in flour and another in cornstarch. The cornstarch provided a thin and brittle coating, not unlike tempura, that was the tasters' favorite. We found that thoroughly drying the chicken with paper towels prior to tossing it with the cornstarch and seasonings ensured crisp skin and no gumminess.

Now we were ready to tackle the sauce. Most recipes we found agreed that authentic Buffalo wing sauce, as made at the Anchor Bar, is nothing but Frank's Louisiana Hot Sauce and butter or margarine, blended in a 2-to-1 ratio. Most recipes also suggest intensifying the sauce's heat with a bit of Tabasco or other hot pepper sauce because, on its own, Frank's is not quite spicy enough. While we liked this simple sauce, most tasters wanted something a little more dynamic. We included brown sugar to round out the flavors. A little cider vinegar balanced out the sugar and added a pleasing sharpness.

Creamy blue cheese dressing and carrot and celery sticks are the classic accompaniments to Buffalo wings. For our dressing, we picked a mild blue cheese and combined it with buttermilk and sour cream for tang and richness and with mayonnaise for body. A little white wine vinegar brightened the flavors, a pinch of sugar added just the right touch of sweetness, and garlic powder, which we normally shy away from, added a subtle background note rather than the assertive bite that comes with fresh garlic. (For the complete story on our development of this recipe, see page 80.)

Our final Buffalo wings buck tradition just a bit, but only in the service of delivering a close-to-foolproof and tasty recipe for a crowd-pleasing favorite.

CUTTING UP CHICKEN WINGS

1. With a chef's knife, cut into the skin between the larger sections of the wing until you hit the joint.

2. Bend back the two sections to pop and break the joint.

3. Cut through the skin and flesh to completely separate the two meaty portions.

4. Hack off the wingtip and discard.

Buffalo Wings

SERVES 6 TO 8

Frank's Louisiana Hot Sauce is not terribly spicy. We like to combine it with a more potent hot sauce, such as Tabasco, to bring up the heat. You will need to double the ingredients in the blue cheese dressing recipe.

SAUCE

4	tablespoons (1/2 stick) unsalted butter
1/2	cup Frank's Louisiana Hot Sauce
2	tablespoons hot pepper sauce, plus more to taste
1	tablespoon dark brown sugar
2	teaspoons cider vinegar

WINGS

1–2	quarts peanut oil for frying
1	teaspoon cayenne pepper
1	teaspoon ground black pepper
1	teaspoon salt
3	tablespoons cornstarch
18	chicken wings (about 3 pounds), wingtips removed and remaining wings separated into 2 parts at joint (see the illustrations on page 27)

VEGETABLES AND DRESSING

4	medium celery ribs, cut into thin sticks
2	medium carrots, peeled and cut into thin sticks
1 1/2	cups Blue Cheese Dressing (page 80)

1. FOR THE SAUCE: Melt the butter in a small saucepan over low heat. Whisk in the hot sauces, brown sugar, and vinegar until combined. Remove from the heat and set aside.

2. FOR THE WINGS: Heat the oven to 200 degrees. Line a baking sheet with paper towels. Heat 2½ inches of the peanut oil in a large Dutch oven over medium-high heat to 360 degrees. While the oil heats, mix the cayenne, black pepper, salt, and cornstarch together in a small bowl. Dry the chicken with paper towels and place the pieces in a large mixing bowl. Sprinkle the spice mixture over the wings and toss with a rubber spatula until evenly coated. Fry half the chicken wings until golden and crisp, 10 to 12 minutes.

With a slotted spoon, transfer the fried chicken wings to the baking sheet. Keep the first batch of chicken warm in the oven while frying the remaining wings.

3. TO SERVE: Pour the sauce mixture into a large bowl, add the chicken wings, and toss until the wings are uniformly coated. Serve immediately with the celery and carrot sticks and the blue cheese dressing on the side.

TOMATO AND MOZZARELLA TART

MORE ELEGANT THAN PIZZA AND EASIER TO eat out of hand than quiche, tomato and mozzarella tart makes a great hors d'oeuvre. We envisioned a simple construction of tomatoes and cheese shingled across a plain, prebaked sheet of puff pastry. Unwilling to make puff pastry from scratch for this recipe, we grabbed some store-bought pastry (we found Pepperidge Farm to be the most available; two pieces of dough come in a single box) and started cooking.

The winning recipe from our first taste test consisted of a flat sheet of puff pastry with a thin border to contain the topping (tomatoes easily slip off a flat sheet of anything) and a thick glaze of egg wash to seal the dough tight against the seeping tomatoes. We trimmed thin strips of dough from the edges of a single rectangular sheet of puff pastry and cemented them with some beaten egg to the top of the sheet to create a uniform 1-inch border. This single tart shell looked large enough for two to three servings. With scarcely any more effort, we found we could serve twice as many by joining the two pieces of dough that came in the box (we sealed the seam tightly with egg wash and rolled it flat) and making a long rectangular version, roughly 18 by 9 inches. Once assembled, the tart was heavily brushed with egg wash.

From prior kitchen tests, we knew that prebaking the crust would be essential to give it a fighting chance against the moisture from the tomatoes. Following the recipe on the back of the Pepperidge Farm box, we baked our tart shell at 400 degrees until it was golden brown. Now we ran into our first problem. The shell was too frail to support a heavy, wet filling. Baked at 350 degrees, the shell was noticeably squatter and drier—and so better suited to a heavy filling—but it was also unpleasantly tough and chewy. We wondered if a two-step baking method might be more successful: a high temperature for initial lift and browning, then a lower temperature to dry out the shell for maximum sturdiness. Our first test—400 degrees reduced to 350 degrees once the dough had risen—proved positive, so we fiddled with temperature pairings until the crust was ideal. When baked at 425 degrees until puffed and light golden (about 15 minutes) and finished at 350 degrees until well browned (15 minutes longer), the crust was flaky yet rigid enough so that we could pick up a piece of tart at one end and hold it aloft.

Now we had half-solved the problem of the soggy crust, but there was still work to do. The egg wash coating had proven only deflective, not impermeable. Liquid from the tomatoes soaked through to the puff pastry, albeit at a slower rate than with uncoated pastry. Egg wash was part of, but not the whole, solution.

Our first thought was to use tomatoes with a relatively low water content. We limited our tests to standard beefsteak (round) and Roma (plum) tomatoes because they are the most readily available. A quick side-by-side test ruled out beefsteaks as excessively high in liquid. As we had suspected, Romas were the better choice for this recipe.

As for extracting the tomatoes' juices, salting—a step common to Mediterranean cooking and one the test kitchen has put to good use in other recipes—worked well but not perfectly. We sprinkled sliced tomatoes with salt and left them to drain on paper towels for 30 minutes. The underlying towels were soaked through, but the tomatoes were still juicy to the touch. Increasing the amount of salt and time accomplished frustratingly little. A little gentle force, however, worked magic: We sandwiched the salted slices between paper towels and pressed down with enough force to extrude any remaining juices (and the seeds) but not enough to squish the slices flat. They were as dry as could be, yet still very flavorful.

Baked quick and hot to melt the cheese and preserve the tomatoes' meaty texture (425 degrees turned out to be the best temperature), the tart

looked ready for the cover of a magazine, especially when slicked with a garlic-infused olive oil and strewn with fresh basil leaves. But just a few minutes from the oven, the horrible truth revealed itself: The

ASSEMBLING A TOMATO TART

1. Brush some of the beaten egg along one edge of one sheet of puff pastry. Overlap with the second sheet of dough by 1 inch and press down to seal the pieces together.

2. With a rolling pin, smooth out the seam. The dough rectangle should measure about 18 by 9 inches. Use a pizza wheel or knife to trim the edges straight.

3. With the pizza wheel or knife, cut a 1-inch strip from the long side of the dough. Cut another 1-inch strip from the same side.

4. With the pizza wheel or knife, cut a 1-inch strip from the short side of the dough. Cut another 1-inch strip from the same side.

5. Transfer the large piece of dough to a parchment-lined baking sheet and brush with more beaten egg. Gently press the long strips of dough onto the 2 long sides of the dough. Brush the long strips of dough with beaten egg. Gently press the short strips of dough onto the 2 short sides. Brush the short strips of dough with beaten egg.

6. With the pizza wheel or knife, trim any excess dough from the corners. The dough is now ready to be sprinkled with the Parmesan.

crust was soggy. Despite the egg wash, the melted mozzarella, and drained and pressed tomatoes, the tart continued to suffer the ills of moisture.

Discouraged but not undone, we remembered those prebaked supermarket pizza crusts and wondered if, as on those crusts, a solid layer of crisply baked Parmesan, on top of the egg wash but beneath the mozzarella, would seal the base of our tart more permanently. We sprinkled finely grated Parmesan over the tart shell for the prebake and crossed our fingers. The cheese melted to such a solid (and deliciously nutty-tasting) layer that liquid rolled right off, like rain off a duck's back.

After baking a whole tart, we were stunned by the results: Slices could be lifted freely and consumed like pizza, even hours from the oven. Rich in flavor and sturdy in form, it had character to match its good looks—and it was quick, too.

Tomato and Mozzarella Tart
SERVES 4 TO 6

The baked tart is best eaten warm within 2 hours of baking. If you prefer to do some advance preparation, the tart shell can be prebaked through step 1, cooled to room temperature, wrapped in plastic wrap, and kept at room temperature for up to 2 days before being topped and baked with the mozzarella and tomatoes. Use low-moisture, shrink-wrapped supermarket cheese rather than fresh mozzarella. To keep the frozen pastry from cracking, it's best to let it thaw slowly in the refrigerator overnight.

	Flour for dusting the work surface
1	(1.1-pound) box frozen puff pastry (Pepperidge Farm), thawed in the box in the refrigerator overnight
1	large egg, beaten
1	ounce Parmesan cheese, freshly grated (1/2 cup)
1	pound Roma tomatoes (3 to 4 medium), cored and cut crosswise into 1/4-inch-thick slices Salt
2	medium garlic cloves, minced or pressed through a garlic press
2	tablespoons extra-virgin olive oil Ground black pepper

| 8 | ounces low-moisture whole-milk mozzarella, shredded (2 cups) |
| 2 | tablespoons coarsely chopped fresh basil |

1. Adjust an oven rack to the lower-middle position and heat the oven to 425 degrees. Dust the work surface with flour and unfold both pieces of puff pastry onto the work surface. Follow the illustrations on page 29 to form 1 large sheet with a border, using the beaten egg as directed. Sprinkle the Parmesan evenly over the bottom of the shell; using a fork, uniformly and thoroughly poke holes in the bottom. Bake 15 minutes, then reduce the oven temperature to 350 degrees; continue to bake until golden brown and crisp, 15 to 17 minutes longer. Transfer to a wire rack; increase the oven temperature to 425 degrees.

2. While the shell bakes, place the tomato slices in a single layer on 2 layers of paper towels and sprinkle evenly with 1/2 teaspoon salt; let stand 30 minutes. Place 2 more layers of paper towels on top of the tomatoes and press firmly to dry the tomatoes. Combine the garlic, olive oil, and a pinch each of salt and pepper in a small bowl; set aside.

3. Sprinkle the mozzarella evenly over the bottom of the warm (or cool, if made ahead) baked shell. Shingle the tomato slices widthwise on top of the cheese (about 4 slices per row); brush the tomatoes with the garlic oil. Bake until the shell is deep golden brown and the cheese is melted, 15 to 17 minutes. Cool on a wire rack 5 minutes, sprinkle with the basil, slide onto a cutting board or serving platter, cut into pieces, and serve.

➤ VARIATIONS
Tomato and Mozzarella Tart with Prosciutto
Follow the recipe for Tomato and Mozzarella Tart, laying 2 ounces thinly sliced prosciutto in a single layer on top of the mozzarella before arranging the tomato slices.

Tomato and Smoked Mozzarella Tart
This variation requires just 6 ounces of mozzarella.
Follow the recipe for Tomato and Mozzarella Tart, substituting 6 ounces smoked mozzarella for the whole-milk mozzarella.

2
SOUPS

NOT SURPRISINGLY, THE DIFFERENCES IN flavor between soup from a can and homemade are immeasurable. What is surprising is that homemade soup need not be a complicated affair.

Two kinds of soup are covered in this chapter—soups that rely on homemade chicken or beef stock and soups that are made with water or canned broth. How do you know which soups should be made with homemade stock and which can be made successfully with canned broth or water?

In general, we find that brothy soups with few ingredients must be made with homemade stock. Chicken noodle soup made with canned broth is not nearly as good as the same soup made with homemade stock. To save time and work, we have developed recipes for chicken and beef stock that also yield meat that can be used in soups.

On the other hand, we find that soups with complex seasonings (such as Asian noodle soups loaded with fish sauce and ginger) or soups with richly flavored ingredients (such as onion soup with caramelized onions and cheese croutons) can be made with canned broth or water. In these cases, we have successfully devised methods for punching up the flavor of the liquid. Of course, you can use homemade stock in these recipes. However, when we find that the quality of a soup made without homemade stock is quite high, we are happy to take this shortcut.

We have also discovered innovative ways to impart great flavor to stock and soup without spending hours over a hot stove. We have found the richest chicken stock is made by first sautéing the chicken parts to extract as much flavor as possible and we also learned that great beef stock isn't all about the bones—it takes meat to add real beefy flavor.

In developing our soups, we learned that eking out as much flavor from key ingredients was the secret to their success. For our butternut squash soup, sautéing the squash seeds and fibers from butternut squash add an incomparable intensity of flavor (the seeds and fibers are later strained out). We developed a richly flavorful *pasta e fagioli* by adding spent Parmesan rinds

(they impart a wonderful flavor boost) along with minced anchovies (the secret ingredient, which adds a remarkable complexity to this otherwise staid Italian-American favorite). Corn chowder is all about the corn, so we focused on squeezing out as much flavor from the corn as possible by first grating the kernels off the cobs and then scraping off the remaining sweet milky pulp so that every bit of corn flavor made it into our soup.

Stock and soup can be prepared in even the most primitive kitchen. You can certainly make each with just a pot for cooking, a spoon for stirring, and a ladle for serving, but there are a few pieces of choice equipment we recommend for optimal results. See pages 34–35 for more information.

Lastly, one of the beauties of soup is the fact that it holds up so well. Many of the soups in this chapter can be made on the weekend and enjoyed several times during the week. See page 41 for tips on storing and reheating soup.

CHICKEN STOCK

MOST STANDARD CHICKEN STOCKS ARE NOT flavorful enough for a robust chicken soup. They are fine if ladled into risotto, but we wanted a stock that really tasted like chicken. We knew that the conventional method—simmering chicken parts and aromatics, such as onions, carrots, and celery, in water for hours—was part of the problem. This method takes too long (at least three hours) to extract flavor from the chicken. We wanted to see if we could do better, and in less time.

We tried blanching a whole chicken, on the theory that blanching keeps the chicken from releasing foam during cooking. The blanched chicken was then partially covered with water and placed in a heatproof bowl over a pan of simmering water. Cooked this way, the chicken never simmered, and the resulting stock was remarkably clear, refined, and full-flavored. The only problem: it took four hours for the stock to take on sufficient flavor. We also noted that our four-pound chicken was good for nothing but the garbage bin after being cooked for so long.

A number of recipes promote roasting chicken bones or parts and then using them to make stock. The theory, at least, is that roasted parts will flavor stock in minutes, not hours. We gave it a try several times, roasting chicken backs, necks, and bones—with and without vegetables. We preferred the stock made with roasted chicken parts and vegetables, but the actual chicken flavor was too tame.

Finally, we tried a method described by Edna Lewis in her book *In Pursuit of Flavor* (Knopf, 1988). She sautés a chicken that's been hacked into small pieces with an onion until the chicken loses its raw color. The pot is then covered and the chicken and onion cook over low heat until they release their rich, flavorful juices, which takes about 20 minutes. Only at that point is the water added, and the stock is simmered for just 20 minutes longer.

We knew we were onto something as we smelled the chicken and onions sautéing, and the finished stock confirmed what our noses had detected. The stock tasted pleasantly sautéed, not boiled. We had some refining to do, though. For once, we had made too strong a brew.

We substituted chicken backs and wingtips for the whole chicken and used more water. The stock was less intense, but just the right strength to make a base for some of the best chicken soup we've ever tasted. We made the stock twice more—once without onion and once with onion, celery, and carrot. The onion added a flavor dimension we liked; the extra vegetables neither added nor detracted from the final soup, so we left them out.

After much trial and error, we had a recipe that delivered liquid gold in just 40 minutes. While this recipe requires more hands-on work (hacking up parts; browning an onion, then chicken parts), it is ready in a fraction of the time required to make stock by traditional methods.

So where do you find the useless chicken parts necessary for this stock? The Buffalo chicken wing fad has made wings more expensive than legs and thighs. For those who can buy chicken backs, this is clearly an inexpensive way to make stock for soup. Our local grocery store usually sells them for almost nothing, but in many locations they may be difficult to find.

Luckily, we found that relatively inexpensive whole legs make an incredibly full-flavored stock for soup. In a side-by-side comparison of a stock made from backs and from whole legs, we found the whole-leg stock was actually more full-flavored than the all-bone stock. Just don't try to salvage the meat from the legs. After 5 minutes of sautéing, 20 minutes of sweating, and another 20 minutes of simmering, the meat is void of flavor.

If you are making a soup that needs some chicken meat, use a whole chicken as directed in the recipe Chicken Stock with Sautéed Breast Meat. The breast is removed in two pieces, sautéed briefly, and then added with the water to finish cooking. The rest of the bird—the legs, back, wings, and giblets—is sweated with the onions and discarded when the stock is done. However, the breast meat is perfectly cooked, ready to be skinned and shredded when cool. We particularly liked the tidiness of this method: One chicken yields one pot of soup.

One note about this method. We found it necessary to cut the chicken into pieces small enough to release their flavorful juices in a short period of time. A meat cleaver, a heavy-duty chef's knife, or a pair of heavy-duty kitchen shears makes the task fairly simple. Cutting up the chicken for stock doesn't require precision. The point is to chop the pieces small enough to release their flavorful juices in a short period of time.

To cut up a whole chicken, start by removing the whole legs and wings from the body; set them aside. Separate the back from the breast, then split the breast and set the halves aside. Hack the back crosswise into three or four pieces, then halve each of these pieces. Cut the wing at each joint to yield three pieces. Leave the wingtip whole, then halve each of the remaining joints. Because of their larger bones, the legs and thighs are most difficult to cut. Start by splitting the leg and thigh at the joint, then hack each to yield three or four pieces.

Tips for Making Better and Quicker Homemade Stock and Soup

Restaurant chefs adhere to time-consuming, involved routines for making chicken and beef stocks. Bones, meat, and mirepoix (onions, carrots, and celery) are first oven-roasted or sautéed on the stovetop. A bouquet garni (a bundle of several fresh herbs) and water are added, and the stock simmers, uncovered, for hours, with the cook periodically skimming off impurities. To clarify the stock, a raft (beaten egg whites and sometimes ground meat) might then be added to trap sediment. Finally, the stock is strained, cooled, and defatted.

This method is fine for professional cooks, and it does yield rich, deeply flavored stock. But most home cooks don't want (or need) to follow such a complicated regimen. We've developed new techniques and helpful tips for making stock with great flavor, stock that requires fewer ingredients, less work, and less time than the classic method.

USING THE RIGHT EQUIPMENT

You don't need to make a huge investment in equipment to produce a good stock, but a few tools make the process easier.

Strainer: A stock made with hacked bones will contain minute bone particles and splinters and must be strained. A fine-mesh strainer is ideal for this job. Liquids must be strained into a clean bowl or pot. The sturdy, deep, relatively narrow bowl of a standing mixer is a perfect receptacle.

Dutch oven or stockpot: Stock should be made in a pot large enough to accommodate plenty of bones, meat, aromatics, and water. Whether you use a Dutch oven or stockpot, choose a lidded pot with a capacity of at least 8 quarts.

Colander: Before straining the stock, transfer the bones and large pieces of meat to a colander. This helps to prevent splashing when pouring the liquid through the strainer. Any type of colander will do—just be sure to place it over a bowl.

Meat cleaver: Hacking chicken parts into small pieces allows their flavorful juices to release quickly into the stock, significantly reducing the total simmering time. Rather than risk damaging your chef's knife, use a meat cleaver, which is designed to cut through bones.

Skimmer: A skimmer is a wide, flat, perforated spoon with a long handle. It is the best tool for skimming impurities and foam that rise to the surface of a stock as it cooks. If a skimmer is not available, a large slotted spoon works well, too.

USING THE RIGHT INGREDIENTS

Choosing Chicken

In kitchen tests, we found that stocks made with kosher or premium chickens (we like Bell & Evans) tasted better and had more body than stocks made with mass-market birds. Our advice: If you have a favorite chicken for roasting, use it for stock.

Cutting up chicken parts: Chicken hacked into small pieces with a meat cleaver will give up its flavor in record time. To cut through bone, place your hand near the far end of the meat cleaver handle, curling your fingers securely around it in a fist. Handle the cleaver the way you would a hammer, holding your wrist stiff and straight and letting the weight of the blade's front tip lead the force of the chop. If you cannot chop the bone in one strike, place the cleaver in the groove of the first chop, then strike the blade's blunt edge with a heavy mallet.

Choosing Beef

We made six stocks with six different cuts of beef, including the chuck, shanks, round, arm blades, oxtails, and short ribs. We added marrowbones to the boneless cuts to establish an equal meat-to-bone ratio in each pot and simmered the bone-in cuts as is. Tasters liked the stock made from shanks best. In addition to using the right cut, we found that the best stock is made with a lot of beef. Most recipes skimp on the beef, but we found that a full six pounds of shanks is required to make two quarts of rich-tasting stock.

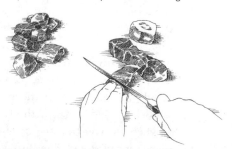

Cutting meat from shank bones: Cut the meat away from the shank bone into large 2-inch chunks.

QUICKER CHICKEN OR BEEF STOCK, STEP BY STEP

FREEZING STOCK EFFICIENTLY

1. Sauté. Onions are a must for any stock, but cooking tests proved that carrots and celery aren't vital.

2. Sweat. Browning the chicken or beef and then sweating it (cooking over low heat in a covered pot) allows the meat to release its rich, flavorful juices quickly, thus reducing the simmering time greatly.

3. Simmer. Add boiling water (to jump-start the cooking process), bay leaves (other herbs don't add much flavor), and salt.

4. Skim. Skimming away the foam that rises to the surface of beef stock significantly improves its flavor. Skimming chicken stock will make it clearer, but the flavor improvement is less noticeable.

5. Strain. Once the flavor has been extracted from the stock ingredients, a skimmer or slotted spoon can be used to remove them to a colander. Then pour the stock through a fine-mesh strainer or a colander lined with cheesecloth.

6. Defat. After stock has been refrigerated, the fat hardens on the surface and is very easy to remove with a spoon. To defat hot stock, we recommend using a ladle or a fat separator.

Ladle cooled stock into nonstick muffin tins and freeze. When the stock is frozen, twist the muffin tin just as you would twist an ice tray. Place the frozen blocks in a zipper-lock plastic bag and seal it tightly. Store the bag in the freezer.

1. An alternative is to pour stock into a coffee mug lined with a quart-size plastic zipper-lock bag.

2. Place the filled bags flat in a large, shallow roasting pan and freeze. Once the stock is solidly frozen, the bags can be removed from the pan and stored in the freezer.

Chicken Stock

MAKES ABOUT 2 QUARTS

If you use a cleaver, you will be able to cut up the chicken parts quickly. A chef's knife or kitchen shears will also work, albeit more slowly. See the illustration and tips on page 34 for using a cleaver.

I   tablespoon vegetable oil
I   medium onion, cut into medium dice
4   pounds chicken backs and wingtips or whole legs, hacked with a meat cleaver into 2-inch pieces
2   quarts boiling water
2   teaspoons salt
2   bay leaves

1. Heat the oil in a large stockpot or Dutch oven. Add the onion; sauté until colored and softened slightly, 2 to 3 minutes. Transfer the onion to a large bowl.

2. Add half the chicken pieces to the pot; sauté until no longer pink, 4 to 5 minutes. Transfer the cooked chicken to the bowl with the onion. Sauté the remaining chicken pieces. Return the onion and chicken pieces to the pot. Reduce the heat to low, cover, and cook until the chicken releases its juices, about 20 minutes.

3. Increase the heat to high; add the boiling water, salt, and bay leaves. Return to a simmer, then cover and barely simmer until the stock is rich and flavorful, about 20 minutes.

4. Strain the stock into a container and discard the solids. Skim the fat and reserve for later use in soups or other recipes, if desired. (The stock can be covered and refrigerated for up to 2 days or frozen for several months.)

➤ VARIATION

Chicken Stock with Sautéed Breast Meat
Make this stock when you want to have some breast meat to add to soup. This recipe starts with a whole chicken.

I   tablespoon vegetable oil
I   whole chicken (about 3½ pounds), breast removed, split, and reserved; remaining chicken hacked with a meat cleaver into 2-inch pieces

I   medium onion, cut into medium dice
2   quarts boiling water
2   teaspoons salt
2   bay leaves

1. Heat the oil in a large stockpot or Dutch oven. When the oil shimmers, add the chicken breast halves; sauté until browned on both sides, about 5 minutes. Remove the chicken breast pieces and set aside. Add the onion to the pot; sauté until colored and softened slightly, 2 to 3 minutes. Transfer the onion to a large bowl.

2. Add half the chicken pieces to the pot; sauté until no longer pink, 4 to 5 minutes. Transfer the cooked chicken to the bowl with the onion. Sauté the remaining chicken pieces. Return the onion and chicken pieces (excluding the breasts) to the pot. Reduce the heat to low, cover, and cook until the chicken releases its juices, about 20 minutes.

3. Increase the heat to high; add the boiling water, the reserved sautéed chicken breasts, the salt, and bay leaves. Return to a simmer, then cover and barely simmer until the chicken breasts are cooked through and the stock is rich and flavorful, about 20 minutes.

4. Remove the chicken breasts from the pot; when cool enough to handle, remove the skin from the breasts, then remove the meat from the bones and shred into bite-size pieces; discard the skin and bones. Strain the stock into a container and discard the solids. Skim the fat and reserve for later use in soups or other recipes. (The shredded chicken and stock can be covered and refrigerated separately for up to 2 days.)

Chicken Noodle Soup

SERVES 6 TO 8

Once we figured out how to make good chicken stock, making chicken noodle soup was incredibly easy.

2   tablespoons chicken fat (reserved from making stock) or vegetable oil
I   medium onion, cut into medium dice
I   large carrot, peeled and sliced ¼ inch thick
I   celery rib, sliced ¼ inch thick
½   teaspoon dried thyme

1 recipe Chicken Stock with Sautéed Breast
   Meat (page 36)
2 cups (3 ounces) wide egg noodles
¼ cup minced fresh parsley leaves
   Ground black pepper

1. Heat the chicken fat in a large stockpot or Dutch oven over medium-high heat. Add the onion, carrot, and celery; sauté until softened, about 5 minutes. Add the thyme, along with the stock and shredded chicken meat; simmer until the vegetables are tender and the flavors meld, 10 to 15 minutes.

2. Add the noodles and cook until just tender, about 5 minutes. Stir in the parsley and pepper to taste, adjust the seasonings, and serve.

➤ VARIATIONS

Chicken Soup with Orzo and Spring Vegetables

Follow the recipe for Chicken Noodle Soup, replacing the onion with 1 medium leek, rinsed thoroughly, quartered lengthwise, and sliced thin crosswise. Substitute ½ cup orzo for the egg noodles. Along with the orzo, add ¼ pound asparagus, trimmed and cut into 1-inch lengths, and ¼ cup fresh or frozen peas. Substitute 2 tablespoons minced fresh tarragon leaves for the parsley.

Chicken Soup with Shells, Tomatoes, and Zucchini

Follow the recipe for Chicken Noodle Soup, adding 1 medium zucchini, cut into medium dice, with the onion, carrot, and celery, and increase the sautéing time to 7 minutes. Add ½ cup chopped tomatoes (fresh or canned) with the stock. Substitute 1 cup small shells or macaroni for the egg noodles and simmer until the pasta is cooked, about 10 minutes. Substitute an equal portion of minced fresh basil leaves for the parsley. Serve with freshly grated Parmesan, if desired.

RICH BEEF STOCK

BEEF STOCK SHOULD TASTE LIKE BEEF—almost as intense as pot roast jus or beef stew broth—and be flavorful enough to need only a few vegetables and a handful of noodles or barley to make a good soup. We didn't want a stock that demanded a trip to the butcher, nor did we want to spend all day making it.

We began our testing by making a traditional stock, using four pounds of beef bones fortified with a generous two pounds of beef, as well as celery, carrot, onion, tomato, and fresh thyme, all covered with four quarts of water. Our plan was to taste the stock after 4, 6, 8, 12, and 16 hours of simmering.

At hours 4, 6, and even 8, our stock was weak and tasted mostly of vegetables. And while the texture of the 12- and 16-hour stocks was richly gelatinous, the flavors of vegetables and bones (not beef) predominated. Not willing to give up on this method quite yet, we found a recipe that instructed us to roast and then simmer beef bones, onions, and tomatoes—no celery and carrots—for 12 hours. During the last three hours of cooking, three pounds of beef were added to the pot. This, we thought, could be our ideal—a stock with great body from the bones, minimal vegetable flavor, and generous hunks of beef to enhance the rich, reduced stock. Once again, however, the stock was beautifully textured, but with very little flavor; the vegetal taste was gone, but there was no real, deep beef flavor in its place. Time to move on.

Knowing now that it was going to take more meat than bones to get great flavor, we started our next set of tests by making stocks with different cuts of meat, including chuck, shank, round, arm blade, oxtail, and short ribs. We browned two pounds of meat and one pound of small marrow-bones (or three pounds bone-in cuts like shank, short ribs, and oxtails), along with an onion. We covered the browned ingredients and let them sweat for 20 minutes. We added only a quart of water to each pot and simmered them until the meat in each pot was done.

With so little added water, these stocks were more braise-like than stock-like. But because more traditional methods yielded bland stocks, we decided to start with the flavor we were looking for and add water from there.

After a 1½-hour simmer, our stocks were done, most tasting unmistakably beefy. Upon a blind tasting of each, we all agreed that the shank broth was our favorite, followed by the marrowbone-enhanced brisket and chuck. Not only was the stock rich, beefy, and full of body, but the shank meat was soft and gelatinous, perfect for shredding and adding to a pot of soup. Because it appeared that our stock was going to require a generous amount of meat, brisket's high price ($3.99 per pound compared with $1.99 for both the shank and chuck) knocked it out of the running.

Though not yet perfect, this stock was on its way to fulfilling our requirements. What we sacrificed in vegetables, however, we were apparently going to have to compensate for in meat. Our two pounds of meat were yielding only one quart of stock. But now that we had a flavor we liked, we decided to see if we could achieve an equally beefy stock with less meat.

To stretch the meat a bit further, we increased the amount of meat and bones by 50 percent and doubled the amount of water. Unfortunately, the extra water diluted the meat flavor, and though this stock was better than many we had tried, we missed the strong beef flavor of our original formula. To intensify the flavor, we tried adding a pound of ground beef to the three pounds of meat, thinking we would throw away the spent meat during straining. But ground beef only fattened up the stock, and its distinctive hamburger flavor muddied the waters. Also, fried ground beef does not brown well, and this burger-enhanced version confirmed that browning the meat-and-bones combination not only deepened the color but beefed up the flavor as well.

We went back to the original proportions, doubling both the meat and bones as well as the water. Not surprisingly, the stock was deeply colored, richly flavored, and full-bodied. We were finally convinced that a good beef stock requires a generous portion of meat. Though our stock required more meat than was necessary for the soup, the leftover beef was delicious, good for sandwiches and cold salads.

At this point, our richly flavored stock needed enlivening. Some recipes accomplished this with a splash of vinegar, others with tomato. Although we liked tomatoes in many of the soups we developed, they didn't do much for our stock. And while vinegar was an improvement, a modest one-half cup red wine, added to the kettle after browning the meat, made the final product even better. At last, we'd achieved our goal: richly flavored beef stock using cuts of beef from the supermarket (instead of a special trip to the butcher), just one pot, and just under 2 hours (rather than all day) at the stove.

SCIENCE: So Much Beef, So Little Flavor

Before we actually began testing, we would not have believed how much meat was required to make a rich, beef-flavored stock. Why, we wondered, did a good beef soup require six pounds of beef and bones when a mere three-pound chicken could beautifully flavor the same size pot of soup?

Though we had always thought of beef as the heartier-flavored meat, we began to understand chicken's strength when making beef stocks. In one of our timesaving beef stock experiments, we used the four pounds of beef called for in the recipe, but substituted two pounds of quicker-cooking hacked-up chicken bones for the beef bones. The result was surprising. Even with twice as much meaty beef as chicken bones, the chicken flavor predominated.

So what's happening here? Appearances aside, the flavor compounds in chicken are very strong, possibly stronger than those of beef. It's the browning or searing that contributes much of the robust beefy flavor to a good steak or stew. (Think how bland boiled beef tastes.) Skin and bones may be another reason why less chicken is required to flavor a stock. Chicken skin, predominantly fat, tastes like the animal. Beef fat, on the other hand, tastes "rich" but not beefy, as evidenced by French fries cooked in beef tallow. In addition, chicken bones, filled with rich, dark marrow, also contribute flavor. Beef bones, on the other hand, lend incredible body to stocks and broths, but their flavor is predominantly and unmistakably that of bone, not of beef.

Finally, according to the U.S. Department of Agriculture, chicken contains more water than beef—61 percent in chuck compared with 77 percent in drumsticks and 73 to 74 percent for wings and backs. This means that when simmered, chicken is releasing 11 to 16 percent more liquid—and flavor—into the pot.

Rich Beef Stock

MAKES ABOUT 2 QUARTS

If using shanks for your stock, cut the meat away from the bones in the largest possible pieces. See page 34 for tips on cutting the meat. Both meat and bones contribute flavor to the final product. You will use only half the meat in the recipes that follow. Refrigerate the remaining meat in an airtight container and use it in sandwiches or cold salads.

1–2	tablespoons vegetable oil
6	pounds beef shanks, meat cut from the bones in large chunks, or 4 pounds chuck and 2 pounds small marrowbones
1	large onion, halved
1/2	cup dry red wine
2	quarts boiling water
1/2	teaspoon salt

1. Heat 1 tablespoon oil in a large stockpot or Dutch oven over medium-high heat; brown the meat, bones, and onion halves on all sides in batches, making sure not to overcrowd the pan and adding additional oil to the pan if necessary. Remove the contents and set aside. Add the red wine to the empty pot; cook until reduced to a syrup, 1 to 2 minutes. Return the browned bones, meat, and onion to the pot. Reduce the heat to low, then cover and sweat the meat and onion until they have released about 3/4 cup dark, very intensely flavored liquid, about 20 minutes. Increase the heat to medium-high and add the water and salt; bring to a simmer, reduce the heat to very low, partially cover, and barely simmer until the meat is tender, 1 1/2 to 2 hours.

2. Strain the stock into a container, discard the bones and onion, and set the meat aside, reserving half of the meat for another use. (At this point, the stock and remaining meat that will be used in the soup can be cooled to room temperature and covered and refrigerated for up to 5 days.) Let the stock stand until fat rises to the top; skim the fat and discard. When the meat is cool enough to handle, shred into bite-size pieces for use in soup.

BEEF NOODLE SOUP

BEEF NOODLE SOUP IS A LOT LIKE CHICKEN Noodle Soup (page 36). Once you've made home-made stock (and reserved the cooked meat), you've done 90 percent of the work involved in making the soup. We assumed the noodle issues here would be similar to those covered in our discussion of chicken noodle soup but wondered if the vegetable choices might be different.

As with chicken noodle soup, sautéed onion, carrot, and celery proved to provide an excellent base for beef noodle soup. Sautéing the vegetables brought out their flavors and gave the soup more depth.

Thyme and parsley, the duo that worked so successfully in chicken noodle soup, played the same role in this soup. The thyme was added early in the process so its robust flavor could infuse the stock evenly. The parsley was added just before serving to preserve its freshness.

Many beef soups contain some canned diced tomatoes. We found that the tomatoes add complexity and some acidity, which helps balance the richness of the beef stock. While tomatoes can take over in chicken noodle soup, they act as a team player in beef soup when used in moderation.

As expected, we liked dried egg noodles best in this soup. Dried linguine and spaghetti were too chewy, and fresh fettuccine lacked the wavy ridges needed to trap bits of vegetables. While fine, extra-broad, or home-style noodles work well in chicken noodle soup, depending on your inclination, hearty beef soup calls out for extra-broad or home-style noodles. The large chunks of meat work better with the wider noodles.

As with chicken noodle soup, we found that the noodles taste best when cooked in the beef soup rather than in a separate pot of salted water. Although you can make the stock for this soup weeks in advance, it's best to assemble beef noodle soup at the last minute. The pasta doesn't hold well and will absorb most of the liquid if you try to keep the soup to reheat at another time.

Beef Noodle Soup

SERVES 6

Our beef stock is the basis of this quick noodle soup. The soup is best served as soon as the noodles are tender. Don't try to refrigerate leftovers. With time, the noodles will absorb more liquid and make the soup more like a stew. If you plan on having leftovers, prepare the recipe through step 1, reserve the portion you want to save for another day, and then cook a portion of the noodles in the remaining soup.

1	tablespoon vegetable oil
1	medium onion, chopped medium
2	medium carrots, chopped medium
1	celery rib, chopped medium
1/2	teaspoon dried thyme
1/2	cup drained canned diced tomatoes
2	quarts Rich Beef Stock (page 39), strained and skimmed of fat, plus 2 cups meat shredded into bite-size pieces
2	cups (3 ounces) extra-broad or home-style egg noodles
1/4	cup minced fresh parsley leaves
	Salt and ground black pepper

1. Heat the oil in a large stockpot or Dutch oven over medium-high heat. Add the onion, carrots, and celery and sauté until softened, about 5 minutes. Add the thyme, tomatoes, stock, and meat. Bring to a boil, reduce the heat, and simmer until the vegetables are tender and the flavors meld, 10 to 15 minutes.

2. Stir in the noodles and cook until just tender, about 8 minutes. Stir in the parsley and salt and pepper to taste. Serve immediately.

➤ VARIATIONS

Beef Noodle Soup with Spinach and Mushrooms

Cremini mushrooms add more flavor than button mushrooms, but either can be used.

Follow the recipe for Beef Noodle Soup, omitting the celery and sautéing the onion and carrots. After 5 minutes, when the vegetables have softened, add 1 more tablespoon oil and 12 ounces thinly sliced mushrooms to the pan. Sauté the vegetables until the mushrooms soften and the liquid they throw off evaporates, 4 to 5 minutes. In step 2, when the noodles have finished cooking, stir in 10 ounces finely chopped spinach leaves and cook until the spinach just wilts, about 1 minute.

Beef Noodle Soup with Peas and Parsnips

Diced parsnips and a handful of frozen peas add sweetness and color to the basic combination.

Follow the recipe for Beef Noodle Soup, substituting 1/2 cup medium-chopped parsnips for the celery. In step 2, cook the noodles until almost tender, about 6 minutes, then add 1 cup thawed frozen peas and cook until the noodles are just tender and the peas are heated through, about 2 minutes.

Beef Barley Soup with Mushrooms

This thick soup often includes fresh dill. If you like, substitute 1 to 2 tablespoons minced fresh dill for the parsley.

Follow the recipe for Beef Noodle Soup, omitting the celery and sautéing the onion and carrots. After 5 minutes, when the vegetables have softened, add 1 more tablespoon oil and 12 ounces thinly sliced cremini or white mushrooms to the pan. Sauté until the mushrooms soften and the liquid they throw off evaporates, 4 to 5 minutes. Add the thyme, tomatoes, stock, meat, and 1/2 cup pearl barley. Bring to a boil, reduce the heat, and simmer until the vegetables and barley are tender, about 45 minutes. Omit the noodles and proceed as directed.

SOUTHEAST ASIAN RICE NOODLE SOUP WITH BEEF

A GOOD SOUTHEAST ASIAN NOODLE SOUP (the kind you get in a Vietnamese or Thai restaurant) starts with a homemade stock flavored with Asian spices and sauces. The stock is rich but not heavy and is filled with fettuccine-width rice noodles, maybe some paper-thin and barely cooked slices of beef, angled scallion slices, crisp bean sprouts, and lots of whole fresh mint, basil, and/or cilantro leaves.

This kind of soup is a terrific strategy for an everyday, home-cooked, one-pot meal that tastes anything but everyday. But we kept running into the inescapable fact that a stock of this caliber is impractical because it has to cook for several hours.

Faced with this dilemma in Western-style soups, it's often possible to substitute canned broth, even though it's no match for homemade. Western soups, like many of those in this book, are typically set up like a stew—sauté aromatics, add liquid and whatever major ingredient, season with herbs, and simmer for at least half an hour to cook the ingredients through and marry the flavors. By the time the soup is cooked, the flavor of the liquid has been substantially transformed by the ingredients cooked in it.

Unfortunately, this model doesn't work for Southeast Asian soups, which are generally collections of raw and cooked ingredients added to the bowl at the last minute, like a garnish, with little or no secondary cooking. So whereas the ingredients of a leek and potato soup are cooked until the edges of the flavors soften and merge, Southeast Asian soups are structured in a way that allows the flavorings to remain distinct and separate, just as they do in a stir-fry.

It seemed to us that the Southeast Asian model might be well suited to the use of canned broth, but for entirely different reasons. What if we cooked strong flavorings, such as garlic and ginger, in the broth before it was ladled into bowls? Could we punch up and disguise the pallid flavor of the canned broth? It was time to put our research to the test in the kitchen.

From past tastings, we knew that canned chicken broth is superior to canned beef broth. Starting with chicken broth, we added chopped garlic and fresh ginger and simmered it for 20 minutes. The flavor of the broth was immeasurably improved, but we wanted to do less work. So instead of chopping, we merely crushed medallions of ginger and whole garlic cloves with the side of a chef's knife before simmering them in the canned broth; the result tasted just as good.

With this base to build on, we experimented with other ingredients to figure out how to get the taste we were looking for. We found that soy and fish sauces added much-needed body and depth of flavor; fish sauce, in particular, added just the right combination of salt and a musky sweetness. Cinnamon sticks and star anise were also appropriate and tasty additions, especially when paired with beef.

TIPS ON STORING AND REHEATING SOUPS

Unless otherwise specified, all the soups in this book can be refrigerated for several days or frozen for several months. Store soup that has been cooled to lukewarm in an airtight container. When ready to serve, reheat only as much soup as you need at that time. You can reheat soup in the microwave or in a covered saucepan set over medium-low heat. Because the microwave heats unevenly, this method is best for single servings. Just heat the soup right in the serving bowl or mug. Larger quantities of soup are best reheated on the stovetop.

You may find that the soup has thickened in the refrigerator or freezer. (As soups cool, liquid evaporates in the form of steam.) Simply thin out the soup with a little water to achieve the proper texture

While most soups can be cooled, then reheated without harm, some will suffer, especially in terms of texture. Soups with rice and pasta are best eaten immediately; when refrigerated, rice and pasta become mushy and bloated as they absorb the liquid in the soup. If you plan on having leftovers, cool the soup before adding the rice or pasta, which is often the last step in most recipes. Add a portion of the rice or pasta to the soup you plan on eating immediately, then add the rest when you reheat the remaining soup.

Typically, soups with seafood also fail to hold up well when stored. For instance, clams will almost always overcook and become tough when reheated. Anticipate serving seafood soups as soon as they are done.

Lastly, pureed soups made from green vegetables will look their best if served immediately upon completion as well. Reheating breaks down the chlorophyll in some green vegetables (asparagus is especially prone to this problem). A soup that is bright green can turn drab army green if stored for several hours and then reheated. These soups will still taste delicious, but their visual appeal will be greatly diminished.

Satisfied with the broth, we turned our attention to the noodles. We found that boiled noodles, especially thin rice vermicelli, had a tendency to get mushy and, if left in the hot soup for any length of time, broke apart. Ultimately, we settled on soaking the noodles in boiling water—a fine distinction that did not overcook them. We drained the noodles when they had softened to the point that they were tender but still had tooth. Thin rice vermicelli requires just 5 or 10 minutes of soaking. Thicker rice noodles (about the width of linguine or narrow fettuc-cine) take 10 to 15 minutes to soften.

Southeast Asian Rice Noodle Soup with Beef

SERVES 4

For this soup, be sure to have all the vegetables and herbs at hand ready for serving. Although the broth can be made in advance, the soup must be served as soon as the recipe is completed.

BROTH

5   cups low-sodium chicken broth
4   medium garlic cloves, smashed
    and peeled
I   (2-inch) piece fresh ginger, peeled, cut
    into 1/8-inch rounds, and smashed
2   (3-inch) cinnamon sticks
2   star anise pods

2   tablespoons fish sauce
I   tablespoon soy sauce
I   tablespoon sugar

SOUP

6   ounces thick rice noodles
12 ounces flank steak, sliced across the grain
    into 1/4-inch strips (see the illustrations
    below)
    Salt and ground black pepper
I   tablespoon vegetable oil
2   cups mung bean sprouts
I   medium jalapeño chile, stemmed, seeded, and
    sliced thin
2   scallions, white and green parts, sliced thin on
    the diagonal
1/3 cup loosely packed basil leaves, torn in half if
    large
1/2 cup loosely packed fresh mint leaves, torn in
    half if large
1/2 cup loosely packed fresh cilantro leaves
2   tablespoons chopped unsalted roasted
    peanuts
    Lime wedges

1. FOR THE BROTH: Bring all of the ingredients to a boil in a medium saucepan over medium-high heat. Reduce the heat to low and simmer, partially covered, to blend the flavors, about 20 minutes. Remove the solids with a slotted spoon and dis-card. Cover to keep warm, then set aside while

SLICING FLANK STEAK

1. To make cutting flank steak easier, place the meat in the freezer for 15 minutes. Once the meat is firm, slice it lengthwise into 2-inch-wide pieces.

2. Cut each 2-inch piece across the grain into very thin slices, not more than 1/4 inch thick.

you prepare the soup or refrigerate in an airtight container for up to 1 day.

2. FOR THE SOUP: Bring 4 quarts water to a boil in a large pot. Off the heat, add the rice noodles and let stand, stirring occasionally, until tender, 10 to 15 minutes. Drain and distribute the noodles among 4 soup bowls.

3. If necessary, reheat the broth in a medium saucepan. Cover and keep warm over low heat.

4. Season the steak slices with salt and pepper to taste. Heat the oil in a medium skillet over medium-high heat until shimmering. Add half of the steak slices in a single layer and sear until well browned, 1 to 2 minutes on each side; set aside. Repeat with the remaining slices.

5. Divide the bean sprouts and beef among the soup bowls. Ladle the hot broth into the bowls and sprinkle with the chile, scallions, herbs, and peanuts. Serve immediately, passing the lime wedges separately.

FRENCH ONION SOUP

FRENCH ONION SOUP SHOULD HAVE A DARK, rich broth, intensely flavored by a plethora of seriously cooked onions and covered by a slice of French bread that is broth-soaked beneath and cheesy and crusty on top. Unfortunately over the years, we had consumed many crocks of flavorless onions floating in hypersalty beef bouillon and topped with globs of greasy melted cheese. We also had eaten weak, watery soups. We set out to develop a soup to obliterate these bad memories.

The first obstacle to success is the base. This soup is most commonly made with homemade beef stock. If the right stock is used (see Rich Beef Stock on page 39), the results can be delicious. But making beef stock takes at least three hours. We wondered if there was a way to get around this step.

We tested soups made with homemade chicken stock (which takes considerably less time to prepare than beef stock) and canned broth. Both were, well, too chickeny and just not right. Soups made with canned beef broth were terrible. Commercial beef broth does not have enough flavor to carry

the day alone. After experimentation, we devised a formula for what we call "cheater" broth. By combining canned beef and chicken broths with red wine (the secret ingredient here), we came up with a broth that has enough good, rich flavor to make an excellent soup base.

The next obvious step was to examine the onion factor. We found Vidalias to be disappointingly bland and boring, white onions to be candy-sweet and one-dimensional, and yellow onions to be only mildly flavorful, with just a slight sweetness. Red onions ranked supreme. They were intensely oniony, sweet but not cloying, with subtle complexity and nuance.

It was exasperating that the onions took so long—nearly an hour—to caramelize. On top of that, they required frequent stirring to keep them from sticking to the bottom of the pot and burning. We found that adding salt to the onions as they began to cook helped draw out some of the water and shaved about 10 minutes off the cooking time, but this didn't seem to be our answer. We also tried roasting the onions, thinking that the even, constant heat of the oven might be the answer. Wrong again. Going in and out of the oven to stir the onions is an incredible hassle.

It was inattentiveness that caused us to let the drippings in the pot of a batch of onions go a little too far. The onions themselves weren't thoroughly caramelized, but all the goo stuck on the pot was. We were sure that the finished soup would taste burnt, but we were surprised to find that it was, in fact, as sweet, rich, and flavorful as the soups we had been making with fully caramelized onions. To refine the technique we had stumbled on, we decided that medium-high heat was the way to go and that the drippings should be very, very deeply browned. There's no way around frequent stirring, but this method cut about another 10 minutes off the onion-cooking time, bringing it down to just over 30 minutes.

With all those wonderful, tasty drippings stuck on the bottom of the pot, the deglazing process of adding the liquid and scraping up all the browned bits is crucial. Once the broth is added to the onions, a simmering time of 20 minutes is needed to allow the onion flavor to permeate the broth and the flavors to meld.

Many French onion soup recipes call for herbs. A couple of sprigs of fresh parsley, some thyme, and a bay leaf simmered in the soup rounded out the flavors and imparted freshness. Having arrived at a soup that was rich, well-balanced, and full of fabulous onion flavor, it was time to move on to the bread and the cheese.

Some recipes call for placing the bread in the bottom of the bowl and ladling the soup over it. We disagree. We opt to set the bread on top, so that only the bottom of the slice is moistened with broth while its top is crusted with cheese. The bread can then physically support the cheese and prevent it from sinking into the soup. To keep as much cheese as possible on the surface, we found it best to use two slices of bread to fill the mouth of the bowl completely. A baguette can be cut on the bias as necessary to secure the closest fit in the bowl.

Traditionally, French onion soup is topped with Swiss, Gruyère, or Emmentaler. We also ventured across the border to try Asiago. Plain Swiss cheese was neither outstanding nor offensive. It was gooey, bubbly, and mild in characteristic Swiss flavor. Both Gruyère and Emmentaler melted to perfection and were sweet, nutty, and faintly tangy, but they also were very strong and pungent, overwhelming many tasters' palettes.

We surprised ourselves by favoring the subdued Italian Asiago. Its flavor, like that of Gruyère and Emmentaler, was sweet and nutty, but without the pungent quality.

Asiago is a dry, not a "melting," cheese, so although we were leaning toward it in flavor, we were left wanting in texture. The obvious answer

was to combine cheeses. We tried a layer of Swiss topped with a grating of Asiago: a winning combination, hands down, of chewy goodness and nutty sweetness.

The final coup that weakens knees and makes French onion soup irresistible is a browned, bubbly, molten cheese crust. The quickest way to brown the cheese is to set the bowls on a baking sheet under the broiler, making heat-safe bowls essential. Bowls or crocks with handles make maneuvering easier. This is no soup for fine china.

French Onion Soup
SERVES 6

For a soup that is resplendent with deep, rich flavors, use 8 cups of Rich Beef Stock (page 39) in place of the canned chicken and beef broths and red wine. Tie the parsley and thyme sprigs together with kitchen twine so they will be easy to retrieve from the soup pot. Slicing the baguette on the bias will yield slices shaped to fill the mouths of the bowls.

SOUP
2	tablespoons unsalted butter
5	medium red onions (about 3 pounds), sliced thin
	Salt
6	cups low-sodium chicken broth
1¾	cups low-sodium beef broth
¼	cup dry red wine
2	sprigs fresh parsley
1	sprig fresh thyme
1	bay leaf
1	tablespoon balsamic vinegar
	Ground black pepper

SCIENCE: Why Do Onions Make You Cry?

The problem is caused by the sulfuric compounds in onions. When an onion is cut, the cells that are damaged in the process release sulfuric compounds as well as various enzymes, notably one called sulfoxide lyase. Those compounds, which are separated in the onion's cell structure, activate and mix to form the real culprit, a volatile new compound called thiopropanal sulfoxide. When thiopropanal sulfoxide evaporates into the air, it irritates the eyes, causing us to cry.

To combat this problem in the test kitchen, we found that protecting our eyes, covering them with goggles (yes, we know that sounds silly) or contact lenses, worked. The goggles and contact lenses form a physical barrier that keeps the gases from irritating our eyes. Introducing a flame from either a lit candle or a gas burner will also change the activity of the thiopropanal sulfoxide by completely oxidizing it.

CHEESE-TOPPED CRUSTS

1   baguette, cut on the bias into ¾-inch slices
    (2 slices per serving)
4½ ounces Swiss cheese, sliced ¹/₁₆ inch thick
3   ounces Asiago cheese, freshly grated (about
    1½ cups)

1. FOR THE SOUP: Melt the butter in a large stockpot or Dutch oven over medium-high heat; add the sliced onions and ½ teaspoon salt and stir to coat the onions thoroughly with the butter. Cook, stirring frequently, until the onions are reduced and syrupy and the inside of the pot is coated with a very deep brown crust, 30 to 35 minutes. Stir in the chicken and beef broths, red wine, parsley, thyme, and bay leaf, scraping the pot bottom with a wooden spoon to loosen the browned bits, and bring to a simmer. Simmer to blend the flavors, about 20 minutes, and discard the herbs. Stir in the balsamic vinegar and adjust the seasonings with salt and pepper. (The soup can be cooled to room temperature and refrigerated in an airtight container for up to 2 days; return to a simmer before finishing the soup with the bread and cheese.)

2. FOR THE CRUSTS: Adjust an oven rack to the upper-middle position; heat the broiler. Set heat-safe soup bowls or crocks on a baking sheet; fill each with about 1½ cups soup. Top each bowl with 2 baguette slices and divide the Swiss cheese slices, placing them in a single layer, if possible, on the bread. Sprinkle with about 2 tablespoons grated Asiago and broil until well browned and bubbly, about 10 minutes. Cool 5 minutes and serve.

CREAM OF TOMATO SOUP

FEW OF US REALLY EAT CANNED TOMATO SOUP these days, but some of us do share nostalgia for Campbell's cream of tomato soup. Our vision was a soup of Polartec softness, rich color, and a pleasing balance of sweetness and acidity.

To get a good dose of reality, we opened a can of Campbell's. Though rich and tomatoey, it was also cloyingly sweet, not unlike a cream of ketchup soup. So we moved on to developing a soup that would actually be as good as we remembered.

We began our testing with canned tomatoes, wanting this to be a soup that could be made any time of the year, not just during the two months of the year when fresh tomatoes are in their prime. We selected fine canned organic diced tomatoes and added shallots, a bit of flour to give the finished product some body, a spoonful of tomato paste and canned chicken broth to enrich the flavor, a splash of heavy cream and sherry for refinement, and a pinch of sugar for good measure. Though the resulting soup was OK, it failed to make the cut; the flavor simply wasn't robust enough.

How do you get bigger flavor from canned tomatoes? If they were fresh and ripe, you might roast them: The caramelization of sugar in the skins that occurs during roasting concentrates and intensifies the flavors. In the test kitchen, where any experiment is considered worth trying, we decided to roast canned tomatoes. We hoped that intense dry heat might evaporate the surface liquid and concentrate the flavor.

Leaving the above recipe otherwise unchanged, we switched from diced to whole tomatoes for ease of handling, drained and seeded them (reserving the juice for later), and then arranged them on a foil-covered rimmed baking sheet and sprinkled them with brown sugar, which we hoped would induce a surface caramelization. Only minutes after sliding our tray of tomatoes into a 450-degree oven, the test kitchen was filled with real tomato fragrance, and we knew we had done something right. The roasting made an extraordinary difference, intensifying the tomato flavor and mellowing the fruit's acidity. The rest of the soup could be prepared while the tomatoes roasted, knocking down the overall preparation time to about 20 minutes.

Only one minor visual detail marred our efforts. The intense flavor we'd achieved by roasting the tomatoes was not mirrored in the soup's color. The deep coronation red we admired while the soup simmered on the stovetop gave way to a faded circus orange following a round in the blender. The mechanical action of combining solids and liquids had aerated the soup and lightened the color. This wouldn't do. We decided to leave the rich tomato broth behind in the saucepan while pureeing the solids with just enough liquid to result in a soup of perfect smoothness. A finish of heavy cream and our vision of tomato soup had come to life.

Cream of Tomato Soup

SERVES 4

Make sure to use canned whole tomatoes that are not packed in puree; you will need some of the juice to make the soup. Buttered or Garlic Croutons on page 48 make a nice accompaniment, as does a grilled cheese sandwich for a heartier meal.

2	(28-ounce) cans whole tomatoes packed in juice, drained, 3 cups juice reserved
1½	tablespoons dark brown sugar
4	tablespoons (½ stick) unsalted butter
4	large shallots, minced
1	tablespoon tomato paste
	Pinch ground allspice
2	tablespoons all-purpose flour
1¾	cups low-sodium chicken broth
½	cup heavy cream
2	tablespoons brandy or dry sherry
	Salt and cayenne pepper

1. Adjust an oven rack to the upper-middle position and heat the oven to 450 degrees. Line a rimmed baking sheet with foil. Seed the tomatoes and spread in a single layer on the foil (see the illustrations below). Sprinkle evenly with the brown sugar. Bake until all the liquid has evaporated and the tomatoes begin to color, about 30 minutes. Let the tomatoes cool slightly, then peel them off the foil; transfer to a small bowl and set aside.

2. Heat the butter in a large saucepan over medium heat until foaming. Add the shallots, tomato paste, and allspice. Reduce the heat to low, cover, and cook, stirring occasionally, until the shallots are softened, 7 to 10 minutes. Add the flour and cook, stirring constantly, until thoroughly combined, about 30 seconds. Whisking constantly, gradually add the chicken broth; stir in the reserved tomato juice and the roasted tomatoes. Cover, increase the heat to medium, and bring to a boil. Reduce the heat to low and simmer, stirring occasionally, to blend the flavors, about 10 minutes.

3. Strain the mixture into a medium bowl; rinse out the saucepan. Transfer the tomatoes and solids in the strainer to a blender; add 1 cup of the strained liquid and puree until smooth. Combine the pureed mixture and remaining strained liquid in the saucepan. Add the cream and warm over low heat until hot, about 3 minutes. Off the heat, stir in the brandy and season with salt and cayenne to taste. Serve immediately. (The soup can be refrigerated in an airtight container for 2 days. Warm over low heat until hot; do not boil.)

PREPARING TOMATOES FOR ROASTING

1. With your fingers, carefully open the whole tomatoes over a strainer set in a bowl and push out the seeds, allowing the juices to fall through the strainer into the bowl.

2. Arrange the seeded tomatoes in a single layer on a foil-lined rimmed baking sheet. The foil is essential; it keeps the tomatoes from scorching and sticking to the baking sheet. Let the roasted tomatoes cool slightly before trying to remove them from the foil.

CREAMY SWEET PEA SOUP

CLASSIC SWEET PEA SOUP WAS ORIGINALLY prepared by stewing fresh blanched peas, leeks, and tendrils of lettuce briefly in butter, moistening them with veal stock, and passing them through a fine-mesh strainer. The soup was then finished with cream and seasoned with fresh chervil.

We wanted to come up with a quick and delicious version of this sophisticated soup, minus the laborious techniques. Flavor, color, and texture all bear equally on the success or failure of this soup. Our challenge was to cook the peas quickly enough to preserve their vivid color and to achieve a puree of spectacular smoothness without incurring the loss of flavor sometimes associated with sieving away vegetable bits in short-cooked soups.

The obvious starting point was the pea itself. For those of us without gardens, the long-awaited season of fresh peas is often disappointing. Grocery-store pods can conceal tough, starchy pellets worthy of neither the price they command nor the effort they occasion. So when we began this recipe, we headed not down the garden path but up the frozen foods aisle. (For more information on frozen peas, see page 48.)

From the pea, we ventured to aromatics. Because the flavor of the peas is delicate and easily overwhelmed, we wanted to minimize any additions. Experimenting with onions, leeks, and shallots sautéed in butter (unquestionably the most pea-compatible fat in terms of flavor), we found onions a bit too strong but shallots and leeks equally agreeable—delicate and sweet, like the peas themselves.

The means of introducing peas to the soup now became critical. The fun of eating whole peas—breaking through the crisp, springy hull to the sweet pea paste—goes missing in a smooth pea soup, where the listless hulls become an impediment to enjoyment and so must be removed altogether. Simmering peas first to soften their skins, we invariably overcooked them. Additions such as sugar snap peas or snow peas sounded interesting but actually added little flavor.

It occurred to us that if we pureed the peas

before putting them into the soup and infused them briefly in the simmering liquid, we might get to the heart of the pea right off. Toward that end, we processed partially frozen peas in a food processor and simmered them briefly in the soup base to release their starch and flavor quickly. At this juncture, finding the puree a trifle thin, we doubled back and added two tablespoons of flour to the sautéed aromatics to give the base a little body. A few ounces of Boston lettuce added along with the peas gave the soup a marvelous frothy texture when pureed. (To achieve optimal texture, the soup still needed to be passed through a strainer.) A bit of heavy cream, salt, and pepper were the only finishing touches required.

Creamy Sweet Pea Soup
SERVES 4 TO 6

Remove the peas from the freezer just before starting the soup so that when you are ready to process them, as the stock simmers, they will be only partially thawed. To preserve its delicate flavor and color, this soup is best served immediately. A few croutons (page 48) are the perfect embellishment.

4 tablespoons (1/2 stick) unsalted butter
8 large shallots, minced (about 3/4 cup), or 2 medium leeks, cleaned (see the illustrations on page 51), white and light green parts chopped fine
2 tablespoons unbleached all-purpose flour
3 1/2 cups low-sodium chicken broth
1 1/2 pounds frozen peas (about 4 1/2 cups), partially thawed at room temperature for 10 minutes (see note)
12 small leaves Boston lettuce (about 3 ounces) from 1 small head, washed and dried
1/2 cup heavy cream
Salt and ground black pepper

1. Heat the butter in a large saucepan over low heat until foaming. Add the shallots and cook, covered and stirring occasionally, until softened, 8 to 10 minutes. Add the flour and cook, stirring constantly, until thoroughly combined, about 30 seconds. Stirring constantly, gradually add the

47

chicken broth. Increase the heat to high and bring to a boil. Reduce the heat to medium-low and simmer 3 to 5 minutes.

2. Meanwhile, in a food processor fitted with the steel blade, process the partially thawed peas until coarsely chopped, about 20 seconds. Add the peas and lettuce to the simmering broth. Increase the heat to medium-high, cover, and return to a simmer; simmer for 3 minutes. Uncover, reduce the heat to medium-low, and continue to simmer 2 minutes longer.

3. Working in batches, puree the soup in a blender until smooth. Strain the soup through a chinois or fine-mesh strainer into a large bowl; discard the solids. Rinse out and wipe the saucepan clean. Return the pureed mixture to the saucepan and stir in the cream. Warm the soup over low heat until hot, about 3 minutes. Season with salt and pepper to taste and serve immediately.

INGREDIENTS: Frozen Peas

Throughout the testing of this soup, we came to depend on frozen peas. Not only are they more convenient than their fresh, in-the-pod comrades, but they taste better. Test after test, we found frozen peas to be tender and sweet while fresh peas tasted starchy and bland. Trying to understand this curious finding, which barked in the face of common sense, we looked to the frozen food industry for some answers.

Green peas lose a substantial portion of their nutrients within 24 hours of being picked. This rapid deterioration is the reason for the starchy, bland flavor of most "fresh" peas found at the grocery store. These not-so-fresh peas might be several days old, depending on where they came from and how long they were kept in the cooler. Frozen peas, on the other hand, are picked, cleaned, sorted, and frozen within several hours of harvest, which helps preserve their delicate sugars and flavors. Fittingly enough, when commercially frozen vegetables first began to appear in the 1920s and 1930s, green peas were among them.

After tasting peas from the two major national frozen food purveyors, Birds Eye and Green Giant, along with some from a smaller organic company, Cascadian Farm, our panel of tasters found little difference among them. All of the peas were sweet and fresh-tasting, with a bright green color. So unless you grow your own or know a reputable local farm stand, you're better off cruising up the frozen food aisle for a bag of frozen peas.

Buttered Croutons
MAKES ABOUT 3 CUPS

The crisp, crunchy texture of croutons offers a pleasant contrast with the smooth, velvety texture of a rich pureed soup. Although tasters preferred the flavor of croutons made with butter, olive oil was a close second. If you like, replace the melted butter with an equal amount of extra-virgin olive oil. Be sure to use regular or thick-sliced bread.

6   slices (about 6 ounces) white bread, crusts removed and slices cut into 1/2-inch cubes (about 3 cups)
    Salt and ground black pepper
3   tablespoons unsalted butter, melted

1. Adjust an oven rack to the upper-middle position and heat the oven to 400 degrees. Combine the bread cubes and salt and pepper to taste in a medium bowl. Drizzle with the butter and toss well with a rubber spatula to combine.

2. Spread the bread cubes in a single layer on a rimmed baking sheet or in a shallow baking dish. Bake, turning at the halfway mark, until the croutons are golden brown and crisp, 8 to 10 minutes. Cool and store in an airtight container or plastic bag for up to 3 days.

➤ VARIATION
Garlic Croutons

Finely mince 2 large garlic cloves or press them through a garlic press. Combine with 3 tablespoons extra-virgin olive oil in a small bowl. Let stand 20 minutes, then pour through a fine-mesh strainer; discard the garlic. Follow the recipe for Buttered Croutons, replacing the melted butter with the garlic-flavored oil. Proceed as directed.

BUTTERNUT SQUASH SOUP

MANY SQUASH SOUPS DO NOT LIVE UP TO their potential. Rather than being lustrous, slightly creamy, and intensely "squashy" in flavor, they are vegetal or porridge-like, and sometimes taste more like a squash pie than a squash soup.

Knowing that our basic method would be to cook the squash and then puree it with a liquid, our first test focused on how to cook the squash for the soup. Some recipes suggest boiling the squash in a cooking liquid, others roasting it in the oven, others sautéing it on the stovetop.

We tried boiling the squash, but having to peel the tough skin away before dicing it seemed unnecessarily tedious. We eliminated the sauté technique for the same reason. While the roasting was infinitely more simple than our attempts at boiling or sautéing (all we had to do was slice the squash in half, scoop out the seeds, and roast it on a rimmed baking sheet), it produced a caramel-flavored soup with a gritty texture. Roasting also took at least one hour—too long for what should be a quick, no-nonsense soup.

In an effort to conserve time without sacrificing the quick preparation we liked from the roasting test, we decided to try steaming the squash. In a large Dutch oven, we sautéed shallots in butter (we tried garlic and onion but found them too overpowering and acrid with the sweet squash), then added water to the sautéed shallots and brought the mix to a simmer. We seeded and quartered the squash and placed it into a collapsible steaming insert, then added the squash and insert to the Dutch oven. We covered the pan and let the squash steam for 30 minutes until it was tender enough to show no resistance to a long-pronged fork. This method proved to be successful. We liked it because all of the cooking took place in just one pot and, as a bonus, we ended up with a squash-infused cooking liquid that we could use as liquid for the soup.

But there was a downside. Essentially, steaming had the opposite effect of roasting: whereas roasting concentrated the sugars and eliminated the liquid in the squash (which is what made the roasted squash soup gritty), steaming added liquid to the squash and diluted its flavor.

As we were preparing squash one morning, it occurred to us that we were throwing away the answer to more squash flavor—the seeds and fibers. Instead of trashing the scooped-out remnants, we added them to the sautéed shallots and butter. In a matter of minutes, the room became fragrant with an earthy, sweet squash aroma, and the butter in our Dutch oven turned a brilliant shade of saffron. We added the water to the pan and proceeded with the steaming preparation. After the squash was cooked through, we strained the liquid of seeds, fibers, and spent shallot, then blended the soup.

To intensify the sweetness of the squash (but not make the soup sweet), we added a teaspoon of dark brown sugar to the blender jar. Not only was this batch of squash soup brighter in flavor, but it was more intense in color as well. To round out the flavor and introduce some richness to the soup we added ½ cup of heavy cream. Now the soup was thick, rich, and redolent with pure squash flavor.

As is true with many creamed soups, texture is almost as important as flavor. We found blending the squash in batches with just enough liquid to make a thick puree worked best—the thicker base provided more friction and made it easier for the blender to smooth out any lumps or remaining squash fibers. Once all the squash was pureed to a silken texture, we added the remaining liquid and cream and briefly pulsed the soup to combine. We heated the soup briefly over a low flame and stirred in a little freshly grated nutmeg. In under one hour

PUREEING SOUP SAFELY

Many vegetable soups are best pureed in a blender to create a smooth texture. Blending hot soup can be dangerous, though. To prevent mishaps, don't fill the blender jar past the halfway point, and hold the lid in place with a folded kitchen towel.

and with only one pot, we made a squash soup that offered nothing less than autumn in a bowl.

Butternut Squash Soup

SERVES 4 TO 6

If you don't own a collapsible metal steaming basket, substitute the removable insert from a pasta pot. Other squash varieties that work well in this soup are delicata and carnival. Delicata is shaped like a zucchini and can be yellow or white with long green stripes. Carnival is shaped like an acorn squash but has a yellow skin with green and orange stripes.

Appealing accompaniments to this soup are lightly toasted pumpkin seeds, a drizzle of aged balsamic vinegar, or a sprinkle of paprika.

4	tablespoons (½ stick) unsalted butter
1	large shallot, chopped fine
3	pounds butternut squash (about 1 large squash), cut in half lengthwise (see the illustrations on page 203), each half cut in half widthwise; seeds and strings scraped out and reserved
6	cups water
	Salt
½	cup heavy cream
1	teaspoon dark brown sugar
	Pinch freshly grated nutmeg

1. Melt the butter in a large, heavy-bottomed stockpot or Dutch oven over medium-low heat until foaming. Add the shallot and cook, stirring frequently, until translucent, about 3 minutes. Add the seeds and strings from the squash and cook, stirring occasionally, until the butter turns a saffron color, about 4 minutes.

2. Add the water and 1 teaspoon salt to the pot and bring to a boil over high heat. Reduce the heat to medium-low, place the squash cut-side down in a steamer basket, and lower the basket into the pot. Cover and steam until the squash is completely tender, about 30 minutes. Take the pot off the heat and use tongs to transfer the squash to a rimmed baking sheet. When cool enough to handle, use a large spoon to scrape the flesh from the skin. Reserve the squash flesh in a bowl and discard the skin.

3. Strain the steaming liquid through a mesh strainer into a second bowl; discard the solids in the strainer. (You should have 2½ to 3 cups liquid.) Rinse and dry the pot.

4. Puree the squash in batches in the blender, pulsing on low and adding enough reserved steaming liquid to obtain a smooth consistency. Transfer the puree to the clean pot and stir in the remaining steaming liquid, the cream, and brown sugar. Warm the soup over medium-low heat until hot, about 3 minutes. Stir in the nutmeg and adjust the seasonings, adding salt to taste. Serve

---

TECHNIQUE: Pureeing Soups

The texture of a pureed soup should be as smooth and creamy as possible. With this in mind, we tried pureeing these soups in a food mill, in a food processor, with a hand-held immersion blender, and in a regular countertop blender.

Forget using the food mill for this purpose. We tried all three blades (coarse, medium, and fine), and, in each case, the liquid ran right through the blade as we churned and churned only to produce baby food of varying textures. The liquid and pureed solids were separated and could not be combined with a whisk.

The food processor does a decent job of pureeing, but some small bits of vegetables can be trapped under the blade and remain unchopped. Even more troubling is the tendency of a food processor to leak hot liquid. Fill the workbowl more than halfway and you are likely to see liquid running down the side of the food processor base. Even small quantities of soup must be pureed in batches, and that's a hassle.

The immersion blender has more appeal since this tool can be brought directly to the pot and there is no ladling of hot ingredients. However, we found that this kind of blender also leaves some chunks behind. If you don't mind a few lumps, use an immersion blender.

For perfectly smooth pureed soups, use a standard blender. As long as ample headroom is left at the top of the blender, there is never any leaking, and the blade on the blender does an excellent job with soups because it pulls ingredients down from the top of the container. No stray bits go untouched by the blade. The recipes we've presented here can be pureed in a single batch in a standard seven-cup blender.

immediately. (The soup can be refrigerated in an airtight container for several days. Warm over low heat until hot; do not boil.)

➤ VARIATIONS

Curried Squash Soup

If you like your curry spicy, choose madras curry powder for this soup.

Mix 4 tablespoons plain yogurt, 2 tablespoons minced fresh cilantro leaves, 1 teaspoon lime juice, and ⅛ teaspoon salt together in a small bowl. Refrigerate until needed. Follow the recipe for Butternut Squash Soup, adding 2 teaspoons curry powder to the blender when pureeing the squash and liquid. Finish the soup as directed and ladle it into individual bowls. Spoon some of the cilantro-yogurt mixture into each bowl and serve immediately.

Squash Soup with Cinnamon-Sugar Croutons

A sprinkle of spicy but sweet croutons is a nice foil for the rich soup.

Adjust an oven rack to the middle position and heat the oven to 350 degrees. Remove the crusts from 4 slices of white sandwich bread and cut the bread into ½-inch cubes (you should have about 2 cups). Toss the bread cubes with 2 tablespoons melted butter in a medium bowl. In a small bowl, combine 4 teaspoons sugar and 1 teaspoon ground cinnamon; sprinkle over the bread cubes and toss to combine. Spread the bread cubes in a single layer on a parchment-lined baking sheet and bake until crisp, 8 to 10 minutes. (The croutons can be stored in an airtight container for several days.) Follow the recipe for Butternut Squash Soup, sprinkling some of the croutons over the bowls of soup just before serving.

RUSTIC POTATO-LEEK SOUP

WE HAVE ALWAYS LIKED THE CLASSIC CREAMY soup that French cooks make from potatoes and leeks. But sometimes this recipe seems a little too refined. At times we want these two ingredients at their most basic; we want to eat them while resting our elbows on a scarred, wooden table, a crusty piece of bread in one hand. So we decided to part company with the creamy French classic and take on the challenge of a more peasant-style, chunky French soup.

Ironically, the two ingredients that should make this soup great (potatoes and leeks) can also be its downfall. The potatoes should actually play only a supporting role; the leeks, gritty and time-consuming to clean though they are, are the real star of this soup. Cooking time is also crucial. Undercook the soup and the flavors will not meld; cook it too long and you will have a mixture of broken-down bits with little flavor or bite. These were the challenges we bore in mind when we set out.

We tested the potatoes first. Quickly eliminating high-starch, low-moisture baking potatoes,

CLEANING LEEKS

Leeks are often quite dirty and gritty, so they require thorough cleaning. There are two ways to do this. Both methods require that you first cut the dark green portion into quarters lengthwise, leaving the root end in tact.

A. Hold the leek under running water and shuffle the cut layers like a deck of cards.

B. Slosh the cut end of the leek up and down in a bowl of water.

which broke down immediately, we duly rejected the flavorful, medium-starch Yukon Gold as well. These potatoes broke down, too—just not as quickly. We settled on waxy, low-starch Red Bliss potatoes, which held their texture and did not become waterlogged during cooking. Then we reduced the proportion of potatoes altogether, giving the leeks the leading role.

Next we wanted to pump up the flavor of the soup. We decided to use not only the white part of the leek but also the light green part (the very dark green part is tough and should be discarded), and we left the chopped pieces large enough to create textural interest. A whopping 4 pounds of leeks used this way provided nonstop flavor. Water wasn't dynamic enough to stand up to it, so we used chicken broth instead.

But our real breakthrough came in the province of technique. We knew that potatoes and leeks would need different simmering times. Stewing the leeks over a low flame to coax out as much flavor as possible, we added the potatoes later, with the chicken broth, then simmered them until almost tender. At that point, we removed the pot from the heat, allowing the potatoes to finish cooking in the hot broth so they would not overcook and become mushy. The result: a soup with perfectly cooked potatoes, sweet and tender leeks, and an outspoken leek flavor. Because the potatoes were not cooked long enough to release their starch and thicken the broth, we added a little flour to cook with the leeks, giving the broth just the right amount of body to pull everything together.

Rustic Potato-Leek Soup
SERVES 6 TO 8

This soup is hearty enough to serve as a main course, accompanied by crusty bread and preceded or followed by salad. Leeks vary in size. If the ones you bought have large desirable white and light green sections, use 4 pounds of leeks; if they're short on these parts, go with 5 pounds. Either way, leeks can be very gritty, so be sure to clean them thoroughly. See the tips on page 51 for cleaning leeks.

4–5	pounds leeks (see note)
6	tablespoons (¾ stick) unsalted butter
I	tablespoon all-purpose flour
5¼	cups low-sodium chicken broth
I	bay leaf
1¾	pounds red potatoes (about 5 medium), peeled and cut into ¾-inch dice
	Salt and ground black pepper

1. Cut off the roots and tough dark green portion of the leeks, leaving the white portion and about 3 inches of the light green portion. Slice the leeks in half lengthwise and chop into 1-inch pieces. (You should have about 11 cups.)

2. Heat the butter in a large stockpot or Dutch oven over medium-low heat until foaming. Stir in the leeks, increase the heat to medium, cover, and cook, stirring occasionally, until the leeks are tender but not mushy, 15 to 20 minutes; do not brown the leeks. Sprinkle the flour over the leeks and stir to coat evenly. Cook until the flour dissolves, about 2 minutes.

3. Increase the heat to high; whisking constantly, gradually add the broth. Add the bay leaf and potatoes, cover, and bring to a boil. Reduce the heat to medium-low and simmer, covered, until the potatoes are almost tender, 5 to 7 minutes. Remove the pot from the heat and let stand, covered, until the potatoes are tender and the flavors meld, 10 to 15 minutes. Discard the bay leaf and season with salt and pepper to taste. Serve immediately. (The soup can be refrigerated in an airtight container for a day or two. Warm over low heat until hot; do not boil.)

➤ VARIATIONS
Rustic Potato-Leek Soup with Kielbasa
Eight ounces of cooked ham, cut into ½-inch dice, can be substituted for the sausage, if desired. Whichever you choose, season the soup with care, since both ham and kielbasa are fully seasoned.

Follow the recipe for Rustic Potato-Leek Soup, stirring in 8 ounces kielbasa sausage, cut into ½-inch slices, just before removing the pot from the heat in step 3. Proceed as directed.

Rustic Potato-Leek Soup with White Beans

Follow the recipe for Rustic Potato-Leek Soup, reducing the potatoes to 2 medium (about ¾ pound). Just before removing the pot from the heat in step 3, stir in 1 cup hot water and 1 cup canned cannellini beans, drained and rinsed well. Proceed as directed.

HEARTY VEGETABLE SOUP

IT SEEMS THAT MOST FAMILIES WHO MAKE vegetable soup do so when the refrigerator crisper drawer is overflowing and the vegetables are a few days away from rotting. The recipe goes something like this: Dissolve a few bouillon cubes in a pot of water, fill it with vegetables, and simmer away. Yes, the method is easy, but the result is a soup with a bland, thin broth and dull, mismatched vegetables.

We wanted just the opposite—a rich, hearty, satisfying soup—though we admit that hearty isn't a usual descriptor for vegetables. They're more often designated as light, healthful, and colorful. Still, we wanted to go all out and develop an exceptional vegetable soup. It didn't have to be quick—perfection can take time—but it had to be good. Really good.

In the test kitchen, we often make stock by "enhancing" canned broth. Herbs and vegetables are simmered in broth and then strained out before fresh vegetables are added to create a soup. We prepared four stocks by simmering aromatics (carrots, celery, onions, and garlic) and herbs (parsley, thyme, and bay leaves) in various liquids: water, canned beef broth, canned low-sodium chicken broth, and canned vegetable broth. The stock made with water was, well, watery. The beef broth was tinny, salty, and artificial-tasting. Tasters were split when it came to the chicken and vegetable broths. Chicken broth produced a stock with clean, balanced flavors, while stock made with vegetable broth had sweeter, tomatoey undertones.

Our basic stock recipe was fine, but we wanted something exceptional. We tried sautéing the aromatic vegetables before simmering them in the broth. This stock was better, but not great. A spoonful of tomato paste improved things, but the stock was still not good enough to stand as "the ultimate" stock. Our next thought was to roast the vegetables for the stock, hoping that caramelization would contribute the richness we were after. This was indeed the case, so we then experimented with the vegetables. Fennel, leeks, and shallots were out; onions, garlic, carrots, celery, and portobello mushrooms were in. The mushrooms were particularly important. They added meaty, deep notes unlike any of the other vegetables.

Our stock was improving, but now we wondered what could be added to the roasted vegetables to punch up the flavor. The green part of leeks was a winner. (We reserved the white part for the soup itself.) And, having had success with roasted mushrooms, we tried dried porcini, which pushed the stock toward perfection. Their meaty, mellow flavor created a stock with superior, intense flavor. Pressing on the spent vegetables when straining the stock squeezed out the last of their flavor.

Now that we had mastered the stock, it was time to move on to the vegetables for the soup itself. Our initial list included russet potatoes, carrots, canned tomatoes, and the white part of the leeks we'd used for the stock. Unimpressed with this mixture, we thought to add more interesting choices. Root vegetables like parsnips and turnips were too potent, as were cruciferous vegetables like broccoli and Brussels sprouts. Green beans and peas were right for a spring or summer soup, but lima beans were just right for this heartier recipe. (Because some tasters disliked limas, we made them optional.) Celery was too unsubstantial, but its starchy, heartier cousin, celeriac, was perfect. Celeriac has bold celery flavor that can hold its own in a complex soup. For visual and textural contrast, we wanted to add leafy greens. Among the greens we tried, bitter, quick-cooking escarole came out on top, adding bright color and flavor.

As a final flourish, we added some chopped parsley and crostini (garlicky toasts). Now we had a soup with multidimensional flavor and a great texture—we'd incorporated sweet, earthy, bright, and even bitter notes, all in the same pot.

Hearty Vegetable Soup

SERVES 4 TO 6 AS A MAIN COURSE

The enhanced broth, called stock below, can be refrigerated for up to 3 days or frozen in an airtight container for up to 2 months. If you can get "petite cut" canned diced tomatoes, they can be used straight away after draining, without any additional chopping. The garlicky crostini (or croutons on page 48) add another dimension of flavor and texture to the soup, but if you're pressed for time, simply serve the soup with crusty bread or crackers.

STOCK

1	large carrot, peeled and chopped medium
1	celery rib, chopped medium
1	medium onion, chopped medium
3	medium portobello mushrooms, roughly chopped
1	medium garlic head, outer papery skins removed and top third of head cut off and discarded
3	tablespoons olive oil
1	heaping tablespoon tomato paste
9	cups low-sodium chicken or vegetable broth
2	medium leeks (about 1 pound), cleaned (see the illustrations on page 51), green parts chopped, white parts sliced thin crosswise
10	sprigs fresh parsley
4	sprigs fresh thyme
2	bay leaves
1/2	ounce dried porcini mushrooms, rinsed

CROSTINI AND SOUP

8–12	baguette slices (1/2 inch thick, cut on the bias)
1	large garlic clove, peeled
	Extra-virgin olive oil
	Salt and ground black pepper
1	(14.5-ounce) can diced tomatoes, drained and chopped coarse
12	ounces russet potatoes (about 2 small), peeled and cut into 1/2-inch cubes
2	medium carrots, peeled and cut into 1/2-inch cubes
12	ounces celeriac (about 1/2 medium), peeled and cut into 1/2-inch cubes
12	ounces escarole (1 small head), washed, stemmed, and leaves cut into 1-inch pieces
1	cup (6 ounces) frozen baby lima beans, thawed (optional)
2	tablespoons minced fresh parsley leaves
	Salt and ground black pepper

1. FOR THE STOCK: Adjust an oven rack to the middle position; heat the oven to 450 degrees. Put the carrot, celery, onion, portobellos, and garlic head on a rimmed baking sheet; drizzle with the oil and toss to coat. Add the tomato paste and toss again until evenly coated. Spread the vegetables in an even layer, setting the garlic head cut-side up; roast until the vegetables are well browned, 25 to 30 minutes.

2. Combine the roasted vegetables, broth, leek greens, parsley, thyme, bay leaves, and porcini in

---

TASTING: **Vegetable Broth**

We gathered nine popular brands of vegetable broth and tasted them three different ways: warmed, in our enhanced broth base for vegetable soup, and in asparagus risotto. The winner of the straight broth tasting was Swanson, which had one of the highest sodium levels, with 970 mg per cup, compared with 330 mg per cup for Kitchen Basics, which had the lowest sodium level. Pitting the winner (Swanson) against the loser (Kitchen Basics), the vegetable soup tasting yielded mixed results. Swanson eked out a win, but neither soup was bad. In the asparagus risotto, we threw in what we thought would be a ringer—Swanson reduced-sodium chicken broth, the winner of our canned chicken broth tasting—to compete against the Swanson and Kitchen Basics vegetable broths. Swanson

vegetable broth was the tasters' favorite. The chicken broth came in second, and Kitchen Basics ended up in last place. Which vegetable broth should you buy? Swanson's is the winner, but the differences among brands when used in cooking (rather than tasting them straight) are more subtle than we would have thought.

THE BEST VEGETABLE BROTH

Swanson Vegetable Broth had the most flavor of the nine brands we tested. It also contains the most sodium, which partly explains its strong showing in our tasting.

a large Dutch oven; cover and bring to a simmer over medium-high heat, then reduce the heat to medium-low and simmer, partially covered, for 30 minutes. Remove the garlic head; using tongs, squeeze the garlic head at the root end until the cloves slip out of their skins. Using a fork, mash the garlic to a paste in a small bowl and set aside. Strain the stock through a large fine-mesh strainer into a container, pressing on the solids to extract as much liquid as possible; discard the solids in the strainer.

3. FOR THE CROSTINI: Adjust an oven rack to the middle position; heat the oven to 400 degrees. Place the baguette slices on a baking sheet; bake until dry and crisp, about 10 minutes, flipping the slices halfway through baking. While still hot, rub one side of each slice with the garlic, then drizzle lightly with olive oil and sprinkle with salt and pepper to taste. Set aside.

4. FOR THE SOUP: Rinse out the Dutch oven and wipe dry; add the tomatoes, potatoes, carrots, celeriac, reserved whites of the leeks, the strained broth, and garlic paste to the pot and bring to a simmer over medium-high heat. Reduce the heat to medium-low and simmer, partially covered, until the vegetables are tender when poked with a skewer or paring knife, about 25 minutes. With the back of a wooden spoon, mash some of the potatoes against the side of the pot to thicken the soup. Stir in the escarole and lima beans (if using); cook until the escarole is wilted and the limas are heated through, about 5 minutes. Stir in the parsley; adjust the seasonings with salt and pepper to taste. Serve immediately in bowls, with the reserved crostini floated on the soup.

HEARTY LENTIL SOUP

LENTIL SOUP IS CHEAP TO MAKE, QUICK TO make, and when made well, tastes great—maybe even better—the next day. We were determined to develop a recipe for our cold weather repertoire that would be a keeper. We wanted a hearty lentil soup worthy of a second bowl—not the tasteless variety we have so often encountered.

We started by preparing five representative recipes, and two discoveries came quickly to light. First, garlic, herbs, onions, and tomatoes are common denominators. Second, texture is a big issue. None of our tasters liked the soup that was brothy or, at the other extreme, the one that was as thick as porridge. They also gave a big thumbs down to those that looked like brown split pea soup. Consequently, recipes that included carrots, tomatoes, and herbs were rewarded for their brighter colors (and flavors). There was also a clear preference for the subtle, smoky depth meat provides. The next step was to determine which lentils to buy and how to cook them.

Brown, green, and red lentils are the most common choices on supermarket shelves. At specialty markets and natural food stores, you can also find black lentils and French green lentils (*lentilles du Puy*), the latter being the darling of chefs everywhere. In addition to color differences, lentils can be divided according to their size—large or small—and to whether they are split, like peas, or not. Ordinary brown and green lentils are large, while red, black, and lentils du Puy are small. Red lentils are often sold split and are used most frequently in Indian dishes such as dal.

To make some sense of all of this, we made five pots of lentil soup, each one using a different-colored lentil. Red lentils were out—they disintegrated when simmered. All four of the

A GOOD SWEAT (MAKES A DIFFERENCE)

Firm Lentils

Mushy Lentils

Sweating the lentils with salt and an acidic component (from the canned tomatoes) retards the conversion of pectin-like compounds to a gel. Once sweated, these lentils easily remain intact during a long simmer in broth (top) while becoming tender on the inside. Lentils simmered without first being sweated fall apart (bottom) if overcooked.

remaining choices produced an acceptable texture, but tasters preferred, as expected, the earthy flavor and firm texture of the lentils du Puy. To our surprise, however, the larger green and brown lentils fared reasonably well, exceeding the low expectations of the test kitchen.

Next, we set out to test cooking methods. Some lentils, especially the large brown and green varieties, have a greater tendency to fall apart if overcooked, even for just a few minutes. Searching for a way to avoid this problem, we employed a common Indian culinary trick: sweating the lentils in a covered pan with aromatic vegetables prior to adding the liquid. Using brown lentils, we cooked up two batches, and, bingo, we had solved the problem! The sweated lentils remained intact, while the unsweated lentils had broken down. And we discovered that sweating the lentils with bacon, canned tomatoes, and salt (as well as aromatic vegetables and herbs) not only ensured an ideal texture but boosted the flavor of the legumes as well.

One issue concerning texture remained. Tasters wanted a chunkier soup and did not like the brothy base. We tried pureeing a few cups of the soup and then adding it back to the pot. Tasters praised the contrast of the now creamy base with the whole lentils and found the entire soup more interesting.

Pork was the meat of choice in all of the recipes we examined. We found that the lentils cooked too quickly to extract the smoky flavor that a ham bone or hock can impart. Prosciutto and pancetta were too mild. Tasters preferred the smoky flavor of bacon and liked the textural addition of the bacon bits. Another advantage bacon offered was rendered fat. We used it to sauté the vegetables and aromatics, which further infused the soup with smoky flavor. Bay leaves, thyme, and parsley rounded out the other flavors and added a touch of bright green to the pot.

Last, but not least, was the question of liquids. 'e prepared two batches, one with water and with chicken broth. Neither was ideal. Water ed a soup that was not as rich in flavor as while the broth-only version tasted too hicken soup. After several more tests,

we concluded that a mix of 3 parts broth to 1 part water produced a hearty depth of flavor without being overpowering.

Many recipes called for the addition of vinegar or lemon juice just before the soup is served. We stirred a touch of balsamic vinegar into the pot at completion, and tasters gave this soup a perfect 10.

With our recipe complete, we developed a few variations. Stirring a hefty amount of spinach into the pot at the end of cooking created a popular version: lentil soup with greens. For a spicier and more exotic rendition, we added some of the aromatic spices used in North African cooking—cumin, coriander, cinnamon, and cayenne—and substituted cilantro for the parsley and lemon juice for the vinegar.

Hearty Lentil Soup

MAKES ABOUT 2 QUARTS, SERVING 4 TO 6

Lentils du Puy, sometimes called French green lentils, are our first choice for this recipe, but brown, black, or regular green lentils are fine, too. Note that cooking times will vary depending on the type of lentils used. Lentils lose flavor with age, and because most packaged lentils do not have expiration dates, try to buy them from a store that specializes in natural foods and grains. Before use, rinse and then carefully sort through the lentils to remove small stones and pebbles.

3	slices (about 3 ounces) bacon, cut into 1/4-inch pieces
1	large onion, chopped fine
2	medium carrots, peeled and chopped medium
3	medium garlic cloves, minced or pressed through a garlic press
1	(14.5-ounce) can diced tomatoes, drained
1	bay leaf
1	teaspoon minced fresh thyme leaves
1	cup (7 ounces) lentils, rinsed and picked over
1	teaspoon salt
	Ground black pepper
1/2	cup dry white wine
4 1/2	cups low-sodium chicken broth
1 1/2	cups water
1 1/2	teaspoons balsamic vinegar
3	tablespoons minced fresh parsley leaves

1. Fry the bacon in a large stockpot or Dutch oven over medium-high heat, stirring occasionally, until the fat is rendered and the bacon is crisp, 3 to 4 minutes. Add the onion and carrots; cook, stirring occasionally, until the vegetables begin to soften, about 2 minutes. Add the garlic and cook until fragrant, about 30 seconds. Stir in the tomatoes, bay leaf, and thyme; cook until fragrant, about 30 seconds. Stir in the lentils, salt, and pepper to taste; cover, reduce the heat to medium-low, and cook until the vegetables are softened and the lentils have darkened, 8 to 10 minutes.

2. Uncover, increase the heat to high, add the wine, and bring to a simmer. Add the chicken broth and water; bring to a boil, cover partially, and reduce the heat to low. Simmer until the lentils are tender but still hold their shape, 30 to 35 minutes; discard the bay leaf.

3. Puree 3 cups of the soup in a blender until smooth, then return to the pot. Stir in the vinegar and heat the soup over medium-low until hot, about 5 minutes. Stir in 2 tablespoons parsley and serve, garnishing each bowl with some of the remaining parsley.

➤ VARIATIONS

Hearty Lentil Soup with Spinach
Follow the recipe for Hearty Lentil Soup, replacing the parsley with 5 ounces baby spinach. Continue to heat the soup, stirring frequently, until the spinach is wilted, about 3 minutes; serve.

Hearty Lentil Soup with Fragrant Spices
Follow the recipe for Hearty Lentil Soup, adding 1 teaspoon ground cumin, 1 teaspoon ground coriander, 1 teaspoon ground cinnamon, and ¼ teaspoon cayenne pepper along with the garlic; substitute lemon juice for the balsamic vinegar and minced fresh cilantro leaves for the parsley.

HAM AND SPLIT PEA SOUP

WE LOVE SPLIT PEA SOUP MADE WITH HAM BROTH, but times have changed. Except for the occasional holiday, most cooks rarely buy a bone-in ham, opting more often for the thin-sliced deli meat. We wondered if we could duplicate this wonderful soup without buying a huge ham.

To confirm or disprove our belief that ham broth is crucial to split pea soup, we made several pork broths and pork-enhanced canned chicken broths. In addition to making broth the old-fashioned way from a meaty ham bone, we made broths from smoked pork necks, pork hocks (fresh and smoked), and smoked ham shanks.

Broths made with hocks—fresh as well as smoked—were more greasy than flavorful. In addition, the hocks gave up very little meat, making it necessary to purchase an additional portion of ham to fortify the soup. Ham shanks, which include the hock, made a pleasant but lightweight broth that was a tad greasy and salty—both fixable problems had the broth been stellar. Pork necks, which are not widely available, made a fairly flavorful but salty broth.

Not surprisingly, the broth made from the bone of a big ham was the winner. It was meaty and full flavored, rich but not greasy, well seasoned without being overly salty, and smoky without tasting artificial. Unlike any of the other broths, this one sported bits of meat. And not just good meat—great meat. The tender pieces of ham that fell away from the bone during cooking were not just a nice byproduct of the broth. They were the glory of our split pea soup.

But was there a way around buying half a ham (with an average weight of about 8 pounds) just to make a pot of soup?

After checking out the ham and smoked pork cases at several different stores, we discovered the picnic ham from the pork shoulder. Unlike what we generally refer to as ham, which comes from the back legs of the animal, the picnic comes from the shoulder and front legs. Smaller than a ham, the half-picnic weighs only 4½ pounds. After making a couple of more pots of soup, we found that the picnic ham—with its bones, fat, rind, and meat—made outstanding stock, and after two hours of simmering, the meat was meltingly tender yet still potently flavorful.

Since we did not need the full picnic half for our pot of soup, we pulled off and roasted two of its meatier muscles and used the remaining meat, bone, fat, and rind to make the soup. At around 99 cents a pound, a picnic ham is usually cheaper than a regular ham, and often cheaper than pork hocks, shanks, and neck bones as well. Here, we thought, was the modern solution. Rather than buy a ham for eating (and eating and eating) with a leftover bone for soup, instead purchase a picnic ham for soup and roast the remaining couple of pounds for eating.

There are several ways to make ham and split pea soup. You can throw all the ingredients—ham bone, peas, and diced vegetables—into a pot and simmer until everything is tender. Or you can sauté the vegetables, then add the remaining ingredients and cook the soup until the ham and peas are tender. Alternatively, you can cook the ham bone and peas (or give the ham bone a little bit of a head start) until both ham and peas are tender and then add raw, sautéed, or caramelized vegetables to the pot, continuing to cook until the vegetables are tender and the flavors have blended.

Although we had hoped to keep the soup a straightforward one-pot operation, we found out pretty quickly that dumping everything in at the same time resulted in gloppy, overcooked peas and tired, mushy vegetables by the time the ham was tender. For textural contrast in this smooth, creamy soup, we ultimately preferred fully—not overly—cooked vegetables.

Our best soups were those in which the vegetables spent enough time in the pot for their flavors to blend but not so long that they had lost all of their individual taste. Of the soups with vegetables added toward the end of cooking, we preferred the one with the caramelized vegetables. The sweeter vegetables gave this otherwise straightforward meat and starch soup a richness and depth of flavor that made the extra step and pan worth the trouble. Many pea soup recipes call for an acidic ingredient—such as vinegar or lemon juice—to

bring balance to an otherwise rich, heavy soup. We found ourselves drawn to balsamic vinegar, whose mildly sweet, mildly acidic flavor perfectly complemented the soup. Some tasters also liked a bit of crunchy raw red onion sprinkled over the soup, but we leave the choice up to you.

Ham and Split Pea Soup
SERVES 6

Use a small smoked picnic ham if you can find one. Otherwise, buy a half-picnic ham and remove some meat, which you can save for use in sandwiches, salads, or omelets.

- 3 quarts water
- 1 piece (about 2½ pounds) smoked, bone-in picnic ham
- 4 bay leaves
- 1 pound (2½ cups) split peas, rinsed and picked over
- 1 teaspoon dried thyme
- 2 tablespoons extra-virgin olive oil
- 2 medium onions, chopped medium
- 2 medium carrots, chopped medium
- 2 medium celery ribs, chopped medium
- 1 tablespoon unsalted butter
- 2 medium garlic cloves, minced or pressed through a garlic press
  Pinch sugar
- 3 small new potatoes, scrubbed and cut into medium dice
  Ground black pepper
  Minced red onion (optional)
  Balsamic vinegar

1. Bring the water, ham, and bay leaves to a boil in a large soup kettle, covered, over medium-high heat. Reduce the heat to low and simmer until the meat is tender and pulls away from the bone, 2 to 2½ hours. Remove the ham meat and bone from the broth; add the split peas and thyme and simmer until the peas are tender but not dissolved, about 45 minutes. Meanwhile, when the ham is cool enough to handle, shred the meat into bite-size pieces and set aside. Discard the rind and bone.

2. While the ham is simmering, heat the oil in a

large skillet over high heat until shimmering. Add the onions, carrots, and celery; sauté, stirring frequently, until most of the liquid evaporates and the vegetables begin to brown, 5 to 6 minutes. Reduce the heat to medium-low; add the butter, garlic, and sugar. Cook the vegetables, stirring frequently, until deeply browned, 30 to 35 minutes; set aside.

3. Add the sautéed vegetables, potatoes, and shredded ham to the soup; simmer until the potatoes are tender and the peas dissolve and thicken the soup to the consistency of light cream, about 20 minutes more. Season with pepper to taste. Ladle the soup into bowls, sprinkle with the red onion, if using, and serve, passing the balsamic vinegar separately.

➤ VARIATION

Ham and Split Pea Soup with Caraway
Toast 1½ teaspoons caraway seeds in a small skillet over medium-high heat, stirring frequently, until fragrant and browned, about 4 minutes. Follow the recipe for Ham and Split Pea Soup, substituting the toasted caraway seeds for the dried thyme.

PASTA E FAGIOLI

PASTA FAZOOL, THE ITALIAN-AMERICAN VERSION of Italy's pasta and bean soup (pasta e fagioli) is hearty, thick, almost stew-like, and always orange-red in color from the presence of tomatoes. Each spoonful is laden with pasta and beans, and the soup is full of harmonious flavors, with no one taste standing out. The vegetables are cut small and used as accents to the pasta. Typically, in mediocre pasta fazool, the beans have no flavor, the pasta is mushy, the broth is too tomatoey, and the soup is bland. We wanted to make a pasta fazool that would make any Italian-American family proud.

We began by preparing a half dozen recipes, most of which followed a similar procedure. First the aromatics (vegetables and often some pork product) were sautéed in olive oil. Then the tomatoes and broth went into the pot, followed by the beans and, finally, the pasta. Almost all of these recipes produced bland soups with mushy pasta. The soup with

the best flavor took more than four hours to prepare and used dried beans. Although the long hours at the stove paid off, the speed with which some other recipes came together was certainly appealing. So the challenge became clear. Could we make a really good soup using canned beans, a shortcut that would save hours of cooking time?

Many recipes for pasta e fagioli contain pancetta (unsmoked Italian bacon), while completely Americanized recipes call for regular bacon. The simplest recipes avoid the pork and use only olive oil. Our first test showed that even a small amount of a pork product added much flavor to the soup, so we sautéed 3 ounces finely diced pancetta in 1 tablespoon olive oil. We served this batch to tasters alongside a version made with the same amount of bacon and oil. The pancetta gave the soup a subtler pork flavor, but tasters did not mind the stronger, smokier flavor of regular bacon. (Pancetta is preferred, but you can use either.)

Most Italian recipes use the same quartet of aromatic vegetables: onions, celery, carrots, and garlic. Tasters liked the onions, celery, and garlic but were divided over the sweetness of the carrots. We decided to omit carrots from the recipe.

In most recipes, the aromatics are sautéed, and then the pan is deglazed with either tomatoes or broth. For the tomatoes, we tried crushed, diced, and sauce. The crushed tomatoes and tomato sauce were overpowering, but the diced tomatoes worked well, helping to intensify the flavors of the aromatics. We also tested chicken broth, a close second to the tomatoes (we would add the broth later), and white wine, the latter simply turning the soup sour.

Cranberry beans, a beautiful pink-and-white mottled variety, are popular in Italy but hard to find in this country. We tested two common substitutes, pinto and red kidney beans. Neither had the sweet, delicate flavor of a cranberry bean, so we tried cannellini beans, also known as white kidney beans. Tasters found these oval-shaped beans to be sweet and creamy and most like cranberry beans. Smaller white beans (navies and Great Northerns) did not have quite enough heft for this soup but are certainly fine if that's what you have on hand.

Although a taste test (see page 61) revealed some good choices among canned beans, we wanted to find a way to boost their flavor. Our first thought was to add the beans to the tomato mixture, a step that might infuse them with the flavors of the pancetta, oil, and vegetables. We prepared two batches of soup—one with beans and broth added simultaneously and one with beans added to the tomatoes and cooked for 10 minutes prior to adding the broth. The results were black and white. The beans added to the tomato mixture adopted its flavors readily, easily beating out the bland beans added later in the recipe.

The makeup of the broth was also critical. Although chicken broth is standard in many recipes, tasters felt that the resulting pasta fazool tasted like chicken soup. We tried water instead of chicken broth, adding some Parmesan rind to boost the flavor. This test was a success, but we went on to try a 60/40 combination of broth and water, retaining the cheese rind. This soup was the winner: good body, good flavor, and not too "chickeny."

For additional flavorings, we added oregano and red pepper flakes to the pot with the aromatic vegetables; tasters approved. Parsley is typically added at the end of cooking, and it took just one test to show that it brightened the flavor and color of the soup. The last flavor-enhancing idea—a long shot, perhaps—was a teaspoon of minced anchovy fillet. Tasters could not identify what was different about the batch with anchovy, but everyone agreed that it was more complex and fuller in flavor.

Our tests showed that pastas with relatively small shapes are best in this soup. Larger shapes, like elbows and shells, crowded out the other ingredients and soaked up too much broth. Tiny pastas, such as stars and pastina, were lost next to the more sizable beans and tomatoes.

Italian Pasta and Bean Soup (Pasta e Fagioli)
SERVES 8 TO 10

This soup does not hold well because the pasta absorbs the liquid, becomes mushy, and leaves the soup dry. The soup can, however, be made in two stages. Once the beans are simmered with the tomatoes, before the broth and water are added, the mixture can be cooled and refrigerated for up to 3 days. When ready to complete the soup, discard the Parmesan rind (otherwise it will become stringy), add the liquid, bring the soup to a boil, and proceed with the recipe.

1	tablespoon extra-virgin olive oil, plus more for drizzling
3	ounces pancetta or bacon (3 slices), chopped fine
1	medium onion, chopped fine
1	celery rib, chopped fine
4	medium garlic cloves, minced or pressed through a garlic press
1	teaspoon dried oregano
1/4	teaspoon red pepper flakes
3	anchovy fillets, minced to a paste
1	(28-ounce) can diced tomatoes

FOUR BEST PASTAS FOR SOUP

DITALINI These "little thimbles" are ½ inch square when cooked, about the same size as the beans and tomatoes. They create the chunkiest soup.

TUBETINI These "tiny tubes" are similar in shape to ditalini but not even half the size when cooked. The soup will have a more brothy appearance.

CONCHIGLIETTE These "small shells," the largest of the recommended pasta shapes, are close to ¾ inch square when cooked.

ORZO This rice-shaped pasta cooks up thinner than the beans but has a similar shape and length, making the soup look a bit more refined.

1 piece Parmesan cheese rind, about 5 by 2 inches

2 (15.5-ounce) cans cannellini beans, drained and rinsed

3½ cups low-sodium chicken broth

2½ cups water
Salt

8 ounces small pasta shape (see "Four Best Pastas for Soup" on page 60)

¼ cup chopped fresh parsley leaves
Ground black pepper

3 ounces Parmesan cheese, freshly grated (about 1½ cups)

1. Heat the oil in a large, heavy-bottomed stockpot or Dutch oven over medium-high heat until shimmering. Add the pancetta and cook, stirring occasionally, until it begins to brown, 3 to 5 minutes. Add the onion and celery; cook, stirring occasionally, until the vegetables are softened, 5 to 7 minutes. Add the garlic, oregano, red pepper flakes, and anchovies; cook, stirring constantly, until fragrant, about 1 minute. Add the tomatoes with their liquid, scraping up any browned bits from the pan bottom. Add the cheese rind and beans; bring to a boil, then reduce the heat to low and simmer to blend the flavors, 10 minutes. Add the chicken broth, water, and 1 teaspoon salt; increase the heat to high and bring to a boil. Add the pasta and cook until tender, about 10 minutes (refer to the package instructions to better estimate the pasta cooking time).

2. Discard the cheese rind. Off the heat, stir in 3 tablespoons of the parsley; adjust the seasonings with salt and pepper to taste. Ladle the soup into individual bowls; drizzle each serving with olive oil and sprinkle with a portion of the remaining parsley. Serve immediately, passing the grated Parmesan separately.

➤ VARIATION

Italian Pasta and Bean Soup with Orange and Fennel

Ditalini and orzo are especially good pasta shapes for this variation.

Trim 1 medium fennel bulb of the stalks and fronds; trim the bottom ½ inch. Halve the bulb

TASTING: Canned White Beans

We sampled four canned white beans in our search for the best beans for this soup. Because so few brands of canned cannellini beans (our favorite for this soup) are distributed nationwide, we broadened our taste test to include alternative white beans with widespread distribution. We tasted each contender twice: straight from the can (after being drained and rinsed) and prepared in our recipe for pasta e fagioli made without the pasta. Here are the two that came out on top:

THE BEST CANNED WHITE BEANS

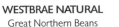

WESTBRAE NATURAL	PROGRESSO
Great Northern Beans	Cannellini Beans
Tasters liked the "earthy" flavor and "creamy" texture of these beans. A bit small for this soup.	Tasters praised their "sweet, slightly salty" flavor.

lengthwise and, using a paring knife, remove the core. Slice the bulb lengthwise into ¼-inch-thick strips, then chop fine. Follow the recipe for Italian Pasta and Bean Soup, cooking the fennel along with the onion and celery and adding 2 teaspoons grated orange zest and ½ teaspoon fennel seeds along with the garlic, oregano, pepper flakes, and anchovies. Proceed as directed.

BLACK BEAN SOUP

BLACK BEANS, ALSO CALLED TURTLE BEANS, are widely eaten in Latin America, and they often are served up in black bean soup. This peasant-style soup is robust, hearty, and earthy-tasting. Black beans have a wonderful creamy texture and a distinctive flavor. Their dark color provides a beautiful backdrop for a colorful array of garnishes.

We wanted to figure out how to build enough flavor to turn these beans into a satisfying bowl of soup. While we focused on flavor, we also paid close attention to texture. The perfect bean was tender without being mushy, with enough tooth to make a satisfying chew.

In pursuit of this perfect texture, we discovered that it was important to cook the beans in enough water; too little water and the beans on the top cooked more slowly than the beans underneath, and the whole pot took forever to cook. (Thirteen cups is sufficient water to cook 1 pound of beans.)

We did some further testing by comparing beans that had been soaked overnight with a batch of unsoaked, as well as with a batch softened by a "quick-soak" method in which the beans were brought to a boil, simmered two minutes, and then covered to let stand for one hour off the heat. The quick-soak method caused a large percentage of the beans to burst during cooking. This reduced the chew we were after, so we nixed that method. Contrary to our expectations, overnight soaking decreased the cooking time by only about half an hour and didn't improve the texture. Because we are rarely organized enough to soak the night before, we no longer soak.

Now that we had discovered how to cook beans with the texture we wanted, it was time to discover the best way to build more layers of flavor onto this base without drowning the earthy flavor of the beans.

We determined that meat gave the beans a necessary depth of flavor. We tested cooking the beans with a ham hock, bacon, ham, and pork loin. We liked all four, and each gave the beans a slightly different flavor; the ham hock provided a smooth background taste, while bacon and ham produced a more assertive and salty flavor. Pork loin was the most subtle of the four choices. Since ham hocks are so inexpensive and one hock flavors a whole pot of soup, we decided to use them in our recipe. We would include bacon in a variation.

In many Caribbean recipes, a sofrito is added to the cooked beans for flavor. Chopped vegetables—usually onion, garlic, and bell pepper—are sautéed in olive oil until soft and then stirred into the beans. We found that this mixture added another layer of fresh flavor without overpowering the flavor of the beans.

We ran several more experiments with flavorings. We tried adding sugar and found that we didn't like the additional sweetness. We also experimented with the cumin, the traditional spice for black beans, simmered in with the beans or mixed into the sofrito. The flavor of the spice got lost when simmered with the beans; we decided to save the cumin for the sofrito.

Black bean soup should be thick, not soupy. Some recipes use a blender or food processor to puree some of the beans and cooking liquid to create a thick texture. A few recipes blend all of the beans and essentially create a soup that is a thick puree, and others rely on some type of starch for thickening. At the outset, we decided we wanted our soup to have whole beans in it, so we dismissed the puree-only version. We did, however, try mashing beans into the sofrito; pureeing some of the beans (we tested various amounts) in the blender; breaking apart some of the beans in the food processor (we tested various amounts); and thickening with starch.

When either the blender or food processor was used, the resulting soup had a grayish brown color that was not as desirable as the more black color of the nonprocessed soups. These approaches also created more work, since the blender/food processor needed cleaning afterward. We found that it's simpler and easier to mash some of the beans with the sofrito using a potato masher. The soup also looked better. However, there was a limit to how many beans could go in the sauté pan at once for mashing.

We considered combining the mashed beans with other classic approaches to thickening. A few recipes add flour to the sofrito, but we did not like this approach. The soup often cooked up too thick and was hard to manage. Cornstarch added at the end of the cooking seemed like a better option. The first time we tested cornstarch, the results were fabulous. Not only did the soup thicken to a pleasing silky consistency, but the color was outstanding. The blackish brown color of the beans appeared deeper and acquired an attractive sheen.

Finally, we found that acids can play a key role in flavoring black beans. We tested red wine, balsamic, and cider vinegars, as well as lime juice and lemon juice. We liked all of these additions except for the cider vinegar, which we found harsh.

Black Bean Soup

SERVES 6

This soup is best if made a day ahead of serving so the flavors can meld. It will hold for 3 days in the refrigerator. Although the ham hock will probably hold just a tablespoon or two of meat, it's worth taking the time to remove this meat from the hock and add it back to the soup. For a slightly different effect, garnish the soup with shredded Monterey Jack cheese, diced seeded tomatoes, and minced jalapeño chile. Cornbread would make an excellent accompaniment to either version. For a meatier soup, make the variation with bacon that follows.

BEANS

1	pound (2¼ cups) dried black beans, rinsed and picked over
1	smoked ham hock (about ⅔ pound), rinsed
1	medium green bell pepper, cored, seeded, and quartered
3	quarts plus 1 cup water
1	medium onion, minced
6	medium garlic cloves, minced or pressed through a garlic press
2	bay leaves
1½	teaspoons salt

SOFRITO

2	tablespoons olive oil
1	medium onion, minced
1	small red bell pepper, cored, seeded, and minced
¾	teaspoon salt
8	medium garlic cloves, minced or pressed through a garlic press
2	teaspoons dried oregano
1	tablespoon ground cumin

FINISHING THE SOUP

2	tablespoons cornstarch
2	tablespoons cold water
1	tablespoon juice from 1 lime
¼	cup sour cream
¼	cup roughly chopped fresh cilantro leaves
½	small red onion, minced
	Hot pepper sauce (optional)

1. FOR THE BEANS: Place the beans, ham hock, green pepper, and water in a large stockpot or Dutch oven. Bring to a boil over medium-high heat, reduce the heat to low, and skim the surface as scum rises. Stir in the onion, garlic, bay leaves, and salt and bring back to a simmer. Cook, partially covered, until the beans are tender but not splitting (taste several, as they cook unevenly), about 2 hours. Remove the ham hock from the pot. When cool enough to handle, remove and cut the meat into bite-size pieces, discarding the bone, skin, and fat. Stir the meat back into the pot of beans.

2. FOR THE SOFRITO: Meanwhile, heat the oil in a large skillet over medium heat. Add the onion, red pepper, and salt and sauté until the vegetables soften, 8 to 10 minutes. Add the garlic, oregano, and cumin and sauté until fragrant, 1 minute longer.

3. TO FINISH THE SOUP: Scoop 1½ cups beans and 2 cups cooking liquid into the pan with the sofrito. Mash the beans with a potato masher or fork until smooth. Simmer, uncovered, over medium heat until the liquid is reduced and thickened, about 5 minutes. Return the sofrito mixture to the bean pot. Simmer, uncovered, until the flavors meld, about 15 minutes.

4. Blend the cornstarch and water together in a small bowl to form a smooth paste. Stir the paste into the soup and simmer until thickened, about 5 minutes. (The soup can be refrigerated in an airtight container for up to 3 days. To reheat, bring the soup to a simmer over low heat.) To serve, remove and discard the green pepper and bay leaves. Stir in the lime juice and adjust the seasonings. Ladle the soup into individual bowls and garnish each bowl with a spoonful of sour cream, a generous sprinkling of cilantro, and some red onion. Serve immediately, passing the hot pepper sauce at the table, if desired.

➤ VARIATION

Black Bean Soup with Balsamic Vinegar and Bacon

For optimum flavor, cook the ham hock with the beans, but don't bother trying to rescue the meat from the spent hock. The fried bits of bacon are more than sufficient.

Although you can garnish this variation with sour cream, cilantro, and red onion, you might try finely chopped hard-boiled eggs and parsley instead.

Fry 4 slices (about 4 ounces) bacon, cut into ¼-inch strips, in a large skillet over medium heat until crisp and brown, about 5 minutes. Transfer the bacon with a slotted spoon to a paper towel–lined plate; reserve the bacon fat in the skillet. Follow the recipe for Black Bean Soup, discarding the ham hock once the beans are tender in step 1 and cooking the sofrito in bacon fat instead of olive oil in step 2. Add the cooked bacon to the beans with the cornstarch slurry in step 4 and substitute balsamic vinegar for the lime juice.

CORN CHOWDER

WHILE IT IS MOST EASILY APPRECIATED ON the cob, fresh corn also lends itself well to another American favorite: corn chowder. The ingredients in most corn chowder recipes are relatively standard: corn and other vegetables, usually potatoes and onions at minimum; liquids such as water or corn or chicken stock enriched with some sort of dairy; and some sort of fat, be it butter, bacon, or the traditional favorite, salt pork. Most recipes also have in common a reliance on the time-honored technique of first cooking the onions in fat to develop flavor and then adding the liquids and vegetables. Comfortable with this basic approach, we decided to build our recipe from the ground up.

We knew from the outset that we wanted our chowder to be loaded with fresh corn flavor. What became apparent after testing a few recipes is that the texture and flavor of the base (the dairy-enriched liquid) are also critical to a great chowder. The first contributor to that flavor is fat. Because lots of people haven't cooked with salt pork and some shy away from bacon, we were hoping that butter or oil would prove to be adequate substitutes, but tests proved otherwise. Chowders prepared with corn oil were bland and insipid. Butter was better, but it failed to add complexity of flavor to the chowder. Somewhat surprisingly, rendered bacon fat also failed to add much interesting flavor.

Tradition, in the form of salt pork, served the chowder best, giving the base a deep, resonant flavor. Salt pork comes from the pig's belly and consists mostly of fat, striated with thin layers of meat. It can be confused with fatback, which is pure fat and comes from the pig's back. Make sure that what you buy at the market is salt pork; because it's both salted and cured and also contains meat, salt pork is more flavorful than fatback. (For more information on salt pork, see page 229.)

The next question concerning the fat was how to use it. What was the best way to render the fat? Was it necessary (or better) to cut up the salt pork into small pieces? Should the salt pork be removed from the pan after rendering, or is there an advantage to leaving it in the pot? The chowder developed a truly delectable flavor when the salt pork stayed in the pot throughout cooking. Cutting it into bits, though, proved to be undesirable; we found those little pieces to be tough and chewy. Our solution was to use two big chunks that could be removed easily at the end of cooking. One shortcoming of this technique is that the same amount of salt pork cut into a couple of big pieces produces less fat than all of those small pieces, and it wasn't quite enough to sweat the onions. We compensated by adding a little butter to the pan.

With this first important building block of flavor in place, we could go on to consider how best to infuse the chowder base with the flavor of corn.

REMOVING KERNELS FROM THE COB

Tapered ears of corn can wobble on cutting boards, and kernels can fly around the kitchen. To work safely and more neatly, we cut the ear in half crosswise and then stand the half ears on their cut surfaces, which are flat and stable.

Corn stock, corn puree, corn juice, and corn pulp were all possibilities.

We made two quick stocks with corncobs and husks, using water in one and chicken broth in the other. Although both brews had some corn flavor, their overall effect on the chowder was minimal; making corn stock was clearly not worth the effort. We did learn, though, that water diluted the flavor of the chowder, while chicken broth improved it; this would be our liquid of choice for the base.

Looking for a quick and easy solution, we next tried pureeing the corn kernels and dumping them into the chowder. This wasn't going to work: the hulls made for an unpleasantly rough texture.

In our research, we identified grating and scraping as a good means of extracting flavor from corn to be used for chowder. This approach is time-consuming and messy, but the result convinced us that it is worth the effort. Here was one of the secrets to great corn chowder. The pulp is thick, lush, smooth-textured, and full of corn flavor. When added to the chowder, it improved both flavor and texture dramatically.

Our next concern was the dairy, and, as it turned out, the thickener to be used. A problem with the dairy component of chowder is its tendency to curdle when heated, with lower-fat products such as 2 percent milk more likely to curdle than high-fat products such as heavy cream. It's the protein component of dairy that causes curdling, and heavy cream is not susceptible because it has so much (about 40 percent) fat; the protein molecules are thus completely surrounded by fat molecules, which keep the proteins from breaking down. But we would not be able to rely entirely on heavy cream to prevent curdling, as our tasters rejected this version. In their collective opinion, it tasted "like hot corn ice cream."

While some heavy cream was needed to give the base some depth of character, whole milk, which is wonderfully neutral and therefore capable of being infused with corn flavor, would make up the larger part of the dairy. This composition gave us some concern about curdling, which is where the thickening factor came in. We realized that the most practical thickener to use would be flour, which is known to help stabilize dairy proteins and thereby prevent curdling. Having a dual objective of both thickening the base and stabilizing the dairy made our work easier. To prevent curdling, the flour has to be in the pot before the dairy is added. The logical choice of technique, then, would be to make a roux, stirring the flour into the fat and onions at the beginning of the cooking process.

Determining the chowder solids was a relatively simple matter. Onions, potatoes, and corn kernels were a given; the questions were what variety of onion and potato and how much of each. All-purpose onions and leeks were serviceable, but Spanish onions proved best, adding flavor without dominating the other ingredients. The favorite potatoes were red potatoes, which remained firm and looked great with their skins left on. Whole corn kernels add authenticity to the chowder, and we learned that adding the kernels after the potatoes have been cooked till tender, then cooking the kernels just briefly, results in a fresh-from-the-cob corn flavor. A bit of garlic added some depth and fullness, while thyme, parsley, and a bay leaf helped to round out the flavors.

MILKING CORN

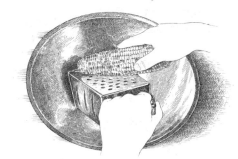

1. Start by grating the corn ears on a box grater.

2. Finish by firmly scraping any remaining kernels off the cob with the back of a butter knife.

Corn Chowder
SERVES 6

Be sure to use salt pork, not fatback, for the chowder. Streaks of lean meat distinguish salt pork from fatback; fatback is pure fat. (See page 229 for more details.) We prefer Spanish onions for their sweet, mild flavor, but all-purpose yellow onions will work fine, too.

10	medium ears fresh yellow corn, husks and silk removed
3	ounces salt pork, trimmed of rind and cut in half
1	tablespoon unsalted butter
1	large onion, preferably Spanish, chopped fine
2	medium garlic cloves, minced or pressed through a garlic press
3	tablespoons all-purpose flour
3	cups low-sodium chicken broth
2	medium red potatoes (about 12 ounces), scrubbed and cut into 1/4-inch dice
1	medium bay leaf
1	teaspoon minced fresh thyme leaves or 1/4 teaspoon dried thyme
2	cups whole milk
1	cup heavy cream
2	tablespoons minced fresh parsley leaves
1 1/2	teaspoons salt
	Ground black pepper

1. Following the illustrations on page 64, use a chef's knife to cut the kernels from 4 ears of corn.

TRIMMING SALT PORK

Salt pork is usually sold with the rind attached, and you must remove the tough rind before slicing or chopping. Steady the salt pork with one hand, and with the other hand slide the blade of a sharp chef's knife between the rind and the fat, using a wide sawing motion to cut away the rind in one piece.

Transfer the kernels to a medium bowl and set aside. (You should have about 3 cups.) Following the illustrations on page 65, grate the kernels from the remaining 6 ears on the large holes of a box grater, then firmly scrape any pulp remaining on the cobs with the back of a butter knife. (You should have 2 generous cups of kernels and pulp.) Transfer the grated corn and pulp to a separate bowl and set aside.

2. Sauté the salt pork in a Dutch oven over medium-high heat, turning with tongs and pressing down on the pieces to render the fat, until the cubes are crisp and golden brown, about 10 minutes. Reduce the heat to low, stir in the butter and onion, cover the pot, and cook until softened, about 12 minutes. Remove the salt pork and reserve. Add the garlic and sauté until fragrant, about 1 minute. Stir in the flour and cook, stirring constantly, about 2 minutes. Whisking constantly, gradually add the broth. Add the potatoes, bay leaf, thyme, milk, reserved grated corn and pulp, and reserved salt pork; bring to a boil. Reduce the heat to medium-low and simmer until the potatoes are almost tender, 8 to 10 minutes.

3. Add the reserved corn kernels and heavy cream and return to a simmer; simmer until the corn kernels are tender yet still slightly crunchy, about 5 minutes longer. Discard the bay leaf and salt pork. (The chowder can be refrigerated in an airtight container for up to 2 days. Warm over low heat until hot; do not boil.) Stir in the parsley, salt, and pepper to taste and serve immediately.

NEW ENGLAND CLAM CHOWDER

WE LOVE HOMEMADE CLAM CHOWDER ALMOST as much as we love good chicken soup. But we must confess that many cooks (including some who work in our test kitchen) don't make their own chowder. While they might never buy chicken soup, they seem willing to make this compromise. We wondered why.

Time certainly isn't the reason. You can actually prepare clam chowder much more quickly than you can a pot of good chicken soup. The reason why many cooks don't bother making their own clam chowder is the clams. First of all, clams can be expensive. Second, clams are not terribly forgiving—you must cook them soon after their purchase (chickens can be frozen), and then the soup itself must be quickly consumed (again, chicken soup can be frozen or at least refrigerated for another day). Last, chowders are more fragile (and thus more fickle) than other soups. Unless the chowder is stabilized in some way, it curdles, especially if the soup is brought to a boil.

Our goals for this soup, then, were multiple but quite clear. We wanted to develop a delicious, traditional chowder that was economical, would not curdle, and could be prepared quickly. Before testing chowder recipes, we explored our clam options (see below for more information). Chowders are typically made with hard-shell clams, so we purchased (from smallest to largest) cockles, littlenecks, cherrystones, and chowder clams, often called quahogs (pronounced ko-hogs).

Although they made delicious chowders, we eliminated littlenecks and cockles, both of which were just too expensive to toss into a chowder pot. Chowders made with the cheapest clams, however, weren't really satisfactory, either. The quahogs we purchased for testing were too large (4 to 5 inches in diameter), tough, and strong-flavored.

Though only a little more expensive than quahogs, cherrystones offered good value and flavor. The chowder made from these slightly smaller clams was distinctly clam-flavored, without an inky aftertaste. Because there are no industry sizing standards for each clam variety, you may find some small quahogs labeled as cherrystones or large cherrystones labeled as quahogs. Regardless of designation, clams much over 4 inches in diameter will deliver a distinctly metallic, inky-flavored chowder.

Some recipes suggest shucking raw clams and then adding the raw clam bellies to the soup pot. Other recipes steam the clams open. We tested both methods and found that steaming clams open is far easier than shucking them. After seven to nine minutes over simmering water, the clams open as naturally as budding flowers. Ours did not toughen up as long as we pulled them from the pot as soon as they opened and didn't let them cook

INGREDIENTS: Clams

Clams are easy enough to cook. When they open, they are done. However, perfectly cooked clams can be made inedible by lingering sand. Straining the juices through cheesecloth after cooking will remove the grit, but it's a pain. Plus, you lose some of the juices to the cheesecloth. Worse still, careful straining will not remove bits of sand still clinging to the clam meat. Rinsing the cooked clams washes away flavor.

That's why so many clam recipes start by soaking clams in cold salt water for several hours. We tried various soaking regimens—such as soaking in water with flour, soaking in water with baking powder, soaking in water with cornmeal, and scrubbing and rinsing in five changes of water. If the clams were dirty at the outset, none of these techniques really worked. Even after soaking, many clams needed to be rinsed and the cooking liquid strained.

However, during the coarse of this testing, we noticed that some varieties of clams were extremely clean and free of grit at the outset. A quick scrub of the shell exterior and these clams were ready for the cooking pot, without any tedious soaking.

The cooked clams were free of grit, and the liquid was clean. If you want to ensure that your clams will be clean (and that your chowder will be free of grit), you must shop carefully.

Clams can be divided into two categories—hard-shell varieties (such as quahogs, cherrystones, and littlenecks) and soft-shell varieties (such as steamers and razor clams). Hard-shells live along sandy beaches and bays; soft-shells live in muddy tidal flats. We have found that a modest shift in location makes all the difference in the kitchen.

When harvested, hard-shells remain tightly closed. In our tests, we found the meat inside to be sand-free. The exterior should be scrubbed under cold running water to remove any caked-on sand, but otherwise these clams can be cooked without further worry about gritty broths.

Soft-shell clams gape when they are alive. We found that they almost always contain a lot of sand. While it's worthwhile to soak them in several batches of cold water to remove some of the sand, you can never get rid of it all. In the end, you must strain the cooking liquid. It's a good idea to rinse the cooked clams, too.

too long in the finished chowder.

Although many chowder recipes instruct the cook to soak the clams in salt water spiked with cornmeal or baking powder to remove grit, we found the extra step of purging or filtering hard-shell clams to be unnecessary (see page 67 for more details). All of the hard-shells we tested were relatively clean, and what little sediment there was sank to the bottom of the steaming liquid. Getting rid of the grit was as simple as leaving the last few tablespoons of broth in the pan when pouring it from the pot. If you find that your clam broth is gritty, strain it through a coffee filter.

At this point, we turned our attention to texture. We wanted a chowder that was thick but still a soup rather than a stew. Older recipes call for thickening clam chowder with crumbled biscuits; bread crumbs and crackers are modern stand-ins.

Bread crumb–thickened chowders failed to impress. We wanted a smooth, creamy soup base for the potatoes, onions, and clams, but no matter how long the chowder was simmered, bread crumbs or crackers never completely dissolved into the cooking liquid. Heavy cream alone, by contrast, did not give the chowder enough body. We discovered fairly quickly that flour was necessary, not only as a thickener but as a stabilizer, because unthickened chowders separate and curdle. Of the two flour methods, we opted to thicken at the beginning of cooking rather than at the end. Because our final recipe was finished with cream, we felt the chowder didn't need the extra butter that would be required to add the flour in a paste to the finished soup.

For potatoes, we found that waxy red boiling potatoes are best for creamy-style chowders. They have a firm but tender texture, and their red skins look appealing.

We now had two final questions to answer about New England clam chowder. First, should it include salt pork or bacon, and, if the latter, did the bacon need to be blanched? Second, should the chowder be enriched with milk or cream?

Salt pork is the more traditional choice in chowder recipes, although bacon has become popular in recent decades, no doubt because of its availability. We made clam chowder with both salt pork and bacon, and tasters liked both versions. Frankly, we ended up using such small amounts of pork in our final recipe that either salt pork or bacon is fine. Bacon is more readily available and, once bought, easier to use up. Blanching the bacon makes it taste more like salt pork, but we rather liked the subtle smokiness of the chowder made with unblanched bacon.

As for the cream versus milk issue, we found that so much milk was required to make the chowder look and taste creamy that it began to lose its clam flavor and became more like a mild bisque or the clam equivalent of oyster stew. Making the chowder with almost all clam broth (5 cups of the cooking liquid from steaming the clams), then finishing the stew with a cup of cream, gave us what we were looking for—a rich, creamy chowder that tasted distinctly of clams.

STEAMING CLAMS FOR CHOWDER

1. Steam clams until they just open, as seen on the left, rather than completely open, as shown on the right.

2. Carefully use a paring knife to open the clams, holding each over a bowl to catch any juices that are released.

3. Discard the top shell and use the knife to sever the muscle that connects the clam to the bottom shell.

New England Clam Chowder

SERVES 6

If desired, replace the bacon with 4 ounces of finely chopped salt pork. See page 229 for information on salt pork. Note that the chowder is best served at once. Reheating will make the clams tough and chewy.

7	pounds medium hard-shell clams, such as cherrystones, washed and scrubbed clean
4	slices (about 4 ounces) thick-cut bacon, cut into 1/4-inch pieces
1	large Spanish onion, chopped medium
2	tablespoons all-purpose flour
1 1/2	pounds red potatoes (about 3 medium), scrubbed and cut into 1/2-inch dice
1	large bay leaf
1	teaspoon minced fresh thyme leaves or 1/4 teaspoon dried thyme
1	cup heavy cream
2	tablespoons minced fresh parsley leaves Salt and ground black or white pepper

SCIENCE:
Buying Clams by Weight or Number

Judging by most recipes, there is no consistent or accurate method of designating the amount of clams needed for a given chowder. Some recipes call for some amount of shucked clams, giving the cook no idea how many whole clams to buy. Other recipes call for "X" number of "hard-shell clams," apparently not taking into account the size differences between a quahog and a littleneck. Likewise, there are no industry sizing standards for each clam variety. Clam size and name vary from source to source, so that one company's cherrystone clam might be another company's quahog.

We wondered if calling for "X" pounds of clams, regardless of size, would yield similar quantities of meat and liquid. Working with 1 1/2-pound quantities, we shucked quahogs, cherrystones, and littlenecks. Although the number of clams per pound varied greatly (two of our quahogs equaled 1 1/2 pounds, while it took 2 dozen littlenecks to equal the same weight). So, even though clams are usually sold by the piece at the fish market, we find it more accurate to measure them by weight rather than quantity. Just ask your fish market to weigh the clams as they count them. Regardless of clam size, you'll need 7 to 8 pounds to make our clam chowder recipes.

1. Bring 3 cups water to a boil in large stockpot or Dutch oven. Add the clams and cover with a tight-fitting lid. Cook for 5 minutes, uncover, and stir with a wooden spoon. Quickly cover the pot and steam until the clams just open, 2 to 4 minutes (see the illustration on page 68). Transfer the clams to a large bowl; cool slightly. Open the clams with a paring knife, holding the clams over a bowl to catch any juices (see the illustration on page 68). With the knife, sever the muscle that attaches the clam to the shell (see the illustration on page 68) and transfer the meat to a cutting board. Discard the shells. Mince the clams; set aside. Pour the clam broth into a 2-quart Pyrex measuring cup, holding back the last few tablespoons of broth in case of sediment; set the clam broth aside. (You should have about 5 cups. If not, add bottled clam juice or water to make this amount.) Rinse and dry the stockpot or Dutch oven, then return the pot to the burner.

2. Fry the bacon in the empty pot over medium-low heat until the fat is rendered and the bacon is crisp, 5 to 7 minutes. Add the onion and cook, stirring occasionally, until softened, about 5 minutes. Add the flour and stir until lightly colored, about 1 minute. Gradually whisk in the reserved clam broth. Add the potatoes, bay leaf, and thyme and simmer until the potatoes are tender, about 10 minutes. Add the reserved minced clams, the cream, parsley, and salt (if necessary) and pepper to taste; bring to a simmer, but do not boil. Remove the pan from the heat, discard the bay leaf, and serve immediately.

VARIATION
Quick Pantry New England Clam Chowder

From late summer through winter, when clams are plentiful, you'll probably want to make fresh clam chowder. But if you're short on time or find clams scarce and expensive, the right canned clams and bottled clam juice deliver a chowder that's at least three notches above canned chowder in quality. We tested seven brands of minced and small whole canned clams and preferred Doxsee Minced Clams teamed with Doxsee clam juice, as well as Snow's Minced Clams and Snow's clam juice.

Follow the recipe for New England Clam Chowder, substituting for the fresh clams 4 (6.5-ounce) cans minced clams, juice drained and reserved, along with 1 cup water and 2 (8-ounce) bottles clam juice in a medium bowl, and clam meat reserved in a small bowl. Add the reserved clam juice and clam meat at the same points in step 2 that the fresh clam broth and meat are added.

SHRIMP BISQUE

THOUGH A BISQUE BY IMPLICATION IS ANY soup that is rich, velvety, and smooth, by definition it contains shellfish, cream, and the classic French aromatic trio of celery, carrot, and onion known as mirepoix. Shrimp bisque, in particular, should be a rich, blushing pastel—delicate in character but deeply intense—with an almost sweet shrimp essence and an elusive interplay of other flavors. Its texture must run unfettered and silky over the tongue. If you are very lucky, there will be tender pieces of poached shrimp and shatteringly crisp, buttery croutons.

The fundamental challenge in making a shrimp bisque is extracting flavor from the shrimp and shells. The recipes we tested did this in a couple of ways. Some recipes we tried pureed the shrimp meat into the base and left it there; others simmered the shrimp in the base until spent and then strained them out. The bisques made with pureed shrimp were grainy with shrimp curds; the ones in which the shrimp were strained out achieved the velvety texture properly associated with a bisque.

Because the shrimp flavor resides more in the shells than in the meat, a bisque made with shrimp alone is weak and unsatisfying. But trying to deal with shells and meat to the advantage of each tends to induce procedural overkill. The recipes that we tested got carried away by having several pots and pans active at once (here a little pot of simmering aromatics, here fish stock simmering with shells and rice, there a pan to sauté shrimp) rather than proceeding one step at a time in logical sequence.

We talked strategy in the test kitchen. The shrimp were key; other ingredients must add background depth and nuance. Fresh shell-on shrimp are virtually unavailable in the United States; those that are not frozen are usually not fresh but simply thawed. Size was not an issue because the shrimp are in effect sacrificed to the bisque. We thought it reasonable to recommend whatever variety of shell-on shrimp could be found in the freezer case. (Though differences in shrimp varieties did not prove overwhelming, as it turned out, the nicest bisques were produced with Mexican or Gulf White shrimp. For more information on shrimp and how they are sized, see page 520.)

We began by taking 2 pounds of shrimp, shelling 8 ounces' worth, and putting them aside to use later as a garnish. We then heated a splash of oil in a heavy Dutch oven. Working in two batches, we sautéed the remaining shell-on shrimp until they reached a blistering pink. To wring every drop of flavor from the shells, we then flambéed the shrimp in brandy. Next we took the sautéed shrimp, dumped them into a food processor, and

TWO WAYS TO FLAMBÉ SHRIMP

A. To flambé on a gas stove, add the warmed brandy to the pan with the shrimp and shells, tilting the pan toward the flame to ignite it and then shaking the skillet.

B. To flambé on an electric stove, add the warmed brandy to the pan with the shrimp and shells, waving a lit match over the pan until the brandy ignites and then shaking the skillet.

ground them to a pulp. Because we knew the shrimp and the shells were destined to be strained from the bisque, a food processor was the fastest way to unlock the shrimp's flavor potential.

Our next step was to sauté the shrimp pulp with a mirepoix in the same Dutch oven. After five minutes, we stirred in a bit of flour, preferring its convenience to the rice or bread suggested for thickening in some recipes. Next came white wine, drained diced tomatoes, and some clam juice. After 20 minutes or so, we strained the fragrant base through a cheesecloth-lined strainer, pressing to extract every drop. It looked like flowing silk shantung.

Back on the stove, we offered the soup base a bit of cream, a couple of drops of lemon juice, a sprig of fresh tarragon, and then the remaining shrimp, cut into pieces. A brief simmer poached the shrimp garnish and brought the flavors into harmony. We removed the tarragon sprig and added a splash of sherry. This bisque possessed everything we demanded of it: flavor in spades and a peerless texture and color.

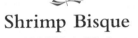

Shrimp Bisque

SERVES 4 TO 6

Shrimp shells contribute a lot of flavor to the bisque, so be sure to purchase shell-on shrimp. A good size to use is extra-large shrimp (21 to 25 per pound; see the ingredient box on page 520 for more information on how shrimp are sized). If your food processor is small and your shrimp are jumbo (16 to 20 per pound), process them in two batches. For straining the bisque, if you do not own a chinois, use a china cap or large, sturdy mesh strainer lined with a double layer of damp cheesecloth (see page 72 for more information). Because this recipe contains chunks of shrimp, it cannot be prepared in advance. If you like, you can prepare the soup up to the point that the base is strained through the chinois and then refrigerate the strained base and the shelled shrimp for several hours. When ready to serve the soup, heat the soup base along with the tarragon, cream, lemon juice, and cayenne and proceed as directed.

2	pounds extra-large shell-on shrimp (21 to 25 per pound), preferably Mexican or Gulf Whites
3	tablespoons olive oil
1/3	cup brandy or cognac, warmed
2	tablespoons unsalted butter
1	small carrot, minced (about 3 tablespoons)
1	small celery rib, minced (about 3 tablespoons)
1	small onion, minced (about 6 tablespoons)
1	medium garlic clove, minced or pressed through a garlic press
1/2	cup all-purpose flour
1 1/2	cups dry white wine
4	(8-ounce) bottles clam juice
1	(14.5-ounce) can diced tomatoes, drained
1	small sprig fresh tarragon
1	cup heavy cream
1	tablespoon juice from 1 small lemon
	Pinch cayenne pepper
2	tablespoons dry sherry or Madeira
	Salt and ground black pepper

1. Peel ½ pound of the shrimp, reserving the shells; cut each peeled shrimp into thirds and reserve. With paper towels, thoroughly pat dry the remaining 1½ pounds shrimp and the reserved shells.

2. Heat a 12-inch heavy-bottomed skillet over high heat until very hot, about 3 minutes. Add 1½ tablespoons of the olive oil and swirl to coat the pan bottom. Add half of the remaining shell-on shrimp and half of the reserved shells; sauté until the shrimp are deep pink and the shells are lightly browned, about 2 minutes. Transfer the shrimp and the shells to a medium bowl and repeat with the remaining oil, shell-on shrimp, and shells. Return the first browned batch to the shrimp in the skillet. Pour the warmed brandy over the shrimp and flambé, shaking the pan (see the illustrations on page 70). When the flames subside, transfer the shrimp and shells to a food processor fitted with the steel blade and process until the mixture resembles fine meal, about 10 seconds.

3. Heat the butter in a large stockpot or Dutch oven over medium heat until foaming. Add the carrot, celery, onion, garlic, and ground shrimp; cover and cook, stirring frequently, until the vegetables are slightly softened and the mixture is fragrant, about 5 minutes. Add the flour and cook, stirring constantly, until combined thoroughly, about 1 minute. Stir in the wine, clam juice, and tomatoes, scraping the pan bottom with a wooden spoon to loosen any browned bits. Cover, increase the heat

to medium-high, and bring to a boil; reduce the heat to low and simmer, stirring frequently, until thickened and the flavors meld, about 20 minutes.

4. Strain the bisque through a chinois or fine-mesh strainer into a medium container, pressing on the solids with the back of a ladle to extract all the liquid. Wash and dry the Dutch oven; return the strained bisque to the Dutch oven and stir in the tarragon, cream, lemon juice, and cayenne. Bring to a simmer over medium-high heat; add the reserved peeled and cut-up shrimp and simmer until the shrimp are firm but tender, about 1½ minutes. Discard the tarragon sprig; stir in the sherry, season with salt and pepper to taste, and serve immediately.

GAZPACHO

GAZPACHO IS HIGH SUMMER IN A BOWL. Popular on both sides of the Atlantic, this ice-cold, uncooked vegetable soup, made principally of tomatoes (whole and juice), cucumbers, bell peppers, and onions and seasoned with olive oil and vinegar, is sometimes referred to as "liquid salad" in its native Spain. That slang name may

A CHINOIS VERSUS A CHINA CAP

A chinois is covered with fine woven mesh and will trap all solids, even small bits. It's ideal for producing a perfectly smooth pureed soup or bisque.

A china cap has the same conical shape as a chinois but consists of metal perforations rather than a mesh screen. It's best for straining hot, thin liquids through bones and vegetables; it will allow tiny solids to pass through. We use it to strain solids from stock.

be more apt on these shores, though, as many American gazpacho recipes instruct the cook to simply puree all the vegetables together in the blender. The resulting mixture is more a thin vegetable porridge with an anonymous vegetal flavor, whereas we were looking for a soup with clearly flavored, distinct pieces of vegetable in a bracing tomato broth.

With our preference for a chunky-style soup established, we had to figure out the best method for preparing the vegetables. Although it was a breeze to use, the blender broke the vegetables down beyond recognition, which was not at all what we wanted. The food processor fared somewhat better, especially when we processed each vegetable separately. This method had distinct pros and cons. On the pro side were ease and the fact that the vegetables released some juice as they broke down, which helped flavor the soup. The cons were that no matter how we finessed the pulse feature, the vegetable pieces were neither neatly chopped nor consistently sized. This was especially true of the tomatoes, which broke down to a pulp. The texture of the resulting soup was more along the lines of vegetable slush, which might be acceptable given the ease of preparation, but still not ideal. On balance, the food processor is a decent option, especially if you favor speed and convenience, so we've included a variation.

Needless to say, we still pressed on to the old-fashioned, purist method of hand chopping the vegetables. It does involve some extra work, but it went much more swiftly than we'd imagined, and the benefits to the gazpacho's texture were dazzling. Because the pieces were consistent in size and shape, they not only retained their individual flavors but also set off the tomato broth beautifully, adding immeasurably to the whole. This was just what we were after.

One last procedural issue we investigated was the resting time. Gazpacho is best served ice-cold, and the chilling time also allows the flavors to develop and meld. We found that four hours was the minimum time required for the soup to chill and the flavors to blossom.

Several of the key ingredients and seasonings also bore some exploration. Tomatoes are a star player here, and we preferred beefsteak over plum because they were larger, juicier, and easier to chop. Gazpacho is truly a dish to make only when local tomatoes are plentiful. We made several batches using handsome supermarket tomatoes, but the flavor paled in comparison to those batches made with perfectly ripe, local, farm-stand tomatoes. We considered skinning and seeding them, but not a single taster complained when we didn't, so we skipped the extra steps.

When it came to peppers, we preferred red over green for their sweeter flavor. But red was less popular in the onion department; tasters rejected red onions, as well as plain yellow, as too sharp. Instead, they favored sweet onions, such as Vidalia or Maui, and shallots equally. We did note, however, that any onion was overpowering if used in the quantities recommended in most recipes (especially in the leftovers the next day), and the same was true of garlic, so we dramatically reduced the quantity of both. To ensure thorough seasoning of the whole mixture, we marinated the vegetables briefly in the garlic, salt, pepper, and vinegar before adding the bulk of the liquid. These batches had more balanced flavors than the batches that were seasoned after all the ingredients were combined.

The liquid component was also critical. Most recipes called for tomato juice, which we sampled both straight and mixed in various amounts with water and canned low-sodium chicken broth. The winning ratio was 5 cups of tomato juice thinned with 1 cup of water to make the 6-cup total we needed. The water cut the viscosity of the juice just enough to make it brothy and light, but not downright thin. Given our preference for ice-cold gazpacho, we decided to add ice cubes instead of straight water. The ice cubes helped chill the soup while providing water as they melted. We also conducted a blind tasting of tomato juices in which Welch's showed very well.

DICING THE VEGETABLES FOR GAZPACHO

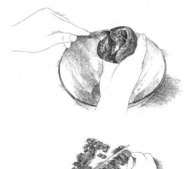

TOMATOES

1. Core the tomatoes, halve them pole to pole, and working over a bowl to catch all the juices, scoop out (and reserve) the inner pulp and seeds with a dinner spoon. Cut the pulp into ¼-inch dice.

2. Cut the empty tomato halves into ¼-inch slices. Turn the slices 90 degrees and cut into even ¼-inch pieces.

PEPPERS

1. Slice a ¾-inch section off both the tip and stem ends of the peppers. Make one slice through the wall of each pepper, lay the pepper skin-side down on a board, and open the flesh, exposing the seeds and membranes.

2. Cut away and discard the seeds and membranes. Cut the flesh into ¼-inch strips. Turn the strips 90 degrees and cut them into even ¼-inch pieces. Also, cut the tips and tops into even ¼-inch dice.

CUCUMBERS

1. Cut a ¾-inch section off both ends of the cucumbers. Halve the cucumbers lengthwise and scoop out the seeds with a dinner spoon. Cut each seeded half lengthwise into ¼-inch strips.

2. Turn the strips 90 degrees and cut into even ¼-inch pieces.

Finally, a word about the two primary seasonings, vinegar and olive oil. Spain is a noted producer of sherry, so it follows that sherry vinegar is a popular choice for gazpacho. When we tasted it, along with champagne, red wine, and white wine vinegars, the sherry vinegar was our favorite by far, adding not only acidity but also richness and depth. If you find that your stock of sherry vinegar has run dry, white wine vinegar was the runner-up and can be substituted. The oil contributes both flavor and a lush mouthfeel to this simple soup, and only extra-virgin will do. Liquid or not, would you dress a beautiful summer salad with anything less?

Classic Gazpacho
SERVES 8 TO 10

This recipe makes a large quantity because the leftovers are so good, but it can be halved if you prefer. For the tomato juice in our gazpacho, we prefer Welch's. If Fresh Samantha juices are available in your grocery store, the company's Veggie Cha Cha vegetable juice also makes an excellent gazpacho—use it in place of the tomato juice. Traditionally, diners garnish their own bowls with more of the same diced vegetables that are in the soup. If that appeals to you, cut some extra vegetables while you prepare those called for in the recipe. Additional garnish possibilities include croutons (page 48), chopped pitted black olives, chopped hard-boiled eggs (page 122), and finely diced avocado.

3	medium, ripe beefsteak tomatoes (about 1¹/₂ pounds), cored and cut into ¹/₄-inch dice, following the illustrations on page 73
2	medium red bell peppers (about 1 pound), cored, seeded, and cut into ¹/₄-inch dice, following the illustrations on page 73
2	small cucumbers (about 1 pound), one peeled and the other with skin on, both seeded and cut into ¹/₄-inch dice, following the illustrations on page 73
¹/₂	small sweet onion, such as Vidalia, Maui, or Walla Walla, or 2 large shallots, minced
2	medium garlic cloves, minced or pressed through a garlic press
2	teaspoons salt
¹/₃	cup sherry vinegar
	Ground black pepper
5	cups tomato juice, preferably Welch's
1	teaspoon hot pepper sauce (optional)
8	ice cubes
	Extra-virgin olive oil for serving

1. Combine the tomatoes, bell peppers, cucumbers, onion, garlic, salt, vinegar, and black pepper to taste in a large (at least 4-quart) nonreactive bowl. Let stand until the vegetables just begin to release their juices, about 5 minutes. Stir in the tomato juice, hot pepper sauce (if using), and ice cubes. Cover tightly and refrigerate to blend the flavors, at least 4 hours and up to 2 days.

2. Adjust the seasonings with salt and pepper to taste and remove and discard any unmelted ice cubes. Serve cold, drizzling each portion with about 1 teaspoon extra-virgin olive oil and topping with the desired garnishes (see note).

➤ VARIATIONS

Quick Food Processor Gazpacho

Using the same ingredients and quantities as for Classic Gazpacho, core and quarter the tomatoes and process them in a food processor until broken down into ¹/₄- to 1-inch pieces, about twelve 1-second pulses; transfer to a large bowl. Cut the cored and seeded peppers and seeded cucumbers into rough 1-inch pieces and process them separately until broken down into ¹/₄- to 1-inch pieces, about twelve 1-second pulses; add to the bowl with the tomatoes. Add the onion, garlic, salt, vinegar, and black pepper to taste; proceed with the recipe as directed.

Spicy Gazpacho with Chipotle Chiles and Lime

A garnish of finely diced ripe avocado is a must with this variation.

Follow the recipe for Classic or Quick Food Processor Gazpacho, omitting the optional hot pepper sauce and adding 2¹/₂ tablespoons minced canned chipotle chiles in adobo sauce, ¹/₄ cup minced fresh cilantro leaves, 6 tablespoons lime juice, and 2 teaspoons grated lime zest along with the tomato juice and ice cubes.

3
SALADS

WHAT DO SALADS MADE WITH LEAFY GREENS have in common with potato salad or coleslaw? The answer is dressing. There are two main types of cold sauces typically used to dress salads. Vinaigrette is a relatively thin emulsion made of oil, vinegar, and seasonings. Mayonnaise is a thick, creamy emulsion of egg yolk and oil with a little acid and some seasonings.

An emulsion is a mixture of two things that don't ordinarily mix, such as oil and water or oil and vinegar. The only way to mix them is to stir or whisk so strenuously that the two ingredients break down into tiny droplets. Many of these droplets will continue to find each other and recoalesce into pure fluid. (This is what happens when the emulsion breaks.) Eventually, one of the fluids (usually the less plentiful one) will break entirely into droplets so tiny that they remain separated by the opposite fluid.

The liquid in the droplet form is called the dispersed phase (vinegar in a vinaigrette, oil in mayonnaise) because the droplets are dispersed throughout the emulsion. The liquid that surrounds the droplets is the continuous phase (oil in a vinaigrette, egg in mayonnaise). Because the continuous phase forms the surface of the emulsion, that's what the mouth and tongue feel and taste first.

Constructing the perfect leafy salad is not difficult, but there are things to watch out for. From battered greens to acidic vinaigrettes, simple salads can suffer from a variety of ills. Good salad begins with clean greens. See our instructions on page 82 for washing, drying, and dressing greens.

Although salad can be nothing more than a simple dressing and a single kind of green, it can also be a more involved affair, with multiple greens, vegetables, meat, seafood, chicken, and/or cheese. The recipes in this chapter fall into four basic categories: basic salads with just greens and dressing; slightly more elaborate leafy salads, meant to be served as first courses; side-dish salads (many made with vegetables and/or pasta rather than leafy greens), meant to be served on the dinner plate with something from the grill or sauté pan; and main-course salads that combine leafy greens and protein and can be served on their own or as a sandwich filling.

MAYONNAISE

MAYONNAISE IS USED TO DRESS VEGETABLE salads—especially potato salad and coleslaw. It acts as a creamy binder and adds richness to any salad. The science of mayonnaise is fairly complex and unusual. Whisking transforms three thin liquids—vegetable oil, lemon juice, and egg yolk—into a thick, creamy sauce. In mayonnaise, the egg yolk and lemon juice are the continuous phase (that's why something that is 95 percent oil doesn't taste greasy) and the oil is the dispersed phase that must be broken into tiny droplets.

Mayonnaise works because an egg yolk is such a good emulsifier and stabilizer. But sometimes mayonnaise can "break," as the ingredients revert back to their original liquid form. To keep mayonnaise from breaking, it is first necessary to whisk the egg yolk and lemon juice thoroughly (the egg yolk itself contains liquid and fat materials that must be emulsified). It is equally important to add the oil slowly to the egg yolk. Remember, 2 tablespoons of yolk and lemon juice must be "stretched" around ¾ cup of oil.

We like the flavor of corn oil in our basic mayonnaise. It produces a dressing that is rich and eggy with good body. Canola oil makes a slightly lighter, more lemony mayo. We find that extra-virgin olive oil can be harsh and bitter, especially if used alone in mayonnaise. While pure olive oil produces a mellower mayonnaise, it costs more than corn or canola oil and does not deliver better results.

While homemade mayonnaise is a delicious addition to salads, many cooks prefer the convenience and safety of commercial brands made without raw eggs. See our tasting of commercial brands of mayonnaise on page 77.

Mayonnaise

MAKES ABOUT ¾ CUP

Each time you add oil, make sure to whisk until it is thoroughly incorporated. It's fine to stop for a rest or to measure the next addition of oil. If the mayonnaise appears grainy or beaded after the last addition of oil, continue to whisk until smooth.

1	large egg yolk
¼	teaspoon salt
¼	teaspoon Dijon mustard
1½	teaspoons juice from 1 lemon
1	teaspoon white wine vinegar
¾	cup corn oil

1. Whisk the egg yolk vigorously in a medium bowl for 15 seconds. Add all of the remaining ingredients except for the oil and whisk until the yolk thickens and the color brightens, about 30 seconds.

2. Add ¼ cup of the oil in a slow, steady stream, continuing to whisk vigorously until the oil is incorporated completely and the mixture thickens, about 1 minute. Add another ¼ cup oil in the same manner, whisking until incorporated completely, about 30 seconds more. Add the remaining ¼ cup oil all at once and whisk until incorporated completely, about 30 seconds more. Serve. (The mayonnaise can be refrigerated in an airtight container for several days.)

➤ VARIATIONS

Lemon Mayonnaise

Follow the recipe for Mayonnaise, adding 1½ teaspoons grated lemon zest along with the lemon juice.

Dijon Mayonnaise

Follow the recipe for Mayonnaise, whisking 2 tablespoons Dijon mustard into the finished mayonnaise.

Tarragon Mayonnaise

Follow the recipe for Mayonnaise, stirring 1 tablespoon minced fresh tarragon leaves into the finished mayonnaise.

Food Processor Mayonnaise

MAKES ABOUT 1½ CUPS

Use 1 whole large egg and double the quantities of the other ingredients in the recipe for Mayonnaise. Pulse all of the ingredients except the oil in a food processor three or four times to combine. With the machine running, add the oil through the feed tube in a thin, steady stream until incorporated completely.

INGREDIENTS: Mayonnaise

Although we love homemade mayonnaise on occasion, we realize that it's not always convenient to whip up a batch, so we set up a tasting of seven nationally available brands of commercially prepared mayonnaise along with Kraft Miracle Whip. Even though the U.S. Food and Drug Administration does not recognize Miracle Whip as a real mayonnaise, we included it in our tasting because of its resounding popularity. Why is Miracle Whip considered a salad dressing and not a mayonnaise? The FDA defines mayonnaise as an emulsified semisolid food that is at least 65 percent vegetable oil by weight, is at least 2.5 percent acidifying ingredient (vinegar and/or lemon juice) by weight, and contains whole eggs or egg yolks. Miracle Whip, which is also sweeter than regular mayo, weighs in with only 40 percent soybean oil. (Water makes up the difference.)

A good mayonnaise will have clear egg flavor and a touch of acidity to offset the significant amount of fat from the added oil. Our tasters liked Hellmann's for having that balance, and Kraft was thought to be "flavorful but not overpowering." Which one should you buy? We recommend Hellmann's, but the difference between the two contenders is not overwhelming.

Finally, is it possible for a light mayo to be as flavorful as the full-fat original? We put five brands to the test: Kraft Light Mayonnaise, Hellmann's Light Mayonnaise, Miracle Whip Light Salad Dressing, Spectrum Light Canola Mayonnaise, and Nayonaise (a soy-based sandwich spread), all with a fat content of 3 to 5 grams per serving. We also threw the winner of the full-fat tasting into the mix (Hellmann's Real Mayonnaise, 11 grams of fat per serving).

The results? Last place went to Nayonaise. Tasters were unanimous in thinking it bore no resemblance to mayonnaise. Miracle Whip and Spectrum didn't fare much better. Tasters thought Kraft was too sweet. Hellmann's Light came in second place, very nearly beating out the winner, Hellmann's Real Mayonnaise. Although the light version had a pastier texture than regular Hellmann's, the bright, balanced flavors were similar.

THE BEST MAYONNAISE

Hellmann's (left), which is known as Best Foods west of the Rockies, took top honors in our tasting. Among the five brands of reduced-fat mayonnaise tested, Hellmann's Light (right) was the clear winner and rated nearly as well as its full-fat cousin.

RANCH DRESSING

RANCH DRESSING WAS MADE FAMOUS IN THE 1950s at the Hidden Valley Guest Ranch in Santa Barbara, California. The recipe was so popular that it was bought and marketed by a large corporation, which proceeded to introduce the herbed buttermilk dressing to the rest of the country in both a powdered and bottled form. Although the stuff made from a powdered mix or picked up in a bottle at the supermarket is still what many of us think of as ranch dressing, it doesn't compare with freshly made.

Most recipes call for buttermilk, thickened with either mayonnaise or sour cream, along with an array of herbs and seasonings. We tried to follow a strictly buttermilk/mayonnaise or buttermilk/sour cream path but found that neither sufficed. While the mayonnaise gave the dressing a nice, round sweetness, the sour cream was a good thickener and also added tartness to the buttermilk—too much tartness when used alone with the buttermilk. By using all three ingredients, however, we gave the dressing a nice balance of flavors, a pleasing consistency, and a good buttermilk kick.

To season this buttermilk base, we tried a number of ingredients called for in other recipes, including Worcestershire sauce, Dijon mustard, lime juice, red wine vinegar, celery seeds, and a host of dried herbs. In the end, we found that fresh herbs and seasonings were the keys to a bright, authentic flavor. Fresh parsley and cilantro, accented by scallion, shallot, and garlic, were the southern California flavors we were looking for. We found it best to mash the garlic into a paste, allowing the garlic flavor to blend quickly and smoothly with the other ingredients. We added minced red pepper for crunch and color and lemon juice to brighten all the flavors.

On a final note, we discovered that this dressing worked best over sturdy greens, such as romaine, iceberg, green leaf lettuce, and spinach. Softer lettuces, such as Boston or Bibb, wilted quickly under the weight of the creamy mixture. Several tasters liked the way the tartness of the buttermilk accented the bitterness of arugula and radicchio.

Ranch Dressing

MAKES ABOUT ¾ CUP

Three-quarters cup of this relatively thick dressing will coat 3 quarts (6 servings) of salad greens. Sturdy greens such as romaine and iceberg are ideal partners with this dressing. See the illustrations below for tips on mincing a shallot.

½	small garlic clove, minced to a paste with ¼ teaspoon salt (see the illustrations on page 626)
¼	small red bell pepper, minced (about 1 tablespoon)
1	medium scallion, white and green parts, minced
1	small shallot, minced (about 2 tablespoons)
1½	teaspoons minced fresh parsley leaves
1½	teaspoons minced fresh cilantro leaves
½	teaspoon juice from 1 small lemon
	Pinch ground black pepper
¼	cup buttermilk
¼	cup mayonnaise
2	tablespoons sour cream

Mix the garlic paste, bell pepper, scallion, shallot, parsley, cilantro, lemon juice, and black pepper together in a medium bowl. Add the buttermilk,

MINCING A SHALLOT

1. Place the peeled bulb flat-side down and make several slices parallel to the work surface, almost to (but not through) the root end. Then make a number of very closely spaced parallel cuts through the top of the shallot down to the work surface.
2. Finish the mincing by making very thin slices perpendicular to the lengthwise cuts.

mayonnaise, and sour cream and whisk until smooth. (The dressing can be refrigerated in an airtight container for up to 4 days.)

THOUSAND ISLAND DRESSING

RECIPES SIMILAR TO THOUSAND ISLAND dressing can be found dating back to the 1900s. While the details of its history are sketchy, the recipe seems to have taken its name from the Thousand Islands region in upstate New York and Canada that borders Lake Ontario and the St. Lawrence River. Some sources suggest that Thousand Island is an adaptation of Russian dressing, the difference being in the peppers, olives, and pickles added to Thousand Island (which some say represent the region's thousand islands). This thick, salmon-colored dressing is often used as a condiment on sandwiches and burgers as well as a dressing for salads (it can be especially good poured over a wedge of iceberg lettuce and some tomatoes).

Most recipes for Thousand Island dressing call for a mixture of mayonnaise and ketchup garnished with bits of chopped olives, sweet pickles, and hard-boiled egg. We found these dressings too sweet and one-dimensional.

Some recipes called for chili sauce as opposed to ketchup, and our tasters preferred it for its spicy tang. However, mayonnaise rather than ketchup or chili sauce should take the lead. More than 2 tablespoons of chili sauce per ½ cup mayonnaise made the dressing too red and tomatoey. By adding a few aromatics (such as garlic, parsley, and lemon juice), we brightened this otherwise heavy dressing, then punctuated it with a bit of heady garlic paste.

To the fine points: We realized that the dressing tasted better when the garnishes (olives, pickles, and egg) were mixed together and seasoned with the garlic, salt, ground black pepper, and lemon juice before being bound with the mayonnaise and chili sauce. This ensured that the garnishes, rather than just the mayonnaise, were able to absorb the seasonings, resulting in a more deeply flavored and lively dressing.

Last, we found that most Thousand Island dressings (including our working recipe at this point) are too thick to pour easily over salad greens. A little water thins the dressing out to the correct consistency.

We tried this dressing on several types of lettuce and liked it best on mild greens such as iceberg, Boston, Bibb, and romaine. Spicier greens such as radicchio and chicory clashed with the sweet elements that are part of this dressing's charm.

In the end, we had a fresh-tasting, well-seasoned Thousand Island dressing able to dress up everything from the most basic salad greens to a pastrami sandwich and a cheeseburger.

Thousand Island Dressing
MAKES ABOUT I CUP

Because this dressing is thick, 1 cup of it will coat only about 3 quarts (or about 6 servings) of salad greens. It works best with mild greens.

I	small garlic clove, minced to a paste with ¼ teaspoon salt (see the illustrations on page 626)
I	tablespoon green olives with pimentos, minced (3 to 4 olives)
¼	cup minced sweet pickle
½	hard-boiled egg (page I22), peeled and minced
I	tablespoon minced fresh parsley leaves
I	teaspoon juice from I small lemon
	Pinch ground black pepper
½	cup mayonnaise
2	tablespoons chili sauce
I	tablespoon water

Mix the garlic paste, olives, pickle, egg, parsley, lemon juice, and pepper together in a medium bowl. Add the mayonnaise, chili sauce, and water and stir until combined. (The dressing can be refrigerated in an airtight container for up to 3 days.)

BLUE CHEESE DRESSING

PRETTY GOOD BLUE CHEESE DRESSING, LIKE that served in many steakhouses, is creamy and tangy, with a hint of sweetness and a few crumbles of blue cheese. It isn't as good as it could be because it isn't cheesy enough. But even at that, it is miles better than bottled blue cheese dressings from the grocery store. To us, those bottled brews are virtually inedible. Harsh, mayonnaise-like concoctions, they are either as sweet as candy or painfully vinegary and sour. In both cases, the result is a one-dimensional dressing completely lacking in that necessary blue cheese punch. We decided it was time to do a little research and development in the test kitchen.

We gathered our recipes and tried them one by one. After much tasting, we concluded that three creamy ingredients were necessary: mayonnaise to give the dressing body, sour cream to supply tang, and buttermilk to both thin out the dressing and support the role of the sour cream. Our challenge was to find the right balance of the three to achieve both good flavor and the right consistency. We tinkered around, and where some recipes called for as much as ½ cup of mayonnaise to ½ cup of crumbled blue cheese, we found only 2 tablespoons of mayonnaise to be necessary. That, taken in combination with 3 tablespoons of sour cream and 3 tablespoons of buttermilk, and our dressing was just right. A combined total of ½ cup of sour cream, buttermilk, and mayonnaise to ½ cup of crumbled blue cheese made for a truly cheesy dressing with a pleasant, creamy tang and enough fluidity to gently coat sturdy, leafy greens.

At this point, our dressing was good but just a bit dull. We added a smidgen of sugar for sweetness and garlic powder and white wine vinegar for a little zing. That was it. The dressing now had high and low notes that titillated the taste buds, was jam-packed with blue-cheesy flavor, and was delicious when eaten not just on a salad but on a chicken wing or as a dip for crudités. (For information on crudités, see pages 9–11.)

Our next step was to investigate different kinds of blue cheese. We were surprised to find that a cheese that made a good dressing didn't necessarily make for good eating. A dressing made with an inexpensive domestic blue cheese—not a $17-per-pound French Roquefort—was our final choice. In general, we found that any rich, creamy blue cheese makes a good dressing. Really pungent cheeses, such as Spanish Cabrales, should be avoided.

Finally, we had to decide on a mixing method. Some of the recipes we researched called for making the dressing in a blender or food processor, but we wanted to make our dressing in the simplest way possible with the fewest number of dirty dishes. We took to mashing the crumbled blue cheese and buttermilk together with a fork to break up the cheese a bit. This was an easy means of getting the texture we liked—creamy, with a few small crumbles of cheese, just enough to give the dressing some tooth.

~

Blue Cheese Dressing

MAKES ABOUT ¾ CUP

In a pinch, whole milk can be used in place of buttermilk. The dressing will be a bit lighter and milder in flavor, but will still taste good. Remember that aggressive seasoning with salt and pepper is necessary because the dressing will be dispersed over greens. Serve this dressing over romaine or curly leaf lettuce. This recipe yields enough dressing to coat 10 cups loosely packed salad greens.

2½	ounces blue cheese, crumbled (about ½ cup)
3	tablespoons buttermilk
3	tablespoons sour cream
2	tablespoons mayonnaise
2	teaspoons white wine vinegar
¼	teaspoon sugar
⅛	teaspoon garlic powder
	Salt and ground black pepper

Mash the blue cheese and buttermilk in a small bowl with a fork until the mixture resembles cottage cheese with small curds. Stir in the remaining ingredients. Taste and adjust the seasonings with salt and pepper to taste. (The dressing can be refrigerated in an airtight container for up to 1 week.)

INGREDIENTS: Salad Greens

The following glossary starts with the four main varieties of lettuce and then covers the most commonly available specialty greens (called mesclun or mesclun mix when sold in combination). When substituting one green for another, try to choose greens with a similar intensity. For example, peppery arugula could be used as a substitute for watercress or dandelion greens, but not for red leaf lettuce, at least not without significantly altering the flavor of the salad.

Main Varieties of Lettuce

BUTTERHEAD LETTUCES Boston and Bibb are among the most common varieties of these very mild-tasting lettuces. A head of butterhead lettuce has a nice round shape and loose outer leaves. The color of the leaves is light to medium green (except, of course, in red-tinged varieties) and the leaves are extremely tender.

LOOSELEAF LETTUCES Red leaf, green leaf, red oak-leaf, and lolla rossa are the most common varieties. These lettuces grow in a loose rosette shape, not a tight head. The ruffled leaves are perhaps the most versatile because their texture is soft yet still crunchy and their flavor is mild but not bland.

ROMAINE LETTUCE The leaves on this lettuce are long and broad at the top. The color shades from dark green in outer leaves (which are often tough and should be discarded) to pale green in the thick, crisp heart. Also called Cos lettuce, this variety has more crunch than either butterhead or looseleaf lettuces and a more pronounced earthy flavor. Romaine lettuce is essential in Caesar salad, when the greens must stand up to a thick, creamy dressing.

ICEBERG LETTUCE Iceberg is the best-known variety of crisphead lettuce. Its shape is perfectly round, and the leaves are tightly packed. A high water content makes iceberg especially crisp and crunchy but also robs it of flavor.

Specialty Greens

ARUGULA Also called rocket, this tender, dark green leaf can be faintly peppery or downright spicy. Larger, older leaves tend to be hotter than small, young leaves, but the flavor is variable, so taste arugula before adding it to a salad. Try to buy arugula in bunches with the stems and roots still attached—they help keep the leaves fresh. Arugula bruises and discolors quite easily. If possible, keep stemmed leaves whole. Very large leaves can be torn just before they are needed.

WATERCRESS With its small leaves and long stalks, watercress is easy to spot. It requires some patience in the kitchen because the stalks are really quite tough and must be removed one at a time. Like arugula, watercress usually has a mildly spicy flavor.

DANDELION GREENS Dandelion greens are tender and pleasantly bitter. The leaves are long and have ragged edges. The flavor is similar to that of arugula or watercress, both of which can be used interchangeably with dandelion greens. Tougher, older leaves that are more than several inches long should be cooked and not eaten raw.

MIZUNA This Japanese spider mustard has long, thin, dark green leaves with deeply cut, jagged edges. Sturdier than arugula, watercress, or dandelion greens, it can nonetheless be used interchangeably with these slightly milder greens in salads when a strong peppery punch is desired. Note that larger, older leaves are better cooked, so choose small "baby" mizuna for salads.

TATSOI This Asian green has thin white stalks and round, dark green leaves. A member of the crucifer family of vegetables that includes broccoli and cabbage, tatsoi tastes like a mild Chinese cabbage, especially bok choy. However, the texture of these miniature leaves is always delicate.

RADICCHIO This most familiar chicory was almost unknown in this country two decades ago. The tight heads of purple leaves streaked with prominent white ribs are now a supermarket staple. Radicchio has a decent punch but is not nearly as bitter as other chicories, especially Belgian endive.

BELGIAN ENDIVE With its characteristic bitter chicory flavor, endive is generally used sparingly in salads. Unlike its cousin radicchio, endive is crisp and crunchy, not tender and leafy. The yellow leaf tips are usually mild-flavored, while the white, thick leaf bases are more bitter. Endive is the one salad green we routinely cut rather than tear. Remove whole leaves from the head and then slice them crosswise into bite-size pieces.

CHICORY Chicory, or curly endive, has curly, jagged leaves that form a loose head. The leaves are bright green and their flavor is usually fairly bitter. The outer leaves can be tough, especially at the base. Inner leaves are generally more tender.

ESCAROLE Escarole has smooth, broad leaves bunched together in a loose head. With its long ribs and softly ruffled leaves, it looks a bit like leaf lettuce. As a member of the chicory family, escarole can have an intense flavor, although not nearly as strong as that of endive or chicory.

SPINACH Of all the cooking greens, spinach is the most versatile in salads because it can be used in its miniature or full-grown form. Flat-leaf spinach is better than curly-leaf spinach in salads because the stems are usually less fibrous and the spade-shaped leaves are thinner, more tender, and sweeter. Curly spinach is often dry and chewy, while flat-leaf spinach, sold in bundles rather than in cellophane bags, is usually tender and moist, more like lettuce than a cooking green.

Leafy Salad 101

CLEANING GREENS

The first step in making any salad is cleaning the greens. (Unwashed greens should be carefully stowed away in the crisper and the rubber band or twist tie removed, as the constriction encourages rotting.) Our favorite way to wash small amounts of lettuce is in the bowl of a salad spinner; larger amounts require a sink. Make sure there is ample room to swish the leaves about and rid them of sand and dirt. The dirt will sink to the bottom. Exceptionally dirty greens (spinach and arugula often fall into this category) may take at least two changes of water. Do not run water directly from the faucet onto the greens as the force of the water can bruise them. When you are satisfied that the leaves are grit-free, spin them dry in a salad spinner. Greens must be quite dry; otherwise, the vinaigrette will slide off and taste diluted.

1. Using your hands, gently move the greens about underwater to loosen grit, which should fall to the bottom of the salad spinner bowl.

2. If you own a crank-style salad spinner, place it in the corner of your sink. This increases your leverage by pushing the spinner down to the sink floor and into the sink walls, thereby stabilizing it.

3. Line the salad spinner with paper towels, then layer in the greens, covering each layer with additional towels. In this manner, the greens will keep for at least 2 days.

4. To store greens for up to a week, loosely roll the greens in paper towels and then place the rolled greens inside a large zipper-lock bag and place in the refrigerator.

BEST SALAD SPINNERS

When we tested eight salad spinners, we had a two-way tie between spinners made by Zyliss and Oxo Good Grips. They both excelled at drying greens, though they had minor trade-offs: The Zyliss finished the task nominally faster, but the Oxo had a more ergonomic handle and a nonskid bottom, a big bonus. The design enhancements lifted the Oxo's price to $26, $5 more than the Zyliss.

ZYLISS   OXO

TOSSING GREENS AND DRESSING

We found that an ideal salad bowl is wide-mouthed and relatively shallow, so that the greens become evenly coated with vinaigrette quickly. A wide bowl also facilitates gentle handling of the greens. The bowl should be roughly 50 percent larger than the amount of greens to make sure there is adequate room for tossing. For example, a salad with 4 quarts of greens should be tossed in a 6-quart bowl. Whatever utensils you choose to toss the salad—wooden spoons, hands (our favorite method), or tongs—a light touch is crucial. A roughly tossed salad will wilt much faster than a lightly tossed salad.

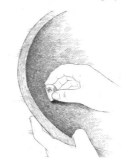 

1. Add mild garlic flavor: Peel and cut a clove of garlic. With the cut side down, rub the interior of your salad bowl.

2. Measure the greens: Loosely pack the greens into a large measuring cup, figuring on 2 cups per serving.

3. Tear the greens: If the greens are too large, tear them gently into manageable pieces with your hands just before serving the salad. If torn ahead of time, they will discolor and wilt.

4. Shake the dressing: Just before adding the dressing, give it a quick shake to make sure that it is fully combined and that the solid ingredients, like shallots, are evenly dispersed.

5. Drizzle the dressing: To prevent overdressed greens, add the dressing in small increments as you toss the salad.

6. Toss the salad: Coat the greens by gently "fluffing" them, adding more vinaigrette only when you are certain the greens need it.

PAIRING VINAIGRETTES WITH SALAD GREENS

The following vinaigrette recipes yield ¼ cup dressing, or enough for 2 quarts greens, about 4 servings. When making smaller or larger amounts of salad, figure on 2 tablespoons of dressing per quart of greens. Vinaigrettes do not store well, so they should be made close to the time they are to be used.

Most salad greens fall into one of three categories: mellow, spicy, or bitter. The following vinaigrettes are paired with a complementary green. Feel free to mix and match greens from within each category to change the flavor, color, and texture of each salad.

Whole fresh herb leaves, like parsley, basil, thyme, oregano, marjoram, and chervil, may also be added to any variety of salad green for a burst of flavor.

Red Wine Vinaigrette for Mellow Salad Greens

Mellow-flavored greens include Boston, Bibb, red and green leaf, red oak, lolla rossa, and iceberg lettuce, as well as flat-leaf spinach. Their mild flavors are easily overpowered and are best complemented by a simple dressing, such as this classic red wine vinaigrette.

3	tablespoons extra-virgin olive oil
2	teaspoons red wine vinegar
⅛	teaspoon salt
	Pinch ground black pepper
2	quarts washed and dried mellow greens

Combine all of the dressing ingredients in a jar, seal the lid, and shake vigorously until emulsified, about 20 seconds.

Creamy Garlic Vinaigrette for Bitter Salad Greens

Escarole, chicory, Belgian endive, radicchio, frisée, and young dandelion greens all fall into this category. A creamy, assertive vinaigrette tempers the astringency of bitter greens.

2	tablespoons extra-virgin olive oil
1	tablespoon sour cream or yogurt
1½	teaspoons white wine vinegar
1½	teaspoons juice from 1 small lemon
1	teaspoon Dijon mustard
½	small garlic clove, minced to a puree
⅛	teaspoon salt
	Pinch ground black pepper

Combine all of the dressing ingredients in a jar, seal the lid, and shake vigorously until emulsified, about 20 seconds.

Mustard and Balsamic Vinaigrette for Spicy Salad Greens

Spicy greens include arugula, watercress, mizuna, and baby mustard greens. They easily stand up to strong flavors, like mustard, shallots, and balsamic vinegar.

3	tablespoons extra-virgin olive oil
2	teaspoons balsamic vinegar
1½	teaspoons Dijon mustard
½	teaspoon finely minced shallot
⅛	teaspoon salt
	Pinch ground black pepper

Combine all of the dressing ingredients in a jar, seal the lid, and shake vigorously until emulsified, about 20 seconds.

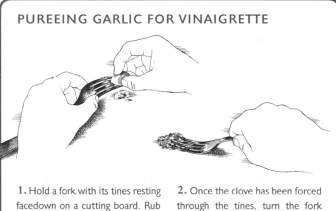

PUREEING GARLIC FOR VINAIGRETTE

1. Hold a fork with its tines resting facedown on a cutting board. Rub a peeled clove of garlic rapidly back and forth against the tines, close to their points.

2. Once the clove has been forced through the tines, turn the fork over and mash any large chunks to make a smooth puree.

CHOOSING VINEGAR AND OIL

All vinegars are not created equal. Some, like red and white wine vinegars, have a searingly high acidity of 5 to 7 percent. Lemon juice, in comparison, is milder, about 4 percent. And depending on its age and quality, balsamic vinegar's acidity can vary a good deal (the cheap stuff being nothing more than caramel-colored red wine vinegar). We adjust the ratio of oil to vinegar to suit the vinegar's strength; the oil mellows the acidity. For example, a red wine–based vinaigrette requires 4 parts oil to 1 part vinegar, but a vinaigrette made with lemon juice requires just 3 parts oil to 1 part juice. Extra-virgin olive oil is our top choice for salads because it tastes good with all greens and vinegars. For results from the tastings the test kitchen has conducted on oil and vinegars, see page 86 for extra-virgin olive oil and page 106 for red wine vinegar.

GREEK SALAD

MOST PIZZA-PARLOR VERSIONS OF GREEK salad consist of iceberg lettuce, chunks of green pepper, and a few pale wedges of tomato, sparsely dotted with cubes of feta and garnished with one forlorn olive of questionable domain. The accompanying dressing is loaded with musty dried herbs. How could we make this pizzeria staple worthy of the dinner table?

We started by testing different vinaigrette recipes, with ingredients ranging from vinegar and lemon juice to yogurt and mustard. Tasters thought that the yogurt-based dressing overwhelmed the salad and that the mustard and cider vinegar versions were just "wrong." Lemon juice was harsh and distilled white vinegar was dull, but a dressing that combined lemon juice and red wine vinegar had the balanced flavor we were looking for. There was no place for dried herbs in this salad. Fresh herbs typically used in Greek cuisine include dill, oregano, parsley, mint, and basil. Tasters loved the idea of mint and parsley, but they lost their zip when mixed with the vinaigrette. Oregano's bold flavor stood up well to the vinegar and lemon juice and was the clear favorite. Pure olive oil and extra-virgin olive oil worked equally well, and the addition of a small amount of garlic gave the dressing the final kick it needed.

The next ingredients up for scrutiny were the vegetables. Although lettuce is not commonly found in traditional Greek salad, it is a main ingredient in the American version. The iceberg lettuce had to go. Romaine, which has the body and crunch of iceberg but also more color and flavor, was the natural choice. Tomatoes were also essential, and only the ripest ones would do. Green bell pepper got a unanimous thumbs down. Everyone preferred the sweeter red variety, which was improved even further by being roasted. In the interest of saving time, we also tried jarred roasted red peppers, which tasters liked even better. The jarred peppers are packaged in a vinegary brine and have more depth of flavor than freshly roasted peppers.

Onion was next. When the pungency of the raw onion sent some tasters running for breath mints, someone suggested soaking the onion in water to eliminate its caustic bite. We took that idea one step further: Why not marinate the onion in the vinaigrette? On a whim, we included some cucumber as well. The results were striking. The cucumber, which had been watery and bland just minutes before, was bright and flavorful, and the onion had lost its unpleasant potency.

Now the vinaigrette recipe was finalized and the vegetables selected, but something was still missing. We returned to the mint and parsley that had been eliminated from the vinaigrette. Instead, we simply mixed them with the vegetables, tossed this mixture together with the onion and cucumber marinating in the vinaigrette, generously sprinkled the salad with feta and Kalamata olives, and offered it all to tasters. It was a hit. This was a Greek salad worthy of being served on china—not in an aluminum takeout container.

❧

Greek Salad
SERVES 6 TO 8

Marinating the onion and cucumber in the vinaigrette tones down the onion's harshness and flavors the cucumber. For efficiency, prepare the other salad ingredients while the onion and cucumber marinate. Use a salad spinner to dry the lettuce thoroughly after washing; any water left clinging to the leaves will dilute the dressing.

VINAIGRETTE
- 3 tablespoons red wine vinegar
- 1 1/2 teaspoons juice from 1 lemon
- 2 teaspoons minced fresh oregano leaves
- 1/2 teaspoon salt
- 1/8 teaspoon ground black pepper
- 1 medium garlic clove, minced or pressed through a garlic press (about 1 teaspoon)
- 6 tablespoons olive oil

SALAD
- 1/2 medium red onion, sliced thin
- 1 medium cucumber, peeled, halved lengthwise, seeded (see illustration 1 on page 91), and cut into 1/8-inch-thick slices (about 2 cups)
- 2 romaine hearts, washed, dried thoroughly, and torn into 1 1/2-inch pieces

2   medium vine-ripened tomatoes (10 ounces total), each tomato cored, seeded, and cut into 12 wedges

¼   cup loosely packed torn fresh parsley leaves

¼   cup loosely packed torn fresh mint leaves

6   ounces jarred roasted red peppers, cut into 2 by ½-inch strips (about 1 cup)

20   large Kalamata olives, each olive pitted and quartered lengthwise

5   ounces feta cheese, crumbled (1 cup)

1. FOR THE VINAIGRETTE: Whisk all of the ingredients together in a large bowl until combined. Add the onion and cucumber and toss; let stand to blend the flavors, about 20 minutes.

2. FOR THE SALAD: Add the romaine, tomatoes, parsley, mint, and peppers to the bowl with the onion and cucumber; toss to coat with the dressing.

3. Transfer the salad to a wide, shallow serving bowl or platter; sprinkle the olives and feta over the salad. Serve immediately.

➤ VARIATION
Country-Style Greek Salad

This salad, made without lettuce, is served throughout Greece, where it is known as country or peasant salad. It is excellent with garden-ripe summer tomatoes.

Follow the recipe for Greek Salad, reducing the red wine vinegar to 1½ tablespoons and the lemon juice to 1 teaspoon in the vinaigrette. Omit the romaine and use 2 medium cucumbers, peeled, halved lengthwise, seeded, and cut into ⅛-inch-thick slices (about 4 cups), and 6 medium tomatoes (about 2 pounds), each tomato cored, seeded, and cut into 12 wedges.

SALAD WITH HERBED BAKED GOAT CHEESE AND VINAIGRETTE

WARM GOAT CHEESE SALAD HAS BEEN A FIXTURE on restaurant menus for years, featuring artisanal cheeses, organic baby field greens, barrel-aged vinegars, and imported oils. Marketing being what it is, the jargon is often more intriguing than the execution: tepid, crumb-dusted cheese on overdressed designer greens at a price that defies reason. When we've tried to prepare this salad at home, the results have been equally disappointing, albeit less expensive. We've usually ended up with flavorless warm cheese melted onto the greens. What we wanted was quite different: creamy cheese rounds infused with flavor and surrounded by crisp, golden breading, all cradled in lightly dressed greens.

Coating and heating the cheese is clearly the major challenge of this recipe. Techniques uncovered in the recipes we researched included pan-frying, broiling, and baking. We began by coating portions of goat cheese in herbs (thyme and chives), then dipping the goat cheese rounds in beaten egg (with a little Dijon mustard added for bite), and finally fresh bread crumbs (the most common option for coating). We tried pan-frying (the most common option in cookbook recipes and the classic restaurant technique). Although the bread crumbs crisped up nicely after a short stay in the hot oil, several problems arose. The interior of the cheese rounds began to melt while the first side was browning, which made turning the disks a nightmare.

Nevertheless, we continued to pursue this method, chilling the rounds in the refrigerator for 30 minutes before they hit the oil, which we hoped would prevent the centers from overheating before the crust had crisped, but this, too, failed. One recipe suggested broiling the goat cheese rounds, but the rounds simply melted under the intense heat of the broiler.

It was time to try baking. Baking the cheese at temperatures ranging from 300 to 400 degrees for 4 to 7 minutes resulted in pallid, soggy crusts across the board, with varying degrees of unpleasant melting. Curious whether higher temperatures would yield the crust we were searching for, we turned the oven up to 475 degrees and ended up with goat cheese fondue.

Logic (or stubbornness) had persuaded us that higher temperatures had the potential to produce a crisp crust, but reality had shown that we needed a more durable breading. Then we hit upon the idea of using Melba toasts—perhaps these extremely dry (and extremely hard) crackers would work. We pulverized them, dunked the cheese in beaten egg, and then coated the rounds in the sandy crumbs. Appearing to fuse with the egg, the Melba crumbs formed a cohesive, shell–like barrier in the oven. Finally, our crust was crisp, although there still was some oozing of the cheese.

Theorizing that if the oven were blistering hot and the cheese arctic cold we would get a crispy crust and no oozing cheese, we place our goat cheese rounds in the freezer rather than the refrigerator for 30 minutes. Baking our "frozen" cheese at 475 degrees for 7 minutes, we struck gold. Although a few kitchen naysayers found the Melba crust a bit dry, we found that a quick brush of olive oil onto the exterior of the breaded and chilled rounds solved this problem.

It was time to add the baked goat cheese

INGREDIENTS: Supermarket Extra-Virgin Olive Oils

When you purchase an artisanal oil in a high-end shop, certain informational perks are expected (and paid for). These typically include written explanations of the character and nuances of the particular oil as well as the assistance of knowledgeable staff. But in a supermarket, it's just you and a price tag (usually $8 to $10 per liter). How do you know which supermarket extra-virgin oil best suits your needs? To provide some guidance, we decided to hold a blind tasting of the nine best-selling extra-virgin oils typically available in American supermarkets.

The label extra-virgin denotes the highest quality of olive oil, with the most delicate and prized flavor. (The three other grades are virgin, pure, and olive pomace. Pure oil, often labeled simply olive oil, is the most commonly available.) To be tagged as extra-virgin, an oil must meet three basic criteria. First, it must contain less than 1 percent oleic free fatty acids per 100 grams of oil. Second, the oil must not have been treated with any solvents or heat. (Heat is used to reduce strong acidity in some nonvirgin olive oils to make them palatable. This is where the term *cold-pressed* comes into play, meaning that the olives are pressed into a paste using mechanical wheels or hammers and are then kneaded to separate the oil from the fruit.) Third, it must pass taste and aroma standards as defined by groups such as the International Olive Oil Council (IOOC), a Madrid-based intergovernmental olive oil regulatory committee that sets the bar for its member countries.

Tasting extra-virgin olive oil is much like tasting wine. The flavors of these oils range from citrusy to herbal, musty to floral, with every possibility in between. And what one taster finds particularly attractive—a slight briny flavor, for example—another might find unappealing. Also like wine, the flavor of a particular brand of olive oil can change from year to year, depending on the quality of the harvest and the olives' place of origin.

We chose to taste extra-virgin olive oil in its most pure and unadulterated state: raw. Tasters were given the option of sampling the oil from a spoon or on neutral-flavored French bread and were asked to eat a slice of green apple—for its acidity—to cleanse the palate between oils. The olive oils were evaluated for color, clarity, viscosity, bouquet, depth of flavor, and lingering of flavor.

Whereas in a typical tasting we are able to identify a clear winner and loser, in this case we could not. In fact, the panel seemed to quickly divide itself into those who liked a gutsy olive oil with bold flavor and those who preferred a milder, more mellow approach. Nonetheless, in both camps—one oil clearly had more of a following than any other—the all-Italian-olive Davinci brand. Praised for its rounded and buttery flavor, it was the only olive oil we tasted that seemed to garner across-the-board approval with olive oil experts and in-house staff alike. Tasters in the mild and delicate camp gave high scores to Pompeian and Whole Foods oils. Among tasters who preferred full-bodied, bold oils, Colavita and Filippo Berio also earned high marks.

THE BEST ALL-PURPOSE OLIVE OIL
Davinci Extra-Virgin Olive Oil was the favorite in our tasting of leading supermarket brands. It was described as "very ripe," "buttery," and "complex."

THE BEST MILD OIL
Pompeian Extra-Virgin Olive Oil was the favorite among tasters who preferred a milder, more delicate oil. It was described as "clean," "round," and "sunny."

THE BEST FULL-BODIED OIL
Colavita Extra-Virgin Olive Oil was the favorite among tasters who preferred a bolder, more full-bodied oil. It was described as "heavy," "complex," and "briny."

rounds to a salad. Most tasters preferred a mix of heartier greens, such as arugula and frisée, and all tasters preferred a classic vinaigrette, as this dressing echoed and complemented the flavors of the goat cheese rounds. Given the fat in the cheese, we found that it's important to dress the greens lightly. Hundreds of goat cheese rounds later, we had developed an easy if unorthodox recipe that could give any bistro a run for its money.

Salad with Herbed Baked Goat Cheese and Vinaigrette

SERVES 6

The baked goat cheese should be served warm. Prepare the salad components while the cheese is in the freezer, then toss the greens and vinaigrette while the cheese cools a bit after baking.

GOAT CHEESE

3	ounces white Melba toasts (about 2 cups)
1	teaspoon ground black pepper
3	large eggs
2	tablespoons Dijon mustard
1	tablespoon chopped fresh thyme leaves
1	tablespoon chopped fresh chives
12	ounces firm goat cheese
	Extra-virgin olive oil

SALAD

2	tablespoons red wine vinegar
1	tablespoon Dijon mustard
1	teaspoon finely minced shallot
1/4	teaspoon salt
6	tablespoons extra-virgin olive oil
	Ground black pepper
18	ounces mixed hearty greens (about 14 cups), washed and dried

1. FOR THE CHEESE: In a food processor, process the Melba toasts to fine, even crumbs, about 1½ minutes; transfer the crumbs to a medium bowl and stir in the pepper. Whisk the eggs and mustard in another medium bowl until combined. Combine the thyme and chives in a small bowl.

2. Using dental floss or kitchen twine, divide the cheese into 12 equal pieces (see page 6 for more information). Roll each piece of cheese into a ball; roll each ball in the combined fresh herbs to coat lightly. Transfer 6 pieces to the egg mixture, turn each piece to coat; transfer to the Melba crumbs and turn each piece to coat, pressing the crumbs into the cheese. Flatten each ball gently with your fingertips into a disk about 1½ inches wide and 1 inch thick and set on a baking sheet. Repeat with the remaining 6 pieces of cheese. Transfer the baking sheet to the freezer and freeze the rounds until firm, about 30 minutes. (The cheese rounds may be wrapped tightly in plastic wrap and frozen for up to 1 week.) Adjust an oven rack to the uppermost position; heat the oven to 475 degrees.

3. MEANWHILE, PREPARE THE SALAD: Combine the vinegar, mustard, shallot, and salt in a small bowl. Whisking constantly, drizzle in the olive oil; season with pepper to taste. Set aside.

4. Remove the cheese from the freezer and brush the tops and sides evenly with olive oil. Bake until the crumbs are golden brown and the cheese is slightly soft, 7 to 9 minutes (or 9 to 12 minutes if the cheese is completely frozen). Using a thin metal spatula, transfer the cheese to a paper towel–lined plate and cool 3 minutes.

5. Place the greens in a large bowl, drizzle the vinaigrette over them, and toss to coat. Divide the greens among individual plates; place 2 rounds of goat cheese on each salad. Serve immediately.

GETTING THE CHEESE RIGHT

PAN-FRIED   BAKED AT 350°   BAKED AT 475°

Pan-fried goat cheese develops a crisp crust, but it's very tricky to turn the rounds over without crushing the melting interior and causing the cheese to ooze out. Goat cheese coated with bread crumbs and baked in a 350-degree oven is soggy and pale. Goat cheese coated with ground Melba toasts, partially frozen, and baked at 475 degrees is crisp, it doesn't "ooze," and it maintains its shape. It has all the benefits of pan-frying with none of the disadvantages.

WILTED SPINACH SALAD

MANY COOKS CONSIDER WILTED SPINACH salad—in which a warm, fragrant dressing gently wilts fresh spinach leaves—to be a restaurant indulgence. While these elegant salads are surprisingly easy to make at home, there are potential problems. After sampling several recipes in the test kitchen, tasters concurred that these salads can disappoint in two major ways—with greasy, dull-tasting dressings and with spinach reduced to mush in puddles of dressing as deep as a fish pond.

The first hurdle—having to wash, dry, and trim mature curly spinach—was easily overcome. Kitchen tests determined that prewashed, bagged baby spinach works well in this salad, as it is both more tender and sweet than the mature variety.

Next, we wanted to identify the best type of oil to use in these salads. Though dressings made with pure olive oil were fine—use it if that's what you have on hand—the flavor nuances of extra-virgin oil gave the dressings more depth and dimension.

When it came to the acidic component, tasters favored fresh lemon juice for its bright, tangy flavor. We discovered that dressings in which the lemon juice was added early and heated through lacked brightness. The punch was restored when we swirled in the lemon juice after the oil and other ingredients had been heated.

We also tested the ratio of oil to acid. The ratio we use for most vinaigrettes, 4 parts oil to 1 part acid, produced greasy dressings. Mindful that we didn't want too much oil overpowering the tender spinach, we scaled back the ratio to 3 parts oil to 1 part acid. A little extra acid made the dressings sharp and fresh-tasting.

Several of us in the test kitchen had in the past encountered wilted salads swimming in dressing, which gave the greens a decidedly drowned, slimy texture. After tasting salads tossed with various quantities of dressing, our tasters settled on just ¼ cup of dressing for 6 cups of greens. The ¼ cup coated the greens generously yet allowed them to retain enough structural integrity to leave these wilted salads with a slight but satisfying crunch.

Serve these salads without delay to enjoy the best of their singular texture.

Wilted Spinach Salad with Goat Cheese, Olives, and Lemon Vinaigrette
SERVES 4
If you prefer, use feta in place of the goat cheese.

5	ounces baby spinach (about 6 cups)
3	tablespoons extra-virgin olive oil
1	medium shallot, minced (about 3 tablespoons)
1	medium garlic clove, minced or pressed through a garlic press (about 1 teaspoon)
1	teaspoon minced fresh oregano leaves
¼	teaspoon salt
⅛	teaspoon ground black pepper
⅛	teaspoon sugar
1	tablespoon juice from 1 lemon
2	ounces goat cheese, cut into small chunks
6	black olives, sliced thin

Place the spinach in a large bowl. Cook the oil, shallot, garlic, oregano, salt, pepper, and sugar in a small skillet over medium heat until the shallot is slightly softened, 2 to 3 minutes. Add the lemon juice and swirl to incorporate. Pour the warm dressing over the spinach, add the cheese and olives, and toss gently with tongs to wilt. Serve immediately.

➤ VARIATIONS
Wilted Spinach Salad with Oranges, Radishes, and Citrus Vinaigrette
See the illustrations on page 95 for tips on segmenting the oranges.

Follow the recipe for Wilted Spinach Salad with Goat Cheese, Olives, and Lemon Vinaigrette, substituting ¼ teaspoon grated orange zest for the oregano and adding it with the oil, shallot, garlic, salt, pepper, and sugar. After pouring the warm dressing over the spinach, replace the cheese and olives with 2 medium seedless oranges, divided into segments, and ⅓ cup grated radishes (about 4 medium).

Wilted Spinach Salad with Bacon Dressing

SERVES 4 TO 6

We prefer thick-cut bacon for the dressing, finding that it offers more presence and textural interest than thin-cut. (Slab bacon can also be used, but it fries up chewy, not crispy.) The easiest way to achieve substantial, uniform pieces (and avoid tiny Baco-style bacon bits) is to cut the strips before frying them rather than crumbling them afterward. This salad comes together quickly, so have the ingredients ready before you begin cooking. When adding the vinegar mixture to the skillet, step back from the stovetop—the aroma is quite potent.

6	ounces baby spinach (about 8 cups)
3	tablespoons cider vinegar
1/2	teaspoon sugar
1/4	teaspoon ground black pepper
	Pinch salt
10	ounces (about 8 slices) thick-cut bacon, cut into 1/2-inch pieces
1/2	medium red onion, chopped medium (about 1/2 cup)
1	small garlic clove, minced or pressed through a garlic press (about 1/2 teaspoon)
3	hard-boiled eggs (page 122), peeled and quartered lengthwise

1. Place the spinach in a large bowl. Stir the vinegar, sugar, pepper, and salt together in a small bowl until the sugar dissolves; set aside.

2. Fry the bacon in a medium skillet over medium-high heat, stirring occasionally, until crisp, about 10 minutes. Using a slotted spoon, transfer the bacon to a paper towel–lined plate. Pour the bacon fat into a heatproof bowl, then return 3 tablespoons bacon fat to the skillet. Add the onion to the skillet and cook over medium heat, stirring frequently, until slightly softened, about 3 minutes. Stir in the garlic and cook until fragrant, about 15 seconds. Add the vinegar mixture, then remove the skillet from the heat. Working quickly, scrape the bottom of the skillet with a wooden spoon to loosen the browned bits. Pour the hot dressing over the spinach, add the bacon, and toss gently with tongs until the spinach is slightly wilted. Divide the salad among individual plates, arrange the egg quarters over each, and serve immediately.

ROASTED PEAR SALAD

ONE OF OUR FAVORITE WINTER SALADS IS THIS roasted pear salad, which features the classic combination of sweet pears, salty Parmesan, bitter arugula, and crunchy walnuts. Our defining parameters for this simple roasted pear salad were elementary: the roasted pears should be slightly al dente, sweet but not syrupy, and caramel-colored on both sides. We first needed to narrow down our playing field—which pear would beget the best roasting results? We roasted one batch each of Anjou, Bartlett, and Bosc (chosen for their availability during the winter). While tasters were torn between Anjou (delicate pear flavor with a grainy texture and good bite) and Bartlett (soft texture with a floral pear essence), the big loser was Bosc (mealy, dry, and flat-tasting).

Determining that either Bartlett or Anjou could be used, we turned to the question of slicing. Too thin a slice and the pear wouldn't hold up to the roasting process, but, if too thickly cut, the pear would be awkward to bite into, especially in a salad. We found our solution at a thickness of about 1/3 inch, or roughly five slices per half.

Next we tossed the thinly sliced pears with various brews of fats, oils, wines, and broths and roasted them for 20 minutes at 425 degrees. Even though butter bestowed the highest glories on the pear, the flavor and color were still slack. So we upped the oven temperature to 500 degrees, decreased the roasting time by five minutes, and decided to turn the pears three quarters of the way through roasting (at halfway through, the pears hadn't browned enough on their first side). To help draw out their untapped sweetness, we sprinkled some sugar onto the butter-coated pears prior to roasting. Not only were these roasted pears sweet and juicy, but, with the help of sugar to accelerate the caramelization process, they positively glistened.

Arugula and Roasted Pear Salad with Walnuts and Parmesan Cheese

SERVES 4 TO 6

The pears may be roasted up to 3 hours in advance, but keep them at room temperature until serving time because refrigeration adversely affects their texture. Warm pears work nicely in this salad, too.

ROASTED PEARS
4 firm Anjou or Bartlett pears (about 2 pounds)
1 tablespoon unsalted butter, melted
2 tablespoons sugar

VINAIGRETTE
1½ tablespoons extra-virgin olive oil
2 teaspoons white wine vinegar
½ teaspoon salt
Ground black pepper

SALAD
2 bunches arugula, stems removed, leaves washed, dried, and torn into bite-size pieces (about 7 cups)
4 ounces Parmesan cheese, shaved with a vegetable peeler (see the illustration on page 134)
1 cup walnuts, chopped coarse and toasted in a small dry skillet over medium heat until lightly browned and fragrant, about 3 minutes

1. Adjust an oven rack to the lower-middle position, place a baking sheet or broiler pan bottom on the rack, and heat the oven to 500 degrees.

2. FOR THE PEARS: Peel and halve each pear lengthwise. With a paring knife or melon baller, remove the core. Set each half cut-side down and slice lengthwise into fifths. Put the slices in a large bowl and toss with the butter; add the sugar and toss again to combine. Spread the pears in a single layer on the preheated baking sheet, making sure each slice lies flat. Roast until browned on the bottom, about 10 minutes. Flip each slice and roast until tender and deep golden brown, about 5 minutes longer. Remove from the oven and set aside to cool.

3. FOR THE VINAIGRETTE: Whisk the oil, vinegar, salt, and pepper to taste together in a small bowl.

4. FOR THE SALAD: Combine the arugula, reserved roasted pear slices, and cheese in a large serving bowl. Add the vinaigrette and toss gently to combine; sprinkle with the chopped walnuts. Serve immediately.

TOMATO, MOZZARELLA, AND BASIL SALAD

THIS ITALIAN-STYLE END-OF-SUMMER SALAD highlights the flavors of fresh mozzarella, ripe tomatoes, and fragrant basil. Although it seemed silly to research a recipe for such a simple dish, we wondered if there were any tricks in its preparation that might make a difference.

Obviously, this salad is meant to be made with only fully ripened tomatoes and a good-quality fresh mozzarella packed in water. If either the tomatoes or mozzarella are unripe and bland, the flavor of the salad will suffer significantly. Tasters preferred the salad made with equal amounts of tomato and mozzarella.

Some recipes we researched called for minced red onion and red wine vinegar; however, we liked the salad without them. Unadorned, the acidity of the tomatoes and the delicate flavor of the mozzarella can shine through. As for the basil, it was best when roughly chopped and sprinkled over the salad as opposed to the way it is oftentimes treated: whole leaves inserted between the slices of mozzarella and tomato. The leaves are simply too big and too chewy. Lastly, we noted the importance of using a high-quality extra-virgin olive oil and coarse salt. Both pure olive oil and table salt tasted too heavy and dense for this light, aromatic salad.

Although it is difficult not to eat the salad right away, allowing the platter to sit for a few minutes lets the flavors meld.

Tomato, Mozzarella, and Basil Salad

SERVES 4 TO 6

Served as an appetizer, light lunch, or snack, this salad is best eaten with a crust of bread to help sop up the tasty tomato-flavored dressing that pools in the bottom of the platter. For the best presentation, discard the first and last slice from each tomato.

4   medium, very ripe tomatoes (about 1¹/₂ pounds), cored and cut into slices ¹/₄ inch thick

1   pound fresh mozzarella cheese, cut into slices ¹/₄ inch thick

2   tablespoons roughly chopped fresh basil leaves

¹/₄   teaspoon kosher salt or sea salt

¹/₈   teaspoon ground black pepper

¹/₄   cup extra-virgin olive oil

Layer the tomatoes and mozzarella alternately and in concentric circles on a medium platter. Sprinkle the tomatoes and cheese with the basil, salt, and pepper. Drizzle the oil over the platter and allow the flavors to meld for 5 to 10 minutes. Serve immediately.

CUCUMBER SALAD

WATER IS THE ENEMY WHEN MAKING cucumber salad. The standing recommendation for ridding watery vegetables such as cucumbers, zucchini, and eggplant of unwanted moisture is to salt them. The salt creates a higher concentration of ions (tiny, charged particles) at the surface of the vegetable than exists deep within its cells.

To equalize the concentration levels, the water within the cells is drawn out through permeable cell walls. In the case of cucumbers, this leaves them wilted, yet very crunchy. Of course, some culinary questions remain: How much salt should be used? Should the cucumber slices be weighted, or pressed, to squeeze out the liquid? How long should they drain?

To find out if pressing salted cucumbers really squeezes out more liquid, we trimmed and seeded six cucumbers to 8 ounces each, sliced them on the bias, and tossed each batch with a teaspoon of salt in its own colander set over a bowl. Three of them had zipper-lock freezer bags filled with 1 quart of water placed on top of them; no additional weight was added to the other three. Then we left them all to drain, measuring the liquid each had released after 30 minutes and after 1, 2, 3, and 12 hours. At each time point, the weighted cucumbers had released about 1 tablespoon more liquid than the unweighted cucumbers; 3 versus 2 after 30 minutes, 4 versus 3 after 1 hour, and so on. Interestingly, the weighted cukes gave off no more liquid after 12 hours than they had after 3 (7 tablespoons at both points). So weighting the cucumbers is worthwhile, but forget about draining the cucumbers overnight; it's not necessary.

At the one-hour mark, we could not detect an appreciable difference in flavor or texture between

SEEDING, SLICING, SALTING, AND DRAINING CUCUMBERS

1. Peel and halve each cucumber lengthwise. Use a small spoon to remove the seeds and surrounding liquid from each cucumber half.

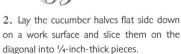

2. Lay the cucumber halves flat side down on a work surface and slice them on the diagonal into ¹/₄-inch-thick pieces.

3. Toss the cucumbers and salt (1 teaspoon for each cucumber) in a colander set in a bowl. Place a gallon-size plastic bag filled with water on top of the cucumbers to weight them down and force out the liquid. Drain for at least 1 hour or up to 3 hours.

weighted and unweighted cukes. But we wanted to see how they would perform in salads with dressing. We mixed one batch each of the weighted and unweighted cucumbers with two different creamy dressings and allowed each to sit at room temperature for one hour. This is where the true value of better-drained cucumbers became obvious; every single taster preferred the salads made with pressed cucumbers for their superior crunch and less diluted dressings.

As for the amount of salt, some cooks recommend simply using the quantity you would normally use to season the cucumbers, while others say you should use more, up to 2 tablespoons per cucumber, and then rinse off the excess before further use. We tried a few cucumbers, prepared exactly as those described above except with 2 tablespoons of salt. The cucumbers with 2 tablespoons did give up about one more tablespoon of liquid within the first hour than those drained with one teaspoon had, but they also required rinsing and blotting dry with paper towels. And despite this extra hassle, they still tasted much too salty in the salads. We would advise forgoing the extra salt.

Yogurt–Mint Cucumber Salad
SERVES 4

Known as raita, this creamy salad traditionally serves as a cooling contrast with curry dishes.

I	cup plain low-fat yogurt
2	tablespoons extra-virgin olive oil
1/4	cup minced fresh mint leaves
2	small garlic cloves, minced or pressed through a garlic press (I heaping teaspoon)
	Salt and ground black pepper
3	medium cucumbers (about 1 1/2 pounds), seeded, sliced, salted, and drained (page 91)

Whisk the yogurt, oil, mint, garlic, and salt and pepper to taste in a medium bowl. Add the cucumbers; toss to coat. Serve chilled, adjusting the seasonings if necessary.

Creamy Dill Cucumber Salad
SERVES 4

Salting and draining the onion along with the cucumbers in this recipe removes the sharp sting of raw onion.

I	cup sour cream
3	tablespoons cider vinegar
I	teaspoon sugar
1/4	cup minced fresh dill
	Salt and ground black pepper
3	medium cucumbers (about 1 1/2 pounds), seeded, sliced, salted, and drained (page 91)
1/2	medium red onion, sliced very thin, salted and drained with cucumbers

Whisk the sour cream, vinegar, sugar, dill, and salt and pepper to taste in a medium bowl. Add the cucumbers and onion; toss to coat. Serve chilled, adjusting the seasonings if necessary.

ASPARAGUS SALADS

ASPARAGUS ARE THE FASHION MODELS OF the salad world—long, graceful spears draped over a bed of tossed, moist greens. But the beauty of these salads is often only skin-deep. Either bland or overseasoned, mushy or nearly raw, this first-course tease can prove to be an unsatisfying encounter. We wanted some recipes for asparagus salad that combined good taste with good looks.

We knew that boiling or steaming asparagus would diminish their flavor. Grilling or broiling would add flavor, but these were unwanted added steps. We soon found that quickly sautéing and browning the asparagus over high heat was the easiest way to enrich flavor. This method also let me add other ingredients right to the pan, where the flavors could meld.

The vinaigrette was about balance. Adding the bold flavors of shallots, garlic, and fresh herbs, or even tart cornichons and salty capers, made for zesty dressings that contrasted nicely with the mellow asparagus. To offset the leanness of the lettuce and vegetables and the sharpness of the dressing, we added cheese or hard-boiled eggs, making the salads more substantial as well as flavorful.

Asparagus, Red Pepper, and Spinach Salad with Sherry Vinegar and Goat Cheese
SERVES 4 TO 6

6   tablespoons extra-virgin olive oil
1   red bell pepper, cored, seeded, and cut into 1 by ¼-inch strips
1   pound asparagus, tough ends snapped off (see the illustration on page 130) and cut on the diagonal into 1-inch pieces
    Salt and ground black pepper
1   medium shallot, sliced thin
1   tablespoon plus 1 teaspoon sherry vinegar
1   medium garlic clove, minced or pressed through a garlic press (about 1 teaspoon)
6   ounces baby spinach (about 8 cups)
4   ounces goat cheese, cut into small chunks

1. Heat 2 tablespoons of the oil in a 12-inch nonstick skillet over high heat until beginning to smoke; add the bell pepper and cook until lightly browned, about 2 minutes, stirring only once after 1 minute. Add the asparagus, ¼ teaspoon salt, and ⅛ teaspoon pepper; cook until the asparagus is browned and almost tender, about 2 minutes, stirring only once after 1 minute. Stir in the shallot and cook until softened and the asparagus is tender-crisp, about 1 minute, stirring occasionally. Transfer to a large plate and cool 5 minutes.

2. Meanwhile, whisk the remaining 4 tablespoons oil, the vinegar, garlic, ¼ teaspoon salt, and ⅛ teaspoon pepper together in a medium bowl until combined. In a large bowl, toss the spinach with 2 tablespoons of the dressing and divide the spinach among salad plates. Toss the asparagus mixture with the remaining dressing and place a portion of it over the spinach; divide the goat cheese among the salads and serve.

Asparagus and Mesclun Salad with Capers, Cornichons, and Hard-Boiled Eggs
SERVES 4 TO 6

5   tablespoons extra virgin olive oil
1   pound asparagus, tough ends snapped off (see the illustration on page 130) and cut on the diagonal into 1-inch pieces
    Salt and ground black pepper
2   tablespoons white wine vinegar
1   small shallot, minced (about 2 tablespoons)
2   tablespoons minced cornichons
1   teaspoon chopped rinsed capers
2   teaspoons chopped fresh tarragon leaves
6   ounces mesclun (about 12 cups)
3   hard-boiled eggs (page 122), peeled and chopped medium

1. Heat 1 tablespoon of the oil in a 12-inch nonstick skillet over high heat until beginning to smoke. Add the asparagus, ¼ teaspoon salt, and ¼ teaspoon pepper; cook until browned and tender-crisp, about 4 minutes, stirring once every minute. Transfer to a large plate and cool 5 minutes.

2. Meanwhile, whisk the remaining 4 tablespoons oil, the vinegar, shallot, cornichons, capers, tarragon, and ¼ teaspoon pepper together in a medium bowl until combined. In a large bowl, toss the mesclun with 2 tablespoons of the dressing and divide among salad plates. Toss the asparagus with the remaining dressing and place a portion of it over the mesclun; sprinkle the chopped eggs evenly over the salads and serve.

THREE-BEAN SALAD

IF YOUR MOTHER MADE THREE-BEAN SALAD, it probably featured a sweet, vinegary dressing mixed with canned green, yellow, and kidney beans and a bite of red onion. This salad was good but never great. We wondered if this classic American recipe could be improved with modern ingredients and techniques.

Our goal was a fresh taste (something other

than canned beans came to mind) and a light, sweet, and tangy dressing that united the subtle flavors of the beans without overpowering them. To that end, our testing divided itself into three categories: improving the flavor and the texture of the beans; determining the right mix of vinegar and oils for the marinade; and addressing the question of sweetness, which was handled differently in almost every recipe we looked at. (Although we did find a few recipes that did not include a sweetener, sugar in one form or another seemed to differentiate three-bean salad from a simple oil and vinegar vegetable salad.)

We decided to first test boiling, blanching, and steaming the green and yellow beans. Not surprisingly, the less time the beans are cooked, the better they stand up in the dressing. Our 10- and 20-minute boiled beans were soft and flavorless, but those blanched for one and two minutes each weren't cooked enough. We eventually settled on boiling the beans for five minutes. This was long enough to remove their waxy exterior and thereby allow the marinade to penetrate, but not long enough to break down their cell structure and make them mushy. After draining the beans, we plunged them into cold water to stop the cooking. Steamed beans held up fairly well, but they didn't have the crunch of the boiled and shocked beans.

Next we moved on to the kidney beans. None of the recipes recommended cooking dried beans—they all called for canned. Just to be sure, we cooked up two batches of dried beans, then marinated them overnight. Not only were the canned beans a lot easier to use, but they tasted just as good.

With the beans ready for dressing, we moved on to the marinade. After testing eight oil varieties and seven types of vinegar, we found that we preferred canola oil for its mild flavor and red wine vinegar for its tang.

We were ready to test types of sugar. We also wanted to test an idea we had run across in several recipes—cooking the sugar, vinegar, and oil together. We quickly realized that cooking the sugar, vinegar, and oil dramatically improved the flavor of the dressing. We tried cooking vinegar mixed with brown sugar, with honey, and with white sugar over medium heat. The white sugar

version won hands down: The cooking process created a syrup with its own unique flavor—sweet and tangy at the same time. It turns out that both heat and the type of sugar used make all the difference between a so-so marinade and a tasty one.

Three-Bean Salad
SERVES 8 TO 10

This recipe is the all-American classic—the variation gives the salad a Southwestern spin. Prepare this salad at least 1 day before you plan on serving it: The beans taste better after marinating in the dressing.

1	cup red wine vinegar
3/4	cup sugar
1/2	cup canola oil
2	medium garlic cloves, minced or pressed through a garlic press (about 2 teaspoons)
	Salt and ground black pepper
8	ounces green beans, cut into 1-inch pieces
8	ounces yellow wax beans, cut into 1-inch pieces
1	(15.5-ounce) can red kidney beans, drained and rinsed
1/2	medium red onion, chopped medium
1/4	cup minced fresh parsley leaves

1. Heat the vinegar, sugar, oil, garlic, 1 teaspoon salt, and pepper to taste in a small nonreactive saucepan over medium heat, stirring occasionally, until the sugar dissolves, about 5 minutes. Transfer to a large nonreactive bowl and cool to room temperature.

2. Bring 3 quarts water to a boil in a large saucepan over high heat. Add 1 tablespoon salt and the green and yellow beans and cook until the beans are crisp-tender, about 5 minutes. Meanwhile, fill a medium bowl with ice water. When the beans are done, drain and immediately plunge them into the ice water to stop the cooking process; let sit until chilled, about 2 minutes. Drain well.

3. Add the green and yellow beans, kidney beans, onion, and parsley to the vinegar mixture and toss well to coat. Cover and refrigerate overnight to let the flavors meld. Let stand at room temperature 30 minutes before serving. (The salad can be covered and refrigerated for up to 4 days.)

➤ VARIATION

Three-Bean Salad with Cumin, Cilantro, and Oranges

Separate 2 medium oranges into segments, remove the membranes from the sides of each segment, then cut each segment in half lengthwise. Set aside. Follow the recipe for Three-Bean Salad, substituting ¼ cup lime juice for ¼ cup of the red wine vinegar, and heating 1 teaspoon ground cumin with the vinegar mixture. Substitute minced fresh cilantro leaves for the parsley and add the halved orange segments to the vinegar mixture along with the beans and onion.

LENTIL SALAD

COMMON ON FRENCH BISTRO MENUS, LENTIL salad is a tasty, toothsome dish whose popularity in the home kitchen is long overdue. We began our research with the main ingredient: the lentil, of which there are several varieties. Not surprisingly, *lentilles du Puy* (French green lentils) turned out to be the best legume for this salad. Fully cooked and tossed with dressing, they held their shape nicely compared to the common brown lentils, which turned mushy after being tossed with dressing, and the red split lentil, which disintegrated before we could even pour on the dressing.

Although we had settled on the kind of lentil, tasters felt that the green ones we had chosen were a little bland. Many of us in the test kitchen had been warned against salting legumes during cooking because it supposedly toughened their skins. Because the lentils were definitely lacking in flavor, we decided to challenge this unwritten rule. Much to our surprise, it seemed this rule was meant to be broken. While the salted lentils took slightly longer to cook, the taste was markedly better. They tasted more robust and earthier than the lentils cooked in plain water.

With the question of how to cook the lentils behind us, we next focused on developing the seasonings for the recipe. Given that we were using French lentils, we narrowed our search to primarily French cookbooks. Many of the recipes we found employed similar cooking methods

SEGMENTING AN ORANGE

1. Start by slicing a ½-inch-thick piece off the top and bottom of the orange.

2. With the fruit resting flat against the work surface, use a very sharp paring knife to slice off the rind, including all of the bitter white pith. Try to follow the contours of the fruit as closely as possible.

3. Working over a bowl to catch the juices, slip the blade between a membrane and one section of fruit and slice to the center, separating one side of the section.

4. Turn the blade of the knife so that it is facing out and is lined up along the membrane on the opposite side of the section. Slide the blade from the center out along the membrane to free the section completely. Continue until all of the sections are removed.

and flavorings. Most called for simmering lentils, draining them, and then tossing them, still warm, with vinaigrette. More often than not, the vinaigrette contained walnut oil, wine vinegar, and other aromatics. Armed with this information, we made several batches of lentil salad. Generally, these salads were good, but there was room for improvement.

Tasters raised several issues about the vinaigrette; some felt it lacked punch, and others disliked the walnut oil. Figuring that the vinegar (everyone liked sherry vinegar best in this recipe) in the dressing lost potency when mixed with the warm lentils, we decreased the ratio of oil to vinegar. While this improved the brightness of the salad, it didn't improve it enough to meet our standards. By doubling the amount of Dijon mustard in the vinaigrette, we gave the dressing a little more bite, which in turn satisfied the problem of dull flavors. Another change we made to the vinaigrette was to omit the walnut oil, which tended to overpower the salad. Even in small amounts, its slight bitterness muted the other flavors. But keeping walnuts in mind, we moved to another issue—texture.

Many of the salads we made tasted fine but were rather one-dimensional. They needed crunch. Topping the salad with a sprinkling of toasted walnuts improved the salad greatly, both adding texture and accentuating the earthiness of the lentils. Introducing scallions to the mix also improved the overall texture and provided pungency. The final ingredient, roasted red peppers, sweetened the salad and rounded out the other flavors.

Lentil Salad with Walnuts and Scallions

SERVES 4

This salad is a natural with grilled sausages; with the addition of lettuce leaves or other greens, it also can be served as a light vegetarian entrée. French lentils du Puy are green lentils sold in many gourmet markets and some supermarkets. They are smaller than common brown lentils, and their color is army green. If you can't find green lentils, use common brown lentils and reduce the simmering time in step 1 by 5 to 7 minutes. See page 16 for information about jarred roasted red peppers.

1	cup lentils du Puy, rinsed and picked over
½	medium onion, halved
2	bay leaves
1	large sprig fresh thyme
	Salt
2	tablespoons sherry vinegar
2	teaspoons Dijon mustard
⅛	teaspoon ground black pepper
6	tablespoons extra-virgin olive oil

½	cup coarsely chopped walnuts, toasted in a dry skillet over medium heat until fragrant, about 3 minutes, and cooled
2	scallions, white and green parts, sliced thin
½	cup drained jarred roasted red peppers, diced

1. Bring the lentils, onion, bay leaves, thyme, ½ teaspoon salt, and 4 cups water to a boil in a medium saucepan over medium-high heat. Reduce the heat and simmer until the lentils are tender but still hold their shape, 25 to 30 minutes.

2. Whisk the vinegar, mustard, ¼ teaspoon salt, the pepper, and oil together in a small bowl; set aside.

3. Drain the lentils through a fine-mesh strainer and discard the onion, bay leaves, and thyme. Transfer the lentils to a medium bowl. Toss the warm lentils with the vinaigrette and cool to room temperature, about 15 minutes. Stir in the walnuts, scallions, and roasted red peppers and serve immediately.

BUTTERMILK COLESLAW

THERE ARE TWO THINGS ABOUT COLESLAW with buttermilk dressing that can be bothersome: the pool of watery dressing that appears at the bottom of the bowl after a few hours, and the harsh flavor of buttermilk. Not only did we want to find a way to keep the cabbage from watering down the dressing, but we wanted to figure out how to make the salad piquant without tasting too sharp and one-dimensional.

To tackle the watery dressing, we tested a number of popular methods for treating cabbage. While most recipes instruct the cook to toss the shredded cabbage immediately with dressing, a few add an extra step. Either the shredded (or merely quartered) cabbage is soaked in ice water for crisping and refreshing, or it is salted, drained, and allowed to wilt.

We soaked cabbage in ice water and found it to be crisp, plump, and fresh. If looks were all that mattered, this cabbage would have scored high next to the limp, salted cabbage in the neighboring colander. But its good looks were deceiving.

Even though we drained the cabbage and dried it thoroughly, the dressing didn't really adhere. Furthermore, within minutes, the cabbage shreds started to lose their recently acquired water, making for not a small but a large puddle of water to dilute the creamy dressing. The stiff cabbage shreds were strawlike, making them difficult to fork and even more difficult to get into the mouth without leaving a creamy trail.

Quite unlike the ice-water cabbage, the salted shreds lost most of their liquid while sitting in the salt, leaving the cabbage wilted but pickle-crisp. Since the cabbage had already lost most of its liquid, there was little or no liquid left for the salt to draw into the dressing. We had found the solution to the problem of watery dressing. In addition, we found that this cabbage, having less water in it, took on more of the dressing's flavors, and, unlike the stiff shreds of ice-water cabbage, this limp cabbage was easier to eat.

We did discover that the salting process leaves the cabbage a bit too salty, but a quick rinse washes away the excess salt. After the cabbage has been rinsed, just pat it dry with paper towels and refrigerate until ready to combine it with the dressing. If the coleslaw is to be eaten immediately, rinse the cabbage quickly in ice water rather than tap water, then pat it dry. Coleslaw is best served cold.

Having figured out how to keep the cabbage from watering down the dressing, we were ready to tackle the dressing itself. While many recipes simply call for buttermilk seasoned with a few spices and herbs, we found the flavor of the buttermilk itself needed to be tempered. By adding both a little mayonnaise and sour cream, we were able to round out its tart, dairy flavor without losing the buttermilk's distinctive bite. The mayonnaise and sour cream also added body to the dressing, helping it cling to the cabbage.

After trying a variety of flavorings and vegetables, we found fresh carrot, shallot, and parsley seasoned with mustard, vinegar, and a pinch of sugar turned the buttermilk-cabbage mixture into a fresh and authentic-tasting coleslaw that doesn't weep.

Coleslaw with Buttermilk Dressing

SERVES 4

See the illustrations below for how to shred cabbage for slaw. Serve this tangy classic with grilled foods, sandwiches, or burgers.

1	pound red or green cabbage (about ½ medium head), shredded fine or chopped (about 6 cups)
	Salt
1	medium carrot, peeled and shredded
½	cup buttermilk
2	tablespoons mayonnaise
2	tablespoons sour cream

SHREDDING CABBAGE

1. Cut a whole head of cabbage into quarters. Cut away the piece of hard core attached to each quarter.

2. Separate the cored cabbage quarters into stacks of leaves and press down on them lightly to flatten.

3. Use a chef's knife to cut each stack of cabbage diagonally into long, thin pieces. Alternatively, roll the stacked leaves crosswise to fit them into the feed tube of a food processor fitted with the shredding disk.

1	small shallot, minced (about 2 tablespoons)
2	tablespoons minced fresh parsley leaves
1/2	teaspoon cider vinegar
1/4	teaspoon Dijon mustard
1/2	teaspoon sugar
1/8	teaspoon ground black pepper

1. Toss the shredded cabbage and 1 teaspoon salt in a colander or large-mesh strainer set over a medium bowl. Let stand until the cabbage wilts, at least 1 hour or up to 4 hours. Rinse the cabbage under cold running water (or in a large bowl of ice water if serving immediately). Press, but do not squeeze, to drain; pat dry with paper towels. Combine the wilted cabbage and the carrot in a large bowl.

2. Stir the buttermilk, mayonnaise, sour cream, shallot, parsley, vinegar, mustard, sugar, 1/4 teaspoon salt, and the pepper in a small bowl. Pour the buttermilk dressing over the wilted cabbage and refrigerate, covered, until ready to serve. (The coleslaw can be refrigerated for up to 3 days.)

➤ VARIATIONS

Buttermilk Coleslaw with Scallions and Cilantro

Follow the recipe for Coleslaw with Buttermilk Dressing, substituting 1 tablespoon minced fresh cilantro leaves for the parsley and 1 teaspoon lime juice for the cider vinegar, omitting the mustard, and adding 2 scallions, sliced thin.

Buttermilk Coleslaw with Lemon and Herbs

Follow the recipe for Coleslaw with Buttermilk Dressing, substituting 1 teaspoon lemon juice for the cider vinegar and adding 1 teaspoon fresh thyme leaves and 1 tablespoon minced fresh chives to the dressing.

AMERICAN POTATO SALAD

WHAT'S A SUMMER PICNIC OR BACKYARD barbecue without potato salad? This dish should be easy to make well, but all too often the potatoes are bland, and they fall apart under the weight of the dressing.

We decided to focus on a simple mayonnaise-based salad with hard-boiled eggs, pickles, and celery. We first wanted to know what type of potato to use and how to cook it. Recipe writers seemed split down the middle between starchy potatoes (like russets) and waxy potatoes (like Red Bliss), with starchy praised for being more absorbent and waxy admired for their sturdiness. When making potato salad, we have always just boiled potatoes with the skin on, but steaming, microwaving, roasting, and baking were all options worth trying.

Next, should the potatoes be peeled? If so, when? Some recipes called for cooking potatoes with the skin on, then peeling and seasoning them immediately, working on the assumption that hot potatoes absorb more flavor than cold ones. We wondered if the extra step of seasoning the cooked potatoes with vinegar, salt, and pepper first made any difference. Could we instead just toss all the ingredients together at the same time?

After boiling, steaming, baking/roasting, and microwaving four different varieties of potatoes—Red Bliss, russets, all-purpose, and Yukon Golds—we found Red Bliss to be the potato of choice and boiling to be the cooking method of choice. Higher-starch potatoes—all-purpose and Yukon Golds as well as russets—are not sturdy enough for salad. They fall apart when cut, making for a sloppy-looking salad.

Next, we wanted to see if we could boost flavor at the cooking stage by boiling the potatoes in chicken broth or in water heavily seasoned with bay leaves and garlic cloves. The chicken broth might just as well have been water—there wasn't a hint of evidence that the potatoes had been cooked in broth. The bay leaves and garlic smelled wonderful as the potatoes cooked, but the potatoes were still bland.

The fact that nothing seemed to penetrate the potatoes got us wondering: Does the potato skin act as a barrier? We performed an experiment by cooking two batches of unpeeled potatoes, the first in heavily salted water and the second in unsalted water. We rinsed them quickly under cold running water and tasted. Sure enough, both batches of potatoes tasted exactly the same. We tried boiling peeled potatoes, but they were waterlogged compared with their unpeeled counterparts.

We found the paper-thin skin of the boiled red potato not unpleasant to taste and certainly pleasant to look at in what is often a monochromatic salad. Although this saved the peeling step, we found the skin tended to rip when the potato was cut. Because the skin was particularly susceptible to ripping when the potatoes were very hot, we solved the problem in two ways. First, we cut the potatoes with a serrated knife, which minimized ripping, and second, we let them cool before cutting them.

Now, it was on to our last step. To find out if the now-cool potatoes would have the capacity to absorb seasoning, we made two salads, letting one cool completely before dressing with vinegar, salt and pepper, and mayonnaise and letting the other cool just until warm and preseasoning it with vinegar and salt and pepper well before adding the mayonnaise. (We found the potatoes could still be cut cleanly as long as they were warm but not hot.) The results were clear. The salad made with potatoes seasoned when still warm was zesty and delicious. The other salad was bland in comparison.

American Potato Salad with Hard-Boiled Eggs and Sweet Pickles

SERVES 4 TO 6

Use sweet pickles, not relish, for the best results.

2	pounds red potatoes (about 6 medium or 18 small), scrubbed
1/4	cup red wine vinegar
	Salt and ground black pepper
3	hard-boiled eggs (page 122), peeled and cut into 1/2-inch dice
1	medium celery rib, minced (about 1/2 cup)
2	tablespoons minced red onion
1/4	cup sweet pickles, minced
1/2	cup mayonnaise
2	teaspoons Dijon mustard
2	tablespoons minced fresh parsley leaves

1. Cover the potatoes with 1 inch water in a stockpot or Dutch oven. Bring to a simmer over medium-high heat. Reduce the heat to medium and simmer, stirring once or twice to ensure even cooking, until the potatoes are tender (a thin-bladed paring knife or metal cake tester can be slipped into and out of the center of the potatoes with no resistance), 25 to 30 minutes

SCIENCE: Keeping Potato Salad Safe

Mayonnaise has gotten a bad reputation, being blamed for spoiled potato salads and upset stomachs after many summer picnics and barbecues. You may think that switching from a mayonnaise-based dressing to a vinaigrette will protect your potato salad (and your family) from food poisoning. Think again.

The main ingredients in mayonnaise are raw eggs, vegetable oil, and an acid (usually vinegar or lemon juice). The eggs used in commercially made mayonnaise have been pasteurized to kill salmonella and other bacteria. The acid is another safeguard; because bacteria do not fare well in acidic environments, the lemon juice or vinegar inhibits bacterial growth. Mayonnaise, even when homemade, is rarely the problem. It's the potatoes that are more likely to go bad.

The bacteria usually responsible for spoiled potato salad are *Bacillus cereus* and *Staphylococcus aureus* (commonly known as staph). Both are found in soil and dust, and they thrive on starchy foods like rice, pasta, and potatoes. If they find their way to your potato salad via unwashed vegetables, an unwashed cutting board, or contaminated hands, they can wreak havoc on your digestive system.

Most food-borne bacteria grow well at temperatures between 40 and 140 degrees Fahrenheit. This is known as the temperature danger zone, and if contaminated food remains in this zone for too long, the bacteria can produce enough toxins to make you sick. The U.S. Food and Drug Administration recommends refrigerating food within two hours of its preparation, or one hour if the room temperature is above 90 degrees.

Although the high acid content of the vinaigrette for our French potato salad might slow bacteria growth, it's best to play it safe and follow the FDA's guidelines. Don't leave any potato salad out for more than two hours, and promptly refrigerate any leftovers in a covered container.

for medium potatoes or 15 to 20 minutes for small potatoes.

2. Drain; cool the potatoes slightly and peel if you like. Cut the potatoes into ¾-inch cubes (use a serrated knife if they have skins) while still warm, rinsing the knife occasionally in warm water to remove the starch.

3. Place the warm potato cubes in a large bowl. Add the vinegar, ½ teaspoon salt, and ¼ teaspoon pepper and toss gently. Cover the bowl with plastic wrap and refrigerate until cool, about 20 minutes.

4. When the potatoes are cool, toss with the remaining ingredients and season with salt and pepper to taste. Serve immediately or cover and refrigerate for up to 1 day.

FRENCH POTATO SALAD

HAVING LITTLE IN COMMON WITH ITS American counterpart, French potato salad is served warm or at room temperature and is composed of sliced potatoes glistening with olive oil, white wine vinegar, and plenty of fresh herbs.

We expected quick success with this seemingly simple recipe—how hard could it be to boil a few potatoes and toss them in vinaigrette? We sliced the potatoes, dressed them while they were still warm (warm potatoes are more absorbent than cool ones), and then served them up to our tasters. The salad looked mangled, as the warm potatoes consistently broke apart upon slicing.

Our first task was to put a stop to homely salads with jagged, broken potatoes and ripped skins. We tried shocking the whole potatoes after cooking (reasoning that the ice-cold water might somehow set the skin—it didn't), slicing the potatoes with a serrated knife (this helped a little bit, but the results were inconsistent), and starting the potatoes in boiling instead of cold water (this made absolutely no difference). It was proving impossible to slice a just-cooked potato without having it fall apart.

We reevaluated our cooking technique: Boil the potatoes whole—generally the standard in the test kitchen, the idea being that the skins

prevent potato starch from leaching out into the water—then slice while warm. On a whim, we boiled some potatoes that we sliced before cooking. This, surprisingly, did the trick. The potato slices emerged from the water unbroken and with their skins intact. They had a clean (not starchy) taste, were evenly cooked, and held together perfectly, unlike those that had been cooked whole before slicing. (We still prefer boiling potatoes in their skins for American potato salad. French potato salad is served warm, so the potatoes must be dressed as soon as they are cooked. American potato salad is served chilled, so you can let the potatoes cool before cutting them. Also, although it is difficult to thinly slice hot potatoes for French potato salad, cooler potatoes are easily cut into large cubes for American-style potato salad.)

This one simple change in technique offered multiple benefits. First, the frustrating (and sometimes painful) task of slicing hot potatoes was eliminated. Second, we now had no need to find uniformly sized potatoes to ensure even cooking. (We just needed to cut the potatoes into slices of uniform thickness.) Third, we found we could perfectly season the cut potatoes while they cooked by adding a hefty 2 tablespoons of salt to the cooking water.

We now shifted our focus to the vinaigrette and its usual ingredients: olive oil, white wine vinegar, herbs, mustard, minced onion, chicken stock, and white wine. Because our initial tests had produced relatively dull salads, we decided to experiment with each component until we found a surefire way to pump up the flavor. The first improvement came by using slightly more vinegar than the test kitchen standard of 4 parts oil to 1 part vinegar. These bland potatoes could handle extra acid. We loved the sharp flavor notes added by champagne vinegar but found that white wine vinegar works well, too. As for the olive oil, extra-virgin or pure olive oil makes an equally good base for the dressing; tasters found little distinction between the two (the former being more flavorful than the latter), presumably because of the other potent ingredients in the vinaigrette. However, expensive fruity olive oils were rejected for their overpowering nature.

We liked the extra moisture and layer of complexity that chicken stock (or broth) and wine added (salads made strictly with oil and vinegar were a tad dry), but it seemed wasteful to uncork a bottle or open a can only to use a few tablespoons. We found a solution to this problem and a revelation when we consulted Julia Child's *The Way to Cook* (Knopf, 1989). She suggests adding some of the potato cooking water to the vinaigrette, a quick and frugal solution that also added plenty of potato flavor and a nice touch of saltiness. Two teaspoons of Dijon mustard and a sprinkle of freshly ground black pepper perked things up, while the gentle assertiveness of minced shallots and a blanched garlic clove (raw garlic was too harsh) added even more depth. As for the fresh herbs, we made salads with all manner of them, including chives, dill, basil, parsley, tarragon, and chervil. But an inherently French *fines herbes* mixture seemed appropriate in theory and was heavenly in reality. Chives, parsley, tarragon, and chervil make up this classic quartet, with its anise undertones.

The last but not least fine point: How to toss the cooked, warm potatoes with the vinaigrette without damaging the slices? The solution was simple. We carefully laid the potatoes in a single layer on a rimmed baking sheet, then poured the vinaigrette over them. Spreading out the potatoes in this way also allowed them to cool off a bit, preventing residual cooking and potential mushiness. While we let the vinaigrette soak into the potatoes, we had just enough time to chop the herbs and shallot before sprinkling them on the finished salad. Adding the herbs just before serving guards against wilting and darkening.

French Potato Salad

SERVES 6

If fresh chervil isn't available, substitute an additional ½ tablespoon of minced parsley and an additional ½ teaspoon of minced tarragon. For best flavor, serve the salad warm, but to make ahead, follow the recipe through step 2, cover with plastic wrap, and refrigerate. Before serving, bring the salad to room temperature, then add the shallot and herbs.

2	pounds red potatoes (about 6 medium or 18 small), scrubbed and cut into ¼-inch-thick slices
2	tablespoons salt
1	medium garlic clove, peeled and threaded on a skewer
1½	tablespoons champagne vinegar or white wine vinegar
2	teaspoons Dijon mustard
¼	cup olive oil
½	teaspoon ground black pepper
1	small shallot, minced (about 2 tablespoons)
1	tablespoon minced fresh chervil leaves
1	tablespoon minced fresh parsley leaves
1	tablespoon minced fresh chives
1	teaspoon minced fresh tarragon leaves

1. Place the potatoes, 6 cups cold water, and the salt in a large saucepan. Bring to a boil over high heat, then reduce the heat to medium. Lower the skewered garlic into the simmering water and partially blanch, about 45 seconds. Immediately run the garlic under cold tap water to stop the cooking; remove the garlic from the skewer and set aside. Simmer the potatoes, uncovered, until tender but still firm (a thin-bladed paring knife can be slipped into and out of the center of a potato slice with no resistance), about 5 minutes. Drain the potatoes, reserving ¼ cup cooking water. Arrange the hot potatoes close together in a single layer on a rimmed baking sheet.

2. Press the garlic through a garlic press or mince by hand. Whisk the garlic, reserved potato cooking water, vinegar, mustard, oil, and pepper together in a small bowl until combined. Drizzle the dressing evenly over the warm potato slices; let stand 10 minutes.

3. Meanwhile, toss the shallot and herbs gently together in a small bowl. Transfer the potatoes to a large serving bowl. Add the shallot-herb mixture and mix lightly with a rubber spatula to combine. Serve immediately.

➤ VARIATIONS

French Potato Salad with Arugula, Roquefort, and Walnuts

Follow the recipe for French Potato Salad, omitting the herbs and tossing the dressed potatoes with ½ cup walnuts, toasted and chopped coarse; 4 ounces Roquefort cheese, crumbled; and 1 small bunch arugula, washed, dried, and torn into bite-size pieces (about 2½ cups), along with the minced shallot in step 3.

French Potato Salad with Radishes, Cornichons, and Capers

Follow the recipe for French Potato Salad, omitting the herbs and substituting 2 tablespoons minced red onion for the shallot. Toss the dressed potatoes with 2 medium red radishes, sliced thin (about ⅓ cup); ¼ cup capers, rinsed; and ¼ cup cornichons, sliced thin, along with the red onion in step 3.

GERMAN POTATO SALAD

SERVED HOT OR WARM, PUNGENTLY TANGY from its vinegar dressing, and chock-full of bacon flavor, German potato salad should be a welcome change from the cold comfort of American-style potato salad. But a recent tasting of German potato salad recipes brought about quite different results. These were the comments, across the board: tasteless, broken-down potatoes; unbalanced, flavorless vinaigrettes; and greasy. It was time to take this recipe into the 21st century.

Starting with the potatoes, we chose low-starch red potatoes. We decided to cut the potatoes before boiling, thus dramatically reducing their cooking time. Using heavily salted water ensured that the potatoes were also well seasoned.

The beauty of the dressing for this potato salad is the foundation of rendered bacon fat (vegetable and olive oils were tested and flatly rejected). However, we knew that we wanted to eschew the usual overly greasy vinaigrette. We fried up pounds of bacon, increasing the amount of bacon fat (and crumbled bacon pieces) until tasters were satisfied. Half a pound of bacon was the right amount for 2 pounds of potatoes, with plenty of bacon to bite into. It also produced a hefty ⅓ cup of bacon fat for the dressing. Tasty? Yes. Light? No way. This heavy dressing was just what we were trying to avoid. Part of the solution to the greasiness problem is to spoon off some excess bacon fat. Two pounds of potatoes require a dressing with just ¼ cup of bacon fat. Any more and the salad is just too fatty.

Choosing the right vinegar to balance the bacon fat is also key. Along with cider vinegar (the usual choice in most recipes), we also tested white wine, red wine, distilled white, and rice vinegars. Surprisingly, tasters preferred the distilled white vinegar, which is often the last choice in the test kitchen owing to its bland flavor. But in this case, that was exactly what we needed—clean acidity without much personality of its own to mask the flavor of the bacon. One cup of vinegar made the right quantity of dressing (the hot potatoes soaked up an amazing amount), but now tasters' palates were assaulted with a harsh, unbalanced dressing. We diluted the acidity with some of the potato cooking water, a trick we picked up when researching our French Potato Salad (page 100).

Sautéed onion was a must (raw onion was too harsh), and after trying red, white, and yellow, we found that you really can't go wrong with any of them. Mustard appears in some German potato salad recipes, but certainly not all. After starting out with salads made with no mustard, tasters were receptive to its addition. We first tried Dijon mustard (both smooth and cracked varieties), but tasters weren't crazy about the wine flavor that it added. Brown mustard was neither here nor there. Whole-grain German-style mustard (of course) proved the best bet. Dotted with flecks of whole mustard seeds, the salad now had both the right flavor and a rustic appearance. A half teaspoon of sugar offset the tartness of the vinegar and mustard, and some chopped parsley added freshness.

Mixing the dressing and potatoes in a big serving bowl is typically how the salad is combined. We found, though, that the potatoes lost most of their heat that way. Instead, we dumped the potatoes right into the skillet where the vinaigrette was waiting, giving them a quick toss right in the hot pan before piling the whole thing into a serving dish. Nice and warm, tangy and full of flavor, this was German potato salad at its very best.

German Potato Salad

SERVES 6 TO 8

Unlike a nonstick skillet, a traditional skillet will allow the bacon to form caramelized bits on the pan bottom. This will result in a richer-tasting dressing and a more flavorful salad.

2 pounds small to medium red potatoes (1 to 2 inches in diameter), scrubbed and halved if small or quartered if medium
   Salt

8 ounces (about 8 slices) bacon, cut crosswise into ½-inch pieces

1 medium onion, chopped fine

½ teaspoon sugar

½ cup distilled white vinegar

1 tablespoon whole-grain German-style mustard

¼ teaspoon ground black pepper

¼ cup chopped fresh parsley leaves

1. Place the potatoes, 1 tablespoon salt, and water to cover in a large saucepan or Dutch oven; bring to a boil over high heat, then reduce the heat to medium and simmer until the potatoes are tender (a thin-bladed paring knife can be slipped into and out of the potatoes with little resistance), about 10 minutes. Reserve ½ cup potato cooking water, then drain the potatoes; return the potatoes to the pot and cover to keep warm.

2. While the potatoes are cooking, fry the bacon in a large skillet over medium heat, stirring occasionally, until browned and crisp, about 5 minutes. With a slotted spoon, transfer the bacon to a paper towel–lined plate; pour off all but ¼ cup bacon grease. Add the onion to the skillet and cook, stirring occasionally, over medium heat until softened and beginning to brown, about 4 minutes. Stir in the sugar until dissolved, about 30 seconds. Add the vinegar and reserved potato cooking water; bring to a simmer and cook until the mixture is reduced to about 1 cup, about 3 minutes. Off the heat, whisk in the mustard and pepper. Add the potatoes, parsley, and bacon to the skillet and toss to combine; adjust the seasonings with salt to taste. Transfer to a bowl and serve immediately, while still warm.

GRAINY MUSTARDS: WHAT'S THE DIFFERENCE?

WHOLE-GRAIN
This German-style mustard has whole seeds and a pure mustard flavor that tasters preferred.

CRACKED
This Dijon-style mustard has flecks of cracked seeds but a strong white wine flavor that tasters did not like.

MACARONI SALAD

MACARONI SALAD IS AN AMERICAN DELI staple. For many people, it's hard to imagine a picnic or summer barbecue without this salad of tender elbow noodles and creamy dressing. Although relatively easy to make, it is also easy to make it badly. Few dishes are less appetizing than a bowl of underseasoned, overcooked noodles accompanied by flavorless, limp celery, killer-sweet pickle relish, and an excess of mayonnaise. Good macaroni salad, however, is dreamy when made with perfectly cooked, well-seasoned noodles and crisp vegetables dressed lightly in mayonnaise.

To start, we focused on the pasta. We tried cooking it al dente, and although we prefer a slightly resistant texture in hot pasta, we found it overly toothsome and stiff when cold. Thoroughly cooked pasta, which offered no resistance when eaten hot, took on a pleasantly yielding and bouncy texture when cool and was also able to maintain its shape without becoming mushy. Pasta that was overcooked even just slightly tasted mushy and slimy and tore into pieces when tossed with the other ingredients.

One trick we picked up was how to turn the hot pasta into a cold salad quickly. When the hot pasta was allowed to cool on its own, it clumped together into a starchy mass and began to overcook as the residual heat from the pasta further softened the noodles. Going against all we had learned about how to cook pasta, we rinsed the pasta under cold water, which both stopped it from further cooking and washed away some of the extra starch. (When serving pasta hot with sauce, this starch is a good thing, because it helps the sauce cling to the pasta.) We then spread the pasta out on paper towels to help drain off this extra water (see the illustrations bottom right). If we skipped this step, water was caught in the curves of the macaroni and turned the dressing watery.

We found the pasta was best mixed with the classic assortment of fresh vegetables and seasonings: celery, red onion, hard-boiled eggs, and sweet pickles. Fresh parsley added a clean, herbal flavor, and a little mustard provided some kick. Wary of burying this fresh-tasting mixture with too much mayonnaise, we started off using only ½ cup per pound of pasta, but found the pasta readily soaked up mayonnaise until we hit 1 cup. Although many recipes call for vinegar, we preferred the light, fresh acidity of lemon juice. The salad tastes best when allowed to cool for at least an hour in the refrigerator. The seasonings mellow substantially, so use a liberal hand with salt and pepper.

Macaroni Salad

SERVES 8 TO 10

Make sure to drain the cooked and rinsed pasta thoroughly.

	Salt
1	pound elbow macaroni
1	celery rib, minced
¼	small red onion, minced (2 to 3 tablespoons)
3	hard-boiled eggs (page 122), peeled and diced small
¼	cup minced sweet pickles
¼	cup minced fresh parsley leaves
¼	cup juice from 1 or 2 large lemons
1	cup mayonnaise
2	teaspoons Dijon mustard
	Ground black pepper

1. Bring 4 quarts water to a boil in a large pot and add 1 tablespoon salt. Stir in the macaroni and cook until thoroughly done, 10 to 12 minutes. Drain the macaroni in a colander and rinse with cold water until cool. Shake the macaroni dry in the colander and spread it in an even layer on a rimmed baking sheet lined with paper towels. Let the macaroni dry for 3 minutes.

2. Roll the macaroni in paper towels to blot any remaining moisture and transfer the drained macaroni to a large bowl. Toss with the remaining ingredients and season liberally with salt and pepper to taste. Refrigerate the macaroni salad for at least 1 hour or up to 1 day.

➤ VARIATIONS

Macaroni Salad with Curried Apples
Follow the recipe for Macaroni Salad, replacing the hard-boiled eggs, sweet pickles, parsley, and mustard with 1 medium Granny Smith apple, cored and cut into ¼-inch dice (about 1½ cups), and ¼ cup minced fresh basil leaves. Mix 1 tablespoon curry powder into the mayonnaise. Proceed with the recipe as directed.

DRYING MACARONI

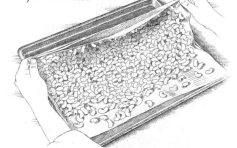

1. Shake the macaroni dry in the colander and spread it in an even layer on a rimmed baking sheet lined with paper towels. Let the macaroni dry for 3 minutes.

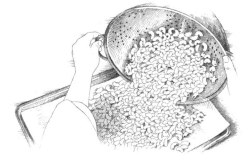

2. Roll the macaroni in paper towels to blot any remaining moisture and transfer the drained macaroni to a large bowl.

Macaroni Salad with Chipotles and Cilantro

Toast 1½ cups frozen corn kernels and 2 medium garlic cloves, unpeeled, in a nonstick skillet set over high heat until the corn turns spotty brown, about 5 minutes; peel and mince the garlic. Follow the recipe for Macaroni Salad, replacing the hard-boiled eggs, sweet pickles, parsley, and mustard with the corn, minced garlic, 3 scallions, minced (about ¼ cup), 1 cup cherry tomatoes, quartered, and ¼ cup minced fresh cilantro leaves. Mix 1 tablespoon minced chipotle chiles in adobo sauce into the mayonnaise. Proceed with the recipe as directed.

ITALIAN-STYLE PASTA SALAD

WE LOVE A GOOD MACARONI SALAD, BUT sometimes we like to trade in our backyard barbecue version for a lighter pasta salad dressed with vinaigrette—that can stand on its own or be served as a light entrée on a hot summer evening.

Our research turned up a dizzying number of recipes for pasta salad. We quickly decided to narrow our focus. Because pasta salad is a summery dish, recipes that featured tomatoes seemed a natural choice.

As we started making pasta salads with tomatoes, we repeatedly encountered the same problem. The tomatoes made the salad too watery and wouldn't allow the flavors of the salad to meld. We tried different sizes of pasta in hopes of capturing the tomatoes. We also tried cutting the tomatoes into different shapes and sizes, but the problem persisted. How to obtain a sweet tomato flavor in a cohesive pasta salad? The answer, surprisingly enough, was sun-dried tomatoes. Granted, we lost the freshness of garden-fresh tomatoes, but using sun-dried tomatoes had several benefits. First, the problem of watery salad was eliminated. Second, as we were using tomatoes packed in olive oil, we could use that oil in our vinaigrette, thus giving the salad a double shot of tomato flavor. Last, we did not need perfectly ripe summer tomatoes to make pasta salad.

One drawback of sun-dried tomatoes is that their concentrated flavor is sometimes too sweet. We tempered this sweetness by adding green olives to our salad; the pleasant brininess of the olives balanced the tastes in the dish.

One small consideration remained: how to integrate all the ingredients in the salad. As it was, all the flavorful stuff fell to the bottom of the bowl, leaving the pasta alone at the top. Thinking back to good pasta salads we've had, they all had one ingredient in common: a leafy green. Thus, we tried adding some arugula. It was a breakthrough. The leaves gave the flavorful ingredients something to stick to, and they were large enough so they didn't fall to the bottom of the bowl. Essentially, the arugula acted as a bridge between the pasta and the other ingredients in the salad. With our ingredients well-balanced and evenly mixed, we finished the salad by tossing in cubed fresh mozzarella.

Pasta Salad with Arugula and Sun-Dried Tomato Vinaigrette
SERVES 6 AS A SIDE DISH OR
4 AS A LIGHT MAIN DISH

We like the assertive flavor of red wine vinegar in this recipe. See page 106 for more information about our testing of leading brands.

	Salt
1	pound fusilli
1	tablespoon extra-virgin olive oil
1	(8-ounce) jar sun-dried tomatoes packed in olive oil
2	tablespoons red wine vinegar
1	large garlic clove, minced or pressed through a garlic press
¼	teaspoon salt
⅛	teaspoon ground black pepper
1	bunch arugula, washed, dried, and torn into bite-size pieces (about 4 cups lightly packed)
½	cup green olives, pitted and sliced
6	ounces fresh mozzarella cheese, cut into ½-inch cubes

1. Bring 4 quarts water to a boil in a large pot over high heat. Add 1 tablespoon salt and the pasta to the boiling water. Cook until al dente. Drain, rinsing the pasta well with cold water. Drain the cold pasta well, transfer it to a large mixing bowl, and toss it with the olive oil. Set aside.

2. Drain the sun-dried tomatoes, reserving the oil. (You should have ⅓ cup oil. If necessary, make up the difference with extra-virgin olive oil.) Coarsely chop the tomatoes. Whisk the reserved oil from the tomatoes together with the vinegar, garlic, salt, and pepper in a small bowl.

3. Add the arugula, olives, mozzarella, and chopped sun-dried tomatoes to the pasta. Pour in the tomato vinaigrette, toss gently, and serve immediately.

INGREDIENTS: Red Wine Vinegar

The source of that notable edge you taste when sampling any red wine vinegar is acetic acid, the chief flavor component in all vinegar and the byproduct of the bacterium *Acetobacter aceti,* which feeds on the alcohol in wine. The process of converting red wine to vinegar once took months, if not years, but now, with the help of an acetator (a machine that speeds the metabolism of the *Acetobacter aceti*), red wine vinegar can be made in less than 24 hours.

Does this faster, cheaper method—the one used to make most supermarket brands—produce inferior red wine vinegar? Or is this a case in which modern technology trumps Old World craftsmanship, which is still employed by makers of the more expensive red wine vinegars? To find out, we included in our tasting vinegars made via the fast process (acetator) and the slow process (often called the Orléans method, after the city in France where it was developed).

We first tasted 10 nationally available supermarket brands in two ways: by dipping sugar cubes in each brand and sucking out the vinegar (a method professionals use to cut down on palate fatigue) and by making a simple vinaigrette with each and tasting it on iceberg lettuce. We then pitted the winners of the supermarket tasting against four high-end red wine vinegars.

Although no single grape variety is thought to make the best red wine vinegar, we were curious to find out if our tasters were unwittingly fond of vinegars made from the same grape. We sent the vinegars to a food lab for an anthocyanin pigment profile, a test that can detect the 10 common pigments found in red grapes. Although the lab was unable to distinguish specific grape varieties (Cabernet, Merlot, Pinot Noir, Zinfandel, and the like), it did provide us with an interesting piece of information: Some of the vinegars weren't made with wine grapes (known as *Vitus vinifera*) but with less expensive Concord-type grapes, the kind used to make Welch's grape juice.

Did the vinegars made with grape juice fair poorly, as might be expected? Far from it. The taste-test results were both shocking and unambiguous: Concord-type grapes not only do just fine when it comes to making vinegar, they may be a key element in the success of the top-rated brands in our tasting. Spectrum, our overall winner, is made from a mix of wine grapes and Concord grapes. Pompeian, which came in second among the supermarket brands, is made entirely of Concord-type grapes.

What else might contribute to the flavor of these vinegars? One possibility, we thought, was the way in which the acetic acid is developed. Manufacturers that mass-produce vinegar generally prefer not to use the Orléans method because it's slow and expensive. Spectrum red wine vinegar is produced with the Orléans method, but Pompeian is made in an acetator in less than 24 hours.

What, then, can explain why Spectrum and Pompeian won the supermarket tasting and beat the other gourmet vinegars? Oddly enough, for a food that defines sourness, the answer seems to lie in its sweetness. It turns out that Americans like their vinegar sweet (think balsamic vinegar).

The production of Spectrum is outsourced to a small manufacturer in Modena, Italy, that makes generous use of the Trebbiano grape, the same grape used to make balsamic vinegar. The Trebbiano, which is a white wine grape, gives Spectrum the sweetness our tasters admired. Pompeian vinegar is finished with a touch of sherry vinegar, added to give the red vinegar a more fruity, well-rounded flavor. Also significant to our results may be that both Spectrum and Pompeian start with wines containing Concord grapes, which are sweet enough to be a common choice when making jams and jellies.

When pitted against gourmet vinegars, Spectrum and Pompeian still came out on top. Which red wine vinegar should you buy? Skip the specialty shop and head to the supermarket.

THE BEST RED WINE VINEGARS

Spectrum vinegar (left) and Pompeian vinegar (right) are available in supermarkets and bested gourmet brands costing eight times as much.

BREAD SALAD

BREAD SALAD MAY SOUND ODD, BUT PAIR
cubes of rustic bread with flavorful ripe tomatoes,
fresh herbs, like basil, parsley, and oregano, and
high-quality extra-virgin olive oil, and very little
else is needed. Thrift may have been the imperative for this Mediterranean treat, but heavenly,
rich aromas and flavor are the results.

Which brings us to the quality of the main
ingredient: the bread. Not surprisingly, sliced
white bread or airy supermarket bread that is
highly refined and becomes rock-hard within a
few days won't do. Ideally, the proper bread for
bread salads should not contain sugar or sweeteners
of any kind, which would conflict with the savory
nature of the other ingredients. Nor should the loaf
have raisins or nuts. What the bread should have is
a sturdy texture and a good wheaty flavor.

Depending on how stale the bread is, it may
need to be dampened with a little water. The
amount is determined by the dryness of the bread;
if the bread receives too much dampening, it will
collapse into a soggy mess when the dressing is
added. Therefore, when assembling the salad, see
how much the bread softens and then adjust the
texture by sprinkling with water as needed, waiting a minute or two between additions to allow
the bread to absorb the water.

Because the bread becomes soggy fairly quickly,
neither of the salads that follow should be made
much in advance of serving. (See the individual
recipes for suggested make-ahead times.) The best
approach is to prepare all of the salad ingredients,
then combine them just before serving.

Bread Salad with Tomatoes, Herbs, and Red Onion

SERVES 4

1   pound day-old coarse peasant bread or sturdy Italian bread, crusts removed, cut or torn into 1-inch cubes (about 6 cups)
1/2 cup extra-virgin olive oil
3   tablespoons red wine vinegar
2   large, ripe round tomatoes or 4 plum tomatoes (about 1 pound total), cored, seeded, and cut into medium dice
1/2 small red onion, sliced very thin
2   tablespoons torn fresh basil or mint leaves
2   teaspoons whole fresh oregano leaves
1   tablespoon minced fresh parsley leaves
1/2 teaspoon salt
1/4 teaspoon ground black pepper

Place the bread cubes in a shallow bowl. Mix the
oil, vinegar, tomatoes, onion, and half of the herbs
together in a medium bowl. Let stand to allow the
flavors to develop, about 10 minutes. Pour the dressing over the bread, add the remaining herbs, and toss
well. Season with the salt and pepper, adding more
or less to taste. If the bread still seems dry, sprinkle
it with 1 to 2 tablespoons water to soften it a bit and
toss again. Serve. (If sturdy bread is used, the salad
can be covered and set aside for up to 2 hours.)

Bread Salad with Roasted Peppers and Olives

SERVES 4 TO 6

*Sourdough or a sturdy peasant bread is needed for this
salad. Airy, unsubstantial bread will quickly become
soggy and is not an option here.*

1   pound sturdy Italian bread, crusts removed, cut or torn into 1-inch cubes (about 6 cups)
2   bell peppers, 1 red and 1 yellow, roasted (page 177), cut into 1/2-inch strips
1/2 cup extra-virgin olive oil
1/4 cup cider vinegar
1   small red or white onion, quartered and sliced thin
1   medium scallion, sliced thin, including 2 inches of green part
3   tablespoons pitted and sliced green olives
1   tablespoon minced fresh oregano leaves
1/2 teaspoon salt
1/4 teaspoon ground black pepper

1. Mix the bread cubes and pepper strips
together in a large bowl; set aside.
2. Mix the oil, vinegar, onion, scallion, olives,

oregano, salt, and pepper together in a medium bowl; let stand to allow the flavors to develop, about 10 minutes. Add the dressing to the bread and peppers; toss to combine. If the bread still seems dry, sprinkle it with 1 to 2 tablespoons water to soften it a bit and toss again. Serve. (If sturdy bread is used, the salad can be covered and set aside for up to 2 hours.)

TABBOULEH

PERHAPS THE BEST-KNOWN ARAB DISH IN THE United States is tabbouleh. However, the tabbouleh typically served here is very different from the original. In its Middle Eastern home, this dish is basically a parsley salad with bulgur, rather than the bulgur salad with parsley that is frequently found here.

In addition to finely minced parsley, a perfect tabbouleh includes morsels of bulgur—crushed, parboiled wheat—tossed in a penetrating, minty lemon dressing with bits of ripe tomato. While these principal ingredients remain the same, a variety of preparation techniques exist, each Arab cook being convinced that his or her method produces the finest version.

We tried processing the bulgur in the five most commonly used ways. First we rinsed the grain, combined it with the minced tomato, and set it aside to absorb the tomato juices. With this method, the bulgur remained unacceptably crunchy.

Next we marinated the bulgur in a lemon juice and olive oil dressing. This approach produced bulgur that was tasty but slightly heavy. The third method, soaking the grain in water until fluffy and then squeezing out the excess moisture, produced an equally acceptable—but equally heavy—nutty-flavored wheat.

Next we soaked the wheat in water for about five minutes, then drained the liquid and replaced it with the lemon–olive oil dressing. We discovered that the wheat's texture was good and the flavor superior.

But the all-out winner came as a surprise. We first rinsed the bulgur, then mixed it with fresh lemon juice. We then set the mixture aside to allow the juice to be absorbed. When treated in this way, bulgur acquires a fresh and intense flavor, but without the heaviness that the added olive oil produces.

To complete the dish, combine the bulgur with the parsley, finely chopped scallions, fresh mint, and tomatoes. Toss with the remaining dressing ingredients and serve within a few hours. Letting the mixture sit for an hour or so blends the flavors nicely, but after five or six hours the scallions tend to become too strong and overpower the other flavors.

The final question is the proportion of parsley to bulgur. Although some Lebanese restaurateurs present a 9-to-1 ratio of parsley to bulgur, we find that the wholesome goodness of the wheat is lost unless it is in a more harmonious balance. We recommend that the finished dish contain 5 parts parsley to 3 or 4 parts wheat.

Tabbouleh
SERVES 4 TO 6
Middle Eastern cooks frequently serve this salad with crisp inner leaves of romaine lettuce, using them as spoons to scoop the salad from the serving dish. Fine-grain bulgur is best in this recipe, but medium-grain will work; avoid coarse-grain bulgur, which must be cooked.

- ½ cup fine-grain bulgur wheat, rinsed under running water and drained
- ⅓ cup juice from 2 lemons
- ⅓ cup extra-virgin olive oil
  Salt
- ⅛ teaspoon Middle Eastern red pepper or cayenne pepper (optional)
- 2 cups minced fresh parsley leaves
- 2 medium tomatoes, halved, seeded, and cut into very small dice
- 4 medium scallions, green and white parts, minced
- 2 tablespoons minced fresh mint leaves or 1 rounded teaspoon dried mint

1. Mix the bulgur wheat with ¼ cup of the lemon juice in a medium bowl; set aside until the grains are tender and fluffy, 20 to 40 minutes, depending on the age and type of the bulgur.

2. Mix the remaining lemon juice, the olive oil, salt to taste, and red pepper (if using) together in a small bowl. In a large bowl, combine the bulgur, parsley, tomatoes, scallions, and mint; add the dressing and toss to combine. Cover and refrigerate to let the flavors blend, 1 to 2 hours. Serve.

CHICKEN CAESAR SALAD

SINCE ITS DEBUT IN THE 1920S, CAESAR salad has suffered at the hands of chefs and home cooks alike. The Caesar was conceived as a salad of whole lettuce leaves, cloaked with a rich dressing made from such unlikely partners as egg, Worcestershire sauce, lemon juice, garlic, and Parmesan cheese and garnished with garlic croutons. Over time, it has been subjected to such oddball additions as chickpeas, palm hearts, and barbecued ribs.

We wanted to bring Caesar salad back to its roots. We were struck, however, by the not inconsiderable effort required to make the salad. Given this investment of time and effort, we decided to make our Caesar not a first course but a light main dish by adding one untraditional (but now familiar) ingredient: sliced chicken breast. We wanted the chicken to add heft to the salad without disturbing the underlying magic of the dressing.

Most Caesar salad dressings have at least one of two common problems. The first is texture, which should be thick and smooth, not thin or gluey. The second is lack of balance among the dressing's key flavors—lemon, Worcestershire, and garlic (and often anchovies)—which are frequently so out of whack that they assault your palate with a biting surplus of garlic or lip-sucking profusion of lemon.

We took on texture first. The classic thickening agent in this olive oil–based dressing is egg, which is either added raw or simmered in the shell very briefly in a process called coddling. The recipes we dug up in our research also included dressings that relied on mayonnaise and sour cream for thickening, but tasters summarily rejected both, finding that the former seemed better suited to a sandwich topping and the latter to a party dip. In side-by-side tests of raw and coddled eggs, tasters preferred the noticeably smoother consistency of the coddled-egg dressing. The brief exposure to heat caused the yolk to thicken slightly, thereby giving the dressing a creamier texture. Many tasters wanted the dressing to be thicker still, so we decided to discard the egg white, which contributed extra liquid, and to double the number of yolks to two. Keep in mind, however, that such a brief exposure to heat does not render the egg as safe as if it were cooked fully; you are still essentially consuming raw egg, which may be of concern to some diners.

A series of tests led us to a well-balanced dressing. Based on an oil quantity of ⅓ cup and our 2 coddled yolks, tasters favored just under 2 tablespoons of lemon juice and a modest teaspoon each of Worcestershire sauce and garlic. The last touch was anchovy, which tasters felt gave the dressing a welcome flavor dimension.

As for the lettuce, romaine is the standard choice. Our tasters stuck to it for its pleasantly sweet flavor and crunchy texture.

The chicken added to Caesar salad in restaurants is often dry and leathery. For our Caesar, we wanted chicken that was moist, well seasoned, and quick and easy to prepare.

Skinless, boneless breasts were the overwhelming choice of tasters, who felt that dark meat tasted out of place. With our eye cocked toward speed and ease, we tested three cooking methods: grilling, sautéing, and broiling. Grilling was too much work for a simple salad. Sautéing was eliminated because it required an extra step (flouring the chicken) and produced (believe it or not) chicken that was too flavorful for this purpose. Broiling, on the other hand, gave us what we wanted—a quick, simple cooking method and chicken that would blend right into the landscape of an already full-flavored salad.

We tried making croutons from various types of white bread and determined that any type made without sweetener tasted fine. Buy a baguette or country white loaf instead of sliced sandwich bread, as the latter usually contains added sugar.

We tested three different methods of making croutons, including toasting, sautéing, and baking the bread cubes, and we tried each method with and without oil and garlic. We quickly learned that infusing olive oil with garlic flavor—rather than using minced garlic—was a key step. Whereas the minced garlic became burnt and bitter in the oven, allowing raw garlic to steep in olive oil for 20 minutes produced a pleasantly garlicky flavor. In the end, we simply tossed raw bread cubes with the seasoned oil and baked them until crisp and golden.

Chicken Caesar Salad

SERVES 4 AS A LIGHT MAIN DISH

Turn this main-dish salad into a first course by omitting the chicken and reducing the total amount of dressing used to ⅔ cup. Both the croutons and the dressing can be made 1 day in advance of serving.

GARLIC CROUTONS

2   large garlic cloves, minced or pressed through a garlic press

¼   teaspoon salt

3   tablespoons extra-virgin olive oil

3   cups ¾-inch bread cubes from 1 baguette or country loaf

BROILED CHICKEN BREASTS

4   boneless, skinless chicken breast halves (about 6 ounces each), trimmed of excess fat

    Salt and ground black pepper

CAESAR DRESSING

2   large eggs

1   tablespoon plus 2 teaspoons juice from 1 lemon

1   teaspoon Worcestershire sauce

    Salt

    Ground black pepper

1   medium garlic clove, minced or pressed through a garlic press (about 1 teaspoon)

4   anchovy fillets, minced to a paste (about 1½ teaspoons)

⅓   cup extra-virgin olive oil

SALAD

2   medium heads romaine lettuce (large outer leaves removed) or 2 large romaine hearts, washed, dried, and torn into 1½-inch pieces (about 10 cups lightly packed)

⅓   cup freshly grated Parmesan cheese

1. FOR THE CROUTONS: Adjust an oven rack to the middle position and heat the oven to 350 degrees. Mix the garlic, salt, and oil in a small bowl; let stand 20 minutes to infuse the flavors, then pour through a fine-mesh strainer into a medium bowl. Add the bread cubes and toss to coat. Spread the bread cubes in an even layer on a rimmed baking sheet; bake, stirring occasionally, until golden, 12 to 15 minutes. Cool on the baking sheet to room temperature. (The croutons can be covered and stored at room temperature for up to 24 hours.)

2. FOR THE CHICKEN: Season the chicken with salt and pepper. Adjust an oven rack to 6 inches from the broiler element; heat the broiler. Spray the broiler pan top with vegetable cooking spray; place the chicken breasts on top and broil until lightly browned, 4 to 8 minutes. Using tongs, flip the chicken over and continue to broil until the thickest part is no longer pink when cut into and registers about 160 degrees on an instant-read thermometer, 6 to 8 minutes. Transfer the chicken to a plate and set aside.

3. FOR THE DRESSING: Bring 2 inches water to a boil in a small saucepan over high heat. Lower the eggs into the water and cook 45 seconds; remove with a slotted spoon. When cool enough to handle, crack the eggs open; reserve the yolks in a small bowl and discard the whites. Add the lemon juice, Worcestershire, ¼ teaspoon salt, ⅛ teaspoon pepper, the garlic, and anchovies; whisk until smooth. Whisking constantly, add the oil in a slow, steady stream. Adjust the seasonings with salt and pepper to taste. (The dressing can be refrigerated in an airtight container for up to 1 day; shake before using.)

4. TO FINISH THE SALAD: In a large bowl, toss the lettuce, Parmesan, and about two thirds of the dressing to coat; divide evenly among individual plates. Remove the tenderloins from the chicken breasts; place in the bowl used to dress the lettuce

along with the remaining dressing. Cut the chicken breasts crosswise into ½-inch slices, add to the bowl, and toss to coat. Divide the dressed chicken evenly among the plates, arranging the slices on the lettuce. Sprinkle each plate with a portion of the croutons and serve immediately.

CLASSIC COBB SALAD

CREATED IN THE 1920S AT THE FAMOUS Hollywood hangout the Brown Derby, a classic cobb salad depends up a large supporting cast for flavor and texture—cool, crunchy greens (both mild and spicy), tender chicken, buttery avocado, juicy tomato, crisp, smoky bacon, and tangy blue cheese—to produce a vibrant salad that is substantial enough to satisfy the hankerings for a main course yet still be light and fresh-tasting.

Cobb salad's classic vinaigrette dressing is both the tie that binds the dish together and its biggest problem. Unifying the disparate elements of this salad is a lot to ask of any dressing. This notion was confirmed when we tested a half dozen recipes and, in each case, the vinaigrette didn't pass its screen test. More often than not, the flavors were dull and muted, with the salad components either drowned in inch-deep puddles of liquid or sitting high and unhappily dry. We wanted a dressing that both stood up to and integrated cobb's multitude of flavors and textures and a method of applying it that would season every ingredient lightly yet thoroughly.

Most of the dressing recipes we consulted called for a quartet of flavorings—garlic, lemon juice, Worcestershire sauce, and mustard—in addition to the basic red wine vinegar, olive oil, salt, and pepper. In an attempt to streamline the formula, we systematically eliminated each of the first four items, but tasters protested. Each one contributed a necessary dimension to the dressing. In fact, we ended up adding a tiny amount of sugar to help soften the double punch of the two acids—lemon juice and vinegar—and to balance the piquancy of the savory ingredients.

The recipes disagreed, however, over the particulars of those four ingredients. Recipes called

for mustard in various forms, although dry was the most common choice. In side-by-side tastings of dry, spicy brown (like Gulden's), and Dijon mustards, we preferred the Dijon for its winey complexity. In addition, it is more of a staple ingredient in home kitchens than mustard powder.

Another common addition that we ultimately rejected was water, which made the dressing, well, watery. The third point of contention was oil. All of the recipes specified olive oil (we liked extra-virgin best), but a number of them cut it with plain vegetable oil. Rather like the water, the vegetable oil diluted the dressing's flavor, so we skipped it. The last big question was about blue cheese, which is a standard component of the salad. Some recipes included it in the dressing, others simply added it to the salad itself. Our tasters agreed that the cheese, when incorporated in the dressing, hogged the spotlight in what should be an ensemble performance.

For the greens, we tasted four common mild salad greens—iceberg, Boston, Bibb, and romaine lettuce—and voted unanimously in favor of the romaine for its combination of flavor and crunch. That hearty crunch provided a nice backdrop for the copious toppings, so we used it in greater proportion than the spicy greens. The tasting of spicy salad greens—chicory, curly endive, arugula, and watercress—was less cut-and-dry. Each had its supporters, but watercress won out because it is the traditional choice.

Cooking the chicken with a minimum of fuss was another concern. For sheer ease, broiling won out over grilling, sautéing, and braising.

We also made slight adjustments to several other ingredients. First, we switched from pale, tasteless supermarket beefsteak tomatoes to cherry tomatoes (the small, sweet, widely available grape tomatoes were our favorites), which taste better at any time but the few last weeks of summer when local tomatoes are in season. The bacon and chives, both classic cobb salad additions, remained untouched, but we doubled the quantity of another key ingredient, avocado, from one to two, because otherwise there wasn't enough to go around.

The typical blueprint for cobb salad is to lay

down a bed of lettuce, arrange the chicken, tomatoes, eggs, and avocado in rows on top, sprinkle the whole arrangement with crumbled bacon, blue cheese, and chives, and toss it together at the table. It was the last step that lost us, as the individual character of each element was compromised when they were flung about in the bowl into one indistinguishable tangle. We tried drizzling the dressing over the composed salad, but that method failed to season the separate elements evenly. Tasters encountered dry spots with no dressing right next to other spots drowning in puddles of the stuff. The best method by far was to dress each ingredient independently, before arranging it on the platter. To do this without dirtying every bowl in the kitchen, we used the same one over and over, dressing and plating each ingredient as we went. This guaranteed that each morsel of each ingredient would be correctly seasoned. By dint of their delicate structures, only the eggs and avocados were exempted from this routine. Instead, we drizzled a bit of dressing evenly over them.

Classic Cobb Salad

SERVES 6 TO 8 AS A MAIN DISH

You'll need a large platter or wide, shallow pasta bowl to accommodate this substantial salad. Avocado discolors quickly, so prepare it at the last possible minute, just before assembling the salad. Though watercress is traditional in cobb salad, feel free to substitute an equal amount of arugula, chicory, curly endive, or a mixture thereof. Use more blue cheese if your taste dictates.

VINAIGRETTE

- 1 teaspoon Dijon mustard
- 1 medium garlic clove, minced or pressed through a garlic press (about 1 teaspoon)
- 1/4 teaspoon sugar
- 1/2 teaspoon salt
- 1/8 teaspoon ground black pepper
- 1 teaspoon Worcestershire sauce
- 2 teaspoons juice from 1 lemon
- 2 tablespoons red wine vinegar
- 1/2 cup extra-virgin olive oil

SALAD

- 3 boneless, skinless chicken breast halves (about 6 ounces each), trimmed of excess fat Salt and ground black pepper
- 1 large head romaine lettuce, washed, dried, and torn into bite-size pieces (about 8 cups)
- 1 bunch watercress (about 4 ounces), washed, dried, and stemmed (about 4 cups)
- 1 pint cherry tomatoes, preferably grape tomatoes (about 10 ounces), each tomato halved
- 3 hard-boiled eggs (page 122), peeled and cut into 1/2-inch cubes
- 2 medium, ripe avocados, preferably Hass (about 8 ounces each), pitted and cut into 1/2-inch cubes (see the illustrations on pages 25–26)
- 8 slices bacon (about 8 ounces), cut crosswise into 1/4-inch pieces; fried in a medium skillet over medium heat until crisp, about 7 minutes; and drained on a paper towel–lined plate
- 2 ounces blue cheese, crumbled (about 1/2 cup)
- 3 tablespoons minced fresh chives

1. FOR THE VINAIGRETTE: Whisk all the ingredients together in a medium bowl until well combined (alternatively, shake vigorously in a tight-lidded jar); set aside. (The dressing may be refrigerated in an airtight container for 1 day; bring to room temperature and shake well before using.)

2. FOR THE SALAD: Meanwhile, season the chicken with salt and pepper. Adjust an oven rack to 6 inches from the broiler element; heat the broiler. Spray the broiler pan top with vegetable cooking spray; place the chicken breasts on top and broil until lightly browned, 4 to 8 minutes. Using tongs, flip the chicken over and continue to broil until the thickest part is no longer pink when cut into and registers about 160 degrees on an instant-read thermometer, 6 to 8 minutes. When cool enough to handle, cut the chicken into 1/2-inch cubes and set aside.

3. TO FINISH THE SALAD: Toss the romaine and watercress with 5 tablespoons of the vinaigrette in a large bowl until coated; arrange on a very large, flat serving platter. Place the chicken in the now-empty bowl, add 1/4 cup of the vinaigrette, and toss to coat; arrange in a row along one edge of

the greens. Place the tomatoes in the now-empty bowl, add 1 tablespoon of the vinaigrette, and toss gently to combine; arrange on the opposite edge of the greens. Arrange the reserved eggs and avocados in separate rows near the center of the greens and drizzle with the remaining vinaigrette. Sprinkle the bacon, cheese, and chives evenly over the salad and serve immediately.

SALADE NIÇOISE

ALONG THE FRENCH RIVIERA, SALADE niçoise, the famous composed salad from the city of Nice, is commonplace. Unfortunately for many Americans, the salade niçoise most of us encounter in this country is bland and lifeless—little more than a bed of lettuce on which lazily strewn piles of overcooked, underseasoned green beans and potatoes, off-ripe tomatoes, rubbery eggs, and soggy tuna drown in a sea of dull dressing.

The components of salade niçoise seldom vary from the aforementioned lettuce, beans, potatoes, eggs, tomatoes, and tuna. These are joined by slivered red onion and piquant Mediterranean garnishes—always olives and sometimes capers and anchovies—as well as the occasional sweet bell pepper, cucumber, and artichoke heart and

perhaps a few whole herb leaves. After trying a few salades niçoise in the test kitchen, we dismissed those platters crowded with an unwieldy collection of ingredients and focused on three basic elements that we considered key (beyond the quality of the produce itself): the dressing, the manner in which the salad components are dressed and assembled, and the tuna, which is what gives the dish its main-course status.

Clearly, the dressing plays a crucial role in flavoring the salad, so we investigated it thoroughly. The importance of extra-virgin olive oil cannot be overstated here, and the fruitier the better. Our tasters preferred the tang of lemon juice over vinegar as the acidic element in the dressing and shallots over garlic to add a mild bite. A little mustard was also welcome in the vinaigrette for the depth of flavor it contributed, and, as another flavor boost, we replaced the standard parsley with the flavorful trio of fresh thyme, basil, and oregano.

Just as important as the ingredients in the dressing, we learned, was how we applied the dressing to the salad. Though we were rooting for the simplest approach—pouring the dressing carefully over the ingredients after they had been placed on the platter—this method won no fans. Because this salad is not tossed, the dressing was never perfectly distributed, so some bites were seasoned while others were

---

INGREDIENTS: Tuna Packed in Olive Oil

Given our preference for tuna packed in olive oil for salade niçoise, we wondered if all brands are created equal. The six we found in grocery stores fell into three categories: light (made from bluefin, yellowfin, or skipjack tuna, or a mixture thereof), white (made from albacore tuna), and imported "white tuna" (made from bonito tuna).

Our panel of tasters did not care for light tuna. The representative brands, Cento Solid Pack Light Tuna and Pastene Fancy Light Tuna, were thought to have "potent" and "metallic" flavors with a "bitter finish," as well as "chewed" and "unpleasant" textures. Surprisingly, our albacore contender, Dave's Albacore Fillets, came in dead last. "It's like eating nothing" was the comment that summed up all others.

The three best-tasting tunas were made by Ortiz, a small Spanish company. Ortiz cans primarily northern bonito white tuna fished off the coast of Spain, a tuna not used by American packers.

Europeans consider this tuna to be of the highest quality because of its extremely white meat, tender texture, and full, clean flavor. The superior flavor is attributed to the migratory nature of the bonito tuna, a high-energy fish. High energy is equated with a high oil content, which in turn is equated with flavor—and lots of it. Although each of the three Ortiz tunas consists of the same ingredients—*bonito del norte,* olive oil, and salt—they have markedly different textures, and it was this characteristic that distinguished them and produced a winner.

THE BEST TUNA PACKED IN OLIVE OIL

ORTIZ BONITO DEL NORTE
The "flaky," "tender," and "pleasant" texture of this "intense and delicious" tuna was perfect for salade niçoise.

not. At this point, we took a cue from some classic French recipes in which each ingredient is dressed individually before being added to the platter. Dressing the components separately paid off, guaranteeing that every bite of each ingredient was fully and evenly seasoned. The downside of this method was the parade of bowls it occasioned—seven in all. After several experiments with the process, however, we decreased the number of bowls by three, and everyone here in the test kitchen agreed that they would happily wash four bowls to achieve such a harmonious salad.

Many authorities consider tuna a defining element of salade niçoise, so we tested several types. Tasters were enthusiastic about grilled fresh tuna, but not every cook would fire up the grill for this dish, so we did not pursue that option for our recipe. By way of canned tuna, we sampled it packed in olive oil (see Tuna Packed in Olive Oil on page 113), vegetable oil, and water. Without exception, tasters preferred the tuna packed in olive oil for its rich flavor and meaty, silky texture. We were surprised, though, that the second choice was tuna packed in water, which tasted clean and allowed the flavors of the dressing to come through loud and clear. Tuna packed in vegetable oil, with its faded, faintly rancid flavor, was nobody's favorite.

We tested various ratios of the salad components and found them to be a matter of taste, provided they were in relative balance and were plentiful enough to afford every diner with a generous taste of each. What mattered more was the precise nature of the ingredients. For instance, butterhead lettuces, such as Boston and Bibb, were more tender than romaine, red leaf, or green leaf. And Red Bliss potatoes had better integrity and texture when boiled than russets.

As we found in the end, this salad, when prepared with the right ingredients and some attention to detail, would give even a native of Nice a moment of pause.

Salade Niçoise

SERVES 4 TO 6 AS A MAIN DISH

Prepare all of the vegetables before you begin cooking the potatoes and this salad will come together very easily. The classic garnish of tiny, briny, piquant niçoise olives is a hallmark of salade niçoise. If they're not available, substitute another small, black, brined olive (do not use canned olives). Anchovies are another classic garnish, but they met with mixed reviews from our tasters, so they are optional. If you cannot find tuna packed in olive oil, substitute water-packed solid white tuna, not tuna packed in vegetable oil. (Among water-packed tunas, StarKist solid white took top honors in our tasting of 10 leading brands.) Compose the salad on your largest, widest, flattest serving platter. Do not blanket the bed of lettuce with the other ingredients; leave some space between the mounds of potatoes, tomatoes and onions, and beans so that leaves of lettuce peek through.

VINAIGRETTE
1/2	cup juice from 2 or 3 large lemons
3/4	cup extra-virgin olive oil
1	medium shallot, minced (about 3 tablespoons)
1	tablespoon minced fresh thyme leaves
2	tablespoons minced fresh basil leaves
2	teaspoons minced fresh oregano leaves
1	teaspoon Dijon mustard
	Salt and ground black pepper

SALAD
1 1/4	pounds red potatoes (about 10 small), each potato scrubbed and quartered
	Salt
2	tablespoons dry vermouth
	Ground black pepper
2	medium heads Boston or Bibb lettuce, leaves washed, dried, and torn into bite-size pieces (about 8 cups loosely packed)
2	(6-ounce) cans olive oil–packed tuna (or three 4-ounce cans), drained
3	small vine-ripened tomatoes (about 14 ounces), each cored and cut into eighths
1	small red onion, sliced very thin
8	ounces green beans, stem ends trimmed and each bean halved crosswise
4	hard-boiled eggs (page 122), peeled and quartered lengthwise

¼ cup niçoise olives
10–12 anchovy fillets (optional)
2 tablespoons capers, rinsed (optional)

1. FOR THE VINAIGRETTE: Whisk the lemon juice, oil, shallot, thyme, basil, oregano, and mustard together in a medium bowl; season with salt and pepper to taste and set aside.

2. FOR THE SALAD: Bring the potatoes and 4 quarts cold water to a boil in a large Dutch oven or stockpot over high heat. Add 1 tablespoon salt and cook until the potatoes are tender when poked with a paring knife, 5 to 8 minutes. With a slotted spoon, gently transfer the potatoes to a medium bowl (do not discard the cooking water). Toss the warm potatoes with the vermouth and salt and pepper to taste; let stand 1 minute. Toss in ¼ cup of the vinaigrette; set aside.

3. While the potatoes cook, toss the lettuce with ¼ cup of the vinaigrette in a large bowl until coated. Arrange a bed of lettuce on a very large, flat serving platter. Place the tuna in the now-empty bowl and break up with a fork. Add ½ cup of the vinaigrette and stir to combine; mound the tuna in the center of the lettuce. Toss the tomatoes, red onion, 3 tablespoons of the vinaigrette, and salt and pepper to taste in the now-empty bowl; arrange the tomato-onion mixture in a mound at the edge of the lettuce bed. Arrange the reserved potatoes in a separate mound at the edge of the lettuce bed.

4. Fill a large bowl with ice water. Return the water used to cook the potatoes to a boil; add 1 tablespoon salt and the green beans. Cook until tender but crisp, 3 to 5 minutes. Drain the beans, transfer to the ice water, and let stand until just cool, about 30 seconds; dry the beans well on a triple layer of paper towels. Toss the beans, 3 tablespoons of the vinaigrette, and salt and pepper to taste in the now-empty bowl; arrange in a separate mound at the edge of the lettuce bed.

5. Arrange the eggs, olives, and anchovies (if using) in separate mounds at the edge of the lettuce bed. Drizzle the eggs with the remaining 2 tablespoons vinaigrette, sprinkle the entire salad with the capers (if using), and serve immediately.

SESAME NOODLE SALAD WITH SHREDDED CHICKEN

GOOD SESAME NOODLE SALADS CAN BE addictive: They may appear as just a humble bowl of cold noodles, but don't be fooled—just one bite and you're hooked on these Chinese wheat noodles with shreds of tender chicken, all tossed with a fresh sesame sauce. Once you get the craving, good versions of the dish are hard to find. The cold noodles have a habit of turning gummy, the chicken often dries out, and the sauce is notorious for turning bland and pasty. We wanted a recipe that could not only quell a serious craving but do it in less time than it would take to grab a bus to Chinatown.

Though immediately drawn to the softer texture and milder flavor of fresh Chinese egg noodles, we conceded that dried spaghetti could serve as a second-string substitute. The trouble with both types of noodles, however, was that after being cooked and chilled, they gelled into a rubbery skein. After trying a number of ways to avoid this problem, we found it necessary to rinse the noodles under cold tap water directly after cooking. This not only cooled the hot noodles immediately but washed away much of their sticky starch. To further forestall any clumping, we tossed the rinsed noodles with a little toasted sesame oil; this kept them slack and separated for hours.

Boneless, skinless chicken breasts are quick to cook and easy to shred; the real question is how to cook them. Cooking the chicken under the broiler, our method of choice for Chicken Caesar Salad (page 110) and Classic Cobb Salad (page 112), worked perfectly here, too.

To be authentic, the sesame sauce should be made with an Asian sesame paste (not to be confused with Middle Eastern tahini), but most recipes substitute peanut butter because it's easier to find. Somewhat surprisingly, tasters preferred chunky peanut butter over smooth, describing its flavor as fresh and more peanutty. We had been making the sauce in a blender and realized that the chunky bits of peanuts were being freshly ground into the sauce, resulting in the cleaner, stronger flavor. We found the flavors of both fresh garlic and ginger necessary, along with soy sauce, rice vinegar, hot pepper sauce, and brown sugar. We then stumbled on the obvious way to keep the sauce from being too thick or pasty: Thin it with water.

Although the sauce was good, tasters still complained that there was not enough sesame flavor. We tried adding toasted sesame seeds. Blended into the sauce along with the peanut butter, the sesame seeds added the final kick of authentic sesame flavor we were all hankering for.

Sesame Noodle Salad with Shredded Chicken

SERVES 4 TO 6 AS A MAIN COURSE

In our experience, chicken takes longer to cook in a gas broiler than in an electric one, which is why the cooking times in the recipe range widely. Although our preference is for fresh Chinese egg noodles, we found that dried spaghetti works well, too. Because dried pasta swells so much more than fresh pasta during cooking, use 12 ounces of dried spaghetti, not 1 pound.

¼	cup sesame seeds
¼	cup chunky peanut butter
2	medium garlic cloves, minced or pressed through a garlic press (about 2 teaspoons)
1	tablespoon minced fresh ginger
5	tablespoons soy sauce
2	tablespoons rice vinegar
1	teaspoon hot pepper sauce
2	tablespoons lightly packed light brown sugar
	Hot water
1	tablespoon salt
1	pound fresh Chinese egg noodles or 12 ounces dried spaghetti
2	tablespoons toasted sesame oil
4	boneless, skinless chicken breast halves (1½ pounds), trimmed of excess fat
4	scallions, sliced thin on the diagonal
1	medium carrot, peeled and grated on the large holes of a box grater (about ⅔ cup)

1. Toast the sesame seeds in a medium skillet over medium heat, stirring frequently, until golden and fragrant, 7 to 10 minutes. Reserve 1 tablespoon sesame seeds in a small bowl. In a blender or food processor, puree the remaining 3 tablespoons sesame seeds, the peanut butter, garlic, ginger, soy sauce, vinegar, hot pepper sauce, and brown sugar until smooth, about 30 seconds. With the machine running, add hot water 1 tablespoon at a time until the sauce has the consistency of heavy cream, about 5 tablespoons; set the mixture aside (it can be left in the blender jar or food processor workbowl).

2. Bring 6 quarts water to a boil in a stockpot. Add the salt and noodles to the boiling water; boil the noodles until tender, about 4 minutes for fresh and 10 minutes for dried. Drain, then rinse under cold running water until cool to the touch; drain again. In a large bowl, toss the noodles with the sesame oil until evenly coated. Set aside.

3. Meanwhile, adjust an oven rack to 6 inches from the broiler element; heat the broiler. Spray the broiler pan top with vegetable cooking spray; place the chicken breasts on top and broil until lightly browned, 4 to 8 minutes. Using tongs, flip the chicken over and continue to broil until the thickest part is no longer pink when cut into and registers about 160 degrees on an instant-read thermometer, 6 to 8 minutes. Transfer to a cutting board and let rest 5 minutes. Using 2 forks, shred the chicken into bite-size pieces. Add the shredded chicken, scallions, carrot, and sauce to the prepared noodles; toss to combine. Divide among individual bowls, sprinkle each bowl with some of the reserved sesame seeds, and serve.

➤ VARIATION

Sesame Noodle Salad with Sweet Peppers and Cucumbers

Core, seed, and cut into ¼-inch slices 1 medium red bell pepper; peel, halve lengthwise, seed, and cut crosswise into ⅛-inch slices 1 medium cucumber. Follow the recipe for Sesame Noodle Salad with Shredded Chicken, omitting the chicken, adding the bell pepper and cucumber to the noodles along with the sauce, and sprinkling each bowl with a portion of 1 table-spoon chopped fresh cilantro leaves along with the sesame seeds.

THAI-STYLE BEEF SALAD

IN THAI CUISINE, SALADS ARE NORMALLY A mixture of crunchy raw vegetables with the simple addition of a single protein; they are quick to prepare and require little cooking. In addition, they are healthy to eat, as they contain little or no fat.

The most important part of a Thai salad is the dressing. This is where balance plays an important role. If any of the flavors is out of sync with the others, you end up with a dressing that is too sweet, too sour, or too salty.

Thai salads are normally dressed with nam pla, a fish-based sauce mixed with ginger, garlic, chiles, sugar, and lime juice. The question we faced when creating a new recipe was whether we could achieve a balanced and traditional-tasting dressing without using so many ingredients. This required some experimentation, but we believe we've succeeded.

Even before we began, we knew we had to base the dressing on fish sauce. A salty, briny liquid made from fermented fish, fish sauce is, culinarily, the Thai equivalent of Chinese soy sauce. Lime juice would provide the sour component, and we found that an equal amount of lime juice and fish sauce struck the right balance. We tried several sweeteners, including granulated sugar, honey, and brown sugar. The granulated sugar gave the dressing a slightly artificial flavor, and even small amounts of honey were too strong, tending to accent the dressing inappropriately with a floral tinge. Brown sugar, however, provided a subtle, pleasant sweetness, complementing the sour and the salty flavors. For spiciness, we considered chiles, but we found it hard to control the heat of the chiles from one salad to another. So we settled on a small amount of red pepper flakes. While this approach is not authentic, we nevertheless achieved a consistent heat level—and we saved ourselves some time.

With our dressing done, we moved on to the vegetables. Because the focus of the salad is seared beef, we wanted to find a balance of flavors and textures that complemented and contrasted with the beef. We looked for vegetables that would cut the richness of the beef, which we felt would benefit the salad. Cucumber was a good choice due to its crispness and mild flavor. Thinly sliced red onion also worked well, adding pungency and crunch. Bibb lettuce lightened the salad. It wouldn't be a Thai salad without a hefty amount of fresh herbs; this job was filled by a duo of cilantro and mint, both of which added a bright, clean flavor. Topped with a sprinkling of chopped peanuts, our Thai-style salad was now complete.

Thai-Style Beef Salad

SERVES 4 AS A MAIN DISH

See the illustrations on page 91 for information about seeding and slicing the cucumber. If you prefer, omit the oil and grill the steak.

1	tablespoon vegetable oil
1¼	pounds flank steak, trimmed of excess fat and patted dry with paper towels
	Salt and ground black pepper
¼	cup fish sauce
¼	cup juice from 2 limes
4	teaspoons brown sugar
¼	teaspoon red pepper flakes
½	medium cucumber, peeled, seeded, and sliced thin
½	small red onion, sliced thin
1	tablespoon packed torn fresh cilantro leaves
1	tablespoon packed torn fresh mint leaves
1	head Bibb or Boston lettuce, leaves washed, dried, and torn into pieces (4 cups lightly packed)
½	cup unsalted dry-roasted peanuts, chopped coarse

1. Heat the oil in a heavy-bottomed 12-inch skillet over medium-high heat until it begins to smoke. Season the steak liberally with salt and pepper, lay it in the pan, and sauté, not moving it until it is well browned, 4 to 5 minutes. Turn the steak over with tongs and reduce the heat to medium.

Continue to cook until the steak is browned on the second side, about 5 minutes. Transfer the steak to a plate and let rest for 10 minutes.

2. Whisk the fish sauce, lime juice, brown sugar, and red pepper flakes together in a medium bowl until the sugar is dissolved. Remove half of the dressing from the bowl and set it aside in a large bowl. Cut the steak across the grain on the diagonal into ⅛-inch-thick slices. Halve the longer slices into roughly 3-inch lengths. Add the steak to the smaller bowl with the dressing, toss to coat, and let marinate for 5 minutes.

3. Remove the steak from the dressing and discard the marinade. Toss the steak, cucumber, onion, cilantro, and mint with the reserved dressing in the larger bowl. Arrange the Bibb lettuce on a large serving platter or individual plates. Spoon the steak and vegetables over the lettuce. Drizzle the salad with any dressing left in the bowl and sprinkle it with the peanuts. Serve immediately.

TUNA SALAD

GRADE-SCHOOL LUNCHES, HOSPITAL CAFETERIAS, and second-rate delis have given tuna salad a bad name with mixtures that are typically mushy, watery, and bland. But these poor examples should not cause cooks to lose hope for this old standard. We recently tackled tuna salad in the test kitchen and came up with three simple preparation and flavoring tricks that guarantee a tuna salad that is evenly moist, tender, flaky, and well seasoned every time.

A first-rate tuna salad begins with the best canned tuna. All tasters favored solid white tuna over chunk light for its meaty texture and delicate flavor. Among the five brands we tried, StarKist reigned supreme, so we made it the basis of all our subsequent testing.

In a dish as simple as tuna salad, the finer points of preparation make a real difference. For instance, most cooks simply squeeze out a bit of the packing water by pressing the detached can lid down lightly on the fish. Tasters consistently deemed all of the salads made with tuna prepared in this manner as "soggy" and "watery." Taking the minor

extra step of draining the tuna thoroughly in a colander before mixing it with other ingredients gave the salads a toothsome, less watery texture.

Breaking the tuna apart with a fork was another standard procedure we dumped. In salads

INGREDIENTS:
Canned Tuna in Water

We selected the 10 best-selling chunk light and solid white tunas packed in water and assembled 25 tasters in the test kitchen. We drained each can of tuna and lightly blended it with mayonnaise but added no seasonings.

In most of our blind taste tests, taste has predictably reigned. But when it came to canned tuna, texture set the pace. Most canned tunas are bland—that's why tuna salad is so heavily seasoned.

Chunk light was the least expensive of the two varieties in our tasting, costing about 41 cents a can less than solid white. This may explain why it is also the top-selling type of canned tuna. Certainly, our tasting results do not explain it, since tasters found only one of the five chunk light samples (Geisha) acceptable. In general, chunk light tuna is made of skipjack or yellowfin tuna or both; skipjack contributes a stronger flavor than yellowfin. Each can contains several small pieces of tuna as well as some flakes.

While our tasters were not wild about the more pronounced flavor of chunk light (which often included an aftertaste of tin), what really upset the balance between the white and light tunas was texture. White tuna you could eat, even pierce, with a fork; the light version was more appropriately scooped with a spoon. When blended with mayonnaise, the small flakes of chunk light tuna quickly broke down even further, taking on a texture that reminded many tasters of cat food. Tasters not only disliked this lack of chew but found that the small shreds of fish held moisture too well, which created a sopping, mushy consistency.

Solid white, on the other hand, consists of one large piece of loin meat from albacore tuna. Though known as "white" tuna, albacore can vary from nearly white to light pink or even beige. Solid white was the tuna of choice among tasters for its mild flavor, milky white appearance, and chunky texture. StarKist took top honors, followed by 3 Diamonds, Chicken of the Sea, Bumble Bee, and Geisha.

THE BEST CANNED TUNA

StarKist Solid White Tuna in Water beat out other brands for "most balanced flavor" and "true tuna taste."

made with tuna prepared this way, we'd invariably bite into a large, dry, unseasoned chunk that the fork had missed. With the tuna in the colander, we decided to break down the larger chunks with our fingers until the whole amount was fine and even in texture. This gave the finished salad a smooth, even, flaky texture that all of our tasters appreciated.

Seasoning was the last consideration we addressed. All too often, tuna salad tastes dull and lifeless because of careless seasoning or, even worse, no seasoning at all. Salt and pepper were critical to making the most of tuna's delicate flavor. An acidic seasoning, such as lemon or lime juice or vinegar, was equally important, adding some much-needed brightness to the flavor. We also found that the order in which we mixed the ingredients made a difference. We first tried mixing the basic seasoning and garnishes with the tuna alone before adding the mayonnaise. Next we tried adding the seasonings, garnishes, and mayonnaise all at once. Our tasters agreed that preseasoning the tuna resulted in a more deeply flavored, lively tuna salad.

After settling on these three basic techniques, we were unanimous in finding mayonnaise to be the binder of choice and found other salad ingredients to be largely a matter of taste. We nonetheless agreed that trace amounts of garlic and mustard added dimension to the overall flavor and that a modest amount of minced pickle provided a touch of piquancy, not to mention a link to tradition. In fact, tuna takes well to a wide range of flavorings; see some of our variations for inspiration.

Classic Tuna Salad

MAKES ABOUT 2 CUPS,
ENOUGH FOR 4 SANDWICHES

See page 118 for information on brands of tuna packed in water and the one we recommend.

2	(6-ounce) cans solid white tuna in water
2	tablespoons juice from 1 lemon
1/2	teaspoon salt
1/4	teaspoon ground black pepper
1	small celery rib, minced (about 1/4 cup)
2	tablespoons minced red onion
2	tablespoons minced dill or sweet pickles
1/2	small garlic clove, minced or pressed through a garlic press (about 1/8 teaspoon)
2	tablespoons minced fresh parsley leaves
1/2	cup mayonnaise
1/4	teaspoon Dijon mustard

Drain the tuna in a colander and shred with your fingers until no clumps remain and the texture is fine and even. Transfer the tuna to a medium bowl and mix in the lemon juice, salt, pepper, celery, onion, pickles, garlic, and parsley until evenly blended. Fold in the mayonnaise and mustard until the tuna is evenly moistened. (The salad can be covered and refrigerated for up to 3 days.)

➤ VARIATIONS

Tuna Salad with Balsamic Vinegar and Grapes

Follow the recipe for Classic Tuna Salad, omitting the lemon juice, pickles, garlic, and parsley and adding 2 tablespoons balsamic vinegar, 6 ounces seedless red grapes, halved (about 1 cup), 1/4 cup lightly toasted slivered almonds, and 2 teaspoons minced fresh thyme leaves to the tuna along with the salt and pepper.

Curried Tuna Salad with Apples and Currants

Follow the recipe for Classic Tuna Salad, omitting the pickles, garlic, and parsley and adding 1 medium, firm, juicy apple, cut into 1/4-inch dice (about 1 cup), 1/4 cup currants, and 2 tablespoons minced fresh basil leaves to the tuna along with the lemon juice, salt, and pepper; mix 1 tablespoon curry powder into the mayonnaise before folding it into the tuna.

CHICKEN SALAD

CLASSIC CHICKEN SALAD CONSISTS OF tender breast meat, pulled apart by hand rather than cubed with a knife and bound loosely with mayonnaise. There's a little celery for texture, some parsley or tarragon for flavor, and a squeeze of lemon juice for freshness. We often make this salad from leftover roast or poached chicken, and we put it together intuitively, by taste and sight.

So what didn't we know about chicken salad? After a little thought, we had only one question. When making the classic version from scratch, and not from leftover meat, how should we cook the chicken?

Although there were many choices, they basically fell into two camps, wet cooking and dry cooking. The wet cooking methods included poaching, steaming, roasting in foil, and, in a method new to us, dropping the chicken into simmering aromatic water and then removing it from the heat and letting it cool to room temperature. Unfortunately, chicken cooked by each of these methods had a bland, unmistakably boiled flavor. Chicken cooked in the microwave also had that wet-cooked taste.

As for the dry-cooking methods, broiled was good, but for this salad, where we wanted the chicken to take center stage, roast chicken won hands down. Even after the skin and bones were removed, the meat tasted roasted, and the resulting chicken salad was superb.

Classic Creamy Chicken Salad

SERVES 6 AS A MAIN COURSE

The chicken can be prepared ahead. Once the chicken breasts have cooled to room temperature, remove and discard the skin. At this point, you may wrap the breasts in plastic and refrigerate them for up to 2 days.

In addition to the parsley leaves, you can flavor the salad with 2 tablespoons of minced fresh tarragon or basil leaves. You may use leftover meat from a roast chicken if desired. Serve the salad in rolls as sandwiches or over greens for a light main course.

CHICKEN

2   large whole, bone-in, skin-on chicken breasts (at least 1½ pounds each)
1   tablespoon vegetable oil
    Salt

SALAD

2   medium celery ribs, cut into small dice
2   medium scallions, white and green parts, minced
¾   cup mayonnaise
2   tablespoons juice from 1 lemon
2   tablespoons minced fresh parsley leaves
    Salt and ground black pepper

1. FOR THE CHICKEN: Adjust an oven rack to the middle position and heat the oven to 400 degrees. Set the breasts on a small, foil-lined rimmed baking sheet. Brush with the oil and sprinkle generously with salt to taste. Roast until a meat thermometer inserted into the thickest part of the breast registers 160 degrees, 35 to 40 minutes. Cool to room temperature. Remove the skin and bones and discard; shred the meat according to the illustrations below. Set aside.

SHREDDING CHICKEN BREASTS

1. Slice along the center bone to separate the two pieces of breast meat. Insert your fingers into the cut made by the knife and gently pry the breast meat off the bone in two pieces.

2. Cut each breast piece into thirds.

3. Use your hands to pull apart each breast piece and shred it into small chunks.

2. FOR THE SALAD: Mix the reserved shredded chicken and all the salad ingredients together in a large bowl, including salt and pepper to taste. Serve. (The salad can be refrigerated in an airtight container for up to 1 day.)

➤ VARIATIONS

Waldorf Chicken Salad

Follow the recipe for Classic Creamy Chicken Salad, adding 1 large crisp apple, cored and cut into medium dice, and 6 tablespoons chopped toasted walnuts.

Curried Chicken Salad with Raisins and Honey

Follow the recipe for Classic Creamy Chicken Salad, adding 6 tablespoons golden raisins, 2 teaspoons curry powder, and 1 tablespoon honey. Replace the parsley with an equal amount of cilantro.

EGG SALAD

EGG SALAD IS ONE OF THOSE SIMPLE, spur-of-the-moment comfort foods that should be easy to make. Yet sometimes it turns out pasty, the overall flavor can be drab, the mayonnaise excessive, or the onions too biting. The hardest part, though, is cooking the eggs properly.

We have always considered hard-boiling an egg to be a crapshoot. There's no way to watch the proteins cook under the brittle shell of an uncracked egg, and you certainly can't poke it with an instant-read thermometer, as you would with so many other foods. Often the eggs are overcooked, with rubbery whites and chalky yolks. Of course, undercooked eggs without fully set yolks are even more problematic, especially when you're trying to make egg salad.

There are two general methods for boiling eggs—starting them in cold water and bringing them to a simmer, and lowering them into already simmering water. The first method is not terribly precise. When do you start the clock—when the eggs go into the water, when the water starts to boil? Also, what temperature is right for

simmering? Everyone knows what boiling water looks like (and the temperature is always 212 degrees at sea level), but simmering water can be 180, 190, or even 200 degrees. We never developed a reliable timing mechanism with this technique.

Lowering eggs into simmering water is not easy either, because the eggs are likely to crack. Some sources suggest poking a thumbtack through the large end of the egg where the air hole typically sits, but we had inconsistent results with this "trick." Again, the issue of defining "simmering water" proved problematic.

Not satisfied with either method, we tried a third method—starting the eggs in cold water, bringing the water to a boil, and then turning off the heat. The pan is covered and the eggs are set aside to cook by residual heat for 10 minutes. There's no need to define "simmer" with this method. As long as you can recognize when water is at a boil and can time 10 minutes, you are guaranteed hard-boiled eggs with bright, creamy yolks and tender whites.

With our eggs perfectly boiled, it was time to make salad. We quickly found that both a fork and a pastry blender mashed the eggs so much that, when blended with mayonnaise, they became unpleasantly pasty. In addition to being reminiscent of baby food, this egg salad was quick to ooze out from between the slices of bread in a sandwich. After experimenting with various options, we found that eggs diced into small cubes (just under ½ inch) gave the salad the full mouthfeel we had been seeking and also held up well in a sandwich.

Although most egg salad recipes call for binding the eggs with mayonnaise, we found recipes that called for combining the mayonnaise with cream cheese, yogurt, light cream, cottage cheese, sour cream, or even buttermilk. Thankfully, we liked plain mayonnaise the best. Some lemon brightened things up, while a bit of mustard added depth. We preferred the sweetness of red onion for the classic recipe but also liked scallions and shallots for some of the variations. Yellow onion was simply too harsh. Minced celery and parsley added an element of freshness, and we finally had an egg salad that was truly a source of comfort rather than disappointment.

Foolproof Hard-Boiled Eggs

MAKES 6

You can double or triple this recipe as long as you use a pot large enough to hold the eggs in a single layer, covered by 1 inch of water.

6   large eggs

1. Place the eggs in a medium saucepan, cover with 1 inch water, and bring to a boil over high heat. Remove the pan from the heat, cover, and let sit for 10 minutes. Meanwhile, fill a medium bowl with 1 quart water and 1 tray ice cubes (or the equivalent).

2. Transfer the eggs to the ice-water bath with a slotted spoon and let sit 5 minutes. Tap each egg all over against the counter surface to crack the shell, then roll it gently back and forth a few times. Begin peeling from the air-pocket (wider) end. The shell should come off in spiral strips attached to the thin membrane.

Classic Egg Salad

MAKES ABOUT 2¹/₂ CUPS,
ENOUGH FOR 4 SANDWICHES

The egg salad can be refrigerated in an airtight container for up to 1 day.

6   hard-boiled eggs, peeled and diced
¹/₄ cup mayonnaise
2   tablespoons minced red onion
1   tablespoon minced fresh parsley leaves
¹/₂ medium celery rib, chopped fine
2   teaspoons Dijon mustard
2   teaspoons juice from 1 lemon
¹/₄ teaspoon salt
     Ground black pepper

Mix all of the ingredients together in a medium bowl, including pepper to taste. Serve.

➤ VARIATIONS

Egg Salad with Radishes, Scallions, and Dill
Follow the recipe for Classic Egg Salad, substituting 1 tablespoon minced fresh dill for the parsley and 1 medium scallion, sliced thin, for the red onion, and adding 3 medium radishes, minced.

Curried Egg Salad
Follow the recipe for Classic Egg Salad, substituting 1 tablespoon minced fresh cilantro for the parsley and adding 1½ teaspoons curry powder. Omit the salt.

Creamy Egg Salad with Capers and Anchovy
Follow the recipe for Classic Egg Salad, adding 1 small garlic clove, minced, 2 tablespoons chopped rinsed capers, and 1 anchovy fillet, minced. Omit the salt.

Creamy Egg Salad with Bacon, Shallots, and Watercress
In medium skillet over medium heat, fry 4 slices bacon (about 4 ounces), cut into ¼-inch pieces, until browned and crisp, about 5 minutes. Transfer the bacon with a slotted spoon to a plate lined with paper towels; pour off all but 1 tablespoon of the fat from the pan. Add 2 large shallots, chopped medium, and sauté until softened and browned, about 5 minutes. Follow the recipe for Classic Egg Salad, omitting the celery and salt, substituting the sautéed shallots for the red onion, and adding the bacon and ¼ cup watercress leaves, chopped coarse.

PEELING HARD-BOILED EGGS

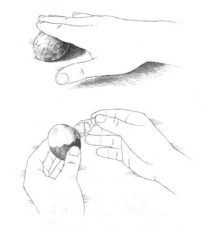

1. Tap the egg against the counter surface, then roll it gently back and forth a few times on the counter to crack the shell all over.
2. Begin peeling from the air pocket (the wider end) of the egg. The shell should come off in spiral strips attached to a thin membrane.

4
VEGETABLES

THIS CHAPTER CONSISTS OF OUR FAVORITE vegetable recipes—the ones we make over and over again in our own home kitchens. There are plenty of "newer" recipes, like grilled corn, as well as plenty of old favorites, such as mashed potatoes and Southern-style greens. We've also breathed life into several popular dishes that have fallen on hard times due to the widespread use of canned convenience products. For instance, our green bean casserole (made with fresh, not frozen, beans and a home-made sauce rather than one from a can) is a revela-tion. When made right, this dish is truly worthy of a holiday table. And, we revamped the 1950s army green stuffed bell pepper—into a bright, beautiful dish good enough to serve to company.

A number of cooking techniques are used in this chapter. Here is an explanation of each method.

BOILING means cooking in an abundant amount of boiling water, at least enough to cover the vegetables by several inches. When referring to vegetables, the term "blanching" (which means cooking in boiling water until partially but not fully done) is often used. If the water is salted during boiling or blanching, the vegetables will be nicely seasoned. Blanched vegetables are often sautéed to finish the cooking process; this is also when more seasoning can be added. Avoid boiling porous vegetables such as cauliflower and broc-coli, which can become waterlogged and mushy when boiled.

STEAMING means cooking in a collapsible basket set over boiling water in a covered con-tainer. With steaming, there is no possibility of seasoning vegetables with salt as they cook. Also, since the vegetables are suspended above water as they steam, they absorb less liquid than they would if boiled.

BRAISING refers to cooking in a covered pan with a small amount of liquid. Often a braise starts with sautéing the vegetables in some fat before adding the liquid. Steam from this liquid cooks the vegetables through and eventually becomes a sauce that seasons the vegetables.

DEEP-FRYING We limit our deep-frying to potatoes for French fries. We use a Dutch oven filled with a fair amount of oil (enough to sub-merge the potatoes). The goal here is to promote the development of an especially crisp exterior.

GRILLING The intense heat of the grill caramelizes the exterior of vegetables and concen-trates their flavors by driving off water. Vegetables should be brushed lightly with oil before grilling, and the grill surface should be scraped meticu-lously clean to prevent delicate vegetables from picking up off flavors. Vegetables should be grilled over a medium-hot fire—you should be able to hold your hand five inches above the cooking sur-face for four seconds.

BROILING is similar to grilling. The intense heat of the broiler browns the exterior of veg-etables and causes water to be expelled and evapo-rated. Vegetables should be lightly oiled, then placed in a single layer on a rimmed baking sheet for broiling.

SAUTÉEING AND STIR-FRYING Most vegetables can be cooked in a hot pan with a little oil or butter. Sautéeing generally occurs over a moderate temperature using a regular or nonstick skillet with either butter or oil; stir-frying relies on oil (not butter) and uses very high temperatures.

One cooking method that can be applied to vegetables that we did not include in this chapter (with the exception of Faster Baked Potatoes on page 182) is microwaving. We can appreciate the value of convenience, but microwaves vary from model to model. One microwave's "medium-high" might be another microwave's "high." Although we found some success cooking small amounts of vegetables in the microwave, we ran into complications when increasing the quanti-ties of vegetables to fit the yields in this chapter (about 4 to 6 servings). In our opinion, there is nothing convenient about cooking vegetables in the microwave only to have them dry out or cook unevenly.

ARTICHOKES

ARTICHOKES ARE COMMONLY MARKETED IN three sizes: small (2 to 4 ounces each), medium (8 to 10 ounces each), and large (12 ounces or more each). Surprisingly, different-size artichokes simultaneously bud on the same plant; the artichokes that grow on the plant's center stalk are the largest, and those that grow at the juncture between the plant's leaves and the stem are the smallest. After preparing, cooking, and eating all three sizes, we found that we preferred the small and medium artichokes to the large, which can be tough and fibrous.

When selecting fresh artichokes at the market, follow these rules of thumb. The artichokes should be tight and compact, like a flower blossom (which they are), and unblemished bright green, and they should "squeak" when you rub the leaves together—evidence that the artichoke still retains much of its moisture. If you tug at a leaf, it should cleanly snap off. If it bends, it's old. Also be on the watch for leaves that look dried out and feathery about the edges—a sure sign of an over-the-hill artichoke.

There are two basic approaches to artichokes: leave them whole (with minimal trimming before cooking) and let your dinner guests eat them leaf-by-leaf at the table, or trim them to the heart before cooking (removing all inedible portions) and let your guests reap the benefit of your labor. Medium artichokes can be left whole or trimmed to the heart. Because of their size, small artichokes are best trimmed to the heart.

Whether you are working with small or medium artichokes, leaving them whole or trimming them to the heart, artichokes will turn brown almost as soon as they are cut. It is crucial to submerge them in acidulated water, which neutralizes the enzymes responsible for oxidation. We tried a variety of acids to prevent oxidation, including white wine vinegar, cider vinegar, and lemon juice, and were most pleased with lemon juice because of its bright yet neutral flavor. Simply add the juice of a lemon per quart of water. Once cleaned, drop the artichokes into the bowl of acidulated water.

Medium artichokes are our favorite for serving whole because they are easy to prepare and each artichoke conveniently serves one person.

After experimenting with a variety of methods for cooking whole artichokes, including boiling, steaming, and microwaving, we concluded that steaming is the best choice. Steamed artichokes had the deepest, most pronounced flavor. We discovered that artichokes steam nicely when set on top of thick-sliced onion rings (see the illustration on page 126), which protects them from becoming waterlogged. If you do not have onions on hand, a steaming rack also works. After steaming, allow the artichokes to cool down for at least 15 minutes before serving. It is easy to burn your fingers on them as the dense artichokes retain a lot of heat. Steamed artichokes can also be chilled and eaten cool if you prefer.

In the test kitchen, we find that small artichokes are best roasted, in part because there's no choke to remove. Roasting concentrates the

INGREDIENTS:
What's Edible and What's Not

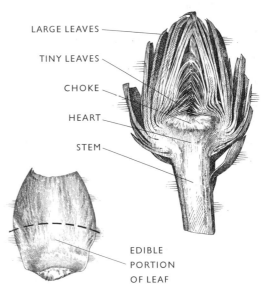

Much of an artichoke is inedible. The entire exterior (including several layers of leaves) as well as the fuzzy choke and tiny inner leaves in the center cannot be eaten. Only the heart and the bottom portions of the inner leaves become meaty and tender when cooked. The cooked heart can be eaten with a knife and fork. The edible portion at the bottom of the leaves is best scraped off with your teeth.

delicate artichoke flavor and lightly crisps the exterior. This cooking method also intensifies the nuttiness of artichokes. The inedible outer portions must be trimmed, but otherwise small artichokes can be roasted as is. To promote browning (and prevent the edges from burning), we found it best to coat the trimmed baby artichokes with olive oil. A 400-degree oven promotes maximum browning but does not run the risk of charring the artichokes, which can happen at higher temperatures.

Steamed Artichokes
SERVES 4

Artichokes steam nicely when set on top of thickly sliced onion rings, which keep the artichokes from becoming waterlogged. If you don't have onions on hand, a steaming rack works as well.

I	lemon, cut in half
4	medium artichokes (8 to 10 ounces each)
2	medium onions

1. Squeeze the lemon juice into a large bowl filled with cold water. Drop the spent lemon halves into the water.

2. Prepare the artichokes according to illustrations 1 through 3 below. Drop the trimmed artichokes into the acidulated water. Cut two 1½-inch-thick slices from the middle of each onion; using your fingers, pop out the outer three or four rings from the rest of each slice. Space the onion rings evenly across the bottom of a large pot or Dutch oven and set one trimmed artichoke on top of each ring (see illustration 4 below).

3. Fill a large pot with water to ½ inch below the top of the onion rings. Bring the water to a boil over medium-high heat. Cover and cook until the outer leaves release easily when pulled, about 30 minutes. Check the pot periodically to make sure the water has not boiled away.

4. With tongs, carefully remove the artichokes from the pot and cool for at least 15 minutes before serving. Steamed artichokes can also be chilled and eaten cool. Serve with one of the following vinaigrettes.

Mustard-Tarragon Vinaigrette
MAKES ABOUT ½ CUP

Although the vinaigrettes can be made ahead, the herbs should be added just before serving to preserve their fresh flavor.

PREPARING ARTICHOKES FOR STEAMING
Medium artichokes (each weighing 8 to 10 ounces) are the best choice for steaming.

1. Removing the pin-sharp thorns from the tips of the leaves makes for easier handling and a more attractive presentation. Grasp the artichoke by the stem and hold it horizontal to the work surface. Use kitchen shears to trim the tips off the leaves row by row, skipping the top two rows.

2. Rest the artichoke on a cutting board. Holding the stem in one hand, cut off the top quarter (the top two rows) of the artichoke with a sharp chef's knife.

3. With the sharp thorns and leaf tips removed, the stem can now be cut flush with the base of the bulb. Drop the trimmed artichoke into a bowl of acidulated water.

4. Set one trimmed artichoke on each thick onion ring.

EQUIPMENT: Chef's Knives

A good chef's knife is probably the most useful tool any cook owns. Besides chopping vegetables, it can be used for myriad tasks, including cutting up poultry, mincing herbs, and slicing fruit. So what separates a good knife from an inferior one? To understand the answer to this question, it helps to know something about how knives are constructed.

The first pieces of cutlery were made about 4,000 years ago with the discovery that iron ore could be melted and shaped into tools. The creation of steel, which is 80 percent iron and 20 percent other elements, led to the development of carbon steel knives—the standard for 3,000 years. Although this kind of steel takes and holds an edge easily, it also stains and rusts. Something as simple as cutting an acidic tomato or living in the salt air of the seacoast can corrode carbon steel.

Today, new alloys have given cooks better options. Stainless steel, made with at least 4 percent chromium and/or nickel, will never rust. Used for many cheap knives, stainless steel is also very difficult to sharpen. The compromise between durable but dull stainless steel and sharp but corrodible carbon steel is a material called high-carbon stainless steel. Used by most knife manufacturers, this blend combines durability and sharpness.

Until recently, all knives were hot drop forged—that is, the steel was heated to 2,000 degrees, dropped into a mold, given four or five shots with a hammer, and then tempered (cooled and heated several times to build strength). This process is labor-intensive (many steps must be done by hand), which explains why many chef's knives cost almost $100.

A second manufacturing process feeds longs sheets of steel through a press that punches out knife after knife, much like a cookie cutter slicing through dough. Called stamped blades, these knives require some hand finishing but are much cheaper to produce because a machine does most of the work.

While experts have long argued that forged knives are better than stamped ones, our testing did not fully support this position. We liked some forged knives and did not like others. Likewise, we liked some stamped knives and did not like others. The weight and shape of the handle (it must be comfortable to hold and substantial but not too heavy), the ability of the blade to take an edge, and the shape of the blade (we like a slightly curved blade, which is better suited to the rocking motion often used to mince herbs or garlic than a straight blade) are all key factors in choosing a knife.

When shopping, pick up the knife and see how it feels in your hand. Is it easy to grip? Does the weight seem properly distributed between the handle and blade? In our testing, we liked knives made by Henckels and Wüsthof. An inexpensive knife by Forschner, with a stamped blade, also scored well.

Buying a good knife is only half the challenge. You must keep the edge sharp. To that end, we recommend buying an electric knife sharpener. Steels are best for modest corrections, but all knives will require more substantial sharpening at least several times a year, if not more often if you cook a lot. Stones are difficult to use because they require that you maintain a perfect 20-degree angle between the stone and blade. An electric knife sharpener (we like models made by Chef's Choice) takes the guesswork out of sharpening and allows you to keep edges sharp and effective.

THE BEST CHEF'S KNIVES

The Henckels Four Star (right) and Wüsthof-Trident Grand Prix (center) are top choices, but expect to spend about $80 for one of these knives. The Forschner (Victorinox) Fibrox (left) is lighter but still solid and costs just $30.

6   tablespoons extra-virgin olive oil
I   tablespoon red wine vinegar
I   tablespoon Dijon mustard
I   tablespoon minced fresh tarragon leaves
I   medium garlic clove, minced or pressed
    through a garlic press
    Salt and ground black pepper

Whisk all of the ingredients, including salt and pepper to taste, together in a medium bowl until thoroughly blended. Serve with steamed artichokes.

Lemon-Mint Vinaigrette

MAKES ABOUT 1/2 CUP

Basil can be substituted for the mint.

6   tablespoons extra-virgin olive oil
I   teaspoon grated zest and 2 tablespoons juice
    from I lemon
I   tablespoon minced fresh mint leaves
I   medium shallot, minced
1/2 teaspoon honey
    Salt and ground black pepper

Whisk all of the ingredients, including salt and pepper to taste, together in a medium bowl until thoroughly blended. Serve with steamed artichokes.

Roasted Baby Artichokes

SERVES 4

Plan on roughly 4 small (or baby) artichokes per serving.

I   lemon, cut in half
16 small artichokes (2 to 4 ounces each)
2   tablespoons extra-virgin olive oil
    Salt and ground black pepper

1. Adjust the oven racks to the upper-middle and lower-middle positions and heat the oven to 400 degrees.

2. Squeeze the lemon juice into a large bowl filled with cold water. Drop the spent lemon halves into the water.

3. Cut off the top quarter of each artichoke and snap off the fibrous outer leaves until you reach the inner leaves (see illustration 1 on page 129). With a paring knife, trim the dark green exterior from the base of the artichoke as well as the exterior of the stem. Trim a thin slice from the end of the stem, then cut the artichoke in half, slicing from tip to stem (see illustration 2 on page 129). Drop the trimmed artichoke into the bowl of acidulated water until ready to cook.

4. Drain the artichokes and toss them in a large bowl with the olive oil. Place the oiled artichokes cut-side down on 2 rimmed baking sheets. Season the artichokes lightly with salt and pepper to taste. Roast for 15 minutes. Using tongs, turn the artichokes. Reverse the position of the baking sheets, from top to bottom and front to back. Roast until the artichokes can be pierced easily with a skewer, about 10 minutes longer. Season with additional salt and pepper to taste, if desired, and serve.

> VARIATION

Roasted Baby Artichokes with Roasted Garlic Aïoli

Aïoli is France's renowned garlicky mayonnaise.

I   lemon, cut in half
16 small artichokes (2 to 4 ounces each)
I   head garlic, cloves separated, skins left on
I   cup extra-virgin olive oil
    Salt and ground black pepper
1/2 teaspoon dry mustard
    Pinch cayenne pepper
I   large egg yolk

1. Adjust the oven racks to the upper-middle and lower-middle positions and heat the oven to 400 degrees.

2. Reserve 1½ teaspoons juice from the lemon and set aside for the aïoli. Squeeze the rest of the lemon juice into a large bowl filled with cold water. Drop the spent lemon halves into the water.

3. Cut off the top quarter and snap off the fibrous outer leaves of each artichoke until you reach the inner leaves (see illustration 1 on page 129). With a paring knife, trim the dark green exterior from the base of the artichoke as well as the exterior of the stem. Trim a thin slice from the end of the stem, then cut the artichoke in half, slicing from tip to

stem (see illustration 2 below). Drop the trimmed artichoke into the bowl of acidulated water until ready to cook.

4. Drizzle the garlic cloves with 1 tablespoon of the oil and wrap the oiled cloves in aluminum foil. Drain the artichokes and toss them in a large bowl with 3 tablespoons of the oil; toss to coat. Place the foil-wrapped garlic and the oiled artichokes cut-side down on 2 rimmed baking sheets. Season the artichokes lightly with salt and pepper to taste. Roast for 15 minutes. Using tongs, turn the artichokes. Reverse the position of the baking sheets, from top to bottom and front to back. Roast until the artichokes can be pierced easily with a skewer and the garlic cloves are soft, about 10 minutes longer.

5. When the garlic is cool enough to handle, squeeze the cloves from the skins into a small non-reactive bowl and press or mince the cloves finely. Add the dry mustard, cayenne, egg yolk, and lemon juice and whisk together thoroughly. Add the remaining ¾ cup oil in a thin, steady stream while whisking constantly until a thick emulsion forms. Season with salt and pepper to taste and serve with the roasted artichokes.

PREPARING ARTICHOKES FOR ROASTING

Small artichokes (each weighing 2 to 4 ounces) are the best choice for roasting.

1. After cutting off the top quarter of the artichoke, snap off the fibrous outer leaves until you reach the yellow leaves.

2. With a paring knife, trim the dark green exterior from the base of the artichoke as well as the exterior of the stem. Trim a thin slice from the end of the stem and cut the artichoke in half, slicing from tip to stem. Drop the trimmed artichoke into a bowl of acidulated water.

ASPARAGUS

ASPARAGUS PRESENTS ONE MAIN PREPARATION issue—should the spears be peeled, or is it better to discard the tough, fibrous ends entirely? In our tests, we found that peeled asparagus have a silkier texture, but we preferred the contrast between the crisp peel and tender inner flesh. Peeling also requires a lot of work. We prefer to simply snap off the tough ends and proceed with cooking.

Asparagus can be cooked in numerous ways. We first investigated moist-heat cooking methods—namely, boiling and steaming—both of which yielded similar results. Although some sources suggest boiling asparagus, we found that steaming is equally appealing (and easy) and leaves the tips just a bit crisper. Simply arrange the trimmed spears in a steamer basket above boiling water and cook until the asparagus is tender but not mushy, a process that will take four to five minutes. Steamed asparagus is pretty bland. At the very least, we found that it should be drizzled with good olive oil and sprinkled with salt and pepper. More flavorful dressings are another good option.

A second option for asparagus is stir-frying. Many recipes for stir-fried asparagus begin by steaming or blanching the spears. The asparagus is then quickly stir-fried with the sauce ingredients. There are two problems with this scenario. First, two cooking methods mean two dirty pots. Second, the flavor of the asparagus is diluted during the first cooking step and then the asparagus doesn't spend enough time with the sauce ingredients to absorb much of their character.

We wanted to solve these problems and knew that skipping the precooking part of the recipe would be necessary. But would this work? The answer is yes, as long as you follow a few rules. First, try to use thinner asparagus that can cook through strictly by stir-frying. If thicker spears are what you have on hand, cut them in half lengthwise so they will cook more quickly.

The second key to success is heat, and plenty of it. Asparagus, even thin spears, will be crunchy if stir-fried for just a minute or two. We found that medium spears cut into 1½-inch lengths need five minutes over intense heat to soften properly. All this heat ensures that the asparagus browns, which improves its flavor. Also, use a skillet large enough to hold the asparagus in a single layer. We also discovered that adding a fairly liquidy sauce (which will reduce quickly to a syrup) helps finish the cooking process.

Another cooking option, and one that most cooks don't consider, is grilling or broiling. The intense dry heat concentrates the flavor of the asparagus, and the exterior caramelization makes the spears especially sweet. The result is asparagus with a heightened and, we think, delicious flavor.

The two primary questions related to broiling concerned the thickness of the stalks and the distance they should be kept from the heat source as they cook. In our tests with thicker asparagus, anywhere from ¾ to 1 inch in diameter, the peels began to char before the interior of the spears became fully tender. When we used thinner spears (no thicker than ⅝ inch), the interior was tender by the time the exterior was browned.

We then focused on how far to keep the spears from the heating element. At 3 inches, the asparagus charred a bit. At 5 inches, the asparagus took a little too long to cook, and they failed to caramelize properly. The middle ground, 4 inches, proved perfect for cooking speed, control, and browning.

As with broiling, we found that thicker spears will char before they become tender on the grill. Stick with spears ⅝ inch in diameter (or smaller) and the asparagus will be tender by the time the exterior is

TRIMMING TOUGH ENDS FROM ASPARAGUS

In our tests, we found that the tough, woody part of the stem will break off in just the right place if you hold the spear the right way. With one hand, hold the asparagus about halfway down the stalk; with the thumb and index fingers of the other hand, hold the spear about an inch up from the bottom. Bend the stalk until it snaps.

lightly charred. Grilled and broiled asparagus should be lightly oiled before cooking—use extra-virgin olive oil for the most flavor. After cooking, grilled and broiled asparagus can be tossed or drizzled with a vinaigrette for even more flavor.

Steamed Asparagus
SERVES 4

To steam asparagus, you will need a collapsible steamer basket that fits into the pot. Make sure the asparagus is above the water level and keep the pot covered. If you are using asparagus with thicker stalks, add a few minutes to the cooking time. You can flavor steamed asparagus with a drizzle of extra-virgin olive oil and salt and pepper, but the recipes that follow use more flavorful vinaigrettes for better results. If the asparagus is not going to be served right away, plunge the asparagus in ice water to stop the cooking process. The cooled and drained asparagus can be covered and refrigerated overnight.

1½ pounds asparagus, preferably with thin stalks about ½ inch in diameter, tough ends snapped off (see the illustration at left)
Extra-virgin olive oil
Salt and ground black pepper

1. Place the steamer basket in a large pot or Dutch oven. Add enough water so that the water barely reaches the bottom of the steamer basket. Turn the heat to high and bring the water to a boil. Add the asparagus, cover, and reduce the heat to medium-high. Steam until the asparagus bends slightly when picked up and the stalks yield slightly when squeezed, 4 to 5 minutes.

2. Using tongs, transfer the asparagus to a platter. Drizzle with olive oil and sprinkle with salt and pepper to taste. Serve immediately.

➤ VARIATIONS
Steamed Asparagus with Lime-Ginger Vinaigrette
See the illustrations on page 131 for mincing fresh ginger.

2 tablespoons juice and 1 teaspoon grated zest from 1 lime
1½ teaspoons minced fresh ginger

½ teaspoon sugar

1 tablespoon chopped fresh cilantro leaves

6 tablespoons canola or vegetable oil
Salt and ground black pepper

1 recipe Steamed Asparagus (without the olive oil, salt, and pepper)

1. Whisk the lime juice, lime zest, ginger, sugar, and cilantro together in a medium bowl. Whisk in the oil until thoroughly combined. Season with salt and pepper to taste.

2. Arrange the steamed asparagus on a platter and drizzle with the dressing. Serve warm or at room temperature.

Steamed Asparagus with Ginger-Hoisin Vinaigrette

Hoisin sauce is a sweet and spicy condiment used in Chinese cooking. Look for it in Asian markets and the Asian aisle of most well-stocked supermarkets. You will find rice vinegar typically shelved along with the other vinegar varieties.

2½ tablespoons rice vinegar

1½ tablespoons hoisin sauce

2½ teaspoons soy sauce

MINCING GINGER

Ginger is highly fibrous, which makes it tricky to mince. A sharp knife is a must.

1. Slice the peeled knob of ginger into thin rounds, then fan the rounds out and cut them into thin, matchstick-like strips.

2. Chop the matchsticks crosswise into a fine mince.

1½ teaspoons minced fresh ginger (see the illustrations below)

1½ tablespoons canola oil

1½ teaspoons toasted sesame oil

1 recipe Steamed Asparagus (without the olive oil, salt, and pepper)

1. Whisk the vinegar, hoisin sauce, soy sauce, and ginger together in a medium bowl. Whisk in the oils until thoroughly combined.

2. Arrange the steamed asparagus on a platter and drizzle with the dressing. Serve warm or at room temperature.

Steamed Asparagus with Roasted Red Pepper Vinaigrette

The roasted red peppers are packed in a vinegary brine that lends a bright flavor to the vinaigrette. See page 16 for more information about buying jarred peppers.

¼ cup jarred roasted red peppers

1 tablespoon red wine vinegar

2 medium garlic cloves, minced or pressed through a garlic press

6 tablespoons extra-virgin olive oil

1 tablespoon minced fresh parsley leaves
Salt and ground black pepper

1 recipe Steamed Asparagus (without the olive oil, salt, and pepper)

1. Combine the peppers, vinegar, garlic, and olive oil in a food processor. Pulse until thoroughly combined, about 10 seconds. Scrape the dressing into a small bowl. Stir in the parsley and season with salt and pepper to taste.

2. Arrange the steamed asparagus on a platter and drizzle with the dressing. Serve warm or at room temperature.

Stir-Fried Asparagus

SERVES 4

Thicker stalks should be halved lengthwise, then cut into 1½-inch pieces to ensure that the centers cook through. The flavors of chicken broth and garlic are basic; the variations are more intriguing.

½ cup low-sodium chicken broth

½ teaspoon salt

¼ teaspoon ground black pepper

2½ tablespoons peanut oil

1½ pounds asparagus, tough ends snapped off (see the illustration on page 130) and cut on the bias into 1½-inch pieces

3 medium garlic cloves, minced or pressed through a garlic press

1. Mix the chicken broth, salt, and pepper together in a small bowl.

2. Heat 2 tablespoons of the oil in a large, nonstick heavy-bottomed skillet over high heat until almost smoking. Add the asparagus and cook, stirring frequently, until well browned, about 5 minutes.

3. Clear a space in the center of the pan, add the garlic, and drizzle with the remaining ½ tablespoon oil. Cook until fragrant, about 30 seconds, then mix with the asparagus. Add the chicken broth mixture and toss to coat the asparagus. Cook until the sauce is syrupy, about 30 seconds. Serve immediately.

➤ VARIATIONS

Stir-Fried Asparagus with Black Bean Sauce

Chinese fermented black beans are available in Asian food shops. They should be moist and soft to the touch. Don't buy beans that are dried out or shriveled. Quality fermented beans should not taste overly salty.

3 tablespoons dry sherry

2 tablespoons low-sodium chicken broth

1 tablespoon soy sauce

1 tablespoon toasted sesame oil

1 tablespoon chopped fermented black beans

1 teaspoon sugar

¼ teaspoon ground black pepper

2½ tablespoons peanut oil

1½ pounds asparagus, tough ends snapped off (see the illustration on page 130) and cut on the bias into 1½-inch pieces

3 medium garlic cloves, minced or pressed through a garlic press

1½ teaspoons minced fresh ginger

2 medium scallions, white and green parts, sliced thin on the bias

1. Mix the sherry, chicken broth, soy sauce, sesame oil, black beans, sugar, and pepper together in a small bowl.

2. Heat 2 tablespoons of the peanut oil in a large, nonstick heavy-bottomed skillet over high heat until almost smoking. Add the asparagus and cook, stirring frequently, until well browned, about 5 minutes.

3. Clear a space in the center of the pan, add the garlic and ginger, and drizzle with the remaining ½ tablespoon peanut oil. Cook until fragrant, about 30 seconds, then mix with the asparagus. Add the black bean mixture and toss to coat the asparagus. Cook until the sauce is syrupy, about 30 seconds. Sprinkle with scallions and serve immediately.

Stir-Fried Asparagus with Soy Sauce, Maple Syrup, and Scallions

Here is an imaginative way to use maple syrup in an Asian sauce to achieve the always-sought-after balance of sweet and salty flavors.

1½ tablespoons soy sauce

1½ tablespoons maple syrup

1 tablespoon dry sherry

2½ tablespoons peanut oil

1½ pounds asparagus, tough ends snapped off (see the illustration on page 130) and cut on the bias into 1½-inch pieces

3 medium garlic cloves, minced or pressed through a garlic press

2 medium scallions, white and green parts, sliced thin on the bias

1. Mix the soy sauce, maple syrup, and sherry together in a small bowl.

2. Heat 2 tablespoons of the oil in a large, nonstick heavy-bottomed skillet over high heat until almost smoking. Add the asparagus and cook, stirring frequently, until well browned, about 5 minutes.

3. Clear a space in the center of the pan, add the garlic, and drizzle with the remaining ½ tablespoon

oil. Cook until fragrant, about 30 seconds, then mix with the asparagus. Add the soy sauce mixture and toss to coat the asparagus. Cook until the sauce is syrupy, about 30 seconds. Sprinkle with the scallions and serve immediately.

Stir-Fried Asparagus and Red Pepper with Garlicky Oyster Sauce

To turn this into an entrée serving 3 or 4, add 1 cup diced firm tofu, drained well, with the red bell pepper in step 2 and serve with steamed rice or Chinese egg noodles.

2	tablespoons oyster sauce
1	tablespoon soy sauce
1	teaspoon toasted sesame oil
2	tablespoons dry sherry
2½	tablespoons peanut oil
1	medium red bell pepper, cored, seeded, and cut into 1 by ¼-inch strips
1½	pounds asparagus, tough ends snapped off (see the illustration on page 130) and cut on the bias into 1½-inch pieces
6	medium garlic cloves, minced or pressed through a garlic press
1	teaspoon minced fresh ginger

1. Mix the oyster sauce, soy sauce, sesame oil, and sherry together in a small bowl.

2. Heat 2 tablespoons of the peanut oil in a large, nonstick heavy-bottomed skillet over high heat until almost smoking. Add the red pepper and cook, stirring frequently, until the strips start to brown, about 2 minutes. Add the asparagus and cook, stirring frequently, until well browned, about 5 minutes.

3. Clear a space in the center of the pan, add the garlic and ginger, and drizzle with the remaining ½ tablespoon peanut oil. Cook until fragrant, about 30 seconds, then mix with the vegetables. Add the oyster sauce mixture and toss to coat the vegetables. Cook until the sauce is syrupy, about 30 seconds. Serve immediately.

INGREDIENTS: Soy Sauce

Few condiments are as misunderstood as soy sauce, the pungent, fragrant, fermented flavoring that's a mainstay in Asian cooking. Its simple, straightforward composition—equal parts soybeans and a roasted grain, usually wheat, plus water and salt—belies the subtle, sophisticated contribution it makes as an all-purpose seasoning, flavor enhancer, tabletop condiment, and dipping sauce.

The three products consumers are likely to encounter are regular soy sauce, light soy sauce (made with a higher percentage of water and hence lower in sodium), and tamari (made with fermented soybeans, water, and salt—no wheat). Tamari generally has a stronger flavor and thicker consistency than soy sauce. It is traditionally used in Japanese cooking.

In a tasting of leading soy sauces, we found that products aged according to ancient customs were superior to synthetic sauces, such as La Choy's, which are made in a day and almost always contain hydrolyzed vegetable protein. Our favorite soy sauce, Eden Selected Shoyu Soy Sauce (*shoyu* is the Japanese word for soy sauce), is aged for three years. Tasters also liked products made by San-J and Kikkoman.

THE BEST SOY SAUCE
Eden Selected Shoyu Soy Sauce was described by tasters as "toasty, caramel-y, and complex." The saltiness was pronounced but not overwhelming. Among the 12 brands tested, it was the clear favorite

Broiled Asparagus
SERVES 4 TO 6
Choose asparagus no thicker than ⅝ inch for this recipe.

2	pounds thin asparagus, tough ends snapped off (see the illustration on page 130)
1	tablespoon olive oil
	Salt and ground black pepper

Adjust an oven rack to the uppermost position (about 4 inches from the heating element) and heat the broiler. Toss the asparagus with the oil and salt and pepper to taste, then arrange the stalks in a single layer on a heavy rimmed baking sheet. Broil, shaking the pan halfway through to turn the spears, until the asparagus is tender and lightly browned, 8 to 10 minutes. Cool the asparagus for 5 minutes and arrange it on a platter.

MAKING PARMESAN SHAVINGS

Thin shavings of Parmesan can be used to garnish vegetable dishes as well as salad. Simply run a sharp vegetable peeler along the length of a piece of cheese to remove paper-thin curls.

➤ VARIATIONS

Broiled Asparagus with Balsamic Glaze and Parmesan Shards

The balsamic glaze can be made ahead; it will keep in the refrigerator, covered, for up to a week.

¾	cup balsamic vinegar
1	recipe Broiled Asparagus
¼	cup extra-virgin olive oil
¼	cup shaved Parmesan cheese (see the illustration above)

Bring the vinegar to a boil in an 8-inch skillet over medium-high heat. Reduce the heat to medium and simmer slowly until the vinegar is syrupy and reduced to ¼ cup, 15 to 20 minutes. Arrange the asparagus on a platter. Drizzle the balsamic glaze and olive oil over the asparagus. Scatter the cheese shavings on top and serve immediately.

Broiled Asparagus with Soy-Ginger Vinaigrette

Putting the garlic through a press ensures that the pieces are very fine. If you don't own a press, mince the garlic to a paste with a knife (see the illustration on page 626).

2	medium scallions, white and green parts, minced
1	tablespoon minced fresh ginger
2	small garlic cloves, minced or pressed through a garlic press
3	tablespoons toasted sesame oil
3	tablespoons soy sauce
¼	cup juice from 2 large limes
1	tablespoon honey
1	recipe Broiled Asparagus

Whisk the scallions, ginger, garlic, sesame oil, soy sauce, lime juice, and honey together in a small bowl. Arrange the asparagus on a platter. Drizzle the vinaigrette over the asparagus and serve immediately.

Grilled Asparagus
SERVES 4

Thick stalks will burn on the surface before they cook through. Purchase asparagus no thicker than ⅝ inch.

1½	pounds asparagus, tough ends snapped off (see the illustration on page 130)
1	tablespoon extra-virgin olive oil
	Salt and ground black pepper

1. Toss the asparagus with the oil in a medium bowl or on a heavy rimmed baking sheet.

2. Grill the asparagus over a medium-hot fire (you should be able to hold your hand 5 inches above the cooking grate for 3 to 4 seconds), turning once, until tender and streaked with light grill marks, 5 to 7 minutes. Transfer the asparagus to a platter. Season with salt and pepper to taste. Serve hot, warm, or at room temperature.

➤ VARIATIONS

Grilled Asparagus with Grilled Lemon Vinaigrette

Grilling the lemon not only mellows its flavors but also helps to release its juices.

1	lemon, cut in half crosswise
6	tablespoons extra-virgin olive oil
1	medium shallot, minced
½	teaspoon minced fresh thyme leaves
	Salt and ground black pepper
1	recipe Grilled Asparagus

1. Place the lemon halves on the grill cut–side down and grill until tender and streaked with light grill marks, about 3 minutes. When the lemon is cool enough to handle, squeeze and strain the juice into a medium nonreactive bowl; you should have about 2 tablespoons. Whisk in the olive oil, shallot, and thyme. Season with salt and pepper to taste.

2. Arrange the asparagus on a platter and drizzle with the dressing. Serve immediately.

Grilled Asparagus with Orange–Sesame Vinaigrette

Tahini, a paste made from ground sesame seeds, is used in Middle Eastern cooking. If tahini is unavailable, increase the sesame seeds to 3 tablespoons and the sesame oil to 1 teaspoon; instead of whisking the ingredients together, pulse them in a food processor for 10 seconds.

I   tablespoon sesame seeds
I   teaspoon tahini
I   teaspoon grated zest and I tablespoon juice from I orange
I   tablespoon rice vinegar
I   teaspoon soy sauce
½   teaspoon minced fresh ginger (see the illustrations on page 131)
½   teaspoon toasted sesame oil
6   tablespoons extra-virgin olive oil
    Salt and ground black pepper
I   recipe Grilled Asparagus

1. Toast the sesame seeds in a dry skillet over medium heat until fragrant, 7 to 10 minutes. Combine the toasted sesame seeds, orange zest and juice, rice vinegar, soy sauce, ginger, and oils in a medium bowl and whisk thoroughly to combine. Season with salt and pepper to taste.

2. Arrange the asparagus on a platter and drizzle with the dressing. Serve immediately.

Grilling Vegetables at a Glance

Use this chart as a guide to grilling the following vegetables. Lightly toss the vegetables or brush them on both sides with olive oil, preferably extra-virgin, before grilling. Unless otherwise specified, vegetables should be cooked over a medium fire.

VEGETABLE	PREPARATION	GRILLING DIRECTIONS
Asparagus	Snap off tough ends.	Grill over a medium-low fire, turning once, until tender and streaked with light grill marks, 5 to 7 minutes.
Corn	Remove all but last layer of husk.	Grill, turning every 1½ to 2 minutes, until husk chars and begins to peel away at tip, exposing some kernels, 8 to 10 minutes.
Eggplant	Remove ends. Cut into ³/₄-inch-thick rounds or ³/₄-inch-thick strips.	Grill, turning once, until flesh is darkly colored, 8 to 10 minutes.
Endive	Cut in half lengthwise through stem end.	Grill, flat-side down, until streaked with dark grill marks, 6 to 8 minutes.
Fennel	Remove stalks and fronds. Slice vertically through base into ½-inch-thick pieces.	Grill, turning once, until streaked with dark grill marks and quite soft, 10 to 15 minutes.
Mushrooms, white and cremini	Clean with a damp towel and trim thin slice from stems.	Grill on a vegetable grid, turning several times, until golden brown, 6 to 7 minutes.
Mushrooms, portobello	Clean with a damp towel and remove stems.	Grill, with gill-like underside facing up, until cap is streaked with grill marks, 8 to 10 minutes.
Onions	Peel and cut into ½-inch-thick slices.	Grill, turning occasionally, until lightly charred, 5 to 6 minutes.
Peppers	Core, seed, and cut into large wedges.	Grill, turning once, until streaked with dark grill marks, 9 to 10 minutes.
Tomatoes, cherry	Remove stems.	Grill on a vegetable grid, turning several times, until streaked with dark grill marks, about 3 minutes.
Tomatoes, plum	Cut in half lengthwise and seed.	Grill, turning once, until streaked with dark grill marks, about 8 minutes.
Zucchini and Summer Squash	Remove ends. Slice lengthwise into ½-inch-thick strips.	Grill, turning once, until streaked with dark grill marks, 8 to 10 minutes.

GREEN BEANS

FOR THOSE OF US WHO ARE 11TH-HOUR cooks, the usual rigmarole for cooking green beans—boiling, shocking in ice water, drying with paper towels, and, finally, reheating in a separately made sauce—simply takes too long and dirties too many dishes. We wanted a streamlined technique that would yield tender beans and a flavorful sauce that was worthy of a holiday spread and yet speedy enough for a last-minute supper.

Our plan was to steam the beans in a covered skillet with a little water, remove the lid partway through cooking to evaporate the water, and then build a quick pan sauce around the beans as they finished cooking. The beans, however, steamed in only eight minutes, leaving little time to make a decent sauce after the water had evaporated. Switching the cooking order around, we then tried making the sauce first. Building good flavor and texture by sautéing aromatics and a little flour, we then added to the pan some fresh herbs, the beans, and some chicken broth instead of just plain water. We covered the skillet and cooked the lot until the beans were almost tender. At that point, we removed the lid to thicken the sauce, and this also allowed us to monitor the progress of the green beans.

When made in a nonstick skillet, these beans are easy to gussy up with some toasted bread crumbs or glazed nuts. By making the toppings first, you can simply wipe the skillet clean with paper towels and return it to the stovetop. We have also included a recipe for the holiday favorite, green bean casserole, whose flavor will surpass the canned souped-up version that so many of us remember from childhood.

~

Garlic-Lemon Green Beans with Toasted Bread Crumbs

SERVES 8

Reduce the amount of garlic if you prefer more subtle flavoring.

2   slices high-quality sandwich bread, each slice torn into quarters
3   tablespoons unsalted butter
      Salt and ground black pepper
2   tablespoons freshly grated Parmesan cheese
6   medium garlic cloves, minced or pressed through a garlic press
2   teaspoons all-purpose flour
1/8   teaspoon red pepper flakes
1   teaspoon minced fresh thyme leaves
1 1/2 pounds green beans, ends trimmed
1   cup low-sodium chicken broth
1   tablespoon juice from 1 lemon

1. Process the bread in a food processor to even, fine crumbs, about ten 1-second pulses. Heat 1 tablespoon of the butter in a 12-inch nonstick skillet over medium-high heat; when melted, add the bread crumbs and cook, stirring frequently, until golden brown, 3 to 5 minutes. Transfer to a medium bowl and stir in 1/4 teaspoon salt, 1/8 teaspoon pepper, and the cheese; set aside.

2. Wipe out the skillet. Add the remaining 2 tablespoons butter, the garlic, and 1/4 teaspoon salt; cook over medium heat, stirring constantly, until the garlic is golden, 3 to 5 minutes. Stir in the flour, red pepper flakes, and thyme, then toss in the green beans. Add the chicken broth and increase the heat to medium-high; cover and cook until the beans are partly tender but still crisp at the center, about 4 minutes. Uncover and cook, stirring occasionally, until the beans are tender and the sauce has thickened slightly, about 4 minutes. Off the heat, stir in the lemon juice and adjust the seasonings with salt and pepper to taste. Transfer to a serving dish, sprinkle evenly with the bread crumbs, and serve.

~

Green Beans with Orange Essence and Toasted Maple Pecans

SERVES 8

The flavors in this dish work well as part of Thanksgiving dinner.

3/4   cup pecans, chopped coarse
3   tablespoons unsalted butter
2   tablespoons maple syrup
      Salt
2   medium shallots, minced

½ teaspoon grated zest plus ⅓ cup juice from
1 large orange
Pinch cayenne pepper
2 teaspoons all-purpose flour
1½ pounds green beans, ends trimmed
⅔ cup low-sodium chicken broth
1 teaspoon minced fresh sage leaves
Ground black pepper

1. Toast the pecans in a 12-inch nonstick skillet over medium-high heat, stirring occasionally, until fragrant, about 3 minutes. Off the heat, stir in 1 tablespoon of the butter, the maple syrup, and ⅛ teaspoon salt. Return the skillet to medium heat and cook, stirring constantly, until the nuts are dry and glossy, about 45 seconds; transfer to a plate.

2. Wipe out the skillet. Heat the remaining 2 tablespoons butter in the skillet over medium heat; when the foaming subsides, add the shallots, orange zest, and cayenne and cook, stirring occasionally, until the shallots are softened, about 2 minutes. Stir in the flour until combined, then toss in the green beans. Add the chicken broth, orange juice, and sage; increase the heat to medium-high, cover, and cook until the beans are partly tender but still crisp at the center, about 4 minutes. Uncover and cook, stirring occasionally, until the beans are tender and the sauce has thickened slightly, about 4 minutes. Off the heat, adjust the seasonings with salt and pepper to taste. Transfer to a serving dish, sprinkle evenly with the pecans, and serve.

Quick Green Bean "Casserole"

SERVES 8

For best results, avoid substituting a lower-fat dairy in place of the heavy cream.

3 large shallots, sliced thin
Salt and ground black pepper
3 tablespoons all-purpose flour
5 tablespoons vegetable oil
10 ounces cremini mushrooms, stems discarded, caps wiped clean and sliced ¼ inch thick
2 tablespoons unsalted butter
1 medium onion, minced (about 1 cup)

2 medium garlic cloves, minced or pressed through a garlic press
1½ pounds green beans, ends trimmed
3 sprigs fresh thyme
2 bay leaves
¾ cup heavy cream
¾ cup low-sodium chicken broth

1. Toss the shallots with ¼ teaspoon salt, ⅛ teaspoon pepper, and 2 tablespoons of the flour in a small bowl; set aside. Heat 3 tablespoons of the oil in a 12-inch nonstick skillet over medium-high heat until smoking; add the shallots and cook, stirring frequently, until golden and crisp, about 5 minutes. Transfer the shallots with the oil to a baking sheet lined with a triple layer of paper towels.

2. Wipe out the skillet and return it to medium-high heat. Add the remaining 2 tablespoons oil, the mushrooms, and ¼ teaspoon salt; cook, stirring occasionally, until browned, about 8 minutes. Transfer to a plate and set aside.

3. Wipe out the skillet. Heat the butter in the skillet over medium heat; when the foaming subsides, add the onion and cook, stirring occasionally, until the edges begin to brown, about 2 minutes. Stir in the garlic and remaining 1 tablespoon flour; toss in the green beans, thyme, and bay leaves. Add the cream and chicken broth, increase the heat to medium-high, cover, and cook until the beans are partly tender but still crisp at the center, about 4 minutes. Return the reserved mushrooms to the skillet and continue to cook, uncovered, until the green beans are tender and the sauce has thickened slightly, about 4 minutes. Off the heat, discard the bay leaves and thyme; adjust the seasonings with salt and pepper to taste. Transfer to a serving dish, sprinkle evenly with the reserved shallots, and serve.

BEETS

THE BEETS MOST OF US REMEMBER FROM CHILDhood are the canned version or the pickled kind (the ones in the giant jars nestled among pink pickled eggs). Freshly cooked beets are altogether different, with sweet, earthy flavors and a firm, juicy texture.

In order to find the best way of cooking fresh beets, we tried three methods: boiling, steaming, and roasting. Boiled beets were diluted in flavor. Looking at the pink water, it was clear that some of that flavor had escaped into the cooking water. Steaming proved to be a slightly better method, but the flavors weren't as concentrated as we would have liked. Roasting was the next option. We tried wrapping the beets in foil as well as leaving them unwrapped. The unwrapped beets dried out and became leathery, but the wrapped beets were juicy and tender and had the concentrated sweetness we were looking for. There was another significant advantage with the wrapped beets: The roasting pan remained stain-free.

Roasted beets can be peeled after cooking (the skins can be rubbed off with a paper towels), which further reduces the mess. We found that an oven temperature of 400 degrees delivered good results. Medium beets were done in 45 minutes to 1 hour. Smaller beets will take less time. We don't recommend roasting very large beets because they can be woody.

Roasted Beets

SERVES 4

To keep your hands from turning a shocking shade of pink, use a paper towel when skinning the beets. Cradle the roasted beet in a paper towel, pinch the skin between the thumb and forefinger, and peel it off. If the beets do stain your hands or cutting board, see the illustration at right for tips on removing these stains. Serve roasted beets as is or flavor them with a vinaigrette or flavored butter.

    4   **medium beets (about I pound without greens)**
    2   **tablespoons extra-virgin olive oil**
          Salt and ground black pepper

1. Adjust an oven rack to the middle position and heat the oven to 400 degrees. Trim all but about 1 inch of the stems from the beets. Wash the beets well and remove any dangling roots. Wrap the beets in aluminum foil and place the wrapped beets on a shallow roasting pan or a rimmed baking sheet. Roast until a skewer inserted in a beet comes out easily, 45 minutes to 1 hour.

2. Remove the beets from the oven and carefully open the foil packet (make sure to keep your hands and face away from the steam). When the beets are cool enough to handle, carefully peel the skins from the beets. Slice the beets ¼ inch thick and place in a medium bowl. Add the olive oil and salt and pepper to taste and toss together gently. Serve warm or at room temperature.

➤ VARIATIONS
Roasted Beets with Dill-Walnut Vinaigrette
Dill and beets are a combination frequently found in Russian cuisine. Because dill quickly loses its fresh flavor when heated, it's best suited for cold preparations such as vinaigrettes and dips.

   ½   **cup chopped walnuts**
   I   **tablespoon red wine vinegar**
   2   **teaspoons juice from I lemon**
   I   **medium shallot, minced**
 I½   **tablespoons minced fresh dill**
   6   **tablespoons extra-virgin olive oil**
        Salt and ground black pepper
   I   **recipe Roasted Beets (without the olive oil, salt, and pepper)**

1. Place the walnuts in a skillet and toast over medium heat, stirring frequently, until fragrant, about 3 minutes. Set aside.

2. Whisk the vinegar, lemon juice, shallot, dill, and oil together in a small bowl until thoroughly combined. Add salt and pepper to taste. Toss the dressing, sliced beets, and walnuts together in a medium bowl. Serve immediately.

REMOVING BEET STAINS

When cut, beets can stain everything they touch, including hands and cutting boards. To help remove these stains, sprinkle the stained area with salt, rinse, and then scrub with soap. The salt crystals help lift the beet juices away.

Roasted Beets with Ginger Butter and Chives

To cut the ginger into matchsticks, first slice it into ⅛-inch-thick rounds. Stack the rounds on top of each other and cut them into thin sticks.

4	tablespoons (½ stick) unsalted butter
1	1-inch piece fresh ginger, peeled and cut into matchsticks (see note)
1	tablespoon minced fresh chives
1	recipe Roasted Beets (without the olive oil, salt, and pepper)
	Salt and ground black pepper

Melt the butter in a small skillet over medium heat. When the foaming subsides, add the ginger and cook until the ginger is fragrant and crisp, 3 to 4 minutes. Add the chives. Toss the butter mixture, sliced beets, and salt and pepper to taste together in a medium bowl. Serve immediately.

BROCCOLI

BROCCOLI REQUIRES A MOIST-HEAT COOKING method to keep the florets tender and to cook the stalks. We tested boiling, blanching then sautéing, and steaming. Boiled broccoli is soggy-tasting and mushy, even when cooked for just two minutes. The florets absorb too much water. We found the same thing happened when we blanched the broccoli for a minute and then finished cooking it in a hot skillet.

Delicate florets are best cooked above the water in a steamer basket. We found that the stalk may be cooked along with the florets as long as it has been peeled and cut into small chunks. Broccoli will be fully cooked after about five minutes of steaming. At this point, it may be tossed with a flavorful dressing. A warning: Cook broccoli just two or three minutes too long and chemical changes cause this vegetable to lose color and texture.

A second option is to sauté the broccoli for several minutes in hot oil, add some liquid ingredients (chicken broth is ideal), cover, and let the steam from the liquid finish cooking the broccoli. The advantage to the sauté-then-steam method is that all the cooking takes place in a single pot. In contrast, traditional stir-frying requires two pots—one to steam the broccoli and one to stir-fry it.

Steamed Broccoli

SERVES 4 TO 6

Cutting the florets and peeled stalks into equal-size pieces ensures that they will all cook at the same rate. The sweet flavor of the steamed broccoli pairs well with bold, bright flavors. Serve it with best-quality olive oil or your favorite vinaigrette, or try one of the vinaigrette recipes that follow. For maximum absorption, toss steamed broccoli with the oil or dressing when hot. The broccoli can be served immediately or cooled to room temperature.

1½	pounds broccoli (about 1 medium bunch), prepared according to the illustrations below (about 8 cups)
2	tablespoons extra-virgin olive oil
	Salt and ground black pepper

PREPARING BROCCOLI

1. Place the head of broccoli upside down on a cutting board and with a large knife trim off the florets very close to their heads. Cut the florets into 1-inch pieces.

2. The stalks may also be trimmed and cooked. Stand each stalk up on the cutting board and square it off with a large knife. This will remove the outer ⅛-inch from the stalk, which is quite tough. Now cut the stalk in half lengthwise and into 1-inch pieces.

Fit a wide saucepan with a steamer basket. Add water, keeping the water level below the basket. Cover and bring the water to a boil over high heat. Add the broccoli to the basket. Cover and steam until the broccoli is just tender, 4½ to 5 minutes. Transfer the broccoli to a serving bowl and toss with the oil and salt and pepper to taste. Serve hot or at room temperature.

➤ VARIATIONS

Steamed Broccoli with Sesame Vinaigrette

Sesame seeds can be found in any supermarket but are usually much less expensive where they are often sold in volume—at Asian grocery stores or natural food stores.

¼	cup sesame seeds
1	tablespoon soy sauce
1½	tablespoons rice vinegar
1	tablespoon sugar
1	teaspoon toasted sesame oil
6	tablespoons vegetable or canola oil
1	recipe Steamed Broccoli (without the olive oil, salt, and pepper)

1. Toast the sesame seeds in a dry skillet over medium heat, shaking the pan occasionally, until the seeds are light golden and fragrant, 7 to 10 minutes.

2. Process the sesame seeds, soy sauce, vinegar, sugar, and oils in a food processor until the sesame seeds are ground and the vinaigrette is well blended, about 15 seconds.

3. Toss the dressing with the broccoli in a serving bowl. Serve hot or at room temperature.

Steamed Broccoli with Balsamic-Basil Vinaigrette

Use a good-quality balsamic vinegar for the vinaigrette.

2	tablespoons balsamic vinegar
6	tablespoons extra-virgin olive oil
1	tablespoon minced fresh basil leaves
1	medium garlic clove, minced or pressed through a garlic press
1	small shallot, minced
	Salt and ground black pepper
1	recipe Steamed Broccoli (without the olive oil, salt, and pepper)

Mix the vinegar, oil, basil, garlic, shallot, and salt and pepper to taste together in a medium bowl until well blended. Toss the dressing with the steamed broccoli in a serving bowl. Serve hot or at room temperature.

Stir-Fried Broccoli

SERVES 4 TO 6

We tried stir-frying broccoli without precooking it and found that the florets started to fall apart long before the stems were tender. While blanching and then stir-frying helped the broccoli to cook more evenly, the florets were soggy. We found that partially cooking the broccoli in a steamer basket and then adding it to a stir-fry pan was the solution. This technique is best used when you want to sauce broccoli rather than dress it with vinaigrette.

½	cup low-sodium chicken broth
½	teaspoon salt
	Ground black pepper
1½	tablespoons plus 1 teaspoon peanut oil
1	recipe Steamed Broccoli (page 139), cooked just 2½ minutes and removed from the steamer
3	medium garlic cloves, minced or pressed through a garlic press

1. Mix the broth, salt, and pepper to taste together in a small bowl.

2. Heat the 1½ tablespoons oil in a large nonstick skillet over high heat until shimmering. Add the partially steamed broccoli and cook, stirring every 30 seconds, until fully cooked and heated through, about 2½ minutes.

3. Clear the center of the pan, add the garlic, and drizzle with the remaining 1 teaspoon oil. Mash the garlic with the back of a spatula. Cook 10 seconds, then mix the garlic with the broccoli. Add the chicken broth mixture and cook until the sauce is syrupy, about 30 seconds. Serve immediately.

Stir-Fried Broccoli with Hot-and-Sour Sauce

Adjust the heat in this dish as desired by increasing or decreasing the amount of chile.

3	tablespoons cider vinegar
1	tablespoon low-sodium chicken broth
1	tablespoon soy sauce
2	teaspoons sugar
1½	tablespoons plus 1 teaspoon peanut oil
1	recipe Steamed Broccoli (page 139), cooked just 2½ minutes and removed from the steamer
2	teaspoons minced fresh ginger
1	tablespoon minced jalapeño chile

1. Mix the vinegar, chicken broth, soy sauce, and sugar together in a small bowl.

2. Heat the 1½ tablespoons oil in a large nonstick skillet over high heat until shimmering. Add the partially steamed broccoli and cook, stirring every 30 seconds, until fully cooked and heated through, about 2½ minutes.

3. Clear the center of the pan, add the ginger and chile, and drizzle with the remaining 1 teaspoon oil. Mash the ginger and chile with the back of a spatula. Cook 10 seconds, then mix the ginger and chile with the broccoli. Add the vinegar mixture and cook until the sauce is syrupy, about 30 seconds. Serve immediately.

Stir-Fried Broccoli with Spicy Black Bean Sauce

Black bean sauce is a salty mixture made from small fermented black soybeans and garlic. It can be found in the Asian food section of most large grocery stores.

½	cup low-sodium chicken broth
2	tablespoons black bean sauce
1	tablespoon dry sherry
1	teaspoon toasted sesame oil
1	tablespoon sesame seeds
1½	tablespoons peanut oil
1	recipe Steamed Broccoli (page 139), cooked just 2½ minutes and removed from the steamer
1	teaspoon red pepper flakes

1. Mix the broth, black bean sauce, sherry, and sesame oil together in a small bowl.

2. Place the sesame seeds in a large nonstick skillet and toast over medium heat, shaking the pan occasionally, until lightly browned, 7 to 10 minutes. Transfer the seeds to another small bowl.

3. Add the peanut oil to the empty skillet and raise the heat to high. When the oil is shimmering, add the partially steamed broccoli and pepper flakes and cook, stirring every 30 seconds, until fully cooked and heated through, about 2½ minutes. Add the broth mixture and cook until the sauce is syrupy, about 1 minute. Sprinkle with the toasted sesame seeds and serve immediately.

Sautéed Broccoli
SERVES 4 TO 6

Adding broth to the sautéing broccoli and steaming it lightly eliminates the need to blanch the broccoli beforehand. This cooking method is well suited to Italian flavors.

2	tablespoons olive oil
1½	pounds broccoli (about 1 medium bunch), prepared according to the illustrations on page 139 (about 8 cups)
½	cup low-sodium chicken broth
	Salt and ground black pepper

Heat the oil in a large nonstick skillet over medium-high heat until shimmering. Add the broccoli and cook, stirring frequently, until it turns bright green, 2 to 3 minutes. Increase the heat to high and add the broth. Cover and cook until the broccoli begins to become tender, about 2 minutes. Uncover and cook, stirring frequently, until the liquid has evaporated and the broccoli is tender, 3 to 4 minutes longer. Season with salt and pepper to taste and serve immediately.

➤ VARIATION

Sautéed Broccoli with Garlic, Pine Nuts, and Parmesan

The rich flavors in this recipe work with pizzas and chicken dishes.

2 1/2	tablespoons olive oil
1/4	cup pine nuts
1 1/2	pounds broccoli (about 1 medium bunch), prepared according to the illustrations on page 139 (about 8 cups)
4	medium garlic cloves, sliced thin
1/4	cup low-sodium chicken broth
1/4	cup dry white wine
1/4	cup freshly grated Parmesan cheese
2	tablespoons thinly sliced fresh basil leaves
	Salt and ground black pepper

1. Heat 2 tablespoons of the oil in a large nonstick skillet over medium-high heat until shimmering. Add the pine nuts and cook, stirring often, until golden, about 2 minutes.

2. Add the broccoli and cook, stirring frequently, until it turns bright green, 2 to 3 minutes. Clear a space in the center of the pan and add the garlic and remaining 1/2 tablespoon oil. Cook until the

garlic is fragrant, about 1 minute. Increase the heat to high and add the broth and wine. Stir, cover, and cook until the broccoli begins to become tender, about 2 minutes. Uncover and cook, stirring frequently, until the liquid has evaporated and the broccoli is tender, 3 to 4 minutes longer. Sprinkle with the cheese and basil and season with salt and pepper to taste. Serve immediately.

SCIENCE:
Why Broccoli Turns Olive Green

We've found that broccoli has an internal clock that starts ticking once the broccoli has steamed for seven minutes. At this point, chemical changes begin to occur, which cause an initial undesirable loss of color and texture. This loss intensifies as cooking continues. By nine minutes, the broccoli has become discolored and mushy, and it begins to take on a sulfurous flavor.

This deterioration is due to two distinct actions: heat and acid. As broccoli is heated during cooking, the chlorophyll begins to break down, resulting in a change of color and texture. In addition, all vegetables contain acids that leach out during cooking and create an acidic environment, further contributing to the breakdown of the chlorophyll. None of this is an issue as long as the steaming time does not exceed seven minutes. We find that broccoli actually has the best texture, color, and flavor after steaming for just five minutes, which also happens to provide the cook with a decent cushion before this chemical reaction begins.

BROCCOLI RABE

A PERFECT PLATE OF BROCCOLI RABE SHOULD be intensely flavored but not intensely bitter. You want to taste the other ingredients and flavors in the dish. So we set our sights on developing a dependable, quick method of cooking that would deliver less bitterness and a rounder, more balanced flavor.

Parcooking any bitter greens helps to rid them of some bitter flavor. We found that steaming produced little change in the broccoli rabe—it was still very intense. When blanched in a small amount of salted boiling water (1 quart of water for about 1 pound of broccoli rabe), the rabe was much better. But the bitterness was still overwhelming, so we increased the boiling salted water to three quarts. Sure enough, the broccoli rabe was delicious; it was complex, mustardy, and peppery as well as slightly bitter, and the garlic and olive oil added later complemented rather than competed with its flavor. Depending on personal taste, you can reduce the amount of blanching water for stronger flavor, or, to really tone down the bitterness, increase the amount of water.

After considerable testing, we found that the lower two inches or so of the stems were woody and tough, while the upper portions of the stems were tender enough to include in the recipes. When we used only the upper portions, there was no need to go through the laborious task of peeling the stems. Cutting the stems into pieces about an inch long made them easier to eat and allowed them to cook in the same amount of time as the florets and the leaves.

Once the broccoli rabe has been blanched, it should be shocked in cool water to stop the cooking process and then dried well. It can be dressed with a vinaigrette or quickly sautéed with flavorful ingredients.

Blanched Broccoli Rabe

SERVES 4

Using a salad spinner makes easy work of drying the cooled, blanched broccoli rabe. See page 82 for tips on buying a salad spinner.

1   **bunch broccoli rabe (about 14 ounces), bottom 2 inches of stems trimmed and discarded, remainder cut into 1-inch pieces (see the illustrations below)**
2   **teaspoons salt**

1. Bring 3 quarts water to a boil in a large saucepan. Stir in the broccoli rabe and salt and cook until wilted and tender, 2 to 3 minutes. Drain the broccoli rabe and set aside.

2. Cool the empty saucepan by rinsing it under cold running water. Fill the cooled saucepan with cold water and submerge the broccoli rabe to stop the cooking process. Drain again; squeeze well to dry and proceed with one of the following variations.

➤ VARIATIONS

Broccoli Rabe with Balsamic Vinaigrette

This sweet vinaigrette complements the bitter, mustardy flavors of broccoli rabe.

2   **tablespoons balsamic vinegar**
1   **tablespoon maple syrup**
1   **medium shallot, minced**
1/4   **teaspoon dry mustard**

6   **tablespoons extra-virgin olive oil**
    Salt and ground black pepper
1   **recipe Blanched Broccoli Rabe**

Whisk the vinegar, maple syrup, shallot, mustard, and oil together in a medium bowl until well blended. Season with salt and pepper to taste. Add the broccoli rabe and toss to combine. Serve at room temperature.

Broccoli Rabe with Red Bell Pepper, Olives, and Feta

Sweet red bell peppers and briny olives complement peppery broccoli rabe both in color and flavor.

3   **tablespoons extra-virgin olive oil**
1   **medium red bell pepper, cored, seeded, and diced**
1   **recipe Blanched Broccoli Rabe**
10   **Kalamata olives, pitted and chopped coarse**
1   **teaspoon minced fresh oregano leaves**
    Salt and ground black pepper
1/4   **cup crumbled feta cheese**

Heat the oil in a large skillet over medium-high heat until shimmering. Add the red bell pepper and cook until barely tender, about 3 minutes. Add the broccoli rabe, olives, and oregano and cook, stirring to coat with oil, until the broccoli rabe is heated through, about 1 minute. Season with salt and pepper to taste, sprinkle with the feta, and serve immediately.

PREPARING BROCCOLI RABE

1. The thick stalk ends on broccoli rabe should be trimmed and discarded. Use a sharp knife to cut off the thickest part (usually the bottom 2 inches) of each stalk.

2. Cut the remaining stalks and florets into bite-size pieces, about 1 inch long.

GRATING GINGER

Most cooks who use fresh ginger have scraped their fingers on the grater when the piece of ginger gets down to a tiny nub. Instead of cutting a small chunk of ginger off a larger piece and then grating it, try this method. Peel a small section of the large piece of ginger. Grate the peeled portion, using the rest of the ginger as a handle to keep fingers safely away from the grater.

Broccoli Rabe with Asian Flavors

Although we think of broccoli rabe mainly in terms of Italian cooking, its strong flavor works well with Asian flavorings, too. See the illustration above for tips on grating ginger.

I	tablespoon soy sauce
I¹/₂	teaspoons rice vinegar
I	teaspoon toasted sesame oil
I	teaspoon sugar
2	tablespoons peanut oil
3	medium garlic cloves, minced or pressed through a garlic press
¹/₂	teaspoon grated fresh ginger
¹/₄	teaspoon red pepper flakes
I	recipe Blanched Broccoli Rabe
	Salt

INGREDIENTS: Sesame Oil

Toasted sesame oil, also known as dark or Asian sesame oil, is an aromatic brown oil used as a seasoning in sauces. Because of its low smoke point, it is not used for cooking. Do not substitute regular sesame oil, which is pressed from untoasted seeds and meant for salad dressings and cooking.

Japanese brands of sesame oil are commonly sold in American supermarkets and are generally quite good. Sesame oil tends to go rancid quickly, so store it in a cool cabinet or refrigerate an opened bottle if you will not use it up within a couple of months.

1. Mix the soy sauce, vinegar, sesame oil, and sugar together in a small bowl.

2. Heat the peanut oil, garlic, ginger, and red pepper flakes in a large skillet over medium heat until the garlic starts to sizzle. Increase the heat to medium-high and add the broccoli rabe and the soy sauce mixture. Cook, stirring to coat the broccoli rabe with the other ingredients, until heated through, about 1 minute. Season with salt to taste and serve immediately.

BRUSSELS SPROUTS

THE TASTE OF BRUSSELS SPROUTS IS OFTEN maligned simply because the sprouts are not prepared properly. True, they can be bitter and limp if overcooked, but they can also be crisp, tender, and nutty-flavored when handled right.

We began our testing with boiling and steaming, the two most popular methods of cooking vegetables. Since bringing water to a boil can take up to 20 minutes, the added cooking time of eight to 10 minutes—to reach just the right tenderness—meant that boiled Brussels sprouts could take up to 30 minutes to prepare. That would be acceptable had the result been spectacular. We found, however, that boiling produced only a waterlogged, olive-green-colored, bitter sprout.

Steaming was next. Certainly, steaming is a great way to cook vegetables—fewer nutrients are washed away in the water, the vegetables keep their vibrant colors, and, since less boiled water is used, the cooking time is dramatically reduced. We were convinced that this would be the ideal cooking method for these "little cabbages." However, after several trials, we found that steamed Brussels sprouts still had quite a bitter taste rather than the nutty flavor we sought, even when we were very careful not to overcook them.

Braising, which refers to cooking food with a small amount of liquid in a tightly covered pan, was the next and last cooking method we tried. We braised one pound of sprouts on top of the stove, using only half a cup of water and cooking them until they were just tender enough to be pierced easily by the tip of a knife, about eight to 10 minutes. This method met all the criteria we had established for perfectly cooked Brussels sprouts by producing a tender, nutty-flavored, bright green vegetable.

Since braising in water was so successful, we decided to try braising in other liquids as well. First, we tried cooking the sprouts in unsalted butter, but found that it was difficult to regulate the heat with the lid on and still keep the butter from burning. They came out tasting fine but took longer to cook and required too much attention. Adding broth to the butter helped reduce the attention needed and produced a very green vegetable, but the taste was merely acceptable. Braising in chicken broth produced sprouts that didn't taste much different from the ones braised in water.

Overall, the tastiest Brussels sprouts we cooked came from braising them in heavy cream, a classic French technique for cooking vegetables. We streamlined the preparation by simply placing the cleaned sprouts in a covered pan with the cream. Lightly seasoned with salt, pepper, and nutmeg, the finished sprouts absorbed most of the cream, creating a slightly sweet, nutty flavor that was in no way bitter. Because the results were so tasty, we almost hesitate to offer any additional ideas for preparing Brussels sprouts. Alas, cooking this healthy vegetable in cream on a regular basis simply goes against the healthy-lifestyle conscience. Save this method for the holidays when you can throw caution to the wind. For everyday, you can still produce wonderful sprouts by braising them in water. The braised sprouts should be drained and then seasoned, either simply with just butter or olive oil and salt and pepper, or in slightly more complex sauces (several recipes follow).

The best Brussels sprouts are available in late fall through early winter, peaking in late November. They are often associated with the holidays because of their short season. When buying Brussels sprouts, choose those with small, tight heads, no more than 1½ inches in diameter, for the best flavor. Larger sprouts can often be trimmed of loose leaves along the stem and still be quite good. However, because these larger sprouts are more robust, they cook best when cut in half.

Look for firm, compact, bright green Brussels sprouts. Yellow or brown-tipped leaves usually indicate that they are older. Once purchased, keep the sprouts in a vented container in the refrigerator for no longer than four to five days.

Braised Brussels Sprouts
SERVES 4

Serve these tender Brussels sprouts seasoned simply with ground black pepper and either butter or extra-virgin olive oil. Or use braised Brussels sprouts in one of the following variations.

I	pound small Brussels sprouts, stem end trimmed with a knife and discolored leaves removed by hand
½	teaspoon salt

Bring the sprouts, ½ cup water, and salt to a boil in a 2-quart saucepan over medium-high heat. Cover and simmer (shaking the pan once or twice to redistribute the sprouts) until a knife tip inserted into the center of a sprout meets no resistance, 8 to 10 minutes. Drain well and season (see note) or use in one of the following recipes.

➤ VARIATIONS

Glazed Brussels Sprouts with Chestnuts
If chestnuts are unavailable, substitute ½ cup toasted chopped hazelnuts.

3	tablespoons unsalted butter
I	tablespoon sugar
I	(16-ounce) can peeled chestnuts in water, drained (about 1½ cups)
I	recipe Braised Brussels Sprouts
	Salt and ground black pepper

1. Heat 2 tablespoons of the butter and the sugar in a medium skillet over medium-high heat until the butter melts and the sugar dissolves. Stir in the chestnuts. Reduce the heat to low and cook, stirring occasionally, until the chestnuts are glazed, about 3 minutes.

2. Add the remaining 1 tablespoon butter and the sprouts and cook, stirring occasionally, to heat through, about 5 minutes. Season with salt and pepper to taste. Serve immediately.

Brussels Sprouts with Cider and Bacon

Stay away from maple-flavored bacon; it will give an unpleasant flavor to this dish. To keep the bacon crisp, add the cooked bacon to the Brussels sprouts immediately before serving.

3	ounces (about 3 slices) bacon, cut into ¹/₂-inch pieces
2	medium garlic cloves, minced or pressed through a garlic press
¹/₂	teaspoon minced fresh thyme leaves
³/₄	cup apple cider or apple juice
¹/₈	teaspoon ground black pepper
I	recipe Braised Brussels Sprouts

1. Cook the bacon in a large skillet over medium-high heat until crisp, about 5 minutes. Transfer the bacon to a paper towel–lined plate to drain.

2. Add the garlic and thyme to the bacon drippings in the skillet (there should be 2 to 3 tablespoons) and cook until fragrant, about 1 minute.

Add the cider and pepper and cook until the liquid is reduced by half, about 4 minutes. Add the sprouts and cook until heated through, about 1 minute. Sprinkle with the reserved bacon and serve immediately.

Brussels Sprouts Braised in Cream

This rich dish is perfect for the holidays. Don't drain the sprouts after braising—the cream reduces to a sublime sauce.

I	pound small Brussels sprouts, stem end trimmed with a knife and discolored leaves removed by hand
I	cup heavy cream
¹/₂	teaspoon salt
	Pinch freshly grated nutmeg
	Ground black pepper

Bring the sprouts, cream, and salt to a boil in a 2-quart saucepan over medium-high heat. Cover and simmer, shaking the pan once or twice to redistribute the sprouts, until a knife tip inserted into the center of a sprout meets no resistance, 10 to 12 minutes. Season with nutmeg and pepper to taste. Serve immediately.

SCIENCE: Does "X" Mark the Spot?

What about that age-old idea of cutting a small "X" in the stem end of each Brussels sprout before cooking? The idea behind this technique is to produce faster, more even cooking throughout by allowing the water or steam to penetrate the thicker stem end. If you have ever practiced this technique, you know that it is time-consuming to cut that little "X," especially since the sprouts are small and round and tend to roll away from the knife. We thought it would be worthwhile to see if this extra step was really necessary.

We carved an "X" into the bottom of half of each batch of Brussels sprouts we tested—whether boiled, steamed, or braised. While monitoring cooking times, we tested one sprout with an "X" and one without. Interestingly, we found that the sprouts with an "X" cut in the stem end did, indeed, seem to be more evenly cooked

when tested early in the cooking, before the sprout was completely tender. However, by the time the sprout top was cooked through, it was impossible to tell the difference in the tenderness or cooking evenness between the marked and unmarked sprouts.

Further tests showed that the same result held true for other vegetables commonly carved with an "X" for even cooking: broccoli stems and pearl onions. Pearl onions cooked at exactly the same rate whether they had been marked or not, while carved broccoli stalks tested slightly faster up to the three-minute point, after which they showed no difference at all.

In other words, the notorious "X" appears to be a tenet of kitchen wisdom based on myth. Cutting an "X" into the stem end of a Brussels sprout, broccoli stalk, or pearl onion has no effect on producing evenly cooked, tender vegetables.

CABBAGE

COOKED PROPERLY, CABBAGE IS PLIANT AND mildly sweet. When overcooked, it turns mushy and has an unpleasant aroma. We set out to find the best way to cook this surprisingly fickle vegetable, reasoning that quick cooking would minimize the negative side effects.

Focusing on green cabbage, we chose to shred it for the quickest cooking and also to provide the greatest surface area for flavoring. We began with the fastest possible method, blanching. Plunging cabbage into boiling water for exactly one minute produced the desired crisp-tender texture and pleasant, mild flavor, but this technique also left the cabbage waterlogged.

Steaming turned out to be a better solution to the problem of water uptake, but cooking times varied too much: four to six minutes with an electric steamer appliance; two to four minutes on the stovetop in a basket insert; less time for tender specimens, more time for fibrous heads. With steaming, there is a thin line between delicious cabbage and the wan, flavorless, mealy kind.

We were not optimistic about the remaining options. We had heard that cabbage sautés terribly, and we went on to find truth in the rumor. Sautéed cabbage scorched before it could soften. In addition, cooking fat remained resolutely on the surface and contributed nothing to flavor other than an oily taste.

But we were perplexed by the many cabbage recipes we came upon that refer to sautéing. Perhaps these cookbook authors, we reasoned, actually had a quick braise-sauté in mind. While braising usually refers to cooking slowly in a covered pan using a small quantity of fat or water-based liquid, we would describe a braise-sauté as a quicker process that employs the fat and the water-based liquid in combination. We hoped this gentle method would preserve texture while encouraging the development of more complex flavor.

We tried braising in cream, a strategy consistent with the notion of braise-sautéing because cream is basically an emulsion of butterfat and milk. Seven minutes later, we had found our ideal. For the first time, we could taste a subtle mix of flavors, complemented by a slight residual crunch. The cream also provided the perfect vehicle for both sweet and savory flavor variations. The only problem is the inherent decadence of cream in an everyday cooking method.

But the quick braise-sauté also worked with every combination of four water-based liquids (white wine, chicken broth, apple juice, or tomato juice) and three common fats (butter, bacon fat, or vegetable oil). In each case, the cabbage cooked in liquid alone tasted characterless, while the addition of fat lent significant extra depth to its flavor and also improved its texture.

The quantity of fat required is less than a teaspoon per serving. You can obviously use more, but there is a lower limit, as we learned when we tried using dairy products that were lower in fat than cream. Light cream worked almost as well as heavy cream, but it started to scorch toward the end of cooking. Half-and-half and milk showed a greater affinity for the bottom of the pan than for the cabbage, and the cabbage cooked with them was porous and had an insipid taste.

Contrary to the common advice to buy a tight, heavy head of cabbage, we had better success with smaller, looser heads that were covered with thin outer leaves.

Braised Cabbage with Parsley and Thyme
SERVES 4

This dish is delicate and simple. For additional richness, increase the amount of butter.

1	tablespoon unsalted butter
1/4	cup low-sodium chicken broth
1	pound green cabbage (1/2 medium head), shredded (see the illustrations on page 97)
1/4	teaspoon minced fresh thyme leaves
1	tablespoon minced fresh parsley leaves
	Salt and ground black pepper

Melt the butter in a large skillet over medium-high heat. Add the broth, and then the cabbage and thyme. Bring to a simmer, cover, and cook, stirring occasionally, until the cabbage is wilted but still bright green, 7 to 9 minutes. Sprinkle with the parsley and season with salt and pepper to taste. Serve immediately.

Cabbage and Apples Braised in Cider

Because Granny Smith apples maintain their shape during cooking, they are the best choice for this recipe. McIntosh apples are not an option, as they will turn to mush.

2	tablespoons unsalted butter
1	Granny Smith apple, peeled, cored, and cut into $1/2$-inch dice (about 1 cup)
$1/2$	cup apple cider
1	teaspoon minced fresh thyme leaves
1	teaspoon caraway seeds
1	pound green cabbage ($1/2$ medium head), shredded (see the illustrations on page 97)
	Salt and ground black pepper

Melt the butter in a large skillet over medium-high heat. When the foaming subsides, add the apple and cook until it just begins to brown, about 5 minutes. Add the cider, thyme, and caraway seeds and simmer until the cider is slightly reduced, about 3 minutes. Add the cabbage, stir to combine, cover, and simmer until the cabbage is wilted but still bright green, 7 to 9 minutes. Season with salt and pepper to taste. Serve immediately.

GLAZED CARROTS

GLAZING IS PROBABLY THE MOST POPULAR way to prepare carrots. However, glazed carrots are often saccharine and ill-suited as a side dish on a dinner plate. These defamed vegetables, adrift in a sea of syrup, often lie limp and soggy from overcooking or retain a raw, fibrous resistance from undercooking. Most recipes for glazed carrots are hopelessly dated. These recipes never deliver what we hope for in glazed carrots: fully tender, well-seasoned carrots with a glossy, clingy, yet modest glaze.

We began with how to prepare the carrots for cooking. Matchsticks were out from the get-go—we were looking for simplicity, not to improve our knife skills. A bag of "baby" carrots unceremoniously emptied into a pan for cooking revealed pieces of wildly different girth, with some more than twice as big around as others. Surely these would cook unevenly, so we halved the large pieces lengthwise. Gone was the convenience of this product. Once cooked, tasters remarked that these baby carrots were shy on both carrot flavor and good looks. We peeled regular bagged carrots and cut them on the bias into handsome oblong shapes. Once cooked, these comely carrots earned much praise for their good flavor. Slender bunch carrots (sold with their tops on and at a higher price), also cut on the bias, were no more flavorful, and their diminutive size lacked presence. Regular bagged carrots it was.

Most recipes suggest that the carrots need to be steamed, parboiled, or blanched prior to glazing, resulting in a battery of dirtied utensils. Instead, we put the carrots with a bit of liquid in a skillet (nonstick, for the sake of easy cleanup), along with some salt and sugar for flavor, covered the skillet, and simmered. Mission accomplished: The carrots were cooked through without much ado. Chicken broth as a cooking liquid lent the carrots savory backbone and a full, round flavor, whereas water left them hollow and wine turned them sour and astringent. We tried swapping the sugar for more compelling sweeteners but found brown sugar too muddy-flavored, maple syrup too assertive, and honey too floral (but good for a variation, we noted). We stood by clean, pure, easy-to-measure granulated sugar.

We moved on to finessing the glaze. After the carrots simmered for a few minutes, when just on the verge of tender (they would see more heat during glazing, so we simmered them shy of done), we lifted the lid from the skillet, stepped up the heat, and let the liquid reduce down. (If the liquid is not reduced, it is thin and watery.) Finally, we added butter (cut into small pieces for quick melting) and a bit more sugar to encourage glaze formation and to favorably increase sweetness. All of this resulted in a light, clingy glaze that with a few more minutes of high-heat cooking took on a pale amber hue and a light caramel flavor. A sprinkle of fresh lemon juice gave the dish sparkle, and a twist or two of freshly ground black pepper provided depth. We were surprised, as were our tasters, that glazed carrots could be this good and this easy.

Glazed Carrots

SERVES 4

Glazed carrots are a good accompaniment to roasts of any kind—beef, pork, lamb, or poultry. A nonstick skillet is easier to clean, but this recipe can be prepared in any 12-inch skillet with a cover.

I	pound carrots (about 6 medium), peeled and sliced ¼ inch thick on the bias (see the illustration below)
½	teaspoon salt
3	tablespoons sugar
½	cup low-sodium chicken broth
I	tablespoon unsalted butter, cut into 4 pieces
2	teaspoons juice from I lemon
	Ground black pepper

1. Bring the carrots, salt, 1 tablespoon of the sugar, and the broth to a boil in a 12-inch nonstick skillet, covered, over medium-high heat. Reduce the heat to medium and simmer, stirring occasionally, until the carrots are almost tender when poked with the tip of a paring knife, about 5 minutes.

SLICING CARROTS ON THE BIAS

Cut the carrots on the bias into rounds about ¼ inch thick and 2 inches long.

Uncover, increase the heat to high, and simmer rapidly, stirring occasionally, until the liquid is reduced to about 2 tablespoons, 1 to 2 minutes.

2. Add the butter and remaining 2 tablespoons sugar to the skillet. Toss the carrots to coat and cook, stirring frequently, until the carrots are completely tender and the glaze is light gold, about 3 minutes. Off the heat, add the lemon juice and toss to coat. Transfer the carrots to a serving dish, scraping the glaze from the pan into the dish. Season with pepper to taste. Serve immediately.

➤ VARIATIONS

Glazed Carrots with Bacon and Pecans

Granulated sugar works best in our traditional glazed carrots, but in this variation light brown sugar was the best choice. Its rich caramel flavor goes well with the bacon and pecans.

3	ounces (about 3 slices) bacon, cut into ½-inch pieces
⅓	cup chopped pecans
I	pound carrots (about 6 medium), peeled and sliced ¼ inch thick on the bias (see the illustration at left)
½	teaspoon salt
3	tablespoons light brown sugar
½	cup low-sodium chicken broth
½	teaspoon minced fresh thyme leaves
I	tablespoon unsalted butter, cut into 4 pieces
2	teaspoons juice from I lemon
	Ground black pepper

1. Cook the bacon in a 12-inch nonstick skillet over medium-high heat until crisp. Transfer the bacon to a paper towel–lined plate to drain.

2. Remove all but 1 tablespoon of the bacon drippings from the pan. Add the pecans and cook until fragrant and lightly browned, about 3 minutes. Transfer to the plate with the bacon.

3. Add the carrots, salt, 1 tablespoon of the brown sugar, the broth, and thyme to the skillet. Bring to a boil, covered, over medium-high heat. Reduce the heat to medium and simmer, stirring occasionally, until the carrots are almost tender when poked with the tip of a paring knife, about 5 minutes. Uncover, increase the heat to high,

and simmer rapidly, stirring occasionally, until the liquid is reduced to about 2 tablespoons, 1 to 2 minutes.

4. Add the butter and remaining 2 tablespoons brown sugar to the skillet. Toss the carrots to coat and cook, stirring frequently, until the carrots are completely tender, about 3 minutes. Off the heat, add the reserved bacon-pecan mixture and the lemon juice, and toss to coat. Transfer the carrots to a serving dish, scraping the glaze from the pan into the dish. Season with pepper to taste and serve immediately.

Glazed Carrots with Orange and Cranberries

Dried cherries can be used in place of the cranberries if you prefer.

I	pound carrots (about 6 medium), peeled and sliced ¼ inch thick on the bias (see the illustration on page 149)
¼	cup dried cranberries
½	teaspoon salt
2	tablespoons sugar
¼	cup low-sodium chicken broth
½	teaspoon grated zest and ¼ cup juice from I orange
I	tablespoon unsalted butter, cut into 4 pieces Ground black pepper

1. Bring the carrots, cranberries, salt, 1 table-spoon of the sugar, the broth, and orange zest and juice to a boil in a 12-inch nonstick skillet, covered, over medium-high heat. Reduce the heat to medium and simmer, stirring occasionally, until the carrots are almost tender when poked with the tip of a paring knife, about 5 minutes. Uncover, increase the heat to high, and simmer rapidly, stirring occasionally, until the liquid is reduced to about 2 tablespoons, 1 to 2 minutes.

2. Add the butter and remaining 1 tablespoon sugar to the skillet. Toss the carrots to coat and cook, stirring frequently, until they are completely tender, about 3 minutes. Transfer the carrots to a serving dish, scraping the glaze from the pan into the dish. Season with pepper to taste and serve immediately.

ROASTED CARROTS

THE SUBLIME NATURE OF ROASTED CARROTS lies in their rustic charm. Simple, sweet, and pure, their perfectly caramelized outer layer gently gives way to a smooth, tender interior—unless they are undercooked and have a crisp, bitter center or, on the opposite end of the spectrum, are subjected to such intense heat that they become wan, limp, and utterly unpalatable. Our ideal roasted carrot recipe, we decided, would be one that would let us throw a couple of ingredients together, toss the carrots into the oven, and let them roast until they were done—a tasty, simple, and effortless side dish.

We started with the basic question of what type of carrot to use. We tested bunch carrots (those with greens still attached), bagged carrots, and bagged baby carrots. The bagged whole carrots were too toothy, fibrous, and bitter. Baby and bunch carrots were the best—sweet and tender. While the flavor and presentation of bunch carrots edged out the bagged babies (bunch carrots were breathtaking when roasted whole with just a nub of green stem left attached), the baby carrots needed no peeling, trimming, or chopping. They were effortless and easy, just what we had in mind.

Still, without a little help from a fatty cohort, we knew that the glossy, bronzed carrots we envisioned would not be possible. So we tossed batches of carrots with vegetable oil, olive oil, extra-virgin olive oil, butter, and clarified butter and roasted them. We were surprised to discover that our favorite was plain olive oil; it neither masked the carrots' sweetness, as did extra-virgin olive and vegetable oils, nor changed their texture, as did the butter.

We next examined possible roasting methods, times, and temperatures. We tried covering the broiler pan with foil to help keep the carrots moist and hasten the roasting, but when we pulled these carrots out from their sealed bed, they had become reminiscent of cafeteria carrots: slightly bitter, pale, and soggy. Carrots covered for only part of the roasting time fared little better. The best batch was the most straightforward: roasted at 475 degrees, uncovered, for 20 minutes, until the carrots were brown and caramel colored.

We proceeded to roast carrots in different sorts of pans to see which would give us the best color and the easiest cleanup. After pitting broiler pan bottoms against rimmed baking sheets and roasting pans against Pyrex dishes and nonstick aluminum pans, we found the broiler pan bottom to be the best for browning the carrots without burning them.

During this testing, we came to wonder just what a baby carrot is. Bagged baby carrots are made by taking long, thin carrots (usually carrot varieties grown for their high sugar and beta carotene content, which makes them sweet and bright in color) and forcing them through a carrot-trimming machine that peels the carrots and cuts them down to their ubiquitous baby size.

Real baby carrots are varieties of carrots that are miniature in size when mature; contrary to popular belief, they are not carrots of the standard length that are picked early. Unfortunately, real baby carrots are available only through specialty produce purveyors that sell to restaurants and other professional kitchens. If you are lucky enough to spy true, greens-still-attached, tapered baby carrots in your grocery store or farmers' market, buy them in the cooler months and roast according to our recipe. Baby carrots harvested in the warmer spring and summer months tend to be less sweet.

Roasted Carrots

SERVES 8

Inspect your bag of baby carrots carefully for pockets of water. Carrots taken from the top of the supermarket's carrot pile are often waterlogged. This not only makes carrots mealy, it also dashes any hopes of caramelization in the oven.

2	pounds baby carrots (two 16-ounce bags)
2	tablespoons olive oil
1/2	teaspoon salt

Adjust an oven rack to the middle position and heat the oven to 475 degrees. Toss the carrots, oil, and salt in the broiler pan bottom. Spread the carrots in a single layer and roast for 12 minutes. Shake the pan to toss the carrots. Continue roasting, shaking the pan twice more, until the carrots are browned and tender, about 8 minutes longer. Serve immediately.

➤ VARIATIONS

Roasted Baby Carrots with Rosemary, Thyme, and Shallots

Follow the recipe for Roasted Carrots, tossing 1 tablespoon minced fresh rosemary leaves, 2 teaspoons minced fresh thyme leaves, and 2 shallots, sliced, with the carrots, oil, and salt.

Roasted Baby Carrots with Sage and Walnuts

Toast the walnuts in a small skillet over medium heat until fragrant, about 5 minutes, then cool and chop.

Follow the recipe for Roasted Carrots, tossing 1 tablespoon minced fresh sage leaves with the carrots, oil, and salt. Just before serving, sprinkle the roasted carrots with 1/3 cup chopped toasted walnuts.

Roasted Maple Carrots with Browned Butter

Follow the recipe for Roasted Carrots, decreasing the oil to 1½ teaspoons. After the carrots have roasted for 10 minutes, heat 1 tablespoon butter in a small saucepan over medium heat, swirling the pan occasionally, until deep gold, about 1 minute. Off the heat, stir in 1 tablespoon maple syrup. Drizzle the maple-butter mixture over the carrots after 12 minutes of roasting. Shake the pan to coat and continue roasting as directed.

Roasted Carrots with Ginger-Orange Glaze

Follow the recipe for Roasted Carrots. After the carrots have roasted for 10 minutes, bring 1 heaping tablespoon orange marmalade, 1 tablespoon water, and ½ teaspoon grated fresh ginger to a simmer in a small saucepan over medium-high heat. Drizzle the marmalade mixture over the carrots after 12 minutes of roasting. Shake the pan to coat and continue roasting as directed.

CAULIFLOWER

MANY OF US IN THE TEST KITCHEN GREW UP eating soggy, overcooked cauliflower cloaked in a thick layer of congealing neon-yellow cheese. Some of us ate the cheesy sauce, but no one remembers liking (or eating) the cauliflower. With time (and experience), we have learned that cauliflower doesn't have to be prepared this way. When properly cooked and imaginatively flavored, cauliflower can be nutty, slightly sweet, and absolutely delicious.

We started our testing by trying to develop a quick stovetop method for cooking cauliflower. During our first round at the stove, we made two important observations. First, we noticed that cauliflower is very porous. This can work to cauliflower's advantage or disadvantage, depending on what the cauliflower absorbs during cooking. We identified two basic cooking methods that went hand in hand with this observation. In the first method, the cauliflower is fully cooked (boiled or steamed), then flavored. In this scenario, keeping the water out is key. In the second method, the cauliflower is flavored as it cooks, which means that you want to get the liquid in. Our new goal was to test the variables for both methods and devise two master recipes with plenty of creative variations.

We first worked on perfecting the "cook first, flavor later" technique. In this method, the cauliflower is fully cooked by boiling, steaming, or microwaving, then tossed with a light vinaigrette or sautéed briefly in butter or oil with simple flavorings.

We began by comparing boiling, steaming, and microwaving. The boiled cauliflower tasted watery; regardless of how long we boiled it, from underdone to overcooked, the first flavor to reach our taste buds was the cooking water. Steaming the cauliflower for seven to eight minutes, on the other hand, produced evenly cooked florets with a clean, bright, sweet flavor.

To verify our strong impression that steamed cauliflower was less watery than the boiled version, we compared the raw and cooked weights of cauliflower cooked by each method. With steaming, there was no weight increase. With boiling,

the cauliflower gained approximately 10 percent of its original weight.

Next we moved to the "flavor while cooking" approach. The basic technique was braising, which involves cooking with a small amount of liquid in a covered container. We hoped that the cooking liquid—our foe in the previous method—would now become our friend. But we were curious as to how this was best done. Should the cauliflower simply be braised with no previous cooking? Or should it be sautéed first, then finished by braising? Or what about partially cooking via the steaming method and then braising?

After testing these three methods, we immediately realized the benefits of sautéing the cauliflower first, then adding some flavorings and liquids and braising the vegetable until tender. Braising the dense vegetable with no precooking simply took too long. Not only did we have to stand over the stove to make sure that it did not overcook, this method also created some of the same problems of liquid absorption that we had found when boiling. When we partially cooked the cauliflower by steaming it and then braising it, the taste was lackluster and flat. Sautéing it for seven minutes on medium-high heat and then braising it, however, intensified the cauliflower's naturally mild flavors. Not only did the cauliflower absorb the flavors from the braising liquid, but the browned cauliflower also tasted wonderfully smoky and earthy.

Cooking cauliflower too long can release unpleasant sulfur-containing compounds in the vegetable that break down when exposed to heat. To avoid this problem, we found it best to cut the cauliflower into 1-inch pieces that will cook uniformly and quickly. With the brown-and-braise method, we also liked how the cut surface of the florets lay flat in the sauté pan. Those cut surfaces browned beautifully, and the sweetness of those florets was pronounced.

We also discovered that just because the tip of a knife slipped in and out of the stem of the cauliflower easily, the cauliflower was not necessarily done. The best way to test for doneness is, quite simply, to sample a piece.

Steamed Cauliflower

SERVES 4

The best complements to the fresh, delicate flavor of steamed cauliflower are mild herbs, nuts, citrus, or simple flavor combinations such as those below. Steamed cauliflower can also be served as is, with just a drizzle of extra-virgin olive oil and a sprinkle of salt.

| 1 | medium head cauliflower (about 2 pounds), prepared according to the illustrations below |

Fit a large saucepan with a steamer basket. Fill the pan with enough water to reach just below the bottom of the basket. Cover and bring the water to a boil over high heat. Add the florets to the basket, reduce the heat to medium, cover, and steam until the cauliflower is tender but firm, about 7 minutes. Remove the cauliflower from the basket and serve, or finish with one of the variations.

➤ VARIATIONS

Steamed Cauliflower with Browned Butter, Walnuts, and Crispy Sage

4	tablespoons (1/2 stick) unsalted butter
1/4	cup walnuts, chopped coarse
1	tablespoon thinly sliced fresh sage leaves
1	recipe Steamed Cauliflower
	Salt and ground black pepper

Heat the butter in a small, heavy-bottomed saucepan over medium heat and cook, swirling frequently, until the butter begins to brown, 3 to 4 minutes. Add the walnuts and cook, stirring constantly, until the nuts become fragrant, about 1 minute longer. Add the sage and cook until the sage becomes crispy, about 30 seconds. Toss the cauliflower gently with the browned butter mixture in a serving bowl. Season with salt and pepper to taste. Serve immediately.

Steamed Cauliflower with Cheddar-Mustard Cream Sauce

Because this sauce does not include flour (therefore eliminating the need for the sauce to boil), it is lighter in texture and quicker to make than most other cheese sauces. The combination of cheddar cheese and mustard goes well with the cauliflower.

1	cup heavy cream
4	ounces cheddar cheese, shredded (about 1 cup)
1	tablespoon whole-grain mustard
	Pinch cayenne pepper
	Salt and ground black pepper
1	recipe Steamed Cauliflower

Place the cream in a small saucepan and bring to a bare simmer over medium heat. When the cream is steaming and just starting to bubble around the edge of the pan, turn off the heat and add the cheese, mustard, and cayenne. Whisk together until smooth. Season with salt and pepper to taste.

PREPARING CAULIFLOWER

  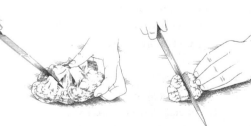

1. Start by pulling off the outer leaves and trimming off the stem near the base of the head.

2. Turn the cauliflower upside down so the stem is facing up. Using a sharp knife, cut around the core to remove it.

3. Using the tip of a chef's knife, separate the florets from the inner stem.

4. Cut the florets in half, or in quarters, if necessary, so that individual pieces are about 1 inch square.

Toss the cauliflower gently with the cheese sauce in a serving bowl. Adjust the seasonings and serve immediately.

Steamed Cauliflower with Bread Crumbs, Capers, and Chopped Egg

2	tablespoons unsalted butter
3	tablespoons dry bread crumbs
1	recipe Steamed Cauliflower
1½	tablespoons juice from 1 lemon
2	tablespoons minced fresh parsley leaves
2	tablespoons capers, rinsed
1	large hard-boiled egg (see page 122), pressed through a sieve to crumble very fine (see the illustration at right)
	Salt and ground black pepper

Heat the butter in a large skillet over medium heat until foaming, about 1½ minutes. Add the bread crumbs and cook, stirring occasionally, until lightly browned, about 5 minutes. Add the cauliflower and cook to heat through, about 1 minute. Add the lemon juice, parsley, capers, and egg and toss lightly to distribute. Season with salt and pepper to taste and serve immediately.

Braised Cauliflower with Garlic and Tomatoes

SERVES 4

We found that you can braise cauliflower in almost any liquid—broth, canned tomatoes, wine, or coconut milk. This preparation is fairly simple and pretty close to a master recipe.

2½	tablespoons olive oil
1	medium head cauliflower (about 2 pounds), prepared according to the illustrations on page 153
3	medium garlic cloves, minced or pressed through a garlic press
¼	teaspoon red pepper flakes
1	(14.5-ounce) can diced tomatoes
2	tablespoons minced fresh basil leaves
	Salt

CRUMBLING HARD-BOILED EGGS

For very fine pieces of hard-boiled egg, press the egg through a mesh sieve.

1. Heat 2 tablespoons of the oil in a large skillet over medium-high heat until shimmering. Add the cauliflower and cook, stirring occasionally, until the florets begin to brown, 6 to 7 minutes. Clear a space in the center of the pan and add the garlic, red pepper flakes, and remaining ½ tablespoon oil. Mash and stir the garlic mixture in the center of the pan until the mixture becomes fragrant, about 1 minute. Stir to combine the garlic mixture and cauliflower and cook 1 minute longer.

2. Add the tomatoes, cover, and cook until the cauliflower is tender but still offers some resistance to the tooth when sampled, 4 to 5 minutes. Add the basil and season with salt to taste. Serve immediately.

Braised Cauliflower with Anchovies, Garlic, and White Wine

SERVES 4

Adjust the amount of red pepper flakes to increase the heat of this dish. See the illustrations on page 266 for tips on mincing the anchovies.

2½	tablespoons olive oil
1	medium head cauliflower (about 2 pounds), prepared according to the illustrations on page 153
2	medium anchovy fillets, minced to a paste

3 medium garlic cloves, minced or pressed through a garlic press
1/2 teaspoon red pepper flakes
1/3 cup dry white wine
1/3 cup low-sodium chicken broth
2 tablespoons minced fresh parsley leaves
Salt

1. Heat 2 tablespoons of the oil in a large skillet over medium-high heat until shimmering. Add the cauliflower and cook, stirring occasionally, until the florets begin to brown, 6 to 7 minutes. Clear a space in the center of the pan and add the anchovies, garlic, red pepper flakes, and remaining ½ tablespoon oil. Mash and stir the garlic mixture in the center of the pan until the mixture becomes fragrant, about 1 minute. Stir to combine the garlic mixture and cauliflower and cook 1 minute longer.

2. Add the white wine and broth, cover, and cook until cauliflower is tender but still offers some resistance to the tooth when sampled, 4 to 5 minutes. Add the parsley and season with salt to taste. Serve immediately.

CORN

DESPITE FARM-STAND SIGNS ACROSS THE COUNTRY announcing "butter and sugar" corn for sale, no one really grows old-time butter and sugar corn anymore. Nor does anybody grow most of the other old-fashioned nonhybrid varieties. These bygone varieties of corn have disappeared for a reason. They converted sugar into starch so rapidly once picked that people literally fired up their kettles before going out to gather the corn. Corn has since been crossbred to make for sweeter ears that have a longer hold on their fresh flavor and tender texture.

Basically, there are three hybrid types: normal sugary, sugar enhanced, and supersweet. Each contains dozens of varieties, with fancy names such as Kandy Korn, Double Gem, and Mystique. Normal sugary types, such as Silver Queen, are moderately sweet, with traditional corn flavor. The sugars in this type of corn convert to starch rapidly after being picked. The sugar-enhanced types are more tender and somewhat sweeter, with a slower conversion of sugar to starch. Supersweet corn has heightened sweetness, a crisp texture, and a remarkably slow conversion of sugar to starch after being picked. It is a popular type for growers who supply distant markets and require a product with a longer shelf life. Any corn sold in your supermarket during the off-season is likely a variety of supersweet.

Beyond the above generalizations, it's impossible to tell which kind of corn you have unless you taste it. With that in mind, we developed cooking methods that would work with all three kinds of corn hybrids. Boiling is probably the most all-purpose cooking method. To increase sweetness, we tried adding milk to the water but found it muddied the corn flavor. Salt toughens the corn up a bit and is best added at the table. Sugar can be added to the water to enhance the corn's

DRY-TOASTING GARLIC

Toasting garlic cloves in a dry skillet tames their harsh flavor and loosens the skins for easy peeling. The garlic does not become soft and creamy like garlic roasted in the oven.

1. Place the unpeeled garlic cloves in a dry skillet over medium-high heat. Toast, shaking the pan occasionally, until the skins are golden brown, about 5 minutes. Transfer the toasted cloves to a cutting board and cool.

2. When cooled, the once-clingy skins peel off readily. The garlic can now be sliced, chopped, or minced as you normally would, but it will have far less bite.

sweetness, but when we tried this with supersweet corn, it tasted too sweet, almost like dessert.

Grilling is our other preferred method for cooking corn. The ideal grilled corn retains the juiciness of boiled corn without sacrificing the toasty caramelization and smoke-infused graces of the grill. We started our tests with the bare ear cooked directly over a medium-high fire. The outcome seemed too good to be true. The lightly caramelized corn was still juicy, but with a toasty hit of grilled flavor and a sweet essence to chase it down. In fact, it was too good to be true. The variety of corn we used was fittingly called Fantasy, which is a supersweet variety. When we tried grilling a normal sugary corn variety with the husks off, the outcome was a flavorless, dry, gummy turnoff. The end result was no better with sugar-enhanced corn. The direct heat was just too much for the fleeting flavors and tender texture of the normal sugary and sugar-enhanced corn types.

We went on to test another popular grilling technique: throw the whole ear on the grill, husks and all, as is. We tried this with all three sweet corn types at various heat levels. Half of the ears of corn were soaked beforehand; the other half were not. In sum, the husks-on method makes for a great-tasting ear of corn, and a particularly crisp, juicy one. But if it were not for the sticky charred husks that must be awkwardly peeled away at the table if you are to serve the corn hot, you would think you were eating boiled corn. The presoaked corn, in particular, just steams in the husks and picks up absolutely no grilled flavor.

Since grilling with the husks off was too aggressive for nonsupersweet varieties and grilling with the husks on was no different from boiled corn, we turned to a compromise approach. We peeled off the outer layers of husks but left the final layer that hugs the ear. This layer is much more moist and delicate than the outer layers, so much so that you can practically see the kernels through the husk. When cooked over a medium-high fire, this gave the corn a jacket heavy enough to prevent dehydration yet light enough to allow a gentle toasting of the kernels. After about eight minutes (rolling the corn one-quarter turn every

FLAVORED BUTTERS FOR BOILED CORN

Lime-Cilantro Butter

6 tablespoons (¾ stick) unsalted butter, softened
1½ teaspoons grated zest from 1 lime
1 tablespoon minced fresh cilantro leaves
Pinch cayenne pepper

Using a fork, beat the butter in a small bowl until light and fluffy. Beat in the lime zest, cilantro, and cayenne until well combined.

Roasted Garlic and Herb Butter

Dry-toasting garlic is a good option when you want to mellow the punch of raw garlic but don't want to take the time to roast a whole head of garlic in the oven. See the illustrations on page 155 for more information.

10 medium garlic cloves, skins left on, dry-toasted and then peeled according to the directions on page 155
6 tablespoons (¾ stick) unsalted butter, softened
1 tablespoon minced fresh parsley leaves
1 tablespoon minced fresh basil leaves
⅛ teaspoon ground black pepper

1. Mince the garlic cloves with a chef's knife or press through a garlic press.
2. Using a fork, beat the butter in a small bowl until light and fluffy. Beat in the garlic, herbs, and pepper until thoroughly combined.

two minutes), we could be certain that the corn was cooked just right, because the husks picked up a dark silhouette of the kernels and began to pull back at the corn's tip.

Boiled Corn
SERVES 8

If you want to serve more corn, bring a second pot of water to a boil at the same time, or cook the corn in batches in just one pot. If you know that you have supersweet corn, omit the sugar.

4   teaspoons sugar (optional)
8   ears fresh corn, husks and silk removed
    Salt and ground black pepper
    Plain butter or flavored butter (see page 156; optional)

Bring 4 quarts water and the sugar, if using, to a boil in a large pot. Add the corn, return to a boil, and cook until tender, 5 to 7 minutes. Drain the corn and season with salt and pepper to taste. Serve immediately, with butter if desired.

PREPARING CORN FOR GRILLING

1. Remove all but the innermost layer of husks. The kernels should be covered by, but visible through, the innermost layer.

2. Use scissors to snip off the tassel, or long silk ends, at the tip of the ear.

JUDGING WHEN GRILLED CORN IS DONE

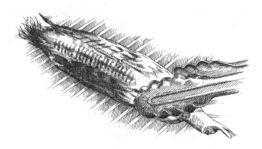

As soon as the husk picks up the dark silhouette of kernels and begins to pull away from the tip of the ear, the corn is ready to come off the grill.

Grilled Corn
SERVES 8

While grilling husks-on corn delivers great pure corn flavor, it lacks the smokiness of the grill; essentially, the corn is steamed in its protective husks. By leaving only the innermost layer, we were rewarded with perfectly tender corn graced with the grill's flavor. Prepared in this way, the corn does not need basting with oil. See the illustration above for tips on judging when the corn is ready to come off the grill.

8   ears fresh corn, prepared according to the illustrations at left
    Salt and ground black pepper
    Butter (optional)

1. Grill the corn over a medium-hot fire (you should be able to hold your hand 5 inches above the cooking grate for 3 to 4 seconds), turning the ears every 1½ to 2 minutes, until the dark outlines of the kernels show through the husk and the husk is charred and beginning to peel away from the tip to expose some kernels, 8 to 10 minutes.

2. Transfer the corn to a platter. Carefully remove and discard the charred husks and silk. Season the corn with salt and pepper to taste and butter, if desired. Serve immediately.

➤ VARIATIONS
Grilled Corn with Spicy Chili Butter

Sautéing the spices with the butter and garlic brings out their flavor. Because salt does not dissolve readily in butter, it's best to serve the salt on the side.

> 6 tablespoons (¾ stick) unsalted butter
> I garlic clove, minced or pressed through a garlic press
> I teaspoon chili powder
> ½ teaspoon ground cumin
> ½ teaspoon paprika
> ⅛ teaspoon cayenne pepper
> 8 ears fresh corn, prepared according to the illustrations on page 157
> I lime, cut into 8 wedges
> Salt

1. Melt the butter in a 10-inch skillet over medium heat. When the foaming subsides, add the garlic, chili powder, cumin, paprika, and cayenne and cook until fragrant, about 1 minute. Turn off the heat and set aside.

2. Grill the corn over a medium-hot fire (you should be able to hold your hand 5 inches above the cooking grate for 3 to 4 seconds), turning the ears every 1½ to 2 minutes, until the dark outlines of the kernels show through the husks and the husks are charred and beginning to peel away from the tip to expose some kernels, 8 to 10 minutes.

3. Transfer the corn to a platter. Carefully remove and discard the charred husks and silk. Using tongs, take each ear of corn and roll it in the spicy butter. Serve immediately, with lime wedges and salt to taste.

Grilled Corn with Garlic Butter and Cheese

> 6 tablespoons (¾ stick) unsalted butter
> I garlic clove, minced or pressed through a garlic press
> 8 ears fresh corn, prepared according to the illustrations on page 157
> ¼ cup freshly grated Parmesan cheese
> Salt

1. Melt the butter in a 10-inch skillet over medium heat. When the foaming subsides, add the garlic and cook until fragrant, about 30 seconds. Remove the pan from the heat.

2. Grill the corn over a medium-hot fire (you should be able to hold your hand 5 inches above the cooking grate for 3 to 4 seconds), turning the ears every 1½ to 2 minutes, until the dark outlines of the kernels show through the husks and the husks are charred and beginning to peel away from the tip to expose some kernels, 8 to 10 minutes.

3. Transfer the corn to a platter. Carefully remove and discard the charred husks and silk. Using tongs, take each ear of corn and roll it in the garlic butter. Sprinkle each ear with a portion of cheese and serve immediately with salt to taste.

Grilled Corn with Soy-Honey Glaze

Corn grilled with soy sauce is a familiar sight at summer fairs and festivals in Japan. Returning the glazed ears of corn to the grill caramelizes the sugar in the sauce and gives the corn a deep, smoky flavor.

> ⅓ cup honey
> ⅓ cup soy sauce
> 8 ears fresh corn, prepared according to the illustrations on page 157

1. Mix the honey and soy sauce together in a 10-inch skillet. Bring to a simmer over medium-high heat. Reduce the heat to medium and simmer until slightly syrupy and reduced to about ½ cup, about 5 minutes. Turn off the heat and set aside.

2. Grill the corn over a medium-hot fire (you should be able to hold your hand 5 inches above the cooking grate for 3 to 4 seconds), turning the ears every 1½ to 2 minutes, until the dark outlines of the kernels show through the husks and the husks are charred and beginning to peel away from the tip to expose some kernels, 8 to 10 minutes.

3. Transfer the corn to a platter. Carefully remove and discard the charred husks and silk. Using tongs, take each ear of corn and roll it in the soy mixture. Return the glazed corn to the grill for an additional 1 to 2 minutes, turning once. Serve immediately.

CREAMED CORN

ALTHOUGH CREAMED CORN IS AVAILABLE any time of year out of the can, it doesn't compare with the clean, sweet flavor of late-summer corn gently simmered with fresh cream. But if you don't handle the fresh corn and cream correctly, you wind up with that overcooked, just-out-of-the-can flavor you were trying to avoid.

Many recipes start by boiling the corn on the cob, then cutting the kernels off the cob and mixing them with a cream sauce. This technique, however, loses much of the sweet, delicate corn flavor to the cooking water. We quickly rejected this method in favor of recipes that simmer the corn kernels (which are first cut free from the cobs) directly in the cream. This technique releases their sugary, summery flavor into the sauce, which is where you want it to be.

Simply simmering fresh corn kernels in cream, however, wasn't enough. It produced a thin, lumpy mixture that lacked the thickened, spoonable texture we desired. Scraping the pulp out of the spent cobs helped a bit, but we wanted the sauce a bit thicker. Flour and cornstarch just made the sauce gummy and overwhelmed the flavor of the corn. We then tried grating a few of the ears, which broke down some of the kernels into smaller pieces. This did the trick. By grating some of the raw kernels off the cob, we were able to release more of the corn's natural thickener. We found that grating about half of the corn in our recipe thickened the sauce sufficiently.

After making a few batches of this recipe with different types of corn, we realized that the cooking times can differ, depending on the corn's variety and age. While some kernels cooked perfectly in only 10 minutes, others needed five minutes longer. We also found that as the corn and cream cook and thicken, the heat needs to be adjusted to keep the mixture at a simmer to prevent the bottom from burning.

As for the other ingredients, we tried using half-and-half instead of heavy cream, but tasters missed the luxurious flavor and heft provided by the latter. A little shallot, garlic, and fresh thyme complemented the delicate flavor of the corn, while a pinch of cayenne added a little kick.

Creamed Corn
SERVES 6 TO 8

For the best texture and flavor, we like a combination of grated corn, whole kernels (cut away from the cobs with a knife), and corn milk (scraped from all the ears with the back of a knife). See the illustrations on pages 64–65 for tips on cutting the kernels off some ears of corn and grating (milking) the rest of the corn.

5	medium ears fresh corn, husks and silk removed
2	tablespoons unsalted butter
I	medium shallot, minced
I	medium garlic clove, minced or pressed through a garlic press
I½	cups heavy cream
½	teaspoon minced fresh thyme leaves
	Pinch cayenne pepper
	Salt and ground black pepper

1. Cut the kernels from 3 ears of corn and transfer them to a medium bowl. Firmly scrape the cobs with the back of a butter knife to collect the pulp and milk in the same bowl. Grate the remaining 2 ears of corn on the coarse side of a box grater set in the bowl with the cut kernels. Firmly scrape these cobs with the back of a butter knife to collect the pulp and milk in the same bowl.

2. Melt the butter in a medium saucepan over medium-high heat. When the foaming subsides, add the shallot and cook until softened but not browned, 1 to 2 minutes. Add the garlic and cook until aromatic, about 30 seconds. Stir in the corn kernels and pulp as well as the cream, thyme, cayenne, ¼ teaspoon salt, and ⅛ teaspoon pepper. Bring the mixture to a simmer and cook, adjusting the heat as necessary and stirring occasionally, until the corn is tender and the mixture has thickened, 10 to 15 minutes. Remove the pan from the heat, adjust the seasonings with salt and pepper to taste, and serve immediately.

➤ VARIATION

Creamed Corn with Bacon and Blue Cheese
Use your favorite kind of blue cheese for this variation. Gorgonzola works as well. Because of the saltiness of the bacon and blue cheese, adding salt may not be necessary.

5   medium ears fresh corn, husks and silk removed

4   ounces (about 4 slices) bacon, cut into
     1/2-inch pieces

1   medium shallot, minced

1   medium garlic clove, minced or pressed
     through a garlic press

1 1/2 cups heavy cream

1/2 teaspoon minced fresh thyme leaves
     Pinch cayenne pepper

2   ounces blue cheese, crumbled (about 1/2 cup)
     Salt and ground black pepper

1. Cut the kernels from 3 ears of corn and transfer them to a medium bowl. Firmly scrape the cobs with the back of a butter knife to collect the pulp and milk in the same bowl. Grate the remaining 2 ears of corn on the coarse side of a box grater set in the bowl with the cut kernels. Firmly scrape these cobs with the back of a butter knife to collect the pulp and milk in the same bowl.

2. Cook the bacon in a large nonstick skillet over medium-high heat until crisp and browned, about 5 minutes. Transfer the bacon to a paper towel–lined plate to drain.

3. Remove and discard all but 2 tablespoons of the bacon drippings from the pan. Add the shallot and cook until softened but not browned, 1 to 2 minutes. Add the garlic and cook until aromatic, about 30 seconds. Stir in the corn kernels and pulp, as well as the cream, thyme, and cayenne. Bring the

SCIENCE: Corn Storage

While the general rule of thumb is to buy and eat corn the same day it has been harvested (as soon as the corn is harvested, the sugars start converting to starches and the corn loses sweetness), most of us have been guilty of trying to break that rule for one reason or another. We tried a variety of methods for overnight storage using Silver Queen corn, one of the more perishable varieties. We found that the worst thing you can do to corn is to leave it sitting out on the counter. Throwing it into the refrigerator without any wrapping is nearly as bad. Storing in an airtight bag helps, but the hands-down winner entailed wrapping the corn (husks left on) in a wet paper bag and then in a plastic bag (any shopping bag will do). After 24 hours of storage, we found the corn stored this way to be juicy and sweet—not starchy—and fresh-tasting.

mixture to a simmer and cook, adjusting the heat as necessary and stirring occasionally, until the corn is tender and the mixture has thickened, 10 to 15 minutes. Remove the pan from the heat and stir in the cheese. Adjust the seasonings with salt and pepper to taste and serve immediately.

EGGPLANT

EGGPLANT CAN BE PREPARED IN SEVERAL ways, including sautéing, grilling, and stir-frying. The biggest challenge that confronts the cook when preparing eggplant is excess moisture. While the grill will evaporate this liquid and allow the eggplant to brown nicely, this won't happen under the broiler or in a hot pan. The eggplant will steam in its own juices. The result can be an insipid flavor and mushy texture.

Salting is the classic technique for drawing moisture out of the eggplant before cooking. We experimented with both regular table salt and kosher salt and preferred kosher salt because the crystals are large enough to wipe away after the salt has done its job. Finer table salt crystals dissolved into the eggplant flesh and had to be flushed out with water. Although traditional recipes call for letting the salted eggplant drain in a colander, we had better results when we placed the salted eggplant on a baking sheet lined with paper towels. In a colander, the eggplant juices tended to fall from one piece to another. On the paper towel–lined baking sheet, the juices were absorbed as soon as they were drawn out of the eggplant. And to further absorb any moisture, we also lightly press the eggplant with paper towels.

The eggplant must then be thoroughly dried, especially if it has been diced for sautéing. We prefer to dice eggplant that will be sautéed to increase the surface area that can brown and absorb flavorings.

When grilling, you want thicker slices that won't fall apart on the cooking grate. We found ¾-inch rounds perfect for grilling. And because the liquid can fall onto the coals, there's no need to salt eggplant destined for the grill.

Stir-frying is basically the same as sautéing except that the finished dish is saucier. In this case, liquid from the eggplant is not such a problem. The eggplant is browned and then sauced quite generously so its texture will correctly be soft rather than crisp or firm. In addition, stir-fry sauces often contain soy sauce and are quite salty. For all these reasons, we found it best to skip salting eggplant when using it in a stir-fry. However, stir-frying works best with small, firm eggplants (sometimes labeled Asian eggplants in markets). Rather than dicing the eggplant (as we do for sautéing), we had the best results when we cut small eggplants in half lengthwise and then crosswise into ½-inch-thick half-moons.

Sautéed Eggplant

SERVES 4

Very small eggplants (weighing less than 6 ounces each) may be cooked without salting. However, we found that larger eggplants generally have a lot of moisture, which is best removed before cooking.

- I   large eggplant (about 1½ pounds), ends trimmed, cut into ¾-inch cubes
- I   tablespoon kosher salt
- 2   tablespoons extra-virgin olive oil
      Ground black pepper
- I   medium garlic clove, minced or pressed through a garlic press
- 2   tablespoons minced fresh parsley leaves or finely shredded fresh basil leaves

1. Place the eggplant cubes on a paper towel–lined rimmed baking sheet and sprinkle the cubes with the salt, tossing to coat them evenly. Let the eggplant stand for at least 30 minutes. Using additional paper towels, gently press any excess moisture from the eggplant.

2. Heat the oil in a heavy-bottomed 12-inch skillet over medium-high heat until shimmering. Add the eggplant cubes and cook until they begin to brown, about 4 minutes. Reduce the heat to medium-low and cook, stirring occasionally, until the eggplant is fully tender and lightly browned, about 10 minutes. Stir in pepper to taste and add the garlic. Cook to blend the flavors, about 2 minutes. Off the heat, stir in the parsley. Serve immediately.

➤ VARIATIONS

Sautéed Eggplant with Cumin and Garlic

Sautéing the spices in the oil makes their flavors bloom.

- I   large eggplant (about 1½ pounds), ends trimmed, cut into ¾-inch cubes
- I   tablespoon kosher salt
- 2   tablespoons vegetable oil
- I   teaspoon ground cumin
- ½   teaspoon chili powder
- 2   medium garlic cloves, minced or pressed through a garlic press
- I   teaspoon sugar
- I   tablespoon minced fresh parsley leaves

1. Place the eggplant cubes on a paper towel–lined rimmed baking sheet and sprinkle the cubes with the salt, tossing to coat them evenly. Let the eggplant stand for at least 30 minutes. Using additional paper towels, gently press any excess moisture from the eggplant.

2. Heat the oil in a heavy-bottomed 12-inch skillet over medium high-heat until shimmering. Add the cumin and chili powder and cook until fragrant, about 20 seconds. Add the eggplant cubes and cook until they begin to brown, about 4 minutes. Reduce the heat to medium-low and cook, stirring occasionally, until the eggplant is fully tender and lightly browned, about 10 minutes. Stir in the garlic and sugar. Cook to blend the flavors, about 2 minutes. Off the heat, stir in the parsley. Serve immediately.

Sautéed Eggplant with Pancetta and Rosemary

Pancetta is unsmoked Italian bacon (for more information, see page 255). It can be found in the deli section of most large grocery stores. If pancetta is unavailable, bacon can be substituted.

- I   large eggplant (about 1½ pounds), ends trimmed, cut into ¾-inch cubes
- I   tablespoon kosher salt
- 3   ounces pancetta, diced fine
- I   small onion, halved and sliced thin
- ½   teaspoon minced fresh rosemary leaves
      Ground black pepper

THE EFFECTS OF SALTING EGGPLANT

BEFORE SALTING   AFTER SALTING

Salting and pressing eggplant collapses the cell walls, eliminating air pockets that would otherwise soak up fat during cooking.

1. Place the eggplant cubes on a paper towel–lined rimmed baking sheet and sprinkle the cubes with the salt, tossing to coat them evenly. Let the eggplant stand for at least 30 minutes. Using additional paper towels, gently press any excess moisture from the eggplant.

2. Cook the pancetta in a heavy-bottomed 12-inch skillet over medium-high heat until crisp, about 5 minutes. Use a slotted spoon to transfer the pancetta to a plate. Add the onion and rosemary to the rendered fat in the pan and cook, stirring frequently, until golden, about 4 minutes. Add the eggplant cubes and cook until they begin to brown, about 4 minutes. Reduce the heat to medium-low and cook, stirring occasionally, until the eggplant is fully tender and lightly browned, about 10 minutes. Stir in the pancetta and pepper to taste. Serve immediately.

Grilled Eggplant

SERVES 4

There's no need to salt eggplant destined for the grill. The intense grill heat will vaporize excess moisture.

3   tablespoons extra-virgin olive oil
2   medium garlic cloves, minced or pressed through a garlic press
2   teaspoons minced fresh thyme or oregano leaves
     Salt and ground black pepper
1   large eggplant (about 1½ pounds), ends trimmed, cut crosswise into ¾-inch-thick rounds

1. Combine the oil, garlic, thyme, and salt and pepper to taste in a small bowl. Place the eggplant on a platter and brush both sides with the oil mixture.

2. Grill the eggplant over a medium-hot fire (you should be able to hold your hand 5 inches above the cooking grate for 3 to 4 seconds), turning once, until both sides are marked with dark stripes, 8 to 10 minutes. Serve hot, warm, or at room temperature.

➤   VARIATIONS

Grilled Eggplant with Basil Oil

Make sure to cook the garlic until it is barely starting to sizzle. The oil will then be just hot enough to slightly wilt the basil when processed together.

¼   cup extra-virgin olive oil
1   medium garlic clove, minced or pressed through a garlic press
½   cup packed fresh basil leaves
     Salt and ground black pepper
1   recipe Grilled Eggplant

1. Place the oil and garlic in a skillet and turn the heat to medium. Cook until the garlic just starts to sizzle and becomes fragrant, about 2 minutes.

2. Place the basil in a food processor. Very carefully pour the hot oil over the basil. Process until the mixture is fragrant and almost smooth, about 30 seconds. Season with salt and pepper to taste.

3. Transfer the grilled eggplant to a platter and drizzle with the basil oil. Serve immediately.

Grilled Eggplant with Cherry Tomato and Cilantro Vinaigrette

Grape tomatoes can also be used in this recipe. Choose the ripest tomatoes for the best, most flavorful vinaigrette.

½   pint cherry tomatoes, each tomato quartered (about 1 cup)
¼   teaspoon salt
     Pinch cayenne pepper
1   medium shallot, minced
2   tablespoons minced fresh cilantro leaves
2   tablespoons juice from 1 lime
6   tablespoons olive oil
1   recipe Grilled Eggplant

1. Mix the tomatoes, salt, cayenne, shallot, cilantro, lime juice, and oil together in a medium bowl. Let stand at room temperature until the tomatoes are juicy and seasoned, about 20 minutes.

2. Transfer the grilled eggplant to a platter. Pour the vinaigrette over the eggplant and serve immediately.

Stir-Fried Eggplant
SERVES 4

Stir-frying eggplant is basically the same as sautéing it except that the finished dish is saucier. Stir-fry sauces typically contain soy sauce and are quite salty. Because of that, we found it best to skip the salting step for eggplant when using it in a stir-fry. Small, firm eggplants, sometimes labeled Asian eggplants, work best in this stir-fry. Rather than dicing the eggplants, we had the best results when we cut them in half lengthwise and then crosswise into ½-inch-thick half-moons. Buy eggplants that weigh about 8 ounces each.

¼	cup low-sodium chicken broth
2	tablespoons soy sauce
1½	teaspoons toasted sesame oil
1	tablespoon plus 1 teaspoon peanut oil
2	small eggplants (about 8 ounces each), ends trimmed, cut in half lengthwise, and cut crosswise into ½-inch-thick half-moons
1	medium garlic clove, minced or pressed through a garlic press
1	teaspoon minced fresh ginger
2	medium scallions, sliced thin

1. Whisk the broth, soy sauce, and sesame oil together in a small bowl.

2. Heat the 1 tablespoon peanut oil in a 12-inch, nonstick heavy-bottomed skillet over high heat until shimmering. Add the eggplant and cook, stirring frequently, until browned, about 3 minutes. Clear a space in the center of the pan and add the garlic, ginger, and remaining 1 teaspoon peanut oil. Cook until fragrant, about 10 seconds. Stir the garlic mixture into the eggplant and add the broth mixture. Cover, reduce the heat to medium, and cook until the sauce has thickened and the eggplant has softened, about 3 minutes. Garnish with the scallions and serve immediately.

➤ VARIATION
Stir-Fried Eggplant with Ground Pork and Peanut Sauce

Although this dish is intended as a side dish for 4, with rice it could feed 2 or 3 as a main course.

⅔	cup low-sodium chicken broth
1	tablespoon hoisin sauce
1	tablespoon soy sauce
2	tablespoons smooth peanut butter
1	tablespoon plus 2 teaspoons peanut oil
6	ounces ground pork
2	small eggplants (about 8 ounces each), ends trimmed, cut in half lengthwise, and cut crosswise into ½-inch-thick half-moons
1	medium garlic clove, minced or pressed through a garlic press
1	teaspoon minced fresh ginger
¼	teaspoon red pepper flakes
2	medium scallions, sliced thin

1. Whisk the broth, hoisin sauce, soy sauce, and peanut butter together in a medium bowl. (The peanut butter will not totally dissolve until it is added to the skillet.)

2. Heat 1 teaspoon of the oil in a 12-inch, nonstick heavy-bottomed skillet over high heat until shimmering. Add the ground pork and cook, stirring to break up the meat, until thoroughly cooked, about 3 minutes. Transfer the pork to a plate and set it aside.

3. Add the 1 tablespoon oil to the empty pan, swirl to coat the pan, and add the eggplant. Cook, stirring frequently, until browned, about 3 minutes. Clear a space in the center of the pan and add the garlic, ginger, pepper flakes, and remaining 1 teaspoon oil. Cook until fragrant, about 10 seconds. Stir in the cooked pork and sauce. Cover, reduce the heat to medium, and cook until the sauce has thickened and the eggplant has softened, about 4 minutes. Garnish with the scallions and serve immediately.

RATATOUILLE

THE WORD *RATATOUILLE* IS DERIVED FROM the French verb *touiller,* meaning "to stir." When it comes to interpretation of the method, there are two schools of thought. Included in the testing were the classic French preparation, in which vegetables are sautéed in olive oil in batches and combined at the last minute with minimal stirring, and a typical American ratatouille, in which everything is tossed into the pot at once and stewed until tender. In American-style ratatouille, it was difficult to distinguish eggplant from zucchini, and the whole amalgamation tasted like watery tomatoes. The batch-cooked ratatouille fared much better, although it was oily from the more than one cup of olive oil needed to keep the vegetables from sticking to the pan. On the plus side, the vegetables remained relatively intact, and the stew carried the flavors particular to each component. So we set out to deal with each vegetable individually, hoping to maximize texture and flavor while minimizing the amount of oil. We began with the eggplant, which is notorious for soaking up oil like a sponge; to minimize the oil, we decided to turn to high-heat cooking.

Because high heat draws out liquid and intensifies flavor, we started with the broiler. Still using the salting/pressing preparation for the eggplant, but this time pressing the eggplant more firmly to draw out even more moisture, we tossed the chunks with a little oil and slipped them under the broiler. The results were less than satisfying. The extreme heat from the broiler caused the eggplant to burn before the pieces were sufficiently dehydrated.

We then set our oven at 500 degrees, thinking that it would present no direct threat from the broiler element. Eureka! The eggplant was firm and toothy, with no sign of sponginess, and the flavor was rich and intense. Next we tried the zucchini (which was simply cut into chunks and lightly oiled) and found that it also benefited from the oven-roasting method. It was toothsome and flavorful. Left undisturbed in the oven, the zucchini retained its shape, and the chunky pieces gave the stew a fresh appearance.

Any hopes of making this an entirely in-oven operation came to a screeching halt when we tested roasting the onions, garlic, and tomatoes. If the onions were to roast evenly, they would have to be sliced rather than chopped, and tasters found the long strands texturally unappealing. Chopping and then sautéing them until caramel-colored and soft gave them a delicate flavor that blended well with the sweet tomatoes. Garlic also performed better in the sauté pan. But rather than subject it to the same slow caramelization as the onions, we found that a quick blast of heat best allowed the flavor to bloom. There was no mistaking its presence in the ratatouille. Finally, the roasted plump tomatoes turned to mush well before any increase in flavor occurred. We found that it was much better to add the tomatoes near the end of cooking, giving them just enough time to start breaking down and supply a bit of moisture to hold the stew together.

Although the test kitchen usually prefers canned tomatoes to most produce aisle specimens, this is one recipe in which the real thing is mandatory, for authenticity as well as for texture and flavor. In fact, buying the right tomato and preparing it correctly can make or break a ratatouille. First we tried the compact Roma tomato, but its lack of liquid gave the stew the appearance of thick chutney. Round tomatoes, especially the rugged beefsteak variety, worked exceptionally well. Their robust flavor, substantial size, and abundance of fleshy meat added just the right amount of texture and freshness to the mélange.

ANY EGGPLANT WILL DO

GLOBE   ITALIAN   JAPANESE

Some ratatouille recipes call for Japanese or Italian eggplant, each of which is thought to be superior to globe eggplant in flavor and texture. In a head-to-head comparison of the three in our recipe, we found that neither the Japanese nor the Italian eggplant had anything on the common globe eggplant.

We found it necessary to first peel the tomatoes, a process that goes quickly by dropping them in boiling water for a few seconds, followed by shocking them in ice water. But no matter what kind of tomato we used, we found that it was better to leave the seedbed in place. The seeds carry quite a bit of liquid, so removing them resulted in a dry ratatouille.

At last, we tested the herbs. Fresh herbs are an important part of Provençal cookery, and this dish is no exception. Basil is by far the herb called for most often in ratatouille, due in no small part to its growing schedule, which is simultaneous with that of the other ingredients. In the end, we chose to combine chopped fresh basil with bright green parsley and woody-flavored thyme. We also found that the full-flavored vegetables demanded a bounty of herbs—more than one quarter cup in total! Adding the herbs just before serving ensures that they will remain bright in color and flavor and complement the vegetables perfectly.

Ratatouille

SERVES 4 TO 6

For the best-flavored ratatouille, we recommend very ripe beefsteak tomatoes. See page 243 for tips on peeling the tomatoes.

2	large eggplants (2 to 2½ pounds), ends trimmed, cut into 1-inch cubes
	Kosher salt
2	large zucchini (about 1½ pounds), scrubbed and cut into 1-inch cubes
¼	cup olive oil
1	large onion, chopped large
2	medium garlic cloves, minced or pressed through a garlic press
3	medium, ripe tomatoes (about 1 pound), cored, peeled, and cut into 2-inch cubes
2	tablespoons chopped fresh parsley leaves
2	tablespoons chopped fresh basil leaves
1	tablespoon minced fresh thyme leaves
	Ground black pepper

1. Place the eggplant in a large colander set over a large bowl. Sprinkle the eggplant with 1 tablespoon salt and toss to distribute the salt evenly. Let the eggplant stand at least 1 hour or up to 3 hours. Rinse the eggplant well under running water to remove the salt and spread it in an even layer on a triple thickness of paper towels. Cover with another triple thickness of paper towels. Press firmly on the eggplant with your hands until the eggplant is dry and feels firm and compressed (see the photograph on page 162).

2. Adjust one oven rack to the upper-middle position and the second rack to the lower-middle position and heat the oven to 500 degrees. Line 2 rimmed baking sheets with foil.

3. Toss the eggplant, zucchini, and 2 tablespoons of the oil together in a large bowl. Divide the vegetables evenly between the prepared baking sheets, spreading them in a single layer on each sheet. Sprinkle with salt to taste and roast, stirring every 10 minutes, until well browned and tender, 30 to 40 minutes, rotating the baking sheets from top to bottom halfway through the roasting time. Set the roasted eggplant and zucchini aside.

4. Heat the remaining 2 tablespoons oil in a heavy-bottomed Dutch oven over medium heat until shimmering. Add the onion, reduce the heat to medium-low, and cook, stirring frequently, until softened and golden brown, 15 to 20 minutes. Stir in the garlic and cook until fragrant, about 30 seconds. Add the tomatoes and cook until they release their juices and begin to break down, about 5 minutes. Add the roasted eggplant and zucchini, stirring gently but thoroughly to combine. Cook until just heated through, about 5 minutes. Stir in the parsley, basil, and thyme and adjust the seasonings with salt and pepper to taste. Serve hot or warm. (The ratatouille can be refrigerated in an airtight container for up to 3 days.)

EGGPLANT PARMESAN

TRADITIONAL RECIPES FOR EGGPLANT Parmesan fry breaded eggplant in copious amounts of oil, usually resulting in greasy eggplant with a sodden, unappealing bread-crumb crust. We wanted a fresher, lighter take on this classic Italian dish. Could we eliminate the frying, streamline the dish, and make it taste better than the original?

Most recipes begin by purging (salting) the eggplant to expel bitter juices and prevent the porous flesh from soaking up excess oil. To double-check this theory, we baked some unsalted eggplant. Oil absorption wasn't a problem, but the eggplant did taste bitter, and it had a raw, mealy texture. Thirty minutes of salting and a firm press with paper towels remedied the problem. For efficiency's sake, we chose good-size globe eggplants; we didn't want to multiply the number of slices we'd have to prepare. For the best appearance, taste, and texture, we settled on unpeeled, ¼-inch-thick crosswise slices, not lengthwise planks.

In our first effort to sidestep deep-frying, we dispensed with the breading altogether, baking naked, salted eggplant slices on a baking sheet coated with cooking spray. (This method is often employed in low-calorie recipes for eggplant Parmesan.) The resulting eggplant earned negative comments from tasters. We concluded that breading was essential and ticked off a list of possibilities. Flour alone wasn't substantial enough. Eggplant swathed in mayonnaise and then bread crumbs turned slimy. Eggplant coated in a flour and egg batter and then bread crumbs was thick and tough. A standard single breading (dipping the eggplant first in egg, then in bread crumbs) was too messy—the egg slid right off the eggplant, leaving the crumbs with nothing to adhere to.

A double, or bound, breading proved superior. Dipping the eggplant first in seasoned flour, then egg, then bread crumbs created a substantial (but not heavy) and crisp coating that brought the mild flavor and tender, creamy texture of the eggplant to the fore. The initial coating of flour in a bound breading creates a dry, smooth base to which the egg can cling. We seasoned the bread crumbs with generous amounts of Parmesan, salt, and pepper.

We'd been using fresh bread crumbs and wondered whether could get away with using store-bought crumbs. The answer was no. Store-bought crumbs were so fine that they disappeared under blankets of tomato sauce and cheese.

After considerable experimentation, we found that the best way to achieve a crisp coating is to bake the breaded slices on two preheated baking sheets, each coated with a modest 3 tablespoons of vegetable oil (olive oil tasted sour), rotating the pans and flipping the slices partway through. At 425 degrees, the slices sizzled during cooking and became fully tender in 30 minutes. Using this technique, we turned out crisp, golden brown disks of eggplant, expending a minimum of effort (and using very little oil). And now (seeing that we weren't busy frying up four batches of eggplant in hot oil), we had time to grate cheese and whip up a quick tomato sauce while the eggplant baked.

Eggplant Parmesan couldn't be called such without Parmesan cheese, so that was a given. We'd already used some for breading the eggplant,

EGGPLANT: Following a Trail of Crumbs
We prepared eggplant in nearly a dozen ways. Below are some failed samples, with tasters' harsh comments.

BAKED NAKED
"Nasty"

FLOUR ALONE
"Insubstantial"

BATTER & CRUMBS
"Thick and tough"

EGG & CRUMBS
"Too messy"

• A WINNING COMBINATION •

FLOUR, EGG, & CRUMBS
Dipping the eggplant in flour, then egg, then bread crumbs created a substantial (but not heavy) and crisp coating.

and a little extra browned nicely on top of the casserole. Mozzarella is another standard addition. A modest amount (8 ounces) kept the casserole from becoming stringy.

A few cloves of minced garlic, a sprinkling of red pepper flakes, and some olive oil started off a quick tomato sauce, followed by three cans of diced tomatoes, with just two of them pureed in the food processor to preserve a chunky texture. A handful of fresh basil leaves (we reserved some basil for garnish, too) plus salt and pepper were the final flourishes.

Because breading softens beneath smothering layers of sauce and cheese, we left most of the top layer of eggplant exposed. This left us with about one cup of extra sauce, just enough to pass at the table. Another benefit of this technique was that without excess moisture, the casserole would be easy to cut into tidy pieces. With the eggplant fully cooked, the dish needed only a brief stay in a hot oven to melt the cheese.

Eggplant Parmesan

SERVES 6 TO 8

Use kosher salt when salting the eggplant. The coarse grains don't dissolve as readily as the fine grains of regular table salt, so any excess can be easily wiped away. It's necessary to divide the eggplant into two batches when tossing it with the salt. To be time-efficient, use the 30 to 45 minutes during which the salted eggplant sits to prepare the breading, cheeses, and sauce.

EGGPLANT

2 pounds globe eggplants (2 medium eggplants), cut crosswise into 1/4-inch-thick rounds
1 tablespoon kosher salt
8 slices high-quality white sandwich bread (about 8 ounces), each slice torn into quarters
2 ounces Parmesan cheese, freshly grated (1 cup)
Salt and ground black pepper
1 cup unbleached all-purpose flour
4 large eggs
6 tablespoons vegetable oil

TOMATO SAUCE

3 (14.5-ounce) cans diced tomatoes
2 tablespoons extra-virgin olive oil
4 medium garlic cloves, minced or pressed through a garlic press
1/4 teaspoon red pepper flakes
1/2 cup coarsely chopped fresh basil leaves
Salt and ground black pepper

8 ounces whole-milk or part-skim mozzarella cheese, shredded (2 cups)
1 ounce Parmesan cheese, freshly grated (1/2 cup)
10 fresh basil leaves, torn, for garnish

1. FOR THE EGGPLANT: Toss half of the eggplant slices and 1½ teaspoons of the kosher salt in a large bowl until combined; transfer the salted eggplant to a large colander set over a bowl. Repeat with the remaining eggplant and remaining 1½ teaspoons kosher salt, placing the second batch on top of the first. Let stand until the eggplant releases about 2 tablespoons liquid, 30 to 45 minutes. Spread the eggplant slices on a triple thickness of paper towels; cover with another triple thickness of paper towels. Press firmly on each slice to remove as much liquid as possible, then wipe off the excess salt.

2. While the eggplant is draining, adjust the oven racks to the upper- and lower-middle positions, place a rimmed baking sheet on each rack, and heat the oven to 425 degrees. Pulse the bread in a food processor to fine, even crumbs, about fifteen 1-second pulses (you should have about 4 cups). Transfer the crumbs to a pie plate and stir in the cheese, ¼ teaspoon salt, and ½ teaspoon pepper; set aside. Wipe out the bowl (do not wash) and set aside.

3. Combine the flour and 1 teaspoon pepper in a large zipper-lock bag; shake to combine. Beat the eggs in a second pie plate. Place 8 to 10 eggplant slices in the bag with the flour; seal the bag and shake to coat the slices. Remove the slices, shaking off the excess flour; dip in the eggs, letting the excess run off; and coat evenly with the bread crumb mixture. Set the breaded slices on a wire rack set over a baking sheet. Repeat with the remaining eggplant.

4. Remove the preheated baking sheets from the oven; add 3 tablespoons oil to each sheet,

tilting to coat evenly with the oil. Place half of the breaded eggplant slices on each sheet in a single layer; bake until the eggplant is well browned and crisp, about 30 minutes, switching and rotating the baking sheets after 10 minutes, and flipping the eggplant slices with a wide spatula after 20 minutes. Do not turn off the oven.

5. FOR THE SAUCE: While the eggplant bakes, process 2 cans of the diced tomatoes in a food processor until almost smooth, about 5 seconds. Heat the olive oil, garlic, and red pepper flakes in a large, heavy-bottomed saucepan over medium-high heat, stirring occasionally, until fragrant and the garlic is light golden, about 3 minutes; stir in the processed tomatoes and the remaining 1 can diced tomatoes. Bring the sauce to a boil, then reduce the heat to medium-low and simmer, stirring occasionally, until slightly thickened and reduced, about 15 minutes (you should have about 4 cups). Stir in the basil and season with salt and pepper to taste.

6. TO ASSEMBLE: Spread 1 cup of the tomato sauce in the bottom of a 13 by 9-inch baking dish. Layer in half of the eggplant slices, overlapping the slices to fit; distribute 1 more cup of the sauce over the eggplant; sprinkle with half of the mozzarella. Layer in the remaining eggplant and dot with 1 more cup of the sauce, leaving the majority of eggplant exposed so it will remain crisp; sprinkle with the Parmesan cheese and the remaining mozzarella. Bake until bubbling and the cheese is browned, 13 to 15 minutes. Cool 10 minutes, scatter the basil over the top, and serve, passing the remaining tomato sauce separately.

GREENS

MANY COOKS THINK THEY CAN TREAT ALL leafy greens the same way, even though some are delicate enough for salads while others seem as tough as shoe leather. After cleaning, stemming, and cooking more than 100 pounds of leafy greens, we found that they fell into two categories, each of which is handled quite differently.

Spinach (which is also good in salads; see page 88), beet greens, and Swiss chard are tender and rich in moisture. They require no additional liquid during cooking. They taste of the earth and minerals but are still rather delicate. Kale and mustard, turnip, and collard greens are tougher and require the addition of some liquid as they cook. Their flavor is much more assertive, even peppery in some cases, and can be overwhelming.

We tested boiling, steaming, and sautéing tender greens. Boiling produced the most brilliantly colored greens, but they were also very mushy and bland. The water cooked out all their flavor and texture. Steamed greens were less mushy, but clearly these tender greens did not need any liquid. Damp greens that were tossed in hot oil (which could be flavored with aromatics and spices) wilted in just two to three minutes in a covered pan. Once wilted, we found it best to remove the lid so the liquid in the pan would evaporate. This method has the advantage of flavoring the greens as they cook.

Tougher greens don't have enough moisture to be wilted in a hot pan; they scorch before they wilt. Steaming these greens produces a better texture but does nothing to tame their bitter flavor. Oddly, it turned them an unattractive jaundice green. It was clear to everyone in the test kitchen that tough greens benefit from cooking in some water, which will wash away some of their harsh notes.

We tested boiling two pounds of greens in an abundant quantity of salted water and what might be called shallow-blanching in several cups of salted water. Greens blanched in larger quantities of salted water had a lot going for them. They were tender, brilliantly colored, and less bitter than those cooked by other methods; also the salt had rounded out their flavor. However, blanching greens this way was not ideal. Once boiled, drained, rinsed, and squeezed, the greens had lost much of their individual character and tasted rather pallid. Cooking the greens in lots of water diluted their flavor too much.

So we tried cooking these assertive greens in small quantities of water. We started by cooking leaves from one pound of greens in one cup salted water, checking at five and then again at seven minutes. The five-minute leaves had a sharp, raw bite and were starting to acquire that dull look.

The seven-minute greens were fully cooked but still tasted bitter. We decided to double the water from one to two cups. The greens cooked in this quantity of water weren't as grossly bitter as those cooked in only one cup of liquid, but they were still a bit too bold. On the verge of settling for conventional blanching, we gave this shallow-cook method one more shot, by once again doubling the water from 2 cups to a quart and cooking

PREPARING LEAFY GREENS

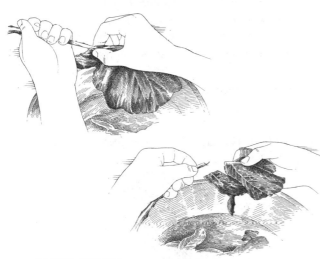

SWISS CHARD, KALE, AND COLLARD AND MUSTARD GREENS

To prepare Swiss chard, kale, and collard and mustard greens, hold each leaf at the base of the stem over a bowl filled with water and use a sharp knife to slash the leafy portion from either side of the thick stem.

TURNIP GREENS

1. Turnip greens are most easily stemmed by grasping the leaf between your thumb and index finger at the base of the stem and stripping it off by hand.
2. When using this method with turnip greens, the very tip of the stem will break off along with the leaves. It is tender enough to cook along with the leaves.

the greens the full seven minutes. The resulting greens offered the perfect balance we wanted: good color, full flavor without bitterness, and a tender green, ready for a quick, final cooking to unite them with other flavorful ingredients.

When you think about it, it stands to reason that a shallow blanch would work best with assertive greens. The more water you use when blanching porous vegetables, the more diluted the flavor of the vegetable becomes. That's one reason why steaming is the preferred way to cook so many vegetables—you want as little of the flavor as possible to escape into the cooking liquid. Assertive greens are different. You want to rid them of some of the bitterness, but not all of it. A shallow blanching erases enough bitterness to make these greens palatable but not so much as to rob them of their character.

Shallow blanching not only preserves the color and flavor, but it also saves time. We were surprised to learn that a gallon of water takes almost 20 minutes to boil. Two quarts (the amount you need to cook greens for four) can be brought to a boil in half the time.

We found that cut leaves cook faster than whole ones, but the leaves are much easier to cut when cooked. Tediously stacking two pounds of leaves in batches, rolling them up like big cigars, and cutting them into ribbons seemed a waste of time when the same leaves boiled down to just two cups seven minutes later. We found it simpler to rough-chop them before blanching. Then, after blanching, it was easy to cut the dramatically shrunken greens as fine as we liked. Once the blanched greens have been cut, they can be quickly cooked with seasonings.

Sautéed Tender Greens

SERVES 4

To stem spinach and beet greens, simply pinch off the leaves where they meet the stems. A thick stalk runs through each Swiss chard leaf, so it must be handled differently; see the illustration at left for information on this technique. A deep Dutch oven or soup kettle is best for this recipe. The greens should be moist but not soaking when they go into the pot.

3   tablespoons extra-virgin olive oil

2   medium garlic cloves, minced or pressed
    through a garlic press

2   pounds damp tender greens, such as spinach,
    beet greens, or Swiss chard, stemmed, washed
    in several changes of cold water, shaken to
    remove excess water, and chopped coarse
    Salt and ground black pepper
    Lemon wedges (optional)

Heat the oil and garlic in a Dutch oven or other deep pot over medium-high heat until the garlic sizzles and turns golden, 1 to 2 minutes. Add the wet greens, cover, and cook, stirring occasionally, until the greens wilt completely, 2 to 3 minutes. Uncover and season with salt and pepper to taste. Raise the heat to high and cook until the liquid evaporates, 2 to 3 minutes. Serve immediately, with lemon wedges if desired.

➤ VARIATIONS

Sautéed Tender Greens with Pine Nuts and Currants

Raisins (either dark or golden) can be used in place of the currants.

3   tablespoons extra-virgin olive oil

1   medium garlic clove, minced or pressed
     through a garlic press

1/4 cup pine nuts, chopped coarse

2   tablespoons currants

2   pounds damp tender greens, such as spinach,
     beet greens, or Swiss chard, stemmed, washed
     in several changes of cold water, shaken to
     remove excess water, and coarsely chopped
     Salt and ground black pepper

Heat the oil, garlic, and pine nuts in a Dutch oven or other deep pot over medium-high heat until the garlic and nuts sizzle and turn golden, 1 to 2 minutes. Add the currants and wet greens, cover, and cook, stirring occasionally, until the greens wilt completely, 2 to 3 minutes. Uncover and season with salt and pepper to taste. Raise the heat to high and cook until the liquid evaporates, 2 to 3 minutes. Serve immediately.

Sautéed Tender Greens with Bacon and Red Onion

This dish also makes a great filling for omelets.

2   ounces (about 2 slices) bacon, cut crosswise
     into 1/2-inch strips

1/2 small red onion, minced

1   medium garlic clove, minced or pressed
     through a garlic press

1/2 teaspoon minced fresh thyme leaves

2   pounds damp tender greens, such as spinach,
     beet greens, or Swiss chard, stemmed, washed
     in several changes of cold water, shaken to
     remove excess water, and chopped coarse
     Salt and ground black pepper

1. Cook the bacon in a Dutch oven or other deep pot over medium heat until the bacon is crisp, about 5 minutes. Transfer the bacon to a paper towel–lined plate to drain, leaving the bacon drippings in the pot.

2. Raise the heat to medium-high. Add the onion to the drippings and cook, stirring frequently, until golden brown, about 3 minutes. Stir in the garlic and cook until fragrant, about 1 minute longer. Add the thyme and wet greens, cover, and cook, stirring occasionally, until the greens wilt completely, 2 to 3 minutes. Uncover and season with salt and pepper to taste. Raise the heat to high and cook until the liquid evaporates, 2 to 3 minutes. Garnish with the reserved bacon and serve immediately.

DRAINING LEAFY GREENS

Many recipes for greens recommend adding them to the cooking pot with a little water from their washing still clinging to their leaves. To keep the damp leaves from turning your work surface into a watery mess, let them drain in an empty dish rack next to the sink.

Blanched Assertive Greens

MAKES ABOUT 2 CUPS

Once the greens have been blanched and drained, they can be used in either of the recipes that follow.

1½ teaspoons salt
2   pounds assertive greens, such as kale or collard, mustard, or turnip greens, stemmed, washed in 2 or 3 changes of cold water, and chopped coarse

Bring 2 quarts water to a boil in a Dutch oven or large, deep sauté pan. Add the salt and greens and stir until wilted. Cover and cook until the greens are just tender, about 7 minutes. Drain into a colander. Rinse the Dutch oven or pan with cold water to cool, then refill with cold water. Pour the greens into the cold water to stop the cooking process. Gather a handful of greens, lift out of the water, and squeeze dry. Repeat with the remaining greens. Roughly cut each bunch of greens and proceed with one of the following recipes.

➤ VARIATIONS

Assertive Greens with Bacon and Onion

SERVES 4

The strong flavors of bacon and sautéed onion make a good match with assertive greens.

2   ounces (about 2 slices) bacon, cut crosswise into thin strips
    Vegetable oil
½   medium onion, chopped fine
2   medium garlic cloves, minced or pressed through a garlic press
1   recipe Blanched Assertive Greens
¼   cup low-sodium chicken broth
2   teaspoons cider vinegar
    Salt

1. Fry the bacon in a large sauté pan over medium heat until crisp, about 5 minutes. Transfer the bacon to a plate lined with paper towels.

2. If necessary, add oil to the bacon drippings in the pan to make 2 tablespoons. Add the onion

DRAINING BLANCHED GREENS

Assertive greens should be blanched, drained, and then sautéed with seasonings. After blanching, it's important to squeeze out as much water as possible. Here's an unusual but quick way to accomplish this task.

1. Instead of squeezing the greens by hand, place them in the hopper of a potato ricer.
2. Close the handle and squeeze the water from the greens. Don't squeeze harder than is necessary or you could puree the greens.

and cook until softened, about 3 minutes. Add the garlic and cook until fragrant, about 30 seconds. Add the greens and stir to coat them with the fat. Add the broth, cover, and cook until the greens are heated through, about 2 minutes. If any excess liquid remains, remove the lid and continue to simmer until the liquid has thickened slightly, about 1 minute longer. Sprinkle the greens with the vinegar and bacon bits and season with salt to taste. Serve immediately.

Assertive Greens with Shallots and Cream

SERVES 4

The sweetness of shallots and the richness of cream mellow the bitterness of the greens.

2   tablespoons unsalted butter
2   medium shallots, chopped fine
1   recipe Blanched Assertive Greens
¼   cup heavy cream
½   teaspoon sugar
½   teaspoon minced fresh thyme leaves

⅛ teaspoon freshly grated nutmeg
Salt and ground black pepper

Melt the butter in a large sauté pan over medium heat. When the foaming subsides, add the shallots and cook, stirring frequently, until golden brown, 3 to 4 minutes. Add the greens and stir to coat them with the fat. Stir in the cream, sugar, thyme, and nutmeg. Cover and cook until the greens are heated through, about 2 minutes. If any excess liquid remains, remove the lid and continue to simmer until the cream has thickened slightly, about 1 minute longer. Season with salt and pepper to taste and serve immediately.

Peas

THERE ARE THREE VARIETIES OF PEAS SOLD IN most markets—shell peas, sugar snap peas, and snow peas. We find that shell peas are generally mealy and bland. Frozen peas are usually sweeter and more flavorful, and therefore the better option. Frozen peas are best blanched and then buttered or sauced. Nothing could be simpler.

The flat, light green snow pea has a long history, especially in the Chinese kitchen. The peas are immature and the pod is tender enough to eat. Sugar snap peas are a relatively recent invention, which date back just 20 years. They are a cross between shell peas and snow peas. The sweet, crisp pod is edible and holds small, juicy peas. Good sugar snaps look like compact fresh garden peas in the shell. They are firm and lustrous with barely discernible bumps along the pods. Expect to find robust fresh peas from late spring through summer.

Sugar snap and snow peas should be cooked quickly so that they retain some crunch and color. Stir-frying works well with snow peas, which have a fairly sturdy pod. However, sugar snap peas are too delicate for such intense heat. We found the pods will become mushy by the time the peas inside are actually heated through.

Steaming yielded tender sugar snap peas, but they tasted flat. We found that sugar snaps benefit greatly from the addition of some salt as they cook, something that can only be done if the peas are blanched.

Although blanching yielded peas with excellent taste and texture, we found that the blanched peas tended to shrivel or pucker a bit as they cooled. We solved this problem by plunging the cooked peas into ice water as soon as they were drained. This also helped set their bright color and prevent further softening from residual heat.

Once blanched and shocked, the peas can be held for up to an hour before seasoning. Here you have two options—a quick sauté with butter or oil and other flavorful ingredients (garlic, herbs, nuts) or dressed with a warm, creamy sauce.

Buttered Peas
SERVES 4

Frozen peas may just be the perfect vegetable. Not only are they inexpensive, but they require no washing, stemming, or chopping, and they cook in a matter of minutes.

1 (16-ounce) bag frozen peas
Salt
1 tablespoon unsalted butter
Ground black pepper

1. Bring 2 quarts water to a boil in a large saucepan. Add the peas and 1 teaspoon salt and cook until the peas are bright green, about 2 minutes. Drain the peas and set aside.

2. Melt the butter in a 10-inch skillet over medium-high heat. When the foaming subsides, add the peas and cook, stirring frequently, until the peas are coated with butter and hot, about 2 minutes. Season with salt and pepper to taste and serve immediately.

➤ VARIATION

Frozen Peas and Ham with Béchamel Sauce
Use thick-cut ham or ham steaks for this combination.

1 (16-ounce) bag frozen peas
Salt
2 tablespoons unsalted butter

6 ounces ham, cut into ¼-inch dice (about 1 cup)
2 teaspoons all-purpose flour
⅔ cup whole milk
Cayenne pepper

1. Bring 2 quarts water to a boil in a large saucepan. Add the peas and 1 teaspoon salt and cook until the peas are bright green, about 2 minutes. Drain the peas and set aside.

2. Melt 1 tablespoon of the butter in a 10-inch skillet over medium-high heat. When the foaming subsides, add the ham and cook, stirring frequently, until the ham is lightly browned, about 3 minutes. Transfer the ham to a plate.

3. Reduce the heat to medium and add the remaining 1 tablespoon butter. Sprinkle the flour into the pan. Using a wooden spoon, stir until the flour is incorporated. Add the milk and continue to stir until no lumps remain. Bring to a simmer and cook until the sauce thickens, about 1 minute. Add the peas and ham, stir, and cook until the peas are hot, about 1 minute. Season with salt and cayenne to taste and serve immediately.

Blanched Sugar Snap Peas
SERVES 4
Have a bowl of ice water ready to shock the drained peas and prevent further softening and shriveling. Snow peas can be used in any of the following recipes, although they are probably best stir-fried (see page 174).

Salt
1 pound sugar snap peas (about 4 cups), stems snapped off and strings removed if needed
1 tablespoon unsalted butter
Ground black pepper

1. Bring 6 cups water to a boil in a large saucepan. Add 1 teaspoon salt and the peas and cook until crisp-tender, 1½ to 2 minutes. Drain the peas, shock them in ice water, and drain again. Dry the peas well on a rimmed baking sheet lined with paper towels.

2. Place the butter in a large skillet and turn the heat to medium-high. When the foaming subsides, add the peas and cook, stirring frequently,

until the peas are heated through, 1 to 2 minutes. Season with salt and pepper to taste and serve immediately.

➤ VARIATIONS
Sugar Snap Peas with Pine Nuts and Garlic
Nuts burn very easily. Keep a sharp eye on the pine nuts in the pan and adjust the heat as necessary.

Salt
1 pound sugar snap peas (about 4 cups), stems snapped off and strings removed if needed
1 tablespoon extra-virgin olive oil
¼ cup pine nuts, chopped coarse
1 medium garlic clove, minced or pressed through a garlic press
Ground black pepper

1. Bring 6 cups water to a boil in a large saucepan. Add 1 teaspoon salt and the peas and cook until crisp tender, 1½ to 2 minutes. Drain the peas, shock them in ice water, and drain again. Dry the peas well on a rimmed baking sheet lined with paper towels.

2. Heat the oil in a large skillet over medium heat until shimmering. Add the pine nuts and cook, stirring frequently, until they are light golden brown, 1 to 2 minutes. Stir in the garlic and cook until fragrant, 30 seconds. Add the peas and cook, stirring frequently, until the peas are heated through, 1 to 2 minutes. Season with salt and pepper to taste and serve immediately.

Sugar Snap Peas with Sesame Seeds
There are two different kinds of sesame oil: toasted and plain. Toasted sesame oil is golden in color and has a distinct, nutty aroma; it is the one you want to use here. See page 144 for more information about sesame oil.

Salt
1 pound sugar snap peas (about 4 cups), stems snapped off and strings removed if needed
2 teaspoons vegetable oil
2 tablespoons sesame seeds
1 teaspoon toasted sesame oil
Ground black pepper

1. Bring 6 cups water to a boil in a large sauce-pan. Add 1 teaspoon salt and the peas and cook until crisp-tender, 1½ to 2 minutes. Drain the peas, shock them in ice water, and drain again. Dry the peas well on a rimmed baking sheet lined with paper towels.

2. Heat the vegetable oil in a large skillet over medium heat until shimmering. Add the sesame seeds and cook, shaking the pan occasionally, until the seeds are light golden brown and begin to pop, 1 to 2 minutes. Add the sesame oil and peas and cook, stirring frequently, until the peas are heated through, 1 to 2 minutes. Season with salt and pepper to taste and serve immediately.

Sugar Snap Peas with Asian Dressing

To mingle the flavors, you can let the peas and dressing stand for up to 10 minutes. Longer than that and the peas will start to lose their bright green color.

2	teaspoons sesame seeds
2	tablespoons orange juice
2	tablespoons rice vinegar
1	teaspoon honey
½	teaspoon soy sauce
1	medium scallion, sliced thin
½	teaspoon grated fresh ginger
2	tablespoons peanut oil
1	teaspoon toasted sesame oil
	Salt and ground black pepper
1	pound sugar snap peas (about 4 cups), stems snapped off and strings removed if needed

STRINGING SNOW PEAS

Snap off the tip of the snow pea and at the same time pull down along the flat side of the pod to remove the string.

1. Toast the sesame seeds over medium heat in a small skillet, shaking the pan often to promote even cooking, until lightly browned and fragrant, 7 to 10 minutes.

2. Meanwhile, combine the orange juice, vinegar, honey, soy sauce, scallion, and ginger in a small bowl. Whisk in the oils. Season with salt and pepper to taste. Stir in the sesame seeds. (The dressing can be set aside for several hours.)

3. Bring 6 cups water to a boil in a large sauce-pan. Add 1 teaspoon salt and the peas and cook until crisp-tender, 1½ to 2 minutes. Drain the peas, shock them in ice water, and drain again. Dry the peas well on a rimmed baking sheet lined with paper towels.

4. Toss the peas with the dressing, adjust the seasonings with salt and pepper to taste, and serve immediately.

Stir-Fried Snow Peas
SERVES 4

Snow peas are sturdier than sugar snap peas and hold up well when stir-fried.

¼	cup low-sodium chicken broth
¼	teaspoon salt
	Ground black pepper
1	tablespoon plus 1 teaspoon peanut oil
1	pound snow peas (about 4 cups), tips pulled off and strings removed (see the illustration at left)
2	medium garlic cloves, minced or pressed through a garlic press
½	teaspoon minced fresh ginger

1. Mix the chicken broth, salt, and pepper to taste together in a small bowl.

2. Heat the 1 tablespoon oil in a 12-inch non-stick skillet over high heat until shimmering. Add the snow peas and cook, stirring frequently, until bright green, about 2 minutes. Clear the center of the pan, add the garlic and ginger, and drizzle with the remaining 1 teaspoon oil. Mash the garlic and ginger with the back of a spatula. Cook for 10 seconds, then mix with the snow peas. Off the heat, add the chicken broth mixture (it should immediately reduce down to a glaze). Serve immediately.

➤ VARIATION

Stir-Fried Snow Peas with Tofu

Be sure to drain the tofu well and pat it dry with paper towels before adding it to the skillet; otherwise, the moisture from the tofu will cause the hot oil to splatter.

1	tablespoon hoisin sauce
1	tablespoon Worcestershire sauce
1	tablespoon soy sauce
3	tablespoons dry sherry
1	teaspoon toasted sesame oil
2	tablespoons peanut oil
8	ounces tofu, drained, dried well with paper towels, and cut into 1 by 1 by $1/2$-inch pieces
1	pound snow peas (about 4 cups), tips pulled off and strings removed (see the illustration on page 174)
2	medium garlic cloves, minced or pressed through a garlic press
$1/2$	teaspoon minced fresh ginger

1. Mix the hoisin sauce, Worcestershire sauce, soy sauce, sherry, and sesame oil together in a small bowl. Set aside.

2. Heat 1 tablespoon of the peanut oil in a 12-inch nonstick skillet over high heat until shimmering. Add the tofu and cook until golden brown, 1 to 2 minutes. Flip the tofu and cook until the other side is golden brown, 1 to 2 minutes longer. Transfer the tofu to a plate.

3. Add 2 teaspoons of the peanut oil to the now-empty skillet and swirl to coat. Add the snow peas and cook, stirring frequently, until bright green, about 2 minutes. Clear the center of the pan, add the garlic and ginger, and drizzle with the remaining 1 teaspoon peanut oil. Mash the garlic and ginger with the back of a spatula. Cook for 10 seconds, then mix with the snow peas. Add the tofu and the sauce, stir, and cook for 1 minute. Serve immediately.

ROASTED BELL PEPPERS

WHEN ROASTED, SWEET RED BELL PEPPERS assume a whole new layer of complex, smoky flavor. In testing the many different methods of roasting peppers, we sought the most efficient way to achieve a tender but not mushy flesh, smoky flavor, and skin that would peel off easily.

After flaming (over a gas burner), broiling, baking, and steaming dozens of peppers, we found that oven-broiling is clearly superior. It's neater and faster, and the peppers are delicious. To reach this conclusion, we roasted dozens of peppers. We found that you must take care not to over-roast the peppers. When the skin of the pepper just puffs up and turns black, you have reached the point at which flavor is maximized and the texture of the pepper flesh is soft but not mushy. After this point, continued exposure to heat will result in darkened flesh that is thinner, flabbier-textured, and slightly bitter.

Some details from our testing. The first method we tested was the stovetop gas burner. The one benefit of this method is that whole peppers retain the liquid that would be released during roasting by other methods. The disadvantages, however, are many. The peppers require constant tending and must be turned with tongs after each exposed area of flesh has charred. The clever tong manipulation doesn't end there, as both ends of the pepper need to be charred to promote even peeling. Also, only two peppers can be roasted at a time, unless you want to try to double this number by using two burners at a time. That, however, requires two pairs of tongs and deft eye-hand coordination and invites both arm-scorching and over-roasting. Forget about using a long-handled fork instead of tongs. After three or four minutes, we found that the softened pepper will fall off the fork right onto the burner flame.

The second approach we tested was oven-roasting at 550 degrees. Whether the peppers are kept whole or split open and flattened, this method takes longer, usually from 12 to 15 minutes, which in turn creates overcooked, soggy flesh. Lower oven temperatures also yielded overcooked peppers and required even longer cooking times—up to 1 hour at 325 degrees.

Broiling peppers does present some challenges, although it is certainly better than either the flame-roasting or oven-roasting methods. The broiler element in most ovens is approximately three inches away from the upper rack, which means that whole peppers usually touch the element. A lower rack level takes too long and cooks the flesh too much. After some trial and error, we found that the answer is to cut the peppers. This method yields less juice (some does collect in the bowl as the peppers steam), but that's an easy trade-off given the many benefits of this method. Primary among these is the fact that the peppers consistently achieved a meaty texture and rich flavor. In addition, peppers that have been cut open and roasted under the broiler are easier to peel than peppers roasted by any other method. The skin blackens and swells up like a balloon and lifts off in whole sections. By comparison, flame-roasting results in small patches of skin peeling off, at best.

Peppers should not be rubbed with oil before they are roasted. The skins will char and blister faster without the oil coating. It does help to line the baking pan with foil. Without foil, sticky, dark spots formed on the baking sheet the where the juices dripped and evaporated during roasting.

Unless you have asbestos fingers, roasted peppers need time to cool before handling, and steaming during this time does make the charred skin a bit easier to peel off. The ideal steaming time is 15 minutes—any less and the peppers are still too hot to work with comfortably. Any more time (we tested lengths up to one hour) provided no discernible advantage. The best method is to use a heat-resistant bowl (glass, ceramic, or metal) with a piece of plastic wrap secured over the top to trap the steam. The wrap holds in the heat, creating more intense steam.

Seeding the peppers before roasting makes it possible to peel the pepper without having to

PREPARING BELL PEPPERS FOR ROASTING

1. Slice ¼ inch from the top and bottom of the bell pepper, then gently remove the stem from the top lobe.

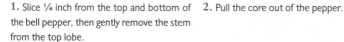

2. Pull the core out of the pepper.

3. Make a slit down one side of the pepper, then lay it flat, skin-side down, in one long strip. Slide a sharp knife along the inside of the pepper and remove all ribs and seeds.

4. Arrange the strips of peppers and the top and bottom lobes skin-side up on a foil-lined baking sheet. Flatten the strips with the palm of your hand.

5. Adjust an oven rack to the top position. If the rack is more than 3½ inches from the heating element, set a rimmed baking sheet, bottom up, on the rack under the baking sheet. Roast until the skin of the peppers is charred and puffed up like a balloon but the flesh is still firm.

6. Remove the baking sheet from the oven. You may steam the peppers at this point or not, as you wish. When the peppers are cool enough to handle, start peeling where the skin has charred and bubbled the most. The skin will come off in large strips.

rinse them to wash away the seeds. If you are still tempted to rinse, notice the rich oils that accumulate on your fingers as you work. It seems silly to rinse away those oils rather than savoring them later with your meal.

The way peppers are treated after they are peeled will determine how long they will keep. Unadorned and wrapped in plastic wrap, peppers will keep their full, meaty texture only about two days in the refrigerator. Drizzled with a generous amount of olive oil and kept in an airtight container, peppers will keep about one week without losing texture or flavor.

Roasted Red Bell Peppers

MAKES 4 ROASTED PEPPERS, ENOUGH TO SERVE 8 AS AN APPETIZER

Cooking times vary, depending on the broiler, so watch the peppers carefully as they roast. You will need to increase the cooking time slightly if your peppers are just out of the refrigerator instead of at room temperature. Yellow and orange peppers roast faster than red ones, so decrease their cooking time by 2 to 4 minutes. Do not roast green or purple peppers—their flavor is bitter and not worth the effort.

4   medium-to-large red bell peppers (6 to 9 ounces each), prepared according to illustrations 1–4 on page 176
    Extra-virgin olive oil
    Salt

1. Adjust an oven rack to the top position. The oven rack should be 2½ to 3½ inches from the heating element. If it is not, set a rimmed baking sheet, turned upside down, on the oven rack to elevate the pan (see illustration 5 on page 176). Turn the broiler on and heat for 5 minutes. Broil the peppers until spotty brown, about 5 minutes. Reverse the pan in the oven and roast until the skin is charred and puffed but the flesh is still firm, 3 to 5 minutes longer.

2. Remove the pan from oven and let the peppers sit until cool enough to handle. (To facilitate peeling, transfer the peppers right out of the oven to a large heat-resistant bowl, cover it with plastic wrap, and steam for 15 minutes.) Peel and discard the skin from each piece (see illustration 6 on page 176).

3. To serve, slice the peppers and arrange them on a platter. Drizzle with oil just until lightly moistened and sprinkle with salt to taste.

STUFFED BELL PEPPERS

MENTION STUFFED PEPPERS TO MOST PEOPLE and they think of an army green shell crammed with leftovers from the school cafeteria. Although the classic 1950s sweet pepper filled with rice and beef and topped with ketchup may sound mediocre, this recipe can be delicious if prepared properly.

To get going, we tried a few classic recipes. Although these trial runs produced nothing as

INGREDIENTS: Bell Peppers

We had long wondered whether color makes a difference when it comes to roasting bell peppers. After roasting five kinds of bell peppers, we can now say that the answer is an unequivocal yes.

Red peppers gave the best and most even results. Yellow peppers were generally more delicate, their flesh thinner and more prone to overcooking, which gave it a brownish hue. Since they are also more expensive than red peppers, we only roast them if the yellow color is important to a dish. Orange peppers are equally delicate and need careful watching. With both yellow and orange varieties, wait for the skin to just char and lift up, making sure the edges are slightly blistered. At this point,

remove these delicate peppers from the broiler. You have more leeway with red peppers and can let them char a bit more, which makes peeling easier.

Based on our kitchen tests, we can confidently say that purple peppers are a waste of money. They lost their color when roasted (or when cooked in any manner), turning a muddy green. Their flavor was bitter, like that of green peppers, not sweet like that of the red, yellow, and orange varieties. Lastly, don't bother roasting green peppers, either. Green peppers, which are simply unripened red peppers, are not sweet and gain nothing by being roasted.

bad as what we remembered from childhood, they were far from perfect. First off, the peppers themselves varied greatly in degree of doneness. Some were so thoroughly cooked that they slumped onto their sides, unable to support their stuffed weight. On the other end of the spectrum, barely cooked peppers added an unfriendly crunch and bitter flavor to the mix. To be a success, the stuffed peppers would have to yield a tender bite yet retain enough structure to stand up proudly on the plate.

None of the fillings hit home, either. An all-rice version was uninteresting, while another stuffed with all meat was leaden and greasy. One recipe called for small amounts of so many varied ingredients that it made us think its creator just wanted to clean out her refrigerator. We came

KEEPING STUFFED PEPPERS UPRIGHT

Here are four novel ways to keep stuffed peppers from spilling their contents as they bake.

A. Reserve the tops of the peppers, which you have cut off to open the peppers for stuffing, and insert them between the stuffed peppers in the pan for added stability.

B. Instead of cooking peppers in a baking dish, as specified in most recipes, put them in a tube pan. The snug fit makes the pepper sit right up.

C. Place the peppers in the cups of a muffin tin; the sides of the cups hold the peppers firmly in place.

D. Place each stuffed pepper in an individual ovenproof custard cup. This is a great system when you want to cook only a couple of peppers instead of a whole batch.

away from this first round of tests wanting a simple yet gratifying filling, neither humdrum nor packed with odd ingredients.

To start, we needed a solid pepper venue with minimal crunch. So we steamed, roasted, and blanched a round of peppers and lined them up for everyone in the test kitchen to examine. The steamed were bland in both color and flavor. We tried roasting in an uncovered dish filled with a little water, an uncovered dish with no water, and a covered dish. Each procedure produced a bitter, subpar pepper. We knew that if we allowed the peppers to roast a little longer, their sugars would caramelize and the peppers would turn sweet. But at that point their texture would also have disintegrated into that of an Italian sandwich ingredient. Tasters unanimously preferred the vibrant color, sturdiness, and overall sweeter flavor of the blanched peppers; the hot water actually seemed to have washed away some of their bitterness.

Usually, a freshly blanched vegetable is plunged immediately into an ice-cold water bath in a process known as shocking. The point is to halt the cooking process at just the right moment while stabilizing the vegetable's brightened color. We find water baths to be a real pain, especially in a kitchen where counter space is prime property. Although the shocked peppers had a slightly brighter hue than those that had been blanched but not shocked, they took much longer to heat through in the oven. So we abandoned shocking and instead fussed with blanching times, being careful to remove the peppers a little early and then allow the residual heat to finish their cooking. We found that a three-minute dip in boiling water followed by a cooling period on the countertop yielded the perfect balance of structure and chew.

Even with a pepper that's cooked to perfection, everyone knows that in this dish the stuffing is the real star of the show. The options for stuffing ingredients are many, including couscous, polenta, and a number of interesting and unusual grains. But we landed on rice. A universal pantry ingredient, it is a classic in American recipes for stuffed peppers.

Because we wanted these stuffed peppers to work as a quick midweek meal, our goal was to keep the rice-based filling simple and satisfying, with a streamlined ingredient list and preparation method. Tasters did not care much for sausage, heavy seasonings, or a mix of too many ingredients. To our surprise, they were big fans of the classic 1950s version of a pepper stuffed with rice and ground beef. Sautéed onion and garlic rounded out the flavors, while tomatoes added a fresh note and some color. Bound together with a little cheese and topped with ketchup, this retro pepper is a model of "make it from what you have in the pantry" simplicity.

Now we had a pepper, and we had a filling. All we had to do was figure out the best way to get them together. The first trick is to use the boiling water from the blanched peppers to cook the rice. While the peppers cool and the rice cooks, the onions, garlic, and beef can be sautéed quickly. Then filling and peppers can be assembled and heated through in the oven. The result? Stuffed peppers that take only 45 minutes from start to finish—and that are also truly worth eating.

Stuffed Bell Peppers

SERVES 4 AS A LIGHT MAIN DISH
OR SIDE DISH

When shopping for bell peppers to stuff, it's best to choose those with broad bases that will allow the peppers to stand up on their own. It's easier to fill the peppers after they have been placed in the baking dish because the sides of the dish will hold the shells steady. In testing, we found it best to drain the peppers cut-side up. When we drained them cut-side down, the hot water draining from the peppers continued to steam them, making the peppers soggy.

    Salt
4   medium red, yellow, or orange bell peppers (about 6 ounces each), $1/2$ inch trimmed off tops, cores and seeds discarded
$1/2$ cup long-grain white rice
$1 1/2$ tablespoons olive oil
1   medium onion, chopped fine
12   ounces ground beef, preferably ground chuck

3   medium garlic cloves, minced or pressed through a garlic press
1   (14.5-ounce) can diced tomatoes, drained, $1/4$ cup juice reserved
5   ounces Monterey Jack cheese, shredded (about $1 1/4$ cups)
2   tablespoons chopped fresh parsley leaves
    Ground black pepper
$1/4$ cup ketchup

1. Bring 4 quarts water to a boil in a large stockpot or Dutch oven over high heat. Add 1 tablespoon salt and the bell peppers. Cook until the peppers just begin to soften, about 3 minutes. Using a slotted spoon, remove the peppers from the pot, drain off the excess water, and place the peppers cut-side up on paper towels. Return the water to a boil; add the rice and boil until tender, about 13 minutes. Drain the rice and transfer it to a large bowl; set aside.

2. Adjust an oven rack to the middle position and heat the oven to 350 degrees.

3. Meanwhile, heat the oil in a 12-inch heavy-bottomed skillet over medium-high heat until shimmering. Add the onion and cook, stirring occasionally, until softened and beginning to brown, about 5 minutes. Add the ground beef and cook, breaking the beef into small pieces with a spoon, until no longer pink, about 4 minutes. Stir in the garlic and cook until fragrant, about 30 seconds. Transfer the mixture to the bowl with the rice and stir in the tomatoes, 1 cup of the cheese, the parsley, and salt and pepper to taste.

4. Stir the ketchup and reserved tomato juice together in a small bowl.

5. Place the peppers cut-side up in a 9-inch square baking dish. Using a soup spoon, divide the filling evenly among the peppers. Spoon 2 tablespoons of the ketchup mixture over each filled pepper and sprinkle each with 1 tablespoon of the remaining cheese. Bake until the cheese is browned and the filling is heated through, 25 to 30 minutes. Serve immediately.

POTATOES

DOZENS OF POTATO VARIETIES ARE GROWN in this country, and at any time you may see as many as five or six in your supermarket. Some potatoes are sold by varietal name (such as Yukon Gold), but others are sold by generic name (baking, all-purpose, and so on). To make sense of this confusion, we find it helpful to group potatoes into three major categories, based on the ratio of solids (mostly starch) to water. The categories are high-starch/low-moisture potatoes, medium-starch potatoes, and low-starch/high-moisture potatoes.

The high-starch/low-moisture category includes baking, russet, and white creamer potatoes. (The formal name for the russet is russet Burbank potato, named after its developer, Luther Burbank of Idaho. This type of potato is also known as the Idaho. In all of our recipes, we call them russets.) These potatoes are best for baking and mashing. The medium-starch/medium-moisture category includes all-purpose, Yukon Gold, Yellow Finn, and purple Peruvian potatoes. These potatoes can be mashed or baked, but are generally not as fluffy as the high-starch potatoes. The low-starch/high-moisture category includes Red Bliss, red creamer, new, white rose, and fingerling potatoes. These potatoes, which are often called waxy potatoes, are best roasted or boiled and used in salad.

Within each category, you can safely make substitutions, but cross-category substitutions can result in poor results. For instance, if you try to fry red potatoes rather than the recommended russet potatoes, you will get poor results.

In addition to categorizing potatoes by starch content, it is useful to divide them into two groups based on how they have been handled after harvesting. Most potatoes are cured after harvesting to toughen their skins and protect the flesh. They are then held in cold storage, often for months. These potatoes are called storage potatoes. Almost all of the potatoes in the supermarket fall into this category.

Occasionally, potatoes are harvested before they have developed their full complement of starch. New potatoes are always low in starch and high in moisture, even if they are actually a high-starch variety. Although all new potatoes are small, not all small potatoes are new. You can pick out a true new potato by examining the skin. If the skin feels thin and you can rub it off with your fingers, you are holding a new potato. New potatoes have a lot of moisture, and their flesh is almost juicy when cut.

BAKED POTATOES

IN THE WORLD OF JUNE CLEAVER, POTATOES were baked at 350 degrees because they were put into the oven along with the roast, which cooked at 350 degrees. The world has changed a lot since Wally and Beav sat down to dinner. We wondered if there was a quicker or better route to perfect baked potatoes.

SCIENCE: Starch in Potatoes

Potatoes are composed mostly of starch and water. The starch is in the form of granules, which in turn are contained in starch cells. The higher the starch content of the potato, the more packed the cells. In high-starch potatoes (russets are a good example), the cells are completely full—they look like plump little beach balls. In medium-starch (Yukon Golds) and low-starch (Red Bliss) potatoes, the cells look more like underinflated beach balls. The space between these less-than-full cells is taken up mostly by water.

In our tests, we found that the full starch cells of high-starch potatoes are most likely to maintain their integrity and stay separate when mashed, giving the potatoes a delightfully fluffy texture. In addition, the low water content of these potatoes allows them to absorb milk, cream, and/or butter without becoming wet or gummy. Starch cells in lower-starch potatoes, on the other hand, tend to clump when cooked and break more easily, allowing the starch to dissolve into whatever liquid is present. The broken cells and dissolved starch tend to produce sticky, gummy mashed potatoes.

However, the high moisture content of red potatoes makes them an excellent choice for dishes such as potato salad, where you want the potatoes to hold their shape. Because they contain a fair amount of moisture, they don't absorb much water as they boil. In contrast, low-moisture russets suck up water when boiled and fall apart. The resulting potato salad tastes starchy and looks sloppy.

SCRUBBING POTATOES

Buy a rough-textured bathing or exfoliating bath glove especially for use in the kitchen. The glove cleans dirt away from potatoes and other root vegetables, but it's relatively gentle and won't scrub away the skin.

We baked all-purpose potatoes, Yukon Golds, and Idaho-grown russets. We tried baking them poked and unpoked, greased and ungreased, with ends dipped in salt, microwaved all the way, microwaved and finished in the oven, baked with gadgets that are supposed to decrease cooking time, and baked at various temperatures. And, against the wishes of all the potato experts we spoke with, we also tried baking them in foil.

After all this experimentation, we discovered that the traditional slow-baking method is best, mainly because of the effect it had on the skin. The skin of a potato baked at 350 degrees for an hour and 15 minutes simply has no peer. Just under the skin, a well-baked potato will develop a substantial brown layer. This is because the dark skin absorbs heat during cooking, and the starch just inside the skin is broken down into sugar and starts to brown. If you love baked potato skin, this is definitely the best method.

Potatoes cooked at 400 and 450 degrees will indeed cook faster—at 450 degrees they may even cook in 45 minutes—but because they cook for a shorter time, the inner browned layer isn't as even or as flavorful as it is with the slower roast method. In addition, the skin isn't quite as thick and chewy. Cooked long enough to develop chewy skin at these higher temperatures, the inner, browned layer becomes thick and unpleasant and somewhat overbrowned.

We also tried starting potatoes at 500 degrees for 10 minutes and then lowering the oven to 350 degrees, but again this method failed to promote even browning. The microwave does a decent job of shortening the overall cooking time and yields decent flesh. What's missing is the delicious browned layer under the skin and the chewy, dry skin that skin lovers covet. We found that cooking the potatoes for half the recommended microwave time, then finishing them in a 450-degree oven produced fluffy, dry flesh, some browning, and pretty good skin. If you're in a hurry, this half-and-half method works best.

As for some of our more unusual tests: Oiling the skin caused a potato to cook somewhat more quickly, but, frankly, the skin was not as good. We found that the expensive metal pokers that you stick into potatoes to decrease cooking time did not seem to have that effect. Cutting the ends off a potato and dipping them in salt made for crusty, salty ends but didn't measurably alter baking time. Finally, poking the potato before baking did not noticeably affect the amount of moisture retained after baking. The flesh of a potato that had been poked was just as dry as one that had not been poked. However, it is a good idea to poke a hole or two in any potato you are going to microwave, since unpoked potatoes can explode when microwaved.

If slow-baking is essential to good skin, the consistency of the flesh also requires some attention. Letting the potato sit awhile after baking without opening it up will steam the potato and cause the flesh to become more dense. For fluffy potatoes, create a wide opening as soon as the potatoes come out of the oven to let the steam escape.

And what about foil-wrapped potatoes? They are a notion perpetuated by mediocre steakhouses that want to keep potatoes warm indefinitely. Foil is an insult to potatoes—it holds the steam in, causing limp, damp skins and dense flesh.

Baked Potatoes

SERVES 4

We found no benefit or harm was done to the potatoes by poking them with the tines of a fork before putting them in the oven. Do use a fork to open the skins as soon as the potatoes come out of the oven.

4 medium russet potatoes (7 to 8 ounces each), scrubbed
Butter
Salt

Adjust an oven rack to the middle position and heat the oven to 350 degrees. Place the potatoes directly on the rack and bake for 1¼ hours. Remove the potatoes from the oven and pierce them with a fork to create a dotted X on the top of each potato (see illustration 1 below). Press in at the ends of each potato to push the flesh up and out (see illustration 2 below). Serve immediately with butter and salt.

➤ VARIATION

Faster Baked Potatoes
This half-and-half method (which takes 35 minutes, start to finish) produces far superior results than straight microwaving. By the time you have scrubbed and microwaved the potatoes, the oven will be preheated. To cook fewer potatoes by this method, plan on 2 minutes total cooking time in the microwave for each potato.

4 medium russet potatoes (7 to 8 ounces each), scrubbed
Butter
Salt

1. Adjust an oven rack to the middle position and heat the oven to 450 degrees.

2. Microwave the potatoes on high power for 4 minutes. Turn the potatoes over and microwave them on high power for another 4 minutes.

3. Transfer the potatoes to the hot oven and cook until a skewer glides easily through the flesh, about 20 minutes. Remove the potatoes from the oven and pierce them with a fork to create a dotted X on the top of each potato (see illustration 1 at left). Press in at the ends of each potato to push the flesh up and out (see illustration 2 at left). Serve immediately with butter and salt.

OPENING A BAKED POTATO

To ensure that the flesh does not steam and become dense, it's imperative to open a baked potato as soon as it comes out of the oven. This technique maximizes the amount of steam released and keeps the potato fluffy and light.

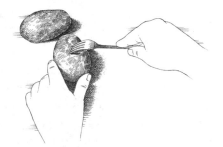

1. Use the tines of a fork to make a dotted X on the top of each potato.

2. Press in at the ends of the potato to push the flesh up and out. Besides releasing steam quickly, this method helps trap and hold on to bits of butter.

TWICE-BAKED POTATOES

THIS SIMPLE DISH—ESSENTIALLY BAKED RUSSET potatoes from which the flesh has been removed, mashed with dairy ingredients and seasonings, mounded back in the shells, and baked again— offers a good range of both texture and flavor in a single morsel. Done well, the skin is chewy and substantial without being tough, with just a hint of crispness to play off the smooth, creamy filling. In terms of flavor, cheese and other dairy ingredients make the filling rich and tangy, a contrast to the mild, slightly sweet potato shell.

Because twice-baked potatoes are put in the oven twice, we found it best to bake them for just an hour, rather than the usual 1¼ hours we bake plain potatoes. Oiling the skins before baking promotes crispness, not something you necessarily want in plain baked potatoes but a trait we came to admire in creamy twice-baked potatoes.

Our favorite baked potato recipe underscores the importance of opening the potatoes right after baking to release as much steam as possible. For twice-baked potatoes, it's advisable to wait a few minutes for the potatoes to cool before slicing them apart and emptying out the flesh; cooled potatoes are much easier to handle, and, because the flesh is mixed with wet ingredients, any compromise to the texture from unreleased moisture is negligible.

Once we had emptied the potato halves of their flesh, we noticed they got a little flabby sitting on the counter waiting to be stuffed. Because the oven was still on and waiting for the return of the stuffed halves, we decided to put the skins back in while we prepared the filling. This worked beautifully, giving the shells an extra dimension of crispness.

Pleased with our chewy, slightly crunchy skins, we now had to develop a smooth, lush, flavorful filling that would hold up its end of the bargain. (Lumpy, sodden, and dull-tasting would not do.) Twice-baked potatoes usually are filled with a mixture of well-mashed potato, shredded cheese, and other dairy ingredients, including one or more of the usual suspects: butter, sour cream, cream cheese, yogurt, ricotta, cottage cheese, milk, cream, and buttermilk. Various herbs and spices also often show up, as well as diced meats and sautéed vegetables.

To get an idea of how we wanted to flavor our filling, we prepared ten different recipes with various ingredient combination. In a rare display of accord, all our tasters agreed on a few general observations. First, everyone preferred tangy dairy products, such as sour cream, yogurt, and buttermilk, to sweet ones, such as milk, cream, and ricotta. Second, the use of only one dairy ingredient produced a rather dull, one-dimensional filling. A second ingredient added depth of flavor and complexity. Third, nobody favored too fatty a mouthfeel, a preference that left the addition of large amounts of butter (some recipes use up to a full stick for four potatoes) and cream cheese out of the running. Dozens of further tests helped us refine our filling to a rich, but not killer, combination of sharp cheddar, sour cream, buttermilk, and just two tablespoons of butter. We learned to season the filling aggressively with salt and pepper; for herbs, the slightly sharp flavor of scallions was best.

With the filling mixed and mounded back into the shells, our last tests centered on the final baking. We wanted to do more than just heat the filling through; we were intent on forming an attractive brown crust on it as well. Broiling turned out to be the easiest and most effective method. After about 10 minutes, the potatoes emerged browned, crusted, and ready for the table.

⤝ Twice-Baked Potatoes

SERVES 6 TO 8

To vary the flavor a bit, try substituting other types of cheese, such as Gruyère, fontina, or feta, for the cheddar. Yukon Gold potatoes, though slightly more moist than our ideal, gave our twice-baked potatoes a buttery flavor and mouthfeel that everyone liked, so we recommend them as a substitution for the russets.

4	medium russet potatoes (7 to 8 ounces each), scrubbed, dried, and rubbed lightly with vegetable oil
4	ounces sharp cheddar cheese, shredded (about 1 cup)
1/2	cup sour cream
1/2	cup buttermilk
2	tablespoons unsalted butter, softened
3	medium scallions, sliced thin
1/2	teaspoon salt
	Ground black pepper

SLICING BAKED POTATOES

This way
NOT this way

Most potatoes have two relatively flat, blunt sides and two curved sides. Halve the baked potatoes lengthwise so the blunt sides are down once the shells are stuffed, making them much more stable on the baking sheet during the final baking.

1. Adjust an oven rack to the upper-middle position and heat the oven to 400 degrees. Bake the potatoes on a foil-lined baking sheet until the skin is crisp and deep brown and a skewer easily pierces the flesh, about 1 hour. Setting the baking sheet aside, transfer the potatoes to a wire rack and let cool slightly, about 10 minutes.

2. Using an oven mitt or a folded kitchen towel to handle the hot potatoes, cut each potato in half so that the long, blunt sides rest on a work surface (see the photograph on page 183). Using a small spoon, scoop the flesh from each half into a medium bowl, leaving ⅛ to ¼ inch of the flesh in each shell. Arrange the shells on the lined baking sheet and return them to the oven until dry and slightly crisped, about 10 minutes. Meanwhile, mash the potato flesh with a fork until smooth. Stir in the remaining ingredients, including pepper to taste, until well combined.

3. Remove the shells from the oven and increase the oven setting to broil. Holding the shells steady on the baking sheet with an oven mitt or towel-protected hand, spoon the mixture into the crisped shells, mounding it slightly at the center, and return the potatoes to the oven. Broil until spotty brown and crisp on top, 10 to 15 minutes. Cool for 10 minutes. Serve warm.

➤ VARIATIONS

Twice-Baked Potatoes with Chipotle Chiles and Onion

For a slightly smoky aftertaste with just a hint of heat, limit the chipotles to 1 tablespoon. For more heat, increase the chipotles to 1½ tablespoons.

Heat 2 tablespoons butter in a medium skillet over medium heat. Add 1 medium onion, chopped fine, and cook until soft, 3 to 4 minutes. Follow the recipe for Twice-Baked Potatoes, omitting the butter and adding 1 to 1½ tablespoons minced canned chipotle chiles in adobo sauce, the sautéed onion, and 2 tablespoons chopped fresh cilantro leaves to the filling mixture in step 2. Proceed as directed.

Twice-Baked Potatoes with Blue Cheese and Thyme

Follow the recipe for Twice-Baked Potatoes, substituting 3 ounces crumbled blue cheese (about ½ cup) for the cheddar and 1 teaspoon finely minced fresh thyme leaves for the scallions.

Twice-Baked Potatoes with Monterey Jack and Pesto

Follow the recipe for Twice-Baked Potatoes, substituting Monterey Jack cheese for the cheddar, reducing the buttermilk to ¼ cup, omitting the butter, and adding ¼ cup prepared pesto to the filling mixture. Proceed as directed.

Twice-Baked Potatoes with Indian Spices and Peas

Heat 2 tablespoons butter in a medium skillet over medium heat. Add 1 medium onion, chopped fine, and cook until soft, 3 to 4 minutes. Add 1 teaspoon finely grated ginger, 3 medium garlic cloves, minced, 1 teaspoon each ground cumin and ground coriander, and ¼ teaspoon each ground cinnamon, ground turmeric, and ground cloves; cook until fragrant, about 30 seconds more, taking care not to brown the garlic or ginger. Off the heat, stir in 1 cup thawed frozen peas; set aside. Follow the recipe for Twice-Baked Potatoes, omitting the cheese and butter and stirring the spiced peas into the filling mixture in step 2. Proceed as directed.

ROASTED POTATOES

THE PERFECT ROASTED POTATO IS CRISP AND deep golden brown on the outside, with moist, velvety, dense interior flesh. The potato's slightly bitter skin is intact, providing a contrast to the sweet, caramelized flavor that the flesh develops during the roasting process. It is rich but never greasy, and it is accompanied by the heady taste of garlic and herbs.

To start, we roasted several kinds of potatoes. We liked high-starch/low-moisture potatoes (we used russets) the least. They did not brown well, their dry, fluffy texture was more like baked than roasted potatoes, and their flavor reminded us of raw potatoes. The medium-starch all-purpose potatoes (we used Yukon Golds) produced a beautiful golden crust, but the interior flesh was still rather dry. The best roasting potatoes came from the low-starch/high-moisture category (we used Red Bliss). These potatoes emerged from the oven with a light, delicate crust and a moist, dense interior that had a more complex, nutty flavor than the others, with hints of bitterness and tang.

After choosing the Red Bliss potatoes, we began to test oven temperatures. At 425 degrees, the result was an even-colored, golden brown potato with a thin, crisp crust and an interior that was soft and dense, although still slightly dry.

While researching, we came across some recipes that called for parboiling the potatoes before roasting them. Hoping that this approach would produce a texturally superior potato that retained more of its moisture after cooking, we tried boiling the potatoes for seven minutes prior to roasting. This produced a potato closer to our ideal, but preparation required considerable attention owing to the additional step.

We then tried covering the potatoes for a portion of their roasting time. We were especially drawn to this technique because it provided a way to steam the potatoes in their own moisture that required little extra effort on the cook's part. The results were perfect. The crisp, deep golden brown crust was perfectly balanced by a creamy, moist interior. These potatoes had a sweet and nutty caramelized flavor, with just a hint of tang from the skin. This simplest of methods produced the very best roasted potatoes.

FLIPPING ROASTED POTATOES

Press the metal spatula against the roasting pan as you slide it under the potatoes to protect the crisp crust. Flip the potatoes so that the other cut sides come into contact with the hot pan.

The next step in the process was figuring out how to add garlic flavor, which makes a good variation on the standard roasted potatoes. If we added minced garlic during the last five minutes of cooking, it burned almost instantly; coating the potatoes with garlic-infused oil failed to produce the strong garlic flavor that we were after; and roasting whole, unpeeled garlic cloves alongside the potatoes and squeezing the pulp out afterward to add to the potatoes was too tedious. The best method turned out to be both simple and flavorful. Mash raw garlic into a paste, place it in a large stainless steel bowl, put the hot roasted potatoes in the bowl, and toss. This method yields potatoes with a strong garlic flavor yet without the raw spiciness of uncooked garlic.

Roasted Potatoes

SERVES 4

To roast more than two pounds of potatoes at once, use a second pan rather than crowding the first. If your potatoes are small, as new potatoes, cut them into halves instead of wedges and turn them cut-side up during the final 10 minutes of roasting.

2 pounds red or other low-starch potatoes, scrubbed, halved, and cut into ¾-inch wedges
3 tablespoons extra-virgin olive oil
Salt and ground black pepper

1. Adjust an oven rack to the middle position and heat the oven to 425 degrees. Toss the potatoes and oil in a medium bowl to coat; season generously with salt and pepper and toss again.

2. Place the potatoes flesh-side down in a single layer in a shallow roasting pan. Cover tightly with aluminum foil and cook for 20 minutes. Remove the foil and roast until the side of the potato touching the pan is crusty and golden brown, about 15 minutes more. Remove the pan from the oven and, with a metal spatula, carefully turn the potatoes. (Press the spatula against the pan as it slides under the potatoes to protect the crusts; see the illustration at left.) Return the pan to the oven and roast until the side of the potato now touching the pan is crusty and golden brown

and the skins have raisin-like wrinkles, 5 to 10 minutes more. Transfer the potatoes to a serving dish (again, using a metal spatula and extra care not to rip the crusts) and serve hot or warm.

➤ VARIATIONS

Roasted Potatoes with Garlic and Rosemary

Follow the recipe for Roasted Potatoes. While the potatoes roast, mince 2 medium garlic cloves with ⅛ teaspoon salt until a paste forms (see illustration on page 626). Transfer the garlic paste to a large bowl; set aside. In the last 3 minutes of roasting time, sprinkle 2 tablespoons chopped fresh rosemary leaves evenly over the potatoes. Immediately transfer the finished potatoes to the bowl with the garlic, toss, and serve warm.

Roasted Potatoes with Lemon-Chive Butter

Lemon and chives are a classic combination. Add the chives at the end of cooking to preserve their delicate flavor.

Follow the recipe for Roasted Potatoes. While the potatoes roast, combine 2 tablespoons unsalted butter, melted, 1 tablespoon minced fresh chives, 1 teaspoon grated lemon zest, and 2 tablespoons lemon juice in a large bowl. Transfer the roasted potatoes to the bowl with the lemon-chive butter, toss, and serve immediately.

Roasted Potatoes with Southwestern Spices

Serve these potatoes with barbecued ribs and grilled corn.

Follow the recipe for Roasted Potatoes. While the potatoes roast, melt 2 tablespoons unsalted butter in a small skillet over medium heat. When the butter starts to sizzle, add 1 teaspoon ground cumin, 1 teaspoon chili powder, 1 teaspoon dry mustard, ⅛ teaspoon cayenne pepper, and 1 medium garlic clove, minced, and cook until fragrant, 30 seconds to 1 minute. Transfer the roasted potatoes to a serving bowl. Pour the spiced butter over the potatoes, toss, and serve immediately.

MASHED POTATOES

MOST OF US WHO MAKE MASHED POTATOES would never consider consulting a recipe. We customarily make them by adding chunks of butter and spurts of cream until our conscience—or a back-seat cook—tells us to stop. Not surprisingly, we produce batches of mashed potatoes that are consistent only in their mediocrity.

For us, the consummate mashed potatoes are creamy, soft, and supple, yet with enough body to stand up to the sauce or gravy from an accompanying dish. As for flavor, the sweet, earthy, humble potato comes first, then the buttery richness that keeps you coming back for more. In addition, we wanted to develop mashed potato variations spiked with complementary flavors, like the garlic mashed potatoes we've eaten in restaurants over the years.

We quickly determined that high-starch potatoes, such as russets, are best for mashing. Next we needed to address the simple matter of the best way to cook the potatoes. We started by peeling and cutting some potatoes into chunks to expedite their cooking while cooking others unpeeled and whole. Even when mashed with identical amounts of butter, half-and-half (recommended by a number of trustworthy cookbooks), and salt, the two batches were very different. The potatoes that had been peeled and cut made mashed potatoes that were thin in taste and texture and devoid of potato flavor, Peeling and cutting before simmering increases the surface area of the potatoes, through which they lose soluble substances such as starch, proteins, and flavor compounds, to the cooking water. The greater surface area also enables lots of water molecules to bind with the potatoes' starch molecules. Combine these two effects and you've got bland, thin, watery mashed potatoes. The potatoes cooked whole and peeled after cooking yielded mashed potatoes that were rich, earthy, and sweet.

Next were the matters of butter and dairy. Working with 2 pounds of potatoes, which serve four to six, we stooped so low as to add only 2 tablespoons of butter. The potatoes ultimately deemed best in flavor by tasters contained 8 tablespoons. They were rich and full and splendid.

When considering dairy, we investigated both the kind and the quantity. Heavy cream made heavy mashed potatoes that were sodden and unpalatably rich, even when we scaled back the amount of butter. On the other hand, mashed potatoes made with whole milk were watery, wimpy, and washed-out. Half-and-half, which we'd used in our original tests, was just what was needed, and 1 cup was just the right amount. The mashed potatoes now had a lovely, light suppleness and a full, rich flavor that edged toward decadent.

The issues attending butter and dairy did not end there. We had heard that the order in which they are added to the potatoes can affect texture. As it turns out, when the butter goes in before the dairy, the result is a silkier, creamier, smoother texture than when the dairy goes in first; by comparison, the dairy-first potatoes were pasty and thick. Also, using melted rather than softened butter made the potatoes even more creamy, smooth, and light.

When the half-and-half is stirred into the potatoes before the butter, the water in it works with the starch in the potatoes to make the mashed potatoes gluey and heavy. When the butter is added before the half-and-half, the fat coats the starch molecules, inhibiting their interaction with the water in the half-and-half added later and thereby yielding silkier, creamier mashed potatoes. The benefit of using melted butter results from its liquid form, which enables it to coat the starch molecules quickly and easily. This buttery coating not only affects the interaction of the starch molecules with the half-and-half, it also affects the starch molecules' interaction with each other. All in all, it makes for smoother, more velvety mashed potatoes. (Melting the butter, as well as warming the half-and-half, also serves to keep the potatoes warm.)

There is more than one way to mash potatoes. In our testing, we had been using either a ricer or a food mill. We preferred the food mill because its large hopper accommodated half of the potatoes at a time. A ricer, which resembles an oversize garlic press, required processing in several batches. Both, however, produced smooth, light, fine-textured mashed potatoes.

A potato masher is the tool of choice for making chunky mashed potatoes, but it cannot produce smooth mashed potatoes on a par with those processed through a food mill or ricer. With a masher, potatoes mashed within an inch of their lives could not achieve anything better than a namby-pamby texture that was neither chunky nor perfectly smooth. Since the sentiment among our tasters was that mashed potatoes should be either smooth or coarse and craggy, a masher is best left to make the latter.

There are two styles of potato mashers—one is a disk with large holes in it, the other a curvy wire loop. We found the disk to be more efficient for reducing both mashing time and the number of lumps in the finished product.

Mashed Potatoes

SERVES 4 TO 6

Russet potatoes make slightly fluffier mashed potatoes, but Yukon Golds have an appealing buttery flavor and can be used if you prefer. Mashed potatoes stiffen and become gluey as they cool, so they are best served piping hot. If you must hold mashed potatoes before serving, place them in a heatproof bowl, cover the bowl tightly with plastic wrap, and set the bowl over a pot of simmering water. Be sure to occasionally check the water level in the pan. The potatoes will remain hot and soft-textured for 1 hour. This recipe can be increased by half or doubled as needed. It yields smooth mashed potatoes. If you don't mind (or prefer) lumps, use a potato masher, as directed in the variation.

2   pounds russet potatoes, scrubbed
8   tablespoons (1 stick) unsalted butter, melted
1   cup half-and-half, warmed
1½   teaspoons salt
     Ground black pepper

1. Place the potatoes in a large saucepan with cold water to cover by about 1 inch. Bring to a boil over high heat, reduce the heat to medium-low, and simmer until the potatoes are just tender when pricked with a thin-bladed knife, 20 to 30 minutes. Drain the potatoes.

2. Set a food mill or ricer over the now-empty

but still-warm saucepan. Following the illustrations on page 189 for using a food mill, spear each potato with a dinner fork, then peel back the skin with a paring knife. Working in batches, cut the peeled potatoes into chunks and drop them into the hopper of a food mill. To use a ricer, halve the potatoes and place cut-side down in the ricer. Process or rice the potatoes into the saucepan.

3. Stir in the melted butter with a wooden spoon until incorporated. Gently whisk in the half-and-half, salt, and pepper to taste. Serve immediately.

➤ VARIATIONS

Mashed Potatoes with Garlic

The garlic can be peeled after toasting, when the skins will slip right off. Just make sure to keep the heat low and to let the garlic stand off the heat until fully softened.

Toast 22 small to medium-large garlic cloves (about ⅔ cup), skins left on, in a small covered skillet over the lowest possible heat, shaking the pan frequently, until the cloves are dark spotty brown and slightly softened, 22 minutes. Remove the pan from the heat and let stand, covered, until the cloves are fully softened, 15 to 20 minutes.

ALL-PURPOSE GRAVY FOR MASHED POTATOES

Gravy, by definition, is a thickened sauce made of meat juices and pan drippings, usually left over from a roast. But what if you don't have a roast on hand and want gravy for some mashed potatoes? What if you are limited to just some canned broth and a few vegetables? The problem is that a roast provides concentrated flavor through the *fond,* the browned bits at the bottom of the roasting pan. After extensive testing, we found that gravy can be made very simply with canned broth and a few vegetables. The key is to brown the vegetables to eke out their roasted, somewhat meaty flavor.

All-Purpose Gravy
MAKES 2 CUPS

This gravy can be served with almost any type of meat and with mashed potatoes as well. The recipe can be doubled. If doubling it, use a Dutch oven so that the vegetables brown properly, and increase the cooking times by roughly 50 percent.

1	small carrot, peeled and chopped into rough ½-inch pieces (about ½ cup)
1	small celery rib, chopped into rough ½-inch pieces (about ½ cup)
1	small onion, chopped into rough ½-inch pieces (about ¾ cup)
3	tablespoons unsalted butter
¼	cup unbleached all-purpose flour
2	cups low-sodium chicken broth
2	cups low-sodium beef broth
1	bay leaf
¼	teaspoon dried thyme
5	whole black peppercorns
	Salt and ground black pepper

1. In a food processor, pulse the carrot until broken into rough ¼-inch pieces, about five 1-second pulses. Add the celery and onion; pulse until all the vegetables are broken into ⅛-inch pieces, about five 1-second pulses.

2. Heat the butter in a large, heavy-bottomed saucepan over medium-high heat. When the foaming subsides, add the vegetables and cook, stirring frequently, until softened and well browned, about 7 minutes. Reduce the heat to medium; stir in the flour and cook, stirring constantly, until thoroughly browned and fragrant, about 5 minutes. Whisking constantly, gradually add the broths; bring to a boil, skimming off any foam that forms on the surface. Reduce the heat to medium-low and add the bay leaf, thyme, and peppercorns. Simmer, stirring occasionally, until thickened and reduced to 3 cups, 20 to 25 minutes.

3. Strain the gravy through a fine-mesh strainer into a clean saucepan, pressing on the solids to extract as much liquid as possible; discard the solids. Adjust the seasonings with salt and pepper to taste. Serve hot.

Peel the cloves and, using a paring knife, cut off the woody root ends. Follow the recipe for Mashed Potatoes through step 1, dropping the peeled garlic cloves into the food mill or ricer with the peeled potatoes and continue as directed.

Mashed Potatoes with Scallions and Horseradish

Follow the recipe for Mashed Potatoes through step 2. Stir the butter into the potatoes until just incorporated. Sprinkle the salt and pepper over the potatoes. Whisk ¼ cup grated fresh horseradish and the green parts of 3 scallions, minced, into the warm half-and-half; add the mixture to the mashed potatoes and stir until just combined. Serve immediately.

Mashed Potatoes with Smoked Cheddar and Grainy Mustard

If you can't find smoked cheddar, plain cheddar is good in this dish, too.

MAKING MASHED POTATOES

WITH A FOOD MILL

1. Hold the drained potato with a dinner fork and peel off the skin with a paring knife.
2. Cut the peeled potato into rough chunks and drop the chunks into the food mill.

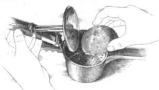

WITH A RICER

Cut each potato in half and place it cut-side down in the ricer. Press down with the handle of the ricer to force the flesh through the holes. The skin will remain in the hopper. Discard the skin and repeat with the remaining potato half.

Follow the recipe for Mashed Potatoes through step 2. Stir the butter into the potatoes until just incorporated. Sprinkle salt and pepper over the potatoes; add the warm half-and-half, 2 tablespoons grainy mustard, and 3 ounces smoked cheddar cheese, shredded (about ¾ cup); stir until just combined. Serve immediately.

BOILED POTATOES

MOST OFTEN, WE BOIL POTATOES FOR SALAD (see pages 98–103 for potato salad recipes). However, freshly dug baby or new potatoes can be boiled, buttered, and served hot as a side dish. In many ways, this simple preparation is the best way to highlight the flavor of really good potatoes. That said, much can go wrong with this dish. The potatoes can split open and become soggy. The key is to cook the potatoes until they are just tender and then drain and butter them immediately.

From our initial tests, we concluded that having potatoes of varying sizes in the pot was problematic. The small potatoes overcooked and their skins split open while we waited for the larger potatoes to cook through. (The best test for doneness is a paring knife or skewer; it should glide easily through the potato without causing it to fall apart.)

While larger potatoes are fine for salad, we found that the best potatoes for boiling and buttering are small—less than 2½ inches in diameter and preferably smaller. These potatoes cooked more evenly. Larger potatoes tended to get a bit mushy right under the skin by the time the center was cooked through.

From previous tests, we knew that you must boil potatoes with their skins on to prevent them from becoming watery. However, we found that the flesh on a boiled potato must be exposed at some point so that it can soak up the butter and seasonings. When we tossed drained, whole, skin-on potatoes with butter, the butter just stayed in the bowl—it could not penetrate the skin.

We tried peeling a thin band around the center of each potato before boiling to eliminate the need to cut them after cooking. This test failed. Once the potatoes were cooked, the skin that had been left on started to break away from the flesh, and the flesh, too, was breaking apart.

For the best results, we found it necessary to cut the potatoes in half after boiling. Although a bit tedious, we found that holding the hot potatoes one at a time with a pair of tongs and then slicing them with a knife worked well. Once all of the potatoes were cut in half, we immediately added them to the bowl with the butter. As soon as the potatoes are coated with fat, the seasonings can be added.

Boiled Potatoes with Butter

SERVES 4

The cooking time will vary depending on the size of the potatoes. For potatoes that measure 2 to 2½ inches in diameter (you will need 12 to 17 potatoes to make 2 pounds), plan on 15 to 18 minutes of cooking time. For potatoes that measure 1½ to 2 inches in diameter (you will need 18 to 24 potatoes to make 2 pounds), plan on 12 to 15 minutes of cooking time. For potatoes that measure 1 to 1½ inches in diameter (you will need 25 to 31 potatoes to make 2 pounds), plan on 10 to 12 minutes of cooking time. For potatoes that measure less than 1 inch in diameter (you will need 32 or more potatoes to make 2 pounds), plan on 8 to 10 minutes of cooking time.

   3   tablespoons unsalted butter
   2   pounds small red or new potatoes, scrubbed
         Salt and ground black pepper

1. Place the butter in a medium serving bowl and set aside to soften while you prepare and cook the potatoes.

2. Place the potatoes and 1 tablespoon salt in a Dutch oven and fill with enough cold water to cover the potatoes by about 1 inch. Bring to a boil over high heat, cover, reduce the heat to medium-low, and simmer, stirring once or twice, until the potatoes are just tender when pierced with a thin-bladed knife or skewer, 8 to 18 minutes depending on the size of the potatoes. Drain the potatoes.

3. Cut the potatoes in half (see the illustration above). Place the halved potatoes in the bowl with the butter and toss to coat. Season with salt and pepper to taste and toss again. Serve immediately.

HANDLING HOT BOILED POTATOES

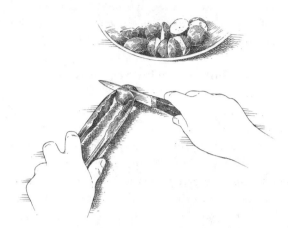

Potatoes should be boiled whole and unpeeled so that they don't become soggy. After boiling, however, the potatoes should be cut in half because the fleshy portion of the potato absorbs butter and seasonings far better than the skin. To halve a hot potato, steady it with a pair of tongs while cutting with a sharp knife.

➤ VARIATIONS

Boiled Potatoes with Butter and Chives
Follow the recipe for Boiled Potatoes with Butter, adding 3 tablespoons thinly sliced fresh chives along with the salt and pepper in step 3.

Boiled Potatoes with Lemon, Parsley, and Olive Oil
Follow the recipe for Boiled Potatoes with Butter, replacing the butter with 3 tablespoons extra-virgin olive oil. Add the minced zest from 1 lemon and 3 tablespoons chopped fresh parsley leaves along with the salt and pepper in step 3.

Boiled Potatoes with Shallots and Sage
Melt 3 tablespoons butter in a small skillet over medium-high heat. When the foaming subsides, add 1 medium shallot, minced, and cook until golden, 2 to 3 minutes. Add 1 tablespoon minced fresh sage leaves and cook until fragrant, about 1 minute. Scrape this mixture into a medium serving bowl and proceed with the recipe for Boiled Potatoes with Butter from step 2.

SCALLOPED POTATOES

TRADITIONALLY RESERVED FOR HOLIDAYS and special events, scalloped potatoes are luxuriously waist-defying. Cooked in fantastic amounts of heavy cream, butter, and cheese, their richness is hardly suitable for your average supper (or diet).

We wanted a lighter, more convenient recipe, but we also wanted a recipe that would taste good (and not come out of a box).

To begin, we made several standard scalloped potato recipes. We rubbed shallow dishes with garlic, sliced potatoes and laid them in rows,

---

EQUIPMENT: Mandolines and V-Slicers

What's cheaper than a food processor and faster (if not also sharper) than a chef's knife? A mandoline. This hand-operated slicing machine comes in two basic styles—the classic stainless steel model, supported by legs, and the plastic hand-held model, often called a V-slicer. We put both types of machines—ranging in price from $8.99 to $169—to the test. To determine the winners, we sliced melons, cut carrots into julienne (matchstick pieces), cut potatoes into batonets (long, skinny French fry pieces), and sliced potatoes into thin rounds. Then we evaluated three aspects of the mandolines: ease of use, including degree of effort, adjustment ease, grip/handle comfort, and safety; quality, including sturdiness and uniformity/cleanliness of slices; and cleanup.

The Progressive Mandoline Multi Slicer ($8.99) and the Target Mandoline Slicer ($9.99) are plastic V-slicers with similar designs. Testers gave these models high marks for safety, handle comfort, and blade sharpness, which helped them whip through melon and potato slices. Interchangeable blade platforms cut respectable batonet and julienne, though these cuts required more effort on the part of testers.

The two other V-slicers tested were the Börner V-Slicer Plus ($34.95) and the Joyce Chen Asian Mandoline Plus ($49.95). The latter produced flawless melon slices, carrot julienne, and potato batonet but got low marks for its small, ineffective

safety mechanism and tricky blade adjustment. Testers also downgraded the poorly designed and not very sturdy base. The Börner unit sliced melons and carrots with little effort, but the potato slices were inconsistent and required more effort to produce. The Börner's well-designed safety guard, however, kept hands away from blades, and its adjustments were quick and easy to make. In the end, testers preferred the cheaper V-slicers made by Progressive and Target to either of these more expensive options.

We also tested two classic stainless steel mandolines. The deBuyer mandoline from Williams-Sonoma ($169) was controversial. Shorter testers had difficulty gaining leverage to cut consistently; some melon slices were 1/8 inch thicker on one side. However, the safety mechanism, sturdiness, and adjustment mechanism were lauded by taller testers. With some practice, all testers were able to produce perfect slices, julienne, and batonet with the Bron Coucke mandoline ($99). This machine has fewer parts to clean and switch out than its plastic counterparts and requires less effort to operate once the user becomes familiar with it. Still, the quality comes at an awfully high price.

THE BEST V-SLICERS
Plastic mandolines (also called V-slicers) may not be as sturdy as stainless steel versions, but their quality far exceeds the minimal dollar investment. Among the four models tested, we liked the Progressive and Target slicers, which are similar in design.

THE BEST CLASSIC MANDOLINE
Of the two stainless steel mandolines tested, we preferred this model made by Bron Coucke. Note, however, that it costs 10 times more than a good V-slicer.

topped them with heavy cream and cheese, and baked them off. The ingredient lists were similar in their inclusion of garlic, cream, and sliced russets, but some also called for half-and-half or milk, while others called for butter and flour. All of the recipes were unabashedly rich and took as long as 1½ hours to make from start to finish. Several tasted pasty from the flour (used as a thickener for the sauce), and nearly all were a bit dull from the sheer lack of aromatics beyond garlic. Not only did these stodgy potato dishes need to be lightened up considerably, but they begged for more flavor, as well as a realistic midweek cooking time.

Starting with the potatoes, we cooked russet, all-purpose, and Yukon Gold varieties side by side in basic scalloped fashion. While Yukon Gold and all-purpose potatoes weren't bad, tasters found them a bit waxy. The traditional russets, with their tender bite and earthy flavor, were the unanimous favorite. The russets also formed tighter, more cohesive layers owing to their higher starch content.

Heavy cream is the obvious, diet-crushing ingredient in traditional scalloped potatoes, so we figured it was probably to blame for their usual heft. To relieve some of the heaviness, we tried replacing the heavy cream with a number of less fatty liquids. We tried half-and-half, but the sauce curdled as it bubbled away in the oven. Half-and-half, as it turns out, doesn't have enough fat to keep the dairy proteins from coagulating under high heat. Supplementing some of the heavy

cream with whole milk worked well (no curdling), but the potatoes still tasted a bit heavy and dairy-rich for an everyday meal. Next we tried replacing some of the heavy cream with chicken broth. The broth effectively mitigated some of the cream's heaviness. After trying a variety of broth-to-cream ratios, we landed on a 50-50 split.

With the sauce lightened up, it was time to tweak its flavor. While the delicate flavor of shallots was easily overpowered, a little sautéed onion and garlic worked wonders. Throwing in leaves of fresh thyme and dried bay also helped to spruce up the sauce with an herbaceous flavor that was neither showy nor distracting.

Up until now, we had been using the tiresome technique of layering the raw potatoes and sauce in a shallow dish and baking them in the oven for 1½ hours. To speed things up, we tried parboiling the potatoes in water first, then combining them with a sauce (thickened with flour to achieve a saucy consistency in less time), and finishing them in the oven. Although this did shave nearly 45 minutes off the cooking time, the potatoes had a hollow flavor, the sauce tasted gummy and flat, and we spent much of the time we had saved washing dirty pots.

Next we tried par-cooking the sliced potatoes in the chicken broth and cream in a covered pot on top of the stove before dumping it all into a shallow casserole dish and finishing it in the oven. Here was our solution. This technique gave the potatoes a head start on the stovetop, where they released some of their starch into the sauce. This starch, a natural thickening agent, transformed the consistency of the cooking liquid into a rightful sauce, negating the need for flour.

When slowly simmered on the stovetop for 10 minutes, at which time the potatoes were about halfway cooked, the casserole required only 15 minutes in a 425-degree oven to finish. We sprinkled a handful of cheddar over the top, and the potatoes emerged from the oven as a bubbling inferno with a golden crown. Although the ripping-hot potatoes and sauce make for a sloppy casserole straight out of the oven, a rest of 10 minutes is all that's needed for them to cool off a bit and cohere.

PROPERLY SLICED POTATOES

When the potatoes were cut thicker than ⅛ inch (left), they slid apart when served. Yet when cut much thinner (right), the layers melted together, producing a mashed potato–like texture. At exactly ⅛ inch (center), the potatoes held their shape yet remained flexible enough to form tight, cohesive layers. Although it is possible to cut ⅛-inch slices by hand, it is far easier when using a food processor or mandoline.

Scalloped Potatoes

SERVES 4 TO 6

The quickest way to slice the potatoes is in a food processor fitted with an ⅛-inch slicing blade. If the potatoes are too long to fit into the feed tube, halve them crosswise and put them in the feed tube cut-side down so that they sit on a flat surface. If the potato slices discolor as they sit, put them in a bowl and cover with the cream and chicken broth. A mandoline or V-slicer (see page 191) is the other option. Don't try to slice the potatoes with a knife; you won't get them thin enough. If you like, use Parmesan instead of cheddar.

2	tablespoons unsalted butter
1	medium onion, minced
2	medium garlic cloves, minced or pressed through a garlic press
1	tablespoon chopped fresh thyme leaves
1¼	teaspoons salt
¼	teaspoon ground black pepper
2½	pounds (about 5 medium) russet potatoes, peeled and sliced ⅛ inch thick
1	cup low-sodium chicken broth
1	cup heavy cream
2	bay leaves
4	ounces cheddar cheese, shredded (1 cup)

1. Adjust an oven rack to the middle position and heat the oven to 425 degrees.

2. Melt the butter in a Dutch oven over medium-high heat. When the foaming subsides, add the onion and cook, stirring occasionally, until soft and lightly browned, about 4 minutes. Add the garlic, thyme, salt, and pepper and cook until fragrant, about 30 seconds. Add the potatoes, broth, cream, and bay leaves and bring to a simmer. Cover, reduce the heat to medium-low, and simmer until the potatoes are almost tender (a paring knife can be slipped into and out of a potato slice with some resistance), about 10 minutes. Discard the bay leaves.

3. Transfer the mixture to an 8-inch square baking dish (or other 1½-quart gratin dish). Sprinkle evenly with the cheese. Bake until the cream is bubbling around the edges and the top is golden brown, about 15 minutes. Cool 10 minutes before serving.

> VARIATIONS

Scalloped Potatoes with Chipotle Chile and Smoked Cheddar Cheese

Follow the recipe for Scalloped Potatoes, adding 1 large chipotle chile in adobo sauce, minced (about 1½ tablespoons), along with the garlic and substituting smoked cheddar cheese for the regular cheddar.

Scalloped Potatoes with Mushrooms

Slice 8 ounces cremini mushrooms ½ inch thick; trim the stems off 4 ounces fresh shiitake mushrooms and slice the caps ¼ inch thick. Follow the recipe for Scalloped Potatoes, adding the mushrooms to the butter along with the onion. Cook until the moisture released by the mushrooms has evaporated, about 5 minutes. Proceed as directed.

Scalloped Potatoes with Fontina and Artichokes

Fontina is a semisoft cow's milk cheese with a mild, nutty flavor.

Thoroughly drain 4 ounces jarred or canned artichoke hearts and cut them into ½-inch pieces. (You should have about 1 cup.) Follow the recipe for Scalloped Potatoes, adding the artichokes with the potatoes in step 2. Proceed as directed, replacing the cheddar with an equal amount of shredded fontina cheese.

FRENCH FRIES

THE IDEAL FRENCH FRY IS LONG AND CRISP, with right-angle sides and a nice crunch on the outside. It should taste of earthy potato, with just a hint of the oil in which it was created. A French fry should definitely not droop, and its coloring should be two-tone, blond with hints of brown.

Obviously, a good French fry requires the right potato. Would it be starchy or waxy? We tested two of the most popular waxy (low-starch/high-moisture) potatoes, and neither was even close to ideal, both being too watery. During the frying, water evaporated inside the potato, leaving hollows that would fill with oil, so the finished fries were greasy. Next we tested the starchy potato most readily available nationwide, the russet. This potato turned out to be ideal, frying up with all the qualities that we were looking for.

Because these are starchy potatoes, it is important to rinse the starch off the surface after you cut the potato into fries. To do this, simply put the cut fries in a bowl, place the bowl in the sink, and run cold water into it, swirling with your fingers until the water runs clear. This might seem like an unimportant step, but it makes a real difference. When we skipped the starch rinse, the fries weren't quite right, and the oil clouded.

At this point, you take the second crucial step: Fill the bowl with clear water, add ice, and refrigerate the potatoes for at least 30 minutes. That way, when the potatoes first enter the hot oil, they are nearly frozen; this allows a slow, thorough cooking of the inner potato pulp. When we tried making fries without this chilling, the outsides started to brown well before the insides were fully cooked.

Our preference is to peel potatoes for French fries. A skin-on fry keeps the potato from forming those little airy blisters that we prefer. Peeling the potato also allows home cooks to see—and remove, if they want to—any imperfections and greenish coloring.

What is the right fat for making perfect French fries? To find out, we experimented with lard, vegetable shortening, canola oil, corn oil, and peanut oil. Lard and shortening make great fries, but we figured that many cooks won't want to use these products. We moved on to canola oil, the ballyhooed oil of the '90s, now used in a blend with safflower oil by McDonald's, which produces 4 million pounds of finished fries a day. But we were unhappy with the results: bland, almost watery fries.

Corn oil was the most forgiving oil in the test kitchen. It rebounded well from temperature fluctuations and held up very well in subsequent frying, and the fries tasted marvelous. A potato fried in peanut oil is light, and the flavor is rich but not dense. The earthy flavor of the potato is there, as with corn oil, but is not overbearing. At this point, we were very close, and yet there was still something missing. The high flavor note, which is supplied by the animal fat in lard, was lacking.

We tried a dollop of strained bacon grease in peanut oil, about two generous tablespoons per quart of oil. The meaty flavor came through, but without its nasty baggage. To be certain of this, we added bacon grease to each of the oils, with these results: canola oil, extra body, but still short on flavor; corn oil, more body, more flavor, nearly perfect; peanut oil, flavor, bite, and body. At last, an equivalent to lard.

Now it was time to get down to the frying, which actually means double-frying. First, we par-fried the potatoes at a relatively low temperature to release their rich and earthy flavor. The potatoes are then quick-fried at a higher temperature until nicely browned and immediately served.

CUTTING POTATOES FOR FRYING

REGULAR FRIES
Slice the peeled potatoes lengthwise into ovals about ¼ inch thick. Stack several ovals on top of each other and slice them into ¼-inch-thick lengths.

STEAK FRIES
1. Cut each potato in half lengthwise. Place the potato half flat-side down and cut into thirds lengthwise.

2. Cut each piece of potato in half lengthwise to yield 12 wedges that measure about ¾ inch across on the skin side.

The garden-variety cookbook recipe calls for par-frying at 350 degrees and final frying at 375 to 400 degrees. But we found these temperatures to be far too aggressive. We prefer an initial frying at 325 degrees, with the final frying at 350 degrees. Lower temperatures allowed for easier monitoring; with higher temperatures, the fries can get away from the cook.

For the sake of convenience, we also attempted a single, longer frying. Like many cooks before us, we found that with standard French fries (as opposed to the much thinner shoestring fries), we could not both sear the outside and properly cook the inside with a single visit to the hot fat. When we left them in long enough to sear the outside, we wound up with wooden, overcooked fries.

French Fries

SERVES 4

For those who like it, flavoring the oil with a few tablespoons of bacon grease adds a subtle, meaty flavor to the fries. Their texture, however, is not affected if the bacon grease is omitted. See the illustrations on page 194 for tips on cutting the potatoes.

4	large russet potatoes (about 10 ounces each), peeled and cut into lengths 1/4-inch thick
2	quarts peanut oil
1/4	cup strained bacon grease (optional)
	Salt and ground black pepper

1. Rinse the cut fries in a large bowl under cold running water until the water turns from milky-colored to clear. Cover with at least 1 inch water, then cover with ice. Refrigerate at least 30 minutes. (The potatoes can be refrigerated up to 3 days ahead.)

2. In a 5-quart pot or Dutch oven fitted with a clip-on candy thermometer, or in a larger electric fryer, heat the oil over medium-low heat to 325 degrees. As the oil heats, add the bacon grease, if using. (The oil will bubble up when you add the fries, so be sure you have at least 3 inches of room at the top of the pot.)

3. Pour off the ice and water, quickly wrap the potatoes in a clean kitchen towel, and pat thoroughly dry. Increase the heat to medium-high and add the fries, a handful at a time, to the hot oil. Fry, stirring with a Chinese skimmer or large-hole slotted spoon, until the potatoes are limp and soft and start to turn from white to blond, 6 to 8 minutes. (The oil temperature will drop 50 to 60 degrees during this frying.) Use the skimmer or slotted spoon to transfer the fries to a triple thickness of paper towels to drain; let rest at least 10 minutes. (The fries can stand at room temperature for up to 2 hours or be wrapped in paper towels, sealed in a zipper-lock bag, and frozen for up to 1 month.)

4. When ready to serve the fries, reheat the oil to 350 degrees. Using a paper bag as a funnel, pour the potatoes into the hot oil. Fry the potatoes, stirring fairly constantly, until golden brown and puffed, about 2 to 5 minutes. Transfer the fries to another triple thickness of paper towels and drain again. Season with salt and pepper to taste. Serve immediately.

➤ VARIATION

Spicy Fries

Combine 1 teaspoon chili powder, 1 teaspoon paprika, 1/2 teaspoon ground cumin, and 1/8 to 1/4 teaspoon cayenne pepper in a small bowl. Follow the recipe for French Fries, using this mixture in place of the black pepper (and with the salt) in step 4.

DISPOSING OF OIL NEATLY

Deep-fried foods, such as French fries, are a real treat, but cleaning up after frying is not. Disposing of the spent oil neatly and safely is a particular challenge. Here's how we do it. First we allow the oil to cool completely. Then we make a quadruple- or quintuple-layered bag using four or five leftover plastic grocery bags. With someone holding the layered bags open over a sink or in an outdoor area, we carefully pour the cooled frying oil from the pot into the innermost bag. We tie the bag handles shut and dispose of the oil in the garbage.

STEAK FRIES

STEAK FRIES ARE THE RUSTIC COUNTRY cousin to French fries. With their skin left on and their shape determined largely by the shape of the potato, these wedge-shaped fries are easier to prepare and less wasteful than the typical French fry, where much effort is expended to obtain ruler-perfect consistency. Much like good French fries, however, good steak fries should be crisp on the outside and tender on the inside. They should not be oily, dry, mealy, or soggy.

As with regular French fries, we found that starchy russets fried up beautifully. Their dense, starchy texture cooked to a consistently tender interior, while the thick skin fried up good and crisp. Russets we bought in 5-pound bags, however, came in various sizes and were difficult to cut into uniform wedges. We found russets that are sold loosely are more consistent in size and are easier to cut into same-size wedges for more consistent cooking times. After cooking up fries of various thicknesses, we preferred wedges with an outside edge that measures ¾ inch wide (this works out to one large potato cut into 12 wedges). Any thicker or thinner and the ratio of tender interior to crisp exterior was thrown off.

Many recipes for deep-fried potatoes suggest refrigerating the raw wedges before frying them, and we found this step to be crucial. Cooling the potatoes down before plunging them into the hot oil allows them to cook more slowly and evenly. By soaking the wedges in a bowl of ice water in the refrigerator for at least 30 minutes, we were able to ensure that the inner pulp was fully cooked before the outside turned overly brown.

Like most people who've fried potatoes before us, we found that simply dunking the chilled, raw fries in hot oil and cooking them until they are done will not produce a good fry. By the time the inside of the fry is cooked and the outside is well browned, the fry itself is wooden and overcooked. We first par-fried them at a relatively low temperature to help them cook through without much browning. We then gave them a brief repose to cool off before refrying them quickly in oil at a higher temperature until nicely browned. In combination with the ice-water bath, this technique worked like a dream. The thick wedges of potato were evenly cooked, with tender middles and crisp, browned exteriors.

Steak Fries
SERVES 4

See the illustrations on page 194 for tips on cutting potatoes for steak fries.

4	large russet potatoes (about 10 ounces each), scrubbed and cut lengthwise into ¾-inch-thick wedges (about 12 wedges per potato)
2	quarts peanut oil
	Salt and ground black pepper

1. Place the cut fries in a large bowl, cover with cold water by at least 1 inch, and then cover with ice cubes. Refrigerate at least 30 minutes or up to 3 days.

2. In a 5-quart pot or Dutch oven fitted with a clip-on candy thermometer, or in a large electric fryer, heat the oil over medium-low heat to 325 degrees. (The oil will bubble up when you add the fries, so be sure you have at least 3 inches of room at the top of the pot.)

3. Pour off the ice and water, quickly the wrap potatoes in a clean kitchen towel, and pat them thoroughly dry. Increase the heat to medium-high and add the fries, one handful at a time, to the hot oil. Fry, stirring with a Chinese skimmer or slotted spoon, until the potatoes are limp and soft and have turned from white to gold, about 10 minutes. (The oil temperature will drop 50 to 60 degrees during this frying.) Use the skimmer or slotted spoon to transfer the fries to a triple thickness of paper towels to drain; let rest at least 10 minutes. (The fries can stand at room temperature for up to 2 hours or be wrapped in paper towels, sealed in a zipper-lock bag, and frozen for up to 1 month.)

4. When ready to serve the fries, reheat the oil to 350 degrees. Using the paper towels as a funnel, pour the potatoes into the hot oil. Discard the paper towels and line a wire rack with another triple thickness of paper towels. Fry the potatoes, stirring fairly constantly, until medium brown and puffed, 7 to 10 minutes. Transfer the fries to the paper towel–lined rack to drain. Season with salt and pepper to taste. Serve immediately.

OVEN FRIES

LOW FAT IS NEVER A GOOD EXCUSE FOR lousy food, and oven fries should be no exception. Abysmal flavor and texture just aren't worth the savings in calories, especially when these "lite" fries taste like over-roasted potatoes with thick, leathery crusts and hollow interiors. In other cases, they are limp, whitish, mealy, and bland—a complete failure in all respects. Yet easy and clean oven-cooking—as opposed to deep-frying in a pot of hot, splattering oil—is such an engaging proposition that we decided to enlist temporarily in the low-fat army to see if we could make an oven fry worth eating on its own terms. If it didn't have a golden, crisp crust and a richly creamy interior, we were going back to the deep fryer.

First off, we tested russet, Yukon Gold, and boiling potatoes. Tasting wimpy and sporting spotty crusts, both the Yukon Gold and boiling potatoes couldn't hold a candle to the russets, with their hearty flavor and facility for turning golden brown. Equally obvious were the results of the peeled-versus-unpeeled-potato test. The unpeeled fries were tougher and had the distinct flavor of baked potatoes, whereas the peeled fries—unanimously preferred by tasters—had a clean and more characteristically "French" fry flavor. Tasters also liked the ample size and easy preparation of potatoes cut into wedges, as opposed to the fussy and wasteful option of trimming potatoes down into squared, fast-food-fry wannabes.

Next we baked the fries at 400, 425, 450, 475, and 500 degrees. At lower temperatures, the fries didn't brown sufficiently. The 500-degree oven was a bit too hot and burned the fries at the edges. Baking at 475 degrees was best, but the fries still needed a deeper golden color and a crispier texture. Adjusting the oven rack to the lower-middle position was only moderately helpful, but moving it to the lowest position made for a significant improvement in the fries. The intense heat from the bottom of the oven browned them quickly and evenly, which, in turn, prevented the interiors from overcooking and melding into the crust (thereby becoming the unlikable hollow fry). Lightweight baking sheets can't handle this extreme temperature, so a heavy pan is a must (see "A Weighty Matter" below).

Up until now, we had been simply tossing the potatoes with oil, salt, and pepper before spreading them out on the baking sheet. Turning our attention to the amount of oil, we found the differences between 1 and 6 tablespoons to be astounding. Any fewer than 5 tablespoons left some of the fries uncoated and caused them to bake up dry and tough; any more than 5 tablespoons made them disagreeably greasy. Exactly 5 tablespoons, however, ensured that each wedge was evenly coated with oil as it baked. To guarantee even distribution of oil, we found it best to spread 4 tablespoons on the baking sheet and to toss the raw fries with the fifth. Slightly glistening as they emerge from the oven, the fries require a brief drain on paper towels to keep them from tasting oily. Although 5 tablespoons is much less oil than the couple of quarts or more called for when deep-frying potatoes, we felt our oven fries no longer qualified as "low fat." Then again, neither did they qualify as pale, soggy, or dry.

Olive oil tasted slightly bitter and out of place, while the mild flavor of vegetable oil and the slight nuttiness of peanut oil (which we prefer to use when deep-frying) both worked well. Although the fries

A WEIGHTY MATTER

HEAVYWEIGHT PAN: EVEN BROWNING

LIGHTWEIGHT PAN: SPOTTY BROWNING

The top pan makes all the difference when baking oven fries. A lightweight pan yields fries that are either pale or burnt. A heavy-duty baking sheet conducts heat better and ensures that the fries color evenly and deeply.

were now sticking to the pan far less than before, we were still plagued by the occasional stuck-on fry until we discovered one last trick. Rather than tossing the potatoes with salt and pepper, we sprinkled the seasonings over the oiled baking sheet. Acting like little ball bearings, the grains of salt and pepper kept the potatoes from sticking to the pan without getting in the way of browning.

Even though we had nailed down the basic method for cooking the fries, they were still beset with crusts that were too thick and interiors that were unappealingly mealy. Wondering what would happen if we steamed the fries before baking them (a technique we'd seen in a few other recipes), we steamed one batch on top of the stove in a steamer basket and another in the oven by covering the baking sheet tightly with foil. This seemingly odd method delivered just the thing we had been after: an oven fry with the creamy, smooth core of an authentic French fry. Steaming on the stovetop had been a counter-clogging, time-consuming affair, but wrapping a baking sheet with foil was easy. The foil trapped the potatoes' natural moisture as they steamed themselves in the oven, and it then came off so the crusts could crisp for the balance of cooking. Five minutes of steaming was just right, turning the dry, starchy centers of the fries to a soft, creamy consistency without interfering with browning.

Now the only problem remaining was the crust. Steaming, although beneficial for the interior, turned the already thick crust even tougher; this was a far cry from the thin, brittle crust of a good French fry. To solve this problem, we decided to try the techniques of rinsing and soaking, which are often employed when making French fries. Rinsing the raw fries under running water made for a slightly more delicate crust, but soaking them for about an hour in cold tap water was pure magic. Slowly turning the water cloudy as they soaked, the fries emerged from the oven with thin, shatteringly crisp crusts and interiors more velvety than any oven fry we had tasted (for more information, see "The Power of Soaking" below). But perhaps the biggest surprise came when we tried soaking the fries in water at different temperatures: ice-cold, cold from the tap, and hot from the tap. The ice water took hours to become cloudy, the cold tap water took about 1 hour, and the hot tap water took a convenient 10 minutes, which meant that we could peel, cut, and soak the potatoes in roughly the same time it took to heat up the oven.

Oven Fries
SERVES 3 TO 4

Take care to cut the potatoes into even wedges so that all of the pieces will cook at about the same rate. Although it isn't required, a nonstick baking sheet works particularly well for this recipe. It not only keeps the fries from sticking but, because of its dark color, encourages deep and even browning. Whether you choose a nonstick baking sheet or a regular baking sheet, make sure that it is heavy-duty. The intense heat of the oven may cause lighter pans to warp.

3 russet potatoes (about 8 ounces each), peeled, each potato cut lengthwise into 10 to 12 even wedges

5 tablespoons vegetable or peanut oil
   Salt and ground black pepper

SCIENCE: The Power of Soaking

Experts agree (just ask McDonald's or our test cooks) that russet potatoes are the best variety for frying—either in a vat of bubbling oil or on a baking sheet in the oven. Unlike other potato varieties, russets produce fries with light, ethereal centers. But they are not perfect.

Russets can produce excessively thick crusts and somewhat dry interiors. The thick crust is caused by the browning of simple sugars in the russet, and the best way to remove some of the surface sugar is to soak the potatoes in water. The water has an added benefit. Potato starches gelatinize completely during cooking. The water introduced during soaking improves the creaminess and smoothness by working its way between the strands of gelatin starch. The final result is a fry that has a good surface crunch married to a smooth interior.

---

1. Adjust an oven rack to the lowest position; heat the oven to 475 degrees. Place the potatoes in a large bowl and cover with hot tap water; soak 10 minutes. Meanwhile, coat an 18 by 12-inch heavy-duty rimmed baking sheet with 4 tablespoons of the oil and sprinkle evenly with ¾ teaspoon salt and ¼ teaspoon pepper; set aside.

2. Drain the potatoes. Spread the potatoes out on a triple thickness of paper towels and pat thoroughly dry with additional paper towels. Rinse and wipe out the now-empty bowl; return the potatoes to the bowl and toss with the remaining 1 tablespoon oil. Arrange the potatoes in a single layer on the prepared baking sheet; cover tightly with foil and bake 5 minutes. Remove the foil and continue to bake until the bottoms of the potatoes are spotty golden brown, 15 to 20 minutes, rotating the baking sheet after 10 minutes. Using a metal spatula and tongs, scrape to loosen the potatoes from the pan, then flip each wedge, keeping the potatoes in a single layer. Continue baking until the fries are golden and crisp, 5 to 15 minutes longer, rotating the pan as needed if the fries are browning unevenly.

3. Transfer the fries to a second baking sheet lined with paper towels to drain. Season with additional salt and pepper to taste and serve immediately.

BAKED SWEET POTATOES

SWEET POTATOES HAVE BEEN HIDING UNDER the bushel basket of holiday meals long enough. They have wonderful flavor, and they're available all year, so why not bake and eat one anytime, just like a potato?

We believe we should do just that, so we set out to find the best way to bake sweet potatoes. We were looking for evenly cooked, moist flesh and softened, slightly caramelized, delicious skin. In trying to reach this goal, we considered and tested 23 individual variables.

Oven variables included temperature, rack level, and whether a baking sheet worked better than just laying the potatoes on the oven rack. We found that the best oven temperature was 400 degrees. Lower temperatures took longer with no improvement, while higher temperatures left burned spots on the bottom of the potatoes.

Similarly, the best rack position was the center. Placing the rack either higher or lower resulted in blackening of the potatoes' thin skins. When we placed the potatoes directly on the rack, sticky juice oozed straight down and burned, so we use a baking sheet lined with foil.

We also tested oven tricks, like placing the potatoes on unglazed oven tiles and beds of rock salt, but neither proved productive. We even tried cooking the potatoes halfway in the microwave and then transferring them to the oven, but the skin did not soften and there was no caramelization. We also tried baking the potatoes wrapped in foil, which turned out to be just what we suspected—a school cafeteria abomination that holds heat in soggy, overbaked potatoes.

We also did a number of tests to find the best way to deal with the skin, which is thin and very delicious when cooked properly. Uncoated skin stayed tough and unappealing, but coating it with butter tended to cause burning. Lightly rubbing it with vegetable or olive oil, though, softened the skin just the right amount.

Piercing the skin, we found, was essential to prevent the infamous exploding potato. But our big payoff in the search for tasty skin was the discovery that you should not turn the potatoes during baking. This method resulted in a perfectly browned bottom skin that was beautifully caramelized.

⌁

Baked Sweet Potatoes
SERVES 4

This recipe is for the moist, orange-fleshed varieties of sweet potatoes that generally show up in supermarkets. If you have white-fleshed sweet potatoes, increase the baking time by 10 minutes and use plenty of butter to moisten their drier flesh. You can cook up to 6 potatoes at one time without altering the cooking time. Buying potatoes of the same size is a good idea because it standardizes cooking time. As with regular baked potatoes, we find it best to open the baked sweet potatoes as wide as possible so that steam can quickly escape; this ensures that the flesh is fluffy rather than dense.

4   small sweet potatoes (about 2 pounds),
    scrubbed and lightly pricked with a fork

2 tablespoons vegetable or olive oil
Salt and ground black pepper
Unsalted butter

1. Adjust an oven rack to the center position and heat the oven to 400 degrees. Rub the potatoes with the oil, then arrange them on a foil-lined baking sheet as far apart from each other as possible.

2. Bake until a knife tip slips easily into the center of a potato, 40 to 50 minutes. Remove the sweet potatoes from the oven and pierce them with a fork to create a dotted X on the top of each potato (see illustration 1 on page 182). Press in at the ends of each sweet potato to push the flesh up and out (see illustration 2 on page 182). Season with salt and pepper to taste. Dot with butter to taste and serve immediately.

MASHED SWEET POTATOES

MASHED SWEET POTATOES ARE OFTEN OVER-dressed in a Willy Wonka–style casserole topped with marshmallows and whipped cream, but when it comes to flavor, this candied concoction doesn't hold a candle to an honest sweet potato mash. With a deep, natural sweetness that requires little assistance, the humble sweet potato, we thought, would taste far better if prepared with a minimum of ingredients.

Yet even with a simple recipe, mashed sweet potatoes can pose problems. Nailing a fork-friendly puree every time is a form of cooking roulette. Mashed sweet potatoes often turn out thick and gluey or, at the other extreme, sloppy and loose. We also found that most recipes overload the dish with pumpkin pie seasonings that obscure the potato's natural flavor. We wanted a recipe that pushed that deep, earthy sweetness to the fore and that reliably produced a silky puree with enough body to hold its shape on a fork. We decided to focus first on the cooking method, then test the remaining ingredients, and finally fiddle with the seasonings.

To determine the best cooking method, we tested a variety of techniques: baking potatoes unpeeled, boiling them whole and unpeeled, boiling them peeled and diced, steaming them peeled and diced, and microwaving them whole and unpeeled. Adding a little butter and salt to the potatoes after mashing, we found, yields a huge improvement in texture, flavor, and ease of preparation.

The baked sweet potatoes produced a mash with a deep flavor and bright color, but the potatoes took more than an hour to bake through, and handling them hot from the oven was risky. Boiling whole sweet potatoes in their skins yielded a wet puree with a mild flavor. When we used a fork to monitor the potatoes as they cooked, we made holes that apparently let the flavor seep out and excess water seep in. Steaming and boiling pieces of peeled potato produced the worst purees, with zero flavor and loose, applesauce-like textures. The microwave,

INGREDIENTS: Sweet Potatoes

It's an age-old culinary question: What is the difference between a yam and a sweet potato? Answer: It depends on where you live. In U.S. markets, a "yam" is actually a mislabeled sweet potato. If you can get a glimpse of the box it's shipped in, you'll see the words "sweet potato" printed somewhere, as mandated by the U.S. Department of Agriculture. In other parts of the world, "yam" refers to a true yam, a vegetable having no relation to the sweet potato.

Sold under the label "ñame" (ny-AH-may) or "igname" here in the United States, a true yam has a hairy, off-white or brown skin and white, light yellow, or pink flesh. This tuber is usually sold in log-shaped chunks that weigh several pounds each. Unlike a sweet potato, a true yam tastes bland and has an ultra-starchy texture. It cannot be used as a substitute for sweet potatoes.

Once you get the sweet potatoes home, remove them from any plastic produce bag. Do not wash the sweet potatoes until you are ready to use them because this exposes the vulnerable skin and causes them to go bad more quickly. Refrigeration is also a no-no; it causes the core of the potato to gradually change texture until it resembles a soft, damp cork. The best storage is a dark, well-ventilated spot.

although fast and easy, was also a disappointment. The rate of cooking was difficult to control, and the difference between undercooked and overdone was only about 30 seconds. Overmicrowaving the potatoes, even slightly, produced a pasty mouth-feel and an odd plastic flavor. By all accounts, this first round of testing bombed. Yet it did end up pointing us in a promising direction.

We had certainly learned a few facts about cooking sweet potatoes. First, their deep, hearty flavor is surprisingly fleeting and easily washed out. Second, the tough, dense flesh reacts much like winter squash when it's cooked, turning wet and sloppy. We also found it safer to peel the sweet potatoes when raw and cold rather than cooked and hot. Taking all of this into account, we wondered if braising the sweet potatoes might work. If cut into uniform pieces and cooked over low heat in a covered pan, the sweet potatoes might release their own moisture slowly and braise themselves.

Adding a little water to the pan to get the process going, we found the sweet potatoes were tender in about 40 minutes. We then simply removed the lid and mashed them right in the pot. To our delight, they were full of flavor because they cooked, essentially, in their own liquid. We tried various pots and heat levels and found that a medium pot (accommodating two or three layers of potatoes) in combination with low heat worked best.

Up to this point, we had been adding only butter to the mash; we wondered what the typical additions of cream, milk, or half-and-half would do. Making four batches side by side, we tasted mashes made with only butter, with butter and milk, with butter and half-and-half, and with butter and heavy cream. Tasters found the butter-only batch tasted boring, while milk turned the mash bland and watery. The batch made with half-and-half came in second, with heartier flavor and fuller body, but the heavy cream stole the show.

As we had now made this recipe many times, a glaring oversight became obvious. Why didn't we replace the small amount of water used to cook the potatoes with the butter and heavy cream?

Curious about how the recipe would react without the water, we were gratified when this stream-lined technique produced the ultimate mash. The puree stood up on a fork, with a luxurious texture that was neither loose nor gluey. Further, with the water out of the picture, the sweet potato flavor was more intense than ever.

Mashed Sweet Potatoes
SERVES 4

Cutting the sweet potatoes into slices of even thickness is important in getting them to cook at the same rate. The potatoes are best served immediately, but they can be covered tightly with plastic wrap and kept relatively hot for 30 minutes. This recipe can be doubled and prepared in a Dutch oven; the cooking time must be doubled as well.

4	tablespoons unsalted butter, cut into 4 pieces
2	tablespoons heavy cream
1/2	teaspoon salt
1	teaspoon sugar
2	pounds sweet potatoes (about 2 large or 3 medium), peeled, quartered lengthwise, and cut crosswise into 1/4-inch-thick slices
	Pinch ground black pepper

1. Combine the butter, cream, salt, sugar, and sweet potatoes in a 3- to 4-quart saucepan. Cover and cook over low heat, stirring occasionally, until the potatoes fall apart when poked with a fork, 35 to 45 minutes.

2. Off the heat, mash the sweet potatoes in the saucepan with a potato masher. Stir in the pepper and serve immediately.

➤ VARIATION

Mashed Sweet Potatoes with Ginger and Brown Sugar
If you like, garnish these potatoes with chopped crystallized ginger.

Follow the recipe for Mashed Sweet Potatoes, replacing the sugar with 1½ tablespoons light or dark brown sugar and adding 2 teaspoons minced or grated fresh ginger along with the sweet potatoes in step 1.

Winter Squash

THERE ARE MANY WAYS TO COOK WINTER squash, but the ideal method for one kind may not necessarily be the best for another. We quickly discovered this when we set out to find the optimum way to cook the two most common winter squash, acorn and butternut. After only a few tests, we found that they responded very differently. We figured that we should develop several basic cooking methods, then recommend the kinds of squash for each method.

One thing that all winter squash have in common is that, counter to the current fashion for al dente vegetables, they must be cooked until well-done to develop their sweetest flavor and smoothest texture. With this as the only given, we tried cooking various kinds of squash by baking, roasting, steaming, and boiling.

After some experimentation, we found that baking the unpeeled and seeded halves cut-side down gave a slightly better texture than cut-side up. We found it best to cook the squash on a foil-lined baking sheet that had been oiled. The oil promoted better browning and reduced the risk of sticking, and the foil made cleanup easy.

Although this method was a success, when we began thinking about serving the squash, we realized that a baked squash half was fine if you could find relatively small squash, but what about those times when the market has only 3-pound butternut squashes. Roasting chunks of peeled squash proved to be a much more successful way to cook such big squash.

We peeled the squash and cut it into 1-inch cubes, then roasted it uncovered at varying oven temperatures. The squash became quite caramelized, with a good chewy texture and a much sweeter and more pronounced flavor. The ideal temperature turned out to be 425 degrees. At lower temperatures, the squash was no better and took much longer to cook, and at higher temperatures it burned on the outside before it was fully cooked inside. A few sources suggested parboiling the cubed squash in lightly salted water for five to six minutes, until it was about half-cooked, then roasting it. Squash cooked this way was bland, so we discarded this idea.

Since sautéing also caramelizes, we decided to try sautéing diced squash in butter and oil until it became lightly caramelized and tender. This process took about 20 minutes and produced very satisfactory squash. But we found the flavor not as deep as the roasted squash, and roasting also had the advantage of requiring less attention during cooking. Adding some liquid and seasonings to the pan, and thus turning the sauté into a braise, was an easy way to add more flavor to the squash. Braising became our third method for handling squash, along with roasting halves and roasting smaller peeled chunks of squash.

Roasted Winter Squash Halves
SERVES 4

This recipe can be made with acorn, buttercup, butternut, or delicata squash. The cooking time will vary depending on the kind of squash you use. Start checking for doneness after the first 30 minutes. For an efficient way of seeding winter squash, see page 204.

2   tablespoons extra-virgin olive oil
I   medium or 2 small winter squash (about 2 pounds total), halved lengthwise and seeded (see the illustrations on pages 203–204)
    Salt and ground black pepper

1. Adjust an oven rack to the lower-middle position and heat the oven to 400 degrees. Line a rimmed baking sheet with aluminum foil. Brush the oil on the foil and the cut sides of the squash. Place the squash cut-side down on the foil. Roast until a skewer inserted in the squash meets no resistance, 40 to 50 minutes.

2. Remove the squash from the oven and turn cut-side up. If necessary, cut large pieces in half to yield 4 pieces. Season the squash with salt and pepper to taste and serve immediately.

➤ VARIATIONS

Roasted Winter Squash with Browned Butter and Sage
The warm flavors of sage and winter squash complement each other beautifully. Serve with roast turkey or chicken.

2   tablespoons extra-virgin olive oil

I   medium or 2 small winter squash (about
     2 pounds total), halved lengthwise and
     seeded (see the illustrations below and
     on page 204)

6   tablespoons (¾ stick) unsalted butter

6   medium fresh sage leaves, sliced thin
     Salt and ground black pepper

1. Adjust an oven rack to the lower-middle position and heat the oven to 400 degrees. Line a rimmed baking sheet with aluminum foil. Brush the oil on the foil and the cut sides of the squash. Place the squash cut-side down on the foil. Roast until a skewer inserted in the squash meets no resistance, 40 to 50 minutes.

2. When the squash is almost done, melt the butter in a small skillet over medium heat. Add the sage and cook, swirling the pan occasionally, until the butter is golden brown and the sage is crisp, 4 to 5 minutes. Remove the skillet from the heat.

3. Remove the squash from the oven and turn cut-side up. If necessary, cut large pieces in half to yield 4 pieces. Season the squash with salt and pepper to taste, drizzle with the sage butter, and serve immediately.

CUTTING UP BUTTERNUT SQUASH

With its thick skin and odd shape, butternut quash is notoriously difficult to cut, even with the best chef's knife. We prefer to use a cleaver and mallet.

1. Set the squash on a damp kitchen towel to hold it in place. Position the cleaver on the skin of the squash.

2. Strike the back of the cleaver with a mallet to drive the cleaver deep into the squash. Continue to hit the cleaver with the mallet until the cleaver cuts completely through the squash.

Roasted Winter Squash Halves with Soy and Maple

Soy sauce and squash may sound like an unlikely combination, but the salty flavor of the soy sauce and the sweetness of the squash enhance each other. This recipe works especially well with kabocha or acorn squash. Given the strong flavors of soy and maple, we find it best to brush the squash with vegetable oil, rather than olive oil, before roasting.

2   tablespoons vegetable oil

I   medium or 2 small winter squash (about
     2 pounds total), halved lengthwise and
     seeded (see the illustrations below and
     on page 204)

3   tablespoons maple syrup

2   tablespoons soy sauce

½   teaspoon minced or grated fresh ginger
     Salt and ground black pepper

1. Adjust an oven rack to the lower-middle position and heat the oven to 400 degrees. Line a rimmed baking sheet with aluminum foil. Brush the oil on the foil and the cut sides of the squash. Place the squash cut-side down on the foil. Roast until a skewer inserted in the squash meets no resistance, 40 to 50 minutes. Do not turn off the oven.

2. While the squash is in the oven, mix the maple syrup, soy sauce, and ginger together in a small bowl.

3. Remove the squash from the oven and turn cut-side up. Brush the cut sides of the squash with the maple-soy mixture and return the squash to the oven. Roast until the cut sides of the squash begin to caramelize, about 5 minutes. Remove the squash from the oven. If necessary, cut large pieces in half to yield 4 pieces. Season the squash with salt and pepper to taste and serve immediately.

Roasted Winter Squash
SERVES 4

Peeled and cut squash pieces (usually butternut) are available in the produce section of most grocery stores. It is preferable to peel and cut your own, but if you are short on time, the bagged variety is an acceptable substitute. One whole 2-pound squash yields about 1½ pounds of trimmed pieces. This recipe is best with butternut, buttercup, or kabocha squash. If peeling the squash yourself, use a heavy-duty vegetable peeler that will remove a thick layer of the skin and tough greenish flesh right below the skin. With most squash, it's easiest to cut the squash in half, remove the seeds, and then start peeling.

- 2   pounds winter squash, peeled, seeded (see pages 203–204), and cut into 1-inch cubes
- 1   medium shallot, minced
- 2   tablespoons olive oil
- 2   teaspoons minced fresh thyme leaves
      Salt and ground black pepper

Adjust an oven rack to the lower-middle position and heat the oven to 425 degrees. Toss the squash, shallot, oil, thyme, and salt and pepper to taste in a large bowl. Spread the squash pieces on a rimmed baking sheet large enough to hold them without crowding. Roast, shaking the pan every 10 minutes, until the squash is tender and evenly browned, 25 to 35 minutes. Adjust the seasonings, adding salt and pepper to taste. Serve immediately.

➤ VARIATION
Roasted Winter Squash with Parsley, Sage, Rosemary, and Thyme
This isn't just a great song, it's also a delicious combination of herbs. To preserve the parsley's fresh flavor, add it at the end of the recipe. Serve with roast chicken or turkey.

- 2   pounds winter squash, peeled, seeded (see pages 203–204), and cut into 1-inch cubes
- 2   tablespoons olive oil
- 1   teaspoon minced fresh thyme leaves
- 1   teaspoon minced fresh sage leaves
- ½   teaspoon minced fresh rosemary leaves
      Salt and ground black pepper
- 1   tablespoon minced fresh parsley leaves

Adjust an oven rack to the lower-middle position and heat the oven to 425 degrees. Toss the squash, oil, thyme, sage, rosemary, and salt and pepper to taste together in a large bowl. Spread the squash pieces on a rimmed baking sheet large enough to hold them without crowding. Roast, shaking the pan every 10 minutes, until the squash is tender and evenly browned, 25 to 35 minutes. Stir in the parsley and adjust the seasonings, adding salt and pepper to taste. Serve immediately.

Braised Winter Squash
Serves 4

This simple recipe is a great way to cook squash quickly. Braise the squash until it just begins to fall apart and absorb the juicy braising liquid. The recipe is best with butternut, buttercup, or delicata squash. Cooking times may differ depending on the type of squash you are using.

- 2   tablespoons unsalted butter
- 1   medium shallot, minced
- 2   pounds winter squash, peeled, seeded (see pages 203–204), and cut into 1-inch cubes
- ½   cup low-sodium chicken broth

REMOVING SQUASH SEEDS

Use an ice cream scoop with a curved bowl to cut out all the seeds and strings without damaging the flesh. Because the edge on this kind of scoop is very sharp, it cuts easily, and because the scoop is larger than a spoon, it can remove more seeds in a single swipe.

1   teaspoon minced fresh thyme leaves
    Salt and ground black pepper

Heat the butter in a Dutch oven or large sauce-pan over medium-high heat. When the foaming subsides, add the shallot and cook, stirring occasionally, until golden, about 4 minutes. Add the squash, broth, thyme, and salt and pepper to taste. Stir, cover, reduce the heat to medium, and cook until the squash is very tender, 16 to 20 minutes. Adjust the seasonings, adding salt and pepper to taste. Serve immediately.

➤ VARIATION
Braised Winter Squash with Asian Flavors
Buttercup squash, also called kabocha, is often used in braises and stews in Asian cooking and is the most traditional choice for this dish.

2   tablespoons vegetable oil
1   small onion, diced
2   pounds winter squash, peeled, seeded (see pages 203–204), and cut into 1-inch cubes
½   cup low-sodium chicken broth
1   tablespoon soy sauce
1   tablespoon mirin (Japanese sweet rice wine)
    Salt and ground black pepper
1   medium scallion, sliced thin

Heat the oil in a Dutch oven or large saucepan over medium-high heat until shimmering. Add the onion and cook, stirring occasionally, until golden, about 4 minutes. Add the squash, broth, soy sauce, mirin, and salt and pepper to taste. Bring to a simmer, cover, and reduce the heat to medium-low. Simmer until the squash is tender, 16 to 20 minutes. Remove the lid and simmer until the liquid thickens, 2 to 3 minutes. Adjust the seasonings, adding salt and pepper to taste. Sprinkle with the scallion and serve immediately.

ZUCCHINI AND SUMMER SQUASH

GARDENS OVERFLOW WITH ZUCCHINI AND other summer squash every summer, but cooks are often at a loss for ideas for using this bounty. The biggest problem that confronts the cook when preparing zucchini is its wateriness. This vegetable is about 95 percent water and becomes soupy if just thrown into a hot pan. If zucchini cooks in its own juices, it won't brown (and because it is fairly bland, zucchini really benefits from browning). Clearly, some of the water must be removed before sautéing.

The first precautions against wateriness must take place in the supermarket. Size and firmness are the most important factors when purchasing zucchini. After extensive testing, we found that smaller zucchini are more flavorful and less watery. Smaller zucchini also have fewer seeds. Look for small to medium zucchini no larger than eight ounces and preferably just six ounces each. Mammoth zucchini may look impressive in the garden (or supermarket), but they will only cause problems in the kitchen.

Even if you've bought small zucchini, you still need to remove moisture before cooking it. Many sources recommend salting sliced zucchini before cooking it. We tested salting to draw off some water and found that sliced and salted zucchini sheds about 20 percent of its weight after sitting for 30 minutes. One pound of sliced zucchini threw off almost three tablespoons of liquid, further confirmation that salting works. We tested longer periods and found that little additional moisture is extracted after 30 minutes.

Another quick-prep option is the grill. The intense heat quickly expels excess moisture in zucchini, and that moisture harmlessly drops down on the coals rather than sitting in the pan. We found that so much evaporation occurs during grilling that salting is not necessary.

Sautéed Zucchini or Summer Squash

SERVES 4

If you like browned zucchini, you must salt it before cooking. Salting drives off excess water and helps the zucchini sauté rather than stew in its own juices. Coarse kosher salt does the best job and can be wiped away without rinsing. Do not add more salt when cooking or the dish will be too salty.

- 4 medium zucchini or summer squash (about 1½ pounds), trimmed and sliced crosswise into ¼-inch-thick rounds
- 1 tablespoon kosher salt
- 3 tablespoons extra-virgin olive oil
- 1 small onion, minced
- 1 teaspoon grated zest and 1 tablespoon juice from 1 lemon
- 1–2 tablespoons minced fresh chives or parsley, basil, mint, or tarragon leaves
  Ground black pepper

1. Place the zucchini slices in a colander and sprinkle with the salt. Set the colander over a bowl until about ⅓ cup water drains from the zucchini, about 30 minutes. Remove the zucchini from the colander and pat dry with a clean kitchen towel or several paper towels, wiping off any remaining salt crystals.

2. Heat the oil in a large skillet over medium heat. Add the onion and cook until almost softened, about 3 minutes. Increase the heat to medium-high and add the zucchini and lemon zest. Cook until the zucchini is golden brown, about 10 minutes. Stir in the lemon juice and fresh herb of choice and season with pepper to taste. Serve immediately.

➤ VARIATION

Sautéed Zucchini or Summer Squash with Olives and Oregano

Follow the recipe for Sautéed Zucchini or Summer Squash, adding ¼ cup chopped Kalamata olives with the lemon juice and using 1 teaspoon minced fresh oregano leaves as the herb.

Grilled Zucchini or Summer Squash

SERVES 4

Excess water evaporates over hot coals, so salting the zucchini before cooking is not necessary. If you like, drizzle the zucchini with a little balsamic vinegar just before serving.

- 4 medium zucchini or summer squash (about 1½ pounds), trimmed and sliced lengthwise into ½-inch-thick strips (see the illustrations below)
- 2 tablespoons extra-virgin olive oil
  Salt and ground black pepper

1. Lay the zucchini slices on a large baking sheet and brush both sides with the oil. Sprinkle generously with salt and pepper to taste.

2. Grill the zucchini over a medium-hot fire (you should be able to hold your hand 5 inches above the cooking grate for 3 to 4 seconds), turning once, until marked with dark stripes, 8 to 10 minutes. Serve hot, warm, or at room temperature.

SLICING ZUCCHINI OR SUMMER SQUASH FOR THE GRILL

1. Cut a thin slice from each end of the zucchini or summer squash. Slice the trimmed squash lengthwise into ½-inch-thick strips.

2. For aesthetic reason, you may want to trim the peel from the outer slices so they match the others. The flesh also cooks better when directly exposed to the heat.

5

RICE, GRAINS, AND BEANS

THIS CHAPTER COVERS THE TWO MOST popular grains in the American kitchen today—rice and cornmeal—as well as beans: white beans, black beans, and red beans.

When buying rice, it is imperative that you pay attention to the size of the grains. Rice can be classed as long-, medium-, or short-grain. Long-grain rice is about four times as long as it is wide. Medium-grain rice is twice as long as it is wide. Short-grain rice is round. In general, long-grain rice cooks up fluffy and separate, while the grains of medium- and short-grain rice tend to clump or become starchy. This is due to the ratio of the two main starches in rice, amylose and amylopectin.

Long-grain rice contains between 23 and 26 percent amylose, a starch that does not gelatinize during cooking. With such a high amylose content, properly cooked long-grain rice remains dry and separate. Medium-grain has an average amylose content between 18 and 26 percent, and short-grain rice falls between 15 and 20 percent. As these numbers indicate, individual lots of rice will behave differently, and our tests with different brands proved this.

We found medium-grain rice a favorite for risotto, where we want some starchiness but not too much. When making plain steamed rice or pilafs, we prefer long-grain rice because individual grains cook up separately.

Cornmeal also comes in three different styles: fine-, medium-, and coarse-grind. We prefer medium-grind cornmeal (about the texture of granulated sugar) when making polenta.

As for dried beans, be sure to purchase beans from a shop or supermarket with a high turnover. (One way to tell if a store has high turnover is to check to see if the bags are dusty—a sure sign of old beans.) No matter how long you cook them, stale beans will never soften.

Although most of the recipes in this chapter are for side dishes, some recipes, such as Chicken and Shrimp Jambalaya (page 221) and Polenta with Meat Ragù (page 226) make complete main courses.

WHITE RICE

FEW FOODS ARE AS SATISFYING AS PERFECTLY cooked rice. But this elemental food can be temperamental—it can resist the cook and be a pot of true grit or dissolve into an unpleasant, gummy mess. Advertisements stress perfect rice, but package instructions are unreliable when you want a tasty bowl of fluffy rice with separate grains. We wanted to find an easy method for making really great long-grain white rice.

We started our tests by following the package directions on four brands of long-grain rice. The technique was a variation on a simmer-covered method, with 1 cup rice to 2 to 2½ cups water. Some of the directions called for salt, some didn't, and there were recipes with and without butter. All the recipes were disappointing—the results mostly insipid, with mushy, frayed grains. There was gritty rice, there was chalky rice, but there was no rice we liked.

Next we tried a method popular with French and Indian cooks—boiling the rice in a generous quantity of salted water as if cooking pasta. Cooked this way, all types of rice came to the table evenly done, with individual grains, but also waterlogged and bland-tasting.

Then we experimented with baking the rice in casseroles, with 1¾ to 2½ parts water to 1 part rice, some with butter, some salted and unsalted. Boiling water was poured over the rice, then the pots were sealed with foil and baked for 25 to 30 minutes. The rice made with less water and salt was better. This result was somewhat beside the point, however, because baked rice, while slightly creamy, did not have the well-defined grains we wanted.

The perfect method was still eluding us, but we had discerned a pattern: Less water and an even, gentle heat worked better. So we tried a pilaf method, because pilaf recipes generally use less water and produce distinct grains of rice. First we sautéed the rice in 2 teaspoons butter or oil, with the amount of water added varying from 1 to 2 cups. After the water came to a boil, we covered the pan and let the rice simmer for 15 minutes, then removed it from the heat and let it rest a bit prior to serving. With this method, the rice cooked up light and tender but not mushy or clumped, with the sautéing adding a rich dimension of flavor.

No matter the variety of rice, we preferred the ratio of 1 cup rice to 1½ cups water. The grains should be sautéed and stirred until some have become milky white. For stronger, nutty flavors, the raw rice can be fried to a toasted golden brown.

We were curious to try the same formula (1 cup rice, 1½ cups water, ½ teaspoon salt) without sautéing. Fluffed with a fork, rice cooked in this manner was almost as fluffy as the pilaf-method rice, with a mild flavor that brings out the subtly floral, "ricey" aromatics. At a small sacrifice of texture, this is the ideal rice for many chicken stews and fish dishes.

There was some flexibility in cooking time, as long as the rice was allowed to rest, covered, after cooking. We got the most consistent results with a cooking time of 15 to 18 minutes from when the pot was sealed to the time the rice was done, with a 15-minute rest on the turned-off burner. (Don't pull the cover off the pot to peek—you want the pot to hold in the heat.) Before serving, fluff the rice with a fork.

White Rice

SERVES 4

This recipe is designed for 1 cup of raw rice in a tight-lidded pot. As you cook more rice, you should reduce the proportion of water. With 2 cups of rice, you can get these results with 2½ to 2¾ cups of water. It is very hard to get a reliable result with less than a cup of rice, however, so we do not advise halving the recipe.

2	teaspoons unsalted butter or vegetable or olive oil
1	cup long-grain white rice (not converted)
1½	cups water
½	teaspoon salt

1. Heat the butter in a 2-quart medium sauce-pan over medium heat. Add the rice; cook, stirring constantly, for 1 to 3 minutes, depending on the desired amount of nutty flavor. Add the water and salt; bring to a boil, swirling the pot to blend the ingredients.

2. Reduce the heat to low, cover tightly, and cook until the water is absorbed, about 15 minutes.

3. Turn off the heat; let the rice stand on the burner, still covered, to finish cooking, about 15 minutes longer. Fluff with a fork and serve.

RICE PILAF

ACCORDING TO MOST CULINARY SOURCES, rice pilaf is long-grain rice that has been cooked in hot oil or butter before being simmered in hot liquid, typically either water or stock. At its most basic, pilaf is a simple rice dish, made rich and flavorful from the sauté in fat and the addition of an aromatic such as onion or garlic. In Middle Eastern cuisines, the term *pilaf* also refers to a more substantial dish in which the rice is cooked in this manner and then flavored with other ingredients—spices, nuts, dried fruits, and/or chicken or other meat. To avoid confusion, we decided to call the simple master recipe for our dish "pilaf-style" rice, designating the flavored versions as rice pilaf.

The logical first step in this process was to isolate the best type of rice for pilaf. We immediately limited our testing to long-grain rice, since medium- and short-grain rice inherently produce a rather sticky, starchy product and we were looking for fluffy, separate grains.

Plain long-grain white rice worked well in our pilaf, but basmati rice was even better: Each grain was separate, long, and fluffy, and the rice had a fresh, delicate fragrance. That said, we would add that you can use plain long-grain rice if basmati is not available.

Most sources indicate that the proper ratio of rice to liquid for long-grain white rice is 1 to 2, but many cooks use less water. After testing every possibility, from 1:1 to 1:2, we found that we got the best rice using 1⅔ cups of water for every cup of rice. To make this easier to remember, as well as easier to measure, we increased the rice by half to 1½ cups and the liquid to 2½ cups.

With our rice-water ratio set, we were ready to test the traditional method, which called for rinsing the rice before cooking it. Each recipe declared one of these preparatory steps to be essential in producing rice with distinct, separate grains that were light and fluffy. Rinsing the rice made a substantial difference, particularly with basmati rice. We simply covered 1½ cups of rice with water, gently moved the grains around using our fingers, and drained the water from the rice. We repeated this process four or five times until the rinsing water was clear enough for us to see the grains distinctly. We then drained the rice and cooked it in oil and liquid. The resulting rice was less hard and more tender, and it had a slightly shinier, smoother appearance.

We allowed the rice to steam for 10 minutes after being removed from the heat to ensure that the moisture was distributed throughout. We wondered if a longer or shorter steaming time would make much of a difference in the resulting pilaf. We made a few batches of pilaf, allowing it to steam for 5 minutes, 10 minutes, and 15 minutes. The pilaf that steamed for 5 minutes was heavy and wet. The batch that steamed for 15 minutes was the lightest and least watery. We also decided to try placing a clean kitchen towel between the pan and the lid right after we took the rice off the stove. We found this produced the best results of all, while reducing the steaming time to only 10 minutes. It seems that the towel (or two layers of paper towels) prevents condensation and absorbs the excess water in the pan during steaming, producing dryer, fluffier rice.

From previous kitchen tests, we knew that sautéing the rice was essential for a light, nutty flavor and tender texture, but we were surprised to see that many Middle Eastern recipes called for as much as ¼ cup butter per cup of rice. Adding butter (since we like the extra flavor and richness that it lends to the rice), we tried from one to four tablespoons per 1½ cups rice. Three tablespoons turned out to be optimal. The rice was buttery and rich without being overwhelmingly so, and each grain was shinier and more distinct than when cooked with less fat.

The addition of flavorings, seasonings, and other ingredients is what gives pilaf its distinctive character. We found that dried spices, minced ginger, and onion and garlic, for example, are best sautéed briefly in the fat before the raw rice is added to the pan. Saffron and dried herbs are best added to the liquid as it heats up, while fresh herbs and toasted nuts should be added to the pilaf just before serving to maximize freshness, texture (in the case of nuts), and flavor. Dried fruits such as raisins, currants, or figs can be incorporated just before steaming the rice, which gives them enough time to heat through and plump up without becoming soggy.

~

Basic Pilaf–Style Rice
SERVES 4

If you like, olive oil can be substituted for the butter depending on what you are serving with the pilaf. For the most evenly cooked rice, use a wide-bottomed saucepan with a tight-fitting lid.

1½	cups basmati or long-grain rice
2½	cups water
1½	teaspoons salt
	Ground black pepper
3	tablespoons unsalted butter
1	small onion, minced

1. Place the rice in a medium bowl and add enough water to cover the rice by 2 inches; using your hands, gently swish the grains to release excess starch. Carefully pour off the water, leaving the rice in the bowl. Repeat 4 or 5 times, until the water runs almost clear. Using a colander or fine-mesh strainer, drain the water from the rice; place

STEAMING RICE

After the rice is cooked, cover the pan with a clean kitchen towel, replace the lid, and allow the pan to sit for 10 minutes.

the colander over the bowl and set aside.

2. Bring the 2½ cups water to a boil, covered, in a small saucepan over medium-high heat. Add the salt and season with pepper to taste; cover to keep hot. Meanwhile, heat the butter in a large saucepan over medium heat until the foam begins to subside; add the onion and sauté until softened but not browned, about 4 minutes. Add the rice and stir to coat the grains with butter; cook until the edges of the grains begin to turn translucent, about 3 minutes. Stir the hot seasoned water into the rice; return to a boil, then reduce the heat to low, cover, and simmer until all the water is absorbed, 16 to 18 minutes. Off the heat, remove the lid, and place a clean kitchen towel folded in half over the saucepan (see the illustration on page 210); replace the lid. Let stand 10 minutes; fluff the rice with a fork and serve.

➢ VARIATIONS

Rice Pilaf with Currants and Pine Nuts
When toasting the pine nuts, note that they can go from toasted to burnt and inedible very quickly.

Toast ¼ cup pine nuts in a small dry skillet over medium heat until golden and fragrant, about 5 minutes; set aside. Follow the recipe for Basic Pilaf-Style Rice, adding ½ teaspoon turmeric, ¼ teaspoon ground cinnamon, and 2 medium garlic cloves, minced or pressed through a garlic press, to the sautéed onion; cook until fragrant, about 30 seconds longer. When the pilaf is off the heat, before covering the saucepan with the kitchen towel, sprinkle ¼ cup currants over the rice in the pan (do not mix in). When fluffing the rice with a fork, toss in the toasted pine nuts.

Indian-Spiced Rice Pilaf with Dates and Parsley
Follow the recipe for Basic Pilaf-Style Rice, adding 2 medium garlic cloves, minced or pressed through a garlic press, 2 teaspoons grated fresh ginger, ⅛ teaspoon ground cinnamon, and ⅛ teaspoon ground cardamom to the sautéed onion; cook until fragrant, about 30 seconds longer. When the rice is off the heat, before covering the saucepan with the kitchen towel, add ¼ cup chopped dates and 2 tablespoons chopped fresh parsley leaves (do not mix in). Let stand and fluff as directed.

Rice Pilaf with Vermicelli
Break 4 ounces vermicelli into 1-inch pieces (you should have about 1 cup); set aside. Follow the recipe for Basic Pilaf-Style Rice, increasing the water to 3½ cups and melting only 1½ tablespoons butter in a saucepan over medium heat; add the vermicelli and cook, stirring occasionally, until browned, about 3 minutes. Remove to a small bowl and set aside. Sauté the onion in the remaining 1½ tablespoons butter in the now-empty saucepan; add 2 medium garlic cloves, minced or pressed through a garlic press, ½ teaspoon ground cumin, ½ teaspoon ground coriander, and a pinch allspice to the sautéed onion; cook until fragrant, about 30 seconds longer. Add the vermicelli along with the rice; proceed with the recipe as directed.

FRIED RICE

LEFTOVERS ARE AN INCREDIBLE BOON TO THE busy cook—as long as you know what to do with them. When faced with the question of what to do with leftover rice, we say, "Fry it."

A sample from your local suburban Chinese restaurant, though, might give you pause. There the norm is often a heavy dish doused with so much soy sauce that you can hardly tell the mushrooms from the chicken. But this is no more representative of the virtues of this dish than a fast-food burger is of a great home-grilled version. We wanted a dish with both firm, distinct grains of rice and light, distinctive flavors. We also knew that the success of the dish would depend on the answers to four questions: what to add, how much to add, when to add it, and when to leave it alone.

Fried rice was created as a way to put leftover rice to good, tasty use. Unlike Chinese restaurants, however, most American cooks are unlikely to have leftover rice on hand, so we decided to experiment by making the dish from freshly cooked, still-warm rice. It was a disaster. The grains gelled together in large clumps, and the whole dish was very wet. Rice freshly cooked and then allowed to cool to room temperature fared little better, still turning out wet and unappealing fried rice. What produced by far the best fried rice was rice that had been cooked and then chilled in the refrigerator overnight. The grains were more separate and evenly coated with oil, and the overall dish was much drier.

But we wanted to see if we could avoid overnight refrigeration. We tried spreading the cooked rice on a baking sheet to cool it down to room temperature rapidly, then placed the pan in the refrigerator to chill completely. The resulting fried rice was drier and the clumps of rice much smaller than in versions prepared with fresh-cooked rice, making this method an option for cooks who want to make fried rice as quickly as possible from freshly cooked rice. But leftover rice is still the best option, as we found when we tried refrigerating cooked rice for different amounts of time. While rice kept in the refrigerator for four hours was acceptable, a whole night in the refrigerator produced the driest, most separate grains and, therefore, the best fried rice.

We tested various types of rice, including extra-long-, long-, medium-, and short-grain. All are suitable for fried rice after an overnight stay in the refrigerator. But don't try making fried rice with store-bought rice that has been precooked, parboiled, or converted. These processed rices become soggy and wet, and the grains quickly begin to break down and disintegrate during frying.

Despite the preference of many Chinese-American restaurants for large quantities of soy sauce in their fried rice, a quick look through many Chinese cookbooks revealed salt as the preferred seasoning. When tested, this rice tasted very clean and light, but tasters longed for a more substantial flavor. We went back to the soy sauce, but the large amount (nearly six tablespoons) needed to fully season the dish caused the rice to turn soggy and ugly. We wanted to find a seasoning with enough flavor intensity to be used sparingly.

The answer was oyster sauce. More appropriately referred to as oyster-flavored sauce, this condiment is a highly concentrated combination of soy sauce, brine, and oyster extracts. It is very thick, salty, and potent in taste. Fried rice made with this sauce was well seasoned and full of distinctive flavor, but not soggy.

In the process of all this testing, we also figured out how best to add the usual egg and vegetables to the rice. To get the eggs the right texture, we scrambled them lightly, then removed them from the pan, reserving them to be added back to the pan at the end of cooking for a quick warm-up. Similarly, we found that moisture from vegetables such as peas, mushrooms, green beans, and asparagus caused the rice to clump when added to the pan along with it. Sautéing the vegetables alone in oil first allows sufficient moisture to cook off, producing a drier dish with better-flavored vegetables. More tender vegetables, such as bean sprouts and scallions, along with herbs, hold their texture and flavor better if they are added at the end of the cooking process.

The odd thing about fried rice is that it's not truly fried. When food is fried, it is cooked in a large amount of fat, usually enough to cover the food (think of fried chicken). What we call fried rice is actually pan-fried or sautéed, which means it is cooked over relatively high heat in a much smaller amount of fat (in this case, oil). We needed to figure out exactly how much oil would be necessary, and we knew that the pan we used would determine the amount. Because we wanted to make a large quantity of fried rice, we limited our testing to large (12-inch) skillets—nonstick and regular—and a 14-inch wok.

The wok held plenty of rice, but the sloped sides and small 6-inch bottom allowed only a small portion of the rice to cook at one time. The wok also required a great deal of oil. The rice on the bottom continually absorbed what was added. The flat surface of the skillet provided a larger cooking area, and the rice sautéed more quickly and evenly. Choosing between regular and nonstick was easy. The regular skillet required much more oil to keep the rice from sticking, making the dish greasy. We preferred the nonstick skillet for the lighter rice it produced.

Even using a nonstick pan, we found that a moderate amount of oil—nearly ¼ cup—was required to keep the rice grains separate. Too little oil caused the rice grains to clump together during sautéing.

Fried Rice with Shrimp, Ham, and Shiitakes

SERVES 4 TO 6

This classic combination can be served as a main course. To cool the rice for the recipe, spread the cooked rice in an even layer on a parchment-lined baking sheet; cool to room temperature, about 30 minutes; and then refrigerate, uncovered, until completely dry and the grains easily separate, at least 4 hours or up to 24 hours.

1/2	ounce dried shiitake mushrooms (5 to 6 medium)
1/4	cup oyster sauce
1	tablespoon soy sauce
3 1/2	tablespoons peanut or vegetable oil
2	large eggs, beaten lightly
8	ounces small shrimp, peeled and deveined
1	cup frozen peas, preferably baby peas, thawed
8	ounces sliced smoked ham, cut into 1/2-inch pieces
2	medium garlic cloves, minced or pressed through a garlic press
5	cups cold cooked white rice, large clumps broken up with fingers (see note)
1	cup bean sprouts
5	medium scallions, white and green parts, sliced thin (about 1/2 cup)

1. Cover the dried shiitakes with 1 cup hot tap water in a small microwave-safe bowl; cover with plastic wrap, cut several steam vents with a paring knife, and microwave on high power for 30 seconds. Let stand until the mushrooms soften, about 5 minutes. Lift the mushrooms from the liquid with a fork, trim off and discard the stems, and slice into 1/4-inch strips; set the mushrooms aside

2. Combine the oyster sauce and soy sauce in a small bowl; set aside.

3. Heat a 12-inch nonstick skillet over medium heat until hot. Add 1 1/2 teaspoons of the oil and swirl to coat the pan bottom. Add the eggs and cook without stirring, until they just begin to set, about 20 seconds, then scramble and break into small pieces with a wooden spoon; continue to cook, stirring constantly, until the eggs are cooked through but not browned, about 1 minute longer. Transfer the eggs to a small bowl and set aside.

4. Return the skillet to medium heat and heat until hot; add 1 1/2 teaspoons of the oil and swirl to coat the pan bottom. Add the shrimp and cook, stirring constantly, until opaque and just cooked through, about 30 seconds. Transfer to the bowl with the eggs and set aside.

5. Return the skillet to the burner, increase the heat to high, and heat the skillet until hot; then add the remaining 2 1/2 tablespoons oil and swirl to coat the pan bottom. Add the peas, mushrooms, and ham; cook, stirring constantly, for 1 minute. Stir in the garlic and cook until fragrant, about 30 seconds. Add the rice and oyster sauce mixture; cook, stirring constantly and breaking up rice clumps, until the mixture is heated through, about 3 minutes. Add the eggs, shrimp, bean sprouts, and scallions; cook, stirring constantly, until heated through, about 1 minute. Serve immediately.

Fried Rice with Peas and Bean Sprouts

SERVES 4 TO 6

This lighter vegetarian recipe is best served as a side dish.

1/4	cup oyster sauce
1	tablespoon soy sauce
3	tablespoons peanut or vegetable oil
2	large eggs, beaten lightly
1	cup frozen peas, preferably baby peas, thawed
2	medium garlic cloves, minced or pressed through a garlic press
6	cups cold cooked white rice, large clumps broken up with fingers (see note on previous recipe)
1	cup bean sprouts
5	medium scallions, white and green parts, sliced thin (about 1/2 cup)

1. Combine the oyster sauce and soy sauce in a small bowl; set aside.

2. Heat a 12-inch nonstick skillet over medium

heat until hot; add 1½ teaspoons of the oil and swirl to coat the pan bottom. Add the eggs and cook without stirring, until they just begin to set, about 20 seconds, then scramble and break into small pieces with a wooden spoon; continue to cook, stirring constantly, until the eggs are cooked through but not browned, about 1 minute longer. Transfer the eggs to a small bowl and set aside.

3. Return the skillet to the burner, increase the heat to high, and heat the skillet until hot; add the remaining 2½ tablespoons oil and swirl to coat the pan bottom. Add the peas and cook, stirring constantly, for 30 seconds; stir in the garlic and cook until fragrant, about 30 seconds. Add the rice and oyster sauce mixture; cook, stirring constantly and breaking up rice clumps, until the mixture is heated through, about 3 minutes. Add the eggs, bean sprouts, and scallions; cook, stirring constantly, until heated through, about 1 minute. Serve immediately.

BROWN RICE

BROWN RICE SHOULD BE SLIGHTLY STICKY, with a hint of chew and a nutty flavor. An ideal version should be easy to come by: Just throw rice and water in a pot and set the timer, right? Yet cooks who have attempted to prepare brown rice know it isn't that simple. Most cooks make the mistake (born of impatience) to crank up the flame in an effort to hurry along the slow-cooking grains (brown rice takes roughly twice as long to cook as white), which inevitably leads to a burnt pot and crunchy rice. Adding plenty of water isn't the remedy, either; excess liquid swells the rice into a gelatinous, wet mass.

We used an expensive, heavy-bottomed pot with a tight-fitting lid (many recipes caution against using inadequate cookware), fiddled with the traditional absorption method (cooking the rice with just enough water), and eventually landed on a workable recipe. Yet, when we tested the recipe with less than ideal equipment—namely, a flimsy pan with an ill-fitting lid—we were back to burnt, underdone rice. With the very best pot and a top-notch stove, it is possible to cook brown rice properly on top of the stove, but we wanted a surefire method that would work no matter the cook, no matter the equipment.

We rarely use the microwave, but thought it might work well in this instance, given that it cooks food indirectly, without a burner. Sadly, it delivered inconsistent results, with one batch turning brittle and another, prepared in a different microwave, too sticky. A rice cooker yielded faultless brown rice on the first try, but many Americans don't own one.

We set out to construct a homemade cooker that would approximate the controlled, indirect heat of a rice cooker. We started with an everyday collapsible vegetable steamer, lined the steamer basket successively with cheesecloth, a coffee filter, and a thin kitchen towel. In each case, it was impossible to stir neatly and consistently during cooking, and the result was irregularly cooked rice. A long-handled fine-mesh strainer used in place of the steamer also failed; the strainer's handle precluded a tight seal between pot rim and lid, and the rice was still raw after two hours.

We then began to consider the merits of cooking the rice in the oven. We'd have more precise temperature control and thought that the oven's encircling heat would eliminate the risk of scorching. Our first try yielded extremely promising results: With the pan tightly covered in aluminum foil, the rice steamed to near-perfection. Fine-tuning the amount of water, we settled on a ratio similar to that used for the white rice recipe: 2⅓ cups of water to 1½ cups of rice, falling well short of the 2:1 water-to-rice ratio advised by most rice producers and nearly every recipe we consulted. Perhaps that is why so much brown rice turns out sodden and overcooked.

Our next task was to spruce up the recipe by bringing out the nutty flavor of the otherwise plain grains. Adding a small amount (2 teaspoons) of either butter or oil to the cooking liquid added mild flavor while keeping the rice fluffy.

To reduce what was a long baking time of 90 minutes at 350 degrees, we tried starting with boiling water instead of cold tap water and raising the oven temperature to 375 degrees. These steps reduced the baking time to a reasonable one hour.

Oven-Baked Brown Rice

SERVES 4 TO 6

Base your decision on whether to use oil or butter in the recipe on the dish the rice will accompany; for example, if you are serving a stir-fry, use oil for the rice. To minimize any loss of water through evaporation, cover the saucepan as the water is heating, and use the water as soon as it reaches a boil. If you own an 8-inch ceramic baking dish with a lid, use it instead of the glass baking dish and foil. To double the recipe, use a 13 by 9-inch baking dish; the baking time need not be increased.

1½	cups long-, medium-, or short-grain brown rice
2⅓	cups water
2	teaspoons unsalted butter or vegetable oil
½	teaspoon salt

1. Adjust an oven rack to the middle position and heat the oven to 375 degrees. Spread the rice in an 8-inch square glass baking dish.

2. Bring the water and butter to a boil, covered, in a medium saucepan over high heat; once boiling, immediately stir in the salt and pour the water over the rice. Cover the baking dish tightly with a double layer of foil. Bake the rice 1 hour, until tender.

3. Remove the baking dish from the oven and uncover. Fluff the rice with a dinner fork, then cover the dish with a clean kitchen towel; let the rice stand 5 minutes. Uncover and let the rice stand 5 minutes longer; serve immediately.

➤ VARIATIONS

Brown Rice with Parmesan, Lemon, and Herbs

We like this Italian-style variation served alongside a simple roast chicken or a rich leg of lamb.

2	tablespoons unsalted butter
1	small onion, chopped medium
1½	cups long-, medium-, or short-grain brown rice
2⅓	cups low-sodium chicken broth
⅛	teaspooon salt
⅛	teaspoon ground black pepper
¼	cup minced fresh parsley leaves
¼	cup chopped fresh basil leaves
1	ounce Parmesan cheese, freshly grated (about ½ cup)
1	teaspoon grated zest and ½ teaspoon juice from one lemon

1. Heat the butter in a medium nonstick skillet over medium-high heat until foaming; add the onion and cook, stirring occasionally, until translucent, about 3 minutes.

2. Adjust an oven rack to the middle position; heat the oven to 375 degrees. Spread the rice in an 8-inch square glass baking dish.

3. Bring the chicken broth to a boil, covered, in a medium saucepan over high heat; once boiling, immediately stir in the salt and pour the broth over the rice. Cover the baking dish tightly with a double layer of foil. Bake the rice 1 hour and 10 minutes, until tender.

4. Remove the baking dish from the oven, uncover, and fluff the rice with a fork. Stir in the pepper, parsley, basil, Parmesan, lemon zest, and lemon juice. Cover the dish with a clean kitchen towel; let the rice stand 5 minutes. Uncover and let the rice stand 5 minutes longer; serve immediately.

Curried Brown Rice with Tomatoes and Peas

2	tablespoons unsalted butter
1	small onion, chopped medium (about ⅔ cup)
1½	teaspoons hot curry powder
1	tablespoon minced fresh ginger
1	medium garlic clove, minced or pressed through a garlic press
	Salt
1	(14.5-ounce) can diced tomatoes, drained
1½	cups long-, medium-, or short-grain brown rice
2⅓	cups low-sodium vegetable broth
½	cup frozen peas, thawed

1. Heat the butter in a medium nonstick skillet over medium-high heat until foaming; add the onion and cook, stirring occasionally, until translucent, about 3 minutes. Add the curry powder, ginger, garlic, and ¼ teaspoon salt; cook until fragrant, about 1 minute. Add the tomatoes and

cook until heated through, about 2 minutes; set the skillet aside.

2. Adjust an oven rack to the middle position; heat the oven to 375 degrees. Spread the rice in an 8-inch square glass baking dish.

3. Bring the vegetable broth to a boil, covered, in a medium saucepan over high heat; once boiling, immediately stir in ⅛ teaspoon salt and pour the broth over the rice. Stir the tomato mixture into the rice and spread the rice-tomato mixture in an even layer. Cover the baking dish tightly with a double layer of foil. Bake the rice 1 hour and 10 minutes, until tender.

4. Remove the baking dish from the oven, uncover, and stir in the peas. Cover the dish with a clean kitchen towel; let the rice stand 5 minutes. Uncover and let the rice stand 5 minutes longer; serve immediately.

WILD RICE PILAF

PROPERLY COOKED WILD RICE IS A STUDY IN contrasts: chewy yet tender and cottony—like popcorn. Ideally, the cooked grains remain discreet, doubling to quadrupling in size from their uncooked state. Undercooked rice is tough and, quite literally, hard to chew. At the other end of the spectrum, overcooked wild rice is gluey.

To find the best cooking method, we first tried steaming and boiling, but both methods produced poorly cooked wild rice. Research revealed the best approach to be slow simmering, although the timing varied from batch to batch. The key is to stop the cooking process at just the right moment; otherwise, the texture goes quickly from tough to gluey. The solution? Once the rice had simmered for 35 minutes, we checked it for doneness every couple of minutes.

Developing good flavor was another story. Plain water made for distinctly bad-tasting rice, and the addition of wine only accentuated the off flavor. Beef broth was overwhelming, but chicken broth was a revelation. Mild yet rich, the chicken broth tempered the rice's muddy flavor to a pleasant earthiness and affirmed its subdued nuttiness. Bay leaves and thyme added finesse and complexity.

Although it was now perfectly cooked, tasters found the wild rice alone to be overwhelming. Perhaps it could be better appreciated if complemented by a mellower grain, such as brown or white rice. Brown rice offered too little contrast, so we quickly settled on white. Cooking both rices in the same pot (adding the white rice midway through the simmer) caused the texture of the white rice to suffer, so an additional pot was called for. To make the most of this second saucepan, we decided to add flavoring ingredients in the style of a pilaf—a simple technique that guarantees flavorful, fluffy rice. Aromatics are first softened in oil or butter, and then the rice is lightly toasted in the pan, after which the liquid is added and the rice simmered until tender. The winning pilaf ingredients turned out to be onions, carrots, dried cranberries, and toasted pecans.

Wild Rice Pilaf with Pecans and Dried Cranberries

SERVES 6 TO 8

Wild rice goes quickly from tough to pasty, so begin testing the rice at the 35-minute mark and drain the rice as soon as it is tender.

1¾	cups low-sodium chicken broth
2½	cups water
2	bay leaves
8	sprigs fresh thyme, divided into 2 bundles, each tied together with kitchen twine
1	cup wild rice, rinsed well and picked over
1½	cups long-grain white rice
3	tablespoons unsalted butter
1	medium onion, chopped fine
1	large carrot, chopped fine
	Salt
¾	cup sweetened or unsweetened dried cranberries
¾	cup pecans, toasted in a small dry skillet over medium heat until fragrant and lightly browned, about 5 minutes, then chopped coarse
1½	tablespoons minced fresh parsley leaves
	Ground black pepper

1. Bring the broth, ¼ cup of the water, the bay leaves, and 1 bundle thyme to a boil in a medium saucepan over medium-high heat. Add the wild rice, cover, and reduce the heat to low; simmer until the rice is plump and tender and has absorbed most of the liquid, 35 to 45 minutes. Drain the rice in a mesh strainer to remove the excess liquid. Return the rice to the now-empty saucepan; cover to keep warm and set aside.

2. While the wild rice is cooking, place the white rice in a medium bowl and cover with 2 inches water; gently swish the grains to release excess starch. Carefully pour off the water, leaving the rice in the bowl. Repeat about 5 times, until the water runs almost clear. Drain the rice in a mesh strainer.

3. Heat the butter in a medium saucepan over medium-high heat until the foaming subsides, about 2 minutes. Add the onion, carrot, and 1 teaspoon salt; cook, stirring frequently, until softened but not browned, about 4 minutes. Add the rinsed white rice and stir to coat the grains with the butter; cook, stirring frequently, until the grains begin to turn translucent, about 3 minutes. Meanwhile, bring the remaining 2¼ cups water to a boil in a small saucepan or a microwave. Add the boiling water and the remaining thyme bundle to the white rice; return to a boil, then reduce the heat to low, sprinkle the cranberries evenly over the rice, and cover. Simmer until all of the liquid is absorbed, 16 to 18 minutes. Off the heat, fluff the rice with a fork.

4. Combine the wild rice, white rice mixture, pecans, and parsley in a large bowl; toss with a rubber spatula. Adjust the seasonings with salt and pepper to taste; serve immediately.

INGREDIENTS: Wild Rice

Wild rice (*Zizania palustris*) and traditional cultivated rice (*Oryza sativa*) are both members of the grass family (as are wheat, corn, oats, barley, and rye). Truly "wild" wild rice is native to the northern Great Lakes, where it is still harvested. But most so-called wild rice is now cultivated on farms in California. Cultivated wild rice grown in man-made paddies costs between $3 and $5 per pound, while hand-harvested rice from lakes and streams in Minnesota and Canada costs about $9 per pound.

RISOTTO

RISOTTO IS A SIMPLE RICE DISH ELEVATED TO ambrosia by the presence of a simple starchy sauce. Encouraged by judicious additions of wine and stock, the starch in the rice is transformed into a velvety, creamy sauce that clings to the toothsome grains.

Obviously, the rice is the key to a texturally flawless risotto. We found that medium-grain rice is the best choice for risotto, where we want some starchiness but not too much. But not all medium-grain rice is the same. In our kitchen tests, we found that the risotto technique may be used with non-Italian medium-grain rice, but the finished texture will pale in comparison to risotto made with Italian rice, which provides the best contrast between supple sauce and firm, toothsome rice. We think Italian rice is a must.

The Italian rice used for risotto comes in two grades: *superfino* and *fino*. These varieties include Arborio (the most widely available), Carnaroli, and Vialone Nano. In a side-by-side taste test of Arborio, Carnaroli, and Vialone Nano, tasters were split evenly between the Arborio and Carnaroli; those liking firmer rice grains chose Arborio, and those liking softer, creamier rice chose Carnaroli. Vialone was deemed too soft and had a "pasty" texture, as if the grains lacked a firm center. One source suggested that Vialone Nano is most popular in and around Venice, where a decidedly loose, soupy texture is the desired consistency for risotto.

Luckily, risotto is so popular that most markets carry at least one brand of Italian rice, generally Arborio. Because this rice is so widely available, we call for it in our recipes. If you like a softer, creamier rice and can find Carnaroli, buy it; it can be used in all the risotto recipes in this chapter.

Having good-quality rice is only half the battle; cooking is the rest. After countless batches with minute variations, we were certain about a few points. First, slowly cooking the diced onion until it yielded its juices and firm form was imperative to the final flavor and texture. The sweetness of properly cooked onion lent depth to this dish, and the softened onion melted into the risotto by serving time. The next step was

217

sautéing the rice, which prompted the starches in the rice to turn translucent—a good visual clue for adding liquid. When we did not cook the rice prior to adding liquid, the risotto was mushy and chalky, and the rice grains lacked their distinctive toothsomeness.

Once the rice is toasted, the liquids are added. The wine must be added before the broth so the boozy flavor has a chance to cook off. Otherwise, we found the alcohol punch was too much. Virtually all risottos are made with a light, dry white wine (although there are some regional specialties made with red wine). Risotto made without wine lacked dimension and tasted bland, so don't skip this step.

The recipes we researched offered a wide range of options for broth, from plain water to veal stock. Water did little for us, and veal stock is rare in all but the best-provisioned professional kitchens. Straight beef broth and chicken broth proved too intense, but diluting chicken broth with an equal amount of water was just right. The chicken broth added richness and depth without taking over. We found that homemade stock was preferable to commercial broth, but the latter still makes a good risotto.

On an interesting note, several prominent cookbook authors suggested using bouillon cubes, but we found the cubes muddied the risotto's clean flavor. We can only assume that the quality of Italian bouillon cubes is superior than what we found on our grocer's shelves.

Although this is contrary to conventional wisdom and the instructions in most cookbooks, we discovered that constant stirring is unnecessary. We added half the broth once the wine had cooked off and allowed the rice to simmer for about 10 minutes, or half the cooking time, with little attention. The rice floated freely, individual grains suspended by the bubbling broth. During this period, we stirred the rice infrequently—about every three minutes—to ensure that it was not sticking to the bottom of the pan. Once all the broth was absorbed by the rice, we added more, a scant half cup at a time. For this period, stirring every minute or so was important; if we did not, the rice stuck to the bottom of the pan.

There is quite a bit of controversy surrounding the doneness of risotto. Some insist it should have a chalky, solid bite, while others feel it should be soft to the core. Tasters expressed individual preferences quite strongly, so you must taste as the rice nears completion and decide for yourself. Generally, we began tasting our rice after about 20 minutes of cooking; you can always cook it longer for a softer texture, but you can never bring back bite.

For the final touch, Parmesan goes in at the very end, to preserve its distinctive flavor and aroma. Grated cheese proved best, as it melted almost instantaneously. The quality of the cheese is paramount, as its taste is so prominent. This is the perfect occasion for buying authentic Parmesan freshly cut from the wheel, with its branded trademark boldly displayed on the rind.

Parmesan Risotto
SERVES 6

This is risotto at its simplest. It can accompany a variety of meals, from grilled or braised cuts to a mélange of roasted vegetables. Parmesan risotto is also appropriate as a first course. Don't fret if you have broth left over once the rice is finished cooking; different brands of rice all cook differently, and we prefer to err on the side of slightly too much broth rather than too little. If you do use all the broth and the rice has not finished cooking, add hot water.

3½	cups low-sodium chicken broth
3	cups water
4	tablespoons (½ stick) unsalted butter
I	medium onion, diced fine
	Salt
2	cups Arborio rice
I	cup dry white wine
2	ounces Parmesan cheese, freshly grated (I cup)
	Ground black pepper

1. Bring the broth and water to a simmer in a medium saucepan over medium-high heat. Reduce the heat to the lowest possible setting to keep the broth warm.

2. Melt the butter in a 4-quart saucepan over medium heat. Once the foaming subsides, add the

onion and ½ teaspoon salt and cook, stirring occasionally, until the onion is very soft and translucent, about 9 minutes. Add the rice and cook, stirring frequently, until the edges of the grains are transparent, about 4 minutes. Add the wine and cook, stirring frequently, until the wine is completely absorbed by the rice, about 2 minutes. Add 3 cups of the warm broth and, stirring infrequently (about every 3 minutes), simmer until the liquid is absorbed and the bottom of the pan is dry, 10 to 12 minutes.

3. Add more of the broth, ½ cup at a time, as needed, to keep the pan bottom from becoming dry (every 3 to 4 minutes); cook, stirring frequently, until the grains of rice are cooked through but still somewhat firm in the center, 10 to 12 minutes. Stir in the cheese, season with salt and pepper to taste, and serve immediately in warmed shallow bowls.

➤ VARIATIONS

Saffron Risotto

Also known as risotto alla Milanese in honor of the city of Milan, saffron risotto is one of the simplest and best variations on basic risotto. While this risotto is the traditional accompaniment to Osso Buco (page 432), it is just as good on its own or with roast pork, veal, or poultry.

Follow the recipe for Parmesan Risotto. In step 2, just after you add the rice to the pot, crumble ¼ teaspoon saffron threads over the rice. Proceed as directed.

Asparagus Risotto with Lemon and Mint

The flavors in this dish are light, making it a suitable accompaniment to broiled or poached salmon or a simple roast chicken. It is essential to use thin asparagus for this recipe, so that it cooks through by the time the rice is done.

Snap the tough ends off 1 pound thin asparagus (see the illustration on page 130). Cut the spears on the bias into ½-inch lengths. Follow the recipe for Parmesan Risotto through step 2. In step 3, add the broth to the rice and stir as directed. After 5 minutes, stir in the asparagus and continue as directed. When adding the Parmesan to the rice, stir in ½ teaspoon grated lemon zest and 2 tablespoons minced fresh mint leaves. Accompany each serving of risotto with a lemon wedge.

MUSHROOM RISOTTO

A FAVORITE MAIN-COURSE RISOTTO DISH OF ours is one packed with earthy, robust flavor courtesy of myriad wild mushrooms—puffballs, hen-of-the-woods, *trompettes-de-la-mort*. These are mushrooms with fanciful names to match their exotic flavor. The trouble is, these exotically flavored wild mushrooms are both elusive and expensive. We wondered if we could approximate (even surpass) that paragon of risottos with supermarket mushrooms and a bit of test kitchen determination.

Most of the mushroom risotto recipes we found were divided into two camps: authentic recipes using wild mushrooms, and workaday ones using cultivated mushrooms. But there was a small third group of recipes that relied largely on dried porcini mushrooms for flavor. Sold by the ounce and packing a punch, dried porcini are both robustly flavored and aromatic—just the thing for that earthy edge we craved. We prepared several of these recipes to mixed reviews. Tasters appreciated the porcini flavor but missed the firm texture and visual presence of fresh mushrooms. Some combination of the two, then, looked to be the best tack to take.

As far as fresh mushrooms go, experience has taught us that they are at their best when cooked via the dry, intense heat of a smoking skillet or a fiery oven. Moist cooking, such as simmering in risotto, renders them rubbery and bland. A preliminary test of roasted mushrooms versus sautéed showed little difference, so we opted for the skillet to keep things on the stovetop. We sautéed the three most common supermarket mushrooms—the standard button, the brown-capped, meaty cremini, and the cremini's larger though similarly flavored sibling, the portobello—and added them to separate batches of the porcini-flavored risotto.

Tasters found the button mushrooms mild and better appreciated the fuller flavor and meatier texture of the cremini and portobellos. Cremini were easier to prepare than portobellos, as the latter's feathery gills must be trimmed before cooking lest they stain the risotto inky black. Tasters favored larger-size pieces over slices, so we opted to quarter the mushrooms. Over medium-high heat and lightly sprinkled with salt, the mushrooms first shed their liquid, then browned deeply. To preserve their texture and flavor, we didn't add the mushrooms to the risotto until the rice was fully cooked.

The hot skillet and a knob of butter (which tasters preferred to olive oil) did wonders for the mushrooms' flavor, but we wanted more. With onions prepped for the rice, we purloined a portion to sauté with the mushrooms. This step proved successful, as the onions lent both sweetness and piquancy. On a roll, we added a couple of cloves of minced garlic and scored again: These mushrooms were good enough to eat on their own.

The risotto's flavor was emphatically mushroomy but one-dimensional and in need of refinement. We added ½ cup more wine to bring some much-needed acidity to the fore. As for herbs, thyme pairs well with mushrooms, so we added 1 teaspoon minced thyme and then, heeding tasters' demands, minced parsley as well. We kept the Parmesan cheese to 1 cup.

Even with these changes, the risotto still fell short of our expectations, being milder and less dynamic than we wanted. We wondered if we were missing obvious flavor-enhancements, hemmed in by the confines of Italian cooking. Throwing tradition out the window, we turned to a cuisine known for its deft touch with mushrooms: Chinese. A quick thumbing through several Chinese cookbooks inspired us to try replacing the chicken broth with mushroom broth. We combined the dried porcini with the cremini's trimmed stems, bundled herbs, and chicken broth cut with water and simmered the mixture until the mushrooms were tender, about 15 minutes (time enough to prep the other ingredients). We then strained the fungi from the broth and finely minced them before returning them to the rice. The results were promising: The risotto was much fuller-flavored than before, and we had cut preparation time. The cremini's stems appeared to add little besides bulk, so we ended up excluding them for the sake of convenience.

Borrowing again from the Chinese palette, we added soy sauce to the broth. Sweet, salty, and earthy, soy sauce has a galvanizing effect on the flavor of mushrooms that we sensed might pay off in the risotto. The scantest splash rounded out the broth's flavor and gave it indescribable depth. Tasters couldn't detect the soy sauce in the finished risotto, but everyone commented on the dish's fuller, earthier flavor.

Mushroom Risotto

SERVES 6 AS A MAIN COURSE OR
8 AS A FIRST COURSE

If cremini mushrooms are not available, button mushrooms make a fine, though somewhat less flavorful, substitute.

2	bay leaves
6	sprigs fresh thyme
4	sprigs fresh parsley
1	ounce dried porcini mushrooms, rinsed in a mesh strainer under running water
3½	cups low-sodium chicken broth
2	teaspoons soy sauce
3¾	cups water
6	tablespoons (¾ stick) unsalted butter
1¼	pounds cremini mushrooms, stems discarded, caps wiped clean, and cut into fourths if small or sixths if larger
2	medium onions, chopped fine (about 2 cups)
	Salt
3	medium garlic cloves, minced or pressed through a garlic press
2	cups Arborio rice
1	cup dry white wine or dry vermouth
2	ounces Parmesan cheese, freshly grated (1 cup)
2	tablespoons finely chopped parsley leaves
	Ground black pepper

1. Tie the bay leaves, thyme sprigs, and parsley sprigs together with kitchen twine. Bring the bundled herbs, porcini mushrooms, broth, soy sauce, and 3½ cups of the water to a boil in a medium saucepan over a medium-high heat; reduce the heat to medium-low and simmer until the dried mushrooms are softened and fully hydrated, about 15 minutes. Remove and discard the herb bundle and strain the broth through a fine-mesh strainer set over a medium bowl (you should have about 6½ cups strained liquid); return the liquid to the

saucepan and keep warm over low heat. Finely mince the porcini and set aside.

2. Adjust an oven rack to the middle position and heat the oven to 200 degrees. Heat 2 tablespoons of the butter in a 12-inch nonstick skillet over medium-high heat. When the foaming subsides, add the cremini mushrooms, 1 cup of the onions, and ½ teaspoon salt; cook, stirring occasionally, until the moisture released by the mushrooms evaporates and the mushrooms are well browned, about 7 minutes. Stir in the garlic until fragrant, about 1 minute, then transfer the mushrooms to an ovensafe bowl and keep warm in the oven. Off the heat, add the remaining ¼ cup water to the now-empty skillet and scrape with a wooden spoon to loosen any browned bits on the pan bottom; pour the liquid from the skillet into the saucepan with the broth.

3. Heat 3 tablespoons of the butter in a large saucepan over medium heat. When the foaming subsides, add the remaining 1 cup onions and ¼ teaspoon salt; cook, stirring occasionally, until the onions are softened and translucent, about 9 minutes. Add the rice and cook, stirring frequently, until the edges of the grains are transparent, about 4 minutes. Add the wine and cook, stirring frequently, until the rice absorbs the wine. Add the minced porcini and 3½ cups of the broth and cook, stirring every 2 to 3 minutes, until the liquid is absorbed, 9 to 11 minutes. Stir in an additional ½ cup broth every 2 to 3 minutes until the rice is cooked through but the grains are still somewhat firm at the center, 10 to 12 minutes (the rice may not require all of the broth). Stir in the remaining 1 tablespoon butter, then stir in the cremini (and any accumulated juices), cheese, and chopped parsley. Adjust the seasonings with salt and pepper to taste; serve immediately.

➤ VARIATION

Mushroom Risotto with Pancetta and Sage

Follow the recipe for Mushroom Risotto through step 2, omitting the thyme from the broth. Cook 2 ounces finely chopped pancetta and 1 tablespoon unsalted butter in a large saucepan over medium heat, stirring frequently, until the pancetta has rendered some fat, about 5 minutes. Add the remaining 1 cup onions, cooking the onions until softened and translucent, about 7 minutes; continue with the recipe, adding and cooking the rice as in step 3 and adding 1 tablespoon minced fresh sage leaves along with the chopped parsley.

JAMBALAYA

WITH CHICKEN, SAUSAGE, SHRIMP, RICE, tomatoes, and a long list of herbs and spices, jambalaya may sound more like a weekend project than a weeknight dinner. But done right, jambalaya is a one-pot meal that can be on the table in about an hour. Like New Orleans, the city from which it came, jambalaya has a combination of sweet, spice, and smoke that makes it a standout. But when poorly executed, jambalaya can be nothing more than gummy rice, overcooked shrimp, and tough, dry chicken.

We started by testing a half dozen recipes, all of which followed the same protocol: In a large Dutch oven, brown the chicken and remove; brown the sausage and remove; sauté the vegetables; add the cooking liquid, tomatoes, seasonings, and rice; return the chicken and sausage to the pot; and, finally, add the shrimp when the rice is about half-done. Our conclusion? We wanted fluffier rice, more succulent chicken, more delicate shrimp, a more modest amount of tomato, and fresher flavors. In addition, we wanted a streamlined method that would bring the dish together easily in a home kitchen.

Although most jambalaya recipes call for a whole chicken cut up into parts, we opted to use chicken thighs instead. We knew this would save us the time it takes to cut up a chicken, but we also thought that using thighs, which are composed of relatively fatty dark meat, might solve the problem of dry chicken, as white meat is more apt to dry out.

We started by searing both sides of the chicken (with the skin on to provide extra fat to flavor the dish) in just 2 teaspoons of hot vegetable oil, then removed it from the pot, set it aside to cool, and

EQUIPMENT: Large Saucepans

In the test kitchen (and at home), most of us reach for a three- to four-quart saucepan more than any other because its uses go beyond boiling water. Which begs an obvious question: Does the brand of pan matter? With prices for these large saucepans ranging from $24.99 for a Revere stainless steel model with thin copper cladding at the base up to $140 for an All-Clad pan with a complete aluminum core and stainless steel interior and exterior cladding, a lot of money is riding on the answer. To let us offer guidance, we tested eight models, all between three and four quarts in size, from well-known cookware manufacturers.

The tests we performed were based on common cooking tasks and designed to highlight specific characteristics of the pans' performance. Sautéing minced onions illustrated the pace at which the pan heats up and sautés. Cooking white rice provided a good indication of the pan's ability to heat evenly as well as how tightly the lid sealed. Making pastry cream let us know how user-friendly the pan was—was it shaped such that a whisk reached into the corners without trouble, was it comfortable to pick up, and could we pour liquid from it neatly? These traits can make a real difference when you use a pan day in and day out.

Of the tests we performed, sautéing onions was the most telling. In our view, onions should soften reliably and evenly (and with minimal attention and stirring) when sautéed over medium heat. In this regard, the All-Clad, Calphalon, KitchenAid, and Sitram pans all delivered. The Chantal and Cuisinart pans sautéed slightly faster, necessitating a little more attention from the cook, but still well within acceptable bounds. Only the Revere and Farberware Millennium sautéed so fast that we considered them problematic.

Incidentally, the Revere and Farberware pans that sautéed onions too fast for us were the lightest pans of the bunch, weighing only 1 pound 10 ounces and 2 pounds 6 ounces, respectively. This indicates that they were made from thinner metal, which is one reason they heat quickly. On the flip side of the weight issue, however, we found that too heavy a pan, such as the 4-pound Calphalon, could be uncomfortable to lift when full. The ideal was about 3½ pounds; pans near this weight, including the All-Clad, KitchenAid, Chantal, Sitram, and Cuisinart, balanced good heft with easy maneuverability.

While none of the pans failed the rice test outright, there were performance differences. In the Sitram, Revere, and Farberware pans, the rice stuck and dried out at the bottom, if only a little bit. Although this did not greatly affect the texture, the flavor, or the cleanup, we'd still choose a pan for which this was not an issue.

Every pan in the group turned out perfect pastry cream. During this test, we did observe one design element that made it easy to pour liquid from the pan neatly, without dribbles and spills. A rolled lip that flares slightly at the top of the pan helped control the pour. Only two pans in the group did not have a rolled lip: the All-Clad and the Calphalon.

So which pan do you want to buy? That depends largely on two things: your budget and your attention span. Based on our tests, we'd advise against really inexpensive pans—those that cost less than $50. For between $50 and $100, you can get a competent pan such as the Chantal, Sitram, or Cuisinart. The only caveat is that you may have to watch them carefully; they offer less room for error than our favorite pans, made by All-Clad, Calphalon, and KitchenAid.

THE BEST LARGE SAUCEPAN

The All-Clad (left), Calphalon (center), and KitchenAid (right) saucepans are our favorites, but they are not flawless. The Calphalon ($110) is heavy, both it and the All-Clad pan ($140) lack rolled lips, and the KitchenAid pan ($119) has a relatively short curved handle. However, these three pans provide moderate, steady heat, even when you are distracted.

peeled off the skin (chicken skin becomes soggy and unappetizing when cooked in liquid). Rice and liquid went into the pot, followed by the chicken, and, after just 25 minutes, the chicken and rice were perfectly cooked through. But there was something clumsy about eating the chicken off the bone. For our next test, we tried cooking the chicken in exactly the same way, but instead of serving the thighs whole, we shredded them. Now the dish looked and tasted much more appealing, offering a bite of chicken in every forkful and no cumbersome bones to remove.

Next, we took on the sausage. After comparing the classic choice, andouille, with tasso, chorizo, and linguiça, we decided that nothing tastes like andouille—a Cajun sausage that infuses the other ingredients in the pot with spice and smoke. We browned ¼-inch pieces of andouille in the chicken fat and then set them aside, planning to add them back to the pot along with the liquid, rice, and chicken.

Vegetables were the next item on our roster. Because the trio of minced bell pepper, onion, and celery is key to Cajun cooking, we included all three in our recipe. However, after sampling bitter-tasting green peppers (the classic choice) side by side with sweet red peppers, we unabashedly chose the red. We also decided to add 2 tablespoons of minced garlic to give the jambalaya more punch.

Now approaching our tenth test, we began to dread the task of chopping and mincing the vegetables and garlic. It just took too much time. So we took out the food processor and gave the vegetables a whirl. What a difference! Not only did the food processor get the job done in seconds, but the vegetables were cut into smaller pieces, and so they sautéed more quickly in the pan and contributed more flavor.

Chicken broth, not water, is traditionally used in jambalaya, but we needed to find the right ratio between liquid and rice. We started with 1½ cups of chicken broth to 1 cup of rice (the water-to-rice ratio in our White Rice recipe on page 209), but our rice was a little dry and there wasn't enough to go around. We increased the rice to 1½ cups and experimented with the various amounts

of broth until deciding 2¼ cups was just right. This rice was the perfect compromise between fluffy pilaf (too light for jambalaya) and sticky risotto (too heavy).

Although the texture was perfect, we needed to punch up the flavor a bit. We tried combining clam juice with the chicken broth, hoping that it might bring out the sweetness of the shrimp. Although the clam juice–chicken broth duo was pleasing and delicate, the rice was still lacking. In an effort to boost the flavor, we substituted ¼ cup of tomato juice (from a can of diced tomatoes) for an equal amount of broth. Now the rice was perfect: flavorful and cohesive without being gummy, heavy, or sticky.

Our last step was to find a way to keep the shrimp tender and sweet. We seared the shrimp in a hot pan, set them aside, and then added them back to the jambalaya when the chicken was halfway done. This batch was a failure. The shrimp were tough, and they took on a smoky flavor from the searing that provided little contrast with the andouille. For the next test, we added the raw shrimp just five minutes before the chicken and rice were finished. After removing the lid, we could see that the shrimp were perfectly cooked to a blushing pink, still tender and succulently sweet.

Chicken and Shrimp Jambalaya
SERVES 4 TO 6
Because andouille varies in spiciness, we suggest tasting a piece of the cooked sausage and then adjusting the amount of cayenne in the jambalaya to suit your taste. If you can't find andouille, try tasso, chorizo, or linguiça;

PROPERLY CUT VEGETABLES

Using the pulse button on a food processor yields finely chopped vegetables in seconds. Don't overprocess or puree the vegetables— they should remain in distinct pieces.

if using chorizo or linguiça, consider doubling the amount of cayenne. The onion, celery, bell pepper, and garlic can be chopped by hand instead of in a food processor. The shrimp don't need to be deveined, but you can do so if you prefer. If you're serving only four people, you may choose to skip the shredding step and serve each person one piece of chicken on the bone.

1   medium onion, trimmed and quartered lengthwise
1   medium celery rib, cut crosswise into quarters
1   medium red bell pepper, cored, seeded, and quartered lengthwise
5   medium garlic cloves, peeled
2   teaspoons vegetable oil
4   bone-in, skin-on chicken thighs
8   ounces andouille sausage, halved lengthwise and cut into 1/4-inch pieces
1 1/2   cups long-grain white rice
1   teaspoon salt
1/2   teaspoon minced fresh thyme leaves
1/4   teaspoon cayenne pepper (see note)
1   (14.5-ounce) can diced tomatoes, drained, 1/4 cup juice reserved
1   cup bottled clam juice
1 1/2   cups low-sodium chicken broth
2   large bay leaves
1   pound large shrimp (31 to 40 per pound), peeled and deveined, if desired (see pages 19–20)
2   tablespoons minced fresh parsley leaves

1. In a food processor, pulse the onion, celery, bell pepper, and garlic until chopped fine, about six 1-second pulses, scraping down the sides of the bowl once or twice. Do not overprocess; the vegetables should not be pureed (see the photo on page 223).

2. Heat the oil in a large, heavy-bottomed Dutch oven over medium-high heat until shimmering but not smoking. Add the chicken, skin-side down, and cook until golden brown, about 5 minutes. Using tongs, turn the chicken and cook until golden brown on the second side, about 3 minutes longer. Transfer the chicken to a plate and set aside. Reduce the heat to medium and add the andouille; cook, stirring frequently, until browned, about 3 minutes. Using a slotted spoon, transfer the sausage to a paper towel–lined plate and set aside.

3. Reduce the heat to medium-low, add the chopped vegetables, and cook, stirring occasionally and scraping the bottom of the pot with a wooden spoon, until the vegetables have softened, about 4 minutes. Add the rice, salt, thyme, and cayenne; cook, stirring frequently, until the rice is coated with fat, about 1 minute. Add the tomatoes, reserved tomato juice, clam juice, broth, bay leaves, and browned sausage to the pot; stir to combine. Remove and discard the skin from the chicken; place the chicken, skinned-side down, on the rice. Bring to a boil, reduce the heat to low, cover, and simmer for 15 minutes. Stir once, keeping the chicken on top, skinned-side down. Replace the cover and continue to simmer until the chicken is no longer pink when cut into with a paring knife, about 10 minutes more; transfer the chicken to a clean plate and set aside. Scatter the shrimp over the rice, cover, and continue to cook until the rice is fully tender and the shrimp are opaque and cooked through, about 5 minutes more.

4. While the shrimp are cooking, shred the chicken with your fingers into thin strands. When the shrimp are cooked, discard the bay leaves. Off the heat, stir in the parsley and shredded chicken; serve immediately.

POLENTA

NOTHING MORE THAN CORNMEAL MUSH, polenta is made from dried, ground corn cooked in liquid until the starches in the corn hydrate and swell into soft, balloon-like structures. For many purposes, this soft stage is the most delicious way to serve polenta.

The stiff polenta you often see in restaurants starts out as a soft mass but is spread into a thin layer on a baking sheet or marble surface, cooled until stiff, sliced, and then sautéed, fried, or grilled until it resembles a crouton. These crisp rectangles are rarely more than a garnish. However, a smooth, piping-hot mound of soft polenta can be a meal. More commonly, soft polenta is used as a filler to stretch out meager servings of small game birds, like quail, or to cut the richness of sausages. Most stews and braised dishes—everything from osso buco to braised rabbit—can be ladled over a bowl of soft polenta.

Although making polenta sounds easy, the traditional Italian method for cooking it is a lot of work. The polenta must be slowly added to boiling salted water and stirred constantly (to prevent scorching) during the entire 30- to 40-minute cooking time. Thirty minutes of such constant stirring can seem like an eternity.

Of course, this assumes that you have avoided the biggest pitfall of all, the seizing problem at the beginning of the cooking process. Cornmeal is a starch, and starch thickens when mixed with water and heated. If this happens too quickly, the cornmeal seizes up into a solid, nearly immovable mass.

We tested adding cornmeal to cold water, using more water, using less water, and using different grinds of cornmeal, all to no avail. Yes, we learned how to prevent seizing (add the cornmeal very slowly), but we still needed to stir constantly for at least 30 minutes to prevent scorching.

This testing did, however, reveal some important information. We found that medium-grind cornmeal makes the best polenta. Finely ground cornmeal, such as the Quaker brand sold in many supermarkets, is too powdery and makes gummy polenta. Cornmeal with a texture akin to granulated sugar, not table salt, makes the best polenta. We also discovered that a ratio of 4 parts water to 1 part cornmeal delivers the right consistency. As for salt, 1 teaspoon is the right amount for 1 cup of cornmeal.

At this point in our testing, we started to explore alternative cooking methods. The microwave was a bust, yielding sticky, raw-tasting polenta. The pressure cooker was even worse; the polenta took a long time to cook and then stuck firmly to the pot. We finally got good results when we prepared polenta in a double boiler. The polenta is cooked over simmering water, so it cannot scorch or seize up the way it can when cooked over direct heat. It emerges with a soft, light texture and sweet corn flavor. There is only one drawback, and it is a big one: time.

While a double boiler produced undeniably rich, creamy polenta, the cooking time was prohibitively long. Even with the minimum attention that the technique required, 1½ hours of cooking was simply impractical. We wondered whether we could produce similar results via more conventional methods. The double-boiler method proved to us that slow, very gentle heat, not vigilant stirring, was the key to unlocking cornmeal's smooth texture. Could we approximate a double boiler's low heat with a conventional saucepan?

We could. A heavy-bottomed saucepan on the stove's lowest possible setting (or in conjunction with a heat tamer; see note on page 226) shielded the polenta from cooking too rapidly and allowed for the starches to be released and the flavor of the cornmeal to develop. Keeping the cover on the pot held in moisture and reduced the risk of scorching the polenta, even when we stirred infrequently rather than constantly. Within 30 minutes, a third of the time it took in the double boiler, we had creamy polenta ready for the table. We did find, however, that with the slightly higher temperature, stirring was a more significant issue. When we left the polenta unheeded for more than seven minutes, it tended to stick to the pot bottom and corners, where it remained until washing. Stirring vigorously every five minutes prevented that mishap.

INGREDIENTS: Instant Polenta

After testing dozens of ways to prepare polenta, we still had one question: what about quick-cooking, or instant, polenta? We tested several brands (all imported from Italy) and found that instant polenta is a great way to make polenta in a hurry. The flavor is good (although not nearly as good as our basic polenta), and it takes no more than 10 minutes.

Quick polenta, like quick grits and instant rice, has been cooked before, then dried. All you need to do is reconstitute it with boiling water. Quick polenta costs at least three times as much as regular cornmeal and doesn't have the smooth texture and full corn flavor of regular polenta. However, instant polenta is easy to prepare (just add to boiling water and simmer for several minutes), and the result is pretty good.

Basic Polenta

SERVES 4 TO 6

If you do not have a heavy-bottomed saucepan, you may want to use a flame tamer to manage the heat. A flame tamer can be purchased at most kitchen supply stores. It's easy to tell whether you need a flame tamer or not. If the polenta bubbles or sputters at all after the first 10 minutes, the heat is too high, and you need a flame tamer. Properly heated polenta will do little more than release wisps of steam. When stirring the polenta, make sure to scrape the sides and bottom of the pan to ensure even cooking. Use this polenta as a base for any stew or braise, especially lamb shanks (page 490) or osso buco (page 432), or for cooked leafy greens (page 169).

6	cups water
	Salt
1½	cups medium cornmeal, preferably stone-ground
3	tablespoons unsalted butter, cut into large chunks
	Ground black pepper

1. Bring the water to a boil in a heavy-bottomed 4-quart saucepan over medium-high heat. Once boiling, add 1½ teaspoons salt and pour the cornmeal into the water in a very slow stream from a measuring cup, all the while stirring in a circular motion with a wooden spoon (see the illustration at right).

2. Reduce the heat to the lowest possible setting and cover. Cook, vigorously stirring the polenta once for about 10 seconds every 5 minutes and making sure to scrape clean the bottom and corners of the pot, until the polenta has lost its raw cornmeal taste and becomes soft and smooth, about 30 minutes. Stir in the butter, season with salt and pepper to taste, and serve immediately.

➤ VARIATIONS

Polenta with Parmesan and Butter
Follow the recipe for Basic Polenta, stirring in 1½ ounces grated Parmesan cheese, freshly grated (¾ cup), with the butter. Divide the polenta among individual bowls and top each with a small pat of butter. Sprinkle generously with more grated Parmesan to taste and serve immediately.

Polenta with Gorgonzola
SERVES 4 TO 6 AS A FIRST COURSE

Choose a Gorgonzola dolce or other mild, creamy blue cheese such as Saga blue. Do not use an aged Gorgonzola for this dish. Other aged blue cheeses will also be too salty, crumbly, and pungent.

Follow the recipe for Basic Polenta, dividing the finished polenta among individual bowls. Top each bowl with a 1-ounce slice of Gorgonzola cheese and serve immediately.

Polenta with Meat Ragù
SERVES 4 TO 6 AS A MAIN COURSE

Instead of tossing slow-simmering Bolognese sauce with pasta, ladle it over mounds of soft polenta, sprinkle it with grated Parmesan cheese, and serve it as a hearty main course.

Prepare Bolognese Sauce (page 255) and keep it warm over low heat. Follow the recipe for Basic Polenta, dividing the finished polenta among individual bowls. Ladle some Bolognese sauce into each bowl and sprinkle with freshly grated Parmesan cheese to taste. Serve immediately, passing more grated Parmesan at the table.

Polenta with Wild Mushroom Sauté
SERVES 4 TO 6 AS A MAIN COURSE

Mushrooms have a natural affinity with polenta, as their chewy, meaty texture and flavor is sharply contrasted by the creamy cornmeal. Refer to the illustrations on page 227 for tips on soaking dried mushrooms. Start the

MAKING POLENTA

When the water comes to a boil, add the salt, then pour the polenta from a measuring cup into the water in a very slow stream, all the while stirring in a circular motion with a wooden spoon to prevent clumping.

polenta before beginning to cook the mushrooms. If the polenta is ready before the mushrooms are, keep it warm over very low heat; leave the cover on and stir every 5 minutes or so. The polenta can be held this way for at least 15 minutes.

1/3	ounce dried porcini mushrooms
1/2	cup water
3	tablespoons unsalted butter
2	tablespoons extra-virgin olive oil
1	sprig fresh rosemary
1	pound portobello mushrooms, stems discarded, caps halved and cut crosswise into 1/2-inch-thick slices
1	pound cremini mushrooms, stems discarded, caps wiped clean and halved
	Salt
2	medium garlic cloves, minced or pressed through a garlic press
1	tablespoon minced fresh parsley leaves
	Ground black pepper
1/2	cup dry red wine
1	recipe Basic Polenta (page 226)

1. Rinse the dried porcini mushrooms in a small strainer under cool running water; drain. Add the mushrooms and water to a small microwave-safe bowl. Cover with plastic wrap, cut several steam vents in the plastic wrap with a paring knife, and microwave on high power for 30 seconds. Let stand until the mushrooms soften, about 5 minutes. Following the illustrations at right, lift the mushrooms from the liquid with a fork and mince. Pour the liquid through a small strainer lined with a coffee filter or a single sheet of paper towel set over a measuring cup. Reserve the mushrooms and strained soaking liquid separately.

2. Heat 1 tablespoon of the butter with the oil and the rosemary sprig in a large skillet over medium-high heat. Once the foaming subsides, add the portobello and cremini mushrooms and 1/2 teaspoon salt and cook, stirring occasionally, until the mushrooms have shed their liquid and the cut surfaces have browned, about 10 minutes. Reduce the heat to medium-low and add the garlic and minced porcini. Cook, stirring frequently, until aromatic, about 1 minute. Remove and discard

the rosemary, stir in the parsley, and season with salt and pepper to taste. Transfer the mushrooms to a bowl and tent with foil to keep warm.

3. Return the pan to the stove and increase the heat to medium-high. Add the porcini liquid and red wine to the skillet and scrape the pan bottom to loosen any browned bits. Simmer until the liquid has reduced to about 1/3 cup, 6 to 8 minutes. Remove the pan from the heat and whisk in the remaining 2 tablespoons butter until completely

REHYDRATING DRIED PORCINI MUSHROOMS

We find that the microwave cuts soaking time from 20 minutes at room temperature to just 5 minutes. Place the dried porcini in a small strainer and rinse under cool running water. Transfer the porcini to a microwave-safe bowl, add tap water, and cover with plastic wrap. Cut several steam vents in the plastic wrap and microwave on high power for 30 seconds. Remove the bowl from the microwave and let stand, covered, until the mushrooms soften, about 5 minutes. Here's how to remove the softened mushrooms from the liquid and leave the sand behind.

1. When soaking dried porcini mushrooms, most of the sand and dirt will fall to the bottom of the bowl. Use a fork to lift the rehydrated mushrooms from the liquid without stirring up the sand. If the mushrooms still feel gritty, rinse them briefly under cool running water.

2. The soaking liquid is quite flavorful and should be reserved. To remove the grit, pour the liquid through a small strainer lined with a coffee filter or a single sheet of paper towel and set over a measuring cup.

incorporated. Season with salt and pepper to taste.

4. Divide the polenta among individual bowls. Divide the mushrooms among the bowls and drizzle a little sauce over each portion. Serve immediately.

BOSTON BAKED BEANS

HEADY WITH SMOKY PORK AND BITTERSWEET molasses, authentic Boston baked beans are both sweet and savory, a unique combination of the simplest ingredients, unified and refined during a long simmer—a fine example of the whole being greater than the sum of the parts.

A close reading of recipes—and there are thousands out there—made it clear that authentic Boston baked beans are not about fancy seasonings; they are about developing intense flavor by means of the judicious employment of canonical ingredients (beans, pork, molasses, mustard, and sometimes onion) and slow cooking. Tasters quickly rejected recipes with lengthy lists of untraditional ingredients and short cooking times.

The most important item on the shopping list is, of course, the beans, the classic choice being standard dried white beans in one of three sizes: small white beans, midsize navy or pea beans, or large Great Northern beans. While the latter two choices were adequate, tasters preferred the small white beans for their dense, creamy texture and their ability to remain firm and intact over the course of a long simmer. (The two larger sizes tended to split.) Per the test kitchen's previous findings, we found that there is no need to soak beans before cooking, so we gladly skipped that step. We did test canned white beans and were not impressed by their lackluster performance. Within two hours of baking, they had turned to mush and lacked the full flavor of the dried beans.

Next came the meat. Some type of cured pork is essential for depth of flavor and lush texture, though its flavor should never dominate. While traditionalists swear by salt pork, we first tried fleshier pork brisket, which is a meatier version of salt pork. Its flavor was enjoyable, but tasters felt the beans lacked richness—the brisket was too lean. Not surprisingly, salt pork scored high with tasters, although some felt the flavor was too mild. Bacon, a more modern choice, was deemed "too smoky and overwhelming" for most, though the heartier pork flavor was appreciated. On a whim, we put both salt pork and bacon into the pot and found the perfect solution. The bacon brought the desired depth to the beans, and the salt pork muted the bacon's hickory tang. Twice as much salt pork as bacon proved the right balance.

In traditional recipes, the salt pork is cast raw into the beans (often as a large piece) and melts into the sauce, but during tests it failed to render completely. Gelatinous chunks of fatty pork bobbing among the beans left even the most carnivorous taster cold. We first diced the pork into smaller bits, but this was only a partial success; unmelted fat remained. Next, we browned it in the Dutch oven prior to adding the beans, and the results were surprising: This simple step (and one not recommended in any of the recipes we'd found) made the flavor of the beans significantly fuller and better than anything we had yet tasted. Apparently, the melted fat more readily flavored the cooking liquid, and the browned bits of meat tasted richer.

While yellow onion was a controversial ingredient in classic recipes, we sensed its flavor could be important, and our intuition proved right. Tasters loved its sweetness and the full flavor it lent the beans, especially once sautéed in the rendered pork fat. Tasters favored a fine dice so that the onion all but disappeared by the time the beans were ready.

Next we tackled the final two ingredients: mustard and molasses. Dry mustard, the classic choice, had worked fine up until now, but most of the test kitchen felt home cooks were more likely to have prepared mustard on hand and that it provided a perk—vinegar—to cut the beans' sweetness. We tested several varieties, including Dijon, German whole-grain, "yellow," and "brown." They all brought a unique angle to the beans, but brown mustard—Gulden's brown mustard, in particular—was best, imparting a pleasant sharpness without calling attention to itself. Even with the mustard's tang, though, we found it necessary to add vinegar for acidity. Most classic recipes include cider vinegar from the start of the cooking time (if at all), but we found the acidity stayed sharper when it was added to the beans once finished. A scant teaspoon proved enough to cut the molasses's sweetness and accent the other flavors.

The molasses, we discovered, would take some finessing, as its brutish flavor and intense sweetness dominated the beans when added carelessly. After tasting batches made with mild, full-flavored (also known as "robust"), and blackstrap varieties, most tasters preferred the subtler tones of the mild variety. We settled on just ½ cup baked with the beans for a balance of moderate sweetness and palate-cleansing bitterness. A tablespoon added after cooking gently reemphasized its character.

All that was left to do now was tweak the cooking time. For testing purposes, we had cooked the beans at 250 degrees for six to seven hours. While pleased with the results, we were curious to see what other temperatures might accomplish. We knew that, to a certain extent, flavor and texture were in opposition. The longer the beans cooked, the better the sauce's flavor, but past a certain crucial moment of equilibrium, time worked against the beans, turning them to mush.

We tested cooking temperatures in increments of 25 degrees between 200 and 350 degrees and met with interesting results. At 200 degrees, the beans took upward of eight hours to cook and were still on the crunchy side. At 350 degrees, the beans percolated vigorously and exploded. Midpoints of 275 and 300 degrees were more successful. The beans were creamy-textured and the sauce full-flavored. With little difference in the outcome when either temperature was used, we chose 300 degrees, which made the beans cook faster, finishing in just about five hours—less time than we had thought possible.

While pleased with the texture and flavor, we still wanted a thicker sauce—soupy beans were not acceptable. We discovered that it was not simply a matter of reducing the volume of water, however, as this led to unevenly cooked beans. We had been cooking the beans start to finish covered with a lid, which had prevented the cooking liquid from reducing effectively. When we removed the lid for the last hour in the oven, we got the results we were looking for—the sauce had reduced to a syrupy, intensified state that perfectly napped the beans.

Boston Baked Beans

SERVES 4 TO 6

The beans can be made ahead. After cooking, cool them to room temperature and refrigerate in an airtight container for up to 4 days.

4	ounces salt pork, trimmed of rind and cut into ½-inch cubes
2	ounces (2 slices) bacon, cut into ¼-inch pieces
1	medium onion, chopped fine
½	cup plus 1 tablespoon mild molasses
1½	tablespoons prepared brown mustard, such as Gulden's
1	pound (about 2½ cups) dried small white beans, rinsed and picked over (see the illustration on page 232)
	Salt
9	cups water
1	teaspoon cider vinegar
	Ground black pepper

BUYING SALT PORK

FATTY

LEAN

The salt pork shown at top has a high ratio of fat to meat and is preferable in this recipe to leaner, meatier salt pork, like the piece shown at bottom.

Adjust an oven rack to the lower-middle position and heat the oven to 300 degrees. Add the salt pork and bacon to a large Dutch oven; cook over medium heat, stirring occasionally, until lightly browned and most of the fat is rendered, about 7 minutes. Add the onion and continue to cook, stirring occasionally, until the onion is softened, about 8 minutes. Add the ½ cup molasses, the mustard, beans, 1¼ teaspoons salt, and the water; increase the heat to medium-high and bring to a boil. Cover the pot and set in the oven. Bake until the beans are tender, about 4 hours, stirring once after 2 hours. Remove the lid and continue to bake until the liquid has thickened to a syrupy consistency, 1 to 1½ hours longer. Remove the beans from the oven; stir in the remaining 1 tablespoon molasses, the vinegar, and additional salt and pepper to taste. Serve. (The beans can be refrigerated in an airtight container for up to 4 days. Warm over medium-low heat before serving.)

> VARIATION

Barbecued Baked Beans

Barbecued baked beans are slow-simmered, oven-cooked beans that are similar to Boston baked beans. Barbecued baked beans are a bit brasher in flavor, however, so they stand up better to the big flavors of grilled and barbecued foods.

4	ounces (about 4 slices) bacon, diced
I	medium onion, diced
4	medium garlic cloves, minced or pressed through a garlic press
I	pound (about 2½ cups) dried navy beans, rinsed and picked over (see illustration on page 232)
I	cup strong black coffee
¼	cup packed dark brown sugar
I	tablespoon mild molasses
1½	tablespoons prepared brown mustard, such as Gulden's
½	cup plus I tablespoon barbecue sauce
½	teaspoon hot pepper sauce
	Salt
8	cups water
	Ground black pepper

1. Adjust an oven rack to the lower-middle position and heat the oven to 300 degrees. Heat a large Dutch oven over medium heat for 2 minutes, add the bacon, and cook until lightly browned and most of the fat is rendered, 5 to 6 minutes. Stir in the onion and continue to cook until the onion has softened, about 8 minutes. Add the garlic and cook until fragrant, about 30 seconds. Add the beans, coffee, brown sugar, molasses, mustard, ½ cup barbecue sauce, hot sauce, 2 teaspoons salt, and the water. Increase the heat to high; once boiling, cover the pot and place it in the oven.

2. Cook, stirring once every hour, until the beans are thoroughly soft, about 4 hours. Remove the lid and continue to cook until the liquid has thickened to a syrupy consistency, 1 to 1½ hours. Remove from the oven and stir in the remaining 1 tablespoon barbecue sauce and salt and pepper to taste. (The beans can be refrigerated in an airtight container for several days. Warm over medium-low heat before serving.)

WHITE BEANS WITH TOMATOES, GARLIC, AND SAGE

THE COMBINATION OF WHITE BEANS WITH tomatoes, garlic, and sage is a ubiquitous dish in Florence, much like Boston and its trademark baked beans. We find the combination of flavors delicious, but we thought this traditional dish could benefit from a little fine-tuning of both technique and flavor.

The traditional Tuscan method for cooking beans is romantic but impractical for the modern home cook. The dried beans are placed in a *fiasco,* the bulbous wine bottle used for Chianti, with some liquid, a sprig of sage, and a few garlic cloves, and then the bottle is sealed and nestled into the embers of the household fire to cook slowly through the night. By the morning, the beans are plump and ready to eat.

Needless to say, we did not try cooking our beans in a fiasco or dying embers. A large, heavy-bottomed saucepan or Dutch oven was our choice as it retained heat well, an important attribute when cooking beans.

To add flavor to the beans as they cooked, we added an onion and a carrot, as well as a whole head of garlic with its top lopped off so that its flavor would permeate the liquid. To most tasters, the traditional handful of garlic cloves added little flavor. While the carrot and onion were discarded after cooking, the garlic cloves were squeezed from their skins and returned to the beans, lending a sweet, mild garlic flavor. We saved a portion of the highly seasoned cooking liquid to moisten the beans.

With the beans cooked, it was time to combine them with the tomatoes, garlic, and sage. Not out to reinvent the wheel, we did not change the flavorings outside of how they were added to the beans. Traditionally, the flavorings are stirred directly into the cooked beans and briefly simmered, but we found that garlic and sage had a better flavor if they were first sautéed in olive oil. When the garlic was lightly toasted, it had a mellower flavor that emphasized the sweetness of the beans. Cooking the sage with the garlic tempered the brash herb to a pleasant background note.

Diced canned tomatoes were preferred over pureed, which made the beans too soupy. Once the juices of the tomatoes evaporated, we added the beans and some of their cooking liquid and simmered until the flavors melded and the bean cooking liquid evaporated.

~~~

White Beans with Tomatoes, Garlic, and Sage

SERVES 6 AS A MAIN DISH OR 8 TO 10
AS A SIDE DISH

Traditionally, the beans receive a liberal dousing of the finest extra-virgin olive oil prior to serving, but use your discretion; some tasters felt the beans were overwhelmed by the pungency of the oil. The amount of oil also depends on its flavor. Although this recipe yields a large quantity, the beans keep for several days and reheat well. We strongly recommend cooking dried beans for the best flavor, but we do offer a canned bean version.

1   pound (about 2½ cups) dried cannellini beans (or Great Northern or navy beans), rinsed and picked over (see the illustration on page 232)

1   medium onion, unpeeled and halved through the root end
1   medium carrot, cut into 2-inch lengths
1   garlic head, top quarter cut off and loose papery skins removed
    Salt
2   bay leaves
6   cups water
¼   cup extra-virgin olive oil, plus more for drizzling
4   medium garlic cloves, sliced thin
¼   cup roughly chopped fresh sage leaves
1   (28-ounce) can diced tomatoes, drained
2   tablespoons minced fresh parsley leaves
    Ground black pepper

1. Bring the beans, onion, carrot, garlic head, 1 teaspoon salt, the bay leaves, and water to a boil in a large saucepan or Dutch oven over medium-high heat. Reduce the heat to low, partially cover, and simmer, stirring occasionally, until the beans are almost tender, 1 to 1¼ hours, adding more liquid if necessary. Remove the pot from the heat, completely cover, and let stand until the beans are fully tender, 30 to 60 minutes. Drain the beans, reserving 1 cup of the cooking liquid. Remove and discard the onion, carrot, and bay leaves. With a slotted spoon, transfer the head of garlic to a cutting board. Using tongs, squeeze the cloves out of the skins and return the softened cloves to the pot with the beans; discard the skins.

2. Heat the olive oil, sliced garlic, and sage in a 12-inch skillet over medium heat. As the oil begins to sizzle, shake the pan back and forth so that the garlic does not stick (stirring with a wooden spoon will cause the garlic to clump). Cook until the garlic turns very pale gold and the sage darkens, about 4 minutes. Add the tomatoes and ½ teaspoon salt and simmer, stirring occasionally, until the tomato juices have evaporated and the tomatoes look shiny, about 10 minutes.

3. Stir in the beans and reserved cooking liquid. Simmer, stirring occasionally, until the liquid has evaporated, 18 to 20 minutes. Off the heat, stir in the parsley and season with salt and pepper to taste. Serve immediately, accompanied by extra-virgin olive oil for drizzling at the table.

➤ VARIATION

Quick White Beans with Tomatoes, Garlic, and Sage

With canned beans, this variation can be made from start to finish in about half an hour.

Follow the recipe for White Beans with Tomatoes, Garlic, and Sage, omitting step 1. In step 3, add 4 (15-ounce) cans cannellini beans, drained and rinsed, along with 1 cup low-sodium chicken broth. Proceed as directed.

BLACK BEANS

BLACK BEANS AS MADE IN LATIN AMERICA ARE more than a side dish. They are flavorful enough to serve as a main course with rice. We wanted to figure out how to build enough flavor to make beans a satisfying main course. While we focused on flavor, we also paid close attention to texture. The perfect bean was tender without being mushy, with enough tooth to make a satisfying chew.

In pursuit of this perfect texture, we discovered that it was important to cook the beans in enough water; too little water and the beans on top cooked more slowly than the beans underneath, and the whole pot took forever to cook. (Twelve cups is a sufficient amount of water to cook one pound of beans.) We did some further testing by comparing beans that had been soaked overnight with a batch of unsoaked,

SORTING DRIED BEANS WITH EASE

It is important to rinse and pick over dried beans to remove any stones or debris before cooking. To make this task easier, sort dried beans on a white plate or cutting board. The neutral background makes any unwanted matter easy to spot and discard.

as well as with a batch softened by a "quick-soak" method in which the beans were brought to a boil, simmered 2 minutes, and then covered to let stand 1 hour off the heat. The quick-soak method caused a large percentage of the beans to burst during cooking. This reduced the chew we were after, so we nixed that method. Contrary to our expectations, overnight soaking decreased the cooking time by only about half an hour and didn't improve the texture. Because we are rarely organized enough to soak the night before, we no longer soak.

Now that we had discovered how to cook beans with the texture we wanted, it was time to discover the best way to build more layers of flavor onto this base without drowning the earthy flavor of the beans.

We determined that meat gave the beans a necessary depth of flavor. We tested cooking beans with a ham hock, bacon, ham, and pork loin. We liked all four, and each gave the beans a slightly different flavor. The ham hock provided a smooth background taste, while bacon and ham produced a more assertive flavor. Pork loin was the most subtle.

In many Caribbean recipes, a sofrito is added to the cooked beans for flavor. Chopped vegetables—usually onion, garlic, and green bell pepper—are sautéed in olive oil until soft and then stirred into the beans. This mixture adds another layer of fresh flavor to beans without overwhelming them.

Some recipes suggest pureeing the sofrito with some of the beans, while others call for mashing some beans with the sofrito. We found that pureeing intensified the flavor of the vegetables enough to almost overwhelm the beans. Simply mashing some beans and the sofrito by hand gets the job done.

We experimented with cumin, the traditional spice for black beans, simmered with the beans or mixed into the sofrito. The flavor of the spice got lost when simmered with the beans; we decided to save the cumin for the sofrito.

Black Beans
SERVES 6

Serve with White Rice (page 209) and garnish with a spoonful of sour cream, minced red onion, and a dash or two of hot pepper sauce.

BEANS

12	cups water
I	pound (about 2½ cups) dried black beans, picked over and rinsed (see the illustration on page 232)
I	smoked ham hock (about ⅔ pound), rinsed
I	green bell pepper, cored, seeded, and quartered
I	medium onion, minced
6	medium garlic cloves, minced or pressed through a garlic press
2	bay leaves
I½	teaspoons salt

SOFRITO

2	tablespoons extra-virgin olive oil
I	medium onion, minced
I	small green bell pepper, cored, seeded, and minced
8	medium garlic cloves, minced or pressed through a garlic press
2	teaspoons dried oregano
¾	teaspoon salt
I½	teaspoons ground cumin
I	tablespoon juice from I medium lime
½	cup chopped fresh cilantro leaves
	Salt and ground black pepper

1. FOR THE BEANS: Bring all the bean ingredients to a boil over medium-high heat in a large, heavy-bottomed saucepan or Dutch oven, skimming the surface as the scum rises. Reduce the heat to low and simmer, partially covered, adding more water if the cooking liquid reduces to the level of the beans, until the beans are tender but not splitting (taste several, as they cook unevenly), about 2 hours. Remove the ham hock. When cool enough to handle, remove the ham from the bone, discard the bone and skin, and cut the meat into bite-size pieces; set aside. Remove and discard the bay leaves.

2. FOR THE SOFRITO: Meanwhile, heat the oil in a large skillet over medium heat; add the onion, bell pepper, garlic, oregano, and salt; sauté until the vegetables soften, 8 to 10 minutes. Add the cumin; sauté until fragrant, about 1 minute longer.

3. TO FINISH THE DISH: Scoop 1 cup of the beans and 2 cups cooking liquid into the pan with the sofrito; mash the beans with a potato masher or fork until smooth. Simmer over medium heat until the liquid is reduced and thickened, about 6 minutes. Return the sofrito mixture with the meat from the ham hock to the bean pot; simmer until the beans are creamy and the liquid thickens to a sauce consistency, 15 to 20 minutes. Add the lime juice; simmer 1 minute longer. Stir in the cilantro, adjust the seasonings with pepper and salt, if necessary, and serve hot over white rice. (The beans can be refrigerated in an airtight container for several days. To reheat, thin with water, if necessary, and warm over medium-low heat.)

➤ VARIATIONS

Black Beans with Dry Sherry
Follow the recipe for Black Beans, adding 1 teaspoon ground coriander to the sofrito along with the cumin, substituting dry sherry for the lime juice, and omitting the cilantro.

Black Beans with Bacon, Balsamic Vinegar, and Sweet Pepper
Fry 8 ounces (about 8 slices) bacon, cut into ½-inch strips, in a medium skillet over medium heat until crisp and browned, about 5 minutes. Transfer with a slotted spoon to a paper towel–lined plate. Follow the recipe for Black Beans, omitting the ham hock and substituting bacon fat for the olive oil and 1 medium red bell pepper for the green bell pepper in the sofrito. Add the cooked bacon to the beans with the sofrito and substitute 2 teaspoons balsamic vinegar for the lime juice.

REFRIED BEANS

AUTHENTIC REFRIED BEANS ARE LEFTOVER stewed beans cooked in copious quantities of lard until they soften to a smooth paste; they are served garnished with toppings like sharp, crumbly cheese, scallions, bacon, and jalapeño chiles. The texture is sinfully lush and the flavor unbeatably rich and satisfying. Delicious, yes—but healthy? We wanted to revise traditional refried beans to make them both healthier and faster—quick enough to cook a skilletful with time left in the hour to chop garnishes, assemble burritos, or fry eggs to serve with the beans for a platter of huevos rancheros.

The beans were the first hurdle to overcome. Canned beans are undeniably convenient, but in flavor and texture they are generally pale compared to dried beans cooked slowly with aromatics. In this case, the canned beans were to be smashed smooth, so texture wasn't an issue. But flavor was paramount, as most refried bean recipes have few ingredients outside of the beans, lard, a little onion, and salt. In preliminary testing, we tried a few traditional recipes with canned beans filling in for dried, and the flavors were boring. Clearly, we needed to boost the dish with additional flavors. First, however, we needed to identify a cooking method that would break down the beans quickly (the traditional recipes took up to an hour) and a fat to replace the lard.

The standard procedure we came across most often involved simply mashing the beans in the pan as they cooked, with a wooden spoon or potato masher. The method was labor-intensive and yielded mediocre results; the chunky mash was punctuated with bits of tough, leathery bean skins. Canned beans apparently have tougher skins than dried beans. It was apparent we needed more force than that generated by a potato masher and an arm—like a food processor or blender. The food processor did a miraculous job. The skins virtually disappeared, and the resulting puree was completely smooth.

With our beans pureed, it was time to fry them. Lard is a tough act to follow; we tried corn, canola, vegetable, and olive oil, and the latter won for its full flavor and rich mouthfeel—mild compared to lard but infinitely healthier. We tried every quantity from a scant tablespoon (unnoticeable) to ½ cup (overkill) for three cans of beans and settled on 5 tablespoons, which is generous but not hedonistic.

The last task was to choose seasonings that would deepen the flavor of the otherwise plain-tasting beans. Onions, which are traditional, added depth and body as well as sweetness. Jalapeño chiles brought a hint of heat and a vegetal edge that tasters liked. Garlic and cumin rounded out the seasonings. We cooked the flavorings in the olive oil and added the bean puree; within 10 minutes, the beans were rich-tasting and smooth.

Refried Beans

SERVES 4 TO 6

If you have a spice grinder, you can enjoy freshly ground whole cumin seeds. The flavor is markedly better than that of store-bought ground cumin. Simply toast the seeds in a skillet for a couple of minutes or until fragrant, then grind them until finely processed. If you like your beans on the spicy side, don't bother to seed the chile. Refried beans can be served with a variety of garnishes, including tortilla chips, salsa, pickled jalapeño chiles (sold in cans in most supermarkets), sliced scallions, shredded Monterey Jack or cheddar cheese, and sour cream.

3   (15-ounce) cans red kidney beans, drained and rinsed

1   cup water

5   tablespoons olive oil

1   medium onion, chopped fine

1   large jalapeño chile, stemmed, seeded, and minced
     Salt

2   medium garlic cloves, minced or pressed through a garlic press

1   teaspoon ground cumin (see note for using ground cumin seeds)

½   cup coarsely chopped fresh cilantro leaves (optional)
     Hot pepper sauce

1. Process the beans and water in a food processor until smooth, scraping down the sides of the workbowl with a rubber spatula as necessary, about 30 seconds; set aside.

2. Put the oil, onion, chile, and ½ teaspoon salt in a large nonstick skillet over medium-high heat. Cook, stirring occasionally, until the onion softens and just begins to brown, about 5 minutes. Add the garlic and cumin and cook, stirring frequently, until aromatic, about 30 seconds. Stir in the bean mixture until thoroughly combined, then reduce the heat to medium. Cook, stirring occasionally, until the beans have thickened and the flavors have blended, about 10 minutes. Stir in the cilantro, if using, and adjust the seasonings with salt and hot pepper sauce to taste. Serve immediately.

6

PASTA AND NOODLES

FEW FOODS RIVAL PASTA IN TERMS OF EITHER speed or convenience. Pasta is almost always on hand, it cooks in minutes, and it can serve as the basis for literally hundreds of one-dish meals. That said, many cooks (even experienced ones) have questions about preparing pasta. How much water do you need to cook a pound of pasta? Is salt necessary in the cooking water? How about oil? How thoroughly do you drain the pasta? What happens if you rinse the pasta after draining?

Many cooks tend to skimp on water, for the obvious reason that the less you use, the faster it comes to a boil. To test this variable, we cooked 1 pound of pasta in 2 quarts of water and discovered two major problems straight off. First, the water tends to foam and boil over the pan edges. Second, the pieces of pasta are more inclined to stick together than when more water is used.

When we talked to Dr. Patricia Berglund, director of the Northern Crops Institute in Fargo, North Dakota, she explained that pasta consists primarily of starch but also contains about 10 percent protein. For dried pasta to make the change from its brittle state to a tender, toothsome noodle, the starch granules must absorb enough hot water to make them burst, thereby giving pasta its tenderness, while the small amount of protein sets up

to provide the noodle with its characteristic bite. We noticed that between absorption and evaporation, 1 quart or more of water can be lost in the process of cooking a pound of pasta. During cooking, a lot of starch also leaches into the cooking water. Without enough water to dilute the leached starch, Berglund said, the pieces of pasta are likely to stick together and the water to foam, which is precisely what we observed. Thus, we recommend you not skimp on the water—use at least 4 quarts per 1 pound of pasta.

While ample water proved key to preventing pasta from sticking, we also found (no great surprise) that frequent stirring makes a difference. It is particularly important to stir the moment the pasta goes into the water. Otherwise, pasta can get remarkably comfortable stuck to the pan bottom or nestled up against its kind. In most cases, any kind of spoon or even a pair of tongs will do for stirring. For long noodles, like spaghetti, we found the tines of a pasta fork most effective in separating the strands. We prefer plastic or stainless steel pasta forks; wood forks can split with use.

Of course, what many people do to prevent sticking is add oil to the boiling water. We tried this repeatedly and determined that oil definitely did not minimize pasta's sticking potential while

MATCHING PASTA SAUCES AND SHAPES

SHORT PASTAS

Short tubular or molded pasta shapes do an excellent job of trapping chunky sauces. Sauces with very large chunks are best with rigatoni or other large tubes. Sauces with small chunks make more sense with fusilli or penne. Clockwise from top right, the shapes shown are penne, shells, farfalle, orecchiette, rigatoni, and fusilli.

STRAND PASTAS

Long strands are best with smooth sauces or sauces with very small chunks. In general, wider noodles, such as pappardelle and fettuccine, can support slightly chunkier sauces (such as pasta primavera) than can very thin noodles. Clockwise from top right, the shapes shown are fettuccine, linguine, spaghetti, capellini, and pappardelle.

cooking. What best keeps noodles from sticking is not oil but cooking in a large quantity of water—and the method of saucing. Americans tend to fill a bowl with pasta and glop the sauce on top. Italians toss the just-cooked pasta and the sauce together. The Italian method evenly distributes the sauce and, in effect, prevents sticking.

As with oil, opinions vary widely about whether or not salt should be added to the cooking water. Other than contributing to flavor, salt had no discernible effect on the pasta or the cooking process itself; in fact, the small amounts of salt we added to the water never increased the boiling point (a plus suggested by several sources). As for flavor, every participating taster found the addition of 2 tablespoons salt over-the-top once the pasta was tossed with an already seasoned sauce. While a couple of tasters preferred 1½ teaspoons salt in the water, the overall opinion was that 1 tablespoon salt to 4 quarts water worked best to round out the pasta flavor.

Most important to the cooking process is determining when the pasta is done, or al dente. We cooked up a number of pasta types made by a variety of manufacturers and found that, overall, the cooking time given in the box instructions is too long. We also found that the old, curious trick of tossing a noodle against the wall (which applies to spaghetti or fettuccine noodles only) isn't accurate. The surefire test is simply biting into the pasta about three minutes before the package directions indicate doneness. Undercooked pasta has a clearly visible white core and is crunchy in the center. When pasta is cooked al dente, which translates as "to the tooth," it should have some bite but still be tender throughout. The white core may be just faintly visible.

While there is no exact science to determining doneness and each person has a different doneness preference, taste-testing the pasta once or twice every minute during the last few minutes of cooking helps the cook gain a better sense of when pasta is just right. The pasta will continue to soften a bit as you drain and sauce it, so pull it off the flame about 30 seconds before you think it will be perfectly cooked.

The only time you might want to rinse drained pasta is if you plan to make pasta salad. (Also, some Asian noodles are best rinsed to remove excess starch.) Rinsing flushes starch from the surface of the noodles, which causes two problems. First, starch helps the sauce adhere to the pasta; without it, the sauce can drain off and pool at the bottom of the bowl. Second, rinsing cools the noodles, which are best served hot.

Finally, some pasta aficionados warn against shaking the strainer after draining the pasta. As with the recommendation against rinsing, there is some cause for this. Shaking drains off some of the starchy moisture that helps the sauce cling to the pasta. But don't worry if by impulse you shake the strainer; it is no grave offense. We found that you lose only about two tablespoons liquid. (Many of our recipes suggest reserving some pasta cooking water to moisten the pasta as it is tossed with the sauce.)

It is important to match the sauce with the right pasta shape. A chunky sauce is better with shells or rigatoni than spaghetti because the short shapes can trap and hold pieces of the sauce, while large chunks of vegetables, for instance, just sit on top of long, thin noodles. The idea is to eat sauce and pasta in the same mouthful. The illustrations on page 236 give additional specific examples.

Once the pasta is sauced, it must be served

RESERVING PASTA WATER TO THIN A SAUCE

In that last flurry of activity before saucing the pasta, it's easy to forget to save a bit of the pasta cooking water. Here's an easy way to make sure you always have some pasta cooking water when you need it. Before cooking the pasta, set up the colander in the sink and place a measuring cup inside the colander. The cup will nudge your memory to scoop out some cooking water before draining the pasta.

immediately. You may want to warm the serving bowls, either with the hot cooking water or by placing them in a very low oven.

The first two thirds of this chapter deals with Italian-style pasta, and the recipes call for dried semolina pasta as well as fresh pasta. (For our tasting of major brands of each type, see pages 244 and 276.) The chapter concludes with several Asian noodle recipes. These noodles require slightly different cooking methods. Information about each type is given with the appropriate recipe.

PASTA WITH GARLIC AND OIL

PASTA WITH GARLIC AND OIL, OR *AGLIO E OLIO* in Italian, is among the most satisfying (and simple) dishes on earth. At first, we wondered why anyone would need a recipe for this dish. You take spaghetti or capellini, perfume it straight from its bath with high-quality olive oil and as much fresh garlic as decency allows, add a dusting of hot red pepper flakes, a small fistful of parsley, and there it is, pasta aglio e olio. And yet, who hasn't ordered it in a restaurant to find its fresh scent tormented by burnt garlic or its noodles gripped in a starchy skein dripping with oil? Clearly, there was much to learn.

We found general agreement on ingredients among recipes: all those mentioned above, along with a splash of the hot pasta cooking water to keep the components in motion. Beyond the basics were regional variations that included a selection of fresh herbs, savory accents such as capers and anchovies, and bread crumbs. We first pursued the perfect garlic flavor, working down the list of possibilities from whole crushed cloves to grated raw garlic and using a pound of pasta for each test. We didn't care for sautéed whole or slivered garlic, whether ultimately removed from the dish or left in. In fact, no one cared for browned garlic at all—it was acrid and one-dimensional. Raw minced or grated garlic alone was zingy and metallic. We needed a third way.

We knew of a technique associated with Mexican cookery in which a large amount of minced garlic is sautéed slowly until it turns golden and mellow, thus producing a garlic flavor far more complex than does a simple sauté. We tried this with a full head of garlic (about ¼ cup minced) and were delighted to discover that the garlic, given low heat and constant stirring, became sticky and straw-colored, with a flavor that was butter-nutty and rich, adding a pronounced depth to the dish. But alone, this slow-sautéed garlic lacked brightness. We decided to combine the forces of cooked and raw by reserving a tablespoon of raw garlic, then stirring it into the fully cooked, candied garlic off the heat to release its perfume and spicy sharpness. The effect of this one-two garlic punch was outstanding, causing waves of flavor to resonate within the dish.

While conducting garlic experiments, it became obvious that other ingredient ratios—for example, the amount of oil—had to be established contiguously. Too much oil removed the silky mouthfeel we wanted for the pasta, but too little left the garlic mute. The amount of oil necessary varied with the diameter of the pasta as well—thicker strands, such as spaghetti, required more oil, even when the total weight of each batch of pasta was the same. In fact, the diameter of the pasta strands altered the behavior of the recipe to such a degree that we decided to work with just one type of pasta—spaghetti, which, unlike some thinner pastas, is available in every grocery store.

Olive oil contributes much of the freshness and

COMBATING ODORIFEROUS INGREDIENTS

After working with pungent ingredients such as garlic, onions, or fish, many cooks use a little lemon juice to wash away any lingering odors from their hands. But sometimes the smell is stronger than the citrus. When that's the case, try washing your hands with a couple of tablespoons of mouthwash.

verve to this dish; extra-virgin is a must. We settled on 6 tablespoons: 3 to sauté the garlic, 3 tossed into the pasta at the end for flavor.

Parmesan cheese is not conventional in this dish, but we liked the nutty depth of flavor it added. Resist, by all means, an urge to pour the contents of a little green cylinder on this dish—it will be forever ruined. A very modest sprinkle of coarsely grated Parmigiano-Reggiano, on the other hand, improves it. (Be sure to do your grating on the larger holes of a box grater; this will discourage the cheese from getting into a sticking contest with the pasta.)

We liked parsley for its freshness but didn't want it slipping around on the noodles like mower clippings; 3 tablespoons did the trick. Gentle seasoning improvements were effected with a touch of lemon juice and sea salt flakes—the bright citrus notes and wee crunch made a big difference.

Finally, sequence and timing matter greatly with this dish. Perhaps to a larger degree than other pastas, pasta aglio e olio suffers from being dumped into cold serving bowls or waiting around for diners to make their way to the table. The most familiar pasta tool, a set of tongs, cannot be recommended for tossing; bits of garlic get stuck in its craw, right where you don't want them. We recommend that you toss the hot strands with a heatproof spatula and use tongs only to transfer the pasta to bowls.

Pasta with Garlic and Oil

SERVES 4 TO 6

For a twist on pasta with garlic and oil, try sprinkling toasted fresh bread crumbs over individual bowls, but prepare the crumbs before proceeding with the pasta recipe. We like the crunch of Maldon sea salt flakes (found in gourmet shops and well-stocked supermarkets) for this dish, but ordinary table salt is fine as well. Given the large amount of garlic in this recipe, you may want to mince it in a small food processor. A garlic press and a chef's knife are other options.

6 tablespoons extra-virgin olive oil
12 medium garlic cloves, minced or pressed
    through a garlic press (about ¼ cup)

   Salt (see note)
1 pound spaghetti
¾ teaspoon red pepper flakes
3 tablespoons chopped fresh parsley
   leaves
2 teaspoons juice from 1 lemon
1 ounce Parmesan cheese, freshly grated
   (½ cup), optional

1. Adjust an oven rack to the lower-middle position, set a large heatproof serving bowl on the rack, and heat the oven to 200 degrees. Bring 4 quarts water to a rolling boil in a large pot.

2. While the water is heating, combine 3 tablespoons of the oil, 3 tablespoons of the garlic, and ½ teaspoon salt in a heavy-bottomed nonstick 10-inch skillet. Cook over low heat, stirring constantly, until the garlic foams and is sticky and straw-colored, 10 to 12 minutes. Meanwhile, add 1 tablespoon salt and the pasta to the boiling water, stir to separate the noodles, and cook until al dente; reserve ⅓ cup pasta cooking water and drain the pasta.

3. Off the heat, add the remaining 1 tablespoon raw garlic to the skillet along with the red pepper flakes, parsley, lemon juice, and 2 tablespoons of the reserved pasta cooking water and stir well to keep the garlic from clumping.

4. Transfer the drained pasta to the warm serving bowl; add the remaining 3 tablespoons olive oil and the remaining pasta cooking water and toss to coat. Add the garlic mixture and ¾ teaspoon salt; toss well to combine. Serve immediately, sprinkling individual bowls with a portion of the Parmesan, if desired.

PASTA WITH PESTO

IN OUR EXPERIENCE WITH PESTO, THE BRIGHT herbal fragrance of basil always hinted at more flavor than it really delivered. Also, although we love garlic, the raw article can have a sharp, acrid taste that overwhelms everything else in the sauce. So our goals were clear when developing a recipe for this simple sauce—heighten the flavor of the basil and subdue the garlic.

Traditionally, pesto is made in a mortar and pestle, which yields an especially silky texture and intense basil flavor. The slow pounding of the basil leaves (it takes 15 minutes to make pesto this way) releases their full flavor.

By comparison, blender and food-processor pestos can seem dull or bland, but if required to choose between the two, we prefer a food processor for several reasons. In a blender, ingredients tend to bunch up near the blade and do not become evenly chopped. Also, to keep solids moving in a blender, it is necessary to add more oil than is really needed to make pesto.

Because most Americans don't own a mortar and pestle (and those who do are unlikely to invest 15 minutes of pounding when the sauce can otherwise be made in seconds), we decided to focus on improving flavor in food-processor pesto. We tested chopping, tearing, and bruising basil leaves to release more of their flavor. In the end, we settled on packing basil leaves in a plastic bag and bruising them with a meat pounder or rolling pin (see the illustration below).

We tried several approaches to taming the garlic—roasting, sautéing, and infusing oil with garlic flavor—but found them all lacking. What we did like was toasting whole cloves in a warm skillet. This tamed the harsh garlic notes and loosened the skins from the cloves for easy peeling.

To bring out the full flavor of the nuts, we toasted them in a dry skillet before processing.

BRUISING HERB LEAVES

Bruising herb leaves, especially basil, in a zipper-lock plastic bag with a meat pounder (or rolling pin) is a quick but effective substitute for hand pounding with a mortar and pestle, and it helps release the herbs' flavor.

(We then toasted the garlic in the empty pan.) Almonds are sweet but fairly hard, so they give pesto a coarse, granular texture. Walnuts are softer but still fairly meaty in texture and flavor. Pine nuts yield the smoothest, creamiest pesto. The choice is yours.

Pasta with Classic Pesto
SERVES 4

Don't limit yourself to just making pesto for pasta—use it to add a boost of flavor to soups, sandwiches, and pizza. Note that the pesto recipe alone yields ¾ cup.

Choose a long, thin pasta or a shape, like fusilli (corkscrews), that can trap bits of the pesto. Basil often darkens in pesto, but you can brighten the color by adding parsley. For sharper flavor, substitute 1 tablespoon finely grated Pecorino cheese for 1 tablespoon of the Parmesan.

CLASSIC PESTO

¼	cup pine nuts, walnuts, or almonds
3	medium garlic cloves, unpeeled
2	cups packed fresh basil leaves
2	tablespoons fresh parsley leaves (optional)
7	tablespoons extra-virgin olive oil
	Salt
¼	cup freshly grated Parmesan cheese
1	tablespoon salt
1	pound pasta (see note)

1. FOR THE PESTO: Toast the nuts in a small, heavy skillet over medium heat, stirring frequently, until just golden and fragrant, 4 to 5 minutes. Transfer the nuts to a plate.

2. Add the garlic to the empty skillet. Toast, shaking the pan occasionally, until fragrant and the color of the cloves deepens slightly, about 7 minutes. Let the garlic cool, then peel and chop.

3. Combine the basil and parsley (if using) in a heavy-duty gallon-size zipper-lock plastic bag. Pound the bag with the flat side of a meat pounder or rolling pin until all the leaves are bruised (see the illustration at left).

4. Place the nuts, garlic, pounded herb(s), oil, and ½ teaspoon salt in a food processor. Process until smooth, stopping as necessary to scrape down

Suzanne

Thank you
for letting me
borrow this book.
It so interesting.
Now — Will I ever make
one of the delicious
recipes?

Dona

the sides of the workbowl. Transfer the mixture to a small bowl, stir in the Parmesan, and adjust the salt to taste. (The surface of the pesto can be covered with a sheet of plastic wrap or a thin film of oil and refrigerated for up to 3 days.)

5. Bring 4 quarts water to a rolling boil in a large pot. Add the tablespoon salt and pasta to the boiling water and stir to separate the noodles. Cook until al dente. Reserve ½ cup pasta cooking water, drain the pasta, and return it to the pot.

6. Stir ¼ cup of the reserved pasta cooking water into the pesto. Toss the hot pasta with the thinned pesto, adding the remaining pasta cooking water as needed. Serve immediately or let cool to room temperature.

➤ VARIATIONS

Pasta with Mint Pesto

Follow the recipe for Pasta with Classic Pesto, replacing the basil with an equal amount of mint leaves and omitting the parsley.

Pasta with Creamy Basil Pesto

The addition of ricotta cheese makes pesto mild and creamy. The pesto is fairly thick and clings nicely to the curves on the fusilli.

Follow the recipe for Pasta with Classic Pesto, adding ¼ cup ricotta cheese at the same time as the Parmesan. Toss well to combine.

Pasta with Creamy Arugula Pesto

Follow the recipe for Pasta with Classic Pesto, replacing the basil with 1 cup packed fresh arugula leaves and increasing the parsley to 1 cup packed. Reduce the Parmesan cheese to 2 tablespoons and add ⅓ cup ricotta cheese when adding the Parmesan.

FRESH TOMATO SAUCE

WHEN TOMATOES ARE GOOD, NOTHING QUITE compares with their taste, a study in subtly contrasting sweet and tart flavors. The best fresh tomato sauces for pasta capture this complexity. Another consideration when making fresh tomato sauce is texture; the best of them are hearty and dense. Too many fresh tomato sauces are watery or mealy and have little fresh tomato flavor. If you are going to bother with fresh tomatoes, the sauce should be at least as good (if not better) than one you could make by opening a can.

We began by culling about 60 recipes for tomato sauce and analyzing the variables. Most sources followed a simple pattern: Heat the oil (and, usually, garlic), add the tomatoes, simmer until the tomatoes have broken down into a thick sauce, add the seasonings, and toss with the pasta.

In some cases, the tomatoes were simply chopped before being added to the oil, but most sources recommended peeling and seeding them before chopping. A few recipes called for seeding the tomatoes but leaving the skins on.

Working with a basic recipe that contained just olive oil, diced fresh tomatoes, and salt, we prepared three batches of sauce—one with tomatoes that we peeled and seeded before dicing, one with tomatoes that we only seeded and diced, and one with tomatoes we neither seeded nor peeled. The results were surprisingly different. The sauce made with peeled and seeded tomatoes was by far the best. It had the best consistency—dense and hearty—as well as the brightest, freshest flavor. Both sauces made with unpeeled tomatoes contained hard, unappetizing bits of curled-up skin (the skin had separated from the individual tomato cubes as the tomatoes cooked). In addition, these sauces were less fresh-tasting.

We also found that the sauce made with peeled and seeded tomatoes cooked more quickly than the other two sauces. It took just 10 minutes in a sauté pan for peeled and seeded tomatoes to fall apart to the proper consistency. When we left the skins on the tomato cubes, they took 18 minutes to collapse; clearly, the skins helped the tomatoes hold their shape. Tasters did not object to the seeds themselves, but they made the chopped tomatoes more watery and thus increased the cooking time. We had uncovered a key element to great fresh tomato sauce: short cooking time. Peeling and seeding speeds cooking and is necessary for this reason, not to mention the fact that the skins mar the texture of the finished sauce.

We were pretty sure about our findings but felt

that our hypothesis—that long cooking destroys fresh tomato flavor—needed more testing. After all, many Italian grandmothers (as well as countless Italian cookbook authors) insist on simmering tomato sauce for at least an hour, if not longer. We prepared three more sauces with peeled, seeded, and diced tomatoes. We cooked one for 10 minutes (the minimum time necessary for the tomatoes to break down into a sauce), one for 30 minutes, and one for an hour. The sauce that cooked for 10 minutes had the best flavor. The others reminded tasters of tomato puree; they were dense and smooth but left us wondering where the tomato flavor had gone.

In the process of doing this testing, we found that it worked best to use a wide pan (a 10-inch pan is right for a single batch of sauce) to promote quick evaporation. When we tried cooking two pounds of prepared tomatoes in a three-quart saucepan, we had to pile the tomatoes on top of one another because of the smaller surface area. As a result, they took an extra 10 minutes to thicken

and did not taste as fresh. As for the type of pan, we prefer a sauté pan with relatively high (3-inch) sides rather than a skillet with sloped sides. The reason is simple—less splattering. Keep the cover off as the sauce cooks to allow the tomato liquid to evaporate, and cook the sauce over brisk medium heat.

Now we knew how to handle the tomatoes to keep their flavor lively: peel, seed, and chop, then cook them quickly in a sauté pan with oil. Next we had to figure out the other components of the sauce. We tried sautéing various aromatic vegetables in the oil before adding the tomatoes and found that a little garlic (heated with the oil so it would not burn) was the best choice. Onion was good as well (especially when we wanted to play up the sweetness in the sauce), but garlic was our first choice. We found leeks, carrots, and celery too distracting.

Our recipe now contained olive oil (we found that extra-virgin olive oil makes a real difference here), garlic, and tomatoes. Of course, the sauce needed salt, and we thought an herb would round out the flavors. Basil is the natural choice for this

---

EQUIPMENT: Paring Knives

A paring knife is useful for coring tomatoes, slivering garlic, and trimming artichokes. But which paring knife is best? Prices range from a modest $5 plus change to a grand $50, which invites the obvious question for a home cook: Is the most expensive knife really 10 times better than the cheapest model? To find out, we put seven all-purpose paring knives through a series of kitchen tests, including peeling and slicing shallots, peeling and slicing apples and turnips, coring tomatoes, peeling and mincing fresh ginger, and slicing lemons and limes.

The way the knives were made (by forging or stamping) wasn't much of a factor in our ratings of paring knives. By definition, a paring knife is used for light tasks where weight and balance are not terribly important (it doesn't take huge effort to peel an apple). The way the handle felt in testers' hands was much more important. Most testers preferred medium-size, ergonomically designed plastic handles. Slim wooden handles were harder to grasp.

Testers also preferred paring knives with flexible blades, which make it easier to work in tight spots. Peeling turnips or sectioning oranges is much easier with a flexible than a stiff blade. Stiffer blades are slightly better at mincing and slicing, but

these are secondary tasks for paring knives. Among the knives tested, expensive forged knives from Wüsthof and Henckels performed well, as did an inexpensive stamped knife made by Forschner.

THE BEST PARING KNIVES

The Wüsthof-Trident Grand Prix (top) is extremely agile and was the clear favorite of our testers. The Forschner (Victorinox) Fibrox (center) is quite light, and the blade is very flexible. The Henckels Four Star (bottom) has an especially comfortable handle, but the blade is a bit less flexible and somewhat less sharp than the blades on our other top picks. Note that the Forschner knife costs just $6, while you should expect to spend about $20 for the Henckels and about $28 for the Wüsthof.

seasonal sauce, but parsley is appropriate as well.

We saved some of the cooking water from the pasta to help spread the dense tomato sauce over the pasta, and we added a little olive oil to the pasta and sauce for a hit of fresh olive flavor. The result was a sauce that celebrated the flavor of tomatoes, plain and simple.

Pasta and Fresh Tomato Sauce with Garlic and Basil

SERVES 4

Any type of tomato may be used in this recipe—just make sure to choose the ripest, most flavorful ones available. Short tubular or curly pasta shapes such as penne and fusilli are well suited to this chunky sauce. Alternatively, before adding the basil, the sauce may be pureed in a blender or food processor so it will coat strands of spaghetti or linguine. The recipe may be doubled in a 12-inch skillet. The sauce freezes well, but add the basil when reheating. See the illustrations at right for tips on peeling tomatoes and the illustrations on page 248 for tips on seeding them.

3	tablespoons extra-virgin olive oil
2	medium garlic cloves, minced or pressed through a garlic press
2	pounds ripe tomatoes, cored, peeled, seeded, and cut into 1/2-inch pieces
2	tablespoons chopped fresh basil leaves
	Salt
1	pound pasta (see note)

1. Bring 4 quarts water to a rolling boil in a large pot.

2. Meanwhile, heat 2 tablespoons of the oil and the garlic in a medium skillet over medium heat until the garlic is fragrant but not browned, about 2 minutes. Stir in the tomatoes; increase the heat to medium–high and cook until any liquid given off by the tomatoes evaporates and the tomato pieces lose their shape to form a chunky sauce, about 10 minutes. Stir in the basil and salt to taste; cover to keep warm.

3. Add 1 tablespoon salt and the pasta to the boiling water and stir to separate the noodles. Cook until the pasta is al dente. Reserve 1/4 cup

pasta cooking water and drain the pasta. Transfer the drained pasta to the cooking pot. Add the reserved pasta cooking water, tomato sauce, and remaining 1 tablespoon oil; toss well to combine. Serve immediately.

➤ VARIATIONS

Pasta and Fresh Tomato Sauce with Chile Pepper and Basil

Follow the recipe for Pasta and Fresh Tomato Sauce with Garlic and Basil, heating 3/4 teaspoon red pepper flakes with the oil and garlic in step 2.

Pasta and Fresh Tomato Cream Sauce with Onion and Butter

This rich sauce is especially good with fresh fettuccine or cheese ravioli.

Follow the recipe for Pasta and Fresh Tomato Sauce with Garlic and Basil, substituting melted butter for the olive oil and 1 medium onion,

PEELING TOMATOES

1. Place the cored tomatoes a pot of boiling water, no more than five at a time. Boil until the skins split and begin to curl around the cored area of the tomato, about 15 seconds for very ripe tomatoes and up to 30 seconds for firmer tomatoes. Remove the tomatoes from the water with a slotted spoon and place them in a bowl of ice water to stop the cooking process and cool the tomatoes.

2. With a paring knife, peel the skins away using the curled edges at the core as your starting point. (The bowl of ice water fulfills a helpful second function—the skins will slide right off the blade of the knife if you dip the blade into the water.)

minced, for the garlic; sauté the onion until golden, about 5 minutes. Continue with the recipe, adding ½ cup heavy cream to the tomatoes after the chunky sauce has formed; simmer until the cream thickens slightly, 2 to 3 minutes longer. Toss the pasta with the sauce and pasta cooking water, omitting the additional oil.

Pasta and Quick Tomato Sauce

DAY IN, DAY OUT, WE FIND THAT CANNED TOMATOES make the best sauce. (The exception might be at the height of the local tomato season, but even then, good canned tomatoes can compete.) To make our sauce, we wanted to use the fewest ingredients possible, so we selected the key players—tomatoes, oil, garlic, and salt—and eliminated nonessentials, such as carrots, meat, wine, and so forth. This immediately eliminated a whole category of longer-cooked, full-bodied sauces. The sauce we were looking for also had to be easy to make—done in 20 minutes or less from pantry to table. Finally, it had to taste first and foremost of tomatoes, with a hint of acidity and a light, fresh flavor.

With this fairly narrow mission statement formed, a number of fundamental issues came to mind. What sort of canned tomatoes are best: whole, chopped, or crushed, packed in puree or juice? How do you get a hint of garlic without overpowering the sauce? How does cooking time affect flavor? Do you need sugar to boost tomato flavor? What about tomato paste?

To get a better sense of the possibilities, we went into the kitchen and cooked up different sauces from our favorite Italian cooks. To our surprise, there was considerable agreement among the staff as to what worked and what didn't. Butter tended to dull the bright, slightly acidic flavor of the tomatoes. Nobody was enthusiastic about the rather one-dimensional flavor of tomato paste. More than two cloves of garlic and three tablespoons of olive oil for one 28-ounce can of tomatoes were too much.

In general, shorter cooking times of 10 to 15 minutes produced a fresher, brighter tomato flavor. A large sauté pan was preferred to a saucepan because it speeded the cooking.

We also came to some conclusions about overall flavor. The sauces we preferred tasted predominantly of tomatoes, not garlic, basil, or any other ingredient. The better recipes also had a nice balance between sweetness and acidity to give the sauce some depth. Sauces made with a little sugar

---

INGREDIENTS: Dried Pasta

In the not-so-distant past, American pasta had a poor reputation, and rightly so. It cooked up gummy and starchy, and experts usually touted the superiority of Italian brands. We wondered if this was still the case.

To find out, we tasted eight leading brands of spaghetti—four American and four Italian. American brands took two of the three top spots, while two Italian brands landed at the bottom of the rankings. It seems that American companies have mastered the art of making pasta.

American-made Ronzoni was the top finisher, with tasters praising its "nutty, buttery" flavor and superb texture. Mueller's, another American brand, took third place. Tasters liked its "clean," "wheaty" flavor.

DeCecco was the highest-scoring Italian brand, finishing second in the tasting. It cooked up "very al dente" (with a good bite) and was almost chewy. Other Italian brands did not fare quite so well. Martelli, an artisanal pasta that costs nearly $5 a pound, finished in next-to-last place, with comments like "gritty" and "mushy" predominating on tasters' score sheets. Another Italian brand, Delverde, sank to the bottom of the ratings.

Our conclusion: Save your money and don't bother with most imported pastas—American pastas are just fine. If you must serve Italian pasta in your home, stick with DeCecco.

THE BEST DRIED PASTA

Ronzoni won tasters over with its firm texture and nutty, buttery flavor.

(no more than ¼ teaspoon) tasted more complex and had a better balance between sweet and tart.

With these decisions made, we compiled a master recipe using 1 teaspoon of minced garlic, 3 tablespoons of olive oil, 1 can of diced tomatoes, 8 chopped basil leaves, ¼ teaspoon of sugar, and salt to taste. This made enough to sauce 1 pound of pasta.

We also tested whether all of the olive oil should be added at the beginning of cooking or if some should be withheld and added at the end to provide a burst of fresh flavor. As we suspected, it was best to use two tablespoons of olive oil for cooking and a third tablespoon at the end to finish the sauce. Not surprisingly, we preferred a high-quality extra-virgin oil because it delivered a pleasant hint of fresh olives.

Now we were ready to taste the sauce on pasta. Much to our surprise, we found that it did not cling properly to the noodles. Our first fix was to return ¼ cup of the pasta cooking water to the drained pasta once it was back in the pot. This dramatically improved the consistency of the sauce to cling to the pasta and, as an added bonus, also improved the flavor. As a final note, we found that adding the tomato sauce, stirring to coat the pasta, and then heating everything for one minute was the most effective saucing method, giving the sauce better distribution and overall consistency.

Pasta and Quick Tomato Sauce

SERVES 4

If you use whole canned tomatoes, avoid those packed in sauce or puree, which results in a dull, relatively flavorless sauce without the interplay of sweetness and acidity. If you choose diced tomatoes, use the can's entire contents, without discarding any liquid. The pasta and sauce quantities can be doubled, but you will have to simmer the sauce for an extra 5 to 6 minutes to thicken it. If you do not have a garlic press, mince the garlic very fine.

I (28-ounce) can diced or whole tomatoes packed in juice

3 tablespoons extra-virgin olive oil

2 medium garlic cloves, minced or pressed through a garlic press

3 tablespoons coarsely chopped fresh basil

¼ teaspoon sugar

   Salt

I pound pasta (any shape)

1. If using diced tomatoes, go to step 2. If using whole tomatoes, drain and reserve the liquid. Dice the tomatoes either by hand or in a food processor (three or four ½-second pulses). The tomatoes should be coarse, with ¼-inch pieces visible. If necessary, add reserved liquid to the tomatoes to total 2⅔ cups.

2. Heat 2 tablespoons of the oil and the garlic in a 10-inch sauté pan over medium heat until fragrant but not browned, about 2 minutes. Stir in the tomatoes; simmer until thickened slightly, about 10 minutes. Stir in the basil, sugar, and ½ teaspoon salt.

3. Meanwhile, bring 4 quarts water to a rolling boil in a large pot. Add 1 tablespoon salt and the pasta to the boiling water, stir to separate the noodles, and cook until al dente; reserve ¼ cup cooking water and drain the pasta. Return the pasta to the pot. Mix in the reserved pasta cooking water, tomato sauce, and remaining 1 tablespoon oil; cook together over medium heat for 1 minute, stirring constantly, and serve immediately.

➤ VARIATIONS

Pasta and Tomato Sauce with Bacon and Parsley

In a medium skillet, fry 4 ounces (about 4 slices) bacon, cut into ½-inch pieces, over medium-high heat until crisp and browned, about 5 minutes. Transfer with a slotted spoon to a paper towel–lined plate; pour off all but 2 tablespoons of the fat from the pan. Follow the recipe for Pasta and Quick Tomato Sauce, omitting the olive oil and heating the garlic and ½ teaspoon red pepper flakes in the reserved bacon fat until fragrant but not browned, about 2 minutes. Continue with the recipe, substituting 2 tablespoons chopped fresh parsley leaves for the basil and adding the reserved bacon with the parsley.

Pasta and Tomato Sauce with Vodka and Cream

Follow the recipe for Pasta and Quick Tomato Sauce, adding ¼ teaspoon red pepper flakes with the garlic. Halfway through the 10-minute simmering time, add ½ cup vodka. Continue with the recipe, adding 1 cup heavy cream and ground black pepper to taste along with the remaining seasonings. Transfer the sauce to a food processor and pulse to a coarse puree. Return the sauce to the pan; simmer over medium heat to thicken, 2 to 3 minutes.

INGREDIENTS: Canned Tomatoes

Canned whole tomatoes are the closest product to fresh. Whole tomatoes, either plum or round, are steamed to remove their skins and then packed in tomato juice or puree. We prefer tomatoes packed in juice; they generally have a fresher, livelier flavor than tomatoes packed in puree, which has a cooked tomato flavor that imparts a slightly stale, tired taste to the whole can.

Diced tomatoes are simply whole tomatoes that have been roughly chopped during processing and then packed with juice. For pasta sauces, we prefer diced tomatoes because they save time and effort. Why chop canned tomatoes (a messy proposition at best) if you don't have to?

To find the best canned whole tomatoes, we tasted eight brands, both straight from the can and in a simple tomato sauce. Muir Glen (an organic brand available in most supermarkets and natural food stores) finished at the head of the pack, along with S&W, a West Coast brand, and Redpack (called Redgold on the West Coast).

BEST CANNED TOMATOES

The winners of our diced canned tomato tasting are packed in juice, not puree, and are recipe-ready.

MUIR GLEN
Organic Diced
Tomatoes

S&W
Ready-Cut
Premium, Peeled
Tomatoes

REDPACK
Ready-Cut Diced
Tomatoes (Redgold
on the West Coast)

PASTA WITH NO-COOK TOMATO SAUCES

ONE OF THE CORNERSTONES OF ITALIAN cooking is the ability to take a few fresh, flavorful ingredients, prepare them with minimal effort, and create simple but exceptional dishes. Raw tomato sauces typify this kind of Italian cooking. These sauces can be made in the time it takes to boil water and cook pasta. A word of wisdom, however: Making these sauces in mid-January with supermarket tomatoes will be disappointing. Only the freshest summer-ripe tomatoes are good enough for these sauces.

The most perplexing question we faced when developing recipes for uncooked tomato sauces was how to prepare the tomatoes. After consulting many leading Italian cookbooks, we found that opinions truly varied. Some chefs preferred to use peeled and seeded tomatoes, other called for seeded but unpeeled tomatoes, and several simply used the whole tomato—peel, seeds, and all.

With tomatoes in hand, we set out to try all possible methods. Our first test was to peel and seed the tomatoes before making the sauce. The process of peeling and seeding was time-consuming, and the results were mediocre. Some of the tomatoes we bought at the farmers' market had thin skins, and trying to peel them resulted in maiming them. Also, once peeled and added to the pasta, the tomatoes didn't hold up well, providing the sauce little body.

Our next test was to seed but not peel the tomatoes, and the results were promising. With the skin left on, the tomatoes held their shape and provided the sauce with a rich presence; the tomato flavor stayed in the foreground rather than disappearing into the pasta as it did with the sauces made with peeled tomatoes. Also, scooping out the seeds was much easier than peeling and seeding.

We also tried to make our sauce with tomatoes that were neither peeled nor seeded. The sauce made in this way was clearly not what we wanted. Once the sauce sat for several minutes, it became watery, and when mixed with pasta, the high amount of liquid diluted the flavors of the pasta, making the dish bland. In the end, we opted to make our sauces with unpeeled, seeded tomatoes.

Once we had determined how to prepare our tomatoes, we focused on other flavors for our sauces. In addition to tomatoes, we thought olive oil should be the other main ingredient. Not only does the oil provide moisture, but it also helps coat the pasta and join the pasta and sauce together. Because these sauces are raw, extra-virgin olive oil is a vital ingredient. In addition to olive oil, we found dozens of ingredients (including herbs, cheese, red pepper flakes, olives, and capers) to add to these sauces for variations. As long as the ingredients are fresh and flavorful and don't require cooking, the possibilities are nearly endless.

Fusilli with No-Cook Tomato Sauce and Fresh Mozzarella

SERVES 4

For maximum creaminess, use fresh mozzarella packed in water rather than the shrink-wrapped cheese sold at supermarkets.

	Salt
1	pound fusilli
1½	pounds ripe tomatoes, cored, seeded, and cut into ½-inch dice
¼	cup extra-virgin olive oil
1	medium garlic clove, minced or pressed through a garlic press
3	medium scallions, sliced thin
	Ground black pepper
8	ounces fresh mozzarella cheese, cut into ½-inch cubes

1. Bring 4 quarts water to a rolling boil in a large pot. Add 1 tablespoon salt and the pasta to the boiling water, stir to separate the noodles, and cook until al dente. Drain and return the pasta to the pot.

2. While the pasta is cooking, prepare the sauce. Combine the tomatoes, oil, garlic, scallions, ½ teaspoon salt, and ¼ teaspoon pepper in a medium bowl. Add the tomato mixture and mozzarella to the pasta in the pot and toss to combine. Adjust the seasonings with salt and pepper to taste and serve immediately.

Farfalle with No-Cook Tomato Sauce, Olives, and Feta

SERVES 4

Add the feta after the tomatoes have been tossed with the pasta to prevent the cheese from melting.

	Salt
1	pound farfalle
1½	pounds ripe tomatoes, cored, seeded, and cut into ½-inch dice
¼	cup extra-virgin olive oil
1	tablespoon chopped fresh mint leaves
½	cup Kalamata olives, pitted and chopped coarse
	Ground black pepper
6	ounces feta cheese, crumbled (about 1½ cups)

1. Bring 4 quarts water to a rolling boil in a large pot. Add 1 tablespoon salt and the pasta to the boiling water, stir to separate the noodles, and cook until al dente. Drain and return the pasta to the pot.

2. While the pasta is cooking, combine the tomatoes, oil, mint, olives, ½ teaspoon salt, and ¼ teaspoon pepper in a medium bowl. Add the tomato mixture to the pasta in the pot and toss. Add the feta and toss again. Adjust the seasonings with salt and pepper to taste and serve immediately.

HOW TO PREVENT A WATERY SAUCE

UNSEEDED   **SEEDED**

The tomatoes on the left were not seeded and exuded ¼ cup of liquid, which would make the pasta sauce watery. The tomatoes on the right were seeded and exuded just 1 tablespoon of liquid—not enough to have an adverse effect on the sauce.

Orecchiette with No-Cook Tomato Sauce, Fennel, and Parmesan

SERVES 4

See the illustration below for coring fennel.

Salt
1 pound orecchiette
1½ pounds ripe tomatoes, cored, seeded, and cut into ½-inch dice
1 small fennel bulb, trimmed of stalks and fronds, halved, cored, and sliced thin
¼ cup extra-virgin olive oil
¼ cup chopped fresh basil leaves
Ground black pepper
2 ounces Parmesan cheese, shaved with a vegetable peeler (see the illustration on page 134)

1. Bring 4 quarts water to a rolling boil in a large pot. Add 1 tablespoon salt and the pasta to the boiling water, stir to separate the noodles, and cook until al dente. Drain and return the pasta to the pot.

2. While the pasta is cooking, combine the tomatoes, fennel, oil, basil, ½ teaspoon salt, and ¼ teaspoon pepper in a medium bowl. Add the tomato mixture to the pasta in the pot and toss to combine. Adjust the seasonings with salt and pepper to taste and serve immediately, garnishing individual bowls with some of the shaved Parmesan.

CORING FENNEL

Fennel bulbs contain a hard core that should be removed when using the fennel raw in a pasta sauce. Cut the trimmed bulb in half through the base; then use a paring knife to cut out the pyramid-shaped piece of the core in each half. The fennel can now be sliced thin.

SEEDING TOMATOES

Because of their different shapes, round and plum (also called Roma) tomatoes are seeded differently.

ROUND TOMATOES

Halve the cored tomato along its equator. Gently squeeze each half and shake out the seeds and gelatinous material. Use your finger to scoop out any seeds that remain.

PLUM TOMATOES

Halve the cored tomato lengthwise, cutting through the core end. Scoop out the seeds and gelatinous material with your finger.

PASTA AND PUTTANESCA SAUCE

PUTTANESCA IS A PASTA SAUCE WITH ATTITUDE. Most home cooks buy this lusty sauce by the jar or know it as restaurant fare—a slow-cooked tomato sauce with garlic, red pepper flakes, anchovies, capers, and black olives tossed with spaghetti. But those of us familiar with puttanesca are often disappointed. Chock-full of high-impact ingredients, puttanesca is often overpowered by one flavor; it is too fishy, too garlicky, too briny, or just plain salty and acidic. It can also be unduly heavy and stew-like, or dull and monochromatic. We were searching for a simple, satisfying sauce with aggressive but well-balanced flavors.

We started our testing by tossing all of the ingredients—minced garlic, minced olives, whole capers, minced anchovies, and red pepper flakes—into a base of canned tomatoes and simmering the lot for 25 minutes. The result was a dull sauce with undeveloped flavors. Our first revision began with sautéing the garlic in olive oil to deepen the garlic flavor—but, as we found out, the garlic should not be allowed to brown; when it did, the sauce quickly became bitter. To rectify the problem, we mixed a bit of water with the garlic before it went into the pan. The water slowed the cooking, making the garlic less likely to brown and burn.

Deciding how to prepare and cook the olives was the next task. After several tests, we decided to toss coarsely chopped olives into the sauce at the very last minute, allowing the residual heat of the tomatoes to warm them. This preserved their flavor, their texture, and their independence. As for which olives worked best, we started with Neapolitan Gaeta olives—small, black, earthy, and herbaceous. For good measure, we also tested Alphonso, Kalamata, and canned black olives in place of the Gaetas. Tasters unanimously rejected the canned olives but liked both the Alphonso and Kalamata olives.

Capers were the least of our worries. Of all the ingredients, they were the most resilient, well able to retain their shape, texture, and flavor. Rinsing them thoroughly, whether salt- or brine-cured, and adding them at the end of cooking along with the olives proved best.

Up to this point, the anchovies in the sauce, added along with the tomatoes to simmer, tasted flat and salty and gave the sauce a funky, fishy taste. We tried mashing whole fillets into the oil with a fork and found the process tedious and ineffective; stray chunks were left behind and inevitably ended up offending anchovy-sensitive tasters. What worked best was mincing the anchovies to a fine paste and adding them to the oil in the pan with the garlic. In two or three minutes,

the anchovies melted into the oil on their own (no fork necessary), and their characteristically full, rich flavor blossomed.

Blooming an ingredient in oil is a technique often used to develop flavor. Because it worked so well with the garlic and anchovies, we decided to try it with the red pepper flakes instead of simmering them with the tomatoes, as we had in the original test. As they cooked with the garlic and anchovies, their flavor permeated the oil.

As for the tomatoes, we tested crushed tomatoes, canned whole tomatoes (chopped by hand), canned diced tomatoes, and fresh. The canned diced tomatoes were the winner. They had a sweet flavor and clung nicely to the pasta.

One last discovery improved the sauce still further. In the test kitchen, we are in the habit of reserving a little pasta cooking water to toss with the finished pasta to keep the sauce from drying out. On a whim, we decided to substitute some of the drained tomato juice for the water, which gave the sauce a brighter, livelier flavor.

Spaghetti Puttanesca

SERVES 4

The pasta and sauce cook in just about the same amount of time. If you like the fruitiness of extra-virgin olive oil, toss 1 tablespoon into the sauced pasta before serving.

	Salt
I	pound spaghetti
4	medium garlic cloves, minced or pressed through a garlic press
I	tablespoon water
2	tablespoons olive oil
I	teaspoon red pepper flakes
4	teaspoons minced anchovies (8–10 fillets)
I	(28-ounce) can diced tomatoes, drained, 1/2 cup juice reserved
3	tablespoons capers, rinsed
1/2	cup black olives, such as Gaeta, Alphonso, or Kalamata, pitted and chopped coarse
1/4	cup minced fresh parsley leaves

1. Bring 4 quarts water to a rolling boil in a large pot. Add 1 tablespoon salt and the pasta to

MINCED VERSUS CHOPPED OLIVES

Minced olives (left) produced a muddy sauce and purple spaghetti. Coarsely chopped olives (right) won't dye the pasta and taste better.

the boiling water and stir to separate the noodles.

2. While the pasta is cooking, mix the garlic and water together in a small bowl. Immediately heat the oil, garlic mixture, red pepper flakes, and anchovies in a large skillet over medium heat. Cook, stirring frequently, until the garlic is fragrant but not browned, 2 to 3 minutes. Stir in the tomatoes and simmer until slightly thickened, about 8 minutes.

3. Cook the pasta until al dente. Drain and return it to the pot. Add ¼ cup of the reserved tomato juice and toss to combine.

4. Stir the capers, olives, and parsley into the sauce. Pour the sauce over the pasta and toss to combine, adding more of the remaining tomato juice to moisten if necessary. Adjust the seasonings with salt to taste and serve immediately.

SPAGHETTI ALLA CARBONARA

A PASTA DISH QUINTESSENTIALLY ROMAN IN nature, carbonara taunts us with food taboos. It begins with a sauce made from eggs and cheese that cooks into velveteen consistency only from the heat of the just-drained pasta that it drapes. Shards of Italian bacon punctuate the dish with enough presence to make one give silent thanks to the pig. And just when you think that it can't get any better, the bright punch of hot garlic announces itself.

But too often, this dish is far from the heavenly marriage of sauce and pasta, but rather a lackluster dish of pasta smothered in an unctuous, congealed mass of cheese, eggs, and bacon. We wanted smooth, silky sauce.

In reviewing recipes for carbonara, we noticed they deviated little in the ingredient list, and the technique was similar throughout: Make a raw sauce with eggs and cheese, render the bacon, cook the pasta, add the hot pasta to the sauce and bacon, and toss until the mixture is hot and creamy. The only noticeable difference we found was in the ratio of ingredients, especially the eggs and cheese. That ratio, we reasoned, must be the key to a successful carbonara.

Eggs form the base of the lush, smooth sauce that binds the other ingredients to the slender strands of pasta. Only the heat from the cooked pasta is necessary to cook the eggs to the right consistency, so we knew a precise amount of egg would be critical to both the texture and the richness of the dish. Basing our recipe on 1 pound of pasta, we started out with 2 eggs. Mixed with 1 cup of grated cheese, this sauce was thick and clumped when introduced to the hot pasta. Four eggs made a sauce too soupy and wet to stick to the pasta. Three eggs were just right. The sauce was silky in texture, had the fortitude to cling to the spaghetti, and was moist and rich.

Next the cheese. When in Rome, the cheese of choice is Pecorino Romano, an aged sheep's milk cheese with a distinctly sharp, tangy flavor. On its own, 1 cup of Pecorino Romano proved too strong for our taste. We tried substituting a cup of Parmigiano-Reggiano for the Pecorino Romano. While the Parmigiano-Reggiano gave the dish a sweet, nutty flavor that was well received, tasters now longed for a little of the potency from the Pecorino Romano. We found that a blend of the cheeses—¼ cup Pecorino Romano and ¾ cup Parmesan—brought out just the right amount of flavor from both. It also made for a perfect ratio of cheese to eggs to create the smooth, creamy sauce we'd been seeking.

Many carbonara recipes include the addition of ½ cup heavy cream to the sauce. Our tasters immediately rejected this lack of discretion. The heavy cream dulled the mouth with a fatty coating, and it deadened the flavor of the cheeses.

On the other hand, the sweet punch of garlic was a welcome addition. At first we sautéed a few minced cloves in a little olive oil before adding it to the sauce, but this sautéed garlic lacked the strength to shoulder the heavy weight of the eggs and cheese. Adding raw garlic to the mixture was just the trick. With just a brief introduction to heat via the hot pasta, the garlic flavor bloomed and gave the dish a pleasing bite.

We focused next on the bacon. In Italy, carbonara is traditionally made with *guanciale*—salt-cured pork jowl. You can't buy this product in the United States, so we centered the testing on available bacons—pancetta (Italian bacon) and American bacon. Pancetta, like American bacon, comes from the belly of the pig, but rather than being smoked, pancetta is cured only with salt, pepper, and spice, usually cloves. American bacon is recognizably smoked and has a distinct sweetness from the sugar that's added during the curing process.

The pancetta gave the carbonara a substantial pork flavor. It was distinctly seasoned with the salt and pepper of the cure. But tasters weren't crazy about its meaty texture. Even though the pancetta was thinly sliced and fried until crisp, the pieces became chewy after a short time in the sauce. The American bacon managed to retain much of its crisp texture, and it added a pleasantly sweet and smoky flavor to the dish that tasters preferred overwhelmingly.

In Italy, you can start a heated argument over whether or not to use wine in carbonara. In an effort to find the absolutely best carbonara, we tried a dry red wine (a common ingredient in authentic recipes), vermouth (which appeared in only one recipe but piqued our interest), and a dry white wine, which was favored by the majority of the recipes we had found. It was no surprise that tasters chose the carbonara with white wine, as it created the most impact and resonance. It was full-flavored, and the acidic nature of the wine cut through the taste of the bacon, brightening the flavor of the dish. When testing how much to add, we found that a modest amount wouldn't do. To bring the wine's full presence to the table, we needed to use at least one-half cup. We also found that adding the white wine to the bacon as it sautéed deepened the flavor of the dish overall.

Up to this point, we had been making the carbonara in the traditional method. We mixed the eggs and cheese in the bottom of the serving bowl along with the fried bacon, then dumped the hot, drained pasta on top and tossed the mixture thoroughly. But this method had flaws. It was difficult to distribute the egg and cheese mixture evenly throughout the pasta, and, try as we might to keep the bacon pieces afloat, gravity pulled them back to the bottom of the bowl.

Mixing the eggs and cheese together in a separate bowl, then pouring the mixture over the hot pasta ensured even coverage. In addition, by removing the eggs and cheese from the bottom of the serving bowl, we were able to preheat the bowl—a step that keeps the pasta warm. Finally, we found that tossing the hot pasta with the egg mixture first, then gently tossing in the bacon, worked best. The bacon adhered nicely to the sticky coating of sauce.

We found that carbonara will not maintain its creamy consistency if the cooked pasta is allowed too much time to drain. We ultimately allowed it to sit in the colander for only a few seconds before mixing it with the sauce. (To ensure that proper moisture from the pasta was not lost, we found it good practice to reserve ⅓ cup of the pasta cooking water to add if the noodles became dry or sticky.) Even with these precautions, the carbonara thickened up considerably if left to cool for even a short time. It's best for hungry diners to wait for the carbonara, not the other way around.

Spaghetti alla Carbonara
SERVES 4 TO 6

Add regular table salt to the pasta cooking water, but use sea salt flakes, if you can find them, to season the dish. We like the full flavor they bring to the carbonara. Note that while either table salt or sea salt can be used when seasoning in step 3, they are not used in equal amounts.

¼	cup extra-virgin olive oil
8	ounces bacon (about 8 slices), slices halved lengthwise, then cut crosswise into ¼-inch pieces
½	cup dry white wine
3	large eggs
1¾	ounces Parmesan cheese, freshly grated (¾ cup)
½	ounce Pecorino Romano cheese, freshly grated (¼ cup)
3	small garlic cloves, minced or pressed through a garlic press
1	pound spaghetti
	Salt (see note)
	Ground black pepper

1. Adjust an oven rack to the lower-middle position, set a large heatproof serving bowl on the rack, and heat the oven to 200 degrees. Bring 4 quarts water to a rolling boil in a large pot.

2. While the water is heating, heat the oil in a large skillet over medium heat until shimmering but not smoking. Add the bacon and cook, stirring occasionally, until lightly browned and crisp, about 8 minutes. Add the wine and simmer until the alcohol aroma has cooked off and the wine is slightly reduced, 6 to 8 minutes. Remove from the heat and cover to keep warm. Beat the eggs, cheeses, and garlic together with a fork in a small bowl; set aside.

3. When the water comes to a boil, add 1 tablespoon table salt to the pasta and stir to separate the noodles. Cook until al dente; reserve ⅓ cup pasta cooking water and drain the pasta for about 5 seconds, leaving the pasta slightly wet. Transfer the drained pasta to the warm serving bowl; if the pasta appears dry, add some of the reserved pasta cooking water and toss to moisten. Immediately pour the egg mixture over the hot pasta and sprinkle with 1 teaspoon sea salt flakes or ¾ teaspoon table salt; toss well to combine. Pour the bacon mixture over the pasta, season generously with black pepper, and toss well to combine. Serve immediately.

SPAGHETTI AND MEATBALLS

MANY COOKS THINK OF MEATBALLS AS HAMburgers with seasonings (cheese, herbs, garlic) and a round shape. This is partly true. However, unlike hamburgers, which are best cooked rare or medium-rare, meatballs are cooked through until well-done—at which point they've often turned into dry, tough hockey pucks. When this is the case, the dish can be so heavy that Alka-Seltzer is the only dessert that makes sense. Our goal was to create meatballs that were moist and light. We also wanted to develop a quick tomato sauce that was loaded with flavor. We focused on the meatballs first.

Meatballs start with ground meat but require additional ingredients to keep them moist and lighten their texture. Meatballs also require

binders to keep them from falling apart in the tomato sauce. A traditional source of moisture in meatballs is egg. We tested meatballs made with and without egg and quickly determined that egg was a welcome addition. It made the meatballs both moister and lighter.

The list of possible binders included dried bread crumbs, fresh bread crumbs, ground crackers, and bread soaked in milk. We found that bread and cracker crumbs soaked up any available moisture, making the meatballs harder and drier when cooked to well-done. In comparison, the meatballs made with bread soaked in milk were moist, creamy, and rich. Milk was clearly an important part of the equation.

We liked the milk but wondered if we could do better. We tried adding yogurt (which works well in our favorite meat loaf recipe) but had to thin it with milk in order to mix it with the bread. Meatballs made with thinned yogurt were even creamier and more flavorful than those made with plain milk. We also tried buttermilk; the results were just as good, with no need to thin the liquid.

With the dairy now part of our working recipe, we found the meatball mixture a tad sticky and hard to handle. By eliminating the egg white (the yolk has all the fat and emulsifiers that contribute smoothness), we eliminated the stickiness.

It was finally time to experiment with the crucial ingredient: the meat. Ground round was too lean; we preferred fattier chuck in this recipe. We tried blending in ground veal but decided it was not worth the bother; these meatballs tasted bland. Ground pork was another matter. It added a welcome flavor dimension.

With our ingredients in order, it was time to test cooking methods. We tried roasting, broiling, and the traditional pan-frying. Roasting yielded dry, crumbly meatballs, while broiling was extremely messy and also tended to produce dry meatballs. Pan-frying produced meatballs with a rich, dark crust and moist texture.

We wondered if we could save cleanup time and build more flavor into the tomato sauce by making it in the same pan used to fry the meatballs. We emptied out the vegetable oil used to fry the meatballs (olive oil is too expensive for this task and doesn't contribute much flavor), then added a little fresh olive oil (olive oil is important to the flavor of the sauce) before adding garlic and tomatoes. Not only did this method prove convenient, but it also gave the sauce depth, as the browned bits that had formed when the meatballs were fried loosened from the pan bottom and dissolved in the sauce.

Meatballs need a thick, smooth sauce—the kind produced by canned crushed tomatoes. Sauces made with whole or diced tomatoes were too chunky and liquidy; they didn't meld with the meatballs but did make them soggy.

Spaghetti and Meatballs

SERVES 4 TO 6

The shaped meatballs can be covered with plastic wrap and refrigerated for several hours ahead of serving time, if you like. Fry the meatballs and make the sauce at the last minute.

MEATBALLS

2	slices good-quality white sandwich bread, crusts removed and slices torn into small pieces
1/2	cup buttermilk or 6 tablespoons plain yogurt thinned with 2 tablespoons whole milk
1	pound ground meat, preferably 3/4 pound ground chuck and 1/4 pound ground pork
1/4	cup freshly grated Parmesan cheese
2	tablespoons minced fresh parsley leaves
1	large egg yolk
1	small garlic clove, minced fine or pressed through a garlic press
3/4	teaspoon salt
	Ground black pepper
1–1 1/2	cups vegetable oil for pan-frying

SMOOTH TOMATO SAUCE

2	tablespoons extra-virgin olive oil
1	small garlic clove, minced fine or pressed through a garlic press
1	(28-ounce) can crushed tomatoes
1	tablespoon minced fresh basil leaves

	Salt and ground black pepper
1	pound spaghetti
	Freshly grated Parmesan cheese for serving

1. FOR THE MEATBALLS: Combine the bread and buttermilk in a small bowl. Let sit for 10 minutes, mashing occasionally with a fork, until a smooth paste forms.

2. Place the ground meat, cheese, parsley, egg yolk, garlic, salt, and pepper to taste in a medium bowl. Add the bread-milk mixture and combine until evenly mixed. Shape 3 tablespoons of the mixture into a 1 1/2-inch round meatball. (When forming meatballs, use a light touch. If you compact the meatballs too much, they can become dense and hard.) You should be able to form about 14 meatballs.

3. Pour the vegetable oil into a 10- or 11-inch sauté pan to a depth of 1/4 inch. Turn the heat to medium-high. After several minutes, test the oil with the edge of a meatball. When the oil sizzles, add the meatballs in a single layer. Fry, turning several times, until nicely browned on all sides, about 10 minutes (see the illustration on page 254). Regulate the heat as needed to keep the oil sizzling but not smoking. Transfer the browned meatballs to a plate lined with paper towels and set aside.

4. Meanwhile, bring 4 quarts water to a rolling boil in a large pot.

5. FOR THE SAUCE: Discard the oil in the pan, but leave behind any browned bits. Add the olive oil and garlic and sauté, scraping up the browned bits, just until the garlic is golden, about 30 seconds. Add the tomatoes, bring to a simmer, and cook until the sauce thickens, about 10 minutes. Stir in the basil and salt and pepper to taste. Add the meatballs and simmer, turning them occasionally, until heated through, about 5 minutes. Keep warm over low heat.

6. Add 1 tablespoon salt and the pasta to the boiling water and stir to separate the noodles. Cook until al dente, drain, and return to the pot. Ladle several large spoonfuls of the sauce (without meatballs) over the spaghetti and toss until the noodles are well coated. Divide the pasta among individual bowls and top each with a little more tomato sauce and 2 or 3 meatballs. Serve immediately, passing the cheese separately.

➤ VARIATION
Spaghetti and Chicken Meatballs

If you want to trim some fat from this recipe, ground chicken is a decent alternative to ground beef and pork. We found that meatballs made from chicken are a tad soft, so they must be refrigerated for an hour before frying to keep them from sticking to the pan or falling apart.

Follow the recipe for Spaghetti and Meatballs, replacing the ground meat with 1 pound ground chicken. After shaping the meatballs in step 2, place them on a platter, cover with plastic wrap, and refrigerate until firm, about 1 hour. Proceed as directed.

PASTA WITH BOLOGNESE SAUCE

BOLOGNESE SAUCE GETS ITS BIG FLAVOR FROM the braising of ground meat and softened vegetables in slowly reducing liquids—most often milk and wine—and then, finally, tomatoes. The process is often given as much as three hours, but the result is a bold, meaty pasta sauce with sweet

BROWNING MEATBALLS

We found that meatballs taste best when browned evenly on all sides. Their round shape makes this a challenge. Our solution is to brown the two broader sides of the meatballs first, then use tongs to stand the meatballs on their ends.

resonance and ultra-tender meat.

Try to shortcut the process and you'll be left with bits of rubbery meat floating in a subpar tomato sauce. We wanted to make Bolognese sauce weeknight-friendly. If perfect, it would be everything that we expected from the long-cooked sauce, but we wanted this sauce on the table in less than an hour.

There is not exactly a wealth of "quick" Bolognese recipes. We found only two, one of them no more than ground beef and jarred tomato sauce. We decided to take the test kitchen's favorite Bolognese sauce, which uses the traditional slow-cooking technique, and try to pare down the cooking time.

The original test kitchen recipe calls for equal parts ground beef, pork, and veal, and, unfortunately, we found all three to be necessary. We were, however, able to avoid buying several packages of meat by purchasing the trusty supermarket "meat loaf mix," made from equal parts of each. To boost the flavor of our quick-cooked sauce, we tested additions such as pancetta, prosciutto, and even porcini mushrooms. Prosciutto was out, owing to its salty flavor and big price tag, but pancetta was a perfect fit—a little went a long way. Porcini mushrooms had such an amazingly beefy impact on the sauce that we just couldn't refuse them.

Vegetables were next under the microscope. Our favorite three-hour recipe called for celery, carrots, and onion, but we found celery could go by the wayside. Garlic found a home, but tasters thought herbs were distracting. Either butter or olive oil can be used to sauté the vegetables, but we chose butter for its richer flavor.

Tomatoes add sweetness to the sauce, and their juice is used to braise the meat. We tried all kinds—crushed, diced, sauce—and in the end liked the juicier canned whole tomatoes best because they come packed in so much juice. To provide some deeper, slow-cooked tomato flavor, we added some tomato paste.

Now hold on a minute! Our goal was to shorten this recipe, not to complicate it with an epic ingredient list. We could already count at least 10 minutes of prep time. The solution? We whipped out a food processor and used it to chop just about everything: carrots, onions, mushrooms, tomatoes, even the pancetta. Only the garlic was spared from the food processor (it never chopped up completely), but a garlic press made quick work of that step, too. Now what had been taking 10 minutes was being accomplished in less than two.

In a true Bolognese, liquids are reduced slowly one at a time to tenderize the meat and develop the characteristic sweetness of the sauce. Because we didn't have all day, we had to find a quicker method. To sweeten the sauce, we added a pinch of sugar. But it wasn't until we started thinking outside the box and tried sweeter white wines like Riesling and Gewürztraminer in place of the traditional dry Sauvignon Blanc that our sauce achieved the proper sweetness. We even tried a white Zinfandel—the "other" white wine—often snubbed for its grapey-sweet flavor. Guess what? It worked beautifully.

Now all we had to do was get around that slow simmer. Sure, cooking everything at a raging boil was an obvious option, but the meat (which was still tough) became downright springy when boiled. Our trick for minimizing cooking time was to reduce the wine on the side in a separate skillet; 1¼ cups went down to 2 tablespoons in 20 minutes.

Now meaty, sweet, and fast, this 45-minute sauce had everything going for it—well, almost. The meat still presented itself in the form of little rubber pellets, and no sauce, however good, could mask that.

GETTING IT RIGHT:
The Pan Matters

When the sauce is simmered in a Dutch oven, it doesn't reduce quickly enough, and the consistency is watery (left). When the sauce is simmered in a 12-inch skillet, the texture is thicker, and the sauce reduces more quickly (right).

COOKED IN DUTCH OVEN   **COOKED IN SKILLET**

A hint of an answer came when we thought about the milk. In Italian cooking, milk and meat are often braised together, producing very tender results. What if we soaked the ground meat in milk before cooking? We tried it. After sautéing the vegetables, we added the milk-soaked meat to the hot pan and watched as the meat disintegrated into grainy, mushy bits. OK, this was not the perfect solution, but at least the meat wasn't tough.

Next we added the meat directly to the pan along with the milk (no soaking). Same as before, the meat fell apart into bits, but this time, no mush. Sure that we were on the right track, the next time we added the meat to the pan, we quickly broke it into large pieces with a wooden spoon (letting it spend no more than a minute in the pan alone) and then added the milk. We stirred the two together to break up the meat and—success! This meat was incredibly tender. Actually, it made sense. As any fan of steak tartare will tell you, raw ground meat is already tender. Because we weren't browning the meat, it never obtained that tough crust that takes hours upon hours to return to its tender state and, as a result, made a sauce that was rich and meaty, sweet and bold, luxuriously tender, and on the table in 45 minutes.

Pasta with Bolognese Sauce
SERVES 4 TO 6

Sweet white wines such as Gewürztraminer, Riesling, and even white Zinfandel work especially well in this sauce. To obtain the best texture, be careful not to break up the meat too much when cooking it with the milk in step 4. With additional cooking and stirring, it will continue to break up. Just about any pasta shape complements this meaty sauce, but spaghetti and linguine are the test kitchen favorites. If using pancetta that has been sliced thin rather than cut into 1-inch chunks, reduce the processing time in step 3 from 30 seconds to about 5 seconds.

½	ounce dried porcini mushrooms
½	cup water
1¼	cups sweet white wine (see note)
½	small carrot, peeled and chopped into rough ½-inch pieces
½	small onion, chopped into rough ½-inch pieces
3	ounces pancetta, cut into 1-inch pieces
1	(28-ounce) can whole tomatoes
1½	tablespoons unsalted butter
1	small garlic clove, minced or pressed through a garlic press
1	teaspoon sugar
1¼	pounds meat loaf mix or equal amounts 80 percent lean ground beef, ground veal, and ground pork
1½	cups whole milk
2	tablespoons tomato paste
	Salt
⅛	teaspoon ground black pepper
1	pound pasta
	Freshly grated Parmesan cheese for serving

1. Rinse the dried porcini mushrooms in a small strainer under cool running water; drain. Add the mushrooms and water to a small microwave-safe bowl. Cover with plastic wrap, cut several steam vents in the plastic wrap with a paring knife, and microwave on high power for 30 seconds. Let stand until the mushrooms soften, about 5 minutes. Lift the mushrooms from the liquid with a fork and mince. Pour the liquid through a small strainer lined with a coffee filter or a single sheet of paper towel set over a measuring cup. Reserve the mushrooms and strained soaking liquid separately.

2. Bring the wine to simmer in a 10-inch nonstick skillet over medium heat; reduce the heat to low and simmer until the wine is reduced to 2 tablespoons, about 20 minutes. Set aside.

3. Meanwhile, pulse the carrot in a food processor until broken down into rough ¼-inch pieces, about ten 1-second pulses. Add the onion; pulse until the vegetables are broken down into ⅛-inch pieces, about ten 1-second pulses. Transfer the vegetables to a small bowl. Process the softened porcini until well ground, about 15 seconds, scraping down the bowl if necessary. Transfer the porcini to the bowl with the carrot and onion. Process the pancetta until the pieces are no larger than ¼ inch, 30 to 35 seconds, scraping down the bowl if necessary; transfer to a small bowl. Pulse the tomatoes with their juice until chopped fine, six to eight 1-second pulses.

4. Heat the butter in a 12-inch skillet over medium-high heat; when the foaming subsides, add the pancetta and cook, stirring frequently, until well browned, about 2 minutes. Add the carrot, onion, and porcini; cook, stirring frequently, until the vegetables are softened but not browned, about 4 minutes. Add the garlic and sugar; cook until fragrant, about 30 seconds. Add the ground meat, breaking the meat into 1-inch pieces with a wooden spoon, about 1 minute. Add the milk and stir to break the meat into ½-inch bits; bring to a simmer, reduce the heat to medium, and continue to simmer, stirring to break up the meat into small pieces, until most of the liquid has evaporated and the meat begins to sizzle, 18 to 20 minutes. Stir in the tomato paste and cook until combined, about 1 minute. Add the tomatoes, reserved porcini

SCIENCE: Why Does Milk Make Meat Tender?

Browning adds flavor, but it also causes the protein molecules in ground meat to denature (unwind). As the proteins unwind, they link up to create a tighter network and squeeze out some of the water in the meat. Long simmering allows some of that liquid to be reabsorbed. But if you skip the browning and cook the meat in milk (or any other liquid) at the outset, you limit the temperature of the meat to about 212 degrees (browning occurs in dry heat and at higher temperatures). As a result, meat cooked in milk does not dry out and toughen but remains tender. This means you can simmer the sauce just until the liquid has reduced to the right consistency rather than waiting for the meat to soften.

soaking liquid, ¼ teaspoon salt, and the pepper; bring to a simmer over medium-high heat, then reduce the heat to medium and simmer until the liquid is reduced and the sauce is thickened but still moist, 12 to 15 minutes. Stir in the reduced wine and simmer to blend the flavors, about 5 minutes.

5. Meanwhile, bring 4 quarts water to a rolling boil in a large pot. Add 1 tablespoon salt and the pasta to the boiling water and stir to separate the noodles. Cook until al dente. Drain, reserving ¼ cup pasta cooking water and return the pasta to the pot. Add 2 cups sauce and 2 tablespoons of the reserved pasta cooking water to the pasta; toss well, adding the remaining pasta cooking water, if necessary, to help distribute the sauce. Divide the pasta among individual bowls and top each portion with about ¼ cup of the remaining sauce. Serve immediately, passing the Parmesan separately.

PASTA WITH MEATY TOMATO SAUCE

NOTHING COULD BE SIMPLER (OR MORE WELCOME on a cold night) than a rustic pasta sauce made from canned tomatoes and a richly flavored piece of meat. The meat (often a pork chop) is browned, the fat drained, and the sauce built in the empty pan. The browned meat is added back to the sauce, the pan covered, and the sauce simmered slowly until the meat is fall-off-the-bone tender. The meat is then shredded and stirred into the sauce, at which point it is served over rigatoni with a good sprinkling of grated cheese.

When we began testing this sauce, it soon became clear that the choice of meat was the most important issue. We tried pork chops from the blade, loin, and sirloin. Even the fattiest chops were dry and tough after braising. We wanted the meat to almost melt when added to the tomato sauce. We needed a piece of meat with more marbling so that it would not dry out during braising.

We thought about a cut from the shoulder—either picnic or Boston butt—because this part of the pig has more fat than the loin, where most chops come from. The problem with these shoulder roasts was their size; the smallest at the market was four pounds. Nevertheless, we cut a pound of this meat into stew-like chunks and proceeded. This meat was more yielding when cooked and had a better flavor. However, the sauce tasted a bit wan; the meat had not done a really good job of

---

INGREDIENTS: Tomato Paste

A celebrated ingredient in its post-WWII heyday, when the long-cooked tomato sauce was king, tomato paste has fallen by the wayside as discerning cooks have favored fresher, more brightly flavored tomato sauces. These days, our use of tomato paste comes with a more conservative hand. We reserve it for occasions when a deep tomato flavor is warranted, such as in a chili or our Bolognese sauce.

Given this limited use, we wondered if it mattered which brand we used. To find out, we went to local supermarkets to gather seven brands for a tasting: six American brands in small cans and an Italian import in a toothpaste-like tube. We asked our tasters to taste the tomato paste as is—no cooking, no sauce.

Every brand did well in providing a big tomato punch, but the Amore brand, imported from Italy, was the unanimous winner, owing to its "intense" and "fresh" flavor. Amore is the only tomato paste tested that contains fat, which could account for its bigger flavor. The Amore brand also scored points because of its tube packaging. Just squeeze out what you need and store the rest in the refrigerator. No fuss, no waste.

How did the flavor of this tomato paste hold up in cooking? We tasted it, along with Hunt's, the brand that came in last, in our Bolognese recipe, to see if we could detect a difference. We did indeed pick out (and downgrade) the distinct dried herb flavor of the Hunt's paste. On the other hand, we liked the sauce made with the Amore tomato paste for its deep, round tomato flavor.

THE BEST TOMATO PASTE

An Italian import, Amore was our tasters' favorite brand. They described this paste-in-a-tube as "intense" and "fresh." The no-fuss, no-waste packaging is also appealing.

flavoring the tomato sauce.

At this point, we turned to spareribs, which are fattier than roasts from the shoulder. The braised meat from spareribs was better than the Boston butt—it was unctuous, almost gelatinous. Best of all, the tomato sauce really tasted meaty. The bones had flavored the sauce in a way that meat alone couldn't. But spareribs are sold in an entire rack that weighs three or more pounds. We needed only four or five ribs for a batch of sauce. That meant spending $9 on a rack of ribs and using half for the sauce and freezing the rest. Was there a more economical way to make this peasant sauce?

We paid $1.99 per pound for country-style ribs and were able to find a small packet with just 1½ pounds of ribs—enough for one batch of sauce, with no leftovers. The sauce made with country-style ribs was similar to the spareribs sauce.

Next we wondered if this sauce could be made with beef. Short ribs are roughly equivalent to spareribs and country-style ribs. (On the cow, ribs cut from the belly, called the plate, as well as those cut from the back are called short ribs.) The sauce made with short ribs was delicious, too. It's just important to remember that short ribs must be simmered longer than pork ribs because they are thicker.

Pasta and Rustic Slow-Simmered Tomato Sauce with Meat

SERVES 4

This sauce can be made with either beef or pork ribs. Depending on their size, you will need 4 or 5 ribs. (See page 259 for information on buying pork ribs.) To prevent the sauce from becoming greasy, trim all external fat from the ribs and drain off most of the fat from the skillet after browning. This thick, rich sauce is best with tubular pasta, such as ziti, or penne. Pass grated pecorino or Parmesan cheese at the table. The sauce can be covered and refrigerated for up to 4 days or frozen for up to 2 months.

- 1 tablespoon olive oil
- 1½ pounds beef short ribs or pork spareribs or country-style ribs, trimmed of fat
- Salt and ground black pepper
- 1 medium onion, minced
- ½ cup dry red wine
- 1 (28-ounce) can diced tomatoes
- 1 pound pasta (see note)
- Freshly grated Pecorino Romano or Parmesan cheese for serving

1. Heat the oil in a heavy-bottomed 12-inch skillet over medium-high heat until shimmering. Season the ribs with salt and pepper and brown on all sides, turning occasionally with tongs, 8 to 10 minutes. Transfer the ribs to a plate; pour off all but 1 teaspoon of fat from the skillet. Add the onion and sauté until softened, 2 to 3 minutes. Add the wine and simmer, scraping the pan bottom with a wooden spoon to loosen the browned bits, until the wine reduces to a glaze, about 2 minutes.

2. Return the ribs and accumulated juices to the skillet; add the tomatoes and their juice. Bring to a boil, then reduce the heat to low, cover, and simmer gently, turning the ribs several times, until the meat is very tender and falling off the bones, 1½ hours (for pork spareribs or country-style ribs) to 2 hours (for beef short ribs).

3. Transfer the ribs to a clean plate. When cool enough to handle, remove the meat from the bones and shred it with your fingers, discarding the fat and bones. Return the shredded meat to the sauce in the skillet. Bring the sauce to a simmer over medium heat and cook, uncovered, until heated through and slightly thickened, about 5 minutes. Adjust the seasoning with salt and pepper.

4. Meanwhile, bring 4 quarts water to a rolling boil in a large pot. Add 1 tablespoon salt and the pasta to the boiling water and stir to separate the noodles. Cook until al dente. Drain and remove to a large serving bowl. Toss the pasta with the sauce. Serve immediately, passing the cheese separately.

➤ VARIATIONS

Pasta and Tomato-Pork Sauce with Rosemary and Garlic

Follow the recipe for Pasta and Rustic Slow-Simmered Tomato Sauce with Meat, using pork spareribs or country-style ribs. Substitute 3 medium garlic cloves, minced, for the onion, and add 2 teaspoons minced fresh rosemary leaves to the skillet along with the garlic; sauté until softened and fragrant, about 30 seconds. Proceed as directed.

Pasta and Tomato–Beef Sauce with Cinnamon, Cloves, and Parsley

Follow the recipe for Pasta and Rustic Slow-Simmered Tomato Sauce with Meat, using beef short ribs and adding ½ teaspoon ground cinnamon, a pinch ground cloves, and 2 tablespoons minced fresh parsley leaves to the softened onion; sauté until the spices are fragrant, about 30 seconds longer. Proceed as directed.

PASTA PRIMAVERA

UNLIKE MOST DISHES, PASTA PRIMAVERA HAS a clear pedigree—and despite the name, this popular recipe originated in the United States, not Italy. Pasta primavera was created at Le Cirque, New York's famed French restaurant, in the 1970s. Patrons told restaurateur Sirio Maccioni that they wanted healthier, lighter dishes, so he created a pasta dish loaded with fresh vegetables. He dubbed his invention spaghetti primavera—*primavera* is Italian for "spring"—and it quickly became a New York sensation.

If you've ever made this dish, you probably loved the flavor. It's a sure winner with company, but for the cook, this recipe is a labor of love. For one thing, it calls for blanching each green vegetable in a separate pot to retain its individual character; if the same pot is used for each vegetable, this first step takes almost an hour. If that weren't enough bother, once the vegetables are blanched, you need five more pots: one to cook the vegetables in garlicky olive oil, one to sauté mushrooms, one to make a fresh tomato sauce flavored with basil, one to make a cream sauce with butter and Parmesan, and one to cook the pasta. None of the tasks involved is difficult, but the timing is complicated and better suited to a professional kitchen, where several cooks can handle different jobs. But we love this dish. We wanted to find out if we could simplify the cooking process while keeping the fresh vegetable flavors.

PORK RIBS

SPARERIBS

COUNTRY-STYLE RIBS

Spareribs come from the belly of the hog. Country-style ribs come from the backbone of the animal, where the shoulder and loin meet. Either can be used in our meaty tomato sauce, although country-style ribs are usually sold in packets with four or five ribs and are more convenient to use than spareribs, which are sold in racks of 10 or more ribs.

The first issue was to decide which vegetables were essential for primavera sauce and which could be dropped. Despite its name, this dish as originally conceived contains many nonspring vegetables, including broccoli, green beans, and zucchini. Only the peas, snow peas, and asparagus are truly spring vegetables.

We began testing other spring vegetables and soon realized why they were not included. Artichokes were way too much work to prepare, and leeks tasted better when sautéed rather than blanched, which meant an extra pan and more work. We usually like fennel, but its sweet, anise flavor overwhelmed that of the other vegetables. We also decided to jettison the broccoli (tasters liked this vegetable the least in this sauce) and snow peas (the pea family was already represented by shelled peas). We were left with four spring/summer vegetables—asparagus, peas, zucchini, and green beans. We went still further and tried eliminating a couple of these vegetables and increasing the quantity of those remaining, but this compromise did not save any time, and tasters felt that the name "primavera" connotes many vegetables, not just two or three.

We found we could blanch all the green vegetables together in a single pot. We had to add them

259

at different times to make sure each was properly cooked, but after some trial and error we devised a cooking regimen—adding the green beans first, followed by the asparagus, then the zucchini, and ending with the peas. Because we were cooking all the vegetables together, we needed a larger pot, which we found we could reuse (without washing) to cook the mushrooms and tomatoes.

We tried adding the cooked vegetables directly to the drained pasta, but they were watery and bland. Clearly, they needed to be sautéed to build flavor. A couple of minutes in a hot skillet with some garlicky butter proved essential.

In the original recipe, the mushrooms are sautéed, then added to the green vegetables, then sautéed again. We wondered if we could instead keep the mushrooms in the pan and build the tomato sauce on top of them. This worked fine. We tried cooking the mushroom-tomato sauce (as well as the green vegetables) in butter and in olive oil. Tasters preferred the sweet, rich flavor of the butter, which worked better with the cream.

Next we focused on the tomatoes. We concluded that this dish would need fresh tomatoes for flavor and juiciness. Plum tomatoes are not as watery as fresh round tomatoes and are best in this dish. We found it unnecessary to seed them, but the peels had to go because they separated from the chopped tomatoes and curled up into unappetizing bits.

Finally, we found that the separate cream sauce (with butter, cheese, and cream) could be combined with the mushroom-tomato sauce. We reduced some cream over the mushroom-tomato mixture and discovered that this worked perfectly well. There was plenty of butter in the sauce already, and we found that cheese could just as easily be sprinkled on at the table. So instead of three pans—one for mushrooms, one for tomato sauce, and one for cream sauce—we had cooked them together in one pan.

At this point, our recipe was just as delicious as the original, and we were down to just three pans, not six. We had also reduced total preparation and cooking time by more than half. This pasta primavera may not be Tuesday night supper, but when you want a fancy pasta dish, there's no reason to run screaming in the other direction when someone suggests primavera sauce.

SHREDDING BASIL

For larger herb leaves such as basil or mint, a cut called a chiffonade is the most attractive and bruise-free way to slice them.

1. Stack 3 or 4 clean, dry leaves.

2. Roll the stack up tightly, like a cigar; slice thin.

Pasta Primavera

SERVES 6 AS A MAIN COURSE
OR 8 TO 10 AS A FIRST COURSE

This dish requires careful timing so that the three main elements—the cooked pasta, the green vegetables, and the sauce—come together at the right time.

	Salt
6	ounces green beans, cut into 3/4-inch pieces
12	medium asparagus spears, tough ends snapped off (see the illustration on page 130), halved lengthwise, and cut on the diagonal into 3/4-inch pieces
1	medium zucchini, cut into 1/2-inch dice
1	cup frozen peas, thawed
6	tablespoons (3/4 stick) unsalted butter
8	ounces white mushrooms, sliced thin
4	large plum tomatoes (about 1 pound), cored, peeled, and chopped medium
1/4	teaspoon red pepper flakes (optional)

½ cup heavy cream

1 pound dried egg fettuccine (see page 276)

2 medium garlic cloves, minced or pressed through a garlic press

¼ cup shredded fresh basil leaves

1½ tablespoons juice from 1 lemon

Freshly grated Parmesan cheese for serving

1. Bring 4 quarts water to a rolling boil in a large pot for the pasta. Bring 3 quarts water to a rolling boil in a large saucepan for the green vegetables; add 1 tablespoon salt. Fill a large bowl with ice water; set aside. Add the green beans to the boiling water in the saucepan; cook 1½ minutes. Add the asparagus; cook 30 seconds. Add the zucchini; cook 30 seconds. Add the peas; cook 30 seconds. Drain the vegetables and immediately plunge them into the ice-water bath to stop the cooking; let sit until chilled, about 3 minutes. Drain well and set aside.

2. Heat 3 tablespoons of the butter in the now-empty saucepan over medium-high heat until foamy. Add the mushrooms and sauté until browned, 8 to 10 minutes. Add the tomatoes and red pepper flakes (if using), reduce the heat to medium, and simmer until the tomatoes begin to lose their shape, about 7 minutes. Add the cream and simmer until slightly thickened, about 4 minutes; cover to keep warm and set aside.

3. Add 1 tablespoon salt and the pasta to the boiling water in the pot and stir to separate the strands. Cook until al dente. While the pasta is cooking, heat the remaining 3 tablespoons butter in a large skillet over medium heat until foamy. Add the garlic and sauté until fragrant and very lightly colored, about 1 minute. Add the blanched vegetables and cook until heated through and infused with garlic flavor, about 2 minutes. Season with salt to taste; set aside. Meanwhile, bring the mushroom-tomato sauce back to a simmer over medium heat.

4. Drain the pasta and return it to the now-empty cooking pot. Add the mushroom-tomato sauce to the pasta and toss well to coat over low heat. Add the vegetables, basil, and lemon juice; season with salt to taste and toss well. Divide the pasta among individual bowls. Serve immediately, passing the cheese separately.

> VARIATION
Lighter Pasta Primavera
While not as delectably rich as the previous version, this primavera, with considerably less saturated fat, is still delicious.

Follow the recipe for Pasta Primavera, replacing 4 tablespoons of the butter with olive oil, using 2 tablespoons to sauté the mushrooms in step 2 and 2 tablespoons to sauté the garlic in step 3. Substitute low-sodium chicken broth for the heavy cream, swirling 2 tablespoons softened butter into the mushroom-tomato sauce before pouring it over the pasta.

PASTA WITH ASPARAGUS SAUCE

ASPARAGUS IS A NATURAL STARTING POINT when trying to make a vegetarian pasta sauce. First, we focused on how to cook the asparagus. We ruled out boiling or steaming because the residual water diluted the flavor. Grilling added bold and smoky characteristics, and broiling also concentrated the flavors, but we wanted a simpler method, one that would also allow for the easy introduction of other flavors. The answer, it turned out, was a quick sauté.

We cut the asparagus into 1-inch pieces and sautéed it with other ingredients over high heat. The asparagus caramelized just a bit, and the heat also brought out the flavors of the other ingredients, such as onions, walnuts, garlic, and shallots. To finish off each dish, we tried a variety of additions, including balsamic vinegar, basil leaves, lemon juice, blue cheese, and arugula. The key, we discovered, is not to overpower the asparagus with too much of one bold ingredient. What's wanted instead is a good balance of salty, sweet, and sour ingredients that allows the asparagus flavor to prevail.

Campanelli with Asparagus, Basil, and Balsamic Glaze
SERVES 4 TO 6
Campanelli is a frilly trumpet-shaped pasta that pairs nicely with this sauce. If you cannot find it, fusilli works well, too.

Salt

1   pound campanelli (see note)

¾   cup balsamic vinegar

5   tablespoons extra-virgin olive oil

1   pound asparagus, tough ends snapped off (see
     the illustration on page 130), spears halved
     lengthwise if larger than ½ inch in diameter
     and cut into 1-inch lengths

1   medium-large red onion, halved and sliced thin

½   teaspoon ground black pepper

¼   teaspoon red pepper flakes

1   cup chopped fresh basil leaves

1   tablespoon juice from 1 lemon

2   ounces Pecorino Romano cheese, shaved with
     a vegetable peeler (see the illustration on
     page 134)

1. Bring 4 quarts water to a rolling boil in a large pot. Add 1 tablespoon salt and the pasta to the boiling water and stir to separate the noodles. Cook until al dente. Drain and return the pasta to the pot.

2. Meanwhile, bring the balsamic vinegar to a boil in an 8-inch skillet over medium-high heat; reduce the heat to medium and simmer slowly until syrupy and reduced to ¼ cup, 15 to 20 minutes.

3. While the vinegar is reducing, heat 2 tablespoons of the oil in a 12-inch nonstick skillet over high heat until it begins to smoke. Add the asparagus, onion, black pepper, red pepper flakes, and ½ teaspoon salt and stir to combine. Cook, without stirring, until the asparagus begins to brown, about 1 minute, then stir and continue to cook, stirring occasionally, until the asparagus is tender-crisp, about 4 minutes longer.

4. Add the asparagus mixture, basil, lemon juice, ½ cup of the cheese, and remaining 3 tablespoons oil to the pasta and toss to combine. Serve immediately, drizzling 1 to 2 teaspoons of the balsamic glaze over each serving and passing the remaining cheese separately.

Cavatappi with Asparagus, Arugula, Walnuts, and Blue Cheese

SERVES 4 TO 6

Cavatappi is a short, tubular corkscrew-shaped pasta. Penne is a fine substitute. If you prefer the mild flavor of spinach to the peppery flavor of arugula, substitute an equal amount of baby spinach leaves. The grated apple, added just before serving, balances the other flavors in this dish.

Salt

1   pound cavatappi (see note)

5   tablespoons extra-virgin olive oil

1   pound asparagus, tough ends snapped off (see
     the illustration on page 130), spears halved
     lengthwise if larger than ½ inch in diameter
     and cut into 1-inch lengths

½   teaspoon ground black pepper

1   cup walnuts, chopped

4   cups lightly packed arugula leaves, washed and
     dried thoroughly

6   ounces strong blue cheese, preferably
     Roquefort, crumbled (about 1½ cups)

2   tablespoons cider vinegar

1   Granny Smith apple, peeled, for grating over
     the pasta

1. Bring 4 quarts water to a rolling boil in a large pot. Add 1 tablespoon salt and the pasta to the boiling water and stir to separate the noodles. Cook until al dente. Drain and return the pasta to the pot.

2. Meanwhile, heat 2 tablespoons of the oil in a 12-inch nonstick skillet over high heat until it begins to smoke. Add the asparagus, pepper, and ½ teaspoon salt and cook, without stirring, until the asparagus begins to brown, about 1 minute. Add the walnuts and continue to cook, stirring frequently, until the asparagus is tender-crisp and the nuts are toasted, about 4 minutes longer. Toss in the arugula and cook until wilted.

3. Add the asparagus mixture, blue cheese, vinegar, and remaining 3 tablespoons oil to the pasta and toss to combine. Serve immediately, grating some of the apple over each serving.

PASTA WITH MUSHROOMS

TRANSFORMING AN ORDINARY BOX OF PASTA and a package of mushrooms into something special is weeknight cooking at its best: quick, simple, and delicious. All we need is the right recipe.

Our first step was to choose the mushrooms. Not willing to shell out $18 per pound on exotic mushrooms, we limited ourselves to cultivated mushrooms that could be purchased for modest prices at the supermarket. The list included white button mushrooms, portobellos, cremini, and shiitakes. A quick taste test confirmed the obvious: White button mushrooms have the least flavor of the group. We also found that portobellos are tasty, but they darken sauces unless the gills are removed, a tedious process. We settled on a combination of cremini and shiitakes; tasters enjoyed the rich and meaty nature of cremini, while shiitakes have a hearty flavor and a pleasant chewy texture.

From experience, we knew the basics of mushroom cookery: They leach liquid a few minutes after exposure to high heat and then, after the moisture evaporates, they begin to brown. We cranked the heat on the stove and threw in a chunk of butter, followed by very thinly sliced mushrooms. The mushrooms quickly absorbed all of the butter and burned slightly. We started anew, adding a good drizzle of olive oil to reduce the risk of burning, but keeping some butter for flavor, and slicing the mushrooms thicker. This time, they cooked the way we expected them to, ending up lightly browned.

We turned to other variables in order to refine our technique. Salt draws moisture out of vegetables, and we suspected it might do the same with mushrooms. In a side-by-side test, mushrooms salted at the onset of sautéing released more liquid than an unsalted batch, which was a bonus. The more juices that were released, the more deeply the mushrooms browned (dry food always browns more readily than moist). Because shiitakes contain more moisture than cremini, we gave them a two-minute head start in the pan. (Note that it is possible to overcook mushrooms; we learned to keep them in the skillet just until they are browned; any longer and they become tough and rubbery.) A traditional skillet is our usual choice for sautéing, but we wondered if a nonstick pan was better for delicate mushrooms. A head-to-head test proved that the traditional skillet was better since the resulting *fond* (the browned bits on the bottom of the pan) contributes flavor to the sauce. (Nonstick skillets produce little fond.) When we added dried porcini, the resulting sauce was richer, but rehydrating dried

MUSHROOM COOKING 101

RAW

1. Raw mushrooms initially soak up all the fat in a pan. Don't give in to temptation and add more oil and butter.

AFTER 4 MINUTES

2. After several minutes, the mushrooms begin to release a significant amount of liquid, which will evaporate with continued cooking.

AFTER 8 MINUTES

3. The liquid has evaporated, and the mushrooms turn golden brown. They are done.

mushrooms complicated this otherwise simple recipe, and the fresh shiitakes and cremini on their own were just fine.

Garlic and thyme have a natural affinity with mushrooms, so we added generous amounts of both, saving other herbs for variations. Adding the thyme after the mushrooms were fully cooked preserved its pungency. We also experimented with a variety of choices from the onion family and settled on mild shallots, which didn't compete with the mushrooms.

We knew from the first recipes tested that we wanted a light, creamy sauce. We removed the mushrooms from the skillet and made a quick pan sauce by deglazing the pan with chicken broth and then tested a few additions. Sour cream caused the sauce to separate, and it was too tangy. A swirl of heavy cream, however, did the trick, creating a smooth, mild sauce. However, with ½ cup chicken broth and ½ cup cream, the pasta turned dry within minutes of saucing. We added more chicken broth in ¼ cup increments and ended up using quite a bit more than we had expected; 1¼ cups creates a saucy, but not soupy, consistency. An acidic element (alcohol, citrus, or vinegar) is often the key ingredient in a recipe—it sharpens and refines competing flavors. We tried small amounts of white wine,

vermouth, Marsala, sherry, Madeira, balsamic vinegar, and lemon juice, the latter being the test kitchen favorite.

Chunky sauces pair well with stubby, molded pasta shapes that have crevices in which the sauce can nestle. We found the best choices to be an unusual, frilly, flower-shaped pasta called campanelli and the readily available farfalle (bow ties). Rather than reducing the sauce and tossing it with the pasta, we simmered al dente pasta in the sauce for a couple of minutes. This way, the pasta and sauce became fully integrated, with the pasta absorbing a good amount of flavor. The sauce also thickens slightly during this step as the pasta leaches starch. As with many pasta dishes, this one is improved by a handful of grated Parmesan cheese, a speck of black pepper, and chopped fresh parsley.

❧

Pasta with Sautéed Mushrooms and Thyme

SERVES 4 AS A MAIN COURSE
OR 6 TO 8 AS SIDE DISH

Vegetable broth can be substituted for the chicken broth to make this dish vegetarian. If you add the pasta to the boiling water at the same time the cremini go into the skillet, the pasta and sauce will be finished at the same time.

SCIENCE: Why Are Shiitake Stems So Tough?

Forget to remove the stems from shiitakes before cooking, and you'll spend a good part of the dinner hour picking inedible, chewy bits from your plate. Seasoned cooks know to either discard the stems or save them for stock, but most learned this lesson the hard way. Why are shiitake stems so tough, while the stems of white button and other cultivated mushrooms are tender?

Many of the experts we contacted suggest that a sturdy stem with a tightly packed cellular structure evolved over time to support the shiitake's wide cap, which can range from the size of a quarter to 5 inches in diameter. Two experts—Judy Rogers, mycologist and executive secretary of the North American Mycological Association, and David Ellis, associate professor of mycology at the University of Adelaide in Australia—concur that the way shiitakes are grown also contributes to the

sturdy composition of their stems. Shiitakes are cultivated on either natural hardwood logs or on man-made sawdust logs. Mushrooms grown this way are called wood-decomposing fungi, a family of mushrooms in which tough, woody stems are characteristic. For these mushrooms, woody stems are a necessity; a tender, flimsy stem would not be able to establish growth in the tough environment of a log. (This hardiness amounts to more long-lived mushrooms, too; shiitakes exist in nature for several weeks without rotting.)

Common white button mushrooms, on the other hand, are raised in composted and sterilized manure. These materials decompose quickly by nature, and the mushrooms grown in them are significantly more delicate with respect to texture and longevity; all but the very ends of their stems are perfectly edible.

2	tablespoons unsalted butter
2	tablespoons extra-virgin olive oil
3–4	large shallots, chopped fine (about 1 cup)
3	medium garlic cloves, minced or pressed through a garlic press
10	ounces shiitake mushrooms, stems discarded, caps wiped clean and sliced 1/4 inch thick
10	ounces cremini mushrooms, wiped clean and sliced 1/4 inch thick
	Salt
1	tablespoon plus 1 teaspoon minced fresh thyme leaves
1 1/4	cups low-sodium chicken broth
1/2	cup heavy cream
1	tablespoon juice from 1 lemon
	Ground black pepper
1	pound campanelli or farfalle
2	ounces Parmesan cheese, freshly grated (1 cup)
2	tablespoons minced fresh parsley leaves

1. Bring 4 quarts water to a rolling boil in a large pot.

2. Meanwhile, heat the butter and oil in a 12-inch skillet over medium heat until foaming. Add the shallots and cook, stirring occasionally, until softened and translucent, about 4 minutes. Add the garlic and cook until fragrant, about 30 seconds. Increase the heat to medium-high; add the shiitakes and cook, stirring occasionally, for 2 minutes. Add the cremini and 1/2 teaspoon salt; cook, stirring occasionally, until the moisture released by the mushrooms has evaporated and the mushrooms are golden brown, about 8 minutes. Stir in the thyme and cook 30 seconds. Transfer the mushrooms to a bowl and set aside. Add the chicken broth to the skillet and bring to a boil, scraping up the browned bits on the bottom of the pan; off the heat, stir in the cream, lemon juice, and salt and pepper to taste.

3. Add 1 tablespoon salt and the pasta to the boiling water and stir to separate the noodles. Cook until just shy of al dente. Drain and return the pasta to the pot.

4. Add the mushrooms, chicken broth–cream mixture, cheese, and parsley to the pasta. Toss over medium-low heat until the cheese melts and the pasta absorbs most of the liquid, about 2 minutes. Serve immediately.

➤ VARIATIONS

Pasta with Mushrooms, Peas, and Camembert

Follow the recipe for Pasta with Sautéed Mushrooms and Thyme, omitting the thyme and adding 1 cup frozen peas, thawed, to the skillet along with the chicken broth; substitute 6 ounces Camembert, cut into 1/2-inch cubes (do not remove the rind) for the Parmesan, and 2 tablespoons finely chopped chives for the parsley. Proceed as directed.

Pasta with Mushrooms, Pancetta, and Sage

Cook 4 ounces pancetta, cut into 1/4-inch cubes, in 2 tablespoons olive oil, stirring occasionally, until lightly browned and crisp, about 6 minutes. Using a slotted spoon, transfer the pancetta to a paper towel–lined plate. Follow the recipe for Pasta with Sautéed Mushrooms and Thyme, substituting the fat in the skillet for the butter and olive oil and an equal amount of minced fresh sage leaves for the thyme; add the pancetta to the pasta along with the sautéed mushrooms in step 4. Proceed as directed.

PASTA WITH BROCCOLI SAUCE

BROCCOLI AND PASTA MAKE A HANDSOME PAIRING. The crisp texture and hearty flavor of broccoli marry well with the mild wheaty tones and tender texture of pasta. The problem is figuring out how to properly cook the broccoli. Generally, we are subjected to broccoli's extremes: mushy and overcooked, or undercooked and bland. We set out to find broccoli's happy medium—crisp, sweet, and tender.

First we tried boiling the broccoli in the pasta water. Picking the vegetables from the water was a bit awkward and beat up the broccoli quite a bit, so we rejected that option. Next we steamed the broccoli in a steaming basket, then sautéed it with extra-virgin olive oil and lots of garlic. The results were good, but working with the two pans was a bother. We wondered if we could simply sauté the florets and stalks in a frying pan with oil, but we found that the relatively dry heat took a while to penetrate and cook the vegetables. We were able to speed things up by adding water to the pan. When the cold water hit the hot pan, it turned into steam, and the moisture quickly turned the broccoli bright green and tender. The combination of both dry and moist heat did the trick.

As far as flavorings go, broccoli has an affinity for garlic and anchovies but also works well with sausage and peppers.

Spaghetti with Broccoli, Garlic, and Anchovies

SERVES 4 TO 6

The garlic can be reduced if you desire a less potent dish.

	Salt
1	pound spaghetti
4	tablespoons extra-virgin olive oil
5	anchovy fillets, minced to a paste (2 teaspoons)
9	medium garlic cloves, minced or pressed through a garlic press (3 tablespoons)
1/2	teaspoon red pepper flakes
2	pounds broccoli (about 1 large bunch), florets cut into 1-inch pieces; stalks peeled, halved lengthwise, and cut into 1/4-inch pieces
1/2	cup water
3	tablespoons chopped fresh parsley leaves
2	ounces Parmesan cheese, freshly grated (1 cup)

1. Bring 4 quarts water to a rolling boil in a large pot. Add 1 tablespoon salt and the pasta to the boiling water and stir to separate the noodles. Cook until al dente.

2. Meanwhile, combine 2 tablespoons of the oil, the minced anchovies, garlic, red pepper flakes, and 1/2 teaspoon salt in a 12-inch nonstick skillet. Cook, stirring constantly, over medium-high heat until fragrant, about 3 minutes. Increase the heat to high, add the broccoli and water, cover, and cook until the broccoli begins to turn bright green, 1 to 2 minutes. Uncover and cook, stirring frequently, until the water has evaporated and the broccoli is tender, 3 to 5 minutes longer.

3. Drain the pasta and return it to the pot.

4. Add the broccoli mixture, the remaining 2 tablespoons oil, the parsley, and cheese to the pasta and toss to combine. Serve immediately.

Orecchiette with Broccoli, Sausage, and Roasted Peppers

SERVES 4 TO 6

Orecchiette is small, ear-shaped pasta. Small shells also work well with this chunky sauce.

	Salt
1	pound orecchiette
4	ounces sweet Italian sausage, casings removed
9	medium garlic cloves, minced or pressed through a garlic press (3 tablespoons)
1	cup jarred roasted red peppers, cut into 1/2-inch squares
1/2	teaspoon ground black pepper
2	pounds broccoli (about 1 large bunch), florets cut into 1-inch pieces; stalks peeled, halved lengthwise, and cut into 1/4-inch pieces

MINCING ANCHOVIES

Anchovies often stick to the side of a chef's knife, making it hard to cut them into small bits. Here are two better ways to mince them.

A. Use a dinner fork to mash delicate anchovy fillets into a paste. Mash the fillets on a small plate to catch any oil the anchovies give off.

B. A garlic press will turn anchovies into a fine puree. This method is especially handy when you have already dirtied the press with garlic.

½   cup water
1   tablespoon extra-virgin olive oil
2   ounces Pecorino Romano cheese, freshly
     grated (1 cup)

1. Bring 4 quarts water to a rolling boil in a large pot. Add 1 tablespoon salt and the pasta to the boiling water and stir to separate the noodles. Cook until al dente. Drain and return the pasta to the pot.

2. While the pasta is cooking, cook the sausage in a 12-inch nonstick skillet over medium-high heat, breaking it into small pieces with a spoon, until browned, about 5 minutes. Stir in the garlic, roasted red peppers, ½ teaspoon salt, and the black pepper. Cook, stirring constantly, until fragrant, about 2 minutes. Increase the heat to high, add the broccoli and water, cover, and cook until the broccoli begins to turn bright green, 1 to 2 minutes. Uncover and cook, stirring frequently, until the water has evaporated and the broccoli is tender, 3 to 5 minutes longer.

3. Add the broccoli mixture, oil, and cheese to the pasta and toss to combine. Serve immediately.

EQUIPMENT: Cheese Graters

In the old days, you grated cheese on the fine teeth of a box grater. Now cheese graters come in several distinct designs. Unfortunately, many of them don't work all that well. With some designs, you need Herculean strength to move the cheese over the teeth with sufficient pressure for grating; with others, you eventually discover that a large portion of the grated cheese has remained jammed in the grater instead of going where it belongs, on your food. Whether you are dusting a plate of pasta or grating a full cup of cheese to use in a recipe, a good grater should be easy to use and efficient.

We rounded up 15 models and set about determining which was the best grater. We found five basic configurations. Four-sided box graters have different-size holes on each side to allow for both fine grating and coarse shredding. Flat graters consist of a flat sheet of metal that is punched through with fine teeth and attached to some type of handle. With rotary graters, you put a small chunk of cheese in a hopper and use a handle to press it down against a crank-operated grating wheel. Porcelain dish graters have raised teeth in the center and a well around the outside edge to collect the grated cheese. We also found a model that uses an electric motor to push and rotate small chunks of cheese against a grating disk.

After grating more than 10 pounds of Parmesan cheese, we concluded that success was due to a combination of sharp grating teeth, a comfortable handle or grip, and good leverage for pressing the cheese onto the grater. Our favorite model was a flat grater based on a small, maneuverable woodworking tool called a rasp. Shaped like a ruler, but with lots and lots of tiny, sharp raised teeth, the Microplane Grater (as it is called) can grate large quantities of cheese smoothly and almost effortlessly. The black plastic handle, which we found more comfortable than any of the others, also earned high praise. Other flat graters also scored well.

What about traditional box graters? Box graters can deliver good results and can do more than just grate hard cheese. However, if grating hard cheese is the task at hand, a box grater is not our first choice.

We also had good results with rotary graters made from metal, but we did not like flimsy versions made from plastic. A metal arm is rigid enough to do some of the work of pushing the cheese down onto the grating drum. The arms on the plastic models we tested flexed too much against the cheese, thus requiring extra pressure to force the cheese down. Hand strain set in quickly. A rotary grater can also chop nuts finely and grate chocolate.

The two porcelain dish graters we tested were duds; the teeth were quite ineffective. And the electric grater was a loser of monumental proportions. True, the grating effort required was next to nothing, but so were the results. A child could have grated cheese faster and more efficiently.

THE BEST GRATER

The Microplane Grater has very sharp teeth and a solid handle, which together make grating cheese a breeze. This grater also makes quick work of ginger and citrus zest.

SPAGHETTI WITH CLAM SAUCE

TOO OFTEN, SPAGHETTI WITH CLAM SAUCE IS A soggy mess of canned clams tossed with over-cooked pasta. We knew we could do better, especially if we used fresh clams.

First we decided to identify the best clams and figure out the best way to cook them. In Italy, tiny clams are often used for this dish, but we couldn't find these clams in the United States unless we begged them from chefs. So we began by buying the tiniest littlenecks we could find. This helped somewhat, but with clams selling for about $5 a dozen regardless of size, a simple pasta dish for four quickly became an extravagance.

We tried the larger cherrystones and even giant quahogs (they're all the same species, just increasingly bigger specimens), lightly steamed and chopped into pieces. But no matter how long or short we cooked them, they were tough, and they lacked the distinctive, fresh brininess of littlenecks. However, we did learn something: Large, less palatable, and far less expensive clams gave us the same kind of delicious clam juice—the backbone of this dish—as small clams.

Then we found cockles, which are almost as small as the baby clams you find in Italy. Because they are sold by the pound, not the dozen, and because they are small, cockles are less expensive than littlenecks. They are also quite delicious. Unfortunately, they're not nearly as widely available as littlenecks. As for choosing littlenecks, the littler, the better, and at least six (preferably eight or more) per person.

Because we still favored using all littlenecks, our dish remained quite expensive. So we resolved that if we were going to pay a small fortune for the dish, we would make sure that it would be uniformly wonderful each time we cooked it. There were three problems with our original recipe, we thought. One was that the clam meat tended to become overcooked in the time it took to finish the sauce; another was that there was often not enough clam juice; finally, we thought that the sauce itself could use another dimension of flavor.

Solving the first problem was easy: We cooked

TWO TYPES OF CLAMS

Quahogs (left) flavor the broth, but littlenecks (right) provide the meat for the pasta sauce.

the clams first, only until they gave up their juices. Then we recombined the clams with the sauce at the last minute, just enough to reheat them.

Next we turned to the occasional dearth of clam juice. When we were too cheap to buy enough littlenecks or couldn't find cockles, we combined a couple dozen littlenecks with about six large quahogs, which we could often buy for just a few dollars. Because it was the juice we were after—not the clam meat—this worked out fine; we simply discarded the quahog meat after cooking it.

We liked the flavor of white wine mixed with clam juice, but we did not like using more than ½ cup or so because its distinctive flavor was somewhat overwhelming. Cutting back on the wine, though, robbed the dish of needed acidity. We added just a little bit of diced plum tomato, barely enough to color the sauce. The benefits were immediate: Not only was the flavor balanced, but another welcome texture was added to the dish.

Satisfied at last, we pronounced ourselves done. With the final recipe, you can steam the clams open while bringing the pasta water to a boil and preparing the other ingredients. Once the clams are done, begin browning the garlic; five minutes later, put in the pasta and finish the sauce. The timing is perfect, and perfectly easy.

Spaghetti with Fresh Clam Sauce

SERVES 4

You can save money by using large, inexpensive quahogs, which provide plenty of liquid for a briny, brothy dish, for about half the price of littlenecks. Because quahogs are so cheap, discard the steamed meat without guilt and dine on the sweet, tender littlenecks with the pasta.

24	littleneck clams (the smaller the better), scrubbed thoroughly (see illustration 1 below)
6	quahog or chowder clams (the larger the better), scrubbed thoroughly
1/2	cup dry white wine
	Pinch cayenne pepper
1/4	cup extra-virgin olive oil
2	medium garlic cloves, minced or pressed through a garlic press
1	large or 2 small plum tomatoes, peeled, seeded, and minced
	Salt
1	pound spaghetti, linguine, or other long-strand pasta
1/3	cup chopped fresh parsley leaves

1. Bring 4 quarts water to a rolling boil in a large pot.

2. Meanwhile, bring the clams, wine, and cayenne to a boil in a deep 10- to 12-inch covered skillet over high heat. Boil, shaking the pan occasionally, until the littlenecks just begin to open (try to catch the clams before they open completely), 3 to 5 minutes. Transfer the littlenecks with a slotted spoon to a medium bowl; set aside. Re-cover the pan and continue cooking the quahogs until their liquid is released, about 5 minutes longer. Discard the quahogs; strain the liquid in the pan through a paper towel–lined sieve into a large measuring cup (see illustration 2 at left). Add enough water to make 1 cup; set aside. Wipe clean the skillet.

3. Heat the oil and garlic in the cleaned skillet over medium-low heat until the garlic turns pale gold, about 5 minutes. Add the tomatoes, raise the heat to high, and sauté until the tomatoes soften, about 2 minutes longer. Add the littlenecks and cover; cook until all the clams open completely, 1 to 2 minutes longer.

4. Meanwhile, add 1 tablespoon salt and the pasta to the boiling water and stir to separate the noodles. Cook until al dente, 7 to 9 minutes. Drain the pasta, transfer it to the skillet with the sauce, and toss. Add the reserved clam liquid and cook until the flavors meld, about 30 seconds. Stir in the parsley, adjust the seasonings, and serve immediately.

PREPARING CLAMS FOR SAUCE

1. Scrub the clams with a soft brush under running water to remove any sand from their shells.

2. To remove any grit from the clam cooking liquid, strain it through a sieve lined with a single layer of paper towel (or a coffee filter) and set over a measuring cup. If desired, moisten the towel first so that it does not absorb any precious clam juice.

SHRIMP FRA DIAVOLO

FRA DIAVOLO, WITH ITS ABUNDANCE OF HOT red pepper and attendant fiery nature, may be named for the devil—its literal translation from the Italian is "brother devil"—but it can do an angel's work for home cooks. How so? Shrimp fra diavolo, a seriously garlicky, spicy, winey tomato sauce studded with shrimp and served over pasta, takes less than 30 minutes to prepare from start to finish. It's a standard restaurant dish that easily makes the transition to home cooking.

That's not to say that this dish doesn't have its challenges, as we discovered after dining on shrimp fra diavolo in restaurants all over Boston's Italian neighborhood, the North End, and then trying published recipes back in the test kitchen. Overall, the sauces we sampled lacked depth and unity of flavor—backbone, if you will. The shrimp contributed little to the overall flavor of the sauce, serving merely as a bulky, lifeless garnish. Ditto the garlic, the flavor of which was often unpleasantly sharp, even acrid. In our ideal fra diavolo, not only would the shrimp themselves be firm, sweet, and well seasoned, but they would commit their flavor to the sauce as well.

Determined as we were to maximize the flavor of the shrimp, they seemed like the natural starting point for our investigation. We made sauces with several species of shrimp (all large, or 31 to 40 shrimp to the pound), and, as we had found in earlier tests with other shrimp dishes, we preferred Mexican and Gulf Whites equally, followed by Black Tiger shrimp, which are the most widely available.

We learned during testing that the way the shrimp are cooked does have a tremendous effect not just on their texture and flavor but also on the overall flavor of the sauce. Most fra diavolo recipes we encountered add plain raw shrimp to the almost finished sauce; in effect, this means the shrimp are braised in the sauce. While these shrimp do remain tender, our tasters agreed that their flavor was barely developed. We tried seasoning the shrimp with olive oil, salt, and red pepper flakes, searing them quickly in a very hot pan, and then adding them to the sauce just before serving. Every taster noted that the shrimp themselves—and therefore the sauce—had a stronger, more unified flavor. The sear also benefited the red pepper flakes, as they now contributed an earthy, toasty note in addition to heat.

Though the searing helped, we wanted to coax still more flavor from the shrimp. Several of the fra diavolo recipes we consulted included cognac.

We added cognac to the pan with the seared shrimp and flambéed it for a minute until the flame petered out. The combined forces of cognac and flame made a difference in the flavor. Not only did many tasters detect the spirit's own complexity, but they also felt that the shrimp tasted a little stronger. This sauce had backbone, which we'd missed in the restaurant versions. All this and drama, too, in an easy, one-minute step.

Curious about why the shrimp flambéed in cognac tasted better, we contacted Dr. Susan Brewer in the department of food science and human nutrition at the University of Illinois in Urbana. She noted that brandy contains hundreds of compounds that undergo profound changes at the roughly 400-degree temperatures of a flambé. The reason for this change is isomerization, a process in which heat changes the structure of sugar molecules. A session with the infrared thermometer in our test kitchen confirmed that the flame does burn at more than 400 degrees. We went on to test Brewer's suggestion by tasting side by side sauces in which the shrimp and cognac had been flambéed and not. Indeed, tasters noted a slightly fuller, sweeter flavor in the sauce in which the shrimp and cognac had been flambéed.

Fra diavolo's satanic associations arise from its liberal doses of garlic and spicy chile heat. We wanted enough garlic to make the devil proud, and we were frankly surprised to find that tasters agreed, preferring sauces that packed the wallop of almost an entire head, or about eight large cloves, over those with lesser amounts. But there was a caveat: Though we wanted the flavor of browned garlic, we had to mitigate the bitterness that often comes with it. We experimented with cutting the garlic in slices and slivers, grating it, pureeing it, and adding it to the sauce at various times, none of which eliminated the bitterness completely. Then we borrowed the stellar technique from our recipe for Pasta with Garlic and Oil (page 239), wherein a similar quantity of garlic is sautéed slowly over low heat until it becomes golden, sticky, mellow, and nutty. What was good for aglio e olio proved good for fra diavolo; the bitterness was gone, and the sauce acquired a sweeter, deeper dimension.

Taking another cue from the aglio e olio recipe, we reserved a tablespoon of raw garlic to add to the sauce at the end of cooking, along with a splash of raw olive oil. The tasters appreciated the bright, fruity, high flavor notes of these raw ingredients, which complemented the bass notes grounding the sauce.

Chile adds fiery heat to fra diavolo. Traditionally, red pepper flakes get the job done, but we also tested cayenne and hot pepper sauce, alone and in various combinations. Though tasters did not detect significant flavor differences, neither cayenne nor pepper sauce bested the traditional pepper flakes, so we stuck with the tried and true.

Our last tests focused on fra diavolo's two remaining major components: tomatoes and wine. We tested canned diced tomatoes (drained of excess liquid), canned crushed tomatoes, canned whole tomatoes (which we chopped by hand), and fresh tomatoes. The winner was drained canned diced tomatoes. The tasters were likewise united behind white wine over its rivals, red wine and white vermouth. The red wine was judged "muddy" and "sour" and the vermouth too herbal. We had been bothered by the compounded acidity of the tomatoes and wine, so we tried adding a little bit of sugar, which balanced the acidity perfectly. We finally had a top-notch shrimp fra diavolo—and the devil by the nose.

Shrimp Fra Diavolo with Linguine

SERVES 4 TO 6

One teaspoon of red pepper flakes will give the sauce a little kick, but add more to suit your taste.

1	pound large shrimp (31 to 40 per pound), peeled and deveined, if desired
1	teaspoon red pepper flakes
6	tablespoons extra-virgin olive oil
	Salt
1/4	cup cognac or brandy
12	medium garlic cloves, minced or pressed through a garlic press (about 1/4 cup)
1/2	teaspoon sugar
1	(28-ounce) can diced tomatoes, drained
1	cup medium-dry white wine, such as Sauvignon Blanc
1/4	cup minced fresh parsley leaves
1	pound linguine or spaghetti

1. Bring 4 quarts water to a rolling boil in a large pot.

2. Meanwhile, heat a heavy-bottomed 12-inch skillet over high heat until the pan is very hot. Toss the shrimp, 1/2 teaspoon of the red pepper flakes, 2 tablespoons of the oil, and 3/4 teaspoon salt in a medium bowl. Add the shrimp to the skillet and quickly spread out in a single layer. Cook without stirring until the bottoms of the shrimp turn spotty brown, 30 to 45 seconds. Off the heat, stir to turn the shrimp, then add the cognac. Let stand off the heat until the cognac warms slightly, about 5 seconds, then return the pan to high heat. Wave a lit match over the skillet until the cognac ignites. Shake the skillet until the flames subside, then transfer the shrimp to a medium bowl and set aside.

3. Off the heat, cool the now-empty skillet for 2 minutes. Return the skillet to the burner and reduce the heat to low. Add 3 tablespoons of the oil and 3 tablespoons of the garlic. Cook, stirring constantly, until the garlic foams and is sticky and straw-colored, 7 to 10 minutes. Add the remaining 1/2 teaspoon red pepper flakes, 3/4 teaspoon salt, the sugar, tomatoes, and wine. Increase the heat to medium-high and simmer until thickened and fragrant, about 8 minutes.

4. While the sauce simmers, add the linguine and 1 tablespoon salt to the boiling water and stir to separate the noodles. Cook until al dente. Reserve 1/3 cup of the pasta cooking water and drain the pasta. Return the pasta to the pot, add about 1/2 cup sauce and 2 to 3 tablespoons of the reserved pasta cooking water, and toss to coat.

5. Stir the reserved shrimp and accumulated juices, remaining 1 tablespoon garlic, and the parsley into the sauce and simmer until the shrimp are heated through, about 1 minute longer. Off the heat, stir in the remaining 1 tablespoon oil. Divide the pasta among warmed individual bowls, top with a portion of the sauce and shrimp, and serve immediately.

➤ VARIATION
Scallops Fra Diavolo with Linguine
The scallops leave more flavorful drippings in the skillet than do the shrimp, and these drippings can make the garlic appear straw-colored before it is done cooking. Make sure that the garlic is fragrant, looks sticky, and has cooked for the full 7 to 10 minutes.

Follow the recipe for Shrimp Fra Diavolo with Linguine, replacing the shrimp with 1 pound sea scallops, tendons removed.

FRESH PASTA

SOME SAUCES (ESPECIALLY THOSE WITH cream) require fresh egg pasta. Filled pasta (such as ravioli) starts with homemade pasta. We wanted to develop a foolproof recipe for basic fresh egg pasta. This meant figuring out the proper ratio of eggs to flour as well as the role of salt and olive oil in the dough. Most recipes start with all-purpose flour, but we figured it was worth testing various kinds of flour. Perhaps most important, we wanted to devise a kneading method that was quick and easy.

Before beginning to develop our pasta dough recipe, we wanted to settle on a basic technique. Pasta dough can be made three ways. Traditionally, the dough is made by hand on a clean counter. The flour is formed into a ring, the eggs are cracked into the center, and the flour is slowly worked into the eggs with a fork. When the eggs are no longer runny, hand-kneading begins. The whole process takes at least 20 minutes and requires a lot of hand strength.

Another option is an electric pasta maker that kneads the dough and cuts it into various shapes. Although these machines have some limited appeal, they are quite expensive. We find that a food processor makes pasta dough much more quickly than the old-fashioned hand method. As most cooks already own a food processor, we recommend it for making fresh pasta dough.

Most recipes for fresh egg pasta start with three eggs and then add various amounts of flour. A three-egg dough will produce about one pound of fresh pasta, so this seemed like a good place to start our working recipe. We saw recipes that called for as little as ½ cup of flour per egg. Other recipes called for as much as ¾ cup of flour per egg. After several tests, we settled on ⅔ cup of flour per egg, or 2 cups of all-purpose flour for 3 eggs.

In most tests, this ratio produced perfect pasta dough without adjustments. However, on a few occasions, the dough was a bit dry. This seemed to happen on dry days, but it also could be that slight variations in egg size threw off the ratio. It

PASTA DOUGH DONE RIGHT

Pasta dough can be a bit tricky to get just right. Higher-protein flour will absorb the eggs more readily than lower-protein flour, and the resulting dough may be dry. During the summer, flour holds more moisture, so the dough may turn out a bit wet. Here's how to judge the consistency of the pasta dough and make adjustments in the food processor.

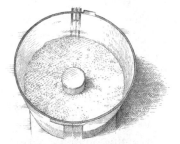

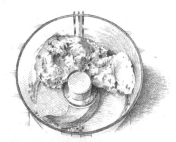

DRY DOUGH
If after 30 seconds of processing the dough resembles small pebbles, it is too dry. With the motor running, add ½ teaspoon water. Repeat one more time, if necessary.

WET DOUGH
If the dough sticks to the sides of the workbowl, it is too wet. Add 1 tablespoon flour at a time until the dough is no longer tacky.

PERFECT DOUGH
Dough that has the right amount of moisture will come together in one large mass. To incorporate the small bits in the workbowl, turn the contents onto a floured surface and knead them together.

was easy enough to add a little water to bring the dough together. The dough was almost never too wet, which was a good thing. It's much harder to add flour to a sticky dough than it is to add a little water to a dry, crumbly dough.

Once the dough came together, we found it beneficial to knead it by hand for a minute or two. Besides, the motor on our food processor started to labor before the dough was smooth enough. Taking the dough out as soon as it came together prevented our food processor from overheating.

At this point, we had a recipe and a method for making pasta dough that we liked a lot. It seemed time to start testing additional flavorings. We found no benefit from adding salt to the dough. If the pasta is cooked in salted water or stock, it will taste well seasoned. Adding olive oil makes fresh

pasta a bit slick, and the olive oil flavor seems out of place in many recipes.

We had been using unbleached all-purpose flour in our tests. We then tested several brands of bleached all-purpose flour and found only minimal differences in the way each flour absorbed the egg. We could not detect any significant differences in flavor. On the other hand, high-protein bread flour and low-protein cake flour had disastrous effects. Bread flour produced a very tough dough that was hard to handle. Pasta dough should be supple and elastic, not stiff and difficult to stretch. At the opposite end of the spectrum, pasta made with cake flour was too soft and crumbly; the dough did not have enough structure. Cake flour also has a sour chemical flavor that is obscured by sugar and butter in cake but comes through loud and clear in pasta.

ROLLING OUT PASTA DOUGH

1. Cut about one sixth of the dough from the ball and flatten in into a disk. Run the disk through the rollers set to the widest position.

2. Bring the ends of the dough toward the middle and press down to seal.

3. Feed the open side of the pasta through the rollers. Repeat steps 1 and 2.

4. Without folding again, run the pasta through the widest setting twice, or until the dough is smooth. If the dough is at all sticky, lightly dust it with flour.

5. Begin to roll the pasta thinner by putting it through the machine repeatedly, narrowing the setting each time. Roll until the dough is thin and satiny, dusting with flour if sticky. You should be able to see the outline of your hand through the pasta. Lay the pasta on a clean kitchen towel and cover it with a damp cloth. Repeat with the other pieces of dough.

6. To make fettuccine, run each sheet through the wide cutter on the pasta machine. Each noodle will measure ⅛ to ¼ inch across.

273

With our dough made, it was time to test rolling techniques. Many Italian sources tout the superiority of hand-rolled pasta. However, every time we rolled pasta dough with a pin, it was too thick. Although thick fettuccine is not an abomination, pasta for tortellini, with its doubled edges, must be thin. Perhaps after years of practice we could roll pasta dough thin enough, but for now we prefer a hand-cranked manual pasta machine. We tested the Imperia and Atlas pasta machines—the two major brands in Italy and widely available in cookware shops in the United States—and found them equally good at turning dough into thin, smooth, satiny sheets of pasta.

Fresh Egg Pasta
MAKES ABOUT I POUND

Although the food processor does most of the work, you must finish kneading this dough by hand. Keep pressing and folding the dough until it is extremely smooth. For more detailed information on making the pasta dough, see page 272.

2   cups (10 ounces) unbleached all-purpose flour
3   large eggs, beaten

1. Pulse the flour in a food processor fitted with a steel blade to distribute and aerate it evenly. Add the eggs; process until the dough forms a rough ball, about 30 seconds. (If the dough resembles small pebbles, add water, ½ teaspoon at a time; if the dough sticks to the side of the workbowl, add flour, 1 tablespoon at a time, and process until the dough forms a rough ball.)

2. Turn the dough ball and small bits out onto a dry work surface; knead until the dough is smooth, 1 to 2 minutes. Cover with plastic wrap and set aside for at least 15 minutes or up to 2 hours to relax. (The pasta dough can also be wrapped well in plastic wrap and kept refrigerated up to 1 day before rolling out.)

3. Using a manual pasta machine, roll out the dough (see illustrations 1 through 5 on page 273). Leave the pasta as is for use in filled pastas. Cut the pasta sheets into long strands to make fettuccine (see illustration 6 on page 273).

PASTA WITH BUTTER AND CHEESE

SAUCES THAT DERIVE MOST OF THEIR FLAVOR from butter and/or cheese are among the simplest in any cook's repertoire. They require minimal work and can usually be prepared in the time it takes to bring four quarts of water to a boil and cook the pasta.

It goes without saying that pasta with butter and cheese is the simplest version of this sauce. We recommend using unsalted butter in this pasta dish (and all your cooking, for that matter). Salted butter does not have the same fresh dairy flavor as sweet butter. Also, manufacturers add varying amounts of salt, which makes it difficult to judge how much more salt a dish might require. We prefer to add salt directly to a dish, not through the butter.

Many butter and cheese sauces are traditionally served over fresh pasta. We wanted to understand the logic behind the recommendation, so we tested a simple butter and Parmesan sauce with both fresh and dried pasta. We felt that fresh pasta was far superior to dried pasta. Fresh noodles absorbed some of the butter, which slid off dried noodles. Also, the egg flavor of good fresh pasta melded better with the butter and cheese, making for more complex dishes.

Unless you plan to flavor the butter (with herbs, for instance), there's no reason to melt it. Simply toss the drained pasta and sauce over low heat to give the noodles a chance to absorb the butter and cheese. Softened butter is a must, but otherwise this sauce requires no planning or cooking.

As for the ratio of ingredients, our tests found that 6 tablespoons butter and ½ cup freshly grated Parmesan cheese made the best sauce.

Fettuccine with Butter and Parmesan
SERVES 4

One of the simplest and best pasta dishes, this should be made with fresh egg noodles. When we tested this dish with dried pasta, we were quite disappointed. The sauce slid off the dried noodles and pooled in the bottom of each serving bowl. In contrast, the fresh noodles absorbed some sauce (and thus tasted better), and the remaining sauce clung to these noodles much more tenaciously.

     Salt
1   recipe Fresh Egg Pasta (page 274), cut into fettuccine
6   tablespoons (³⁄₄ stick) unsalted butter, softened
1   ounce Parmesan cheese, freshly grated (¹⁄₂ cup), plus more for serving

Bring 4 quarts water to a rolling boil in a large pot. Add 1 tablespoon salt and the pasta to the boiling water and stir to separate the noodles. Cook just until al dente. Drain the pasta and return it to the cooking pot. Add the butter and Parmesan and cook over low heat, tossing to combine the ingredients, for 1 minute. Adjust the seasonings, adding salt to taste. Serve immediately, passing more Parmesan at the table.

➤ VARIATION

Fettuccine with Sage Butter

Other fresh, highly aromatic herbs, such as rosemary and thyme, may be used similarly. We found it best to let the herbs steep in the melted butter for 5 minutes, enough time for the butter to be perfumed with—but not overwhelmed by—the flavor of the sage.

Place 5 tablespoons butter and 2 tablespoons minced fresh sage leaves in a sauté pan large enough to accommodate the cooked pasta. Heat over low until the butter is melted. Turn off the heat and set aside for 5 minutes to allow the sage to flavor the butter. Cook the fresh pasta as directed in the recipe for Fettuccine with Butter and Parmesan. Drain and add the pasta to the sauté pan. Add the Parmesan cheese and cook over low heat, tossing to combine the ingredients and flavors, 1 to 2 minutes. Adjust the seasonings and serve immediately, passing more cheese at the table.

FETTUCCINE ALFREDO

THE MOST FAMOUS CREAM SAUCE FOR PASTA is commonly called Alfredo. When fettuccine Alfredo is good, it is worth every calorie, but the sauce is often thick and gloppy; at other times, it is too runny and just sits at the bottom of the bowl. We wanted to develop a foolproof sauce that was thick enough to coat pasta from end to end without becoming dry or lumpy.

We started out with a composite recipe and decided to test cooking methods first. Some sources suggest reducing the cream to thicken its texture. Others merely heat the cream. Some just pour room-temperature cream over drained pasta. We found problems with all three methods.

If all the cream is reduced, the sauce becomes too thick and does not easily coat the noodles. However, if the cream is just warmed (or left unheated), it remains too liquidy and pools around the pasta. We decided to test reducing part of the cream to give the sauce enough body to cling to the pasta, then adding the remaining cream to the sauce along with the cooked pasta. This worked beautifully. After several tests, we settled on a total of 1⅔ cups cream for one pound of pasta and bringing most of the cream (1⅓ cups) to a simmer to reduce it slightly. Once the cream comes to a bare simmer, remove the pan from the heat to prevent the cream from cooking down too much.

In the spirit of trying weird suggestions, we experimented with a few recipes that called for whipping the cream lightly instead of reducing it to give it body. As might be expected, this did not work. The sauce was fluffy and odd on pasta. Save whipped cream for dessert.

Because the butter must be melted for this sauce, we decided to add it directly to the cream. We tested as little as two tablespoons and as much as two sticks. Five tablespoons was just right, providing the right amount of lubrication to the pasta and a good, buttery flavor. To round out the sauce, we settled on a cup of freshly grated Parmesan cheese and some salt, pepper, and nutmeg.

We tested our working recipe with ultrapasteurized as well as pasteurized cream. Ultrapasteurized cream is the standard in most markets. It is subjected to high temperatures during pasteurization to promote a longer shelf life. This process gives the cream a slightly cooked flavor, which we could taste in a blind test against a sauce made with pasteurized

INGREDIENTS: Fresh Pasta

While you cannot get any fresher than homemade pasta—which is surprisingly simple to do—few home cooks are willing to make pasta from scratch. The alternatives include shopping at a market that makes pasta fresh on-site or purchasing the "fresh" packaged pasta at the supermarket. You can also forgo the fresh approach and purchase dried egg pasta, which is manufactured under numerous brand names and sold in supermarkets and specialty stores. Which option, we wondered, is the best?

As expected, the homemade pasta in our tasting stood out for its soft, delicate chew and clean flavor. Also relatively agreeable to our panel of tasters were a couple of brands of fresh refrigerator pasta and a common supermarket brand of dried egg pasta. Tasters gave decent marks to refrigerated fresh fettuccine made by Contadina Buitoni (which is available nationwide) as well as Monterey Pasta Company (available mostly in California). They also liked Ronzoni dried egg fettuccine, which is available nationwide.

In the process of doing this tasting, though, we found that fresh is a relative term. Unlike homemade fresh pasta, with its two ingredients, the "fresh" refrigerator egg pasta found in supermarkets, as well as the dried egg pasta, are hybrids, made with the semolina flour and water ordinarily used for dried pasta, but with eggs added in. The higher-protein semolina flour, which can absorb more liquid than all-purpose flour, automatically compromises the delicacy of the noodles' consistency. That is not to say, however, that they had the chew of eggless dried pasta; they simply could not compare with the delicacy of homemade. Also, the addition of water to these noodles (and the fact that some contain egg whites rather than whole eggs) seemed to dilute the fresh egg flavor usually associated with homemade pasta. This was particularly true with the dried egg pasta.

Perhaps our biggest quibble with fresh refrigerator pasta, though, is that it is not really fresh at all. Unless your supermarket has a high rate of turnover, you may be buying a product that has been sitting on the shelf for weeks.

Fresh pasta is extremely perishable because it is high in moisture, which provides an ideal breeding ground for bacteria. Naturally occurring enzymes also exist that will, over time, discolor the pasta as well as modify its fats. These changes in the fats produce off flavors, according to Jim Jacobs, technical director at Northern Crops Institute, a learning center in Fargo, North Dakota, devoted to the study of the use of wheats, including durum, in food products. Consequently, the majority of fresh pasta products sold in supermarkets are both pasteurized and sealed in something called modified atmosphere packaging so as to extend their shelf life. This packaging method involves extracting air from inside the package and substituting it with another gas, typically a mix of carbon dioxide and nitrogen. This inhibits the growth of bacteria and helps extend the pasta's shelf life by 25 to 120 days, depending on the product as well as the specific technology used.

Even though a fresh refrigerated pasta product can be safe to eat for as many as four months after its manufacture, this does not mean that time does not take its toll; it is possible that the pasta will have sat long enough for its texture to degrade from tender and soft to mushy.

One last point, regarding the price. Most packages are just 9 ounces. Because most recipes call for either 12 or 16 ounces of fresh pasta, you end up buying two packages and spending nearly $6. Besides the expense, you inevitably have a few ounces left over. A 1-pound package of dried pasta serves four to six for about $1. If money is really a concern, set aside a few hours on a Saturday afternoon to make your own homemade noodles (the actual hands-on time is less than an hour) and serve your guests genuinely fresh pasta for pennies.

THE BEST FETTUCCINE

HOMEMADE FETTUCCINE
The clear favorite, with springy yet resilient texture and pure flavor.

CONTADINA BUITONI FETTUCCINE
This supermarket brand is a decent second choice with good chew but little egg flavor.

MONTEREY PASTA COMPANY FETTUCCINE
This pasta, found mostly in supermarkets in California, is a bit thicker than the others and tastes more like wheat than eggs.

RONZONI FETTUCCINE
This dried pasta is made with eggs and has a clean, almost sweet flavor. The noodles are thicker and heartier than homemade.

cream. Pasteurized cream won hands-down.

Pasteurized cream is heated during processing, but to a lower temperature that kills bacteria but doesn't prolong shelf life. In our tests, it had a fresher, sweeter cream flavor, and we think it is worth searching out this product when making cream sauces. (It also makes great whipped cream.) Many organic creams are pasteurized, so check out the organic dairy section in your supermarket or visit a natural food store.

Until this point, we had been using our own homemade fettuccine in tests. We decided to test store-bought fresh fettuccine as well as dried fettuccine with our Alfredo sauce.

Dried fettuccine was a disappointment. When cooked, dried pasta is much less porous than fresh, and the cream sauce did not adhere well to the noodles. When we finished eating, there still was sauce in the bottom of the bowls.

The package of mass-market fresh fettuccine from the supermarket refrigerator case cooked up a bit gummy (a common problem with these products) and did not have much flavor. This pasta would do in a pinch, but it was a far cry from homemade. On the other hand, store-bought fettuccine that had been freshly made at a local gourmet shop was quite good, holding on to every drop of sauce and adding a nice egg flavor to the dish.

Some sources suggest cooking the fresh pasta a little firmer than usual and then finishing the cooking process right in the cream sauce. We tested this method against pasta that was fully cooked and sauced and much preferred it. The sauce really penetrates the noodles, and the combination of creamy sauce and fresh egg pasta is unbeatable.

Some final observations. The dish may look a bit soupy as you divide it among individual serving bowls. However, the pasta will continue to absorb sauce as it sits in the bowls. In fact, pasta that looks perfect going into bowls will be too dry by the time you start eating. Lukewarm cream sauces are not appetizing, so heating the pasta bowls is a must. Fettuccine Alfredo is also very rich. We prefer to serve it in small portions as an appetizer. A few bites more than satisfy any longing for creamy richness.

Finally, this basic sauce lends itself to numerous variations. We tested several possibilities, and tasters responded most favorably to lemon, Gorgonzola, and prosciutto (separately, not together). We developed variations for each of these ingredients.

Fettuccine Alfredo
SERVES 6 AS AN APPETIZER

Do not cook the sauce over too high a flame or for too long, or it will be gluey instead of creamy. Fresh egg pasta is a must here; dried pasta can't stand up to the richness of the Alfredo ingredients. You can substitute one pound of high-quality purchased fresh fettuccine for our homemade pasta. Make sure to cook your pasta extra-firm, as it will cook further (and absorb some of the butter and cream) when added to the sauce.

1²/₃	cups heavy cream, preferably not ultrapasteurized
5	tablespoons unsalted butter
	Salt
1	recipe Fresh Egg Pasta (page 274), cut into fettuccine
2	ounces Parmesan cheese, freshly grated (1 cup)
	Ground black pepper
	Pinch freshly grated nutmeg

1. Bring 4 quarts water to a rolling boil in a large pot.

2. Combine 1⅓ cups of the cream and the butter in a sauté pan large enough to accommodate the cooked pasta. Heat over low until the butter is melted and the cream comes to a bare simmer. Turn off the heat and set aside.

3. When the water comes to a boil, add 1 tablespoon salt and the pasta to the boiling water and stir to separate the noodles. Cook until almost al dente. Drain the pasta and add it to the sauté pan. Add the remaining ⅓ cup cream, the Parmesan, ½ teaspoon salt, pepper to taste, and the nutmeg. Cook over very low heat, tossing to combine the ingredients, until the sauce is slightly thickened, 1 to 2 minutes. Serve the fettuccine immediately in heated pasta bowls.

Fettuccine with Lemon and Cream

Follow the recipe for Fettuccine Alfredo, heating ¼ cup fresh lemon juice with the cream and butter in step 2 and tossing 2 teaspoons grated lemon zest with the pasta and sauce in step 3.

Fettuccine with Gorgonzola and Cream

Sweet Gorgonzola, sometimes labeled Gorgonzola dolce, is milder than the harder, drier aged Gorgonzola and makes for a slightly piquant but still creamy variation on Alfredo sauce. It is available at cheese shops, Italian delis, and many supermarkets.

Follow the recipe for Fettuccine Alfredo, stirring 4 ounces sweet Gorgonzola cheese, crumbled, into the heated cream and butter mixture in step 2. Proceed as directed.

Fettuccine with Prosciutto and Cream

For this recipe, we like prosciutto cut into ¼-inch-thick slices and then diced; prosciutto sliced paper-thin seems to disappear into the sauce and noodles.

Follow the recipe for Fettuccine Alfredo, cooking ¼ pound prosciutto, cut into ¼-inch dice, in the butter just until softened, about 2 minutes. Add the cream and bring to a bare simmer. Proceed as directed.

RAVIOLI

RAVIOLI, AS ARE ALL FILLED PASTAS, ARE AMONG the rare treats that the home cook is best equipped to execute properly. Commercial ravioli are tough and doughy, not supple and tender like homemade versions. Ravioli made by hand at a gourmet pasta shop or Italian market can be every bit as good as those made at home, but, in our experience, you are well-advised to walk past packages of ravioli in the supermarket refrigerator case.

Of course, making filled pasta strikes fear into many home cooks, who expect the job to be impossibly difficult and time-consuming. After making countless batches of ravioli, we must admit that these fears are at least partially true. Ravioli need not be difficult to prepare, but they are time-consuming to make. Each piece must be

shaped by hand, and that takes time.

We don't make this statement lightly. We're certainly not averse to shortcuts and were more than willing to try the various ravioli-making gadgets sold in any well-stocked kitchen shop. Sadly, we must report that the gimmicks we tried for making quick ravioli don't really work.

We began with the attachments that can be fitted onto a manual pasta machine to turn out ravioli. It looks so easy. Take two sheets of pasta, some filling, and turn out hundreds of ravioli in minutes. Unfortunately, we had problems with the pasta sticking together and can't recommend these attachments. We threw away at least half the ravioli we made because they were misshapen or broken.

Likewise, we were disappointed with the metal molds sometimes used by pasta shops. They seemed more trouble than they are worth, as the pasta sheets must be cut precisely to fit in the molds. The other choice is to waste a lot of fresh pasta, but, given the amount of time and effort it takes to make the pasta, that doesn't make much sense. In the end, we found that cutting and shaping the pasta dough by hand is the most straightforward and foolproof way to make filled pasta.

Because ravioli have doubled edges where the pasta is folded over the filling and sealed together, we found that the pasta sheets must be rolled as thin as possible. Otherwise, the edges may remain too chewy when the rest of the pasta shape is already cooked through. Use the last setting on a manual pasta machine for the best results.

The biggest problem most home cooks encounter when making ravioli is that the pieces sometimes open up when they are boiled. There's nothing worse than seeing all the filling floating around the pot, so it's imperative to seal the edges of each piece properly. We tried brushing the edges of the dough with water and with lightly beaten egg. We found that both made the dough sticky and harder to handle. We had the best results when we used the pasta sheet as quickly as possible, when it was still moist and pliable. Pasta sheets that have been left out to dry (even for just 20 to 30 minutes) will be too brittle to manipulate. If your dough has become dry, brushing the edges lightly with water is best. (Eggs just make a sticky mess.) Just be careful to brush the edges lightly, or the dough will become very tacky.

To guarantee that the pasta does not dry out, we recommend that you roll one sheet of dough at a time, then fill and shape it. Once the first batch of ravioli is made, start over again with another piece of pasta dough, running it through the pasta machine and then cutting and filling it as directed.

Don't overload the pasta with filling, which might cause the pasta shape to burst in the boiling water. A rounded teaspoon of filling is more than enough for a medium ravioli. As an added precaution, cook the pasta in water that is at a low boil. Highly agitated water may actually rip open delicate pasta shapes.

To prevent the ravioli from sticking together in the pot, we found it necessary to cook the pasta in two batches. While the second batch is in the pot, you can sauce the first batch and bring it to the table. Warmed pasta bowls will keep the pasta hot while you finish cooking the remaining pasta. If you prefer, brings two pots of water to a boil and divide the pasta between the two pots to cook it all at one time.

Given the work involved, we wanted to be able to shape the ravioli in advance and then cook them as desired. (You don't want to be shaping ravioli while dinner guests wait.) We found it best to transfer shaped ravioli to a lightly floured baking sheet. (The flour helps prevent sticking.) If you are not going to cook the pasta right away, stash the baking sheets in the refrigerator for up to two hours. After that, we found, the pasta dried out. For longer storage, we discovered that the freezer is the best place for ravioli. Place the floured baking sheets in the freezer until the pasta shapes are frozen solid, about two hours. Transfer the frozen pastas to a large zipper-lock plastic bag and freeze them for up to a month. Don't defrost frozen pasta; simply drop it into boiling water and add a minute or two to the cooking time.

MAKING RAVIOLI

1. Use a pizza wheel or sharp knife to cut one fresh pasta sheet at a time into long rectangles measuring 4 inches across. Place small balls of filling (about 1 rounded teaspoon each) in a line 1 inch from the bottom of the pasta sheet. Leave 1¼ inches between the balls of filling.

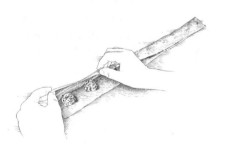

2. Fold over the top of the pasta and line it up with the bottom edge. Seal the bottom and the two open sides with your finger.

3. Use a fluted pastry wheel to cut along the two sides and bottom of the sealed pasta sheet.

4. Run the pastry wheel between the balls of filling to cut out the ravioli.

Most any finely chopped or ground meat, seafood, poultry, or vegetable can be turned into a filling for ravioli, but there are a couple of guidelines. Most fillings have cheese to add flavor and a creamy texture. Fillings also contain egg yolk, which helps bind the ingredients. When we tested fillings without egg yolk, they tended to be runny and thin. We found it best to add just the yolk, which has most of the egg's thickening powers, and omit the watery white.

A liquidy filling will become even runnier when the pasta is cooked, so juices from vegetables should be cooked off, and some very loose ingredients, such tomatoes, are best not included in fillings. For these reasons, we think a plain cheese and herb filling, or one made with ground meat, is the easiest to work with. We decided to offer both choices.

We find that simple sauces are best with filled pastas. You don't want to overwhelm the filling, which you have worked hard to make and should be the focal point for your taste buds. Ravioli is delicious with melted butter and a sprinkling of grated Parmesan cheese. When you want to sauce the pasta a bit more elaborately, a fairly smooth tomato sauce that will stick to the pasta (not slide off) is best. Tasters liked a tomato sauce made with butter; the butter flavor complemented the fresh egg pasta. Minced carrot and onion give this sauce a sweetness that contrasts nicely with both the cheese and the meat filling.

Ravioli

SERVES 4 TO 6 AS A MAIN COURSE
OR 8 AS A FIRST COURSE

This recipe produces 2-inch-square ravioli with 3 cut edges and 1 folded edge. The folded edge may be trimmed with a fluted pastry wheel, if you like. For a smooth, more refined sauce, puree the mixture in a food processor or blender, return the pureed sauce to the pan, stir in ½ cup heavy cream, and cook, stirring constantly, until the sauce thickens, about 2 minutes.

RAVIOLI

- 1 recipe Fresh Egg Pasta (page 274)
- 1 recipe Parsley and Ricotta Filling or Meat and Ricotta Filling (recipes follow)

SIMPLE TOMATO SAUCE

- 3 tablespoons unsalted butter
- 1 small onion, minced
- 1 medium carrot, peeled and minced
- 1 (28-ounce) can diced tomatoes
  Salt
- 2 tablespoons minced fresh basil or parsley leaves

- 1 tablespoon salt
  Freshly grated Parmesan cheese for serving

1. FOR THE RAVIOLI: Follow the illustrations on page 279 to form and fill the ravioli.

2. FOR THE SAUCE: Melt the butter in a medium saucepan. Add the onion and carrot; cook over medium heat until the vegetables soften but are not browned, about 10 minutes. Stir in the tomatoes with their juice and ½ teaspoon salt; simmer until thickened slightly, about 10 minutes. Stir in the basil and adjust the seasonings.

3. TO COOK AND SAUCE THE RAVIOLI: Bring 4 quarts water to a rolling boil in a large pot. Add the salt and half the ravioli and stir gently to separate. Cook, lowering the heat if necessary to keep the water at a gentle boil, until the doubled edges are al dente, 4 to 5 minutes. With a slotted spoon, transfer the ravioli to warmed serving bowls or plates; add some sauce. Meanwhile, put the remaining ravioli in the boiling water and repeat the cooking and saucing process. Serve immediately, passing the Parmesan cheese separately.

Parsley and Ricotta Filling

MAKES ABOUT 2½ CUPS

The simplest pasta filling, as it requires no cooking. Other herbs—basil or mint—may be substituted.

- 1 cup whole-milk ricotta cheese
- 1½ ounces Parmesan cheese, freshly grated (¾ cup)
- 1 large egg yolk
- ½ cup minced fresh parsley leaves
- ½ teaspoon salt
  Ground black pepper

Combine the ricotta, Parmesan, egg yolk, parsley, salt, and pepper to taste in a medium bowl. (The filling can be covered and refrigerated overnight.)

Meat and Ricotta Filling
MAKES ABOUT 2 1/2 CUPS
This filling is delicious with ground beef, veal, and/or pork. Use any combination of these meats.

I	tablespoon extra-virgin olive oil
2	medium garlic cloves, minced or pressed through a garlic press
1/2	pound ground meat (see note)
I	cup whole-milk ricotta cheese
1/4	cup freshly grated Parmesan cheese
I	large egg yolk
1/4	cup minced fresh basil leaves
1/2	teaspoon salt
	Ground black pepper

1. Heat the oil in a medium skillet. Add the garlic and sauté until lightly colored, about 1 minute. Add the meat; cook over medium-high heat, stirring to break up larger pieces, until the liquid evaporates and the meat browns, 3 to 4 minutes. Drain off the fat; transfer the meat mixture to a medium bowl. Cool slightly.

2. Stir in the remaining ingredients, including pepper to taste. (The filling can be covered and refrigerated overnight.)

HEARTY MEAT LASAGNA

MOST FAMILIES HAVE HOMEMADE LASAGNA once, maybe twice a year, on holidays (especially if you are Italian) or birthdays. Lasagna is not enjoyed more frequently because it takes the better part of a day to boil the noodles, slow-cook the sauce, prepare and layer the ingredients, and then finally bake it off. Although this traditional method does produce a superior dish, we were interested in an Americanized version, one that could be made in two hours or less from start to finish. We would have to sacrifice some of the rich flavors of a traditional recipe, but we were hoping to produce a lasagna good enough for a family gathering. A bland, watery casserole just wouldn't do.

We knew from the start that to expedite the lasagna-making process, we would have to use no-boil lasagna noodles. After a few initial tests, we discovered that the secret of no-boil noodles in this lasagna is to leave your tomato sauce a little on the watery side. The noodles can then absorb liquid without drying out the dish overall. With all this in mind, we got to work on the other components of the lasagna.

Italian cooks build the sauce from the meaty browned bits left in the pan from the meatballs and Italian sausages they cook and later layer into the lasagna. By combining top-quality tomato products with a four-hour simmer, they make a rich, thick, and complex-tasting sauce. We were after the same depth of flavor, but, as time was of the essence, meatballs and a slow simmer were out of the question. We began by concentrating on different kinds of ground meat.

Working with a base of sautéed aromatics (onions and garlic), an all-beef sauce turned out to be one-dimensional and dull. Adding ground pork was an improvement and certainly made the combination more interesting. Although the pairing of beef and sweet Italian sausage (removed from its casing and browned with the beef) was even better, tasters were still left wanting. Finally, we turned to meat loaf mix, a combination of equal parts ground beef, pork, and veal sold in one package at most supermarkets. The flavor of the sauce this trio produced was robust and sweet. The texture wasn't right, though; it was still too loose and taco-like. We wanted something richer, creamier, and more cohesive, so our thoughts turned to Bolognese (see page 254), the classic meat sauce enriched with dairy. Borrowing the notion of combining meat and dairy, we reduced a quarter cup of cream with the meat before adding the tomatoes. The ground meat soaked up the sweet cream, and the final product was rich and decadent. Even better, at this point we had been at the stove for only 12 minutes.

Because no-boil noodles rely primarily on the liquid in the sauce to rehydrate and soften, we had to get the moisture content just right. If the sauce was too thick, the noodles would be dry and crunchy; too loose and they would turn flaccid, limp, and lifeless. We started building the sauce with two 28-ounce cans of pureed tomatoes, but tasters found this sauce too heavy for the lasagna, overwhelming the other flavors. Two 28-ounce cans of diced tomatoes yielded too thin a sauce. We settled on one 28-ounce can of each. The combination of pureed and diced tomatoes yielded a luxurious sauce, with soft but substantial chunks of tomatoes. We added the tomatoes to the meat mixture, warmed it through (no reduction necessary), and in just 15 minutes on the stove the meat sauce was rich, creamy, ultra-meaty, and ready to go.

Most Americans like their lasagna to be cheesy. It was a given that we would sprinkle each layer with mozzarella cheese—the classic lasagna cheese—and, after a test of whole versus part-skim, we found that whole-milk mozzarella was the best for the job. It had a more intense flavor than its part-skim counterpart and nicer melting qualities, which are crucial to this dish. We also tested shredded, bagged mozzarella, but because it has a very low moisture content, it melted oddly and was somewhat dry, not to mention unappetizing. Shredding a 1-pound block of whole-milk mozzarella on a box grater or in the food processor is the ticket.

Ricotta was the next cheese up for scrutiny. As it turned out, it made little difference whether we used whole-milk or part-skim ricotta. Each was characteristically creamy and rich, and tasters gave them both a thumbs up.

For added sharpness, we tested the ricotta mixture with Parmesan and Pecorino Romano. Tasters unanimously rejected the Pecorino for giving the lasagna a "sheepy" and "gamey" flavor. Grated Parmesan added a nice little kick to the mild, milky ricotta. An egg helped to thicken and bind this mixture, and some chopped basil added flavor and freshness. Tucked neatly between the layers of lasagna, this ricotta mixture was just what we were after.

With all the components of the lasagna decided, it was time to concentrate on the layering procedure. Smearing the entire bottom of a

13 by 9-inch glass dish with some of the sauce was the starting point. Next came the first layer of no-boil noodles, which we topped with ricotta, then mozzarella, and, finally, meat sauce. We built two more layers using this same formula. For the fourth and final layer, we covered the pasta with the remaining meat sauce and remaining mozzarella and then sprinkled the top with grated Parmesan.

In our tests, we found that covering the lasagna with foil from the outset of baking prevented the loss of moisture and helped soften the noodles properly. Removing the foil for the last 25 minutes of baking ensured that the top layer of cheese turned golden brown. An oven temperature of 375 degrees proved ideal. By the time the top was browned, the noodles had softened.

We found that lasagna made with no-boil noodles takes a little longer in the oven than conventional lasagna. The real time savings is in the preparation. Start to finish, the meat and tomato lasagna took about 1½ hours to make: 40 minutes prep time, 40 minutes in the oven, and 10 minutes to rest. Measuring the final product against an authentic Italian lasagna may not be entirely fair, but having the time to make it on a weeknight, or whenever the craving strikes, is satisfying beyond compare.

Hearty Meat Lasagna

SERVES 6 TO 8

If you can't find meat loaf mix for the sauce, or if you choose not to eat veal, substitute ½ pound ground beef and ½ pound sweet Italian sausage, casings removed, for the meat loaf mix. The assembled, unbaked lasagna, if wrapped tightly in plastic wrap and then in foil, will keep in the freezer for up to 2 months. To bake, defrost it in the refrigerator for a day or two and bake as directed, extending the baking time by about 5 minutes.

TOMATO-MEAT SAUCE

1	tablespoon olive oil
1	medium onion, chopped fine
6	medium garlic cloves, minced or pressed through a garlic press

I	pound meat loaf mix or $^1/_3$ pound each ground beef chuck, ground veal, and ground pork (see note)
$^1/_2$	teaspoon salt
$^1/_2$	teaspoon ground black pepper
$^1/_4$	cup heavy cream
I	(28-ounce) can pureed tomatoes
I	(28-ounce) can diced tomatoes, drained

RICOTTA, MOZZARELLA,
AND PASTA LAYERS

15	ounces whole-milk or part-skim ricotta cheese ($1^3/_4$ cups)
$2^1/_2$	ounces Parmesan cheese, freshly grated ($1^1/_4$ cups)
$^1/_2$	cup chopped fresh basil leaves
I	large egg, lightly beaten
$^1/_2$	teaspoon salt
$^1/_2$	teaspoon ground black pepper
12	no-boil lasagna noodles
I	pound whole-milk mozzarella cheese, shredded (4 cups)

1. Adjust an oven rack to the middle position and heat the oven to 375 degrees.

2. FOR THE SAUCE: Heat the oil in a large, heavy-bottomed Dutch oven over medium heat until shimmering but not smoking, about 2 minutes; add the onion and cook, stirring occasionally, until softened but not browned, about 2 minutes. Add the garlic and cook until fragrant, about 2 minutes. Increase the heat to medium-high and add the ground meat, salt, and pepper; cook, breaking the meat into small pieces with a wooden spoon, until the meat loses its raw color but has not browned, about 4 minutes. Add the cream and simmer, stirring occasionally, until the liquid evaporates and only the fat remains, about 4 minutes. Add the pureed and drained diced tomatoes and bring to a simmer; reduce the heat to low and simmer slowly until the flavors are blended, about 3 minutes; set the sauce aside. (The sauce can be cooled, covered, and refrigerated for 2 days; reheat before assembling the lasagna.)

3. FOR THE LAYERS: Mix the ricotta, 1 cup of the Parmesan, the basil, egg, salt, and pepper in a

medium bowl with a fork until well combined and creamy; set aside.

4. Smear the entire bottom of a 13 by 9-inch baking dish with ¼ cup of the meat sauce (avoiding large chunks of meat). Place 3 noodles in the baking dish to create the first layer. Drop 3 tablespoons of the ricotta mixture down the center of each noodle and level the domed mounds by pressing with the back side of a measuring spoon. Sprinkle the layer evenly with 1 cup of the shredded mozzarella cheese. Spoon 1½ cups of the meat sauce evenly over the cheese. Repeat the layering of noodles, ricotta, mozzarella, and sauce two more times. Place the 3 remaining noodles on top of the sauce, spread the remaining sauce over the noodles, sprinkle with the remaining 1 cup mozzarella, then with the remaining ¼ cup Parmesan. Lightly spray a large sheet of foil with nonstick cooking spray and cover the lasagna.

5. Bake 15 minutes, then remove the foil. Return the lasagna to the oven and continue to bake until the cheese is spotty brown and the sauce is bubbling, about 25 minutes longer. Cool the lasagna about 10 minutes; cut into pieces and serve.

SPINACH LASAGNA

IN NORTHERN ITALY, WHERE TRADITIONAL spinach lasagna has its roots, cooks keep things simple, combining layers of homemade pasta, fresh spinach, béchamel (white sauce), and cheese. Given its delicate flavors and straightforward ingredient list, it makes an ideal entrée for informal dinner parties. Yet the Americanized recipes we've encountered invariably fail.

The problem (but not the solution) is simple enough. Most American cookbook authors call for convenient no-boil (also called oven-ready) noodles, whereas traditional Italian recipes use homemade fresh pasta. Lasagna made with fresh pasta, which cooks in an instant, requires only a brief stay in the oven to give the separate layers a chance to bind. No-boil noodles are a different story. No matter what the brand, the instructions on the back of the box—which we confirmed in the test kitchen—insist on at least 45 minutes of baking. This long stint in the oven robs the spinach of its vibrancy, rendering it greenish gray and lifeless. The other complication is that béchamel—made with only milk, flour, and butter and serving as the necessary glue that holds the layers together—usually exhibits little more flavor than a squirt of Elmer's glue.

We knew we could rescue the spinach from ruin by shortening the baking time of the lasagna. As an interim solution, we used conventional lasagna noodles, cooked al dente, so that we could prepare test batches with 20-minute baking times. We dismissed frozen spinach because tasters consistently gave it low marks during preliminary tests. As for fresh spinach, two types are available at the market: tender baby leaves and the mature, crinkly variety. Though we generally favor the former, for this application the heartier crinkly spinach proved ideal; baby spinach was too fragile to withstand the punishing heat of the oven. We then made four lasagnas, preparing the crinkly spinach differently for each. Sautéed spinach took on a muddy flavor and baked up slimy. Finely chopped raw spinach retained a brilliant green color after baking but tasted grassy and underdone. Raw spinach that we wilted in the hot béchamel sauce didn't work; it took on an unappealingly wet texture. Blanching (dunking in boiling salted water, then shocking in an ice-water bath) was the solution, as it allowed the spinach to retain its verdant color and pure flavor. We wrapped the spinach in a kitchen towel and forcefully wrung out excess liquid to guard against soggy lasagna.

Béchamel is a classic milk sauce thickened with a roux. Because the sauce thickens considerably in the oven (as the noodles leach starch), we needed a béchamel on the lighter side, finally settling on 5 tablespoons butter, ¼ cup flour, and 3½ cups milk. Then we needed to add some flavor. A lone bay leaf plus seasoning with salt and pepper did little. Replacing part of the milk with chicken stock wasn't the answer—the resulting sauce was watery and salty. Lemon juice and lemon zest were rejected as well, judged by tasters as too acidic. We regrouped and sautéed a cup of minced shallots (they're sweeter and less harsh than onions) and plenty of garlic in butter before whisking in the

flour for the roux. To infuse the sauce with even more flavor, we added two potent bay leaves (kept fresh in the freezer, as is our custom in the test kitchen) and freshly grated nutmeg and then finished by stirring in some grated Parmesan cheese. Sprinklings of salt and pepper were the only other refinements we needed for a luxurious sauce that would complement, but not obliterate, the flavor of the spinach.

Most recipes for spinach lasagna call for both ricotta and mozzarella, but we wanted to try other options as well. Whole-milk ricotta was declared slightly heavy and grainy by the tasters. When we covertly added scoops of cottage cheese (pureed with an egg to smooth out its curds), not one taster could identify the mystery ingredient. Although heretical to any "real" northern Italian cook, it provided a pleasing tang and extra creaminess without the distinct, somewhat dry layer created by the ricotta. Finally, we tried replacing bland mozzarella with fontina, a creamy, semifirm Italian cheese with buttery, nutty tones. Its complex flavor was a welcome addition, and it also melts beautifully.

With approximately 40 lasagnas under our belts, we'd grown tired of the slick, cooked conventional noodles draped over every colander and bowl in the kitchen. We were determined to find a way to use no-boil noodles, despite our misgivings about their lengthy baking time. We covered a lasagna made with no-boil noodles with aluminum foil to trap the heat and cranked up the dial on the oven, but the lasagna still took too long to cook—the spinach was overdone, while the noodles remained chewy. Next we par-cooked no-boil noodles by soaking them in boiling water and met with some success, although it seemed ridiculous to be boiling water for no-boil noodles. The simpler solution—and the key to this recipe—was to soak the noodles in hot tap water for just 5 minutes. After only 20 minutes in a 425-degree oven, the noodles were perfectly cooked and, just as important, the spinach had maintained its vitality. The only cooking left to do involved a quick trip to the broiler to brown the cheese.

Spinach Lasagna

SERVES 6 TO 8

It's necessary to soak the no-boil lasagna noodles in this recipe because the lasagna doesn't bake as long as the Hearty Meat Lasagna on page 282. Be sure to use Italian fontina rather than bland and rubbery Danish or American fontina; if it is not available, substitute whole-milk mozzarella. To make the cheese easier to shred, freeze it for 30 minutes to firm it up. Because the lasagna is broiled at the end of cooking to brown the surface, make sure to use a baking dish that is broiler-safe.

SPINACH

1	tablespoon salt
2	(10-ounce) bags curly spinach, stemmed and rinsed

BÉCHAMEL

5	tablespoons unsalted butter
5	large shallots, minced (about 1 cup)
4	medium garlic cloves, minced or pressed through a garlic press (generous 1 tablespoon)
1/4	cup unbleached all-purpose flour
3 1/2	cups whole milk
2	bay leaves
3/4	teaspoon freshly grated nutmeg or 1/2 teaspoon ground nutmeg
1/2	teaspoon salt

1/4	teaspoon ground black pepper
1	ounce Parmesan cheese, freshly grated (1/2 cup)

CHEESES AND PASTA

8	ounces whole-milk cottage cheese
1	large egg
1/4	teaspoon salt
12	no-boil lasagna noodles from 1 box
1	tablespoon unsalted butter
2	ounces Parmesan cheese, freshly grated (1 cup)
8	ounces Italian fontina cheese, shredded (2 cups)

1. FOR THE SPINACH: Fill a large bowl with ice water. Bring 4 quarts water to a rolling boil in a large Dutch oven or stockpot over high heat; add the salt and spinach, stirring until the spinach is just wilted, about 5 seconds. Using a skimmer or fine-mesh strainer, transfer the spinach to the ice water and let stand until completely cool, about 1 minute, then drain the spinach and transfer it to a clean kitchen towel. Wrap the towel tightly around the spinach to form a ball and wring until dry. Chop the spinach medium and set aside.

2. FOR THE BÉCHAMEL: Melt the butter in a medium saucepan over medium heat until foaming; add the shallots and garlic and cook, stirring frequently, until the shallots are translucent,

---

BÉCHAMEL 101

Béchamel is a simple white sauce made with flour and butter (the roux) and milk. Béchamel is the base for a number of creamy dishes, including gratins, macaroni and cheese, and creamed spinach. For a proper béchamel, the flour must be adequately cooked to eliminate its raw taste and the milk slowly whisked in to prevent lumps.

1. Melt the butter until foaming, then whisk in the flour to make a white roux. Cook the roux for 1 1/2 to 2 minutes to eliminate any raw, floury flavor, but do not let brown.

2. Whisking constantly, slowly add the milk to the roux. (There's no need to scald the milk, as most recipes in our research direct.)

3. Bring the sauce to a low boil, whisking often, and let simmer about 10 minutes. The finished béchamel should be glossy, with the consistency of heavy cream.

about 4 minutes. Add the flour and cook, stirring constantly, for about 1½ minutes; do not brown. Gradually whisk in the milk. Bring the mixture to a boil over medium-high heat. Whisk in the bay leaves, nutmeg, salt, and pepper; reduce the heat to low and simmer 10 minutes, whisking occasionally. Whisk in the Parmesan and discard the bay leaves. Transfer the sauce to a bowl, press a piece of plastic wrap directly against the surface, and set aside.

3. FOR THE CHEESES, PASTA, AND ASSEMBLY: Blend the cottage cheese, egg, and salt in a food processor or blender until very smooth, about 30 seconds. Transfer to a bowl and set aside. Adjust an oven rack to the middle position and heat the oven to 425 degrees. Place the noodles in a 13 by 9-inch broiler-safe baking dish and cover with hot tap water; let soak 5 minutes, agitating the noodles occasionally to prevent sticking. Remove the noodles from the water and place in a single layer on a clean kitchen towel. Wipe the baking dish dry and coat with the butter. Use a rubber spatula to spread ½ cup of the béchamel over the bottom of the baking dish; position 3 noodles on top of the sauce. Stir the spinach into the remaining béchamel in the bowl, mixing well to break up the clumps of spinach (you should have about 4 cups spinach-béchamel mixture). Spread 1 cup of the spinach mixture evenly over the noodles, sprinkle evenly with the Parmesan, and top with 3 more noodles. Spread 1 cup spinach mixture evenly over the noodles, sprinkle evenly with 1 cup of the fontina, and top with 3 more noodles. Spread 1 cup spinach mixture evenly over the noodles, followed by the cottage cheese mixture. Finish with the remaining 3 noodles, the remaining 1 cup spinach mixture, and the remaining 1 cup fontina. Lightly spray a large sheet of foil with nonstick cooking spray and cover the lasagna. Bake until bubbling, about 20 minutes, then remove the foil. Remove the lasagna and adjust the oven rack to the uppermost position (about 6 inches from the heating element) and heat the broiler. Broil the lasagna until the cheese is spotty brown, 4 to 6 minutes. Cool 10 minutes, then cut into pieces and serve.

➤ VARIATIONS
Spinach Lasagna with Prosciutto

Follow the recipe for Spinach Lasagna through step 1. Heat 2 tablespoons of the butter for the béchamel in a medium saucepan over medium heat until foaming; add 2 ounces thinly sliced prosciutto, chopped medium, and cook, stirring frequently, until slightly crisp, about 4 minutes. Using a slotted spoon, remove the prosciutto to a small bowl. Add the remaining 3 tablespoons butter for the béchamel to the saucepan and continue with the recipe from step 2. When assembling the lasagna, sprinkle the prosciutto evenly over the cottage cheese mixture. Proceed as directed.

Spinach Lasagna with Mushrooms

Follow the recipe for Spinach Lasagna through step 1. Heat 2 tablespoons butter in a medium saucepan over medium heat until foaming; add 8 ounces white mushrooms, wiped clean, trimmed, and sliced ¼ inch thick. Cook the mushrooms until lightly browned, about 8 minutes; using a slotted spoon, transfer the mushrooms to a small bowl. Continue with the recipe from step 2, using the same saucepan used to cook the mushrooms to make the béchamel. When assembling the lasagna, distribute the mushrooms evenly over the cottage cheese mixture. Proceed as directed.

SOAKING NO-BOIL NOODLES

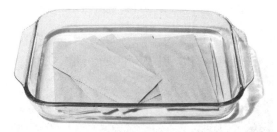

A five-minute soak in hot tap water dramatically reduces the baking time for the no-boil noodles in our Spinach Lasagna, allowing the spinach to remain fresh-looking and tasting. We tested five brands of no-boil noodles for that recipe and found them all to be adequate. We did, however, notice differences in various brands. Our favorite, Barilla, consists of very thin noodles that resemble fresh pasta; Barilla is available in supermarkets nationwide.

MACARONI AND CHEESE

WITH THE POSSIBLE EXCEPTION OF MEAT LOAF and fried chicken, few dishes are as personal as macaroni and cheese. Baked or stovetop, custard-based or little more than white sauce and pasta, with or without toasted bread crumbs, there must be a million recipes out there—surely enough to satisfy nearly everyone. Unfortunately, no one of these recipes can satisfy everyone at the same time. Sure, the kids would be fine with the contents of the blue-box brand, but for most adults this ready-mix mac and cheese lost its appeal soon after we learned how to boil water. Conversely, decadent recipes replete with cream, eggs, and a who's-who list of pungent cheeses are decidedly adults-only; just try to serve them to the kids and you'll get upturned noses and pushed-back plates.

To get our bearings, we scoured the aforementioned million recipes (or at least 40), starting with *Cook's* own recipe, published in January/February 1997. A custard-style macaroni and cheese, this recipe uses eggs and evaporated milk (as opposed to the more traditional whole milk) to prevent the custard from curdling (a common occurrence in recipes with eggs). Although a long-standing test kitchen favorite, this dish is incredibly rich. We wanted something simpler—but, as our next test revealed, not too simple. When we layered cooked pasta and cheese into a casserole dish, poured milk over the lot, and put the dish in the oven, the fat from the cheese separated and the result was a greasy mess. We concluded that the cheese needs some sort of binder—either eggs or flour.

We were now left with the path chosen by the vast majority of recipe writers: béchamel sauce. Béchamel is a white sauce made by cooking flour and butter to form a light roux. Milk is gradually whisked in and the béchamel is cooked until it thickens. Combined with cheese and partially cooked noodles, the mix is then poured into a casserole dish and baked.

Traditional recipes incorporate the cheese into the béchamel before stirring in par-cooked pasta and then baking until the sauce is bubbling hot and thick. It sure sounds easy. But no matter how much attention we paid, we just couldn't pull a great baked macaroni and cheese out of the oven. Sometimes the pasta was overcooked—a result of just one minute too many of boiling on the stovetop. Even worse were the batches made with undercooked noodles. We tried to remedy these by keeping the dishes in the oven longer (anywhere from 20 to 30 minutes), but after a while the bubbling cheese began to separate and the dishes took on an oily, grainy feel.

Frustrated, we pushed the idea of using the oven aside (to heck with tradition) and started working solely on the stovetop. Maybe we could better prevent the overcooking (and undercooking) of the pasta.

We made the next batch of sauce and boiled the pasta on the side. We cooked the pasta until it was a few minutes shy of being done, tossed it in with the sauce and cheese, and simmered it until the pasta was tender, which took a good 10 minutes. To our dismay, this batch had begun to separate, just like our oven-baked experiments, and the par-cooked pasta released its starch to the sauce, giving it a gritty feel. Next we cooked the pasta until very tender and quickly mixed it with the cheese and sauce. This time tasters thought that the noodles needed more time to absorb the sauce. We needed to cook the pasta less at the outset. Boiled until just past al dente, the noodles still had enough structure to stand up to the heat of the sauce for a few minutes without turning mushy, and the cheese sauce filled every nook and cranny.

We now decided to work on the correct proportions of butter to flour to milk, reasoning that the winning combination would provide the desired silky sauce. Béchamel recipes that used more butter than flour lacked cohesion. Those using equal parts butter and flour seemed heavy and dull. We had much better luck using slightly more flour than butter (6 tablespoons to 5 tablespoons, respectively). Just this little change cut enough of the richness that we were trying to avoid, and, when we added 5 cups of whole milk, there was plenty of sauce to smother the noodles.

Technically speaking, as soon as we added

cheese to the white sauce, it turned from béchamel to Mornay. We knew that choosing the right cheese (and using the right amount) would affect not only the flavor of the dish but also its texture. Indeed, an unpleasant grainy feel was introduced by hard cheeses such as Parmesan, Gruyère, and some aged cheddars, to say nothing of their overly distinct flavor. On the other hand, incredibly mild, soft cheeses such as mascarpone and ricotta contributed no flavor, and their creamy texture pushed the macaroni and cheese right back into sickly territory. In the end, what worked best were two cheeses—sharp cheddar for flavor and Monterey Jack for creaminess.

How much cheese to use? Many recipes called for twice as much cheese as pasta (we were using 1 pound of pasta). The result was a sticky, stringy macaroni and cheese that was off the charts in

SCIENCE: Two Cheeses Are Better Than One

Why are some cheese sauces velvety smooth while others have a texture like grit followed by a grease chaser? Because macaroni and cheese is nothing absent a great sauce, this question had to be answered. In testing various cheeses for our recipe, we came upon a dichotomy: Monterey Jack could provide appealing texture but only modest flavor, while cheddar brought the best flavor but rough texture. Curious about this, we started digging for answers.

A major distinction between Monterey Jack and cheddar is moisture content. Government regulations allow Jack cheese to have 5 percent more total moisture than cheddar, and more moisture makes a cheese easier to blend into a liquid. Moreover, cheddar cheese has more fat than Jack cheese. Aside from fat and water content, age also has a profound effect on how a cheese behaves when melted. Monterey Jack is never aged for more than a few months, but cheddar can be aged for years. As cheddar ages, casein, the primary protein in cheese, breaks down, and the strong flavor compounds we associate with good cheddar develop.

What does this difference in age mean for cheese sauce? Cheddar, particularly older cheddar, is gritty because the casein structure has been broken down. In contrast, Monterey Jack is creamy because the casein structure is more intact and therefore better able to retain fat and moisture. We learned that the combination of young Jack cheese with moderately aged cheddar gives both good texture and good flavor.

terms of richness. More frugal recipes seemed designed around an impending cheese shortage, using merely ½ pound of cheese to 1 pound of pasta. The result was more macaroni and milk than macaroni and cheese. We found that 1 pound of cheese was the perfect amount for 1 pound of pasta. Just the right texture and flavor, and easy to remember, too.

We were done, right? Wrong. Many of the tasters wanted at least the option of adding a toasty, golden topping of bread crumbs—a flashback to the baked versions. To keep to our stovetop commitment, we tossed homemade bread crumbs with melted butter and toasted them on the stovetop, then portioned them out over individual servings in generous amounts. But these crumbs seemed more like an afterthought than part of the dish. We weren't about to go back to baking the macaroni and cheese, but wondered if using the broiler instead for a quick blast of heat would work. We placed fresh buttered bread crumbs on top of the next batch of macaroni and cheese and placed it under the broiler. This was it. The broiler concentrated the heat right on the bread crumbs, turning them a deep, golden brown. Better still, the process took only a few minutes—yet it was just enough time to let the bottom of the crumbs sink into the cheese sauce and seem baked right in.

Classic Macaroni and Cheese

SERVES 6 TO 8 AS A MAIN COURSE
OR 10 TO 12 AS A SIDE DISH

It's crucial to cook the pasta until tender—that is, just past the "al dente" stage. In fact, it's better to overcook rather than undercook the pasta. Whole, low-fat, and skim milk all work well in this recipe. The recipe may be halved and baked in an 8-inch, square, broiler-safe baking dish. If desired, offer celery salt or hot sauce (such as Tabasco) for sprinkling at the table.

BREAD CRUMB TOPPING

6   slices (about 6 ounces) good-quality white
    sandwich bread, torn into rough pieces

3   tablespoons cold unsalted butter, cut into
    6 pieces

SOME FAILED EXPERIMENTS

OILY AND SEPARATED

CURDLED AND CLUMPY

RICH AND CLOYING

Some early tests revealed common problems with this recipe. When we layered the noodles, milk, and cheese (without first cooking them together) in the pan, the fat separated from the cheese and the macaroni and cheese was oily (top). When we added eggs to the recipe, they curdled and produced a lumpy sauce (center). Too much cheese made the macaroni so rich you could eat only two or three spoonfuls (bottom).

PASTA AND CHEESE

1	pound elbow macaroni
	Salt
5	tablespoons unsalted butter
6	tablespoons all-purpose flour
1½	teaspoons dry mustard
¼	teaspoon cayenne pepper (optional)
5	cups milk (see note)
8	ounces Monterey Jack cheese, shredded (2 cups)
8	ounces sharp cheddar cheese, shredded (2 cups)

1. FOR THE BREAD CRUMBS: Pulse the bread and butter in a food processor until the crumbs are no larger than ⅛ inch, ten to fifteen 1-second pulses. Set aside.

2. FOR THE PASTA AND CHEESE: Adjust an oven rack to the lower-middle position and heat the broiler. Bring 4 quarts water to a rolling boil in a Dutch oven over high heat. Add the macaroni and 1 tablespoon salt and stir to separate the noodles.

Cook until the pasta is tender. Drain in a colander and set aside.

3. In the now-empty Dutch oven, heat the butter over medium-high heat until foaming. Add the flour, mustard, and cayenne (if using) and whisk well to combine. Continue whisking until the mixture becomes fragrant and deepens in color, about 1 minute. Whisking constantly, gradually add the milk; bring the mixture to a boil, whisking constantly (the mixture must reach a full boil to fully thicken), then reduce the heat to medium and simmer, whisking occasionally, until thickened to the consistency of heavy cream, about 5 minutes. Off the heat, whisk in the cheeses and 1 teaspoon salt until the cheeses are fully melted. Add the pasta and cook over medium-low heat, stirring constantly, until the mixture is steaming and heated through, about 6 minutes.

4. Transfer the mixture to a broiler-safe 13 by 9-inch baking dish and sprinkle evenly with the bread crumbs. Broil until the crumbs are deep golden brown, 3 to 5 minutes, rotating the pan if necessary for even browning. Cool about 5 minutes, then serve.

➤ VARIATIONS

Macaroni and Cheese with Peas and Ham

Cut 8 ounces baked deli ham, sliced ¼ inch thick, into 1-inch squares. Follow the recipe for Classic Macaroni and Cheese, adding the chopped ham and 1 cup frozen peas to the cheese sauce along with the pasta. Proceed as directed.

Macaroni and Cheese with Kielbasa and Mustard

Cut 8 ounces smoked kielbasa lengthwise into quarters, then cut each quarter crosswise into ½-inch slices. Follow the recipe for Classic Macaroni and Cheese; in step 3, add 1 medium onion, chopped fine, to the foaming butter and cook, stirring occasionally, until the onion begins to brown, about 6 minutes. Add the flour to the onion and continue with the recipe, reducing the salt in the sauce to ½ teaspoon and adding the sliced kielbasa and 4 teaspoons whole-grain Dijon mustard to the cheese sauce along with the pasta. Proceed as directed.

BAKED FOUR-CHEESE PASTA

WE LOVE CLASSIC MACARONI AND CHEESE, BUT sometimes we get a hankering for the Italian version, *pasta ai quattro formaggi*. This hearty casserole is a silky-smooth blending of pasta and four cheeses that is rich but not heavy. In reality, however, it often turns into an inedible mess: tasteless, stringy, heavy, and greasy. We wanted to discover what made this dish great in the first place, delivering a pasta dinner that lived up to its sophisticated reputation.

Of course, the cheese was the first issue in terms of both flavor and texture. We were committed to Italian cheeses, but this barely diminished the choices—research turned up varying combinations and amounts (1 cup to 6½ cups cheese per 1 pound pasta) of Asiago, fontina, Taleggio, Pecorino Romano, mascarpone, mozzarella, Gorgonzola, Parmesan, and ricotta. Initial testing reduced the scope quickly: Mascarpone and ricotta added to neither flavor nor texture, and Asiago was bland. Pasta tossed with mozzarella was gooey and greasy, whereas Taleggio was not only difficult to obtain but also made the pasta too rich and gluey. After testing numerous combinations of the remaining cheeses, tasters favored a 2½-cup combination of Italian fontina (which is creamier and better-tasting than versions of this cheese made elsewhere), Gorgonzola, Pecorino Romano, and Parmesan.

Both heating the cheeses and cream together and adding the cheeses separately to the hot pasta produced nasty messes. Each attempt caused the cheeses to curdle, separate, and/or turn greasy. Some recipes solved this problem by beginning with a *besciamella* (known in French as a *béchamel*). This basic white sauce is made by cooking butter and flour and then adding milk or cream. The cheeses can then be added to the white sauce, which because of the flour doesn't separate. The white sauce did keep the sauce from breaking, but it also had an unintended side effect: The flavors of the cheeses were diminished. The solution was to radically reduce the amount of flour and butter to two teaspoons each (instead of the usual three to four tablespoons

each). Now the sauce was silky and smooth, and the flavors of the cheeses stood out.

After making this recipe a half dozen more times, we were bothered by the notion of heating the cheeses ahead of time with the béchamel. We wanted to cook the cheeses as little as possible for the best flavor, so we put the shredded/crumbled/grated cheeses in a large bowl and added the hot pasta and hot béchamel. A quick toss melted the cheeses without cooking them. We had now both simplified the recipe and produced a cleaner-tasting, more flavorful dish.

Tubular pasta shapes (we found penne to be ideal) allow the sauce to coat the pasta inside and out and are the best choice. Many recipes suggest cooking the pasta fully and then baking it for 20 to 30 minutes. This is a recipe for mushiness. To keep the pasta from overcooking, we found it necessary to drain the pasta several minutes before it was al dente and then minimize the baking time. Just seven minutes in a 500-degree oven (the pasta heats more quickly in a shallow baking dish) is enough to turn the pasta and sauce into a casserole.

Many recipes add a bread crumb topping that browns and crisps in the oven. We tried this casserole with and without the crumb topping, and tasters unanimously voted for the topping. It contrasts nicely with the creamy pasta and helps balance the richness of the sauce.

❧

Baked Four-Cheese Pasta

SERVES 4 TO 6 AS A MAIN COURSE
OR 6 TO 8 AS A SIDE DISH

BREAD CRUMB TOPPING

3–4	slices white sandwich bread, each slice torn into quarters
¼	cup freshly grated Parmesan cheese
¼	teaspoon salt
⅛	teaspoon ground black pepper

PASTA AND CHEESE

1	pound penne
	Salt
4	ounces Italian fontina cheese, shredded (about 1 cup)

3 ounces Gorgonzola cheese, crumbled (about ¾ cup)

1 ounce Pecorino Romano cheese, freshly grated (½ cup)

½ ounce Parmesan cheese, freshly grated (¼ cup)

2 teaspoons unsalted butter

2 teaspoons all-purpose flour

1½ cups heavy cream

¼ teaspoon ground black pepper

1. FOR THE TOPPING: Pulse the bread in a food processor until the mixture resembles coarse crumbs, about ten 1-second pulses (you should have about 1½ cups). Transfer to a small bowl; stir in the Parmesan, salt, and pepper. Set aside.

2. FOR THE PASTA: Adjust an oven rack to the middle position and heat the oven to 500 degrees. Bring 4 quarts water to a rolling boil in a large pot. Add the pasta and 1 tablespoon salt to the boiling water and stir to separate the pasta. While the pasta is cooking, combine the cheeses in a large bowl; set aside.

3. Melt the butter in a small saucepan over medium-low heat; whisk the flour into the butter until no lumps remain, about 30 seconds. Gradually whisk in the cream, increase the heat to medium, and bring to a boil, stirring occasionally; reduce the heat to medium-low and simmer 1 minute to ensure that the flour cooks. Stir in ¼ teaspoon salt and the pepper; cover the cream mixture to keep hot and set aside.

4. When the pasta is very al dente (when bitten into, the pasta should be opaque and slightly underdone at the very center), drain about 5 seconds, leaving the pasta slightly wet. Add the pasta to the bowl with the cheeses; immediately pour the cream mixture over, then cover the bowl with foil or a large plate and let stand 3 minutes. Uncover the bowl and stir with a rubber spatula, scraping the bottom of the bowl, until the cheeses are melted and the mixture is thoroughly combined.

5. Transfer the pasta to a 13 by 9-inch baking dish and sprinkle evenly with the reserved bread crumbs, pressing down lightly. Bake until the topping is golden brown, about 7 minutes. Serve immediately.

➤ VARIATIONS

Baked Four-Cheese Pasta with Tomatoes and Basil

Follow the recipe for Baked Four-Cheese Pasta, adding one (14.5-ounce) can diced tomatoes, drained, to the pasta along with the cream mixture and stirring in ¼ cup coarsely chopped fresh basil leaves just before transferring the pasta to the baking dish. Proceed as directed.

Baked Four-Cheese Pasta with Prosciutto and Peas

Follow the recipe for Baked Four-Cheese Pasta, omitting the salt from the cream mixture and adding 4 ounces prosciutto, chopped, and 1 cup frozen peas to the pasta along with the cream mixture. Proceed as directed.

TURKEY TETRAZZINI

TURKEY TETRAZZINI CAN BE AN INTERESTING blend of toasted bread crumbs, silky sauce, and a modicum of turkey meat, all bound together by one of our favorite foods, spaghetti. Or it can taste like cafeteria food. The downside of most casseroles—in which the fusion of individual tastes and textures diminishes them—can hold true here as well. We wondered if a basic noodle casserole could be reengineered so that this eminently practical American dish could be made worthy of a well-laid table.

A bit of culinary sleuthing solved the most pressing problem, the fact that the ingredients are double-cooked. (Most casserole recipes are three-step affairs: Cook the ingredients, mix them together, and then bake them in a casserole.) In *American Cookery* (Little, Brown & Co., 1972), James Beard suggests using a shallow baking dish rather than a deep casserole. Paired with a very hot (450-degree) oven, this reduces the baking time to a mere 15 minutes, a fraction of the time suggested by most cookbooks. Tasted against longer baking times and slower ovens, this quick method won hands down; with its fresher-tasting vegetables, it easily avoided the wretched, overcooked dullness of cafeteria cuisine.

Next we adjusted the sauce. The traditional choice is béchamel, a sauce in which milk is added to a roux, a paste made from flour and hot fat. We decided to use a velouté, a sauce based on chicken stock rather than dairy. This brightened up both the texture and the flavor, since dairy tends to dampen other flavors. We also played around with the amount of sauce, trying larger and smaller quantities, and found that more sauce overran the taste of the other ingredients. In this case, less was more. It still needed punctuation—so we spruced it up with a shot of sherry and a little lemon juice and nutmeg; a bit of Parmesan cheese provided tang and bite; and fresh thyme contributed singular aroma.

Most recipes do not toast the bread crumbs before baking. Doing so does complicate things by adding an extra step (in a pinch, you can skip the toasting), but it also adds to the flavor and texture of the dish; it's worth the minimal effort required. Tossing the toasted bread crumbs with a bit of grated Parmesan also helps.

Turkey Tetrazzini

SERVES 8

Tetrazzini is also great with leftover chicken. Using a shallow baking dish without a cover and a very hot oven will improve both texture and flavor. Don't skimp on the salt and pepper; this dish needs aggressive seasoning.

BREAD CRUMB TOPPING

1/2	cup fresh bread crumbs
	Pinch salt
1 1/2	tablespoons unsalted butter, melted
1/4	cup freshly grated Parmesan cheese

PASTA

6	tablespoons (3/4 stick) unsalted butter, plus more for the baking dish
8	ounces white button mushrooms, wiped clean, stems trimmed, and sliced thin
2	medium onions, chopped fine
	Salt and ground black pepper
12	ounces spaghetti or other long-strand pasta, strands snapped in half
1/4	cup all-purpose flour
2	cups low-sodium chicken broth
3	tablespoons dry sherry
1 1/2	ounces Parmesan cheese, freshly grated (3/4 cup)
1/4	teaspoon freshly grated nutmeg
2	teaspoons juice from 1 lemon
2	teaspoons minced fresh thyme leaves
2	cups frozen peas, thawed
4	cups cooked skinless, boneless turkey or chicken meat, cut into 1/4-inch pieces

1. FOR THE TOPPING: Adjust an oven rack to the middle position and heat the oven to 350 degrees. Mix the bread crumbs, salt, and butter in a small baking dish; bake until golden brown and crisp, 15 to 20 minutes. Cool to room temperature and mix together with the Parmesan in a small bowl. Set aside.

2. FOR THE PASTA: Increase the oven temperature to 450 degrees. Heat 2 tablespoons of the butter in a large skillet over medium heat until the foaming subsides; add the mushrooms and onions and sauté, stirring frequently, until the onions soften and the liquid from the mushrooms evaporates, 12 to 15 minutes. Season with salt and pepper to taste; transfer to a medium bowl and set aside.

3. Meanwhile, bring 4 quarts water to a rolling boil in a large pot. Add 1 tablespoon salt and the pasta to the boiling water and stir to separate the noodles. Cook until al dente. Reserve 1/4 cup of the pasta cooking water, drain the spaghetti, and return it to the pot with the reserved liquid.

4. Melt the remaining 4 tablespoons butter in a clean skillet over medium heat. When the foam subsides, whisk in the flour and cook, whisking constantly, until the flour turns golden, 1 to 2 minutes. Whisking constantly, gradually add the chicken broth. Increase the heat to medium–high and simmer until the mixture thickens, 3 to 4 minutes. Off the heat, whisk in the sherry, Parmesan, nutmeg, lemon juice, thyme, and 1/2 teaspoon salt. Add the sauce, sautéed mushroom mixture, peas, and turkey to the cooked pasta and mix well; adjust the seasonings to taste.

5. Turn the mixture into a buttered 13 by 9-inch baking dish (or other shallow ovenproof dish of similar size), sprinkle evenly with the reserved

bread crumbs, and bake until the crumbs brown and the mixture is bubbly, 13 to 15 minutes. Serve immediately.

TUNA NOODLE CASSEROLE

IS TUNA NOODLE CASSEROLE AN AMERICAN institution or a national nightmare? In most cases, the answer is both, no doubt because most versions of this dish are so bad. Most often made from a canned soup base—cream of mushroom, cream of celery, and cream of chicken are the usual choices—mixed with soggy noodles, canned tuna, and a few stray vegetables from the crisper drawer, tuna noodle casserole delivers little in flavor or texture, save for the sometimes crunchy topping of bread crumbs. We wanted our tuna noodle casserole to possess a silky sauce, tasty, firm chunks of vegetables, and properly cooked noodles. We also wanted to figure out how to add some brightness to the dish.

First the vegetables. Many recipes use a lot of celery, which adds crunch but almost no flavor. Interestingly enough, our tasters preferred no celery at all. Bell peppers held a similar fate. Green peppers were rejected immediately, and while red peppers performed slightly better, tasters preferred to do without them altogether. Onions were included for their subtle aromatic flavor; in fact, two were necessary to make their presence known. Mushrooms, a must in any tuna noodle casserole, were also included. After testing cremini and white button mushrooms, tasters could find no appreciable difference, so we went with the more available white button. We sautéed both the onions and the mushrooms to give them a slightly caramelized flavor and to allow the moisture in the mushrooms to evaporate so as not to water down the sauce. Peas were added for color and the sake of tradition. We found that frozen peas would not turn soggy if we added them right before baking. A little fresh thyme and parsley brought out even more freshness and color.

On to the tuna. Many of the oil-packed tunas tested had little textural appeal out of the can. Imported olive oil–packed tuna was a little better but didn't hold much of its shape when mixed in the casserole. Water-packed solid chunk tuna was much better. We were able to flake it, right out of the can, into big chunks that held their shape in the casserole. (For information on specific brands of tuna, see page 118.)

While many recipes call for elbow macaroni, we

BREAKING LONG STRANDS OF PASTA NEATLY

Though we usually don't recommend breaking strand pasta that we plan to sauce and eat, broken spaghetti or linguine is good in some casseroles, such as turkey Tetrazzini. Here's a neat way to break the spaghetti in half without causing short strands to fly every which way in the kitchen.

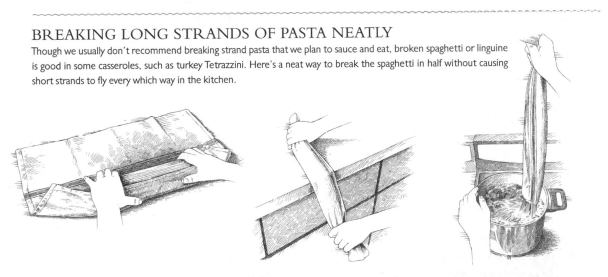

1. Roll up the bundle of spaghetti in a kitchen towel that overlaps the pasta by 3 or 4 inches at both ends.

2. Holding both ends firmly, center the rolled bundle over the edge of a counter. Push down with both hands to break the pasta in the middle of the bundle.

3. Holding the bundle vertically over the pot of boiling water, release the bottom of the towel so that the pasta slides neatly into the pot.

found it too starchy and thick. We chose fettuccine instead for its toothsome texture and big structural presence. To make the dish easier to eat, we broke the strands into thirds so that there was no need to wind the pasta around a fork. (Our tip on page 293 illustrates how to break the strands neatly.)

If not using a canned soup base, most cooks turn to a béchamel, a sauce made from a roux (hot fat and flour) and milk, but tasters were not satisfied. Next we tried a velouté, a similar sauce based on chicken broth instead of dairy that was so successful in our Turkey Tetrazzini (page 292). This produced the velvety sauce we were looking for. We then added a small amount of milk to give the sauce a little creaminess and just enough lemon juice to wake up the other ingredients.

As for the topping, we realized right off that store-bought bread crumbs, often stale and sandy, did not work. Instead, we used fresh bread crumbs, which we tossed with a little butter and toasted in the oven.

Tuna Noodle Casserole

SERVES 6

See page 118 for the results of our tasting of various brands of canned tuna.

BREAD CRUMB TOPPING

1	cup fresh bread crumbs
	Pinch salt
1½	tablespoons unsalted butter, melted

PASTA

6	tablespoons (¾ stick) unsalted butter, plus more for the baking dish
	Salt
12	ounces dried fettuccine, noodles broken into thirds
10	ounces white button mushrooms, stems discarded, caps wiped clean, and sliced ¼ inch thick
2	medium onions, minced
	Ground black pepper
¼	cup unbleached all-purpose flour
2	cups low-sodium chicken broth
¾	cup whole milk
1	tablespoon juice from 1 lemon
¼	cup minced fresh parsley leaves
1½	tablespoons chopped fresh thyme leaves
2	(6-ounce) cans water-packed solid white tuna, drained and flaked into 1-inch pieces with a fork
1½	cups frozen peas, thawed

1. FOR THE TOPPING: Set an oven rack to the middle position and heat the oven to 350 degrees. Mix the bread crumbs, salt, and butter in a small baking dish; bake until golden brown and crisp, 15 to 20 minutes. Cool to room temperature and transfer to a bowl.

2. FOR THE PASTA: Increase the oven temperature to 450 degrees. Butter a shallow casserole or 13 by 9-inch baking dish.

3. Bring 4 quarts water to a rolling boil in a large pot. Add 1 tablespoon salt and the pasta to the boiling water and stir to separate the noodles. Cook until al dente. Reserve ¼ cup of the pasta cooking water, drain the pasta, and return it to the pot with the reserved liquid.

4. Heat 2 tablespoons of the butter in a large skillet over medium heat until the foaming subsides. Add the mushrooms and onions, season with salt and pepper to taste, and sauté, stirring frequently, until the onions soften and the mushroom liquid evaporates, 7 to 10 minutes. Check the seasonings, transfer to a medium bowl, and set aside.

5. Melt the remaining 4 tablespoons butter in a clean skillet over medium heat. When the foam subsides, whisk in the flour and cook, whisking constantly, until the flour turns golden, 1 to 2 minutes. Whisking constantly, gradually add the chicken broth and milk. Raise the heat to medium-high and cook until the mixture thickens, about 5 minutes. Off the heat, whisk in ½ teaspoon salt, the lemon juice, parsley, and thyme.

6. Add the sauce, mushroom mixture, tuna, and peas to the pasta and mix well. Adjust the seasonings to taste.

7. Turn the mixture into the buttered baking dish, sprinkle evenly with the reserved bread crumbs, and bake until the crumbs brown and the mixture is bubbly, about 10 minutes. Serve immediately.

PAD THAI

PAD THAI IS A REMEDY FOR A DEAD, JADED palate. Hot, sweet, and pungent Thai flavors tangled in an un-Western jumble of textures awaken all of the senses that have grown weary of the usual grub. We have downed numerous platefuls of pad thai, many from an excellent Thai restaurant only a few blocks away from our test kitchen. What we noticed was that from one order to the next, pad thai prepared in the same reliable restaurant kitchen was inconsistent. If it was perfect, it was a symphony of flavors and textures. It balanced sweet, sour, and spicy, and the tender, glutinous rice noodles ensnared curls of shrimp, crisp strands of bean sprouts, soft curds of fried egg, and sturdy bits of tofu. Sometimes, however, it tasted weak and flat, as if seasoned too timidly. At its worst, pad thai suffers from indiscriminate amounts of sugar, from slick, greasy noodles, or from sticky, lifeless strands that glom onto one another to form a chaotic skein.

We have become so enamored of pad thai and so tired of disappointment that we have attempted it several times in the test kitchen with only moderate success, and that we attribute to luck. The recipes were unclear, the ingredient lists daunting, and we stumbled through the steps only to produce dry, undercooked noodles and unbalanced flavors. Happily, though, our pad thai was loaded with plump, sweet shrimp (not the paltry four or five per typical restaurant order), and the flavors tasted clean and fresh. Our goal was to build on these positives and produce a consistently superlative pad thai.

Rice sticks, the type of noodles used in pad thai, are often only partially cooked, particularly when used in stir-fries. We found three different methods of preparing them: soaking them in room-temperature water, soaking them in hot tap water, and boiling. We began with boiling and quickly realized that this was bad advice. Drained and waiting in the colander, the noodles glued themselves together. When we managed to stir-fry them, they wound up soggy and overdone. Noodles soaked in room-temperature water remained fairly stiff. After lengthy stir-frying, they eventually became tender, but longer cooking made this pad thai drier and stickier. Finally, we tried soaking the rice sticks in hot tap water for about 20 minutes. They "softened," turning limp and pliant, but were not fully tender. Drained, they were loose and separate, and they cooked through easily with stir-frying. The result? Noodles that were at once pleasantly tender and resilient.

Sweet, salty, sour, and spicy are the flavor characteristics of pad thai, and none should dominate; they should coexist in harmony. Although the cooking time is short, the ingredient list isn't, and many components will appear foreign to some. Fish sauce supplies a salty-sweet pungency, sugar gives sweetness, the heat comes from ground chiles, vinegar provides acidity, and tamarind rounds out the dish with its fruity, earthy, sweet-tart molasses-tinged flavor. Garlic and sometimes shallots contribute their heady, robust flavors. Some recipes call for ketchup (sounded dubious but probably worth trying), and some require soy sauce.

With these ingredients in hand, we set off to find out which ones were key to success and how much of each to use to achieve balanced flavor. For 8 ounces of rice sticks, 3 tablespoons of fish sauce and the same amount of sugar were ideal. Three-quarters of a teaspoon of cayenne (many recipes call for Thai chiles, but for the sake of simplicity, we opted not to use them) brought a low, even heat—not a searing burn—and 1 tablespoon of rice vinegar (preferred in pad thai for its mild acidity and relatively complex fermented-grain flavor) greatly vivified the flavors.

Tasters liked the garlic at 1 tablespoon minced. Shallots had a surprising impact on flavor. Just one medium shallot (about 3 tablespoons minced) produced such a round, full sweetness and depth of flavor that we just couldn't say no. To coax the right character out of these two aromatics, we found that cooking them to the point of browning was critical; they tasted mellow, sweet, and mildly toasty.

Tamarind was the most enigmatic ingredient on our list. Tamarind is a fruit that grows as a round brown pod about five inches long and is often sold as a paste (a hard, flat brick) or as a sticky concentrate. (For more information, see page 296.) Although we eschew hard-to-find ingredients in the test kitchen, we came to the conclusion that tamarind is central—if not essential—to the unique flavor of pad thai. Testing showed that tamarind paste has a fresher, brighter, fruitier flavor than concentrate, which tasted dull by comparison. For those who cannot obtain either tamarind paste or concentrate, we worked out a

INGREDIENTS: Tamarind

Sweet-tart, brownish red tamarind is a necessary ingredient for a rendition of pad thai that looks and tastes authentic. Tamarind is commonly sold in paste (also called pulp) and in concentrate form. But don't fret if neither is available—you can still make a very good pad thai using lime juice and water. Here are your three options.

TAMARIND PASTE OR PULP

Tamarind paste, or pulp, is firm, sticky, and filled with seeds and fibers. We favored this product because it had the freshest, brightest flavor. To use it in the pad thai recipe, soak 2 tablespoons in ¾ cup boiling water for about 10 minutes, then push it through a mesh strainer to remove the seeds and fibers and extract as much pulp as possible.

TAMARIND CONCENTRATE

Tamarind concentrate looks more like a scary pomade than a food-stuff. It's black, thick, shiny, and gooey. Its flavor approximates that of tamarind paste, but it tastes less fruity and more "cooked," and it colors the pad thai a shade too dark. To use in the pad thai recipe, mix 1 tablespoon with ⅔ cup hot water.

LIME JUICE AND WATER SUBSTITUTE

If tamarind is out of the question, combine ⅓ cup lime juice and ⅓ cup water and use it in its place; use light brown sugar instead of granulated to give the noodles some color and a faint molasses flavor. Because it will already contain a good hit of lime, do not serve this version of pad thai with lime wedges.

formula of equal parts lime juice and water as a stand-in. This mixture produces a less interesting and less authentic dish, but we polished off several such platefuls with no qualms.

We tried a little ketchup, but its vinegary tomato flavor was out of place. As for soy sauce, even just a mere tablespoon was a big bully—its assertive flavor didn't play nicely with the others.

The other ingredients in pad thai are sautéed shrimp, scrambled eggs, chopped peanuts, bean sprouts, and scallions. For more textural intrigue and to achieve authentic pad thai flavor, dried shrimp and Thai salted preserved radish are worthy embellishments (both sold in Asian grocery stores). Dried shrimp are sweet, salty, and intensely shrimpy, and they add tiny bursts of incredible flavor. We used 2 tablespoons of the smallest dried shrimp we could find and chopped them up finer still, because tasters asked that their firm, chewy texture be mitigated. Thai salted preserved radish is brownish yellow in color, dry, and a bit wrinkled, and it is sold in long sections (think daikon radish) folded into a flimsy plastic package. Two tablespoons of chopped salted radish added piquant, savory bits with a good crunch.

Oddly, after consuming dozens of servings of pad thai, we did not feel glutted. We were addicted. These days, if we order it in a restaurant, we prepare ourselves for disappointment. We've come to think that pad thai is not unlike chocolate chip cookies: It's always best homemade.

Pad Thai
SERVES 4

A wok might be the implement of choice in restaurants and the old country, but a large 12-inch skillet (nonstick makes cleanup easy) is more practical for home cooks. Although pad thai cooks very quickly, the ingredient list is long, and everything must be prepared and within easy reach at the stovetop when you begin cooking. For maximum efficiency, use the time during which the tamarind and noodles soak to prepare the other ingredients. Tofu is a good and common addition to pad thai. If you like, add 4 ounces of extra-firm tofu or pressed tofu (available in Asian markets), cut into ½-inch cubes (about 1 cup), to the noodles along with the bean sprouts.

2 tablespoons tamarind paste or substitute (see page 296)

¾ cup boiling water

3 tablespoons fish sauce

1 tablespoon rice vinegar

3 tablespoons sugar

¾ teaspoon cayenne pepper

4 tablespoons peanut or vegetable oil

8 ounces dried rice stick noodles, about ¼ inch wide

2 large eggs
Salt

12 ounces medium (40 to 50 per pound) shrimp, peeled and deveined, if desired (see the illustrations on pages 19–20)

3 garlic cloves, minced or pressed through a garlic press

1 medium shallot, minced

2 tablespoons dried shrimp, chopped fine (optional)

2 tablespoons chopped Thai salted preserved radish (optional)

6 tablespoons chopped unsalted roasted peanuts

3 cups (6 ounces) bean sprouts

5 medium scallions, green parts only, sliced thin on a sharp diagonal

¼ cup loosely packed cilantro leaves (optional)
Lime wedges for serving

1. Rehydrate the tamarind paste in the boiling water (see the instructions on page 296). Stir the fish sauce, rice vinegar, sugar, cayenne, and 2 tablespoons of the oil into the tamarind liquid; set aside.

2. Cover the rice sticks with hot tap water in a large bowl; soak until softened, pliable, and limp but not fully tender, about 20 minutes. Drain the noodles and set aside. Beat the eggs and ⅛ teaspoon salt in a small bowl; set aside.

3. Heat 1 tablespoon of the oil in a 12-inch skillet (preferably nonstick) over high heat until just beginning to smoke. Add the shrimp and sprinkle with ⅛ teaspoon salt; cook, tossing occasionally, until the shrimp are opaque and browned about the edges, about 3 minutes. Transfer the shrimp to a plate; set aside.

4. Off the heat, add the remaining 1 tablespoon oil to the skillet and swirl to coat; add the garlic and shallot, set the skillet over medium heat, and cook, stirring constantly, until light golden brown, about 1½ minutes. Add the beaten eggs to the skillet and stir vigorously with a wooden spoon until scrambled and barely moist, about 20 seconds. Add the rice noodles, dried shrimp, and salted radish (if using) to the eggs; toss with 2 wooden spoons to combine. Pour the fish sauce mixture over the noodles, increase the heat to high, and cook, tossing constantly, until the noodles are evenly coated. Scatter ¼ cup of the peanuts, the bean sprouts, all

SOAKING THE NOODLES

STIFF NOODLES
Soaking the rice sticks in room-temperature water yields hard noodles that take too long to stir-fry.

STICKY NOODLES
Fully cooking the rice sticks in boiling water results in soft, sticky, gummy, overdone noodles.

PERFECT NOODLES
Soaking the rice sticks in hot water yields softened noodles. When stir-fried, they are tender but resilient.

THE NEW BEST RECIPE

but ¼ cup of the scallions, and the cooked shrimp over the noodles; continue to cook, tossing constantly, until the noodles are tender, about 2½ minutes (if not yet tender, add 2 tablespoons water to the skillet and continue to cook until tender).

5. Transfer the noodles to a serving platter, sprinkle with the remaining scallions, the remaining 2 tablespoons peanuts, and the cilantro (if using). Serve immediately, passing the lime wedges separately.

SPICY SICHUAN NOODLES

SPICY SICHUAN NOODLES ARE A MEAL IN A bowl. To make them, you top the noodles with a rich, savory sauce—a mélange of browned ground pork, aromatic ginger and garlic, salty soy sauce, and nutty peanut butter in a chicken broth base. All this is set ablaze by the heat of chiles and finished with a sprinkling of sliced scallions and bean sprouts.

This dish is absent from restaurant menus. By all accounts, it is street food in China, the equivalent of sausage and onions from a curbside cart in New York. Because we could not sample prepared versions, we researched Sichuan noodles in cookbooks, but turned up only a handful of recipes. Ground pork, peanut butter or sesame paste, chiles (in the form of oil, paste, or flakes), chicken broth, and soy sauce were common denominators. Other flavorings and ingredients, such as oyster sauce, were a tossup.

The sauce for spicy Sichuan noodles is built simply. Ground pork, marinated briefly in soy sauce and sherry, is browned either by sautéing it in a skillet with just a little oil or by deep-frying it in a cup or so of oil. The pork is then removed from the skillet, the oil drained off, and the ginger and garlic briefly cooked. Next the chicken broth is added, then the peanut butter or sesame paste. In a simpler rendition, the ginger and garlic are omitted and the other sauce ingredients are simmered right in the skillet with the pork. In both versions, the mixture of pork and sauce is simply poured over noodles and served.

We quickly determined that deep-frying the pork was not worth the trouble or waste of oil. Browning could be accomplished easily in only 1 tablespoon of oil.

Fresh ginger and garlic spike the dish with aromatic piquancy, but in equal amounts their potencies vied for dominance, and the pairing was not harmonious. Tasters voted garlic to the fore, relegating ginger to second position. Soy sauce brought a savory quality, while oyster sauce added depth and sweetness that rounded out the flavors. Rice vinegar cut the richness of the sauce and livened things up. Asian sesame paste (not Middle Eastern tahini sesame paste) is typically called for in spicy Sichuan noodle recipes, with peanut butter a recommended substitute. We were inclined to use peanut butter because of its availability, and it produced perfectly good results. Two tablespoons, the amount recommended in many recipes, was too little to contribute much flavor or to thicken the amount of chicken broth needed to coat a pound of cooked fresh noodles. We doubled the amount to ¼ cup, enough to add rich nutty flavor and to adequately thicken the sauce. Any more and the sauce became intolerably rich as well as overly thick.

Next we tried Asian sesame paste in place of peanut butter. Its flavor is mysterious, and it yields an intriguing sauce with an earthy, smoky flavor and a faintly bitter edge. If an Asian grocer is nearby, we recommend seeking out sesame paste. The consistency varies from brand to brand— some are thin and pourable, like honey, while others are spreadable—so we found it necessary to compensate by making minor adjustments in the amount of chicken broth in the sauce.

While you're shopping for sesame paste, look for Sichuan peppercorns. These berries from a prickly ash tree native to Asia bring to the dish a woodsy flavor, with a hint of star anise.

Chinese grocery stores are stocked with a dizzying array of noodles, fresh as well as dried. A couple of recipes recommended fresh egg noodles, so that's where we began. In the refrigerator section of a major Chinatown market we chose two types of fresh noodles, lo mein and the descriptively named "plain noodles." From the local supermarket, we purchased—for nearly twice the cost—a few packages of "Asian-style noodles" in wide-cut and narrow-cut versions. Cooked, these three types of noodles were different from one another, but all were a better match for the sauce than the other noodles. The spaghetti-shaped lo mein didn't give the sauce much noodle surface to cling to, and their very yielding texture was unremarkable. The plain noodles, shaped like fat, squared-off strands of spaghetti, were as soft and gummy as a piece of Bazooka; this pleased some and annoyed others. The wide-cut Azumaya brand noodles had good chew, too, but to a lesser degree. Their fettuccine-like shape was perfect for the sauce; the broad surfaces were easily sauced and could buoy up bits of pork.

Fresh noodles are not always an option, so we also looked into dried. Sturdier non-egg noodles, with their chewy and more substantial presence, were a superior match. In fact, for those who prefer noodles with a lower "mush" quotient, dried Asian noodles are better than fresh.

And for those for whom neither fresh nor dried Asian noodles are options, dried linguine is an acceptable substitute. Most tasters polished off an entire bowl. One note: If you're using pasta, abandon the notion of "al dente"—Asian noodles are cooked until they submit readily to the tooth. When we cooked them al dente and dressed them, the combination was unpleasant. Once the noodles are cooked and drained, it's best to serve them immediately; give them a few idle minutes and they will fuse together. The only remedy is a hot-water rinse to help disentangle the mass.

Common practice with Italian pasta is to toss the sauce with the cooked and drained pasta in the pot in which the pasta was cooked, giving the mix a little additional heat to help form a loose union. Noodles for this dish, however, look and hold up better when simply divided among bowls, ladled with sauce, and then sprinkled with a garnish. It is then up to the diner to toss, swirl, and slurp down the noodles with chopsticks . . . or a fork.

Spicy Sichuan Noodles with Pork
SERVES 4

If you cannot find Asian noodles, linguine may be substituted. If you are using natural peanut butter or Asian sesame paste that has a pourable rather than a spreadable consistency, use only 1 cup of chicken broth. Also note that the amount of sauce will coat 1 pound of fresh noodles but only 12 ounces of dried noodles, which bulk up during boiling.

8	ounces ground pork
3	tablespoons soy sauce
2	tablespoons dry sherry
	Ground white pepper
2	tablespoons oyster sauce
1/4	cup peanut butter or Asian sesame paste
1	tablespoon rice vinegar
1–1 1/4	cups low-sodium chicken broth (see note)
1	tablespoon peanut oil
1	tablespoon minced fresh ginger
6	medium garlic cloves, minced or pressed through a garlic press
3/4	teaspoon red pepper flakes
1	tablespoon toasted sesame oil
12	ounces dried Asian noodles or 1 pound fresh Asian noodles (width between linguine and fettuccine), or 12 ounces dried linguine
3	medium scallions, sliced thin
2	cups bean sprouts (optional)
1	tablespoon Sichuan peppercorns, toasted in a small dry skillet until fragrant, then ground (optional)

1. Combine the pork, 1 tablespoon of the soy sauce, the sherry, and a pinch white pepper in a small bowl; stir well with a fork and set aside while preparing the other ingredients. Whisk together the oyster sauce, remaining soy sauce, peanut butter, vinegar, and a pinch white pepper in a medium bowl. Whisk in the chicken broth and set aside.

2. Bring 4 quarts water to a rolling boil in a large pot.

3. Meanwhile, heat a 12-inch skillet over high heat until hot, about 2 minutes. Add the peanut

oil and swirl to coat the pan bottom. Add the pork and cook, scraping along the pan bottom and breaking up the pork into small pieces with a wide metal or wooden spatula, until the pork is in small, well-browned bits, about 5 minutes. Stir in the ginger, garlic, and red pepper flakes; cook until fragrant, about 1 minute. Add the peanut butter–chicken broth mixture; bring to a boil, whisking to combine, then reduce the heat to medium-low and simmer to blend the flavors, stirring occasionally, about 3 minutes. Stir in the sesame oil.

4. While the sauce simmers, add the noodles to the boiling water and stir to separate. Cook until tender (refer to the package directions, but use them only as a guideline and be sure to taste for doneness). Drain the noodles; divide them among individual bowls, ladle a portion of the sauce over them, and sprinkle with the scallions, bean sprouts, and ground Sichuan peppercorns (if using). Serve immediately.

➤ VARIATION
Spicy Sichuan Noodles with Pork and Shiitake Mushrooms

Soak 8 small dried shiitake mushrooms in 1 cup boiling water until softened, 15 to 20 minutes; drain, reserving ½ cup of the soaking liquid. Trim and discard the stems; cut the caps into ¼-inch slices and set aside. Follow the recipe for Spicy Sichuan Noodles with Pork, substituting the reserved mushroom liquid for an equal amount of chicken broth and stirring the sliced mushrooms into the sauce along with the sesame oil in step 3.

Lo Mein

LO MEIN IS A SIMPLE DISH—BASICALLY A STIR-fry with boiled noodles. So why is lo mein so often poorly executed? The lo mein served in many Chinese restaurants is frequently oily and uninteresting; the noodles are often a tasteless mass. We wanted something different—flavorful strands of noodles coated in a light, tangy sauce.

Most lo mein recipes call for fresh Chinese egg noodles, which are somewhat different from their Italian counterparts. Most fresh Chinese noodles are more tender and chewier and absorb flavors more readily than fresh Italian pasta. After testing both kinds of fresh noodles, we preferred the authentic Chinese-style noodles, which were significantly more substantial. However, these larger noodles often congealed in a huge mass as they cooled. Up to this point, we had been cooking the noodles until al dente, draining them, and then holding them before adding them to the stir-fry. We obviously needed to change this procedure.

We started by cooking our noodles less, a move that showed promise. By draining the noodles about a minute before they were al dente, we found we could avoid the sticky mass problem, and the noodles stayed toothsome rather than overcooked in the finished dish. In addition to undercooking the noodles slightly, we rinsed the drained noodles with cold water and tossed them with a little bit of sesame oil. Sure enough, rinsing the noodles rid them of excess starch. Tossing them with oil further prevented the noodles from sticking together, and the sesame oil enhanced the

KEEPING BEAN SPROUTS CRISP AND FRESH

The bagged bean sprouts sold in supermarkets often contain more than enough for a single recipe. Once you open the bag, however, the sprouts are liable to lose their crunch. To keep leftover sprouts crisp, submerge the sprouts in a container of cold water. The sprouts will stay crisp for up to five days.

flavor of the completed dish.

Now that we had solved the noodle problems, we moved on to the sauce. Our thought was to generate the greatest flavor with the fewest ingredients. We also wanted to keep the sauce light and therefore an improvement on the goopy Chinese takeout sauces. Switching from fresh shiitake mushrooms (the common choice in many recipes) to dried shiitakes allowed us to use the rehydrating liquid as a base for the sauce. This was perfect; it deepened the flavors and kept the sauce from being too thick. (In the beef lo mein variation, chicken broth had the same results.) Soy sauce was another essential component; we found that a light-bodied soy did the job. The darker, sweeter soy sauces were too cloying and sweet and not well suited for our purposes. To finish the dish, we chose oyster sauce. While not exactly a household staple, it was listed in most of the recipes we consulted. We found, and tasters agreed, that the oyster sauce gave the lo mein an interesting brininess and an appealing gloss.

Vegetable Lo Mein
SERVES 4

Look for fresh Chinese egg noodles in the produce section of your supermarket. If you cannot find fresh noodles, you can substitute dried noodles, either Asian or Italian. If you do so, choose a noodle the thickness of spaghetti.

8	dried shiitake mushrooms (about 2 ounces)
1/2	cup hot water
1	tablespoon salt
12	ounces fresh Chinese egg noodles
1	tablespoon toasted sesame oil
2	tablespoons oyster sauce
2	tablespoons soy sauce
1 1/2	tablespoons vegetable oil
1/2	small head napa cabbage, sliced crosswise into 1/8-inch strips (about 3 cups)
4	medium scallions, green parts only, cut into 1-inch pieces
1	tablespoon minced fresh ginger
1	cup bean sprouts

1. Cover the mushrooms with the water in a small microwave-safe bowl. Cover with plastic wrap, cut several steam vents with a paring knife, and microwave on high power for 30 seconds. Let stand until the mushrooms soften, about 5 minutes. Carefully lift the mushrooms from the liquid with a fork; pour the soaking liquid through a small strainer lined with a single layer of paper towels and placed over a measuring cup. Set aside 1/4 cup of the strained liquid. Trim and discard the mushroom stems and slice the caps into 1/4-inch strips.

2. Bring 4 quarts water to a rolling boil in a large pot. Add the salt and noodles and stir to separate the noodles. Cook until the noodles are slightly underdone, about 2 minutes. Drain thoroughly, rinse the noodles under cold running water, and drain again. Toss with the sesame oil in a large bowl and set aside.

3. Mix the reserved mushroom liquid, oyster sauce, and soy sauce in a small bowl; set aside.

4. Heat a 12-inch nonstick skillet over high heat for 3 minutes. Add 1 tablespoon of the oil and swirl to coat the bottom of the pan evenly. Add the mushrooms and stir-fry until seared and three-quarters cooked, about 2 minutes. Add the cabbage and stir-fry until just wilted, about 1 minute. Clear the center of the pan and add the scallions, ginger, and remaining 1/2 tablespoon oil. Cook until fragrant, about 10 seconds, then stir the aromatics into the vegetables.

5. Add the noodles, sprouts, and mushroom liquid mixture to the pan. Stir-fry and toss to combine all the ingredients until the noodles are heated through, about 1 minute. Serve immediately.

Beef and Pepper Lo Mein
SERVES 4

For information about preparing flank steak for a stir-fry, see page 42.

1	tablespoon salt
12	ounces fresh Chinese egg noodles
1	tablespoon toasted sesame oil
1/4	cup low-sodium chicken broth

2   tablespoons oyster sauce
1   tablespoon soy sauce
2½   tablespoons vegetable oil
8   ounces flank steak, trimmed and sliced thin
     across the grain on the bias
½   small head napa cabbage, sliced crosswise into
     ⅛-inch strips (about 3 cups)
1   medium red bell pepper, cored, seeded, and
     sliced thin
4   medium scallions, green parts only, cut into
     1-inch pieces
1   tablespoon minced fresh ginger
1   cup bean sprouts

1. Bring 4 quarts water to a rolling boil in a large pot. Add the salt and noodles to the boiling water and stir to separate the noodles. Cook until the noodles are slightly underdone, about 2 minutes. Drain thoroughly, rinse the noodles under cold running water, and drain again. Toss with the sesame oil in a large bowl and set aside.

2. Mix the chicken broth, oyster sauce, and soy sauce in a small bowl; set aside.

3. Heat a 12-inch nonstick skillet over high heat for 3 minutes. Add 1 tablespoon of the oil and swirl to coat the bottom of the pan evenly. Add the flank steak and stir-fry until seared and three-quarters cooked, about 2 minutes. Transfer the steak to a bowl. Heat 1 tablespoon of the oil in the now-empty pan until shimmering. Add the cabbage and bell pepper and stir-fry until softened slightly, about 1 minute. Clear the center of the pan and add the scallions, ginger, and remaining ½ tablespoon oil. Cook until fragrant, about 10 seconds, then stir the aromatics into the vegetables.

4. Add the noodles, beef (and any accumulated juices), sprouts, and chicken broth mixture to the pan. Stir-fry and toss to combine all the ingredients until the noodles are heated through, about 1 minute. Serve immediately.

CUTTING SCALLIONS

Slicing or chopping scallions with a knife often crushes their natural tube configuration, which not only adds to preparation time but also spoils their appearance. Use this method with scallions as well as chives.

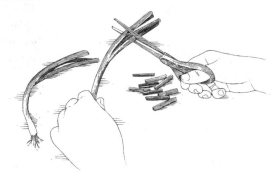

Starting at the green end, use scissors to cut neat, intact pieces of scallion.

7

POULTRY

IN MOST KITCHENS (AND OURS IS NO DIFFERENT), poultry means chicken or turkey. Chicken has become America's favorite weeknight entrée. Quick to prepare, chicken is a tasty and typically healthful choice for today's family. Turkey (with all the fixings) remains the top pick for holiday gatherings. In addition to its popularity, poultry also takes to a wide variety of cooking methods including sautéing, frying, broiling, and roasting. (For information on grilling chicken, see chapter 14.)

Convenience and versatility aside, cooking these birds, especially the whole bird, can be a challenge, and the result is often disappointing. Who hasn't served a turkey with sawdust-dry breast meat or a chicken with soggy skin? These problems stem from the very anatomy of these birds. Breast meat has very little fat and is prone to drying out. Overcooking is a constant threat for white meat. Dark meat, on the other hand, takes more time to cook; it has a fair amount of fat that must be rendered, or melted, and released from the bird if the meat is to be palatable. In addition to these competing interests, you have to deal with the skin. In most cases, you want the skin on all parts of the bird to crisp.

With these challenges in mind, we offer our best poultry recipes, along with the accompaniments (stuffings, gravies, and sauces) that go with them.

Poultry also includes duck, and we have included a recipe for a classic duck preparation in this chapter. Keeping breast meat tender is not an issue when preparing duck since all the meat on this bird is dark. The biggest challenge is the fat—there's too much of it—and the skin can be flabby if duck is not cooked properly.

Even more important than ensuring that the poultry you eat is tasty is ensuring that it is safe. It's probably best to assume that the chicken you buy is contaminated, given the prevalence of bacteria in the poultry supply. We suggest that you follow some simple precautionary measures whenever you prepare poultry.

When handling poultry, make sure to wash hands, knives, cutting boards, and counters (and anything else that has come into contact with the raw poultry, its juices, or your hands) with hot, soapy water. Be especially careful not to let the poultry, its juices, or your unwashed hands touch foods (like salad ingredients) that will be eaten raw.

Finally, cook poultry to an internal temperature high enough to ensure that any bacteria have been killed. (Use an instant-read thermometer to gauge when poultry is done.) Temperatures vary between white and dark meat and among the types of poultry, so it is important to follow the guidelines provided in individual recipes.

SIMPLEST ROAST CHICKEN

COOKING A CHICKEN WOULD APPEAR TO BE a simple task. The meat is not tough by nature. The dark meat is relatively forgiving in terms of cooking time. The breast meat is not particularly thick, which means that the outer layers are less likely to dry out while you are attempting to properly cook the center of the bird.

Yet most home-cooked chickens are either grossly overcooked or so underdone that they resemble an avian version of steak tartare. To solve this problem once and for all, we decided to set our sights on devising a recipe for roast chicken that would give us perfectly crisp and well-seasoned skin, juicy and tender white meat with just a hint of chew, and fully cooked dark meat—all the way to the bone.

To begin, we developed a series of tests based on a few simple observations. First, chicken is made up of two totally different types of meat: white and dark. The white meat is inevitably overcooked and dry even as the dark meat is still little more than raw next to the bone. Second, chicken, unlike beef, has skin, which should be nicely browned and crispy. As we found during the testing process, crisp skin is not always consistent with perfectly cooked meat. Finally, chicken is an odd amalgam of meat and bones. The drumsticks and wings stick out, the thigh meat is on the side of the bird, and the breast meat is on the top (at least when the chicken is roasted whole). The home cook is dealing with a complex three-dimensional structure, quite different from a brisket or a pot roast. The anatomy of the chicken presents a more complex set of cooking considerations. In search of these, we ended up roasting chickens 14 different ways.

We started our tests with the most pertinent question: What is the best oven temperature for roasting a chicken? Our first bird went into a 450-degree oven and cooked for 44 minutes. When it emerged, the skin was dark and crispy, but we encountered the classic problem with high-heat meat cookery: While the dark meat was fine, the outer portion of the white meat was overcooked and on the tough side even as the internal thigh temperature registered 160 degrees, the temperature we generally consider best for white meat. (Dark meat really tastes best cooked to 165 or 170 degrees.)

We then went to the other extreme and tested a bird in a 275-degree oven for an hour and 35 minutes, raising the heat to 425 degrees for the last 10 minutes to crisp the skin. The white meat was not quite as juicy as the dark, but not dry, either. The skin, however, was a light gold, not a rich sienna, and it was chewy and not very tasty—obviously, not browned enough.

Finally, we tried a simple, classic approach: We roasted the bird at 375 degrees for one hour. The skin was golden and slightly crispy. At 160 degrees internal temperature, the juices ran clear, but the dark meat was still not properly cooked near the bone. We continued cooking until the thigh meat reached an internal temperature of about 170 degrees. At this point, the breast meat was close to 180 degrees, but it was still juicy. This was an interesting discovery. While the breast meat of chicken roasted at 450 degrees was a bit dry when the thigh registered 160 degrees, the bird roasted at 375 degrees still had juicy breast meat when the thigh registered close to 170 degrees. We also found that the commonly held indication of doneness, "until the juices run clear," is an imprecise measure—the white meat will be cooked, but the dark meat can still be a little bloody at the bone, a sight that we would prefer to leave to B movies rather than the dinner plate.

In an attempt to get crispier skin, we tried preheating the oven to the higher temperature of 450 degrees and turning the heat down to 350 degrees upon putting in the chicken. The bird cooked in 53 minutes, and the skin was pale gold and slightly chewy—not much different from the chicken roasted at 375 degrees and not quite as good overall. Next, we roasted a bird at 375 degrees for 30 minutes, then raised the heat to 450 degrees. This method delivered the best results—perfectly cooked meat and crisp skin.

We were happy with these results, but there remained a couple of techniques often recommended for roasting chicken that we wanted to test. The first was basting. We started with butter and basted every 15 minutes. The results were appalling. Despite a nice brown color, the skin was chewy and greasy. The next bird was basted with oil, which turned out a crispier skin, but the color was off—a pale gold. We then brushed a bird with butter before roasting and shoved it in the oven without any further basting. This was the best method. Great color and great crispy texture. Essentially, the only reason to brush a chicken with butter is to advance the color of the skin. The oven heat turns the milk solids in the butter brown, and, in the process, the skin develops more flavor as well.

The second often-recommended technique we wanted to test was trussing, which is said to promote more even cooking. We trussed a bird according to the best French method and cooked it for what seemed a long time, 1½ hours. The white meat was overcooked, but the dark meat was just right. It was also interesting to note that the cooking time was so long. We concluded that trussing makes it more difficult to cook the inner part of the thigh properly—because it is less exposed to the heat, it needs more oven time. Voilà!—overcooked white meat. An untrussed bird took only one hour to cook, and the white and dark meat were both nicely roasted.

Having figured out that continuous basting and trussing were both unnecessary, we were hoping to find that the bird need not be turned, either. But even cooking is crucial to chicken cookery, and a couple of tests were in order.

305

INGREDIENTS: Chicken

Picking out a quality chicken at the supermarket is a guessing game. The terms fresh, organic, free-range, all-natural, and lean rarely indicate good flavor or texture, and neither does price. In our 1994 chicken tasting, the only dependable sign of quality we found was brand, with Bell & Evans and Empire taking top honors. Several years later, we wondered if these companies would win a second tasting and if, at long last, we could find a reliable, nonbranded measure of quality.

We identified and investigated a long list of genetic and environmental factors that might help the consumer purchase a high-quality, tasty bird. Our first stop was genetic engineering. Birds are bred to meet the goals of a particular producer. Murray's chickens, for example, are engineered for a high yield of breast meat and a low yield of fat. (Tasters found them "tough" and "dry.") Perdue chickens are bred for a high ratio of meat to bone. (We found this means big breasts but scrawny legs.) It seemed to us, at least at first pass, that few, if any, producers were engineering birds for flavor.

More toothsome meat can simply be the result of a chicken's age. The older the chicken (an older broiler/fryer is seven to nine weeks old rather than the more typical six to seven weeks), the more distinct its flavor. Free-range birds, whose diet is less intense and less controlled than that of indoor chickens (because free-range birds have unrestricted access to the outdoors, it is impossible to keep them from eating random grasses and insects), take longer to reach their proper weight and are older when they are processed. Yet the "free-range" moniker is no indication of superior flavor. The two free-range birds we tasted, Eberly and D'Artagnan, had both fans and critics.

Processing factors that can affect the flavor and appearance of a chicken include how the chicken was rinsed and chilled prior to packaging. Antimicrobial agents, such as sodium triphosphates, are sometimes added to the final rinse water to cut down on contamination by bacteria like salmonella. (Some tasters can detect traces of this chemical. It is usually described as "metallic.") Some rinsing methods cause excess water to build up under the skin, and this can lead to a shriveled appearance after cooking. After slaughtering and rinsing, the chickens are quickly chilled to a temperature of about 28 degrees Fahrenheit, or just above their freezing point. If the chickens are chilled too quickly, the meat can get spongy and watery. If chilled too slowly, the meat can dry out and develop an off color. None of these effects could be confirmed in our tasting because we could not be certain about how a particular bird was processed.

Our first solid clue to any possible connection between processing method and flavor emerged when we discovered that Empire, the only kosher chicken in our tasting, was also the best-tasting. (Murray's birds are not kosher but are processed under similar conditions in accordance with Muslim law.) Both Empire and Murray's birds are hand-slaughtered rather than killed by machine, which ensures both a clean kill and a quick and efficient "bleed-out." Industry experts indicated that machine-processed chickens are more likely to be subject to improper slaughtering, which can cause blood to clot, resulting in tough meat or a livery flavor.

Because tasters far preferred the Empire chicken to Murray's, however, it followed that more was at work here than slaughtering technique. For one thing, kosher chickens like Empire's are dunked in cold water to remove feathers after slaughter. Cold water firms both the skin and the fat layer beneath it. In contrast, most other producers scald birds in hot water to remove the feathers. The experts we talked to said that scalding can "solubilize" the chicken's fat, leading to excessive moisture loss and a wrinkled appearance in the chicken skin after cooking. Uneven scalding can also cause "barking," or a blotchy appearance in the skin.

Appearance aside, perhaps the most noticeable difference between the Empire bird and the others we tasted is that the Empire bird tasted juicy and well seasoned. In keeping with kosher law, the chickens are buried in salt for one hour to draw out impurities and are then rinsed in cold spring water. The combination of salt and water acts like a brine, encouraging the fiber in the meat to open and trap the salt and water, leading to a juicier, more flavorful bird. This single factor, more than any other, seems to have put the Empire bird ahead of the pack.

If you are looking for advice on purchasing a high-quality, good-tasting chicken, we recommend kosher. All the other descriptives—free-range, natural, lean, organic, and the like—don't necessarily translate into a better-tasting chicken. Empire, the brand that won our contest, was followed by Bell & Evans, winner of our 1994 tasting. You can't go wrong with either. Let it also be noted that Tyson, a mass-produced bird priced at just $1.29 per pound, came in third, ahead of birds costing more than twice as much. One last word of advice: Out of eight birds in the tasting, Perdue finished dead last, with tasters describing the meat as "pithy," "chalky," and "stringy," with sour notes as well.

First we roasted a bird for 15 minutes on each side and then put it on its back. This chicken, weighing close to 3¼ pounds, took just 50 minutes to cook. The skin was golden and crunchy, the white and dark meat perfectly cooked, and the overall presentation superb. To make this process a bit easier, we tried roasting another bird breast-side down for 20 minutes and then turned it breast-side up. This chicken was good, but the skin was less crispy, and, at the point at which the white meat was perfect, the dark meat was a bit undercooked. Thus, unfortunately, two turns proved crucial.

After we had roasted half a dozen birds according to our basic method (375 degrees for 30 minutes, then 450 degrees for the rest of the cooking time, with two turns for even cooking), we made an interesting discovery. The thigh that was facing up during the second 15 minutes of roasting ended up lower in temperature than the thigh that started off facing up. Why? The thigh that started off facing the roasting pan was facing a cold pan that reflected little heat. When the thigh that started by facing up was turned facedown, the pan was hot and was radiating plenty of heat. To even things out, we decided to preheat the roasting pan.

Having roasted 14 chickens, we had finally arrived at the best method: Roast the untrussed chicken on its side at 375 degrees in a preheated pan, turning it on its other side after 15 minutes. After another 15 minutes, turn the chicken breast-side up and cook at 450 degrees until the thigh has reached an internal temperature of 165 to 170 degrees and the breast registers 160 degrees. Easy, straightforward, and guaranteed (or as guaranteed as cooking methods can be) to produce a truly satisfying roast chicken.

Simplest Roast Chicken
SERVES 3 TO 4

A 3½-pound bird should roast in 55 to 60 minutes, while a 4-pound bird requires 60 to 65 minutes. We recommend using a V-rack (see right), but be sure to grease it so the chicken does not stick to it. If you don't have a V-rack, set the bird on a regular roasting rack and use balls of aluminum foil to keep the roasting chicken

propped up on its side. Although we recommend kosher chicken for this recipe, you can also brine your chicken with similar results; see the variation that follows the recipe for instructions on brining chicken.

I   whole kosher chicken (3½ to 4 pounds; see the box on page 306 for guidelines on selecting the best-tasting chicken), rinsed and patted dry, giblets removed and reserved for another use

2   tablespoons unsalted butter, melted
Salt and ground black pepper
Vegetable oil for the V-rack

1. Place a shallow roasting pan in the oven and heat the oven to 375 degrees. Brush the chicken with the butter and sprinkle liberally with salt and pepper to taste.

2. Remove the heated pan from the oven and set the oiled V-rack in it. Place the chicken on the rack, wing-side up. Roast 15 minutes. Rotate the chicken so that the other wing side is up. Roast 15 minutes, then rotate the chicken, breast-side up. Turn the oven to 450 degrees. Roast until an instant-read thermometer inserted in the breast registers 160 degrees and in the thigh registers between 165 and 170 degrees, 20 to 25 minutes longer. Transfer the chicken to a cutting board; let rest 10 minutes. Carve and serve.

➤ VARIATION
Simplest Brined Roast Chicken
We do not recommend brining kosher chicken because it's already salted, and the brining will make the meat unpalatably salty. Use this recipe for brining when you can't find kosher chicken. This recipe uses table salt (not

EQUIPMENT: V-Racks

As the name suggests, a V-rack is a V-shaped metal roasting rack that serves to hold a chicken (or turkey) at the same time as it elevates it, allowing for complete air circulation, resulting in even cooking. We recommend purchasing a fixed V-rack (as opposed to an adjustable one) because we've found that the adjustable V-racks are not as sturdy as the fixed ones and are prone to collapse, especially after turning the bird.

kosher) in its brine. If you'd like to use kosher salt, whose large flakes measure differently from fine-grained table salt, see page 312 for conversion information.

Dissolve ½ cup table salt in 2 quarts cold water in a large bowl, stockpot, or Dutch oven. Immerse the chicken in the brine and refrigerate for 1 hour. Remove the chicken from the brine and pat dry with paper towels. Proceed with the recipe for Simplest Roast Chicken.

GARLIC–ROSEMARY ROAST CHICKEN

IN THE TUSCAN TRADITION, GARLIC AND ROSEMARY add flavor to a roast chicken. Indeed, they render it heady and robust, but garlic and rosemary are often bullies, overly aggressive and assertive. This explains why an exceptional garlic and rosemary roast chicken is even more of a rarity than a plain one.

An assessment of several recipes revealed a nearly universal approach to this dish: the simple application of a garlic-rosemary mixture beneath the skin before roasting. The recipes that we tried yielded, for the most part, overroasted chickens with tough, parched breast meat, and just one bite filled the mouth with the astringent, resinous flavor of rosemary and a vaguely raw and very sharp garlickiness that could be tasted for days. The task at hand was to harness the flavors of garlic and rosemary and unite them with a perfectly roasted chicken with tender and moist breast and thigh meat.

Good garlic-rosemary roast chicken begins with the roasting method. We wanted the garlic and rosemary seasoning to penetrate the meat (not just be a flavor accent to the skin), so we turned to brining. From previous tests, the kitchen has found that brining, or soaking in a saltwater solution, adds moisture and seasoning to meat, so that's where we began. For our flavored brine, we crushed 10 garlic cloves and 3 sprigs of rosemary with ½ cup salt, stirred the mixture into a pint of hot tap water to allow the flavors to bloom, then added cold water to cool the mixture before adding the chicken. The difference this time, in using the brine, was notable. This roast chicken was subtly flavored and perfumed with garlic and rosemary.

Past kitchen tests have shown that starting a bird breast-side down helps with even cooking (the legs get heat exposure and a head start, while the breast is shielded), and our findings concurred with these tests. We also agreed that dividing the roasting time (about one hour for a 4-pound bird) between two oven temperatures (375 and 450 degrees) yielded tender, moist meat and nice browning, two antithetical objectives. But we reversed the order. We started the chicken breast-side down at 450 and finished it breast-side up at 375. This way, the part of the bird that bore the brunt of the heat was the sturdier dark meat of the legs, not the delicate white breast meat, which proved to be more tender when exposed to more moderate temperatures.

Tasters agreed that a *jus* (a light sauce) was essential for adding more garlic and rosemary flavor to this dish. Liquid added to the roasting pan at the halfway point prevented the drippings from scorching so that a jus could be made from them. We made a minor adjustment by adding a greater amount of liquid to reduce the risk of complete evaporation and then singeing. Though the liquid could be added at the outset instead of at the midpoint, it was unnecessary simply because it was not until the latter portion of roasting that the drippings tended to burn. Liquid in the roasting pan meant that the skin would not be ultracrisp, but there seemed little point in crisping the skin when a sauce would be moistening it just before serving.

Applying a garlic and rosemary mixture beneath the skin in the style of most recipes is the best method of incorporating flavor (tossing whole garlic cloves and rosemary sprigs into the cavity did not work), but questions remained. First, should the garlic-rosemary mixture include a fat element, either butter or olive oil? It should. A fruity, aromatic olive oil (butter seemed out of place) helped in the distribution of the garlic and rosemary and also added flavor. We next tried preparing the garlic for the paste in a few different ways. To our surprise, the simplest method—calling for a modest 2 teaspoons of raw garlic—was pleasantly punchy and the uncontested favorite. Responding to comments that the rosemary was too pungent and piney, we pared it back to just 2 teaspoons minced and made the necessary adjustments to the amounts of olive oil, salt, and pepper. We distributed just a portion of this modest amount of aromatic paste under the skin of the breast and thigh areas. The remainder we rubbed into the cavity of the chicken to season the drippings that gathered within, which would flavor the jus. This judicious seasoning was key: The chicken met with success.

The chicken was good, but the resulting jus was lacking in depth. Chicken broth and a small amount of white wine helped, but, in keeping with the theme of this dish, a bit of garlic and rosemary was also required. Once again, we prepared the garlic in a number of different ways: We toasted it, sliced and sautéed it, minced and sautéed it, and incorporated raw garlic into the jus. Sweet, mellow slowly roasted garlic mashed to a paste took the honors. To circumvent roasting the garlic separately under its own cover, we tried tossing unpeeled cloves (about 10) into the roasting pan and roasting them beneath the chicken. There they became soft and creamy, and because they sat for some time in the liquid and drippings, their flavors permeated the jus. The only problem was that the garlic cloves were too darkly colored in spots, but that was easily remedied by adding the cloves to the roasting pan 15 minutes into cooking, giving them just 15 minutes of dry heat to brown before adding the liquid. As for the rosemary, one sprig added to the simmering liquid and discarded before serving provided just the right amount of flavor.

Garlic-Rosemary Roast Chicken with Jus

SERVES 3 TO 4

See the box on page 306 for guidelines on selecting the best-tasting chicken. This recipe uses table salt (not kosher) in its brine. If you'd like to use kosher salt, whose large flakes measure differently from fine-grained table salt, see page 312 for conversion information.

If the roasting pan is considerably larger than the chicken, keep an eye on the pan drippings; the greater surface area may mean more rapid evaporation and a risk of burnt drippings. Add water to the pan as necessary if the liquid evaporates.

CHICKEN

1/2	cup table salt
10	garlic cloves, unpeeled
3	sprigs fresh rosemary
1	whole chicken (3 1/2 to 4 pounds), trimmed of excess fat, chicken rinsed and patted dry, giblets removed and reserved for another use

GARLIC-ROSEMARY PASTE

2	teaspoons minced fresh rosemary leaves
2	medium garlic cloves, minced or pressed through a garlic press
1/8	teaspoon salt
	Ground black pepper
2	tablespoons extra-virgin olive oil

JUS

10	medium-large garlic cloves, unpeeled
1/2	teaspoon extra-virgin olive oil
1 3/4	cups low-sodium chicken broth
1/2	cup water
1/4	cup dry white wine or vermouth
1	sprig fresh rosemary
	Salt and ground black pepper

1. FOR THE CHICKEN: Combine the salt, garlic, and rosemary in a zipper-lock bag; seal, pressing out the air. With a meat pounder or rolling pin, pound the garlic cloves until crushed. Transfer the mixture to a large bowl, stockpot, or Dutch oven and stir in 2 cups hot tap water; let stand 10 minutes to release the flavors. Add 1½ quarts cold water and stir until the salt is dissolved. Immerse the chicken in the brine, cover, and refrigerate 1 hour.

2. Remove the chicken from the brine and pat dry with paper towels. Adjust an oven rack to the lower-middle position and heat the oven to 450 degrees. Set a V-rack in a small roasting pan and lightly spray the rack with nonstick cooking spray.

3. FOR THE PASTE: Stir the rosemary, garlic, salt, ¼ teaspoon pepper, and 1 tablespoon of the oil together in a small bowl. Rub about 1½ teaspoons

of the paste in the cavity of the chicken. Carefully loosen the skin over the breast and thigh on each side; slip half of the remaining paste under the skin on each side of the breast, then, using your fingers, distribute the paste over the breast and thigh by rubbing the surface of the skin (see the illustrations below). Tie the ends of the drumsticks together with kitchen twine and tuck the wings behind the back. Rub all sides of the chicken with 2 teaspoons of the oil and season with pepper. Set the chicken breast-side down on the prepared V-rack and roast 15 minutes.

4. FOR THE JUS: While the chicken is roasting, toss the garlic cloves with the oil; after the chicken has roasted 15 minutes, scatter the garlic cloves in the pan and continue to roast 15 minutes.

5. Remove the roasting pan from the oven; decrease the oven temperature to 375 degrees. Using tongs or wads of paper towels, rotate the chicken breast-side up; brush the breast with the remaining 1 teaspoon oil. Add 1 cup of the broth and the water to the pan and continue to roast until the chicken is medium golden brown and an instant-read thermometer inserted into the thickest part of the breast and thigh registers about 160 and 170 degrees, respectively, 20 to 25 minutes, adding more water to the roasting pan if the liquid evaporates. Tip the V-rack to allow the juices in the cavity to run into the roasting pan. Transfer the chicken to a large plate.

6. Remove the garlic cloves to a cutting board. Using a wooden spoon, scrape up the browned bits in the roasting pan and pour the liquid into a 2-cup liquid measuring cup. Allow the liquid to settle; meanwhile, peel the garlic and mash to a paste with a fork. Using a soup spoon, skim the fat off the surface of the liquid (you should have about ⅔ cup skimmed liquid; if not, supplement with water). Transfer the liquid to a small saucepan, then add the wine, rosemary sprig, remaining ¾ cup broth, and garlic paste; simmer over medium-high heat until reduced to about 1 cup, about 8 minutes. Add the accumulated juices from the chicken and discard the rosemary sprig; adjust the seasonings with salt and pepper to taste. Carve the chicken and serve with the jus.

➤ VARIATION

Garlic-Rosemary Roast Chicken with Potatoes

In this variation, the jus is omitted and the potatoes roast in the flavorful drippings. The roasted garlic can be spread on bread and eaten alongside the chicken.

Follow the recipe for Garlic-Rosemary Roast Chicken with Jus through step 3, omitting the jus ingredients (and step 4). During the first 15 minutes of roasting, quarter 1½ pounds 2-inch red or Yukon Gold potatoes; toss the potatoes, 10 medium-large unpeeled garlic cloves, 1½ tablespoons extra-virgin olive oil, and ¼ teaspoon each salt and pepper in a medium bowl. After the chicken has roasted 15 minutes, scatter the potatoes and garlic in a single layer in the roasting pan; roast for another 15 minutes. Continue with the

APPLYING THE PASTE

 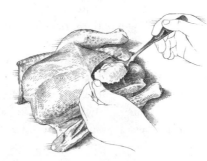 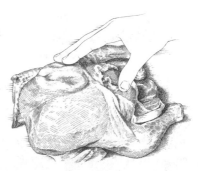

1. With your fingers, carefully loosen the skin over the breast and thigh.

2. Spoon some garlic-rosemary paste under the skin on each side of the breast.

3. With your fingers on top of the skin, work the paste to distribute it evenly over the breast and thigh.

recipe from step 5, omitting the addition of the liquid to the roasting pan and stirring the potatoes after rotating the chicken. When the chicken is done, do not tip the V-rack with the roast chicken to allow the juices to run into the roasting pan. While the chicken rests, transfer the potatoes and garlic to a large paper towel–lined plate and pat with additional paper towels. Carve the chicken and serve with the potatoes and garlic.

CHICKEN WITH 40 CLOVES OF GARLIC

POULET À QUARANTE GOUSSES D'AIL, OR "chicken with 40 cloves of garlic," is a classic Provençal dish that entered into the American culinary consciousness several decades ago, when our interest in French gastronomy was sparked. But since its introduction, chicken with 40 cloves of garlic has failed to make it onto many dinner tables or into many cooks' repertoires—and not without reason.

Recipes for chicken with 40 cloves of garlic involve a whole or cut-up chicken. Sometimes the chicken is browned, sometimes not. It is put into a pot along with raw garlic cloves (most often unpeeled), some liquid (usually wine and/ or chicken broth), sometimes onions and other aromatic vegetables and herbs, and then the lot is cooked, covered, for an hour or more. The garlic becomes soft and spreadable, but its flavor is spiritless, not like that of sweet, sticky roasted garlic. With such prolonged cooking, the chicken becomes tender, but the breast meat takes on a dry, chalky quality, and the flavor of the chicken in general is vapid, as if it has been washed out into the liquid. In addition, as cannot be helped in moist-heat cookery, the chicken skin is soggy, flabby, and wholly unappealing, even if the chicken had first been browned.

A diagnostic test of several recipes found all tasters in agreement. We all sought richer, more concentrated flavors like those imparted by roasting, not braising. We wanted the chicken browned, full-flavored, and crisp-skinned, the garlic browned, sweet, and nutty. And we wanted a savory sauce to unite the elements.

Our first decision was to use a cut-up chicken rather than a whole bird because it cooks faster and more evenly. We brined the chicken, browned it in a large skillet, tossed in the unpeeled garlic cloves from three medium heads (42 cloves, so pretty true to the name), and slipped the skillet into a hot oven. About 12 minutes later, the chicken was fully cooked; we removed the chicken pieces, leaving the garlic in the skillet, and made a pan sauce with the drippings, wine, chicken broth, and butter. The gravest offense of this attempt came from the garlic: The cloves were far from done. Although they were browned, they were neither creamy nor spreadable, and they had a raw, fiery flavor. The second problem was that the chicken, though flavorful and crisp-skinned, seemed divorced from the other elements. Third, the sauce lacked depth and tasted of neither the

DEVELOPING THE FLAVOR OF THE GARLIC

Remove the outer papery skins from three heads of garlic and separate but do not peel the individual cloves (far left). Lightly oil the cloves and roast them in a pie plate covered with foil; remove the foil (second from left) and continue to roast until the cloves are fully tender. Add the roasted cloves to the braising liquid in the skillet (center), return the chicken to the pan, and place the skillet in the oven. When the chicken is done, remove a dozen garlic cloves and use a rubber spatula to push them through a mesh sieve to remove the skins to obtain a smooth paste (second from right). Whisk the garlic paste into the pan sauce just before serving (right).

Brining Poultry 101

Why are some chickens and turkeys dry as sawdust while others boast meat that's firm, juicy, and well seasoned? The answer is brining. Soaking a chicken or turkey in a brine—a solution of salt (and often sugar) and a liquid (usually water)—provides it with a plump cushion of seasoned moisture that will sustain it throughout cooking. The bird will actually gain a bit of weight—call it, for lack of a better phrase, water retention—that stays with it through the cooking process. This weight gain translates into moist meat; the salt and sugar in the brine translate into seasoned, flavorful meat. For a complete understanding of the process, read on.

SCIENCE: WHY BRINING WORKS

Many have attributed the added juiciness of brined chicken to osmosis—the flow of water across a barrier from a place with a higher water concentration (the brine) to a place with a lower one (the chicken). We decided to test this explanation. If osmosis is, in fact, the source of the added juiciness of brined meat, we reasoned, then a bucket of pure unsalted water should add moisture at least as well as a brine, because water alone has the highest water concentration possible: 100 percent. After soaking one chicken in brine and another in water for the same amount of time, we found that both had gained moisture, about 6 percent by weight. Satisfied that osmosis was indeed the force driving the addition of moisture to meat during brining, we roasted the two birds, along with a third straight out of the package. We would soon discover that osmosis was not the only reason why brined meat cooked up juicy.

During roasting, the chicken taken straight from the package lost 18 percent of its original weight, and the chicken soaked in water lost 12 percent of its presoak weight. Remarkably, the brined bird shed a mere 7 percent of its starting weight. Looking at the test results, we realized that the benefit of brining could not be explained by osmosis alone. Salt, too, was playing a crucial role by aiding in the retention of water.

Table salt is made up of two ions, sodium and chloride, that are oppositely charged. Proteins, such as those in meat, are large molecules that contain a mosaic of charges, negative and positive. When proteins are placed in a solution containing salt, they readjust their shape to accommodate the opposing charges. This rearrangement of the protein molecules compromises the structural integrity of the meat, reducing its overall toughness. It also creates gaps that fill up with water. The added salt makes the water less likely to evaporate during cooking, and the result is meat that is both juicy and tender.

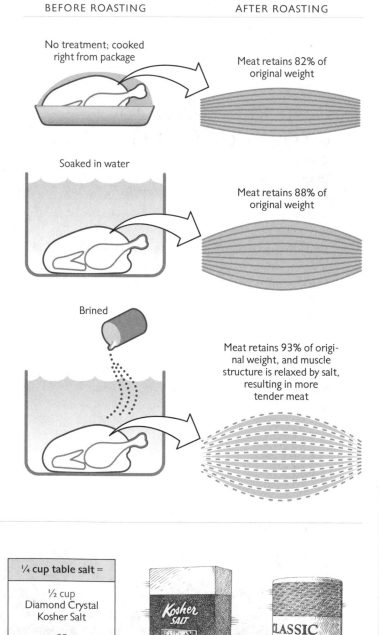

BEFORE ROASTING — AFTER ROASTING

No treatment; cooked right from package

Meat retains 82% of original weight

Soaked in water

Meat retains 88% of original weight

Brined

Meat retains 93% of original weight, and muscle structure is relaxed by salt, resulting in more tender meat

TWO TYPES OF SALT FOR BRINING

You can use either kosher or regular table salt for brining. Kosher salt is ideal because its large, airy crystals dissolve so quickly in water. Unfortunately, the salt crystals of the two major brands of kosher salt—Morton and Diamond Crystal—are not equally airy, and therefore measure differently. This inconsistency between the two brands makes precise recipe writing a challenge. Because there's no accounting for which brand of kosher salt you might have on hand, we list table salt in our brining recipes. If you use kosher salt in your brine, keep in mind the following when making the conversions from table salt in our brining recipes:

¼ cup table salt =
½ cup Diamond Crystal Kosher Salt
—or—
¼ cup plus 2 tablespoons Morton Kosher Salt

KOSHER SALT   TABLE SALT

TOOLS OF THE TRADE

From zipper-lock plastic bags that fit on the shelf of the refrigerator to a self-contained cooler chilled with ice packs and stored in a cool garage or cellar, brining vessels come in all shapes and sizes. When brining in coolers or large containers, it may be necessary to weight the food down with a wide, heavy object such as a dinner plate or soup bowl. This helps keep the food fully immersed in the brine.

ZIPPER-LOCK PLASTIC BAGS
Use for: Chicken or turkey parts

COOLER OR WASHTUB
Use for: Turkey

LARGE BOWL, SOUP POT, OR DUTCH OVEN
Use for: Cornish hen (whole or butterflied), chicken (whole or butterflied)

ICE PACKS
The refrigerator keeps a brine at the ideal temperature of 40 degrees. Ice packs keep the temperature down when refrigerator space is at a premium or the brining vessel is especially large.

TWO WAYS TO RINSE BRINED POULTRY

Some recipes call for rinsing brined chicken or turkey of the excess salt on its surface. However, this step can make a soggy mess of your countertop. Using your sink to contain the mess and a wire rack or colander to hold the meat will streamline the process.

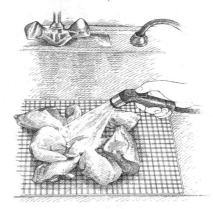

Place the chicken or turkey on a wire rack or in a colander. Set the rack or colander in an empty sink and use the sink sprayer or tap to wash off the meat. Then blot the meat dry with paper towels.

HANGING IT OUT TO DRY

Brining does have one negative effect on chicken and turkey: Adding moisture to the skin as well as the flesh can prevent the skin from crisping when cooked. We found that air-drying, a technique used in many Chinese recipes for roast duck, solves this problem. Letting brined chicken and turkey dry uncovered in the refrigerator allows surface moisture to evaporate, making the skin visibly more dry and taut, thereby promoting crispness when cooked. Although this step is optional, if crisp skin is a goal, it's worth the extra time. For best results, air-dry whole brined birds overnight. Brined chicken parts can be air-dried for several hours.

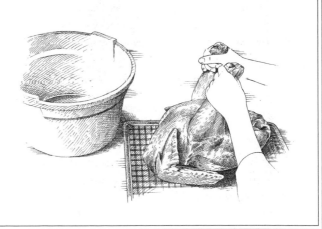

Transfer the brined bird to a heavy-duty cooling rack set over a rimmed baking sheet, pat the bird dry with paper towels, and refrigerate. The rack lifts the bird off the baking sheet, allowing air to circulate freely under the bird.

chicken nor the garlic. Despite its demerits, this technique showed enough promise that we were compelled to pursue it.

We grappled with the garlic first. We knew that to soften and gain color, the cloves would have to roast in dry heat, but they would require considerably more time to roast than was built into the pan-roasting technique. Hence, they would need to be at least partially roasted by the time they joined the chicken. Some tests later, we arrived at roasting the garlic cloves, tossed with a little olive oil, salt, and pepper, in a small baking dish for 40 minutes in a 400-degree oven. For the first 30 minutes, they cooked under foil to speed things along. For the final 10 minutes, they went uncovered to finish browning. At this point, the garlic cloves were soft, sweet, and mellow but could still withstand some additional cooking with the chicken and sauce. Because the garlic could be roasted while the chicken was being brined and browned, this step did not add time to the recipe.

We then focused on refining the cooking technique. In a braise, the chicken cooks half-submerged in simmering liquid, and an exchange of flavors thereby occurs to the benefit of both the chicken and the liquid that becomes the sauce. This made us decide to modify the pan-roasting

technique. After we browned the chicken, we poured off the rendered fat, added chicken broth and dry vermouth (we came to use vermouth because it is herbaceous, slightly sweet, and more flavorful than most white wines of the same price), added the roasted garlic cloves, returned the chicken skin-side up, and then put the skillet in the 400-degree oven from which the garlic had emerged. Things were slightly improved with this pan-roasting/braising technique. The sauce had better flavor, although it was still mousy, especially in texture, and the chicken seemed to be more a part of the dish. The skin, however, had turned soggy from the moisture.

To counter the effects of the moisture, we tried increasing the oven temperature to 450 degrees. This produced acceptably crisp skin. The ultimate solution, however, was a quick blast of broiler heat, which crisped the skin very nicely in less than five minutes. Because cooks with drawer-type gas broilers might find this step inconvenient, if not impossible, we made it optional. We were nonetheless pleased with the results of this hybrid pan-roasting/braising technique.

Now a different issue came into play. The brined chicken, cooked in the liquid that eventually becomes the sauce, seemed to exude juices

---

INGREDIENTS: Garlic

Garlic falls into two primary categories: hardneck and softneck. The garlic that most of us cook with is softneck, so called because its neck is soft and braidable. Softneck garlic contains a circle of plump cloves shrouding a second circle of smaller cloves, all enveloped by many papery layers. Because softneck garlic is heat-tolerant and produces and stores well, it has become the favored commercial garlic. Supermarket garlics are almost invariably softneck.

Hardneck, which is the original cultivated garlic variety, is distinguished by its stiff center staff, around which large uniform cloves hang. Hardneck garlic has a relatively sparse parchment wrapper that makes it easier to peel (and damage) than softneck. It is considered superior in flavor—more complex and intense than softneck. Its thinly wrapped cloves lose moisture quickly, however, and do not winter over, as do the cloves of the robust softneck.

We tasted eight garlic varieties, softneck and hardneck, raw and cooked, and found a wide range of flavors. We enjoyed several softneck and hardneck varieties, but our favorites were Porcelain Zemo and Rocambole Carpathian, both of which are hardnecks.

TWO TYPES OF GARLIC

HARDNECK GARLIC   **SOFTNECK GARLIC**

Hardneck garlic has a stiff center staff around which its large, uniformly sized cloves hang. Softneck garlic, the kind found most commonly in supermarkets, has cloves of varying sizes (larger on the outside, smaller near the center) and no central staff.

---

that resulted in an overseasoned sauce, even for those tasters who love salt. We pulled back on the salt in the brine until we were using only ¼ cup of table salt per 2 quarts of water. Unsure that this small amount was of any benefit to the dish as a whole, we compared it with a batch made with unbrined chicken. Even this weak brine improved the flavor and juiciness of the cooked chicken.

Finally, we worked on the flavor of the sauce. Inspired by those recipes that included onions, we roasted some shallots—milder in flavor than onions—with the garlic cloves to see if they would affect the flavor of the sauce. Indeed they did. The sauce tasted fuller and rounder. Some tasters even found the roasted shallots to be good eating. Herbs—thyme, rosemary, and bay—all had pleasing effects on the flavor of the sauce, offering depth and complexity.

We had seen in another recipe the recommendation of mashing a few of the garlic cloves and adding them back to the sauce. Using a mesh sieve and a rubber spatula, we made a paste of a dozen or so peeled garlic cloves and whisked it into the sauce. (Peeling the cloves and then mashing them on a cutting board with the back of a fork is another effective method.) What an extraordinarily good idea. The garlic paste endowed the sauce with the velvety texture of a well-made gravy, and the sauce was now richly flavored with garlic as well as chicken and wine. Last, several tablespoons of butter to enrich the sauce met with applause.

Chicken with 40 Cloves of Garlic

SERVES 3 TO 4

Try not to purchase heads of garlic that contain enormous cloves; if unavoidable, increase the foil-covered baking time to 40 to 45 minutes so that the largest cloves soften fully. A large Dutch oven can be used in place of a skillet, if you prefer. See the box on page 306 for guidelines on selecting the best-tasting chicken. This recipe uses table salt (not kosher) in its brine. If you'd like to use kosher salt, whose large flakes measure differently from fine-grained table salt, see page 312 for conversion information. Broiling the chicken for a few minutes at the end of cooking crisps the skin but is optional. Serve the dish with slices of crusty baguette; you can dip them into the sauce or spread them with the roasted garlic cloves.

I	whole chicken (3½ to 4 pounds), trimmed of excess fat, chicken rinsed and patted dry, giblets removed and reserved for another use
¼	cup table salt
	Ground black pepper
3	medium garlic heads, outer papery skins removed, cloves separated and unpeeled
2	medium shallots, peeled and quartered
I	tablespoon olive oil
	Salt
2	sprigs fresh thyme
I	sprig fresh rosemary
I	bay leaf
¾	cup dry vermouth or white wine
¾	cup low-sodium chicken broth
2	tablespoons unsalted butter

1. Adjust an oven rack to the middle position and heat the oven to 400 degrees. Following the illustrations on page 329, cut the chicken into 8 pieces (4 breast pieces, 2 thighs, 2 drumsticks), discarding the wings. Dissolve the salt in 2 quarts cold water in a large bowl, stockpot, or Dutch oven; immerse the chicken pieces in the brine and refrigerate until fully seasoned, about 30 minutes. Rinse the chicken pieces under running water and thoroughly pat dry with paper towels. Season both sides of the chicken pieces with pepper.

2. Meanwhile, toss the garlic and shallots with 2 teaspoons of the olive oil and salt and pepper to taste in a 9-inch pie plate; cover tightly with foil and roast until softened and beginning to brown, about 30 minutes, shaking the pan once to toss the contents after 15 minutes (the foil can be left on during tossing). Uncover, stir, and continue to roast, uncovered, until browned and fully tender, 10 minutes longer, stirring once or twice. Remove from the oven and increase the oven temperature to 450 degrees.

3. Using kitchen twine, tie together the thyme, rosemary, and bay leaf; set aside. Heat the remaining 1 teaspoon olive oil in a 12-inch heavy-bottomed ovenproof skillet over medium-high heat until

beginning to smoke; swirl to coat the pan with oil. Brown the chicken pieces, skin-side down, until deep golden, about 5 minutes; using tongs, turn the chicken pieces and brown until golden on the second side, about 4 minutes longer. Transfer the chicken to a large plate and discard the fat; off the heat, add the vermouth, chicken broth, and herbs to the skillet, scraping the bottom with a wooden spoon to loosen the browned bits. Set the skillet over medium heat, add the garlic-shallot mixture, and return the chicken, skin-side up, to the pan, nestling the pieces on top of and between the garlic cloves.

4. Place the skillet in the oven and roast until an instant-read thermometer inserted into the thickest part of the breast registers about 160 degrees, 10 to 12 minutes. If desired, increase the heat to broil and broil to crisp the skin, 3 to 5 minutes. Using potholders or oven mitts, remove the skillet from the oven and transfer the chicken to a serving dish. Remove 10 to 12 garlic cloves to a mesh sieve and reserve; using a slotted spoon, scatter the remaining garlic cloves and shallots around the chicken and discard the herbs. With a rubber spatula, push the reserved garlic cloves through the sieve into a bowl; discard the skins. Add the garlic paste to the skillet. Bring the liquid to a simmer over medium-high heat, whisking occasionally to incorporate the garlic. Adjust the seasoning with salt and pepper to taste. Whisk in the butter until incorporated. Pour the sauce into a sauceboat and serve with the chicken.

HIGH-ROAST CHICKEN

AT THE PINNACLE OF SIMPLE FOOD IS ROAST chicken—the easy answer to any weeknight cooking conundrum. Our basic roast chicken fits that bill of fare perfectly.

But occasionally we want something different. We'd heard mentioned the "high-roasting" technique for chicken in which the bird is roasted at temperatures in excess of 450 degrees. The method is reputed to produce a better bird, with crisp skin tanned to a deep golden hue. The only drawback we could foresee was that the breast meat might be prone to overcooking at such high temperatures.

In her book *Roasting: A Simple Art* (Morrow, 1995), Barbara Kafka suggests roasting a 5- to 6-pound bird at 500 degrees for about an hour. While cooking a chicken in that manner seemed to verge on pyromaniacal, we had heard several people swear by the method. So along with roasting birds at 425 and 450 degrees, we gave it a go. However, we decided to use 3½- to 4-pound birds because they are the size most commonly found in grocery stores.

When the birds came out of the oven, the differences between them were marked. The 500-degree bird was a looker, with beautiful, deep brown, crisp skin. The other two were splotchy and only mildly attractive. And, of course, the inevitable had occurred: The breast meat on all the birds had been torched; as the thighs sauntered up to the finish line, the more delicate breast meat overcooked. And, worst of all, with 450- and 500-degree oven temperatures, we chased everyone, coughing and hacking, out of the kitchen filled with billows of smoke.

To remedy the uneven cooking, we tried several adjustments, from preheated roasting pans to different configurations of oven temperatures, all to no avail. The obvious solution was to rotate the bird so that the breast would spend some time shielded from the intense oven heat while the thighs would receive the exposure they needed to catch up. After trying this technique, however, we vetoed it. We were after deep browning and crisp skin, neither of which was produced by this method. For that, the bird needs to spend all or at least most of the roasting time breast up.

We suspected that the fix lay in butterflying the chicken—that is, removing the backbone, then opening and flattening the bird. This method would give the thighs greater exposure to the heat, increasing the odds that they would cook at the same rate as the breast. In addition, all areas with skin would be faceup to facilitate even browning and crisping. We tried it, and it worked like a charm. The thighs actually raced ahead of the breast meat and finished first.

While butterflying a chicken is actually an easy task—it takes all of a couple of minutes—we wondered if that wasn't too much to ask of the home cook on a weeknight. And yet the results had been so good. Tasters concurred that butterflied roast chicken was roast chicken elevated to a whole new level in terms of both appearance and doneness. Consequently, we put our hesitations aside and concentrated on determining the best roasting temperature for a butterflied bird. Again, for the best-browned, most crispy, and nicest-looking bird, 500 degrees was the optimal temperature.

But there was still that smoking problem. We tried putting water in the pan under the bird (set on a rack), but this steamed the chicken and prevented the skin from crisping. We tried bread slices, soaked wood chips, and even uncooked rice to catch the drippings, but they all turned to charcoal before the chicken was done. Then we tried potatoes. They burned in spots, dried out in others, and stuck to the pan, but they also showed mouthwatering potential; tasters lined up for any morsel of crispy potato that could be salvaged. Even better, by creating a butter and absorbing some of the drippings, the potatoes kept the

fat from hitting the hot pan bottom, where it would normally sizzle and burn on contact. We knew that with some finessing, the answer to the smoking problem could also provide a great side dish.

We assumed that the potatoes would need some protection as they cooked to keep them from burning and drying out. A broiler pan came to the rescue. With its slotted top and its ample bottom pan, which nicely accommodated the potatoes, it was just what the chicken and potatoes ordered. The potatoes in the broiler pan had turned a deep brown and were as crisp as potato chips but far tastier. A foil lining on the pan bottom helped with potato removal and cleanup, and that was that. Not surprisingly, the potatoes won their own fans, who, waiting for the daily potato call, began to regard the chicken as the side dish.

Now that we had solved the major problems of high-roast chicken, we began to wonder if we could take this method to further new heights. Though the butterflied chickens had

BUTTERFLYING A CHICKEN

1. Cut through the bones on either side of the backbone, then remove and discard the backbone.

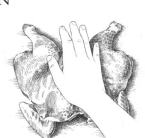

2. Flip the chicken over as shown and use the heel of your hand to flatten the breastbone.

3. If using a flavored butter, slip your fingers between skin and breast, loosening the membrane.

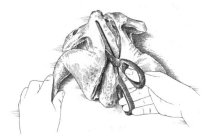

4. Scoop some of the butter onto a spoon, slide it under the breast skin, and push it off with your fingers.

5. Work the butter under the skin to cover the breast evenly. Repeat steps 4 and 5 with each drumstick and thigh.

6. Transfer the chicken to a broiler pan rack and push each leg up to rest between thigh and breast.

been emerging from the oven with crisp skin, we noticed that as they sat waiting to be carved, the breast skin became soggy. We began searching for a way to keep it crisp. We tried basting with oil, basting with butter, putting butter under the skin, putting chicken fat under the skin, and finishing the cooking under the broiler, but we found only one thing that worked. When other colleagues heard what it was, they rolled their eyes: drying the chicken uncovered overnight in the refrigerator. We borrowed the technique from recipes for crispy-skin Chinese roasted duck. Letting the bird dry uncovered in the fridge allows surface moisture to evaporate; the skin becomes dry and taut and so crisps more readily in the heat of the oven. It took a couple of side-by-side tastings to convince tasters that air-drying worked and was worth the effort. And even though we agreed that it is worth the trouble, it remains an option—that is, you can skip it and still have a great roast chicken.

EQUIPMENT: Kitchen Shears

A pair of kitchen shears is not an essential kitchen implement. But when you need to butterfly or trim chicken, there is no tool better suited than kitchen shears. To test their versatility, we also used kitchen shears to cut lengths of kitchen twine, trim pie dough, and cut out parchment paper rounds. We found two pairs to recommend.

Wüsthof Kitchen Shears ($28) made easy, smooth cuts even through small chicken bones and completed all tasks flawlessly. The size and proportion of the shears felt ideal—the blades could open wide for large jobs and to achieve more forceful cutting, but the shears were also suited to smaller, more detailed tasks such as snipping pieces of twine. These shears boasted heft, solid construction, and textured handles that were comfortable, even when wet and greasy. They were also suitable and comfortable for left-handed users.

Messermeister Take Apart Kitchen Shears ($17) were also great performers, though the blades didn't have quite the spread of those on the Wüsthof. These shears, too, made clean, easy cuts and accomplished all tasks without hesitation. The soft, rubber-like handles proved extremely comfortable, but lefties take note: These scissors were clearly designed for right-handed users.

The other step in preparation for roasting that makes a significant improvement in the flavor and texture of the bird is brining. The salt in the brine permeates the chicken, so the meat is evenly seasoned and full-flavored. Brining also keeps the breast meat moist and tender, providing a cushion if it overcooks a bit (though there's little chance of that happening with a butterflied bird). Brining solutions are formulated in concentrations to fit the duration of the brine; we chose to go with a very concentrated one-hour brine that can be done the evening you intend to roast the bird or, if you plan ahead, the night before, so that the bird can dry overnight in the refrigerator. But there is also a quick solution. In the course of testing different types of birds, we were glad to discover that kosher chickens, which are salted during processing to draw out fluids, provide an excellent alternative to brining for those cooks with time constraints.

With technique resolved, we wanted to work flavorings into the roast chicken. Clearly, anything on the surface of the chicken would burn at 500 degrees. Instead, garlic, herbs, and other bold flavors mixed with some softened butter and placed under the chicken skin before roasting added subtle, welcome flavor not only to the chicken but to the potatoes below as well.

When all was said and done, we had roasted four dozen chickens and more than 60 pounds of potatoes. But we had accomplished what we had set out to do: We had four-star, perfectly browned roast chicken with spectacular skin—and potatoes, too.

Crisp-Skin High-Roast Butterflied Chicken with Potatoes

SERVES 3 TO 4

See the box on page 306 for guidelines on selecting the best-tasting chicken. This recipe uses table salt (not kosher) in its brine. If you'd like to use kosher salt, whose large flakes measure differently from fine-grained table salt, see page 312 for conversion information. Because the brine contains sugar and you'll be cooking the chicken under high heat, it's important that you rinse it thoroughly before proceeding—otherwise, the sugar remaining on the skin will caramelize and ultimately burn. For extra-crisp skin, after applying the flavored butter (if using), let the chicken dry uncovered in the refrigerator for 8 to 24 hours. For this cooking technique, russet potatoes offer the best potato flavor, but Yukon Golds develop a beautiful color and better retain their shape after cooking. Either works well in this recipe. A food processor makes quick and easy work of slicing the potatoes.

½   cup table salt

½   cup sugar

I   whole chicken (3½ to 4 pounds), trimmed of excess fat, chicken rinsed and patted dry, giblets removed and reserved for another use
Vegetable cooking spray

I   recipe flavored butter for placing under skin (optional; recipes follow)

2½   pounds russet or Yukon Gold potatoes (4 or 5 medium), peeled and sliced ⅛ to ¼ inch thick

1½   tablespoons olive oil

¾   teaspoon salt (for potatoes)
Ground black pepper

1. Dissolve the salt and sugar in 2 quarts cold water in a large bowl, stockpot, or Dutch oven. Immerse the chicken in the brine, cover, and refrigerate until fully seasoned, about 1 hour. Meanwhile, adjust an oven rack to the lower-middle position and heat the oven to 500 degrees. Line the bottom of a broiler pan with foil and spray with vegetable cooking spray. Remove the chicken from the brine and rinse thoroughly under cold running water. Following the illustrations on page 317, butterfly the chicken and flatten the breastbone. Apply the flavored butter (if using) by slipping your fingers underneath the skin of the breast and legs to loosen the membrane and rub the mixture beneath the skin. Position the chicken on the broiler pan rack and push each leg up to rest between the thigh and breast; thoroughly pat dry with paper towels.

2. Toss the potatoes with 1 tablespoon of the olive oil, the salt, and pepper to taste in a medium bowl. Spread the potatoes in an even layer in the foil-lined broiler pan bottom. Place the broiler pan rack with the chicken on top. Rub the chicken with the remaining ½ tablespoon oil and sprinkle with pepper to taste.

3. Roast the chicken until spotty brown, about 20 minutes. Rotate the pan and continue to roast until the skin has crisped and turned deep brown and an instant-read thermometer registers 160 degrees in the thickest part of the breast, 20 to 25 minutes longer. Transfer the chicken to a cutting board. With potholders, remove the broiler pan rack; soak up excess grease from the potatoes with several sheets of paper towels. Remove the foil liner with the potatoes from the broiler pan bottom and invert the foil and potatoes onto a baking sheet or second cutting board. Carefully

CARVING A BUTTERFLIED CHICKEN

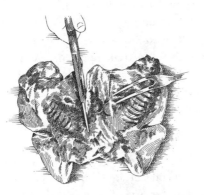

1. Place chicken skin-side down and use kitchen shears to cut through the breastbone. (Since the breastbone is broken and the meat is flattened during pounding, this should be easy.)

2. Once the breast has been split, only the skin is holding the portions together. Separate each leg and thigh from each breast and wing.

peel back the foil, using a metal spatula to help scrape the potatoes off the foil as needed. With additional paper towels, pat off the remaining grease. Cut the chicken into serving pieces and serve with the potatoes.

Chipotle Butter with Lime and Honey

MAKES ABOUT 3 TABLESPOONS

2   tablespoons unsalted butter, softened
1   medium garlic clove, minced or pressed through a garlic press
1   teaspoon honey
1   teaspoon very finely grated lime zest
1   medium chipotle chile in adobo sauce, minced to a paste, plus 1 teaspoon adobo sauce

Mash all of the ingredients together in a small bowl.

Mustard–Garlic Butter with Thyme

MAKES ABOUT 3 TABLESPOONS

2   tablespoons unsalted butter, softened
1   medium garlic clove, minced or pressed through a garlic press
1   tablespoon Dijon mustard
1   teaspoon minced fresh thyme leaves
    Ground black pepper

Mash all of the ingredients, including pepper to taste, together in a small bowl.

PAN-ROASTED CHICKEN BREASTS

THE BEST WAY TO COOK BONE-IN CHICKEN breasts is over a live fire on a hot grill. But during the colder months of the year, cooking them becomes a challenge. Oven-roasting whole chicken breasts fails to impress us because the delicate white meat cooks faster than the skin can crisp. This cut of chicken is also difficult to sauté or cook through

on the stovetop because it has great girth on one end and is thin and tapered on the other. If overcooked, it becomes dry and takes on the texture of overchewed bubble gum. And last, this piece of chicken has a mild—some might say bland—flavor that could certainly use a boost.

Our immediate thought was to try pan-roasting, a restaurant technique in which food is browned in a skillet on the stovetop and then placed, skillet and all, in a hot oven to finish cooking. We often employ this technique to cook a whole cut-up chicken and wondered if pan-roasting could be adapted to breasts only, where the meat is thicker and more prone to drying out than in the legs and thighs. The goal was to produce moist, tender, crisp-skinned bone-in chicken breasts.

The first problem we encountered was the packaging and quality of chicken breasts in the supermarket. Curiously, bone-in, skin-on split chicken breasts are often sold three to a package. (This makes no sense from either an anatomical or a culinary perspective.) More problematic are the realities that split chicken breasts are often covered only by shreds of skin and that large portions of the meat near the breastbone are often missing. An additional reason not to buy split chicken breasts is that the pieces within one package can differ greatly in size (we found 9-ounce and 13-ounce pieces in one pack). Obviously, smaller pieces cook more quickly, so when cooking pieces of divergent sizes, we were forced to monitor them closely and pull the smaller breasts out earlier. Not ideal. Consequently, we found we prefer to purchase whole chicken breasts and split them ourselves so that we have more control over their size, quantity, and condition.

With these matters resolved, we tried brining the chicken—soaking it in a saltwater solution—before cooking it. It was no surprise that this chicken was superior—more moist and better seasoned than unbrined chicken. Brining also mitigated the dryness and blandness typical of chicken breasts. For the sake of convenience, we went with a quick and concentrated brine—½ cup of table salt dissolved in 2 quarts of water—and a brine time of 30 minutes. The sugar that the test kitchen typically likes in brines was omitted from this recipe because

EQUIPMENT: Large Skillets

The choices in material, weight, brand, and price of skillets—from $10 to $140—are dizzying. Preliminary tests on a lightweight discount store special selling for $10 confirmed our suspicions that cheap was not the way to go. But how much do you need to spend on this vital piece of kitchen equipment? To find out what more money buys, we zeroed in on a group of eight pans from well-known manufacturers, ranging in price from $60 to more than twice that, and sautéed our way to some pretty surprising conclusions.

All of the pans tested had flared sides, a design that makes it easier to flip foods in the pan (accomplished by jerking the pan sharply on the burner). Oddly, this design feature has created some confusion when it comes to nomenclature. Different manufacturers have different names for their flare-sided pans, including sauté pan, skillet, frypan, chef's pan, and omelette pan. In the test kitchen, we refer to flare-sided pans as skillets and to pans with straight sides (and often lids as well) as sauté pans. All of the pans tested also fall into a category we refer to as traditional—that is, none of the pans were nonstick. Most had uncoated stainless steel cooking surfaces, which we prize for promoting a *fond* (the browned, sticky bits that cling to the interior of the pan when food is sautéed and that help flavor sauces).

The pans tested measured 12 inches in diameter (across the top) or as close to that as we could get from each manufacturer. We like this large size in a skillet because it can accommodate a big steak or all of the pieces of a cut-up 3½-pound chicken. Because the pan walls slope inward, the cooking surface of each pan measures considerably less than 12 inches. In fact, we found that even ¼ inch less cooking space could determine whether all of the chicken pieces fit without touching and therefore how well they would brown. (If a pan is too crowded, the food tends to steam rather than brown.) For instance, the All-Clad, with its 9¼-inch cooking surface, accommodated the chicken pieces without incident, whereas the 9-inch cooking surface of the Viking caused the pieces to touch.

Skillet construction also varies, and our group included two popular styles: clad and disk bottom. The All-Clad, Viking, Calphalon, Cuisinart, and KitchenAid units are clad, which means that the whole pan body, from the bottom up through the walls, is made from layers of the same metal that have been bonded under intense pressure and heat. These layers often form a sandwich, with the "filling" made of aluminum—which has the third-highest thermal conductivity of all metals, behind silver and copper—and each slice of "bread" is made of stainless

steel—which is attractive, durable, and nonreactive with acidic foods, but is a lousy heat conductor on its own.

In the disk-bottom construction style, only the pan bottom is layered, and the walls are thus thinner than the bottom. In our group, the Farberware has an aluminum sandwich base, and the Emerilware has disks of both aluminum and copper in its base.

Although some manufacturers tout the benefits of cladding, our kitchen testing did not support this. The two skillets with disk bottoms, the Farberware and the Emerilware, did heat up a little faster than the rest of the field, but it was easy to accommodate this difference by adjusting the stovetop burner. Both of these pans also performed well in cooking tests.

The weight of the pans turned out to be more important than construction, especially in our solder tests. The lightweight (1 pound, 1 ounce) aluminum budget pan was the quickest to reach 361 degrees, at an average of 2.8 minutes, but the lightweight pan performed poorly in kitchen tests.

We concluded that a range of 3 to 4 pounds is ideal in a 12-inch skillet. The medium-weight pans (especially those from All-Clad, Viking, and Calphalon) brown foods beautifully, and most testers handled them comfortably. These pans have enough heft for heat retention and structural integrity, but not so much that they are difficult to lift or manipulate.

Which skillet should you buy? For its combination of excellent performance, optimum weight and balance, and overall ease of use, the All-Clad was our favorite. But others, such as the Calphalon and Farberware, nearly matched the All-Clad in performance and good handling and did so for less than half the price, making these pans our two best buys.

THE BEST LARGE SKILLETS

The All-Clad Stainless 12-Inch Frypan (left: $125) took top honors in our testing. The Calphalon Tri-Ply Stainless 12-Inch Omelette Pan (top right: $65) and the Farberware Millennium 18/10 Stainless Steel 12-Inch Covered Skillet (bottom right: $70) were rated best buys, costing about half as much as the winning pan.

it caused scorching in the skillet. We also found it necessary to rinse the brined chicken before cooking; otherwise, the skin was unpalatably salty.

When it came to browning, we heated a mere teaspoon of vegetable oil in the skillet until it was smoking and then browned both sides of the chicken before transferring the skillet to the lowest rack in the oven. We tried oven temperatures ranging from 375 up to 500 degrees. Five hundred caused profuse smoking and sometimes singed drippings. Temperatures on the lower end meant protracted cooking times. At 450, however, the skin was handsomely browned and crackling crisp, and the chicken cooked swiftly to the internal temperature of 160 degrees, which translated to about 18 minutes for 12-ounce breasts.

The bonus of pan-roasting is that the skillet is left with caramelized drippings, or *fond*. To let the fond go to waste would be criminal; it is ideal for making a rich, flavorful pan sauce to accompany the chicken. Shallots, wine, chicken broth, herbs, and butter, or a variation on this combination, created pan sauces that added flavor interest and made these crisp-skinned, pan-roasted chicken breasts as good as, if not better than, their grilled incarnations.

Pan-Roasted Chicken Breasts with Sage-Vermouth Sauce

SERVES 4

We prefer to split whole chicken breasts ourselves because store-bought split chicken breasts are often sloppily butchered. However, if you prefer to purchase split chicken breasts, try to choose 10- to 12-ounce pieces with skin intact. If split breasts are of different sizes, check the smaller ones a few minutes early to see if they are cooking more quickly, and remove them from the skillet if they are done ahead. This recipe uses table salt (not kosher) in its brine. If you'd like to use kosher salt, whose large flakes measure differently than fine-grained table salt, see page 312 for conversion information.

CHICKEN
- ½ cup table salt
- 2 whole bone-in, skin-on chicken breasts (about 1½ pounds each), split in half along breast bone and trimmed of rib sections
- Ground black pepper
- 1 teaspoon vegetable oil

SAGE-VERMOUTH SAUCE
- 1 large shallot, minced (about 4 tablespoons)
- ¾ cup low-sodium chicken broth
- ½ cup dry vermouth
- 4 medium fresh sage leaves, each leaf torn in half
- 3 tablespoons unsalted butter, cut into 3 pieces
- Salt and ground black pepper

1. FOR THE CHICKEN: Dissolve the salt in 2 quarts cold water in a large bowl, stockpot, or Dutch oven. Immerse the chicken in the brine, cover, and refrigerate until fully seasoned, about 30 minutes. Remove the chicken from the brine, rinse under cold water, and pat dry with paper towels. Season the chicken with pepper.

2. Adjust an oven rack to the lowest position and heat the oven to 450 degrees.

3. Heat the oil in a heavy-bottomed 12-inch ovenproof skillet over medium-high heat until beginning to smoke; swirl the skillet to coat with the oil. Brown the chicken, skin-side down, until deep golden, about 5 minutes; turn the chicken pieces and brown until golden on the second side, about 3 minutes longer. Turn the chicken skin-side down and place the skillet in the oven. Roast until the juices run clear when the chicken is cut with a paring knife or the thickest part of the breast registers 160 degrees on an instant-read thermometer, 15 to 18 minutes. Using a potholder or oven mitt to protect your hands from the hot skillet handle, remove the skillet from the oven. Transfer the chicken to a platter, and let it rest while making the sauce. (If you're not making a sauce, let the chicken rest 5 minutes before serving.)

4. FOR THE SAUCE: Still using a potholder or oven mitt, pour off most of the fat from the skillet; add the shallot, then set the skillet over medium-high heat and cook, stirring frequently, until the shallot is softened, about 1½ minutes. Add the chicken broth, vermouth, and sage, increase the heat to high, and simmer rapidly, scraping the skillet bottom with a wooden spoon to loosen the browned bits, until slightly thickened and reduced to about ¾ cup,

about 5 minutes. Pour the accumulated chicken juices into the skillet, reduce the heat to medium, and whisk in the butter, one piece at a time, until incorporated. Season with salt and pepper to taste and discard the sage. Spoon the sauce around the chicken breasts and serve immediately.

➤ VARIATIONS

Pan-Roasted Chicken Breasts with Garlic-Sherry Sauce
Peel 7 medium garlic cloves and cut crosswise into very thin slices (you should have about 3 tablespoons). Follow the recipe for Pan-Roasted Chicken Breasts with Sage-Vermouth Sauce, substituting the sliced garlic for the shallots and cooking the garlic until lightly browned, about

1½ minutes. For the sauce, substitute dry sherry for the vermouth and 2 sprigs fresh thyme for the sage leaves. Add ½ teaspoon lemon juice along with the salt and pepper.

Pan-Roasted Chicken Breasts with Sweet-Tart Red Wine Sauce
This sauce is a variation on the Italian sweet-sour flavor combination called agrodolce.

Follow the recipe for Pan-Roasted Chicken Breasts with Sage-Vermouth Sauce, substituting ¼ cup each dry red wine and red wine vinegar for the vermouth and 1 bay leaf for the sage leaves. Add 1 tablespoon sugar and ¼ teaspoon ground black pepper to the skillet with the chicken broth.

SCIENCE: Preheating Skillets

Most home cooks do not properly preheat their skillets, which results in a lack of both crust and flavor development. This may be due in part to the advice of high-quality cookware manufacturers, who often suggest preheating a pan with a film of oil over low heat for only one to two minutes. Overheating, they warn, can cause discoloration. We followed their recommendations and were appalled at the sorry state of the food: pale, crustless, and with feeble browning. In our opinion, richly browned foods are worth risking discoloration, which, by the way, is easily removed with a little elbow grease.

How do you know when your skillet is properly preheated? We began with the common cookbook advice of sprinkling water in the preheated pan. If the droplets immediately bead up and dance on the skillet's surface, the pan is hot enough. Not exactly. Beading and dancing occur even when the skillet is too cool. We held outstretched palms a few inches above the surface of the skillet, but this proved to be a very inaccurate measure. We put bread crumbs, bread slices, sugar, popcorn kernels, rice, salt, ice cubes, and measured amounts of water into cold skillets, turned on the heat, and waited for some sort of sign. Bread crumbs and slices charred and smoked much too soon. Sugar melted, began to caramelize, and made a mess. Popcorn and rice browned unevenly and erratically after a few minutes, before the skillet was hot enough. Salt was lame. It showed no visible changes, even after the skillet was hotter than we cared for. Heated until every trace of water evaporated, ice cubes and measured amounts of water showed some promise, but given

that boiling points vary with elevation, we thought the method a bit unreliable.

It was oil—smoking oil, to be exact—that held the answer. Measured into a cold skillet and heated for a few minutes, oil gives off wisps of smoke that serve as a visual alarm that the skillet is hot and ready. We tested our theory with beef steaks, chicken (skin-on), and fish fillets and steaks. In each case, oil that had just begun to smoke was a good indicator that the skillet was hot enough to produce well-crusted, good-tasting, and good-looking food without overcooking.

That said, not every kind of oil is suitable for high-heat browning and searing. Unrefined oils, such as extra-virgin olive oil, should not be used because their smoke points are low. Refined oils like vegetable, canola, corn, and peanut (be careful of the unrefined peanut oil carried in some grocery stores) work well because their smoke points are high (above 400 degrees). A word to the wise: Using just-smoking oil as a heat indicator is good only for browning and searing in very little oil, no more than a couple of tablespoons. Smoking oil is simply too hot for pan-frying and deep-frying.

A few final words on browning and searing in a white-hot skillet. To minimize splattering and maximize browning, wick away excess moisture on the surface of the food with paper towels. For more serious splatter containment, use a splatter screen. And be prepared to turn on your exhaust fan or crack open a window. The light smoke that will waft from the skillet will dissipate more quickly with some ventilation.

Pan-Roasted Chicken Breasts with Onion and Ale Sauce

Brown ale gives this sauce a nutty, toasty, bittersweet flavor. Newcastle Brown Ale and Samuel Smith Nut Brown Ale are good choices.

Follow the recipe for Pan-Roasted Chicken Breasts with Sage-Vermouth Sauce, substituting ½ medium onion, sliced very thin, for the shallot; cook the onion until softened, about 3 minutes. Use brown ale in place of the vermouth and 1 sprig fresh thyme for the sage leaves. Add 1 bay leaf and 1 teaspoon brown sugar along with the chicken broth. Add ½ teaspoon cider vinegar along with the salt and pepper.

Pan-Roasted Chicken with Shallot and Vermouth Sauce

SERVES 3 TO 4

Pan-roasting a whole chicken doesn't differ much from pan-roasting just the breasts. The bird must, of course, first be cut into serving pieces. Cutting a 3½- to 4-pounder into eight pieces (two each of drumsticks and thighs and four breast pieces) conveniently provides a portion of both white and dark meat for each serving. Note that the skillet handle will be blistering hot after being in the oven, so be sure to use a potholder or oven mitt to remove the skillet from the oven and when handling the skillet as you make the sauce. Dry white wine can be substituted for the vermouth.

See the box on page 306 for guidelines on selecting the best-tasting chicken. This recipe uses table salt (not kosher) in its brine. If you'd like to use kosher salt, whose large flakes measure differently from fine-grained table salt, see page 312 for conversion information.

CHICKEN
- 1 whole chicken (3½ to 4 pounds), trimmed of excess fat, chicken rinsed and patted dry, giblets removed and reserved for another use
- ½ cup table salt
  Ground black pepper
- 1 teaspoon vegetable oil

SHALLOT AND VERMOUTH SAUCE
- 1 large shallot, minced (about 4 tablespoons)
- ¾ cup low-sodium chicken broth
- ½ cup dry vermouth
- 2 sprigs fresh thyme
- 3 tablespoons cold unsalted butter, cut into 3 pieces
  Salt and ground black pepper

1. FOR THE CHICKEN: Following the illustrations on page 329, cut the chicken into 8 pieces (4 breast pieces, 2 thighs, 2 drumsticks), discarding the wings. Dissolve the salt in 2 quarts cold water in a large bowl, stockpot, or Dutch oven. Immerse the chicken in the brine, cover, and refrigerate until fully seasoned, about 30 minutes. Remove the chicken from the brine, rinse, and pat dry with paper towels. Season the chicken with pepper.

2. Adjust an oven rack to the lowest position and heat the oven to 450 degrees.

3. Heat the oil in a heavy-bottomed 12-inch ovenproof skillet over medium-high heat until beginning to smoke; swirl the skillet to coat evenly with the oil. Brown the chicken pieces, skin-side down, until deep golden, about 5 minutes; turn the chicken pieces and brown until golden on the second side, about 4 minutes longer. Turn the chicken skin-side down and place the skillet in the oven. Roast until the juices run clear when the chicken is cut with a paring knife or the thickest part of the breast registers about 160 degrees on an instant-read thermometer and the thickest part of the thighs and drumsticks registers about 170 degrees, about 10 minutes longer. Using a potholder or oven mitt to protect your

CHICKEN PARTS

For Pan-Roasted Chicken with Shallot and Vermouth Sauce (and its variations) and Chicken with 40 Cloves of Garlic, we cut a whole chicken into two drumsticks, two thighs, and four breast pieces. Discard the wings and back or save them for making stock.

hands from the hot skillet handle, remove the skillet from the oven. Transfer the chicken skin-side up to a platter, and let rest while making the sauce. (If not making a sauce, let the chicken rest 5 minutes before serving.)

4. FOR THE SAUCE: Still using a potholder or oven mitt, pour off most of the fat from the skillet, add the shallot, and set the skillet over medium-high heat; cook, stirring frequently, until the shallot is softened, about 1½ minutes. Add the chicken broth, vermouth, and thyme; increase the heat to high and simmer rapidly, scraping the skillet bottom with a wooden spoon to loosen the browned bits. Simmer until slightly thickened and reduced to about ⅔ cup, about 6 minutes. Pour the accumulated chicken juices into the skillet, discard the thyme, and whisk in the butter, one piece at a time, until incorporated. Season the sauce with salt and pepper to taste. Return the chicken pieces, skin-side up, to the skillet and simmer to heat through, about 1 minute. Serve immediately.

➤ VARIATIONS

Pan-Roasted Chicken with Sherry-Rosemary Sauce
Follow the recipe for Pan-Roasted Chicken with Shallot and Vermouth Sauce, substituting dry sherry for the vermouth and 2 sprigs fresh rosemary for the thyme.

Pan-Roasted Chicken with Cognac-Mustard Sauce
Follow the recipe for Pan-Roasted Chicken with Shallot and Vermouth Sauce, substituting ¼ cup each white wine and cognac or brandy for the vermouth and 1 tablespoon Dijon mustard for an equal amount of the butter.

BROILED CHICKEN

ALTHOUGH THEY CERTAINLY DON'T SOUND glamorous, broiled chicken parts can be fabulous when properly prepared: moist, well seasoned, with a lovely caramelized flavor and crispy skin. Broiled chicken can also be made quickly and inexpensively, requiring little attention and the most basic of ingredients, making it the ultimate weeknight dinner.

The difficulties with broiling chicken relate directly back to the level of heat, which is obviously high. If food is placed too close to the heating element, it can easily char on the outside long before it is cooked through at the center. Achieving crispy skin can also be a problem if it is not given time to slowly render its fat. To avoid these problems, we would have to figure out the optimal distance between the oven rack and the heat source, the best way to season the meat, and the parts of the chicken best suited to broiling.

We chose to broil only bone-in, skin-on chicken. First, we like the contrast of crisp skin with broiled chicken meat, and we know that skin helps to keep the meat from drying out. Second, chicken cooked with the bone in seems to have a better, more meaty flavor. Finally, chicken sold this way is always less expensive than parts sold trimmed of skin and bones.

Ultimately, cutting up a whole young chicken yourself is best, but for cooks with little time to spare, packaged chicken thighs are the most appropriate chicken part for broiling; they are perfectly sized and the least likely to dry out of all the different parts of the bird. If you really like white meat, breasts are doable as well.

From prior discoveries in the test kitchen, we knew that we would be brining the chicken for best flavor, so we moved on to finding the best way to broil. We decided to limit ourselves to the modern-style oven broilers in which the distance from the heat can be controlled. Many recipes we found said to broil the bird four to eight inches away from the heating element. This resulted in chicken with thick, charred, rubbery skin and meat that was not always cooked through. We tried broiling chicken at all levels in a wall oven (this one has rungs 4, 7, 10, and 13 inches away from the heating element). We found that chicken cooked on the bottom shelf (about 13 inches from the top of the oven) was best, staying moist and tender. To caramelize the chicken even more after it was almost completely cooked, we moved it up to the second shelf from the top for the final minute or two of broiling. This approach gave us

ENSURING CRISPY SKIN

Make three diagonal slashes in the skin of each chicken piece to help render the fat.

chicken that closely resembled grilled chicken in both appearance and depth of meaty flavor.

Although the skin was now well browned, we still found it a touch too thick for our taste. Remembering a technique used in cooking duck, we tried slashing the skin a few times before placing it in the oven to broil. This worked quite well. The skin rendered just a little more fat because of the extra surface area exposed to the heat of the broiler. We also discovered that starting the chicken skin-side down was key to getting a thin, crisp skin. This way, we could finish the chicken skin-side up, so it could crisp under the direct heat of the broiler.

Broiled chicken is delicious plain, but it's also easy to jazz it up. We offer recipes for a garlicky herb rub and a spicy dipping sauce. You can also add barbecue sauce in the last few minutes of the cooking process (the high sugar content in most sauces will burn under the heat of the broiler if the sauce is put on at the beginning).

⇥ Broiled Chicken

SERVES 3 TO 4

Though we recommend brining, you may bypass this step if pressed for time. Simply skip step 1 and season the chicken generously with salt and pepper before broiling. See the box on page 306 for guidelines on selecting the best-tasting chicken. This recipe uses table salt (not kosher) in its brine. If you'd like to use kosher salt, whose large flakes measure differently from fine-grained table salt, see page 312 for conversion information. This

recipe will work only in broilers with adjustable racks, not fixed-height broilers. If you're making either the garlic rub or the dipping sauce (recipes follow) to flavor the chicken, prepare it while the chicken is brining.

- 6 tablespoons table salt
- ½ cup sugar
- I whole chicken (3½ to 4 pounds), trimmed of excess fat, chicken rinsed and patted dry, giblets removed and reserved for another use Ground black pepper

1. Dissolve the salt and sugar in 1 quart cold water in a large bowl, stockpot, or Dutch oven. Meanwhile, following illustrations 1 through 8 on page 329, cut the chicken into 6 pieces (2 thighs, 2 drumsticks, and 2 breast pieces), discarding the wings. Immerse the chicken in the brine and cover; refrigerate until fully seasoned, about 1 hour. Remove the chicken from the brine, rinse well, and dry thoroughly with paper towels.

2. Meanwhile, adjust an oven rack to the lowest position and the other rack to the upper-middle position (the top rack should be about 5 inches from the heating element; the bottom rack should be 13 inches away); heat the broiler. Line the bottom of the broiler pan with foil and fit with the slotted broiler pan top. Following the illustration at left, make three diagonal slashes in the skin of each chicken piece with a sharp knife (do not cut into meat). Season both sides of the chicken pieces with pepper and place, skin-side down, on the broiler pan top.

3. Broil the chicken on the bottom rack of the oven until just beginning to brown, 12 to 16 minutes. Using tongs, turn the chicken skin-side up and continue to broil on the bottom rack until the skin is slightly crisp and the thickest part of the breast meat registers 160 degrees on an instant-read thermometer, about 10 minutes (if some chicken parts are browning too quickly, cover only those pieces with small pieces of foil). Transfer the breast pieces to a plate and cover with foil to keep warm. Continue to broil the thighs and drumsticks on the bottom rack until the thickest part of the meat registers 165 degrees on an instant-read thermometer, about 5 minutes longer. Return the breast

pieces, skin-side up, to the pan and move the pan to the upper rack; broil until the chicken is dark spotty brown and the skin is thin and crisp, about 1 minute. Serve immediately.

➤ VARIATIONS

Broiled Chicken Breasts

Follow the recipe for Broiled Chicken through step 2, substituting 4 bone-in, skin-on chicken breast halves (about 3 pounds) for the cut-up whole chicken. Broil the chicken breasts on the bottom rack until just beginning to brown, 12 to 16 minutes. Using tongs, turn the breasts skin-side up and continue to broil on the bottom rack until the skin is slightly crisp and the thickest part of the meat registers 160 degrees on an instant-read thermometer, about 10 minutes. Move the pan to the upper rack; broil until the chicken is dark spotty brown and the skin is thin and crisp, about 1 minute. Serve immediately.

Broiled Chicken Thighs

Follow the recipe for Broiled Chicken through step 2, substituting 8 bone-in, skin-on chicken thighs (about 3 pounds) for the whole cut-up chicken. Broil the chicken thighs on the bottom rack until just beginning to brown, 12 to 16 minutes. Using tongs, turn the chicken skin-side up and continue to broil on the bottom rack until the skin is slightly crisp and the thickest part of the meat registers 165 degrees on an instant-read thermometer, about 15 minutes. Move the pan to the upper rack; broil until the chicken is dark spotty brown and the skin is thin and crisp, about 1 minute. Serve immediately.

Garlic, Lemon, and Rosemary Rub

5 medium garlic cloves, minced or pressed through a garlic press
2 teaspoons grated zest and 1/4 cup juice from 2 lemons
1 tablespoon minced fresh rosemary leaves
 Ground black pepper
3 tablespoons extra-virgin olive oil

Combine the garlic, lemon zest, rosemary, and pepper to taste in a small bowl. Combine the lemon juice and oil in another small bowl. Follow the recipe for Broiled Chicken, Broiled Chicken Breasts, or Broiled Chicken Thighs, spreading a portion of the garlic rub under the skin before slashing the skin. Broil as directed, but before moving the chicken to the upper rack to crisp the skin, brush the chicken with the lemon juice and oil mixture.

Spicy Jamaican Jerk Dipping Sauce

1/4 cup juice from 2 limes
1/4 cup lightly packed brown sugar
1 medium garlic clove, unpeeled
1 medium habanero chile
2 medium scallions, white and green parts, minced
1/2 medium onion, minced
4 teaspoons minced fresh ginger
1/2 teaspoon dried thyme
 Pinch ground allspice

1. Stir together the lime juice and brown sugar until dissolved in a small bowl; set aside. Meanwhile, toast the garlic and habanero in a small dry skillet over medium heat, shaking the pan frequently, until blistered, about 8 minutes. Peel and mince the garlic; seed and mince the habanero. Combine the garlic, habanero, scallions, onion, ginger, thyme, and allspice in another small bowl and stir in 2 tablespoons of the lime–brown sugar mixture; set aside as a dipping sauce for the cooked chicken.

2. Follow the recipe for Broiled Chicken, Broiled Chicken Breasts, or Broiled Chicken Thighs, brushing the chicken pieces with the remaining lime–brown sugar mixture before moving them to the upper oven rack to crisp the skin. Serve the chicken, passing the dipping sauce separately.

FRIED CHICKEN

WHAT MAKES FRIED CHICKEN GREAT? THERE'S NO doubt about it: the crust. Crisp and crackling with flavor, the crust must cleave to the chicken itself, not balloon away or flake off in chips like old radiator paint. In addition, it should carry a deep, uniform mahogany color, without spots or evidence of greasiness. As for the chicken itself, tender, moist, and flavorful are the descriptors of the day. Served hot, it should be demonstrably juicy; served room temperature, it should be moist. On no account should it be punishingly dry or require a saltshaker as a chaperone.

The truth is that frying chicken at home is a daunting task, a messy tableau of buttermilk dip and breading, hot fat, and splatters one hopes will end at the stove's edge. The results are often tantamount to the mess: greasy, peeling chicken skin and dry, unseasoned meat that's a long way from Grandma's.

It was no surprise to us that the chicken we were frying had to be premium quality to be worth the effort. Packaged chicken parts were irregular and disappointing, containing mismatched pieces in shabby dress with tattered skin, cut without a nod to basic anatomy. Given this situation, we thought it wise to spend a few minutes cutting a whole 3½-pound broiler into 12 manageable pieces (see page 329).

In our first stove-side excursion, we fried up several batches of chicken with different coatings, oils, and so on. But our real interest resided beneath the skin: half of the chickens had been brined for two hours; the other half had not. A brine is at minimum a mixture of salt and water; sugar is often added as well. When soaked in brine, chicken (as well as other poultry and meat) absorbs some of the salt and some of the water, thereby becoming more flavorful and more juicy once cooked. The tasting results bore out these benefits of brining: However glorious the crust, however perfectly fried the piece, the unbrined chicken earned marks far below its brined competition. Who wants to bite through a crisp, rich, seasoned crust only to hit dry, white Styrofoam? Another benefit of brining presented itself during cooking. Our brined chicken parts fried at equal rates, relieving us of the need to baby-sit the white meat or pull the wings out of the fat early.

While brining per se may not be common practice when preparing fried chicken, soaking the chicken pieces in some kind of liquid—particularly buttermilk—is traditional. This process is thought to tenderize the meat (a mistaken assumption) and add flavor. We examined a number of soaking solutions and found the bright acidic flavor and clinging viscosity of buttermilk to produce the best flavor accents and richest browning during cooking.

Appreciating the tang of a buttermilk soak but unwilling to forgo the succulence of brined chicken, we found ourselves whispering "buttermilk brine." Instead of soaking the chicken in buttermilk alone, why not add the saline blast of a brine, doubling the rewards and minimizing the number of steps? To get a leg up on the idea, we made it a flavored brine, adding a mountain of crushed garlic, a couple of crushed bay leaves, and some sweet paprika.

This remarkable "twofer" won high marks indeed, well above those garnered by a unilateral soak or brine. The buttermilk and paprika showed spirit, garlic and bay leaves crept into the crust, and the meat was tender and seasoned. We also spiked the brine with ¼ cup of sugar—not enough to sweeten but enough to bring other flavors out of hiding.

Fried foods taste irresistibly good when dressed in crumbs or flour not only because their insides are protected from damaging temperatures but also because hot, enveloping fat performs minor miracles on the flavor of the flour or crumbs. But what kind of coating is best?

To find out, we tested straight flour against a panoply of contenders: matzo crumbs, ground saltines, cornflakes, Melba toast, cornmeal, and panko (Japanese-style) bread crumbs. In the end, plain flour that necessitated no seasoning whatsoever, as the chicken had been brined, surpassed all other options for the integrity and lightness of the crust it produced.

Many fried chicken recipes use a single breading process in which the chicken is dipped first into beaten egg, then into flour or crumbs. A double, or bound, breading dips the chicken into flour first, then into egg, and finally into flour or crumbs. In side-by-side tests, we found that the double breading offered a superior base coat that was more tenacious in its grip, more protective in its bearing, without being overly thick or tough.

Another practice that has made its way into many fried chicken recipes is that of air-drying the breaded chicken before frying it. Rather than becoming soggy in the refrigerator, as might be expected, the breading toughens up over time to produce a fried chicken of superior crispiness.

We were also curious about the effect of air-drying on unbreaded chicken. We have come to favor the laser-crisp and taut skin of roasted birds that have been air-dried and wanted to see if an

CUTTING UP A CHICKEN

Chicken destined for the fry pot should be cut into fairly small pieces. Instead of the standard eight pieces (two breasts, two wings, two thighs, and two legs), we cut each breast piece in half and sever the wing at the main joint (the skin cooks better when thus separated, and the wing pieces are easier to eat) to yield a total of 12 pieces.

1. With a sharp chef's knife, cut through the skin around the leg where it attaches to the breast.

2. Using both hands, pop the leg joint out of its socket.

3. Use a chef's knife to cut through the flesh and skin to detach the leg from the body.

4. A line of fat separates the thigh and drumstick. Cut through the joint at this point. Repeat steps 1 through 4 with the other leg.

5. Bend the wing out from the breast and use a boning knife to cut through the joint. Repeat with the other wing.

6. Cut through cartilage around wingtip to remove it. Discard the tip. Cut through joint to split it. Repeat with other wing.

7. Using poultry shears, cut along the ribs to completely separate the back from the breast. Discard the backbone.

8. Place the knife on the breastbone, then apply pressure to cut through and separate the breast into halves.

9. Cut each breast in half crosswise into two pieces.

analogous effect could be achieved by refrigerating our brined, unbreaded chicken on a rack for a couple of hours. We were reasonably confident this would allow the buttermilk to dry just enough to maintain a protective and flavorful posture and the chicken to bread nicely without first being dabbed or dried, frying up dry and crisp.

We tested the effects of air-drying the chicken before and after breading and compared the results with chicken that underwent no air-drying. Both air-dried versions were superior in terms of crust, but each was distinctly different from the other. The chicken that was breaded and then air-dried had a heartier, more toothsome crust—crunchy to some, hard to others. The chicken that was air-dried and then breaded was lighter and crispier—flaky, more shattery. We preferred this traditionally Southern crust. Though it initially seemed ideal, we noticed that its delicate crispiness succumbed to sandiness and porosity over the course of a few hours. This was not acceptable.

The memory of a particularly light but resilient crust on a chicken-fried steak recipe we had made persuaded us to add baking soda and baking powder to an egg wash bolstered with buttermilk. We hoped the sandiness in the crust that developed over time might thus be offset. Stirred into the wash, ½ teaspoon of soda and 1 teaspoon of powder produced just enough carbon dioxide to lighten the breading to perfection. Not only did it bronze to a shattery filigree in the hot fat, it also remained crisp as it cooled.

One of the most important requirements of fat as a frying medium is that it offers nothing of its own flavor and, in fact, has none to offer. This means that the oil must be refined—in other words, cleansed and sanitized. Another requirement is that the oil perform at temperatures below its smoke point (the temperature at which it emits smoke and acrid odors) to maintain thermal stability. With the relatively moderate temperatures required by our recipe, all refined vegetable oils stayed well below their smoke points. In the end, peanut oil edged out Crisco shortening by virtue of its marginally more neutral and clean flavor.

A cast-iron Dutch oven covered during the first half of the frying reduced splatters to a fine spray, maintained the oil temperature impeccably, and fried the chicken through in about 15 minutes total versus the 20 minutes per side recommended in many recipes.

Drying the gleaming, bronzed statuettes was the most satisfying test. Paper bags are simply not porous enough to keep the chicken out of a gathering pool of grease. We found that paper towels absorbed excess fat quickly and that rolling the pieces over onto a bare rack thereafter kept them crisp.

Crispy Fried Chicken
SERVES 4 TO 6

Maintaining an even oil temperature is key to the success of this recipe. Use an instant-read thermometer with a high upper range; a clip-on candy/deep-fry thermometer is fine, too, though it can be clipped to the pot only for the uncovered portion of frying.

See the box on page 306 for guidelines on selecting the best-tasting chicken. This recipe uses table salt (not kosher) in its brine. If you'd like to use kosher salt, whose large flakes measure differently from fine-grained table salt, see page 312 for conversion information.

CHICKEN
- ½   cup table salt
- ¼   cup sugar
- 2   tablespoons paprika
- 3   medium garlic heads, cloves separated
- 3   bay leaves, crumbled
- 7   cups buttermilk
- I   whole chicken (3½ to 4 pounds), trimmed of excess fat, chicken rinsed and patted dry, giblets removed and reserved for another use, chicken cut into 12 pieces (see the illustrations on page 329)

COATING
- 4   cups unbleached all-purpose flour
- I   large egg
- I   teaspoon baking powder
- ½   teaspoon baking soda
- I   cup buttermilk

- 3–4   cups refined peanut oil or vegetable shortening for frying

1. FOR THE CHICKEN: In a gallon-size zipper-lock plastic bag, combine the salt, sugar, paprika, garlic cloves, and bay leaves. With a rubber mallet or flat meat pounder, smash the garlic into the salt and spice mixture thoroughly. Pour the mixture into a large nonreactive bowl, stockpot, or Dutch oven. Add the buttermilk and stir until the salt is completely dissolved. Immerse the chicken in the brine, cover with plastic wrap, and refrigerate until fully seasoned, 2 to 3 hours. Remove the chicken from the buttermilk brine and shake off any excess; place it in a single layer on a large wire rack set over a rimmed baking sheet. Refrigerate uncovered for 2 hours. (After 2 hours, the chicken can be covered with plastic wrap and refrigerated up to 6 hours longer.)

2. FOR THE COATING: Measure the flour into a large, shallow dish. Beat the egg, baking powder, and baking soda in a medium bowl; stir in the buttermilk (the mixture will bubble and foam). Working in batches of three, drop the chicken pieces in the flour and shake the dish to coat. Shake the excess flour from each piece, then, using tongs, dip the chicken pieces into the egg mixture, turning to coat well and allowing the excess to drip off. Coat the chicken pieces with flour again, shake off the excess, and return to the wire rack.

3. Adjust an oven rack to the middle position, set a second wire rack over a second rimmed baking sheet, and place it on the oven rack; heat the oven to 200 degrees. Line a large plate with a double layer of paper towels. Meanwhile, heat the oil (which should have a depth of 2½ inches in the pan) in a large cast-iron Dutch oven with a diameter of about 12 inches over medium-high heat to 375 degrees on an instant-read thermometer. Place half of the chicken pieces, skin-side down, in the oil, cover, reduce the heat to medium, and fry until deep golden brown, 6 to 8 minutes; after about 3 minutes, lift the chicken pieces with tongs to check for even browning; rearrange if some pieces are browning faster than others. (Spot-check the oil temperature; after the first 6 minutes of frying, the oil should be about 325 degrees. Adjust the burner if necessary.) Turn the chicken pieces over and continue to fry, uncovered, until they

are deep golden brown on the second side, 6 to 8 minutes longer. Using tongs, transfer the chicken to the paper towel–lined plate; let stand 2 minutes to drain, then transfer to the rack in the warm oven. Replace the paper towel lining on the plate. Return the oil to 375 degrees and fry the remaining chicken pieces, transferring the pieces to the towel-lined plate to drain, then transferring them to the wire rack (now removed from the oven) with the other chicken pieces. Cool the chicken pieces on the wire rack about 5 minutes and serve.

OVEN-FRIED CHICKEN

WE'VE ALWAYS THOUGHT OF OVEN-FRIED chicken as ersatz fried chicken—only for those who were afraid to mess up their kitchens or consume too much fat. Depending on the liquid or crumb coating, this chicken could be bland, soggy, rubbery-skinned, greasy, artificially flavored, dry, or crumbly. Was it possible, we wondered, to make a decent alternative to the real thing?

After looking at scores of recipes, we realized that the coatings—both the moist one that helps the crumbs stick and the dry one that provides texture and crunch—were the key issues to examine.

We started with the moist coating. Before testing, we assumed this wet dunk did little more than help the crumbs adhere to the chicken. After testing, however, it became clear that this initial coat plays a larger role. A good first coat, we discovered, should offer flavor, attract the right proportion of crumbs to form an impressive, uniform crust, and, finally, help the crust stay crunchy during baking.

To find the best moist coating, we baked 13 drumsticks, keeping the dry coating constant while varying the moist coating: water, whole milk, evaporated milk, cream, buttermilk, yogurt, sour cream, milk beaten with egg, egg beaten with lemon juice, and egg with Dijon mustard. In addition, we tried legs coated with ranch dressing, mayonnaise, and butter.

Because many recipes for oven-fried chicken start by rolling chicken parts in butter, we thought the fat coatings would perform well. Not so. All of them—butter, mayonnaise, and ranch dressing—

created a slick surface that prevented the crumbs from adhering properly. In addition, none of the fats did anything to crisp the crumbs.

With the exception of buttermilk and evaporated milk, moreover, none of the dairy coatings impressed us. Buttermilk and evaporated milk did attract decent crusts and give a subtle flavor dimension to the chicken, but they didn't result in the crispness we wanted.

The egg beaten with lemon did result in a crisp coating. Unfortunately, it also contributed too much lemon flavor with an overcooked egg aftertaste. But a change of just one ingredient made all the difference. Chicken coated with beaten egg and Dijon mustard was our favorite. This not-too-thick, not-too-thin moistener not only attracted a uniform, impressive layer of crumbs, it also gave the meat a wonderfully subtle flavor. Unlike many of the wet coatings, which made the crumbs either soggy or barely crisp, this one took the crumbs to an almost crunchy level.

Up until this point, we had been using dry bread crumbs in our tests. With our tests of wet coatings concluded, it was time to focus on other dry coating options. We started with 20 dry coatings or combinations thereof, all from published recipes. After baking and tasting them all, there wasn't a single one we thought was perfect.

Of the cereal coatings, cornflakes were the best, offering good color and crunch, but they also had too much sweet corn flavor. Ditto for bran flakes, but their distinct flavor was even more pronounced. Unprocessed bran looked like kitty litter, while Grape-Nuts looked like hamster food.

Crackers didn't work, either. Both saltines and Ritz were too soft; the Ritz, in addition, were too sweet. Cracker meal delivered a bland blond shell. In the bread department, stuffing mix scored well in crunch but struck out in flavor. Fresh bread crumbs, on the other hand, tasted great but lacked the crunch we had come to like.

The meals and flours, as to be expected, did not show well. Cornmeal tasted raw, and it chipped off the chicken like flecks of old paint. Our grocery store's house brand of Shake 'n Bake was vile, tasting of liquid smoke and bad hot dogs.

Although this first round of tests did not produce a strong winner, it did help us to clarify what it was that we wanted—a coating that was crunchy (not just crisp) and flavorful (but not artificial-tasting) and that baked up a rich copper brown. With a clear ideal in mind, we found a whole new range of coating possibilities in the specialty/international cracker section of our grocery store, including Melba toast, *pain grillé* (French crisp toast), Swedish crisps, lavash (crisp flat bread), bread sticks, bagel chips, Italian toasts, and pita chips. This series of tests delivered oven-fried chicken that was much closer to our ideal. The rather surprising winner, it turned out, was Melba toast. It scored the best in all three major categories—texture, flavor, and color.

Over the course of testing, we found that we much preferred legs and thighs to breasts because they don't dry out as quickly. As expected, the buttermilk brine that worked so well in our crispy fried chicken recipe did wonders here, too. The meat was more moist and better seasoned after a two-hour brine. We also discovered that we didn't like the skin on oven-fried chicken. Unlike fried chicken, in which hot oil causes the fat to render and the skin to crisp, oven heat simply softens the skin and makes it rubbery. We decided to remove the skin before coating the pieces.

Oven temperature was a simple matter. We started baking at 400 degrees, and all of the chicken pieces were cooked through and rich golden brown in about 40 minutes. A wire rack set over a foil-covered rimmed baking sheet or shallow baking pan allows heat to circulate around the chicken during baking, letting the chicken crisp without being turned. The foil, of course, protects the pan, making cleanup a breeze.

Oven-Fried Chicken
SERVES 4

See the box on page 306 for guidelines on selecting the best-tasting chicken. This recipe uses table salt (not kosher) in its brine. If you'd like to use kosher salt, whose large flakes measure differently from fine-grained table salt, see page 312 for conversion information.

To make Melba toast crumbs, place the toasts in a heavy-duty plastic freezer bag, seal, and pound with a meat pounder or other heavy, blunt object. Leave some crumbs the size of pebbles in the mixture, but most should resemble coarse sand.

CHICKEN

½	cup table salt
¼	cup sugar
2	tablespoons paprika
3	medium garlic heads, cloves separated
3	bay leaves, crumbled
7	cups low-fat buttermilk
4	whole chicken legs, drumsticks and thighs separated (see illustration 4 on page 329) and skin removed

COATING

¼	cup vegetable oil
1	box (about 5 ounces) plain Melba toast, crushed (see note)
2	large eggs
1	tablespoon Dijon mustard
1	teaspoon dried thyme
¾	teaspoon salt
½	teaspoon ground black pepper
½	teaspoon dried oregano
¼	teaspoon garlic powder
¼	teaspoon cayenne pepper (optional)

1. FOR THE CHICKEN: In a gallon-size zipper-lock plastic bag, combine the salt, sugar, paprika, garlic cloves, and bay leaves. With a rubber mallet or flat meat pounder, smash the garlic into the salt and spice mixture thoroughly. Pour the mixture into a large nonreactive bowl, stockpot, or Dutch oven. Add the buttermilk and stir until the salt is completely dissolved. Immerse the chicken in the brine and refrigerate until fully seasoned, 2 to 3 hours. Remove the chicken from the brine and shake off the excess; place the chicken pieces in a single layer on a large wire rack set over a rimmed baking sheet. Refrigerate uncovered for 2 hours. (After 2 hours, the chicken can be covered with plastic wrap and refrigerated up to 6 hours longer.)

2. Adjust an oven rack to the upper-middle position and heat the oven to 400 degrees. Line a baking sheet with foil and set a large wire rack over the pan.

3. FOR THE COATING: Drizzle the oil over the Melba toast crumbs in a shallow dish or pie plate; toss well to coat. Mix the eggs, mustard, thyme, salt, pepper, oregano, garlic powder, and cayenne (if using) with a fork in a second shallow dish or pie plate.

4. Working with one piece at a time, coat the chicken on both sides with the egg mixture. Set the chicken in the Melba crumbs, sprinkle the crumbs over the chicken, and press to coat. Turn the chicken over and repeat on the other side. Gently shake off the excess and place the chicken on the rack in the pan. Bake until the chicken is a deep nutty brown and the juices run clear, about 40 minutes. Serve.

BREADED CHICKEN CUTLETS

TENDER BONELESS CHICKEN BREAST, PAN-fried with a cloak of mild-flavored crumbs, has universal appeal. Almost every cuisine has such a dish. Though simple, this dish can fall prey to a host of problems. The chicken itself may be rubbery and tasteless, and the coating—called a bound breading and arguably the best part of the dish—often ends up uneven, greasy, pale, or even burnt.

For a breaded chicken cutlet to be great, the chicken itself must hold up its end of the bargain. Because the test kitchen is fiercely devoted to the benefits of brining poultry, we wondered what effect soaking the cutlets in a mixture of salt, sugar, and water would have. The brined cutlets were a hit, exceptionally juicy and seasoned all the way to the center. The brining step is easy to execute and takes just 30 minutes, during which time you can pull together other components of the recipe. It's not often that so little work yields such big benefits. (For cutlet recipes with a sauce, such as Marsala and piccata, the sauce adds plenty of moisture, and there's no need to brine the chicken.)

Throughout the first series of tests, we noticed that the thin tip of the cutlet and the opposite end, which was much more plump, cooked at different rates. This problem was a cinch to fix; all we had to do was pound the chicken breasts gently to an even ½-inch thickness with a meat pounder (see bottom right) or the bottom of a small saucepan. To promote even cooking, we also found it best to remove the floppy tenderloin from the underside of each cutlet before pounding.

The ideal breading should taste mild and comforting but not dull and certainly not greasy. To explore the possibilities, we pan-fried cutlets coated with fine, fresh bread crumbs (made from fresh sliced white sandwich bread ground fine in the food processor) and dry bread crumbs. The dry bread crumbs had an unmistakably stale flavor. The fresh bread crumbs swept the test, with a mild, subtly sweet flavor and a light, crisp texture. We went on to test crumbs made from different kinds of white bread, including premium sliced sandwich bread, Italian, French, and country-style. The sandwich bread was the sweetest and appealed to tasters in this recipe. That said, fresh crumbs made from all of these breads were good.

During the crumb testing, we made several important observations about the breading process. First, we learned that the cutlets had to be thoroughly dried after brining. We also learned that we could not dispense with the coating of flour that went onto the chicken before the egg wash and crumbs. If the cutlets were even slightly moist, or if we skipped the flour coat, the breading would peel off the finished cutlets in sheets. Dry cutlets also produced the thinnest possible coating of flour, which eliminated any floury taste when the cutlets were cooked and served. In addition, we found that it was essential to press the crumbs onto the cutlets to ensure an even, thorough cover. Finally, we discovered that it was best to let the breaded cutlets rest for about five minutes before frying them, again to help bind the breading to the meat.

The bread crumbs are attached to the floured cutlets by means of a quick dip in beaten eggs. But beaten eggs are thick and viscous, and they tend to form too heavy a layer on the meat, giving the breading a thick, indelicate quality. Thinning the eggs with oil, water, or both is a common practice that allows any excess to slide off the meat more easily, leaving a thinner, more delicate coat. We tried all three routines, and honestly, we couldn't

REMOVING THE TENDERLOIN

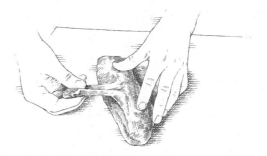

The tenderloin (the long narrow piece of meat attached to each cutlet) tends to fall off during pounding, so it is best removed and reserved for another use, such as a stir-fry.

TRIMMING CUTLETS

Most cutlets have a little yellow or white fat still attached to the breast meat. Lay each cutlet tenderloin side down and smooth the top with your fingers. Any fat will slide to the edge of the cutlet, where it can be trimmed with a knife.

POUNDING CUTLETS

Place the cutlets, smooth-side down, on a large sheet of plastic wrap. Cover with a second sheet of plastic wrap and pound gently. The cutlets should already be thin; you simply want to make sure that they have the same thickness from end to end.

detect much difference in the flavor or texture of the finished breading. In repeated tests, we did notice that the breading made with oil-thinned egg wash seemed to brown a little more deeply than that made with water-thinned wash, so we added a tablespoon of oil to our two beaten eggs and moved on.

Last, we explored the details of pan-frying. In any breaded preparation, the oil in the pan should reach one third to one half of the way up the food for thorough browning. Which fat should be used for sautéing the cutlets? Cutlets sautéed in olive oil were markedly better than those sautéed in vegetable oil.

Breaded Chicken Cutlets

SERVES 4

This recipe uses table salt (not kosher) in its brine. If you'd like to use kosher salt, whose large flakes measure differently from fine-grained table salt, see page 312 for conversion information. When coating the cutlets with the bread crumb mixture, use your hands to pat a thorough, even coating onto the chicken to make sure the crumbs adhere. The chicken is cooked in batches of two because the crust is noticeably more crisp if the pan is not overcrowded. See the illustrations on page 336 for tips on breading cutlets.

4	boneless, skinless chicken breasts (5 to 6 ounces each), tenderloins removed and reserved for another use, fat trimmed (see the illustrations on page 334)
1/4	cup table salt
	Ground black pepper
1 1/2	cups homemade bread crumbs (see the illustrations below)
3/4	cup unbleached all-purpose flour
2	large eggs
1	tablespoon plus 3/4 cup olive oil
	Lemon wedges for serving

1. Use a meat pounder, rubber mallet, or rolling pin to pound the chicken breasts to an even ½-inch thickness. Dissolve the salt in 1 quart cold water in a gallon-size zipper-lock plastic bag. Add the cutlets and seal the bag, pressing out as much air as possible. Refrigerate until the cutlets are fully seasoned, 30 minutes. Line a baking sheet with a triple layer of paper towels.

2. Remove the cutlets and lay them in a single layer on the baking sheet. Cover with another triple layer of paper towels and press firmly to absorb the moisture. Allow the cutlets to dry for 10 minutes. Carefully peel the paper towels off the cutlets; sprinkle the cutlets with pepper to taste and set them aside.

3. Adjust an oven rack to the lower-middle

MAKING FRESH BREAD CRUMBS

Fresh bread crumbs are far superior to bland, overly fine commercial crumbs. Any stray hunk of good-quality bread (preferably made without sweetener, seeds, or other extraneous ingredients) can be turned into fresh crumbs. Country white bread, plain Italian bread, and baguettes are ideal. Slightly stale bread is easier to cut, but crumbs can be made from fresh bread. You can use the crumbs as is or toast them in a dry skillet over medium heat until golden brown.

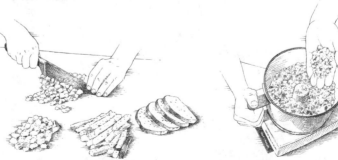

1. Slice off and discard the bottom crust of the bread if it is tough and overbaked.

2. Slice the bread into ⅜-inch-thick pieces. Cut these slices into ⅜-inch strips, then cut these into cubes and chop until you have small pieces about the size of a lemon seed.

3. To make the crumbs in a food processor, cut the trimmed loaf into 1½-inch cubes, then pulse the cubes in a food processor to the desired crumb size.

position, set a large heatproof plate on the rack, and heat the oven to 200 degrees. Place the bread crumbs in a shallow dish or pie plate. Spread the flour in a second shallow dish. Beat the eggs with the 1 tablespoon olive oil in a third shallow dish. Place a wire rack over a baking sheet.

4. Working with one at a time, dredge the cutlets thoroughly in the flour, shaking off the excess. Using tongs, dip both sides of the cutlets in the egg mixture, taking care to coat them thoroughly and allowing the excess to drip back into the dish to ensure a very thin coating. Dip both sides of the cutlets in the bread crumbs, pressing the crumbs with your fingers to form an even, cohesive coat. Place the breaded cutlets in a single layer on the wire rack and allow the coating to dry for about 5 minutes.

5. Meanwhile, heat 6 tablespoons of the remaining oil in a heavy-bottomed 10-inch nonstick skillet over medium-high heat until shimmering but not smoking, about 2 minutes. Lay two cutlets gently in the skillet and cook until deep golden brown and crisp on the first side, gently pressing down on the cutlets with a wide metal spatula to help ensure even browning, about 2½ minutes. Using tongs, turn the cutlets, reduce the heat to medium, and continue to cook until the meat feels firm when pressed gently and the second side is deep golden brown and crisp, 2½ to 3 minutes. Line the warmed plate with a double layer of paper towels and set the cutlets on top; return the plate to the oven.

6. Discard the oil in the skillet and wipe the skillet clean using tongs and a large wad of paper towels. Repeat step 5, using the remaining 6 tablespoons oil and the now-clean skillet to cook the remaining cutlets. After draining on paper towels, serve all the cutlets with the lemon wedges.

BREADING CUTLETS

1. Dredge the cutlets thoroughly in flour, shaking off the excess.

2. Using tongs, dip both sides of the cutlets in the egg mixture, taking care to coat them thoroughly and allowing the excess to drip back into the dish to ensure a very thin coating. Tongs keep the breading from coating your fingers.

3. Dip both sides of the cutlets in the bread crumbs, pressing the crumbs on with your fingers to form an even, cohesive coat.

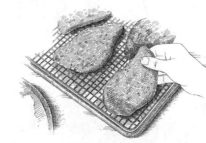

4. Place the breaded cutlets in a single layer on a wire rack set over a baking sheet and allow the coating to dry for about 5 minutes. This drying time stabilizes the breading so that it can be sautéed without sticking to the pan or falling off.

Parmesan Breaded Chicken Cutlets

Follow the recipe for Breaded Chicken Cutlets, replacing ¼ cup of the bread crumbs with ¼ cup freshly grated Parmesan cheese.

Breaded Chicken Cutlets with Garlic and Oregano

Follow the recipe for Breaded Chicken Cutlets. Beat 3 tablespoons very finely minced fresh oregano leaves and 8 medium garlic cloves, minced or pressed through a garlic press, into the egg mixture in step 3.

CHICKEN PARMESAN

CHICKEN PARMESAN—BREADED CHICKEN CUTLETS topped with cheese and tomato sauce—is beloved by many American families. Although the dish has its roots in Italy, the execution and the excess are purely American. The chicken is usually covered with way too much cheese and sauce, and it is served with a full portion of spaghetti.

We wanted to remain true to the hearty nature of this dish, but we also wanted to use some restraint. At the outset, we made several decisions. First, the chicken would take center stage, and the pasta portions would be modest. (We figured on eight ounces of dried spaghetti for four servings, not the pound called for in many recipes.) Second, we would cover the chicken with a modest amount of cheese and tomato sauce. You spend a lot of time breading and cooking the chicken; why bury it under a mountain of molten cheese and sauce? We also wanted to avoid a problem common with this dish: soggy cutlets.

Based on our experience with breaded chicken cutlets, we knew the best way to bread and cook a cutlet. However, we wondered if sautéing would be the right route here, as the cheese that coats the cooked cutlets would be melted under the broiler or in the oven. We figured it was worth trying to cook the chicken under the broiler and save a step. Unfortunately, broiling resulted in inconsistently and unimpressively browned cutlets. In contrast,

sautéing produced a beautiful, evenly golden brown color and rich, satisfying flavor.

Some recipes, especially older ones, instruct the reader to top cooked cutlets with mozzarella cheese and bake them on a bed of tomato sauce, covered, until the cheese melts. As far as we are concerned, this step not only added several minutes to the preparation time, it also destroyed the crisp, delicious coating and turned the cutlets into soggy mush. We simply sprinkled the cooked cutlets with mozzarella and Parmesan (3 tablespoons mozzarella and 1 tablespoon Parmesan per cutlet were sufficient) and broiled them until the cheeses melted and turned spotty brown. They were now ready for tomato sauce and the accompanying pasta.

As for the sauce, chicken Parmesan requires a smooth, thick sauce that goes together in a flash. Crushed tomatoes were the obvious choice. We found that a little garlic and herbs enlivened their flavor and kept the recipe simple.

~

Chicken Parmesan
SERVES 4

Timing is key here. The spaghetti should go into the boiling water at the same time the first batch of breaded cutlets goes into the oil.

SMOOTH TOMATO SAUCE
2   medium garlic cloves, minced or pressed
      through a garlic press
¼   cup extra-virgin olive oil
1   (28-ounce) can crushed tomatoes
½   teaspoon dried basil
¼   teaspoon dried oregano
¼   teaspoon sugar
      Salt and ground black pepper

CHICKEN AND PASTA
1   recipe Breaded Chicken Cutlets (page 335)
2   teaspoons salt
8   ounces spaghetti or linguine
3   ounces mozzarella cheese, shredded (¾ cup)
¼   cup freshly grated Parmesan cheese, plus more
      for serving

1. FOR THE SAUCE: Heat the garlic and oil together in a large saucepan over medium-high heat until the garlic starts to sizzle. Stir in the tomatoes, basil, oregano, sugar, a pinch of salt, and 2 grinds of pepper and bring to a simmer. Continue to simmer until the sauce thickens a bit and the flavors meld, 10 to 12 minutes. Taste the sauce, adjusting the salt if necessary. Cover and keep warm.

2. Bring 3 quarts water to a boil in a large pot. Adjust an oven rack to the top position and heat the broiler.

3. Meanwhile, bread the chicken cutlets, place them in a single layer on a wire rack set over a baking sheet, and allow the coating to dry about 5 minutes (see step 4 of the recipe on page 336).

4. Add the salt and spaghetti to the boiling water and stir to separate the noodles. At the same time, cook the chicken cutlets according to step 5 of the recipe on page 336. When the cutlets are done, transfer them to a clean wire rack set over a clean baking sheet. Top each cutlet with 3 tablespoons mozzarella and 1 tablespoon Parmesan. Place the baking sheet under the broiler and broil until the cheeses melt and are spotty brown, about 3 minutes.

5. Drain the spaghetti. Transfer a chicken cutlet and a portion of spaghetti to each of 4 plates. Spoon 1 to 2 tablespoons sauce over part of each cutlet, then sauce the spaghetti as desired. Serve immediately, passing more Parmesan separately at the table.

CHICKEN MARSALA

CHICKEN MARSALA IS A CLASSIC ITALIAN restaurant staple. Ideally, this dish should feature tender chicken cutlets napped in a silky Marsala wine—enriched pan sauce. But, after several disappointing encounters with this dish that involved watery sauces, flaccid mushrooms, and pale, stale chicken, we realized that chicken Marsala was in need of a rescue.

While all of the recipes we found listed the same three ingredients—breast of chicken, mushrooms, and Marsala—the cooking methods differed. Some called for simmering the chicken and mushrooms

in Marsala, which resulted in flavors that were waterlogged and bland. Others recommended cooking everything in separate pans, creating not only a messy kitchen but a dish with disjointed flavors. Yet others had the cook sauté everything in the same pan, but sequentially. The clear winner turned out to be the classic approach, in which the meat is sautéed first, then moved to a warm oven while the browned bits left in the pan are splashed with wine and enriched with butter to create a sauce. With this decided, we focused on perfecting the sautéed chicken and developing the sauce.

When sautéing, the most important steps include getting the skillet as hot as possible and patting the chicken dry with paper towels before dusting with a light coating of flour. Using these pointers as a guide, we sautéed with a variety of oils and with butter, to find that vegetable oil was the least likely to burn and splatter.

Our next task was to figure out how to get the mushrooms crisp and brown without burning the drippings left from the sautéed chicken. One way to do this, we thought, would be to add more fat to the pan and scrape the browned bits off the bottom before cooking the mushrooms. We tried adding both fat and flavor by cooking small pieces of pancetta (Italian bacon that has been cured but not smoked) directly after the chicken. Just as we thought, the fat rendered from the pancetta prevented the chicken drippings from burning while providing the oil necessary for sautéing the mushrooms—not to mention adding a meaty, pepper-flavored punch to the sauce.

Because several types and grades of Marsala wine can be found on the market, we conducted a taste test before doing any cooking, trying imported and California brands of both the sweet and dry varieties. We favored an imported wine, Sweet Marsala Fine, for its depth of flavor, smooth finish, and reasonable price tag. By reducing the wine, we found the silky, plush texture we were looking for in the final sauce. Knowing that stock is traditionally added to pan sauces for depth of flavor and body, we tested a variety of stock-to-Marsala ratios. Again and again, tasters preferred a sauce made only from wine, slightly reduced. The stock simply got in the way of the Marsala's distinctive zip.

All we had to do now was round out the final flavors. Lemon juice tempered the Marsala's sweetness, while a garlic clove and a teaspoon of tomato paste rounded out the other flavors. Last, we found that half a stick of unsalted butter whisked in at the end added a dream-like finish and beautiful sheen.

Chicken Marsala

SERVES 4

Our wine of choice for this dish is Sweet Marsala Fine, an Italian wine that gives the sauce body, soft edges, and a smooth finish. See page 394–395 for more information about making a pan sauce. Because these cutlets spend about 15 minutes in the oven while the sauce is being prepared, there's no need to pound the cutlets or remove the tenderloins.

4	boneless, skinless chicken breasts (5 to 6 ounces each), fat trimmed (see the illustration on page 334)
1	cup unbleached all-purpose flour
	Salt and ground black pepper
2	tablespoons vegetable oil
2½	ounces (about 3 slices) pancetta, cut into 1 by ⅛-inch pieces
8	ounces white mushrooms, sliced (about 2 cups)
1	medium garlic clove, minced or pressed through a garlic press
1	teaspoon tomato paste
1½	cups sweet Marsala (see note)
1½	tablespoons juice from 1 large lemon
4	tablespoons (½ stick) unsalted butter, cut into 4 pieces
2	tablespoons minced fresh parsley leaves

1. Adjust an oven rack to the lower-middle position, place a large heatproof dinner plate on the rack, and heat the oven to 200 degrees.

2. Pat the chicken breasts dry. Place the flour in a shallow baking dish or pie plate. Season both sides of the chicken cutlets with salt and pepper to taste. Working with one cutlet at a time, coat both sides with flour. Lift the breast from the tapered end and shake to remove excess flour; set aside.

3. Meanwhile, heat the oil in a 12-inch heavy-bottomed skillet over medium-high heat until shimmering. Place the floured cutlets in a single layer in the skillet and cook until golden brown, about 3 minutes. Using tongs, turn the cutlets and cook on the second side until golden brown and the meat feels firm when pressed with a finger, about 3 minutes longer. Transfer the chicken to the heated plate and return the plate to the oven.

4. Return the skillet to low heat and add the pancetta. Sauté, stirring occasionally and scraping the pan bottom with a wooden spoon to loosen the browned bits, until the pancetta is browned and crisp, about 4 minutes. With a slotted spoon, transfer the pancetta to paper towels to drain.

5. Add the mushrooms to the pan and increase the heat to medium-high. Sauté, stirring occasionally and scraping the pan bottom, until the liquid released by the mushrooms evaporates and the mushrooms begin to brown, about 8 minutes. Add the garlic, tomato paste, and cooked pancetta and cook, stirring constantly, until the tomato paste begins to brown, about 1 minute. Off the heat, add the Marsala. Return the pan to high heat and simmer vigorously, scraping the browned bits from the pan bottom, until the sauce is slightly syrupy and reduced to about 1¼ cups, about 5 minutes. Off the heat, add the lemon juice and any accumulated juices from the chicken. Whisk in the butter, 1 tablespoon at a time, until incorporated. Stir in the parsley and season with salt and pepper to taste. Pour the sauce over the chicken and serve immediately.

CHICKEN PICCATA

CHICKEN PICCATA—SAUTÉED CUTLETS WITH A lemon-caper sauce—is a restaurant classic that translates easily to the home kitchen. We imagined that piccata would be easy to perfect, and it was, after we realized that most recipes miss the point. To begin with, many cookbook authors add extraneous ingredients and thereby ruin the pure simplicity of the dish. The other major problem is blandness. Many recipes contain just a tablespoon of lemon juice and a teaspoon of capers, neither of which provides much flavor. Our goals were simple: to cook the chicken properly and to make a stream-lined sauce that really tastes of lemons and capers.

Many piccata recipes call for flouring or bread-ing the cutlets. As in past tests, we found that floured cutlets browned better and were less likely to stick to the pan. Tasters did not like breaded cutlets; what's the point of developing a crisp crust only to douse it with sauce? We also tried dipping the cutlets in milk as well as beaten eggs before flouring them. Although the crust was a bit thicker when cooked, tasters felt that there was little advantage to this extra step.

With our chicken tests completed, we turned our attention to the sauce. We wanted a strong lemon flavor that wasn't harsh or overly acidic. We also wanted a sauce that was thick enough to nap the sautéed cutlets. We knew we wanted to deglaze the empty skillet used to cook the chicken with some liquid to loosen the flavorful browned bits, then reduce the liquid and thicken it.

Most of the recipes we uncovered in our research called for 1 to 2 tablespoons of lemon juice. All of our tasters agreed that these sauces weren't lemony enough. We found that ¼ cup delivered a nice lemon punch. Recipes that instructed the cook to deglaze the hot pan with lemon juice and then simmer the sauce for sev-eral minutes tasted flat. Adding the lemon juice toward the end of the cooking time helped keep it tasting fresh.

Our caper testing led us to a similar conclusion. You need to use a lot of capers—2 tablespoons is just right—and they should be added when the sauce is nearly done so they retain their structural integrity.

We next focused on the liquid for deglazing the pan. Chicken broth and white wine were the most obvious candidates. The wine seemed like a good idea, but it contributed more acid to the sauce, which it did not need. Broth proved a more neutral base for the lemon juice and capers.

Before deglazing the pan, we sautéed some aromatics in the pan drippings. We tested shallots, onions, scallions, and garlic separately. All were fine, although tasters preferred the shallots and garlic. Just make sure to watch the pan carefully so

that the aromatics don't burn. Add the broth to the pan as soon as the garlic or shallots start to color.

At this point, our sauce was quite good, but we wondered if there was another way to add lemon flavor. In our research, we uncovered several recipes that called for lemon slices. We halved a lemon, then cut it into very thin half circles. We tried adding the lemon slices with the lemon juice, but the slices were too crunchy and numerous. For the next test, we used just half a lemon and added the slices with the broth. They simmered for five minutes and softened considerably. The longer simmering time also allowed oils from the peel to flavor the sauce. We tried replacing the sliced lemon with grated zest but found the slices more appealing and less work.

The last remaining issue for testing was thick-ening the sauce. Some recipes called for a roux (a combination of flour and fat), while others added either softened butter or softened butter mixed with flour once the sauce was cooked. A roux made the sauce too thick. Thickening the sauce at the end seemed more practical. The butter-flour paste gave the sauce a floury taste that dulled the flavors of the lemon and capers. Plain butter proved best. Parsley, added with the butter, gave the sauce some color.

~⊱

Chicken Piccata

SERVES 4

Because this sauce is so light, we find that each person should be served 1½ small cutlets. Serve the cutlets and sauce on a single platter and let each person help him- or herself.

2	large lemons
6	boneless, skinless chicken breasts (5 to 6 ounces each), tenderloins removed and reserved for another use, fat trimmed (see the illustrations on page 334)
	Salt and ground black pepper
½	cup unbleached all-purpose flour
4	tablespoons vegetable oil
1	small shallot, minced, or 1 small garlic clove, minced or pressed through a garlic press
1	cup low-sodium chicken broth

2   tablespoons small capers, rinsed
3   tablespoons unsalted butter, softened
2   tablespoons minced fresh parsley leaves

1. Adjust an oven rack to the lower-middle position, set a large heatproof serving or dinner plate on the rack, and heat the oven to 200 degrees.

2. Halve one lemon pole to pole. Trim the ends from one half and cut it crosswise into slices ⅛ to ¼ inch thick; set aside. Juice the remaining half and whole lemon to obtain ¼ cup juice; reserve.

3. Sprinkle both sides of the cutlets generously with salt and pepper. Measure the flour into a shallow baking dish or pie plate. Working with one cutlet at a time, coat with the flour and shake to remove the excess.

4. Heat 2 tablespoons of the oil in a heavy-bottomed 12-inch skillet over medium-high heat until shimmering. Lay half of the chicken cutlets in the skillet. Sauté the cutlets until lightly browned on the first side, 2 to 2½ minutes. Turn the cutlets and cook until the second side is lightly browned, 2 to 2½ minutes longer. Remove the pan from the heat and transfer the cutlets to the plate in the oven. Add the remaining 2 tablespoons oil to the now-empty skillet and heat until shimmering. Add the remaining chicken cutlets and repeat.

5. Add the shallot to the now-empty skillet and return the skillet to medium heat. Sauté until fragrant, about 30 seconds (10 seconds for garlic). Add the broth and lemon slices, increase the heat to high, and scrape the pan bottom with a wooden spoon or spatula to loosen the browned bits. Simmer until the liquid reduces to about ⅓ cup, about 4 minutes. Add the reserved lemon juice and capers and simmer until the sauce reduces again to ⅓ cup, about 1 minute. Remove the pan from the heat and swirl in the butter until it melts and thickens the sauce. Stir in the parsley and season with salt and pepper to taste. Spoon the sauce over the chicken and serve immediately.

➤ VARIATIONS
Peppery Chicken Piccata
Follow the recipe for Chicken Piccata, adding ½ teaspoon coarsely ground black pepper along with the lemon juice and capers.

Chicken Piccata with Prosciutto
Follow the recipe for Chicken Piccata, adding 2 ounces thinly sliced prosciutto, cut into 1 by ¼-inch pieces, along with the shallot; sauté until the prosciutto is just lightly crisped, about 45 seconds.

Chicken Piccata with Black Olives
Follow the recipe for Chicken Piccata, adding ¼ cup pitted and chopped black olives along with the lemon juice and capers.

COQ AU VIN
WE REMEMBER DISCOVERING COQ AU VIN IN the late 1960s when French food was taking hold in American kitchens. This classic fricassee of cut-up chicken is cooked in a red wine sauce and finished with a garnish of bacon, tiny glazed pearl onions, and sautéed mushrooms At its best, coq au vin should be hugely tasty, the acidity of the wine rounded out by rich, salty bacon and sweet, caramelized onions and mushrooms. The chicken should act like a sponge, soaking up those same dark, compelling flavors. We set about creating a recipe that would satisfy our appetite for a really great coq au vin.

We started out by cooking and tasting a number of recipes from French cookbooks. As we cooked, we noticed that the recipes fell into two categories: those that were simpler and more provincial in character, and one that was more complicated and promised a more refined taste. Tasting these versions, we recognized them as the serviceable renditions of recent memory: The sauces were good but not extraordinary; the chicken tasted mostly like chicken. In short, the recipes weren't special enough to merit the time they demanded.

We moved on to testing a much more complicated recipe from Madeleine Kamman's *The New Making of a Cook* (William Morrow, 1998). This two-day affair was also a brown fricassee, but with a much more elaborate sauce. The recipe began by combining red wine with veal broth and browned vegetables and reducing this mixture by about half. The chicken was then browned and the pan deglazed with the reduced wine mixture (in deglazing, liquid is added to a hot pan to remove the browned bits that remain from the previous round of cooking). Once the chicken was cooked, the sauce was strained, bound first with *beurre manié* (a paste of mashed butter and flour), and then with a bit of chicken liver pureed with heavy cream; the sauce was then finished with flambéed cognac.

Although it was built on the same basic model as the others, this dish was in a whole different league. It was what a good coq au vin ought to be—the sauce beautifully textured, clean-flavored, and rich without being heavy or murky. The chicken was drenched in flavor. Though we were able to make it in just one day instead of the two that Kamman posited, the recipe unquestionably demanded more time, more last-minute fussing, and a lot more dishes (in addition to a blender) than the recipes we'd made before.

As we compared Kamman's recipe with the others, two techniques stood out. First, Kamman bound her sauce differently—with beurre manié and chicken liver—rather than sprinkling the meat or vegetables with flour at the beginning. Kamman also used all chicken legs instead of both legs and breasts as the other recipes did. Finally, Kamman's recipe was the only one that reduced the wine with the stock and aromatics before adding the chicken; the others used raw wine.

We first tested a coq au vin bound with beurre manié and compared it with one in which the vegetables were sprinkled with flour. We liked using the beurre manié far better because it gave us more control over the thickness of the sauce. With the latter technique, we were forced to choose a measurement of flour without knowing what the final measurement of liquid would be.

We found that we also agreed with Kamman's use of legs only. Not only do the legs add more flavor to the sauce because they cook longer than the breasts, but, as Kamman points out, the breasts don't cook long enough in the wine to take on much wine flavor; they taste insipid compared with the legs. Further testing demonstrated that thighs worked as well as whole legs.

Finally, we tested a recipe in which the wine was reduced by half before it was cooked with the chicken against a recipe in which the wine was added to the pan raw and reduced at the end, after the chicken was cooked. There was a readily discernible difference in taste between the two: The first sauce, in which the wine had been reduced early on, was much less astringent, tasting full and round; the other tasted raw and somewhat sweet in comparison. The better sauce tasted more of chicken as well, so the flavor was more interesting and complex. There was even a noticeable difference in the taste of the chicken itself. The chicken in the first test tasted better because it tasted of the cooked, reduced wine; the other had the harsh,

PREPARING FRESH PEARL ONIONS

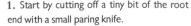

1. Start by cutting off a tiny bit of the root end with a small paring knife.

2. To keep the onions from falling apart, cut an X in the exposed root end of each onion. This will allow the layers to expand but still hold together when sautéed.

3. We find it easier to peel fresh pearl onions after they have been blanched in boiling water for 30 seconds. Use a slotted spoon to transfer the onions to a bowl of ice water. When cool, drain the onions and slip off the skins.

sweet flavor of raw wine. In addition, it was a boon not to have to reduce the sauce at the end when we had other things to do.

Having determined that beurre manié, dark meat, and a preliminary reduction of the wine were key to the success of this dish, we ran some final tests to find out if the addition of cognac, chicken liver, or tomato paste improved the sauce enough to merit the extra trouble. While cognac was a refinement that we could taste, we liked the sauce well enough without it. The chicken liver mellowed the taste of the sauce by balancing the acidity of the wine, and it added body; but since its addition required two more steps and we liked the sauce without it, we nixed the liver. Tomato paste, however, was simple to whisk in, and, as it furnished some of the extra flavor and body that a true veal stock would add, we decided to use it.

Kamman's recipe also called for using pork brisket or pancetta in lieu of bacon, neither of which is smoked, as bacon is; we found it's not worth the extra trouble to find either. Finally, we played with the proportions of chicken broth and wine to arrive at a sauce with a wine flavor that was rich and full but not overpowering.

Coq au Vin

SERVES 4

If you have the time to blanch and skin them, fresh pearl onions are terrific. For more information, see the illustrations on page 342. Serve over buttered egg noodles or mashed potatoes.

I	bottle (750 ml) medium-bodied, fruity red wine, such as Oregon Pinot Noir, Zinfandel, or a light Rhône Valley wine
2½	cups low-sodium chicken broth
6	ounces (about 6 slices) bacon, preferably thick-cut, cut crosswise into ¼-inch pieces
6–7	tablespoons unsalted butter, at room temperature
I	large carrot, chopped coarse
I	large onion, chopped coarse
2	medium shallots, quartered
2	medium garlic cloves, skin on and smashed

4	whole chicken legs, trimmed of excess skin and fat, thighs and drumsticks separated (see illustration 4 on page 329), or 8 bone-in, skin-on chicken thighs (about 3 pounds), trimmed of excess skin and fat
	Salt and ground black pepper
I	teaspoon dried thyme, 10 fresh parsley stems, and I bay leaf tied together in a 6-inch square of cheesecloth to make a bouquet garni (see the illustration on page 546)
I½	teaspoons tomato paste
24	frozen pearl onions (evenly sized), thawed, or fresh pearl onions (see note)
8	ounces white mushrooms, whole if small, halved if medium, quartered if large
2–3	tablespoons unbleached all-purpose flour
2	tablespoons minced fresh parsley leaves

1. Bring the red wine and chicken broth to a boil in a large, heavy nonreactive saucepan, reduce the heat to medium-high, and cook until reduced to about 4 cups, about 20 minutes. Remove the pan from the heat.

2. Meanwhile, fry the bacon in a large Dutch oven over medium heat until the fat is rendered and the bacon is golden brown, about 5 minutes. Transfer the bacon with a slotted spoon to a paper towel–lined plate to drain; set aside. Add 1 tablespoon of the butter to the rendered bacon fat and heat until melted; add the carrot, onion, shallots, and garlic and sauté until lightly browned, 10 to 15 minutes. Press the vegetables against the side of the pan with a slotted spoon to squeeze out as much fat as possible; transfer the vegetables to the pan with the reduced wine mixture. Discard all but 1 tablespoon of the fat from the Dutch oven.

3. Generously sprinkle the chicken pieces with salt and pepper to taste. Place the Dutch oven over medium-high heat and add 1 tablespoon of the butter. When the butter has melted, add half the chicken pieces, skin-side down, and cook, not moving them until the skin is crisp and well browned, about 5 minutes. Using tongs, flip the chicken and brown on the second side, about 5 minutes longer. Transfer the browned chicken to a large plate. Brown the remaining chicken pieces, transfer them to the plate, and set aside.

4. Pour off all the fat from the Dutch oven. Return the pan to the heat and add the wine-vegetable mixture. Bring to a boil, scraping up any browned bits from the pan bottom with a wooden spoon. Add the browned chicken, bouquet garni, and tomato paste. Return the mixture to a boil, then reduce the heat to low and simmer gently, partially covered, until the meat is tender and infused with wine flavor, 45 to 60 minutes. Turn the chicken once during cooking.

5. While the chicken and sauce are cooking, heat 2 tablespoons of the butter in a medium skillet over medium-low heat. Add the pearl onions and cook, stirring occasionally and reducing the heat if the butter starts to brown too fast, until lightly browned and almost cooked through, 5 to 8 minutes. Add the mushrooms, season with salt to taste, cover, increase the heat to medium, and cook until the mushrooms release their liquid, about 5 minutes. Remove the cover, increase the heat to high, and boil until the liquid evaporates and the onions and mushrooms are golden brown, 2 to 3 minutes more. Transfer the onions and mushrooms to the plate with the bacon; set aside.

6. When the chicken is cooked, transfer it to a serving bowl or platter; cover with aluminum foil to keep warm. Strain the sauce through a fine-mesh strainer set over a large measuring cup, pressing on the solids with a wooden spoon to release as much liquid as possible; the sauce should measure 2 to 3 cups. Return the sauce to the pan; skim as much fat as possible off the surface. Counting 1 tablespoon each of butter and flour for each cup of sauce, mash 2 to 3 tablespoons each butter and flour in a small bowl or plate to make a smooth paste (beurre manié). Bring the sauce to a boil and whisk in the beurre manié until smooth. Add the reserved chicken, bacon, onions, and mushrooms. Adjust the seasonings, reduce the heat to medium-low, and simmer very gently to warm through and blend the flavors, about 5 minutes. Check the seasonings one more time and adjust with additional salt and pepper if necessary; add the parsley. Transfer the chicken to a serving platter and pour the sauce over it. Serve immediately.

CHICKEN CACCIATORE

CACCIATORE, WHICH MEANS "HUNTER-STYLE" in Italian, originally referred to a simple method of cooking fresh-killed game. Game hen or rabbit was sautéed along with wild mushrooms, onions, and other foraged vegetables, then braised with wine or broth. Unfortunately, when applied to chicken and translated by American cooks, cacciatore mutated into a generic pasty "red sauce" dish, often featuring sauces that were greasy and overly sweet along with dry, overcooked chicken. We thought it was time for a resurrection. We knew there was a really good version of this dish to be found, and we were determined to discover it.

From the beginning, we knew that we wanted a sauce that was just substantial enough to cling to the chicken; we didn't want the chicken to be swimming in broth, nor did we want a sauce reminiscent of Spackle. Another thing we wanted was a streamlined cooking method. This cacciatore would be easy enough to prepare on a weeknight and, we hoped, would necessitate the use of only one pot.

We began our work with a blind taste test. We gathered an abundance of recipes (every Italian cookbook seems to include some form of cacciatore), then selected what seemed to be the more authentic versions (no boneless, skinless chicken breasts, no jarred tomato sauces) written by prominent Italian cooks. All four of the recipes we chose started with the same basic preparation, one that we would also use for our working recipe. Chicken (a whole chicken cut up in all but one of the recipes) was dredged in flour and sautéed in olive oil, then removed from the pan, which was then deglazed—a process in which a liquid is used to lift the browned bits from the pan bottom—with either wine or broth. Vegetables—most often tomatoes, onions, and mushrooms—were added, the chicken was returned to the pot, and the dish was then left to cook until the meat was fall-apart tender.

As we reviewed the tasters' notes on this trial run, we noticed that two problems were common to all the recipes. For one, tasters found the dishes too greasy (nearly an inch of oil floated at the top of one dish); for another, they disliked the presence of chicken skin in the final product. The skin, which was crisp after the initial sauté, had become soggy and unappealing.

All of the recipes except one had other serious problems as well. One was too vegetal, another included black olives that proved too dominant a flavor, and a third had no tomatoes, an omission that tasters thought took the dish too far from what Americans consider a classic cacciatore. The fourth recipe was much more promising. It started off with chicken thighs rather than a whole cut-up chicken and used a mixture made from equal parts flour and softened butter, known as beurre manié, to thicken the sauce. The dark thigh meat remained much more moist and plump than the fibrous, flavorless breast meat we had ended up with in the other recipes. (It was also much easier to simply buy a package of thighs than to cut up a whole chicken.) The thighs also gave the braising liquid a more intense flavor. Unfortunately, the beurre manié overthickened the sauce, giving it a gravy-like consistency.

From the test results, we derived a few conclusions and devised a working recipe. Chicken thighs were in, but the flabby skin was out—and this, we hoped, would reduce the overabundance of grease in the dish. Wine (whether to use red or white was still to be determined) was the liquid of choice for braising, and the vegetables needed to be kept to a minimum—a combination of onions, mushrooms, and tomatoes would suffice.

We thought that the flabby skin problem could be solved by using skinless chicken thighs, but that assumption proved untrue. A batch made with skinless thighs, while good, lacked the intense flavor of the batches made with skin-on chicken. The rendered fat and juice from the chicken skin caramelized on the pan bottom; this fond, when deglazed, made a big contribution to the flavor of the sauce. In addition, the skin protected the flesh of the chicken from direct contact with the high heat, thereby preventing the formation of a fibrous crust. We needed to lose the chicken skin after its fat had been rendered.

We found that pulling the skin off the thighs after the initial sauté cost the dish none of its flavor while allowing us to serve the dish skinless. Removing the skin before braising also eliminated the problem of excess grease. The fat from the skin is first rendered at a high heat, which helps keep the skin from sticking to the pan bottom. The extra fat is disposed of, but the caramelized bits are left behind for deglazing.

Next came the braising medium. Preliminary testing suggested that red wine would prevail. Most tasters liked its bold presence, although some thought its hearty flavor was a bit too harsh. We tried cutting the wine with small amounts of water, dry vermouth, and chicken broth and found that the latter buffered the strong presence of the wine and rounded out the flavors. (Because some tasters preferred the lighter, brothier taste of the version made with white wine, we decided to offer that as a variation on the master recipe.)

At this point, the sauce was rich in flavor but lacking in substance. Truthfully, it was more like a broth; the vegetables and chicken were lost in liquid. We remembered that the flour used to dredge the chicken thighs had been thrown away with the skin. We would have to reintroduce it somewhere else. The addition of beurre manié was too complicated for this streamlined dish, so we ended up adding a little flour directly to the vegetables as they were finishing their sauté. The sauce was now silky and robust. On a whim, we threw in a piece of Parmesan cheese rind, an option we had noticed in one of the recipes tested earlier. The sauce, very good before, now surpassed all of our expectations. It was substantial, lavish, and amply flavored.

We were finally down to the details of finishing. Portobello mushrooms, bursting with the essence of red wine, added an earthy flavor and meaty chew. We also found that just about any herb would complement the recipe; we chose sage for its woodsy flavor.

Chicken Cacciatore with Portobellos and Sage
SERVES 4

The addition of the Parmesan cheese rind is optional, but we highly recommend it for the robust, savory flavor it lends to the dish. An equal amount of minced fresh rosemary leaves can be substituted for the sage.

345

8   bone-in, skin-on chicken thighs (about
    3 pounds), trimmed of excess skin and fat
    Salt and ground black pepper
1   teaspoon olive oil
1   medium onion, chopped
6   ounces (about 3 medium) portobello
    mushroom caps, wiped clean and cut into
    ¾-inch dice
4   medium garlic cloves, minced or pressed
    through a garlic press
1½ tablespoons unbleached all-purpose flour
1½ cups dry red wine
½   cup low-sodium chicken broth
1   (14.5-ounce) can diced tomatoes, drained
2   teaspoons minced fresh thyme leaves
1   Parmesan cheese rind, about 4 by 2 inches
    (optional)
2   teaspoons minced fresh sage leaves

1. Heat the oven to 300 degrees. Season the chicken liberally with salt and pepper to taste. Heat the olive oil in an ovenproof Dutch oven over medium-high heat until shimmering but not smoking, about 2 minutes. Add 4 of the chicken thighs, skin-side down, and cook, not moving them until the skin is crisp and well browned, about 5 minutes. Using tongs, flip the chicken and brown on the second side, about 5 minutes longer. Transfer the browned chicken to a large plate. Brown the remaining chicken thighs, transfer them to the plate, and set aside. When the chicken has cooled, remove and discard the skin (see the illustration above). With a spoon, remove and discard all but 1 tablespoon of the fat from the pan.

2. Add the onion, mushrooms, and ½ teaspoon salt to the now-empty Dutch oven. Sauté over medium-high heat, stirring occasionally, until the moisture evaporates and the vegetables begin to brown, 6 to 8 minutes. Add the garlic and sauté until fragrant, about 30 seconds. Stir in the flour and cook, stirring constantly, for about 1 minute. Add the wine, scraping the pan bottom with a wooden spoon to loosen the browned bits. Stir in the broth, tomatoes, thyme, Parmesan rind (if using), ½ teaspoon salt (omit salt if using the cheese rind), and pepper to taste. Add the chicken pieces and accumulated juices, submerging the chicken in

SKINNING BROWNED CHICKEN

Once the chicken thighs have been browned and cooled, grasp the skin from one end and pull to separate the skin from the meat. Discard the skin.

the liquid. Bring to a simmer, cover, and place the pot in the oven. Bake until the chicken is done, about 30 minutes. Remove from the oven. (The stew can be covered and refrigerated for up to 3 days. Bring to a simmer over medium-low heat.)

3. Discard the cheese rind, stir in the sage, and adjust the seasonings. Serve immediately.

➤ VARIATION

Chicken Cacciatore with White Wine and Tarragon

Mince 3 large shallots; clean 10 ounces white mushrooms and quarter if large, halve if medium, or leave whole if small. Follow the recipe for Chicken Cacciatore with Portobellos and Sage, substituting the shallots for the chopped onion, the white mushrooms for the portobellos, dry white wine for the red wine, and 2 teaspoons minced fresh tarragon leaves for the sage.

CHICKEN PROVENÇAL

CHICKEN PROVENÇAL—CHICKEN PIECES ON the bone simmered with tomatoes, garlic, herbs, and olives—may represent the best of French peasant cooking, but it is not well-known here in the United States. We soon discovered why. The handful of recipes we tested produced rubbery, dry chicken; dull and muddy flavors; and a sauce that was too thick or too thin, too sweet or too greasy. We wanted a chicken dish that was meltingly tender, moist, and flavorful, napped in an aromatic, garlicky tomato sauce that we could mop up with a good loaf of crusty bread.

The chicken was our starting point. From previous kitchen tests, most notably in our Chicken Cacciatore (page 344), we decided to make the dish with thighs only. Next we addressed the skin. Its flabby texture after cooking made it virtually inedible. When we began with skinless thighs, however, they stuck to the pan, the outer layer of meat becoming tough and dry with browning. The skin, it turns out, acts as a necessary cushion between the meat and the pan, so we left it on for browning and then discarded it. We also wondered if the amount of browning mattered. A side-by-side taste test—one batch made with lightly browned thighs, the other with deeply browned thighs—revealed that more browning renders more fat and results in more chicken flavor. The dish prepared with deeply browned thighs had a rich flavor that was far superior to the blander taste of the other.

We assumed that olive oil was essential to this dish (it is from Provence, after all), but most recipes (which use about three tablespoons) were too greasy. We browned a batch of thighs in a meager single tablespoon of olive oil and found that the skin quickly rendered a couple of additional tablespoons of fat. But even with this reduced amount of fat, tasters still found the final dish to be greasy. Pouring off all but one tablespoon of the fat after browning the chicken eliminated the greasiness, but now the flavor of the sauce was lacking. We were throwing out flavor with the rendered fat. In another test, we used just one teaspoon of oil. Sure enough, using less olive oil at the beginning allowed for a stronger chicken flavor in the final dish because we were discarding less chicken fat. We had one more test in mind—drizzling two teaspoons of extra-virgin olive oil over the finished dish just before serving. Tasters approved of the additional fruity olive flavor.

Our final tests with the chicken focused on the cooking method. Almost by definition, chicken Provençal is braised (browned and then cooked in a tightly covered pot in a small amount of liquid over low heat for a long time). Stovetop braising proved unreliable. The cooking time varied, and, even though we set the flame at the same heat level every time, the heat transfer was not uniform. Braising in a 300-degree oven was much more reliable, producing a predictably even, consistent level of heat. Next, we tested the optimal braising time. Technically, thighs are considered done when they reach an internal temperature of 170 degrees, or after 30 minutes of braising. Unfortunately, 30 minutes of braising produced thighs that were not as meltingly tender as desired, and the chicken did not have enough flavor. We decided to cook them longer, although we were uncertain if a longer cooking time would overcook and dry out the chicken.

To our surprise, after trying longer and longer cooking times, we ended up keeping the dish in the oven for a whopping 1½ hours. At this point, the meat simply fell off the bones; it was exceedingly tender and flavorful, and the thighs did not seem overcooked. Additional tests, however, revealed that slightly less time—1¼ hours, wherein the meat reaches an internal temperature of 210 degrees—is perfect, as the meat then stays on the bone. Why this long cooking time? The long stay in the oven breaks down the connective tissue in the thighs, much as it does in a pot roast, yielding more tender meat. (White meat contains little connective tissue, so there's no benefit to cooking it longer.) In addition, thighs have plenty of fat that keeps them moist as they braise.

Many recipes call for sautéing onions after the chicken is browned and taken out of the pot. Tasters approved of some onion but not a lot, commenting that a modest amount of the onion's pungent flavor was enough to balance the sweetness of the tomatoes. Garlic is most often added next and sautéed briefly to bring forth its flavor. Preliminary tests showed that both dry white wine and dry vermouth work well for deglazing the pan, but the wine turned out to be the favorite among tasters. The vermouth seemed to exaggerate the acidity of the tomatoes.

Crushed and pureed canned tomatoes each produced a thick, sweet, overbearing sauce reminiscent of bad Italian restaurant food. Canned diced tomatoes, though more promising, presented the opposite problem: Even when drained, they contain a fair amount of liquid, and the resulting sauce was too thin. We added a few tablespoons of tomato paste to the diced tomatoes, and the texture improved dramatically—now the sauce coated the chicken without overwhelming it. Chicken broth rounded out the flavors while providing a bit more volume. For a more intense flavor—and better consistency—we ended up reducing the braising liquid after removing the chicken from the pot.

Whole niçoise olives appeared in nearly every recipe, but tasters complained about the pits. Niçoise are so small that pitting by hand with a knife is an awful lot to ask. We tried Kalamatas, Gaetas, and oil-cured olives, but none of them sufficed. The flavors of their brine or oil were too strong and inappropriate. While discussing this predicament among colleagues, a solution surfaced that involved a mallet and clean kitchen towels (see the tip below).

As for seasonings, the combination of dried herbs referred to as herbes de Provence (lavender, marjoram, basil, fennel seed, rosemary, sage, summer savory, and thyme) seemed like a shoo-in. But tasters said that, when used alone, these dried herbs were too strong, giving the sauce a flavor that bordered on medicinal. Fresh thyme, oregano, and parsley with a bay leaf were preferred, and a teaspoon of the dried blend became an optional item.

PITTING NIÇOISE OLIVES

Removing the pits by hand from tiny niçoise olives is not an easy job. We found the following method to be the most expedient. Cover a cutting board with a clean kitchen towel and spread the olives on top, spacing them about 1 inch apart. Place a second clean towel over the olives. Using a mallet, pound the olives firmly for 10 to 15 seconds, being careful not to split the pits. Remove the top towel and, using your fingers, press the pit out of each olive.

A pinch of cayenne balanced the sweet tomatoes. Inspired by one of the better initial recipes tested, we tried adding a teaspoon of minced anchovies before deglazing. Although tasters could not identify the ingredient, everyone agreed the sauce tasted richer and fuller. The final item on our list was lemon zest, a common and, as it turned out, welcome addition.

Chicken Provençal (Braised Chicken with Tomatoes, Garlic, and Olives)

SERVES 4

This dish is often served with rice or crusty bread, but soft polenta is also a good accompaniment. Niçoise olives are preferred; other olives are too potent.

8	bone-in, skin-on chicken thighs (about 3 pounds), trimmed of excess skin and fat
	Salt
1	tablespoon extra-virgin olive oil
1	small onion, chopped fine
6	medium garlic cloves, minced or pressed through a garlic press
1	anchovy fillet, minced (about 1 teaspoon)
1/8	teaspoon cayenne pepper
1	cup dry white wine
1	cup low-sodium chicken broth
1	(14.5-ounce) can diced tomatoes, drained
2 1/2	tablespoons tomato paste
1 1/2	tablespoons chopped fresh thyme leaves
1	teaspoon chopped fresh oregano leaves
1	bay leaf
1	teaspoon herbes de Provence (optional)
1 1/2	teaspoons grated zest from 1 lemon
1/2	cup niçoise olives, pitted (see the illustration at left)
1	tablespoon chopped fresh parsley leaves

1. Adjust an oven rack to the lower-middle position; heat the oven to 300 degrees. Sprinkle both sides of the chicken with salt. Heat 1 teaspoon of the olive oil in a Dutch oven over medium-high heat until shimmering but not smoking. Add 4 of the chicken thighs, skin-side down, and cook without moving them until the skin is crisp and

well browned, about 5 minutes. Using tongs, turn the chicken pieces and brown on the second side, about 5 minutes longer; transfer to a large plate. Brown the remaining 4 chicken thighs, transfer to the plate, and set aside. Discard all but 1 tablespoon of the fat from the pot.

2. Add the onion to the fat in the Dutch oven and cook, stirring occasionally, over medium heat until browned, about 4 minutes. Add the garlic, anchovy, and cayenne; cook, stirring constantly, until fragrant, about 1 minute. Add the wine and scrape up the browned bits on the pan bottom with a wooden spoon. Stir in the chicken broth, tomatoes, tomato paste, thyme, oregano, bay leaf, and herbes de Provence (if using). Remove and discard the skin from the chicken thighs (see page 346), then submerge the chicken in the liquid in the pot and add the accumulated chicken juices. Increase the heat to high, bring to a simmer, cover, and set the pot in the oven. Bake until the chicken offers no resistance when poked with the tip of a paring knife but the meat still clings to the bones, about 1¼ hours.

3. Using a slotted spoon, transfer the chicken to a serving platter and tent with foil. Discard the bay leaf. Set the Dutch oven over high heat, stir in 1 teaspoon of the lemon zest, bring to boil, and cook, stirring occasionally, until the sauce is slightly thickened and reduced to 2 cups, about 5 minutes. Stir in the olives and cook until heated through, about 1 minute. Meanwhile, mix the remaining ½ teaspoon lemon zest with the parsley. Spoon the sauce over the chicken, drizzle the chicken with the remaining 2 teaspoons olive oil, sprinkle with the parsley mixture, and serve.

➤ VARIATION
Chicken Provençal with Saffron, Orange, and Basil
Follow the recipe for Chicken Provençal, adding ⅛ teaspoon saffron threads along with the wine and substituting orange zest for the lemon zest and 2 tablespoons chopped fresh basil for the parsley.

CHICKEN POT PIE
MOST EVERYONE LOVES A GOOD CHICKEN pot pie, though few seem to have the time or energy to make one. Not surprising. Like a lot of satisfying dishes, traditional pot pie takes time. Before the pie even makes it to the oven, the cook must poach a chicken, take the meat off the bone and cut it up, strain the stock, prepare and blanch vegetables, make a sauce, and mix and roll out biscuit or pie dough. Given the many time-consuming steps it can take to make a pot pie, our goal was to make the best one we could as quickly as possible. Pot pie, after all, was intended as weeknight supper food.

Our experiences with making pot pie also made us aware of two other difficulties. First, the vegetables tend to overcook. A filling that is chock-full of bright, fresh vegetables going into the oven looks completely different after 40 minutes of high-heat baking under a blanket of dough. Carrots become mushy and pumpkin-colored, while peas and fresh herbs fade from fresh spring green to olive drab. We wanted to preserve the vegetables' color as long as it didn't require any unnatural acts to do so.

We had also made a number of pot pies that were too juicy. Before baking, the filling was thick and creamy. When cut into after baking, the pie looked like chicken soup en croûte. Although we wanted the pie moist and saucy, we also wanted it thick enough to eat with a fork.

We began by determining the best way to cook the chicken. In addition to making pies with roast chicken and poached chicken, we steamed and roasted whole chickens and braised chicken parts.

Steaming the chicken was time-consuming, requiring about one hour, and the steaming liquid didn't make a strong enough stock for the pot pie sauce. Roast chicken also required an hour in the oven, and by the time we took off the skin and mixed the meat in with the sauce and vegetables, the roasted flavor was lost. We had similar results with braised chicken. It lost its delicious flavor once the browned skin was removed.

Next we tried poaching, the most traditional cooking method. Of the two poaching liquids we tried, we preferred the chicken poached in wine and stock to the one poached in stock alone.

349

The wine infused the meat and made for a richer, more full-flavored sauce. To our disappointment, however, the acidity of the wine sauce caused the green peas and fresh herbs to lose their bright green color in the oven. Vegetables baked in the stock-only sauce kept their bright color, though the bland sauce needed perking up—a problem we'd have to deal with later. Now we were ready to test this method against quicker-cooking boneless, skinless chicken breasts.

Because boneless, skinless breasts cook so quickly, sautéing was another possible cooking method for them. Before comparing our liking for poached parts versus poached breasts, we tried cooking the breasts three different ways. We cut raw breast meat into bite-size pieces and sautéed them; we sautéed whole breasts, shredding the breast meat once it was cool enough to handle; and we poached whole breasts in stock, also shredding the meat.

Once again, poaching was our favorite method. The resulting tender, irregularly shaped chicken pieces mixed well with the vegetables and, much like textured pasta, caused the sauce to cling. The sautéed chicken pieces, however, floated independently in the sauce, their surfaces too smooth to attract sauce. For simplicity's sake, we had hoped to like the sautéed whole breasts. Unfortunately, sautéing caused the outer layer of meat to turn crusty, a texture we did not like in the pie.

Our only concern with the poached boneless, skinless breasts was the quality of the stock. In earlier tests, we found that bone-in parts could be poached in commercially prepared low-sodium broth (rather than homemade stock) without much sacrifice in flavor. We surmised that the bones and skin improved the flavor of the broth during the long cooking time. But how would quick-cooking boneless, skinless breasts fare in the broth? The answer? Not as bad as we feared. In our comparison of the pies made with boneless breasts poached in homemade stock and prepared broth, we found little difference in quality. Evidently, it's not the cooking time of the chicken but the abundance of ingredients in a pot pie that makes it possible to use broth with no ill consequences. Ultimately, we were able to shave half an hour off the cooking time (10 minutes to cook the breasts compared with 40 minutes to cook

the parts). For those who like either dark or a mix of dark and white meat in the pie, boneless, skinless chicken thighs can be used as well.

A good pot pie with fresh vegetables, warm pastry, and full-flavored sauce tastes satisfying. One with overcooked vegetables tastes stodgy and old-fashioned. So we made pies with raw vegetables, sautéed vegetables, and parboiled vegetables. After comparing the pies, we found that the vegetables sautéed before baking held their color and flavor best, the parboiled ones less so. The raw vegetables were not fully cooked at the end of the baking time and gave off too much liquid, watering down the flavor and thickness of the sauce.

Our final task was to develop a sauce that was flavorful, creamy, and of the proper consistency. Chicken pot pie sauce is traditionally based on a roux (a mixture of butter and flour sautéed together briefly), which is thinned with chicken broth and often enriched with cream.

Because of the dish's inherent richness, we wanted to see how little cream we could get away with using. We tried three different pot pie fillings, using ¼ cup cream, ¼ cup half-and-half, and 1½ cups milk, respectively. Going into the oven, all of the fillings seemed to have the right consistency and creaminess; when they came out, however, it was a different story. Vegetable and meat juices diluted the consistency and creaminess of the cream and half-and-half sauces. To achieve a creamy-looking sauce, we would have needed to increase the cream dramatically. Fortunately, we didn't have to try it, because we actually liked the milk-enriched sauce. The larger quantity of milk kept the sauce creamy and tasted delicious.

To keep the sauce from becoming too liquidy, we simply added more flour. A sauce that looks a little thick before baking will become the perfect consistency after taking on the chicken and vegetable juices released during baking.

We had worked out the right consistency, but because we had been forced to abandon the wine for the vegetables' sake, the sauce tasted a little bland. Lemon juice, a flavor heightener we had seen in a number of recipes, had the same dulling effect on the color of the vegetables as the wine. We tried sherry, and it worked perfectly. Because sherry is more intensely flavored and less acidic than wine, it gave us the flavor we were looking for without harming the peas and carrots.

Chicken Pot Pie

SERVES 6 TO 8

You can make the filling ahead of time, but remember to heat it on top of the stove before topping it. Mushrooms can be sautéed along with the celery and carrots, and blanched pearl onions can stand in for the onion.

1	recipe Savory Pie Dough Topping or Fluffy Buttermilk Biscuit Topping (page 352)
1½	pounds boneless, skinless chicken breasts and/or thighs
2	cups low-sodium chicken broth
1½	tablespoons vegetable oil
1	medium-large onion, chopped fine
3	medium carrots, peeled and cut crosswise ¼ inch thick
2	small celery ribs, cut crosswise ¼ inch thick
	Salt and ground black pepper
4	tablespoons (½ stick) unsalted butter
½	cup unbleached all-purpose flour
1½	cups milk
½	teaspoon dried thyme
3	tablespoons dry sherry
¾	cup frozen peas, thawed
3	tablespoons minced fresh parsley leaves

1. Make the pie dough or biscuit topping and refrigerate it until ready to use.

2. Adjust an oven rack to the lower-middle position and heat the oven to 400 degrees. Put the chicken and broth in a small Dutch oven or stockpot over medium heat. Cover, bring to a simmer, and simmer until the chicken is just done, 8 to 10 minutes. Transfer the chicken to a large bowl, reserving the broth in a measuring cup.

3. Increase the heat to medium-high and heat the oil in the now-empty pan. Add the onion, carrots, and celery and sauté until just tender, about 5 minutes. Season with salt and pepper to taste. While the vegetables are sautéing, shred the meat into bite-size pieces. Transfer the cooked vegetables to a bowl with the chicken; set aside.

4. Heat the butter over medium heat in the again-empty pan. When the foaming subsides, add the flour; cook about 1 minute. Whisk in the reserved chicken broth, the milk, any accumulated chicken juices, and the thyme. Bring to a simmer, then continue to simmer until the sauce fully thickens, about 1 minute. Season with salt and pepper to taste and stir in the sherry.

5. Pour the sauce over the chicken mixture and stir to combine. Stir in the peas and parsley. Adjust the seasonings. (The mixture can be covered and refrigerated overnight; reheat before topping with the pastry.) Pour the mixture into a 13 by 9-inch baking pan (or shallow baking dish of similar size) or six 12-ounce ovenproof dishes. Top with the desired pastry (see page 885 for pie dough instructions). Bake until the pastry is golden brown and the filling is bubbling, 30 minutes for the large pot pie and 20 to 25 minutes for the smaller pies. Serve hot.

➤ VARIATIONS

Chicken Pot Pie with Spring Vegetables
Follow the recipe for Chicken Pot Pie, replacing the celery with 18 thin asparagus spears that have been trimmed and cut into 1-inch pieces. Increase the peas to 1 cup.

Chicken Pot Pie with Wild Mushrooms
The soaking liquid used to rehydrate dried porcini mushrooms replaces some of the broth used to poach the chicken and then to enrich the sauce. See page 227 for more information on rehydrating dried mushrooms.

Follow the recipe for Chicken Pot Pie, soaking 1 ounce dried rinsed porcini mushrooms in 2 cups warm tap water until softened, about 20 minutes. (Alternatively, you can combine the mushrooms with 2 cups tap water in a small microwave-safe bowl. Cover with plastic wrap, cut several steam vents in the plastic wrap with a paring knife, and microwave on high power for 30 seconds. Let stand until the mushrooms soften, about 5 minutes.) Lift the mushrooms from the liquid, strain the liquid, and reserve 1 cup. Chop the mushrooms. Use the soaking liquid in place of 1 cup of the chicken broth. Proceed with the recipe, cooking the rehydrated porcini and 12 ounces sliced button mushrooms with the vegetables. Finish as directed.

Chicken Pot Pie with Corn and Bacon
This Southern variation with corn and bacon works especially well with the biscuit topping.

Follow the recipe for Chicken Pot Pie, replacing the oil with 4 ounces (about 4 slices) bacon, cut crosswise into ½-inch strips. Cook over medium heat until the fat is rendered and the bacon is crisp, about 6 minutes. Remove the bacon from the pan with a slotted spoon and drain on paper towels. Cook the vegetables in the bacon fat. Add the drained bacon to the bowl with the chicken and the cooked vegetables. Proceed with the recipe, replacing the peas with 2 cups fresh or frozen corn.

Savory Pie Dough Topping
MAKES ENOUGH FOR I RECIPE
CHICKEN POT PIE
If you like a crust in, not just on top of, your pot pie, tuck the overhanging dough down into the pie, along the side of the pan, instead of fluting the edge.

1½	cups (7½ ounces) unbleached all-purpose flour
½	teaspoon salt
4	tablespoons vegetable shortening, chilled and cut into ¼-inch pieces
8	tablespoons (I stick) cold unsalted butter, cut into ¼-inch pieces
3–4	tablespoons ice water

1. Mix the flour and salt in a food processor. Scatter the shortening over the flour mixture, tossing to coat the shortening with a little of the flour. Cut the shortening into the flour with five 1-second pulses. Add the butter and continue pulsing, cutting in the solids until the flour is pale yellow and resembles coarse cornmeal, with butter bits no larger than small peas, about four more 1-second pulses. Turn the mixture into a medium bowl.

2. Sprinkle 3 tablespoons of the ice water over the mixture. With a rubber spatula, use a folding motion to mix the water in. Press down on the dough mixture with the broad side of the spatula until the dough sticks together, adding up to 1 tablespoon more ice water if the dough will not come together. Shape the dough into a ball, then flatten it into a 4-inch-wide disk. Wrap in plastic wrap and refrigerate 30 minutes or up to 2 days before rolling.

3. When the pie filling is ready, roll the dough on a floured surface to approximate a 15 by 11-inch rectangle about ⅛ inch thick. If making individual pies, roll the dough ⅛ inch thick and cut 6 dough rounds about 1 inch larger than the dish circumference. Place the dough over the pot pie filling, trimming the dough that overhangs to within ½ inch of the pan lip. Tuck the overhanging dough back under itself so the folded edge is flush with the pan lip. Flute the edges all around. Alternatively, don't trim the dough and simply tuck the overhanging portion down into the pie. Cut at least four 1-inch vent holes in a large pot pie or one 1-inch vent hole in smaller pies. Proceed with Chicken Pot Pie recipe.

Fluffy Buttermilk Biscuit Topping
MAKES ENOUGH FOR I RECIPE
CHICKEN POT PIE
For more information about shaping biscuits, see page 711.

1	cup (5 ounces) unbleached all-purpose flour
1	cup (4 ounces) plain cake flour
2	teaspoons baking powder
¼	teaspoon baking soda
1	teaspoon sugar
½	teaspoon salt
8	tablespoons (I stick) cold unsalted butter, quartered lengthwise and cut crosswise into ¼-inch pieces
¾	cup cold buttermilk, plus I to 2 tablespoons if needed

1. Pulse the dry ingredients together in a food processor fitted with the metal blade. Add the butter pieces and pulse until the mixture resembles coarse cornmeal with a few slightly larger butter lumps.

2. Transfer the mixture to a medium bowl and add the buttermilk. Stir with a fork until the

dough gathers into moist clumps. (If the clumps are still dry, add more buttermilk, a tablespoon at a time, up to 2 tablespoons in all.) Transfer the dough to a floured work surface and form into a rough ball. Roll out the dough until it is ½ inch thick. Using a 2½- to 3-inch pastry cutter, stamp out 8 rounds of dough. If making individual pies, cut the dough slightly smaller than the circumference of each dish. (Dough rounds can be refrigerated on a lightly floured baking sheet covered with plastic wrap for up to 2 hours.)

3. Arrange the dough rounds over the warm filling and proceed with the recipe for Chicken Pot Pie.

CHICKEN AND RICE

ALTHOUGH THERE IS NO SPECIFIC AMERICAN tradition for a dish called "chicken and rice," its appeal is obvious: It's a one-dish supper, it's easy, and it's eminently variable. Yet after having made a dozen attempts at perfecting this recipe, we found two major problems. The white meat tends to dry out before the dark meat is cooked, and the rice is often heavy and greasy.

First we tackled the problem of overcooked breast meat. It turned out that the solution was rather simple. By adding the breast meat to the dish 15 minutes after the thighs and legs, both cooked perfectly. Of course, one could make this dish with just dark or light meat, but most cooks are more likely to have a whole chicken on hand than just thighs or breasts.

The texture of the rice was a more vexing issue. Our first thought was to reduce the amount of olive oil in which the chicken and onion are sautéed from two tablespoons to one. But this simply was not enough fat to get the job done, and the resulting rice was only fractionally less greasy. We thought that perhaps the chicken skin was the culprit, but after making this dish with skinless chicken pieces, we were surprised to find that the rice was still heavy and that the chicken, as we had expected, was tough and chewy without the skin to protect it during the initial sautéing.

We then thought that perhaps reducing the amount of liquid would produce less-sodden rice. For 1½ cups of long-grain white rice, we were using an equal amount of chicken stock, plus two cups of water. We tried reducing the stock to a mere half cup; the rice was indeed less sodden, but the layer of rice on top was undercooked and dried out. Fortunately, this problem, too, was rather easily solved. We found that stirring the dish once when adding the breast meat, so that the rice on top was stirred into the bottom, produced more even cooking.

Next we made four different batches using different liquids: chicken stock (heavy rice); water (bland and flat-tasting); a combination of wine and water (the acidity of the wine cut through the fat, producing clean, clear flavors); and a combination of water, canned diced tomatoes, and tomato liquid (the acid in the tomatoes punched up and enriched the flavor). Learning from these tests, we tried a combination of white wine, water, canned diced tomatoes, and tomato liquid, with excellent results.

Finally, we tested different varieties of rice to see which held up best to this sort of cooking. A basic long-grain white rice was fine, with good flavor and decent texture; a medium-grain rice was creamy, with a risotto-like texture and excellent flavor; basmati rice was nutty, with separate, light grains (this was by far the lightest version, but the basmati rice seemed somewhat out of place in such a pedestrian dish; it is, however, well suited to the variation with Indian spices on page 354); and converted rice was absolutely tasteless. So, while medium-grain and basmati rice both provided good results, we preferred basic long-grain white rice for this all-purpose dish.

Chicken and Rice with Tomatoes and White Wine
SERVES 4

If you prefer, substitute 2 pounds of breast meat or boneless thighs for the pieces of a whole chicken.

I   whole chicken (3 to 4 pounds), rinsed and patted dry, giblets and wings removed and reserved for another use, chicken cut into 8 pieces (see the illustrations on page 329)

Salt and ground black pepper

2 tablespoons extra-virgin olive oil

1 medium onion, chopped fine

3 medium garlic cloves, minced or pressed
through a garlic press

1½ cups long-grain white rice

1 (14.5-ounce) can diced tomatoes, drained,
½ cup liquid reserved

½ cup dry white wine

2 cups water

⅓ cup chopped fresh parsley leaves

1. Sprinkle the chicken pieces liberally on both sides with salt and pepper. Heat the oil until shimmering in a large, heavy nonreactive Dutch oven over high heat. Add the chicken pieces, skin-side down, and cook, without moving them, until well browned, about 6 minutes. Turn the chicken pieces with tongs and cook, again without moving them, until well browned on the second side, about 6 minutes longer. Transfer to a plate and set aside.

2. Pour all but 2 tablespoons of the fat from the pan, return it to the burner, and reduce the heat to medium. Add the onion and sauté, stirring frequently, until softened, 3 to 4 minutes. Add the garlic and sauté until fragrant, about 1 minute longer. Stir in the rice and cook, stirring frequently, until coated and glistening, about 1 minute. Stir in the tomatoes with the reserved liquid, the wine, 1 teaspoon salt, and the water, scraping the browned bits off the pot bottom with a wooden spoon. Return the chicken thighs and legs to the pan and bring to a boil. Reduce the heat to low, cover, and simmer gently for 15 minutes. Add the chicken breast pieces and stir the ingredients gently until the rice is thoroughly mixed. Cover and simmer until both the rice and chicken are tender, 10 to 15 minutes longer. Stir in the parsley, cover, and allow the dish to rest for 5 minutes. Serve immediately.

➤ VARIATIONS

Chicken and Rice with Saffron and Peas
Remove the peas from the freezer before beginning the recipe so that they'll be completely thawed when it's time to add them to the dish.

Follow the recipe for Chicken and Rice with Tomatoes and White Wine through step 1. In step 2, add 1 medium green bell pepper, cored, seeded, and cut into medium dice, to the pan with the onion and sauté, stirring frequently, until softened, 3 to 4 minutes. Add 4 teaspoons paprika and ¼ teaspoon saffron threads along with the garlic. Continue with the recipe, adding 1 cup thawed frozen peas to the pan with the parsley. Cover and allow to rest for 5 minute. Serve immediately.

Chicken and Rice with Chiles and Lime
Follow the recipe for Chicken and Rice with Tomatoes and White Wine through step 1. In step 2, add 2 jalapeño chiles, stemmed, seeded, and minced, to the pan with the onion and sauté, stirring frequently, until softened, 3 to 4 minutes. Add 2 teaspoons ground cumin, 2 teaspoons ground coriander, and 1 teaspoon chili powder with the garlic. Continue with the recipe, replacing the parsley with ¼ cup chopped fresh cilantro leaves. With the cilantro, stir in 3 tablespoons lime juice. Cover and allow to rest for 5 minutes. Serve immediately.

Chicken and Rice, Indian Style
This variation is similar to the Indian chicken and rice dish known as biryani.

Follow the recipe for Chicken and Rice with Tomatoes and White Wine through step 1. In step 2, pour all but 2 tablespoons of the fat from the pan, return it to the burner, and reduce the heat to medium. Add a 3-inch cinnamon stick and sauté, stirring with a wooden spoon, until it unfurls, about 15 seconds. Add 1 medium onion, chopped fine, and 2 medium green bell peppers, cored, seeded, and cut into medium dice. Sauté, stirring frequently, until softened, 5 to 6 minutes. Add 1 teaspoon ground turmeric, 1 teaspoon ground coriander, and 1 teaspoon ground cumin with the garlic and sauté until fragrant, about 1 minute longer. Proceed with the recipe as directed.

CHICKEN STIR-FRIES

THE MOST COMMON STIR-FRY OF ALL IS made with chicken. Sounds easy, right? Well, it turns out that a good chicken stir-fry is more difficult to prepare than a beef or pork stir-fry because chicken, which has less fat, inevitably becomes dry and stringy when cooked over high heat. Perfection in a chicken stir-fry, then, requires split-second timing to avoid either under- or over-cooked poultry, neither result being particularly appealing

We were after a stir-fry that featured tender, juicy, bite-size pieces of chicken paired with just the right combination of vegetables in a simple yet complex-flavored sauce. And because this was a stir-fry, we had to do all of this quickly.

Our initial recipe testing revealed one key fact: White meat was preferable to dark meat because chicken thighs are hard (and extremely time-consuming) to clean. When stir-fried, tasters found the dark meat chewy, with bits of connective tissue and fat still attached. On the other hand, breast meat was easy to clean (one pound finished in five minutes flat), and it was effortless to cut. That said, chicken breast has its downside: It is notoriously bland and very easy to overcook.

In the past, we've used a marinade to impart flavor to meat destined for stir-fries. Chicken was no exception. Tossing the pieces of chicken in a simple soy-sherry mixture for 10 minutes before cooking added much-needed flavor but did nothing to improve its texture.

The obvious solution to dry chicken was brining, our favorite method of adding juiciness to poultry. A test of brined boneless breasts did, in fact, confirm that this method solved our cooking problem. However, a half hour or more of brining time followed by 10 minutes of marinating was out of the question; this was supposed to be a quick midweek stir-fry. It seemed redundant to soak the chicken first in one salty solution (brine) and then another (marinade), so we decided to combine the two, using the soy sauce to provide the high salt level in the brine. This turned out to be a key secret to great chicken stir-fry. Now we were turning out highly flavored, juicy pieces of chicken—most of the time. (Given the finicky nature of high-heat cooking, some batches of chicken still occasionally turned out tough because of overcooking.)

Next we turned to a traditional Chinese technique called velveting, which involves coating chicken pieces in a thin cornstarch and egg white or oil mixture, then par-cooking in moderately heated oil. The coating forms a barrier on the chicken that keeps precious moisture inside; that extra juiciness makes the chicken seem more tender. Cornstarch mixed with egg white yielded a cakey coating; tasters preferred the more subtle coating provided by cornstarch mixed with oil. This velveted chicken was supple, but it was also pale, and, again, this method seemed far too involved for a quick weeknight dinner.

PREPARING CHICKEN FOR STIR-FRY

  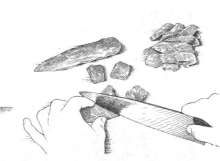

1. Separate the floppy tenderloin from the main part of the breast. Starting at the thick end, cut the chicken into ¼-inch slices. Stop slicing when you reach the tapered end of the breast.

2. With the flat side of the knife, press the chicken to an even thickness of ¼ inch, then cut the piece into 1-inch squares.

3. Use the same technique to cut the tenderloin, flattening it with the side of the knife and then cutting it into 1-inch pieces.

We wondered if the same method—coating in a cornstarch mixture—would work if we eliminated the par-cooking step. It did. This chicken was not only juicy and tender, but it also developed an attractive golden brown coating. Best of all, the entire process took less than five minutes. The only problem was that the coating, which was more of an invisible barrier than a crust, became bloated and slimy when cooked in the sauce.

Our science editor explained that the cornstarch was absorbing liquid from the sauce, which resulted in the slippery finish. We cut the cornstarch with flour, which created a negligible coating—not too thick, not too slimy—that also managed to seal in the chicken juices. Substituting sesame oil for peanut oil added a depth of rich flavor.

After trying everything from pounding to cubing the chicken, tasters voted on simple, flat ¼-inch slices, which were all the more easy to cut after freezing the breasts for 20 minutes. These wide, flat slices of chicken browned easily; we cooked them in two batches, first browning one side, then turning them over to quickly brown the second side rather than constantly stirring (as in "stir"-fry) as many recipes suggest. Although choosing not to stir-fry seemed counterintuitive, we found that the constant motion of that method detracted from the browning of the chicken.

As for the vegetables in our master recipe, we found that a combination of bok choy and red bell pepper worked well with the chicken. Another flavor combination, a pairing of green beans and shiitake mushrooms, also proved to be pleasing. For the sauce, the test kitchen has found that chicken broth, rather than soy or fish sauce, makes the best base because it is not overpowering. Hoisin and oyster sauce are both obvious flavor enhancers. We have also tested the addition of cornstarch to help the sauce coat the meat and vegetables and found that a small amount is necessary. Otherwise, the sauce will be too thin and will not adhere properly to the solids.

The basic stir-fry method was developed several years ago in the test kitchen. After the protein (in this case, the chicken) is cooked and removed from the pan, the vegetables are stir-fried in batches, garlic and ginger (the classic stir-fry combination) are quickly cooked in the center of the pan, and then the chicken is returned to the pan along with the sauce. This final mixture is then cooked over medium heat for 30 seconds to finish.

In the end, a great chicken stir-fry doesn't really take more time to prepare than a bad one. It does, however, require more attention to detail and knowledge of a few quick tricks.

Marinated Velveted Chicken for Stir-Fry

To make the chicken easier to slice, freeze it for 20 minutes, until it is firm but not frozen. Prepare the ingredients for the stir-fry recipes while the chicken marinates.

CHOOSING THE RIGHT PAN

The right pan makes all the difference when stir-frying. A 12-inch nonstick pan (left) is large enough to accommodate food without any steaming or sticking. A flat-bottomed wok (second from left) is better than a regular curved wok but still does not have as much surface area in contact with the stovetop as the completely flat-bottomed skillet. The batter on the chicken sticks and burns in a conventional (not nonstick) 12-inch skillet (second from right). A 10-inch skillet (right) is so small that food steams as it cooks.

THE BEST CHOICE:
Nonstick Skillet

A MEDIOCRE CHOICE:
Flat-Bottomed Wok

A BAD CHOICE:
Traditional Skillet

THE WORST CHOICE:
Small Skillet

¹/₄	cup soy sauce
¹/₄	cup dry sherry
I	cup water
I	pound boneless, skinless chicken breasts, trimmed of excess fat and prepared according to illustrations on page 355
2	tablespoons toasted sesame oil
I	tablespoon cornstarch
I	tablespoon unbleached all-purpose flour

1. Combine the soy sauce, sherry, and water in a medium bowl; add the chicken and stir to break up the clumps. Cover with plastic wrap and refrigerate at least 20 minutes or up to 1 hour.

2. Mix the sesame oil, cornstarch, and flour together in a medium bowl until smooth. Drain the chicken in a mesh strainer. Toss the chicken in the cornstarch–flour mixture until evenly coated. Use immediately in one of the following recipes.

EQUIPMENT: Inexpensive Nonstick Skillets

Our favorite choice for stir-frying is a large nonstick pan. Although one could spend $100 or more on this pan, most cooks would rather buy a cheaper one. This makes sense to us, especially when buying nonstick pans, where the increased browning afforded by heavier and more expensive pans is not an issue. To find the best pan for the job, we rounded up eight inexpensive nonstick skillets, all purchased at hardware or discount stores for no more than $50 apiece.

Every pan in our group received a good score in release ability and cleaning tests, the raisons d'être for nonstick. We tested both traits in a purposefully abusive manner by burning oatmeal into the pans over high heat for 45 minutes. That kind of treatment would trash a traditional pan, but the scorched cereal slid out of our nonstick pans with no fuss, and the pans practically wiped clean.

Most manufacturers recommend using plastic, rubber, coated, or wooden utensils to avoid scratching a nonstick coating (and all caution against using any sharp utensil such as a knife, fork, or beater). Makers of only three of our pans, the Farberware, Innova, and Bialetti, actually sanction the use of metal utensils.

In their new, off-the-shelf condition, all of our pans turned in a reasonable-to-good performance cooking the foods best suited to nonstick cooking: eggs and fish. In fact, every pan but the Revere produced evenly cooked omelets and released them with ease. The omelet made in the Farberware pan was especially impressive. The Farberware also did a particularly nice job searing salmon fillets to an even, crusty, medium brown. (Salmon is much higher in fat than skinless chicken cutlets and therefore browns more easily, even in a nonstick pan.) Overall, however, our tests indicated that any of these pans could easily handle such light-duty tasks as cooking eggs. Low cost does not mean a big trade-off here.

Sauté speed is also an important measure of a pan's performance. We tested this by sautéing 1½ cups of hand-chopped onions over medium heat for 10 minutes in the hope of ending up with pale gold onions that bore no trace of burning. And you know what? For the most part, we did. The Wearever, T-Fal, Innova, and Revere pans, which were all on the light side in terms of weight, turned out the darkest onions, but they were still well within an acceptable color range. Onions sautéed in the Farberware, Meyer, Calphalon, and Bialetti were a shade lighter, indicating a slightly slower sauté speed. The Farberware onions, however, took top honors based on how evenly all the pieces colored.

Of course, construction quality is a concern with any piece of cookware, but especially with inexpensive models. Will the thing hold up, or will you have to replace it in six months? Based on our experience, you may well sacrifice a measure of construction quality with a budget pan. Pans with handles that were welded or riveted onto the pan body, including the Farberware, Innova, Meyer, and Calphalon, all felt solid and permanent. But the heat-resistant plastic (called phenolic) handles on the T-Fal, Revere, Bialetti, and Wearever pans were not riveted in place, and all three of them came loose during testing. That does not bode well for their future.

THE BEST INEXPENSIVE NONSTICK SKILLET

The Farberware Millennium 18/10 Stainless Steel 12-Inch Nonstick Skillet costs around $30 and delivered superior results in our tests. It was heavier than the other inexpensive pans we tested and had the most solid construction, which contributed greatly to its success.

Gingery Stir-Fried Chicken and Bok Choy

SERVES 4 AS A MAIN DISH WITH RICE

¼	cup low-sodium chicken broth
2	tablespoons dry sherry
1	tablespoon soy sauce
1	tablespoon oyster sauce
½	teaspoon toasted sesame oil
1	teaspoon cornstarch
1	teaspoon sugar
¼	teaspoon red pepper flakes
4	teaspoons minced fresh ginger
1	medium garlic clove, minced or pressed through a garlic press
	Peanut or vegetable oil
1	recipe Marinated Velveted Chicken for Stir-Fry
1	small head bok choy (about 1 pound), washed and dried, stalks and greens separated, stalks cut on the bias into ¼-inch slices and greens cut into ½-inch strips
1	small red bell pepper, cored, seeded, and cut into ¼-inch strips

1. Whisk the chicken broth, sherry, soy sauce, oyster sauce, sesame oil, cornstarch, sugar, red pepper flakes, and 2 teaspoons of the minced ginger in a small bowl. Combine the remaining 2 teaspoons ginger, the garlic, and 1 teaspoon peanut oil in another small bowl.

2. Heat 2 teaspoons peanut oil in a 12-inch nonstick skillet over high heat until smoking; add half of the chicken in a flat, even layer. Cook, without stirring but gently separating the pieces, until golden brown on the first side, about 1 minute; turn the chicken pieces and cook until lightly browned on the second side, about 30 seconds. Transfer the chicken to a clean bowl. Repeat with an additional 2 teaspoons peanut oil and the remaining chicken.

3. Add 1 tablespoon peanut oil to the now-empty skillet; heat until just smoking. Add the bok choy stalks and red bell pepper; stir-fry until they begin to brown, about 1 minute. Push the vegetables to the sides of the skillet to clear the center; add the garlic-ginger mixture to the clearing and cook, mashing the mixture with a spoon, until fragrant, 15 to 20 seconds, then stir the mixture into the stalks and continue to cook until the stalks are tender-crisp, about 30 seconds longer. Stir in the bok choy greens and cook until they begin to wilt, about 30 seconds. Return the chicken to the skillet. Whisk the sauce to recombine and add to the skillet. Reduce the heat to medium and cook, stirring constantly, until the sauce is thickened and the chicken is cooked through, about 30 seconds. Transfer to a serving platter and serve immediately.

INGREDIENTS: Peanut Oil

You may think all peanut oils are the same. Think again. Highly refined oils, such as Planters, are basically tasteless. They are indistinguishable from safflower, corn, or vegetable oil. In contrast, unrefined peanut oils (also labeled roasted or cold-pressed peanut oil) have a rich nut fragrance straight from the bottle. When heated, these oils smell like freshly roasted peanuts.

In the test kitchen, we find that unrefined, or roasted, peanut oil is a real plus in simple stir-fries. Like good olive oil, good peanut oil makes many dishes taste better. Three brands that we particularly like are Loriva, Hollywood, and Spectrum.

Spicy Stir-Fried Sesame Chicken with Green Beans and Shiitake Mushrooms

SERVES 4 AS A MAIN DISH WITH RICE

½	cup low-sodium chicken broth
3	tablespoons soy sauce
2	tablespoons dry sherry
1	tablespoon plus 1 teaspoon Asian chili sauce
1	tablespoon plus 1 teaspoon sugar
1	teaspoon cornstarch
1	tablespoon sesame seeds, toasted in a small dry skillet until golden, 7 to 10 minutes
2	teaspoons toasted sesame oil
3	medium garlic cloves, minced or pressed through a garlic press (1 tablespoon)
1	teaspoon minced fresh ginger
	Peanut or vegetable oil

- 1 recipe Marinated Velveted Chicken for Stir-Fry with 1 tablespoon sesame seeds added to the flour mixture
- 1 pound green beans, ends trimmed, and cut on the bias into 1-inch pieces
- 8 ounces shiitake mushrooms, stems discarded, caps sliced $1/8$ inch thick

1. Whisk the chicken broth, soy sauce, sherry, chili sauce, sugar, cornstarch, 2 teaspoons of the toasted sesame seeds, 1 teaspoon of the sesame oil, and 1 teaspoon of the garlic together in a small bowl until combined. Combine the remaining 2 teaspoons garlic, the ginger, and 1 teaspoon peanut oil in a small bowl.

2. Heat 2 teaspoons peanut oil in a 12-inch nonstick skillet over high heat until smoking; add half of the chicken in a flat, even layer. Cook, without stirring but gently separating the pieces, until golden brown on the first side, about 1 minute; turn the chicken pieces and cook until lightly browned on the second side, about 30 seconds. Transfer the chicken to a clean bowl. Repeat with an additional 2 teaspoons peanut oil and the remaining chicken.

3. Add 1 tablespoon peanut oil to the now-empty skillet; heat until just smoking. Add the green beans and cook, stirring occasionally, for 1 minute; add the mushrooms and stir-fry until the mushrooms are lightly browned and softened, about 3 minutes. Push the vegetables to the sides of the skillet to clear the center; add the garlic-ginger mixture to the clearing and cook, mashing the mixture with a spoon, until fragrant and golden brown, 30 to 45 seconds, then stir the mixture into the beans and mushrooms. Continue to stir-fry until the beans are tender-crisp, about 30 seconds longer. Return the chicken to the skillet. Whisk the sauce to recombine, then add to the skillet; reduce the heat to medium and cook, stirring constantly, until the sauce is thickened and the chicken is cooked through, about 30 seconds. Transfer to a serving platter, drizzle with the remaining 1 teaspoon sesame oil, and sprinkle with the remaining 1 teaspoon sesame seeds.

ROAST TURKEY

IS IT POSSIBLE TO ROAST A TURKEY PERFECTLY? Usually, juicy breast meat comes at a price—shocking pink legs and thighs. You have some leeway with the dark meat, which is almost impossible to dry out during normal roasting times. The problem is that the breast, which is exposed to direct heat and finishes cooking at a lower temperature, becomes parched, while the legs and thighs take their time creeping to doneness. Nearly every roasting method in existence tries to compensate for this; few succeed.

We tested dozens of different methods for roasting a turkey, from traditional to idiosyncratic. Our goals were to end up with an attractive bird, to determine the ideal internal temperature, and to find a method that would finish both white and dark meat simultaneously.

Our first roasting experiments used the method most frequently promoted by the National Turkey Federation, the U.S. Department of Agriculture (USDA), and legions of cookbook authors and recipe writers. This method features a moderately low roasting temperature of 325 degrees, a breast-up bird, and an open pan. We tried this method twice, basting one turkey and leaving the other alone. The basted turkey acquired a beautifully tanned skin, while the unbasted bird remained quite pale. Both were cooked to 170 degrees in the leg/thigh. Despite the fact that this was 10 degrees lower than recommended by the USDA and most producers, the breasts still registered a throat-catchingly dry 180 degrees.

We quickly determined that almost all turkeys roasted in the traditional breast-up manner produced breast meat that was 10 degrees ahead of the leg/thigh meat (tenting the breast with heavy-duty foil was the exception; read on). Because white meat is ideal at 160 degrees and dark thigh meat just loses its last shades of pink at about 170 degrees, you might conclude, as we did, that roasting turkeys with their breasts up is a losing proposition.

We also discovered that stuffing a bird makes overcooked meat more likely. Because it slows interior cooking (our tests showed a difference of nearly 30 degrees in internal temperature after an hour in the oven), stuffing means longer oven times, which can translate to bone-dry surface meat. We eventually did develop a method for roasting a stuffed turkey (see page 365), but if the turkey is your priority, we recommend cooking the dressing separately.

Of all the breast-up methods, tenting the bird's breast and upper legs with foil, as suggested by numerous authors, worked the best. The foil deflects some of the oven's heat, reducing the ultimate temperature differential between white and dark meat from 10 to 6 degrees. The bird is roasted at a consistent 325-degree temperature, and during the last 45 minutes of roasting the foil is removed, allowing enough time for lovely browning. If you're partial to open-pan roasting and don't care to follow the technique we developed, try the foil shield; it ran second in our tests.

Amid all these failures and near-successes, some real winners did emerge. Early on, we became fans of brining turkey in a saltwater bath before roasting. When we first removed the brined turkey from the refrigerator, we found a beautiful, milky-white bird. When roasted, the texture of the breast was different from that of the other birds we had cooked; the meat was firm and juicy at the same time. And the turkey tasted fully seasoned; others had required a bite of skin with the meat to achieve the same effect. We experimented with the brining time and found that 4 hours in the refrigerator produces a nicely seasoned turkey without overly salty pan juices. Brining was our first real breakthrough; we now believe it to be essential to achieving perfect taste and texture. But we had yet to discover the way to roast.

Our most successful attempt at achieving equal temperatures in leg and breast came when we borrowed James Beard's technique of turning the turkey as it roasts. In this method, the bird begins breast-side down on a V-rack, then spends equal time on each of its sides before being turned breast-side up. The V-rack is important not just to hold the turkey in place but also to elevate it, affording it some protection from the heat of the roasting pan. This combination of rack and technique produced a turkey with a breast temperature that ran only a few degrees behind the leg temperature.

Because we were using smaller turkeys than Beard had used, we had to fine-tune his method. Large turkeys spend enough time in the oven to brown at 350 degrees; our turkeys were in the 12-pound range and were cooking in as little as two hours, yielding quite pale skin. Clearly, we needed higher heat.

Reviewing our notes, we noticed that the basted birds were usually the evenly browned, beautiful ones. So we turned up the heat to 400 degrees, basted faithfully, and got what we wanted. In an effort to streamline, we tried to skip the leg-up turns, roasting only breast-side down, then breast-side up. But in order for the turkey to brown all over, these two extra turns were necessary. Brining, turning, and basting are work, yes, but the combination produces the best turkey we've ever had.

During our first few tests, we discovered that filling the cavity with aromatic herbs and vegetables made for a subtle but perceptible difference in flavor. This was especially noticeable in the inner meat of the leg and thigh; turkeys with hollow cavities, by contrast, tasted bland. Roasted alongside the turkey, the same combination of carrot, celery, onion, and thyme also did wonders for the pan juices.

Classic Roast Turkey

SERVES 10 TO 12

We prefer to roast small turkeys, no more than 14 pounds gross weight, because they cook more evenly than large birds. If you must cook a large bird, see the recipe on page 374. This recipe uses table salt (not kosher) in its brine. If you'd like to use kosher salt, whose large flakes measure differently from fine-grained table salt, see page 312 for conversion information.

2   cups table salt
1   turkey (12 to 14 pounds gross weight; see the box on page 366 for guidelines on selecting a turkey), rinsed thoroughly; giblets, neck, and tailpiece removed and reserved to make gravy (see page 364)
3   medium onions, chopped coarse
1½   medium carrots, chopped coarse

1½   celery ribs, chopped coarse

6   sprigs fresh thyme

3   tablespoons unsalted butter, melted

1. Dissolve the salt in 2 gallons cold water in a large stockpot or clean bucket. Add the turkey and refrigerate or set in a very cool spot (40 degrees or colder) for 4 hours.

2. Remove the turkey from the brine, rinse well under cool running water, and pat dry inside and out with paper towels. Place the turkey on a meat rack (or sturdy flat rack) set over a rimmed baking sheet. Place the turkey, uncovered, in the refrigerator and air-dry for at least 8 hours or overnight.

3. Adjust an oven rack to the lowest position and heat the oven to 400 degrees. Toss one third of the onions, carrots, celery, and thyme with 1 tablespoon of the melted butter and place this mixture in the body cavity. Bring the turkey legs together and perform a simple truss (see the illustrations on page 362).

4. Scatter the remaining vegetables and thyme over a shallow roasting pan. Pour 1 cup water over the vegetables. Set a V-rack in the pan. Brush the entire breast side of the turkey with half of the remaining butter, then place the turkey, breast-side down, on the V-rack. Brush the entire back-side of the turkey with the remaining butter.

5. Roast for 45 minutes. Remove the pan from the oven (close the oven door); baste with the juices from the pan. With a wad of paper towels in each hand, turn the turkey, leg/thigh-side up. If the liquid in the pan has totally evaporated, add another ½ cup water. Return the turkey to the oven and roast for 15 minutes. Remove the turkey from the oven again, baste, and again use paper towels to turn the other leg/thigh-side up; roast for another 15 minutes. Remove the turkey from the oven one last time, baste, and turn it breast-side up; roast until the breast registers about 165 degrees and the thigh registers 170 to 175 degrees on an instant-read thermometer, 30 to 45 minutes (see the illustrations on page 362). Remove the turkey from the pan to a carving board and let it rest until ready to carve (see page 363), at least 20 minutes. Serve with gravy (recipe follows).

GRAVY

TO A TRADITIONALIST, THE THOUGHT OF A gravyless Thanksgiving dinner is culinary heresy. Good gravy is no mere condiment; it's the tie that binds. But too often gravy is a last-minute affair, thrown together without much advance preparation or thought. Many of us have experienced the result: either dull, greasy gravy or thin, acidic pan juices that are one-dimensional, lacking the body and stature that we expect from a good American gravy.

So we set out to produce a rich, complex sauce with as much advance preparation as possible to avoid that last-minute time pressure, when space is at a premium and potatoes need to be mashed, turkey sliced, water goblets filled, and candles lit.

We began our tests by experimenting with thickeners. In a blind taste test we tried four different options, including cornstarch, beurre manié (a paste made from equal parts by weight of flour and butter), and two flour-based roux—one regular (a mixture of melted butter and flour stirred together over heat) and one dark (in which the butter-flour paste is cooked until it is dark brown).

Although most tasters were pretty sure before the tasting began that the cornstarch-thickened gravy would have inferior texture and flavor, it actually turned out to be quite good. Admittedly, it was a bit thinner in body and more acidic in flavor than the roux-based sauces, but it was acceptable. Overall, though, the dark roux proved to be the best thickener. It added a subtle depth and complexity to the gravy not found with the other options. A roux-based gravy can also be made ahead of time, a slight advantage over the cornstarch and beurre manié options, which require last-minute whisking.

To this dark roux, we added turkey stock made from the neck and giblets. Cooking the sauce over low heat for half an hour or more helped develop the flavor, but the resulting gravy was still pale and lacked punch. We then used a bulb baster to remove fat from the roasting turkey and used this as the base for the roux, instead of the butter. This tasted fine but was not an improvement over the butter version. We soon discovered, however, that the trick was to take this prethickened basic brown sauce and enrich it with pan drippings.

Roast Turkey 101

Most of us roast a turkey only once a year—on Thanksgiving, of course—so why not do things right? From stuffing a turkey (or not) to testing the meat for doneness and carving, follow these illustrated steps for preparing a successful holiday roast.

PREPARING AN UNSTUFFED TURKEY FOR ROASTING

1. Using the center of a 5-foot length of kitchen twine, tie the legs together at the ankles.

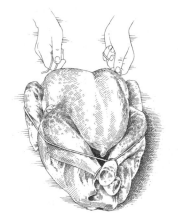

2. Run the kitchen twine around the thighs and under the wings on both sides of the bird and pull it tight.

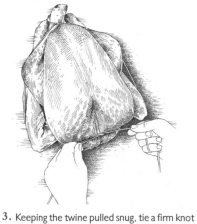

3. Keeping the twine pulled snug, tie a firm knot around the excess flesh at the neck of the bird. Snip off the excess twine.

STUFFING A TURKEY

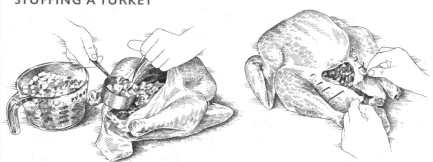

1. Use a measuring cup to place the preheated stuffing in the cavity of the bird. Remember, it's imperative that the stuffing be heated before it is placed in the bird.

2. To keep the stuffing in the cavity, use metal skewers (or cut bamboo skewers) and thread them through the skin on both sides of the cavity.

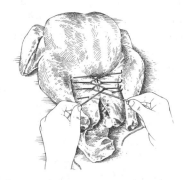

3. Center a 2-foot piece of kitchen twine on the top skewer and then cross the twine as you wrap each end of the twine around and under the skewers. With another short piece of twine, tie the legs loosely together.

4. Flip the bird over onto its breast. Stuff the neck cavity loosely with approximately 1 cup stuffing. Pull the skin flap over and use a skewer to pin the flap to the turkey.

TESTING A TURKEY FOR DONENESS

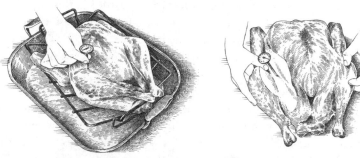

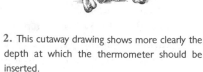

1. When using an instant-read thermometer, measure the temperature of the thickest part of the thigh away from any bone.

2. This cutaway drawing shows more clearly the depth at which the thermometer should be inserted.

CARVING A TURKEY

1. Remove any twine used to truss the bird. Start by slicing the skin between the meat of the breast and the leg.

2. Continue to cut down to the joint, using a fork to pull the leg away from the bird while the tip of the knife severs the joint between the leg and breast.

3. Place the leg/thigh piece skin-side down on a cutting board. Use the blade to locate the joint between the thigh and leg. It's right where the thigh and leg form their sharpest angle. Cut through the joint. If you have properly located it, this should be easy since you are not cutting through bone.

  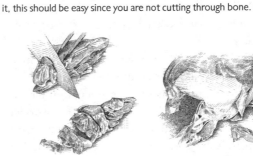 

4. Slice medallions from the leg, turning it so you can cut off all of the meat.

5. Remove the large pieces of meat from either side of the thighbone.

6. Slice these large thigh pieces, leaving a bit of skin attached to each slice.

7. Use a fork to pull the wing away from the body. Cut through the joint between the wing and the breast to separate the wing from the bird.

8. Cut the wing in half for easier eating.

9. With the tip of your knife, cut along the length of the breastbone.

10. Angle the blade of the knife, and slice along the line of the rib cage to remove the entire breast half. Use a fork to pull the breast half away from the cage in a single piece.

11. Cut thin slices from the breast, slicing across the grain of the meat.

WHAT'S A SAFE INTERNAL TEMPERATURE?

Industry standards developed by the U.S. Department of Agriculture and the National Turkey Federation call for whole birds to be cooked to an internal thigh temperature of 180 to 185 degrees. The breast temperature, according to these standards, should be 170 degrees. However, our kitchen tests showed that no meat is at its best at a temperature of 180 to 185 degrees. And breast meat really tastes best closer to 160 to 165 degrees.

While the USDA might have us believe that the only safe turkey is a dry turkey, this just isn't true. The two main bacterial problems in turkey are salmonella and *Campylobacter jejuni*. According to USDA standards, salmonella in meat is killed at 160 degrees, as is campylobacter. Turkey is no different. So why the higher safety standard of 180 degrees?

Part of the problem is that stuffing must reach an internal temperature of 165 degrees to be considered safe. (Carbohydrates such as bread provide a better medium for bacterial growth than do proteins such as meat; hence the extra safety margin of 5 degrees.) The USDA also worries that most cooks don't own an accurate thermometer.

The final word on poultry safety is this: As long as the temperature on an accurate instant-read thermometer reaches 160 degrees when inserted in several places, all unstuffed meat (including turkey) should be bacteria-free. Dark meat is undercooked at this stage and tastes better at 170 to 175 degrees. With our turning method, the breast will reach about 165 degrees when the leg is done.

A temperature of 165 degrees also guarantees that stuffed turkeys are safe. Bacteria in meat cooked to 180 to 185 degrees is certainly long gone—but so are moistness and flavor.

Pan drippings are the source of gravy's allure and also its difficulties. That gorgeous mahogany-colored goo that congeals at the bottom of a roasting pan is one of the best-tasting things on earth, a carnivore's ambrosia. But we found that to get dark brown pan drippings with a complex range of flavors, you need to roast your turkey over aromatic vegetables—chopped onions, carrots, and celery—as well as some fresh thyme sprigs. We also found it necessary to keep an eye on the pan, adding water whenever things started looking too dry.

After deglazing the pan with wine and simmering off the alcohol, we strained the resulting wine sauce into the roux, smashing the remaining herbs and vegetables into the strainer with a wooden spoon to wring the taste out of them. The result was worth the effort. After a quick simmer and an adjustment of the seasonings, we had an intense and richly flavored sauce that had the familiarity and comfort of traditional American gravy but hinted at the sophistication of a fine French brown sauce.

Giblet Pan Gravy

MAKES ABOUT 6 CUPS

The gravy is best made over several hours. Complete step 1 while the turkey is brining. Continue with step 2 once the bird is in the oven. Start step 3 once the bird has been removed from the oven and is resting on a carving board.

I	tablespoon vegetable oil
	Reserved turkey giblets (heart and gizzard), neck, and tailpiece
I	onion, unpeeled and chopped
I¹/₂	quarts homemade turkey or chicken stock or I quart low-sodium chicken broth plus 2 cups water
2	sprigs fresh thyme
8	stems fresh parsley
3	tablespoons unsalted butter
¹/₄	cup all-purpose flour
I	cup dry white wine
	Salt and ground black pepper

1. Heat the oil in a stockpot; add the giblets, neck, and tail; and sauté until golden and fragrant, about 5 minutes. Add the onion and continue to sauté until softened, 3 to 4 minutes longer. Reduce the heat to low, cover, and cook until the turkey and onion release their juices, about 20 minutes. Add the stock and herbs, bring to a boil, and adjust the heat to low. Simmer, uncovered, skimming any scum that may rise to the surface, until the broth is rich and flavorful, about 30 minutes longer. Strain the broth into a large container (you should have about 5 cups) and reserve the neck, heart, and gizzard. When cool enough to handle, shred the neck meat, remove the gristle from the gizzard, and dice the reserved heart and gizzard. Refrigerate the giblets and broth until ready to use.

2. While the turkey is roasting, return the reserved turkey broth to a simmer. Heat the butter in a large, heavy-bottomed saucepan over medium-low heat. Vigorously whisk in the flour (the roux will froth and then thin out again). Cook slowly, stirring constantly, until nutty brown and fragrant, 10 to 15 minutes. Vigorously whisk all but 1 cup of the hot broth into the roux. Bring to a boil, then continue to simmer, stirring occasionally, until the gravy is lightly thickened and very flavorful, about 30 minutes longer. Set aside until the turkey is done.

3. When the turkey has been transferred to a carving board to rest, spoon out and discard as much fat as possible from the roasting pan, leaving the caramelized herbs and vegetables. Place the roasting pan over two burners set on medium-high heat (if the drippings are not a dark brown, cook, stirring constantly, until they caramelize). Return the gravy to a simmer. Add the wine to the roasting pan of caramelized vegetables, scraping up any browned bits with a wooden spoon and boiling until reduced by half, about 5 minutes. Add the remaining 1 cup turkey broth, then strain the pan juices into the gravy, pressing as much juice as possible out of the vegetables. Stir the reserved giblets into the gravy and return to a boil. Adjust the seasonings, adding salt and pepper to taste if necessary. Serve with the carved turkey.

Roast Turkey with Stuffing

THERE IS SOMETHING UNDENIABLY FESTIVE about a stuffed roast turkey, and for many people the holidays just aren't the holidays without one. Every year, though, we are warned that for health and safety reasons, turkeys are best roasted unstuffed. Despite these warnings, many cooks continue to stuff their holiday birds. For the sake of flavorful, moist, turkey-infused stuffing, these cooks sacrifice perfectly cooked breast meat and risk food-borne illness from underdone stuffing.

There must be a way, we thought, to safely and successfully roast a stuffed turkey, keeping the breast meat succulent and ensuring that the stuffing is fully cooked. Before we began, we decided to limit our turkey to a maximum of 15 pounds, because it is just too difficult to safely stuff and roast larger birds.

Our objectives were clear. For health reasons, we wanted to find a means of minimizing the amount of time our stuffing would spend in the danger zone of 40 to 140 degrees, in which bacteria grows most quickly. In addition, we sought to coordinate the cooking of the breast and the thigh. We knew that the breast meat cooks faster than the thigh by about 10 degrees, and because the breast is done at 165 degrees and the thigh at 170 to 175 degrees, this usually results in choke-quality white meat. Introducing stuffing into this equation, we thought, was just asking for trouble; testing had demonstrated that stuffing the turkey slows interior cooking significantly, requiring longer cooking times and producing even drier surface meat.

After a few introductory tests, it became clear that this was exactly the problem we would face. Using high heat or low, the stuffing lagged behind the meat, remaining 5 degrees shy of the 165 we were aiming for, even when both breast and thigh were about 15 degrees higher than we wanted them.

In desperation, we toyed with the idea of sticking hot skewers or a ball of foil into the stuffing in the cavity to help conduct some heat. Suddenly, it occurred to us that if we heated the stuffing for a few minutes in the microwave before filling the cavity, we might give it a head start on cooking.

We tested the prewarmed stuffing hypothesis on a turkey that we roasted at a constant 325 degrees. We heated the stuffing in the microwave to about 120 degrees before stuffing the bird. We opted to roast the bird one hour breast-side down, one hour on each side, then finish with the breast up. As we monitored the temperature of the stuffing, the outlook seemed grim. The stuffing temperature dropped and bottomed out in the first hour at 89 degrees. Gradually, it climbed back up and hit 140 degrees, also free of the danger zone, in 2¼ hours, the best time yet. Most impressively, this time we were waiting for the thigh to finish cooking, not the stuffing! The breast was long gone at 178 degrees, but we knew we were onto something. This was an enormous improvement over the 3½ hours it had taken for the cold stuffing used in previous tests to dawdle its way to 165, while the breast and thigh meat overcooked.

We pursued the prewarming technique and found that the stuffing usually hits its lowest temperature in the bird at the one-hour mark, dropping approximately 20 degrees. In the microwave we were able to heat it to 130 degrees; starting at such a high temperature helps it get out of the danger zone in 2¼ to 2¾ hours. We checked with food scientists to see if this half-hour differential in times presented a bacterial growth problem. We were told no, since very little occurs above 110 degrees. No longer did we have to wait for the stuffing to finish cooking while the breast and thigh overcooked.

With the stuffing issue resolved, we focused on the best way to roast the turkey. It had become clear to us that high heat and even constant moderate heat wreak havoc on the turkey, resulting in parched breast meat. The low-and-slow method is, well, too low and slow—not a safe method for a stuffed turkey. A combination of low heat with high or moderate heat seemed to be the answer.

We also determined that no matter what the cooking temperature, roasting the bird breast-side down for only one hour was not sufficient.

In this position, the breast is shielded and its cooking slowed while the thighs are exposed to the heat needed to speed their cooking. If we rotated the breast up after one or even two hours, the breast was guaranteed to overcook in the remaining time. We abandoned roasting

with each leg-side up to afford the breast more "down time."

We then roasted two turkeys, both started breast-side down. One cooked at a low 250 degrees for three hours, was rotated breast up, cooked for an additional 15 minutes, and then

---

INGREDIENTS: Turkey

Many people purchase a turkey just once during the year. Thanksgiving, of course, would be that occasion. When the moment of purchase arrives, however, the buyer may be somewhat befuddled. The options are many—this brand or that brand, fresh or frozen, flavor-enhanced or not. Then there is the growing number of product disclaimers to plow through—no antibiotics, no animal byproducts, minimal processing, and on and on it goes.

Everyone has priorities and standards when it comes to purchasing turkey. But what it all reduces to for most every cook is whether friends or relatives drive away after the big meal murmuring "That was the best turkey I've ever had" or "Thank goodness there was plenty of gravy and cranberry sauce."

To try to ensure the former response, we decided to do a blind tasting of turkey. We corralled as many turkeys as we have ovens and cooked them all up. We roasted them using exactly the same method (starting breast-side down in a 400-degree oven, then rotating to one side, then the other side, and finally back to breast-side up to finish) and determined doneness at exactly the same internal temperature (175 degrees measured at the thigh). We then held a blind tasting, rating each of the nine birds for flavor, texture, and overall likability.

Because turkey is, for the most part, a regionally distributed product, few national brands are available. Consequently, our lineup consisted primarily of brands found on the East Coast. We selected them carefully, however, in order to represent the range of the types of turkeys found in stores nationwide. This included birds that were fresh and frozen, flavor-enhanced (or "basted," to use the industry term) and minimally processed.

We have found that the best way to cook a turkey is to brine it first—that is, to immerse the turkey overnight in a strong solution of water and salt. Recognizing that not everyone brines their turkeys, though, we did not brine any of the turkeys for the tasting. But a few of the turkeys in the tasting came prepared in a manner that is similar to brining. These had either been injected with a salt solution or, in the case of the kosher bird, rubbed with salt, left to rest so that the salt penetrates, and then rinsed during processing.

All the turkeys in the tasting that were basted or rubbed with salt as part of the manufacturer's processing method were remarkably moist and tender and placed high in our ratings. The reason? As the basting solution penetrates the turkey, the salt unravels the coiled proteins in the uncooked muscle, trapping water between the protein strands. As the meat cooks, the proteins set and form a barrier that prevents moisture from leaking out. The salt also helps to enhance the natural flavors of the turkey.

Commercially basted turkeys can also "fool" you into thinking a turkey is juicier than it is. This is because the basting solutions often contain some kind of fat—usually butter or oil. "In small amounts, fat makes the salivary glands produce saliva, which tricks you into thinking there's more juiciness in the meat," says Dr. Sarah G. Birkhold, assistant professor of poultry science at Texas A&M University.

While the success of the basted and kosher turkeys was not unexpected, what did surprise us was that tasters found no discernible difference between frozen and fresh birds. That came as no surprise to Birkhold, however. She explained that improved technology permits manufacturers to "flash-freeze" birds in freezers where temperatures range around 30 degrees below zero and cold air is blasted at about 60 miles per hour. This prevents the development of large ice crystals that can damage the tissue, causing moisture loss. Home freezers, of course, cannot replicate this process. So if you are buying a turkey in advance of Thanksgiving, you are much better off buying a frozen one than buying and freezing a fresh one.

While prebasted birds might conveniently deliver juicy, tender meat, we still advocate brining a turkey on your own whenever possible. As our results show, a standard U.S. Department of Agriculture (USDA) grade A turkey is a good choice; it can only get better with brining. Note, however, that when brining at home, you should avoid kosher or "basted" birds, which have already been treated with salt. A final advantage to brining your turkey at home is that you can avoid the additives often contained in basted birds.

the temperature was increased to 400 degrees. The breast overcooked as the thigh crept up to 175 degrees. The other turkey we roasted at 400 degrees for one hour, reduced the oven temperature to 250 degrees, flipped it breast-side up after a total of three hours, and then turned the heat back up to 400 degrees and roasted until done. This bird finished as close to perfection as possible: 163 degrees in the breast, 175 degrees in the thigh, and 165 degrees in the stuffing. Clearly, the thigh meat benefited from the initial blast of heat. The only disappointment was the spotty browning of the skin. A few minor adjustments to the time spent breast-side up, and we arrived at a safe, perfectly roasted stuffed turkey.

Roast Stuffed Turkey

SERVES 10 TO 12

A 12- to 15-pound turkey will accommodate approximately half of the stuffing. Bake the remainder in a casserole while the bird rests before carving. This recipe uses table salt (not kosher) in its brine. If you'd like to use kosher salt, whose large flakes measure differently from fine-grained table salt, see page 312 for conversion information.

2	cups table salt
1	turkey (12 to 15 pounds gross weight; see the box on page 366 for guidelines on selecting a turkey), rinsed thoroughly; giblets, neck, and tailpiece removed and reserved to make gravy (see page 364)
2	medium onions, chopped coarse
1	medium carrot, chopped coarse
1	celery rib, chopped coarse
4	sprigs fresh thyme
12	cups prepared stuffing (pages 368–372)
3	tablespoons unsalted butter, plus more for the casserole and foil
¼	cup homemade turkey or chicken stock or low-sodium chicken broth

1. Dissolve the salt in 2 gallons cold water in a very large stockpot, Dutch oven, or clean bucket. Add the turkey and refrigerate or set in a very cool spot (40 degrees or colder) for 4 hours.

2. Remove the turkey from the brine, rinse well under cool running water, and pat dry inside and out with paper towels; set aside. Place the turkey on a meat rack (or sturdy flat rack) set over a rimmed baking sheet. Place the turkey, uncovered, in the refrigerator and air-dry for at least 8 hours or overnight.

3. Adjust an oven rack to the lowest position and heat the oven to 400 degrees. Scatter the onions, carrot, celery, and thyme over a shallow roasting pan. Pour 1 cup water over the vegetables. Set a V-rack in the pan.

4. Place half of the stuffing in a buttered medium casserole dish, dot the surface with 1 tablespoon of the butter, cover with buttered foil, and refrigerate until ready to use. Microwave the remaining stuffing on full power, stirring 2 or 3 times, until very hot (120 to 130 degrees), 6 to 8 minutes (if you can handle the stuffing with your hands, it is not hot enough). Referring to the illustrations in "Stuffing a Turkey" on page 362, spoon 4 to 5 cups of stuffing into the turkey cavity until very loosely packed. Secure the skin flap over the cavity opening with turkey lacers or skewers. Melt the remaining 2 tablespoons butter. Tuck the wings behind the back, brush the entire breast side with half of the melted butter, and place the turkey breast-side down. Fill the neck cavity with the remaining heated stuffing and secure the skin flap over the opening. Place on the V-rack and brush the back with the remaining melted butter.

5. Roast 1 hour, then reduce the temperature to 250 degrees and roast 2 hours longer, adding more water if the pan becomes dry. Remove the pan from the oven (close the oven door) and, with a wad of paper towels in each hand, turn the bird breast-side up and baste (the temperature of the breast should be 145 to 150 degrees). Increase the oven temperature to 400 degrees; continue roasting until the breast registers about 165 degrees, the thigh registers 170 to 175 degrees, and the stuffing registers 165 degrees on an instant-read thermometer, 1 to 1½ hours longer. Remove the turkey from the pan to a carving board and let it rest while you finish the stuffing.

6. Add the stock to the dish of reserved stuffing, replace the foil, and bake at 400 degrees until hot throughout, 20 to 25 minutes. Remove the foil; continue to bake until a golden brown crust forms on the stuffing, about 15 minutes longer.

7. Carve the turkey (see page 363) and serve with stuffing and gravy.

BREAD STUFFINGS FOR TURKEY

IN OUR TESTS, WE FOUND THAT DRIED BREAD cubes are essential when making stuffing because they do a better job of absorbing seasonings and other flavors than fresh cubes. To dry bread, cut a fresh loaf of French or other white bread into half-inch slices, place the slices in a single layer on baking sheets or cooling racks, and allow the slices to sit out overnight. The next day, cut the slices into ½-inch cubes and allow them to dry in a single layer for an additional night.

If you're in a hurry, place the sliced bread in a 225-degree oven for 30 to 40 minutes, or until dried but not browned. Remove the bread from the oven and cut into ½-inch cubes. You will need a 1-pound loaf of bread to obtain the 12 cups of cubes necessary for the following stuffing recipes.

All of these stuffings can be covered and refrigerated for one day. Store the mixture in a 13 by 9-inch or comparable-size ovensafe or microwave-safe pan and reheat in a 325-degree oven or microwave until the stuffing is heated through before packing it into a bird. Place any stuffing that won't fit in the bird in a buttered 8-inch square baking dish. Drizzle ¼ cup stock (turkey or chicken) over the stuffing, dot with pats of butter, and cover with a piece of foil that has been smeared with butter. Bake in a 400-degree oven for 20 to 25 minutes, remove the foil, and continue to bake until a golden brown crust forms on top of the stuffing, about 15 minutes longer.

Bread Stuffing with Sausage, Pecans, and Dried Apricots
MAKES ABOUT 12 CUPS

High-quality sausage is the key to this recipe. Toast the pecans in a 350-degree oven until fragrant, 6 to 8 minutes.

1	pound sweet Italian sausage, removed from casings and crumbled
6	tablespoons (¾ stick) unsalted butter
1	large onion, chopped (about 1½ cups)
4	medium celery ribs, chopped (about 1½ cups)
½	teaspoon each dried sage, dried thyme, and dried marjoram
½	teaspoon ground black pepper
½	cup fresh parsley leaves, chopped fine
2	cups pecans, toasted and roughly chopped
1	cup dried apricots, cut into thin strips
1	teaspoon salt
12	cups dried French or other white bread cubes (see the instructions at left)
1	cup homemade turkey or chicken stock or low-sodium chicken broth
3	large eggs, lightly beaten

1. Cook the sausage in a large skillet over medium heat until browned, about 10 minutes. Transfer the sausage to a large bowl with a slotted spoon. Discard the fat; in the same pan, melt the butter.

2. Add the onion and celery and cook, stirring occasionally, over medium heat until soft and translucent, 6 to 7 minutes. Add the dried herbs and pepper and cook for another minute. Transfer to the bowl with the sausage; add the parsley, pecans, apricots, and salt and mix to combine. Add the bread cubes to the bowl.

3. Whisk the stock and eggs together in a small bowl. Pour the mixture over the bread cubes. Gently toss to distribute the ingredients evenly. Follow the instructions in the recipe Roast Stuffed Turkey on page 367 to stuff the bird and bake extra stuffing.

Bread Stuffing with Ham, Pine Nuts, Mushrooms, and Fennel
MAKES ABOUT 12 CUPS

Light brown cremini mushrooms have more flavor than regular white button mushrooms, but the latter can also be used in this recipe.

6	tablespoons (¾ stick) unsalted butter
1	large onion, chopped (about 1½ cups)
1	large fennel bulb, chopped (about 1½ cups)
10	ounces cremini mushrooms, wiped clean and sliced thin
1½	teaspoons dried basil
½	teaspoon ground black pepper
1	cup pine nuts, toasted
¼	pound thinly sliced prosciutto, cut into thin strips
¼	pound thinly sliced smoked ham, each slice cut in half and then cut crosswise into thin strips
1	ounce Parmesan cheese, freshly grated (½ cup)
½	cup fresh parsley leaves, chopped fine
½	teaspoon salt
12	cups dried French or other white bread cubes (see the instructions under Bread Stuffings for Turkey on page 368)
1	cup homemade turkey or chicken stock or low-sodium chicken broth
3	large eggs, lightly beaten

1. Melt the butter in a large skillet or Dutch oven. Add the onion and fennel and cook, stirring occasionally, over medium heat until soft and translucent, 6 to 7 minutes. Add the mushrooms and cook until the liquid they release has evaporated, about 10 minutes. Add the basil and pepper and cook for another minute. Transfer the contents of the pan to a large bowl.

2. Add the pine nuts, prosciutto, smoked ham, Parmesan, parsley, and salt to the bowl and mix to combine. Add the bread cubes.

3. Whisk the stock and eggs together in a small bowl. Pour the mixture over the bread cubes. Gently toss to distribute the ingredients evenly. Follow the instructions in the recipe Roast Stuffed Turkey on page 367 to stuff the bird and bake extra stuffing.

Bread Stuffing with Bacon, Apples, Sage, and Caramelized Onions
MAKES ABOUT 12 CUPS

For the best flavor, make sure to cook the onions until they are deep golden brown.

1	pound bacon, cut crosswise into ¼-inch strips
6	medium onions, sliced thin (about 7 cups)
	Salt
2	Granny Smith apples, peeled, cored, and cut into ½-inch cubes (about 2 cups)
½	teaspoon ground black pepper
½	cup fresh parsley leaves, chopped fine
3	tablespoons fresh sage leaves, cut into thin strips
12	cups dried French or other white bread cubes (see the instructions under Bread Stuffings for Turkey on page 368)
1	cup homemade turkey or chicken stock or low-sodium chicken broth
3	large eggs, lightly beaten

1. Cook the bacon in a large skillet or Dutch oven over medium heat until crisp and browned, about 12 minutes. Remove the bacon with a slotted spoon and drain on paper towels. Discard all but 3 tablespoons of the rendered fat.

2. Increase the heat to medium-high and add the onions and ¼ teaspoon salt. Cook the onions until golden in color, making sure to stir occasionally and scrape the sides and bottom of the pan, about 20 minutes. Reduce the heat to medium and continue to cook, stirring more often to prevent burning, until the onions are deep golden brown, another 5 minutes. Add the apples and cook 5 minutes. Transfer the contents to a large bowl.

3. Add ¾ teaspoon salt, the pepper, parsley, and sage to the bowl and mix to combine. Add the bread cubes.

4. Whisk the stock and eggs together in a small bowl. Pour the mixture over the bread cubes. Gently toss to distribute the ingredients evenly. Follow the instructions in the recipe Roast Stuffed Turkey on page 367 to stuff the bird and bake extra stuffing.

CORNBREAD STUFFING

CORNBREAD STUFFING IS A SOUTHERN CLASSIC. We set out to make a cornbread stuffing with a toasted top, moist interior, and satisfyingly rich flavor. After a few initial batches, we became aware of the principal problems with this dish. We found that most cornbread stuffings are much too dry. The cornbread turns into stale, loose nuggets that refuse to bind with any of the other ingredients. On the other end of the spectrum are stuffings that are too wet. They simply turn into a damp, sloppy mass. We wanted a moist and cohesive stuffing that wasn't soggy or greasy. While most recipes use stock, butter, and eggs to bind the stuffing ingredients together and add moisture, we wondered if there were other options. Finally, there was quantity. None of the stuffings we had tried made nearly enough to handle a Thanksgiving crowd of 8 to 10 hungry people and provide ample allowance for leftovers.

We decided it would be easiest to begin by finding out which type of cornbread is best suited for stuffing and then figure out how it should be prepared. Although there were differences of opinion, tasters generally preferred the rather fluffy, slightly sweet Northern-style cornbread.

Next we focused our attention on what to do with the cornbread once it was made. We made stuffings from cornbread that was whacked into small crumbs, cut into even-size cubes, and torn into bite-size pieces. The crumbs had a potent cornbread flavor, but the texture was mealy and unattractive. Although the cubed cornbread looked very tidy, it didn't carry the same flavorful punch as the crumbs. Tearing cornbread into bite-size pieces, however, created enough crumbs to release the cornbread flavor, while the bigger pieces were toothsome and made for the most attractive dish.

We now made stuffings using fresh, toasted, and stale cornbread. The fresh cornbread turned soggy and bland, while the flavor of the toasted bread was overpowering. The hands-down winner of the lot was the stuffing made with stale bread, with its potent but not bullish flavor and pleasingly moist texture. (Drying fresh cornbread in a warm oven accomplishes the same thing.) With the main ingredient in the bag, we turned next to the binders.

Turkey or chicken stock, eggs, and pan drippings are the classic ingredients used to help moisten and bind a stuffing. After ruling out turkey drippings, which we use to make gravy, we tested stuffings made with stock and eggs on their own to see exactly how each would fare. As expected, the eggs thoroughly bound the ingredients so that each forkful of stuffing was cohesive. The stock added the necessary moisture and distinct poultry flavor. Obviously, a mixture of these two ingredients was key, but we also wanted to add something to the stuffing that would make it a bit richer and softer without turning it greasy or wet. Recalling an old cornbread pudding recipe, we tried pouring a little half-and-half into the mix. This was the missing link, turning a second-rate side dish into a medal winner. The stuffing took on an extraordinarily full, rich flavor without being oily or sodden.

Soaking stale bread is a classic technique. You are replacing the bread's lost moisture with something more flavorful. Wondering if an adaptation of this idea would move our stuffing along, we soaked the stale cornbread in the egg, stock, and cream mixture overnight. We then baked it and compared it with stuffings baked after an hour-long soak, a 30-minute soak, and no soaking at all.

The differences in the stuffings were remarkable. The unsoaked stuffing tasted absolutely dull and lifeless when compared with the overnighter, and the 30-minute soaker was not nearly as good as the 60-minute one. While there was an obvious difference between the overnighter and the 60-minute version, it was far less than we had expected. Because overnight soaking can be inconvenient, we settled on one hour.

Now all we needed to do was round out the final flavors. Onions, celery, and fresh thyme and sage were shoo-ins. As we had expected, they all needed to be sautéed slightly before being mixed in with the cornbread. We tried adding a little wine or whiskey but found that their boozy flavor meddled with the rich flavor of the cornbread.

Finally, some bulk pork sausage added nice pockets of texture and a meaty punch without overpowering the balance of flavors. Here was a cornbread stuffing that would match that of any Southern grandmother. It almost seems a shame to hide it under a reservoir of gravy.

Cornbread and Sausage Stuffing

MAKES ABOUT 12 CUPS

In this recipe, the stuffing is not baked in the turkey, but in a baking dish. If you want to stuff your turkey with it, prepare the stuffing through step 2, then follow the directions on page 367 for microwaving the stuffing. To make the stuffing a day in advance, increase both the chicken stock and half-and-half by ¼ cup each and refrigerate the unbaked stuffing 12 to 24 hours; before transferring it to the baking dish, let the stuffing stand at room temperature for about 30 minutes so that it loses its chill.

12	cups Golden Cornbread for Stuffing (recipe follows) broken into 1-inch pieces (include crumbs)
3	cups homemade turkey or chicken stock or low-sodium chicken broth
2	cups half-and-half
2	large eggs, lightly beaten
8	tablespoons (1 stick) unsalted butter, plus more for the baking dish
1½	pounds bulk pork sausage, broken into 1-inch pieces
3	medium onions, chopped fine (about 3 cups)
3	celery ribs, chopped fine (about 1½ cups)
2	tablespoons minced fresh thyme leaves
2	tablespoons minced fresh sage leaves
3	small garlic cloves, minced or pressed through a garlic press
1½	teaspoons salt
2	teaspoons ground black pepper

1. Heat the oven to 250 degrees. Spread the cornbread pieces and crumbs in an even layer on 2 baking sheets and dry in the oven for 50 to 60 minutes; cool. Place the cornbread in a large bowl. Whisk the stock, half-and-half, and eggs together in a medium bowl; pour over the cornbread and toss very gently to coat so that the cornbread does not break into smaller pieces. Set aside.

2. Heat a heavy-bottomed 12-inch skillet over medium-high heat until hot, about 1½ minutes. Add 2 tablespoons of the butter and swirl to coat the pan bottom. When the foaming subsides, add the sausage and cook, stirring occasionally, until it loses its raw color, 5 to 7 minutes. With a slotted spoon, transfer the sausage to a medium bowl. Add about half of the onions and celery to the fat in the skillet; sauté, stirring occasionally, over medium-high heat until softened, about 5 minutes. Transfer the onion mixture to the bowl with the sausage. Return the skillet to the heat and add the remaining 6 tablespoons butter; when the foaming subsides, add the remaining celery and onions and sauté, stirring occasionally, until softened, about 5 minutes. Stir in the thyme, sage, and garlic; cook until fragrant, about 30 seconds; add the salt and pepper. Add this mixture along with the sausage mixture to the cornbread and stir gently to combine so that the cornbread does not break into smaller pieces. Cover the bowl with plastic wrap and refrigerate to blend the flavors, at least 1 hour or up to 4 hours.

3. Adjust an oven rack to the lower-middle position and heat the oven to 400 degrees. Butter a 15 by 10-inch baking dish (or two 9-inch square or 11 by 7-inch baking dishes). Transfer the stuffing to the baking dish; pour any liquid that has accumulated in the bottom of the bowl over the stuffing and, if necessary, gently press the stuffing with a rubber spatula to fit it into the baking dish. Bake until golden brown, 35 to 40 minutes.

➤ VARIATION

Golden Cornbread for Stuffing
MAKES ABOUT 12 CUPS CRUMBLED CORNBREAD

3	large eggs
1	cup buttermilk
1	cup milk
1½	cups yellow cornmeal, preferably stone-ground
1½	cups unbleached all-purpose flour
1	tablespoon baking powder

³/₄   teaspoon baking soda
4   teaspoons sugar
³/₄   teaspoon salt
3   tablespoons unsalted butter, melted

1. Adjust an oven rack to the middle position and heat the oven to 375 degrees. Grease a 13 by 9-inch baking dish.

2. Beat the eggs in a medium bowl; whisk in the buttermilk and milk.

3. Whisk the cornmeal, flour, baking powder, baking soda, sugar, and salt together in a large bowl. Push the dry ingredients up the sides of the bowl to make a well, then pour the egg and milk mixture into the well and stir with a whisk until just combined; stir in the melted butter.

4. Pour the batter into the greased baking dish. Bake until the top is golden brown and the edges have pulled away from the sides of the pan, 30 to 40 minutes.

5. Transfer the baking dish to a wire rack and cool to room temperature before using, about 1 hour.

ROAST TURKEY FOR A CROWD

MOST RECIPES RECOMMEND ROASTING 12- TO 14-pound turkeys, a size that is easy to handle and that delivers, according to many tasters, superior flavor. But what if you have more than 10 people coming to dinner? Roasting two turkeys is not an option for most home cooks. We set out to find a way to roast a massive bird, enough to feed the most crowded Thanksgiving table.

Our first step was to select the right brand at the market. Two years ago, the test kitchen conducted a turkey taste test and came up with an interesting—and totally unexpected—result. The frozen Butterball finished ahead of the fresh Butterball entry as well as more than one fresh premium brand. The reason? Frozen Butterball turkeys are injected with a salt solution—in other words, they are brined. Although the flavor of the meat was a bit on the bland side, many tasters commented that this bird "tastes just like Thanksgiving." We performed another taste test just to be sure and

found that the meat was, indeed, moist and tender. So now we had a turkey that had been brined for us, eliminating a step that would be all but impossible with a huge bird.

Other techniques had to be eliminated from the start, given the size of the bird. We chose not to air-dry (another favored *Cook's* technique that would be unworkable with a huge bird) or stuff the turkey (which would add to the already long cooking time). Finally, we wanted to keep this bird as traditional as possible, so we opted not to rub it with spices or massage it with flavored butter.

Our next task was to determine the proper cooking temperature. We roasted it, per the instructions included with the Butterball, at 350 degrees until the thigh registered 170 to 180 degrees, approximately 4½ hours. Although the breast meat was tender, the dark meat was surprisingly fatty and the skin a tad blond and springy. Next we cooked a turkey at 400 degrees. We began it breast-side down and, after an hour, flipped it breast-side up, hoping for a deeply browned showstopper. (This technique yields great results for smaller turkeys. As the fat renders out of the dark meat, it flows down into and bastes the breast.) Although it looked great, the breast meat turned out chalky and parched, as if it had spent the day at the beach.

Because high temperature had yielded a prettier bird and low temperature a more tender one, we decided to try a combination of both. After roasting a dozen or so birds, we finally hit on the right combination of temperatures for a large turkey: 425 degrees for the first hour (breast-side down) and 325 degrees thereafter (breast-side up). The breast meat was firm and juicy, the dark meat rich and tender, and the skin a breathtakingly rosy mahogany brown.

After we had cooked and turned 200 pounds of turkey, a test cook pointed out that her mother would never be able to rotate a turkey of this weight. We tried yet another turkey, with the same combination of high and low heat, but we kept the turkey breast-side up the entire time. It was slightly inferior to the turned bird but still good enough to eat, so those not up to the task can skip this step. (We also tried this same method breast-side down, and the skin turned out mottled and undercooked.)

Although we had opted not to stuff the bird, we wondered if a simple aromatic mix in the cavity might add flavor to the meat. We started with the classic onion, carrot, and celery combination, and, while this turkey was better, something was still missing. Lemon added freshness to the meat closest to the bone and gave the pan juices a cleaner taste. Sprigs of fresh thyme added the scent of Thanksgiving. More vegetables went into the roasting pan to flavor the drippings. We added a little water to ensure that the vegetables didn't dry out.

After roasting several birds, trussed and untrussed, we concluded that trussing added a fussiness we didn't want as well as an unwelcome 15 to 20 minutes in cooking time. (To cook the inner thigh fully, which is hidden by trussing, you inevitably overcook the white meat.) We also investigated the best way to treat the skin, leaving it as is versus brushing it with unsalted butter, olive oil, or vegetable oil. The difference was not appreciable, but the turkey with the butter tasted better and more, well, buttery. The next question was whether

CRANBERRY SAUCES

THE DISTINCTIVE, TART FLAVOR OF CRAN-berries has long made them a favorite accompaniment for game and fowl, particularly the holiday turkey. You can always follow the directions on the bag of cranberries and boil the fruit with some sugar and water. But why make the same old sauce, which is generally too sweet and one-dimensional in flavor?

The best cranberry sauce has a clean, pure cranberry flavor, with enough sweetness to temper the assertively tart fruit but not so much that the sauce is cloying or candylike. The texture should be that of a soft gel, neither too liquidy nor too stiff, cushioning some softened but still intact berries.

Before preparing any of these sauces, sort through the berries carefully. Leave in any berries that are white, but discard any that are bruised, bloated, or soft. Freeze berries right in the bag and use thawed berries in any of these recipes.

Basic Cranberry Sauce

MAKES 2 1/4 CUPS

If you've got frozen cranberries, do not defrost them before use; just pick through them and add about 2 minutes to the simmering time.

3/4	cup water
1	cup sugar
1/4	teaspoon salt
1	(12-ounce) bag cranberries, picked over

Bring the water, sugar, and salt to a boil in a medium nonreactive saucepan over high heat, stirring occasionally to dissolve the sugar. Stir in the cranberries; return to a boil. Reduce the heat to medium; simmer until saucy, slightly thickened, and about two thirds of the berries have popped open, about 5 minutes. Transfer to a nonreactive bowl, cool to room temperature, and serve. (The sauce can be covered and refrigerated for up to 7 days; let stand at room temperature 30 minutes before serving.)

➤ VARIATIONS

Cranberry-Orange Sauce
Orange juice adds little flavor, but we found that zest and liqueur pack the orange kick we were looking for in this sauce.

Follow the recipe for Basic Cranberry Sauce, heating 1 tablespoon grated orange zest with the sugar mixture. Off the heat, stir in 2 tablespoons orange liqueur, such as Triple Sec or Grand Marnier.

Cranberry Sauce with Pears and Fresh Ginger
Peel and core 2 medium, firm, ripe pears and cut into 1/2-inch chunks; set aside. Follow the recipe for Basic Cranberry Sauce, heating 1 tablespoon grated fresh ginger and 1/4 teaspoon ground cinnamon with the sugar mixture and stirring the pears into the liquid along with the cranberries.

regular basting is worth the effort. It turned out that basting actually makes the skin soggy, so we simply brushed the turkey with melted butter once prior to cooking.

Tenting the turkey either during or after roasting was also abandoned: The foil traps the steam and softens the skin. Instead, letting the roasted bird sit at room temperature, uncovered, for 35 to 40 minutes allows the juices, which rise to the surface during cooking, to flow back into the meat. This was more successful than the usually recommended 20 minutes, probably because of the size of the bird.

For those who don't want to buy a Butterball, we wondered if this method would work on another brand of turkey. We tested an organic turkey, which wasn't injected, and a kosher turkey, which is essentially brined by the koshering process. All the testers preferred the Butterball for its juicier meat. The kosher bird came in second, and the organic turkey took last place because the meat was dry. If you prefer to avoid a frozen, injected bird, try a kosher brand.

TECHNIQUE: Defrosting a Frozen Turkey

We had excellent results when roasting a frozen Butterball turkey, but without allowing sufficient time for defrosting, this iceberg of a bird can sink your Thanksgiving dinner faster than you can say "Titanic." It's best to defrost the turkey in the refrigerator, figuring 1 day of defrosting for every 4 pounds of turkey. That means a frozen 20-pound turkey should go into the refrigerator on Saturday morning if it's to be ready by Thursday, Thanksgiving Day.

There is a faster (and more tedious) means of defrosting the turkey if you find yourself on Wednesday morning with a frozen bird. Place the turkey, still in its original wrapper, in a bucket of cold water for about 10 hours (or 30 minutes per pound) and change the water every half hour. Yes, every 30 minutes you will be handling this gargantuan bird, a step necessary to guard against bacterial growth. Since baby-sitting a turkey is not our idea of fun, if faced with a frozen turkey that late in the game, we'd go out and buy a fresh bird.

Roast Turkey for a Crowd
SERVES 20 TO 24

You can use any roasting pan to roast the turkey, even a disposable one, but make sure to use a V-rack to elevate it. Be careful to dry the skin thoroughly before brushing the bird with butter; otherwise, it will have spotty brown skin. Rotating the bird helps produce moist, evenly cooked meat, but for the sake of ease, you may opt not to rotate it. In that case, skip the step of lining the V-rack with foil and roast the bird breast-side up for the entire cooking time. Because we do not brine the bird, we had the best results with a frozen Butterball (injected with salt and water) and a kosher bird (soaked in salt water during processing).

2	medium onions, chopped coarse
2	medium carrots, chopped coarse
2	celery ribs, chopped coarse
1	lemon, quartered
2	sprigs fresh thyme
1	frozen Butterball or kosher turkey (18 to 22 pounds gross weight), rinsed thoroughly; giblets, neck, and tailpiece removed and reserved for gravy (recipe follows)
4	tablespoons (1/2 stick) unsalted butter, melted
2	teaspoons kosher salt or 1 teaspoon table salt
1	teaspoon ground black pepper

1. Adjust an oven rack to the lowest position; remove the remaining racks. Heat the oven to 425 degrees. Line a large V-rack with heavy-duty foil and poke holes in the foil; set the V-rack in a 15 by 12-inch roasting pan.

2. Toss the onions, carrots, celery, lemon, and thyme in a medium bowl; set aside. Brush the turkey breast with 2 tablespoons of the melted butter, then sprinkle with half of the salt and half of the pepper. Set the turkey breast-side down on the V-rack. Brush with the remaining 2 tablespoons butter and sprinkle with the remaining salt and pepper. Fill the cavity with half the onion mixture; scatter the rest in the roasting pan and pour 1 cup water into the pan.

3. Roast the turkey 1 hour; remove the roasting pan with the turkey from the oven. Lower the oven temperature to 325 degrees. Using a clean dish towel or 2 potholders, turn the turkey breast-side up; return the roasting pan with the turkey to the oven and continue to roast until the legs move freely and an instant-read thermometer inserted into the thickest part of the thigh registers 170 to 180 degrees, about 2 hours longer. Remove the turkey from the pan to a carving board and let rest until ready to carve (see page 363), 35 to 40 minutes. Serve with gravy (recipe follows).

Giblet Pan Gravy for a Crowd

MAKES ABOUT 2 QUARTS

The gravy is best made over several hours. Complete step 1 while the turkey is brining. Continue with step 2 once the bird is in the oven. Start step 3 once the bird has been removed from the oven and is resting on a carving board.

Follow the recipe for Giblet Pan Gravy on page 364, making adjustments to the following ingredients: add 3 cups water to 1½ quarts turkey or chicken stock or broth, increase the butter to 5 tablespoons, the flour to ¼ cup plus 2 tablespoons, and the wine to 1½ cups. Proceed as directed in the recipe.

HIGH-ROAST TURKEY

HIGH-ROAST TURKEY IS THE HOLY GRAIL of holiday cookery. Not even two hours goes by before the bird is roasted, and with picture-perfect skin. Yet the potential for the piercing shriek of a smoke alarm and torched breast meat are sufficient reason to approach this recipe with more than a pinch of trepidation.

It all started with Barbara Kafka, who introduced America to the high-roast turkey in her book *Roasting* (Morrow, 1995) with a recipe for turkey roasted in a 500-degree oven. In the past five years, we have performed many tests using the high-roast method with chicken, paying particular attention to the problems that high temperatures present for the home cook. We wondered if this technique could be applied to turkey. For this endeavor, we started by placing a 12-pound bird breast-side up on a V-rack, placing the rack in a roasting pan, and then roasting the turkey undisturbed until the thigh meat registered the optimum temperature of 175 degrees—in this case, just under two hours. As promised, there was crisp skin, but only over the breast meat, probably because the turkey was never rotated in the oven. In addition, the breast meat was overcooked by the time the thighs were cooked. Even worse, the kitchen filled with black smoke caused by burnt pan drippings. Still, despite the seeming failure of this initial attempt, we were encouraged by the terrific-looking skin and the short amount of time needed to roast the turkey.

In their natural form, turkeys are not designed to roast evenly. The vaulted bone structure of the breast promotes faster cooking, while the legs lag behind. We decided a turkey redesign was in order. We butterflied the turkey—a technique in which the backbone is removed and the bird is opened up and then flattened. Logic dictated that with the turkey basically in two dimensions, not three, and all of the meat facing up, the turkey would cook more evenly, and the skin would have equal time to crisp. As it turned out, however, butterflying a turkey is a whole lot harder than butterflying a chicken, a feat we'd accomplished many times with only a little help from a good pair of scissors to cut out the backbone. Because scissors are no match for the sturdier bone structure of a turkey, we found a good-quality chef's knife was necessary to cut along either side of the backbone. Even with a sharp blade, we still needed to apply some serious pressure to cut through the thicker bones, sometimes literally hacking our way through. Once the backbone was removed, we found that the sturdy rib cage would not flatten under pressure from the heel of a hand, as a chicken's does. We reached for a heavy-duty rolling pin, placed the turkey breast-side up, and whacked the breastbone until it flattened—aggressive culinary therapy, if you will. All of this means getting quite physical, but there's no way around it if you want to turn out a perfect high-roast turkey.

We roasted the butterflied bird, and the results were outstanding. As the legs were now in contact with part of the breast, they helped prevent the white meat from overcooking. The thighs, which had been cooking more slowly than the breast meat, zoomed ahead, and by the time the breast meat was up to optimum temperature, 165 degrees, the thighs had reached their target temperature of 175 degrees. If it weren't for the billowing smoke, we would have shouted eureka!

The meat was evenly cooked and the skin was crisp, but what to do about the smoke? Filling the roasting pan with water to keep the fat from hitting the bottom of the hot pan solved the smoke problem but delivered soggy skin. (Much of the water evaporates, creating a humid environment, which is anathema to crisp skin.) After many tests, we finally hit on stuffing as the answer. Placed in the bottom of the roasting pan, where it could soak up the drippings, the stuffing could not only eliminate the smoking problem but also pick up outstanding flavor.

The question now was how best to construct this arrangement. A broiler pan was our first thought, since the slotted top would allow the drippings to reach the stuffing. But while the broiler pan top was the perfect size to hold the turkey, the bottom held only enough stuffing for four—not enough for seconds, not to mention leftovers. After going through the kitchen's battalion of roasting pans to use with the broiler pan top, we finally resorted to a disposable rectangular aluminum roasting pan. It was big enough to hold plenty of stuffing, sturdy enough to support the broiler pan top, and, best of all, easy to clean up—we just threw it away.

The recipe we had been using, Cornbread and Sausage Stuffing (page 371), now needed some fine-tuning. After soaking up the fat and liquid from the drippings, our previously well-balanced recipe had become greasy. We lowered the fat in the recipe by reducing the amount of butter from

BUTTERFLYING A TURKEY

1. Holding the turkey upright with the backbone facing front, use a hacking motion to cut directly to the left of the backbone with a chef's knife.

2. Continue cutting to the left of the backbone until the cut is complete.

3. Holding the backbone with one hand, hack directly to the right of the backbone until the backbone is cut free.

4. Using scissors, cut between the ribs and skin. Then cut out the rib plates and remove any small pieces of bone.

5. Place the turkey breast-side up on the cutting board and cover with plastic wrap. With a large rolling pin, whack the breastbone until it cracks and the turkey flattens.

6. After brining and rinsing, place the turkey breast-side up on the broiler pan top. Tuck the wings under the turkey. Push the legs up to rest on the lower portion of the breast. Tie the legs together with kitchen twine.

8 tablespoons to 2 and by cutting the amount of half-and-half and sausage in half. We also reduced the amount of chicken broth; the stuffing got plenty of moisture from the juices of the turkey.

With the mechanics of high-roast turkey in place, we were able to move on to flavor—or lack thereof. As we often do at *Cook's,* we turned to brining—a process in which the turkey is soaked in a solution of salt, sugar, and water. The salt in the solution makes its way into the meat and seasons it. The brine also adds moisture to the meat, which protects it from the effects of overcooking. But with this moisture comes soggy skin. Air-drying the brined turkey in the refrigerator the night before it was roasted allowed the moisture in the skin to evaporate, and once again the roasted skin was crackling crisp.

So we had great turkey and stuffing, but what about the gravy? We had always made gravy using pan drippings, but now the stuffing soaked up those precious juices. Gravy made only from giblet stock was weak. The solution was the backbone, which we chopped into small pieces and threw into a roasting pan along with the neck and giblets, celery, carrot, onion, and garlic. We roasted the bones and vegetables at 450 degrees until well browned, then placed them in a saucepan along with chicken broth, white wine, and water and made a stock. After the stock cooled down, we skimmed off the fat and reserved it to make a roux—a mixture of flour and fat used to thicken sauces or gravies. This gravy was big on flavor, and, by making it ahead, while the turkey was brining, we were able to cut down the amount of work necessary on Thanksgiving Day. Finally, we had delivered great skin, moist, flavorful meat, and superior dressing, all in less than two hours.

Crisp-Skin High-Roast Butterflied Turkey with Sausage Dressing
SERVES 10 TO 12

If you prefer not to brine your turkey, we recommend a kosher bird. This recipe uses table salt (not kosher) in its brine. If you'd like to use kosher salt, whose large

CARVING A BUTTERFLIED TURKEY

1. With a sharp carving knife, cut both leg quarters off the turkey.

2. Cut both wing pieces off the breast section.

3. Slice straight down along the breastbone. Continue to slice down, with the knife hugging the rib bones, to remove the breast meat.

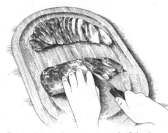

4. Beginning at the narrow end of the breast, slice the meat across the grain, about ¼ inch thick.

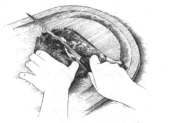

5. Pull the thigh and drumstick apart and locate the joint. Cut through the joint, separating it into two pieces.

6. Remove the largest pieces of meat from the thigh and slice the meat across the grain, about ¼ inch thick.

flakes measure differently from fine-grained table salt, see page 312 for conversion information. The dressing can be made with cornbread, challah, or Italian bread, but note that they are not used in equal amounts. If you don't own a broiler pan top, or if yours does not span the roasting pan, try a sturdy wire rack that rests comfortably on top of a 16 by 12-inch disposable roasting pan. Cover the rack with a large sheet of heavy-duty foil, fold excess foil under, spray it with nonstick cooking spray, and, with a paring knife, cut slits in the foil for fat drainage.

TURKEY

1	cup table salt
1	cup sugar
1	turkey (12 to 14 pounds gross weight), rinsed thoroughly; giblets, neck, and tailpiece removed and reserved for gravy (recipe follows); turkey butterflied following illustrations 1 through 5 on page 376
1	tablespoon unsalted butter, melted

SAUSAGE DRESSING

12	cups cornbread (page 371) broken into 1-inch pieces (include crumbs), or 18 cups 1-inch challah or Italian bread cubes (from about 1½ loaves)
1¾	cups homemade turkey or chicken stock or low-sodium chicken broth
1	cup half-and-half
2	large eggs, lightly beaten
12	ounces bulk pork sausage, crumbled
3	medium onions, chopped fine (about 3 cups)
3	celery ribs, chopped fine (about 1½ cups)
2	tablespoons unsalted butter
2	tablespoons minced fresh thyme leaves
2	tablespoons minced fresh sage leaves
3	medium garlic cloves, minced or pressed through a garlic press
1½	teaspoons salt
2	teaspoons ground black pepper

1. To BRINE THE TURKEY: Dissolve the salt and sugar in 2 gallons cold water in a large stockpot or clean bucket. Add the turkey and refrigerate or set in a very cool spot (not more than 40 degrees) for 4 hours.

2. FOR THE DRESSING: While the turkey brines,

adjust one oven rack to the upper-middle position and the second rack to the lower-middle position and heat the oven to 250 degrees. Spread the bread in even layers on 2 rimmed baking sheets and dry in the oven, 40 to 50 minutes for the challah or Italian bread or 50 to 60 minutes for the cornbread.

3. Place the bread in a large bowl. Whisk together the stock, half-and-half, and eggs in a medium bowl; pour over the bread and toss gently to coat so the bread does not break into smaller pieces. Set aside.

4. Heat a heavy-bottomed 12-inch skillet over medium-high heat until hot, about 1½ minutes. Add the sausage and cook, stirring occasionally, until it loses its raw color, 5 to 7 minutes. With a slotted spoon, transfer the sausage to a medium bowl. Add about half the onions and celery to the fat in the skillet; sauté, stirring occasionally, until softened, about 5 minutes. Transfer the onion mixture to the bowl with the sausage. Return the skillet to the heat and add the butter; when the foam subsides, add the remaining celery and onions and sauté, stirring occasionally, until softened, about 5 minutes. Stir in the thyme, sage, and garlic; cook until fragrant, about 30 seconds; add the salt and pepper. Add this mixture along with the sausage and onion mixture to the bread and stir gently to combine, trying not to break the bread into smaller pieces.

5. Spray a 16 by 12-inch disposable aluminum roasting pan with nonstick cooking spray. Transfer the dressing to the roasting pan and spread in an even layer. Cover the pan with foil and refrigerate until needed.

6. To PREPARE THE TURKEY FOR ROASTING: Set a slotted broiler pan top on the roasting pan with the foil-covered dressing and spray with nonstick cooking spray; set the roasting pan on a baking sheet to support the bottom. Remove the turkey from the brine and rinse well under cool running water. Following illustration 6 on page 376, position the turkey on the broiler pan top; thoroughly pat the surface of the turkey dry with paper towels. Refrigerate the turkey and dressing, uncovered, for 8 to 24 hours.

7. To ROAST THE TURKEY WITH THE DRESSING: Adjust an oven rack to the lower-middle position

and heat the oven to 450 degrees. Remove the broiler pan top with the turkey and remove and discard the foil on the roasting pan. Replace the broiler pan top with the turkey. Brush the turkey with the melted butter. Place the entire assembly in the oven and roast until the turkey skin is crisp and deep brown and an instant-read thermometer reads 165 degrees when inserted in the thickest part of the breast and 175 degrees when inserted in the thickest part of the thigh, 80 to 100 minutes, rotating the pan from front to back after 40 minutes.

8. Transfer the broiler pan top with the turkey to a cutting board and let rest 20 minutes. Meanwhile, adjust an oven rack to the upper-middle position, place the roasting pan with the dressing back in the oven, and bake until golden brown, about 10 minutes. Cool the dressing 5 minutes, then spoon into a bowl or onto a serving platter. Carve the turkey (see page 377) and serve with gravy (recipe follows).

Turkey Gravy

MAKES ABOUT 1 QUART

Because we don't have pan drippings left over from our high-roast turkey (the stuffing soaks them up), we developed this version, which relies on trimmings, the backbone, and a few aromatic vegetables.

To roast the trimmings and vegetables, it's best to use a roasting pan that can sit on the stovetop. If you don't own one, a broiler pan bottom will work; when setting it on the stovetop, however, use medium heat instead of high heat and add only half the amount of chicken broth before scraping up the drippings; add the remaining chicken broth to the saucepan along with the wine.

	Reserved turkey giblets, neck, tailpiece and backbone, hacked into 2-inch pieces
1	medium carrot, cut into 1-inch pieces
1	celery rib, cut into 1-inch pieces
2	small onions, chopped coarse
6	garlic cloves, unpeeled
3½	cups low-sodium chicken broth
2	cups dry white wine
3	cups water
6	sprigs fresh thyme
¼	cup unbleached all-purpose flour
	Salt and ground black pepper

1. Heat the oven to 450 degrees. Place the turkey trimmings, carrot, celery, onions, and garlic in a large flameproof roasting pan. Spray lightly with cooking spray and toss to combine. Roast, stirring every 10 minutes, until well browned, 40 to 50 minutes.

2. Remove the pan from the oven and place on the stovetop over burners set on high heat. Add the chicken broth and bring to a boil, scraping up the browned bits on the pan bottom with a wooden spoon.

3. Transfer the contents of the roasting pan to a large saucepan. Add the wine, water, and thyme and bring to a boil over high heat. Reduce the heat to low and simmer until reduced by half, about 1½ hours. Strain the stock into a large measuring cup or container. Cool to room temperature; cover with plastic wrap and refrigerate until the fat congeals, at least 1 hour.

4. To finish the gravy, skim the fat from the stock using a soup spoon and reserve the fat. To remove the remaining bits of fat in the stock, pour the stock through a fine-mesh strainer into a medium saucepan. Discard the bits in the strainer. Bring the stock to a simmer over medium-high heat. In a second medium saucepan, heat 4 tablespoons of the reserved turkey fat over medium-high heat until bubbling; whisk in the flour and cook, whisking constantly, until combined and honey-colored, about 2 minutes. Continuing to whisk constantly, gradually add the hot stock; bring to a boil, then reduce the heat to medium-low and simmer, stirring occasionally, until slightly thickened, about 5 minutes. Season with salt and pepper to taste and serve with the turkey. (The gravy can be refrigerated for up to 3 days; reheat in a medium saucepan over medium heat until hot, about 8 minutes.)

TURKEY BURGERS

A LEAN, FULLY COOKED TURKEY BURGER, seasoned with salt and pepper, is a weak stand-in for an all-beef burger. Simply put, it is dry, tasteless, and colorless. We wanted a turkey burger with beef burger qualities—dark and crusty on the outside and full-flavored and juicy with every bite.

Finding the right meat was crucial to developing the best turkey burger. According to the National Turkey Federation, there are three options—white meat (with 1 to 2 percent fat), dark meat (over 15 percent fat), and a blend of the two (ranging from 7 to 15 percent fat).

At the grocery store, we found multiple variations on the white meat/dark meat theme, including higher-fat ground fresh turkey on Styrofoam trays or frozen in tubes like bulk sausage, lower-fat ground turkey breasts, and then there were the individual turkey parts we take home and grind up ourselves. We bought them all, took them back to the test kitchen, and fired up a skillet.

The higher-fat (15 percent) ground turkey turned out to be flavorful and reasonably juicy with a decent, burger-like crust. Frankly, these burgers didn't need too much help. But, given that a great beef burger contains only 20 percent fat, a mere 5 percent fat savings didn't seem worth it.

At the other extreme, with only 1 or 2 percent fat, was ground turkey breast. As we were mixing and forming these patties, we knew we had about as much chance of making them look, taste, and feel like real burgers as we did of making vanilla wafers taste like chocolate chip cookies. They needed a binder to keep them from falling apart. They needed extra fat to keep them from parching and extra fat in the pan to keep them from sticking. And they needed flavor to save them from blandness.

With 7 percent fat, lean ground turkey was the most popular style at all the grocery stores we checked. Burgers made from this mix were dry, rubbery, and mild-flavored. With a little help, however, these leaner patties were meaty enough to have real burger potential.

Most flavorful of all and only about 10 percent fat were the boned and skinless turkey thighs we ground ourselves in the food processor. We first tried grinding the skin with the meat but found that it ground inconsistently and we had to pick it out. In the next batch, we left it out and found the result to be equally flavorful and much lower in calories. As a matter of fact, our butcher declared our home-ground skinless turkey almost 90 percent lean when he tested it in his Univex Fat Analyzer.

For all the obvious reasons, we had sworn that even if we liked the outcome, we weren't going to make grind-your-own-turkey part of the recipe, but these burgers—meaty-flavored with a beef-like chew—were far superior to any we made with the commercially ground turkey. If you are willing to take the time, turkey thighs ground up in the food processor cook up into low-fat turkey burgers with great flavor and texture.

For those with little time or energy for this process, we decided to see what we could do to improve the lean commercially ground turkey. To improve texture and juiciness, we started with the obvious—milk-soaked bread. For comparison, we also made burgers with buttermilk- and yogurt-soaked bread. All these additions made the burgers feel too much like meat loaf and destroyed whatever meaty flavor there had been, since turkey is mild to start with. The bread and milk lightened the meat's color unpleasantly, while the sugar in both ingredients caused the burgers to burn easily and made it impossible to develop a good thick crust.

We tried other fillers to improve the texture, including cornmeal mush, mashed pinto beans, and minced tempeh, but their flavors were too distinct. Minced, rehydrated, dried mushrooms added a moist, chewy texture that the burgers desperately needed. They also offered an earthy, meaty, yet not overly distinct flavor. However, the real winner—for flavor, texture, and easy availability—was ricotta cheese. Moist and chewy, it gave the burgers the texture boost they needed and required very little effort.

Finally, we decided to experiment a bit with added flavorings. We wanted only those which would enhance a burger's taste without drawing attention to themselves. We tried more than 25 different flavorings—from fermented black beans to olive paste to teriyaki marinade—and found only two that we liked: Worcestershire sauce and Dijon mustard.

Next we turned to the cooking method. Since turkey burgers must be well-done for safety reasons, cooking them can be a bit tricky—too high a heat and they burn before they're done; too low and they look pale and steamed. We tried several cooking methods, from broiling to roasting, but nothing compared in quality and ease with our stovetop method. Browning the burgers in a heavy-bottomed skillet over medium heat, then cooking them partially covered over low heat gave us a rich-crusted burger that was cooked all the way through.

Although our generous cooking times should ensure a fully cooked burger, as an extra precaution you may want to test for doneness by sticking an instant-read thermometer through the side and into the center of one of them. The burger is done at 160 degrees.

Best Turkey Burgers
SERVES 4

We found that the extra step of grinding fresh turkey thighs ourselves made the most flavorful, best-textured burgers. If you can, buy boneless turkey thighs. Pan-frying develops a good, thick crust on the burgers, while grilling gives them a subtle smoky flavor that we love. Serve the burgers on buns with ketchup and the usual accompaniments.

I	turkey thigh (about 2 pounds), skinned and boned, or 1½ pounds skinless, boneless thighs
½	teaspoon salt
½	teaspoon ground black pepper
2	teaspoons Worcestershire sauce
2	teaspoons Dijon mustard
I	tablespoon vegetable or canola oil

1. Cut the skinned and boned thigh into 1-inch chunks and arrange in a single layer on a baking sheet. Freeze until somewhat firm, about 30 minutes.

2. Working in 3 batches, place the semifrozen turkey chunks in a food processor fitted with the steel blade; pulse until the largest pieces are no bigger than ⅛ inch, twelve to fourteen 1-second pulses.

3. Transfer the ground meat to a medium bowl. Stir in the salt, pepper, Worcestershire sauce, and mustard until blended and divide the meat into 4 portions. Lightly toss one portion from hand to hand to form a ball, then lightly flatten the ball with your fingertips into a 1-inch-thick patty.

Repeat with the remaining portions.

4. Heat a large, heavy skillet (preferably cast iron or stainless steel with an aluminum core) over medium heat until very hot, 4 to 5 minutes. Swirl the oil in the pan to coat the bottom. Add the burgers and cook over medium heat without moving them until the bottom of each is dark brown and crusted, about 5 minutes. Turn the burgers over; continue to cook until the bottom is light brown but not yet crusted, 4 to 5 minutes longer. Reduce the heat to low, position the cover slightly ajar on the pan to allow steam to escape, and continue to cook 5 to 6 minutes longer, or until the center is completely opaque yet still juicy or an instant-read thermometer inserted from the side of the burger into the center registers 160 degrees. Remove from the pan and serve immediately.

Quick Turkey Burgers
SERVES 4

By enriching store-bought lean ground turkey with ricotta cheese, you can produce an excellent burger. Ricotta cheese can burn easily, so keep a close watch on the burgers as they cook.

1¼	pounds 93 percent lean ground turkey
½	cup whole-milk ricotta cheese
½	teaspoon salt
½	teaspoon ground black pepper
2	teaspoons Worcestershire sauce
2	teaspoons Dijon mustard
I	tablespoon vegetable or canola oil

1. Combine the ground turkey, cheese, salt, pepper, Worcestershire sauce, and mustard in a medium bowl until blended. Divide the meat into 4 portions. Lightly toss one portion from hand to hand to form a ball, then lightly flatten the ball with your fingertips into a 1-inch-thick patty. Repeat with the remaining portions.

2. Heat a large, heavy skillet (preferably cast iron or stainless steel with an aluminum core) over medium heat until very hot. Swirl the oil in the pan to coat the bottom. Add the burgers and cook over medium heat without moving them until the bottom of each is dark brown and

crusted, 3 to 4 minutes. Turn the burgers over; continue to cook until the bottom is light brown but not yet crusted, 3 to 4 minutes longer. Reduce the heat to low, position the cover slightly ajar on the pan to allow steam to escape, and continue to cook 8 to 10 minutes longer, flipping once if necessary to promote deep browning, or until the center is completely opaque yet still juicy or an instant-read thermometer inserted from the side of the burger into the center registers 160 degrees. Remove from the pan and serve immediately.

➤ VARIATION
Grilled Turkey Burgers
Follow the recipe for Best Turkey Burgers through step 3, or complete the recipe for Quick Turkey Burgers through step 1. Grill the burgers over a medium-low fire (you can hold your hand about 5 inches above the grill surface for 5 seconds) until dark spotty brown on the bottom, 7 to 9 minutes. Turn the burgers over; continue grilling 7 to 9 minutes longer or until the bottom is dark spotty brown and the center is completely opaque or an instant-read thermometer inserted from the side of the burger registers 160 degrees. Remove from the grill and serve immediately.

ROAST DUCK

GOOD DUCKS ARE DELICIOUS, BUT TOO OFTEN our pleasure in them is ruined because they are just too greasy. It wasn't always this way. Wild ducks are so lean they need to be covered with bacon to keep them from drying out in the oven. But only hunters encounter this problem. Supermarket shoppers must rely on domesticated Pekin (also called Long Island) ducks. And, boy, are these birds fatty. Although the sticker weight may say 4½ pounds, the final weight after roasting can be less than 2 pounds. No wonder a single duck yields two or maybe three servings.

A knockout duck should have crisp skin and moist, flavorful meat. To achieve this goal, we would have to rid the bird of a lot of fat. At the outset, we decided we wanted an old-fashioned

roast duck, cooked through without a trace of pink. Restaurants rely on different duck breeds with large breasts, in particular the muscovy, that can be cooked rare. But consumers must order such ducks by mail, and we wanted to use the duck you find in the supermarket. Since the breast on a Pekin duck is no thicker than half an inch, it can't be cooked rare or medium, especially if you're trying to get the legs to soften up.

Our initial tests demonstrated the need to start getting rid of the fat from the outset. We found that unless the skin rests directly on meat or bone, it will never crisp properly. So before cooking even starts, the large clumps of white fat that line the body and neck cavity must be pulled out by hand and discarded. Any loose skin must also be trimmed away, including most of the flap that covers the neck cavity.

Our next tests centered on roasting methods. Every source we consulted agreed that a roasting rack is necessary to keep the duck elevated above the rendered fat. After that, there was little agreement. Many recipes suggest pricking the skin to help fat escape. We used a fork as well as the tip of a paring knife, and both worked moderately well.

One chef told us he always starts duck in a 500-degree oven to render the fat quickly and then turns down the heat to 350 degrees to cook the duck through. Our instincts told us this approach was problematic, and the billows of smoke that filled the kitchen proved that this method can work only in a kitchen equipped with an extremely powerful exhaust fan.

Next we tried the method advocated by most older sources—cooking in a moderate oven (350 degrees) for two hours, followed by a short burst of higher heat (425 degrees) to crisp the skin. The results were decent. The skin was good, and the breast was fine. However, the legs were still too fatty, and the wings were flabby and totally unappetizing. Tasters devoured the breasts, but they ate around the fat in the legs, and no one would touch the wings.

Many recent sources tout slow roasting followed by a period of moderate roasting to crisp the skin. Of all the traditional methods that we tried, slow roasting and constant turning (so that the fat drips down from all sides) did the best job of getting rid of fat. However, even after four hours in the oven, the legs were still too fatty to eat with gusto. The internal fat, especially the fat that divides the thigh from the leg, was not melting away. And we noticed that the breast meat (which is hard to overcook because of the fatty skin on top) was actually starting to dry out after so many hours in the oven. We had created a problem that duck wasn't supposed to have. Clearly, it was time to switch gears.

Many Asian recipes for duck start with steaming or boiling. The theory is that moist heat melts some of the fat, and it's true. Because moisture transfers heat more efficiently than dry air, moist cooking methods such as steaming cause more fluid loss than dry cooking methods such as roasting. After steaming or boiling, the duck can be roasted to render the rest of the fat and crisp up the skin. We decided to try a two-step cooking process, with moist heat followed by dry heat.

We bought three ducks and steamed one for an hour (a time suggested by several sources), blanched another for one minute, and boiled a third for 15 minutes. The steamed and boiled ducks were already cooked, so we roasted them in a 400-degree oven to crisp the skin. The blanched duck was roasted at a constant 350 degrees for two hours, followed by 425 degrees until the skin was brown and crisp.

The scale told the story here. When we roasted a duck without any treatment with water, we were able to reduce its initial weight by an average of 45 percent. Boiling or blanching pushed this number up to 48 percent and 46 percent, respectively. In contrast, the duck that was steamed lost an astonishing 58 percent of its weight. This duck also tasted less greasy, especially in the breast, and the skin was the thinnest and the crispest.

One problem remained. We still thought the legs were a bit too fatty. We wanted them to be dense, dark, and meaty, like the best confit. Steaming was melting all the fat right underneath the skin, but domesticated birds have a lot of intermuscular fat in the legs and thighs, which is shielded from the steam and the oven heat by the skin, meat, and bones. We tried various steaming

times and roasting regimens, but we just couldn't get the legs degreased.

At this point, we decided to cut the bird into six parts—two wings, two leg/thighs, and two breasts. We figured the fat in the leg/thighs would no longer be protected and would render quickly in the oven. And were we ever right. The difference was dramatic.

When we roasted a whole steamed duck for an hour, only two to three tablespoons of fat were rendered. However, when we roasted the parts from a steamed duck for less time and with far less body weight (we were saving the carcass and back for stock), we were able to coax a full one-third cup of fat out of the six parts. The skin was especially crisp and delicious because we were able to cook the parts skin-side down directly in the pan, not on a rack. (We found it helpful to spoon off the fat when turning the parts.) The breast was moist, the wings were beautifully browned and very crisp, and we finally had a roast duck with legs that everyone at the table was fighting over.

As for the steaming step, we would never roast duck again without doing this first. It doesn't really add any time to the process because the duck roasts for such a short period. It can also be steamed a day in advance. Two-step duck may not be the easiest, but it produces the best results and minimizes last-minute kitchen work.

Crisp Roast Duck with Port Wine Glaze
SERVES 2 TO 3

Pekin ducks, also called Long Island ducks, are the only choice in most supermarkets. Almost always sold frozen, the duck must defrost in the refrigerator for at least one day before cooking. To feed six people, steam one duck after the other and then roast all the pieces together in an oversize roasting pan or large rimmed baking sheet.

PORT WINE GLAZE
1¼	cups port
2	medium garlic cloves, peeled and cut into thin slivers
4	fresh thyme sprigs

CRISP ROAST DUCK
1 whole Pekin duck (about 4½ pounds),
   rinsed thoroughly, neck, giblets, and all
   visible fat discarded
   Salt and ground black pepper

1. FOR THE GLAZE: Bring all the ingredients to a boil in a small saucepan. Reduce the heat to medium-low and simmer until slightly thickened and reduced to a scant ¼ cup, 25 to 30 minutes. Remove and discard the garlic and thyme; set the glaze aside.

2. FOR THE DUCK: Meanwhile, set a V-rack in a large, high-sided roasting pan and position the duck breast-side up on the rack. Add water to just below the bottom of the duck. Bring the water to a boil over high heat, cover the pan tightly with aluminum foil (or the pan cover, if available), adjust the heat to medium (to maintain a slow, steady boil), and steam, adding more hot water to maintain the water level if necessary, until the skin has pulled away from at least one leg. For duck with very moist, tender meat and slightly crisp skin once roasted, steam about 40 minutes. Steam 10 minutes longer for somewhat denser meat and very crisp skin after roasting. Transfer the duck to a carving board and, when cool enough to handle, cut into 6 pieces—2 wings, 2 legs, and 2 breast halves. (The cooled duck, either whole or cut into pieces, can be wrapped in foil and refrigerated overnight. Reserve the back and carcass for another use.)

3. Adjust an oven rack to the bottom position and heat the oven to 425 degrees. Season the pieces on both sides with salt and pepper to taste and position skin-side down in a lightly oiled roasting pan. Roast, carefully pouring off the fat if more than two tablespoons accumulate in the pan, until the skin on the breast pieces is a rich brown color and crisp, about 25 minutes. Transfer the breast pieces to a platter and cover with foil to keep warm. Again, pour off the excess fat from the pan, turn the leg/thigh and wing pieces skin-side up, and continue roasting until the skin on these pieces is deep brown and crisp, 15 to 20 minutes longer. Again, pour off the excess fat from the pan. Return the breast pieces to the pan and brush both sides of every piece with the glaze. Roast until the glaze is hot and richly colored on the duck pieces, 3 to 4 minutes. Serve immediately.

➤ VARIATION
Crisp Roast Duck with Orange Glaze
The lime juice keeps this thick, syrupy glaze from being too sweet.

Follow the recipe for Crisp Roast Duck with Port Wine Glaze, substituting 1 cup freshly squeezed orange juice, 2 tablespoons fresh lime juice, and 2 tablespoons honey for the port and omitting the garlic and thyme.

8

BEEF

BEFORE YOU CHOOSE A PARTICULAR STEAK or roast, it helps to understand something about the anatomy of a cow. Eight different cuts of beef are sold at the wholesale level (see the illustration below). From this first series of cuts, known in the trade as primal cuts, a butcher (usually at a meat-packing plant in the Midwest but sometimes on-site at your local market) will make the retail cuts that you bring home from the market. How you choose to cook a particular piece of beef depends on where the meat comes from on the cow and how it was butchered.

CHUCK/SHOULDER Starting at the front of the animal, the chuck (or shoulder) runs from the neck down to the fifth rib. Three are four major muscles in this region, and meat from the chuck tends to be flavorful and fairly fatty, which is why ground chuck makes the best hamburgers. Chuck also contains a fair amount of connective tissue, so when the meat is not ground, it generally requires a long cooking time to become tender.

RIB Moving back from the chuck, the next primal cut along the top half of the animal is the rib section, which extends from the sixth to the twelfth rib. The prime rib comes from this area, as do rib-eye steaks. Rib cuts have excellent beefy flavor and are quite tender.

SHORT LOIN The short loin (also called the loin) extends from the last rib back through the midsection of the animal to the hip area. It contains two major muscles—the tenderloin and the shell. The tenderloin is extremely tender (it is positioned right under the spine) and has quite a mild flavor. This muscle may be sold whole as a roast or sliced crosswise into steaks, called filets mignons. The shell is a much larger muscle and has a more robust beef flavor as well as more fat. Strip steaks (also called shell steaks) come from this muscle and are our favorite. Two steaks from the short loin area contain portions of both the tenderloin and the shell muscles. These steaks are called the T-bone and porterhouse, and both are excellent choices.

SIRLOIN The next area is the sirloin, which contains relatively inexpensive cuts that are sold both as steaks and roasts. We find that sirloin cuts are fairly lean and tough. In general, we prefer other parts of the animal, although top sirloin makes a decent roast.

ROUND The back of the cow is called the round. Roasts and steaks cut from this area are usually sold boneless and are quite lean and can be tough. Again, we generally prefer cuts from other parts of the cow, although top round can be roasted with some success.

BRISKET/SHANK, PLATE, AND FLANK The underside of the animal is divided into the brisket/shank (near the front of the animal), the plate, and the flank. Thick boneless cuts are removed from these three parts of the cow. The brisket is rather tough and contains a lot of connective tissue. The plate is rarely sold at the retail level (it is used to make pastrami). The flank is a leaner cut that makes an excellent steak when grilled.

THE EIGHT PRIMAL CUTS OF BEEF

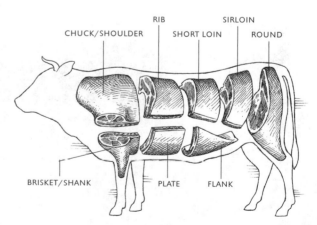

Knowing When Meat Is Done 101

Although professional cooks might rely on the feel of a steak to determine doneness, we find this method much too imprecise. An instant-read thermometer coupled with knowledge of how temperatures relate to desired doneness will ensure success in the kitchen. (The chart below lists these temperatures.)

Know that maximum juiciness and flavor often collides with maximum safety. Health officials generally suggest cooking all meat to 160 degrees in order to ensure that any bacteria or pathogens that may be present have been killed. This is sound advice if food safety is your top concern. However, the reality is that most people (including us) prefer their meat cooked to a lower internal temperature. The reason is simple. Heating causes meat fibers to contract and expel juices. A steak cooked to 160 degrees will be significantly drier than a steak cooked to 130 degrees. In most instances, we cook meat to maximum palatability. If safety is your top concern, you should cook all meat until it is well-done (and the internal temperature registers at least 160 degrees).

Note that these temperatures apply only to lean cuts and dry-heat cooking methods such as grilling and roasting. When braising or stewing fattier cuts, the internal temperature of the meat will climb much higher, but the collagen in these cuts will protect against dryness.

INSTANT-READ THERMOMETERS

There are two types of commonly sold hand-held thermometers: digital and dial face. While they both take accurate readings, we prefer digital thermometers because they register temperatures faster and are easier to read. After testing a variety of digital thermometers, we preferred the Thermapen ($80) for its well-thought-out design—a long, folding probe and comfortable handle—and speed (just 10 seconds for a reading). If you don't want to spend so much money on a thermometer, at the very least purchase an inexpensive dial-face model. There's no sense ruining a $50 roast because you don't own even a $10 thermometer.

THE BEST INSTANT-READ THERMOMETER
The Thermapen ($80) is our top choice for its pinpoint accuracy and quick response time.

CHECKING THE INTERNAL TEMPERATURE

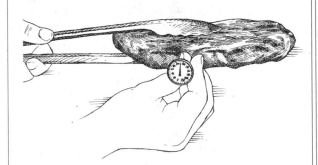

Most instant-read thermometers work best when the tip is stuck at least an inch deep into food. On a thin steak, the tip can go right through the meat if inserted from the top. For the most accurate reading, hold the steak with a pair of tongs and slide the tip of the thermometer through the side of the steak. Make sure that the shaft is embedded in the meat and not touching any bone.

OPTIMUM INTERNAL TEMPERATURES FOR MEAT

The chart below lists optimum internal temperatures, based on maximum juiciness and flavor. For optimum safety, all meat should be cooked until the internal temperature reaches 160 degrees.

To determine internal temperature, insert an instant-read thermometer deep into the meat away from any bone. Take two or three readings to make sure the entire piece of meat has reached the proper temperature.

Note that the temperatures that follow are at serving time. Since the internal temperature of most cuts will rise as the meat rests (the effect is called carry-over cooking), you will want to remove steaks from the grill or a roast from the oven before it hits these temperatures. For instance, a roast that registers 125 degrees on an instant-read thermometer when it comes out of the oven might reach 135 degrees by the time it has rested on the counter for 15 minutes.

Unfortunately, the significance of the carry-over effect will vary from recipe to recipe based on the thickness of the cut (thicker cuts hold on to heat better than thinner cuts and will experience a greater rise in temperature as they rest) as well as the heat level used during the cooking process (a roast that comes out of a 250-degree oven has less heat to hold on to, and the internal temperature won't climb nearly as much as that of a roast that comes out of a 450-degree oven). For this reason, you should follow temperatures in recipes, which have been designed to compensate for the carry-over effect for that specific recipe. Recipes give temperatures at which the meat should be removed from the oven. The numbers below indicate how temperature at serving time correlates with various levels of doneness.

	RARE	MEDIUM-RARE	MEDIUM	MEDIUM-WELL	WELL-DONE
Beef	125°F	130°F	140°F	150°F	160°F
Veal	125°F	135°F	140°F	150°F	160°F
Lamb	125°F	130°F	140°F	150°F	160°F
Pork	*	*	145°F	150°F	160°F

*not recommended

PAN-SEARED PREMIUM STEAKS

STEAKS MUST BE COOKED SO THAT THE ENTIRE surface caramelizes to form a rich, thick crust. The intense heat of the grill makes it easy to obtain such a crust. But sometimes grilling is impractical. We wanted to get the same result from pan-searing.

We decided to focus on boneless steaks. Bone-in steaks, such as T-bones and porterhouses, really should be grilled; when pan-seared it's the bone, not the meat, that makes contact with the pan, and the result is poor coloring and no crust development. We tested a dozen boneless steaks and found two that everyone in the test kitchen could agree on—rib-eye and strip steaks.

Rib steaks are cut from the rib roast (or prime rib) and come with the curved bone attached. More often, you will see boneless steaks from the rib, called rib-eye steaks. Rib eyes are tender and smooth-textured, with a distinctive, robust, beefy taste. They are very rich, with good-size pockets of fat. Rib eye is also known as Delmonico steak in New York or Spencer steak in the West.

The strip steak is cut from the short loin part of the cow. Also called shell, Kansas City strip, New York strip, or top loin, strip steak has a noticeable grain and a moderate amount of chew. The flavor is excellent and the meat a bit less fatty than in rib-eye steaks. Strip steaks are also slightly more expensive than rib eyes.

It was obvious to us from the beginning that the key to browning the steaks was going to be preheating the pan, so that when the steaks hit the pan, the surface would be hot enough to sear the steaks before they overcooked. In this regard, we wondered if different types of pans would heat and cook differently.

We found that a cast-iron skillet did an excellent job of browning the steaks, but we feared pan sauces would suffer. Many sources discourage the use of cast-iron pans because of the iron's tendency to react with acidic foods, giving them a metallic, off flavor. Sure enough, when we prepared a red wine pan sauce in a cast-iron skillet, it tasted tinny.

Next we tried searing steaks in a nonstick skillet, but the browned bits that a good sear leaves behind in the pan and that make sauces so delicious did not materialize. The resulting sauces were anemic and weakly flavored. Pan sauces made in regular nonreactive pans were rich in both flavor and color. We had good results with heavy-bottomed pans made by All-Clad and Calphalon.

We had been searing the steaks over high heat to promote browning, but tasters noticed that the pan sauces tasted bitter. To avoid this problem, we tried heating the pan over high heat and then reducing the heat to medium-high once the steaks went into the pan. This worked fine as long as the pan was fully preheated (three minutes over high heat worked best) before the steaks were added. We found that strip and rib-eye steaks had enough fat to be seared without oil.

Over the course of testing, we noticed a few more factors that ensured a good crust on the steak and richly flavored browned bits in the pan to flavor the sauce. There should be at least ¼ inch of space between the steaks if they are to sear, not steam. At the same time, the pan should not be too large because that encourages burning. A 12-inch skillet is the right size for four steaks. We also noticed that it was not a good idea to move the steaks around in the pan. This interrupted the browning process and resulted in steaks that lacked good caramelization. The steaks browned much better when moved only once, just to turn them over to the other side.

~

Pan-Seared Strip or Rib-Eye Steaks
SERVES 4

Serve these steaks with any of the pan sauces on page 390–392.

4   boneless strip or rib-eye steaks,
    1 to 1¼ inches thick (about 8 ounces each),
    patted dry with paper towels
    Salt and ground black pepper

1. Heat a heavy-bottomed nonreactive 12-inch skillet over high heat until very hot. Meanwhile,

season both sides of the steaks with salt and pepper to taste.

2. Lay the steaks in the pan, leaving ¼ inch of space between them. Reduce the heat to medium-high and cook, not moving the steaks until they are well browned, about 4 minutes. Using tongs, flip the steaks; cook 4 minutes more for rare (120 degrees on an instant-read thermometer), 5 minutes more for medium-rare (125 to 130 degrees), and 6 minutes more for medium (135 to 140 degrees). Transfer the steaks to a large plate, tent loosely with foil, and let rest for 5 minutes while preparing a pan sauce.

PAN SAUCES FOR STEAK

A PAN SAUCE—MADE WITH JUST A HANDFUL of ingredients and in a matter of just a few minutes—can look and taste nearly as rich as a classic, labor-intensive French sauce. The base of a pan sauce is the *fond,* or browned bits, clinging to the bottom of the skillet after sautéing or searing meat. Once the food is removed from the skillet, aromatics such as minced shallots can be sautéed; then, in a process called deglazing, liquid (usually wine, broth, or both) is added, and the fond is scraped up with a wooden spoon. The liquid is simmered and reduced to concentrate the flavors and thicken the texture, and, in a final (and sometimes optional) step, the reduction is enriched and slightly thickened by the addition of butter.

If the recipe calls for canned broth (for the sake of convenience, our recipes always do), use the low-sodium variety because reduction can result in overwhelming saltiness. Also avoid the "cooking wines" sold in grocery stores. They contain considerable amounts of salt and are generally unappealing in flavor.

If you intend to make a pan sauce, opt for a traditional skillet. A nonstick skillet will not develop the fond to the same degree that a traditional skillet will, and, because the fond supplies a pan sauce with richness and depth of flavor, a nonstick skillet will render a less flavorful pan sauce. Also important is the size of the skillet. It should comfortably hold the food being cooked. If it is overcrowded, the food will steam and will fail to create much fond.

If traditional (unenameled) cast iron is your cookware of choice, make sure the pan is well seasoned and free of rust. When tested in our kitchen, a sauce made in a well-seasoned cast-iron pan tasted fine. Poorly maintained cast iron, however, will yield a metallic-tasting sauce.

A great red wine pan sauce starts with the right wine (see page 393). But even the right wine can produce a poor sauce. We found that wine doesn't react well to changes in temperature, making it a tricky ingredient to handle, especially in a pan sauce where it is the dominant flavor. As wine is heated, delicate flavor compounds known as esters break apart, turning fruity flavors and aromas sour and bitter. The higher the heat, the more rapidly the esters break down.

Transferring this knowledge to cooking, it would seem reasonable to assume that low, slow heat is better for wine than hot, fast heat. To test this assumption, we made two classic steak pan sauces, one made with rapidly simmered wine and the other made with slowly reduced wine. The results were so radically different that tasters thought the sauces had been made from different wines altogether. The rapidly simmered wine was tart and edgy, while the slowly reduced wine was smooth and round. This surprised many of us who have learned to cook pan sauces the traditional way.

Classically, wine is added to a hot pan (the same pan in which the meat was just cooked) and reduced quickly over high heat while scraping up the tasty browned bits off the pan's bottom. We found that deglazing the hot pan with stock, not wine, and finishing the sauce with wine that had been slowly reduced in a separate pan made a much better pan sauce—one unlike any we had made before. It was rich and voluptuous, with complex layers of flavor.

As we tested a few more pan sauces using this method, we discovered another trick. The wine reduction takes on an extra dimension and polished texture when small amounts of aromatic vegetables are added. Treating the wine almost like a stock, we steeped shallots, carrots, mushrooms, and herbs in the reducing wine, then strained them out before adding the reduction to the sauce.

However, not all pan sauces with wine benefit from this extra step. For instance, we found that a sauce made with Madeira was just fine when made the conventional way (by adding the wine to the hot pan and letting it reduce).

A shallot butter sauce is even easier to prepare. It makes sense to think of this sauce as a melted version of compound butter. Compound butters are made by rolling butter (seasoned with shallots, herbs, spices, mustard, etc.) into a log, chilling the log, and then slicing off a round to melt over a cooked steak. Although delicious, a compound butter does not take advantage of the browned bits left in the pan used to sear the steaks.

For this reason, we like to add shallots to the empty skillet, then throw in the cold butter to create a quick, light sauce. Some lemon juice and parsley round out the flavor. Make sure the butter is cold when it goes into the pan. We found that cold butter gives a sauce more body than softened butter.

Classic Red Wine Pan Sauce
MAKES ENOUGH FOR 4 STEAKS
Start cooking the steaks when the wine has almost finished reducing. Use smooth, medium-bodied, fruity wine, preferably made from a blend of grapes, such as a Côtes du Rhône. For more information about choosing a red wine for cooking, see page 393. See page 394–395 for tips about making pan sauces.

DOES BRANDING MATTER?

To guarantee quality, more and more people are looking beyond the confines of their local supermarket butcher case and buying their steaks through mail-order sources. These outlets promise all-star beef with a price tag to match. But do the mail-order steaks really outshine the ones you can get around the corner? And is there something you can buy locally that's better than your average supermarket steak?

We gathered seven widely available mail-order strip steaks and two from local supermarkets (Coleman Natural—hormone- and antibiotic-free—from our local Whole Foods Market and choice steak from the regular market). Our candidates included Niman Ranch, a high-end, all-natural restaurant favorite; Peter Luger, a New York steakhouse that many consider to be the best in the country; Omaha, probably the most well-known mail-order steak company, with two steaks in the running (their "private reserve" as well as their standard); Allen Brothers, a Chicago-based company that supplies many of this country's steakhouses; and Lobel's, a New York butcher shop. In addition to Lobel's boneless strip steak, we included Lobel's Wagyu, or Kobe-style, steak from Oakleigh Ranch in Australia. Kobe beef comes from Wagyu cattle raised to certain specifications in Kobe, Japan. Considered the foie gras of beef, the meat is extremely well marbled, tender, and rich. Wagyu is the more generic name for the same type of beef, but not from Japan. Although few of us could afford the hefty $68/pound price tag for Wagyu beef, we wanted to see if it was really worth that much.

Well, it was. After pan-searing three dozen steaks (four of each type for perhaps the largest tasting turnout in the test kitchen), we found that money can buy you happiness, if happiness for you is the best steak you ever ate.

"Wow," wrote one happy taster of our first-place Wagyu steak. "This is unlike any strip that I've had." Others deemed the Wagyu steak "tender like a filet" and "very rich and meaty." But the overwhelming richness—which one taster likened to "foie gras–infused beef"—was not everyone's cup of tea. A minority of tasters agreed with the one who wrote, "This doesn't taste like beef at all."

Three steaks shared the spot for second place: Niman Ranch ($22 per pound), praised for its "good flavor" and "nice texture"; Coleman Natural, deemed "very robust"; and Peter Luger, described as having "strong beef flavor" and "great juiciness."

Unfortunately, the brand most people turn to when ordering steak through the mail took the last two spots in our tasting. The Omaha strip steak had "off flavors" and was "grainy-tasting," while the Omaha Private Reserve (at almost twice the price) finished last, with tasters finding it "a little chewy" and "very dry."

The good news is that you don't have to spend a small fortune (or pay for shipping) to get a great steak. Coleman Natural steak, available at all-natural supermarkets, tied for second place and was a comparative bargain at $14 per pound (just $4 more than the low-ranked Stop & Shop beef). If you want to sample true steak greatness, however, you may want to splurge on the Wagyu beef—at least once.

WINE REDUCTION

I	small carrot, peeled and finely chopped (about 2 tablespoons)
I	small shallot, minced
2	white mushrooms, finely chopped (about 3 tablespoons)
I	small bay leaf
3	sprigs fresh parsley
I	cup red wine

SAUCE

I	small shallot, minced
1/2	cup low-sodium chicken broth
1/2	cup low-sodium beef broth
3	tablespoons cold unsalted butter, cut into 3 pieces
1/2	teaspoon minced fresh thyme leaves
	Salt and ground black pepper

1. FOR THE WINE REDUCTION: Heat the carrot, shallot, mushrooms, bay leaf, parsley, and wine in a nonreactive 12-inch skillet over low heat; cook, without simmering (the liquid should be steaming but not bubbling), until the mixture reduces to 1 cup, 15 to 20 minutes. Strain through a fine-mesh strainer and return to a clean skillet. Continue to cook over low heat, without simmering, until the liquid is reduced to 2 tablespoons, 15 to 20 minutes longer. Transfer the wine reduction to a small bowl.

2. FOR THE SAUCE: To the same skillet used to cook the steaks (do not clean the skillet or discard the accumulated fat unless there's more than 1 tablespoon in the pan), add the shallot and cook over medium-low heat until softened, about 1 minute. Turn the heat to high and add the chicken and beef broths. Bring to a boil, scraping up the browned bits on the pan bottom with a wooden spoon until the liquid is reduced to 2 tablespoons, about 6 minutes. Turn the heat to medium-low and whisk in the reserved wine reduction and any accumulated juices shed by the steaks. Whisk in the butter, one piece at a time, until melted and the sauce is thickened and glossy; add the thyme and season with salt and pepper to taste. Spoon the sauce over the steaks and serve immediately.

Madeira Pan Sauce with Mustard and Anchovies

MAKES ENOUGH FOR 4 STEAKS

This sauce was inspired by one served in a Paris bistro, where the menu includes steak frites *and nothing else. If you do not have Madeira on hand, dry sherry makes a fine substitute. We found no benefit to reducing Madeira slowly, so this recipe comes together much more quickly than the Classic Red Wine Pan Sauce (see preceding recipe).*

I	medium shallot, minced
I	cup Madeira
2	anchovy fillets, minced to a paste (about I teaspoon)
I	tablespoon minced fresh parsley leaves
I	tablespoon minced fresh thyme leaves
I	tablespoon Dijon mustard
I	tablespoon juice from I lemon
3	tablespoons cold unsalted butter, cut into 3 pieces
	Salt and ground black pepper

To the same skillet used to cook the steaks (do not clean the skillet or discard the accumulated fat unless there's more than 1 tablespoon in the pan), add the shallot and cook over medium-low heat until softened, about 1 minute. Add the Madeira; increase the heat to high and scrape the pan bottom with a wooden spoon to loosen the browned bits. Simmer until the liquid is reduced to about 1/3 cup, 6 to 8 minutes. Add any accumulated juices shed by the steaks and reduce the liquid 1 minute longer. Whisk in the anchovies, parsley, thyme, mustard, lemon juice, and butter, one piece at a time, until the butter has melted and the sauce is slightly thickened; season with salt and pepper to taste. Spoon the sauce over the steaks and serve immediately.

Shallot-Butter Pan Sauce

MAKES ENOUGH FOR 4 STEAKS

This sauce requires very little time or effort to prepare.

2	medium shallots, minced (about 1/3 cup)
4	tablespoons (1/2 stick) cold unsalted butter, cut into 4 pieces

1   teaspoon juice from 1 lemon
1   teaspoon minced fresh parsley leaves
     Salt and ground black pepper

To the same skillet used to cook the steaks (do not clean the skillet or discard the accumulated fat unless there's more than 1 tablespoon in the pan), add the shallots and cook over medium-low heat until softened, about 1 minute. Stir in the butter, one piece at a time, scraping up the browned bits on the pan bottom with a wooden spoon. When the butter is just melted, stir in the lemon juice and parsley; season with salt and pepper to taste. Spoon the sauce over the steaks and serve immediately.

Pan-Seared Filets Mignons

WHEN IT COMES TO STEAK, AMERICANS PRIZE tenderness above all—and filet mignon is the most tender steak there is. It is also expensive, and both factors may drive its perennial popularity as a grand, splashy, celebratory restaurant meal. You've probably noticed that in a restaurant, filet mignon (also known as tenderloin steak or simply as filet) is usually served rare, with a deeply seared crust, and adorned with a rich, luxurious pan sauce or flavored butter.

Well, there is no reason to limit the fun to restaurants. Filets are available in any supermarket with a meat case, and they are not difficult to cook. We wanted to replicate the best restaurant filets at home, which meant developing a deeply browned, rich crust on both sides of each steak without overcooking the interior or scorching the drippings in the pan, which would go on to serve as the basis for a luscious sauce. To that end, we investigated the fine points of both the steaks themselves and the cooking process. Is it worth paying top dollar for superthick steaks, or would supermarket filets of any size do? And what about the best cooking method, temperature, and pan?

Filets are thick (usually 1¼ to 2 inches), boneless steaks cut from the slender, supertender, ultralean tenderloin muscle, which rests under the animal's spine. The muscle remains tender because the animal doesn't use it to move about, and it is both lean and mildly flavored because it has little marbling (ribbons of intramuscular fat that melt during cooking to provide flavor and juiciness).

We shopped for filets at six local supermarkets and were not satisfied with the butchering job from a single one. The steaks were usually cut unevenly, with one end noticeably thicker than the other. Beyond that, different steaks in the same package were different sizes and weights. This was far from ideal for expensive, premium steaks. Consistency of size and thickness was important for even cooking within each steak, as well as from steak to steak, in the pan. With that in mind, we purchased a small, roughly 2-pound section of the tenderloin, called a tenderloin roast, and cut our own steaks from it. The process was easy, taking less than two minutes, and our hand-cut filets were uniform. Tenderloin roasts were available wherever we shopped, so if you can get them, too, we recommend this practice. Alternatively, ask the butcher to cut the steaks for you.

To determine the optimal thickness for filets, we cooked steaks cut 1 and 2 inches thick and at ¼-inch intervals in between. Tasters preferred the 1½-inch cut, which made for a generous (but not over-the-top) portion.

Grilling is a good option for filets, but because we also wanted to make a pan sauce, we decided to cook our filets in a pan. The recipes we looked at suggested a couple of alternatives, including broiling, high-roasting (oven-roasting at high heat), and pan-searing (stovetop cooking over high heat), all of which we tried. Pan-searing was our approach of choice because it developed the deep brown, caramelized crust critical to the flavor of both the meat and the sauce. Right off the bat, we confirmed our suspicion that filets are best cooked rare to medium-rare. In our opinion, cooking them to medium begins to compromise their tenderness, which is, after all, their raison d'être.

Our next tests involved searing well-dried filets in a dry pan and in a pan filmed with oil. (Drying the steaks thoroughly with paper towels aids development of a crust.) Not surprisingly for such lean meat, the oil was necessary to produce a deep, dark, satisfying crust, and we found that rubbing the oil right into the steaks reduced the splattering a little.

In our tests of different heat levels, we found that a crust formed over a consistently high flame was better developed than one formed over a medium-high flame. But this approach also created a problem. Over such high heat, the fond (the browned bits left in the pan after the steaks were cooked) was often scorched by the time the meat reached medium-rare, giving the sauce a bitter flavor. We tried out a couple of ideas to remedy the problem.

First, we switched from the 12-inch skillet we'd

INGREDIENTS: Red Wines for Cooking

When a recipe calls for red wine, the tendency is to grab whatever is inexpensive, close at hand, or already open on the counter. But as with any ingredient, the type of wine you cook with can make a big difference. The wrong wine can turn a good sauce bad. Yet because wines range enormously in flavor, body, and astringency, choosing a good one for the kitchen can be a shot in the dark.

What defines a good red cooking wine? It is appropriate for a wide range of recipes, easy to find at the local store, and consistent through the years. To help determine which red wines are good cookers, we set up a series of three cooking tests—a quick tomato sauce, a long-cooked beef stew, and a pan sauce for steak—through which we could test numerous bottles.

Organizing the overwhelming body of red wine into manageable groups, we assigned four categories based on flavor, body, and style: light/fruity, smooth/mellow, hearty/robust, and nondescript jug wine. Ironically, the only type of wine not represented is the "cooking wine" found on most supermarket shelves. In the past, we found that these low-alcohol concoctions have no flavor, a high-pitched acidity, and an enormous amount of salt, which renders them both undrinkable and a very poor choice for cooking.

We began by cooking with a representative from each category: a light/fruity Beaujolais, a smooth/mellow Merlot, a hearty/robust Cabernet Sauvignon, and a jug of Paul Masson Mountain Burgundy. The results were drastically different. The Beaujolais made refreshingly fruity but wimpy sauces, while the Merlot made for balanced sauces with an overcooked, jam-like flavor. The Cabernet Sauvignon produced an astringent, woody bite that bullied other ingredients out of the way, and the Paul Masson made sweet, simple sauces that neither offended nor impressed anyone.

Although none of the four groups "won" this first round of testing, what emerged were some important attributes of a good cooking wine and some characteristics to be wary of. The light wine made weak sauces, and the hearty wine made sauces that were too muscular. Oak flavors (from barrel aging) did not soften as they cooked but wound up tasting bitter and harsh. Fruity characteristics, on the other hand, mingled well with the other sauce ingredients and complemented their flavors.

Narrowing our focus to smooth, fruity, medium-bodied wines with little oak influence, we put four more types of wine through the trio of recipes: a Chianti, a Zinfandel, a Pinot Noir, and a Côtes du Rhône. The Chianti tasted great in the tomato sauce but made an astringent pan sauce and cardboard-tasting stew. The Zinfandel tasted overcooked and jammy in the tomato sauce and turned the pan sauce bitter. While both the Côtes du Rhône and Pinot Noir turned in impressive results across the board, the Côtes du Rhône was stellar. When compared with the sauces made with the Pinot Noir (a wine made from just one type of grape), the Côtes du Rhône (a blend of grapes) had a fuller, more even-keeled flavor. The varietals within the blend compensated for the others' shortcomings. The resulting sauces were potent but well-rounded. Besides Côtes du Rhône, there are many fruity, medium-bodied, blended wines, including wines from the greater Rhône Valley, Languedoc (near the Mediterranean), Australia, and the United States.

We found a strong correlation between price and quality when it comes to red wine. Tests demonstrated that a $5 bottle cooked much differently than bottles costing $10, $20, or $30. As a wine cooks and reduces, it becomes a more intensely flavored version of itself, and defining characteristics become unbearably obvious. The sweet, bland $5 wines cooked down to a candy-like sauce, while the $10, $20, and $30 bottles were increasingly smooth, with multiple layers of flavor. Although the higher-end wines tasted slightly more balanced and refined, none of the tasters thought the flavor difference between the $10 and $20 or $30 bottles was worth the extra money. What's more, limiting the price to around $10 does not restrict your options when shopping. We found plenty of good blends from California, Australia, and France.

Pan Sauces 101

THE SETUP

Because pan sauces cook quickly, before you begin to cook it is essential to complete your mise en place—that is, have all necessary ingredients and utensils collected and ready to use.

Just-seared meat

After searing the meat, transfer it to a plate and tent it loosely with foil while making the sauce. A loose seal will keep any crust that has formed from turning soggy.

Small bowl

Have ready a small empty bowl or container to catch excess fat that might have to be poured off before you begin the sauce.

Aromatics

Aromatics include garlic and onions, but are most often shallots—their flavor is mild, sweet, and complex. If "minced" is specified, make sure they are fine and even; this will cause them to release maximum flavor, and their texture will be less obtrusive in the finished sauce.

Liquids

Leave liquid ingredients (such as wine, broth, and juices) in a measuring cup. Once emptied, keep the measuring cup close at hand; the reduced liquid can be poured back into the measuring cup toward the end of simmering to assess its final volume and to gauge if it is adequately reduced.

Wooden utensil

A wooden utensil works best to scrape up the fond while deglazing because it is rigid (unlike a rubber spatula) and does not screech (like metal on metal). A wooden spatula is ideal because it can cover more of the surface area of the pan than the rounded tip of a spoon.

Herbs and flavorings

Herbs are sometimes used in sprig form, to be removed from the sauce before serving. Delicate herbs such as parsley and tarragon are usually chopped and added to the sauce at the end so that they do not discolor. Other flavorings such as mustard, lemon juice, capers, and chopped olives are often added at the end for maximum flavor impact.

Whisk

For maximum efficiency and easy maneuverability, use a medium-size whisk with flexible wires that can get into the rounded sides of the skillet.

Butter

Cut the butter into tablespoon-size chunks so that it will melt quickly into the sauce. Cold butter is easier to incorporate into a sauce than softened butter, and It makes a sturdier emulsion that is more resistant to separation. Butter can be omitted, but the sauce will be thinner, with little silkiness.

Salt and pepper

Tasting for and correcting seasoning is the last step before serving. Keep salt in a ramekin so that it is easy to measure out in small amounts.

THE EXECUTION
Here's how to make a pan sauce step by step.

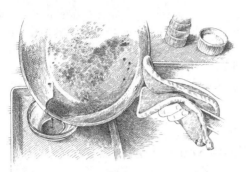

1. Discard excess fat
After removing the seared or sautéed items from the skillet, the first step is to discard most of the fat in the skillet, leaving just enough (several teaspoons) to cook the aromatics. With most steaks, this step is not necessary; with fatty chops, it probably is.

2. Sauté aromatics
Add the aromatics to the skillet and cook them until they soften slightly, usually no more than a couple of minutes, adjusting the heat, if necessary. Be sure not to let the fond scorch, or the finished sauce will taste burnt and bitter.

3. Deglaze
Add the liquid to the skillet—it will sizzle and steam on contact—and scrape up the fond on the bottom of the skillet.

4. Reduce
The most accurate way to check the volume of the reduced liquid is to return it to the measuring cup. Some recipes ask you to reduce the liquid to an exact amount (say, ½ cup). Others recommend reducing the liquid by one half or two thirds.

5. Return juices to skillet
As the meat rests, it will likely release juices; add these juices back to the skillet. If the juices should thin the sauce, allow it to simmer an additional minute or two to restore the proper consistency.

6. Whisk in butter
Whisk in the cold butter, one piece at a time. Grab hold of the butter with the whisk and swirl it around in the skillet until it is melted and incorporated into the sauce. Taste for seasoning before serving.

been using (for four steaks) to a smaller 10-inch model. The decreased surface area between the steaks helped protect the fond. (A heavy-bottomed or cast-iron skillet is essential here; the All-Clad 10-inch skillets we use in the test kitchen weigh about 2½ pounds. Smaller or lighter pans, we found, overheat too easily.) Second, we revisited the high-roasting method, combining it with our searing method by finishing the seared steaks on a preheated rimmed baking sheet in a hot oven. This approach protected the fond from the direct heat of the oven and gave us a head start on the pan sauce while the steaks finished cooking.

Throughout testing, the oven time needed to achieve a given degree of doneness varied continually, as did our thermometer readings. While internal temperature guidelines for varying stages of doneness certainly do exist, it can be difficult to achieve an accurate reading in such a small piece of meat. The reading can be way off depending on where the thermometer probe hits, and it's surprisingly easy to miss dead center when you're working fast and juggling tongs and a hot steak in one hand and a thermometer in the other. In some cases, we had readings as low as 117 degrees and as high as 140 degrees in the same steak. The reading all depended on the position of the probe.

DEALING WITH MISSHAPEN FILETS

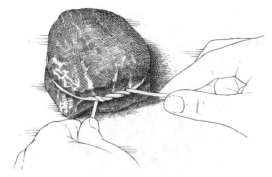

To correct for unevenly or oddly cut filets, tie a 12-inch piece of kitchen twine around each steak. Snip off the excess twine at the knot to make sure it does not ignite on the grill. Adjust the shape of the tied filet by gently rolling or patting it with your hand until it is more uniform in appearance and thickness.

What's a cook to do? Just make a small nick in the steak with the tip of a paring knife and look inside. Be sure to remove the steaks from the heat just before they are done to your liking. They will continue to cook a little off the heat, which should give them a perfect finish. This method never failed to produce steaks cooked just the way we like them.

Pan-Seared Filets Mignons
SERVES 4

If the filets are misshapen or unevenly cut, as supermarket steaks sometimes are, follow the illustration below to tie each one before cooking. Determining when the meat is cooked to your liking is key to a good steak, so pay close attention to the visual cues in step 3. We find that mild filets benefit from potent sauces, including any of the pan sauces on pages 390–392. If you choose to serve the steaks with a pan sauce, have all the sauce ingredients ready before searing the steaks. Begin the sauce while the steaks are in the oven. To cook six steaks instead of four, switch to a 12-inch pan and use 6 teaspoons of olive oil.

- 4   center-cut filets mignons, 1½ inches thick (7 to 8 ounces each), patted dry with paper towels
- 4   teaspoons olive oil
      Salt and ground black pepper

1. Adjust an oven rack to the lower-middle position, place a rimmed baking sheet on the oven rack, and heat the oven to 450 degrees. When the oven reaches 450 degrees, heat a heavy-bottomed 10-inch skillet (not nonstick) over high heat on the stovetop until very hot.

2. Meanwhile, rub each side of the steaks with ½ teaspoon oil and sprinkle generously with salt and pepper to taste. Place the steaks in the skillet and cook, without moving the steaks, until well browned and a nice crust has formed, about 3 minutes. Turn the steaks with tongs and cook until well browned and a nice crust has formed on the second side, about 3 minutes longer. Remove the pan from the heat; using tongs, transfer each steak to the heated baking sheet in the oven.

3. Roast 2 to 4 minutes for very rare (the center

of the steaks will appear cherry red and feel very soft and loose when cut into with the tip of a paring knife), 4 to 6 minutes for rare (the centers will appear red and soft), 6 to 8 minutes for medium-rare (the centers will appear pink and feel firm but juicy), or 8 to 10 minutes for medium (the centers will appear light pink and feel firm and compact). (After transferring the steaks to the oven, prepare a pan sauce in the empty skillet, if desired.) Transfer the steaks to a large plate, tent loosely with foil, and let rest for about 5 minutes before serving.

➤ VARIATION

Bacon-Wrapped Filets Mignons

Wrap 1 slice bacon around the circumference of each filet, overlapping the ends and securing them to the meat with a toothpick. Follow the recipe for Pan-Seared Filets Mignons, holding the filets two or three at a time on their sides with tongs in the skillet to crisp the bacon slightly all the way around the filets before transferring them to the oven.

STEAK AU POIVRE

THERE'S NOTHING COMPLICATED ABOUT STEAK au poivre. When well executed, the slightly sweet, smooth sauce has more than a hint of shallot and brandy, the steak is well browned on the outside and cherry red on the interior, and the crust of cracked peppercorns provides a pungent, slow burn, adding fire and depth to an otherwise simple steak.

That's the good news. A third-rate steak au poivre has peppercorns that fall off the steak only to reveal underbrowned meat. What's more, the peppercorn coat prevents the steak from forming drippings in the skillet that are the foundation of a rich sauce, and few home cooks have beef or veal stock on hand to give the sauce the substance and backbone it needs. Because most steak au poivre recipes make no attempt to solve these problems, the home cook is left aghast at the end result: wan, tasteless steaks covered by an insipid sauce made in a blackened skillet that is headed straight for the trash.

Our first few tests were useful only in determining the best cut of steak for au poivre. Filets were tender but too mild-flavored. Rib eyes, always a favorite in the test kitchen, have abundant fat pockets and pronounced veins of gristle that separate two differently textured muscles. A peppercorn crust obscures these imperfections, requiring scrutiny and maneuvering on the part of the diner to eat around these parts. Strip steaks, however, have external lines of gristle that are easily trimmed before cooking, and their neat, tight, even grain makes them particularly suited to steak au poivre.

We quickly determined peppercorn type. Among black, white, and a four-peppercorn blend of green, pink, black, and white, plain old black was the favorite in the test kitchen. Tasters extolled it for its sharp bite, rich and intense flavor, and elusive smokiness.

The steaks we cooked early on were crusted with a scant teaspoon of peppercorns on each side. Loose pepper fell off the steaks and scorched pitifully in the skillet. The pepper that did stick shielded the surface of the steaks, preventing browning and thereby the formation of a fond (the sticky browned bits left in a pan after sautéing) on which to build the sauce. In addition, most tasters thought we were far too liberal in our peppercorn allotment—the heat was incendiary and vicious. Our first thought was to cut back on the peppercorns, but then a light bulb went on. What if the steaks were coated on one side only? The unpeppered side would brown nicely, producing

PROPERLY GROUND PEPPERCORNS

For steak au poivre, grind or crush whole peppercorns (left) to a very coarse texture (right). If your pepper mill cannot handle this task, see the alternative methods on page 398. In any case, do not use finely ground pepper in this recipe.

more fond for the sauce, and there would be no peppercorns on that side to singe.

Typically, steaks cook over intensely high heat. But for this new approach, we placed the skillet over medium heat until it was hot and, after laying the steaks in the skillet—unpeppered-side down—turned up the heat to medium-high. This technique gave the steaks six minutes to brown on the first side and form a fond. Then the steaks were flipped onto their peppered side and given only three to five minutes (depending on desired doneness) to complete their cooking, this time without scorching the pepper. This method worked like a charm.

The steak was done, so we turned our attention to the sauce. All steak au poivre sauces contain beef or veal stock and brandy. Most sauces contain cream, though some achieve a particular richness from butter only. The stock was the first problem we needed to address. Most home cooks have only canned chicken and beef broth on hand, and the latter has long been considered either artificial-tasting or weakly flavored in the test kitchen.

CRUSHING PEPPERCORNS

If your pepper mill can't produce coarsely crushed peppercorns, you have two alternatives.

A. Use the bottom of a heavy pan and a rocking motion to crush peppercorns.

B. Spread the peppercorns in an even layer in a zipper-lock plastic bag and whack them with a rolling pin or meat pounder.

Using chicken broth alone, we cooked down the liquid to concentrate its flavor, but the sauce still lacked meatiness and depth. We tried to doctor it with dried porcini mushrooms, but the mushroom flavor was too distinct and would have detracted from the beefy flavor of the steak it should be complementing. We tried commercial veal demi-glace (superconcentrated veal stock), but the tomato paste–laden demi-glace looked and tasted unnatural. Finally, we tried low-sodium beef broth straight from the can and reduced it. This sauce was beefier, more substantial, and deeper in color—but it was plagued by the tinny flavor characteristic of canned broth.

On the verge of giving up, we finally hit upon a solution. We reduced almost equal amounts of chicken and beef broths with sautéed shallots to about one quarter of their original volume. Finally— a terrific, full-flavored sauce. But the long simmering time threw a wrench in the works. A typical pan sauce for steak is made by deglazing the skillet in which the steaks were cooked. This usually takes no longer than a few minutes and can be accomplished while the steaks rest. The sauce took well over 10 minutes to make, much longer than you'd want the meat to rest. The solution was straightforward: Reduce the broth mixture before cooking the steaks, then use the resulting liquid to deglaze the skillet.

Introducing brandy to the sauce was no trivial matter. We tried reducing it with the broth mixture to concentrate its flavor. This worked, but because we were also concentrating the sugar in the brandy, the resulting sauce tasted as sweet as butterscotch pudding, with no spirited bite. If we held off adding the brandy until much later in the sauce-making process, it tasted hot and raw. The time to add it was when the reduced broth mixture went into the skillet to deglaze it; the mixture simmers for about five minutes, just long enough for the brandy to reduce a bit, shake its alcoholic harshness, and meld with the broth.

Tasters voted to enrich the sauce with both cream and butter, not just butter alone. Cream made the sauce luxurious and sophisticated and gave its texture substance. Only ¼ cup was needed, and, when added at the same time as the brandy, the cream had a chance to cook down and lend body to the sauce. To finish, butter whisked in at the end brought silkiness, a bit of raw brandy gave a nice bite and fresh brandy flavor, and a teaspoon of lemon juice or champagne vinegar brightened things up.

Steak au Poivre with Brandied Cream Sauce

SERVES 4

To save time, crush the peppercorns and trim the steaks while the broth mixture simmers. Many pepper mills do not have a sufficiently coarse setting. In that case, crush the peppercorns with a sauté pan or rolling pin (see the illustrations on page 398). Finely ground pepper is not a substitute for the crushed peppercorns in this recipe.

SAUCE

4	tablespoons ($^1/_2$ stick) unsalted butter, cut into 4 pieces
I	medium shallot, minced
I	cup low-sodium beef broth
$^3/_4$	cup low-sodium chicken broth
$^1/_4$	cup heavy cream
$^1/_4$	cup plus I tablespoon brandy
I	teaspoon juice from I lemon or I teaspoon champagne vinegar
	Salt

STEAKS

4	strip steaks, $^3/_4$ to I inch thick and no larger than 3 inches at the widest points (8 to 10 ounces each), trimmed of exterior gristle
	Salt
I	tablespoon black peppercorns, crushed

1. FOR THE SAUCE: Heat 1 tablespoon of the butter in a heavy-bottomed 12-inch skillet over medium heat. When the foaming subsides, add the shallot and cook, stirring occasionally, until softened, about 2 minutes. Add the beef and chicken broths, increase the heat to high, and boil until reduced to about ½ cup, about 8 minutes. Set the reduced broth mixture aside. Rinse and wipe out the skillet.

2. FOR THE STEAKS: Meanwhile, sprinkle both sides of the steaks with salt; rub one side of each steak with 1 teaspoon crushed peppercorns and,

using your fingers, press the peppercorns into the steaks to make them adhere.

3. Place the clean skillet over medium heat until hot. Lay the steaks unpeppered-side down in the hot skillet, increase the heat to medium-high, firmly press down on the steaks with the bottom of a cake pan (see the illustration below), and cook the steaks without moving them until well browned, about 6 minutes. Using tongs, flip the steaks, firmly press down on them with the bottom of the cake pan, and cook on the peppered side about 3 minutes longer for rare, about 4 minutes longer for medium-rare, or about 5 minutes longer for medium. Transfer the steaks to a large plate and tent loosely with foil.

4. TO FINISH THE SAUCE: Pour the reduced broth, cream, and ¼ cup brandy into the now-empty skillet; increase the heat to high and bring to a boil, scraping the pan bottom with a wooden spoon to loosen the browned bits. Simmer until deep golden brown and thick enough to heavily coat the back of a metal tablespoon or soup spoon, about 5 minutes. Off the heat, whisk in the remaining 3 tablespoons butter, one piece at a time, the remaining 1 tablespoon brandy, the lemon juice, and any accumulated meat juices. Adjust the seasonings with salt.

5. Set the steaks on individual dinner plates, spoon an equal portion of the sauce over each steak, and serve immediately.

ADHERING THE PEPPER TO THE STEAKS

Pressing down on the steaks with a cake pan or flat pot lid once the steaks have been placed in the hot skillet promotes browning and ensures that the peppercorns adhere.

Chicken-Fried Steak

ALTHOUGH THIS TRUCK-STOP FAVORITE OFTEN gets a bad rap, chicken-fried steak can be delicious when cooked just right. When cooked wrong, the dry, rubbery steaks snap back with each bite and are coated in a damp, pale breading and topped with a bland, pasty white sauce. When cooked well, however, thin cutlets of beef are breaded and fried until crisp and golden brown. The creamy gravy that accompanies the steaks is well seasoned and not too thick.

The first question we encountered on the road to good chicken-fried steak was what type of steak to use. By design, chicken-fried steak is a technique used with only the cheapest of cuts. No one would use strip steaks or filets mignons in this recipe, but steaks from the round, chuck, and sirloin are all contenders. We tested cube, Swiss, top-round, bottom-round, eye-round, chuck, and top-sirloin steaks and came up with one winner.

The cube steak was our favorite. This steak is lean yet tender; most of the other cuts tested were either fatty or difficult to chew.

Cube steak is usually cut from the round and tenderized (cubed) by the butcher, who uses a special machine to give the steak its unique, bumpy texture. We found that this lean, tender steak required little trimming and was easy to pound out to a thin cutlet, about ⅓ inch thick. Regular top-, bottom-, and eye-round steaks, on the other hand, were thick and tough, requiring lots of muscle to pound out and chew. Swiss and chuck steaks, which come from the shoulder, were slightly less tough but still chewy and resilient. Top sirloin tasted great and had a nice texture, but the meat was laced with wide strips of gristle. Trimming the gristle turned this steak into small, awkwardly sized pieces, making for unusual portions and cooking times.

What really makes chicken-fried steak great is

EQUIPMENT: Steak Knives

If you've ever shopped for steak knives, you might have noticed that sets of four can range in price from as little as $40 to as much as $150. We wondered if price really makes a difference when it comes to the performance of these knives, so we bought five sets of knives and cooked up some steaks to find out.

Our favorites were pricey. A set of four Henckels Four Star Steak Knives or Wüsthof-Trident Classic Steak Knives fetches between $140 and $150. Manufactured in the same manner as the other kitchen knives in their high-quality lines, these knives justly demand a high price. Fresh from their boxes, they had razor-sharp blades that sliced effortlessly through crusts and glided through meat, and their handles made them comfortable to use (Henckels got top honors here). But if you are lax in the upkeep of your knives, beware—these knives require regular honing and sharpening to be kept in tiptop shape.

Right behind these big shots were Chicago Cutlery Steak Knives, Walnut Tradition. At $40 for a set of four, it's easy to overlook their slightly less comfortable handles and somewhat flimsier feel but rank them right in with the best. These knives also were sharp, and the gently curved angle of the blades made for simple and smooth slicing. And they look like they belong in a butcher shop—or in the fist of a serious steak eater. Don't forget to steel these knives as well to keep them sharp.

Our least favorite knife sets contained knives with serrated blades. Henckels Gourmet Steak Knives, $40 for a set of four, and Dexter Russell Steakhouse Steak Knives, $30 for a set of four, required a good deal of sawing to cut through a steak and produced rather ragged pieces (not that your taste buds care). The cheaper set of Henckels steak knives felt insubstantial in their construction, whereas the Dexter Russell knives were of mammoth proportions. Neither requires steeling for upkeep.

THE BEST STEAK KNIVES

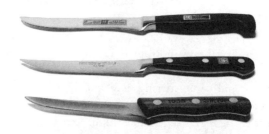

The Henckels Four Star Steak Knives (top) were the top choice of testers, followed closely by the Wüsthof-Trident Classic Steak Knives (middle). At a fraction of the cost, the Chicago Cutlery Steak Knives, Walnut Tradition (bottom), are a great value with good (if not great) performance in our kitchen tests.

the coating and subsequent frying. But what kind of coating is best? To find out, we tested straight flour against various contenders, including cornflakes, Melba toast, cornmeal, matzo crumbs, ground saltines, and panko (Japanese bread crumbs). Straight flour was light and clung well to the steak but was simply too delicate for the toothsome meat and cream gravy. Cornflakes and Melba toast both burned and became tough, while the grittiness of cornmeal was simply out of place. Matzo, saltines, and panko all tasted great but quickly grew soggy under the rich cream gravy.

We figured our single-breading technique might to be blame and decided to try double (or bound) breading. With single breading, meat is dipped into egg and then into flour, while double breading starts off with an initial dip in flour, then into egg, and again into flour (or into a coating such as those we tried with the steak). In side-by-side tests, we were surprised to discover that single breading was actually messier than double. When initially dipped in flour, the meat becomes dry and talcum-smooth, allowing the egg to cling evenly to the surface. The double breading also offered a more substantial base coat on the meat that didn't become overly thick or tough. Seasoned flour and a double-breading technique yielded a much improved crust.

Although this double breading was far superior to any other breading so far, we were still left wanting a heartier and crunchier crust. We wondered if we could bolster the egg wash with some buttermilk, baking soda, and baking powder, something that we knew worked well with fried chicken. Sure enough, these ingredients turned the egg wash into a thick, foamy concoction. This created a wet yet airy layer into which both layers of flour were able to stick and hydrate. This wet-looking, skin-like coating fried up to an impressive, dark mahogany color with a resilient texture that didn't weaken under the gravy. Because the coating is such a big part of the dish, we found it necessary to season it heavily using salt, black pepper, and cayenne.

After frying a few batches of these steaks, we found the flavor of peanut oil preferable to that of vegetable oil or even shortening. Because the steaks are thin, they fry evenly in just one inch of oil. To keep splattering to a minimum, we used a deep Dutch oven. We also noted that the steaks fried to a dark, beautiful brown without tasting too greasy when the oil was heated initially to 375 degrees. Although the thick breading offers substantial protection from the hot oil, the steaks usually cook through completely within the time it takes for the crust to brown, about 2½ minutes per side.

Equally important to the crust is the cream gravy made from the fried drippings. Not wanting to waste any time while the fried steaks were kept warm in the oven, we found it easy to strain the small amount of hot oil used to fry the steaks right away. Adding the strained bits of deep-fried crumbs back to the Dutch oven, we were ready to make gravy. Most recipes simmer the drippings with some milk and thicken it with flour. To avoid making a floury-tasting sauce, we decided to cook the flour in the fat (that is, make a roux) and then add the milk, along with a splash of chicken broth. We found this technique quick and easy, and it produced an authentic-tasting sauce.

We tested recipes using cream, half-and-half, and evaporated milk, but tasters preferred the fresh, clean flavor and lighter texture of whole milk. Onions and cayenne are traditional seasonings for the gravy, but tasters also liked small additions of thyme and garlic (neither of which is authentic). Topped with the light, well-seasoned gravy, this chicken-fried steak is the best any trucker has ever tasted.

Chicken-Fried Steak

SERVES 6

Initially heating the oil to 375 degrees is key to the success of this recipe. An instant-read thermometer with a high upper range is perfect for checking the temperature; a clip-on candy/deep-fry thermometer will also work. If your Dutch oven measures 11 inches across (as ours does), you will need to fry the steaks in two batches.

STEAK

3 cups unbleached all-purpose flour
Salt and ground black pepper

⅛ teaspoon cayenne pepper

1   large egg
1   teaspoon baking powder
1/2 teaspoon baking soda
1   cup buttermilk
6   cube steaks (about 5 ounces each), pounded
    to 1/3-inch thickness
4–5 cups peanut oil

CREAM GRAVY
1   medium onion, minced
1/8 teaspoon dried thyme
2   medium garlic cloves, minced or pressed
    through a garlic press
3   tablespoons unbleached all-purpose flour
1/2 cup low-sodium chicken broth
2   cups whole milk
3/4 teaspoon salt
1/4 teaspoon ground black pepper
    Pinch cayenne pepper

1. FOR THE STEAKS: Measure the flour, 5 teaspoons salt, 1 teaspoon pepper, and the cayenne into a large, shallow dish. In a second large, shallow dish, beat the egg, baking powder, and baking soda; stir in the buttermilk (the mixture will bubble and foam).

2. Set a wire rack over a rimmed baking sheet. Pat the steaks dry with paper towels and sprinkle each side with salt and pepper to taste. Drop the steaks into the seasoned flour and shake the dish to coat. Shake the excess flour from each steak, then, using tongs, dip the steaks into the egg mixture, turning to coat well and allowing the excess to drip off. Coat the steaks with flour again, shake off the excess, and place them on the wire rack.

3. Adjust an oven rack to the middle position, set a second wire rack over a second rimmed baking sheet, and place on the oven rack; heat the oven to 200 degrees. Line a large plate with a double layer of paper towels. Meanwhile, heat 1 inch oil in a large (11-inch-diameter) Dutch oven over medium-high heat to 375 degrees. Place three steaks in the oil and fry, turning once, until deep golden brown on each side, about 5 minutes (oil temperature will drop to around 335 degrees). Transfer the steaks to the paper towel–lined plate to drain, then transfer them to the wire rack in the oven. Bring the oil back to 375 degrees and repeat

the cooking and draining process (use fresh paper towels) with the three remaining steaks.

4. FOR THE GRAVY: Carefully pour the hot oil through a fine-mesh strainer into a clean pot. Return the browned bits from the strainer along with 2 tablespoons of the frying oil back to the Dutch oven. Turn the heat to medium, add the onion and thyme, and cook until the onion has softened and begins to brown, 4 to 5 minutes. Add the garlic and cook until aromatic, about 30 seconds. Add the flour and stir until well combined, about 1 minute. Whisk in the broth, scraping any browned bits off the bottom of the pan. Whisk in the milk, salt, pepper, and cayenne; bring to a simmer over medium-high heat. Cook until thickened (the gravy should have a loose consistency—it will thicken as it cools slightly), about 5 minutes.

5. Transfer the chicken-fried steaks to individual plates. Spoon a generous amount of the gravy over each steak. Serve immediately, passing any remaining gravy in a bowl.

PRIME RIB

A PRIME RIB IS A LITTLE LIKE A TURKEY: YOU probably cook only one a year, usually for an important occasion such as Christmas. Although you know there are alternative cooking methods that might deliver a better roast, they're too risky. You don't want to be remembered as the cook who carved slices of almost-raw standing rib or delayed dinner for hours waiting for the roast to finish cooking. Rather than chance it, you stick with the standard 350 degrees for X minutes per pound. A roast cooked this way, you decide, will at least not embarrass you.

Other than using general terms like juicy and tender, we weren't quite sure how to define perfect prime rib when we started testing, so we had no preconceived ideas about what techniques or methods would deliver a superior roast. In addition to our normal cookbook research, we decided to interview a few of the thousands of chefs who cook prime rib every day. Between what we found in books and what we learned from these chefs, we came up with a dozen or so fairly different

TYING UP PRIME RIB

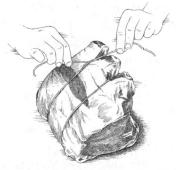

It is imperative to tie prime rib before roasting. If left untied, the outer layer of meat will pull away from the rib-eye muscle and overcook. To prevent this problem, tie the roast at both ends, running the twine parallel to the bone.

methods. Although there were minor issues, such as whether the roast needed to be tied or whether it should be roasted on a rack, one big question needed answering: At what temperature should prime rib be roasted?

We started with oven temperatures. Suggested roasting temperatures ranged from a tepid 250 degrees to a bold 425 degrees. Other recipes recommended an initial high-temperature sear (450 to 500 degrees), then reduced the oven temperature to a more moderate 350 degrees for actual roasting. Wanting to test the full range, we roasted prime ribs at temperatures ranging from 250 to 500 degrees.

All prime ribs roasted at oven temperatures exceeding 300 degrees looked pretty much the same. Each slice of carved beef was well-done around the exterior, medium toward the center, and a beautiful, pink medium-rare at the center. We might have been tempted to report that roasting temperature doesn't much matter if we hadn't tried cooking prime rib at oven temperatures under 300 degrees. The results surprised us, although it certainly wasn't love at first sight.

About halfway through the cooking time of the first roast tested at 250 degrees, we wrote in our notes, "Though the meat looks virtually raw, the internal temperature registers 110 degrees, and very little of its fat has rendered." But we changed our minds quickly as soon as we carved the first slice. This roast was as beautiful on the inside as it

was anemic on the outside. Unlike the roasts that cooked at higher temperatures, this one was rosy pink from the surface to the center—the juiciest and most tender of all the roasts we had cooked. This was restaurant prime rib at its best.

In addition to being evenly cooked, the prime rib roasted in a 250-degree oven had another thing going for it: Its internal temperature increased only a degree or two during its resting period. (Roasts are allowed to rest when they come out of the oven both to distribute the heat evenly and to allow the juices to reabsorb back into the outer layers of the meat.) A roast cooked to 128 degrees, for example, moved only to 130 degrees after a 45-minute rest.

Not so with the roasts cooked at higher temperatures. Their internal temperatures increased much more dramatically out of the oven. As a matter of fact, we noticed a direct correlation between oven temperature and the increase in the temperature of the roast while resting. Prime ribs roasted at moderate temperatures (325 to 350 degrees) increased, on average, 14 degrees during resting. In other words, if pulled from the oven

CARVING PRIME RIB

1. Using a carving fork to hold the roast in place, cut along the rib bones to sever the meat from the bones.

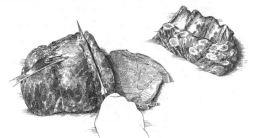

2. Set the roast cut-side down; carve the meat across the grain into thick slices.

at a rare 126-degree internal temperature, these roasts moved up to a solid medium (140 degrees) by the end of the resting period. Meanwhile, the prime rib roasted at 425 degrees increased a whopping 24 degrees (from 119 to 143) during its rest. We considered a smaller increase in postcooking temperature a definite advantage. It let us pull the roast from the oven at the temperature we wanted instead of having to speculate as to how many degrees the temperature would climb during resting.

In addition to its more stable internal temperature, prime rib roasted at 250 degrees lost less weight during cooking than prime rib roasted at higher temperatures. A 6¾-pound roast cooked in a 250-degree oven weighed just over 6¼ pounds when it came out of the oven, a loss of less than half a pound. By contrast, similar roasts cooked in a 325-degree oven lost just more than a pound, while roasts cooked at 350 degrees lost 1½ pounds. The prime rib cooked at 425 degrees lost a shocking 2 pounds. Part of the weight loss is fat, but certainly a good portion is juice. This test confirmed our suspicions that the beef roasted at 250 degrees was indeed juicier than that roasted at higher temperatures.

Because members of the National Cattlemen's

Beef Association would not endorse an oven-roasting temperature below 300 degrees, we decided to check the safety of this low-heat method before getting too sold on it. After conversations with a number of food scientists across the country, we determined that low-temperature roasting is as safe a cooking method as higher-temperature roasting, especially if you brown the roast first, which should kill any bacteria on the exterior. And though the odds of finding bacteria inside a prime rib roast are close to nil, the only way to guarantee a bacteria-free slab of prime rib is to cook it to an internal temperature of 160 degrees, no matter what cooking method is used, low temperature or high. Unfortunately, at 160 degrees, the meat is gray, tough, and unappetizing.

So were we willing to brown the roast first to kill any bacteria on the exterior? Yes; in fact, we thought this step was necessary for other recipes. The only thing that bothered us about the slow-roasted prime rib was its raw-looking, fatty exterior. Searing the meat on top of the stove before low-roasting it gave it a beautiful crusty brown exterior.

As nebulous as the meaning of "perfect prime rib" had been to us at the beginning of our tests, it became crystal clear the moment we carved off that

INGREDIENTS: Two Rib Roasts

A whole rib roast (aka prime rib) consists of ribs 6 through 12. Butchers tend to cut the roast in two. We prefer the cut further back on the cow, which is closest to the loin. This cut is referred to as the first cut, the loin end, or sometimes the small end because the meat and ribs get larger as they move up toward the shoulder. The first cut can include anywhere from two to four ribs. Sometimes we like a large roast for the holidays, and in this case we prefer a roast with four ribs. At other times, a slightly smaller roast, with just three ribs, is fine. When ordering the former, be sure to specify the first four ribs from the loin end—ribs 9 through 12—to receive the first cut. When ordering a three-rib roast, ask for the first three ribs from the loin end—ribs 10 through 12.

Either way, the first cut is more desirable because it contains the large, single rib-eye muscle and is less fatty. The less desirable cut, which is still an excellent roast, is closer to the chuck (or shoulder) end and is sometimes called the second cut. The closer to the chuck, the less tender the roast becomes.

FIRST CUT　　　**SECOND CUT**

first slice of low-roasted prime rib. We immediately recognized it as the beef you get at a great prime rib restaurant. As it turns out, many such restaurants slow-roast their meat. They use special ovens that roast the meat at 250 degrees until it reaches an internal temperature of 120 degrees. At that time, the oven heat is decreased to 140 degrees, causing the meat's internal temperature to increase to 130 degrees and remain there until ready to serve (up to 24 hours later). Unfortunately, few home cooks can use this method since most home oven thermostats do not go below 200 degrees. But by following our recipe, home cooks can very closely approximate the superb prime rib served in the country's best restaurants.

Prime Rib

SERVES 6 TO 8

If you purchase the roast several days ahead of time, you might want to try aging the meat in the refrigerator to improve its flavor and texture. (See page 408 for more information on aging beef.) For information on buying a rib roast, see page 404.

I   (3- or 4-rib) standing rib roast (about 7 pounds), aged up to 4 days (if desired), tied with kitchen twine at both ends, twine running parallel to the bones (see page 403)
    Salt and ground black pepper

1. An hour before cooking, remove the roast from the refrigerator to bring it to room temperature.

2. Adjust an oven rack to the lowest position and heat the oven to 250 degrees. Heat a large, heavy-bottomed roasting pan over two burners set at medium-high. Place the roast in the hot pan and cook on all sides until nicely browned and about ½ cup fat has been rendered, 6 to 8 minutes.

3. Remove the roast from the pan. Set a wire rack in the pan, then set the roast on the rack. Generously season with salt and pepper to taste.

4. Place the roast in the oven and roast until the meat registers 130 degrees (for medium-rare), 3 to 3½ hours. Remove the roast from the oven and tent with foil. Let stand 20 to 30 minutes to allow the juices to redistribute themselves evenly throughout the roast.

5. Remove the twine and set the roast on a cutting board, rib bones at a 90-degree angle to the board. Carve (see the illustrations on page 403) and serve immediately.

ROAST BEEF WITH YORKSHIRE PUDDING

ROAST BEEF WITH YORKSHIRE PUDDING CAN be simple or elaborate. The English tend to make it Sunday afternoon with a cheap cut of beef from the shoulder or round. In America, we use an expensive rib roast and promote it as a holiday recipe. We decided to pursue the latter, assuming that most American cooks would want to save this dish for special occasions.

When we tested a half dozen sample recipes for this dish, however, we were disappointed. Too often the meat was dry, chewy, and unevenly cooked. The accompanying jus was bland, thin, and pale. The recipes for Yorkshire pudding seemed fickle: Sometimes the pudding failed to rise, and its texture was too dense; other times it cooked unevenly. But these tests helped us figure out what we wanted. We envisioned a roast beef with a browned, flavorful exterior complementing an evenly cooked, juicy, tender, and rosy red interior. The ideal jus, made from the beef drippings, would be rich in beef flavor and deep mahogany in color, with plenty of body. As for the perfect Yorkshire pudding, it would be dramatically high and have a crisp and lightly browned outer crust with a tender, moist, and airy interior. Unlike the popover, Yorkshire pudding should be richly flavored with beef fat.

We started with a first-cut rib roast but wondered whether we needed to use a bone-in or boneless roast. A blind taste test revealed the bone-in roast as the unanimous favorite. Tasters said this roast was juicier and had a beefier flavor. In comparison, the boneless roast was chewy and dry. We concluded that the bones must be protecting the nonfatty side of the meat, helping to retain the juices and bringing forth a meatier flavor.

Discussing this discovery with our butcher, he suggested a way to have the best of both worlds—the superior meat from cooking on the bone and the ease of serving a boneless roast. He cut the meat from the bones and tied it back on (most any butcher and many supermarkets will provide this service), and we cooked the whole thing. This was the first important step toward a great roast beef dinner, as we got the flavor we wanted along with quick and easy carving. Just snip the twine after roasting, set the bones aside, and start slicing.

Most roast beef recipes utilize a moderate oven temperature of about 350 degrees. Often the roasting process begins or ends with a blast of high heat—upward of 400 degrees. The intention is to have the high heat brown the outside of the roast and the moderate heat cook the inside. The problem with this standard approach is that the outer layers of meat overcook, while the slices from the middle are unevenly cooked, the center being red and the remainder gray and unappealing. After considerable testing, we found that a boneless roast is like a bone-in prime rib: It benefits from a quick sear on the stovetop to develop the crust and then

EQUIPMENT: Roasting Pans

Though most cooks haul out their roasting pan infrequently, when you do need this large pan, nothing else will do. A roasting pan is a must for prime rib and other roasts.

A roasting pan should promote deep, even browning of food. It should be easy to maneuver in and out of the oven. And it should be able to travel from oven to stovetop, so that you can deglaze the pan and loosen drippings.

Roasting pans can be made from stainless steel, enameled steel, nonstick-coated aluminum, or anodized aluminum, all of which we tested. We decided not to test pans lined with copper, which are prohibitively expensive; cast-iron pans, which when loaded with food are too heavy to lift; and pans made from Pyrex, ceramic, or stoneware, all of which seem better suited to lasagna and casseroles because they can't be used on top of the stove.

We tested eight roasting pans and preferred the materials we like in other cookware—stainless steel and anodized aluminum. These materials are heavy (though not prohibitively so) and produce good browning. Although nonstick coatings made cleanup easier, roasting racks slid around in these pans. For instance, when one test cook tilted a nonstick pan ever so slightly to remove it from the oven, a turkey and rack slid sharply to one side, which threw off her balance and nearly landed the hot turkey in her lap.

Roasting pans generally come in two different styles—upright handles and side handles (see the photos at right). Upright handles tend to be square in shape, while side handles are generally oval loops. We found upright handles to be easier to grip. The problem with side handles is that their position, coupled with the large size of the pan, can cause you to bring your forearms perilously close to the hot oven walls. We tested one pan without handles, which was by far the most difficult to take out of the oven.

We tested pans ranging in length from 16 to 20 inches and in width from 11 to 14 inches. We preferred pans that measured about 16 inches long and 12 to 14 inches across. Larger pans made for an awkward fit in the oven and, because of their large surface area, tended to burn pan drippings more easily.

In terms of weight, heavier pans performed better in all tests, especially on top of the stove. Lightweight pans buckled, and the meat browned quite spottily.

To summarize, heavy-duty pans made from stainless steel or anodized aluminum work best to brown foods, especially if the pan is to be used on top of the stove as well as in the oven, as is the case with our prime rib recipe.

THE BEST ROASTING PANS

The All-Clad Stainless Steel Roti ($200), left, is our favorite roasting pan. The handles on the pan are upright and easy to grasp. More important, this heavy pan conducts heat well and works on both the stovetop and in the oven. The Granite Ware Oval Roaster, right, is the best inexpensive option, priced at just $20. The side handles on this pan are more difficult to grasp than upright handles and seem more likely to cause burns. Also, this lightweight pan does not perform well on the stovetop, often causing foods to burn if the pan is set over high heat. You should sear roasts in a heavy skillet and use the roasting pan only for the oven portion of the cooking process. But given the difference in price, it's worth considering this lightweight option.

a low oven heat of 250 degrees. A roast cooked at 250 degrees will be rosy pink from the surface to the center, juicy, and tender.

A minor obstacle appeared during the searing step when the rendered beef fat melted the twine that held the meat to the bones. We tried again, this time separating the meat from the bones and searing just the fatty top and sides of the meat. We let the meat cool briefly, tied it back onto the bones, and then roasted the meat at 250 degrees. Finally, a perfectly prepared roast beef. The exterior was crusty, browned, and flavorful; the inside juicy, tender, evenly cooked, and brimming with beef flavor.

But still there were problems to contend with. Slow roasting succeeds so well at keeping the juices inside the meat that there were no pan drippings for the jus or rendered beef fat for the Yorkshire pudding. We tried using the fat rendered from the searing on the stovetop, but it was overly seasoned, and the puddings were inedible. Seasoning the meat after searing, which would have produced usable fat, also failed because the low oven temperature did not dissolve the salt into the meat. We now had a perfectly cooked roast beef, but we also had to face the challenges of where to find the flavor for the jus and the fat for the Yorkshire pudding.

Traditionally, a jus is prepared after a roast is cooked. The roasting pan is placed on the stovetop, and some liquid, typically wine, is added to deglaze the pan, a process in which all of the flavorful browned bits get lifted off the pan bottom. Broth is then added to the pan and reduced by simmering to concentrate the flavors and improve the texture. Vegetables and aromatics are often added to the pan prior to roasting to add flavor to a jus, so this is where we began our next batch of tests.

We threw in onions, carrots, celery, thyme, and a bit of water with the roast at the beginning of oven cooking. The vegetables steamed and the jus was terrible. We eliminated the water, but still no browning occurred because of the low oven temperature. (One taster said this jus was like dishwater.) Because browning brings out flavor, we considered using the time that the raw roast rests out of the refrigerator to roast the vegetables at high heat, using the same pan in which we'd cook the beef. This jus was better, but too vegetal-tasting. We tried adding tomatoes and garlic, ingredients that are sometimes added to meat stocks to add richness and base notes. "Where's the beef?" asked one taster, thereby giving us an idea. We tossed in some oxtails (a readily available and inexpensive cut) with the vegetables in the next test. Oxtails are not only loaded with beef flavor but are also very fatty. We had struck gold! Our search for flavor for the jus had also unearthed fat that could be used in the pudding.

PREPARING BONELESS PRIME RIB

1. Position the meat back on the bones exactly from where it was cut. Using 4 individual lengths of twine, tie the meat back onto the bones, running the twine parallel to the bones.

2. Use a metal spatula to push the oxtails and onions to the sides of the pan. Place the roast bone-side down (seared fatty-side up) in the center of the roasting pan.

3. When it comes time to check the temperature of the roast, insert a thermometer through the top of the roast until you reach the center.

It took a few more tests to determine that the jus was actually improved when we used oxtails and onions alone. We had eliminated the carrots and celery because they detracted from the rich beef flavor. The garlic was too strong, and the thyme proved more pleasing if we added it when making the jus on the stovetop. The jury was out on the tomatoes. Some thought they rounded out the flavor, while other tasters thought they were too harsh and acidic. We tried another test, employing a technique used when roasting veal bones for stock: We rubbed the oxtails with a bit of tomato paste. "Wow, what did you do?" the tasters exclaimed. Not only was the rich beefy flavor more intense, but the texture of the jus was now thicker and silkier. Now on a roll, we had one more idea to try. We snipped the twine on the cooked roast

and tossed the rib bones into the simmering jus. Perfection at last.

Finally, we used the fat from the oxtails to create the best Yorkshire pudding. Now we had a superior recipe, albeit one that takes a bit more work than the standard English version. This is a dish worth serving on a special occasion, not just for Sunday dinner.

Prime Rib Roast Beef with Jus
SERVES 10 TO 12

Ask the butcher to cut the meat off the ribs, but make sure to keep the ribs because the meat is tied back onto them for roasting. Letting the roast stand at room temperature for 1 hour before roasting helps it cook evenly. Plan on removing the roast from the refrigerator about 4½ hours before serving.

SCIENCE: Why Aging Tenderizes Beef

Meat is aged to develop its flavor and improve its texture. This process depends on certain enzymes, whose function while the animal is alive is to digest proteins. After the animal is slaughtered, the cells that contain these enzymes start to break down, releasing the enzymes into the meat, where they attack the cell proteins and break them down into amino acids, which have more flavor. The enzymes also break down the muscles, so the tissue becomes softer. This process can take a few days or a few weeks. (For the sake of safety, meat should not be aged for more than four days at home; beyond that time it must be done under carefully controlled conditions.)

Traditionally, butchers have hung carcasses in the meat locker to age their beef. Today, some beef is still aged on hooks (this process is called dry aging), but for the most part beef is wet-aged in vacuum-sealed packets. We wondered if it was worth it to the home cook to go the extra mile for dry-aged beef, so we ordered both a dry-aged and a wet-aged prime rib roast from a restaurant supplier in Manhattan. The differences between the two roasts were clear-cut.

Like a good, young red wine, wet-aged beef tasted pleasant and fresh on its own. When compared with the dry-aged beef, though, we realized its flavors were less concentrated. The meat tasted washed-out. The dry-aged beef, on the other hand, engaged the mouth. It was stronger, richer, and gamier-tasting, with a pleasant tang. The dry-aged and wet-aged beef were equally

tender, but the dry-aged beef had an added buttery texture.

Unfortunately, most butchers don't dry-age beef anymore because hanging the quarters of beef eats up valuable refrigerator space. Dry-aged beef also dehydrates (loses weight) and requires trimming (loses more weight). That weight loss means that less beef costs more money. Wet-aged beef loses virtually no weight during the aging process, and it comes prebutchered, packaged, and ready to sell. Because beef is expensive to begin with, most customers opt for the less expensive wet-aged beef. Why does dry aging work better than wet aging? The answer is simple: air. Encased in plastic, wet-aged beef is shut off from oxygen—the key to flavor development and concentration.

Because availability and price pose problems, you may simply want to age beef yourself. It's just a matter of making room in the refrigerator and remembering to buy the roast ahead of time, up to four days before you plan on roasting it. When you get the roast home, pat it dry and place it on a wire rack set over a paper towel–lined cake pan or plate. Set the racked roast in the refrigerator and let it age until you are ready to roast it, up to four days. (Aging begins to have a dramatic effect on the roast after three days, but we also detected some improvement in flavor and texture after just one day of aging.) Before roasting, shave off any exterior meat that has completely dehydrated. Between the trimming and dehydration, count on a 7-pound roast losing at least half a pound during aging.

1   (4-rib) standing rib roast (about 8 pounds),
    meat removed from the bone, ribs reserved
    (see note), and meat patted dry with paper
    towels

1½ pounds oxtails (4 pieces, each about 3 inches
    in diameter)

1   tablespoon tomato paste

3   medium onions, each cut into eighths

3   tablespoons vegetable oil
    Salt, preferably kosher

2   tablespoons ground black pepper

1   cup medium-bodied red wine, such as a Côtes
    du Rhône

1¾ cups low-sodium beef broth

1¾ cups low-sodium chicken broth

2   sprigs fresh thyme

1. Remove the roast and ribs from the refrigerator and let stand at room temperature for 1 hour. Meanwhile, adjust an oven rack to the lowest position and heat the oven to 400 degrees. Rub the oxtails with the tomato paste and place in a large, heavy-bottomed roasting pan. Toss the onions with 1 tablespoon of the oil, then scatter the onions in the roasting pan. Roast until the oxtails and onions are browned, about 45 minutes, flipping the oxtails halfway through the cooking time. Remove from the oven and set the roasting pan with the oxtails aside; reduce the oven temperature to 250 degrees.

2. When the roast has stood at room temperature for 1 hour, heat a heavy-bottomed 12-inch skillet over medium heat until hot. Meanwhile, rub the ends and fat side of the roast with the remaining 2 tablespoons oil, then sprinkle with 1½ teaspoons kosher salt (or ¾ teaspoon table salt) and the pepper. Place the roast fat-side down in the hot skillet and cook until well browned, 12 to 15 minutes. Using tongs, stand the roast on end and cook until well browned, about 4 minutes. Repeat with the other end. Do not brown the side where the ribs were attached. Place the roast browned-side up on a cutting board and cool 10 minutes. Following illustration 1 on page 407, tie the browned roast to the ribs. Set the roast bone-side down in the roasting pan (illustration 2), pushing the oxtails and onions to the sides of the pan.

3. Roast for 1 hour, then remove from the oven and check the internal temperature; the center of the roast should register about 70 degrees on an instant-read thermometer. (If the internal temperature is higher or lower, adjust the total cooking time.) Return the roast to the oven (prepare the Yorkshire pudding batter now, if making) and cook 1¼ to 1¾ hours longer, until the center of the meat registers about 122 degrees for rare to medium-rare or about 130 degrees for medium-rare to medium (illustration 3). Transfer the roast to a cutting board and tent loosely with foil. If making Yorkshire pudding, increase the oven temperature to 450 degrees.

4. While the roast rests, spoon off the fat from the roasting pan, reserving 3 tablespoons for the Yorkshire pudding; set the roasting pan aside while preparing the puddings for baking. While the pudding bakes, set the roasting pan over 2 burners at high heat. Add the wine to the roasting pan; using a wooden spoon, scrape up the browned bits and boil until reduced by half, about 3 minutes. Add the beef broth, chicken broth, and thyme. Cut the twine on the roast and remove the roast from the ribs; transfer the meat to the cutting board and tent again with the foil. Add the ribs to the roasting pan and continue to cook, stirring occasionally, until the liquid is reduced by two thirds (to about 2 cups), 16 to 20 minutes. Add any accumulated juices from the meat and cook to heat through, about 1 minute longer. Discard the ribs and oxtails; strain the jus through a mesh strainer into a gravy boat, pressing on the onions to extract as much liquid as possible.

5. Set the meat browned-side up on the cutting board and cut into ⅜-inch-thick slices; sprinkle lightly with salt. Serve immediately, passing the jus separately.

YORKSHIRE PUDDING

YORKSHIRE PUDDING IS MADE WITH FLOUR, salt, eggs, milk, and fat rendered from the roast beef, which gives it flavor and distinguishes it from the popover, which is generally made with butter. The eggy batter rises dramatically in the oven, and, as this happens, the center becomes airy and custardy and the crust crisps and browns.

Yorkshire pudding is often prepared in a roasting pan and then cut into individual pieces. Initial tests revealed problems with this approach. The pieces from the center of the pan were squat and lacked enough of the delectable browned crust, while those from the edges of the pan were missing a pleasing amount of the tender, soft, airy interior. Tasters were more smitten by individual puddings. They are uniform in shape, consistent in contrasting components, and much easier to serve. Because a popover pan makes only six and most people do not have one, we decided to try a muffin pan and got excellent results.

With the question of the proper baking pan settled, we focused on several other fine points. The biggest challenge would be getting the right height and texture. Yorkshire pudding can be notoriously fickle, rising beautifully sometimes and other times falling flat. We started our tests by leaving the batter lumpy (a common recipe directive). When this approach failed, we tried the less popular instruction: whisking the ingredients until smooth. These puddings rose higher, and the texture became more airy.

Next we tried the common practice of using room-temperature ingredients and letting the batter rest before baking. This gives the batter a bit of a head start when it enters the oven, having to rise up from a base temperature of about 70 degrees rather than a chilly 40 or 50 degrees. Sure enough, a rested, room-temperature batter enhanced the height and inner texture of the puddings.

Experimenting with oven temperatures was next. We tried constant, moderate oven temperatures ranging from 325 to 375. These puddings looked more like muffins because the large crown was missing. Constant high temperatures ranging from 400 to 450 also failed. These puddings had the desired height, but they were too dark on the outside and undercooked on the inside. Some Yorkshire pudding recipes call for starting with a hot oven (450 degrees in most recipes) and then lowering the heat about halfway through baking (to 350 degrees). We tried this approach, and these puddings were excellent. The intense 450-degree

heat not only browns the puddings nicely but quickly turns the moisture in the batter to steam, causing it to rise. The interior then cooks through at 350 degrees. Curious during the next test, we peeked inside the oven while the puddings were baking, and the inflow of cool air caused the puddings to collapse. (Hence the first rule of making Yorkshire pudding: No peeking!)

Additional testing showed that an accurate oven temperature is essential. If your oven is 25 degrees too high, the outer crust will darken and taste burnt; if it is 25 degrees too low, the inside of the puddings will not cook fully. Since most home ovens are not well calibrated, it makes sense to purchase a good oven thermometer before making this recipe.

Following through on the idea that an initial blast of high heat is good, we also tried preheating the greased muffin tin. The beef fat was smoking hot, and the batter sizzled when it hit the tin. This worked like a charm. We thought we were done until we noticed that the leftovers fell slightly as they sat. Remembering a technique used to preserve popover height, we pierced the next batch of puddings with a skewer as soon as they came out of the oven. This allowed the steam to escape instead of condensing inside the puddings, turning the interiors soft and overly moist, which causes collapse.

As for flavor, recipes for Yorkshire pudding are remarkably consistent in terms of using beef

YORKSHIRE PUDDING, FLAT OR FULL?

If the batter does not rest to give the gluten in the flour time to relax, or if the oven door is opened during baking, the puddings will fall (left). Proper mixing and resting of the batter and an undisturbed bake in the oven ensure huge crowns with crisp, golden brown exteriors and tender, moist, airy interiors (right).

fat, although amounts vary. We prepared a batch using 4 tablespoons of fat from the rendered oxtails. Although these puddings were flavorful, they were dripping in fat. Three tablespoons proved ideal.

Individual Yorkshire Puddings

SERVES 12

Prepare the Yorkshire pudding batter after the beef has roasted for 1 hour, then, while the roast rests, add beef fat to the batter and get the puddings into the oven. While the puddings bake, complete the jus. A hot, accurate oven temperature is key for properly risen and perfectly browned puddings. Work quickly to fill the muffin tin with batter, and do not open the oven door during baking.

   3   large eggs, at room temperature
 1½ cups whole milk, at room temperature
 1½ cups (7½ ounces) unbleached all-purpose flour
 ¾ teaspoon salt
  3 tablespoons beef fat (reserved from the roasting pan)

1. Whisk the eggs and milk together in a large bowl until well combined, about 20 seconds. Whisk the flour and salt together in a medium bowl and add to the egg mixture; whisk quickly until the flour is just incorporated and the mixture is smooth, about 30 seconds. Cover the batter with plastic wrap and let stand at room temperature for at least 1 hour or up to 3 hours.

2. After removing the roast from the oven, whisk 1 tablespoon of the beef fat into the batter until bubbling and smooth, about 30 seconds. Transfer the batter to a 1-quart liquid measuring cup or other pitcher.

3. Measure ½ teaspoon of the remaining 2 tablespoons beef fat into each cup of a standard (12-cup) muffin pan. When the roast is out of the oven, increase the oven temperature to 450 degrees and place the muffin pan in the oven to heat for 3 minutes (the fat will smoke). Working quickly, remove the muffin pan from the oven, close the oven door, and divide the batter evenly among the 12 muffin cups, filling each about two-thirds full.

Immediately return the pan to the oven. Bake, without opening the oven door, for 20 minutes; reduce the oven temperature to 350 degrees and bake until deep golden brown, about 10 minutes longer. Remove the pan from the oven and pierce each pudding with a skewer to release the steam and prevent collapse. Using your hands or a dinner knife, lift each pudding out of the pan. Serve immediately.

ROAST BEEF TENDERLOIN

FOR LARGE HOLIDAY PARTIES, FEW CUTS CAN top beef tenderloin. The tenderloin, which comes from the short loin, starts out very tender and can be cooked at a high oven temperature. This elegant roast thus cooks quickly, and its rich, buttery slices are always fork-tender. Despite its many virtues, however, beef tenderloin is not without its liabilities. Price, of course, is the biggest. Even at a local warehouse-style supermarket, the going rate for a whole beef tenderloin is $7.99 a pound—making for an average sticker price of about $50.

There is good reason for the tenderloin's hefty price. Because it sits up under the spine of the cow, it gets no exercise at all and is therefore the most tender piece of meat. It is one of the two muscles in the ultrapremium steaks known as the porterhouse and T-bone, so when it is removed from the cow as a whole muscle, it is going to sell for an ultrapremium price. We confirmed this by heading to the supermarket and the local butcher and purchasing $550 worth of beef tenderloin—which bought us just 11 roasts.

A whole beef tenderloin can be purchased "unpeeled," with an incredibly thick layer of exterior fat left attached, but it's usually sold "peeled," or stripped of its fat. Because of our many bad experiences with today's overly lean pork and beef, we purchased six of the 11 roasts unpeeled, determined to leave on as much fat as possible. However, after a quick examination of the unpeeled roasts, we realized that the excessively thick layer of surface fat had to go. Not only would such a large quantity of rendering fat smoke up the kitchen, it would also prohibit a delicious crust from forming on the meat. We dutifully peeled the thick layer of fat from the six tenderloins, but even after removing the sheaths of fat, there were still large pockets of fat on the interior as well as significant surface fat.

Does it make sense to buy an unpeeled roast and trim it yourself? We think not. We paid $6.99 a pound at the butcher for our unpeeled tenderloins, each weighing about 8 pounds. After cleaning them up, the peeled tenderloins weighed about 5 pounds, with a whopping 3 pounds of waste. We purchased peeled tenderloins of similar quality from another source for only $7.99 per pound. Clearly, the unpeeled tenderloins were more expensive with no benefits. And although we don't like tenderloins that have been picked clean, right down to the meat, we recommend buying peeled roasts, with their patches of scattered fat, and letting them be.

The tenderloin's sleek, boneless form makes for quick roasting, but its torpedo-like shape—thick and chunky at one end, gradually tapering at the other end—naturally roasts unevenly. For those looking for a range of doneness, this is not a problem, but for cooks who want a more evenly cooked roast, something must be done.

Folding the tip end of the roast under and tying it bulks up the tenderloin center to almost the same thickness as the more substantial butt end. This ensures that the tenderloin cooks more evenly. (Even so, the tip end is always a little more well-done than the butt.) Tying the roast at approximately 1½-inch intervals further guarantees a more uniform shape and consequently more even slices of beef. Snipping the silver skin (the translucent sheath that encases certain cuts of beef) at several points also prevents the meat from bowing during cooking. This occurs when the silver skin shrinks more than the meat to which it is attached.

Over the years, we've come to like slow roasting for large roasts. The lower the heat, we've found, the more evenly the roast cooks. To develop a rich brown crust on these slow-roasted larger cuts, we pan-sear them first or increase the oven temperature for the last few minutes of roasting—or we may do both.

INGREDIENTS: Salt

The food press has exalted exotic sea salts. We wondered if a pinch here or a smidgen there is really worth as much as $36 a pound. Will your food taste better if you spend more money on salt?

To find out, we embarked on a two-month odyssey, testing nine brands of salt in five different kitchen applications. Each was dissolved in spring water, dissolved in chicken stock, dissolved in water used to cook pasta, baked in biscuits, and sprinkled onto pieces of roast beef tenderloin. For each test, we measured salt by weight rather than volume. The results were, to say the least, surprising.

Tasters loved the crunch of the large sea salt flakes or crystals when sprinkled over slices of roast tenderloin. Here, Maldon Sea Salt was the clear winner, followed by Fleur de Sel de Camargue and Light Grey Celtic Sea Salt.

Although tasters had a clear preference in the meat test, we found that all brands and types of salt taste pretty much the same. Why didn't the fancy sea salts beat the pants off plain table salt in these tests? The main reason is dilution. Yes, sea salts sampled right from the box (or sprinkled on meat at the table) did taste better than table salt. But dissolve that salt in a pot of stock or stew and you'll never be able to tell the difference.

One final (and very important) point. Our results should not be taken to mean that all salts behave in the same way in the kitchen. For example, salts with a fine texture may seem saltier than coarse salts because of the way the crystals pack down in a teaspoon when measured. For instance, a teaspoon of coarse Maldon Sea Salt contains just half as much salt as a teaspoon of fine table salt.

What, then, can we conclude from the results of these tests? For one, expensive sea salts are best saved for the table, where their delicate flavor and great crunch can be appreciated. Don't waste $36-a-pound sea salt when making stew. If you like to keep coarse salt in a ramekin next to the stove where you can pick up a pinch, choose a kosher salt, which costs just pennies per pound. If you measure salt by the teaspoon when cooking, you might as well use table salt, which is also the best choice for baking.

But a beef tenderloin is a different proposition. Though relatively large, its long, thin shape would seem to dictate a relatively quick cooking time. To determine the ideal roasting temperature, we started at the two extremes, roasting one tenderloin at 200 degrees, the other at 500. As expected, the roast cooked at 500 degrees not only created a very smoky kitchen from the rendering fat, it was also overcooked at each end and around the perimeter. However, the high oven heat had formed a thick, flavorful crust. A good crust is crucial to this rich yet mild-tasting roast, whose flavor is sometimes barely recognizable as beef. Despite the even, rosy pink interior of the beef cooked at 200 degrees, this roast lacked the all-important crust. Neither oven temperature was ideal, so we kept roasting.

Because the higher roasting temperature provided the rich flavor this roast desperately needs, we decided to roast it at as high a temperature as possible. A 450-degree oven still gave us smoke and uneven cooking, so we moved down to 425 degrees. For comparison, we roasted another

LEARNING TO TIE BUTCHER'S KNOTS

Many cooks have trouble tying roasts properly. If that's the case, practice with a roll of paper towels and strands of kitchen twine. It's a lot neater than practicing on a roast.

tenderloin at 200 degrees, this time increasing the oven temperature to 425 degrees at the end of cooking to develop a crust. Both roasts emerged from the oven looking beautiful, and their meat looked and tasted almost identical. Because the tenderloin roasted at 425 degrees was done in just 45 minutes (compared with the slow-roasted tenderloin, which took just about twice as long), we chose the high-heat method.

PREPARING A BEEF TENDERLOIN

1. To keep the meat from bowing as it cooks, slide a knife under the silver skin and flick the blade upward to cut through the silver skin at five or six spots along the length of the roast.

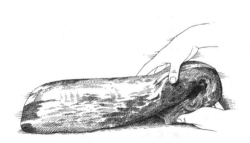

2. To ensure that the tenderloin roasts more evenly, fold the thin tip end of the roast under about 6 inches.

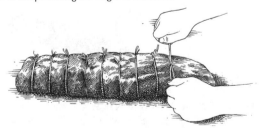

3. For more even cooking and evenly sized slices, use 12-inch lengths of kitchen twine to tie the roast every 1½ inches.

4. Set the meat on a sheet of plastic wrap and rub it all over with oil. Sprinkle with salt and pepper, then lift the plastic wrap up and around the meat to press on the excess. This last step guarantees even coverage.

Although all roasts should rest 15 to 20 minutes after cooking, we found that beef tenderloin improves dramatically if left uncarved even longer. If cut too soon, its slices are soft and flabby. A slightly longer rest—we settled on 30 minutes—allows the meat to firm up to a texture we found much more appealing. Before carving, we preferred removing the big pockets of excess fat, which become more obvious at warm and room temperatures.

≻≻

Roast Beef Tenderloin
SERVES 12 TO 16

To give the tenderloin a more pronounced pepper crust, increase the amount of pepper to 6 tablespoons and use a mixture of strong black and white and mild pink and green peppercorns. Be sure to crush the peppercorns with a mortar and pestle or with a heavy-bottomed saucepan or skillet. Do not use a coffee or spice grinder, which will grind the softer green and pink peppercorns to a powder

before the harder black and white peppercorns begin to break up. Serve with Parsley Sauce with Cornichons and Capers, Salsa Verde, or Chimichurri (page 415). Make a double recipe of the last two sauces to accompany such a large piece of meat.

1   **whole peeled beef tenderloin (5 to 6 pounds), patted dry with paper towels, silver skin cut, tip end tucked under, and tied (see illustrations 1 through 3 on page 413)**
2   **tablespoons olive oil**
1   **tablespoon kosher salt**
2   **tablespoons coarsely ground black pepper (see note)**

1. Remove the tenderloin from the refrigerator 1 hour before roasting to bring the meat to room temperature.

2. Adjust an oven rack to the upper-middle position and heat the oven to 425 degrees. Set the roast on a sheet of plastic wrap and rub it

---

EQUIPMENT: Boning Knives

The slim, flexible blade of a boning knife may look eccentric, but it is perfectly designed to slide nimbly through joints and between bones. It is an essential tool for such tasks as removing cutlets from a whole chicken breast and can also be used to remove fat and silver skin from a beef tenderloin. The slim blade creates less drag through the meat, and the slices made are neater than those possible with the wider blade of a chef's knife.

Because most home cooks are likely to use a boning knife infrequently, we wondered if a cheaper knife would do. To find out, we tested six leading knives with blades between 5 and 7 inches long and prices between $9 and $71. Both large- and small-handed testers used each knife to butcher a whole chicken and to trim beef ribs of fat and silver skin. Each knife was evaluated for handle comfort, slipperiness (hands become very greasy when butchering), agility (including flexibility), and sharpness.

The winning Forschner (Victorinox) Fibrox boning knife, priced at $17.90, received high marks for its uniquely designed ergonomic handle as well as its slim, highly maneuverable blade and razor-sharp edge. The plastic handle nestled comfortably into both large and small hands, and it stayed there even when our hands became slick with fat. The blade was the narrowest of the lot, which made it very agile. And while all the knives arrived

with razor-sharp edges, the Forschner seemed exceptionally keen, gliding effortlessly through tough tendon and thick skin.

The J. A. Henckels Professional S boning knife ($49.99) finished a close second. Its blade was nearly as agile as the Forschner, but the handle was somewhat slippery. The Wüsthof-Trident Grand Prix boning knife ($54) was "fiendishly sharp," but the wide blade was not as agile as those on the top models, and the handle became slippery when coated with chicken fat. The textured metal handle of the Global boning knife ($70.99) received mixed reviews, and testers did not like the boxy handle on the Chicago Cutlery boning knife ($14.99) or the flimsy blade on the Farberware Professional boning knife ($8.99).

THE BEST BONING KNIFE
The Forschner (Victorinox) Fibrox knife boasts a handle that testers found "easy to grip" and a narrow blade that shows "great flexibility around bones." Everyone raved about the "amazing" sharpness of this knife straight out of the box.

SAUCES FOR BEEF

Parsley Sauce with Cornichons and Capers

MAKES ABOUT 1 1/4 CUPS

This sauce pairs perfectly with beef tenderloin (cooked in the oven or on the grill).

- ¾ cup minced fresh parsley leaves
- 12 cornichons, minced (6 tablespoons), plus 1 teaspoon cornichon juice
- ¼ cup drained capers, chopped coarse
- 2 medium scallions, white and light green parts, minced
  Pinch salt
- ¼ teaspoon ground black pepper
- ½ cup extra-virgin olive oil

Mix all of the ingredients together in a medium bowl. (The sauce can be covered and set aside at room temperature for several hours.)

Salsa Verde

MAKES GENEROUS ¾ CUP

Salsa verde is excellent with grilled or roasted meats, such as Roast Beef Tenderloin (page 414). It is best served immediately after it is made, but can be refrigerated in an airtight container for up to 2 days.

- 1 large slice white sandwich bread
- ½ cup extra-virgin olive oil
- 2 tablespoons juice from 1 lemon
- 2 cups lightly packed fresh parsley leaves
- 2 medium anchovy fillets
- 2 tablespoons drained capers
- 1 small garlic clove, minced or pressed through a garlic press (about ½ teaspoon)
- ⅛ teaspoon salt

1. Toast the bread in a toaster at a low setting until the surface is dry but not browned, about 15 seconds. Cut the bread into rough ½-inch pieces (you should have about ½ cup).

2. Process the bread pieces, oil, and lemon juice in a food processor fitted with the steel blade until smooth, about 10 seconds. Add the parsley, anchovies, capers, garlic, and salt. Pulse until the mixture is finely chopped (the mixture should not be smooth), about five 1-second pulses, scraping down the bowl with a rubber spatula after 3 pulses. Transfer the mixture to a small bowl and serve.

Chimichurri

MAKES 1 GENEROUS CUP

Like a loose, fresh salsa in consistency, this mixture is a common accompaniment to sautéed, roasted, and grilled meats in South America. For best results, use flat-leaf parsley. This sauce works well with beef, especially mild filet or tenderloin. Although this sauce tastes best the day it is made, any that is left over can be refrigerated for several days.

- 1 cup packed fresh parsley leaves, preferably flat-leaf parsley
- 5 medium garlic cloves, peeled
- ½ cup extra-virgin olive oil
- ¼ cup red wine vinegar
- 2 tablespoons water
- ¼ cup finely minced red onion
- 1 teaspoon salt
- ¼ teaspoon red pepper flakes

Process the parsley and garlic in a food processor fitted with the steel blade, stopping as necessary to scrape down the sides of the bowl with a rubber spatula, until the garlic and parsley are chopped fine (twenty 1-second pulses); transfer to a medium bowl. Whisk in the remaining ingredients until thoroughly blended. Let stand for 30 minutes to allow the flavors to develop before serving.

all over with the oil. Sprinkle with the salt and pepper and then lift the wrap to press the excess seasoning into the meat (see illustration 4 on page 413).

3. Transfer the prepared tenderloin from the wrap to a wire rack set in a shallow roasting pan. Roast until an instant-read thermometer inserted into the thickest part of the roast registers about 125 degrees (the meat will range from medium-rare to medium in different areas when it finishes resting), about 45 minutes. Remove from the oven and tent loosely with foil. Let stand for about 30 minutes before carving. (The cooled tenderloin can be wrapped in plastic, refrigerated up to 2 days, sliced, and served chilled.)

4. Cut the meat into ½-inch-thick slices. Arrange on a platter and serve.

ANATOMY OF A BEEF TENDERLOIN

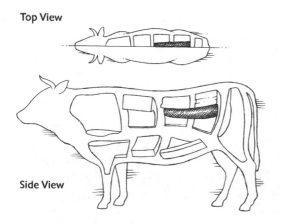

Butt End

Tip End

Center-Cut Chateaubriand

A whole beef tenderloin comprises these sections: The thicker end of the roast is called the butt end; the middle portion—which is virtually an even thickness—is called the center-cut Chateaubriand or short tenderloin; and the tapering tip end is sold as part of the whole tenderloin or removed and sold as tenderloin tips.

LOCATING THE TENDERLOIN

Top View

Side View

The tenderloin muscle is extremely tender because it is never used to move any part of the cow.

BASIC ROAST BEEF

SOMETIMES YOU JUST WANT ROAST BEEF. NOT a bank account–busting holiday rib roast, not a dainty and delicate tenderloin, but an honest, Everyman's slice of Tuesday night beef, served with mashed potatoes, gravy, and green vegetables. Most supermarket meat departments are loaded with inexpensive roasts that would seem to fit the bill, but their labels can be a bit baffling. What's the difference between a bottom rump round roast and a bottom butt sirloin? Lots of these names would make an eight-year-old snicker, but they are not all that helpful.

Determined to get to the bottom of this, we gathered armloads of these cheap roasts and went to work. We decided to develop a technique first and then examine the various cuts that might (or might not) work with our final technique. To start, we cooked five separate roasts, each at a different oven temperature, ranging from 250 to 500 degrees. The results were disappointing, but we learned two things. First, the lowest oven temperature was best. The meat that was roasted at 500 degrees became dry, with most of the outer layers of the meat overcooked. The roast cooked at 250 degrees, however, was more tender and juicy and had better flavor. Second, and most important, we found that the internal temperature of the meat does not necessarily determine the juiciness or texture of the roast. A roast cooked at 250 degrees until it reaches an internal temperature of 120 degrees is definitely more tender and juicy than meat cooked to the same internal temperature in a 500-degree oven. In other words, it's not just where you are going but how you get there.

Why is this true? To fully understand what was happening inside the meat, we examined four different roasts prepared at different temperatures— 250, 350, 400, and 500 degrees. All were cooked to the same internal temperature—130 degrees—and allowed to sit for an additional 10 minutes after they were removed from the oven. The roasts were then cut in half. When we compared the roasts, the answer was immediately apparent. The 500-degree roast was almost entirely overcooked. That is, the center was still red, but 70 percent of the remainder was gray and unappealing. By comparison, the roast cooked at 250 degrees was light red throughout, with only 10 percent of the outer layer gray and overcooked. The roasts cooked at the in-between temperatures varied between these two extremes. Lower oven temperatures allow sufficient time for the even conduction of heat to the center of the roast. At higher oven temperatures, the outside and the inside of the roast have a much larger temperature differential.

The meat developed very little exterior flavor or color when roasted at a constant low temperature, however. Our options for producing the desired crispy brown crust were to crank up the oven, either at the beginning or end of the cooking time, or to sear the roast on the stovetop. We experimented with these methods, alone and in combination, and first eliminated the variations with an initial high oven temperature. Even after turning the temperature back down to 250 degrees, the oven retained enough of the extra heat to spoil our slow, evenly cooked center. Turning the oven up toward the end of the cooking time was much more successful: The meat did not overcook at the edges, but the color was still not as dark as we wanted. When combined with an initial sear in a hot roasting pan or Dutch oven, this method ultimately delivered the best results. The meat had a crisp crust when it went into the oven, and it developed a deeper, more even color during the final blast of oven heat.

The key to making sense of the confusing labels found on supermarket roasts is to identify the larger section, or primal, from which the roast was cut. In this category of inexpensive roasts, the relevant sections are the chuck (or shoulder), round (or back leg), and sirloin (or lower back). Many different roasts can be cut from each of these sections, and butchers in different parts of the country are liable to call the same roast by different names. Thus, every roast is different, but

meat cut from each of these three main sections is similar enough to allow us to make some useful generalizations. While the top round is certainly different from the bottom round, for the purposes of this recipe, we've found that all "round roasts" will behave in much the same way, which is to say differently from "chuck roasts" or "sirloin roasts."

Sirloin roasts were our favorite for this cooking method. They had big, beefy flavor, enough fat to stay juicy, and a tender texture. Cheaper round roasts were decidedly second best: not bad at all, but generally tougher, drier, and less flavorful than the sirloin. Both sirloin and round roasts will sometimes be labeled "rump" roasts; this means that the roast was cut from the area near the dividing line between the round and the sirloin. As such, any kind of rump roast falls somewhere between the two in our ranking: better than a "bottom-round" roast, for example, but not quite as nice as a "top sirloin."

Chuck roasts were a dilemma. We love the flavor of the chuck, and in many cases even preferred it to that of the sirloin. But since the chuck is crisscrossed with so many connective fibers, it is not a pretty roast to look at, and veins of tough gristle can make it tough to chew. Chuck is an excellent choice for pot-roasting and stewing, which allow the connective tissue to break down and dissolve. Since it is scarce in some supermarkets anyway, we recommend choosing one of these other cooking methods when lucky enough to obtain a nice chuck roast.

Slow-Roasted Beef

SERVES 6 TO 8

Our favorite roast for this recipe is the top sirloin, but any roast from the sirloin will work well. Round roasts are also an option, but they are definitely a second choice. If you have time, refrigerate the roast on a wire rack set over a paper towel–covered plate for up to three days. This aging process delivers a tender, more flavorful roast. Make sure, however, that before roasting you trim off the parts of the roast that have dehydrated and turned leathery. Tying the roast makes it compact and promotes even cooking. Leftovers make excellent roast beef sandwiches. This roast works well with All-Purpose Gravy (page 188) and potatoes.

1   boneless beef roast (3 to 4 pounds), preferably from the sirloin, aged, if desired (see note), tied crosswise with twine at 1-inch intervals
    Salt and ground black pepper
1   tablespoon vegetable oil

1. Adjust an oven rack to the lower-middle position and heat the oven to 250 degrees. Season the roast liberally with salt and pepper to taste. Heat the oil in an ovenproof Dutch oven or flame-proof heavy-duty roasting pan over medium-high heat until just smoking. Sear the roast until well browned, about 2 minutes on each side.

2. Transfer the pot to the oven and cook, uncovered, until an instant-read thermometer inserted into the thickest part of the roast registers 110 degrees, 45 minutes to 1 hour. Increase the oven temperature to 500 degrees and cook until the internal temperature reaches 120 degrees for rare, 125 degrees for medium-rare, or 130 degrees for medium, 10 to 20 minutes longer. (Cooking times can vary depending on the size and shape of the roast.) Remove the roast from the pot and transfer to a cutting board. Tent the roast loosely with foil and let stand for 20 minutes. Snip the twine off the roast, cut crosswise into thin slices, and serve.

POT ROAST

POT ROAST, A SLOW-FOOD SURVIVOR OF GENERA-tions past, has stubbornly remained in the repertoire of Sunday-night cookery, but with few good reasons. The meat is often tough and stringy and so dry that it must be drowned with the merciful sauce that accompanies the dish.

A good pot roast by definition entails the transformation of a tough (read cheap), nearly unpalatable cut of meat into a tender, rich, flavorful main course by means of a slow, moist cooking process called braising. It should not be sliceable; rather, the tension of a stern gaze should be enough to break it apart. Nor should it be pink or rosy in the middle—save that for prime rib or steak.

The meat for pot roast should be well marbled with fat and connective tissue to provide the dish

with the necessary flavor and moisture. Recipes typically call for roasts from the sirloin (or rump), round (leg), or chuck (shoulder). When all was said and done, we cooked a dozen cuts of meat to find the right one.

The sirloin roasts tested—the bottom-rump roast and top sirloin—were the leanest of the cuts and needed longer cooking to be broken down to a palatable texture. The round cuts—top round, bottom round, and eye of round—had more fat running through them than the sirloin cuts, but the meat was chewy. The chuck cuts—shoulder roast, boneless chuck roast, cross rib, chuck mock tender, seven-bone roast, top-blade roast, and chuck-eye roast—cooked up the most tender, although we gave preference to three of these cuts (see page 421 for more information). The high proportion of fat and connective tissue in these chuck cuts gave the meat much-needed moisture and superior flavor.

Tough meat, such as brisket, can benefit from the low, dry heat of oven-roasting, and it can be boiled. With pot roast, however, the introduction of moisture by means of a braising liquid is thought to be integral to the breakdown of the tough muscle fibers. (We also tried dry-roasting and boiling pot roast just to make sure. See page 422 to find out why braising was the winner.) It was time to find out what kind of liquid and how much was needed to best cook the roast and supply a good sauce.

Before we began the testing, we needed to deal with the aesthetics of the dish. Because pot roast is traditionally cooked with liquid at a low temperature, the exterior of the meat will not brown sufficiently unless it is first sautéed in a Dutch oven on the stovetop. High heat and a little oil were all that were needed to caramelize the exterior of the beef and boost both the flavor and the appearance of the dish.

Using water as the braising medium, we started with a modest ¼ cup, as suggested in a few recipes. This produced a roast that was unacceptably fibrous, even after hours of cooking. After increasing the amount of liquid incrementally, we found that the moistest meat was produced when we added liquid halfway up the sides of the roast (depending on the cut, this amount could be between 2 and 4 cups). The greater amount of liquid also accelerated the cooking process, shaving nearly one hour off the cooking time needed for a roast cooked in just ¼ cup of liquid. Naively assuming that more is always better, we continued to increase the amount of water, but to no better effect. We also found it necessary to cover the Dutch oven with a piece of foil before placing the lid on top. The added seal of the foil kept the liquid from escaping (in the form of steam) by means of the loose-fitting lid and eliminated any need to add more liquid to the pot.

Next we tested different liquids, hoping to add flavor to the roast and sauce. Along with our old standby, water, we tested red wine, canned low-sodium chicken broth, and canned low-sodium beef broth. Red wine had the most startling effect on the meat, penetrating it with a potent flavor

that most tasters agreed was "good, but not traditional pot roast." However, tasters did like the flavor of a little red wine added to the sauce after the pot roast was removed from the pan. Each of the broths on their own failed to win tasters over completely—the chicken broth was rich but gave the dish a characteristic poultry flavor, while the beef broth tasted sour when added solo. In the end, we found that an equal amount of each did the job, with the beef broth boosting the depth of flavor and the chicken broth tempering any sourness. Because different amounts of liquid would have to be added to the pot depending on the size and shape of each individual roast, we chose to be consistent in the amount of chicken and beef broth used—1 cup each—and to vary the amount of water to bring the liquid level halfway up the sides of the roast.

Trying to boost the flavor of the sauce even

HOW TO TIE A TOP-BLADE ROAST

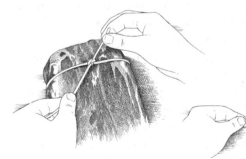

1. Slip a 6-foot piece of kitchen twine under the roast and tie a double knot.

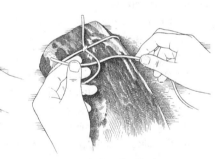

2. Hold the twine against the meat and loop the long end of twine under and around the roast.

3. Run the long end through the loop.

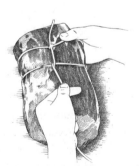

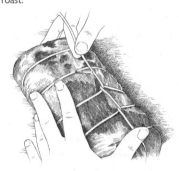

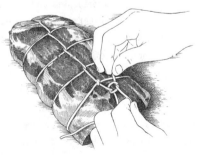

4. Repeat this procedure down the length of the roast.

5. Roll the roast over and run the twine under and around each loop.

6. Wrap the twine around the end of the roast, flip the roast, and tie the twine to the original knot.

more, we added the basic vegetables—carrot, celery, onion, and garlic—to the pot as the meat braised. Unfortunately, the addition of raw vegetables made the pot roast taste more like a vegetable stew. We then tried sautéing them until golden brown and found that the caramelized flavor of the vegetables added another layer of flavor to the sauce. Tomato paste, an ingredient found in several recipes, was not a welcome addition. Tasters appreciated the sweetness it added but not the "tinny" flavor it gave to the sauce. A little sugar (2 teaspoons) added to the vegetables as they cooked gave the sauce the sweetness tasters were looking for.

Some recipes thicken the sauce with a mixture of equal parts butter and flour (*beurre manié*); others use a slurry of cornstarch mixed with a little braising liquid. Both techniques made the sauce more gravy-like than we preferred, and we didn't care

SCIENCE: What's So Special About Collagen?

Collagen is the predominant protein in connective tissue and is quite difficult to chew. It is found in abundance in tough cuts of meat, such as those used to make pot roast. Braising is a slow-cooking technique that is applied to tough cuts of meat. The meat is submerged halfway in cooking liquid, covered, and heated at a low temperature. By the time the meat reaches 150 degrees, the muscle tissue has tightened fully and has expelled a great deal of its moisture into the braising liquid. If the meat is pulled from the pot at this temperature, it will be dry and tough, but the braising liquid will be rich and flavorful.

With further heating, the collagen in the muscle will break down progressively into soft gelatin. The tightened muscle tissue strands can then separate a little, and moisture from the cooking liquid will accumulate between the fibers. Now, though the finished product still is tough muscle tissue, it is more succulent, owing to the conversion of collagen to soft gelatin and to the resultant opening of gaps between the tough strands of muscle.

Since collagen won't completely melt until the internal temperature of the meat reaches 200 degrees, you must really cook tough cuts of meat to make full use of this phenomenon. In fact, when making pot roast, you really can't overcook the meat. Excessive cooking might cause the meat to fall apart, but, in general, the longer the meat is pot-roasted, the more tender it will become.

for the dilution of flavor. We chose to remove the roast from the pot, then reduce the liquid over high heat until the flavors were well concentrated and the texture more substantial.

As for the best cooking method for pot roast, there are two schools of thought: on the stove or in the oven. After a few rounds of stovetop cooking, we felt that it was too difficult to maintain a steady, low temperature, so we began pot-roasting in the oven, starting out at 250 degrees. This method required no supervision, just a turn of the meat every 30 to 40 minutes to ensure even cooking. We then tested higher temperatures to reduce the cooking time. Heat levels above 350 degrees boiled the meat to a stringy, dry texture because the exterior of the roast overcooked before the interior was cooked and tender. The magic temperature turned out to be 300 degrees—enough heat to keep the meat at a low simmer while high enough to shave a few more minutes off the cooking time.

As noted above, pot roast is well-done meat—meat cooked to an internal temperature above 165 degrees. Up to this point, we were bringing the meat to an internal temperature of 200 to 210 degrees, the point at which the fat and connective tissue begin to melt. In a 300-degree oven, the roast came up to that temperature in a neat 2½ hours, certainly by no means a quick meal but still a relatively short time in which to cook a pot roast. But we still had not achieved our goal of fall-apart tenderness. We went back and reviewed our prior testing to see what we might have missed.

Once in a great while in the test kitchen we happen upon a true "Eureka!" moment, when a chance test result leads to a breakthrough cooking technique. Some days before, we had forgotten to remove one of the roasts from the oven, allowing it to cook one hour longer than intended. Racing to the kitchen with our instant-read thermometer, we found the internal temperature of the roast was still 210 degrees, but the meat had a substantially different appearance and texture. The roast was so tender that it was starting to separate along its muscle lines. A fork poked into the meat met with no resistance and nearly disappeared into the flesh. We took the roast out of the pot and "sliced" into it. Nearly all the fat and connective tissue had dissolved into the meat, giving each bite a soft, silky texture and rich, succulent flavor. We "overcooked" several more roasts. Each roast had the same great texture. The conclusion? Not only do you have to cook pot roast until it reaches 210 degrees internally, but the meat has to remain at that temperature for a full hour. In other words, cook the pot roast until it's done—and then keep on cooking!

Simple Pot Roast
SERVES 6 TO 8

Our favorite cut for pot roast is a chuck-eye roast. Most markets sell this roast with kitchen twine tied around the center (see the photo below); if necessary, do this yourself. Seven-bone and top-blade roasts are also good choices for this recipe. Remember to add only enough water to come halfway up the sides of these thinner roasts, and begin checking for doneness after 2 hours. If using a top-blade roast, tie it before cooking (see the illustrations on page 419) to keep it from falling apart. Mashed or boiled potatoes are a good accompaniment.

I	boneless chuck-eye roast (about 3½ pounds), patted dry with paper towels
	Salt and ground black pepper
2	tablespoons vegetable oil
I	medium onion, chopped medium
I	small carrot, chopped medium
I	small celery rib, chopped medium
2	medium garlic cloves, minced or pressed through a garlic press
2	teaspoons sugar
I	cup low-sodium chicken broth
I	cup low-sodium beef broth
I	sprig fresh thyme
I–I½	cups water
¼	cup dry red wine

1. Adjust an oven rack to the middle position and heat the oven to 300 degrees. Sprinkle the roast generously with salt and pepper to taste.

2. Heat the oil in a large ovenproof Dutch oven over medium-high heat until shimmering but not smoking. Brown the roast thoroughly on all sides, reducing the heat if the fat begins to smoke, 8 to 10 minutes. Transfer the roast to a large plate; set aside.

3. Reduce the heat to medium; add the onion, carrot, and celery to the pot and cook, stirring occasionally, until beginning to brown, 6 to 8 minutes. Add the garlic and sugar; cook until fragrant, about 30 seconds. Add the chicken and beef broths and thyme, scraping the pan bottom with a wooden spoon to loosen the browned bits. Return the roast and any accumulated juices on the plate to the pot; add enough water to come halfway up the sides of the roast. Cover with a lid, bring the liquid to a simmer over medium heat, and transfer the pot to the oven. Cook, turning the roast every 30 minutes, until fully tender and a meat fork or

CHUCK ROASTS

SEVEN-BONE POT ROAST　　　**TOP-BLADE POT ROAST**　　　**CHUCK-EYE ROAST**

The seven-bone pot roast (left) is a well-marbled cut with an incredibly beefy flavor. It gets its name from the bone found in the roast, which is shaped like the number seven. Because it is only 2 inches thick, less liquid and less time are needed to braise this roast. Do not buy a seven-bone pot roast that weighs more than 3½ pounds, as it will not fit in a Dutch oven. This roast is also sometimes referred to as a seven-bone steak.

The top-blade pot roast (middle) is also well marbled with fat and connective tissue, which make this roast very juicy and flavorful. Even after thorough braising, this roast retains a distinctive strip of connective tissue, which is not unpleasant to eat. This roast may also be sold as a blade roast.

The chuck-eye roast (right) is the fattiest of the three roasts and the most commonly available. Its high proportion of fat gives pot roast great flavor and tenderness. Because of its thicker size, this roast takes the longest to cook.

sharp knife slips easily in and out of the meat, 3½ to 4 hours.

4. Transfer the roast to a carving board; tent with foil to keep warm. Allow the liquid in the pot to settle about 5 minutes, then use a wide spoon to skim the fat off the surface; discard the thyme sprig. Boil over high heat until reduced to about 1½ cups, about 8 minutes. Add the wine and reduce to 1½ cups, about 2 minutes. Season with salt and pepper to taste.

5. Using a chef's or carving knife, cut the meat into ½-inch-thick slices, or pull apart into large pieces; transfer the meat to a warmed serving platter and pour about ½ cup of the sauce over the meat. Serve, passing the remaining sauce separately.

➤ VARIATION

Pot Roast with Root Vegetables

In this variation, carrots, potatoes, and parsnips are added near the end of cooking to make a complete meal.

1. Follow the recipe for Simple Pot Roast. In step 3, when the roast is almost tender (a sharp knife should meet little resistance), transfer the roast to a cutting board. Pour the braising liquid through a mesh strainer and discard the solids. Return the liquid to the empty pot and let it settle for 5 minutes; use a wide spoon to skim the fat off the surface. Return the roast to the liquid and add 1½ pounds (about 8 medium) carrots, peeled and sliced ½ inch thick (about 3 cups); 1½ pounds small red potatoes, halved if larger than 1½ inches in diameter (about 5 cups); and 1 pound (about 5 large) parsnips, peeled and sliced ½ inch thick (about 3 cups), submerging them in the liquid. Continue to cook until the vegetables are almost tender, 20 to 30 minutes.

2. Transfer the roast to a carving board; tent with foil to keep warm. Add the wine and salt and pepper to taste; boil over high heat until the vegetables are fully tender, 5 to 10 minutes. Using a slotted spoon, transfer the vegetables to a warmed serving bowl or platter; using a chef's or carving knife, cut the meat into ½-inch-thick slices or pull apart into large pieces; transfer to the bowl or platter and pour about ½ cup of the sauce over the meat and vegetables. Serve, passing the remaining sauce separately.

BRAISED BRISKET

BRAISED BRISKET IS A WORKHORSE MEAL. IT is cheap, can serve many people (or just a few with great leftovers), and is usually cooked with straightforward, universally appealing flavors. The all-too-common problem with brisket, however, is that the meat turns out extraordinarily dry and chewy.

Whole briskets weigh roughly 12 to 13 pounds, yet butchers usually sell them cut in half or even smaller. If cut in half, one end of the brisket is called the "first" or "flat" cut and the other is called the "second" or "point" cut. We prefer pieces from the second (point) cut because they tend to be thicker, more tender, and more flavorful. Braising requires that the meat lie flat in a covered pot, and we noted that a three-pound brisket (serving six to eight people) was the largest any of our covered pots could accommodate.

The method for braising brisket is the same as for other stews and braises. The meat is first browned, then set off to the side while the browned bits left

ROASTING VERSUS BRAISING

A distinctive pattern of fat and connective tissue runs through the meat of a chuck roast (left). When cooked in dry heat, or roasted (middle), the fat and sinew do not break down sufficiently, even after many hours in the oven. Cooking the meat in moist heat, or braising (right), promotes a more complete breakdown of the fat and connective tissue, yielding very tender meat.

behind in the pot are used to make a flavorful sauce. The browned beef is nestled back into the pot with the sauce, the liquid is brought to a gentle simmer, and the meat is cooked until tender.

Using this basic method as our starting point, we noted that there are three keys to cooking brisket so that it doesn't taste dry or chewy. First (taking a cue from our pot roast recipe), it is easier to maintain a consistent simmer in a 300-degree oven than on top of the stove. Oven temperatures higher than 300 degrees turn the simmer into a boil (which dries out the meat), while oven temperatures lower than 300 degrees simply added unnecessary hours to the cooking time. Second,

we found it takes several hours of constant simmering for the brisket to turn tender. A three-pound piece of brisket requires 2½ to 3 hours in the oven, at which point, a dinner fork should slide in and out of its center with little resistance. Third, it is necessary to slice the brisket thinly across the grain when serving.

Core to the universal appeal of brisket is the simple flavored sauce that accompanies it. Many brisket recipes we researched base the sauce on the flavor of caramelized onions (the meat is almost smothered by the onions as it cooks). Giving this idea a try, we found it easy to lightly caramelize some onions in the drippings left over from

EQUIPMENT: Dutch Ovens

We find that a Dutch oven (also called a lidded casserole) is almost essential to making stews and braises such as pot roast. A Dutch oven is nothing more than a wide, deep pot with a cover. It was originally manufactured with ears on the side (small, round tabs used for picking up the pot) and a top that had a lip around the edge. The latter design element was important because a Dutch oven was heated by coals placed both underneath and on top of the pot. The lip kept the coals on the lid from falling off. One could bake biscuits, cobblers, beans, and stews in this pot. It was, in the full sense of the word, an oven. This oven was a key feature of chuck wagons and essential in many Colonial American households, where all cooking occurred in the fireplace. This useful pot supposedly came to be called "Dutch" because at some point the best cast iron came from Holland.

Now that everyone in the United States has an oven, the Dutch oven is no longer used to bake biscuits or cobblers. However, it is a requisite for dishes that start on top of the stove and finish in the oven, as many stews do. To make recommendations about buying a modern Dutch oven, we tested 12 models from leading makers of cookware.

We found that a Dutch oven should have a capacity of at least six quarts to be useful. Eight quarts is even better. As we cooked in the pots, we came to prefer wider, shallower Dutch ovens because it's easier to see and reach inside them and they offer more bottom surface area to accommodate larger batches of meat for browning. This reduces the number of batches required to brown a given quantity of meat and, with it, the chances of burning the flavorful pan drippings. Ideally, the diameter of a Dutch oven is twice as great as its height.

We also preferred pots with a light-colored interior finish, such as stainless steel or enameled cast iron. It is easier to judge the caramelization of the drippings at a glance in these pots. Dark finishes can mask the color of the drippings, which may burn before you realize it. Our favorite pot is the eight-quart All-Clad Stainless Stockpot (despite the name, this pot is a Dutch oven). The seven-quart Le Creuset Round French Oven, which is made of enameled cast iron, also tested well. These pots are quite expensive, costing at least $150 even on sale. A less expensive alternative is the seven-quart Lodge Dutch Oven, which is made from cast iron. This pot is extremely heavy (making it a bit hard to maneuver), it must be seasoned (wiped with oil) regularly, and the dark interior finish is not ideal, but it does brown food quite well and costs just $45.

THE BEST DUTCH OVENS

Our favorite pot is the eight-quart All-Clad Stainless Stockpot (left). Despite the name, this pot is a Dutch oven. Expect to spend nearly $200 for this piece of cookware. A less expensive alternative is the seven-quart Lodge Dutch Oven (right), which costs about $45. However, since this pot is made from cast iron, it may react with acidic sauces and is not appropriate for all recipes, especially those that contain significant amounts of tomatoes or wine.

browning the meat. To build a flavorful, well-rounded sauce around the onions, it is important to add both brown sugar and tomato paste to develop their sweet onion flavor. A combination of beef and chicken broth also proved crucial, as did the addition of red wine, garlic, bay leaves, and fresh thyme. Lastly, we refreshened the flavor of this well-simmered sauce by adding a dash of cider vinegar just before serving. With an ample amount of sauce to serve alongside the sliced brisket, no one will ever complain that this version tastes chewy or dry.

Braised Beef Brisket

SERVES 6 TO 8

Make sure to use an ovenproof pot that is large enough so that the brisket lies flat. Leftover brisket can be refrigerated in the sauce for a day or two. Reheat the brisket in the sauce in a covered pot over medium-low heat.

1	beef brisket (about 3 pounds), preferably point cut (see the illustration at right), trimmed of excess fat and patted dry with paper towels
	Salt and ground black pepper
2	tablespoons vegetable oil
3	pounds yellow onions, sliced thin
2	tablespoons brown sugar
6	medium garlic cloves, minced or pressed through a garlic press
1	teaspoon tomato paste
1/4	cup unbleached all-purpose flour
1/2	cup dry red wine
1	cup low-sodium beef broth
1	cup low-sodium chicken broth
4	bay leaves
4	sprigs fresh thyme
1	tablespoon cider vinegar

1. Adjust an oven rack to the middle position and heat the oven to 300 degrees.

2. Sprinkle the brisket generously with salt and pepper to taste. Heat the oil in a large ovenproof Dutch oven over high heat until smoking. Cook the brisket until dark brown on the first side, about 5 minutes. Flip the brisket and cook until well browned on the second side, about 5 minutes longer. Transfer the brisket to a large plate; set aside.

3. Reduce the heat to medium. Add the onions, brown sugar, and 1/4 teaspoon salt. Using a wooden spoon, scrape the browned bits from the pan bottom. Cook, stirring frequently, until the onions are softened and lightly browned, about 10 minutes. Stir in the garlic and tomato paste and cook until fragrant, about 30 seconds. Stir in the flour and cook for 1 minute. Slowly stir in the wine to dissolve the flour and cook until almost dry, about 1 minute. Stir in the beef broth, chicken broth, bay leaves, and thyme. Return the brisket to the pot, nestling it in the liquid, and bring to a simmer. Cover the pot, transfer it to the oven, and cook until a fork slides easily in and out of the center of the roast, 2½ to 3 hours.

4. Transfer the brisket to a cutting board, tent with foil, and let rest for 15 minutes. Remove and discard the bay leaves and thyme from the sauce, stir in the vinegar, and adjust the seasonings with salt and pepper to taste. Slice the brisket thinly across the grain. Arrange the meat on a warmed

LOCATING THE BRISKET

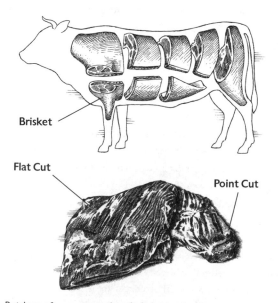

Butchers often separate the whole brisket into two parts, the flat end (left portion) and the point cut (right portion). The point cut is a bit thicker and contains more fat. It is more tender than the flat cut and is our first choice.

platter and spoon some of the sauce over it. Serve, passing the remaining sauce at the table.

➤ VARIATION
Braised Brisket with Sauerkraut and Prunes
This traditional German recipe offers a good balance between sweet and sour.

Follow the recipe for Braised Beef Brisket, reducing the amount of onions to 1½ pounds (about 3 large onions). Stir in 2 pounds packaged sauerkraut, well rinsed and drained (about 3 cups), and 1 cup pitted prunes along with the broths in step 3. Proceed with the recipe as directed.

CORNED BEEF AND CABBAGE

CORNED BEEF AND CABBAGE, THE VENERABLE one-pot meal of boiled corned beef, cabbage, and other winter vegetables (also known in parts of the country as New England boiled dinner), has struck us less as a dish with big flavor and genuine dinner-table appeal than as a symbol of the stalwart Yankee ethics of hard work and thrift. That misconception, however, was the first of several to be busted during our testing. In the course of tasting umpteen dishes of corned beef and cabbage, we came to realize that this dish needn't be mushy, overwhelmingly salty, or one-dimensional, as it had always seemed. Instead, it can be a full-flavored medley of meaty, tender, well-seasoned beef, subtle spices, and sweet, earthy vegetables, each distinct in flavor and texture.

We commenced our research and testing with the usual spate of recipes, most of which were based on a four- to six-pound piece of corned beef. The term *corned* refers to the curing of meat with salt, often used as a method of preservation before refrigeration became widespread. Legend has it that the salt grains were roughly the same size as corn kernels, hence the name corned beef. The cut of beef most commonly corned is boneless brisket, which is a trimmed, 12- to 13-pound piece taken from the front part of the cow's breast. For retail sale, the whole brisket is usually split

into two parts, called the first, or flat, cut and the second, or point, cut. Of the two, the point cut is thicker, fattier, and, to our taste, more flavorful and more tender than the flat cut. Both cuts can be trimmed further into smaller pieces of meat, and both are available as commercially corned beef.

At the supermarket, we found more commercial corned beef options than we had anticipated from reading the recipes we had researched. In addition to "low-sodium" corned beef, there were regular and "gray," each in both flat and point cuts in sizes ranging from three to six pounds. We were told by a representative from Mosey's, a national producer of corned beef, that the gray style is popular only in, and therefore limited to, New England. The difference between regular and gray is made clear on the package. The brine for gray corned beef contains only water and salt, whereas the "regular" corned beef brine also contains sodium nitrite, which helps the meat retain its red color by reacting with purple color pigments and turning them to pink and red.

We brought back an example of each type and took to the stove. Cooking directions on the packages and in our research recipes did not vary by much. Generally, instructions were to cover the meat with one to three inches of water and simmer until tender, anywhere from 2½ to 3 hours, depending on the size of the brisket.

To our surprise, the regular corned beef choices disappointed us across the board. Though they remained an appealing pink even when cooked, our tasters described the flavor of both the full- and low-salt versions as "sharp and somewhat chemical," most likely from the nitrite. In addition, the texture was deemed grainy, with a noticeably chalky mouthfeel. By comparison, the gray corned beef looked, well, gray, because it lacked the color boost given to regular brisket by the nitrite. The flavor, however, was superior, and for that, we'll gladly trade the pink color. Whereas the chemical qualities we noted in the regular versions obscured the flavor of the beef, the gray corned beef tasted cleaner and beefier. The salt had a stronger presence than we preferred, and the spice we look for in ideal corned beef was nonexistent, but we knew we wanted to stick with the gray corned beef for further testing.

But because the nitrite-free corned beef is a product limited to a small region of the country, we decided to try corning our own brisket. We figured that this would also make it easier to control the saltiness. Our research turned up two methods of corning—the wet cure and the dry cure. Both methods require close to a week, but they are also mindlessly easy. All you need to do is prepare the meat and its cure. Beyond that, there is no work whatsoever. We tested each method, using 5-pound fresh briskets in both flat and point cuts.

Because meat preservative is readily available in drugstores in the form of the potassium nitrate called saltpeter, we still had the option of producing regular and gray corned beef. Even in our home-corned beef, though, the preservative added a harshness to the flavor that competed with the taste of the beef. Because the color of the meat was less important to us than the flavor, we dropped the saltpeter from further testing.

Testing the wet method for our gray corned beef involved tasting briskets cured in a brine of 2 cups of salt and 3 quarts of water for 14, 12, 10, 7, and 5 days. Among all of them, we liked the 5-day brisket best, noting a pleasing saltiness alongside the distinctive flavor of beef. We also confirmed our preference for the fattier point cut of brisket. Fat carries flavor in all cuts of meat, and beef brisket is no different. The flat cut is especially lean and therefore less flavorful and moist than the point cut.

At this point, we also gave the dry-cure method a go. Adapting a recipe from Julia Child's *The Way to Cook* (Knopf, 1989), we rubbed our 6-pound, point-cut brisket with ¼ cup salt and a few crushed herbs and spices, placed it in a 2-gallon zipper-lock bag, weighted the meat with a brick, and let it sit for 5 days in the fridge. Lo and behold, the result

Vegetables for Corned Beef and Cabbage

The vegetables listed below are some of our favorites. However, if you love potatoes but cannot abide parsnips, choose vegetables to suit your taste. To make sure that the vegetables are evenly cooked, we trim them all to sizes appropriate for their density and cooking characteristics and add them to the pot in two batches.

CATEGORY 1

Once the meat has been removed from the pot, add the desired selection and quantity of vegetables from this category. Return the liquid to a boil and simmer for 10 minutes before adding vegetables from category 2.

VEGETABLE	PREPARATION
Carrots	Peeled and halved crosswise; thin end halved lengthwise, thick end quartered lengthwise.
Rutabagas (small)	Peeled and halved crosswise; each half cut into six chunks.
White turnips (medium)	Peeled and quartered.
New potatoes (small)	Scrubbed and left whole.

CATEGORY 2

At the 10-minute mark, add selected vegetables from this category, return the cooking liquid to a boil, and continue to simmer until all the vegetables are just tender, 10 to 15 minutes longer.

Boiling onions	Peeled and left whole.
Green cabbage, uncored (small head)	Blemished leaves removed and cut into six to eight wedges.
Parsnips	Peeled and halved crosswise; thin end halved lengthwise, thick end quartered lengthwise.
Brussels sprouts, whole	Blemished leaves removed, stems trimmed, and sprouts left whole.

was the best corned beef of them all, even better than the 5-day wet-cured corned beef, with a concentrated beef flavor, assertive yet not overpowering saltiness, and pleasant spiciness. Curing the brisket for 2 extra days, 7 in total, brought out the flavor of the spices a little more, without affecting the saltiness.

Julia Child's recipe suggested desalting the dry-cured meat by soaking it in several changes of water for at least 24 hours or up to 3 days, depending on the size of the brisket. To be honest, we initially overlooked this step; we simply rinsed the surface of the meat to remove shards of crumbled bay leaf and cracked peppercorns and went ahead with the cooking. When we finally did try the full desalting, we found that the meat tasted slightly richer because of the diminished salt presence, but not so much better that it justified a 24-hour soak as opposed to a quick rinse.

With the corned beef tasting just the way we wanted it, we turned our attention to the cooking method, then to the vegetables. Though most recipes call for cooking corned beef and cabbage on the stove, we did try a couple of tests in the oven. Our advice is to stick to the stove, on which the meat cooked faster and was easier to monitor. Also, we found that adding the vegetables and adjusting the heat to compensate was easier with the pot on top of the stove.

On the stove, we noticed that the meat emerged from the pot tender and flaky if cooked at a lively simmer, as opposed to tight and tough when cooked at a full boil. We also preferred to cook the meat covered to prevent water evaporation and a resulting overconcentration of salt in the broth. We experimented with different quantities of water in the pot, covering the corned beef by ½ inch to 3 inches and found that it makes no difference in terms of the meat or vegetables. The amount of water does matter to the broth, though. The broth produced from covering the meat by inch to an inch (8 to 10 cups over a 4½-pound brisket in our 8-quart pot) and cooking it with the pot lid on was nicely seasoned and suitable for use on its own or in a soup.

The last, though not insignificant, variable was the vegetables. We tested a wide variety of vegetables, from the familiar to the exotic, and settled on the traditional green cabbage, with the added interest of carrots, parsnips, potatoes, turnips, rutabagas, onions, and Brussels sprouts, all borrowed from the New England boiled dinner, as our favorites. We tried cooking the vegetables along with the meat, but there were two distinct disadvantages to this approach. First, it was difficult to judge when the vegetables were properly done. Second, it would require a pot larger than any we had in the test kitchen or in our own homes.

The best method turned out to be removing the meat from the broth when done, then cooking the vegetables in the broth. This not only benefited the vegetables, giving them a full, round flavor from the salt and rendered fat in the broth, but it also allowed us time to let the meat rest before cutting it.

Home-Corned Beef Brisket and Cabbage, New England Style

SERVES 8 WITH LEFTOVERS

If you prefer a leaner piece of meat, feel free to use the flat cut. In fact, we found more flat-cut than point-cut briskets in supermarket meat cases, so you'll probably have to ask the meat department attendant or butcher to bring you a point cut. Leave a bit of fat attached for better texture and flavor. The meat is cooked fully when it is tender, the muscle fibers have loosened visibly, and a skewer slides in with minimal resistance. Serve this dish with horseradish, either plain or mixed with whipped or sour cream, or with grainy mustard. Use any leftover meat to make Corned Beef Hash (page 654).

¼	cup table salt
1	tablespoon black peppercorns, cracked
¾	tablespoon ground allspice
1	tablespoon dried thyme
½	tablespoon paprika
2	bay leaves, crumbled
1	beef brisket (4 to 6 pounds), preferably point cut (see the illustration on page 424), trimmed of excess fat and patted dry with paper towels
7–8	pounds prepared vegetables of your choice (see page 426)

1. Mix the salt and seasonings in a small bowl.

2. Spear the brisket about 30 times per side with a meat fork or metal skewer. Rub each side evenly with the salt mixture; place in a 2-gallon zipper-lock bag, forcing out as much air as possible. Place in a pan large enough to hold it (a rimmed baking sheet works well), cover with a second, similar-size pan, and weight with 2 bricks or heavy cans of similar weight. Refrigerate 5 to 7 days, turning once a day. Rinse the meat and pat dry.

3. Bring the brisket to a boil with water to cover by ½ to 1 inch in a large Dutch oven or stockpot (at least 8 quarts), skimming any impurities that rise to the surface. Cover and simmer until a skewer inserted in the thickest part of the brisket slides out with ease, 2 to 3 hours.

4. Heat the oven to 200 degrees. Transfer the meat to a large platter, ladling about 1 cup of the cooking liquid over it to keep it moist. Cover with aluminum foil and set in the oven.

5. Add the vegetables from category 1 (see page 426) to the pot and bring to a boil; cover and simmer until the vegetables begin to soften, about 10 minutes. Add the vegetables from category 2 (see page 426) and bring to a boil; cover and simmer until all the vegetables are tender, 10 to 15 minutes longer.

6. Meanwhile, remove the meat from the oven and cut it across the grain into ¼-inch slices. Return the meat to the platter.

7. Transfer the vegetables to the meat platter, moisten with additional broth, and serve.

BRAISED SHORT RIBS

IN THE SUPERMARKET MEAT CASE, SHORT RIBS are often overlooked, seldom understood, rather intimidating hunks of meat and bone that are frequently shunned. But braise them, and they become yielding, tender, and succulent. Then douse them with a velvety sauce containing all the rich, bold flavors from the braise, and they are as satisfying as beef stew, but with much more panache. All of this, however, comes at a price: short ribs are outrageously fatty. The challenge is to get them to give up their fat.

The first step in most braises is browning the meat. Browning adds color and flavor, but in the case of short ribs it also presents an opportunity to render some of the fat. We tried browning both on the stovetop and in the oven and quickly became a proponent of oven browning. As long as you own a roasting pan large enough to hold all of the ribs in a single layer, you can use the oven to brown them in just one batch. This eliminates the need to brown in multiple batches on the stove, which can create a greasy, splattery mess and result in burnt drippings in the bottom of the pot. In the oven, the ribs can brown for a good long time to maximize rendering. (Because they can brown unattended, you can use that time to prepare the other ingredients for the braise.) The single inconvenience of oven browning is deglazing the roasting pan on the stovetop, which makes a burner-worthy roasting pan a prerequisite.

Like a beef stew, short ribs need aromatic vegetables. After having made a couple of batches with onions only, we chose to use a combination of onions, carrots, celery, and garlic for full, round flavor.

Braising liquids required only a cursory investigation. Homemade beef stock was out of the question because just about no one makes it. Based on previous tastings in the test kitchen, we also discounted canned beef broth. Canned chicken broth, however, offered sufficient backbone and, when enriched by the flavor and body contributed by the short ribs themselves, made for a rich, robust sauce. We began using a combination of red wine, chicken broth, and water. We eventually eliminated the water, but the sauce, despite the abundance of aromatics and herbs, remained strangely hollow and lacking. All along, we had been using a cheap, hardly potable wine. After stepping up to a good, solid one worthy of drinking, the sauce improved dramatically; it had the complexity and resonance that we were seeking.

If the braising liquid were to transform itself into the sauce we were after, it would need some thickening. After various experiments, we found that adding flour to the sautéed vegetables before pouring in the liquid resulted in a sauce that was lustrous and had the perfect consistency.

As they braise, the browned short ribs continue

to release fat, which means that the braising liquid must be defatted before it is palatable. We found the easiest technique to be a two-day process, necessitating some forethought. Braise the ribs, let them cool in the liquid so that the meat does not dry out, remove them, strain the liquid, and then chill the ribs and the liquid separately. The next day, spoon the solidified fat off the liquid's surface and heat the liquid and the ribs together.

Short Ribs Braised in Red Wine with Bacon, Parsnips, and Pearl Onions

SERVES 6

If braising and serving the ribs on the same day, bypass cooling the ribs in the braising liquid; instead, remove them from the pot straight out of the oven, strain the liquid, and then let it settle so that the fat separates to the top. With a wide, shallow spoon, skim off as much fat as possible and continue with the recipe. Though this recipe and the one that follows call for widely available English-style short ribs, both recipes will also work with flanken-style short ribs. We like to serve these short ribs with mashed potatoes, but they also taste good over egg noodles.

6	pounds bone-in English-style short ribs, trimmed of excess fat and silver skin, or bone-in flanken-style short ribs (see page 430)
	Salt and ground black pepper
3	cups full-bodied dry red wine
3	large onions, chopped medium
2	medium carrots, chopped medium
I	large celery rib, chopped medium
9	medium garlic cloves, chopped
1/4	cup unbleached all-purpose flour
4	cups low-sodium chicken broth
I	(14.5-ounce) can diced tomatoes
1 1/2	tablespoons minced fresh rosemary leaves
I	tablespoon minced fresh thyme leaves
3	medium bay leaves
I	teaspoon tomato paste

BACON, PEARL ONION, AND PARSNIP GARNISH

6	ounces (about 6 slices) bacon, cut into 1/4-inch pieces
8	ounces frozen pearl onions (do not thaw)
4	medium parsnips (about 10 ounces), peeled and cut on the diagonal into 3/4-inch pieces
1/4	teaspoon sugar
1/4	teaspoon salt
6	tablespoons minced fresh parsley leaves

1. Adjust an oven rack to the lower-middle position and heat the oven to 450 degrees. Arrange the short ribs bone-side down in a single layer in a large flameproof roasting pan; season with salt and pepper to taste. Roast until the meat begins to brown, about 45 minutes; drain off all the liquid and fat with a bulb baster. Return the pan to the oven and continue to cook until the meat is well browned, 15 to 20 minutes longer. (For flanken-style short ribs, arrange the ribs in a single layer in a large roasting pan; season with salt and pepper. Roast until the meat begins to brown, about 45 minutes; drain off all the liquid and fat with a bulb baster. Return the pan to the oven and continue to cook until browned, about 8 minutes; using tongs, flip each piece and cook until the second side is browned, about 8 minutes longer.) Transfer the ribs to a large plate; set aside. Drain off the fat to a small bowl and reserve. Reduce the oven temperature to 300 degrees. Place the roasting pan on 2 stovetop burners set at medium heat; add the wine and bring to a simmer, scraping up the browned bits on the pan bottom with a wooden spoon. Set the roasting pan with the wine aside.

2. Heat 2 tablespoons of the reserved fat in a large ovenproof Dutch oven over medium-high heat; add the onions, carrots, and celery. Sauté, stirring occasionally, until the vegetables soften, about 12 minutes. Add the garlic and cook until fragrant, about 30 seconds. Stir in the flour until combined, about 45 seconds. Stir in the wine from the roasting pan, the chicken broth, tomatoes, rosemary, thyme, bay leaves, tomato paste, and salt and pepper to taste. Bring to a boil and add the short ribs, completely submerging the meat in the liquid; return the liquid to a boil, cover the pot, place it in the oven, and simmer until the ribs are tender, 2 to 2½ hours. Transfer the pot to a wire rack and cool, partially covered, until warm, about 2 hours.

3. Transfer the ribs from the pot to a large plate, removing the excess vegetables that may cling to

the meat; discard any loose bones that have fallen away from the meat. Strain the braising liquid into a medium bowl, pressing out the liquid from the solids; discard the solids. Cover the ribs and liquid separately with plastic wrap and refrigerate overnight. (The ribs can be refrigerated for up to 3 days.)

4. To PREPARE THE GARNISH AND FINISH THE DISH: Cook the bacon in a Dutch oven over medium heat until just crisp, 8 to 10 minutes; remove with a slotted spoon to a plate lined with paper towels. Add the pearl onions, parsnips, sugar, and salt to the Dutch oven; increase the heat to high and sauté, stirring occasionally, until

INGREDIENTS: Short Ribs

Short ribs are just what their name says they are: "short ribs," cut from any part along the length of the cow's ribs. They can come from the lower belly section or higher up toward the back, from the shoulder (or chuck) area, or the forward midsection.

When we started testing short ribs, we went to the local grocery store and bought out their supply. What we brought back to the test kitchen were 2- to 4-inch lengths of wide, flat rib bone, to which a rectangular plate of fatty meat was attached (see photo below left). We also ordered short ribs from the butcher. Imagine our confusion when these turned out to be long, continuous pieces of meat, about ¾ inch thick, that had been cut across the ribs and grain and that included two or three segments of rib bone (see photo below right). The former, we learned, are sometimes called English-style short ribs, and the latter are called flanken-style ribs.

We began by braising both types of ribs. The ones from the butcher were favored by most tasters because the relatively thin, across-the-grain cut made the meat more pleasant to eat; the supermarket ribs were a bit stringier because they contained longer segments of "grain." Both types were equally tender and good, but considering the cost ($5.99 versus $2.99 per pound) and effort (special order) required to procure the butcher-cut specimens, we decided to go with the supermarket variety.

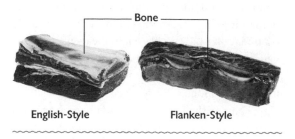

Bone

English-Style   Flanken-Style

browned, about 5 minutes. Meanwhile, spoon off and discard the solidified fat from the reserved braising liquid. Add the defatted liquid to the Dutch oven and bring to a simmer, stirring occasionally; adjust the seasonings with salt and pepper to taste. Submerge the ribs in the liquid and return to a simmer. Reduce the heat to medium and cook, partially covered, until the ribs are heated through and the onions and parsnips are tender, about 5 minutes longer; gently stir in the bacon. Divide the ribs, vegetables, and sauce among individual bowls, sprinkle each with 1 tablespoon of the parsley, and serve.

➤ VARIATION

Porter-Braised Short Ribs with Prunes, Brandy, and Lemon Essence

Brandy-soaked prunes take the place of vegetables here, so this version is particularly suited to a mashed root vegetable or potato accompaniment. Use a dark, mildly assertive beer, not a light lager.

PRUNE, BRANDY, AND
LEMON ESSENCE GARNISH
½   cup brandy
8   ounces pitted prunes, halved
2   teaspoons brown sugar
2   teaspoons grated zest from 1 lemon
6   tablespoons minced fresh parsley leaves

1. Follow the recipe for Short Ribs Braised in Red Wine with Bacon, Parsnips, and Pearl Onions, substituting 3 cups porter for the red wine, eliminating the rosemary, and substituting 2 tablespoons Dijon mustard and 2 teaspoons Worcestershire sauce for the tomato paste. Continue with the recipe through step 3.

2. To PREPARE THE GARNISH AND FINISH THE DISH: Bring the brandy to a boil in a small saucepan; off the heat, add the prunes and let stand until plump and softened, about 15 minutes. Meanwhile, spoon off and discard the solidified fat from the braising liquid. Bring the braising liquid to a boil in a Dutch oven over medium-high heat, stirring occasionally. Add the prunes and brandy and the brown sugar; adjust the seasonings with salt and pepper to taste. Submerge the ribs in the

liquid and return to a simmer. Reduce the heat to medium-low and cook, partially covered, until the ribs are heated through, about 5 minutes longer; gently stir in the lemon zest. Divide the ribs and sauce among individual bowls, sprinkle each with 1 tablespoon parsley, and serve.

Osso Buco

OSSO BUCO, OR ITALIAN BRAISED VEAL SHANKS, is too venerable a recipe to fiddle with. We decided the best way to approach the dish was to perfect (and simplify, if possible) the cooking technique and to extract the most flavor from the simple ingredients: veal shanks (which are browned), aromatics (onions, carrots, and celery, all sautéed), and liquids (a blend of wine, stock, and tomatoes).

To start, we gathered three classic recipes and prepared each in the test kitchen. At the tasting, there was little consensus about the recipes, although white wine was clearly preferred to red wine. Tasters did, however, offer similar ideas as to what constituted the perfect osso buco; it would be rich in flavor and color and somewhat brothy but not stewy. This first goal is the reason why we prefer osso buco to veal stews made with boneless shoulder meat. While shoulder meat can be a bit wan, the shank is robust, and the bone adds tremendous flavor to the stewing liquid. With these traits in mind, we created a rough working recipe and set out to explore the two main components in this dish—the veal shanks and the braising liquid.

Most recipes we reviewed called for shanks from the upper portion of the hind leg, cut into pieces between 1 and 1½ inches thick. We found that purchasing shanks is tricky, even when we special-ordered them. From one market, we received stunning shanks with a lovely pinkish blush, which were ideal except for the weight. Each shank weighed between 12 and 16 ounces—too large for individual servings. Part of the charm of osso buco is receiving an individual shank as a portion. We concluded that shanks should weigh 8 to 10 ounces (with the bone) and no more. At

another market, the shanks were generally in the ideal weight range, but the butchering job was less than perfect. In the same package, shank widths varied from 1 to 2½ inches and were occasionally cut on an extreme bias, making tying difficult (see the explanation below) and searing uneven.

The first step, then, is to shop carefully. We found a thickness of 1½ inches and a weight of 8 ounces ideal. Make sure all the shanks you buy are close to these specifications. Each shank should have two nicely cut, flat sides to facilitate browning.

Preparing the meat for braising was the first step. Most recipes called for tying the shanks and dredging them in flour before searing. We found that tying a piece of kitchen twine around the equator of each shank does prevent the meat from falling apart and makes for a more attractive presentation. When we skipped this step, the meat fell off the bone and floated about in the pot.

Although we do not generally dredge meat in flour before browning, we felt we should at least try it, considering that the majority of osso buco recipes include this step. Tasters felt that the meat floured before searing was gummy and lacked depth. The flour on the meat browns rather than the meat itself, and the flour coating may peel off during the long braising time.

To develop the best flavor in the shanks, we seasoned them heavily with salt and pepper and seared them until a thick, golden brown crust formed. We seared the shanks in two batches (even if they could all fit in the pan at the same time) so that we could deglaze the pan twice with wine, thereby enriching the braising liquid doubly.

The most difficult part of developing this recipe was attaining an ideal braising liquid and sauce. Braising, by design, is a relatively inexact cooking method because the rate at which the liquid reduces can vary greatly. Some of the initial recipes we tried yielded far too much liquid, which was thin in flavor and texture. In other cases, the liquid nearly evaporated by the time the meat was tender. We needed to create a foolproof, flavorful braising liquid and cooking technique that produced a rich sauce in a suitable volume and did not need a lot of last-minute fussing.

We experimented with numerous techniques to attain our ideal liquid, including reductions before braising and after braising (with the aromatics and without) and a reduction of the wine to a syrup during the deglazing process. In the end, we settled on the easiest method: natural reduction in the oven. The seal on most Dutch ovens is not perfectly tight, so the liquid reduces as the osso buco cooks. We found further simmering on the stovetop unnecessary as long as we started with the right amount of liquid in the pot.

The braising liquid traditionally begins with meat stock and adds white wine and tomatoes. As few cooks have homemade meat stock on hand and canned versions are often unappealing, we knew that canned chicken broth would be our likely starting point. Two cups (or one can) seemed the right amount, and tests confirmed this. To enrich the flavor of the broth, we used a hefty amount of diced onion, carrot, and celery. Tasters liked the large amount of garlic in one recipe, so we finely minced about six cloves and added it to the pot prior to the broth. We rounded out the flavors with 2 bay leaves.

We hoped to write the recipe in even amounts, using whole vegetables, one can of stock, one bottle of wine, and so on. But an entire bottle of wine proved overwhelming. The resulting sauce was dominated by acidity. Some testers also felt that the meat was tougher than previous batches with less wine. We scaled the wine back to 2½ cups, about two thirds of a bottle, and were happy with the results. More than half of the wine is used to deglaze the pot between searing batches of veal shanks, and thus the final dish is not as alcoholic or liquidy as it might seem.

With the wine and broth amounts settled, we needed to figure out how to best incorporate the tomatoes. Most tasters did not like too much tomato because they felt it easily overwhelmed the other flavors. Fresh tomatoes are always a gamble outside of the summer months, so we chose canned diced tomatoes, thoroughly drained of their juice. This approach worked out well, and the tomatoes did not overwhelm the sauce.

We still needed to determine the ideal braising time. Several sources suggested cooking osso buco almost to the consistency of pulled pork. Tasters loved the meat cooked this way, but it was less than attractive—broken down and pot roast–like. We wanted compact meat firmly attached to the bone, so we cooked the meat until it was just fork-tender but still clinging to the bone. Two hours in the oven produced veal that was meltingly soft but still attached to the bone. With some of the larger shanks, the cooking time extended to about 2½ hours.

We experimented with oven temperature and found that 325 degrees reduced the braising liquid to the right consistency and did not harm the texture of the meat. While beef stews are best cooked at 300 degrees, veal shanks have so much collagen and connective tissue that they can be braised at a slightly higher temperature.

Just before serving, osso buco is sprinkled with gremolata, a mixture of minced garlic, parsley, and lemon zest. We were surprised to find variations on this classic trio. A number of recipes included orange zest mixed with lemon zest or on its own. Other recipes included anchovies. We tested three gremolatas: one traditional, one with orange zest mixed in equal part with lemon zest, and one with anchovies. Tasters liked all three but favored the traditional version.

In some recipes, the gremolata is used as a garnish, and in others it is added to the pot just before serving. We chose a compromise approach, stirring half the gremolata into the pot and letting it stand for 5 minutes so that the flavors of the garlic, lemon, and parsley permeated the dish. We sprinkled the remaining gremolata on individual servings for a hit of freshness.

Osso Buco

SERVES 6

To keep the meat attached to the bone during the long simmering process, tie a piece of kitchen twine around the thickest portion of each shank before it is browned. Use a zester, vegetable peeler, or paring knife to remove the zest from a single lemon, then mince it with a chef's knife. With the lid on the pot cracked, the braising liquid should reduce to a sauce-like consistency in the oven. Just before serving, taste the liquid and, if it seems too thin, simmer the liquid on the stovetop as you remove the strings from the osso buco and arrange them in bowls. Osso buco is traditionally served with risotto alla Milanese *(page 219), although mashed potatoes and polenta are good options, too.*

OSSO BUCO

6	tablespoons vegetable oil
6	veal shanks, 1½ inches thick (8 to 10 ounces each), patted dry with paper towels and tied around the equator with kitchen twine
	Salt and ground black pepper
2½	cups dry white wine
2	medium onions, cut into ½-inch dice
2	medium carrots, cut into ½-inch dice
2	medium celery ribs, cut into ½-inch dice
6	medium garlic cloves, minced or pressed through a garlic press
2	cups low-sodium chicken broth
2	small bay leaves
1	(14.5-ounce) can diced tomatoes, drained

GREMOLATA

3	medium garlic cloves, minced or pressed through a garlic press (about 1 tablespoon)
2	teaspoons minced lemon zest
¼	cup minced fresh parsley leaves

1. FOR THE OSSO BUCO: Adjust an oven rack to the lower-middle position and heat the oven to 325 degrees. Heat 2 tablespoons of the oil in a large ovenproof Dutch oven over medium-high heat until shimmering. Meanwhile, sprinkle both sides of the shanks generously with salt and pepper to taste. Swirl to coat the pan bottom with the oil. Place 3 shanks in a single layer in the pan and cook until they are golden brown on one side, about 5 minutes. Using tongs, flip the shanks and cook on the second side until golden brown, about 5 minutes longer. Transfer the shanks to a bowl and set aside. Off the heat, add ½ cup of the wine to the Dutch oven, scraping the pan bottom with a wooden spoon to loosen any browned bits. Pour the liquid into the bowl with the browned shanks. Return the pot to medium-high heat, add 2 tablespoons oil, and heat until shimmering. Brown the remaining shanks, about 5 minutes for each side. Transfer the shanks to the bowl. Off the heat, add an additional 1 cup wine to the pot, scraping the bottom to loosen the browned bits. Pour the liquid into the bowl with the shanks.

2. Set the pot over medium heat. Add the remaining 2 tablespoons oil and heat until shimmering. Add the onions, carrots, and celery and cook, stirring occasionally, until soft and lightly browned, about 9 minutes. Add the garlic and cook until lightly browned, about 1 minute longer. Increase the heat to high and stir in the broth, the remaining 1 cup wine, the accumulated veal juices in the bowl, and the bay leaves. Add the tomatoes; return the veal shanks to the pot (the liquid should just cover the shanks). Bring the liquid to a full simmer. Cover the pot, cracking the lid just slightly, and transfer the pot to the oven. Cook the shanks until the meat is easily pierced with a fork but not falling off the bone, about 2 hours. (The shanks can be refrigerated for up to 2 days. Bring to a simmer over medium-low heat.)

3. FOR THE GREMOLATA: Combine the garlic, lemon zest, and parsley in a small bowl. Stir half of the gremolata into the pot, reserving the rest for garnish. Adjust the seasonings with salt and pepper to taste. Let the osso buco stand, uncovered, for 5 minutes.

4. Using tongs, remove the shanks from the pot, cut off and discard the twine, and place 1 veal shank in each of 6 bowls. Ladle some of the braising liquid over each shank and sprinkle each serving with gremolata. Serve immediately.

STIR-FRIED BEEF AND BROCCOLI

ORDER BEEF AND BROCCOLI IN MOST RESTAU-rants and you are served a pile of chewy, gray "beef" surrounded by a forest of giant, overcooked, army-issue broccoli. Worst of all is the thick-as-pudding brown sauce, which, aside from being flavored with burnt garlic, is otherwise tasteless.

We turned to several recipes in cookbooks for help. Although most produced that gloppy, tasteless mass of beef and broccoli that we were trying to avoid, a couple of recipes showed promise. In these recipes, we found that each component of the dish—the beef, the broccoli, and even the sauce—was distinct and cooked to the best of its ability. Grateful for this glimmer of hope, we grabbed a nonstick 12-inch skillet (our pan of choice when it comes to stir-frying because its flat surface perfectly matches the surface of the

American stovetop) and started cooking.

Although flank steak—a chewy cut from the underbelly beneath the loin—is most often called for in this stir-fry, we also tested a few other boneless cuts. Tender and expensive filet mignon (from the tenderloin) was mushy and dull-flavored in this application. Strip steak (from the loin) was good, but not as good as the flank. A blade steak (cut from the shoulder blade area of the chuck) was similar to the tenderloin—too soft and too mild-tasting. Flank steak clearly offered the biggest beefy taste. Slicing the steak thinly across the grain made it tender, but when we used a less-than-razor-sharp knife (like the knives found in most home kitchens), the steak tugged on the blade. We put the steak in the freezer for 20 minutes to stiffen it up enough to make slicing easier.

Having recently discovered that using soy sauce in a marinade aids in tenderizing meat (see Grilled Steak Tips on page 567), we tested one batch of nonmarinated flank steak against batches marinated in soy sauce for two hours, one hour, and ten minutes. The results were dramatic. Two hours was overkill; the steak became gummy and spongy. One hour was perfect. The steak was tender and full of great soy flavor. Just a few minutes of marinating, however, made a big difference, which is good news if you don't have the full hour to marinate the steak.

Cooking the broccoli evenly was the next test, and our first decision here was to get rid of those gargantuan pieces of broccoli we found in both the restaurant and recipe versions of this dish. Fork-friendly 1-inch pieces of broccoli floret seemed right, and by trimming the tough exterior from the broccoli stems and slicing them into thin ⅛-inch slices, we were able to cook the stems right along with the florets.

Most recipes cook the broccoli by either straightforward stir-frying or by steaming or blanching. While the former technique produced unevenly cooked broccoli, steaming or blanching made for tender broccoli every time. Unfortunately, this technique required an additional pan. In an effort to avoid this, we modified our use of the pan we'd already been using. After cooking the beef and removing it from the skillet,

we stir-fried the broccoli for a few seconds, added water to the pan, and covered it tightly in hopes of steaming the broccoli. This greatly simplified the recipe and produced superior broccoli—steamed to perfect tenderness and a brilliant emerald hue.

As for other vegetables, tasters wanted to keep this dish true to its name, save for the addition of red bell pepper, which added sweetness and vivid color. After removing the broccoli, we tossed the peppers into the hot pan and cooked them briefly to retain their crispness.

Garlic was a must, but we had to figure out the best way to add it to the mix. Added to the marinade, the garlic scorched in the skillet as it cooked with the beef. Added with the broccoli, it tasted raw. In the end we added minced garlic (along with some well-received ginger) to the skillet when the red peppers were nearly finished cooking.

Oyster sauce is the typical base for the sauce in this dish. Indeed, in some restaurants, it is referred to as "beef and broccoli in oyster sauce." We found no need to depart from the tradition of oyster sauce, as its deep, earthy notes provided the right flavor base and its thick consistency (think ketchup) added great body to the sauce. Soy sauce was next up for consideration, but we found it to be an unnecessary addition; there was already enough in both the oyster sauce and the beef marinade. Rice vinegar and sherry are common additions, but only the latter was approved for its warm flavor. Chicken broth also passed muster to balance the flavors. Just a little toasted sesame oil and light brown sugar and the sauce took a sweet and nutty turn for the better.

Finally satisfied with the sauce, we added it to the pan with the browned beef and steamed broccoli. We tossed the mixture, but the sauce pooled on the bottom of the skillet. Clearly, the sauce wasn't thick enough, so we reluctantly returned to an often used but frequently troublesome ingredient: cornstarch. While many recipes (including some used in our early failed tests) called for a tablespoon or more of this thickener, we started more modestly. With a tentative hand, we stirred in the cornstarch until we had used only one teaspoon.

And now we had it: a sensuous sauce that barely

Stir-Frying 101

There are six key steps you should follow to turn out a perfect stir-fry. Use a minimum of oil, preferably peanut oil, in each of the steps called for below—no more than one tablespoon and less when possible.

1. Preparing the ingredients in advance is key. While the meat is marinating, whisk the sauce ingredients together in a measuring cup and add a small amount of oil to the garlic and ginger.

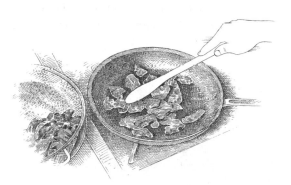

2. Heat the oil in a nonstick 12-inch skillet until smoking. Drain the meat and add half to the pan. Cook until well browned. Remove to a large bowl and repeat with more oil and the remaining meat.

3. Stir-fry long-cooking vegetables—such as broccoli, asparagus, or green beans—in oil in the empty pan; add a little water, cover, and then steam. Once the vegetables are crisp-tender, transfer them to a bowl.

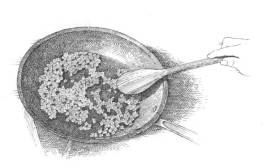

4. Stir-fry short-cooking vegetables—such as peppers, snow peas, or onions—for a minute or two in oil in the empty pan.

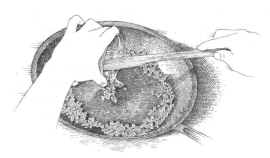

5. When the vegetables are slightly browned, push them to the sides of the pan and add the garlic and ginger to the center of the pan. Cook until fragrant (15 to 20 seconds), then stir the aromatics into the vegetables.

6. Return the meat and long-cooking vegetables to the skillet. Whisk the sauce to recombine, pour it into the skillet, and toss with the meat and vegetables. When all of the ingredients are heated through (30 to 60 seconds), serve immediately.

clung to the deeply browned, tender beef and perfectly cooked jade-green broccoli. The kitchen was awash with the heady aroma of garlic, and we knew that we had brought in Chinatown, just as we'd hoped.

Stir-Fried Beef and Broccoli with Oyster Sauce

SERVES 4 WITH RICE

This basic recipe can be altered in countless ways by changing the vegetables and/or sauce. The variations offer two possibilities.

I	pound flank steak, sliced according to the illustrations on page 42
3	tablespoons soy sauce
I	tablespoon dry sherry
2	tablespoons low-sodium chicken broth
5	tablespoons oyster sauce
I	tablespoon light brown sugar
I	teaspoon toasted sesame oil
I	teaspoon cornstarch
6	medium garlic cloves, minced or pressed through a garlic press
I	tablespoon minced fresh ginger
3	tablespoons peanut or vegetable oil
I¼	pounds broccoli, florets cut into bite-size pieces, stems trimmed, peeled, and cut on the diagonal ⅛ inch thick
⅓	cup water
I	small red bell pepper, cored, seeded, and diced
3	medium scallions, cut on the diagonal ½ inch thick

1. Combine the beef and soy sauce in a medium bowl; cover with plastic wrap and refrigerate at least 10 minutes or up to 1 hour, stirring once. Meanwhile, whisk the sherry, chicken broth, oyster sauce, brown sugar, sesame oil, and cornstarch in a measuring cup. Combine the garlic, ginger, and 1½ teaspoons of the peanut oil in a small bowl.

2. Drain the beef and discard the liquid. Heat 1½ teaspoons of the peanut oil in a nonstick 12-inch skillet over high heat until smoking. Add half of the beef to the skillet and break up the clumps; cook without stirring, 1 minute, then stir

and cook until the beef is browned about the edges, about 30 seconds. Transfer the beef to a medium bowl. Add 1½ teaspoons of the peanut oil to the skillet, heat until just smoking, and repeat with the remaining beef.

3. Add 1 tablespoon of the peanut oil to the now-empty skillet; heat until just smoking. Add the broccoli and cook 30 seconds; add the water, cover the pan, and lower the heat to medium. Steam the broccoli until tender-crisp, about 2 minutes; transfer to a paper towel–lined plate.

4. Add the remaining 1½ teaspoons peanut oil to the skillet; increase the heat to high and heat until just smoking. Add the bell pepper and cook, stirring frequently, until spotty brown, about 1½ minutes.

5. Clear the center of the skillet; add the garlic and ginger mixture to the clearing and cook, mashing the mixture with a spoon, until fragrant, 15 to 20 seconds, then stir the mixture into the peppers. Return the beef and broccoli to the skillet and toss to combine. Whisk the sauce to recombine, then add to the skillet; cook, stirring constantly, until the sauce is thickened and evenly distributed, about 30 seconds. Transfer to a serving platter, sprinkle with the scallions, and serve.

➤ VARIATIONS

Stir-Fried Beef and Eggplant with Oyster Sauce

If you like, add 1 teaspoon minced fresh chile with the garlic and ginger.

Follow the recipe for Stir-Fried Beef and Broccoli with Oyster Sauce through step 2. Omit the broccoli. Add 1 tablespoon peanut oil to the now-empty skillet and heat until just smoking. Add 1 pound eggplant, cut into ¾-inch cubes, and cook, stirring every 30 seconds, until browned and no longer spongy, about 5 minutes; transfer to the bowl with the beef. Proceed with the recipe as directed from step 4, returning the eggplant to the skillet with the beef.

Stir-Fried Beef and Snow Peas with Ginger Sauce

This classic stir-fry has a clean, bright ginger flavor. Snow peas require so little cooking that one pound may be cooked in a single batch.

1 pound flank steak, sliced according to the illustrations on page 42

6 tablespoons soy sauce

1 tablespoon dry sherry

3 tablespoons low-sodium chicken broth

1 teaspoon toasted sesame oil

½ teaspoon sugar

1 teaspoon cornstarch

6 medium garlic cloves, minced or pressed through a garlic press

3 tablespoons minced fresh ginger

2½ tablespoons peanut or vegetable oil

1 pound snow peas, strings removed

1 (8-ounce) can sliced bamboo shoots in water, drained

3 medium scallions, cut on the diagonal ½ inch thick

1. Combine the beef and 3 tablespoons of the soy sauce in a medium bowl; cover with plastic wrap and refrigerate at least 10 minutes or up to 1 hour, stirring once. Meanwhile, whisk the remaining 3 tablespoons soy sauce, sherry, chicken broth, sesame oil, sugar, and cornstarch in a measuring cup. Combine the garlic, ginger, and the 1½ teaspoons of the peanut oil in a small bowl.

2. Drain the beef and discard the liquid. Heat 1½ teaspoons of the peanut oil in a nonstick 12-inch skillet over high heat until smoking. Add half of the beef to the skillet and break up the clumps; cook without stirring, 1 minute, then stir and cook until the beef is browned about the edges, about 30 seconds. Transfer the beef to a medium bowl. Add 1½ teaspoons of the peanut oil to the skillet, heat until just smoking, and repeat with the remaining beef.

3. Add the remaining 1 tablespoon peanut oil to the now-empty skillet; heat until just smoking. Add the snow peas and cook until crisp-tender, about 1 minute. Add the bamboo shoots and cook until sizzling, about 30 seconds.

4. Clear the center of the skillet; add the garlic and ginger mixture to the clearing and cook, mashing the mixture with a spoon, until fragrant, 15 to 20 seconds, then stir the mixture into the snow peas. Return the beef to the skillet and toss to combine. Whisk the sauce to recombine, then add to the skillet; cook, stirring constantly, until the sauce is thickened and evenly distributed, about 30 seconds. Transfer to a serving platter and sprinkle with the scallions. Serve immediately.

CHILI CON CARNE

A STRICTLY TEXAN CHILI, KNOWN AS CHILI con carne, depends on either pureed or powdered ancho chiles; uses beef; excludes tomato, onion, and beans; and features a high proportion of meat to chiles. We wanted a chili that would be hearty, heavy on the meat, and spicy but not overwhelmingly hot. We wanted a creamy consistency somewhere between soup and stew. The flavors would be balanced so that no single spice or seasoning stood out or competed with the chile or beef.

Because chiles are the heart of chili con carne, we had to learn about the different types. After considerable testing and tasting, we settled on a combination of ancho and New Mexico for the dried chiles (for more information on dried chiles, see page 442), with a few jalapeños added for their fresh flavor and bite. Chilis made with toasted and ground whole dried chiles tasted noticeably fuller and warmer than those made with chili powder. The two main toasting methods are oven and skillet, and after trying both, we went with the oven—simply because it required less attention and effort than skillet toasting. The chiles will puff in the oven, become fragrant, and dry out sufficiently after five to six minutes. One caveat, though: Overtoasted chiles can take on a distinctly bitter flavor, so don't let them go too long.

With the chiles chosen and toasted, the next big question was how best to prepare them. The two options here are to rehydrate the toasted chiles in liquid and process them into a puree, or to grind them into a powder. It didn't take long for us to select grinding as the preferred method. It was easier, faster, and much less messy than making the puree, which tasters felt produced a chili that was too rich, more like a Mexican enchilada sauce than a bowl of chili.

This felt like the right time to determine the best ratio of chile to meat. Many of the recipes we looked at in our research suggested that a tablespoon of ground chile per pound of meat was sufficient, but we found these chilis to be bland and watery. Three tablespoons per pound of meat, on the other hand, produced chili with too much punch and richness. Two tablespoons per pound was the way to go.

There was little agreement in the recipes we had collected as to how the chili powder should be added. After running several tests, we found that sautéing the spices, including the chiles, is key to unlocking their flavor. We also discovered that blending the chili powder with water to make a paste keeps it from scorching in the pot; this step is advised.

Since chuck is our favorite meat for stewing, we knew it would work best in chili. Still, there were some aspects of the meat question that still had to be settled. Should the chuck be standard hamburger grind, coarser chili grind, hand-cut into tiny cubes, or a combination? The chili made from cubes of beef was far more appealing than those made from either type of ground beef; they both had a grainy, extruded texture. Most of the recipes we looked at specified that the meat should be cut into ¼-inch cubes. However, we found that larger 1-inch chunks gave the chili a satisfying chew. In addition, cutting a chuck roast into larger chunks was much, much faster and easier than breaking it down into fussy ¼-inch dice.

Next we set out to determine the best type, or types, of liquid for the chili. The main contenders were water, chicken broth, beef broth, beer, black coffee, and red wine. We tried each one on its own, as well as in any combination we felt made sense. The surprise result was that we liked plain water best because it allowed the flavor of the chiles to come through in full force. Both broths, whether on their own, combined in equal parts with each other, or combined with water, muddied the chile flavors. All of the other liquids, used either alone or mixed with an equal part of chicken broth or water, competed with the chile flavor.

Another basic factor to determine was the garlic. Tasters agreed that three cloves were too

few and eight were too many, so we settled on five. We found many recipes that called for powdered garlic rather than fresh. Out of obligation, we tested powdered versus fresh garlic and found fresh to be far superior.

Though common in modern recipes, Texas chili lore leaves tomatoes and onions out of the original formula. These two ingredients may break with tradition, but we found both to be essential. The acidity of the tomato and the sweetness of the onion, both used in small amounts, add interest and dimension to the chili. The batches we tested without them were decidedly dull. We tested various amounts and types of tomato products and determined that more than one cup pushed the flavor of the chili toward that of a spaghetti sauce. Products with a smooth consistency, such as canned crushed tomatoes or plain tomato sauce, helped create the smooth sauce we wanted.

We found that bacon lends the chili a subtly sweet, smoky essence that is most welcome. Other "secret" ingredients fell by the wayside. Coke imparted a sourish, off taste. Brown sugar cut the heat of the chiles too much. An ounce of unsweetened chocolate gave the chili a rounder, deeper flavor, and 2 tablespoons of peanut butter made the sauce creamier and earthy-tasting. Much as we liked both peanut butter and chocolate, we decided they were not essential.

Chili is generally thickened to tighten the sauce and make it smoother. Flour, roux (a paste of flour and melted butter), cornstarch, and masa harina (a flour ground from corn treated with lime, or calcium oxide) are the most common options. Dredging the meat in flour before browning and adding a roux along with the liquid were both effective, but these approaches made it more difficult to finesse the consistency of the finished product because both were introduced early in the cooking process. A roux added at the end of the cooking left a faint taste of raw flour. We did prefer thickening at the end of cooking, though, because we could control the consistency by adding thickener gradually until the chili reached the right consistency. We like chili thick enough to coat the back of a wooden spoon, like the custard base of homemade ice cream.

Our first choice for thickening was masa harina,

added at the end of cooking. Masa both thickened and imparted a slightly sweet, earthy corn flavor to the chili. If masa harina is not available in your grocery store and you'd rather not mail-order it, use a cornstarch and water slurry. It brings no flavor to the chili, but it is predictable, is easy to use, and gives the "gravy" a silky consistency and attractive sheen.

One last note. Time and time again, tasters observed that chili, like many stews, always improved after an overnight rest because the flavors blended and mellowed. If you are able, cook your chili a day ahead. The result will be worth the wait.

Chili Con Carne

SERVES 6

To ensure the best chile flavor, we recommend toasting whole dried chiles and grinding them in a minichopper or spice-dedicated coffee grinder, all of which takes only 10 (very well spent) minutes. Select dried chiles that are moist and pliant, like dried fruit.

To toast and grind dried chiles: Place the chiles on a baking sheet in a 350-degree oven until fragrant and puffed, about 6 minutes. Cool, stem, and seed, tearing the pods into pieces. Place the pieces in a spice grinder and process until powdery, 30 to 45 seconds.

For hotter chili, boost the heat with a pinch of cayenne, a dash of hot pepper sauce, or crumbled pequín chiles near the end of cooking. Serve the chili with any of the following side dishes: warm pinto or kidney beans, cornbread or chips, corn tortillas or tamales, rice, biscuits,

or just plain crackers. Top with any of the following garnishes: chopped fresh cilantro leaves, minced white onion, diced avocado, shredded cheddar or Monterey Jack cheese, or sour cream.

3	tablespoons ancho chili powder, or 3 medium pods (about ½ ounce), toasted and ground (see note)
3	tablespoons New Mexico chili powder, or 3 medium pods (about ¾ ounce), toasted and ground (see note)
2	tablespoons cumin seeds, toasted in a dry skillet over medium heat until fragrant, about 4 minutes, and ground
2	teaspoons dried oregano, preferably Mexican
7½	cups water
4	pounds beef chuck roast, trimmed and cut into 1-inch cubes (see the illustrations on page 540)
	Salt
8	ounces (about 8 slices) bacon, cut into ¼-inch pieces
1	medium onion, minced
5	medium garlic cloves, minced or pressed through a garlic press
4–5	small jalapeño chiles, stemmed, seeded, and minced
1	cup canned crushed tomatoes or plain tomato sauce
2	tablespoons juice from 1 lime
5	tablespoons masa harina or 3 tablespoons cornstarch
	Ground black pepper

EQUIPMENT: Flame Tamer

A flame tamer (or heat diffuser) is a metal disk that can be fitted over an electric or gas burner to reduce the heat output. This device is especially useful when trying to keep a pot at the barest simmer. If you don't own a flame tamer (it costs less than $10 and is stocked at most kitchenware stores), you can fashion one from aluminum foil. Take a long sheet of heavy-duty foil and shape it into a 1-inch-thick ring that will fit on your burner. Make sure that the ring is an even thickness so that a pot will rest flat on it. The foil ring elevates the pot slightly above the flame or electric coil, allowing you to keep a pot of chili or sauce at the merest simmer.

HOMEMADE FLAME TAMER
A homemade flame tamer made with aluminum foil keeps chili and sauces from simmering too briskly.

1. Mix the chili powders, cumin, and oregano in a small bowl and stir in ½ cup of the water to form a thick paste; set aside. Toss the beef cubes with 2 teaspoons salt; set aside.

2. Fry the bacon in a large Dutch oven over medium-low heat until the fat is rendered and the bacon is crisp, about 10 minutes. Remove the bacon with a slotted spoon to a paper towel–lined plate; pour all but 2 teaspoons of the fat from the pot into a small bowl; set aside. Increase the heat to medium-high; sauté the meat in 4 batches until well browned on all sides, about 5 minutes per batch, adding 2 teaspoons additional bacon fat to the pot as necessary. Set the browned meat aside.

3. Reduce the heat to medium and add 3 tablespoons of the bacon fat to the now-empty pan. Add the onion and sauté until softened, 5 to 6 minutes. Add the garlic and jalapeño chiles and sauté until fragrant, about 1 minute. Add the chili mixture and sauté until fragrant, 2 to 3 minutes. Add the reserved bacon and browned beef, the crushed tomatoes, lime juice, and remaining 7 cups water. Bring to a simmer. Continue to cook at a steady simmer until the meat is tender and the juices are dark, rich, and starting to thicken, about 2 hours.

4. Mix the masa harina with ⅔ cup water (or the cornstarch with 3 tablespoons water) in a small bowl to form a smooth paste. Increase the heat to medium, stir in the paste, and simmer until thickened, 5 to 10 minutes. Adjust the seasonings generously with salt and ground black pepper to taste. Serve immediately or, for best flavor, cool slightly, cover, and refrigerate overnight or for up to 5 days. Reheat before serving.

➤ VARIATION

Smoky Chipotle Chili Con Carne
Grill-smoking the meat in combination with chipotle chiles gives this chili a distinct, but not overwhelming, smoky flavor. Make sure you start with a chuck roast that is at least 3 inches thick. The grilling is meant to flavor the meat by searing the surface and smoking it lightly; it is not a way to cook it.

1. To smoke the meat: Puree 4 medium garlic cloves with 2 teaspoons salt. Rub the chuck roast with the puree and sprinkle evenly with 2 to 3 tablespoons New Mexico chili powder; cover and set aside. Meanwhile, build a hot fire in the grill. When you can hold your hand 5 inches above the grill surface for no more than 3 seconds, spread the hot coals to an area about the size of the roast. Open the bottom grill vents, scatter 1 cup soaked mesquite or hickory wood chips over the hot coals, and set the grill rack in place. Place the meat over the hot coals and grill-roast, opening the lid vents three quarters of the way and covering so that the vents are opposite the bottom vents to draw smoke through and around the roast. Sear the meat until all sides are dark and richly colored, about 12 minutes per side. Remove the roast to a bowl; when cool enough to handle, trim and cut into 1-inch cubes, reserving the juices.

2. To make the chili: Follow the recipe for Chili Con Carne, omitting the browning of the beef cubes and substituting 5 chipotle chiles in adobo sauce, minced, for the jalapeño chiles. Add the grill-smoked meat cubes and the juice accumulated in the bowl with the cooked bacon.

BASIC CHILI

LIKE POLITICS, CHILI PROVOKES HEATED DEBATE. Some purists insist that a chili that contains beans or tomatoes is just not chili. Others claim that homemade chili powder is essential or that ground meat is taboo. But there is one kind of chili that almost every American has eaten (or even made) at one time or another. It's the kind of chili you liked as a kid and still see being served at Super Bowl parties. Made with ground meat, tomatoes, and chili powder, this thick, fairly smooth chili is spiced but not spicy. It's basic grub (and it can be great grub) that's not intended to fuel impassioned exchanges over the merits of ancho versus New Mexico chiles.

Although this simple chili should come together easily, it should not taste as if it did. The flavors should be rich and balanced, the texture thick and lush. Unfortunately, many "basic" recipes yield a pot of underspiced, underflavored chili reminiscent of Sloppy Joes. Our goal was to develop a no-fuss chili that tasted far better than the sum of its common parts.

Most of the recipes for this plain-spoken chili begin by sautéing onions and garlic. Tasters liked red bell peppers added to these aromatics but rejected other options, including green bell peppers, celery, and carrots. After this first step, things became less clear. The most pressing concerns were the spices (how much and what kind) and the meat (how much ground beef and whether or not to add another meat). There were also the cooking liquid (what kind, if any) and the proportions of tomatoes and beans to consider.

Our first experiments with these ingredients followed a formula we had seen in lots of recipes: 2 pounds ground beef, 3 tablespoons chili powder, 2 teaspoons ground cumin, and 1 teaspoon each red pepper flakes and dried oregano. Many recipes add the spices after the beef has been browned, but we knew from work done in the test kitchen on curry that ground spices taste better when they have direct contact with hot cooking oil.

EQUIPMENT: Slow Cookers

Slow cookers (better known as Crock-Pots, a name trademarked by the Rival company) may be the only modern kitchen convenience that saves the cook time by using more of it rather than less. To see if these appliances could cook not just slowly but also well, we purchased five of them, all 6-quart oval cookers, a size and shape offering the most options in terms of the amount and type of food that can be prepared. The contestants included three "standard" cookers, the Rival Crock-Pot ($39.99), the Farberware Millennium Slow Cooker ($39.99), and the Hamilton Beach Portfolio Slow Cooker ($34.99); one with a new "programmable" feature, the Rival Smart-Pot ($49.99); and one with a completely revamped design, the West Bend Versatility Cooker ($54.99).

All five models had the standard slow cooker temperature settings of low, high, and keep warm. To test the functioning of each setting, we cooked the pot roast recipe on page 418 on low for eight hours and the basic chili recipe on page 440 on high for four hours; we then set each pot of chili on "keep warm" for two hours. All five cookers produced good renditions of the pot roast and chili, and all five kept the chili plenty warm for two hours. (The lowest temperature reached during warming was a piping-hot 187 degrees, by the West Bend cooker; the other four cookers maintained the chili at close to 200 degrees.)

What do we recommend? In the "standard slow cooker with no fancy features" category, both the Farberware Millennium and the Rival Crock-Pot performed admirably. The Hamilton Beach cooker showed slight scorching of the chili in the bottom corners of the crockery pot and so was slightly downgraded.

How did the two novel cookers fare? Rival's Smart-Pot is the only cooker on the market that lets you select a specific time and heat setting and then automatically shifts to the warm setting when the cooking time is up. Theoretically, this buys you a couple of more hours at the mall or at work before you have to come home and tend the pot. Two hours after switching from high to warm, however, the Smart-Pot had brought the temperature of the chili down by just 10 degrees, from 205 to 195. We're not sure this feature is worth the extra money.

West Bend's Versatility Cooker is a standout because its pot is made from aluminum with a nonstick interior coating, which means you can use it to cook foods on the stovetop, just as you would any other conventional pan. Both our chili and pot roast recipes start out with instructions for browning on the stovetop, and it was nice to brown foods in the same pot we ultimately used for slow cooking. While a crockery-less crockery pot does seem a little odd, this expensive model does get the job done, and then some.

THE BEST SLOW COOKERS
The Farberware Millennium (left) and the Rival Crock-Pot (center) were the best basic models tested. The West Bend Versatility Cooker (right) has a stovetop-worthy pot made of aluminum rather than the classic ceramic.

To see if these results would apply to chili, we set up a test with three pots of chili—one with the ground spices added before the beef, one with the spices added after the beef, and a third in which we toasted the spices in a separate skillet and added them to the pot after the beef. The batch made with untoasted spices added after the beef tasted weak. The batch made with spices toasted in a separate pan was better, but the clear favorite was the batch made with spices added directly to the pot before the meat. In fact, subsequent testing revealed that the spices should be added at the outset—along with the aromatics—to develop their flavors fully.

Although we didn't want a chili with killer heat, we did want real warmth and depth of flavor. Commercial chili powder is typically 80 percent ground dried red chiles, with the rest a mix of garlic powder, onion powder, oregano, ground cumin, and salt. To boost flavor, we increased the amount of chili powder from 3 to 4 tablespoons, added more cumin and oregano, and tossed in some cayenne for heat. We tried some more exotic spices, including cinnamon (which was deemed "awful"), allspice (which seemed "out of place"), and coriander (which "added some gentle warmth"). Only

the coriander became part of our working recipe.

It was now time to consider the meat. The quantity (two pounds) seemed ideal when paired with two 15-ounce cans of beans. Tests using 90 percent, 85 percent, and 80 percent lean ground beef showed that there is such a thing as too much fat. Pools of orange oil floated to the top of the chili made with ground chuck (80 percent lean beef). At the other end of the spectrum, the chili made with 90 percent lean beef was a tad bland—not bad, but not as full-flavored as the chili made with 85 percent lean beef, which was our final choice.

We wondered if another type of meat should be used in place of some of the ground beef. After trying batches of chili made with ground pork, diced pork loin, sliced sausage, and sausage removed from its casing and crumbled, tasters preferred the hearty flavor and creamy texture of an all-beef chili. (The exception was one batch to which we added bacon; many tasters liked its smoky flavor, so we made a version with bacon and black beans as a variation on the master recipe.)

Some of us have always made chili with beer and been satisfied with the results. Nodding to the expertise of others, we tried batches made

---

INGREDIENTS: Dried Chiles

For the most part, chili con carne is based on fairly mild dried chiles. The most common of these are dark, mahogany red, wrinkly-skinned ancho chiles, which have a deep, sweet, raisiny flavor; New Mexico Reds, which have a smooth, shiny, brick-red skin and a crisp, slightly acidic, earthy flavor; California chiles, which are very similar to New Mexico in appearance but have a slightly milder flavor; and long, shiny, smooth, dark brown pasilla chiles. Pasillas, which are a little hotter than the other three varieties, have grapey, herby flavor notes and, depending on the region of the country, are often packaged and sold as either ancho or mulato chiles.

We sampled each of these types, as well as a selection of preblended commercial powders, alone and in various combinations in batches of chili. Though the chilis made with individual chiles tasted much more pure and fresh than any of the premixed powders, they nonetheless seemed one-dimensional on their own. When all was said and done, the two-chile combination

we favored was equal parts ancho, for its earthy, fruity sweetness and the stunning deep red color it imparted to the chili, and New Mexico, for its lighter flavor and crisp acidity.

Chile heat was another factor to consider. Hotter dried chiles that appear regularly in chili include guajillo, de árbol, pequín, japones, and cayenne. Though we did not want to develop a fiery, overly hot chili, we did want a subtle bite to give the dish some oomph. We found that minced jalapeños, added with the garlic to the chili pot, supplied some heat and a fresh vegetal flavor.

with water (too watery), chicken broth (too chickeny and dull), beef broth (too tinny), wine (too acidic), and no liquid at all except for that in the tomatoes (beefy-tasting and by far the best). When we tried beer, we were surprised to find that it subdued that great beefy flavor. Keep the beer on ice for drinking with dinner.

Tomatoes were definitely going into the pot, but we had yet to decide on the type and amount. We first tried two small (14.5-ounce) cans of diced tomatoes. Clearly not enough tomatoes. What's more, the tomatoes were too chunky, and they were floating in a thin sauce. We tried two 28-ounce cans of diced tomatoes, pureeing the contents of one can in the blender to thicken the sauce. Although the chunkiness was reduced, the sauce was still watery. Next we paired one can of tomato puree with one can of diced tomatoes and, without exception, tasters preferred the thicker consistency. The test kitchen generally doesn't like the slightly cooked flavor of tomato puree, but this recipe needed the body it provided. In any case, after the long simmering time, any such flavor was hard to detect.

We tried cooking the chili with the lid on, with the lid off, and with the lid on in the beginning and off at the end. The chili cooked with the lid on was too soupy, that cooked with the lid off too dense. Keeping the lid on for half of the cooking time and then removing it was ideal—the consistency was rich but not too thick. Two hours of gentle simmering was sufficient to meld the flavors; shorter cooking times yielded chili that was soupy or bland—or both.

Most recipes add the beans toward the end of cooking, the idea being to let them heat through without causing them to fall apart. But this method often makes for very bland beans floating in a sea of highly flavorful chili. After testing several options, we found it best to add the beans with the tomatoes. The more time the beans spent in the pot, the better they tasted. In the end, we preferred dark red kidney beans or black beans because both keep their shape better than light red kidney beans, the other common choice.

With our recipe basically complete, it was time to try some of those offbeat additions to the pot that other cooks swear by, including cocoa powder, ground coffee beans, raisins, chickpeas, mushrooms, olives, and lima beans. Our conclusion? Each of these ingredients was either weird-tasting or too subtle to make much difference. Lime wedges, passed separately at the table, both brightened the flavor of the chili and accentuated the heat of the spices. Our chili was now done. Although simple, it is, we hope, good enough to silence any debate.

Beef Chili with Kidney Beans

SERVES 8 TO 10

Good choices for condiments include diced fresh tomatoes, diced avocado, sliced scallions, chopped red onion, chopped cilantro leaves, sour cream, and shredded Monterey Jack or cheddar cheese. The flavor of the chili improves with age; if possible, make it a day or two in advance and reheat before serving. Leftovers can be frozen for up to a month.

2	tablespoons vegetable or corn oil
2	medium onions, chopped fine
1	medium red bell pepper, cored, seeded, and cut into 1/2-inch cubes
6	medium garlic cloves, minced or pressed through a garlic press
1/4	cup chili powder
1	tablespoon ground cumin
2	teaspoons ground coriander
1	teaspoon red pepper flakes
1	teaspoon dried oregano
1/2	teaspoon cayenne pepper
2	pounds 85 percent lean ground beef
2	(15-ounce) cans dark red kidney beans, drained and rinsed
1	(28-ounce) can diced tomatoes
1	(28-ounce) can tomato puree
	Salt
2	limes, cut into wedges

1. Heat the oil in a large Dutch oven over medium heat until shimmering but not smoking. Add the onions, bell pepper, garlic, chili powder, cumin, coriander, pepper flakes, oregano, and cayenne and cook, stirring occasionally, until the vegetables are softened and beginning to brown,

about 10 minutes. Increase the heat to medium-high and add half the beef. Cook, breaking up the chunks with a wooden spoon, until no longer pink and just beginning to brown, 3 to 4 minutes. Add the remaining beef and cook, breaking up the chunks with the wooden spoon, until no longer pink, 3 to 4 minutes.

2. Add the beans, tomatoes, tomato puree, and ½ teaspoon salt. Bring to a boil, then reduce the heat to low and simmer, covered, and stirring occasionally, for 1 hour. Remove the cover and continue to simmer 1 hour longer, stirring occasionally (if the chili begins to stick to the bottom of the pot, stir in ½ cup water and continue to simmer), until the beef is tender and the chili is dark,

rich, and slightly thickened. Adjust the seasonings with additional salt to taste. Serve with the lime wedges and condiments (see note), if desired.

➤ VARIATION

Beef Chili with Bacon and Black Beans
Cut 8 ounces (about 8 slices) bacon into ½-inch pieces. Fry the bacon in a large Dutch oven over medium heat, stirring frequently, until browned, about 8 minutes. Pour off all but 2 tablespoons of the fat, leaving the bacon in the pot. Follow the recipe for Beef Chili with Kidney Beans, substituting the bacon fat in the Dutch oven for the vegetable oil and an equal amount of canned black beans, drained and rinsed, for the dark red kidney beans.

SCIENCE: Why Some Don't Think Hot Peppers Taste Hot

One enduring mystery among those partial to spicy food is why people have such varying tolerances for the heat of chile peppers. As it turns out, there are several reasons why your dinner companion may find a bowl of chili only mildly spicy while the same dish causes you to frantically summon a waiter for a glass of milk to cool the heat before you expire. (Milk, not water, is the thing to drink when you want to cool the fire in your mouth.)

Your dining partner may be experiencing "temporary desensitization." The phenomenon, discovered by Barry Green of the Monell Chemical Senses Institute in Philadelphia, occurs when you eat something spicy hot, then lay off for a few minutes. As long as you keep eating chiles, their effect keeps building. But if you take a break—even for as little as two to five minutes, depending on your individual susceptibility—you will be desensitized when you go back to eating the chiles. In other words, a dish with the same amount of chiles will not seem as hot the second time around.

The more likely explanation, however, is that people who find chiles intensely, punishingly hot simply have more taste buds. According to Linda Bartoshuk, a psychophysicist at the Yale School of Medicine, human beings can be neatly divided into three distinct categories when it comes to tasting ability: unfortunate "nontasters," pedestrian "medium tasters," and the aristocrats of the taste-bud world, "supertasters."

This taste-detection pecking order appears to correspond directly to the number of taste buds a person possesses, a genetically predetermined trait that may vary by a factor of 100. Indeed, so radical is the difference among these three types that Bartoshuk speaks of them inhabiting different "taste worlds."

Bartoshuk and her colleagues discovered the extent of this phenomenon a few years ago when they carried out experiments using a dye that turns the entire mouth blue except for the taste papillae (structures housing taste buds and other sensory receptors). After painting part of subjects' tongues with the dye, they were rather stunned at the differences they saw. One poor taster had just 11 taste buds per square centimeter, while a supertaster had 1,100 in the same area.

Further experiments confirmed that the ability to taste intensely was in direct proportion to the number of taste buds. Researchers found that women were twice as likely as men to be supertasters, while men were nearly twice as likely as women to be nontasters.

What does this have to do with how hot you find chiles? It turns out that every taste bud in the mouth has a pain receptor literally wrapped around it. Along with the extra taste buds comes an extra ability to feel pain. As a result, supertasters have the capacity to experience 50 percent more pain from capsaicin, the chemical that gives chiles their heat.

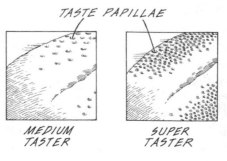

TASTE PAPILLAE

MEDIUM TASTER

SUPER TASTER

HAMBURGERS

AMERICANS PROBABLY GRILL MORE HAMBURGERS than any other food. Despite all this practice, plenty of hamburgers seem merely to satisfy hunger rather than give pleasure. Too bad, because making an exceptional hamburger isn't that hard or time-consuming. Fast-food chains no doubt had good reasons when they decided against selling hand-formed, 100 percent ground-chuck burgers; home cooks, however, do not. If you have the right ground beef, the perfect hamburger can be ready in less than 15 minutes, assuming you season, form, and cook it properly. The biggest difficulty for many cooks, though, may be finding the right beef.

To test which cut or cuts of beef would cook up into the best burgers, we called a butcher and ordered chuck, round, rump, sirloin, and hanging tenderloin, all ground to order with 20 percent fat. (Although we would question fat percentages in later testing, we needed a standard for these early tests. Based on experience, this percentage seemed right.) After a side-by-side taste test, we quickly concluded that most cuts of ground beef are pleasant but bland when compared with robust, beefy-flavored ground chuck. Pricier ground sirloin, for example, cooked up into a particularly boring burger.

So pure ground chuck—the cut of beef that starts where the ribs end and travels up to the shoulder and neck, ending at the foreshank—was the clear winner. We were ready to race ahead to seasonings, but before moving on we stopped to ask ourselves whether cooks buying ground chuck from the grocery store would agree with our choice. Our efforts to determine whether grocery-store ground chuck and ground-to-order chuck were even remotely similar took us along a culinary blue highway from kitchen to packing plant, butcher shop, and science lab.

According to the National Livestock and Meat Board, the percentage of fat in beef is checked and enforced at the retail level. If a package of beef is labeled 90 percent lean, then it must contain no more than 10 percent fat, give or take a point. Retail stores are required to test each batch of ground beef, make the necessary adjustments, and keep a log of the results. Local inspectors routinely pull ground beef from a store's meat case for a fat check. If the fat content is not within 1 percent of the package sticker, the store is fined.

Whether a package labeled ground chuck is, in fact, 100 percent ground chuck is a different story. First, we surveyed a number of grocery-store meat department managers, who said that what was written on the label did match what was in the package. For instance, a package labeled "ground chuck" would have been made only from chuck trimmings. Same for sirloin and round. Only "ground beef" would be made from mixed beef trimmings.

We got a little closer to the truth, however, by interviewing a respected butcher in the Chicago area. At the several grocery stores and butcher shops where he had worked over the years, he had never known a store to segregate meat trimmings. In fact, in his present butcher shop, he sells only two kinds of ground beef: sirloin and chuck. He defines ground sirloin as ground beef (mostly but not exclusively sirloin) that's labeled 90 percent lean, and chuck as ground beef (including a lot of chuck trimmings) that's labeled 85 percent lean.

Only meat ground at federally inspected plants is guaranteed to match its label. At these plants, an

---

EQUIPMENT: Food Processor as Grinder

Even though we have a meat grinder in our test kitchen, we don't regularly grind meat ourselves. The setup, breakdown, and cleanup required for a 2-pound chuck roast is just not worth the effort. Besides, hamburgers are supposed to be impromptu, fast, fun food.

To our surprise, the food processor does a respectable grinding job, and it's much easier to use than a grinder. The key is to make sure the roast is cold, that it is cut into small chunks, and that it is processed in small batches. For a 2-pound roast, cut the meat into 1-inch chunks. Divide the chunks into four equal portions. Place one portion of meat in the workbowl of a food processor fitted with the steel blade. Pulse the cubes until the meat is ground, fifteen to twenty 1-second pulses. Repeat with the remaining portions of beef. Then shape the ground meat as directed in the recipe.

445

inspector checks to make sure that labeled ground beef actually comes from the cut of beef named on the label and that the fat percentage is correct. Most retailers, though, cannot guarantee that their ground beef has been made from a specific cut; they can only guarantee fat percentages. Because the labeling of retail ground beef can be deceptive, we suggest that you buy a chuck roast and have the butcher grind it for you. Even at a local grocery store, we found that the butcher was willing to grind to order. Some meat always gets lost in the grinder, so count on losing a bit (2 to 3 percent).

Because commercially ground beef is at risk for contamination with the bacteria E. coli, we thought it made theoretical sense for home cooks to grind their beef at home, thereby reducing their odds of eating tainted beef. It doesn't make much practical sense, though. Not all cooks own a grinder. And even if they did, we thought home grinding demanded far too much setup, cleanup, and effort for a dish meant to be so simple.

To see if there was an easier way, we tried chopping the meat by hand and grinding it in the food processor. The hibachi-style hand-chopping method was just as time-consuming and even more messy than the traditional grinder. In this method, you must slice the meat thin and then cut it into cubes before going at it with two chef's knives. The fat doesn't distribute evenly, meat flies everywhere, and, unless your knives are razor sharp, it's difficult to chop through the meat. What's worse, you can't efficiently chop more than two burgers at a time. In the end, the cooked burgers can be mistaken for chopped steak.

SHAPING BURGERS THE RIGHT WAY

All too often, burgers come off the grill with a domed, puffy shape that makes it impossible to keep condiments from sliding off. Fast-food restaurants produce burgers that are evenly shaped, but they are also extremely thin. We wondered if we could find a way to produce a meatier burger that would have the same thickness from edge to edge.

We shaped 6-ounce portions of ground beef into patties that were 1 inch, ¾ inch, and ½ inch thick. Once cooked, all of these burgers looked like tennis balls, and it was nearly impossible to anchor ketchup and other goodies on top. After talking to several food scientists, we understood why this happens.

The culprit behind puffy burgers is the connective tissue, or collagen, that is ground up along with the meat. When the connective tissue in a patty heats up to roughly 130 degrees, it shrinks. This happens first on the flat top and bottom surfaces of the burger and then on the sides, where the tightening acts like a belt. When the sides tighten, the interior meat volume is forced up and down, so the burger puffs.

One of the cooks in the test kitchen suggested a trick she had picked up when working in a restaurant. We shaped patties ¾ inch thick but then formed a slight depression in the center of each one so that the edges were thicker than the center. On the grill, the center puffed up to the point where it was the same height as the edges. Finally, a level burger that could hold on to toppings.

1. With cupped hands, toss one portion of meat back and forth from hand to hand to shape it into a loose ball.

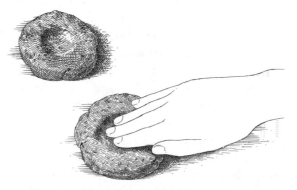

2. Pat lightly to flatten the meat into a ¾-inch-thick burger that measures about 4½ inches across. Press the center of the patty down with your fingertips until it is ½ inch thick, creating a well in the center. Repeat with the remaining portions of meat.

The food processor did a surprisingly good job of grinding the meat. We thought the steel blade would raggedly chew the meat, but the hamburger turned out evenly chopped and fluffy. (For more information, see "Food Processor as Grinder" on page 445.)

We figured the average chuck roast to be about 80 percent lean. To check its leanness, we bought a chuck roast—not too fatty, not too lean—and ground it in the food processor. We then took our ground chuck back to the grocery store and asked the butcher to check its fat content in the Univex Fat Analyzer, a machine the store uses to check each batch of beef it grinds. A plug of our ground beef scored an almost perfect 21 percent fat when tested.

Up to this point, all of our beef had been ground with approximately 20 percent fat. A quick test of burgers with less and more fat helped us to decide that 20 percent fat, give or take a few percentage points, was good for burgers. Any more fat and the burgers are just too greasy. Any less starts to compromise the beef's juicy, moist texture.

When to season the meat with salt and pepper may seem an insignificant detail, but when making a dish as simple as a hamburger, little things matter. We tried seasoning the meat at four different points in the process. Our first burger

TESTING BURGERS FOR DONENESS

It's difficult to get an accurate temperature reading even in the thickest burgers. While we like to hold steaks and chops with tongs and slide an instant-read thermometer through the side, we find this technique can cause delicate burgers to break apart. Instead, we like to slide the tip of the thermometer into the burger at the top edge and push it toward the center.

was seasoned before the meat was shaped, the second burger was seasoned right before cooking, the third after each side was seared, and the fourth after the burger had been fully cooked. Predictably, the burger that had been seasoned throughout was our preference. All the surface seasoned burgers were the same. Tasters got a hit of salt up front, then the burger went bland. The thin surface area was well seasoned, while the interior of the burger was not.

Working with fresh-ground chuck seasoned with salt and pepper, we now moved on to shaping and cooking. To defy the overpacking and overhandling warning you see in many recipes, we thoroughly worked a portion of ground beef before cooking it. The well-done burger exterior was nearly as dense as a meat pâté, and the less-well-done interior was compact and pasty.

It's pretty hard to overhandle a beef patty, though, especially if you're trying not to. Once the meat has been divided into portions, we found that tossing each portion from one hand to the other helped bring the meat together into a ball without overworking it.

We made one of our most interesting discoveries when we tested various shaping techniques for the patties. A well in the center of each burger ensured that they came off the grill with an even thickness instead of puffed up like a tennis ball. (See Shaping Hamburgers on page 446.) To our taste, a four-ounce burger seemed a little skimpy. A six-ounce portion of meat patted into a nicely sized burger fit perfectly in a bun.

Now nearly done with our testing, we needed only to perfect our grilling method. Burgers require a real blast of heat if they are to form a crunchy, flavorful crust before the interior overcooks. While many of the recipes we looked at advise the cook to grill burgers over a hot fire, we suspected we'd have to adjust the heat because our patties were quite thin in the middle. Sure enough, a superhot fire made it too easy to overcook the burgers. We found a medium-hot fire formed a crust quickly, while also providing a wider margin of error for properly cooking the center. Nonetheless, burgers cook quickly—needing only 2½ to 3½ minutes per side. We don't advise walking away from the grill when cooking burgers for this reason.

To keep the burgers from sticking to the grill, we coated it with oil. All you need to do is dip a wad of paper towels in some vegetable oil, hold the wad with long-handled tongs, and rub it on the hot grate just before adding the burgers.

One last finding from our testing: Don't ever press down on burgers as they cook. Rather than speeding their cooking, pressing on the patties serves only to squeeze out their juices and make the burgers dry.

Charcoal-Grilled Hamburgers

SERVES 4

For those who like their burgers well-done, we found that poking a small hole in the center of the patty before cooking helped the burger cook through to the center before the edges dried out. See the illustrations on page 446 for tips on shaping burgers. See page 445 for details about grinding your own meat with a food processor.

- 1½ pounds 80 percent lean ground chuck
- 1 teaspoon salt
- ½ teaspoon ground black pepper
  Vegetable oil for the grill rack
  Buns and desired toppings

FREEZING BURGER PATTIES

If you like the convenience of pulling out frozen burgers, chops, or steaks as you need them, simply separate the meat with sheets of parchment paper, place the meat in freezer bags, and freeze. The paper makes it much easier to pull individual pieces from the frozen package.

1. Light a large chimney starter filled with hardwood charcoal (about 6 quarts) and allow to burn until all the charcoal is covered with a layer of fine gray ash. Spread the coals out evenly over the bottom of the grill. Set the cooking rack in place, cover the grill with the lid, and let the rack heat up, about 5 minutes. Use a wire brush to scrape clean the cooking grate. The grill is ready when the coals are medium-hot. (See how to gauge heat level on page 568.)

2. Meanwhile, break up the chuck to increase the surface area for seasoning. Sprinkle the salt and pepper over the meat; toss lightly with your hands to distribute the seasonings. Divide the meat into 4 equal portions (6 ounces each); with cupped hands, toss one portion of meat back and forth to form a loose ball. Pat lightly to flatten the meat into a ¾-inch-thick burger that measures about 4½ inches across. Press the center of the patty down with your fingertips until it is about ½ inch thick, creating a well, or divot, in the center of the patty. Repeat with the remaining portions of meat.

3. Lightly dip a wad of paper towels in vegetable oil; holding the wad with tongs, wipe the grill rack. Grill the burgers, divot-side up, uncovered and without pressing down on them, until well seared on the first side, about 2½ minutes. Flip the burgers with a wide metal spatula. Continue grilling to the desired doneness, about 2 minutes for rare, 2½ minutes for medium-rare, 3 minutes for medium, and 4 minutes for well-done. Serve immediately in buns with the desired toppings.

➤ VARIATIONS

Gas-Grilled Hamburgers
Preheat the grill with all burners set to high and the lid down until the grill is very hot, about 15 minutes. Scrape the grill grate clean with a grill brush. Leave both burners on high. Follow the recipe for Charcoal-Grilled Hamburgers from step 2 and cook with the lid down.

Grilled Cheeseburgers
We suggest grating cheese into the raw beef as opposed to melting it on top. Because the cheese is more evenly distributed, there's no danger of overcooking the burgers while you wait for the cheese to melt.

Follow the recipe for Charcoal-Grilled Hamburgers or Gas-Grilled Hamburgers, mixing 3½ ounces cheddar, Swiss, Monterey Jack, or blue cheese, shredded or crumbled as necessary, into the ground chuck along with the salt and pepper. Shape and cook the burgers as directed.

Grilled Hamburgers with Garlic, Chipotles, and Scallions

Toast 3 medium unpeeled garlic cloves in a small dry skillet over medium heat, shaking the pan occasionally, until the garlic is fragrant and the color deepens slightly, about 8 minutes. When cool enough to handle, peel and mince the garlic. Follow the recipe for Charcoal-Grilled Hamburgers or Gas-Grilled Hamburgers, mixing the garlic, 1 tablespoon minced chipotle chile in adobo sauce, and 2 tablespoons minced scallions into the meat along with the salt and pepper. Shape and cook the burgers as directed.

Grilled Hamburgers with Cognac, Mustard, and Chives

Mix 1½ tablespoons cognac, 2 teaspoons Dijon mustard, and 1 tablespoon minced fresh chives together in a small bowl. Follow the recipe for Charcoal-Grilled Hamburgers or Gas-Grilled Hamburgers, mixing the cognac mixture into the meat along with the salt and pepper. Shape and cook the burgers as directed.

Grilled Hamburgers with Porcini Mushrooms and Thyme

Cover ½ ounce dried porcini mushroom pieces with ½ cup hot tap water in a small microwave-safe bowl; cover with plastic wrap, cut several steam vents with a paring knife, and microwave on high power for 30 seconds. Let stand until the mushrooms soften, about 5 minutes. Lift the mushrooms from the liquid with a fork and mince, using a chef's knife (you should have about 2 tablespoons). Follow the recipe for Charcoal-Grilled Hamburgers or Gas-Grilled Hamburgers, mixing the porcini mushrooms and 1 teaspoon minced fresh thyme leaves into the meat along with the salt and pepper. Shape and cook the burgers as directed.

COOKING BURGERS INDOORS

NOTHING BEATS A GRILLED HAMBURGER, but weather and circumstance (like living in a high-rise apartment) may not always permit outdoor cooking. So what's the best way to cook hamburgers in the kitchen?

Broiling and pan-searing are the two obvious choices. Even with the burgers very close to the heating element, we found that broiling did not create the kind of thick crust we wanted. We had much better results in a very hot pan (cast iron is ideal). And we didn't even need any fat in the pan to keep the burgers from sticking. All of the variations starting on page 448 can be cooked according to the recipe below.

Pan-Seared Hamburgers

SERVES 4

A well-seasoned cast-iron pan is our first choice for this recipe, but any heavy-bottomed skillet can be used.

- 1½ pounds 80 percent lean ground chuck
- 1 teaspoon salt
- ½ teaspoon ground black pepper
- Buns and desired toppings

1. Break up the chuck to increase the surface area for seasoning. Sprinkle the salt and pepper over the meat; toss lightly with your hands to distribute the seasonings. Divide the meat into 4 equal portions (6 ounces each); with cupped hands, toss one portion of meat back and forth to form a loose ball. Pat lightly to flatten the meat into a ¾-inch-thick burger that measures about 4½ inches across. Press the center of the patty down with your fingertips until about ½ inch thick, creating a well, or divot, in the center. Repeat with the remaining portions of meat.

2. Heat a heavy-bottomed 12-inch skillet over medium-high heat. When the skillet is hot (drops of water flicked into it should evaporate immediately), add the patties divot-side up. Cook the burgers,

turning once, to the desired doneness, about 3 minutes per side for rare, 3½ minutes per side for medium-rare, 4 minutes per side for medium, and 5 minutes per side for well-done. Serve immediately in buns with the desired toppings.

MEAT LOAF

NOT ALL MEAT LOAVES RESEMBLE MAMA'S. IN fact, some ingredient lists look like the work of a proud child or defiant adolescent. Canned pineapple, cranberry sauce, raisins, prepared taco mix, and even goat cheese have all found their way into published recipes. Rather than feud over flavorings, though, we decided to focus on the meatier issues.

To begin with, we narrowed our testing to red meat. We had plenty of questions to answer: What meat or mix of meats delivers good mouthfeel and flavor? Which fillers offer unobtrusive texture? Should the loaf be cooked free-form or in a standard loaf pan, or are the new perforated pans designed for meat loaves worth the money? Should the loaf be topped with bacon, ketchup, both, or neither? Is it better to sauté the onions and garlic before adding them to the meat mix, or are they just as good raw and grated?

To determine which ground meat or meat mix makes the best loaf, we used a very basic meat loaf recipe and made miniature loaves with the following meat proportions: equal parts beef chuck and pork; equal parts veal and pork; equal parts beef chuck, pork, and veal; 2 parts beef chuck to 1 part ground pork and 1 part ground veal; 3 parts beef chuck and 1 part ground bacon; equal parts beef chuck and ham; all ground beef chuck; and all ground veal.

We found out that meat markets haven't been selling meat loaf mix (a mix of beef, pork, and veal, usually in equal proportions) all these years for nothing. As we expected, the best meat loaves were made from the combination of these three meats. Straight ground veal was tender but overly mild and mushy, while the all-beef loaf was coarse-textured, liver-flavored, and tough. Though interesting, neither the beef/ham nor

the beef/bacon loaves looked or tasted like classic meat loaf. Both were firm, dense, and more terrine-like. Also, as bacon lovers, we preferred the bacon's smoky flavor and crispy texture surrounding, not in, the loaf.

Although both of the beef-pork-veal mixtures were good, we preferred the mix with a higher proportion of ground chuck. This amount gave the loaf a distinct but not overly strong beef flavor. The extra beef percentage also kept the loaf firm, making it easier to cut. Mild-tasting pork added another flavor dimension, while the small quantity of veal kept it tender. For those who choose not to special-order this mix or mix it themselves at home, we recommend the standard meat loaf mix of equal parts beef, pork, and veal.

After comparing meat loaves made with and without fillers or binders, we realized that starch in a meat loaf offers more than economy. Loaves made without filler were coarse-textured, dense, and too hamburger-like. Those with binders, on the other hand, had that distinctive meat loaf texture.

But which binder to use? Practically every hot and cold cereal box offers a meat loaf recipe using that particular cereal. We made several meat loaves, each with a different filler. Though there was no clear-cut winner, we narrowed the number from 11 down to three. After tasting all the meat loaves, we realized that a good binder should help with texture but not add distinct flavor. Cracker crumbs, quick-cooking oats, and fresh bread crumbs fit the bill.

Just as we found that we liked the less distinctly flavored fillers, so we preferred sautéed—not raw—onions and garlic in the meat mix. Because the meat loaf cooks to an internal temperature of just 160 degrees, raw onions never fully cook. Sautéing the vegetables is a five-minute detour well worth the time.

We found our meat loaves in need of some liquid to moisten the filler. Without it, the filler robs the meat dry. As with the fillers, we ran across a host of meat loaf moisteners and tried as many as made sense. Tomato sauce made the loaf taste like a meatball with sauce. We liked the flavor of ketchup but ultimately decided that we preferred it baked on top rather than inside. Beer and wine do not make ideal meat moisteners, either. The meat doesn't cook long enough or to a high enough internal temperature to burn off the alcohol, so the meat ends up with a distinctly raw alcohol taste.

As with many other aspects of this home-cooked favorite, we found that there is a good reason why the majority of meat loaf recipes call for some form of dairy for the liquid—it's the best choice. We tried half-and-half, milk, sour cream, yogurt, skim and whole evaporated milk, and even cottage cheese. Whole milk and plain yogurt ended up as our liquids of choice, with the yogurt offering a complementary subtle tang to the rich beef.

Cooks who don't like a crusty exterior on their meat loaf usually prefer to bake it in a loaf pan. We found that the high-sided standard loaf pan, however, causes the meat to stew rather than bake. Also, for those who like a glazed top, there is another disadvantage: The enclosed pan allows the meat juices to bubble up from the sides, diluting and destroying the glaze. Similarly, bacon placed on top of the meat loaf curls and doesn't properly attach to the loaf, and if tucked inside the pan, the bacon never crisps.

For all these reasons, we advise against the use of a standard loaf pan. If you prefer a crustless, soft-sided meat loaf, invest in a meat loaf pan with a perforated bottom and accompanying drip pan. The enclosed pan keeps the meat soft while the perforated bottom allows the drippings to flow to the pan below. While still not ideal for a crispy bacon top, it at least saves the glaze from destruction.

Ultimately, we found that baking a meat loaf free-form on a rimmed baking sheet gave us the results we wanted. The top and sides of the loaf brown nicely, and basting sauces, like the brown sugar and ketchup sauce we developed, glaze the entire loaf, not just the top. Bacon, too, covers the whole loaf. And because its drippings also fall into the pan, the bacon crisps up nicely.

Meat Loaf with Brown Sugar–Ketchup Glaze

SERVES 6 TO 8

If you like, you can omit the bacon topping from the loaf. In this case, brush on half of the glaze before baking and the other half during the last 15 minutes of baking. If you choose not to special-order the mix of meat below, we recommend the standard meat loaf mix of equal parts beef, pork, and veal, available at most grocery stores.

INGREDIENTS: Ketchup

For many people, a burger isn't done until it has been coated liberally with ketchup. Ketchup is also an essential ingredient in many meat loaf recipes, including ours. This condiment originated in Asia as a salty, fermented medium for pickling or preserving ingredients, primarily fish. Early versions were made with anchovies and generally were highly spiced.

Tomato-based ketchup has its origins in nineteenth-century America. We now consume more than 600 million pints of ketchup every year, much of it landing on top of burgers. But as any ketchup connoisseur knows, not all brands are created equal. To find out which is the best, we tasted 13 different samples, including several fancy mail-order ketchups and one we made in our test kitchen.

It wasn't much of a surprise that the winner was Heinz. For all tasters but one, Heinz ranked first or second, and they described it with words like "classic" and "perfect." A tiny bit sweeter than Heinz, Del Monte took second place, while Hunt's (the other leading national brand, along with Heinz and Del Monte) rated third.

What about the mail-order, organic, fruit-sweetened, and homemade ketchups? Most tasters felt these samples were overly thick and not smooth enough. Some were too spicy, others too vinegary. Our homemade ketchup was too chunky, more like "tomato jam" than ketchup. In color, consistency, and flavor, none of these interlopers could match the archetypal ketchup, Heinz.

THE BEST KETCHUP
In a blind taste test, Heinz beat 12 other samples, including several high-priced boutique brands. Panelists described it as "glossy," "balanced," and "smooth."

GLAZE

1/2	cup ketchup or chili sauce
1/4	cup brown sugar
4	teaspoons cider or distilled white vinegar

MEAT LOAF

2	teaspoons vegetable oil
1	medium onion, chopped (about 1 cup)
2	medium garlic cloves, minced or pressed through a garlic press
2	large eggs
1/2	teaspoon dried thyme
1	teaspoon salt
1/2	teaspoon ground black pepper
2	teaspoons Dijon mustard
2	teaspoons Worcestershire sauce
1/4	teaspoon hot pepper sauce
1/2	cup whole milk or plain yogurt
2	pounds meat loaf mix (50 percent ground chuck, 25 percent ground pork, 25 percent ground veal)
2/3	cup crushed saltine crackers (about 16) or quick oats or 1 1/3 cups fresh bread crumbs (page 335)
1/3	cup minced fresh parsley leaves
8	ounces (8 slices) bacon, or more as needed (amount will vary depending on loaf shape)

1. FOR THE GLAZE: Mix all of the ingredients together in a small saucepan; set aside.

2. FOR THE MEAT LOAF: Heat the oven to 350 degrees. Heat the oil in a medium skillet. Add the onion and garlic; sauté until softened, about 5 minutes. Set aside to cool while preparing the remaining ingredients.

3. Mix the eggs, thyme, salt, black pepper, mustard, Worcestershire sauce, hot pepper sauce, and milk in a medium bowl. Add the egg mixture to the meat in a large bowl along with the crackers, parsley, and cooked onion and garlic; mix with a fork until evenly blended and the meat mixture does not stick to the bowl. (If the mixture sticks, add more milk, a couple of tablespoons at a time, until the mixture no longer sticks.)

4. Turn the meat mixture onto a work surface. With wet hands, pat the mixture into a loaf shape approximately 9 by 5 inches. Place on a foil-lined (for easy cleanup) rimmed baking sheet. Brush with half the glaze, then arrange the bacon slices crosswise over the loaf, overlapping them slightly, to completely cover the surface of the loaf. Use a spatula to tuck the bacon ends underneath the loaf.

5. Bake the loaf until the bacon is crisp and the internal temperature of the loaf registers 160 degrees, about 1 hour. Cool at least 20 minutes. Simmer the remaining glaze over medium heat until thickened slightly. Slice the meat loaf and serve with the remaining glaze passed separately.

9.

PORK

IN 1985, AMID GROWING CONCERNS ABOUT saturated fat in the American diet, Congress created the National Pork Board with the goal of helping producers provide consumers with the leaner meat they desired. Working with the board, producers developed new breeding techniques and feeding systems aimed at slimming down pigs. As a result, pigs are now much leaner and more heavily muscled than they were 20 years ago, with an average of 31 percent less fat. This is good news for our waistlines, but much of the meaty flavor, moisture, and tenderness disappeared along with the fat, causing some cuts of pork to taste like diet food. For this reason, choosing the right cut and the right cooking method makes a big difference when preparing today's pork.

A pig is butchered into four primal cuts. The term *primal cuts* refers to the basic cuts made to an animal when it is initially butchered. Butchers turn primal cuts into the chops, roasts, and other cuts sold at the retail level. Retail cuts from the same primal cut generally share similar traits, so when shopping it helps to understand the characteristics of the four primal cuts of pork.

SHOULDER Cuts from the upper portion of the well-exercised front legs (called the blade shoulder) tend to be tough, with a fair amount of fat. The economical arm, or picnic (or ham) shoulder, has characteristics similar to the blade shoulder. Shoulder hocks (used primarily as a flavoring agent in soups, slow-cooked greens, and stews) also come from this part of the pig, while ham hocks come from the hind legs of the animal. All shoulder cuts require long, slow cooking to become fork-tender.

LOIN Butchers divide this area between the shoulder and the leg into some of the most popular cuts of pork, including pork chops, tenderloin, roasts, and ribs. Because the loin area is so lean, these cuts are prone to dryness.

LEG The leg is sometimes referred to as the ham. Ham can be wet- or dry-cured or sold fresh, as a roast.

BELLY The belly, or side, of the pig is, not surprisingly, the fattiest part, home to spareribs and bacon.

THE FOUR PRIMAL CUTS OF PORK

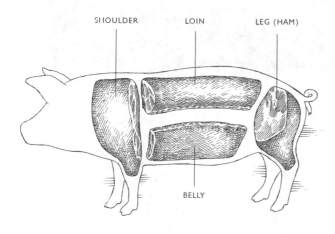

SHOULDER   LOIN   LEG (HAM)

BELLY

INGREDIENTS: Enhanced or Unenhanced Pork?

Because modern pork is remarkably lean and therefore somewhat bland and prone to dryness if overcooked, a product called enhanced pork has overtaken the market. In fact, it can be hard to find unenhanced pork in some areas. Enhanced pork has been injected with a solution of water, salt, sodium phosphates, sodium lactate, potassium lactate, sodium diacetate, and varying flavor agents to bolster flavor and juiciness, with the total amount of enhancing ingredients adding 7 to 15 percent extra weight. Pork containing additives must be so labeled, with a list of the ingredients.

After several taste tests, we have concluded that while enhanced pork is indeed juicier and more tender than unenhanced pork, the latter has more genuine pork flavor. Some tasters picked up unappealing artificial, salty flavors in enhanced pork. Enhanced pork can also leach juices that, once reduced, will result in overly salty pan sauces (see page 464 for more information). If you want to add moisture and flavor to a dry cut while maintaining complete control of flavor and salt levels, we recommend that you buy unenhanced pork and brine it at home (that is, soak the meat in a saltwater solution).

THICK-CUT PORK CHOPS

WHEN WAS THE LAST TIME YOU HAD A REALLY juicy, tender, thick pork chop? These days, it is likely to be something you remember but not something that you've recently enjoyed. In response to American demands for low-fat meat, the pork industry has systematically trimmed down the hefty fat-producing hogs of the past to create today's newer pig, sleek of silhouette and lean of flesh. In fact, today's pork has at least 30 percent less fat than pork had 20 years ago.

In our experience, thick-cut pork chops are less likely to dry out than thinner chops. After testing several options, we settled on rib loin chops 1½ inches thick. Thick chops require a bit more finesse than simple sautéing because the exterior will brown long before the interior comes up to temperature. Our research uncovered two options: cook the chops on the stovetop the entire time (using the cover and regulating the heat levels to produce fully cooked chops that do not burn), or start the chops on the stove and transfer them to the oven to finish cooking through to the bone.

A high-heat sear for two to three minutes per side (depending on the number of chops in the pan) followed by about 10 minutes per side of covered stovetop cooking over reduced heat yielded very good results. But we found these chops to be just slightly less tender than those that we started in the skillet and finished in the oven. There was no demonstrable advantage to using a lower oven temperature (we tried 450, 350, and 250 degrees); the chops simply took longer to cook. In the end, purely for the sake of expediency, we settled on searing the chops in a skillet, then transferring them to a preheated rimmed baking sheet in a 450-degree oven to finish cooking.

We had found the best cooking method, but the chops were still lacking in flavor and moisture. Owing to their relative absence of fat or collagen (those classic suppliers of flavor and moisture), these chops were clearly perfect candidates for brining. Soaking the chops for an hour in a salt and sugar brine yielded a significant improvement in flavor and moisture.

Our final step was to determine the exact relationship between flavor and the internal temperature of the meat. The best-tasting chops we had tried had an internal reading of 140 to 145 degrees. But medium-rare pork? What would our mothers say?

One of the reasons so much pork today reaches the table dry and overcooked is the public's residual fear of the trichinosis parasite. But there is actually

SCIENCE: Cooking Pork Safely

Red meat (beef, lamb, and veal) has traditionally been cooked to a lower internal temperature than pork. Guidelines for cooking pork to temperatures as high as 190 degrees originated decades ago when pork quality was inconsistent and fears of trichinosis ran high. Today, the risk of trichinosis is nearly nonexistent in the United States. According to the Centers for Disease Control and Prevention, only 13 human cases of trichinosis were confirmed in 2002, and the source of contamination for eight of those cases was wild game and for two of them privately raised pigs. What's more, even when the trichina parasite is present, it is killed when the temperature of the meat rises to 137 degrees.

Both the U.S. Department of Agriculture and the National Pork Board recommend cooking pork to a final internal temperature of 160 degrees. The Pork Board advises removing larger cuts from the oven at 150 degrees, resting the meat, and serving it at 160. Unfortunately, given the leanness of today's pork, these recommendations result in dry, tough meat. In the test kitchen, we have found cooking modern pork beyond 150 degrees to be a waste of time and money. We cook thinner cuts of pork such as chops to a slightly rosy 140 to 145 degrees; their temperature will climb about 5 degrees as they rest. We remove large cuts from the oven at about 135 degrees, tent them with foil, and allow the meat to rest, during which time the temperature rises by at least 10 degrees. (Be sure to check the final temperature before serving to make certain that it does reach 145 degrees.) If you are concerned about contamination from salmonella (which is possible in any type of meat, including beef), you must cook the pork to 160 degrees to be certain that all potential pathogens are eliminated.

little cause for concern, because the United States now sees few trichinosis cases (only 230 cases nationwide from 1991 to 1996, some 40 percent of them caused by eating wild game). Moreover, the parasites that cause this disease are destroyed when the pork reaches an internal temperature of 137 degrees. So the notion of medium-rare pork needn't be met with a shudder of alarm.

After fiddling with various options, we committed to the bold maneuver of cooking the chops to a temperature of 125 to 127 degrees. We were able to do this by letting the chops complete their cooking outside the oven, covering them with aluminum foil while they rested to allow the juices to redistribute throughout the meat. After a five-minute rest, the chops' temperature went up to a perfect 145 degrees. Relinquishing a minimum of juice—it mostly stayed in the chops—and retaining the barest whisper of pink on their interior, the chops were succulent and highly flavorful. This was largely due, we felt, to the fact that cooking by residual heat is a gentler and more precise method of reaching the final serving temperature. Chops left to rest uncovered, on the other hand, not only lost heat but showed little escalation in their internal temperature between pan and plate.

To ensure perfectly cooked chops, an instant-read thermometer is absolutely essential. Time estimates will be just that—estimates—and no amount of prodding or poking with your finger will give you a true reading of doneness.

Pan-Seared, Oven-Roasted Thick-Cut Pork Chops

SERVES 4

Be sure to buy chops of the same thickness so that they cook consistently—see the photographs at right for details. If the chops aren't being cooked immediately after brining, simply wipe off the excess brine, place them on a wire rack set on top of a rimmed baking sheet, and refrigerate, uncovered, for up to three hours. This recipe uses table salt (not kosher) in its brine. If you'd like to use kosher salt, whose large flakes measure differently from fine-grained table salt, see page 312 for conversion information.

¾	cup packed light brown sugar
¼	cup table salt
4	bone-in rib pork chops, 1½ inches thick (about 12 ounces each)
½	teaspoon ground black pepper
1	tablespoon vegetable oil

1. Dissolve the brown sugar and salt in 6 cups cold water in a gallon-size zipper-lock plastic bag. Add the pork chops and seal the bag, pressing out as much air as possible. Refrigerate until fully seasoned, about 1 hour. Remove the chops from the brine, rinse, and pat thoroughly dry with paper towels. Season the chops with the pepper.

2. Adjust an oven rack to the lower-middle position, place a shallow roasting pan or rimmed baking sheet on the rack, and heat the oven to 450 degrees. When the oven reaches 450 degrees, heat the oil in a heavy-bottomed 12-inch skillet over high heat until shimmering. Lay the chops in the skillet and cook until well browned and a nice crust has formed on the surface, about 3 minutes. Turn the chops over with tongs and cook until well browned and a nice crust has formed on the second side, 2 to 3 minutes longer.

3. Using the tongs, transfer the chops to the preheated pan in the oven. Roast until an instant-read thermometer inserted into the center of a chop registers 125 to 127 degrees, 8 to 10 minutes, turning the chops over once halfway through the cooking time. Transfer the chops to a platter, tent loosely with foil, and let rest for 5 minutes (use this time to make a pan sauce, if desired). Check the internal temperature; it should register 145 degrees. Serve immediately.

BUY THE RIGHT PORK CHOP

Supermarket chops are often cut thick at the bone and thinner at the outer edge, like the one on the left. With such chops, the thinner periphery will overcook before the thicker meat near the bone is finished. Make sure you buy chops that are of even thickness, like the one on the right.

➤ VARIATIONS
Thick-Cut Pork Chops with Spicy Citrus Pan Sauce

Prepare this sauce in the pan used to brown the chops. Start the sauce once the chops come out of the oven and are resting.

1/2	cup molasses
1 1/2	teaspoons grated zest and 1/4 cup juice from 2 limes
1	cup juice from 2 large oranges
2	medium garlic cloves, chopped
4	chipotle chiles in adobo sauce
1	recipe Pan-Seared, Oven-Roasted Thick-Cut Pork Chops (page 456)
2	tablespoons cold unsalted butter, cut into 2 pieces
	Salt and ground black pepper

1. Combine the molasses, lime zest and juice, orange juice, garlic, and chiles in the workbowl of a food processor fitted with the metal blade and puree until smooth. Transfer the puree to a bowl; set aside.

2. Brine and cook the pork chops as directed; set them aside on a platter and tent loosely with foil.

3. Pour off the fat in the skillet used to brown the chops. Place the skillet over medium-high heat and add the molasses puree, scraping the pan bottom with a wooden spoon to loosen the browned bits. Simmer until thickened and syrupy, about 2 minutes. Whisk in the butter, one piece at a time, until melted. Season the sauce with salt and pepper to taste and spoon the sauce over the chops. Serve immediately.

Thick-Cut Pork Chops with Sweet-and-Sour Pan Sauce and Bacon

Prepare this sauce in the pan used to brown the chops. Start the sauce once the chops go into the oven to roast.

1	recipe Pan-Seared, Oven-Roasted Thick-Cut Pork Chops (page 456)
5	ounces (about 5 slices) bacon, cut into 1/4-inch pieces
2	large shallots, minced (about 1/2 cup)
	Pinch sugar
1	medium garlic clove, minced or pressed through a garlic press
4	medium plum tomatoes, peeled, seeded, and cut into 1/4-inch pieces
1/2	cup balsamic vinegar
1	cup dry Marsala or sweet vermouth
4	tablespoons (1/2 stick) cold unsalted butter, cut into 4 pieces

INGREDIENTS: Modern Versus Old-Fashioned Pork

A few farmers are raising fattier pigs, yielding chops and roasts that are similar to the pork enjoyed by our grandparents. We wondered how this pork would taste to modern cooks raised on leaner modern pork. To find out, we purchased center-cut pork chops from New York farmers who raise heritage breeds the old-fashioned way (the animals are free-roaming and are fed wholesome, natural diets) and tasted them alongside supermarket chops.

Tasters had an interesting response to the farm-raised pork, noting that while it was juicy, with significantly more fat than the supermarket chops, it also had unusual "mineral" and "iron" flavors. Some tasters also found that the extra fat in the old-fashioned pork left behind an unpleasant coating in their mouths. Surprisingly, most tasters favored the more familiar supermarket meat. A few tasters thought that the old-fashioned pork was delicious but definitely an acquired taste.

We wondered just how fatty this old-fashioned pork was and so sent a sample pork butt to a food laboratory to be ground and analyzed for fat content. For comparison, we also sent a supermarket sample of the same cut. As we expected, the old-fashioned pork butt had significantly more fat—50 percent more—than the supermarket butt. Old-fashioned pork chops had 210 percent more fat than the supermarket samples, but this sky-high fat level was probably due to differences in the way the two kinds of pork were trimmed; supermarkets tend to remove most external fat, pork farmers who raise heritage breeds do not.

So is it worth the effort and money to search for a local or mail-order source for old-fashioned pork? The answer may have something to do with your age. If you were raised on old-fashioned pork, you will appreciate its flavor and extra fat. If your palate is accustomed to leaner pork, you are better off shopping at the supermarket.

I   tablespoon chopped fresh parsley leaves
      Salt and ground black pepper

1. Brine and pan-sear the pork chops as directed in steps 1 and 2.

2. As soon as the pork chops go into the oven (step 3), pour off the fat in the skillet used to brown the chops. Place the skillet over medium-high heat and cook the bacon until crisp, about 6 minutes. Transfer the bacon to a paper towel–lined plate; pour off all but 1 tablespoon of the bacon fat. Reduce the heat to low, add the shallots and sugar, and cook until the shallots are softened, about 1 minute (do not brown). Add the garlic and cook until fragrant, about 30 seconds. Increase the heat to medium-high, stir in the tomatoes and vinegar, and scrape the pan bottom with a wooden spoon to loosen the browned bits. Add the Marsala and simmer until reduced by half, about 5 minutes. Whisk in the butter, one piece at a time, until melted. Stir in the parsley and season the sauce with salt and pepper to taste. Spoon the sauce over the chops and serve immediately.

EASIEST PORK CHOPS

WE LOVE OUR THICK-CUT PORK CHOPS (PAGE 456), but they are not the quickest or easier of our chop recipes to prepare. You need to set aside an hour to brine the chops, and then they require a two-step cooking process that starts on the stove and finishes in the oven. They are great when you have the time to brine, sear, and roast, but is there a way to produce a good chop in less time?

First stop was the local supermarket meat counter. We filled a shopping cart with an overwhelming number of chops and went back to the test kitchen to see if any would fit the bill. First to go were boneless chops, which cooked up much drier than their bone-in counterparts. Superthin chops (about ¼ inch thick) were axed, too, because they dried out in the time it took for us to walk them through a hot kitchen. By comparison, 1-inch-thick (or thicker) chops, which were much less apt to dry out, necessitated the use of both the stove and the oven before being fully cooked. This just

SCORING THE CHOPS

Using a sharp knife, cut two slits, about 2 inches apart, through the outer layer of fat and connective tissue. This will keep the chops from curling as they cook.

wasn't quick enough to meet our 20-minute goal. The right thickness for our purposes proved to be ½ to ¾ inch—thin enough to keep the cooking on the stovetop and thick enough to give the chops a fighting chance for a juicy interior. As with our thick-cut pork chops, the rib chops fared best in our tests, followed by center-cut chops.

Pork chop recipes use one of three basic approaches. In the first, the chops are seared over high heat and then cooked uncovered over medium-low. The second method also starts the chops on high heat, then adds stock or water and covers the pan before reducing the heat. The third method again sears the chops over high heat but covers the pan without adding any liquid beforehand. The worst of the lot was leaving the pan uncovered, which produced unevenly cooked chops. Adding liquid and then covering the pan was not much better. After 15 minutes (about the same cooking time the other two methods required), the chops were still tough. The last method, which seared the chops over high heat and covered the pan without first adding liquid, showed the most promise. Although still miles away from our dream of juicy, tender pork chops, we didn't need a gallon of water or the jaw strength of a bear to chew them.

Using the high-heat, covered-pan cooking method, we uncovered a few secrets of pork chop cookery. First, chops should not be cooked to an internal temperature much higher than 140 degrees—cooking them beyond this point results in tough, dry meat. We also found that when we reduced the searing time from three minutes per side to one minute per side, the chops were more moist, albeit not juicy. In fact, we needed only to look in the pan to see the enormous amount of juices that had been released. If the juices were in the pan, they weren't in the chops.

Thinking out loud, a colleague raised an interesting point—perhaps the high heat was causing the problem. Although we usually sear pork roasts and thick chops over high heat to develop flavor, perhaps these thinner chops were too quick to dry out in a hot pan. We raced back to the stove and heated the pan over a more modest medium heat before adding the chops. After a few minutes, we covered the chops and cooked them over medium-low. When we uncovered them, voilà! We found a large reduction in the amount of pan juices. We then cut into what appeared to be a pretty tender chop and happily found the juices right inside the meat, where they belonged. Progress!

Perhaps pushing our luck, we wondered what would happen if the pork chops were introduced to the heat at an even slower pace. If medium heat was good, what about—you guessed it—no heat? Although it seemed strange, we placed the next batch of chops in a cold pan and then turned the heat to medium. After the chops had cooked for a few minutes on each side, we covered them and cooked them through over low heat while uttering a silent prayer. Our hopes ran high when we noticed that there were barely any pan juices in the skillet. We plated a chop, bit down, and were met with the juiciest and most tender chop yet.

The only drawback was color—or lack thereof. Without enough heat to promote browning, these pork chops were as blond as the ubiquitous bombshell. Using a little sugar in addition to salt and pepper to season them went a long way toward helping to color the chops. We also found that instead of splitting the browning time and the sugar evenly between the two sides of the chops, it was better to sugar one side and let it develop a more substantial color. This side, the first side to come in contact with the pan, then became the presentation side.

Although starting meat in a cold pan was odd—if not downright weird—it made quick-cooking a weeknight pork chop almost foolproof. Would these pork chops win any beauty contest? We doubted it. We did know, though, that we didn't have to serve them in a sea of applesauce. It could, and would, be served on the side.

Easy Pork Chops
SERVES 4

In this recipe, "natural" pork chops—that is, pork chops that are not "enhanced"—work best (for more information on enhanced pork, see page 454 and page 464); the liquid injected into enhanced pork inhibits browning. Electric burners are slower to heat than gas burners, so, if using one, begin heating the burner before seasoning the chops. If you don't hear a gentle sizzle after the pork chops have been cooking for two minutes over medium heat, your stovetop is running at a low heat output. Raise the heat to medium-high to cook the pork chops uncovered (as directed in the recipe). Then reduce the heat to medium-low instead of low, cover the chops, and continue with the recipe as directed. When cooking the first side of the chops, use color as an indicator of when to flip them; then, to determine doneness, use an instant-read thermometer—do not go solely by cooking times. Serve these very simple pork chops with chutney or applesauce, or try one of the recipe variations that follow.

4	bone-in rib or center-cut pork chops, $1/2$ to $3/4$ inch thick (about 7 ounces each), patted dry with paper towels and scored according to the illustration on page 458
I	teaspoon vegetable oil
	Salt and ground black pepper
$1/2$	teaspoon sugar

1. If using an electric stove, turn the burner to medium heat. Rub both sides of each chop with ⅛ teaspoon of the oil and sprinkle with salt and pepper to taste. Sprinkle the meat portion on one side of each chop evenly with ⅛ teaspoon of the sugar, avoiding the bone.

2. Place the chops sugared-side down in a nonstick 12-inch skillet, positioning the chops so that the ribs point to the center of the pan. Using your hands, press the meat on each chop into the pan. Set the skillet over medium heat; cook until lightly

browned, 4 to 9 minutes (the pork chops should be sizzling after 2 minutes; if not, see note). Using tongs, flip the chops, positioning them in the same manner, with the ribs pointing to the center of the skillet. Cover the skillet, reduce the heat to low, and cook until the center of each chop registers 140 to 145 degrees on an instant-read thermometer, 3 to 6 minutes (begin checking internal temperature after only 2 minutes); the chops will barely brown on the second side. Transfer the chops to a platter, tent loosely with foil, and let rest for 5 minutes. Do not discard the liquid in the skillet.

3. Add any juices accumulated on the platter to the skillet. Set the skillet over high heat and simmer vigorously until reduced to about 3 tablespoons, 30 to 90 seconds; adjust the seasonings with salt and pepper to taste. Off the heat, return the pork chops to the skillet and turn them to coat with the reduced juices. Serve the chops immediately, browned-side up, pouring any remaining juices over them.

➤ VARIATIONS

Pork Chops with Mustard-Sage Sauce

This sauce and the brandy and prune one that follows both start out thick and are thinned by the juices released by the chops as they rest.

Follow the recipe for Easy Pork Chops; after transferring the chops to a platter and tenting them loosely with foil, pour the pan juices in the skillet into a small bowl and reserve. While the chops rest, add 1 teaspoon vegetable oil and 1 medium garlic clove, minced (about 1 teaspoon), to the now-empty skillet; set the skillet over medium heat and cook until fragrant, about 30 seconds. Add ¼ cup low-sodium chicken broth; increase the heat to high and simmer until reduced to about 2 table-spoons, about 3 minutes. Add the pork chop juices to the skillet. Off the heat, whisk in 1 tablespoon Dijon mustard and 3 tablespoons cold unsalted butter until melted and combined. Stir in 1 teaspoon minced fresh sage leaves and adjust the seasonings with salt and pepper to taste. Spoon the sauce over the chops and serve immediately.

SCIENCE: Low and Slow for Pork Chops

Pork chops, which may go from succulent to leathery with the most minor differences in cooking technique, pose a challenge for the cook. According to one Canadian study, for example, pork cooked to an internal temperature of 180 degrees in a 400-degree oven can lose between two and three times the moisture of pork cooked to 160 degrees in a 250-degree oven. Curious about this and about the unconventional cold-pan method of cooking chops in our recipe, we decided to investigate the effect of heat on pork meat. What we discovered was that the secret to juicy pork resides in the structure of its muscle proteins.

Proteins are long chains of linked amino acids that fold into a huge variety of three-dimensional shapes. Folded muscle protein also holds and immobilizes a considerable amount of water in an ordered fashion. Introduce heat, though, and this organized state of affairs is thrown into disarray as the proteins unfold. Thermal analysis of pork has shown that there are three approximate temperatures at which groups of pork proteins come undone: 126 degrees, 145 degrees, and 168 degrees. As each of these temperatures is reached, more water is freed from the proteins. Meat proteins also tend to compact as they cook, squeezing out the freed-up water.

To better understand these effects, we took cubes of pork and cooked them to 100 degrees, 140 degrees, and 180 degrees. At the highest temperature, the meat not only shrank more, but the muscle fibers became tighter and more pronounced. When we went ahead and seared a cube on one side in a very hot pan, we found that the edge touching the pan contracted and looked similar to the cube cooked to 180 degrees, even though the rest of the cube was raw.

All cooks focus on the temperature reached at the middle of a piece of meat to determine doneness, but this may be too myopic. The means by which the middle gets to that temperature is at least as important. High-heat cooking methods, such as searing, guarantee that the outer layer of meat will be very well-done before the inside is just done. Brining can compensate for this but this method just won't work with regular (unbrined) chops. By keeping the heat level low, water loss on the outside of the chop is minimized, and more of the juice that is bound inside the meat remains there.

Pork Chops with Brandy and Prunes

Cover ⅓ cup chopped pitted prunes with ¼ cup brandy and let stand. Follow the recipe for Easy Pork Chops; after transferring the chops to a platter and tenting them loosely with foil, pour the pan juices in the skillet into a small bowl and reserve. While the chops rest, add 1 teaspoon vegetable oil and 1 medium shallot, minced (about 3 tablespoons), to the now-empty skillet; set the skillet over medium heat and cook, stirring occasionally, until the shallot has softened, about 2 minutes. Off the heat, add the brandy and prunes; set the skillet over medium-high heat and cook until the brandy is reduced to about 2 tablespoons, about 3 minutes. Add the pork chop juices to the skillet. Off the heat, whisk in 2 teaspoons minced fresh thyme leaves and 3 tablespoons cold unsalted butter until melted and combined. Adjust the seasonings with salt and pepper to taste. Spoon the sauce over the chops and serve immediately.

SMOTHERED PORK CHOPS

SMOTHERED PORK CHOPS, A HOMEY DISH OF chops braised in deeply flavored onion gravy, are folksy, not fancy; denim, not worsted wool. The cooking process is straightforward: You brown the chops, remove them from the pan, brown the onions, return the chops to the pan, cover them with the onions and gravy—hence the term *smothered*—and braise them until tender. Inarguably easy, but initial recipe tests produced bland, dry pork and near-tasteless gravies with woeful consistencies ranging from pasty to processed to gelatinous to watery.

Poor texture and shallow flavor rob smothered pork chops of their savory-sweet glory. To get it right, we knew we'd have to identify the best chops and the best way to cook them. And the gravy was no less important.

Some of our research recipes specified sirloin chops, which are cut from the rear end of the loin. Our tasters found this cut a little dry and often unavailable. Blade chops, cut from the far front end of the loin, were juicier but suffered the same spotty availability. Of the two remaining types of chops, center-cut loin and rib, we found the latter to be the juiciest and most flavorful because it had a bit more fat.

We tried rib chops as thick as 1½ inches and as thin as ½ inch and were shocked when tasters unanimously chose the ½-inch chops. Thick chops overwhelmed the gravy, which we believed should share equal billing with the meat. Thin chops also picked up more onion flavor during cooking. We also tried boneless chops, but they cooked up dry, so we decided to stick with bone-in for optimum juiciness.

We skipped brining these chops for two reasons: First, these chops cook in a moist environment provided by the gravy, so why spend time instilling extra moisture? We would not be using the harsh, dry heat of grilling, searing, or roasting, which makes brining a viable and often necessary option. Second, no matter how we adjusted the salinity of the brine, the salt-infused meat caused the gravy to become intolerably salty.

Last we tackled the question of cooking time. Although we prefer to slightly undercook pork to ensure tenderness, this is one application where further cooking was necessary since we wanted to infuse the meat with the flavor of the gravy and onions. After their initial browning, the chops registered a rosy 140 degrees on an instant-read thermometer. They were cooked through and tender, but since they had yet to be smothered, they had none of the onion flavor we wanted. Fifteen minutes of braising in the gravy boosted the flavor but toughened the chops, which now registered almost 200 degrees. At that temperature, the meat fibers have contracted and expelled moisture, but the fat and connective tissue between the fibers, called collagen, have not had a chance to melt fully and turn into gelatin. It is this gelatin that makes braised meats especially rich and tender. Another 15 minutes of braising time solved the problem. At this point, the chops registered 210 degrees; the extra time allowed the fat and collagen to melt completely, so the meat was tender and succulent as well as oniony from the gravy.

It was important that the gravy build on the

flavor of the browned pork chops. The canned condensed soup called for in some of the research recipes produced gravies that tasted processed and gluelike. Water produced a weak, thin gravy, but chicken broth improved the picture, adding much-needed flavor.

For liquid to morph into gravy, it must be thickened. Cornstarch is an easy option, but it resulted in a gelatinous, translucent sauce that looked and felt wrong. Next we tried adding flour, in three different ways. Flouring the chops before browning them turned their exteriors gummy and left the gravy with a chalky mouthfeel. Flouring the onions left the gravy tasting of raw flour. Last, we called upon a roux, a mixture of flour and fat (in this case, vegetable oil) cooked together. This occasioned the need for an extra pan, which we'd hoped to avoid having to use, but the results were fantastic. The roux was simple to make, and it thickened the sauce reliably without adding the taste of raw flour, lending the gravy both a smooth finish and another layer of flavor that was slightly nutty.

The roux was good, but we tried to improve it with two oft-used refinements. First, we fried a couple of slices of bacon and substituted the rendered fat for the vegetable oil in the roux. What a hit! The sweet/salty/smoky bacon flavor underscored and deepened all of the other flavors in the dish. Beyond that, we followed in the footsteps of many a gravy master who has eked out even more flavor from a roux by browning it for five minutes to the shade of peanut butter. Cooking the flour this way unlocks a rich, toasty flavor that builds as the shade deepens.

The onions play a title role in the gravy. We tried them minced, chopped, and sliced both thick and thin. Thin-sliced onions cooked to a melting texture that was our favorite. We tried simply softening the onions until they were translucent versus cooking them for a few more minutes until their edges browned, a winning technique that accentuated their natural sweetness. Perhaps the most important onion test was trying different types, including standard-issue supermarket yellow onions, red onions, and sweet Vidalia onions. The yellow onions triumphed for their "deep brown hue" and "balanced flavor."

The onions cook in the same pan used to brown the chops. We wanted to make sure that the onions released enough moisture to dissolve (or deglaze) the flavorful, sticky browned bits (called *fond*) left in the pan by the chops, so we salted them lightly. The heat and salt worked together to jump-start the breakdown of the onions' cell walls, which set their juices flowing. We also added two tablespoons of water to the pan for insurance.

Our last flavor tweak was an unusual one for us—we eliminated the salt we customarily use to season chops. Tasters agreed that the salt added to the onions, along with the naturally salty bacon and chicken broth and the garlic, thyme, and bay used to build extra flavor in the gravy, seasoned the dish adequately.

Smothered Pork Chops
SERVES 4

Be sure to use low-sodium chicken broth in this recipe; regular chicken broth can result in an overseasoned sauce. Serve smothered chops with a starch to soak up the rich gravy. Simple egg noodles was the test kitchen favorite, but rice or mashed potatoes also work well.

3	ounces (about 3 slices) bacon, cut into 1/4-inch pieces
2	tablespoons unbleached all-purpose flour
1 3/4	cups low-sodium chicken broth
2	tablespoons vegetable oil
4	bone-in rib pork chops, 1/2 to 3/4 inch thick (about 7 ounces each), patted dry with paper towels
	Ground black pepper
2	medium yellow onions, halved and sliced thin (about 3 1/2 cups)
	Salt
2	tablespoons water
2	medium garlic cloves, minced or pressed through a garlic press
1	teaspoon minced fresh thyme leaves
2	bay leaves
1	tablespoon minced fresh parsley leaves

1. Fry the bacon in a small saucepan over medium heat, stirring occasionally, until lightly

browned and the fat is rendered, 8 to 10 minutes. Using a slotted spoon, transfer the bacon to a paper towel–lined plate and reserve, leaving the fat in the pan (you should have 2 tablespoons bacon fat; if not, supplement with vegetable oil). Reduce the heat to medium-low and gradually whisk the flour into the fat until smooth. Cook, whisking frequently, until the mixture is light brown, about the color of peanut butter, about 5 minutes. Whisk in the chicken broth in a slow, steady stream; increase the heat to medium-high and bring to a boil, stirring occasionally. Cover and remove from the heat; set aside.

2. Heat 1 tablespoon of the oil in a 12-inch skillet over high heat until smoking. Meanwhile, sprinkle the pork chops with ½ teaspoon pepper. Brown the chops in a single layer until deep golden on the first side, about 3 minutes. Flip the chops and cook until browned on the second side, about 3 minutes longer. Transfer the chops to a large plate and set aside.

3. Reduce the heat to medium and add the remaining 1 tablespoon oil, the onions, ¼ teaspoon salt, and the water to the now-empty skillet. Using a wooden spoon, scrape up the browned bits on the pan bottom; cook, stirring frequently, until the onions are softened and browned around the edges, about 5 minutes. Stir in the garlic and thyme and cook until fragrant, about 30 seconds. Return the chops to the skillet in a single layer and cover them with the onions. Pour in the reserved sauce and any juices released by the pork chops; add the bay leaves. Cover, reduce the heat to low, and simmer until the

pork is tender and a paring knife inserted into the chops meets very little resistance, about 30 minutes.

4. Transfer the chops to a warmed serving platter and tent with foil. Increase the heat to medium-high and simmer the sauce rapidly, stirring frequently, until thickened to a gravy-like consistency, about 5 minutes. Discard the bay leaves, stir in the parsley, and adjust the seasonings with salt and pepper to taste. Cover the chops with the sauce, sprinkle with the reserved bacon, and serve immediately.

➤ VARIATIONS

Smothered Pork Chops with Cider and Apples
Follow the recipe for Smothered Pork Chops, substituting apple cider for the chicken broth and 1 large or 2 small Granny Smith apples, peeled, cored, and cut into ⅓-inch wedges, for 1 onion, and increasing the salt to ½ teaspoon in step 3.

Smothered Pork Chops with Spicy Collard Greens
Follow the recipe for Smothered Pork Chops, increasing the oil in step 3 to 2 tablespoons, omitting 1 onion, and increasing the garlic to 4 cloves. Just before returning the browned chops to the pan in step 3, add 4 cups thinly sliced collard greens and ½ teaspoon red pepper flakes.

MAPLE-GLAZED PORK ROAST

SWEET MAPLE, WITH ITS DELICATE FLAVOR NOTES of smoke, caramel, and vanilla, makes an ideal foil for pork, which has a faint sweetness of its own. The result of this marriage is a glistening maple-glazed pork roast, which, when sliced, combines the juices from tender, well-seasoned pork with a rich maple glaze to create complex flavor in every bite.

When we tested five different recipes, however, we found that this dish often falls short of its savory-sweet promise. Of course, many of the roasts turned out dry (a constant concern when cooking today's lean pork), but we were surprised

SLICING ONIONS THIN

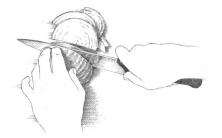

Orb-shaped foods like onions are difficult to slice whole because they do not sit stable on a flat side. Unless whole sliced onion rings are the goal, to slice an onion, halve it pole to pole, peel it, set it on a cut side, and then slice.

to discover that the glazes presented even bigger problems. Most of them were too thin to coat the pork properly, some were so sweet that they required a hotline to the dentist's office, and none of them had a pronounced maple flavor.

Good maple-glazed roast pork starts out as good plain roast pork. We wanted a boneless cut and tested four options. Tasters preferred the blade-end loin roast for its flavor and juiciness, which it receives in part from a deposit of fat that separates the two muscle sections at one end of the roast. As with our basic recipe for roasting this cut, we found that brining was not necessary but that a stovetop sear followed by roasting in a moderate oven was key.

With the roast in the oven, it was time to get serious about developing maple flavor. The recipes we had researched touted dozens of glaze concoctions and methods for marrying them to the pork. Most of the flavoring ingredients added to the maple syrup either diluted it (so that it was too thin to use as a glaze) or were simply unwelcome. This list included soy sauce, vinegar, lemon juice, cranberry juice, cider, and bourbon for liquid ingredients and herbs, spices, jams, jellies, brown sugar, maple sugar, mustards, and chiles for flavor boosters. (We reserved the best of these flavorings for recipe variations). Everyone agreed, however, that small amounts of complementary spices added subtle dimension to the maple, thus cinnamon, ground cloves, and cayenne all found their way into the glaze recipe. Still, we wanted more maple flavor and a glaze that would really stick to the meat. We even tried brining one loin in maple syrup and wrapping another with maple-flavored bacon. The former added no discernible maple flavor, while the latter tasted mildly artificial. We finally hit upon a simple solution to enhance flavor when we reduced the maple syrup in a saucepan. But we were frustrated when it dripped down off the roast onto the bottom of the roasting pan and burned.

Then we had an idea. Remember the hot pan we had left from searing the roast? How about putting it to additional use? We decided to use it to flash-reduce the maple syrup. We removed the loin from the pan after searing, poured off the excess fat, added the syrup, and let it heat for 30 seconds. This allowed us to use the drippings that had formed in the pan

when the meat seared and also eliminated the extra pan we had been using to reduce the syrup. Next we decided to lose the roasting pan (and basting brush, which we invariably trashed with the sticky glaze) in favor of the same skillet. Instead of pouring the glaze mixture over the pork in the roasting pan, where it would run to the edges and scorch, we returned the seared loin to the skillet with the syrup, twirled the pork around in the glaze a couple of times with tongs, and popped the whole thing into the oven, with the skillet serving as the roasting pan.

The smaller surface area of the skillet prevented the glaze from spreading out and burning. This pan also made it easier to coat the pork thoroughly because it was sitting right in the glaze, like a belle in her bath. The roast emerged from the oven with a thick, uniform, glistening coating of glaze and an impressive, concentrated maple flavor. We had the best results with fairly small roasts (about 2½ pounds); the sauce tended to burn when we tried to cook through larger roasts. An oven temperature of 325 degrees (which is 25 degrees higher than our standard roasting temperature for this cut of meat) was fine given the small size of the roast, and it helped speed up the roasting time a bit, too.

In the end, we had managed to turn this into a one-pan dish by searing, reducing the glaze, and roasting all in the same skillet. And there was yet

THE PROBLEM WITH ENHANCED PORK

**JUICES LOST FROM
ENHANCED PORK**   **JUICES LOST FROM
REGULAR PORK**

Many markets sell enhanced pork, which has been injected with a water–salt–sodium phosphate solution meant to season the meat and improve juiciness. During testing, we found that an enhanced roast exuded nearly one and a half times as much liquid as a regular roast when carved. We recommend buying regular pork.

another bonus. Starting with a hot skillet shaved a little time off the whole process. This skillet-roasted, burnished beauty was now out of the oven in 45 minutes or less.

Maple-Glazed Pork Roast

SERVES 4 TO 6

A nonstick ovenproof skillet will be much easier to clean than a traditional one. Whichever you use, remember that the handle will be blistering hot when you take it out of the oven, so be sure to use a potholder or oven mitt. Note that you should not trim the pork of its thin layer of fat. The flavor of grade B maple syrup (sometimes called "cooking maple") is stronger and richer than that of grade A, but grade A syrup will work well, too. This dish is unapologetically sweet, so we recommend side dishes that take well to the sweetness. Garlicky sautéed greens, braised cabbage, and soft polenta are good choices.

1/3	cup maple syrup, preferably grade B
1/8	teaspoon ground cinnamon
	Pinch ground cloves
	Pinch cayenne pepper
I	boneless blade-end pork loin roast (about 2 1/2 pounds), tied at even intervals along the length with 5 pieces kitchen twine and patted dry with paper towels
3/4	teaspoon salt
1/2	teaspoon ground black pepper
2	teaspoons vegetable oil

1. Adjust an oven rack to the middle position and heat the oven to 325 degrees. Stir the maple syrup, cinnamon, cloves, and cayenne together in a measuring cup or small bowl; set aside. Sprinkle the roast evenly with the salt and pepper.

2. Heat the oil in a heavy-bottomed ovenproof nonstick 10-inch skillet over medium-high heat until just beginning to smoke. Place the roast fat-side down in the skillet and cook until well browned, about 3 minutes. Using tongs, rotate the roast one-quarter turn and cook until well browned, about 2½ minutes; repeat until the roast is well browned on all sides. Transfer the roast to a large plate. Reduce the heat to medium and pour off the fat from the skillet; add the maple syrup

mixture and cook until fragrant, about 30 seconds (the syrup will bubble immediately). Off the heat, return the roast to the skillet; using tongs, roll to coat the roast with glaze on all sides.

3. Transfer the skillet to the oven and roast until the center of the roast registers about 135 degrees on an instant-read thermometer, 35 to 45 minutes, using tongs to roll the roast to coat with glaze twice during the roasting time. Transfer the roast to a carving board; set the skillet aside to cool slightly and thicken the glaze, about 5 minutes. Pour the glaze over the roast and let rest for 15 minutes (the center of the roast should register 145 to 150 degrees). Snip the twine off the roast, cut into ¼-inch slices, and serve immediately.

➤ VARIATIONS

Maple-Glazed Pork Roast with Rosemary

Follow the recipe for Maple-Glazed Pork Roast, substituting 2 teaspoons minced fresh rosemary leaves for the cinnamon, cloves, and cayenne.

Maple-Glazed Pork Roast with Orange Essence

Follow the recipe for Maple-Glazed Pork Roast, adding 1 tablespoon grated orange zest to the maple syrup along with the spices.

Maple-Glazed Pork Roast with Star Anise

Follow the recipe for Maple-Glazed Pork Roast, adding 4 star anise pods to the maple syrup along with the spices.

Maple-Glazed Pork Roast with Smoked Paprika

Follow the recipe for Maple-Glazed Pork Roast, adding 2 teaspoons smoked hot paprika to the maple syrup along with the spices.

ROAST PORK LOIN

UNASSUMING AND SIMPLE TO PREPARE, A BONE-less pork roast is hearty weeknight fare for a casual family feast. The practical advantages of this supermarket cut are many: It is affordable and widely available; the mild, sweet flavor of roast pork pairs well with most any side dish; and left-overs make great sandwiches.

The two types of boneless roasts from the loin are the common center loin roast, which contains a lean, unbroken eye of meat, and the blade-end loin roast, which has a section of the shoulder's blade muscle attached. Both are fine, although tasters preferred the flavor and juiciness of the blade-end roast, which benefits from a deposit of fat that separates the two muscles. A blade-end roast is also thicker and shorter in length than a center loin roast of equal weight, which means a center loin roast may cook unevenly due to its elongated shape.

As is the custom in our test kitchen, we tried brining the meat (soaking it in a saltwater solution to season and boost juiciness), and brining did, indeed, yield tender, juicy, well-seasoned pork. On the other hand, the unbrined pork was almost as good (as long as we took care not to overcook it), and it was nice to dispense with the 2½-hour brining time. (Serving the roast with a pan sauce, which was our plan, also made brining less impera-tive.) We also ran a series of tests using "enhanced" pork, a common supermarket product that has been injected with a solution of water, salt, and sodium phosphate to season the meat and add moisture. Tasters were put off by the flood of liquid these roasts released when they were sliced, as well as by the overly wet, spongy texture of the meat.

Today's leaner pork may be pleasing to health-conscious carnivores, but its low fat content makes it exceptionally prone to overcooking. Pork is best served at a temperature of 145 to 150 degrees, rather than the 160 degrees (or higher) recommended by many older recipes. If, however, you take the roast out of the oven once it reaches this temperature, it will be overcooked. The temperature of the roast will continue to rise, by as much as 15 degrees, once it has been taken out of the oven. The thing to do is to remove the roast when it registers 135 degrees, and then let it rest on the cutting board before slicing.

Just as important as the final temperature of the roast is how quickly it gets there. We roasted pork loins at a variety of oven temperatures and found that roasting slow and low is the key to juicy, evenly cooked meat. Roasts cooked at high temperatures were dried out near the edges before the center was done. However, even large roasts (where the dispar-ity in cooking rates between the exterior and inte-rior is greatest) were tender and juicy throughout when cooked in a 300-degree oven.

Innumerable tests have proven that roasts with a deep brown, caramelized crust both look and taste better than those without. Trying to brown the meat using high oven heat at the beginning or end of the roasting produced marginal results, so we decided to sear it on the stovetop. Because the meat was tied into a neat bundle, it fit well in a skil-let on the stovetop, which gave us great browning and lots of control over the process. Tying a roast may seem fussy to some, but we discovered that this small investment of time is amply rewarded. The uniform shape of a tied roast promotes even cook-ing and yields attractive round slices.

After searing the roast on the stovetop, there were plenty of drippings and crusty browned bits, or fond, left over in the skillet—perfect for making a quick pan sauce. After searing several roasts, however, we discovered that the amount and color of the fond varied greatly. Sometimes the pan was quite dark, almost black in spots, and the resulting sauce tended to be bitter. Other times there was very little stuck

TYING A PORK LOIN

Straight from the supermarket packaging, most pork loins will lie flat in the pan and cook unevenly (left). Tying the roast not only yields more attractive slices but ensures that the roast will have the same thickness from end to end so that it cooks evenly (right).

to the pan, and the sauce turned out pale and bland. By adjusting the heat as needed during the searing process, we were able to keep the pan from burning, but how could we make sure enough fond would stick to the pan in the first place? The key was to control the amount of fat in the skillet. Pork loin roasts have a layer of fat on just one side, which is usually presented as the "top." When we placed the roast in the skillet with the fat side down first, as we were naturally inclined to do, much of that fat layer quickly rendered into the pan and prevented the meat from sticking to the surface. The meat browned, but the pan stayed fairly clean. Conversely, when we browned the fat side last, the other sides had plenty of time to brown in a relatively dry pan, and thus left behind lots of fond for our sauce.

Roast Pork Loin

SERVES 4 TO 6

This recipe can be made with roasts as large as 4½ pounds, which should serve 8 to 10 people. It makes enough jus for a larger roast. Because of the addition of vegetables, the variations will accommodate only a 2½-pound roast. A thin (⅛-inch) layer of fat will result in a delicious crispy crust, but this recipe will also work with a roast that has been completely trimmed.

ROAST
1   boneless blade-end pork loin roast (about 2½ pounds), tied at even intervals along the length with 5 pieces kitchen twine and patted dry with paper towels
    Salt and ground black pepper
1   tablespoon vegetable oil

JUS
    Vegetable oil (if needed)
2   small shallots, minced (about ¼ cup)
2   cups low-sodium chicken broth
2   bay leaves
2   sprigs fresh thyme
¼   teaspoon sugar
2   teaspoons juice from 1 lemon

1. Adjust an oven rack to the middle position and heat the oven to 300 degrees. Sprinkle the roast evenly with salt and pepper. Heat the oil in a 12-inch skillet over medium-high heat until smoking. Add the roast, fat-side up, and brown on all sides (fat side last), 8 to 10 minutes, lowering the heat to medium if necessary to prevent the roast from burning. Transfer the roast to a V-rack set inside a roasting pan, but do not wash the skillet.

2. Transfer the roasting pan to the oven and cook until an instant-read thermometer inserted into the center of the roast registers 135 degrees, 45 to 55 minutes. (If cooking a larger roast, increase the time to 65 to 75 minutes.) Remove the roast from the oven and transfer it to a cutting board. Tent lightly with foil and let rest 15 to 20 minutes (the center of the roast should register 145 to 150 degrees).

3. While the roast is resting, make the jus. Either pour off fat or add oil to the skillet so that there is about 1 tablespoon of fat in the pan. Heat the skillet over medium heat until the oil is shimmering. Add the shallots and cook, scraping the browned bits from the pan bottom, until softened, 4 to 5 minutes. Add the broth, bay leaves, thyme, and sugar and simmer until reduced by half, about 15 minutes. Remove the pan from the heat and stir in the lemon juice. Discard the bay leaves and thyme and adjust the seasonings with salt and pepper to taste.

4. Snip the twine off the roast and cut the pork crosswise into thin slices. Serve immediately with the jus.

➤ VARIATIONS

Roast Pork Loin with Carrots, Fennel, and Honey

Toss 2 medium fennel bulbs (about 1½ pounds), halved, cored, and cut into ½-inch-thick pieces, and 1½ pounds carrots, peeled and cut on the bias into 1½-inch pieces, with 2 tablespoons melted butter, 2 tablespoons honey, ½ teaspoon salt, and ⅛ teaspoon ground black pepper in a large roasting pan. Place a V-rack in the pan over the vegetables. Follow the recipe for Roast Pork Loin, placing the seared roast on the rack in the pan with the vegetables. After the roast is removed from the oven in step 2, return the roasting pan with the vegetables to the oven, increase the temperature to 500 degrees, and roast the vegetables, stirring occasionally, until browned, 15 to 20 minutes longer.

467

Prepare the jus as directed in step 3, replacing the sugar with ¼ teaspoon honey. Serve the roasted vegetables with the pork.

Roast Pork Loin with Potatoes and Sage

Toss 3 pounds large red potatoes, cut into 1-inch wedges, with 2 tablespoons olive oil, 1 teaspoon salt, and ¼ teaspoon ground black pepper in a large roasting pan. Place a V-rack in the pan over the potatoes. Follow the recipe for Roast Pork Loin, placing the seared roast on the rack in the pan with the potatoes. After the roast is removed from the oven, add 2 teaspoons chopped fresh sage leaves to the potatoes, increase the oven temperature to 500 degrees, and roast the potatoes, stirring occasionally, until browned and crisp, 15 to 20 minutes. Serve the roasted potatoes with the pork.

SAUTÉED PORK TENDERLOIN MEDALLIONS

THERE'S NO REASON PORK TENDERLOIN NEEDS to be roasted whole. Sometimes we prefer tenderloin cut into medallions, sautéed, and then finished with a pan sauce.

We started our testing by cutting the tenderloin into 1-inch-thick slices and pounded them down to ¾ inch with the flat side of a chef's knife blade (to increase the surface area for searing). We then sautéed the medallions in a bit of sizzling oil for about one minute per side. At the end, every single slice was seared beautifully on both sides, and the pan drippings were perfectly caramelized and ready to deglaze for a flavorful, simple sauce. The whole operation, from refrigerator to table, took only 15 minutes. Beneath the seared crust on each slice was juicy, succulent meat that met all our expectations for this extra-tender cut.

While testing and retesting our chosen method, we came up with a few pointers to help ensure successful sautéing. First, trim the pearlescent membrane, called the silver skin, from the tenderloin before cutting the medallions. If left on, the silver skin shrinks in the heat of the pan, pulling the meat up and out of the hot fat, thereby inhibiting browning. Second, do not overcook the meat. There should be just a tinge of pink when you peek into a piece with the tip of a paring knife. The meat will not be completely cooked at the end of the searing time, but that is fine because you later return it to the pan to reheat and meld with the sauce.

There is one drawback to sautéing. We found that sautéing four batches of medallions (the amount derived from two tenderloins) in the same pan caused the pan drippings to burn. We found it best to sauté just two batches of medallions (the amount that one tenderloin yields) and then make the pan sauce. For this reason, sautéing is ideal when cooking for three. You may cook medallions from two tenderloins in two sauté pans at the same time and then make pan sauces in each pan, but grilling or roasting is probably easier when trying to cook pork tenderloin for a crowd.

Sautéed Pork Tenderloin Medallions

SERVES 3 (3 OR 4 SLICES PER PERSON)

To promote even cooking, cut your slices to a uniform thickness. If it helps, lay a ruler in front of the loin and slice at the inch marks. If you've got one, cover the pan with a splatter screen to keep the fat from splattering. Serve with one of the pan sauce variations that follow.

1	teaspoon salt
½	teaspoon ground black pepper
1	pork tenderloin (about 1 pound), trimmed of silver skin (see the illustration on page 586), and cut into 1-inch slices, each pounded to ¾ inch with the flat side of a chef's knife blade
2	tablespoons olive oil

Sprinkle the salt and pepper over both sides of the pork slices. Heat the oil in a large, heavy-bottomed skillet until shimmering. Working in batches of no more than six slices to avoid overcrowding, sear the medallions without moving them until browned on one side, about 80 seconds (the oil should sizzle but not smoke). Turn the medallions with tongs to avoid scraping off the sear; sear until the meat is mostly opaque at the sides, firm to the touch, and well browned, about 80 seconds. Transfer the pork to a plate; continue with one of the pan sauce recipes that follow, using the drippings in the pan as the base for the sauce.

➤ VARIATIONS

Sautéed Pork Tenderloin Medallions with Port, Dried Cherries, and Rosemary

1	recipe Sautéed Pork Tenderloin Medallions (page 468)
1/3	cup port
1/2	cup dried cherries
2/3	cup low-sodium chicken broth
2	teaspoons minced fresh rosemary leaves
	Salt and ground black pepper

1. Prepare the pork as directed and transfer it to a plate.

2. Set the now-empty skillet used to cook the pork over medium-high heat and add the port and cherries. Cook, scraping the pan bottom with a wooden spatula to loosen the browned bits, until the liquid reduces to about 2 tablespoons, 2 to 3 minutes. Increase the heat to high and add the broth, rosemary, and any accumulated pork juices from the plate. Cook until the liquid reaches the consistency of maple syrup, about 2 minutes. Add salt and pepper to taste.

3. Reduce the heat to medium and return the pork to the pan, turning the meat to coat. Simmer to heat the pork through, about 3 minutes. Season with salt and pepper to taste. Transfer the pork to a serving plate and spoon the sauce over the meat. Serve immediately.

Sautéed Pork Tenderloin Medallions with Cream, Apples, and Sage

1	recipe Sautéed Pork Tenderloin Medallions (page 468)
1	tablespoon unsalted butter
1	Granny Smith apple, peeled, cored, and cut into 12 slices
1/2	medium onion, sliced thin (about 1/2 cup)
1/3	cup apple cider
3	tablespoons applejack or brandy
1/2	cup low-sodium chicken broth
2	tablespoons minced fresh sage leaves
1/4	cup heavy cream
	Salt and ground black pepper

1. Prepare the pork as directed and transfer it to a plate.

2. Set the now-empty skillet used to cook the pork over medium-high heat and add the butter. Swirl the pan until the butter melts. Add the apple and onion and sauté until the apple starts to brown, about 4 minutes. Add the cider and applejack and simmer, scraping the pan bottom with a wooden spatula to loosen the browned bits, until the liquid reduces to a glaze, about 2½ minutes. Increase the heat to high and add the broth, sage, and any accumulated pork juices from the plate. Cook until the liquid reaches the consistency of maple syrup, about 3 minutes. Add the cream and cook until reduced by half, about 2 minutes.

3. Reduce the heat to medium and return the pork to the pan, turning the meat to coat. Simmer to heat the pork through and blend the flavors, about 3 minutes. Adjust the seasonings with salt and pepper to taste. Transfer the pork to a serving plate and spoon the sauce over the meat. Serve immediately.

Sautéed Pork Tenderloin Medallions with Red Wine Vinegar, Warm Spices, and Raisins

If you like, currants can be substituted for the raisins.

1	recipe Sautéed Pork Tenderloin Medallions (page 468)
1/2	teaspoon ground cinnamon
1/4	teaspoon ground cloves
1/8	teaspoon cayenne pepper
2	teaspoons sugar
1	tablespoon olive oil
1	medium onion, sliced thin (about 1 cup)
1/4	cup dry sherry
1/4	cup red wine vinegar
1/2	cup low-sodium chicken broth
1/4	cup raisins
	Salt and ground black pepper

1. Prepare the pork as directed and transfer it to a plate.

2. Mix the cinnamon, cloves, cayenne, and sugar in a small bowl; set aside. Set the now-empty skillet used to cook the pork over medium-high heat, add the oil, and heat briefly. Add the onion and sauté until softened and starting to color, about 2 minutes. Add the spice mixture, sherry, and vinegar and cook, scraping the pan bottom with a wooden spatula to loosen the browned bits, until the liquid reduces to a glaze, about 2½ minutes. Increase the heat to high and add the broth, raisins, and any accumulated pork juices from the plate. Cook until the liquid reaches the consistency of maple syrup, about 3 minutes.

3. Reduce the heat to medium and return the pork to the pan, turning the meat to coat. Simmer to heat the pork through and blend the flavors, about 3 minutes. Adjust the seasonings with salt and pepper to taste. Transfer the pork to a serving plate and spoon the sauce over the meat. Serve immediately.

Sautéed Pork Tenderloin Medallions with Orange, Fennel, and Green Olives
See the illustrations on page 248 for tips on coring the fennel.

1	recipe Sautéed Pork Tenderloin Medallions (page 468)
1	tablespoon olive oil
½	medium fennel bulb, fronds and stems discarded, root end trimmed, cored, and sliced thin (about 1 cup)
2	medium garlic cloves, minced or pressed through a garlic press
⅓	cup juice and 1 teaspoon grated zest from 1 large orange
⅔	cup low-sodium chicken broth
¼	cup pitted green olives, sliced
2	tablespoons chopped fresh parsley leaves Salt and ground black pepper

1. Prepare the pork as directed and transfer it to a plate.

2. Set the now-empty skillet used to cook the pork over medium-high heat, add the oil, and heat briefly. Add the fennel and sauté until softened and starting to color, about 2 minutes. Add the garlic and cook until fragrant, about 30 seconds. Add the orange juice and cook, scraping the pan bottom with a wooden spatula to loosen the browned bits, until the liquid reduces to a glaze, about 2½ minutes. Increase the heat to high and add the broth and any accumulated pork juices from the plate. Cook until the liquid reaches the consistency of maple syrup, about 3 minutes.

3. Reduce the heat to medium and return the pork to the pan, turning the meat to coat. Add the orange zest, olives, and parsley and simmer to heat the pork through and blend the flavors, about 3 minutes. Adjust the seasonings with salt and pepper to taste. Transfer the pork to a serving plate and spoon the sauce over the meat. Serve immediately.

PORK STIR-FRIES

FROM A PORK AND VEGETABLE STIR-FRY—homemade or ordered out—we usually expect nothing more than tough, tasteless pork and barely cooked vegetables in a thick, slithery sauce. We set out to make pork and vegetable stir-fries that were both tasty and tender without being labor-intensive.

Pork shoulder is often called for in authentic pork stir-fry recipes, but because pieces weighing less than several pounds can be difficult to find and because most Western cooks would be loath to deal with the accompanying gristle and intramuscular fat, we excluded pork shoulder as a possibility. Instead, we tried stir-frying the more sensible options: boneless loin chops and tenderloin, both cut into strips thin enough to eat with a piece or two of vegetable. The loin chops cooked into dry, tight, tough pieces not unlike shoe leather. The tenderloin was the uncontested winner. Tender and yielding, it had the textural quality of a filet mignon.

The next task was to determine whether marinating the pork was worth the trouble. We tossed one plain batch of tenderloin strips unceremoniously into the skillet; we marinated a second batch with some soy sauce and sherry for a few minutes before cooking. The version with the marinade, which boosted flavor quickly and easily, was the clear winner. But it also dealt us a setback when the pork failed to brown properly, even in the hottest skillet. The reason? Pork tenderloin is almost always sold in shrink-wrapped packages and therefore contains a lot of moisture (and we were adding more). We discovered that the answer was to cook the pork in batches over high heat. This way, the moisture that the pork released evaporated rapidly, and, after it did, the pork was free to take on color. Each batch needed to cook for only two minutes—quite a flash in the pan.

With the pork out of the skillet and set aside in a bowl, we worked on the vegetables and flavorings. Because different vegetables cook at different rates, batch cooking was necessary (batch cooking also prevents overcrowding, so that the vegetables, too,

can brown their way to good flavor). We added various mixes of aromatics (such as garlic and ginger) using our standard stir-fry method (add at the end of cooking to a clearing in the center of the skillet, where they can cook long enough to develop their flavors but not long enough to burn).

We were not after an abundance of sauce, just enough light-bodied liquid to cling to the pork and vegetables and provide succulence. If we added enough soy sauce or fish sauce to provide the bulk of the sauce, saltiness or fishy pungency prevailed. If we added water, the flavor was hollow. Chicken broth was the solution. It provided a liquid element that gave the sauce backbone and did not dilute flavor. We also found that a small addition of acid—lime juice or rice vinegar—did a lot to brighten flavors. Finally, just a teaspoon of cornstarch prompted the sauce to cloak the meat and vegetables lightly instead of pooling at the bottom of the pan.

SLICING PORK TENDERLOIN FOR STIR-FRIES

1. Freeze the tenderloin until firm, 20 to 30 minutes. Cut the tenderloin crosswise into ⅓-inch-thick medallions.

2. Slice each medallion into ⅓-inch-wide strips.

Stir-Fried Pork, Eggplant, and Onions with Garlic and Black Pepper

SERVES 4 WITH RICE

This Thai stir-fry is not for those with timid palates.

12	ounces pork tenderloin, sliced according to the illustrations at left
1	teaspoon plus 2½ tablespoons fish sauce
1	teaspoon plus 2½ tablespoons soy sauce
2	tablespoons low-sodium chicken broth
2	teaspoons juice from 1 lime
2½	tablespoons light brown sugar
1	teaspoon cornstarch
9	medium garlic cloves, minced or pressed through a garlic press (about 3 tablespoons)
2	teaspoons ground black pepper
3½	tablespoons peanut or vegetable oil
1	pound eggplant, cut into ¾-inch cubes
1	large onion, cut into ¼- to ⅜-inch wedges
½	cup loosely packed fresh cilantro leaves, chopped very coarse

1. Combine the pork, 1 teaspoon fish sauce, and 1 teaspoon soy sauce in a small bowl. Whisk the

remaining 2½ tablespoons each fish sauce and soy sauce, the chicken broth, lime juice, brown sugar, and cornstarch in a measuring cup. Combine the garlic, pepper, and 1 tablespoon of the peanut oil in a small bowl.

2. Heat 1½ teaspoons peanut oil in a nonstick 12-inch skillet over high heat until smoking; add half of the pork to the skillet and cook, stirring occasionally and breaking up the clumps, until well browned, about 2 minutes. Transfer the pork to a medium bowl. Repeat with an additional 1½ teaspoons peanut oil and the remaining pork.

3. Add 1 tablespoon peanut oil to the now-empty skillet; add the eggplant and cook, stirring every 30 seconds, until browned and no longer spongy, about 5 minutes; transfer to the bowl with the pork.

4. Add the remaining 1½ teaspoons peanut oil to the skillet; add the onion and cook, stirring occasionally, until beginning to brown and soften, about 2 minutes.

5. Clear the center of the skillet; add the garlic and pepper mixture to the clearing and cook, mashing the mixture with a spoon, until fragrant and beginning to brown, about 1½ minutes, then stir the mixture into the onion. Return the pork and eggplant to the skillet and toss to combine. Whisk the sauce to recombine, then add to the skillet; cook, stirring constantly, until the sauce is thickened and evenly distributed, about 30 seconds. Transfer to a serving platter and sprinkle with the cilantro. Serve immediately.

Stir-Fried Pork, Green Beans, and Red Bell Pepper with Gingery Oyster Sauce

SERVES 4 WITH RICE

See page 144 for more information on sesame oil.

12	ounces pork tenderloin, sliced according to the illustrations on page 471
2	teaspoons soy sauce
2	teaspoons plus 1 tablespoon dry sherry
⅓	cup low-sodium chicken broth
2½	tablespoons oyster sauce
2	teaspoons toasted sesame oil
1	teaspoon rice vinegar
¼	teaspoon ground white pepper
1	teaspoon cornstarch
2	medium garlic cloves, minced or pressed through a garlic press
2	tablespoons grated fresh ginger
3	tablespoons peanut or vegetable oil
12	ounces green beans, cut on the diagonal into 2-inch lengths
¼	cup water
1	large red bell pepper (about 8 ounces), cored, seeded, and cut into ¾-inch squares
3	medium scallions, sliced thin on the diagonal

1. Combine the pork, soy sauce, and 2 teaspoons sherry in a small bowl. Whisk the remaining 1 tablespoon sherry, the chicken broth, oyster sauce, sesame oil, rice vinegar, white pepper, and cornstarch in a measuring cup. Combine the garlic, ginger, and 1½ teaspoons of the peanut oil in a small bowl.

2. Heat 1½ teaspoons peanut oil in a nonstick 12-inch skillet over high heat until smoking; add half of the pork to the skillet and cook, stirring occasionally and breaking up the clumps, until well browned, about 2 minutes. Transfer the pork to a medium bowl. Repeat with an additional 1½ teaspoons peanut oil and the remaining pork.

3. Add 1 tablespoon peanut oil to the now-empty skillet; add the green beans and cook, stirring occasionally, until spotty brown, about 2 minutes. Add the water, cover the pan, and lower the heat to medium. Steam until the beans are tender-crisp, 2 to 3 minutes; transfer the beans to the bowl with the pork.

4. Add the remaining 1½ teaspoons peanut oil to the skillet; add the bell pepper and cook, stirring frequently, until spotty brown, about 2 minutes.

5. Clear the center of the skillet; add the garlic and ginger mixture to the clearing; cook, mashing the mixture with a spoon, until fragrant, about 45 seconds, then stir the mixture into the peppers. Return the pork and green beans to the skillet and toss to combine. Whisk the sauce to recombine, then add to the skillet; cook, stirring constantly, until the sauce is thickened and evenly distributed, about 30 seconds. Transfer to a serving platter and sprinkle with the scallions. Serve immediately.

Spicy Stir-Fried Pork, Asparagus, and Onions with Lemon Grass

SERVES 4 WITH RICE

See the illustrations below for mincing lemon grass.

12	ounces pork tenderloin, sliced according to the illustrations on page 471
1	teaspoon plus 2 tablespoons fish sauce
1	teaspoon soy sauce
⅓	cup low-sodium chicken broth
2	teaspoons juice from 1 lime
1	tablespoon light brown sugar
1	teaspoon cornstarch
2	medium garlic cloves, minced
¼	cup minced lemon grass from 2 stalks
¾	teaspoon red pepper flakes
3½	tablespoons peanut or vegetable oil
1	pound asparagus, cut on the diagonal into 2-inch pieces
¼	cup water
1	large onion, cut into ¼- to ⅜-inch wedges
¼	cup chopped fresh basil leaves

1. Combine the pork, the 1 teaspoon fish sauce, and the soy sauce in a small bowl. Whisk the remaining 2 tablespoons fish sauce, the chicken broth, lime juice, brown sugar, and cornstarch in a measuring cup. Combine the garlic, lemon grass, red pepper flakes, and 1 tablespoon of the peanut oil in a small bowl.

2. Heat 1½ teaspoons peanut oil in a nonstick 12-inch skillet over high heat until smoking; add half of the pork to the skillet and cook, stirring occasionally and breaking up the clumps, until well browned, about 2 minutes. Transfer the pork to a medium bowl. Repeat with an additional 1½ teaspoons peanut oil and the remaining pork.

3. Add 1 tablespoon peanut oil to the now-empty skillet; add the asparagus and cook, stirring every 30 seconds, until lightly browned, about 2 minutes. Add the water, cover the pan, and lower the heat to medium. Steam the asparagus until tender-crisp, about 2 minutes; transfer the asparagus to the bowl with the pork.

4. Add the remaining 1½ teaspoons peanut oil to the skillet; add the onion and cook, stirring occasionally, until beginning to brown and soften, about 2 minutes.

5. Clear the center of the skillet; add the garlic and lemon grass mixture to the clearing and cook, mashing the mixture with a spoon, until fragrant, about 1 minute, then stir the mixture into the onion. Return the pork and asparagus to the skillet and toss to combine. Whisk the sauce to recombine, then add to the skillet; cook, stirring constantly, until the sauce is thickened and evenly distributed, about 30 seconds. Transfer to a serving platter and sprinkle with the basil. Serve immediately.

MINCING LEMON GRASS

Because of its tough outer leaves, lemon grass can be difficult to mince. We like this method, which relies on a sharp knife.

1. Trim all but the bottom 3 to 4 inches of the lemon grass stalk.

2. Remove the tough outer sheath from the trimmed lemon grass. If the lemon grass is particularly thick or tough, you may need to remove several layers to reveal the tender inner portion of the stalk.

3. Cut the trimmed and peeled lemon grass in half lengthwise, then mince finely.

OVEN-ROASTED RIBS

BARBECUED SPARERIBS STRIKE A PRIMITIVE chord deep within all of us, excluding perhaps the most ardent vegetarian. But we are the first to admit that hauling out the grill and stoking the slow fire necessary for sublime ribs can be inconvenient. And forget about barbecuing ribs during the winter in many parts of the country. Is there another way to achieve such bliss?

Most oven-roasted rib recipes we have tried have turned out tough, stringy, and relatively flavorless meat, completely devoid of all the merits of barbecued ribs. Driven by the haunting flavor of great ribs, we thought we might create a recipe for oven-roasted spareribs that placed a close second to our barbecued ribs.

For the meat, there was little choice in the matter. Plain old spareribs provided the best flavor and were the most economical. Two slabs of spareribs, about three pounds each, were enough to feed four people abundantly, and both slabs fit in the oven on one rack. We found that the meat needed little preparation outside of trimming any excess fat.

One of the pluses of cooking ribs indoors is that the only equipment necessary is a pan in which to cook them. After roasting several batches of ribs in roasting pans and on baking sheets, we favored suspending the ribs on a sturdy flat rack over a shallow baking sheet so that no part of the meat would rest in the rendered fat. The baking sheet also allowed for the best circulation of heat.

To flavor the meat, we employed our Dry Rub for Barbecue (page 579). We found that the ribs needed to sit for a minimum of an hour coated in the rub for the spices to penetrate the meat. Refrigerating the spice-rubbed ribs overnight gave the meat the best flavor. If you can plan ahead, letting the rubbed meat rest in the refrigerator overnight is the best way to build flavor.

As any barbecue-pit master will tell you, the key to tender, falling-of-the-bones ribs is a steady fire and slow cooking. On a grill, the ribs are placed on the opposite side of the cooking grate from a small pile of banked coals. The temperature will fluctuate between 250 and 350 degrees—the lower the better. We experimented with oven temperatures ranging from 250 degrees to 350 degrees and found 300 degrees to be best. At 250 degrees, the ribs cooked for close to five hours before the meat had separated from the bones, and the outer meat was leathery. At 350 degrees, the ribs cooked too quickly and were tough and flabby with unrendered fat. At 300 degrees, they were fully done in 3½ hours; the meat had separated from the bones and was quite juicy. A lot of the fat had rendered out, too.

With an ideal oven temperature selected, we experimented with a variety of techniques to see if we could improve on the texture of the meat. Blanching, or parboiling, the ribs is a commonly employed technique that hastens cooking, but we found it yielded surprisingly tough, dry meat. We also tried adding a pan of water to the oven to increase the oven's humidity, but again the meat was tough in comparison with the dry-cooked meat. We then tried wrapping the ribs in foil to trap the steam. The wrapped ribs were paler but juicier than unwrapped ribs. This inspired us to try wrapping the ribs for part of the cooking time and then uncovering them to attain the characteristic dark crust. We found that covering them for only the first hour of cooking yielded moist ribs with a thick, flavorful crust.

The meat was sweet, savory, and succulent, but it lacked the smoky flavor and aroma essential to great ribs. We tried substituting ground chipotle chiles (smoked jalapeño peppers) for the cayenne pepper in our spice rub, but the smokiness of the chiles mysteriously disappeared among the other flavors. We then thought about adding barbecue sauce for its hickory flavor—a sensitive issue considering how quickly sugar-laden sauce burns. We first tried slathering sauce on after we took the foil off, one hour into cooking, and the sauce blackened and turned bitter. We then tried basting the ribs after three hours of cooking, and they remained wet and gummy when pulled from the oven half an hour later. Splitting the difference proved just right. When applied to the ribs after two hours of cooking (so the sauce cooked for 1½ hours), the sauce darkened but did not burn and reduced to a sticky, satisfying glaze.

The ribs disappeared from the test kitchen

within minutes of coming out of the oven, but we were able to save a few and tried wrapping the ribs in foil and sealing them in a paper bag—the trick that had worked so well with our barbecued ribs. As we had expected, the ribs wrapped for an hour were juicier and more tender than ribs that were not wrapped.

Oven-Roasted Spareribs

SERVES 4

While the final step of wrapping the ribs in foil and putting them in a paper bag may seem eccentric, it is well worth it. We found the meat "finished" in this way to be extraordinarily succulent and tender. Although this recipe is very simple to prepare, you will need more than five hours to season, roast, and rest the ribs.

> 2 full racks spareribs (about 6 pounds total), trimmed of excess fat
> 3/4 cup Dry Rub for Barbecue (page 579)
> 3 cups barbecue sauce (see pages 595–597)

1. Rub both sides of the ribs with the dry rub and let stand at room temperature for 1 hour. (For stronger flavor, wrap the rubbed ribs in a double layer of plastic wrap and refrigerate for up to 1 day.)

2. Adjust an oven rack to the middle position and heat the oven to 300 degrees. Place the ribs meaty-side up on a heavy rack on a rimmed baking sheet, then wrap the pan with aluminum foil. Roast for 1 hour and remove the foil. Roast for another hour, then brush the meaty side of the ribs liberally with the barbecue sauce, about 3/4 cup per slab. Cook for another 1½ hours, or until the bones have separated from the meat.

3. Remove the ribs from the oven and wrap each slab completely in foil. Put the foil-wrapped slabs in a brown paper bag and crimp the top of the bag to seal tightly. Allow to rest at room temperature for 1 hour.

4. Unwrap the ribs, cut between the bones, and serve immediately with the remaining barbecue sauce on the side.

SPIRAL-SLICED HAM

WE'VE ALWAYS BEEN FOND OF HAM. WE LOVE its toothy, meaty chew and its unique flavor combination of sweet, salt, and smoke. Despite this devotion, we have to admit that the versions appearing on most holiday tables are far from ideal. Very often they are dry as dust or mushy as a wet paper towel. We decided to find the best possible way to prepare a precooked supermarket ham so that it could live up to its full potential.

Hams vary in terms of the amount of water added during the curing process. A ham that has no added water is labeled just plain "ham." While some manufacturers still make these hams, they are very hard to find in supermarkets. "Ham with natural juices" (as the label would state) has 7 to 8 percent water added; "ham-water added" has 12 to 15 percent water added; and "ham and water product" contains more than 15 percent added water. The more water a ham contains, the less expensive it is per pound. Hams also vary in terms of bone. They may be boneless, semiboneless, or completely bone-in.

Our tasting results were pretty predictable: More bone and less water seemed to make for the tastiest hams. Boneless and semiboneless hams had "compressed" textures that we did not like, and the hams with the most water added had the most diluted ham flavor. Bone-in, spiral-sliced hams with natural juices were the favorite in our tasting. They were neither overly pumped up with water nor packed into a cylindrical loaf shape. They were also the

CHOOSING A HAM

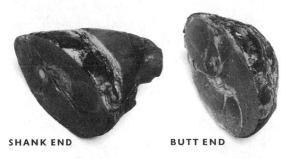

SHANK END **BUTT END**

For easy carving, look for a shank-end ham (left), which has a tapered, pointed end opposite the cut side. The sirloin, or butt, end (right) has a rounded, blunt end.

475

favorite of the test kitchen staff in terms of convenience. After having to carve many of the hams in
the testing, they were quite happy to meet up with
a ham that had been carved for them. Spiral-sliced
hams were hands-down the most convenient of the
bone-in choices.

"Cooking" (really, only heating) these fully
cooked hams is a no-brainer, which is why, we'll
bet, these hams are so popular around the holidays. The problem is that heating instructions for
spiral-sliced hams differ from package to package.
To add to the confusion, there are discrepancies in
recommended final internal temperatures. Such
imprecision wouldn't be such an issue if these hams
didn't readily dry out and turn to jerky when heated
improperly.

One factor that had to be decided at the outset was
the internal temperature to which the ham should
be heated. Spiral-sliced hams are fully cooked, and
so long as the sell-by date hasn't come and gone,
the ham can be served straight out of the package.
While most cooks would still elect to heat the ham
before serving, there is no consensus as to what temperature it should reach before being brought to the
table. The label of one package said 120 degrees. The
National Pork Producers Council said 140 degrees.
Two manufacturers didn't include a temperature in
their heating directions, so we called to inquire and
were told 150 degrees by one and 155 degrees by
the other. This discrepancy is unfortunate, because
heating the ham to the proper internal temperature
is critical to helping it retain its juices.

When we heated a ham to 140 degrees, it lost
a large amount of liquid and was dry. Heating to
130 degrees was an improvement, but we found
that taking the ham to only 100 degrees was better
yet. The outer inch of the ham registered at about
145 degrees, and residual heat caused the internal
temperature to continue rising as the ham rested,
covered, after coming out of the oven. After 40
minutes, it peaked at 115 to 120 degrees, which had
been our original goal. Though this may sound like
a low temperature, the ham was warm to the touch
and, most important, had remained moist and juicy.
And, after all, we are dealing with a precooked cut
of meat here.

Having settled on the final temperature, we

TRIMMING THE OVEN BAG

Use scissors to trim the oven bag, leaving 1 inch above the tie.

needed to figure out exactly how to get there. Our
first task was to determine the proper oven temperature. We quickly found that a high (400-degree) or
even a moderate (325-degree) oven was no good.
Though the hams were covered with foil for protection, when subjected to these temperatures they
lost an astounding amount of liquid (up to 2 cups);
the meat was dry and leathery and the slices curled
and splayed.

We then began experimenting with low oven
temperatures. These worked much better, but the
cooking time now became an issue. At the low end
of the scale, an average nine-pound ham heated in
a 225-degree oven was both juicy and moist and
held its shape, but it took a grueling 3¼ hours to
heat up. In a 250-degree oven, the ham was just as
good, but it heated in 2¾ hours, shaving 30 minutes
off the cooking time.

Although easy, this was still a long process, so
we sought means to speed it up. We tried different
combinations of high and low temperatures, but
they were either detrimental to the moistness of the
ham or did nothing to speed its heating.

Someone in the test kitchen then suggested a
plastic oven bag instead of the foil cover. Quite
to our astonishment, this simple, flimsy-looking
accouterment trimmed a few minutes per pound.
While this may sound insignificant, it can translate
into a 20- to 30-minute differential when cooking
a piece of meat the size of a ham. How did it work?
We posited that the oven bag, wrapped tightly

around the ham, eliminated the air space—an insulation of sorts—formed between the foil and the ham, thereby giving the ham direct exposure to heat and speeding its heating. Another step that speeds the heating process is letting the ham stand at room temperature for 90 minutes before putting it in the oven. This, too, takes off a couple of minutes per pound. By using an oven bag and letting the ham stand at room temperature, we had whittled the heating time down to about 2 hours, with a 40-minute rest out of the oven. Protracted though this process may seem, it's great in that it frees the oven for other last-minute cooking tasks.

With the cooking method in place, we now had two more points to consider: making the sauce and carving the ham. We wanted to come up with something better than the gooey glaze that comes in a packet with many hams. And we wanted to see which of the two cuts of spiral-sliced ham available—the shank or the sirloin—would be easier to carve.

Most spiral-sliced hams come with an enclosed packet of glaze. We tossed them all aside because we have found that glazes, whether prepackaged or homemade, do little to enhance this kind of ham. Instead, they tend to sit on the surface like a layer of gooey candy. Although this may appeal to children, we much prefer to make an interesting, flavorful sauce. The sauce, since it doesn't use any pan drippings, can be made ahead and reheated. It dresses up the ham, making it look and taste more elegant, and it also adds moisture to carved ham slices, which tend to dry out somewhat as they sit uncovered on a serving platter.

We also discovered that the shank end of the ham is substantially easier to carve than the sirloin, or butt, end because of the bone configuration. The packages aren't labeled as such, but the shank can be identified by the tapered, more pointed end opposite the cut side. The sirloin, on the other hand, has a very blunt, rounded end. If you can't find a shank half, however, don't despair; both halves taste equally good. Your knife will just encounter a few more bumps and curves when you carve the sirloin half.

CARVING A SPIRAL-SLICED HAM

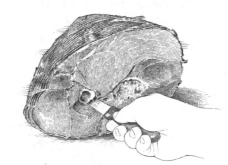

1. With the tip of a paring or carving knife, cut around the bone to loosen the attached slices.

2. Using a long carving knife, slice horizontally above the bone and through the spiral-cut slices, toward the back of the ham.

3. Pull the cut portion away from the bone and cut between the slices to separate them fully.

4. Beginning at the tapered end, slice above the bone to remove the remaining chunk of meat. Flip the ham over and repeat the procedure for the other side.

477

Spiral-Sliced Ham
SERVES 20 TO 30

You can put the ham in the oven cold, bypassing the 90-minute standing time. If you do, add a couple of minutes per pound to the heating time. If using an oven bag, cut slits in the bag so it does not burst. Allow about 3 to 4 servings per pound for a bone-in ham. We recommend buying a shank portion because the bone configuration makes it easier to carve; look for the half ham with a tapered, pointed end.

1	spiral-sliced bone-in half ham (7 to 10 pounds), preferably shank end

1. Unwrap the ham and remove and discard the plastic disk covering the bone. Place the ham in a plastic oven bag, pull tightly for a close fit, tie the bag up, and trim the excess plastic (see the illustration on page 476). Set the ham cut-side down in a 13 by 9-inch baking dish and cut 4 slits in the top of the bag with a paring knife. Alternatively, place the unwrapped ham cut-side down in the baking dish and cover tightly with foil. Let stand at room temperature for 90 minutes.

2. Meanwhile, adjust an oven rack to the lowest position and heat the oven to 250 degrees. Bake the ham until the center registers about 100 degrees on an instant-read thermometer, 1½ to 2½ hours (about 14 minutes per pound if using a plastic oven bag, about 17 minutes per pound if using foil), depending on the size of the ham.

3. Remove the ham from the oven and let it rest in the baking dish in the oven bag or with the foil cover until the internal temperature registers 115 to 120 degrees on an instant-read thermometer, 30 to 40 minutes. Cut open the oven bag or remove the foil, place the ham on a carving board, and slice according to the illustrations on page 477. Serve immediately with one of the following sauces, if desired.

Dried Cherry and Stout Sauce with Brown Sugar and Allspice
MAKES ABOUT 4 CUPS

Stout is a strong, dark beer made from toasted barley. It makes a rich sauce with smoky notes and an appealing bitter finish.

1	cup low-sodium chicken broth
2	tablespoons cornstarch
2	tablespoons unsalted butter
3	medium shallots, chopped fine
⅛	teaspoon ground allspice

INGREDIENTS: Spiral-Sliced Hams

Spiral-sliced hams offer the best combination of flavor, texture, and convenience when it comes to slicing, but are all spiral-sliced hams the same? To find out, we rounded up the five most widely available spiral-sliced bone-in hams. All were heated according to our recipe and served plain (without a sauce or glaze).

We found a wide variety in both flavor and texture. The Cook's Spiral Sliced Hickory Smoked Honey Ham ($2.29 per pound) was the clear winner. Almost all tasters appreciated this ham's clean and meaty flavor, though a few were left wanting stronger sweet, salt, smoke, and spice flavors. Overall, it was declared an "honest ham" that "doesn't seem processed" or "taste as if it's pumped full of chemicals."

The Hillshire Farm Spiral Sliced Brown Sugar Cured Ham ($1.79 per pound) also received mostly positive comments. Most tasters noted a pleasant balance of salt and sweet, but others thought the flavor insubstantial and "lacking much assertion." As for the texture, many found it a bit chewy and dry, while a couple of tasters said these qualities made it a "real man's ham."

The other hams in the tasting did not fare as well. Almost every taster remarked on the pock-marked meat of the Hillshire Farm Spiral Sliced Honey Cured Ham ($1.79 per pound). Its appearance, coupled with the rubbery, wet, very "pumped" texture, made this very sweet ham "look and taste like a sponge." Tasters could not get too enthused about the Colonial Spiral Sliced Ham ($2.69), either, finding it spongy and soft. The most expensive ham in the tasting, the Carando Spiral Sliced Hickory Smoked Ham ($3.99 per pound), landed at the bottom of the rankings. Sold under the Farmland label in the Midwest and on the West Coast, this ham elicited comments such as "sour," "acidic," and "musty" from tasters. The meat verged on dry, with a coarse, crumbly, "fall-apart" quality.

4 cups stout

1/3 cup packed dark or light brown sugar

I cup dried cherries (about 5 ounces)

1 1/2 tablespoons balsamic vinegar

Salt and ground black pepper

1. Whisk the broth and cornstarch together in a small bowl; set aside. Heat the butter in a 12-inch skillet over medium heat until foaming; add the shallots and cook until softened, about 3 minutes. Stir in the allspice; cook until fragrant, about 30 seconds. Add the stout, brown sugar, and dried cherries; increase the heat to medium-high, bring to a simmer, and cook until slightly syrupy, about 10 minutes.

2. Whisk the broth and cornstarch mixture to recombine, then gradually whisk it into the simmering liquid; return to a simmer to thicken, stirring occasionally. Off the heat, stir in the balsamic vinegar; season with salt and pepper to taste. (The sauce can be cooled to room temperature and refrigerated for up to 2 days. Reheat in a medium saucepan over medium-low heat.) Serve with ham.

Mustard Sauce with Vermouth and Thyme

MAKES ABOUT 3 1/2 CUPS

The Dijon mustard lends a creaminess to this sauce, while the whole-grain mustard adds texture and visual appeal.

1 1/2 cups low-sodium chicken broth

2 tablespoons cornstarch

2 tablespoons unsalted butter

3 medium shallots, chopped fine

2 cups dry vermouth

I tablespoon dark or light brown sugar

1/2 cup Dijon mustard

1/4 cup whole-grain mustard

I tablespoon chopped fresh thyme leaves

Salt and ground black pepper

1. Whisk the broth and cornstarch together in a small bowl; set aside. Heat the butter in a 12-inch skillet over medium heat until foaming; add the shallots and cook until softened, about 3 minutes. Stir in the vermouth and brown sugar; increase the heat to medium-high and simmer until the alcohol vapors have cooked off, about 4 minutes.

2. Whisk the broth and cornstarch mixture to recombine, then gradually whisk it into the simmering liquid; return the sauce to a simmer to thicken, stirring occasionally. Off the heat, whisk in the mustards and thyme; season with salt and pepper to taste. (The sauce can be cooled to room temperature and refrigerated for up to 2 days. Reheat in a medium saucepan over medium-low heat.) Serve with ham.

ROAST FRESH HAM

ALTHOUGH THIS ROAST IS CALLED A HAM, IT gains much of its undeniable appeal from the fact that it's not really a ham at all—or at least not what most of us understand the term to mean. It's not cured in the fashion of a Smithfield ham or salted and air-dried like prosciutto. It's not pressed or molded like a canned ham, and it's not smoked like a country ham. In fact, the only reason this cut of pork is called a ham is because it comes from the pig's hind leg.

Even before we began roasting, we had decided that a full fresh ham, weighing in at about 20 pounds, was too much for all but the very largest feast. So we decided to use one of the two cuts into which the leg is usually divided—the sirloin, which comes from the top of the leg, or the shank, from the bottom of the leg (see page 480). We also decided that we wanted our ham skin-on (we couldn't see giving up the opportunity for cracklings). Fortunately, this is how these roasts are typically sold.

From our experiences with other large roasts, we knew what the big problem would be: making sure the roast cooked all the way through while the meat stayed tender and moist. In our first set of tests, then, we wanted to assess not only the relative merits of sirloin and shank but also the best oven temperature and cooking time.

Early on in this process, we determined that the roast needed to be cooked to a lower final internal temperature than some experts recommend. We found that we preferred the roast pulled from the oven at 145 to 150 degrees—at this point, the meat is cooked to about medium and retains a slight blush.

While the roast rests, its residual heat brings the temperature up to approximately 155 to 160 degrees.

That determined, we started testing different oven temperatures. First to come out of the oven was a ham from the sirloin end of the leg that we had roasted at a high temperature, 400 degrees, for its entire stay in the oven. Carving this ham was akin to whittling wood—Olympics-worthy agility with the carving knife was required to cut around the aitchbone (part of the hip), the cracklings were more suited for tap shoes than consumption, and the meat was dry, dry, dry. We moved on to roasting a shank-end ham at a low heat the whole way through. This ham tasted like a wrung-out washcloth, with no cracklings in sight. What we did appreciate was the straightforward bone composition of the shank end, which simplified carving and convinced us to use this end of the fresh ham for the remainder of our tests.

Next we roasted a shank-end ham by starting it at a low temperature (325 degrees) and finishing it at a higher one (400 degrees), hoping to end up with both moist meat and crispy cracklings. To our dismay, this ham was also rather dry, which we attributed to the ham's long stay in the oven, made necessary by the low cooking temperature. What's more, the brief hike in the temperature at the end of cooking didn't help to crisp the skin.

Again, we figured we ought to try the opposite: starting the ham at a high temperature to give the meat a head start and get the skin on its way to crisping, then turning down the heat for the remainder

BUYING FRESH HAM

SHANK END   **SIRLOIN END**

Fresh ham comes from the pig's hind leg. Because a whole leg is too large for most occasions, it is usually cut into two sections. The sirloin, or butt, end is harder to carve than our favorite, the shank end. Either way, make sure to buy a fresh ham with skin, which will protect the meat and keep it moist.

SCORING THE SKIN

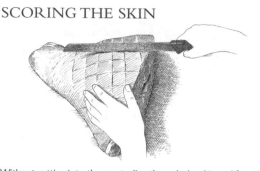

Without cutting into the meat, slice through the skin and fat with a serrated knife, making a 1-inch diamond pattern.

of the roasting time to cook the meat through. Although meat cooked according to this method was slightly chalky and dry, the skin was close to our goal, crispy enough to shatter between our teeth yet tender enough to stave off a trip to the dentist. We decided that this would be our master roasting method.

Hoping to solve the dry meat dilemma, we brined a shank-end ham, immersing it in a solution of salt water and spices to tenderize and flavor it. More than slightly biased from the positive results we achieved in past brining experiments with turkey, chicken, shellfish, and other cuts of pork, we expected brining to make the meat incredibly juicy. The salt in a brine causes the protein structure in meat to unravel and trap water in its fibers; brining also encourages the unwound proteins to gel, forming a barrier that helps seal in moisture. Together, these effects allow the cook to increase the roasting temperature, thus speeding the roasting process without fear of drying out the meat. Our estimations proved accurate: The brined shank emerged from the oven succulent and flavorful, with meat tender enough to fall apart in your mouth.

Just when we thought the ham couldn't possibly get any better, we decided to try roasting one shank facedown on a rack set in a roasting pan rather than letting it sit directly in the pan. This adjustment kept the cut end from becoming tough and leathery from direct contact with the hot pan. Rack roasting also allowed the heat to circulate around the ham constantly, promoting faster and more even cooking.

With our temperature firmly in place, we turned to tweaking the flavor of the roast and obtaining the type of cracklings we had heard of but never really tasted. Not content with the infusion of flavor from the brine, we turned to spice rubs to further develop the flavor of the roast. Fresh thyme, sage, rosemary, garlic, brown sugar, cloves, dry mustard, juniper berries, peppercorns, and salt were all given an equal opportunity to complement the pork. We liked the combination of sage's earthy sweetness and garlic's pungent bite as well as the edge of fresh parsley, peppercorns, and kosher salt. Since our composed rub didn't lean strongly on any one particular spice, we were left with a wide-open field of glazing options.

While some recipes we tried called for simply basting the roast in its own drippings, we veered in the direction of sugary glazes, opting for sugar's ability to crisp, caramelize, and sweeten the skin. But the intermittent encounters between glaze, brush, and ham were still under negotiation: Exactly when should we glaze? Throughout the roasting period? If so, at what intervals? Since part of the beauty of this pork roast is that it can be left in the oven mostly unattended, we didn't want glazing to complicate the process. Starting the ham at 500 degrees negated glazing it at the outset—the sugary glaze would definitely char black before the roast had been in the oven very long. We decided to let the roast cook unglazed at 500 degrees for the first 20 minutes. We then turned the oven temperature down to 350 degrees and began to brush it liberally with glaze. We continued to do so at 45-minute intervals, which amounted to three bastings during the roasting period. This ham was the one: flavorful meat with sweetened, crunchy skin.

More than one person in the test kitchen proclaimed this ham to be the best roast pork they'd ever eaten. Rich and tender, with an underlying hint of sweetness, the meat had the power to quiet a room full of vocal, opinionated cooks and editors. Perhaps even better is the sweet, slightly salty, crisp and crunchy skin that intensifies to a deep crimson by the time the roast is done.

CARVING THE TWO CUTS OF HAM

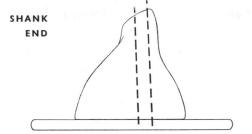

SHANK END

1. Transfer the ham to a cutting board and carve it lengthwise alongside the bone, following the two dotted lines in the illustration above.

2. Lay the large boneless pieces that you have just carved flat on the cutting board and slice into ½-inch pieces.

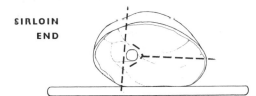

SIRLOIN END

1. Transfer the ham to a cutting board and carve into three pieces around the bones along the dotted lines in the illustration above.

2. Lay the large boneless pieces that you have just carved flat on the cutting board and slice into ½-inch pieces.

Roast Fresh Ham

SERVES 8 TO 10

Fresh ham comes from the pig's hind leg. Because a whole leg is too large for most occasions, it is usually cut into two sections. The sirloin, or butt, end is harder to carve than our favorite, the shank end. If you don't have room in your refrigerator, you can brine the ham in a large insulated cooler or a small plastic garbage can; add 5 or 6 freezer packs to the brine to keep it chilled. This recipe uses table salt (not kosher) in its brine. If you'd like to use kosher salt, whose large flakes measure differently from fine-grained table salt, see page 312 for conversion information.

ROAST

1   fresh bone-in half ham with skin (6 to 8 pounds), preferably shank end, rinsed

BRINE

2   cups table salt

3   cups packed dark or light brown sugar

2   garlic heads, cloves separated, lightly crushed and peeled

10   bay leaves

½   cup black peppercorns, crushed

GARLIC AND HERB RUB

- 1 cup lightly packed sage leaves from 1 large bunch
- 1/2 cup parsley leaves from 1 bunch
- 8 medium garlic cloves, peeled
- 1 tablespoon kosher salt or 1 1/2 teaspoons table salt
- 1 1/2 tablespoon ground black pepper
- 1/4 cup olive oil

GLAZE

- 1 1/3 cups glaze (recipes follow)

1. FOR THE ROAST: Following the illustration on page 480, carefully slice through the skin and fat with a serrated knife, making a 1-inch diamond pattern. Be careful not to cut into the meat.

2. FOR THE BRINE: In a large (about 16-quart) bucket or stockpot, dissolve the salt and sugar in 1 gallon hot tap water. Add the garlic, bay leaves, peppercorns, and 1 gallon cold water. Submerge the ham in the brine and refrigerate 8 to 24 hours.

3. Set a large disposable roasting pan on a baking sheet for extra support; place a flat wire rack in the roasting pan. Remove the ham from the brine. Rinse under cold water and dry thoroughly with paper towels. Place the ham wide cut-side down on the rack. (If using the sirloin end, place the ham skin-side up.) Let the ham stand, uncovered, at room temperature 1 hour.

4. FOR THE RUB: Meanwhile, adjust an oven rack to the lowest position and heat the oven to 500 degrees. In the workbowl of a food processor fitted with the metal blade, process the sage, parsley, garlic, salt, pepper, and oil until the mixture forms a smooth paste, about 30 seconds. Rub all sides of the ham with the mixture.

5. TO BAKE AND GLAZE THE HAM: Roast the ham at 500 degrees for 20 minutes. Reduce the oven temperature to 350 degrees and continue to roast, brushing the ham with glaze every 45 minutes, until the center of the ham registers 145 to 150 degrees on an instant-read thermometer, about 2 1/2 hours longer. Tent the ham loosely with foil and let stand until the center of the ham registers 155 to 160 degrees on the thermometer, 30 to 40 minutes. Carve, following the illustrations on page 481, and serve.

→ VARIATION

Cola Ham

Although cooking with Coke may seem humorous and unsophisticated, you haven't lived until you've tried cola ham. Cola ham was born when one of our staff members mentioned the Southern tradition of Coca-Cola glaze and joked that we should try brining the meat in it. After giving this joke fair consideration, we dumped six liters of Coca-Cola Classic into a brine bucket, added salt, and let the ham soak in this foamy concoction overnight. The next day, we cooked it according to our recipe. The outcome was the talk of the kitchen. It was juicy, it was unusual, it was fantastic. The Coke had added its own unique flavor to the ham while tenderizing the meat even more than our regular brine. The meat was falling off the bone and unbelievably tender throughout.

Follow the recipe for Roast Fresh Ham, substituting 6 liters Coke Classic for both the hot and cold water in the brine, omitting the brown sugar, and reducing the salt to 1 1/2 cups. Proceed as directed, rubbing the ham with the garlic and herb mixture and brushing it with Coca-Cola Glaze with Lime and Jalapeño (page 483).

Apple Cider and Brown Sugar Glaze

MAKES ABOUT 1 1/3 CUPS, ENOUGH TO GLAZE 1 FRESH HAM

- 1 cup apple cider
- 2 cups packed dark or light brown sugar
- 5 whole cloves

Bring the cider, brown sugar, and cloves to a boil in a small nonreactive saucepan over high heat. Reduce the heat to medium-low and simmer until syrupy and reduced to about 1 1/3 cups, 5 to 7 minutes. (The glaze will thicken as it cools between bastings; cook over medium heat about 1 minute, stirring once or twice, before using.)

Spicy Pineapple-Ginger Glaze

MAKES ABOUT 1 1/3 CUPS, ENOUGH TO
GLAZE 1 FRESH HAM

1   cup pineapple juice
2   cups packed dark or light brown sugar
1   tablespoon grated fresh ginger
1   tablespoon red pepper flakes

Bring the pineapple juice, brown sugar, ginger, and red pepper flakes to a boil in a small nonreactive saucepan over high heat. Reduce the heat to medium-low and simmer until syrupy and reduced to about 1⅓ cups, 5 to 7 minutes. (The glaze will thicken as it cools between bastings; cook over medium heat about 1 minute, stirring once or twice, before using.)

Coca-Cola Glaze with Lime and Jalapeño

MAKES ABOUT 1 1/3 CUPS,
ENOUGH TO GLAZE 1 FRESH HAM

1   cup Coca-Cola
1/4 cup juice from 2 limes
2   cups packed dark or light brown sugar
2   medium jalapeño chiles, stemmed, seeded, and cut crosswise into 1/4-inch-thick slices

Bring the Coca-Cola, lime juice, brown sugar, and chiles to a boil in a small nonreactive saucepan over high heat. Reduce the heat to medium-low and simmer until syrupy and reduced to about 1⅓ cups, 5 to 7 minutes. (The glaze will thicken as it cools between bastings; cook over medium heat about 1 minute, stirring once or twice, before using.)

Orange, Cinnamon, and Star Anise Glaze

MAKES ABOUT 1 1/3 CUPS,
ENOUGH TO GLAZE 1 FRESH HAM

1   tablespoon grated zest and 1 cup juice from 2 large oranges
2   cups packed dark or light brown sugar
4   star anise pods
1   (3-inch) cinnamon stick

Bring the orange zest and juice, brown sugar, star anise, and cinnamon to a boil in a small nonreactive saucepan over high heat. Reduce the heat to medium-low and simmer until syrupy and reduced to about 1⅓ cups, 5 to 7 minutes. (The glaze will thicken as it cools between bastings; cook over medium heat about 1 minute, stirring once or twice, before using.)

FRIED HAM STEAK WITH CIDER GRAVY

WITH CRISPY BROWN EDGES AND SWEET, nutty-tasting meat, pan-fried ham steaks are a Southern treat. Luckily, when the craving hits, they cook in minutes. For this version, we chose to gussy ham steaks up a bit with a cider-based gravy—nothing too fancy—just a little something to moisten the meat and to use for dunking biscuits.

Ham steaks are sold in two sizes—small, individual portions and large-size slices obviously cross-cut from a whole ham. Initially, we were attracted to the individual portions, but quickly found that their flavor paled in comparison to the larger steaks. And the texture was significantly tougher. On close inspection, they appeared to be cut from pressed or canned hams (bits of ham trimmings packed together) rather than whole large hams. Clearly, large steaks were the way to go—portioning would be done after cooking. Most large ham steaks weigh in between 1 and 1½ pounds. Some companies do produce extra-thick steaks closer to two pounds, but we found that these are best reserved for other purposes, like baking or grilling, as they take too long to heat through in the skillet. Premium ham steaks (which we recommend) are cut from the center of the ham, the leanest section, though it can be hard to tell unless specifically marked on the package.

Admittedly, frying ham steaks is not rocket science. The meat is already cooked; it is just a matter of heating the meat through and creating a well-browned crust. We tried temperatures from low to high heat and found medium-high yielded the best results, with well-browned, crisp edges. Butter proved a better bet than oil as a frying medium because it made for a richer crust.

With the steak fried and resting in a warm oven, we tackled the gravy. The recipes we found included everything from cider thickened with flour to a complicated sauce worthy of a three-star restaurant. We aimed for a middle ground—full-flavored, but not requiring inordinate effort; it was a simple ham steak after all.

The steak left a thick fond that started the gravy off right. We deglazed the skillet with cider, vigorously scraping the bottom with a spoon to free the browned bits firmly affixed to it. The issues we needed to solve were how much cider to start with and how much to reduce it by. When it boiled down too far, the resulting gravy was sickly sweet to most tasters—more like the base for a dessert sauce. Too little and the gravy was bland. After several tests, we found reducing two cups of cider to one cup yielded a slightly viscous liquid with a strong apple flavor that was not too sweet—just what we wanted. In fact, we had to add a pinch of brown sugar to appease some tasters.

Despite the cider's syrupy texture, most tasters desired a slightly thicker gravy, so we needed to add a thickener. Flour imparted pastiness, but cornstarch was flavorless and added an appealing luster. A scant three-quarters teaspoon packed all the thickening power necessary for a glossy gravy just substantial enough to nap the ham. And to add a little more character to the gravy, we looked for a seasoning or two complementary to the ham's sweet flavor. After sampling a few, tasters agreed on thyme for earthiness and mustard for an assertive punch.

Fried Ham Steak with Cider Gravy
SERVES 3 TO 4
The size of the ham steak ultimately determines the serving size. We were able to feed 4 from 1 large steak (with a couple of side dishes), but feel free to fry 2; you will need to reduce the skillet's temperature to medium for the second steak. You may want to taste a small bite of the cooked ham steak before adjusting the gravy's seasoning to prevent oversalting—some brands of ham steaks are saltier than others. Ideal accompaniments would be biscuits and either a leafy salad or cooked greens.

- 3/4   teaspoon cornstarch
- 1/2   teaspoon brown sugar
- 1   teaspoon Dijon mustard
- 1   tablespoon plus 2 cups apple cider
- 1   tablespoon unsalted butter
- 1   large ham steak (about 1 1/2 pounds), patted dry with paper towels
- 2   sprigs fresh thyme
-     Salt and ground black pepper

1. Adjust an oven rack to the middle position and heat the oven to 200 degrees.

2. Whisk the cornstarch, brown sugar, mustard, and 1 tablespoon cider together in a small bowl.

3. Heat the butter in a 12-inch skillet over medium-high until the foaming subsides. Add the ham steak and cook, without moving, until browned, 3½ to 4 minutes. Using tongs and a large spatula, flip the steak and cook on the second side until browned, about 3 minutes. Transfer the ham steak to an ovenproof plate or baking sheet and place it in the oven.

4. Return the skillet to medium-high heat and add the remaining 2 cups cider and the thyme sprigs, scraping the pan bottom with a wooden spoon to release any browned bits. Cook until the cider is reduced by half, about 6 minutes. Whisk in the cornstarch mixture and cook, stirring frequently, until the sauce is thickened, about 2 minutes. Remove and discard the thyme sprigs and adjust the seasonings with salt and pepper to taste.

5. Cut the ham steak into 3 or 4 pieces and place on individual plates. Spoon some cider gravy over each ham steak and serve immediately.

10

LAMB

LIKE BEEF, LAMB HAS A RICH RED COLOR, BUT the meat is generally stronger-tasting. This is because the muscle itself is quite tasty and because lamb fat has a particularly strong flavor.

Most lamb sold in the supermarket has been slaughtered when 6 to 12 months old. (When the animal is slaughtered past the first year, the meat must be labeled mutton.) Generally, younger lamb has a milder flavor that most people prefer. The only indication of slaughter age at the supermarket is size. A whole leg of lamb weighing nine pounds is likely to have come from an older animal than a whole leg weighing just six pounds. Lamb is initially divided into five primal (or major) cuts.

SHOULDER This area extends from the neck through the fourth rib. Meat from this area is flavorful, although it contains a fair amount of connective tissue and can be tough. Chops, roasts, and boneless stew meat all come from the shoulder.

RIB The rib area is directly behind the shoulder and extends from the fifth to the twelfth rib. The rack (all eight ribs from this section) is cut from the rib. When cut into individual chops, the meat is called rib chops. Meat from this area has a fine, tender grain and a mild flavor.

LOIN The loin extends from the last rib down to the hip area. The loin chop is the most familiar cut from this part of the lamb. Like the rib chop, it is tender and has a mild, sweet flavor.

THE FIVE PRIMAL CUTS OF LAMB

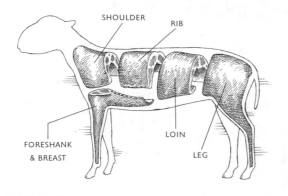

LEG The leg area runs from the hip down to the hoof. It may be sold whole or broken into smaller roasts and shanks (one comes from each hind leg). These roasts may be sold with the bones in, or they may be butterflied and sold boneless.

FORESHANK/BREAST The final primal cut is from the underside of the animal and is called the foreshank and breast. This area includes the two front legs (each yields a shank) as well as the breast, which is rarely sold in supermarkets.

INGREDIENTS: Lamb

Lamb is a hard sell in the United States. According to the American Meat Institute, we eat less than 1½ pounds of lamb per person each year. Lamb gets a much more favorable reception abroad. And we wondered why. Is imported grass-fed lamb that much more tender and less "lamby" than domestic grain-fed lamb?

To find out, we held a blind taste test of imported lamb legs from New Zealand, Australia, and Iceland, along with domestic lamb. Our tasters included both lamb enthusiasts and the lamb-averse.

Tasters didn't find any of the roasts "gamey" or overly tough, and they found all of them to be juicy. The Australian lamb had the strongest lamb flavor. The meat was chewy and dark, indicating older lamb, a trait not offensive to the lamb lovers in our group. The New Zealand lamb had a bold lamb flavor, but some tasters disliked the texture, finding it "stringy" and "more like ham." The domestic lamb was milder in taste; many thought it more reminiscent of roast beef than lamb. Tasters thought that the domestic lamb's texture was a bit chewy, but not unpleasantly so. The lamb from Iceland was the smallest lamb by far. It also had the most delicate flavor—too delicate for those tasters who enjoyed a stronger lamb flavor (one referred to the Icelandic lamb as "lamb lite"). All found the texture of the Icelandic lamb to be the most tender by far. As one taster noted, it "cut like butter."

BRAISED LAMB CHOPS

IN OUR TESTS, WE FOUND THAT GRILLING IS the best method for cooking most lamb chops. They are too fatty for broiling (unless, of course, your kitchen has a professional ventilation system); our kitchen filled with smoke every time we tried this technique. Sautéing is not much better. The chops render so much fat that they are swimming in grease in no time and do not brown all that well since the edges tend to curl up as the chops cook. For best results, we prefer to grill lamb chops.

There are two exceptions to this rule. The other indoor preparation we like for lamb chops calls for braising somewhat chewy shoulder chops, which respond especially well to this cooking method. (Don't braise rib or loin chops; they lose their distinctive flavor when braised.)

Our first test in this arena was a stovetop braise using a minimal amount of liquid that could be quickly reduced and thickened for a sauce. We browned the chops with sliced onion in a deep sauté pan large enough to hold the chops in a single layer. Then we deglazed with white wine, herbs, a little tomato, and water to barely cover the chops and simmered the whole thing, covered, for an hour and a half, until the meat was tender. We were surprised at how long the relatively thin chops took to cook, and the results were disappointing. The lamb had a sticky, gummy quality that we attributed to the scant quantity of liquid.

Next time we switched to red wine (and more of it) and braised the chops just to medium. We decided to try this experiment after it occurred to us that grilled chops are tender when cooked medium—maybe we needn't actually stew the chops at all, just briefly braise them. The red wine improved the flavor, and cooking the meat to a lesser degree of doneness vastly shortened the cooking time. Using chops about ¾ inch thick, we found that we now had a delicious stovetop braise that cooked in just 15 to 20 minutes—a true weeknight supper dish for the winter months.

Braised Shoulder Lamb Chops with Tomatoes and Red Wine
SERVES 4

Because they are generally leaner, round-bone chops, also called arm chops, are preferable for this braise. If available, however, lean blade chops also braise nicely. See the box on page 488 for more information on different shoulder chops.

4   shoulder lamb chops, about ¾ inch thick, trimmed of excess fat
    Salt and ground black pepper
2   tablespoons olive oil
1   small onion, chopped fine
2   small garlic cloves, minced or pressed through a garlic press
⅓   cup dry red wine
1   cup canned diced tomatoes, with their juice
2   tablespoons minced fresh parsley leaves

1. Sprinkle the chops with salt and pepper to taste. Heat 1 tablespoon of the oil in a heavy-bottomed nonreactive 12-inch skillet over medium-high heat. Cooking in batches if necessary to avoid overcrowding, add the chops and sauté until browned on both sides, 4 to 5 minutes. Remove the chops from the pan to a plate and set aside.

2. Pour off the fat in the pan. Return the pan to medium heat and add the remaining 1 tablespoon oil. Add the onion and cook until softened, about 4 minutes. Add the garlic and cook until fragrant, about 1 minute. Add the wine and simmer until reduced by half, scraping the browned bits from the pan bottom with a wooden spoon, 2 to 3 minutes. Stir in the tomatoes, then return the chops to the pan. Reduce the heat to low, cover, and simmer until the chops are cooked through but tender, 15 to 20 minutes.

3. Transfer 1 chop to each of 4 plates. Stir the parsley into the braising liquid in the skillet and simmer until the sauce thickens, 2 to 3 minutes. Adjust the seasonings with salt and pepper, spoon the sauce over the chops, and serve immediately.

➤ VARIATIONS
Braised Shoulder Lamb Chops with Tomatoes, Rosemary, and Olives
Follow the recipe for Braised Shoulder Lamb Chops with Tomatoes and Red Wine, adding 1 tablespoon minced fresh rosemary leaves with the garlic and stirring in ⅓ cup pitted and sliced Kalamata olives with the tomatoes in step 2.

Braised Shoulder Lamb Chops with Red Peppers, Capers, and Balsamic Vinegar
Follow the recipe for Braised Shoulder Lamb Chops with Tomatoes and Red Wine, adding

1 medium red bell pepper, cored, seeded, and diced, with the onion in step 2 and stirring in 2 tablespoons rinsed capers and 2 tablespoons balsamic vinegar with the parsley in step 3.

Braised Shoulder Lamb Chops with Figs and North African Spices

1/3	cup stemmed dried figs
1/3	cup warm water
4	shoulder lamb chops, about 3/4 inch thick, trimmed of excess fat
	Salt and ground black pepper
2	tablespoons olive oil
1	small onion, chopped fine
2	small garlic cloves, minced or pressed through a garlic press
1	teaspoon ground coriander
1/2	teaspoon ground cumin
1/2	teaspoon ground cinnamon
1/8	teaspoon cayenne pepper
1	cup canned diced tomatoes, with their juice
2	tablespoons honey
2	tablespoons minced fresh parsley leaves

1. Place the figs and water in a bowl and soak for 30 minutes. Drain, reserving the water. Cut the figs into quarters and reserve.

2. Sprinkle the chops with salt and pepper to taste. Heat 1 tablespoon of the oil in a heavy-bottomed nonreactive 12-inch skillet over medium-high heat. Cooking in batches if necessary to avoid overcrowding, add the chops and cook until browned on both sides, 4 to 5 minutes. Remove the chops from the pan to a plate and set aside.

3. Pour off the fat in the pan. Return the pan to medium heat and add the remaining 1 tablespoon oil. Add the onion and cook until softened, about 4 minutes. Add the garlic and spices and cook until fragrant, about 1 minute. Add the reserved soaking liquid from the figs and simmer until reduced by half, scraping the browned bits from the pan bottom with a wooden spoon, 2 to 3 minutes. Stir in the tomatoes and honey, then return the chops to the pan. Reduce the heat to low, cover, and simmer until the chops are cooked through but tender, 15 to 20 minutes.

4. Transfer 1 chop to each of 4 plates. Stir the parsley into the braising liquid in the skillet and simmer until the sauce thickens, 2 to 3 minutes. Adjust the seasonings with salt and pepper, spoon the sauce over the chops, and serve immediately.

INGREDIENTS:
Shoulder Lamb Chops

Lamb shoulder is sliced into two different cuts, blade and round-bone chops. You'll find them sold in a range of thicknesses (from about 1/2 inch to more than 1 inch thick), depending on who's doing the butchering. (In our experience, supermarkets tend to cut them thinner, while independent butchers cut them thicker.) Blade chops are roughly rectangular in shape, and some are thickly striated with fat. Each blade chop includes a piece of the chine bone (the backbone of the animal) and a thin piece of the blade bone (the shoulder blade of the animal).

Round-bone chops, also called arm chops, are more oval in shape and as a rule are substantially leaner than blade chops. Each contains a round cross section of the arm bone so that the chop looks a bit like a mini ham steak. In addition to the arm bone, there's also a tiny line of riblets on the side of each chop.

As to which chop is better, we didn't find any difference in taste or texture between the two types except that the blade chops generally have more fat. We grill both blade and round-bone chops. We like the way the fat in the blade chop melts on the grill, flavoring and moistening the meat, and we love the grilled riblets from the round-bone chop. For braising, though, we always prefer round-bone chops because they add less fat to the sauce. That said, blade chops vary quite a bit in fat content; those with little intramuscular fat will work fine if well trimmed.

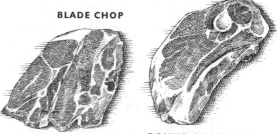

BLADE CHOP

ROUND-BONE CHOP

The blade chop (left) is roughly rectangular in shape and contains a piece of the chine bone and a thin piece of the blade bone. The arm, or round-bone, chop (right) is leaner and contains a round cross section of the arm bone. Both are great on the grill, but for braising we prefer the leaner round chop.

Braised Lamb Shanks

ONE OF THE GREAT PLEASURES OF COOKING is turning relatively tough cuts of meat into meltingly tender dishes. Among the most richly flavored of these tougher cuts is the lamb shank, which is simply the bottom portion of the fore or hind leg of a lamb.

Like other cuts of meat that come from the joints of animals, such as oxtails or short ribs, lamb shanks are extremely flavorful when properly cooked. This is because they contain a high proportion of connective tissue and fat, which break down during cooking and add flavor to the meat.

However, the presence of all this connective tissue and fat means that shanks can only be cooked using a long, slow, moist cooking method that will cause the connective tissue to disintegrate and render the fat without drying out the meat. The only practical cooking method for achieving this goal is braising, which means cooking the meat partially covered in liquid, usually in a closed container. Braising keeps the temperature of the meat relatively low—around the boiling point of water—for a long period, which is exactly what is needed to convert the tough collagen to tender gelatin.

While we obtained satisfactory results by braising shanks on top of the stove, we preferred braising in an oven because of its unique heating properties. With the heat coming from all directions, the meat cooks more evenly. This is a particular advantage, given that many pans have hot spots that cause them to heat unevenly on a burner.

Because of the high fat content of this cut, several straightforward precautions are necessary to keep the level of fat in the final product to a minimum. First, if your butcher has not already done so, take the time to trim the lamb shanks of the excess fat that encases the meat. Even a long, slow braise will not successfully render all of the exterior fat on a lamb shank. Trimming it helps you get a jump on that potential problem.

Browning the shanks well before braising them also helps render some of the exterior fat. Browning also offers the advantage of providing a great deal of flavor to the dish. Be sure to drain the fat from the pan after browning.

The third important step is to remove the fat from the braising liquid after the shanks have been cooked. To do this, take the shanks out of the braising liquid, strain out the vegetables, and allow the sauce to rest undisturbed for a short while. Then, using a ladle, carefully skim the fat that has risen to the surface and discard it. This process can be facilitated by transferring the sauce to a taller, narrower container before setting it aside to rest. If, after skimming the liquid, you find that it still has too much fat, you may repeat this step after 10 more minutes, although with most shanks, this will not be necessary. Further, if the braise is prepared well in advance of serving, you may refrigerate the braising liquid, then lift off the solidified fat from the top of the liquid.

The braising liquid, along with the aromatics you add to it, will greatly enhance the flavor of the entire dish. Stock is the traditional braising liquid because it adds textural richness as well as depth of flavor. As we have said many times before in these pages, making homemade stock is not practical. We recommend, therefore, using canned chicken broth, not beef broth, for this braise. The chicken broth complements the flavor of the lamb shanks.

Wine is a particularly good addition to the braising liquid, adding complexity and acid to the sauce. The acid is particularly important because of the richness of the lamb. Too little acid creates a dull, rather flat-tasting dish. On the other hand, too much acid results in a harsh, off-putting flavor. After trying different ratios, we found that 2 parts wine to 3 parts broth gives the best flavor. We found that either white wine or red works well, the difference being that red wine will give you a richer, deeper finish.

Whatever liquid you use for braising, we discovered, it should cover all but the top inch of the shanks. This is a departure from classic braising, where less liquid is used. We adopted this method after leaving shanks to braise in the oven, then returning some time later to find that the liquid had boiled away and the shanks were burned. Unless you are using a true braising pan with an extremely tight-fitting lid, a fair amount of liquid will escape over the cooking process. Using more liquid prevents the pan from drying out, no matter how loose the seal is.

Lamb shanks need not be served whole, though we prefer them this way for their dramatic appeal. Once the shanks are cooked and cooled, you may remove the meat from the bone before reincorporating it with the vegetables and sauce. The resulting stew-type dish will be less dramatic in presentation but equally delicious. You may also vary the choice of herbs and spices according to your taste; in the following recipes, we have included suggestions.

Lamb Shanks Braised in Red Wine

SERVES 6

If you're using smaller shanks than the ones called for in this recipe, reduce the initial braising time in step 3 from 1½ hours to 1 hour. Serve these braised shanks over mashed potatoes or polenta. If you want to prepare the dish ahead of time, make the recipe through step 3, then cool and refrigerate the shanks and braising liquid (still in the pot) overnight. When ready to serve, remove the solidified fat on the surface, then warm the dish over medium heat.

1	tablespoon extra-virgin olive oil
6	lamb shanks (³⁄₄ to 1 pound each), trimmed of excess fat
	Salt and ground black pepper
2	medium onions, sliced thick
3	medium carrots, cut crosswise into 2-inch pieces
2	celery ribs, cut crosswise into 2-inch pieces
4	medium garlic cloves, peeled
2	tablespoons tomato paste
2	teaspoons minced fresh thyme leaves
2	teaspoons minced fresh rosemary leaves
2	cups dry red wine
3	cups low-sodium chicken broth

1. Adjust an oven rack to the lower-middle position and heat the oven to 350 degrees. Heat the oil in a large ovenproof Dutch oven over medium-high heat until it is shimmering. Meanwhile, sprinkle both sides of the shanks generously with salt and pepper to taste. Swirl to coat the pan bottom with the oil. Place 3 shanks in a single layer in the pan and cook, turning once, until nicely browned all over, about 7 minutes. Transfer the shanks to a plate and set aside. Brown the remaining shanks and transfer them to the plate.

2. Drain all but 2 tablespoons of the fat from the pot. Add the onions, carrots, celery, garlic, tomato paste, herbs, and a light sprinkling of salt. Cook until the vegetables soften slightly, 3 to 4 minutes. Add the wine, then the stock, stirring with a wooden spoon to loosen the browned bits on the pan bottom. Bring the liquid to a simmer. Add the shanks and season with salt and pepper to taste.

3. Cover the pot and transfer it to the oven. Braise the shanks for 1½ hours. Uncover and continue braising until the shank tops are browned, about 30 minutes. Turn the shanks and braise until the other side is browned and the meat is fall-off-the-bone tender, 15 to 30 minutes longer.

4. Remove the pot from the oven and let the shanks rest in the sauce for at least 15 minutes. With tongs, carefully transfer the shanks to individual plates. Arrange a portion of the vegetables around each shank. With a large spoon or ladle, skim the excess fat from the braising liquid and adjust the seasonings. Spoon some of the braising liquid over each shank and serve immediately.

➤ VARIATION

Braised Lamb Shanks with Lemon and Mint

Grate the zest from 1 lemon, then cut the lemon into quarters. Follow the recipe for Lamb Shanks Braised in Red Wine, replacing the thyme and rosemary leaves with 1 tablespoon minced fresh mint leaves and replacing the red wine with dry white wine. Add the quartered lemon to the braising liquid in step 2. Proceed as directed, stirring the lemon zest and an additional 1 tablespoon minced fresh mint leaves into the sauce just before serving.

RACK OF LAMB

THE WORD "MOUTHWATERING" MUST HAVE BEEN coined to describe rack of lamb. The meat is ultratender and luscious-tasting, more refined in flavor than almost any other cut of lamb, but no less satisfying.

But, at $17 to $18 a pound, there's hardly a cut of meat more expensive. And like other simple but fabulous dishes (roast chicken comes to mind), there's nothing to cooking it except that there's no disguising imperfection. You want the meat to be perfectly pink and juicy, the outside intensely browned to boost flavor and provide contrasting texture, and the fat to be well enough rendered to encase the meat in a thin, crisp, brittle shell.

With all of this in mind, we set out to find a foolproof way to roast this extravagant cut. And because it's such a good choice for a party, we wanted a sauce to serve with it. A traditional jus is easy to make from pan drippings if your butcher gives you bones from butchering and trimming the rack. But you don't get bones if you buy a rack from a supermarket or one that's been vacuum-sealed, and two racks on their own, cooked only to medium-rare, just don't produce enough jus for four people. We had to figure out a new way to make a sauce.

Since good exterior caramelization is critical to the taste of any roast meat, we needed to find out whether the rack would brown adequately in the oven or would need to first be browned on top of the stove. We hoped for the former; we like the ease of simply shoving the rack into the oven. So we decided to test four racks that had been trimmed and frenched (rib bones cleaned of meat and fat for an attractive presentation) at four different temperatures in a preheated oven: 425 degrees, 475 degrees, 500 degrees, and, finally, 200 degrees.

Unfortunately, none of the high oven temperatures gave us the quality of crust we were looking for, even when we preheated the roasting pan. We knew that the conditions of our remaining test—roasting at 200 degrees—would not make for a nicely browned lamb; the meat wouldn't form a crust at such a low temperature. So we started this test by searing the fat side of the rack in a little vegetable oil in a skillet on top of the stove to get a crust before putting it in a 200-degree oven. The slow-roast technique was a bust: The meat was no more tender than when cooked at a high heat, it had a funny, murky taste and mushy texture that we didn't like, and it took much too long to cook.

But the searing technique was terrific. The only refinement we needed was to find a way to brown the strip of eye meat that lies below the bones on the bony side of the rack. After some experimentation, we came up with the system of leaning two racks upright one against the other in the pan; this allowed us to brown all parts of the meat before roasting.

Now we went back to testing oven temperatures. Once the rack was seared, we roasted it at 350, 425, and 475 degrees. We ended up taking the middle road. At 425 degrees, the lamb tasted at least as good as (if not better than) it did when cooked at a lower temperature, and there was more room for error than when it cooked at a higher heat.

But now we were running into an unexpected problem. Surprisingly, the racks we were cooking were too fatty. They looked great when they came out of the oven, but once carved the chops were covered with a layer of fat that was browned only on the exterior. Some chops also had a second layer of internal fat, separated by a thin piece of meat, called the cap, that didn't get browned at all. We didn't want to forfeit this little flap of meat (particularly at the price we paid for it), but there seemed no help for it: We needed to get rid of some of the fat. So we trimmed the flap and all the fat underneath it, leaving only a minimal amount at the top of the eye and covering the bones to give the cut its characteristic rounded shape.

BROWNING RACKS OF LAMB

To achieve a good crust on a rack of lamb, brown it on both sides on top of the stove before placing it in the oven in a preheated roasting pan. Start by placing 2 racks in a hot pan with the meat in the center and the ribs facing outward (left). Once browned, stand the racks up in the pan and lean them against each other to brown the bottoms (right).

The meat tasted great, needing only one final adjustment: We removed the silver skin that we had exposed in trimming the fat. (The silver skin is the pearlescent membrane found on certain cuts of meat. It is very tough and, if not removed, can cause meat to curl during cooking.)

Satisfied with our roasting technique, we were now ready to work on a sauce. We wanted a separate sauce, ready just as soon as the lamb was done, so that we weren't starting from scratch with the pan drippings at the last minute. First we made a separate jus (a very concentrated, reduced stock made with meat, onions, carrots, garlic, and a little water), using lamb stew pieces on the bone bought separately at the supermarket. The jus tasted good, but making it was too much work; we didn't want to complicate a simple meal. So we went back to the pan drippings. If we transferred the rack to a second pan after browning on top of the stove, we could make a pan sauce while the lamb roasted. As it turned out, we got the best results by preheating the roasting pan in the oven so that it was hot when the lamb hit it.

Roasted Racks of Lamb

SERVES 4 TO 6

Have your butcher french the racks (that is, remove excess fat from the rib bones) for you; inevitably, the ribs will need some cleaning up, but at least the bulk of the work will be done. Should you choose to make one of the accompanying pan sauces, have all the ingredients ready before browning the lamb on the stovetop and start to make the sauce just as the lamb goes into the oven. This way, the sauce will be ready with the meat. See the photos on page 491 for tips on browning the racks of lamb.

2   (8- or 9-rib) racks of lamb (1¼ to 1½ pounds each), rib bones frenched, meat trimmed of fat and silver skin (see the illustrations at right), and patted dry with paper towels
      Salt and ground black pepper
2   tablespoons vegetable oil

1. Adjust an oven rack to the lower-middle position, place a shallow roasting pan or rimmed baking sheet on the oven rack, and heat the oven to 425 degrees.

2. Season the lamb generously with salt and pepper to taste. Heat the oil in a heavy-bottomed 12-inch skillet over high heat until shimmering. Place the racks of lamb in the skillet, meat-side down in the center of the pan, with the ribs facing outward. Cook until well browned and a nice crust has formed on the surface, about 4 minutes. Using tongs, stand the racks up in the skillet, leaning them against each other to brown the bottoms; cook until the bottoms have browned, about 2 minutes longer.

3. Transfer the lamb to the preheated roasting pan. (Begin a pan sauce, if making.) Roast until

PREPARING RACK OF LAMB

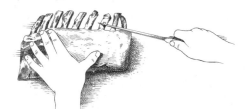

1. Using a boning or paring knife, scrape the ribs clean of any scraps of meat or fat.

2. Trim off the outer layer of fat, the flap of meat underneath it, and the fat underneath that flap.

3. Remove the silver skin by sliding the boning knife between the silver skin and the flesh.

an instant-read thermometer inserted into the center of each rack registers about 125 degrees for medium-rare or 130 degrees for medium, 12 to 15 minutes, depending on the size of the rack. Remove the racks from the oven, cover the meat loosely with foil, and let rest about 10 minutes. Carve, slicing between the ribs into individual chops Serve immediately with an additional sprinkling of salt and pepper or with one of the following sauces.

➤ VARIATIONS

Roasted Racks of Lamb with Red Wine Pan Sauce and Rosemary

See page 78 for illustrations on mincing shallots.

I	recipe Roasted Racks of Lamb
2	medium shallots, minced
I	cup dry red wine
2½	teaspoons minced fresh rosemary leaves
I	cup low-sodium chicken broth
2	tablespoons cold unsalted butter, cut into 2 pieces
	Salt and ground black pepper

1. Prepare the lamb as directed.

2. After transferring the browned lamb to the roasting pan, pour off all but 1½ tablespoons of the fat from the skillet. Add the shallots and place the skillet over medium heat. Sauté the shallots until softened, about 1 minute. Add the red wine and rosemary; increase the heat to medium-high and simmer, scraping up the browned bits on the pan bottom, until dark and syrupy, about 7 minutes. Add the chicken broth and simmer until reduced to about ¾ cup, about 5 minutes longer. Swirl in the butter, one piece at a time, and season with salt and pepper to taste. Serve the sauce with the lamb, passing it separately at the table.

Roasted Racks of Lamb with Sweet-and-Sour Mint Sauce

This simple sauce should be made before you begin cooking the lamb so the sugar has time to dissolve while the lamb cooks.

½	cup loosely packed fresh mint leaves, chopped
¼	cup red wine vinegar
I	tablespoon sugar
	Salt
I	recipe Roasted Racks of Lamb

1. Stir the mint, vinegar, and sugar together in a small bowl. Let stand about 20 minutes to allow the sugar to dissolve. Season with salt to taste.

2. Prepare the lamb as directed. Serve the sauce with the lamb, passing it separately at the table.

Roasted Racks of Lamb with Orange Pan Sauce and Middle Eastern Spices

I	recipe Roasted Racks of Lamb
2	medium shallots, minced
I	teaspoon ground cumin
¼	teaspoon ground black pepper
¼	teaspoon ground cinnamon
¼	teaspoon ground cardamom
⅛	teaspoon cayenne pepper
2	teaspoons sugar
3	tablespoons red wine vinegar
¼	cup juice from I medium orange
1½	cups low-sodium chicken broth
I	tablespoon minced fresh cilantro leaves
	Salt

1. Prepare the lamb as directed.

2. After transferring the browned lamb to the roasting pan, pour off all but 1½ tablespoons of the fat from the skillet. Add the shallots and place the skillet over medium heat. Sauté the shallots until softened, about 1 minute. Stir in the cumin, black pepper, cinnamon, cardamom, cayenne, and sugar; cook until fragrant, about 1 minute. Stir in the vinegar, scraping up the browned bits on the pan bottom. Add the orange juice, increase the heat to medium-high, and simmer until very thick and syrupy, about 2 minutes. Add the chicken broth and simmer until slightly thickened and reduced to about ¾ cup, 8 to 10 minutes. Off the heat, stir in the cilantro and season with salt to taste. Serve the sauce with the lamb, passing it separately at the table.

ROAST LEG OF LAMB

THE MAIN PROBLEM WE HAVE HAD WITH ROAST leg of lamb is that it cooks unevenly. In the past, no matter what we tried, the outer part became dry and gray, while the meat around the bone remained almost raw. The uneven thickness of the leg is the most formidable obstacle to even cooking. At the thicker sirloin end, the meat surrounding the flat, twisting hipbone is very thin. The center of the leg, which consists of the top half of the thigh, is fleshy, but the thigh then tapers dramatically toward the knee joint, and the shank itself is a mere nub of meat.

The only way to deal with this problem is to remove the hipbone and aitchbone entirely and then tie the leg into as compact a shape as possible. Once you have done this, by the way, you will understand why it is not smart to buy the sirloin end of the leg as a separate small roast, no matter how attractive the price. After the hipbone has been removed, there is barely enough meat at the sirloin end to serve two people.

Boning and tying, however, do not by themselves guarantee even cooking, as we discovered. Special procedures must be followed in roasting the leg to ensure that all parts are exposed to the same amount of heat and will thus reach similar internal temperatures at the same time.

We started out by roasting a 7½-pound leg at 400 degrees, with the meat resting directly on the roasting pan. After approximately one hour, the top of the leg, which had been facing up, registered 120 degrees on a meat thermometer, which to our taste is underdone for leg of lamb. The meat around the thighbone, meanwhile, was practically raw, while the bottom of the leg, which had been resting on the hot pan, had reached a temperature of around 135 degrees, which is a little overcooked for our taste.

We have always resisted roasting on a rack because, when cooked only to rare or medium-rare, meat produces virtually no browned bits for gravy unless it rests directly on the pan. With leg of lamb, however, we surmised that a rack might be useful, for it would protect the downward-facing side of the leg from becoming overcooked by the heat of the pan.

To test this theory, we rack-roasted another leg. After cooking it at 500 degrees for 30 minutes (high initial heat promotes browning) and then at 300 degrees for about 45 minutes longer, the leg was done on the top side; the thermometer registered a consistent 130 degrees whether inserted sideways, into the exterior portion of the top side, or poked deep into the middle. Alas, the bottom side of the roast proved undercooked. Evidently the rack had been too effective in keeping the bottom of the leg cool.

But this experiment, while only partially successful, pointed toward a solution. Perhaps turning the leg during cooking would promote more even cooking by allowing the top and the bottom sides equal exposure to both the cool rack and the hot oven roof. We further reasoned that setting the pan on the bottom shelf of the oven would slightly heat up the rack side, which was too cool, while mitigating the glare from the oven roof.

This is how we roasted our next lamb leg, and the results were near perfect. The outermost slices were a little closer to medium than to medium-rare and the bone meat was still a bit underdone, but most of the roast was the way we wanted it, deep pink and juicy.

Roast Leg of Lamb

SERVES 8 TO 12,
DEPENDING ON SIZE OF LEG

Legs come in a variety of sizes. Our recipe starts with a semiboneless (the butcher should remove the hipbone and aitchbone) leg that weighs between 6 and 8 pounds. (The weight of the whole, untrimmed leg is about 1½ pounds more.) Smaller legs have a sweeter, milder flavor, so you may want to search for a petite leg if you don't like a strong "sheepy" flavor. If roasting a smaller leg, reduce the cooking time at 325 degrees by at least 10 minutes.

We find it best to cook lamb by internal temperature. We like our lamb medium-rare, or about 135 degrees when carved. Since the internal temperature will rise while the lamb rests, pull the leg out of the oven when the temperature reaches 130 degrees. If you like lamb on the rarer side, pull it out of the oven at 120 degrees (the temperature will rise to 125 degrees by carving time). If you like lamb more well-done, pull it out at 135 degrees (the temperature will rise above 140 degrees).

Salt and ground black pepper

1 teaspoon finely minced fresh rosemary leaves (omit if making Mint Sauce on page 496)

1 semiboneless leg of lamb (6 to 8 pounds), trimmed of excess fat (see illustrations 1 through 4 below)

3 medium garlic cloves, peeled and cut into thin slivers

2 tablespoons olive oil
   Piquant Caper Sauce or Mint Sauce (recipes follow; optional)

1. Mix 2 teaspoons salt, 2 teaspoons pepper, and the rosemary together in a small bowl.

2. Sprinkle a portion of the rosemary mixture over the inner surface of the cleaned and boned meat. Tie the lamb according to illustrations 5 and 6 below. Cut slits in the roast with the tip of a paring knife. Poke the garlic slivers inside. Brush the exterior with the oil, then rub the remaining seasoning onto all the surfaces of the meat. Place the leg meaty-side up in a roasting pan fitted with a flat rack; let stand 30 minutes. Adjust an oven rack to the lowest position and heat the oven to 450 degrees.

3. Pour ½ cup water into the bottom of the roasting pan. Roast the lamb for 10 minutes. With a wad of paper towels in each hand, turn the leg over. Roast 10 minutes longer. Lower the oven temperature to 325 degrees. Turn the leg meaty-side up and continue roasting, turning the leg every 20 minutes, until an instant-read thermometer inserted in several locations registers 130 degrees for medium, 60 to 80 minutes longer.

PREPARING A LEG OF LAMB FOR ROASTING

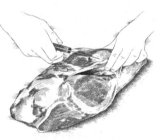

1. The butcher should remove the aitchbone and hipbone (right front); you should save them so you can make stock. If the shank bone has been partially detached by the butcher, remove it with a knife and save it, too, for making stock.

2. Lamb fat is strong-flavored and unpleasant to chew. Remove large pieces of fat, using a knife and your hands to cut and then pull the fat off the leg. It's fine to leave a few streaks of fat to moisten the roast.

3. The strong-tasting lymph node (a ½-inch round, grayish, flat nodule) and surrounding fat should be removed. Set the leg meaty-side up and cut into the area that separates the broad, thin flap of meat on one side of the leg from the thick, meaty lobe.

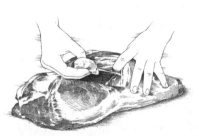

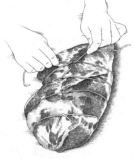

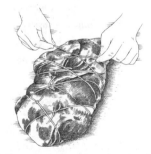

4. Use both hands and the knife to widen the incision, exposing the lymph node and surrounding fat. Reach in and grasp the nugget of fat. Pull while cutting the connective tissue, being very careful not to cut into the gland itself. Pull the fat and other matter free.

5. Set the leg meaty-side up and smooth the flap of meat at the sirloin end so that it folds over and neatly covers the tip of the thighbone. Tie several short lengths of kitchen twine around the leg, placing each piece of twine parallel to the next.

6. Tie several more short lengths of twine around the leg, running pieces of twine perpendicular to those in step 5.

Transfer the roast to another pan; cover with foil and set aside in a warm spot to complete cooking and to allow the juices to reabsorb into the meat, 15 to 20 minutes. Reserve the roasting pan if making the Piquant Caper Sauce.

4. When the sauce is ready, remove the twine from the roast and carve by cutting slices parallel to the bone, each about ¼ inch thick. When the meat on top has been removed, flip the leg over and carve the bottom in the same fashion. To facilitate carving the side of the leg, grasp the narrow end of the leg and hold it perpendicular to the work surface and slice as before. Serve the sliced lamb with either sauce or plain.

Piquant Caper Sauce
MAKES ENOUGH TO ACCOMPANY
I LEG OF LAMB

If making this sauce, ask the butcher for the hipbone and aitchbone and reserve any meat scraps that have come off the lamb during the cleaning process. Make sure to remove the fat from these scraps. You can also use the hinged part of the shank bone. To accommodate the hipbone, you will need a wide saucepan or deep sauté pan. Start the sauce as soon as the lamb goes into the oven.

I	tablespoon olive oil
	Lamb bones and meat scraps (see note)
I	medium onion, chopped coarse
3	cups low-sodium chicken broth
⅓	cup dry white wine or dry vermouth
2	tablespoons unsalted butter, softened
2	tablespoons unbleached all-purpose flour
⅓	cup (3 ounces) small capers, drained, bottling liquid reserved
I	teaspoon balsamic vinegar

1. Heat the oil in a large, heavy-bottomed saucepan over medium heat until shimmering. Add the reserved bones and meat scraps and the onion and sauté, turning the bones several times, until well browned, about 10 minutes. Add the broth, scraping the pan bottom to loosen the browned bits; bring to a boil. Reduce the heat to low; simmer, partially covered, until the bones and meat have given up their flavor to the broth,

about 1 hour. Add a little water if the bones are more than half-exposed during cooking.

2. While the roasted leg of lamb is resting, set the now-empty pan used to roast the lamb over medium heat. Add the wine and scrape with a wooden spoon until the browned bits dissolve. Pour the mixture into the lamb stock, then strain everything into a 2-cup glass measure. Let sit until the fat rises, then skim off the fat. Add water, if necessary, to make 1½ cups of liquid. Pour the liquid back into the saucepan and bring to a boil.

3. Mix the butter and flour in a small bowl to form a smooth paste. Gradually whisk the butter-flour mixture into the stock. Stir in the capers, vinegar, and any juices released by the lamb as it rested. Simmer to blend the flavors, about 3 minutes. Add more vinegar or caper bottling liquid to achieve a piquant, subtly sharp-sweet sauce. Serve the sauce with the lamb, passing it separately at the table.

Mint Sauce
MAKES ENOUGH TO ACCOMPANY
I LEG OF LAMB

This sauce has a refreshing mint flavor without the cloying sweetness of mint jelly. The texture is much thinner than jelly, similar to maple syrup. This sauce is remarkably easy to make and does not require any bones since no stock is necessary. If making this sauce, eliminate the rosemary from the lamb recipe and just rub the meat with olive oil and salt and pepper and stud it with garlic. Mince the mint right before adding it to the sauce to preserve its fresh flavor.

I	cup white wine vinegar
6	tablespoons sugar
¼	cup minced fresh mint leaves

1. Bring the vinegar and sugar to a simmer in a nonreactive medium saucepan over medium heat and cook until slightly syrupy, 8 to 10 minutes. (The liquid should be reduced to about ½ cup.)

2. Remove the pan from the heat, let cool for 5 minutes, and stir in the mint. Pour the sauce into a bowl and cover with plastic wrap. Set aside for at least 1 hour. (The sauce can be set aside for several hours.) Serve at room temperature with the lamb.

11

FISH AND SHELLFISH

BUYING FISH AND SHELLFISH IS AS TRICKY AS cooking it, if not more so. Here are a few general points when purchasing it to keep in mind: Always buy from a trusted source, preferably one with high volume, which should help ensure freshness. That said, what are the visual cues of freshness when it comes to fish and shellfish?

For starters, fish should smell like the sea, not fishy or sour. The flesh should look bright, shiny, and firm, not dull or mushy. When possible, try to get your fishmonger to slice steaks and fillets to order rather than buying precut pieces that may have been sitting for some time and lost fluids. Avoid fish that is shrink-wrapped, since the packaging makes it difficult to examine and smell.

Many shellfish are sold live. This means lobsters should be moving around in the tank, and oysters, clams, and mussels should be tightly shut. If the shellfish doesn't smell or look fresh, it probably isn't. Given the perishability of fish and shellfish, we suggest cooking it on the same day of purchase. And, no matter whether it is fish or shellfish, make sure it has been kept chilled until the minute you buy it. Take it home quickly and refrigerate it at once.

The recipes that follow are our takes on America's favorite seafood dishes, both humble (baked scrod and pan-fried catfish) and elegant (crab cakes and fish meunière).

FISH MEUNIÈRE

FISH MEUNIÈRE IS A DECEPTIVELY EASY FRENCH restaurant dish that ought to serve as a model recipe for home cooking. Ideally, fillets are dredged lightly in flour (no need for eggs or bread crumbs) and cooked on the stovetop until a golden crust forms, leaving the inside moist and flavorful. A browned butter sauce seasoned with lemon is then poured over the fish. What could be simpler, more delicious, or better suited to a Tuesday night dinner? That's what we thought, too, before we cooked a few test batches to get a handle on the technique for making this dish. What we got were plates of pale, soggy fillets in pools of greasy sauce—that is, if the fish hadn't stuck to the pan

or fallen apart as we tried to plate it. Despite these failures (or maybe because of them), one thing did become clear. The simplicity of this dish makes it imperative that everything be prepared and cooked just so.

Taking a closer look at our initial meunière recipes (the term *meunière* refers to "miller's wife," a nod to the flour in the recipe), it was no wonder that we had found little success at the stove. Some recipes called for almost two sticks of butter per two pounds of fish—translated, that makes a scant ½ cup butter per 16 ounces of fish. Who wants to eat fish literally swimming in fat? We certainly didn't. Other recipes failed in browning the fish, and the resulting fillets were soggy and white. It was time to go back to basics.

Whole Dover sole—a variety of white flatfish—is the most authentic choice for preparing à la meunière, but it is hard to come by in the best of fish markets and prohibitively expensive when it can be had, and a whole sole, if it can even be found, presents cleaning and filleting issues. We settled instead on a filleted white flatfish that would be available in most markets, thinking that sole or flounder would be the options. That said, we soon became aware of a veritable parade of choices—gray sole, lemon sole, yellowtail flounder, southern flounder, summer flounder, winter flounder, petrale sole, rex sole, rock sole, and starry flounder. After cooking 20 pounds of flatfish, we discovered that variety didn't much matter (tasters approved of them all); what counted were the thickness of the fillet and its freshness. If the fillet was thinner than ⅜ inch, it was nearly impossible to brown it without overcooking it. Fillets that were ⅜ inch thick or slightly more were perfect. They weighed five to six ounces each and fit easily in a large skillet. Fillets weighing seven to ten ounces also were acceptable, although they required cutting and trimming.

Small things can make a big difference when it comes to cooking fish. For one, a thin coat of flour speeds up the browning, which is a particularly useful thing to know when you've got thin fillets that cook quickly. Straight from the fishmonger's wrapping paper, fillets are typically wet. They must be patted dry, or the flour will

FLIPPING FISH FILLETS

To turn fish fillets without breaking them, use two spatulas—a regular model and an extra-wide version especially designed for fish. (In the test kitchen, we use a spatula that is 8½ inches wide by 3¼ inches deep for this job.) Using the regular spatula, gently lift the long side of the fillet. Then, supporting the fillet with the extra-wide spatula, flip it so that the browned side faces up.

become thick and gluey. Simply dredging the dried fillets in flour presented problems. Excess flour fell off the fish and into the pan, where it burned. Shaking off the extra flour before cooking solves this problem. Still, even after a quick shake, the fillets cooked up with blotchy brown crusts that did nothing for the flavor.

We then tried a technique used by Julia Child, who recommends seasoning the fillets with salt and pepper and letting them sit before dredging. After five minutes, the fillets had begun to glisten with moisture. We dredged them with flour, shook off the excess, and cooked them. "Perfectly seasoned and evenly coated" was the thumbs-up response from tasters. Why does letting the seasoned fish rest for five minutes make such a difference? The salt extracts water from the fish, not so much as to make it wet but just enough to give it a thin coating of moisture that helps to ensure a perfectly even coating of flour. Without "bald spots" in the coating, the fish browns uniformly and tastes better.

The technique of pan-frying necessitates a heavy skillet and a good amount of fat. Food is cooked in a single layer as the cook waits patiently for it to brown, turning it once and then waiting again. The temptation is to lift the food and take a peek, but it is essential to resist the impulse. For maximum browning (and to keep the fish from falling apart), the fish must be left undisturbed as it cooks.

We found that traditional skillets did not work well. No matter how much fat we used, the fish had a tendency to stick. A nonstick skillet, on the other hand, worked well every time, producing beautifully browned fillets and no sticking. A 12-inch skillet is a must, we discovered, and even then only two fillets would fit at a time without overlapping. We wanted our recipe to serve four, but using two skillets side by side seemed unreasonable. Instead, we chose to cook the fish in two batches, using a warmed plate in a preheated 200-degree oven to keep the first batch hot.

Clarified butter, or butter with the milk solids removed, is the traditional fat used by the French. Not only does clarified butter lend a rich flavor to the fish, but it has a higher smoking point (and thus burns less easily) than whole butter. Clarifying butter is easy, but it is too lengthy a process for a quick midweek entrée. Would tasters notice its absence? We cooked one batch with canola oil and another with clarified butter, and even the least discerning tasters noticed the difference. Whole butter burned, but a mixture of oil and butter, a classic combination, did the trick.

Next we experimented with the amount of fat. Although recipes ranged from one to six tablespoons (for two fillets), we found that two tablespoons were ample, especially in a nonstick skillet. At this point, because we were using so little fat, we were technically sautéing rather than pan-frying. We began by cooking the fillets over low heat, but the results were mediocre at best; the fillets did not brown but instead poached in the fat, and the taste was lackluster. High heat turned out to be equally problematic. By the time the interior of each fillet had cooked, some of the exterior had scorched, resulting in a bitter and unappealing taste. Our next try was a winner. We heated the pan over high heat, then lowered the heat to medium-high as soon as we added the fish. The exterior browned beautifully, while the inside remained succulent.

For fillets that were the ideal thickness of ⅜ inch, three minutes on the first side and about two minutes on the second side achieved both a flavorful, nutty-tasting exterior and a moist, delicate interior. Because the side that is cooked

499

first is the most attractive, we found it best to stick to the hard-and-fast rule of cooking for three minutes on the first side and then adjusting the time for the second side. (With flatfish, the side of the fillet that is cooked first also matters. See "Anatomy of a Flatfish Fillet" below.) The question was, how could we tell when a thin fillet was done? Restaurant chefs press the fillets with their fingers—a reliable technique but one that requires practice. Observation eventually indicated that the fillet was done when opaque. Because the fish continues to cook off the heat of the stovetop (and in the gentle heat of the preheated oven), it is imperative to remove it slightly before it's fully done. Instead of using the tip of a knife, a method that tends to damage the fillet, we found that a toothpick inserted into a thick edge worked well.

One last cooking consideration remained to be resolved. Traditionally, the sauce served with meunière is *beurre noisette*, or browned butter, with lemon and parsley added. Crucial to the flavor of

the sauce, which adds a rich nuttiness to the fish, is proper browning of the milk solids in the butter, a task not easily accomplished in a nonstick skillet. The problem is that the dark surface of the pan makes it nearly impossible to judge the color of the butter. The solution was simple: Brown the butter in a medium stainless steel skillet; its shiny bottom makes it easy to monitor the color. We then added lemon juice to the browned butter, sprinkled the fish with parsley, and poured the sauce over the fish.

ANATOMY OF A FLATFISH FILLET

"BONE" SIDE
Rounded indentations run along the
length of the fillet on this side.

"SKIN" SIDE
The fillet is darker and flatter.

Flatfish fillets have two distinct sides, and it makes a difference which one goes into the pan first. The side of the fillet that was facing the bones in the whole fish browns best and makes the most attractive presentation on the plate. The side of the fillet that was facing the skin is darker and doesn't brown as well. When cooking, start the fillets bone-side down, then flip them once a nice crust has formed. When the fillets are cooked through, slide them, bone-side up, onto heated dinner plates.

Fish Meunière with Browned Butter and Lemon

SERVES 4

Try to purchase fillets that are of similar size, and avoid those that weigh less than 5 ounces because they will cook too quickly. When placing the fillets in the skillet, be sure to place them skinned-side up—so that the opposite side, which had bones, will brown first (and make an attractive presentation). A nonstick skillet ensures that the fillets will release from the pan, but for the sauce a traditional skillet is preferable because its light-colored surface will allow you to monitor the color of the butter as it browns.

FISH

1/2   cup unbleached all-purpose flour

4   sole or flounder fillets (5 to 6 ounces each and 3/8 inch thick), patted dry with paper towels
Salt and ground black pepper

2   tablespoons vegetable oil

2   tablespoons unsalted butter, cut into 2 pieces

BROWNED BUTTER

4   tablespoons (1/2 stick) unsalted butter, cut into 4 pieces

I   tablespoon chopped fresh parsley leaves

I1/2   tablespoons juice from I lemon

I   lemon, cut into wedges, for serving

1. FOR THE FISH: Adjust an oven rack to the lower-middle position, set 4 heatproof dinner plates on the rack, and heat the oven to 200 degrees. Place the flour in a large baking dish. Season both sides of each fillet generously with salt and pepper; let stand until the fillets are glistening with moisture,

about 5 minutes. Coat both sides of the fillets with flour, shake off the excess, and place in a single layer on a baking sheet. Heat 1 tablespoon of the oil in a 12-inch nonstick skillet over high heat until shimmering; add 1 tablespoon of the butter and swirl to coat the pan bottom. When the foaming subsides, carefully place 2 fillets skin-side up in the skillet (see the photo on page 500). Immediately reduce the heat to medium-high and cook, without moving the fish, until the edges of the fillets are opaque and the bottom is golden brown, about 3 minutes. Using 2 spatulas, gently flip the fillets (see the illustration on page 499) and cook on the second side until the thickest part of the fillet easily separates into flakes when a toothpick is inserted, about 2 minutes longer. Transfer the fillets, one to each heated dinner plate, keeping them bone-side up, and return the plates to the oven. Wipe out the skillet and repeat with the remaining 1 tablespoon each oil and butter and the remaining fish fillets.

2. FOR THE BROWNED BUTTER: Heat the butter in a 10-inch skillet over medium-high heat until the butter melts, 1 to 1½ minutes. Continue to cook, swirling the pan constantly, until the butter is golden brown and has a nutty aroma, 1 to 1½ minutes; remove the skillet from the heat. Remove the plates from the oven and sprinkle the fillets with the parsley. Add the lemon juice to the browned butter and season to taste with salt; spoon the sauce over the fish and serve immediately with the lemon wedges.

➤ VARIATIONS

Fish Meunière with Toasted Slivered Almonds

Follow the recipe for Fish Meunière with Browned Butter and Lemon, adding ¼ cup slivered almonds to the skillet when the butter has melted in step 2.

Fish Meunière with Capers

Follow the recipe for Fish Meunière with Browned Butter and Lemon, adding 2 tablespoons rinsed capers along with the lemon juice in step 2.

BOSTON BAKED SCROD

NAMED FOR THE OLD BEANTOWN RESTAURANTS that made this dish famous, Boston baked scrod is now a seafood restaurant standard across the country. Every once in a while, this simple recipe turns out great, with sweet, tender pieces of cod lightly seasoned with butter and lemon and topped with crisp toasted crumbs. More often than not, however, it's rubbery and bland and topped off with a soggy crust. Knowing how good it can be and how awful it usually is, we set out to discover what makes Boston baked scrod worth the effort.

The term *scrod,* as we quickly found out when shopping, is somewhat controversial and may be used to refer to several types of small fish (weighing in at less than 2½ pounds or so). It is more accurate to use the term *scrod cod* when buying fish at the local market to make sure the fish you are getting is really cod. A scrod cod fillet weighs about one pound and is enough for two portions. For easy cooking and serving, we found it helpful to cut the strangely shaped fillets in half crosswise. These two pieces, however, are much different in shape and thickness. Knowing that they would not cook at the same rate, we found it necessary to fold the thin tailpiece in half to make it as thick as the piece from the head end of the fish.

After fitting the four pieces of cod in a glass casserole, we baked and broiled several batches. After testing a variety of oven temperatures and positions, we preferred the 14 minutes it took to cook the fish under the broiler. Positioned 6 inches from the element (ours is electric), the fish cooked through evenly with no ill effects on texture or flavor. Because cod is a relatively wet fish, it stands up well to the broiler's intense heat. We did have decent results in a hot (450-degree) oven, but the baking time was longer than the broiling time, and we still needed to switch the broiler on to brown the crumbs, and so broiling it was.

Although we had now developed a good cooking method, these initial tests drove home how bland the flavor of cod really is. No amount of lemon juice squeezed onto the fish at the table could turn it into a tasty meal. In an effort to zip up the bland cod, we tried broiling the fish with both butter and lemon juice. As the fish broiled, it

501

soaked up some of these flavors and released some of its moisture. The fish not only turned out a bit more seasoned, but a flavorful little sauce was created in the pan. By adding some sautéed shallot and garlic and some fresh parsley to the butter and lemon juice, we brought the cod to a new level, where it tasted both impressive and clean. With a heavy-handed dose of salt and black pepper, we had discovered an easy way to make scrod worth eating.

The final component of Boston baked scrod is the toasted crumbs of bread that garnish the top of each portion. Adding both texture and flavor, these crumbs are not only an authentic part of the recipe but help to raise it above the humdrum. Prepackaged bread crumbs were disappointingly bland and heavy, adding only a sandy crunch. Fresh bread crumbs, on the other hand, simply absorbed moisture as the fish cooked, turning wet and sodden instead of toasting. Only toasted homemade bread crumbs contributed the seasoning and texture we were after. Made by processing and toasting several slices of high-quality sandwich bread and then seasoning them with salt, black pepper, and fresh parsley, these crumbs needed only a minute under the broiler to adhere to the fish and heat through. Topped with these crunchy, flavorful crumbs, the well-seasoned fillets of cod and their impromptu sauce are the best representatives of Boston baked scrod we've ever tasted.

Boston Baked Scrod

SERVES 4

Cod fillets average about 1 pound at most markets. If you cut each fillet in half crosswise, you will have enough for 4 servings. To keep the thinner piece from the tail end from overcooking, fold these pieces in half before placing them in the casserole dish.

TOPPING

2	slices high-quality sandwich bread, such as Pepperidge Farm, quartered
1	tablespoon minced fresh parsley leaves
1/4	teaspoon salt
1/8	teaspoon ground black pepper

SCROD

5	tablespoons unsalted butter, melted
1	medium shallot, minced
1	small garlic clove, minced or pressed through a garlic press
1 1/2	tablespoons juice from 1 lemon
1	tablespoon minced fresh parsley leaves
	Salt and ground black pepper
2	skinless scrod cod fillets (about 1 pound each), cut in half crosswise

1. FOR THE TOPPING: Adjust one oven rack to the upper-middle position (about 6 inches from the heat source) and the second rack to the middle position; heat the oven to 400 degrees.

2. Pulse the bread in a food processor until processed into fairly even 1/4-inch pieces (about the size of Grape-Nuts cereal), about ten 1-second pulses. Spread the crumbs evenly on a rimmed baking sheet; toast on the lower rack, shaking the pan once or twice, until golden brown and crisp, 4 to 5 minutes. Toss the bread crumbs, parsley, salt, and pepper together in a small bowl.

3. FOR THE SCROD: Increase the oven setting to broil. Melt the butter in a small skillet over medium-high heat until the foaming has subsided. Reduce the heat to medium and add the shallot and garlic and sauté until slightly softened, about 1 minute. Remove the pan from the heat; add the lemon juice, parsley, 1/4 teaspoon salt, and 1/8 teaspoon pepper and swirl to incorporate. Remove the pan from the heat and set aside.

4. Season the scrod liberally with salt and pepper. Fold the thin tailpieces in half to increase their thickness. Place the fillets in a shallow 13 by 9-inch casserole and pour the melted butter mixture over them. Broil until the fish is completely opaque when gently flaked with a paring knife, 14 to 15 minutes. Baste the fish with the pan drippings and top with the bread crumbs. Continue broiling until the crumbs are golden brown, about 1 minute. Using a metal spatula, transfer the fish to individual plates and pour the basting juices around the edges of the fish (not on top, or the bread crumbs will become soggy). Serve immediately.

PAN-FRIED CATFISH

IT WAS NOT TOO LONG AGO THAT CATFISH, common in the Low Country—the coastal areas of South Carolina and Georgia, where it flourished in local waters—was considered junk fish. Times have changed, and today catfish is highly sought after and expensive. Although we found pan-frying catfish to be very similar to pan-frying other fish, we did stumble upon differences unique to catfish.

First off, most catfish found at the store is farm-raised in fresh water, although ocean catfish (also known as wolffish) can occasionally be found. While the oddly sized fillets of ocean catfish (some are mammoth and others tiny) don't easily lend themselves to pan-frying, we found the average farm-raised freshwater fillets usually weigh in at around three quarters of a pound. Two fillets of farm-raised catfish will easily serve four people, and we found it best to cut each fillet in half down the middle so that each portion has a thin tail end and a thicker middle. This ensures that each half fillet will cook at the same rate and that each person will have the same ratio of crisp, fried tail to tender, flaky flesh. We also discovered that it was necessary to remove the skin and the tissue that lies directly underneath it. While the skin offended no one, the dark fatty tissue was very fishy-tasting and unappealing.

We found that these fillets benefited from being dredged in flour, dipped in an egg wash, and finally coated with a seasoned cornmeal-flour mixture. Also, they browned beautifully and cooked through in only a matter of minutes—great for a weeknight dinner.

Pan-Fried Catfish

SERVES 4

To minimize splatters and maximize safety, use a Dutch oven with sides at least 5 inches high (not a regular skillet) when pan-frying the fish.

I   cup unbleached all-purpose flour
$\frac{1}{2}$ cup fine cornmeal
    Salt and ground black pepper
$\frac{1}{8}$ teaspoon cayenne pepper
2   large eggs
$2\frac{1}{2}$ cups vegetable oil for frying, or as needed
2   catfish fillets (about 12 ounces each), skin and dark fatty flesh just below the skin removed, fillets cut in half lengthwise
    Lemon wedges or one of the dipping sauces on page 529, for serving

1. Set a wire rack over a rimmed baking sheet, place the sheet on the middle oven rack, and heat the oven to 200 degrees. Place ½ cup of the flour in a wide, shallow dish. In a another wide, shallow dish, mix together the remaining ½ cup flour, the cornmeal, 1 teaspoon salt, ¼ teaspoon black pepper, and the cayenne. In a third shallow dish, whisk the eggs with 1 tablespoon of the oil until combined.

2. Pat the fish fillets dry with paper towels and sprinkle each side with salt and pepper to taste. Drop the fish into the flour and shake the dish to coat. Shake the excess flour from each piece, then, using tongs, dip the fillets into the egg mixture, turning to coat well and allowing the excess to drip off. Coat the fillets with the cornmeal mixture, shake off the excess, and lay them on another wire rack set over a rimmed baking sheet.

3. Heat ½ inch oil in a large, heavy-bottomed Dutch oven over high heat until the oil reaches a temperature of 400 degrees. (The oil should not smoke, but it will come close.) Place 2 catfish fillets in the hot oil and fry, turning once, until golden brown, about 4 minutes. Adjust the heat as necessary to keep the oil between 385 and 390 degrees. Remove the fillets from the oil with a slotted spoon and lay them on a plate lined with several layers of paper towels; blot to remove any excess oil. Transfer the fried fish to the wire rack in the warm oven. Bring the oil back to 400 degrees and repeat the cooking process with the remaining fish fillets. Serve the fried fish immediately with either lemon wedges or dipping sauce.

PAN-ROASTED HALIBUT

WITH ITS NATURALLY LEAN, FIRM TEXTURE AND clean, mild flavor, halibut is often preferred braised rather than roasted or sautéed because this moist-heat cooking technique keeps the fish from drying out. The downside, however, is that braising does not develop as much flavor as other methods, producing fish the test kitchen considers lackluster. So we set out to discover a cooking method that not only added flavor but also produced a perfectly cooked, moist, and tender piece of fish.

Before addressing the questions of technique and sauce, we took to the supermarkets and fishmongers to settle on the best cut of halibut with which to proceed. Fillets, we learned, come from smaller fish and are rare, so we ruled them out. By virtue of availability, halibut steaks were a better choice. But steaks vary considerably in size depending on the weight of the particular fish, which typically ranges from 15 to 50 pounds but can reach up to 300 pounds.

After buying more than 40 pounds of halibut, our advice is this: Inspect the steaks in the fish case and choose the two that are closest in size. This approach ensures that the steaks will cook at the same rate, thus avoiding the problem of overcooking the smaller one. We found the best size steak for the home cook to be between 10 and 12 inches in length and roughly 1¼ inches thick (see "Three Kinds of Halibut Steak" on page 506). We did test thinner and thicker steaks, adjusting the cooking time as necessary, and had success on both counts. We also tried halibut steaks that we purchased frozen. The flavor matched that of the fresh fish,

TRIMMING CARTILAGE

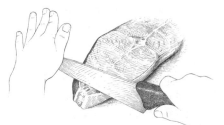

Cutting off the cartilage at the ends of the steaks ensures that they will fit neatly in the pan and diminishes the likelihood that the small bones located there will wind up on your dinner plate.

but tasters were disappointed in the texture, which they found mushy and fibrous.

Keeping in mind that we wanted to brown the fish to develop flavor, we tested two different techniques: skillet-cooking on the stovetop and roasting in the oven at 500 degrees. Neither was ideal. The skillet-seared fish browned nicely but became a little dry. The roasted sample was moist and evenly cooked, but it barely browned and had little flavor; we craved some of the browning from the skillet to intensify the flavor. To achieve this, we chose a common restaurant technique and combined the methods.

First we seared the fish in a heavy-duty, oven-proof skillet on the stovetop, and then we put the whole thing—pan and fish—into the oven to finish cooking. This approach was an improvement, but we still had a problem. Our efforts to brown the fish sufficiently to enhance its flavor usually caused it to overcook.

After much additional testing, we finally hit on the solution. Instead of sautéing the fish on both sides, we seared it on one side only, flipped it in the pan, and then placed it in the oven to finish with the seared side up. This worked beautifully, combining the enhanced flavor of browned fish with the moist interior that came from finishing in the oven's even heat. Finally, moist fish with great sautéed flavor.

Next we explored a few refinements. All home cooks know that fish sticks to the pan, and a nonstick skillet is the common solution to this problem. In this case, however, we feared that many nonstick skillets would not be truly oven-worthy, so we had to solve the sticking problem that came with the use of a traditional skillet. We knew that success would lie in a well-preheated pan. In a skillet preheated over high heat for just one minute, the fish stuck like crazy. After two minutes, it stuck a little bit. What did the trick was 2½ minutes of preheating over high heat, or just until the oil started to smoke.

We also tried searing the halibut in different fats. Butter burned badly, even when combined with oil. The best choice was pure olive oil, the richness of which tasters welcomed over vegetable oil.

Oven temperatures were up next for testing,

and we tried four settings: 425, 450, 475, and 500 degrees. Finding no discernible difference in the fish roasted at any of these temperatures, we opted for 425 degrees because it offered the greatest margin for error. (The slower the oven, the longer the window of time for doneness.) Timing was another key to moist, perfectly cooked fish. For the type and thickness of steaks we were using, we found that six minutes of oven time left the fish a bit underdone. At roughly nine minutes the flakes were opaque, but they had not sacrificed any moisture or tenderness.

In addition to timing, we wanted to determine if there were other reliable clues as to when the fish was done properly. Evie Hansen, director of marketing for National Seafood Educators and author of several seafood cookbooks, noted that for health safety reasons, the U.S. Food and Drug Administration suggests a final internal temperature of 140 degrees on an instant-read thermometer. We tested this suggested temperature and concur.

With the fish seared and roasted properly, all we needed was a sauce or two to accompany it. Though we usually think of making an easy sauce from the drippings left in the pan, in this case that was not an option because the pan was overheated from the hot oven. After trying a variety of relishes, salsas, flavored butters, and vinaigrettes, tasters all agreed that they preferred a sauce with some richness (that is, fat) to complement the lean fish. Flavored butters were easy to prepare and

SERVING HALIBUT STEAKS

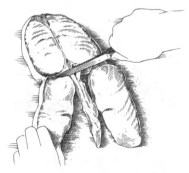

Remove the skin from the cooked steaks and separate each quadrant of meat from the bones by slipping a spatula or knife gently between them. Transfer the pieces of fish to a warm serving platter.

fit the bill in terms of richness, as did vinaigrette because of its olive oil.

Pan-Roasted Halibut Steaks
SERVES 4 TO 6

This recipe calls for a heavy ovenproof skillet. If you plan to serve the fish with one of the flavored butters or the vinaigrette on page 506, prepare it before cooking the fish. Even well-dried fish can cause the hot oil in the pan to splatter. You can minimize splattering by laying the halibut steaks in the pan gently and putting the edge closest to you in the pan first so the far edge falls away from you.

2   tablespoons olive oil
2   (full) halibut steaks (see the photos on
    page 506), about 1¼ inches thick and
    10 to 12 inches long (about 2½ pounds total),
    gently rinsed, dried well with paper towels,
    and trimmed of cartilage at both ends (see
    the illustration on page 504)
    Salt and ground black pepper
    Flavored butter or sauce (recipes follow)

1. Adjust an oven rack to the middle position and heat the oven to 425 degrees. When the oven reaches 425 degrees, heat the oil in a 12-inch heavy-bottomed ovenproof skillet over high heat until the oil just begins to smoke.

2. Meanwhile, sprinkle both sides of both halibut steaks generously with salt and pepper. Reduce the heat to medium-high and swirl the oil in the pan to distribute; carefully lay the steaks in the pan and sear, without moving them, until spotty brown, about 4 minutes (if the steaks are thinner than 1¼ inches, check browning at 3½ minutes; thicker steaks of 1½ inches may require extra time, so check at 4½ minutes). Off the heat, flip the steaks over in the pan using two thin bladed metal spatulas (see the illustration on page 499).

3. Transfer the skillet to the oven and roast until an instant-read thermometer inserted into the steaks reads 140 degrees, and the fish flakes loosen and the flesh is opaque when checked with the tip of a paring knife, about 9 minutes (thicker steaks may take up to 10 minutes). Remove the skillet from the oven and, following the illustration at left,

separate the skin and bones from the fish with a spatula. Transfer the fish to a warm platter and serve immediately with a flavored butter or sauce.

Chipotle-Garlic Butter with Lime and Cilantro

MAKES ABOUT ¼ CUP

4   tablespoons (½ stick) unsalted butter, softened
1   medium chipotle chile in adobo sauce, seeded and minced, plus 1 teaspoon adobo sauce
1   medium garlic clove, minced or pressed through a garlic press
1   teaspoon honey
1   teaspoon grated zest from 1 lime
2   teaspoons minced fresh cilantro leaves
½   teaspoon salt

Beat the butter with a fork until light and fluffy. Stir in the remaining ingredients until thoroughly combined. Dollop a portion of the butter over the pieces of hot cooked fish and allow the butter to melt. Serve immediately.

Anchovy-Garlic Butter with Lemon and Parsley

MAKES ABOUT ¼ CUP

4   tablespoons (½ stick) unsalted butter, softened
1   anchovy fillet, minced to a paste
1   medium garlic clove, minced or pressed through a garlic press
1½ teaspoons juice from 1 lemon
2   tablespoons minced fresh parsley leaves
½   teaspoon salt

Beat the butter with a fork until light and fluffy. Stir in the remaining ingredients until thoroughly combined. Dollop a portion of the butter over the pieces of hot cooked fish and allow the butter to melt. Serve immediately.

Chunky Cherry Tomato–Basil Vinaigrette

MAKES ABOUT 1½ CUPS

½   pint cherry or grape tomatoes, each tomato quartered (about 1 cup)
¼   teaspoon salt
¼   teaspoon ground black pepper
2   medium shallots, minced (about 3 tablespoons)
2   tablespoons minced fresh basil leaves
3   tablespoons juice from 1 lemon
6   tablespoons extra-virgin olive oil

Mix the tomatoes with the salt and pepper in a medium bowl; let stand until juicy and seasoned, about 10 minutes. Whisk the shallots, basil, lemon juice, and oil together in a small mixing bowl, pour the vinaigrette over the tomatoes, and toss to combine. Pour over the pieces of hot cooked fish and serve immediately.

THREE KINDS OF HALIBUT STEAK

Most halibut steaks consist of four pieces of meat attached to a central bone (left). It is not uncommon, however, to encounter a steak with just two pieces, both located on the same side of the center bone (center). These steaks were cut from the center of the halibut, adjacent to the belly cavity. The belly, in effect, separates the two halves. We slightly preferred full steaks with four meat sections; each full steak serves two or three people. If you can find only the belly steaks, you will have to purchase four steaks instead of two to make the recipe. Avoid very small, boneless steaks (right) cut entirely free from the bone and each other. Most boneless steaks won't serve even one person.

PAN-SEARED SALMON

BECAUSE SALMON IS SO RICH AND FLAVORFUL, we wanted a method for preparing it that would exploit the fish's high oil content and natural moistness while also indulging our taste for fish that comes out of the pan with a crisp, even, deeply golden crust. So we zeroed in on exploring the technique of pan-searing over a relatively high heat on the stovetop. Requiring little time and equipment, pan-searing heightens the flavor of the salmon and produces an appealing contrast in texture. Or at least it does when the fish is cooked right. In the past, we have struggled to attain the perfect degree of doneness. Our fish was often overcooked to the point of being dry and chalky as we tried to create a nice crust, or, in an effort to protect against overcooking, we ended up with a poor crust.

The amount and type of fat to use was a real wild card in our research. There were recipes using everything from butter to canola oil, in quantities ranging from five tablespoons down to no fat at all for four fillets.

We chose the extreme first, cooking four fillets with no fat in the pan. Though salmon supplies plenty of its own fat and a nonstick pan eliminates sticking problems, these fillets developed uneven, blotchy, unappealing crusts, especially on the skin side. Some fat in the pan, we thought, would improve matters. So we cooked four fillets in amounts ranging from one to three tablespoons of canola oil, moving in one-half tablespoon increments. These larger amounts might work well for lean fish, but for a fatty fish such as salmon even one tablespoon of oil was too much. Eventually, we found that a mere teaspoon of fat in a large skillet was all we needed to promote a deep, even crust on both sides of the fillets.

We also experimented with different types of fat in our research. To risk repeating, salmon is extremely rich to begin with, and butter simply pushed it over the top (not to mention the fact that it burned). The flavor of olive oil seemed at odds with the fish, and a butter–olive oil combination offered no advantage. Cooking spray was subpar. Peanut oil worked nicely, as did both canola and vegetable oil. Because these two oils are more of a staple than peanut oil and are neutral in flavor, they were our first choice. Some recipes suggested oiling the fillets themselves instead of the pan, but this practice diminished the crust we wanted.

While we were at it, we also tried dredging the fish in a coating meant to cook up crisp, including seasoned flour, bread crumbs, and cornmeal, but we disliked them all for uneven browning, dull flavor, and pasty texture.

Without a doubt, the type of pan would be an important variable. The good news concerning pans was that every one of the four we tried—including a cheap, thin stainless steel model, heavy-bottomed stainless steel and nonstick models, and our faithful cast-iron skillet—produced a decent crust. Though the nonstick pan ensured easy cleanup and no sticking, the crust it developed was marginally less deep than the others, and the necessary preheating of the pan is not kind to the nonstick finish. The heavy stainless steel and cast-iron pans produced exemplary crusts, while the lighter, cheaper pan scorched almost fatally during cooking. While any one of them will work, our favorites were the heavy stainless steel and cast-iron models. Whichever pan you choose, make sure it is large enough to accommodate the fillets comfortably; the edges of the fillets should not touch, as this can cause steaming, instead of searing, to occur. We found a 12-inch skillet to be just right.

Preheating the pan and choosing the right heat for cooking the fish were also critical. We tried preheating for lengths of time ranging from one to five minutes and found that three minutes over high heat did the trick, regardless of whether the stove is gas or electric. But the high heat was too much once the fish was in the pan, cooking it too fast and producing billows of smoke, so we reduced the heat to medium-high. Because the pan loses some heat when the fish is added, we waited about 30 seconds before reducing the flame so the pan could regain some of the lost heat.

Timing, of course, was also crucial. We did not want to overcook the salmon. Because our fillets were consistently 1¼ inches thick, we decided to start by following the old kitchen maxim of 10 minutes per inch of thickness. The fish overcooked. It overcooked at 10 minutes and at nine minutes, too. At eight minutes, though, it undercooked ever so slightly. Fortunately, as with many cuts of meat, we learned that salmon fillets have enough residual heat to continue cooking briefly after they come out of the pan. In fact, we found that a one-minute rest before serving brought the eight-minute fillets to a perfect medium with no danger of overcooking.

Though many sources suggest shaking the pan after adding the salmon to prevent sticking, we found this step to be unnecessary. Provided that the pan is hot enough and the fat is shimmering, we decided it is best to just drop the fillet skin-side down in the pan and leave it be. When the fish turns opaque and milky white from the bottom to about halfway up the fillet, it's time to flip it. Then simply slide a thin, flexible metal spatula between the pan bottom and the skin and flip it quickly so the flesh side is down; make sure not to move the fish for the first two minutes. After that, you can lift it gently at the corner with the spatula to check the bottom crust. We also suggest peeking inside the fillet with the tip of a paring knife. The center should still show traces of bright, translucent orange. If it is completely opaque and the orange color is a little duller, as it is toward the exterior of the fillet, the fish is overcooked.

Pan-Seared Salmon

SERVES 4

With the addition of the fish fillets, the pan temperature drops. Compensate for the heat loss by keeping the heat on high for 30 seconds after adding the fillets to the pan. If cooking 2 or 3 fillets instead of the full recipe of 4, use a 10-inch skillet and medium-high heat for both preheating the pan and cooking the salmon. A splatter screen helps reduce the mess of pan-searing. Serve salmon with chutney (recipe follows), a fresh salsa, an herb-spiked vinaigrette, or lemon or lime wedges.

4	center-cut salmon fillets, 1¼ inches thick (about 6 ounces each), pinbones removed (see the illustration on page 509)
	Salt and ground black pepper
1	teaspoon canola or vegetable oil

1. Heat a 12-inch heavy-bottomed skillet over high heat for 3 minutes. Sprinkle the salmon with salt and pepper to taste.

2. Add the oil to the pan and swirl to coat the bottom. When the oil shimmers (but does not smoke), add the fillets skin-side down and cook, without moving, until the pan regains lost heat, about 30 seconds. Reduce the heat to medium-high; continue to cook until the skin side is well browned and the bottom half of the fillets turn opaque, 4½ minutes. Turn the fillets and cook, without moving them, until they are no longer translucent on the exterior and are firm, but not hard, when gently squeezed: 3 minutes for medium-rare and 3½ minutes for medium. Remove the fillets from the pan to a platter and let stand for 1 minute. Pat the fillets with paper towels to absorb excess fat, if desired. Serve immediately.

➤ VARIATIONS

Pan-Seared Salmon with Sesame Crust
For heightened sesame flavor, rub the fish fillets with toasted sesame oil instead of canola or vegetable oil.

Spread ¼ cup sesame seeds in a pie plate. Follow the recipe for Pan-Seared Salmon, rubbing the fillets with 2 teaspoons canola or vegetable oil, sprinkling them with salt and pepper to taste, and then pressing the flesh sides of the fillets into the sesame seeds to coat. Continue with the recipe, being careful not to break the sesame crust when removing the fillets from the pan.

Sweet-and-Sour Chutney

MAKES ENOUGH FOR 4 SALMON FILLETS

This condiment, which should be served warm or at room temperature, is intensely flavored. Use with discretion.

1	teaspoon fennel seeds
½	teaspoon ground cumin
½	teaspoon ground coriander
¼	teaspoon ground cardamom
¼	teaspoon paprika
¼	teaspoon salt
2	teaspoons olive oil
½	medium onion, chopped fine (about ½ cup)
¼	cup red wine vinegar

1 tablespoon sugar
2 tablespoons water
1 tablespoon minced fresh parsley leaves

Mix the fennel seeds, cumin, coriander, cardamom, paprika, and salt together in a small bowl. Heat the oil in a medium skillet over medium heat, add the onion, and sauté until soft, 3 to 4 minutes. Add the spice mixture and sauté until fragrant, about 1 minute. Increase the heat to medium-high and add the vinegar, sugar, and water; cook until the mixture is reduced by about one third and reaches a syrupy consistency, about 1½ minutes. Stir in the parsley. Remove from the heat and set aside. Serve with pan-seared salmon.

BROILED SALMON

SALMON IS A SUREFIRE CROWD-PLEASER, BUT it's not always easy to make for a crowd. Pan-searing individual portions is not complicated, but it can get cumbersome with too many pieces of fish. So we set out to find the best way of cooking a whole side of salmon, enough to feed eight or more guests, in the oven. We wanted fish that was moist but not soggy, firm but not chalky, and nicely crusted, with golden, flavorful caramelization over its flesh. If we could work some interesting flavors and contrasting textures into the bargain, all the better.

Creating some flavorful caramelization on the flesh of the fish was a key goal, so we focused right away on high-heat cooking. Baking, though it seemed like a natural choice, was out because it implies cooking in a moderate, 350-degree oven, which would never brown the fish. Heating things up from there, we tested roasting at oven temperatures of 400, 450, and 500 degrees. To our surprise, none of them worked well. Even at 500 degrees, on a preheated baking sheet, the fish remained pale owing to the necessarily short (16-minute) cooking time; any more time in the oven, and the fish would overcook. Another source of consternation was moisture—not the lack of it, as we might have expected—but an excess. The abundance of fat and collagen in the

farmed Atlantic salmon we were cooking melted during roasting, giving the fish an overly wet, slippery texture and fatty mouthfeel.

Broiling was the next step up in heat, and here we met with some success. The salmon browned nicely under the intense broiler heat and, as a result, also developed better flavor. Some of the copious moisture evaporated, leaving the fish with a much-improved texture—drier and more firm, yet still juicy. None of the broiling and roasting combinations we went on to try topped broiling from start to finish. We were on the right track to be sure, but plain broiled salmon was not terribly inspiring. If we were going to serve this to a crowd of people at a weekend dinner party, a flavor boost and some textural interest would be absolutely necessary.

The addition of an interesting topping for the fish could, we thought, achieve both goals. Dried bread crumbs came immediately to mind—and departed almost as quickly once we tasted them. The flavor was lackluster and the texture akin to sawdust. Our favorite Japanese panko crumbs were judged too light of flavor and feathery of texture. Fresh bread crumbs were a crisp improvement,

PREPARING THE SALMON

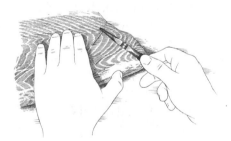

1. Run your fingers over the surface to feel for pinbones, then remove them with tweezers or needle-nosed pliers.

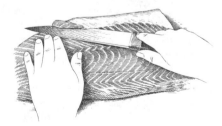

2. Hold a sharp chef's knife at a slight downward angle to the flesh and cut off and discard the whitish, fatty portion of the belly.

and toasted fresh bread crumbs laced with garlic, herbs, and butter were better still. But there were more avenues to explore.

Dry spice rubs, similar to what we might apply to the fish if grilling, met with mixed results. Glazes and spice pastes won praise for their flavor, but since they themselves were wet, they added little in the way of texture.

Potatoes were another topping possibility. Potato crusts on fish are typically engineered by laying paper-thin slices of potato on the fish and sautéing it on the stovetop. Testing proved that the slices would not form a cohesive crust without the direct heat of a hot pan. In addition, we couldn't slice them thin enough without the help of a mandoline. But because tasters loved the potato flavor, we tried some other methods. A crust of grated raw potatoes remained too loose and crunchy. Sautéing the grated potato before applying it to the fish helped some, but not enough, while completely precooking the potatoes robbed them of both flavor and texture.

Clinging tenaciously to the notion of potato flavor while groping for another way to build a crisp, crunchy texture, one test cook smirked and suggested, half in jest, that we try crushed potato chips. Everyone in the test kitchen laughed, but after settling down we looked at one another and said, practically in unison, "Let's try it." Imagine our astonishment, then, at the overwhelming success of chips. Though a bit greasy and heavy on their own, they offered just what we were looking for in a crust: great potato flavor and crunch that wouldn't quit. After lightening the chips up by mixing in some fresh toasted bread crumbs and adding dill for complementary flavor, we found ourselves with an excellent, if unorthodox, topping. We also found that the chips made a rich foil for some of the other flavors we wanted to add.

Because the chips brown under the broiler in a minute—literally—we broiled the fish until it was almost cooked through before adding the topping. This gave us just the texture we wanted. After adding a flavorful wet element (mustard) to help the crumbs adhere to the fish, we knew we had it: a quick, oven-cooked, well-flavored, texturally interesting—and surprising—salmon dinner for eight.

Broiled Salmon with Mustard and Crisp Potato Crust
SERVES 8 TO 10

Heavy-duty foil measuring 18 inches wide is essential for creating a sling that aids in transferring the cooked fillet to a cutting board. Use a large baking sheet so that the salmon will lie flat. If you can't get the fish to lie flat, even when positioning it diagonally on the baking sheet, trim the tail end. If you prefer to cook a smaller 2-pound fillet, ask to have it cut from the thick center of the fillet, not the thin tail end, and begin checking doneness a minute earlier.

SERVING THE SALMON

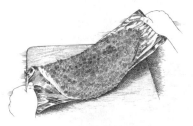

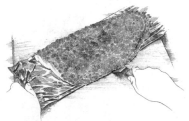

1. Grasp the foil overhang at both ends; lift it carefully and set the fish on the cutting board.

2. Slide an offset spatula under the thick end. Grasp the foil, press the spatula down against the foil, and slide it under the fish down to the thin end, loosening the entire side of the fish.

3. Grasp the foil again, hold the spatula perpendicular to the fish to stabilize it, and pull the foil out from under the fish. Use a moist paper towel to clean the board and serve immediately.

3   slices high-quality sandwich bread, such as
    Pepperidge Farm, crusts removed
4   ounces high-quality plain potato chips,
    crushed into rough 1/8-inch pieces (about
    1 cup)
6   tablespoons chopped fresh dill
1   whole side of salmon fillet (about 3 1/2
    pounds), pinbones removed and belly fat
    trimmed (see the illustrations on page 509)
1   teaspoon olive oil
3/4 teaspoon salt
    Ground black pepper
3   tablespoons Dijon mustard

1. Adjust one oven rack to the uppermost position (about 3 inches from the heat source) and the second rack to the upper-middle position; heat the oven to 400 degrees.

2. Pulse the bread in a food processor until processed into fairly even 1/4-inch pieces about the size of Grape-Nuts cereal (you should have about 1 cup), about ten 1-second pulses. Spread the crumbs evenly on a rimmed baking sheet and toast on the lower rack, shaking the pan once or twice, until golden brown and crisp, 4 to 5 minutes. Toss the bread crumbs, crushed potato chips, and dill together in a small bowl.

3. Increase the oven setting to broil. Cut a piece of heavy-duty foil 6 inches longer than the fillet. Fold the foil lengthwise in thirds and place lengthwise on a rimmed baking sheet; position the salmon lengthwise on the foil, allowing the excess foil to hang over the baking sheet. Rub the fillet evenly with the oil and sprinkle with the salt and pepper to taste. Broil the salmon on the upper rack until the surface is spotty brown and the outer 1/2 inch of the thick end is opaque when gently flaked with a paring knife, 9 to 11 minutes. Remove the fish from the oven, spread evenly with the mustard, and press the bread crumb mixture onto the fish. Return to the lower rack and continue broiling until the crust is deep golden brown, about 1 minute longer.

4. Following the illustrations on page 510, transfer the salmon and foil sling to a cutting board, remove the sling, and serve the salmon from the board.

➤ VARIATIONS

Broiled Salmon with Barbecue Sauce and Crisp Potato Crust

Follow the recipe for Broiled Salmon with Mustard and Crisp Potato Crust, replacing the mustard with 3 tablespoons barbecue sauce.

Broiled Salmon with Horseradish and Crisp Potato Crust

Heat 3 tablespoons unsalted butter in a small skillet over medium heat until foaming; sauté 1/2 cup minced shallots until softened and translucent, about 2 minutes. Off the heat, add 1/2 cup prepared horseradish and 1 tablespoon sugar. Follow the recipe for Broiled Salmon with Mustard and Crisp Potato Crust, substituting 1 tablespoon fresh thyme leaves for the dill and the horseradish mixture for the Dijon mustard.

SALMON CAKES

OUR IDEAL SALMON CAKE IS TOOTHSOME, tender, and moist on the inside; crisp and golden brown on the outside; shapely; and firm and cohesive throughout. But we encountered many potholes on the road to that ideal. Salmon cakes often suffer from a texture that is either dry, overprocessed, and mushy, or wet, loose, and underbound. Fresh salmon flavor may be close to nonexistent, replaced by a distracting amalgam of mismatched seasonings. The exterior coating may be lackluster.

To begin, we started with the fish for our cakes. Based on our experience with three different brands of canned salmon, we wouldn't for a minute consider it. Full of bones and skin that made cleaning a real hassle, all three brands were utterly unappealing in terms of appearance, smell, taste, and texture. When it came to considering leftover cooked fish, we asked around among home cooks. Everyone we interviewed reported buying only as much fish as could be eaten in a single meal; leftover cooked fish is simply not something most people have on hand. That was the first good reason we found to make these salmon cakes with fresh fish.

Despite the break with both tradition and the dictate of most current recipes, it was easy to find other good reasons for using fresh fish. The savings of time and effort were high on the list. We simply couldn't see the point of bringing home a beautiful, fresh salmon fillet and then going to the trouble of cooking it twice, once to make "leftovers" and then again to make cakes. In addition to that, we wanted to take advantage of the collagen, a structural protein found in raw fish (and meat) that melts when cooked and provides natural moisture and binding capacity. Both characteristics would be boons to the cakes' texture that precooking the salmon would eliminate. Last, the raw fish would provide a hedge against overcooking and, consequently, drying out the cakes.

Having decided to use fresh fish, we next tried a couple of methods for breaking it down. Predictably, the food processor ground the fish too finely for our tastes, even when we proceeded with the greatest care. As it turned out, chopping the fish by hand was not difficult, and it provided a far greater margin of error in terms of over-processing than did the food processor.

The collagen in the fish gave us a great head start in binding the cakes, but it couldn't do the job entirely on its own. Without additional binders, the cakes had a chunky, heavy texture and such strong salmon flavor that some tasters were overwhelmed. Common choices for binders included eggs, either whole or yolks alone, and mayonnaise. Of the many egg combinations we tried, the yolks alone worked best. But when we tried mayonnaise, everyone preferred it over the egg yolks. Just 2 tablespoons of mayonnaise for the 1¼ pounds of chopped fish we were using added a noticeable creaminess to the texture and a welcome tang to the flavor.

Starchy products—including cooked potato, crushed crackers, dry and fresh bread crumbs, and bread soaked in milk—made up another category of binders worth testing. The cooked potato produced cakes that were rubbery and dry, and both the crushed crackers and dry bread crumbs became leaden and mushy by absorbing too much moisture from the fish, not to mention the fact

that they gave the cakes a stale flavor. The milk-soaked bread showed well, but best overall were the fresh bread crumbs we made by simply mincing a piece of sturdy white sandwich bread, crusts removed. The bread lightened and softened the texture of the cakes, making them smoother and more refined. The flavor also benefited. On its own, the bread tasted slightly sweet, so it helped to balance out the strong flavor of the salmon and the creamy tang of the mayonnaise.

With the binding just right, we tried the various flavorings listed in our stack of test recipes. Maybe we're just purists, but the herbs, scallions, garlic, mustard, Worcestershire sauce, hot pepper sauce, and Old Bay seasoning all tasted out of place. In the end, the basic combination of onion, lemon juice, and parsley prevailed by providing simple, bright, fresh flavors. Some tasters objected to the crunch of the minced onion, but we quickly solved that problem by grating it to allow for better integration into the fish mixture.

The next step was to find the crisp, light, golden coating of our dreams. Some recipes left out the coating altogether, but the resulting cakes lacked interest. Flour alone soaked right into the fish mixture and became pasty when cooked. Dry bread crumbs alone were OK but uninspiring. Our stellar coating involves a full breading treatment, called anglaise, which consists of flour, beaten egg, and bread crumbs, applied in sequence. Although making the coating does entail some extra work as well as more dirty dishes, the result is well worth it: a toasty, gorgeous coating. A 15-minute stay in the freezer prior to breading, we found, firms the cakes slightly for easier handling and causes some of the surface moisture to evaporate, which helps the breading to adhere.

Perfecting the cooking procedure would be our last step. Temperature and timing were crucial to ensure that the breading browned but did not burn and that the cakes cooked through to the center without overcooking and drying out. Stovetop cooking over a medium-high flame in a large, heavy-bottomed skillet (at least 12 inches in diameter so as to accommodate eight cakes) proved to be our answer. Cooking the cakes in a generous quantity of vegetable oil—it should reach halfway up the cakes in the pan—for just two minutes per side produced a perfect golden crust and moist fish within, cooked just barely to medium. We also experimented with other fats as a cooking medium, including olive oil, butter, clarified butter, and a combination of butter and vegetable oil. But for its safety, ease of use, and convenience, vegetable oil alone remained our cooking medium of choice. Its neutral flavor allowed the balanced flavor of the fish mixture, bright seasonings, and toasty breading of these salmon cakes to really shine.

Pan-Fried Fresh Salmon Cakes

SERVES 4

A big wedge of lemon is the simplest accompaniment, but any one of the dipping sauces on page 529 is an excellent embellishment. If possible, use supercrisp panko crumbs to coat the cakes.

1¼	pounds salmon fillets
1	slice high-quality white sandwich bread, such as Pepperidge Farm, crusts removed and white part chopped very fine (about 5 tablespoons)
2	tablespoons mayonnaise
¼	cup finely grated onion
2	tablespoons chopped fresh parsley leaves
¾	teaspoon salt
1½	tablespoons juice from 1 lemon
½	cup unbleached all-purpose flour
2	large eggs, lightly beaten
1½	teaspoons plus ½ cup vegetable oil
1½	teaspoons water
¾	cup plain dry bread crumbs, preferably panko (Japanese-style bread crumbs)
	Lemon wedges or one of the dipping sauces on page 529 for serving

1. Following the illustration on page 509, locate, remove, and discard any pinbones in the salmon. Using a sharp knife, cut the flesh off the skin and discard the skin. Chop the salmon flesh into ¼- to ⅓-inch pieces and mix in a medium bowl with the chopped bread, mayonnaise, onion, parsley, salt, and lemon juice. Scoop a generous ¼-cup portion of the salmon mixture from the bowl and use your hands to form it into a patty measuring roughly 2½ inches in diameter and ¾ inch thick; place on a parchment-lined baking sheet and repeat with the remaining salmon mixture until you have 8 patties. Place the patties in the freezer until the surface moisture has evaporated, about 15 minutes.

2. Meanwhile, spread the flour in a pie plate or shallow baking dish. Beat the eggs with the 1½ teaspoons vegetable oil and the water in a second pie plate or shallow baking dish, and spread the bread crumbs in a third. Dip the chilled salmon patties, one at a time, in the flour to cover; shake off any excess. Transfer to the beaten egg and, using a slotted spatula, turn to coat; let the excess drip off. Transfer to the bread crumbs; shake the pan to coat the patties completely. Return the now-breaded patties to the baking sheet.

3. Heat the remaining ½ cup vegetable oil in a large, heavy-bottomed skillet over medium-high heat until shimmering but not smoking. Add the salmon patties and cook until medium golden brown, about 2 minutes. Flip the cakes over and continue cooking until medium golden brown on the second side, about 2 minutes longer. Transfer the cakes to a large plate lined with paper towels to absorb any excess oil on the surface, if desired, and let drain about 30 seconds. Serve with lemon wedges or dipping sauce.

➤ VARIATIONS

Pan-Fried Smoked Salmon Cakes

Follow the recipe for Pan-Fried Fresh Salmon Cakes, substituting 8 ounces smoked salmon or lox, chopped into ¼- to ⅓-inch pieces, for 8 ounces of the fresh salmon and reducing the salt to ½ teaspoon.

Pan-Fried Fresh Salmon Cakes with Cheese

Follow the recipe for Pan-Fried Fresh Salmon Cakes, adding 2 tablespoons freshly grated Parmesan or Asiago cheese to the salmon mixture and reducing the salt to ½ teaspoon.

PAN-SEARED TUNA STEAKS

A POPULAR OFFERING ON HIGH-END RES- taurant menus, great pan-seared tuna makes a spectacularly simple dinner entrée. Done well, the fish should have a deeply seared crust that envel- ops a tender, moist, plum-red interior. Now that high-quality tuna is readily available in markets, we turned to mastering pan-seared tuna at home.

The consensus in the test kitchen was to cre- ate a master recipe for four 8-ounce steaks cooked in one pan. We started testing with ¾-inch- thick steaks, the relatively thin ones sold in some supermarkets. The heat from searing these steaks traveled through them too quickly; the tuna lost its rare look, feel, and taste. Next up were steaks cut 1 inch thick. The extra ¼ inch made a big difference; the centers of these steaks were rare when removed from the pan, at which point they registered 110 degrees on an instant-read ther- mometer. Curious about the still-cold-at-the- center tuna served in restaurants, we did another test. Our fishmonger cut 1½-inch steaks, and we cooked them up. The centers of these steaks reg- istered only 75 degrees. If you want the inside of your tuna steaks still cold (we prefer them at least warm), seek out these thicker specimens.

To see which type of tuna would work best, we purchased the four most likely contenders— bigeye, bluefin, yellowfin, and albacore—just one hour after they arrived at a fish market on Martha's Vineyard. (All of the tuna had been caught that day in the waters around the island.) A couple of hours later, 16 experienced (and grateful) home cooks gathered for the most expensive tasting they've ever attended. When the results were tallied, yellowfin was the clear favorite. (See "Fresh Tuna Buying Guide" on page 516 for the details.)

Knowing that a crispy crust would be a chal- lenge without the horsepower of a commercial range, we started with a very hot skillet and 2 tablespoons of oil. Unfortunately, the tuna did not develop the deep brown crust that we were after. Because tuna is such a lean fish, we thought to use more fat. Still no deep brown crust.

THE EFFECTS OF CARRY-OVER COOKING

1 MINUTE AFTER COOKING	10 MINUTES AFTER COOKING

These two tuna steaks were cooked in the same pan for the same amount of time. The piece on the left was cut immediately after it was removed from the pan; the center is rare. The piece on the right was placed on a plate and covered loosely with foil for 10 min- utes before slicing; the center of this steak has cooked to medium because of carry-over cooking. The internal heat that the steak picked up from the pan continues to cook the tuna while it rests. If you want your tuna rare, slice the steak as soon as it is removed from the pan to release the internal heat.

We began to realize that we would need some sort of coating for the steaks and started by testing crushed peppercorns, putting a liberal amount on both sides of the steaks. The flavor of the peppercorns was overpowering, however, and the high heat caused them to burn. We reduced the quantity as well as the heat level (from high to medium-high) and obtained much better results. Or at least we thought so. Some tasters objected to the presence of peppercorns in any quantity, thinking that they competed with the flavor of the tuna. Because several other tast- ers favored the combination, we decided to make it a variation. Now we were looking for a more neutral-flavored coating for our master recipe. But whatever that coating might be, we had at least learned two things from the tests with pep- percorns. First, a nonstick skillet was necessary to prevent scorching and sticking. Second, it was best to rub the tuna with oil to help the coating adhere and then use a bit more oil in the hot pan to cook the fish.

Our next try at a coating was a blend of aro- matic spices, including cumin, coriander, and mustard seeds. Some tasters loved the sweet, hot, spicy blend of flavors, but others thought the flavors were not generic enough for a basic recipe. We then hit on the idea of sesame seeds: simple, easy to find, and neutral enough to pair with a range of other flavorings. Into the pan went another batch of steaks. They browned and formed an exquisite crust. The contrast between the crisp, crunchy, beautifully browned crust and the tender, rare interior was exactly right.

We had already discovered that the cooking time was a function of many variables, including the thickness of the steaks. We were also aware that tuna steaks (like beef) continue to cook from residual heat after they have been removed from the skillet. This allows the home cook to serve diners with different preferences; the more they want it cooked, the longer you let the steaks sit at room temperature. One curious note. While the tuna does rise in temperature as it rests, it does not need to rest, as red meat does, to evenly redistribute its juices. If a steak is done to someone's liking straight from the pan, you can slice right into it.

We tried to determine precise cooking times but concluded, given the variables of pan and stovetop, that providing exact instructions would be impossible. We tried an instant-read thermometer but found it clumsy. By the time you've taken a reading on the first steak, the second one might overcook. The solution? Use a paring knife to peek into the center before you think it is ready. You can either continue cooking or remove it from the pan and let the residual heat do the work (if the fish is almost ready).

We had cooked up more than 50 pounds of tuna to reach the simple conclusions that sesame seeds make the best crust and that the steaks must be at least 1 inch thick to achieve a rare center. As a last step, we created a few fast and flavorful sauces to complement the basic recipe. Ginger and soy headline an Asian-style dipping sauce, while oranges and avocado team up in a winter salsa. Both accompaniments come together in a few minutes and complement the rich flavor of this fish.

Pan-Seared Sesame-Crusted Tuna Steaks

SERVES 4

Most members of the test kitchen staff prefer their tuna steaks rare to medium-rare; the cooking times given in the recipe are for steaks cooked to these two degrees of doneness. For tuna steaks cooked medium, observe the timing for medium-rare, then tent the steaks loosely with foil for 5 minutes before slicing. If you prefer tuna steaks cooked so rare that they are still cold in the center, try to purchase steaks that are 1½ inches thick and cook them according to the timing below for rare steaks. Bear in mind, though, that the cooking times below are estimates; check for doneness by nicking the fish with a paring knife. To cook only two steaks, use half as many seeds, reduce the oil to 2 teaspoons both on the fish and in the pan, use a 10-inch nonstick skillet, and follow the same cooking times.

³/₄	cup sesame seeds
4	tuna steaks, about 1 inch thick (8 ounces each)
2	tablespoons vegetable oil
	Salt and ground black pepper

1. Spread the sesame seeds in a shallow baking dish or pie plate. Pat the tuna steaks dry with a paper towel; use 1 tablespoon of the oil to rub both sides of the steaks, then sprinkle with salt and pepper. Press both sides of each steak in the sesame seeds to coat.

2. Heat the remaining 1 tablespoon oil in a 12-inch nonstick skillet over high heat until just beginning to smoke and swirl to coat the pan. Add the tuna steaks and cook 30 seconds without moving the steaks. Reduce the heat to medium-high and continue to cook until the seeds are golden

SHAPES OF TUNA STEAKS

Steaks of the same thickness will cook differently depending on their shape. Triangular steaks (left) cook more slowly than rectangular steaks (right) because the heat takes longer to travel to the center.

THE NEW BEST RECIPE

brown, about 1½ minutes. Using tongs, flip the tuna steaks carefully and cook, without moving them, until golden brown on the second side, about 1½ minutes for rare (opaque at the perimeter and translucent red and cool at the center when checked with the tip of a paring knife) or 3 minutes for medium-rare (opaque at the perimeter and reddish pink at the center). To serve, cut into ¼-inch-thick slices. Serve with sauce or salsa (recipes follow), if desired.

➤ VARIATION
Pan-Seared Pepper-Crusted Tuna Steaks
Follow the recipe for Pan-Seared Sesame-Crusted Tuna Steaks, omitting the sesame seeds and pressing ½ teaspoon cracked black or white peppercorns onto each side of the oiled tuna steaks.

Ginger-Soy Sauce with Scallions
MAKES I SCANT CUP,
ENOUGH FOR 4 TUNA STEAKS
If available, serve pickled ginger and wasabi, passed separately, with the tuna and this sauce.

¼	cup soy sauce
¼	cup rice vinegar
¼	cup water
2½	teaspoons sugar
1	medium scallion, sliced thin
2	teaspoons minced fresh ginger
1½	teaspoons toasted sesame oil
½	teaspoon red pepper flakes

Combine all of the ingredients together in a small bowl, stirring to dissolve the sugar.

Avocado-Orange Salsa
MAKES ABOUT I CUP,
ENOUGH FOR 4 TUNA STEAKS
To keep the avocado from discoloring, prepare this salsa just before you cook the tuna steaks.

1	large orange, cut into segments (see page 95)
1	ripe avocado, diced medium
2	tablespoons minced red onion
4	teaspoons juice from 1 lime
1	small jalapeño chile, stemmed, seeded, and minced
2	tablespoons minced fresh cilantro leaves
	Salt

Combine all of the ingredients, including salt to taste, together in a small nonreactive bowl.

INGREDIENTS: Fresh Tuna Buying Guide

To find out which of the four varieties of tuna available to consumers in the United States would make the tastiest pan-seared tuna, we held a blind taste test. The samples were lightly salted and cooked in canola oil to provide the purest taste comparisons. The good news is that the most readily available variety—yellowfin—was the clear favorite. The tunas are listed in order of preference.

Yellowfin: The favorite of most tasters. The flavor was the "most complex—not fishy, and almost sweet." "Best texture," wrote one taster, and others agreed. Firm enough so that the pieces held together, yet very tender and smooth, with a melt-in-your-mouth quality.

Bigeye: The most intensely flavored of all the varieties, with an "almost meaty flavor" and the deepest red color. Tasters found the texture tender but "very wet and moist." The high water content created a problem when pan-searing. The fibers of the fish did not hold together well, and it was difficult to create a crust. A puddle of liquid formed on the plate when it was served.

Bluefin: Many tasters found that this variety had an odd aftertaste, "almost metallic," wrote one. The texture was thought to be "chewy," "slippery," and "mushy." Bluefin was even wetter than bigeye. The liquid seeped out of the fish both during pan-searing and while it sat sliced on the serving plate. So much liquid leached out while cooking that it was impossible to form a crust.

Albacore: The only variety that can legally be sold in cans labeled "white-meat" tuna. Most tasters found it bland and somewhat dry. "Best for a sandwich," commented one taster. The texture was firm but not tough. Unlike other varieties, albacore does not have a brilliant red color

PAN-SEARED SCALLOPS

SCALLOPS OFFER SEVERAL POSSIBLE CHOICES for the cook, both when shopping and when cooking. There are three main varieties of scallops—sea, bay, and calico. Sea scallops are available year-round throughout the country and are the best choice in most instances. Like all scallops, the product sold at the market is the dense, disk-shaped muscle that propels the live scallop in its shell through the water. The guts and roe are usually jettisoned at sea because they are so perishable. Ivory-colored sea scallops are usually at least an inch in diameter (and often much bigger) and look like squat marshmallows. Sometimes they are sold cut up, but we found that they can lose moisture when handled this way and are best purchased whole.

Small, cork-shaped bay scallops (about half an inch in diameter) are harvested in a small area from Cape Cod to Long Island. Bay scallops are seasonal—available from late fall through midwinter—and are very expensive, up to $20 a pound. They are delicious but nearly impossible to find outside of top restaurants.

Calico scallops are a small species (less than half an inch across and taller than they are wide) harvested in the southern United States and around the world. They are inexpensive (often priced at just a few dollars a pound) but generally not terribly good. Unlike sea and bay scallops, which are harvested by hand, calicos are shucked by machine steaming. This steaming partially cooks the scallops and gives them an opaque look. Calicos are often sold as "bays," but they are not the same thing. In our test kitchen, we found that calicos are easy to overcook and often end up with a rubbery, eraser-like texture. Our recommendation is to stick with sea scallops, unless you have access to real bay scallops.

In addition to choosing the right species, you should inquire about processing when purchasing scallops. Most scallops (by some estimates up to 90 percent of the retail supply) are dipped in a phosphate and water mixture that may also contain citric and sorbic acids. Processing extends shelf life but harms the flavor and texture of the scallop. Its naturally delicate, sweet flavor can be masked by the bitter-tasting chemicals. Even worse, during processing scallops absorb water, which is thrown off when they are cooked. You can't brown processed scallops in a skillet—they shed so much liquid that they steam.

By law, processed scallops must be identified at the wholesale level, so ask your fishmonger. Also, look at the scallops. Scallops are naturally ivory or pinkish tan; processing turns them bright white. Processed scallops are slippery and swollen and usually sitting in milky white liquid at the store. Unprocessed scallops (also called dry scallops) are sticky and flabby. If they are surrounded by any liquid (and often they are not), the juices are clear, not white.

Besides the obvious objections (why pay for water weight or processing that detracts from their natural flavor?), processed scallops are more difficult to cook. We found that sautéing to caramelize the exterior to a concentrated, nutty-flavored, brown-and-tan crust is the best way to cook scallops. The caramelized exterior greatly enhances the natural sweetness of the scallop and provides a nice crisp contrast with the tender interior.

The most common problem a cook runs into with scallops is getting a nice crust before the scallop overcooks and toughens. We started our tests by focusing on the fat in the pan. Since scallops cook quickly, we knew it would be important to choose a fat that browned efficiently. We tried butter, olive oil, canola oil, a combination of butter and oil, plus cooking in oil with a finish of butter at the end for flavor.

To preserve the creamy texture of the flesh, we cooked the scallops to medium-rare, which means the scallop is hot all the way through but the center still retains some translucence. As a scallop cooks, the soft flesh firms and you can see an opaqueness that starts at the bottom of the scallop, where it sits in the pan, and slowly creeps up toward the center. The scallop is medium-rare when the sides have firmed up and all but about the middle third of the scallop has turned opaque.

The scallops browned well in all the fats we tested, but butter produced the thickest crust and best flavor. The nutty taste of butter complements the sweetness of the scallop without compromising its delicate flavor. We tested various pans, and while the technique worked in both nonstick and regular skillets, we recommend a light-colored regular skillet so you can judge how quickly the butter is browning and regulate the heat if necessary.

Despite the origin of the word *sauté*, which means "to jump" in French, it's critical for the formation of a good crust to leave the scallop alone once it hits the pan. We found the best method for cooking was to place the scallops carefully in the pan, one at a time, with one flat side down for maximum contact with the hot pan. We turned the scallops once and browned the second flat side. The best tool for turning scallops is a pair of tongs, although a spatula can be used in a pinch.

Pan-Seared Scallops

SERVES 4

This recipe was developed for standard sea scallops, about the size of a short, squat marshmallow. If using smaller scallops, turn off the heat as soon as you turn them; they will finish cooking from the residual heat, 15 to 30 seconds longer. For very large scallops, turn the heat to low once they have browned and continue cooking for 1 minute, then turn the scallops, raise the heat to medium, and cook them at least 2 minutes on the second side.

1½   pounds sea scallops (about 30 per pound), small tendons removed (see the illustration at right)
       Salt and ground black pepper
1½   tablespoons unsalted butter

1. Sprinkle the scallops on both sides with salt and pepper to taste. Heat a large sauté pan over medium-high heat until hot, about 1 minute. Add half the butter and swirl to coat the pan bottom. Continue to heat the pan until the butter begins to turn golden brown.

2. Add half the scallops, one at a time, flat-side down. Cook, adjusting the heat as necessary to prevent the fat from burning, until the scallops are well browned, 1½ to 2 minutes. Using tongs, turn the scallops, one at a time. Cook until

medium-rare (the sides have firmed up and all but the middle third of the scallop is opaque), 30 seconds to 1½ minutes longer, depending on size. Transfer the scallops to a warm platter; cover with foil. Repeat the cooking process using the remaining butter and scallops. Serve immediately.

➤ VARIATIONS
Pan-Seared Scallops with Lemon, Shallots, and Capers

1   recipe Pan-Seared Scallops
1   medium shallot, minced
1   cup dry white wine
1   teaspoon grated zest and 1 tablespoon juice from 1 small lemon
2   tablespoons unsalted butter
2   tablespoons minced fresh parsley leaves
1   tablespoon minced capers
     Salt and ground black pepper

After searing the scallops and transferring them to a warm platter, pour off all but 1 tablespoon of the butter in the skillet and sauté the shallot in the fat until softened, 1 to 2 minutes. Add the wine and lemon zest and simmer until reduced to about ⅓ cup, 6 to 7 minutes. Off the heat, stir in the butter, parsley, lemon juice, capers, and salt and pepper to taste. Spoon the sauce over the scallops and serve at once.

REMOVING TENDONS FROM SCALLOPS

The small, rough-textured, crescent-shaped muscle that attaches the scallop to the shell will toughen when cooked. Use your fingers to peel the tendon away from the side of each scallop before cooking.

Pan-Seared Scallops with Sherry, Red Onion, Orange, and Thyme

1	recipe Pan-Seared Scallops
1/3	cup minced red onion
3/4	cup dry sherry
1/4	cup juice and 1 teaspoon grated zest from 2 oranges
1	teaspoon minced fresh thyme leaves
2	tablespoons unsalted butter
1	tablespoon juice from 1 small lemon
	Salt and ground black pepper

After searing the scallops and transferring them to a warm platter, pour off all but 1 tablespoon of the butter in the skillet and sauté the red onion in the fat until softened, 1 to 2 minutes. Add the sherry, orange juice and zest, and thyme and simmer until reduced to about ⅓ cup, 6 to 7 minutes. Off the heat, stir in the butter, lemon juice, and salt and pepper to taste. Spoon the sauce over the scallops and serve at once.

PAN-SEARED SHRIMP

HAVING PREPARED LITERALLY TONS OF SHRIMP in the test kitchen and in our own home kitchens, we have found that pan-searing produces the ultimate combination of a well-caramelized exterior and a moist, tender interior. If executed properly, this cooking method also preserves the shrimp's plumpness and trademark briny sweetness.

That being said, a good recipe for pan-seared shrimp is hard to find. Of the handful of recipes we uncovered, the majority resulted in shrimp that were variously dry, flavorless, pale, tough, or gummy—hardly appetizing. It was time to start some serious testing.

We quickly uncovered a few basic rules. First, tasters unanimously favored shrimp that were peeled before being cooked. Peeled shrimp are easier to eat, and unpeeled shrimp fail to pick up the delicious caramelized flavor that pan-searing provides. Second, the shrimp were best cooked in a 12-inch skillet; its large surface area kept the shrimp from overcrowding the pan and steaming—a surefire way to prevent caramelization. Third, oil was the ideal cooking medium, favored over both a dry pan (which made the shrimp leathery and metallic-tasting) and butter (which tended to burn).

Next, in pan-searing the shrimp, we found that in the time it took to get the shrimp to brown, they turned out tough and overcooked. Looking for another way to promote browning in a shorter time frame, we thought to add a pinch of sugar to the shrimp. Not only did the sugar caramelize into a nice brown crust, it also accentuated the shrimp's natural sweetness, nicely setting off their inherent sea-saltiness.

Even in a 12-inch skillet, 1½ pounds of shrimp must be cooked in two batches, or they will steam instead of sear. The trick was to develop a technique that neither overcooked the shrimp nor let half of them turn cold while the other half finished cooking. To prevent overcooking, we tried searing the shrimp on one side, removing the pan from the flame, and then allowing the residual heat to finish cooking the other side of the shrimp. This worked like a charm. Better yet, the residual heat from the pan also solved the cold shrimp problem. As soon as the second batch finished cooking (the first batch was now near room temperature), we tossed the first batch back into the pan, covered it, and let the residual heat work its magic once again. After about a minute, all of the shrimp were both perfectly cooked and piping hot. Now all we needed were a few ideas for some quick sauces.

We tested sauces made from assertive ingredients such as garlic, ginger, and chipotle chile mixed with plenty of acidity as a foil for the shrimp's richness. The most successful of these sauces were those that clung to the shrimp like a glaze. All of them could easily be made ahead of time and quickly tossed with the shrimp during the last stage of cooking, once the pan was removed from the heat.

Pan-Seared Shrimp

SERVES 4

The cooking times below are for 21 to 25 shrimp (that is, the size of the shrimp is such that there are 21 to 25 in 1 pound). If this size is not available in your market, buy large shrimp—the next size down—and adjust the cooking time slightly. Either a nonstick or traditional skillet will work for this recipe, but a nonstick simplifies cleanup.

2	tablespoons vegetable oil
1½	pounds extra-large shrimp (21 to 25 per pound), peeled and deveined
¼	teaspoon salt
¼	teaspoon ground black pepper
⅛	teaspoon sugar

Heat 1 tablespoon of the oil in a 12-inch skillet over high heat until smoking. Meanwhile, toss the shrimp, salt, pepper, and sugar in a medium bowl. Add half of the shrimp to the pan in a single layer and cook until spotty brown and the edges turn pink, about 1 minute. Remove the pan from the heat. Using tongs, flip each shrimp and let stand until all but the very center is opaque, about 30 seconds. Transfer the shrimp to a large plate. Repeat with the remaining oil and shrimp. After the second batch has stood off the heat, return the first batch to the skillet and toss to combine. Cover the skillet and let stand until the shrimp are cooked through, 1 to 2 minutes. Serve immediately.

➤ VARIATIONS

Pan-Seared Shrimp with Garlic-Lemon Butter

Beat 3 tablespoons softened unsalted butter with a fork in a small bowl until light and fluffy. Stir in 1 medium garlic clove, minced, 1 tablespoon lemon juice, 2 tablespoons chopped fresh parsley leaves, and ⅛ teaspoon salt until combined. Follow the recipe for Pan-Seared Shrimp, adding the flavored butter when returning the first batch of shrimp to the skillet. Serve with lemon wedges, if desired.

Pan-Seared Shrimp with Ginger-Hoisin Glaze

Stir 2 tablespoons hoisin sauce, 1 tablespoon rice vinegar, 1½ teaspoons soy sauce, 2 teaspoons grated fresh ginger, 2 teaspoons water, and 2 scallions, sliced thin, together in a small bowl. Follow the recipe for Pan-Seared Shrimp, substituting an equal amount of red pepper flakes for the black pepper and adding the hoisin mixture when returning the first batch of shrimp to the skillet.

SHRIMP SIZES

Shrimp are sold by size (extra-large, large, medium, and small) as well as by the number needed to make a pound, usually given in a range. Choosing shrimp by the numerical rating is more accurate than choosing by a size label, which varies from store to store. Here's how the two sizing systems generally line up.

SMALL
51 to 60 shrimp
per pound

MEDIUM
40 to 50 shrimp
per pound

LARGE
31 to 40 shrimp
per pound

EXTRA-LARGE
21 to 25 shrimp
per pound

Pan-Seared Shrimp with Chipotle-Lime Glaze

Stir 1 chipotle chile in adobo sauce, minced, 2 teaspoons adobo sauce, 4 teaspoons brown sugar, 2 tablespoons lime juice, and 2 tablespoons chopped fresh cilantro leaves together in a small bowl. Follow the recipe for Pan-Seared Shrimp, adding the chipotle mixture when returning the first batch of shrimp to the skillet.

SHRIMP SCAMPI

ALMOST EVERY ITALIAN RESTAURANT MENU IN the United States features shrimp scampi. The name sounds Italian, but, in reality, it doesn't make much sense. The word *scampi* refers to a species of crayfish found in the Adriatic, not the buttery, herby, garlicky, lemony sauce we think of as a natural partner to sautéed shrimp. Despite the questionable origins of this dish, we love its simplicity and bold flavors.

The perfect shrimp scampi is surrounded by an ample amount of sauce flavored with garlic and lemon. We find that most recipes are too oily and that the garlic (which generally goes into the pan first) burns by the time the shrimp have cooked through. Most sauces are too thin, and there's not near enough to sop up with a chewy piece of bread. In addition, most recipes overcook the shrimp.

To start, we sautéed the shrimp quickly in batches. This prevented them from overcooking and becoming rubbery while helping retain their natural juices so they would not dry out. With the shrimp cooked and reserved, we built a sauce in the empty pan. Beginning with butter, we simply heated the garlic through before adding the lemon juice and a little vermouth, which gave the sauce a nice depth of flavor. Adding the liquid also kept the garlic from burning and turning bitter.

The sauce was delicious but thin. For body, we added more butter and finished it with parsley, then added a pinch of cayenne. We returned the shrimp and their juices to the pan, and the dish was done. Nothing complicated, and perfect.

Shrimp Scampi
SERVES 4 TO 6

Serve scampi with plenty of chewy bread to soak up the sauce.

- 2 tablespoons extra-virgin olive oil
- 2 pounds extra-large shrimp (21 to 25 per pound), peeled and deveined, if desired
- 3 tablespoons unsalted butter
- 4 medium garlic cloves, minced or pressed through a garlic press
- 2 tablespoons juice from 1 lemon
- 1 tablespoon dry vermouth
- 2 tablespoons minced fresh parsley leaves
- Pinch cayenne pepper
- Salt and ground black pepper

1. Heat 1 tablespoon of the oil in a 12-inch skillet over high heat until shimmering. Swirl to coat the pan bottom. Add half the shrimp and cook, stirring occasionally, until opaque and just cooked through, about 2 minutes. Transfer the shrimp to a medium bowl. Repeat with the remaining oil and shrimp.

2. Return the now-empty skillet to medium-low heat. Melt 1 tablespoon of the butter in the pan. When the foaming subsides, add the garlic and cook, stirring constantly, until fragrant, about 30 seconds. Off the heat, add the lemon juice and vermouth. Whisk in the remaining 2 tablespoons butter, add the parsley and cayenne, and season with salt and black pepper to taste. Return the shrimp and accumulated juices to the skillet. Toss to combine and serve immediately.

➤ VARIATIONS

Shrimp Scampi with Cumin, Paprika, and Sherry Vinegar

This dish is deeply flavorful but has slightly less heat than either of the other two versions.

Follow the recipe for Shrimp Scampi, sautéing 1 teaspoon ground cumin and 2 teaspoons paprika with the garlic, substituting an equal amount of sherry vinegar for the lemon juice, and omitting the cayenne.

Shrimp Scampi with Orange Zest and Cilantro

Because it is spicy, this dish is best served with white rice.

Follow the recipe for Shrimp Scampi, sautéing 1 teaspoon finely grated orange zest and ¼ teaspoon hot red pepper flakes with the garlic, substituting 2 tablespoons minced fresh cilantro leaves for the parsley, and omitting the cayenne.

GUMBO

WE HAD LONG KNOWN OF THE LEGENDARY soup/stew of Louisiana that is famous for both its complex flavor and its temperamental nature, but our experience with it was limited. That changed after we took a quick trip to southern Louisiana. In just over 48 hours, we covered a couple of hundred miles of bayou country, downed 15 bowls of gumbo, cooked alongside four native cooks, and interviewed two more. After returning, we dug up and studied about 80 recipes, and before long we learned that gumbo, like all great folk recipes, is open to plenty of individual interpretation. Generally speaking, though, gumbo usually includes some combination of seafood, poultry, or small game along with sausage or some other highly seasoned, cured smoked pork. Also present is the Creole/Cajun "holy trinity" of onion, bell pepper, and celery. Quite often, gumbos are thickened with okra or ground dried sassafras leaves, known as filé (pronounced fee-LAY) powder. Last, but very important, most gumbos are flavored with a dark brown roux. For us, this roux is the heart of a good gumbo.

In classic French cooking, a roux is nothing more than flour cooked gently in some type of fat to form a paste that is used to thicken sauces. If the flour is just barely cooked, you have a white roux; if cooked to a light beige, you have a blond roux. When it reaches the color of light brown sugar, you have a brown roux. Creole and Cajun cooks push that progression to the outer limit. When they make a roux, they keep cooking until the flour reaches a shade of very dark brown, sometimes just short of black. This breaks down the starches in the flour to the point where the roux offers relatively little thickening power. Instead, it imbues gumbo with a complex, toasty, smoky flavor and a deep, rich brown color that define the dish. The problem is that the flour can burn very easily, and the only safeguards against that are relatively low heat and constant stirring. This means that it often takes as long as an hour of constant stirring and careful attention to make a dark roux. Few of the home cooks we asked said they'd be willing to go to this length for the proper-colored roux, so we had to shorten that time if we wanted a more practical recipe for gumbo.

Our goals for this project were falling into place, and there were three. First, the roux was key. We wanted to feature its flavor over the cacophony of other herbs and spices and to streamline its preparation. Once we had mastered the roux, we would have to determine the components and flavorings of the stew. As a starting point, we chose to feature shrimp over chicken or game and to include sausage. Finally, we would have to decide whether to use okra or filé as a thickener, knowing that either would bring not only viscosity but also a distinct flavor to the dish.

The distinctive taste, color, and aroma of a dark roux is a central characteristic of Creole and Cajun food. Most of the recipes we saw called for cooking the roux over low heat while stirring

MAKING A ROUX

A long-handled, straight-edged wooden spatula is the best tool for stirring a roux. Be sure to scrape the pan bottom and reach into the corners to prevent burning. The cooking roux will have a distinctive toasty, nutty aroma. If it smells scorched or acrid, or if there are black flecks in the roux, it has burned.

constantly for anywhere from 40 to 60 minutes. Since the roux truly does need to be stirred constantly as it cooks to avoid burning the flour, which will give the mixture a noticeable bitter taste, time was the first issue we had to tackle. We decided on 20 minutes as our limit for stirring. Any longer than that, we reasoned, and most cooks would probably skip over this dish. Just as important, tasters discerned little difference in flavor between gumbos made with the traditional low-heat, long-cooking roux and those with roux that were cooked faster and hotter.

To hit that 20-minute mark, we knew we'd have to increase the heat and probably preheat the oil before adding the flour. For our testing, we began with the widely used 1-to-1 ratio of all-purpose flour to vegetable oil, using ½ cup of each.

Some cooks recommend heating the oil until it smokes and then cooking the roux over high heat. Though this method produced a very dark roux, about the color of bittersweet chocolate, in less than 10 minutes there was too much sizzle and smoke. The process felt out of control, and the specter of a burned roux loomed large.

We slowed things down a bit, preheating the oil over medium-high heat for only about two minutes (to well below the smoke point) before adding the flour, then lowering the heat to medium to cook the roux. At the 20-minute stopping point, the roux had cooked to a deep reddish brown, about the color of a shelled pecan or a dirty penny. It had started to smoke once or twice, but it cooled fairly quickly when we removed it from the heat, stirred it for a minute, and then returned it to the burner. In all, the process was much less nerve-wracking than the high-heat methods we had tried, and it yielded absolutely acceptable results.

We experimented with a number of fats—including bacon fat, sausage fat, butter, and different types of oil—and ended up preferring the flavor and ease of vegetable oil. We tried different ratios of fat to flour, varying them by as much as six tablespoons up and down from the ½-cup starting point, but none improved on the original 1-to-1 ratio in terms of either taste or performance. Switching the all-purpose flour from a high-protein, unbleached northern brand to a slightly lower-protein, bleached national brand improved the texture of the gumbo slightly, making it a little smoother and more satiny. The gumbo's consistency also improved due to a thorough skimming of the foam on the surface of the liquid, both just after it had come to a boil and throughout the simmering time.

Throughout the roux testing, the occasional separation of the flour and oil upon the addition of the simmering liquid continued to perplex us. All along, we had followed the instructions in most of the recipes we'd studied to add simmering stock, which is about 200 degrees, to a hot roux-vegetable mixture, also about 200 degrees. But there is another, if less popular, school of thought. Food scientist and author of *On Food and Cooking* (Collier, 1984) Harold McGee and legendary New Orleans restaurateur Leah Chase had advised cooling either the roux or the stock before combining them. Sure enough, cooling the stock (which took less time than cooling the roux) did the trick.

After doing some research, we figured out that adding 200-degree stock to 200-degree roux would thus cause instant gelatinization of the starch in the flour. The result is disastrous: The globules of flour stick together in clumps before they can be dispersed throughout the liquid. By adding cooler stock, the roux and the stock have time to blend thoroughly before the whole mixture comes up to temperature and the starch gelatinizes, resulting in the smooth consistency we were seeking.

The rest of the recipe development process focused on testing the wide range of ingredients and flavorings we encountered on our trip and in our research. First we experimented with the liquid. Our testing thus far had been done with a simple shrimp stock made by simmering the shells in water. We tried boiling the shells in chicken stock instead of water, combining equal parts shrimp and chicken stock, adding bottled clam juice to the shrimp stock, and adding small amounts of white wine and beer to the gumbo. The clam juice did the trick, adding a depth of flavor that supplemented the 20-minute roux.

Two big flavoring questions concerned tomatoes—some say that gumbo just isn't gumbo without them—and garlic. Well, our tasters said that gumbo was just fine without tomatoes, but they gave the thumbs up to garlic, six cloves of it, in fact. Other seasonings in gumbo range from elaborate mixtures of herbs, spices, and sauces down to nothing more than salt. We tried what seemed like a hundred seasoning variations and finally settled on a simple combination of dried thyme and bay leaves. Our experiments with different proportions of onion, bell pepper, and celery in the holy trinity notwithstanding, the classic ratio of 1 part celery to 2 parts pepper to 4 parts onion tasted best. We did, however, switch from the traditional green bell pepper to red peppers, preferring their sweeter, fuller flavor.

Next we considered the level of spicy heat, usually provided by either cayenne pepper alone or in combination with a hot pepper sauce such as Tabasco. The gumbos we tasted in Louisiana were only subtly spicy, with the pepper heat very much in the background. We wanted to feel a slight heat in the back of our throats after we had swallowed a couple of spoonfuls. A mere ¼ teaspoon of cayenne did the trick for our tasters, all of whom favored the powder over the vinegary taste of bottled hot sauce.

Last, we considered whether to thicken the gumbo with okra or filé powder. We think both are probably acquired tastes. Thus far, everyone had been satisfied without either, and because both added distinct—and to some unwelcome—flavors, we decided to reserve them for the variations on the master recipe.

Creole-Style Shrimp and Sausage Gumbo

SERVES 6 TO 8

Making a dark roux can be dangerous. The mixture reaches temperatures in excess of 400 degrees. Therefore, use a deep pot for cooking the roux and long-handled utensils for stirring it, and be careful not to splash it on yourself. One secret to smooth gumbo is adding shrimp stock that is neither too hot nor too cold to the roux. For a stock that is at the right temperature when the roux is done, start preparing it before you tend to the vegetables and other ingredients, strain it, and then give it a head start on cooling by immediately adding ice water and clam juice. So that your constant stirring of the roux will not be interrupted, start the roux only after you've made the stock. Alternatively, you can make the stock well ahead of time and bring it back to room temperature before using it. Spicy andouille sausage is a Louisiana specialty that may not be available everywhere; kielbasa or any fully cooked smoked sausage makes a fine substitute. Gumbo is traditionally served over white rice.

1½	pounds small shrimp (51 to 60 per pound), shells removed and reserved
4½	cups water
1	cup bottled clam juice
3½	cups ice water
½	cup vegetable oil
½	cup all-purpose flour, preferably bleached
2	medium onions, chopped fine
1	medium red bell pepper, cored, seeded, and chopped fine
1	medium celery rib, chopped fine
6	medium garlic cloves, minced or pressed through a garlic press
1	teaspoon dried thyme
1	teaspoon salt
¼	teaspoon cayenne pepper
2	bay leaves
1	pound smoked sausage, such as andouille or kielbasa, sliced into ½-inch rounds
½	cup minced fresh parsley leaves
4	medium scallions, white and green parts, sliced thin
	Ground black pepper

1. Bring the reserved shrimp shells and the 4½ cups water to a boil in a stockpot or large saucepan over medium-high heat. Reduce the heat to medium-low and simmer for 20 minutes. Strain the stock into a container and stir in the clam juice and ice water (you should have about 2 quarts of tepid stock, 100 to 110 degrees). Set the stock aside and discard the shells.

2. Heat the oil in a Dutch oven or large, heavy-bottomed saucepan over medium-high heat until it registers 200 degrees on an instant-read

thermometer, 1½ to 2 minutes. Reduce the heat to medium and gradually stir in the flour with a wooden spatula or spoon, working out any lumps that form. Continue stirring constantly, reaching into the corners of the pan, until the mixture has a toasty aroma and is deep reddish brown, about the color of an old copper penny or between the colors of milk chocolate and dark chocolate, about 20 minutes. (The roux will thin as it cooks; if it begins to smoke, remove the pan from the heat

INGREDIENTS: Okra and Filé

In a Creole or Cajun dark roux, most of the starch in the flour breaks down in the cooking, so it does more to flavor the stew than thicken it. That leaves the task to one of two other traditional Southern ingredients, okra and filé powder. (It's also possible, as we do in our master recipe, to go without either one for a slightly thinner stew. Both okra and filé powder are often an acquired taste.) One thing on which most Creole and Cajun cooks agree is that you should never use okra and filé together because the gumbo will get too thick or even gummy.

Okra pods, said to have been brought to the southern United States from Africa by the slave trade, are slender, green, usually about 3 inches in length, ridged in texture, tapered in shape, and often slightly fuzzy. The interior of the pods is sticky and mucilaginous, so once they are cut open, they thicken any liquid in which they are cooked. Okra's flavor is subtle, with hints of eggplant, green bean, and chestnut. In our gumbo testing, we could detect no taste difference between fresh and frozen.

The other possible thickener, filé powder, is made of ground dried sassafras leaves. It is said to have been introduced to the settlers of southern Louisiana by the native Choctaw Indians. Filé, also referred to in Louisiana as gumbo filé, adds both a gelatinous thickness and a subtle, singular flavor to gumbo. Though difficult to describe precisely, the flavor is distinctly earthy, with notes of straw, bay, marjoram, and oregano. Filé is as much a hallmark of authentic Louisiana cooking as a dark roux and the holy trinity of onion, bell pepper, and celery. Filé is used in one of two ways. Diners can sprinkle a little bit onto their portions of gumbo right at the table, or the cook can stir some into the pot at the very last moment of cooking or even once the pot has come off the heat. In our recipe variation, we prefer to add it to the pot, which mellows the flavor somewhat. In stores that carry it, pale green filé powder is generally sold in tall, slender, 1-ounce jars.

and stir the roux constantly to cool slightly.)

3. Add the onions, bell pepper, celery, garlic, thyme, salt, and cayenne to the roux and cook, stirring frequently, until the vegetables soften, 8 to 10 minutes. Add 1 quart of the reserved stock in a slow, steady stream while stirring vigorously. Stir in the remaining stock. Increase the heat to high and bring to a boil. Reduce the heat to medium-low, skim the foam from the surface, add the bay leaves, and simmer, uncovered, skimming any foam that rises to the surface, for about 30 minutes. (The mixture can be covered and set aside for several hours. Reheat when ready to proceed.)

4. Stir in the sausage and continue simmering to blend the flavors, about 30 minutes. Stir in the shrimp and simmer until cooked through, about 5 minutes. Off the heat, stir in the parsley and scallions and adjust the seasonings with salt, black pepper, and cayenne to taste. Serve immediately.

➤ VARIATIONS

Shrimp and Sausage Gumbo with Okra

Fresh okra can be used in place of frozen, though it tends to be more slippery, a quality that diminishes with increased cooking. Substitute an equal amount of fresh okra for frozen; trim the caps, slice the pods ¼ inch thick, and increase the sautéing time with the onions, bell pepper, and celery to 10 to 15 minutes.

Follow the recipe for Creole-Style Shrimp and Sausage Gumbo, adding 10 ounces thawed frozen cut okra to the roux along with the onions, bell pepper, and celery. Proceed as directed.

Shrimp and Sausage Gumbo with Filé

Follow the recipe for Creole-Style Shrimp and Sausage Gumbo, adding 1½ teaspoons filé powder along with the parsley and scallions after the gumbo has been removed from the heat. Let rest until slightly thickened, about 5 minutes. Adjust the seasonings and serve.

SOFT-SHELL CRABS

THERE ARE DOZENS OF SPECIES OF CRABS, but the blue crab, which is found in waters along the East Coast, is the most common variety. Soft-shell crabs are blue crabs that have been taken out of the water just after they have shed their shells. At this brief stage of its life, the whole crab, with its new, soft, gray skin, is almost completely edible and fabulously delicious.

For the cook, soft-shells are a wonderfully immediate experience. Once cleaned, they demand to be cooked and eaten on the spot, so they offer a very direct taste of the sea. Because the crabs must be cooked so quickly after they are killed and cleaned, home cooks have an advantage over restaurants. We're convinced that the best way to enjoy soft-shells is to cook them at home, where you can be sure to eat them within minutes of preparing them.

The whole point of preparing soft-shells is to get them crisp. The legs should crunch delicately, while the body should provide a contrast between its thin, crisp outer skin and the soft, rich interior, which explodes juicily in the mouth. Deep-frying delivers these results, but this method is better suited to restaurants, since air pockets and water in the crab cause a lot of dangerous splattering. For optimum safety, soft-shell crabs should be deep-fried in a very large quantity of oil in a very deep pot, which is not practical at home.

We wanted to develop an alternative method for home cooks. We tried roasting, but the crabs did not get crisp enough. Grilling is not always practical, and broiling did not work well. In the end, we found that pan-frying produces a satisfyingly crisp crab. Crabs still splatter hot fat when cooked this way, but there is less fat to splatter than in deep-frying. To avoid the mess and danger of the splattering fat, we recommend sliding a splatter screen (see page 527) over the pan as the crabs cook.

A coating of some kind helps crisp the crabs. We tried flour, cornmeal, bread crumbs, and even Cream of Wheat coatings and ended up choosing flour. It's a shame to hide the unique, essential flavor of the crabs with a heavy coating, and flour provides a crisp crust without adding flavor. It also has the advantage of being on hand most of the time.

We also tried soaking the crabs in milk for two hours before applying the coating, as we had read that this serves to sweeten crabs. To the contrary, we found that milk takes away from the just-out-of-the-water flavor that we like.

The type of fat you use for frying is largely a matter of personal preference. We tried frying floured crabs in whole butter, clarified butter, vegetable and peanut oils, and a combination of whole butter and olive oil. Whole butter gave the crabs a delicious, nutty taste and browned them well. Clarified butter didn't brown them significantly better and was more work, so it offers no advantage over whole butter. (Clarified butter can be brought to higher temperatures than whole butter because the easily burnt milk solids have been removed.) Vegetable and peanut oils got the

PREPARING A SOFT-SHELL CRAB

1. Cut off the crab's mouth with kitchen scissors; the mouth is the first part of the shell to harden. You can also cut off the eyes at the same time, but this is for purely aesthetic purposes; the eyes are edible.

2. Lift the pointed sides of the crab and cut out the spongy off-white gills underneath; the gills are fibrous and watery and unpleasant to eat.

3. Finally, turn the crab on its back and cut off the triangular, or T-shaped, "apron flap."

crabs a hair crisper than butter and added no flavor; peanut oil crisped the crabs particularly well because it fries very hot without burning. The combination of butter and oil didn't give a better result than either fat used separately, and we were surprised to find that the flavor of butter and even the flavorlessness of the other oils complement crabs better than the olive oil. Our preference is to fry with either peanut oil or butter, depending on the taste we want and the kind of sauce we are making.

Whether you opt for peanut oil, vegetable oil, or butter, crabs fry best in quite a lot of fat. Count on at least one tablespoon of butter per crab depending on the size of the pan; the crabs actually seem to absorb the butter as they cook. When cooking with oil, we add the oil to a depth of ⅛ to ¼ inch. You can cook in any kind of pan, but a cast-iron pan holds heat particularly well and practically guarantees a crispy critter.

Once you've cooked the crabs, they should be sauced and served immediately. In a pinch, you can hold crabs for a few minutes in a 300-degree oven, but they're really better eaten practically out of the pan. Therefore, if you're serving a main course for four (count on two crabs per person), you'll need two pans, each at least 11 inches in diameter, if you expect everyone to sit down to eat together. If you've got only one pan, your best bet is to let two people start on the first batch of crabs when they're cooked, while you start cooking the

---

EQUIPMENT: Splatter Screen

Because they are full of water, soft-shell crabs spit hot fat when they are pan-fried. To protect your hands and face (and to keep your stovetop from becoming covered with grease), we recommend that you slide a splatter screen—a round, flat wire net with a handle—over the skillet with the crabs as they cook. Steam can escape through the netting so the crabs stay crisp (a pan lid would trap steam and make the crabs soggy), but the fat stays in the pan.

A splatter screen can be used whenever you are pan-frying. Just make sure to use a screen that is slightly larger than the skillet. Also, because the handles on many splatter screens are metal, they will become hot and should be handled with an oven mitt.

---

second batch. Or serve crabs as an appetizer—one per person is plenty. Because they're fried, the crabs don't need much of a sauce, just a drizzle of something acidic, such as lemon juice or vinegar.

Pan-Fried Soft-Shell Crabs
SERVES 4

A splatter screen is essential if you want to minimize the mess and the danger to your arms and face. For maximum crispness, you should cook the crabs in two pans, each covered with a splatter screen, so you can serve the crabs as soon as they are cooked. If you are working with just one splatter screen and pan, cook 4 crabs in 4 tablespoons of butter, transfer them to a platter in a 300-degree oven, wipe out the pan, add 4 more tablespoons of butter, and cook the remaining crabs.

1	cup unbleached all-purpose flour
8	medium-to-large soft-shell crabs, prepared (see the illustrations on page 526) and patted dry with paper towels
10	tablespoons (1 stick plus 2 tablespoons) unsalted butter
¼	cup juice from 2 large lemons
2	tablespoons minced fresh parsley leaves
	Salt and ground black pepper

1. Place the flour in a wide, shallow dish. Dredge the crabs in the flour and pat off the excess. Heat two 11- or 12-inch heavy-bottomed skillets over medium-high heat until the pans are quite hot, about 3 minutes. Add 4 tablespoons butter to each pan, swirling the pans to keep the butter from burning as it melts. When the foam subsides, add 4 crabs shell-side down to each pan. Cover each pan with a splatter screen and cook, adjusting the heat as necessary to keep the butter from burning, until the crabs turn reddish brown, about 3 minutes. Turn the crabs with a spatula or tongs and cook until the second side is browned, about 3 minutes more. Drain the crabs on a plate lined with paper towels.

2. Set one pan aside for cleaning. Pour off the butter from the other pan and remove from the heat. Add the lemon juice to deglaze the empty,

hot pan. Cut the remaining 2 tablespoons butter into pieces and add to the skillet. Swirl the pan to melt the butter. Add the parsley and salt and pepper to taste. Arrange 2 crabs on each of 4 plates. Spoon some of the butter sauce over each plate and serve immediately.

➤ VARIATION

Pan-Fried Soft-Shell Crabs with Lemon, Capers, and Herbs

The pan sauce is tart and powerfully flavorful; you need only about 1 tablespoon per serving.

Follow the recipe for Pan-Fried Soft-Shell Crabs, reducing the lemon juice to 3 tablespoons and adding 2 teaspoons sherry vinegar, 1½ teaspoons chopped rinsed capers, and 1 medium scallion, sliced thin, to the pan with the lemon juice in step 2. Proceed as directed, adding 2 teaspoons minced fresh tarragon leaves with the parsley and salt and pepper.

INGREDIENTS: Soft-Shell Crabs

Not surprisingly, considering how perishable they are, soft-shells can be quite difficult to locate. Fresh soft-shells are available only "in season," which used to mean a few short months during the summer. Now the "season" can extend from February all the way through to September, and maybe even into October, depending on the weather. Frozen crabs may also be available, but they are not nearly as good.

Once you buy the crabs, your fishmonger will probably offer to clean them for you. If you like the crabs juicy, you'll be happier if you clean them yourself. The reason is that a crab, like a lobster, grows by shedding its hard shell periodically. After shedding, the crab swells with water to fill out its new skin, and the skin immediately begins to harden into a new, larger shell. When you clean a live crab, juice pours out of it. The longer the crab sits before cooking, the more liquid it loses. We found that a crab that is cooked immediately after cleaning is much plumper and juicier than a crab cleaned several hours before cooking. To prepare a live crab, follow the illustrations on page 526.

We advise against storing soft-shells. Even a live crab won't stay that way very long in your refrigerator; because they can die from the cold temperature in your refrigerator, they're better off at the fish store, where they are kept not cold, but cool.

CRAB CAKES

GOOD CRAB CAKES TASTE FIRST AND FOREMOST of sweet crabmeat. Too many restaurants serve crab-flecked dough balls. That's why the crab cake is especially suited to home cooking.

Great crab cakes begin with top-quality crabmeat. We tested all the various options, and the differences are stark. Canned crabmeat is horrible; like canned tuna, it bears little resemblance to the fresh product. Fresh pasteurized crabmeat is watery and bland. Frozen crabmeat is stringy and wet. There is no substitute for fresh blue crabmeat, preferably "jumbo lump," which indicates the largest pieces and highest grade. This variety costs a couple of dollars a pound more than other types of fresh crab meat, but, since a 1-pound container is enough to make crab cakes for four, in our opinion, it's money well spent.

Fresh lump blue crab is available year-round but tends to be most expensive from December to March. The meat should never be rinsed, but it does need to be picked over to remove any shells or cartilage the processors may have missed.

Once we figured out what type of crab to use, our next task was to find the right binder. None of the usual suspects worked. Crushed saltines were a pain to smash into small-enough crumbs, potato chips added too much richness, and fresh bread crumbs blended into the crabmeat a little too well. We finally settled on fine dry bread crumbs. They have no overwhelming flavor and are easy to mix in. The trickiest part is knowing when to stop; crab cakes need just enough binder to hold them together but not so much that the filler overwhelms the seafood. We started out with ¾ cup crumbs but ended up reducing it down to just 2 to 4 tablespoons for our final recipe. Cooks who economize by padding their pricey seafood with bread crumbs will end up with dough balls, not crab cakes.

The other ingredients we adopted are equally basic. Good, sturdy commercial mayonnaise (we like Hellmann's) keeps the crabmeat moist (a homemade blend can be too liquidy), and a whole egg, unbeaten, makes the crab, crumbs, and seasonings meld together both before and during cooking.

Classic recipes call for spiking crab cakes with everything from Tabasco to Worcestershire sauce, and those are both fine. But we've decided the best blend of tradition and trendiness is Old Bay seasoning combined with freshly ground white pepper and a tablespoon or more of chopped fresh herbs.

Just as essential as careful seasoning is careful mixing. We found a rubber spatula works best, used in a folding motion rather than stirring. This is important because you want to end up with a

chunky consistency. Those lumps aren't cheap.

We were pleased with our basic recipe on most fronts, but we still had trouble keeping the cakes together as they cooked. Our last breakthrough came when we tried chilling the shaped cakes before cooking. As little as half an hour in the refrigerator made an ocean of difference: The cold firmed up the cakes so that they fried into perfect plump rounds without falling apart. We found that formed cakes can be kept, refrigerated and tightly

DIPPING SAUCES FOR SEAFOOD

THESE SAUCES WORK ESPECIALLY WELL WITH PAN-FRIED FRESH SALMON CAKES (PAGE 513), Pan-Fried Catfish (page 503), and Pan-Fried Crab Cakes (page 530). You might also serve one of these sauces with Steamed Lobsters (page 532).

Tartar Sauce
MAKES GENEROUS 3/4 CUP
This is the classic sauce for fried seafood.

- 3/4 cup mayonnaise
- 1 1/2 tablespoons minced cornichons (about 3 large), plus 1 teaspoon cornichon juice
- 1 tablespoon minced scallion
- 1 tablespoon minced red onion
- 1 tablespoon rinsed capers, minced

Mix all of the ingredients together in a small bowl. Cover and refrigerate until the flavors blend, at least 30 minutes. (The sauce can be refrigerated for several days.)

Creamy Lemon Herb Sauce
MAKES GENEROUS 1/2 CUP
This sauce is flavorful, but it won't overpower delicate seafood.

- 1/2 cup mayonnaise
- 2 1/2 tablespoons juice from 1 lemon
- 1 tablespoon minced fresh parsley leaves
- 1 tablespoon minced fresh thyme leaves
- 1 large scallion, white and green parts, minced

- 1/2 teaspoon salt
- Ground black pepper

Mix all of the ingredients, including ground black pepper to taste, together in a small bowl. Cover and refrigerate until the flavors blend, about 30 minutes. (The sauce can be refrigerated for several days.)

Creamy Chipotle Chile Sauce
MAKES ABOUT 1/2 CUP
This sauce is the richest of the three and the most complex.

- 1/4 cup mayonnaise
- 1/4 cup sour cream
- 2 teaspoons minced chipotle chiles in adobo sauce
- 1 small garlic clove, minced or pressed through a garlic press
- 2 teaspoons minced fresh cilantro leaves
- 1 teaspoon juice from 1 lime

Mix all of the ingredients together in a small bowl. Cover and refrigerate until the flavors blend, about 30 minutes. (The sauce can be refrigerated for several days.)

wrapped, for up to 24 hours.

We also tried different cooking methods. After baking, deep-frying, and broiling, we settled on pan-frying in a cast-iron skillet over medium-high heat. This method is fast and also gives the cook complete control over how brown and how crisp the cakes get. We first tried frying in butter, but it burned as it saturated the crab cakes. Cut with vegetable oil, it was still too heavy and made a mess of the pan. The ideal medium turned out to be vegetable oil. It can be heated without burning and smoking, it creates a crisp crust, and it never gets in the way of the crab flavor.

Pan-Fried Crab Cakes

SERVES 4

The amount of bread crumbs you add will depend on the crabmeat's juiciness. Start with the smallest amount, adjust the seasonings, and then add the egg. If the cakes won't bind at this point, add more bread crumbs, 1 tablespoon at a time.

I	pound jumbo lump crabmeat, picked over to remove cartilage or shells
4	scallions, green parts only, minced (about ¹/₂ cup)
I	tablespoon chopped fresh herb, such as cilantro, dill, basil, or parsley leaves
I¹/₂	teaspoons Old Bay seasoning
2–4	tablespoons plain dry bread crumbs
¹/₄	cup mayonnaise
	Salt and ground white pepper
I	large egg
¹/₄	cup unbleached all-purpose flour
¹/₄	cup vegetable oil
	Lemon wedges or one of the dipping sauces on page 529 for serving

1. Gently fold the crabmeat, scallions, herb, Old Bay, 2 tablespoons bread crumbs, and mayonnaise together in a medium bowl, being careful not to break up the lumps of crab. Season with salt and white pepper to taste. Carefully fold in the egg with a rubber spatula until the mixture just clings together. Add more crumbs if necessary.

2. Divide the crab mixture into 4 portions and

shape each into a fat, round cake, about 3 inches across and 1¹/₂ inches high. Arrange on a baking sheet lined with waxed or parchment paper; cover with plastic wrap and chill at least 30 minutes. (The crab cakes can be refrigerated for up to 24 hours.)

3. Put the flour on a plate or in a pie tin. Lightly dredge the crab cakes in the flour. Heat the oil in a large, preferably nonstick skillet over medium-high heat until hot but not smoking. Gently lay the chilled crab cakes in the skillet and pan-fry until the outsides are crisp and browned, 4 to 5 minutes per side. Serve immediately with lemon wedges or dipping sauce.

LOBSTER

AS WITH MOST SEAFOOD, WE FIND THAT KNOWING how to shop for lobster is just as important as knowing how to cook it. Lobsters must be purchased alive. Choose lobsters that are active in the tank, avoiding listless specimens that may have been in the tank too long. Maine lobsters, with their large claws, are meatier and sweeter than clawless rock or spiny lobsters, and they are our first and only choice. Size is really a matter of preference and budget. We found it possible to cook large as well as small lobsters to perfection as long as we adjusted the cooking time (see page 531).

During the initial phase of testing, we confirmed our preference for steamed lobster rather than boiled. Steamed lobster did not taste better than boiled, but the process was simpler and neater, and the finished product was less watery when cracked open on the plate. Steaming the lobster on a rack or steamer basket kept it from becoming waterlogged. (If you happen to live near the ocean, seaweed makes a natural rack.) We found that neither beer nor wine in the pot improved the lobster's flavor, nor did any herbs, spices, or other seasonings. It seems that nothing can penetrate the hard lobster shell.

Although we had little trouble perfecting our cooking method, we were bothered by the toughness of some of the lobster tails we were eating.

HARD-SHELL VERSUS SOFT-SHELL LOBSTERS

To determine whether a lobster has a hard or soft shell, squeeze the side of the lobster's body. A soft-shell lobster will yield to pressure, while a hard-shell lobster will feel hard, brittle, and tightly packed.

No matter how we cooked them, most of the tails were at least slightly rubbery and chewy.

We spent six months talking to research scientists, chefs, seafood experts, lobstermen, and home cooks to see how they tackled the problem of the tough tail. The suggestions ranged from the bizarre (petting the lobster to "hypnotize" it and thus prevent an adrenaline rush at death that causes the tail to toughen, or using a chopstick to kill the lobster before cooking), to the sensible (avoiding really old, large lobsters). But after testing every one of these suggestions, we still didn't have a cooking method that consistently delivered a tender tail.

Occasionally, we would get a nice tender tail, but there did not seem to be a pattern. We then spoke with several scientists who said we were barking up the wrong tree. The secret to tender lobster was not so much in the preparation and cooking as in the selection.

Before working on this topic in the test kitchen, the terms hard-shell and soft-shell lobster meant nothing to us. Unlike crabs, lobsters are not clearly distinguished in this way at the retail level. Of course, we knew from past experience that some lobster claws rip open as easily as an aluminum flip-top can, while others won't crack until you take out your shop tools. We also noticed the small, limp claw meat of some lobsters and the full, packed meat of others. We attributed these differences to the length of time the lobsters had been stored in the tank. It seems we were wrong. These variations are caused by the particular stage of molting that the lobster was in at the time it was caught.

As it turns out, most of the lobsters we eat during the summer and fall are in some phase of molting. During the late spring, as waters begin to warm, lobsters start to form the new shell tissue underneath their old shells. As early as June off the shores of New Jersey and in July or August in colder Maine and Canadian waters, the lobsters shed their hard exterior shell. Because the most difficult task in molting is pulling the claw muscle through the old shell, the lobster dehydrates its claw (hence the smaller claw meat).

Once the lobster molts, it emerges with nothing but a wrinkled, soft covering, much like that on a soft-shell crab. Within 15 minutes, the lobster inflates itself with water, increasing its length by 15 percent and its weight by 50 percent. This extra water expands the wrinkled, soft covering, allowing the lobster room to grow long after the shell starts to harden. The newly molted lobster immediately eats its old shell, digesting the crucial shell-hardening calcium.

Understanding the molt phase clarifies the deficiencies of soft-shell summer lobster. It explains why it is so waterlogged, why its claw meat is so shriveled and scrawny, and why its tail meat is so underdeveloped and chewy. There is also far less meat in a 1-pound soft-shell lobster than in a hard-shell lobster that weighs the same.

Approximate Steaming Times and Meat Yields for Lobster

LOBSTER SIZE	COOKING TIME (IN MINUTES)	MEAT YIELD (IN OUNCES)
1 lb		
SOFT-SHELL	8 to 9	about 3
HARD-SHELL	10 to 11	4 to 4½
1¼ lbs		
SOFT-SHELL	11 to 12	3½ to 4
HARD-SHELL	13 to 14	5½ to 6
1½ lbs		
SOFT-SHELL	13 to 14	5½ to 6
HARD-SHELL	15 to 16	7½ to 8
1¾–2 lbs		
SOFT-SHELL	17 to 18	6¼ to 6½
HARD-SHELL	about 19	8½ to 9

During the fall, the lobster shell continues to harden and the meat expands to fill the new shell. By spring, lobsters are at their peak, packed with meat and relatively inexpensive since it is easier for fishermen to check their traps than it is during the winter. As the tail grows, it becomes firmer and meatier and will cook up tender, not tough. Better texture and more meat are two excellent reasons to give lobsters a squeeze at the market and buy only those with hard shells. As a rule of thumb, hard-shell lobsters are reasonably priced from Mother's Day through the Fourth of July.

Steamed Lobsters

SERVES 4

Hard-shell lobsters are much meatier than soft-shell lobsters, which have recently molted. To determine whether a lobster has a hard or soft shell, see the illustration on page 531. Because hard-shell lobsters are packed with more meat than soft-shell lobsters, you may want to buy slightly larger lobsters if the shells appear to be soft.

4   live lobsters
8   tablespoons (1 stick) unsalted butter, melted
     until hot (optional), for serving
     Lemon wedges for serving

Bring about 1 inch of water to a boil over high heat in a large stock pot set up with a wire rack, pasta insert, or seaweed bed. Add the lobsters, cover, and return the water to a boil. Reduce the heat to medium-high and steam until the lobsters are done (see the chart on page 531). Serve immediately with the warm butter and lemon wedges.

STEAMED CLAMS AND MUSSELS

CLAMS AND MUSSELS ARE BOTH BIVALVES, AND they can be prepared in the same fashion. The main challenge when preparing clams and mussels is getting rid of the grit. These two-shelled creatures are easy to cook: When they open, they are done. However, perfectly cooked clams and mussels can be made inedible by lingering sand.

Straining their juices through cheesecloth after cooking will remove the grit, but it's a pain. Besides being messy, solids such as shallots and garlic are removed. Worse still, careful straining may not remove every trace of grit, especially bits that are still clinging to the clam or mussel meat.

After much trial and error in the test kitchen, we concluded that it is also impossible to remove all the sand from dirty clams or mussels before cooking. We tried various soaking regimens—such as soaking in cold water for two hours, soaking in water with flour, soaking in water with cornmeal, and scrubbing and rinsing in five changes of water. None of these techniques worked. Dirty clams and mussels must be rinsed and scrubbed before cooking, and any cooking liquid must be strained after cooking. Rinsing the cooked clams and mussels is a final guarantee that the grit will be removed, but flavor is washed away as well.

During the course of this testing, we noticed that some varieties of clams and mussels were extremely clean and free of grit. A quick scrub of the shell exterior and these bivalves were ready for the pot. Best of all, the cooking liquid could be served without straining. After talking to seafood experts around the country, we came to this conclusion: If you want to minimize your kitchen work and ensure that your clams and mussels are free of grit, you must shop carefully.

Clams can be divided into two categories—hard-shell varieties (such as littlenecks and cherrystones) and soft-shell varieties (such as steamers and razor clams). Hard-shells grow along sandy beaches and bays, soft-shells in muddy tidal flats. A modest shift in location makes all the difference in the kitchen.

When harvested, hard-shells remain tightly closed. In our test, we found that the meat inside was always free of sand. The exterior should be scrubbed under cold running water to remove any caked-on mud, but otherwise these clams can be cooked without further worry about gritty broths.

Soft-shell clams gape in their natural habitat. We found that they almost always contain a lot of sand. While it's worthwhile to soak them in several batches of cold water to remove some of the sand, you can never get rid of it all. In the end, you must strain the cooking liquid. And sometimes you must rinse the cooked clams after shucking as well.

We ultimately concluded that hard-shell clams (that is, littlenecks or cherrystones) are worth the extra money at the market. Gritty clams, no matter how cheap, are inedible. Buying either littlenecks or cherrystones ensures that the clams will be clean.

A similar distinction can be made with mussels based on how and where they are grown. Most mussels are now farmed either on ropes or along seabeds. (You may also see "wild" mussels at the market. These mussels are caught the old-fashioned way—by dredging along the sea floor. In our tests, we found them extremely muddy and basically inedible.) Rope-cultured mussels can be as much as twice the cost of wild or bottom-cultured mussels, but we found them to be free of grit in our testing. Since mussels are generally inexpensive (no more than a few dollars a pound), we think clean mussels are worth the extra money. Look for tags, usually attached to bags of mussels, that indicate how and where the mussels have been grown.

When shopping, look for tightly closed clams and mussels (avoid any that are gaping, which may be dying or dead). Clams need only be scrubbed. Mussels may need scrubbing as well as debearding. Simply grab onto the weedy protrusion, pull it out from between the shells, and discard. Don't debeard mussels until you are ready to cook them, as debearding can cause the mussels to die. Mussels or clams kept in sealed plastic bags or underwater will also die. Keep them in a bowl in the refrigerator and use them within a day or two for best results.

We tested the four most common cooking methods for clams and mussels: steaming in an aromatic broth (usually with some wine in it), steaming over an aromatic broth, roasting in the oven, and sautéing in some oil on the stove. In our tests, we found that clams or mussels that were sautéed, roasted, or steamed over a broth tasted of pure shellfish, but they also tasted flat and one-dimensional. They cooked in their juices. In contrast, clams and mussels that were steamed in a flavorful broth picked up flavors from the liquid and tasted better.

With steaming in broth as our preferred all-purpose cooking method, we started to test various amounts and types of liquids, including fish stock, water, wine, and beer. We found white wine to be the best choice, although beer worked nicely with the mussels and is given on page 535 as a recipe variation. The bright acidity of white wine balances the briny flavor of clams and mussels. Fish stock and water (even when seasoned with garlic, herbs, and spices) were dull by comparison. While it is possible to steam four pounds of bivalves in just half a cup of liquid (naturally, the pot must be tightly sealed), we like to have extra broth for dunking bread or for saucing rice. We settled on using two cups of white wine to cook four pounds of clams or mussels.

We also made some refinements to the cooking broth. Garlic, shallots, and a bay leaf enrich the flavor of the shellfish. Simmering the broth for three minutes before adding the shellfish is sufficient time for these seasonings to flavor the wine broth. The all-purpose broth can be flavored in numerous ways, as the recipe variations demonstrate.

DEBEARDING MUSSELS

Mussels often contain a weedy beard protruding from the crack between the two shells. It's fairly small and can be difficult to tug out of place. We have found the easiest way to perform this task is to trap the beard between the side of a small paring knife and your thumb and pull to remove it. The flat surface of the knife gives you some leverage to extract the pesky beard.

Steamed Clams or Mussels

SERVES 4

The basic flavorings in this recipe work with all kinds of mussels and with either littlenecks or cherrystone clams. (Really large cherrystones may require 9 to 10 minutes of steaming to open.) Variations below may be better suited to the particular flavors of mussels or clams, as indicated.

2	cups dry white wine
1/2	cup minced shallots
4	medium garlic cloves, minced or pressed through a garlic press
I	bay leaf
4	pounds clams or mussels, scrubbed, debearded if cooking mussels (see the illustration on page 533)
4	tablespoons (1/2 stick) unsalted butter
1/2	cup chopped fresh parsley leaves

1. Bring the wine, shallots, garlic, and bay leaf to a simmer in a large pot. Continue to simmer to blend the flavors for about 3 minutes. Increase the heat to high and add the clams or mussels. Cover and cook, stirring twice, until the clams or mussels open, 4 to 8 minutes, depending on the size of the shellfish and the pot.

2. Use a slotted spoon to transfer the clams or mussels to a large serving bowl; discard any that have not opened. Swirl the butter into the broth in the pan to make an emulsified sauce. Stir in the parsley. Pour the broth over the clams or mussels and serve immediately with warm bread or rice.

➤ VARIATIONS

Steamed Clams or Mussels with White Wine, Curry, and Herbs

2	cups dry white wine
1/2	cup minced shallots
4	medium garlic cloves, minced or pressed through a garlic press
I	bay leaf
I	teaspoon curry powder
4	pounds clams or mussels, scrubbed, debearded if cooking mussels (see the illustration on page 533)
4	tablespoons (1/2 stick) unsalted butter
2	tablespoons chopped fresh parsley leaves
2	tablespoons chopped fresh cilantro leaves
2	tablespoons chopped fresh basil leaves

1. Bring the wine, shallots, garlic, bay leaf, and curry powder to a simmer in a large pot. Continue to simmer to blend the flavors for about 3 minutes. Increase the heat to high and add the clams or mussels. Cover and cook, stirring twice, until the clams or mussels open, 4 to 8 minutes, depending on the size of the shellfish and the pot.

2. Use a slotted spoon to transfer the clams or mussels to a large serving bowl; discard any that have not opened. Swirl the butter into the broth in the pan to make an emulsified sauce. Stir in the parsley, cilantro, and basil. Pour the broth over the clams or mussels and serve immediately with warm bread or rice.

Steamed Mussels with Cream Sauce and Tarragon

2	cups dry white wine
1/2	cup minced shallots
4	medium garlic cloves, minced or pressed through a garlic press
I	bay leaf
4	pounds mussels, scrubbed and debearded (see the illustration on page 533)
3/4	cup heavy cream
1/2	cup chopped fresh parsley leaves
2	teaspoons minced fresh tarragon leaves
I	tablespoon juice from I lemon

1. Bring the wine, shallots, garlic, and bay leaf to a simmer in a large pot. Continue to simmer to blend the flavors for about 3 minutes. Increase the heat to high and add the mussels. Cover and cook, stirring twice, until the mussels open, 4 to 8 minutes, depending on the size of the shellfish and the pot.

2. Use a slotted spoon to transfer the mussels to a large serving bowl; discard any that have not opened. Simmer the broth until reduced to 1/2 cup, about 8 minutes. Add the cream and simmer until thickened, about 2 minutes. Stir in the herbs and

lemon juice. Return the mussels to the pot, heat briefly, and serve immediately with bread.

Mussels Steamed in Beer

2	cups light-colored beer
1/2	cup minced onion
4	medium garlic cloves, minced or pressed through a garlic press
3	sprigs fresh thyme
1	bay leaf
4	pounds mussels, scrubbed and debearded (see the illustration on page 533)
4	tablespoons (1/2 stick) unsalted butter
1/2	cup chopped fresh parsley leaves

1. Bring the beer, onion, garlic, thyme, and bay leaf to a simmer in a large pot. Continue to simmer to blend the flavors for about 3 minutes. Increase the heat to high and add the mussels. Cover and cook, stirring twice, until the mussels open, 4 to 8 minutes, depending on the size of the shellfish and the pot.

2. Use a slotted spoon to transfer the mussels to a large serving bowl; discard any that have not opened. Swirl the butter into the pan liquids to make an emulsified sauce. Stir in the parsley. Pour the broth over the mussels and serve immediately with warm bread or rice.

CLAMBAKE

A CLAMBAKE IS A RITE OF SUMMER ALONG THE East Coast. At this festive beach party, loads of shellfish and a variety of vegetables are steamed in a wide, sandy pit using seaweed and rocks warmed from a nearby campfire. This feast usually takes a day or more to prepare—digging the pit is no small chore—and hours to cook. We wanted to re-create the great flavors of the clambake indoors. Though some may mock the idea of a kitchen clambake, it is nonetheless a simple and efficient way (taking a mere half hour) to prepare a fantastic shellfish dinner—complete with corn, potatoes, and sausage—for a hungry crowd.

An indoor clambake is not a novel idea. We

found dozens of recipes in our cookbook library. While the methods used to put together an indoor clambake vary dramatically, the ingredients, in keeping with tradition, are fairly consistent, including clams, mussels, lobsters, potatoes, corn, onions, and spicy sausage. Some recipes tell the cook to partially cook each ingredient separately and then finish things together on the grill, while others recommend specific systems for layering the ingredients in a stockpot. Some recipes use seaweed or corn husks for extra flavor, while others tout the importance of smoky bacon. The common goal of all these recipes, however, is to manage the process such that the various components are cooked perfectly and ready to serve at the same time. Taking note of these different clambake styles, we began our testing.

It soon became apparent which methods were worthwhile and which simply made a mess. Partially cooking the ingredients separately before combining them on the grill was time-consuming and produced a clambake without that authentic clambake flavor. Layering the various ingredients in a stockpot, on the other hand, was both easy to do and produced tasty results. With the stockpot set over high heat, the components steamed and infused one another with their flavors. This method was not without problems, however, as the onions turned out slimy, and half the ingredients wound up submerged in shellfish-flavored water. Using this pot method as a point of departure, we began to tinker with the method and the ingredients.

Although all of the recipes we uncovered called for adding water to the pot to create steam for cooking, we found the shellfish released enough of their own liquid to make adequate steam. When placed over high heat, the shellfish took only a few minutes to release the moisture needed to steam the whole pot, with a cup or more left over to use a sauce for the clams and mussels. We took advantage of those first few minutes when the pot was dry by lining it with sliced sausage, giving it a chance to sear before the steam was unleashed. We tested several kinds of sausage, and tasters preferred mild kielbasa. The light smoked flavor of this sausage works well with seafood, and the sausage is fairly juicy and fatty, making it perfectly suited to this cooking method.

With the sausage layered on the bottom, we played with the order in which to add the remaining ingredients. We found it best to lay the clams and mussels right on top of the sausage because they provide most of the necessary liquid for the steam and needed to be close to the heat source. Wrapping them loosely in a cheesecloth sack makes them easy to remove when done. Although potatoes actually take the longest to cook, they were best laid on top of the clams and mussels, close to the heat source yet easily accessible with a prodding knife to test their doneness. We shortened their cooking time by cutting the potatoes into 1-inch pieces. Corn, with a layer of husk left on, was placed on top of the potatoes. The husk, we found, protects the delicate corn from becoming infused with too much shellfish flavor. The husk also protects the corn from any foam released by the lobsters, which we placed on top of the corn. We decided to omit the onions, which no one ate; the bacon, which smoked out the delicate flavor of the shellfish; and the seaweed, which was hard to find and unnecessary for flavor.

Layered in this fashion, the clambake took just 17 to 20 minutes to cook through completely over high heat. Surprisingly, the shellfish liquid is quite salty and naturally seasons all the ingredients. After taking a couple of minutes to remove the ingredients from the pot and arrange them attractively on a platter, we had a feast that had been made from start to finish in half an hour.

Indoor Clambake

SERVES 4 TO 6

Choose a large, narrow stockpot in which you can easily layer the ingredients. The recipe can easily be cut in half and layered in an 8-quart Dutch oven, but it should cook in the same amount of time.

2   pounds littleneck or cherrystone clams, scrubbed

2   pounds mussels, scrubbed and debearded (see the illustration on page 533)

1   pound kielbasa, sliced into $1/3$-inch rounds

1   pound small new or red potatoes, scrubbed and cut into 1-inch pieces

4   medium ears corn, silk and all but the last layer of husks removed (see the illustrations on page 157)

2   live lobsters (about $1^1/_2$ pounds each)

8   tablespoons (1 stick) salted butter, melted

1. Place the clams and mussels on a large piece of cheesecloth and tie the ends together to secure; set aside. In a 12-quart heavy-bottomed stockpot, layer the sliced kielbasa, the sack of clams and mussels, the potatoes, the corn, and the lobsters on top of one another. Cover with the lid and place over high heat. Cook until the potatoes are tender (a paring knife can be slipped into and out of the center of a potato with little resistance) and the lobsters are bright red, 17 to 20 minutes.

2. Remove the pot from the heat and remove the lid (watch out for scalding steam). Remove the lobsters and set them aside until cool enough to handle. Remove the corn from the pot and peel off the husks; arrange the ears on a large platter. Using a slotted spoon, remove the potatoes and arrange them on the platter with the corn. Transfer the clams and mussels to a large bowl and cut open the cheesecloth with scissors; discard any clams or mussels that have not opened. Using a slotted spoon, remove the kielbasa from the pot and arrange it on the platter with the potatoes and corn. Pour the remaining steaming liquid in the pot over the clams and mussels. With a kitchen towel in your hand, twist and remove the lobster tails, claws, and legs (if desired). Arrange the lobster parts on the platter. Serve immediately with the melted butter and plenty of napkins.

12

STEWS

THIS CHAPTER COVERS STEWS MADE WITH BEEF, pork, and lamb. (Chicken stews and fish stews are covered in chapters 7 and 11, respectively.) Although each kind of meat and each stew has its own requirements, there are a few general points to keep in mind. First and foremost, start with the right cut of meat.

In our testing, we found that meat from the shoulder area of the animal usually has the best combination of flavor and texture. This meat is well marbled with fat, so it won't dry out during the stewing process. Other cuts are simply too lean to use in stews. They will become tough if cooked this way.

So why does shoulder meat generally make the best stews? Its intramuscular fat and connective tissue make it amenable to long, slow, moist cooking. When cooked in liquid, the connective tissue melts down into gelatin, making the meat tender. The fat in the meat helps as well, in two important ways. Fat carries the chemical compounds that our taste buds perceive as beef, lamb, or pork flavor, and it also melts when cooked, lubricating the meat fibers as it slips between the cells, increasing tenderness.

We found that buying roasts and chops and cutting them up for stew ourselves had distinct advantages over buying precut packages of meat. Packages labeled "stew meat" in supermarkets often contain misshapen parts or small bits of meat. In addition, stew meat packages may have scraps from various parts of the animal. To make sure that you have purchased the proper cut of meat and that it is divided into evenly sized chunks, take the five extra minutes to cut the meat yourself.

Browning the meat well is another key point to keep in mind. Meat stews generally begin with seasoning the chunks of meat with salt and pepper and then sautéing them in a film of oil. Don't rush this step. In our tests, meat that was only spottily browned didn't taste as good. Browning the meat and some of the vegetables, especially onions, adds flavor to the final dish.

How does browning work? In vegetables it is largely sugars and in meat it is the sugars and proteins that caramelize, or brown, making the meat and vegetables taste better. In addition to flavoring the meat, proper browning covers the bottom

of the pan with browned bits called *fond*. When liquid is added to the pot, the fond loosens and dissolves, adding flavor to the stew. This process is called deglazing. Wine and stock are the most common choices for deglazing the pan, but water works, too. Because the foundation of a stew's flavor comes from the fond and deglazing liquid, it is crucial that the meat be browned properly. In most recipes, to ensure proper browning, we sauté the meat in two batches. If all of the meat is put into the pot at once, the pieces crowd one another and steam, thus turning a pallid gray color rather than brown.

Contrary to popular belief, browning does not "seal in" the juices in meat. After browning, when the meat is slow-cooked, more and more juices are expelled as the internal temperature of the meat rises. By the time the meat is fork-tender, it has in fact shed most of its juices. As odd as it sounds, this is the beauty of a stew, since the surrounding liquid, which is served as a sauce, is enriched by these juices.

Our tests revealed that the temperature of the stewing liquid is crucial. We found it essential to keep the temperature of the liquid below 212 degrees. Boiled meat remains tough, and the outside becomes especially dry. Keeping the liquid at a simmer (rather than a boil) allows the internal temperature of the meat to rise slowly. By the time it is actually fork-tender, much of the connective tissue will have turned to gelatin. The gelatin, in turn, helps to thicken the stewing liquid.

To determine whether stews cook best on the stovetop or in the oven, we tried both, simmering a basic beef stew on the stovetop over low heat (with and without a flame-taming device to protect the pot from direct heat) and in a moderate oven. The flame-tamer device worked too well in distancing the pot from the heat; the stew juices tasted raw and boozy. Putting the pot right on the burner worked better, but we found ourselves constantly adjusting the burner to maintain a gentle simmer, and this method is prone to error. We had the most consistent results in the oven. We found that putting a covered Dutch oven in a 300-degree oven ensures that the temperature of the stewing liquid will remain below the boiling point, at about 200 degrees. (The oven must be kept at a temperature higher than 200 degrees because ovens are not completely efficient in transferring heat; a temperature of 300 degrees recognizes that some heat will be lost as it penetrates through the pot and into the stew.)

The recipes in this chapter are conventional stews—large chunks of boneless meat accompanied by vegetables in a thickened sauce. The chapter also includes cassoulet, a classic French dish that combines stewed meat, beans, sausage, and toasted bread. We've radically simplified this recipe, making it possible to prepare this grand dish at home.

A final note about our choice of liquids for use in meat stews. Few home cooks have meat stock on hand. They might make beef stock for beef soup because there's no other alternative, but they generally make only what they need for a particular recipe. In stews, with their many components, the liquid element is usually not as central as it is in soup. Beef stock is too much work for such recipes. We find that low-sodium canned chicken broth (which tastes better than canned beef broth) is a fine option. If you have homemade chicken stock on hand, you can use some in these recipes. However, we have found that the differences between meat stews made with homemade chicken stock and those made with canned chicken broth are minimal.

HEARTY BEEF STEW

BEEF STEW SHOULD BE RICH AND SATISFYING. Our goal in developing a recipe for it was to keep the cooking process simple without compromising the stew's deep, complex flavor. We focused on these issues: What cuts of beef respond best to stewing? How much and what kind of liquid should you use? When and with what do you thicken the stew?

Experts tout different cuts as being ideal for stewing. We browned 12 different cuts of beef, marked them for identification, and stewed them in the same pot. Chuck proved to be the most flavorful, tender, and juicy. Most other cuts were too stringy, too chewy, too dry, or just plain bland.

The exception was rib-eye steak, which made good stew meat but is too expensive a cut for this purpose.

Our advice is to buy a steak or roast from the chuck and cube it yourself. The names given to different cuts of chuck vary, but the most commonly used names for retail chuck cuts include boneless chuck-eye roasts, cross-rib roasts, blade steaks and roasts, shoulder steaks and roasts, and arm steaks and roasts. We particularly like chuck-eye roasts, but all chuck cuts are delicious when cubed and stewed.

Having settled on our cut of beef, we started to explore how and when to thicken the stew. Dredging meat cubes in flour is a roundabout way of thickening stew. The floured beef is browned, then stewed. During the stewing process, some of the flour from the beef dissolves into the liquid, causing it to thicken. Although the stew we cooked this way thickened up nicely, the beef cubes had a "smothered steak" look.

We also tried two thickening methods at the end of cooking—a *beurre manié* (softened butter mixed with flour) and cornstarch mixed with water. Both methods are acceptable, but the beurre manié lightened the stew liquid's color, making it look more like pale gravy than rich stew juices. Also, the extra fat did not improve the stew's flavor enough to justify its addition. For those who prefer thickening at the end of cooking, we found that cornstarch dissolved in water did the job without compromising the stew's dark, rich color.

Pureeing the cooked vegetables is another thickening method. Once the stew is fully cooked, the meat is pulled from the pot and the juices and vegetables are pureed to create a thick sauce. Tasters felt this thickening method made the vegetable flavor too prominent.

Ultimately, though, we opted for thickening the stew with flour at the beginning—stirring it into the sautéing onions and garlic, right before adding the liquid. Stew thickened this way did not taste any better than that thickened at the end with cornstarch, but it was easier. There was no last-minute work; once the liquid started to simmer, the cook was free to do something else.

We next focused on stewing liquids. We tried

water, wine, canned beef broth, canned chicken broth, combinations of these liquids, and beef stock. Stews made with water were bland and greasy. Stews made entirely with wine were too strong. The stew made from beef stock was delicious, but we decided that beef stew, which has many hearty ingredients contributing to its flavor profile, did not absolutely need beef stock, which is time-consuming to make. When we turned to canned broths, the chicken outscored the beef broth. The stew made entirely with chicken broth was good, but we missed the acidity and flavor provided by the wine. In the end, we preferred a combination of chicken broth and red wine.

We tested various amounts of liquid and found that we preferred stews with a minimum of liquid, which helps to preserve a strong meat flavor. With too little liquid, however, the stew may not cook evenly, and there may not be enough "sauce" to spoon over starchy accompaniments. A cup of liquid per pound of meat gave us sufficient sauce to moisten a mound of mashed potatoes or polenta without drowning them. We tested various kinds of wine and found that fairly inexpensive fruity, full-bodied, young wines, such as Chianti or Zinfandel, were best.

To determine when to add the vegetables, we made three different stews, adding carrots, potatoes, and onions to one stew at the beginning of cooking and to another stew halfway through the cooking process. For our final stew, we cooked the onions with the meat but added steamed carrots and potatoes when the stew was fully cooked.

The stew with vegetables added at the beginning was thin and watery. The vegetables had fallen apart and given up their flavor and liquid to the stew. The beef stew with the cooked vegetables added at the last minute was delicious, and the vegetables were the freshest and most intensely flavored. However, it was more work to steam the vegetables separately. Also, vegetables cooked separately from the stew didn't really meld all that well with the other flavors and ingredients. We preferred to add the vegetables partway through the cooking process. They didn't fall apart this way, and they had enough time to meld with the other ingredients. There is one exception to this rule. Peas were added just before serving the stew to preserve their color and texture.

One final note: The meat passes from the tough to tender stage fairly quickly. Often at the 1-hour mark, we found that the meat would still be chewy. Fifteen minutes later, it would be tender. Let the stew go another 15 minutes and the meat starts to dry out. Taste the meat often as the stew nears completion to judge when it's just right.

CUTTING STEW MEAT

For stew meat pieces that are cut from the right part of the animal and regularly shaped, we suggest buying a boneless roast and cutting the meat yourself. A three-pound roast, once trimmed, should yield 2¾ pounds of beef, the maximum amount that can be correctly browned in two batches in a large Dutch oven.

1. Pull apart the roast at its major seams (delineated by lines of fat and silver skin). Use a knife as necessary.

2. With a paring knife, trim off excess fat and silver skin.

3. Cut the meat into cubes or chunks as directed in specific recipes.

Hearty Beef Stew
SERVES 6 TO 8

Make this stew in an ovenproof Dutch oven, preferably one with a capacity of 8 quarts but nothing less than 6 quarts. Choose a Dutch oven with a wide bottom; this will allow you to brown the meat in just 2 batches. See page 542 for information about choosing a red wine for use in this dish.

- 3 pounds beef chuck roast, trimmed and cut into 1½-inch cubes (see the illustrations on page 540)
  Salt and ground black pepper
- 3 tablespoons vegetable oil
- 2 medium onions, chopped coarse (about 2 cups)
- 3 medium garlic cloves, minced or pressed through a garlic press
- 3 tablespoons unbleached all-purpose flour
- 1 cup full-bodied dry red wine
- 2 cups low-sodium chicken broth
- 2 bay leaves
- 1 teaspoon dried thyme
- 4 medium red potatoes (about 1½ pounds), peeled and cut into 1-inch cubes
- 4 large carrots (about 1 pound), peeled and sliced ¼ inch thick
- 1 cup frozen peas (about 6 ounces), thawed
- ¼ cup minced fresh parsley leaves

1. Adjust an oven rack to the lower-middle position and heat the oven to 300 degrees. Dry the beef thoroughly with paper towels, then season it generously with salt and pepper to taste. Heat 1 tablespoon of the oil in a large ovenproof Dutch oven over medium-high heat until shimmering. Add half of the meat so that the individual pieces are close together but not touching. Cook, not moving the pieces until the sides touching the pot are well browned, 2 to 3 minutes. Using tongs, turn each piece and continue cooking until most sides are well browned, about 5 minutes longer. Transfer the beef to a medium bowl, add another 1 tablespoon of the oil to the pot, and swirl to coat the pan bottom. Brown the remaining beef; transfer the meat to the bowl and set aside.

2. Reduce the heat to medium, add the remaining 1 tablespoon oil to the now-empty Dutch oven, and swirl to coat the pan bottom. Add the onions and ¼ teaspoon salt. Cook, stirring frequently and vigorously, scraping the pot bottom with a wooden spoon to loosen the browned bits, until the onions have softened, 4 to 5 minutes. Add the garlic and continue to cook for 30 seconds. Stir in the flour and cook until lightly colored, 1 to 2 minutes. Add the wine, scraping up the remaining browned bits from the bottom and edges of the pot and stirring until the liquid is thick. Gradually add the broth, stirring constantly and scraping the pan edges to dissolve the flour. Add the bay leaves and thyme and bring to a simmer. Add the meat and return to a simmer. Cover and place the pot in the oven. Cook for 1 hour.

3. Remove the pot from the oven and add the potatoes and carrots. Cover and return the pot to the oven. Cook until the meat is just tender, about 1 hour. Remove the pot from the oven. (The stew can be covered and refrigerated for up to 3 days. Bring to a simmer over medium-low heat.)

4. Add the peas, cover, and allow to stand for 5 minutes. Stir in the parsley, discard the bay leaves, adjust the seasonings, and serve immediately.

➤ VARIATION
Beef Goulash

Goulash is like the Merlot of beef stews—mellow, with sweet overtones. If your tastes run more toward Zinfandel, add a pinch of hot paprika or cayenne pepper for a more complex, spicy version. The flavor from the beef fat adds something to this stew, so don't trim the meat too closely. We recommend removing external fat from the chuck roast but leaving internal fat alone unless it is excessively thick. Serve the stew over 1 pound of buttered egg noodles. Try tossing the noodles with 1 tablespoon of toasted caraway seeds for a distinctive and delicious flavor combination. (Caraway is an unusual and authentic touch.)

- 3 pounds beef chuck roast, trimmed and cut into 1½-inch cubes (see the illustrations on page 540)
  Salt and ground black pepper
- 3 tablespoons vegetable oil or lard
- 3 medium-large onions, chopped coarse

6   medium garlic cloves, minced or pressed
     through a garlic press

5   tablespoons sweet paprika

¼   cup unbleached all-purpose flour

3   cups low-sodium chicken broth

2   tablespoons tomato paste

2   bay leaves

1   teaspoon dried marjoram

1   large red bell pepper, cored, seeded, and
     chopped coarse

1   large green bell pepper, cored, seeded, and
     chopped coarse

½   cup sour cream

¼   cup minced fresh parsley leaves

1. Adjust an oven rack to the lower-middle position and heat the oven to 300 degrees. Dry the beef thoroughly with paper towels, then season it generously with salt and pepper to taste. Heat 1 tablespoon of the oil in a large ovenproof Dutch oven over medium-high heat until shimmering. Add half of the meat so that the individual pieces are close together but not touching. Cook, not moving the pieces until the sides touching the pot are well browned, 2 to 3 minutes. Using tongs, turn each piece and continue cooking until most sides are well browned, about 5 minutes longer. Transfer the beef to a medium bowl, add another

DOUBLE DUTY FOR POT LIDS

Most stews start with browning the meat, which must then be removed from the pan so the other ingredients can be browned, occasioning a dirty dish. We suggest that instead of using a clean dish, invert the lid of the pan in which you're cooking over another bowl or pot. The lid, which you need to wash anyway, now serves as a spoon rest and receptacle for the sautéed food.

1 tablespoon of the oil to the pot, and swirl to coat the pan bottom. Brown the remaining beef; transfer the meat to the bowl and set aside.

2. Reduce the heat to medium, add the remaining 1 tablespoon oil to the now-empty Dutch oven, and swirl to coat the pan bottom. Add the onions and ¼ teaspoon salt. Cook, stirring frequently and vigorously, scraping the pot bottom with a wooden spoon to loosen the browned bits, until the onions have softened and browned, about 8 minutes. Stir in the garlic and cook until fragrant, about 30 seconds. Add the paprika and flour and stir until the onions are evenly coated and fragrant, 1 to 2 minutes.

3. Stir in 1½ cups of the broth, scraping the pot bottom with a wooden spoon to loosen the remaining browned bits and stirring until the flour is incorporated and the liquid thickened. Gradually add the remaining 1½ cups broth, stirring constantly and scraping the pan edges to dissolve the flour. Stir in the tomato paste, bay leaves, marjoram, and

INGREDIENTS: Red Wine for Stew

When making a dish that uses red wine, our tendency is to grab whichever inexpensive, dry red is on hand, usually the leftover contents of a recently opened bottle. But we began to wonder what difference particular wines would make in the final dish and decided to investigate.

We called on the advice of several local wine experts, who gave us some parameters to work with when selecting red wines to use in a braise such as Hearty Beef Stew. (The rules are slightly different when making some dishes, such as Beef Burgundy, that traditionally rely on a particular kind of wine. See page 548 for more details on choosing a red wine for this dish.)

When selecting a red wine for a basic stew, look for one that is dry (to avoid a sweet sauce) and with good acidity (to aid in breaking down the fibers of the meat). Keep in mind that any characteristic found in the uncooked wine will be concentrated when cooked.

From tests we ran, we found that softer, fruity wines such as Merlot yielded a "grape jelly" flavor, which most tasters thought was too sweet for beef stew or cacciatore. We also learned that it's best to avoid wines that have been "oaked," usually older wines; the oak flavor tends to become harsh and bitter as the wine is cooked.

¾ teaspoon salt. Add the browned beef and accumulated juices, stir to blend, and submerge the meat under the liquid. Increase the heat to medium, bring to a simmer, cover the pot, and place it in the oven. Cook for 1 hour and 20 minutes.

4. Remove the pot from the oven and stir in the red and green peppers. Cover and return the pot to the oven. Cook until the meat is just tender, about 40 minutes. Remove the pot from the oven. If serving immediately, spoon off the fat that rises to the top. (The stew can be covered and refrigerated for up to 3 days. Spoon off the congealed fat and bring the stew back to a simmer over medium-low heat.)

5. Place the sour cream in a medium bowl and stir in about ½ cup of the hot stewing liquid. Stir the sour cream mixture back into the stew. Stir in the parsley, discard the bay leaves, and season with salt and pepper to taste. Serve immediately.

CARBONNADE

A BASIC BEEF STEW CAN BE ALTERED IN DOZENS of ways, usually by adding more ingredients to the pot. But you can also go the other way and strip beef stew down to its bare bones (to its beef). If you also trade in the carrots and potatoes for a plethora of onions and add a good dose of beer, you've created a Belgian beef stew called *carbonnade à la flamande.*

Beef, beer, and onions have an affinity—they're an ensemble with great appeal (think burger, onion rings, and a beer). In a carbonnade, the heartiness of beef melds with the soft sweetness of sliced onions in a broth that is deep and rich with the malty flavor of dark beer.

We made several versions of carbonnade and found that despite the simple and few ingredients, making a poor one is quite easy to do. We wound up with several batches of tough, tasteless beef and onions in a pale, insipid broth. Not quite what we had in mind.

We used the framework of our recipe for hearty beef stew to arrive at an improved carbonnade. The operations were as follows: The beef is browned in batches and set aside, the onions are sautéed in the empty pot, the flour is sprinkled over the onions, the liquid is added, the beef is returned to the pot, and the covered pot goes into the oven, where it simmers until the beef is fork-tender.

In developing a recipe for carbonnade, the first departure from our beef stew recipe came with the selection of beef. For a basic beef stew, we prefer a chuck roast cut into 1½-inch chunks. A chuck roast is composed of a number of different muscles interwoven with intramuscular fat and connective tissue. This fat and tissue make for good texture and flavor, and the different muscles make for pieces of meat with uneven or differing textures, even when cooked.

The substance of carbonnade is purely beef and onion—there are no chunks of potatoes or carrots with which the beef competes. Consequently, we wanted smaller pieces of beef of a uniform texture that would be a better match for the soft, thinly sliced onions. Enter 1-inch-thick blade steaks (also called top-blade or flatiron steaks)—small, long, narrow steaks cut from the shoulder (or chuck) area of the animal. Most blade steaks have a decent amount of fat marbling, which gives them good flavor as well as a tender texture. One taster described the blade steak in carbonnade as "buttery," a quality that is well suited to this stew. The trade-off is that these smaller steaks are a bit more time-consuming to trim of silver skin and gristle, but they are well worth it.

Onions—and a good deal of them—go into a carbonnade. Two pounds was the right amount in relation to the amount of beef. We tried both white and red onions, but both were cloyingly sweet. Yellow onions tasted the best. After browning the beef, the floor of the pot was crusty with fond (browned bits). Do not underestimate the importance of the fond—it furnishes the stew with color and flavor. As we had done with goulash, we added ¼ teaspoon salt along with the thinly sliced onions to help release their moisture. This assists in keeping the fond from burning and in loosening it from the pot when deglazing. Garlic is not an ingredient in all carbonnade recipes, but we liked its heady essence; a small amount is added to the onions only after they are cooked so that the garlic does not burn.

The right beer is key to achieving a full, robust carbonnade. Beers of the light, lager persuasion, those commonly favored in America, lack guts—they result in light-colored, watery-tasting stews. We tried a number of different beers and found that reasonably dark ales, very dark ales, and stouts made the richest and best-tasting carbonnade. A few of our favorites were Chimay (a Trappist ale from Belgium), Newcastle Brown Ale, Anchor Steam (this beer cannot technically be classified as an ale), Samuel Smith Taddy Porter, and Guinness Extra Stout.

We tried making carbonnade with beer as the only liquid, but they lacked backbone and sometimes had an overwhelming bitterness, depending on the type of beer used. Equal parts chicken stock or canned broth and beer made a deeper, more solid-tasting stew. The addition of dried thyme and a bay leaf added herbal notes that complemented the other flavors. Just a bit of cider vinegar perked everything up, and a bit of dark brown sugar rounded out the flavors.

Carbonnade à la Flamande

SERVES 6 TO 8

To make sure the beef browns well, dry the pieces thoroughly with paper towels. Don't bother making this stew with a light-colored beer—both the color and flavor will be insipid. We particularly liked Newcastle Brown Ale, Anchor Steam, and Chimay. For those who like a heavier beer, with a slightly bitter flavor, porter and stout are good. Top-blade steaks are cut from the shoulder area of the cow. They are tender, but each steak has a line of gristle running down the center that should be removed. Top-blade steaks are often called flatiron steaks or blade steaks.

3–3½	pounds top-blade steaks, gristle removed and steaks cut into 1-inch pieces (see the illustrations at right)
	Salt and ground black pepper
3	tablespoons vegetable oil
2	pounds medium onions, halved and sliced thin
2	medium garlic cloves, minced or pressed through a garlic press
3	tablespoons unbleached all-purpose flour
1½	cups low-sodium chicken broth
1½	cups dark beer (see note)
¾	teaspoon dried thyme
1	bay leaf
1	tablespoon dark brown sugar
1	tablespoon cider vinegar

1. Adjust an oven rack to the lower-middle position and heat the oven to 300 degrees. Dry the beef thoroughly with paper towels, then season it generously with salt and pepper to taste. Heat 1 tablespoon of the oil in a large ovenproof Dutch oven over medium-high heat until shimmering. Add half of the meat so that the individual pieces are close together but not touching. Cook, not moving the pieces until the sides touching the pot are well browned, 2 to 3 minutes. Using tongs, turn each piece and continue cooking until most sides are well browned, about 5 minutes longer. Transfer the beef to a medium bowl, add another 1 tablespoon of the oil to the pot, and swirl to coat the pan bottom. Brown the remaining beef; transfer the meat to the bowl and set aside.

2. Reduce the heat to medium-low, add the remaining 1 tablespoon oil to the now-empty Dutch oven, and swirl to coat the pan bottom. Add the

PREPARING BLADE STEAKS FOR BEEF CARBONNADE

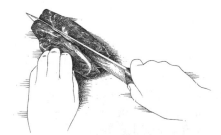

1. Cut each steak in half lengthwise, leaving the gristle attached to one half.

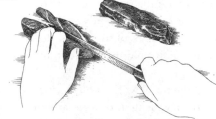

2. Cut away the gristle from the half to which it is still attached and cut the meat into 1-inch pieces.

onions and ¼ teaspoon salt and cook, stirring occasionally and vigorously, scraping the pot bottom with a wooden spoon to loosen the browned bits, until the onions have released some moisture, about 5 minutes. Increase the heat to medium and cook, stirring occasionally and scraping the pot bottom, until the onions are limp, softened, and lightly browned, 12 to 14 minutes. Stir in the garlic and cook until fragrant, about 30 seconds. Add the flour and stir until the onions are evenly coated.

3. Stir in the broth, scraping the pot bottom and edges with a wooden spoon to loosen the browned bits. Gradually add the beer, stirring constantly and scraping the pan edges to dissolve the flour. Add the thyme, bay leaf, sugar, and vinegar along with the browned beef and accumulated juices, pushing down on the beef to submerge the pieces; sprinkle with salt and pepper to taste, bring to a simmer, cover, and place in the oven. Cook until the beef is fork-tender, 1½ to 2 hours. Remove and discard the bay leaf. Adjust the seasonings with salt and pepper to taste and serve. (The stew can be covered and refrigerated for several days. Bring back to a simmer over medium-low heat.)

BEEF BURGUNDY

IF THE LOUVRE WERE JUST A MUSEUM, THEN *boeuf à la bourguignonne* might be just beef stew. Both are French and utterly extraordinary, but only one can be enjoyed at home. We liken beef Burgundy more to a fabulous prime steak napped with a rich, silken red wine reduction sauce than to a mundane beef stew. The beef in beef Burgundy is cut into satisfyingly large chunks that become utterly tender. The braising liquid, brimming with voluptuous wine and infused with aromatic vegetables, garlic, and herbs, is finessed into a sauce of burgundy velvet studded with mushrooms and pearl onions. Beef Burgundy is earthy, big, robust, warm, and welcoming in a brooding sort of way.

At least that's what it is at its best. We have had versions that fell far short of this, with tough meat or a dull sauce with no flavor complexity. We wanted to find a way to bring this classic dish to its full potential in a home kitchen.

Recipes for beef Burgundy are very much alike. Aromatic vegetables (onions, garlic, and carrots), red wine, stock, herbs, mushrooms, and pearl onions are all requisite ingredients; their combinations and proportions and the variations in preparation and technique are where the recipes diverge.

We started by completing four recipes, and from these four we made several important observations. First, marinating the beef in the red wine and herbs that will later go into the braise—a common recommendation in recipes—does not improve the flavor of the cooked meat. Second, the braising liquid requires straining to rid it of bits of aromatic vegetables and herbs so that it may become a silky sauce. We found that bundling in cheesecloth all the goods that must eventually come out of the pot made their extraction possible in one easy step. When wrapped in cheesecloth, however, the aromatic vegetables cannot first be sautéed—a customary step, the omission of which we feared would adversely affect the flavors of the braise. Remarkably, it did not. But perhaps this is why it took such generous amounts of chopped onions, carrots, and garlic, as well as parsley, thyme, peppercorns, and bay leaves, to create a balanced mélange of flavors.

The cut of beef best suited to the long braise of beef Burgundy is a chuck roast. It's the cut that almost every recipe calls for and the one we preferred in a regular beef stew because of its rich, meaty flavor. Because the beef in a beef Burgundy is cut into chunks larger than those in a beef stew—a good 1½ to 2 inches—we found it necessary to take extra care to trim off as much fat and silver skin as possible; larger pieces of beef also mean larger, more detectable bites of these undesirables.

Each and every beef Burgundy begins with either salt pork or bacon cut into lardons, or small strips, and fried to a crisp; the fat that results is used to brown the beef chunks. The crisped pork is added to the pot to simmer alongside the beef so that it can relinquish its flavors to the braise, providing a subtle, sweet underpinning and lending the sauce roundness and depth. We tried both bacon and salt pork and favored the cleaner, purer, more honest flavor of salt pork. Moreover, the thicker, more toothsome strips of salt pork had better texture than the lifeless, thin pieces of bacon. Salt pork can be a challenge to find in grocery stores, so we reasoned that just as blanching salt pork removes excess salt that would otherwise crystallize on the surface during frying, blanching thick-cut bacon ought to calm the smoke and sugar and make it appropriate for beef Burgundy. This worked well. The thick-cut bacon had more textural appeal than regular bacon and was an acceptable substitute for salt pork.

As for the stock that goes into the braise, most recipes call for beef, preferably homemade. Because making beef stock is so time-consuming, we wanted to try canned broth. From past experience, we knew that canned beef broth does not make an acceptable substitute for homemade beef stock. Therefore, in all subsequent tests, we used what we have found to be the next best option—canned chicken broth—with excellent results. Still, beef Burgundy necessitates a good amount of liquid for braising, and too much chicken broth tasted too chickeny. Water was a fine filler, especially since the braising liquid is later reduced to create the sauce. We then tried something a bit unorthodox to boost flavor. Just a small amount of dried porcini mushrooms wrapped into the cheesecloth package brought the meatiness and savory quality that homemade beef stock would conceivably have added. A modicum of tomato

paste added color and sprightliness.

Wine was the next issue. Beef Burgundy does not exist without a healthy dose of it. We concluded after several batches that anything less than a whole bottle left the sauce lacking and unremarkable. After numerous experiments, we had determined that a Burgundy, or at least a decent Pinot Noir, is indeed the wine of choice (see page 548 for more details). Though most recipes indicate that all of the wine should be added at the outset, one recipe, as well as one wine expert, recommended saving just a bit of the wine to add at the very end, just before serving. This late embellishment of raw wine vastly improved the sauce, brightening its flavor, giving it resonance, and making it sing.

Midway through testing, we decided we needed an alternative to browning the meat in the Dutch oven, where it would eventually be braised. Browning in batches took too long, and the drippings, or fond, that are essential flavor providers frequently burned. Evidently, the small cooking surface of even a large Dutch oven was a liability. We took to browning the beef in two batches in a heavy, large 12-inch skillet. To keep the fond from going to waste, we deglazed the pan with a bit of water and poured it directly into the braising pot, where it would eventually marry with the broth and wine.

Next we went to work to find the best means of adding flour to thicken the braising liquid that

MAKING THE VEGETABLE HERB BOUQUET

1. Cut two 22-inch lengths of cheesecloth and unfold each piece once lengthwise so that each forms a 2-ply, 22 by 8-inch piece.

2. Lay the cheesecloth in a medium bowl, stacking the sheets. Place the designated ingredients in the cheesecloth-lined bowl.

3. Gather together the edges of the cheesecloth and fasten them securely with kitchen twine. Trim any excess cheesecloth with scissors if necessary.

must blossom into a velvety sauce. Tossing the beef in flour before browning interfered with the color the beef could attain and ultimately affected its flavor. We found it preferable to make a roux in the skillet and add broth and water to it, then have it join the beef, wine, and vegetable and herb bouquet in the braising pot. This afforded us the opportunity to cook the roux until it achieved a toasty brown color, which made a favorable impact on the flavor of the dish.

With everything assembled in the Dutch oven, into the oven it went, where the constant, all-encompassing heat produced an even simmer that required little attention. This was the time to prepare the mushrooms and pearl onions, both of which would later join the sauce. We embraced already-peeled frozen pearl onions for this dish. A brisk simmer in a skillet with some water, butter, and sugar, and then a quick sauté with the mushrooms, created glazed beauties that were ready to grace the sauce. The final flourish, a little brandy, added richness and warmth to an already magnificent boeuf à la bourguignonne.

Beef Burgundy

SERVES 6

If you cannot find salt pork (see page 229 for more information), thick-cut bacon can be substituted. Cut it crosswise into ¼-inch pieces and treat it just as you would the salt pork, but note that you will have no rind to include in the vegetable and herb bouquet. To make this dish a day or two in advance, see Do-Ahead Beef Burgundy on page 549. Boiled potatoes are the traditional accompaniment, but mashed potatoes or buttered noodles are nice as well.

BEEF BRAISE

6   ounces salt pork, trimmed of rind (see the illustration on page 66), rind reserved and salt pork cut into 1 by ¼ by ¼-inch pieces

10   sprigs fresh parsley, torn into quarters

6   sprigs fresh thyme

2   medium onions, chopped coarse

2   medium carrots, chopped coarse

1   medium garlic head, cloves separated and crushed but unpeeled

2   bay leaves, crumbled

½   teaspoon black peppercorns

½   ounce dried porcini mushrooms, rinsed (optional)

4–4¼   pounds beef chuck roast, trimmed and cut into 2-inch chunks (see the illustrations on page 540)

    Salt and ground black pepper

2½   cups water

4   tablespoons (½ stick) unsalted butter, cut into 4 pieces

⅓   cup unbleached all-purpose flour

1¾   cups low-sodium chicken broth

1   bottle (750 ml) wine, red Burgundy or Pinot Noir

1   teaspoon tomato paste

ONION AND MUSHROOM GARNISH

36   frozen pearl onions (about 7 ounces)

1   tablespoon unsalted butter

1   tablespoon sugar

    Salt

¾   cup water

10   ounces white mushrooms, whole if small, halved if medium, quartered if large

2   tablespoons brandy

3   tablespoons minced fresh parsley leaves

1. FOR THE BRAISE: Bring the salt pork, reserved salt pork rind, and 3 cups water to a boil in a medium saucepan over high heat. Boil 2 minutes, then drain well.

2. Cut two 22-inch lengths of cheesecloth. Following the illustrations on page 546, wrap the parsley, thyme, onions, carrots, garlic, bay leaves, peppercorns, porcini mushrooms (if using), and blanched salt pork rind in the cheesecloth and set in a large ovenproof Dutch oven. Adjust an oven rack to the lower-middle position and heat the oven to 300 degrees.

3. Put the salt pork in a 12-inch skillet and set the skillet over medium heat; sauté until lightly browned and crisp, about 12 minutes. With a slotted spoon, transfer the salt pork to the Dutch oven. Pour off all but 2 teaspoons of the fat and reserve. Dry the beef thoroughly with paper towels, then season it generously with salt and pepper to taste. Increase the heat to high and brown half of the beef

in a single layer, turning once or twice, until deep brown, about 7 minutes; transfer the browned beef to the Dutch oven. Pour ½ cup of the water into the skillet and scrape the pan with a wooden spoon to loosen the browned bits. When the pan bottom is clean, pour the liquid into the Dutch oven.

4. Return the skillet to high heat and add the 2 teaspoons reserved pork fat; swirl to coat the pan bottom. When the fat begins to smoke, brown the remaining beef in a single layer, turning once or twice, until deep brown, about 7 minutes; transfer the browned beef to the Dutch oven. Pour ½ cup more water into the skillet and scrape the pan with a wooden spoon to loosen the browned bits. When the pan bottom is clean, pour the liquid into the Dutch oven.

5. Set the now-empty skillet over medium heat and add the butter. When the foaming subsides, whisk in the flour until evenly moistened and pasty. Cook, whisking constantly, until the mixture has a toasty aroma and resembles light-colored peanut butter, about 5 minutes. Gradually whisk in the broth and the remaining 1½ cups water. Increase the heat to medium-high and bring to a simmer, stirring frequently, until thickened. Pour the mixture into the Dutch oven. Add 3 cups of the wine, the tomato paste, and salt and pepper to taste to the Dutch oven and stir to combine. Set the Dutch oven over high heat and bring to a boil. Cover and place the pot in the oven. Cook until the meat is tender, 2½ to 3 hours.

6. Remove the Dutch oven from the oven and, using tongs, transfer the vegetable and herb bouquet to a mesh strainer set over the pot. Press the liquid back into the pot and discard the bouquet. With a slotted spoon, transfer the beef to a medium bowl; set aside. Allow the braising liquid to settle about 15 minutes, then, with a wide, shallow spoon, skim the fat off the surface and discard.

7. Bring the liquid in the Dutch oven to a boil over medium-high heat on the stovetop. Simmer briskly, stirring occasionally to ensure that the bottom is not burning, until the sauce is reduced to about 3 cups and thickened to the consistency of heavy cream, 15 to 25 minutes.

8. PREPARE THE GARNISH: While the sauce is reducing, bring the pearl onions, butter, sugar, ¼ teaspoon salt, and ½ cup of the water to a boil in a medium skillet over high heat. Cover, reduce the heat to medium-low, and simmer, shaking the pan occasionally, until the onions are tender, about 5 minutes. Uncover, increase the heat to

---

INGREDIENTS: Does It Have to Be Burgundy?

Beef Burgundy is rightfully made with true Burgundy wine. This means a red wine made from the Pinot Noir grape grown in the French province of Burgundy. Characteristically, these wines are medium-bodied but also deep, rich, and complex, with earthy tones and a reticent fruitiness. They are also expensive. Throughout our testing, into each batch of beef Burgundy, we emptied a $12 bottle of Burgundy—the least expensive we could find. Quite frankly, it was making outstanding beef Burgundies. Nonetheless, we tried more costly, higher-quality Burgundies and found that they bettered the dish—a $30 bottle gave a stellar, rousing performance. We thought it worth exploring other wines, but, wanting to remain faithful to the spirit of the dish, we limited ourselves to Pinot Noirs made on the West Coast of the United States, which are slightly less expensive than French Burgundies. We made beef Burgundies with domestic Pinot Noirs at three different price points, and even the least expensive wine—a $9 bottle—was perfectly acceptable, although its flavors were simpler and less intriguing than those of its Burgundian counterpart.

Both the Burgundies and the Pinot Noirs exhibited the same pattern—that is, as the price of the wine increased, so did the depth, complexity, and roundness of the sauce. We can advise with some confidence to set your price, then seek out a wine—either Burgundy or Pinot Noir—that matches it. But if your allegiance is to a true Burgundy, be warned that they can be difficult to find because production is relatively limited. We also caution you to beware of several very inexpensive mass-produced wines from California of questionable constitutions that are sold as "Burgundy." They are usually made from a blend of grape varieties, and whether or not they actually contain so much as a drop of Pinot Noir is a mystery. We made beef burgundy with one of these wines, and it resulted in a fleeting, one-dimensional, fruity, sweet sauce that, though palatable, lacked the deep, lavish flavors we have come to expect in a beef Burgundy.

high, and simmer until all of the liquid evaporates, about 3 minutes. Add the mushrooms and ¼ teaspoon salt. Cook, stirring occasionally, until the liquid released by the mushrooms evaporates and the vegetables are browned and glazed, about 5 minutes. Transfer the vegetables to a large plate and set aside. Add the remaining ¼ cup water to the skillet and stir with a wooden spoon to loosen the browned bits. When the pan bottom and sides are clean, add the liquid to the reducing sauce.

9. When the sauce in the Dutch oven has reduced to about 3 cups and thickened to the consistency of heavy cream, reduce the heat to medium-low. Stir in the beef, mushrooms and onions (and any accumulated juices), the remaining wine, and the brandy. Cover the pot and cook until just heated through, 5 to 8 minutes. Adjust the seasonings with salt and pepper to taste and serve, sprinkling the individual servings with the minced parsley.

➤ VARIATION

Do-Ahead Beef Burgundy

The braise can be made a day or two ahead, and the sauce, along with the onion and mushroom garnish, can be completed the day you intend to serve the dish.

1. Follow the recipe for Beef Burgundy through step 5. Using tongs, transfer the vegetable and herb bouquet to a mesh strainer set over the Dutch oven. Press the liquid back into the pot and discard the bouquet. Let the beef cool to room temperature in the braising liquid in the Dutch oven. (The braise can be kept covered in the refrigerator for 1 to 2 days.)

2. To complete the dish, use a slotted spoon to skim the congealed fat off the top and discard. Set the pot over medium-high heat and bring to a simmer. With the slotted spoon, transfer the beef to a medium bowl and set aside. Simmer the sauce briskly, stirring occasionally to ensure that the bottom is not burning, until reduced to about 3 cups and thickened to the consistency of heavy cream.

3. Continue with the recipe from step 8.

POZOLE

POZOLE IS THE MEXICAN NAME FOR BOTH hominy (dried field corn kernels treated with lime and boiled until tender but still chewy) and the stew made with hominy and pork. The stew is made throughout Mexico, in several quite distinct incarnations. *Pozole blanco* (white pozole) is prepared without any chiles. *Pozole rojo* (red pozole) is made with dried red chiles and *pozole verde* (green pozole) with tomatillos, fresh green chiles, and cilantro. Pozole blanco seems fairly bland compared with the red and green versions, so we decided to focus on the latter two styles.

Whether red or green, pozole should have a complex, richly flavored broth with lots of body. The meat, which is shredded, must be exceedingly tender, while the hominy is toothsome and sweet. A garnish of chopped raw vegetables (lettuce, radishes, and herbs) is added at the table.

Authentic pozole is made with bones from the head, neck, shank, and feet of the pig, supplemented with some boneless meat from the shoulder or loin. We wondered how important bones were to this dish. We prepared one batch with boneless shoulder meat only and another with a bone-in shoulder roast. (We chose the shoulder not only because of availability but also because it has consistently proved to be the best cut for stewing.) The liquid of the pozole prepared without bones was weak in flavor and thin in texture. The version made with the bone-in shoulder roast had a distinctive, satisfying pork flavor. It was obvious to tasters that bones are key to developing rich, full-bodied pork flavor. In addition, the bones released a large amount of gelatin that gave the pozole a voluptuous body.

There are two cuts from the shoulder. Since Boston butt is typically sold without the bone, we decided to use the picnic roast (or picnic ham). We found that a 5-pound roast, once trimmed of its thick skin and fat, yielded just less than 3 pounds of boneless meat—enough for the stew.

Pozole differs from other meat stews in that the meat is shredded rather than cubed. The meat is usually stewed in large chunks until it is tender enough to pull apart by hand. Just to make sure that tradition is best, we trying cubing the meat and then shredding it after cooking, but this process proved quite tedious. We then tried cooking the roast whole, but this increased the cooking time dramatically. Finally, we tried cutting the meat into large chunks, following the natural lines of the muscles as we removed the meat from the bone. This approach worked best—the stewing time was not excessive (two hours did the trick), and the meat was easy to shred. The sizes and shapes of these chunks varied from 3 by 1-inch strips to 4-inch cubes. From a 5-pound roast, we cut eight or nine randomly shaped chunks plus the bones, which had some pieces of meat tightly attached.

Pozole differs from most stews in another regard. Stew meat is typically browned to enhance the flavor of both the meat and the stewing liquid. In many pozole recipes, the meat is simply added raw to the simmering liquid. The reason is simple: Browning inhibits the shredding process and creates a firmer, crustier texture on the outside of each piece of meat. Another choice is to sweat the meat with some onions. We tried both simmering and sweating and found that the latter developed more flavor in the liquid without firming up the texture of the meat. Just make sure to cook the onions first so they will release some liquid and thus prevent the meat from burning or scorching on the outside.

In addition to onion, garlic is the other aromatic ingredient typically added at the outset when making pozole. Once the onion is soft, the garlic goes into the pot and cooks just until fragrant. We found that gentle sweating, rather than browning, works best for the alliums.

Once the meat has been sweated, it's time to add the liquid and other seasonings. We tested water and canned chicken broth (figuring that homemade stock, while always good, wouldn't be necessary in such a highly flavored dish). Although the water was fine, the broth was superior, adding not only depth of flavor but body to the stewing liquid. Tomatoes would also add moisture. Although some versions of red pozole reserve the tomatoes as part of the garnish, our tasters liked the tomatoes cooked right in the stew. The acidity of the tomatoes created a more lively mix. (Note that for green pozole, the tomatoes should be used as a garnish.)

Oregano is another main ingredient in pozole. Several varieties are grown in Mexico, all of which differ from the Mediterranean oregano popular in this country. Mexican oregano does not have the anise compounds found in Mediterranean varieties. Its flavor is more earthy and more potent. We tested pozole with dried Mexican, dried Mediterranean, and fresh Mediterranean oregano. (We were unable to purchase fresh Mexican oregano.) The dried Mediterranean oregano had a strong pizza-parlor flavor that was out of place in pozole. The fresh Mediterranean oregano was a better substitute for the dried Mexican oregano, which we prefer but can be difficult to find.

The final component of the pozole to examine was the chiles. The red color comes from dried chiles, so we tested several possibilities—anchos, New Mexico reds, and pasillas. We removed stems and seeds from the dried chiles, soaked them in boiling water, and then pureed the chiles and soaking liquid to create a thick paste. (We tested toasting the chiles before soaking but found this step added little to this dish.) The paste was added to the pot once the meat was tender. We liked all three chiles but preferred the deep reddish brown color and rich, sweet, raisiny flavor of the anchos.

We also tested chili powder, sprinkling some into the pot once the onions, garlic, and meat had been sweated. Although the results weren't terrible, everyone in the test kitchen agreed that the pozole made with powder instead of a puree of whole chiles was less complex-tasting and less appealing. It's worth spending the extra few minutes soaking and pureeing the anchos as directed in our recipe.

We found that it can be difficult to create a stew that pleases all tasters, especially when it comes to an agreed-upon spiciness. For this reason, we think it makes sense to mix three quarters of the ancho chile puree into the pozole and serve the remaining puree at the table with the garnishes. Those who like spicy food can add more puree; those who don't, won't.

It was time to deal with the hominy. We started by preparing one batch of pozole with freshly rehydrated hominy (which took hours to prepare) and another batch with canned hominy (which took seconds to drain and rinse). The pozole with freshly cooked hominy was superb, but the pozole with canned hominy was pretty good. It was chewy (as hominy should be) and relatively sweet.

After a few more tests, we found that cooking the canned hominy in the stew for 40 to 45 minutes allows the hominy to soak up some of the flavorful broth. Don't try to cook canned hominy any longer. We found that the texture will suffer and the hominy will become soggy if simmered for an hour or more.

Canned hominy comes in white and yellow varieties, depending on the type of field corn used. We tested white and yellow hominy and found that both types are fine. Flavor isn't much of an issue; white and yellow hominy are both sweet and "corny" tasting. In terms of appearance, yellow hominy looks a bit better in green pozole, but the difference is slight. (The chile puree used to make red pozole makes it impossible to tell the difference between white and yellow hominy in this version.)

Our pozole recipe turned out to be remarkably simple—no more than an hour of hands-on work and a start-to-finish time of about three hours. Do take the 10 minutes to prepare all the suggested garnishes. The lettuce, radishes, cilantro, oregano, and lime all brighten the stew and turn it into a one-dish meal.

Pozole Rojo

SERVES 8 TO 10

This earthy-tasting, full-flavored pork and hominy stew originated in Mexico, although it is now extremely popular in the American Southwest. This stew is typically accompanied by an assortment of crunchy toppings (each in a small bowl) and warm tortillas. Ancho chiles (see page 442) are used to create the rich flavor and color in this dish. Mexicans use oregano liberally. If available, use dried Mexican oregano; fresh Mediterranean oregano makes a better substitute than dried Mediterranean oregano.

STEW

1	bone-in picnic shoulder roast (about 5 pounds)
	Salt and ground black pepper
2	tablespoons vegetable oil
2	medium-large onions, chopped coarse (about 3 cups)
5	medium garlic cloves, minced or pressed through a garlic press
1	(14.5-ounce) can diced tomatoes
1	tablespoon chopped fresh oregano leaves or 1 teaspoon dried Mexican oregano
6	cups low-sodium chicken broth
2	ounces dried ancho chiles (about 3 large)
1½	cups boiling water
3	(15-ounce) cans white or yellow hominy, drained and rinsed

GARNISHES

2	limes, cut into quarters
½	head romaine lettuce, sliced crosswise into thin strips
6	medium radishes, sliced thin
1	small onion, minced
	Roughly chopped fresh cilantro leaves
	Chopped fresh oregano leaves or dried Mexican oregano
¼	cup pureed ancho chiles (prepared with the stew)
	Soft flour or corn tortillas, warmed

1. Adjust an oven rack to the lower-middle position and heat the oven to 300 degrees. Trim the thick skin and excess fat from the meat and cut along the muscles to divide the roast into large pieces of various sizes; reserve the bones. Season the meat generously with salt and pepper to taste.

2. Heat the oil in a large ovenproof Dutch oven over medium heat until shimmering. Add the onions and ¼ teaspoon salt. Cook, stirring frequently, until the onions have softened, about 4 minutes. Stir in the garlic and cook until fragrant, about 30 seconds.

3. Add the meat and bones and stir often until it is no longer pink on the outside, about 8 minutes. Add the tomatoes, oregano, broth, and ½ teaspoon salt. Increase the heat to medium-high and bring to a simmer. With a large spoon,

skim off any scum. Cover the pot and place it in the oven. Cook until the meat is very tender, about 2 hours.

4. Meanwhile, remove the stems and seeds from the ancho chiles; soak the chiles in a medium bowl with the boiling water until soft, about 20 minutes. Puree the chiles and soaking liquid in a blender until smooth. Pour the puree through a strainer into a bowl and reserve ¼ cup of the pureed anchos for garnish.

5. Remove the pot from the oven and remove the meat and bones to a cutting board. Stir in the hominy and the remaining ¾ cup ancho chile puree. Cover and bring the stew to a simmer on top of the stove over medium-low heat. Cook until the hominy is hot and the flavors meld, about 30 minutes.

6. When the meat is cool, shred it using your fingers or the tines of 2 forks; discard the bones. Stir the shredded meat into the stew. If serving immediately, spoon off any fat that rises to the top and then simmer until the meat is hot, about 10 minutes. (The stew can be covered and refrigerated for up to 3 days. Spoon off the hardened fat and bring back to a simmer over medium-low heat.) Adjust the seasonings. Ladle the stew into individual bowls and serve immediately with the garnishes.

➤ VARIATION
Pozole Verde

Verde means "green" in Spanish, and green pozole, not surprisingly, is lighter and more refreshing than red pozole. Green pozole is prepared with lots of cilantro, fresh jalapenos, and tomatillos. These ingredients are cooked for a very short time; the flavors are bigger, brighter, and fresher-tasting than pozole with red sauce. A slightly different set of garnishes accompanies green pozole as well: diced tomato, diced avocado, and minced jalapeño. In other words, forgo the cilantro, oregano, and ancho chile puree garnishes suggested for Pozole Rojo.

Follow the recipe for Pozole Rojo, eliminating the tomatoes and ancho chiles. While the pozole is simmering, puree 1 pound tomatillos, husked, washed, and quartered; 3 medium jalapeño chiles, stemmed, seeded, and chopped coarse; ½ small onion, chopped coarse; and ½ cup water in a blender until smooth, 2 to 3 minutes. Add 2 bunches (about 5 cups) fresh cilantro leaves and stems and puree until smooth, about 2 minutes. When the pozole comes out of the oven in step 5, remove the meat and bones and stir in the hominy. Simmer as directed. Stir the tomatillo mixture into the stew along with the shredded cooled meat and simmer until heated through, 10 to 15 minutes. Serve with the suggested garnishes.

CASSOULET

EVERY ONCE IN A WHILE, A DISH COMES AROUND that is so robust, so satisfying to every sense that we deem it comfort food. It warms us from the inside out and assures us that this winter, too, shall pass. Cassoulet is such a dish. But for most cooks, the reasons to eat cassoulet outnumber the reasons to make it. Cassoulet can take three days to make, and the ingredients can be both hard to find and difficult to prepare.

Cassoulet originated in Languedoc, France, and each area of the region touts its recipe as "the real thing." All versions of the dish contain white beans, but that is where the agreement ends. Some prefer pork loin in their cassoulet, others use a shoulder of lamb, while still others use a combination of both. Mutton, duck, pheasant, garlic sausage, and even fish can be found in the different variations.

But the best-known and most often replicated cassoulet comes from Toulouse. This cassoulet must start with the preparation of confit. Meat or poultry, most often goose legs (the region of Toulouse is also home to the foie gras industry, which means that goose is plentiful), is placed in a large container, sprinkled heavily with salt, and cured for 24 to 48 hours. This both preserves and tenderizes the meat. After this, the meat is simmered slowly in its own fat, so that the flavor of the fat penetrates the spaces previously occupied by the juices. The finished confit may be used immediately or stored in an airtight container, covered in its own fat, to prevent contamination.

The challenge of making cassoulet doesn't end with preparing confit, however. Pork loin and mutton must be slow-roasted for hours to become fully tender, and garlic sausages must be freshly made. The beans must be presoaked and then simmered with pork rinds to develop flavor. Finally, the entire mixture has to be combined in an earthenware pot, topped with bread crumbs, and placed in a low-temperature oven to simmer slowly for several hours.

The result is nothing short of divine. But while this classic French peasant dish can be replicated by restaurants, it is definitely not a dish for the casual home cook. The time investment alone is impractical, and it can be difficult to achieve a perfect balance of flavors. On more than one occasion, we have eaten cassoulets that were overwhelmed by salt or swimming in fat, most often because of the confit and sausages. All the same, we love this dish so much that we decided it would be worth the effort to try to streamline it without compromising its essential nature.

We decided to accept the hardest of the challenges first and conquer the confit component. We eliminated the notion of confit made from scratch as far too time-consuming. Assessing our other options, we created three cassoulets. One was prepared with braised duck leg confit (goose leg confit is less widely available) purchased through our butcher. The others we made with no confit at all, starting one version with sautéed and braised duck legs and the other with sautéed and braised chicken legs, which we wanted to use because they're so easy to find in the supermarket. The results were disheartening, although not surprising. The cassoulet made with the purchased confit was the clear favorite. Those made without it produced dishes more reminiscent of duck and chicken stews.

Unfortunately, ready-made confit is not widely available, so we wanted to develop a recipe that wouldn't rely on it. Somewhat ironically, we arrived at the solution to the problem with some help from the confit itself.

Because confit is salt-cured and then cooked in its own fat, it retains an intense duck flavor when added to the cassoulet, contributing a rich, slightly smoky flavor that was noticeably absent from the dishes prepared with the sautéed duck and

chicken. The texture of the dish made with confit was superior as well, the flesh plump with flavor yet tender to the bite; the sautéed and braised duck and chicken became tough and gave up all of their flavor to the broth. Taking an educated guess, we decided to adopt an approach often used in the test kitchen and brine the chicken. Because we had found when making other dishes that brining resulted in poultry that was both more moist and more flavorful, we reasoned that brining the chicken might bring it closer to the tender texture of confit. To approximate the confit's light smokiness, we decided to cook the legs in bacon fat.

We quick-soaked the chicken thighs for one hour in a concentrated salt and sugar solution, sautéed them quickly in rendered bacon fat, and then braised them with the rest of the cassoulet ingredients. What resulted was just what we were hoping for: a suitable substitute for duck confit. The bacon added smoky flavor, and it enhanced the flavors of the pork and sausage added later. The texture and flavor were spot on, the chicken thighs were plump and juicy, and the broth became well seasoned because of the brine. With this "mock" confit in hand, we proceeded.

Our next test involved figuring out which meats to use and how to avoid slow roasting. We knew that we wanted to be true to the original recipe and use either fresh pork or lamb. We decided to try stewing the meat in liquid entirely on top of the stove. This method yielded great results in terms of tenderness, but the meat had none of the depth of flavor that occurs with roasting. Searing the meat in some of the rendered bacon fat that we had used with the chicken thighs took care of that problem.

Because we were now stewing the meat, we needed to use cuts that were appropriate for this method. We tried pork loin, the choice in so many cassoulet recipes, but the loin became waterlogged and tasteless during stewing. A suggestion from our butcher led us to try a blade-end roast, which is the part of the loin closest to the shoulder. The blade-end roast, which has more internal fat than the center loin, retained the moisture and flavor. To facilitate quicker cooking, we cut the roast into 1-inch pieces. We used similar testing with the lamb. Lamb shoulder is the best cut for stewing, but it can be difficult to find in markets. We bought thick shoulder lamb chops instead, which we boned and also cut into 1-inch pieces. Finally, perfectly tender meat—and a choice of meats, at that!—without the effort of roasting.

Cassoulets traditionally use white beans. We wanted to make sure that the beans would retain their shape while adding a soft texture to the dish. Canned beans fell apart quickly, so we opted for dried. We tested four varieties, and the winner was the pale green flageolet bean. These small, kidney-shaped French beans have a creamy, tender texture and delicate flavor that perfectly enhanced the cassoulet. We also cooked the beans on top of the stove along with some bacon and the aromatics to let them absorb as much flavor as possible, an effort to duplicate the depth of flavor in the original dish.

The last major decision we had to make concerned the sausage. After ruling out the use of hard-to-find French sausages (and not willing to take the time to make our own), we found that both kielbasa and andouille sausages intensified the smoky flavor that we so desired.

With the major problems out of the way, we were able to concentrate on streamlining the technique used to cook the dish. This proved to be quite simple. With the chicken, meat, and beans now modified for cooking on the stovetop, oven braising became unnecessary. Cooking the dish entirely on the stove at a low simmer, with a quick finish in the oven to brown the bread crumbs, produced perfect results in a short amount of time. At last, we had it: a quick cassoulet that was worthy of the name.

Simplified Cassoulet with Pork and Kielbasa

SERVES 8

Although this dish can be made without brining the chicken, we recommend that you do so. This recipe uses table salt (not kosher) in its brine. If you'd like to use kosher salt, whose large flakes measure differently from fine-grained table salt, see page 312 for conversion information. To ensure the most time-efficient preparation of the cassoulet, while the chicken is brining and the beans are simmering, prepare the remaining ingredients. Look for dried flageolet beans in specialty food stores. If you can't find a boneless blade-end pork loin roast, a boneless Boston butt makes a fine substitution. Additional salt is not necessary because the brined chicken adds a good deal of it. If you skip the brining step, add salt to taste before serving.

CHICKEN

1/2	cup table salt
1	cup sugar
10	bone-in chicken thighs (about 3 1/2 pounds), trimmed of excess fat

BEANS

1	pound dried flageolet or Great Northern beans, rinsed and picked over (see the illustration on page 232)
1	medium onion, peeled and left whole
1	medium garlic head, papery outer skins removed and top 1/2 inch sliced off
	Salt and ground black pepper
6	ounces (about 6 slices) bacon, chopped medium
1	pound boneless blade-end pork loin roast, trimmed of excess fat and cut into 1-inch pieces
1	small onion, chopped fine
2	medium garlic cloves, minced or pressed through a garlic press
1	(14.5-ounce) can diced tomatoes, drained
1	tablespoon tomato paste
1	large sprig fresh thyme
1	bay leaf
1/4	teaspoon ground cloves
3 1/2	cups low-sodium chicken broth
1 1/2	cups dry white wine
1/2	pound kielbasa, halved lengthwise and cut crosswise into 1/4-inch slices

CROUTONS

6	slices good-quality white sandwich bread, cut into 1/2-inch dice (about 3 cups)
3	tablespoons unsalted butter, melted

1. FOR THE CHICKEN: In a gallon-size zipper-lock plastic bag, dissolve the salt and sugar in 1 quart cold water. Add the chicken, pressing out as much air as possible; seal and refrigerate until fully seasoned, about 1 hour. Remove the chicken from the brine, rinse thoroughly under cold water, and pat dry with paper towels. Refrigerate until ready to use.

2. FOR THE BEANS: Bring the beans, whole onion, garlic head, 1 teaspoon salt, ½ teaspoon pepper, and 8 cups water to a boil in a stockpot or large Dutch oven over high heat. Cover, reduce the heat to medium-low, and simmer until the beans are almost fully tender, 1¼ to 1½ hours. Drain the beans and discard the onion and garlic. Return the cooked beans to the Dutch oven.

3. While the beans are cooking, fry the bacon in another Dutch oven over medium heat until just beginning to crisp and most of the fat is rendered, 5 to 6 minutes. Using a slotted spoon, add half of the bacon to the pot with the beans; transfer the remaining bacon to a paper towel–lined plate and set aside. Increase the heat to medium-high. When the bacon fat is shimmering, add half of the chicken thighs, fleshy-side down; cook until lightly browned, 4 to 5 minutes. Using tongs, turn the chicken pieces and cook until lightly browned on the second side, 3 to 4 minutes longer. Transfer the chicken to a large plate; repeat with the remaining thighs and set aside. Drain off all but 2 tablespoons of the fat from the pot. Return the pot to medium heat; add the pork pieces and cook, stirring occasionally, until lightly browned, about 5 minutes. Add the chopped onion and cook, stirring occasionally, until softened, 3 to 4 minutes. Add the minced garlic, tomatoes, tomato paste, thyme, bay leaf, cloves, and pepper to taste; cook until fragrant, about 1 minute. Stir in the broth and wine, scraping up the browned bits on the pot bottom with a wooden spoon. Add the chicken thighs and any accumulated juices to the pot and submerge the thighs in the liquid. Increase the heat to high and bring to a boil. Then reduce the heat to low, cover, and simmer about 40 minutes. Remove the cover and continue to simmer until the chicken and pork are fully tender, 20 to 30 minutes more. Using tongs

and a slotted spoon, remove and discard the skin on the chicken thighs.

4. FOR THE CROUTONS: While the chicken and pork simmer, adjust an oven rack to the lower-middle position and heat the oven to 400 degrees. Mix the bread and butter in a small baking dish. Bake, tossing occasionally, until light golden brown and crisp, 8 to 12 minutes. Cool to room temperature; set aside.

5. TO FINISH THE CASSOULET: Gently stir the kielbasa, drained beans and bacon, and reserved bacon into the pot with the chicken and pork; remove and discard the thyme sprig and bay leaf and adjust the seasonings with salt and pepper to taste. Sprinkle the croutons evenly over the surface and bake, uncovered, until the flavors have melded and the croutons are deep golden brown, about 15 minutes. Let stand 10 minutes and serve.

➤ VARIATION

Simplified Cassoulet with Lamb and Andouille Sausage

Lamb, with its robust, earthy flavor, makes an excellent substitute for the pork. Andouille sausage adds a peppery sweetness that our tasters loved.

Follow the recipe for Simplified Cassoulet with Pork and Kielbasa, substituting 2 pounds shoulder lamb chops, trimmed, boned, and cut into 1-inch pieces, for the pork, and substituting 8 ounces andouille sausage for the kielbasa.

IRISH STEW

IRISH STEW IS A SIMPLE LAMB STEW THAT HAS sustained countless generations. At its most basic, Irish stew is made with just lamb, onions, potatoes, and water. There's no browning or precooking. The raw ingredients are layered in the pot and cooked until tender.

We prepared several variations of this basic dish and identified a couple of problems. First, by modern standards, it is bland. With no browning and so few ingredients, authentic Irish stew can't even compete with a good bowl of beef stew. Second, the potatoes break down and lose their shape after several hours of simmering. Although the potatoes do thicken the stew, modern palates generally prefer vegetables that are not so overcooked.

Our goals for this recipe were clear. While remaining true to the dish's humble roots—lamb and potatoes—we wanted to pump up the flavors (especially of the lamb) and find a way to thicken the stew without overcooking the potatoes.

We started with boneless lamb shoulder meat, figuring that the equivalent cut had worked well with beef stews. We browned the meat, replaced the water with chicken broth, added carrots and Worcestershire sauce for flavor (this ingredient was suggested in a number of recipes), and thickened everything with flour. The results were better but not great. Browning helped intensify the lamb's flavor, but the chicken broth, carrots, and Worcestershire sauce tended to diminish this effect. The flour was a good idea, though, creating a nicely textured sauce.

For the next test, we browned the chunks of boneless shoulder meat, removed the meat from the pan, added some onions, and cooked them until tender. We added some flour for thickening power and then some water. We returned the meat to the pot and let the stew cook for an hour before adding the potatoes (so they would not overcook). This stew was better—there were few distractions—but the lamb flavor was a bit weak. With so little else in the pot, the lamb has to carry the day, and this meat was not up to the task.

We started to think that shoulder meat was the wrong choice. We tested some boneless leg of lamb (the cut commonly sold as stew meat), and the results were extremely disappointing. The meat cooked up dry, tough, and not very flavorful. This cut has far less fat than the shoulder, making it a poor choice for stewing.

We were ready to throw in the towel when James Beard came to the rescue. In the course of our research, we found his recipe for Irish stew, which called for leaving the meat on the bone. We tested his recipe and were pleasantly surprised. The water and lamb bones had, in fact, created a rich-tasting stock. The meat itself was especially tasty, no doubt because it was cooked on the bone. Cooking whole chops (as Beard suggested) made this dish seem more like

a braise than a stew. Also, Beard did not brown the meat, a step we had grown fond of in earlier tests.

We took a Chinese cleaver and cut shoulder chops into 2-inch pieces. Although this idea seemed promising, the hacked-up bones created some small splinters, which tasters felt were unappealing and even dangerous. Our next idea was to remove the meat from the bones and cut it into stew-size chunks. The meat would be browned and then removed from the pot so that the onions could be cooked. When the meat was added back to the stew pot, we would throw in the uncooked lamb bones as well. As we had hoped, this strategy gave us excellent results.

Cutting the lamb meat into medium-size chunks made this dish seem like a stew. Browning added flavor to the meat as well as the stew. The bones, which still had bits of meat attached to them, created a rich, heady sauce. Some tasters liked to gnaw on the meaty bones; others felt that bones have no place in a finished stew and should be discarded just before serving. The choice is yours.

We found it worthwhile to buy shoulder chops from the butcher. In most supermarkets, shoulder lamb chops are thin—often about ½ inch thick. At this thickness, the stew meat is too insubstantial. Ideally, we like chops cut 1½ inches thick, but 1-inch chops will suffice.

We had a few more tests to run. Although traditional recipes often layer raw onions in the pot with the meat, potatoes, and water, we knew that cooking the onions would be key. Tasters had liked stews made with softened onions, but further tests proved that browning the onions added even more depth to the final dish.

We generally prefer low-starch, red-skinned potatoes in stews because they hold their shape well. However, in this dish the potatoes traditionally act as a thickener. Even though we had added some flour to the browned onions to thicken the sauce, we wondered if a higher-starch potato would be more appropriate in Irish stew. We decided to try this dish with russets and Yukon Golds as well as red potatoes.

Russets fell apart into a soupy mess and were universally panned. The red potatoes were fine, but the Yukon Golds stole the show. Their buttery, rich flavor was appreciated by tasters in this simple stew. Tasters also liked the soft, creamy texture of the Yukon Gold potatoes.

Thyme and parsley are often added to Irish stew, and we saw no need to deviate from tradition. The parsley is best stirred in just before serving to maintain its bright, fresh flavor. At last, a hearty Irish stew worth eating.

Irish Lamb Stew

SERVES 6

The secret to the success of this Irish stew is the addition of lamb bones to the pot. Bone-in shoulder chops weighing 4½ pounds will yield about 2½ pounds of boneless meat as well as a pile of bones. Some meat will cling to the bones, and the choice is yours whether to remove the bones just before serving for a more refined dish or to include them for a casual eating experience. True Irish stew includes just meat and potatoes with some onions. We've added a recipe for a popular variation with carrots and turnips.

4½	pounds shoulder lamb chops, 1 to 1½ inches thick
	Salt and ground black pepper
3	tablespoons vegetable oil
3	medium-large onions, chopped coarse (about 5 cups)
¼	cup unbleached all-purpose flour
3	cups water
1	teaspoon dried thyme
6	medium Yukon Gold or red potatoes (about 2 pounds), peeled and cut into 1-inch cubes
¼	cup minced fresh parsley leaves

1. Adjust an oven rack to the lower-middle position and heat the oven to 300 degrees. Cut the meat from the bones and reserve the bones. Trim the meat of excess fat and cut it into 1½-inch cubes. Season the meat generously with salt and pepper to taste.

2. Heat 1 tablespoon of the oil in a large ovenproof Dutch oven over medium-high heat until shimmering. Add half the meat to the pot so that the individual pieces are close together but not touching. Cook, not moving the pieces until the sides touching the pot are well browned, 2 to 3 minutes. Using tongs, turn each piece and continue cooking until most sides are well browned, about 5 minutes longer. Transfer the meat to a medium bowl, add another 1 tablespoon of the oil to the pot, and swirl to coat the pan bottom. Brown the remaining lamb in the same manner; transfer the meat to the bowl and set aside.

3. Reduce the heat to medium, add the remaining 1 tablespoon oil, and swirl to coat the pan bottom. Add the onions and ¼ teaspoon salt and cook, stirring frequently and vigorously, scraping the pot bottom with a wooden spoon to loosen any browned bits, until the onions have softened, about 5 minutes. Add the flour and stir until the onions are evenly coated, 1 to 2 minutes.

4. Stir in 1½ cups of the water, scraping the pan bottom and edges with the wooden spoon to loosen the remaining browned bits. Gradually add the remaining 1½ cups water, stirring constantly and scraping the pot edges to dissolve the flour. Add the thyme and 1 teaspoon salt and bring to a simmer. Add the bones and then the meat and accumulated juices in the bowl. Return to a simmer, cover the pot, and place it in the oven. Cook for 1 hour.

5. Remove the pot from the oven and place the potatoes on top. Cover, return the pot to the oven, and cook until the meat is tender, about 1 hour. If serving immediately, stir the potatoes into the liquid, wait for 5 minutes, and spoon off any fat that rises to the top. (The stew can be covered and refrigerated for up to 3 days. Spoon off the hardened fat and bring back to a simmer over medium-low heat.)

6. Stir in the parsley and adjust the seasonings. Remove the bones, if desired. Serve immediately.

> VARIATIONS

Irish Lamb Stew with Carrots and Turnips

Follow the recipe for Irish Lamb Stew, substituting ½ pound carrots, peeled and sliced ¼ inch thick, and ½ pound turnips, peeled and cut into 1-inch cubes, for 1 pound of the potatoes. Proceed as directed.

Italian-Style Lamb Stew with Green Beans, Tomatoes, and Basil

This peasant-style lamb stew has its roots in Sicily. The approach to preparing it, though, is identical to that of Irish stew. Garlic, wine, and rosemary add the flavors of the Mediterranean, and tomatoes and green beans replace some of the potatoes to lighten the dish.

4½	pounds shoulder lamb chops, 1 to 1½ inches thick
	Salt and ground black pepper
3	tablespoons vegetable oil
3	medium-large onions, chopped coarse (about 5 cups)
3	medium garlic cloves, minced or pressed through a garlic press
¼	cup unbleached all-purpose flour
½	cup dry white wine
1¾	cups water
1	tablespoon minced fresh rosemary leaves
1	(14.5-ounce) can diced tomatoes
4	medium Yukon Gold or red potatoes (about 1¼ pounds), peeled and cut into 1-inch cubes
¾	pound green beans, ends trimmed and beans halved
¼	cup minced fresh basil leaves

1. Adjust an oven rack to the lower-middle position and heat the oven to 300 degrees. Cut the meat from the bones and reserve the bones. Trim the meat of excess fat and cut it into 1½-inch cubes. Season the meat generously with salt and pepper to taste.

2. Heat 1 tablespoon of the oil in a large oven-proof Dutch oven over medium-high heat until shimmering. Add half of the meat to the pot so that the individual pieces are close together but not touching. Cook, not moving the pieces until the sides touching the pot are well browned, 2 to 3 minutes. Using tongs, turn each piece and continue cooking until most sides are well browned, about 5 minutes longer. Transfer the meat to a medium bowl, add another 1 tablespoon of the oil to the pot, and swirl to coat the pan bottom. Brown the remaining lamb in the same manner; transfer the meat to the bowl and set aside.

3. Reduce the heat to medium, add the remaining 1 tablespoon oil, and swirl to coat the pot bottom. Add the onions and ¼ teaspoon salt and cook, stirring frequently and vigorously, scraping the pot bottom with a wooden spoon to loosen any browned bits, until the onions have softened, about 5 minutes. Add the garlic and cook until fragrant, about 30 seconds. Add the flour and stir until the onions are evenly coated, 1 to 2 minutes.

4. Stir in the wine and 1 cup of the water, scraping the pot bottom and edges with the wooden spoon to loosen the remaining browned bits. Gradually add the remaining ¾ cup water, stirring constantly and scraping the pan edges to dissolve the flour. Add the rosemary, tomatoes, and 1 teaspoon salt and bring to a simmer. Add the bones and then the meat and accumulated juices in the bowl. Return to a simmer, cover the pot, and place it in the oven. Cook for 1 hour.

5. Remove the pot from the oven and place the potatoes and green beans on top. Cover, return the pot to the oven, and cook until the meat is tender, about 1 hour. If serving immediately, spoon off any fat that rises to the top. (The stew can be covered and refrigerated for up to 3 days. Spoon off the hardened fat and bring back to a simmer over medium-low heat.)

6. Stir in the basil and adjust the seasonings. Remove the bones, if desired. Serve immediately.

LAMB TAGINE

TAGINES ARE FUNDAMENTAL TO THE CUISINES of Morocco, Algeria, and other North African countries. The term comes from the earthenware pot with a conical cover that has traditionally been used to prepare stews in this region. Most tagines are highly aromatic and feature a blend of sweet and savory ingredients. Most also contain some sort of fruit (often dried) as well as a heady mixture of ground spices, garlic, and cilantro. Lamb tagines are especially popular, although chicken or vegetable tagines have their advocates, too.

Tagines differ widely from region to region. We decided to start with a classic, slow-simmering recipe typically prepared in Morocco. Our goal was to develop a dish that kept the authentic flavors of Morocco but eliminated most of the fuss.

Many tagine recipes have incredibly long ingredient lists or call for pieces of equipment (such as the above-mentioned earthenware pot) that are unlikely to be found in American kitchens. We wanted to make this dish in a Dutch oven. As for the tagine itself, we wanted the lamb to be moist and succulent. The flavors and aromas would be heady, with a medley of spices blending together harmoniously. A few vegetables and fruits would provide depth and offer the characteristic sweet and savory components.

Given our results with Irish stew, we were leery of using boneless lamb shoulder meat. However, our fears were unfounded. Given the abundance of flavors in this recipe, tasters did not miss the extra oomph provided by the lamb bones we had included in our recipe for Irish stew. Shoulder meat was plenty tasty when seasoned so liberally with the spices of a tagine.

Using our recipe for beef stew as a template, we realized right off that some changes would have to be made. Although we found it necessary to pat the beef dry with paper towels before browning it, the same step caused problems with lamb. Unlike beef, which can be moist, lamb tends to be sticky, and the paper towels "glued" onto it. Picking off the bits of paper was tedious, so we quickly abandoned the step.

Next we focused on the spices. Sweet, warm spices are typically used in North African cooking. Ground cinnamon and ginger were quickly voted in by tasters, as was cumin. Most everyone liked the addition of some fragrant coriander, but tasters were divided about cayenne—some liked a little heat, but others did not. We decided to make this spice optional.

Although some sources suggested tossing the meat with the spices before browning it, we found that this caused the spices to burn. Other recipes add the spices with the liquid, but we found sautéing the spices in a little oil helped to bring out their flavor. It made sense to add the spices to the pot along with the flour—that is, once the onions and garlic were sautéed.

Adding the spices with the flour creates a thick coating on the pan bottom. We found it is essential

to scrape the pan bottom when the liquid is added to incorporate the spices into the stew and develop their full flavor potential.

As for the liquid in a tagine, some traditional recipes call for lamb stock. We wondered how canned chicken broth would perform instead. Thankfully, canned chicken broth proved more than adequate in this dish. It adds body to the stew but doesn't compete with the lamb flavor (the way it did in Irish stew). We also tested water in this recipe, but tasters felt that the stew suffered a bit, especially in terms of body.

Tomatoes are another constant in most tagines. We found that canned diced tomatoes provide an acidic contrast that heightens the other flavors. We tested several other vegetables, including summer squash, sweet potatoes, and potatoes. All are delicious, but none seemed essential in a basic tagine—the tomatoes and onions are more than enough. We did like the addition of chickpeas, another common addition to many tagines. Canned chickpeas are fine in this dish; just make sure to add them near the end of the stewing time to keep them from becoming mushy.

As for fruits, we liked the soft texture and sweet flavor of most every dried fruit tested. Apricots were a unanimous favorite, but prunes, raisins, and currants are other good options.

Finally, we found that it's best to use a strong hand with the seasonings. Plenty of garlic and cilantro punch up the flavor and keep the sweet elements in check.

Lamb Tagine

SERVES 6 TO 8

If you can't find boneless lamb shoulder, you can purchase blade or arm chops and remove the meat yourself. Figure that 4½ pounds of chops will yield the 2½ pounds of boneless meat needed for this recipe. A variety of dried fruits—pitted prunes, dark raisins, golden raisins, or currants—can be substituted for the apricots. Serve this exotic fare over couscous or basmati rice.

2½ pounds boneless lamb shoulder, trimmed and
     cut into 1½-inch cubes
     Salt and ground black pepper

3 tablespoons olive oil
2 medium-large onions, chopped coarse
4 medium garlic cloves, minced or pressed
   through a garlic press
3 tablespoons unbleached all-purpose flour
1½ teaspoons ground cumin
1 teaspoon ground cinnamon
1 teaspoon ground ginger
½ teaspoon ground coriander
⅛ teaspoon cayenne pepper (optional)
2¼ cups low-sodium chicken broth
1 (14.5-ounce) can diced tomatoes
1 cup dried apricots, roughly chopped
2 bay leaves
6 fresh cilantro sprigs (optional)
1 (15-ounce) can chickpeas, drained and rinsed
¼ cup minced fresh cilantro or parsley leaves
¼ cup toasted slivered almonds (optional)

1. Adjust an oven rack to the lower-middle position and heat the oven to 300 degrees. Season the lamb generously with salt and pepper to taste.

2. Heat 1 tablespoon of the oil in a large oven-proof Dutch oven over medium-high heat until shimmering. Add half of the meat so that the individual pieces are close together but not touching. Cook, not moving the pieces until the sides touching the pot are well browned, 2 to 3 minutes. Using tongs, turn each piece and continue cooking until most sides are well browned, about 5 minutes longer. Transfer the meat to a medium bowl, add another 1 tablespoon of the oil to the pot, and swirl to coat the pan bottom. Brown the remaining lamb in the same manner; transfer the meat to the bowl and set aside.

3. Reduce the heat to medium, add the remaining 1 tablespoon oil, and swirl to coat the pan bottom. Add the onions and ¼ teaspoon salt and cook, stirring frequently and vigorously, scraping the pot bottom with a wooden spoon to loosen any browned bits, until the onions have softened, about 5 minutes. Stir in the garlic and cook until fragrant, about 30 seconds. Add the flour, cumin,

cinnamon, ginger, coriander, and cayenne (if using) and stir until the onions are evenly coated and fragrant, 1 to 2 minutes.

4. Gradually add the broth, scraping the pot bottom and edges with the wooden spoon to loosen the remaining browned bits and spices, and stirring until the flour is dissolved and the liquid is thick. Stir in the tomatoes, apricots, bay leaves, and cilantro sprigs (if using) and bring to a simmer. Add the browned lamb and accumulated juices in the bowl, pushing down the meat to submerge the pieces. Return to a simmer, cover the pot, and place it in the oven. Cook for 1¼ hours.

5. Remove the pot from the oven and stir in the chickpeas. Cover and return the pot to the oven. Cook until the meat is tender and the chickpeas are heated through, about 15 minutes. If serving immediately, spoon off any fat that rises to the top. (The stew can be covered and refrigerated for up to 3 days. Spoon off the hardened fat and bring back to a simmer over medium-low heat.)

6. Discard the bay leaves and cilantro sprigs. Stir in the minced cilantro and adjust the seasonings. Serve immediately, garnishing each bowl with almonds, if desired.

CHOPPING DRIED FRUIT

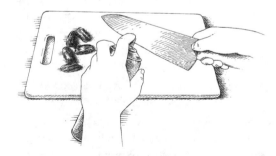

Dried fruit, especially apricots (or dates), very often sticks to the knife when you try to chop it. To avoid this problem, coat the blade with a thin film of vegetable cooking spray just before you begin chopping any dried fruit. The chopped fruit won't cling to the blade, and the knife will stay relatively clean.

13

GRILLING

COOKING FOOD OUTDOORS OFTEN YIELDS the best results, but it can be a challenge for the cook because grilling (quick cooking with a hot fire) and barbecuing (long, slow cooking with a cooler fire) are so imprecise. As long as the thermostat on your oven is properly calibrated, you should have no trouble following recipes that call for roasting at a particular temperature. This chapter includes recipes for grilled beef, pork, lamb, chicken, and fish. Recipes for grilling burgers, both beef and turkey, are found on pages 448 and 382, respectively. This chapter covers the three methods of outdoor cooking.

GRILLING Quickly cooking relatively thin cuts of food (steaks, chops, fish, and chicken parts) directly over a hot or medium-hot fire (around 500 degrees, and in some cases even hotter). Charcoal grilling is always done with the lid off. When cooking with gas, the lid must be kept down to contain the heat.

GRILL-ROASTING An alternative to oven-roasting that involves indirect cooking over moderate heat (300 to 400 degrees) with the lid on. Whole chickens and turkeys and tender cuts such as beef tenderloin and pork loin are grill-roasted.

BARBECUING Slowly smoking tough, thick cuts (ribs, brisket, or pork shoulder rubbed with dry spices) over a low fire (250 to 300 degrees). This method tenderizes the meat and adds authentic smoky barbecue flavor.

In addition to these three cooking methods, the outdoor cook also has a choice of the type of grill used: charcoal grill versus gas. To take as much of the guesswork out of the process as possible, we have assembled instructions and tips for grilling on both charcoal and gas grills on pages 568 and 569.

GRILLED PREMIUM STEAKS

GRILLED PREMIUM STEAKS HAVE MANY ATTRAC-tive qualities: rich, beefy flavor; a thick, caramelized crust; and almost no prep or cleanup for the cook. But sometimes a small bonfire fueled by steak fat can leave expensive steaks charred and tasting of resinous smoke. Other times the coals burn down so low that the steaks end up with pale, wimpy grill marks and almost no flavor at all. In these cases, you probably tried to leave the steaks on the grill long enough to develop flavor, but they just overcooked.

So we went to work, promising ourselves we'd figure out how to use the grill to cook the entire steak perfectly: meat seared evenly on both sides so that the juices are concentrated into a powerfully flavored, dark brown, brittle coating of crust; the juicy inside cooked a little past rare; and the outside strip of rich, soft fat crisped and browned slightly on the edges.

We decided to focus on the steaks from the short loin and rib sections of the animal that we think are the best the cow has to offer—the T-bone and porterhouse, as well as the strip and filet mignon (all from the short loin) and the rib eye (a rib steak without the bone, which is the most common way this cut is sold). We figured these steaks were bound to cook pretty much the same because they were all cut from the same general part of the cow.

Early on in our testing, we determined that we needed a very hot fire to get the crust we wanted without overcooking the steak. We could get that kind of heat by building the charcoal up to within 2 or 2½ inches of the grilling grate. But with this arrangement, we ran into problems with the fat dripping down onto the charcoal and flaming. We had already decided that a thick steak—at least 1¼ inches thick, to be precise—was optimum, because at that thickness we achieved a tasty contrast between the charcoal flavoring on the outside of the steak and the beefy flavor on the inside. The problem was that we couldn't cook a thick steak over consistently high heat without burning it.

After considerable experimentation, we found the answer to this dilemma: We had to build a fire with two levels of heat. Once we realized that we needed a fire with a lot of coals on one side and far fewer coals on the other, we could sear the steak properly at the beginning of cooking, then pull it onto the cooler half of the grill to finish cooking at a lower temperature. We could also use the dual heat levels to cook thin steaks as well as thick ones properly, and the system provided insurance against bonfires as well—if a steak flared up, we simply moved it off the high heat.

We gauged the level of heat on both sides of the fire by holding a hand about five inches over the cooking grate (as explained on page 568). When the medium-hot side of the grill was hot enough for searing, we could stand to hold a hand over the grill only for three or four seconds. For the cooler side of the grill, we could count seven seconds. (This is how we adapted our recipes for a gas grill, using burners set to high and medium.)

A two-level fire is also good for cooking—porterhouse and T-bone, two of our favorite cuts, which are especially tricky to cook properly. Both consist of two muscles (strip and tenderloin) with a T-shaped bone in between. When grilled long enough to cook the strip section perfectly, the lean tenderloin is inevitably overcooked, dry, and flavorless. We found that if we grilled the steak with the tenderloin toward the cooler side of the fire, it cooked more slowly and reached proper doneness at the same time as the strip.

Common cooking wisdom suggests that bringing meat to room temperature before grilling will cause it to cook more evenly and that letting it rest for five minutes after taking it off the grill will both preserve the juices and provide a more even color. We tested the first of these theories by simultaneously grilling two similar steaks, one straight from the refrigerator and a second that had stood at room-temperature for one hour. We noticed no difference in the cooked steaks except that the room-temperature steak cooked a couple of minutes faster than the other. The second test was more conclusive. Letting a cooked steak rest

COMPOUND BUTTERS FOR STEAKS

Roasted Red Pepper and Smoked Paprika Butter

MAKES 4 TABLESPOONS, ENOUGH FOR 4 STEAKS

Serve this butter with any grilled or pan-seared steaks. It is especially good with filets mignons.

- 4 tablespoons (½ stick) unsalted butter, softened
- 2 tablespoons very finely minced jarred roasted red peppers (about 1 ounce)
- 1 tablespoon minced fresh thyme leaves
- ¾ teaspoon smoked paprika
- ½ teaspoon salt
  Ground black pepper

Using a fork, beat all of the ingredients, including ground black pepper to taste, together in a small bowl until combined. Just before serving the steaks, spoon about 1 tablespoon of the butter onto each and serve.

Lemon, Garlic, and Parsley Butter

MAKES 4 TABLESPOONS, ENOUGH FOR 4 STEAKS

This is a variation on maître d'hôtel butter, a classic French accompaniment to meat, fish, and vegetables.

- 4 tablespoons (½ stick) unsalted butter, softened
- ½ teaspoon grated lemon zest
- 1 tablespoon minced fresh parsley leaves
- 1 medium garlic clove, minced or pressed through a garlic press (about 1 teaspoon)
- ½ teaspoon salt
  Ground black pepper

Using a fork, beat all of the ingredients, including ground black pepper to taste, together in a small bowl until combined. Just before serving the steaks, spoon about 1 tablespoon of the butter onto each and serve.

for five minutes does indeed help the meat retain more juices when sliced and promotes a more even color throughout the meat.

We tried lightly oiling steaks before grilling to see if they browned better that way, and tried brushing with butter halfway through grilling to see if the flavor improved. Although the oiled steaks browned a tiny bit better, the difference wasn't significant enough to merit the added ingredient. (The filet mignon cut was an exception; oiling improved browning in this leaner steak.) As for the butter, we couldn't taste any difference.

We did find that proper seasoning with salt and pepper before grilling is essential. Seasonings added after cooking sit on the surface and don't penetrate as well as salt and pepper added before cooking. Be liberal with the salt and pepper. A fair amount falls off during the cooking process. Finally, consider using coarse sea salt or kosher salt. In our tests, tasters consistently preferred steaks sprinkled with coarse salt before grilling compared with those sprinkled with table salt. The larger crystals are more easily absorbed by the meat and sprinkle more evenly. (See page 412 for more information.)

Charcoal-Grilled Strip or Rib Steaks

SERVES 4

Strip and rib steaks, on or off the bone, are our first choice for individual steaks. A steak that's between 1¼ and 1½ inches thick gives you a solid meat flavor as well as a little taste of the grill; cut any thicker and the steak becomes too thick for one person to eat. If your guests are more likely to eat only an 8-ounce steak, grill two 1-pounders, slice them, and serve each person a half steak. To test a steak for doneness, insert an instant-read thermometer through the side of the steak deep into the meat but not touching the bone, so that most of the shaft is embedded in the steak (see the illustration on page 387).

4   strip or rib steaks, with or without the bone,
      1¼ to 1½ inches thick (12 to 16 ounces each),
      patted dry with paper towels
      Salt and ground black pepper

1. Light a large chimney starter filled with hardwood charcoal (about 6 quarts) and allow to burn until all the charcoal is covered with a layer of fine gray ash. Build a two-level fire by stacking most of the coals on one side of the grill and arranging the remaining coals in a single layer on the other side of the grill. Set the cooking rack in place, cover the grill with the lid, and let the rack heat up, about 5 minutes. Use a wire brush to scrape clean the cooking rack. The grill is ready when the pile of coals is medium-hot and the single layer of coals is medium-low. (See how to gauge heat level on page 568.)

2. Meanwhile, sprinkle both sides of the steaks with salt and pepper to taste. Grill the steaks, uncovered, over the hotter part of the fire until well browned on one side, 2 to 3 minutes. Turn the steaks; grill until well browned on the other side, 2 to 3 minutes. (If the steaks start to flame, pull them to the cooler part of the grill and/or extinguish the flames with a squirt bottle filled with water.)

3. Once the steaks are well browned on both sides, slide them to the cooler part of the grill. Continue grilling, uncovered, to the desired doneness, 5 to 6 minutes more for rare (120 degrees on an instant-read thermometer), 6 to 7 minutes for medium-rare on the rare side (125 degrees), 7 to 8 minutes for medium-rare on the medium side (130 degrees), or 8 to 9 minutes for medium (135 to 140 degrees).

4. Remove the steaks from the grill and let rest for 5 minutes. Serve immediately.

> VARIATION
Gas-Grilled Strip or Rib Steaks

Depending on the heat output of your gas grill, you may need to cook the steaks over the cooler part of the grill for an extra minute or two.

Turn on all burners to high, close the lid, and heat the grill until very hot, about 15 minutes. Scrape the grill grate clean with a grill brush. Leave one burner on high and turn the other burner(s) to medium. Follow the recipe for Charcoal-Grilled Strip or Rib Steaks from step 2 and cook with the lid down.

Charcoal-Grilled Filets Mignons

SERVES 4

Filet mignon steaks are cut from the tenderloin, which is, as the name indicates, an especially tender portion of meat. Though tender, the steaks are not extremely rich. To prevent the steaks from drying out on the grill and to encourage browning, we found it helpful to rub each steak lightly with a little oil before grilling. To serve, we suggest that you drizzle the grilled steaks with olive oil and garnish them with lemon wedges, or serve with one of the compound butters on page 563. If the filets are misshapen or unevenly cut, as supermarket steaks sometimes are, follow the illustration on page 396 to tie each one before grilling.

    4   center-cut filets mignons, 1½ to 2 inches thick
         (7 to 8 ounces each), patted dry
    4   teaspoons olive oil
         Salt and ground black pepper

1. Light a large chimney starter filled with hardwood charcoal (about 6 quarts) and allow to burn until all the charcoal is covered with a layer of fine gray ash. Build a two-level fire by stacking most of the coals on one side of the grill and arranging the remaining coals in a single layer on the other side of the grill. Set the cooking rack in place, cover the grill with the lid, and let the rack heat up, about 5 minutes. Use a wire brush to scrape clean the cooking rack. The grill is ready when the pile of coals is medium-hot and the single layer of coals is medium-low. (See how to gauge heat level on page 568.)

2. Meanwhile, lightly rub the steaks with the oil and sprinkle both sides of the steaks with salt and pepper to taste. Grill the steaks, uncovered, over the hotter part of the fire until well browned on one side, 2 to 3 minutes. Turn the steaks; grill until well browned on the other side, 2 to 3 minutes.

3. Once the steaks are well browned on both sides, slide them to the cooler part of the grill. Continue grilling, uncovered, to the desired doneness, 6 minutes more for rare (120 degrees on an instant-read thermometer), 7 minutes for medium-rare on the rare side (125 degrees),

8 minutes for medium-rare on the medium side (130 degrees), or 9 to 10 minutes for medium (135 to 140 degrees).

4. Remove the steaks from the grill and let rest for 5 minutes. Serve immediately.

➤ VARIATION

Gas-Grilled Filets Mignons

Depending on the heat output of your gas grill, you may need to cook the steaks over the cooler part of the grill for an extra minute or two.

Turn on all burners to high, close the lid, and heat the grill until very hot, about 15 minutes. Scrape the grill grate clean with a grill brush. Leave one burner on high and turn the other burner(s) to medium. Follow the recipe for Charcoal-Grilled Filets Mignons from step 2 and cook with the lid down.

Charcoal-Grilled Porterhouse or T-Bone Steaks

SERVES 4

How can you argue with a steak that gives you two different tastes and textures—from the strip and the tenderloin—in one cut, plus the bone? Since T-bone and porterhouse steaks are so large, it's best to have the butcher cut them thick (1½ inches) and let one steak serve two people. The key to keeping the delicate tenderloin from overcooking is to sear the steaks with the strip portions over the hottest coals and the tenderloin portions facing the cooler part of the fire.

    2   porterhouse or T-bone steaks, 1½ inches
         thick (about 1¾ pounds each), patted dry
         Salt and ground black pepper

1. Light a large chimney starter filled with hardwood charcoal (about 6 quarts) and allow to burn until all the charcoal is covered with a layer of fine gray ash. Build a two-level fire by stacking most of the coals on one side of the grill and arranging the remaining coals in a single layer on the other side of the grill. Set the cooking rack in place, cover the grill with the lid, and let the rack heat up, about 5 minutes. Use a wire brush to scrape clean the cooking rack. The grill

is ready when the pile of coals is medium-hot and the single layer of coals is medium-low. (See how to gauge heat level on page 568.)

2. Meanwhile, sprinkle both sides of the steaks with salt and pepper to taste. Position the steaks on the grill so the tenderloin pieces are over the cooler part of the fire but the strip pieces are over the hotter part of the fire (see the illustration below). Grill the steaks, uncovered, until well browned on one side, 2 to 3 minutes. Turn the steaks; grill until well browned on the other side, 2 to 3 minutes. (If the steaks start to flame, pull them to the cooler part of the grill and/or extinguish the flames with a squirt bottle filled with water.)

3. Once the steaks are well browned on both sides, slide them completely to the cooler part of the grill. Continue grilling, uncovered, to the desired doneness, 5 to 6 minutes more for rare (120 degrees on an instant-read thermometer), 6 to 7 minutes for medium-rare on the rare side (125 degrees), 7 to 8 minutes for medium-rare on the medium side (130 degrees), or 8 to 9 minutes for medium (135 to 140 degrees).

4. Remove the steaks from the grill to a cutting board and let rest for 5 minutes. Cut the strip and filet pieces off the bones and slice each piece crosswise about ½ inch thick (see the illustrations at right). Serve immediately.

GRILLING PORTERHOUSE AND T-BONE STEAKS

The delicate, buttery tenderloin portion must be protected when grilling porterhouse and T-bone steaks. Keep the tenderloin (the smaller portion on the left side of the bone on these steaks) over the cooler part of the fire.

➤ VARIATION

Gas-Grilled Porterhouse or T-Bone Steaks

The key to preventing the delicate tenderloin portions of the steaks from overcooking is to sear the steaks with the strip portions over the burner turned to high and to keep the tenderloin facing the burner turned to medium.

Turn on all burners to high, close the lid, and heat the grill until very hot, about 15 minutes.

CARVING PORTERHOUSE OR T-BONE STEAKS

1. Once grilled, let a porterhouse or T-bone steak rest for 5 minutes before slicing. Once the meat has rested, start by slicing close to the bone to remove the strip section.

2. Turn the steak around and cut the tenderloin section off the bone.

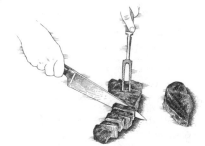

3. Slice each piece crosswise about ½ inch thick. Serve immediately.

Scrape the grill grate clean with a grill brush. Leave one burner on high and turn the other burner(s) to medium. Follow the recipe for Charcoal-Grilled Porterhouse or T-Bone Steaks from step 2 and cook with the lid down.

GRILLED STEAK TIPS

STEAK TIPS HAVE NEVER BEEN ON OUR LIST of favorite meats. It's not that we're premium steak snobs, but we were skeptical about a cut of meat that has long been the darling of all-you-can-eat restaurant chains, where quantity takes precedence over quality. There is also some confusion about what constitutes a steak tip. Some steak tips are sautéed and served with a sauce (these are often called pub-style steak tips); some are marinated and grilled (known as tailgate tips). We were drawn to grilling and so began by testing five such recipes.

The recipes differed in the ingredients used to marinate the meat and in the marinating time. The simplest recipe marinated the tips in a bottled Italian-style salad dressing for 24 hours. The most complex marinated the meat for three days in a mixture that included aromatics and herbs. Despite such variations in time and ingredients, none of these grilled tips was very good. Some were mushy, but most were tough and dry. At this point, steak tips still seemed like a cheap cut of meat, with promising beefy flavor but poor texture.

Thinking that the problem might be the cut of meat, we went to the supermarket only to discover a confusing array of meats—cubes, strips, and steaks—labeled "steak tips." Still more confusing, these cubes, strips, and steaks could be cut from a half dozen different parts of the cow.

After grilling more than 50 pounds of tips, it became clear that the only cut worth grilling is one referred to by butchers as flap meat. (For more information on buying steak tips, see page 571.) When we grilled whole flap meat steaks and then sliced them on the bias before serving, tasters were impressed. Although the meat was still a bit chewy, choosing the right cut was a start.

We now turned to marinades. Given the long-held belief that acidic marinades tenderize tough meat, we created four recipes using four popular acids: yogurt, wine, vinegar, and fruit juice. To determine optimal marination time, we let the meat sit in each marinade for four hours and for 24 hours. Curious about marinades' other claim to fame—flavoring—we added aromatics, spices, and herbs.

The yogurt marinade was the least favorite, producing dry meat that was chewy and tough. Tasters also panned the wine-based marinade. The meat was tough and dry, the flavors harsh and bland. Some tasters liked the complex flavor of the vinegar marinade, but everyone found the tips to be "overly chewy." The marinade prepared with pineapple juice was the favorite. Both the four-hour and 24-hour versions yielded juicy, tender, flavorful meat.

Why did pineapple juice make the best marinade? Our first thought was proteases, enzymes that help to break down proteins. Proteases are found in pineapple, papaya, and other fruits. One of them, papain, from papayas, is the active component of meat tenderizers such as Adolph's. The juice we had been using was pasteurized, however, and the heat of pasteurization is thought to disable such enzymes. To see if proteases were in fact at work, we devised three tests in which we made three more marinades: one with pasteurized pineapple juice from the supermarket; a second with pasteurized pineapple juice heated to the boiling point and then cooled; and a third with fresh pineapple pureed in a food processor.

The result? The fresh juice was a much more aggressive "tenderizer," so much so that it turned the meat mushy on the inside and slimy on the outside. We had learned: Proteases do break down meat, but they don't make it any better (tasters universally disapproved of these tenderized tips); pasteurization does kill this enzyme (the fresh juice was much more powerful than the supermarket variety); and proteases were not responsible for the strong showing made by the original pineapple marinade. Why, then, did tasters prefer the pineapple marinade to those made with yogurt, wine, and vinegar?

Outdoor Cooking 101

LIGHTING A CHARCOAL FIRE

Our favorite way to start a charcoal fire is with a chimney starter, also known as a flue starter. To use this simple device, fill the bottom section with crumpled newspaper, set the starter on the grill grate, and fill the top with charcoal. (A large starter can hold about six quarts of charcoal.) When you light the newspaper, flames will shoot up through the charcoal, igniting it. Match-light charcoal has been soaked in lighter fluid, and we find that it imparts an off flavor to foods. Plain charcoal briquettes are a much better option. We also like hardwood charcoal, also called natural or lump charcoal. Because it burns hotter and quicker than briquettes, we prefer hardwood charcoal when grilling. However, it is too hot to be practical when cooking with indirect heat.

CHARCOAL VERSUS GAS

Our preference when grilling (that is, cooking over direct heat) is to use charcoal. We like the high heat generated and the flavor that food absorbs from hardwood charcoal (our favorite fuel for most recipes). However, when doing indirect cooking—barbecuing or grill-roasting—the differences in flavor between foods cooked over gas and charcoal diminish a bit.

TAKING THE TEMPERATURE OF THE FIRE

Use the chart below to determine the intensity of the fire. The terms *hot fire*, *medium-hot fire*, *medium fire*, and *medium-low fire* are used in all our grilling recipes. When using a gas grill, ignore dial readings such as medium or medium-low in favor of actual measurements of the temperature, as described here.

Intensity of fire	Time you can hold your hand 5 inches above grate
Hot fire	2 seconds
Medium-hot fire	3 to 4 seconds
Medium fire	5 to 6 seconds
Medium-low fire	7 seconds

Once the coals have been spread out in the bottom of the grill, put the cooking grate in place and put the cover on for five minutes to heat up the grate. (On gas grills, preheat with the lid down and all burners on high for 15 minutes.) Scrape the cooking grate clean and then take the temperature of the fire by holding your hand 5 inches above the cooking grate and counting how long you can comfortably leave it in place.

CHECKING THE FUEL LEVEL IN A GAS TANK

There's nothing worse than running out of fuel halfway through grilling. If your grill doesn't have a gas gauge, use this technique to estimate how much gas is left in the tank.

1. Bring a cup or so of water to a boil in a small saucepan or glass measuring cup (if using the microwave). Pour the water over the side of the tank.

2. Feel the metal with your hand. Where the water has succeeded in warming the tank, it is empty; where the tank remains cool to the touch, there is still propane inside.

THREE TYPES OF CHARCOAL FIRES

Single-Level Fire
Arrange all the lit charcoal in an even layer. This kind of fire delivers even heat and is best for quick searing at a moderate temperature.

Two-Level Fire
Spread some of the lit coals in a single layer over half of the grill. Leave the remaining coals in a pile that rises to within 2 or 2½ inches of the cooking grate. This kind of fire permits searing over very hot coals and slower cooking over moderate coals to cook through thicker cuts.

Modified Two-Level Fire
Pile all the lit coals into half the grill to create a hot place for searing, but leave the remaining portion of the grill empty. Some heat from the coals will still cook foods placed over the empty part of the grill, but the heat is very gentle and little browning will occur here.

BARBECUING ON A GAS GRILL

Remove part or all of the cooking grate. Place a foil tray with soaked wood chips on top of the primary burner. Make sure the tray is resting securely on the burner so it will not tip. Replace the grill rack. Light all burners and cover the grill. When you see a lot of smoke (after about 20 minutes), turn off the burner (or burners) without the chips and place the food over it (or them). If the chips flame, douse the fire with water from a squirt bottle. Cover the grill.

BARBECUING ON A CHARCOAL GRILL

1. Pile the lit coals on one half of the grill and leave the other half free of coals.

2. Place soaked and drained wood chunks or a foil packet filled with wood chips on top of the coals. Set the top grate in position, heat briefly, and then scrape the grate clean with a wire brush. You are now ready to cook over the cool part of the fire. Put the food on the grill and set the lid in place. Open the air vents as directed in individual recipes.

3. A grill thermometer inserted through the vents on the lid can tell you if the fire is too hot or if the fire is getting too cool and you need to add more charcoal. You will get different readings depending on where the lid vents are and thus the thermometer is in relation to the coals. Because you want to know the temperature where the food is being cooked, rotate the lid so that the thermometer is close to the food. Make sure, however, that the thermometer stem does not touch the food.

USING WOOD CHIPS ON A CHARCOAL GRILL

1. Place the amount of wood chips called for in the recipe in the center of an 18-inch square of heavy-duty aluminum foil. Fold in all four sides of the foil to encase the chips.

2. Turn the foil packet over. Tear about six large holes (each the size of a quarter) through the top of the foil packet with a fork to allow smoke to escape. Place the packet, with holes facing up, directly on a pile of lit charcoal.

USING WOOD CHIPS ON A GAS GRILL

Buy small, rectangular disposable foil trays to hold wood chips on a gas grill, or fashion your own tray out of aluminum foil.

1. Start with an 18 by 12-inch piece of heavy-duty foil. Make a 1-inch fold on one long side. Repeat three more times, then turn the fold up to create a sturdy side that measures about an inch high. Repeat the process on the other long side.

2. With a short side facing you, fold in both corners as if wrapping a gift.

3. Turn up the inside inch or so of each triangular fold to match the rim on the long sides of the foil tray.

4. Lift the pointed end of the triangle over the rim of foil and fold down to seal. Repeat the process on the other short side.

After rereading the ingredient list in our pineapple marinade, we devised a new theory. The pineapple marinade included soy sauce, an ingredient that is packed with salt and that was not used in any of the other marinades. Was the soy sauce tenderizing the meat by acting like a brine of salt and water? In the past, the test kitchen has demonstrated the beneficial effects of brining on lean poultry and pork.

We then ran another series of tests, trying various oil-based marinades made with salt or soy sauce (in earlier tests, we had determined that oil helped to keep the meat moist and promoted searing). To use salt in a marinade, we first had to dissolve it. Because salt doesn't dissolve in oil, we used water, but the liquid prevented the meat from browning properly. That said, brining did make these steak tips tender and juicy.

We concluded that soy sauce, not pineapple juice, was the secret ingredient in our tasters' favorite marinade. The salt in soy sauce was responsible for the improved texture of the steak tips, and the soy sauce also promoted browning. After experimenting with brining times, we determined that an hour was optimal. It allowed for the thicker parts of the meat to become tender while preventing the thinner sections from becoming too salty.

We then went to work on flavor variations, adding garlic, ginger, orange zest, hot pepper, brown sugar, and scallions for an Asian marinade and making a Southwest-inspired marinade that included garlic, chili powder, cumin, cayenne, brown sugar, and tomato paste. We found that a squeeze of fresh citrus served with the steak provided a bright acidic counterpoint.

Because this relatively thin cut cooks quickly, high heat is necessary to achieve a perfect crust. The uneven thickness of many tips presented a problem, though. The exterior would scorch by the time the thick portions were cooked, and the thin parts would be overcooked. A two-level fire, with more coals on one side of the grill to create hotter and cooler areas, solved the problem. We started the tips over high heat to sear them and then moved them to the cooler area to finish cooking.

We prefer steaks grilled rare, so we were surprised to find that when cooked rare the meat was rubbery, whereas longer cooking gave it a tender chew—without drying out the meat. Even when cooked until well done, the tips were exceptionally juicy. We had the brine to thank again: The salty soy marinade helped the meat hold on to its moisture.

Conventional wisdom prompted one more test. We grilled two more batches of tips and sliced one immediately after it came off the grill and the other five minutes later. Sure enough, the rested tips were both more juicy and more tender. Finally, we had a recipe for steak tips as pleasing to the palate as they are to the pocketbook.

Charcoal-Grilled Steak Tips
SERVES 4 TO 6

A two-level fire allows you to brown the steak over the hot side of the grill, then move it to the cooler side if it is not yet cooked through. If your steak is thin, however, you may not need to use the cooler side of the grill. The times in the recipe below are for relatively even, 1-inch-thick steak tips. When grilling, bear in mind that even those tasters who usually prefer rare beef preferred steak tips cooked medium-rare to medium because the texture is firmer and not quite so chewy. Serve lime wedges with the Southwestern-marinated tips and orange wedges with the tips marinated in garlic, ginger, and soy sauce.

1   recipe marinade (recipes on page 572)
2   pounds flap meat sirloin steak tips, trimmed of
     excess fat
     Lime or orange wedges for serving

1. Combine the marinade and meat in a gallon-size zipper-lock bag; press out as much air as possible and seal the bag. Refrigerate for 1 hour, flipping the bag after 30 minutes to ensure that the meat marinates evenly.

2. About halfway through the marinating time, light a large chimney starter filled with hardwood charcoal (about 6 quarts) and allow to burn until all the charcoal is covered with a layer of fine gray ash. Build a two-level fire by stacking most of

the coals on one side of the grill and arrange the remaining coals in a single layer on the other side of the grill. Set the cooking rack in place, cover the grill with the lid, and let the rack heat up, about 5 minutes. Use a wire brush to scrape clean the cooking rack. The grill is ready when the pile of coals is medium-hot and the single layer of coals is medium-low. (See how to gauge heat level on page 568.)

3. Remove the steak tips from the marinade and pat dry with paper towels. Grill, uncovered, until well seared and dark brown on the first side, about 4 minutes. Using tongs, flip the steak tips and grill until the second side is well seared and the thickest part of the meat is slightly less done than desired, 4 to 5 minutes for medium-rare (about 130 degrees on an instant-read thermometer), 6 to 8 minutes for medium (about 135 degrees); if the exterior of the meat is browned but the steak is not yet cooked through, move the steak tips to the cooler side of the grill and continue to grill to the desired doneness.

4. Transfer the steak tips to a cutting board. Tent the tips loosely with foil and let rest for 5 minutes. Slice the steak tips very thinly on the bias. Serve immediately with the lime or orange wedges.

➤ VARIATION
Gas-Grilled Steak Tips
Follow the recipe for Charcoal-Grilled Steak Tips through step 1. When about 15 minutes of marinating time remains, turn on all burners to high, close the lid, and heat the grill until very hot, about 15 minutes. Scrape the grill grate clean with a grill brush. Leave one burner on high and turn the other burner(s) to medium. Continue with the recipe from step 3 and cook with the lid down.

INGREDIENTS: Steak Tips

Steak tips can come from two different parts of the cow. One type comes from tender, expensive cuts in the middle of the back of the cow, such as the tenderloin. These tips are a superior cut, but not what we consider to be a true steak tip, which should be a more pedestrian cut that is magically transformed into a desirable dish through marinating and cooking. If the steak tips at your market cost $8 to $10 per pound, the meat likely comes from the tenderloin.

True steak tips come from various muscles in the sirloin and round and cost about $5 per pound. After tasting 50 pounds of lower-priced cuts, tasters had a clear favorite: a single muscle that butchers call flap meat, with tips from this cut typically labeled "sirloin tips." A whole piece of flap meat weighs about 2½ pounds. One piece can range in thickness from ½ inch to 1½ inches and may be sold as cubes, strips, or small steaks. It has a rich, deep beefy flavor and a distinctive longitudinal grain.

We found that it's best to buy flap meat in steak form rather than cut into cubes or strips, which are often taken from nearby muscles in the hip and butt that are neither as tasty nor as tender. Because meat labeling is so haphazard, you must visually identify flap meat; buying it in steak form makes this easy.

Steak tips can be cut from a half dozen muscles and are sold in three basic forms: cubes, strips, and steaks. To make sure that you are buying the most flavorful cut (called flap meat sirloin tips by butchers and pictured below), buy whole steaks.

Steaks

Strips

Cubes

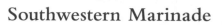

Southwestern Marinade
MAKES ENOUGH FOR 2 POUNDS OF
STEAK TIPS

1/3	cup soy sauce
1/3	cup vegetable oil
3	medium garlic cloves, minced or pressed through a garlic press
1	tablespoon dark brown sugar
1	tablespoon tomato paste
1	tablespoon chili powder
2	teaspoons ground cumin
1/4	teaspoon cayenne pepper

Combine all of the ingredients in a small bowl.

Garlic, Ginger, and Soy Marinade
MAKES ENOUGH FOR 2 POUNDS OF
STEAK TIPS

1/3	cup soy sauce
3	tablespoons vegetable oil
3	tablespoons toasted sesame oil
3	medium garlic cloves, minced or pressed through a garlic press
1	tablespoon minced fresh ginger
2	tablespoons dark brown sugar
2	teaspoons grated zest from 1 orange
1/2	teaspoon red pepper flakes
1	medium scallion, sliced thin

Combine all of the ingredients in a small bowl.

EQUIPMENT: Grill Brushes

To test the brushes, we concocted a "paint"—a mixture of honey, molasses, mustard, and barbecue sauce—that we could burn onto our grates. We coated the grates four times, baking them for one hour in the test kitchen ovens between coats. The result was a charred mess that would be sure to challenge even the hardiest of brushes. The grates were put back on the grills, which were then heated so we could test the brushes under real-life conditions.

The seven brushes we tested were chosen based on the construction and design of the handle and the scrubbing head. The handle of the stainless steel model was decidedly the heaviest and looked to be the most durable, but it absorbed heat at an alarming rate. Plastic performed adequately if you didn't spend too much time in one place on the grill (melting occurred) and if the handle was long enough. One plastic-handled brush, the Grill Pro, with a skimpy 5-inch handle, didn't even make it through the first test. The handle was so short that we couldn't get the brush to the far side of the grill without getting burned. A combination plastic-aluminum brush handle was so flexible it caused burnt knuckles when pressed with any strength. The material of choice for grill brush handles is clearly wood, which is relatively comfortable and durable.

In terms of the scrubbing heads, six of the seven brushes tested had brass bristles. Among these six, those with stiffer bristles fared better than their softer counterparts, but none of them worked all that well. The bristles on most bent after a few strokes and trapped large quantities of gunk, thereby decreasing their efficiency.

In the end, only one brush was able to successfully clean our molten mess down to the grill grate in a reasonable number of strokes. The unusual but incredibly effective Grill Wizard has no brass bristles to bend, break, or clog with unwanted grease and grime. Instead, this brush comes equipped with two large woven mesh stainless steel "scrubbie" pads. The pads are able to conform to any grill grate's spacing, size, and material, including porcelain. Best of all, the pads are detachable, washable, and replaceable. The 14-inch handle, made of poplar, is smooth, with rounded edges (unlike its square-cut competitors) and a hook for easy storage.

THE BEST GRILL BRUSH

The Grill Wizard China Grill Brush ($20) has no bristles; instead, stainless steel "scrubbie" pads are held in place by stainless steel bars. Although it may look a bit odd, it worked far better than the other options we tested.

GRILLED FLANK STEAK

THANKS TO FAJITAS, FLANK STEAK HAS BECOME the darling of Tex-Mex fans from New York to California and everywhere in between. But there are good reasons for the popularity of flank steak in addition to mere culinary fashion. Like other steaks cut from the chest and side of the cow, flank has a rich, full, beefy flavor. Also, because it is thin, it cooks relatively quickly. Because flank steaks are typically too long to fit in a pan, grilling suits this cut.

Although grilling flank steak appeared to be a pretty straightforward procedure, we still had some questions about what was exactly the best way to go about it. We had two very simple goals: creating a good sear on the outside of this thin cut before it overcooked on the inside, and tenderness. We wondered whether the meat should be marinated or rubbed with spices, how hot the fire should be, and how long the meat should be cooked.

Virtually every recipe we found for flank steak called for marinating it. Most sources championed the marinade as a means of tenderizing the meat as well as adding flavor. We found that marinades with a lot of acid eventually made this thin cut mushy and unappealing. If we omitted the acid, we could flavor the meat, but this took at least 12 hours. As for tenderness, when the cooked steaks were sliced thin across the grain, there was virtually no difference between those that had been marinated and those that had not.

With marinades no longer a possibility, we turned to spice rubs. We rubbed one steak with a spice rub eight hours before cooking, one an hour before, and one just before we put it over the flames. One steak, with no spice rub at all, was cooked just like the others. The three spice-rubbed steaks all had about the same amount of flavor and all developed almost identical dark brown, very flavorful crusts. The plain steak did not develop nearly as nice a crust, but cooked in approximately the same amount of time. We noticed no differences in tenderness among the steaks.

Seeing how spice rubs created excellent crust with plenty of intense flavor, they were voted our first choice for flank steak. That said, however, spice rubs are not good for folks who like their flank steak cooked to medium, because if you leave the steak on for that long, the spices burn. (You even have to be a bit careful to keep the spices from burning if you like your steak medium-rare.) But if you don't mind exercising a small degree of attention while grilling, we highly recommend using spice rubs for flank steak. Finally, if you want to cook flank steak beyond medium, we suggest adding flavor by passing a sauce separately at the table.

Every source we checked was in the same camp when it came to cooking flank steak, and it is the right camp. Flank steak should be cooked over high heat for a short period of time. We tried lower heat and longer cooking times, but inevitably the meat ended up being tough. Because flank steak is too thin to be checked with a meat thermometer, you must resort to a primitive method of checking for doneness: Cut into the meat to see if it is done to your liking. Remember that carry-over heat will continue to cook the steak after it comes off the grill. So if you want the steak medium-rare, take it off the heat when it tests rare, and so on.

Most sources were also in the same camp when it came to letting the steak rest after cooking. During cooking, the heat drives the juices to the center of the meat. This phenomenon is particularly noticeable with high-heat cooking. If you cut the meat right after it comes off the heat, much more of the juice spills out than if you allow the meat to rest, during which time the juices become evenly distributed throughout the meat once again. This is common wisdom among cooks, but to be sure it was correct, we cooked two more flank steaks, sliced one up immediately after it came off the fire, and allowed the second to rest for five minutes before slicing it. Not only did the first steak exude almost twice as much juice when sliced as the second, it also looked grayer and was not as tender. So in this case, conventional wisdom prevails: Give your steak a rest.

And when it comes to slicing flank steak, it's important to slice across the grain into thin slices; otherwise the meat will be too chewy.

Charcoal-Grilled Flank Steak

SERVES 4 TO 6

For this recipe, the coals are banked on one side of the grill to create an especially hot fire. Because flank steak is so thin, there's no need to use the cooler part of the grill for cooking the meat through. Also, the thinness of the meat means you have to rely on timing, touch, and/or nick-and-peek, not an instant-read thermometer, to determine doneness.

I   flank steak (about 2½ pounds)
    Salt and ground black pepper

1. Light a large chimney starter filled with hardwood charcoal (about 6 quarts) and allow to burn until all the charcoal is covered with a layer of fine gray ash. Build a modified two-level fire by stacking all of the coals on one side of the grill. Set the cooking rack in place, cover the grill with the lid, and let the rack heat up, about 5 minutes. Use a wire brush to scrape clean the cooking grate. The grill is ready when you have a hot fire. (See how to gauge heat level on page 568.)

2. Sprinkle both sides of the steak generously with salt and pepper to taste. Grill the steak over the coals until well seared and dark brown on one side, 5 to 7 minutes. Using tongs, flip the steak and grill until the interior of the meat when cut into is slightly less done than you want it to be when you eat it, 2 to 5 minutes more for rare or medium-rare (depending on the heat of the fire and the thickness of the steak).

3. Transfer the steak to a cutting board. Tent loosely with foil and let rest for 5 minutes. Slice the steak thinly on the bias across the grain. Adjust the seasonings with additional salt and pepper and serve immediately.

➤ VARIATIONS

Gas-Grilled Flank Steak

Turn on all burners to high, close the lid, and heat the grill until very hot, about 15 minutes. Scrape the grill grate clean with a grill brush. Leave all burners on high. Follow the recipe for Charcoal-Grilled Flank Steak from step 2 and cook with the lid down.

Grilled Flank Steak Rubbed with Latin Spices

Watch the meat carefully as it cooks to ensure that the spice rub darkens but does not burn. If necessary, slide the steak to the cooler part of the charcoal grill (or reduce the heat on a gas grill) to keep the steak from charring.

2   tablespoons ground cumin
2   tablespoons chili powder
I   tablespoon ground coriander

INGREDIENTS: Three Flat Steaks

When it comes to flat steaks, skirt and hanger steaks are most similar to flank steak, and, like flank, have recently become fashionable. The similarities: Hanger and flank both come from the rear side of the animal, while skirt comes from the area between the abdomen and the chest cavity. All are long, relatively thin, quite tough, and grainy, but each has rich, deep, beefy flavor.

We soon came to realize that all flat steaks are not equal. Hanger, a thick muscle that is attached to the diaphragm of the cow, derives its name from the fact that when the animal is butchered, this steak hangs down into the center of the carcass. Because hanger steak is a classic French bistro dish, the cut is highly prized in restaurants and, therefore, difficult to find in butcher shops. We don't think this is a great loss since the hanger steaks we sampled had the toughest texture and was the least flavorful of the three cuts.

On the other hand, flank steak is easy to find in any supermarket. It has great beef flavor and is quite tender if cooked rare or medium-rare and sliced thin across the grain. Because of the popularity of fajitas, flank steak has recently gone steeply up in price, often retailing for $7 a pound.

Last but not least, skirt steak, which was the cut originally used for fajitas, can also be difficult to find in supermarkets and even butcher shops. This is a real pity because skirt steak has more fat than flank steak, which makes it juicier and richer-tasting. At the same time, skirt has a deep, beefy flavor that outshines both hanger or flank steak. If you see skirt steak, buy it, and cook it like flank.

2　teaspoons ground black pepper
½　teaspoon ground cinnamon
½　teaspoon red pepper flakes
1½　teaspoons salt
1　recipe Charcoal-Grilled or Gas-Grilled Flank Steak (page 574)

1. Combine all of the spices and the salt in a small bowl.

2. Follow the Charcoal-Grilled or Gas-Grilled Flank Steak recipe, omitting the salt and pepper in step 2 and rubbing the steak on both sides with the spice mixture instead.

Grilled Flank Steak with Sweet-and-Sour Chipotle Sauce

If you can't find chipotle chiles in adobo sauce, substitute ½ teaspoon liquid smoke mixed with 2 minced jalapeño chiles and 3 tablespoons ketchup.

¼　cup honey
2　tablespoons vegetable oil
3　chipotle chiles in adobo sauce
2　tablespoons balsamic vinegar
2　tablespoons whole-grain mustard
½　cup juice from 3 or 4 limes
2　medium garlic cloves, minced or pressed through a garlic press
1　teaspoon ground cumin
2　tablespoons chopped fresh cilantro leaves
½　teaspoon salt
　　Ground black pepper
1　recipe Charcoal-Grilled or Gas-Grilled Flank Steak (page 574)

1. Combine the honey, oil, chiles, vinegar, mustard, lime juice, garlic, and cumin in a blender jar or the workbowl of a food processor fitted with the steel blade and puree or process until smooth. Transfer to a small bowl and stir in the cilantro, salt, and pepper to taste; set aside. (The sauce can be covered and refrigerated for 3 days.)

2. Follow the Charcoal-Grilled or Gas-Grilled Flank Steak recipe. Remove the steak from the grill and brush both sides generously with the chipotle sauce. Let the steak rest for 5 minutes. Pass the remaining sauce separately with the sliced steak.

Grilled Flank Steak with Spicy Parsley Sauce

This almost-spreadable, spicy herb sauce complements the flavor of grilled flank steak without overwhelming it. The sauce is easy to make and can be prepared in advance.

1　cup minced fresh parsley leaves
3　medium garlic cloves, minced or pressed through a garlic press
1　medium jalapeño chile, stemmed, seeded, and minced
½　cup extra-virgin olive oil
3　tablespoons red wine vinegar
　　Salt and ground black pepper
1　recipe Charcoal-Grilled or Gas-Grilled Flank Steak (page 574)

1. Combine the parsley, garlic, chile, olive oil, vinegar, and salt and pepper to taste in a small bowl. (The sauce can be covered and refrigerated for 3 days.)

2. Follow the Charcoal-Grilled or Gas-Grilled Flank Steak recipe. Serve the parsley sauce, passing it separately, with the sliced steak.

Classic Fajitas
SERVES 8

Although fajitas were originally made with skirt steak (a fattier cut with more flavor), the combination of flank steak and vegetables grilled and then wrapped in warm tortillas is the one that put flank steak on the culinary map in the United States. The ingredients should go on the grill in order: the steak over a hot fire, the vegetables over a medium fire, and the tortillas around the edge of a medium-to-low fire just to warm them. Alternatively, the tortillas can be stacked, then wrapped in a clean, damp dish towel and warmed in a microwave oven at full power for about 3 minutes; keep the tortillas wrapped until serving time. Cover the grilled but unsliced flank steak with foil for the 10 minutes or so it takes for the vegetables and tortillas to cook.

1　recipe Charcoal-Grilled or Gas-Grilled Flank Steak (page 574)
¼　cup juice from 3 or 4 limes
　　Salt and ground black pepper

1 very large onion, peeled and cut into ½-inch
rounds
2 very large red or green bell peppers,
cleaned and cut according to the
illustration below
16 (10- to 12-inch diameter) flour
tortillas
Classic Red Tomato Salsa (page 24) and/or
Chunky Guacamole (page 26)

1. Follow the recipe for either Charcoal-Grilled or Gas-Grilled Flank Steak, sprinkling the meat with the lime juice and salt and pepper to taste before grilling.

2. Remove the steak to a cutting board and tent loosely with foil. When the charcoal fire has died down to medium or the gas grill burners have been adjusted to medium, place the onion rounds and peppers on the grill and grill them, turning them occasionally, until the onions are lightly charred, about 6 minutes, and the peppers are streaked with dark grill marks, about 10 minutes. Remove the vegetables to a cutting board and slice them into thin strips; set aside. Arrange the tortillas around the edge of the grill and heat until just warmed, about 20 seconds per side. (Take care not to let the tortillas dry out, or they will become brittle; wrap the tortillas in a towel to keep them warm, then place them in a basket.)

3. Slice the steak thinly on the bias across the grain. Arrange the sliced meat and vegetables on a large platter. Serve immediately with the tortillas, passing the salsa and/or guacamole separately.

CUTTING PEPPERS FOR THE GRILL

Remove and discard a ¼-inch-thick slice from the top and bottom of each pepper. Reach into the pepper and pull out the seeds in a single bunch. Slice down one side of the pepper, then lay it flat, skin-side down, in a long strip. Slide a sharp knife along the inside of the pepper to remove the white ribs and any remaining seeds. The flattened and cleaned pepper is now ready for grilling.

BARBECUED BRISKET

OUR FAVORITE WAY TO COOK BRISKET IS TO barbecue it. When prepared correctly, the meat picks up a great smoky flavor and becomes fork-tender. Unfortunately, many a barbecued brisket ends up burnt, tough, or chewy. This is because brisket is so tough to begin with. Unless it is fully cooked, the meat is very chewy and practically inedible. Because brisket is so large (a full cut can weigh 13 pounds), getting the meat "fully cooked" can take many hours. Our goal was to make the meat as tender as possible as quickly as possible.

What does "fully cooked" mean when talking about brisket? To find out, we roasted four small pieces to various internal temperatures. The pieces cooked to 160 and 180 degrees were dry and quite tough. A piece cooked to 200 degrees was slightly less tough, although quite dry. A final piece cooked to 210 degrees had the most appealing texture and the most pleasant chew, despite the fact that it was the driest.

So what's going on here? Heat causes muscle proteins to uncoil and then rejoin in a different formation, which drives out juices in the same way that wringing removes moisture from a wet cloth. This process starts in earnest at around 140 degrees, and by the time the meat reaches 180 degrees, most of its juices have been expelled. This explains why a medium-rare steak (cooked to 130 degrees) is much juicier than a well-done steak (cooked to 160 degrees).

With tender cuts, like steak, the lower the internal temperature of the meat, the juicier and less tough the meat will be. However, with cuts that start out tough, like brisket, another process is also at work. Brisket is loaded with waxy-looking connective tissue called collagen, which makes the meat chewy and tough. Only when the collagen has been transformed into gelatin will the meat be tender. Collagen begins to convert to gelatin at 130 to 140 degrees, but the conversion process occurs most rapidly at temperatures above 180 degrees.

When cooking brisket, the gelatinization of collagen must be the priority. Thus, the meat should be cooked as fully as possible, or to an internal temperature of 210 degrees. The muscle juices will be long gone (that's why the sliced meat is served with barbecue sauce), but the meat will be extremely tender because all the collagen will have been converted to gelatin.

It is important to point out that moist-heat cooking methods (such as braising) are appropriate for cooking meats to such high internal temperatures because water is a more efficient conductor of heat than air. Meats cooked in a moist environment heat up faster and can be held at high internal temperatures without burning or drying out.

Given the fact that brisket must be fully cooked and that it can be so big, the meat needs 10 to 12 hours of barbecuing to reach the fork-tender stage. Even when butchers separate the brisket into smaller pieces, as is often the case, the cooking time is astronomical. Most cooks are not prepared to keep a fire going that long. To get around this tending-the-fire-all-day-long problem, we found it necessary to commit barbecue heresy. After much testing, we decided to start the meat on the grill but finish it in the oven, where it could be left to cook unattended.

We wondered how long the meat would have to stay on the grill to pick up enough smoke flavor. In our testing, we found that two hours allowed the meat to absorb plenty of smoke flavor and created a dark brown, crusty exterior. At this point, the meat is ready for the oven. We found it best to wrap the meat in foil to create a moist environment. (Unwrapped briskets cooked up drier, and the exterior was prone to burning.) After barbecuing, a whole brisket requires three hours or so in a 300-degree oven to become fork-tender. Barbecue purists might object to our use of the oven, but this method works, and it doesn't require a tremendous commitment of hands-on cooking time.

Some further notes about our testing. Although many experts recommend basting a brisket regularly as it cooks on the grill to ensure moistness, we disagree. Taking the lid off wreaked havoc with our charcoal fire, and the meat didn't taste any different despite frequent basting with sauce. Likewise, we don't recommend placing a pan filled with water (we also tried beer) on the grill. Some barbecue masters believe that the liquid adds moisture and flavor to the meat, but we couldn't tell any difference between brisket cooked with and without the pan of liquid.

Brisket comes with a thick layer of fat on one side. We tried turning the brisket as it cooked, thinking this might promote even cooking, but we had better results when we barbecued the brisket fat-side up the entire time. This way, the fat slowly melts, lubricating the meat underneath.

Barbecued Beef Brisket on a Charcoal Grill

SERVES 18 TO 24

Cooking a whole brisket, which weighs about 10 pounds, may seem like overkill. However, the process is easy, and the leftovers keep well in the refrigerator for up to 4 days. (Leave leftover brisket unsliced, and reheat the foil-wrapped meat in a 300-degree oven until warm.) Don't worry if your brisket is a little larger or smaller; split-second cooking times are not critical because the meat is eaten very well-done. Still, if you don't want to bother with a big piece of meat, barbecuing brisket for less than a crowd is easy to do. Simply ask your butcher for either the point or flat portion of the brisket (we prefer the point cut; see page 424), each of which weighs about half as much as a whole brisket. Then follow this recipe, reducing the spice rub by half and barbecuing for just 1½ hours. Wrap the meat tightly in foil and reduce the time in the oven to 2 hours. No matter how large or small a piece you cook, it's a good idea to save the juices the meat gives off while in the oven to enrich the barbecue sauce. Hickory and mesquite are both traditional wood choices with brisket.

1	cup Dry Rub for Barbecue (page 579)
1	whole beef brisket (9 to 11 pounds), fat trimmed to ¼-inch thickness
2	(3-inch) wood chunks or 2 cups wood chips
3	cups barbecue sauce (see pages 595–597)

1. Apply the dry rub liberally to all sides of the meat, patting it on firmly to make sure the spices adhere and completely obscure the meat. Wrap the brisket tightly in plastic wrap and refrigerate for 2 hours. (For stronger flavor, refrigerate for up to 2 days.)

2. About 1 hour prior to cooking, remove the brisket from the refrigerator, unwrap, and let it come up to room temperature. Soak the wood chunks in cold water to cover for 1 hour and drain, or place the wood chips on an 18-inch square of aluminum foil, seal to make a packet, and use a fork to create about 6 holes to allow smoke to escape (see the illustrations on page 569).

3. Meanwhile, light a large chimney starter filled a bit less than halfway with charcoal briquettes (about 2½ quarts, or 40 coals) and allow to burn until covered with a thin layer of gray ash. Empty the coals into one side of the grill, piling them up in a mound 2 or 3 briquettes high. Keep the bottom vents completely open. Place the wood chunks

or the packet with the chips on top of the charcoal. Put the cooking grate in place, open the grill lid vents completely, and cover, turning the lid so that the vents are opposite the wood chunks or chips to draw smoke through the grill. Let the grate heat for 5 minutes and then clean it with a wire brush.

4. Position the brisket fat-side up on the side of the grill opposite the fire. Barbecue, without removing the lid, for 2 hours. (The initial temperature will be about 350 degrees and will drop to 250 degrees after 2 hours.)

5. Adjust an oven rack to the middle position and preheat the oven to 300 degrees. Attach 2 pieces of heavy-duty foil, 4 feet long, by folding the long edges together 2 or 3 times, crimping tightly to seal well, to form an approximate 4 by 3-foot rectangle. Position the brisket lengthwise in the center of the foil. Bring the short edges over the brisket and fold down, crimping tightly to seal. Repeat with the long sides of the foil to seal the brisket completely. (See illustrations 1 and 2 on

KEY STEPS TO BARBECUED BRISKET

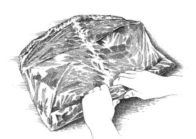

1. After barbecuing, place the brisket on two 4-foot sections of heavy-duty aluminum foil that have been sealed together to make a 4 by 3-foot rectangle. Bring the short ends of the foil up over the brisket and crimp tightly to seal.

2. Seal the long sides of the foil packet tightly up against the sides of the meat. Put the brisket on a rimmed baking sheet and put the sheet in the oven.

3. After the brisket comes out of the oven, use oven mitts to hold the baking sheet and carefully pour the juices into a bowl. Reserve the juices and defat if you like. They make a delicious addition to barbecue sauce.

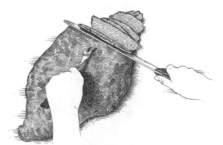

4. Since the grain on the two sections of the brisket goes in opposite directions, separate the cuts before slicing.

5. Carve the brisket on the bias across the grain into long, thin slices.

page 578.) Place the brisket on a rimmed baking sheet. Bake until the meat is fork-tender, 3 to 3½ hours.

6. Remove the brisket from the oven, loosen the foil at one end to release steam, and let rest for 30 minutes. If you like, drain the juices into a bowl (see illustration 3) and defat the juices in a gravy skimmer.

7. Unwrap the brisket and place it on a cutting board. Separate the meat into 2 sections and carve it on the bias across the grain into long, thin slices. Serve with plain barbecue sauce or with barbecue sauce that has been flavored with up to 1 cup of defatted brisket juices.

➤ VARIATION

Barbecued Beef Brisket on a Gas Grill

You will need a pretty large grill to cook a whole brisket. If your grill has fewer than 400 square inches of cooking space, barbecue either the point or flat end, each of which weighs about half as much as a whole brisket. Follow the directions in the note on page 577 for cooking a smaller piece of brisket.

Follow the recipe for Barbecued Beef Brisket on a Charcoal Grill through step 2. Soak the wood chips for 15 minutes in a bowl of water to cover. Place the wood chips in a foil tray (see the illustrations on page 569). Place the foil tray with the soaked wood chips on top of the primary burner (see the illustration on page 569). Turn all burners to high and preheat with the lid down until the chips are smoking heavily, about 20 minutes. Scrape the grate clean with a wire brush. Turn the primary burner down to medium and turn off the other burner(s). Position the brisket fat-side up over the cool part of the grill. Cover and barbecue for 2 hours. (The temperature inside the grill should be a constant 275 degrees; adjust the lit burner as necessary.) Proceed as directed from step 5 of the recipe.

Dry Rub for Barbecue

MAKES ABOUT 1 CUP

You can adjust the proportions of spices in this all-purpose rub or add or subtract a spice, as you wish. For instance, if don't like spicy foods, reduce the cayenne. Or, if you are using hot chili powder, eliminate the cayenne entirely. This rub works well with ribs and brisket, as well as with Boston butt for pulled pork (page 598).

¼	cup sweet paprika
2	tablespoons chili powder
2	tablespoons ground cumin
2	tablespoons dark brown sugar
2	tablespoons salt
1	tablespoon dried oregano
1	tablespoon granulated sugar
1	tablespoon ground black pepper
1	tablespoon ground white pepper
1–2	teaspoons cayenne pepper

Mix all of the ingredients together in a small bowl. (The rub can be stored in an airtight container at room temperature for several weeks.)

GRILLED PORK CHOPS

WE LOVE A JUICY, FLAVORFUL PORK CHOP. TOO bad most pork chops are dry and bland. The pork industry has reduced the fat in pigs by 50 percent since the 1950s. Yes, pork is now the "other white meat," nearly as lean as chicken. But along with all that fat went flavor and juiciness.

The reality of many a grilled pork chop is a burnt exterior, raw interior, tough meat, nary a hint of flavor—the list goes on. We were looking for perfection: a plump, Rubenesque chop with a seared crust reminiscent of chiaroscuro and an interior that would be juicy and flavorful all the way to the bone. We wanted a chop that looked and tasted so good that it transcended the far reaches of backyard grilling and became art.

Thick pork chops usually come from the loin of the pig, which runs from the shoulder to the hip. To determine which cut would be best, we conducted a blind taste test with four different chops, starting with the blade chop, which is from the shoulder end, or front, of the loin. Because the shoulder region of the loin has the most fat and is riddled with connective tissue, tasters found the blade chops to be full of flavor but also tough and chewy. At the hip end of the loin are the sirloin chops. These were dry, somewhat tasteless, and a bit tough. Moving on to the center of the loin, we tested the center-cut chop and the rib chop. Although both were tender and flavorful, tasters preferred the rib chops, which were juicy and well marbled with fat.

Although rib chops are flavorful on their own, we wanted to see if we could boost their flavor by using a spice rub, marinade, or brine. We tested two types of rub: dry and wet. The wet rubs, made with spices and a liquid, gave the chops good flavor but also caused their exterior to turn syrupy. Tasters preferred the dry rubs, which combine potent dried spices with sugar to create big flavor and a crisp crust.

Next we tried marinating the chops in an acidic oil mixture flavored with herbs and garlic. While the marinade succeeded in flavoring the exterior of the chops, it did little for the interior. Moreover, the meat took on a slimy texture that prohibited formation of a good crust.

SCIENCE: Bone-In Chops Are Better

We knew from past experience that bone-in chops taste better than boneless chops, but we wanted to test this notion more systematically. To find out how boneless chops would fare on the grill, we removed the bones from several rib chops, grilled them, and compared them with their bone-in counterparts in a blind taste test. Every taster preferred the meat that had been cooked on the bone. It was much more juicy and had more pork flavor than the meat cooked without the bone. We contacted several food scientists, who offered a few explanations.

First, because bone is a poor conductor of heat, the meat next to the bone doesn't cook as quickly. Although this factor doesn't alter the cooking time significantly, having a section of the pork chop cook at a slightly slower rate contributes to a juicier end product. The bone also insulates the muscle closest to it, protecting it from exposure to the air. In a boneless chop, a larger area of muscle is exposed, so more of the flavorful juices evaporate during grilling. Finally, fat is a crucial source of flavor, and, as it melts during cooking, it also increases the perceived juiciness. In certain cuts, especially ribs and chops, deposits of fat are located next to the bone. When the bone is removed, some fat is removed as well. With less fat, the boneless chops cook up with less pork flavor and seem drier.

Finally, we tried brining, a method we often turn to in the test kitchen, in which lean cuts of meat (usually pork or poultry) are soaked in a solution of water and salt and sometimes sugar. (Brining yields moist, well-seasoned meat and poultry that are hard to overcook, an important factor when grilling.) The brined chops were well seasoned throughout, not just on the surface. They were also extremely juicy—each bite was full of moist, seasoned pork flavor, complemented by the warm crunch of the spice rub.

It was now time to grill. As a preliminary test, we pitted hardwood charcoal against the more traditional charcoal briquettes. After grilling a few chops over each, we found we preferred the hardwood for its intensely hot fire and slightly smoky flavor. As for the fire itself, we always begin testing with a single-level fire—that is, a fire of even and generally high heat made by spreading coals evenly across the grill. We threw the chops over the fire and watched as they browned to a beautiful bronze within minutes. But when we pulled the chops off the grill and cut into one, it was rare at the bone. Moderating the temperature of the fire only drew out the cooking time and sacrificed the deep, caramelized crust we had achieved over high heat.

Moving next to a two-level fire, which is achieved by banking more hot coals on one side of the grill than on the other, we tried a multitude of temperature combinations, each time starting the chops over high heat to develop a nicely browned crust. Moving the chops from high to medium, high to low, and high to no heat were all tested, but none of these combinations produced a thoroughly cooked interior in a reasonable amount of time. Throwing the grill lid back on after the initial sear cooked the chops all the way through—a breakthrough to be sure—but the flavor of the meat was adversely affected. (The inside of most charcoal grill covers is coated with a charcoal residue that readily imparts bitter, spent flavors to foods.) Seizing on the notion of covering the chops for part of the cooking time, we turned to a handy disposable aluminum roasting pan to solve the problem. We threw the pan over the chops after searing them over high heat and moving them to the cooler part of the grill. This time we had a crisp crust, juicy meat, and no off flavors.

In our eagerness to serve these perfect chops, we cut into them right off the grill and watched as the juices ran out onto the plate. We allowed the next round of chops to sit covered under the foil pan for five minutes. When we cut into the chops this time, only a little of the juice escaped. We were surprised, however, to find that these chops were slightly tougher than the chops that did not rest. We took the internal temperature and found that it was now nearly 165 degrees—overcooked in our book. (At 145 degrees, pork is cooked, safe to eat, and still juicy. Temperatures above 150 degrees yield dry, tough meat.) We cooked one more batch of chops and this time took them off the grill earlier, once they had reached an internal temperature of 135 degrees, then let them sit under the foil pan for a good five minutes. Thanks to the residual heat left in the bone, the temperature shot up an average of 10 to 15 degrees, bringing the meat into that desirable range of 145 to 150.

Charcoal-Grilled Pork Chops

SERVES 4

Rib loin chops are our top choice for their big flavor and juiciness. Dry rubs add a lot of flavor for very little effort, but the chops can also be seasoned with pepper alone just before grilling. You will need a large disposable aluminum roasting pan to cover the chops and help them finish cooking through to the bone.

- 6 tablespoons table salt
- 6 tablespoons sugar
- 4 bone-in rib or center-cut pork chops, 1½ inches thick (about 12 ounces each)
- 1 recipe dry rub (page 582) or ground black pepper

1. Dissolve the salt and sugar in 3 quarts cold water in a 2-gallon zipper-lock plastic bag. Add the chops and seal the bag, pressing out as much air as possible. (Alternatively, divide the brine and chops evenly between two 1-gallon zipper-lock bags.) Refrigerate, turning the bag once, until fully seasoned, about 1 hour. Remove the chops from the brine and pat thoroughly dry with paper towels. Coat the chops with the dry

THE BEST CHOP FOR GRILLING

Pork chops come from the loin of the pig. A whole pork loin weighs 14 to 17 pounds and can be cut into blade chops, rib chops, center-cut chops, and sirloin chops. The loin muscle runs the entire length of the backbone. Starting midway back, the tenderloin muscle runs along the opposite side of the backbone. Center-cut and sirloin chops contain both kinds of muscle. (On the center-cut chop, the tenderloin is the small piece of meat on the left side of the bone in the photo below.) We found that the tenderloin cooks more quickly than the loin and can dry out on the grill. This is one reason why we prefer rib chops, which contain only loin meat. Following are tasters' impressions after sampling four different chops cut from the loin. Rib chops were tasters' top choice, followed by center-cut chops.

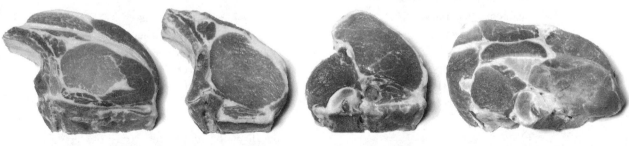

BLADE CHOP
Fattiest, toughest, juiciest, most flavor

RIB CHOP
Some fat, relatively tender, juicy, great flavor

CENTER-CUT CHOP
Little fat, relatively tender, less juicy, good flavor

SIRLOIN CHOP
Tough, quite dry, little flavor

DRY RUBS FOR GRILLED PORK

PORK BENEFITS FROM ASSERTIVE SEASONINGS, ESPECIALLY WHEN IT IS GRILLED AND THERE is no opportunity to make a pan sauce. These four rubs are particularly well suited to chops and tenderloins. Consider serving pork with a fruit salsa (see page 584) for added moisture.

Basic Spice Rub for Grilled Pork

MAKES ENOUGH FOR 4 CHOPS
OR 2 TENDERLOINS

I	tablespoon ground cumin
I	tablespoon chili powder
I	tablespoon curry powder
I	teaspoon ground black pepper
2	teaspoons brown sugar

Combine all of the ingredients in a small bowl.

Indian Spice Rub for Grilled Pork

MAKES ENOUGH FOR 4 CHOPS
OR 2 TENDERLOINS

Serve pork rubbed with this fragrant combination with Mango Salsa (page 584).

I	tablespoon fennel seeds
I	tablespoon ground cumin
I	teaspoon ground coriander
I	teaspoon ground cardamom
I	teaspoon dry mustard
1/2	teaspoon ground cinnamon
1/4	teaspoon ground cloves
2	teaspoons brown sugar

Grind the fennel seeds to a powder in a spice grinder. Transfer to a small bowl and stir in the remaining ingredients.

Chipotle and Ancho Rub for Grilled Pork

MAKES ENOUGH FOR 4 CHOPS
OR 2 TENDERLOINS

A little of this potent rub goes a long way.

I	dried chipotle chile (not in adobo sauce), stemmed, seeded, and broken into I-inch pieces
1/2	medium ancho chile, stemmed, seeded, and broken into I-inch pieces
I	teaspoon dried oregano
1/4	teaspoon garlic powder
1/4	teaspoon salt
2	teaspoons brown sugar

Grind both chiles to a powder in a spice grinder. Transfer to a small bowl and stir in the remaining ingredients.

Herb Rub for Grilled Pork

MAKES ENOUGH FOR 4 CHOPS
OR 2 TENDERLOINS

A little salt is added to this rub to help break the dried herbs down into a powder. Do not salt the meat if using this rub.

1 1/2	teaspoons dried thyme
1 1/2	teaspoons dried rosemary
1 1/2	teaspoons black peppercorns
2	bay leaves, crumbled
2	whole cloves or allspice berries
1/2	teaspoon salt

Grind all of the ingredients to a powder in a spice grinder.

rub or season generously with pepper.

2. Light a large chimney starter filled with hardwood charcoal (about 6 quarts) and allow to burn until all the charcoal is covered with a layer of fine gray ash. Build a two-level fire by stacking most of the coals on one side of the grill and arranging the remaining coals in a single layer on the other side of the grill. Set the cooking rack in place, cover the grill with the lid, and let the rack heat up, about 5 minutes. Use a wire brush to scrape clean the cooking rack. The grill is ready when the pile of coals is medium-hot and the single layer of coals is medium-low. (See how to gauge heat level on page 568.)

3. Grill the chops, uncovered, over the hotter part of the fire until browned on each side, 2½ to 3 minutes per side. Move the chops to the cooler part of the grill and cover with a disposable aluminum roasting pan. Continue grilling, turning once, until an instant-read thermometer inserted through the side of a chop away from the bone registers 135 degrees, 7 to 9 minutes longer. Transfer the chops to a platter, cover with the foil pan, and let rest for 5 minutes. (The internal temperature should rise to 145 degrees.) Serve immediately.

➤ VARIATION
Gas-Grilled Pork Chops
Because gas grill lids don't build up a residue that can impart an off flavor to foods (as charcoal grills do), they can be used to concentrate heat to cook the pork chops through; there's no need, therefore, for a disposable roasting pan.

Follow step 1 of the recipe for Charcoal-Grilled Pork Chops. Turn on all burners to high, close the lid, and heat the grill until very hot, about 15 minutes. Scrape the grill grate clean with a grill brush. Leave one burner on high and turn the other burner(s) to medium-low. Cook the chops as directed in step 3 with the lid down.

GRILLED PORK TENDERLOIN

ALTHOUGH A PORK TENDERLOIN IS TOO SMALL to grill-roast, it is a roast and it can be grilled. In fact, grilling is a terrific way to cook pork tenderloin, a sublimely tender cut that benefits especially from the flavor boost provided by fire. But grilling a tenderloin does have its challenges. The chief problem is how to achieve a rich, golden, caramelized crust without destroying the delicate texture of the meat by overcooking it. What level of heat is best, and exactly how long should a tenderloin cook? Will grilling alone adequately flavor the meat, or should you pull another flavor-building trick from your culinary magic hat?

As the name suggests, tenderness is the tenderloin's main appeal. Anatomically speaking, the tenderloin is a small, cylindrical muscle located against the inside of the pig's rib cage. (In a human being, the equivalent muscle is in the midback area.) Because this muscle doesn't get much use, it remains very tender. Also, because the tenderloin is small, usually weighing 12 to 16 ounces, it cooks very quickly. So it is great for fast, easy weeknight dinners.

Another reason for the tenderloin's popularity is its natural leanness. Though this is good news for diners concerned about fat intake, it can cause problems for the cook. The cut has almost no marbling, the threads of intramuscular fat that contribute a great deal of flavor to meat. Marbling also helps ensure juiciness, since the fat between the muscle fibers melts during cooking. Without that extra measure of protection, the long, slender, quick-cooking tenderloin can overcook and dry out much faster than fattier cuts.

To guard against this possibility, the tenderloin should be cooked to medium so it will retain a slightly rosy hue in the center. The internal temperature should be 145 to 150 degrees, which is just short of the 160 degrees recommended by the U.S. Department of Agriculture. In the time it takes this cut to reach 160 degrees, the meat becomes dry, chewy, grayish white, and unappetizing. (For information on safe internal temperatures when cooking pork, see page 455.)

SALSAS FOR PORK

All of these salsas are great with pork, whether the pork has been grilled or roasted.

Black Bean and Mango Salsa

MAKES ABOUT 2 1/2 CUPS

1/2	cup cooked black beans
1	medium mango, peeled, pitted, and cut into 1/4-inch dice
1/4	medium red bell pepper, cored, seeded, and diced small
1/4	medium green bell pepper, cored, seeded, and diced small
1/4	medium red onion, diced small
6	tablespoons pineapple juice
1/4	cup juice from 2 or 3 limes
1/4	cup chopped fresh cilantro leaves
1	tablespoon ground cumin
1/2	small jalapeño chile, stemmed, seeded, and minced
	Salt and ground black pepper

Mix all of the ingredients, including salt and pepper to taste, together in a medium bowl. Transfer the salsa to an airtight container and refrigerate to blend the flavors at least 1 hour or up to 4 days.

Mango Salsa

MAKES ABOUT 2 CUPS

2	medium mangoes, peeled, pitted, and cut into 1/4-inch dice
1/2	medium red onion, minced
2	scallions, sliced thin
1/2	medium jalapeño chile, stemmed, seeded (if desired), and minced

1	tablespoon juice from 1 lime
2	tablespoons minced fresh cilantro leaves
	Salt and ground black pepper

Mix all of the ingredients, including salt and pepper to taste, together in a medium bowl. (Transfer the salsa to an airtight container and refrigerate for at least 1 hour or up to 4 days.)

Peach Salsa

MAKES ABOUT 2 1/2 CUPS

Nectarines can be substituted for the peaches. In addition to pork, this salsa works well with lamb.

2	ripe but not mushy peaches, pitted and chopped coarse
1	small red bell pepper, cored, seeded, and diced
1	small red onion, diced
1/4	cup chopped fresh parsley leaves
1	medium garlic clove, minced or pressed through a garlic press (about 1 teaspoon)
1/4	cup pineapple juice
6	tablespoons juice from 2 or 3 limes
1	medium jalapeño chile, stemmed, seeded, and minced
	Salt

Mix all of the ingredients, including salt to taste, together in a medium bowl. Transfer the salsa to an airtight container and refrigerate to blend the flavors at least 1 hour or up to 4 days.

Before setting match to charcoal, we reviewed numerous grilled tenderloin recipes and found most to be more confusing than enlightening. Many recipes were vague, offering ambiguous directions such as "grill the tenderloins for 10 to 12 minutes, turning." Those that did provide details disagreed on almost every point, from method (direct or indirect heat, open or covered grill) to heat level (hot, medium-hot, medium, or medium-low), timing (anywhere from 12 to 60 minutes), and internal temperature (from 145 to 160 degrees).

Direct grilling over hot, medium-hot, medium, and medium-low fires constituted our first series of tests. While the meat certainly cooked over all of these fires, it didn't cook perfectly over any of them. The medium-low fire failed to produce the essential crust. Each of the other fires produced more of a crust than we wanted by the time the internal temperature of the tenderloins had reached 145 degrees. Even the medium fire, which took 16 minutes to cook the tenderloin to 145 degrees, charred the crust a little too much by the time the meat had cooked through. The more intense medium-hot and hot fires cooked the meat a little faster, which meant less time on the grill, but the crust was still overly blackened in some spots.

It was clear at this point that building a two-level fire and some indirect cooking on a cooler area of the grill would be necessary to allow the tenderloin to cook through without becoming charred. Cooking over a medium-hot fire seared the meat steadily and evenly in 2½ minutes on each of four sides, but the internal temperature at this point usually hovered around 125 degrees. To finish cooking, we moved the tenderloin to the cooler part of the grill and waited for the internal temperature to climb. And we waited, and waited some more. About 10 seemingly endless minutes and countless temperature checks later, the meat arrived at 145 degrees. Since this took so long, we tried speeding up the process by covering the tenderloin with a disposable aluminum roasting pan.

We seared the meat directly over medium-hot coals for 2½ minutes per side, then moved it to a cooler part of the grill and covered it with a pan.

In just 2½ minutes under the pan, the tenderloin reached 145 degrees internal without picking up additional char on the crust.

The well-developed crust did the tenderloin a world of good, but we knew there were other flavor development methods to try, including marinating, dry and wet flavor rubs, and brining. Marinating, which required at least 2 to 3 hours and often up to 24, simply took too long, especially for an impromptu weeknight meal. Next we tried both dry and wet flavor rubs. Our tasters' favorite dry spice rubs for pork were quick to throw together and gave the tenderloin a fantastic, flavorful crust. We also had good luck with wet rubs. They are also easy to make, have strong flavors, and give the pork a lovely, crusty, glazed effect.

As good as these methods are, though, the meat still lacked seasoning at its center. So we tried brining. Since it takes close to an hour to make a rub and any side dishes, prepare the fire, and heat the grill rack, we reasoned that the tenderloins could spend that time—but no more—sitting in a brine. We started out with a simple saltwater brine, which seasoned the meat nicely throughout. Then, picking up on the subtle sweetness we liked in the dry and wet rubs, we added some sugar to the brine. The results were spectacular.

INGREDIENTS: Preflavored Pork Tenderloin

The fact that today's leaner pork is less flavorful is recognized by the industry as well as by consumers. This development, coupled with sheer convenience, may be why some distributors now offer various superlean cuts, including the tenderloin and the center cut loin filet, vacuum-packed in their own "flavoring solutions." The flavoring choices in our local market were peppercorn and teriyaki for tenderloins and lemon-garlic and honey-mustard for center-cut loin filets.

Curious, we bought one of each and grilled them carefully for a test kitchen tasting. The results fell far short of the mark. Sitting in the flavor solutions for who knows how long obliterated the texture of the meat, making it soft, wet, and spongy. In addition, these flavorings tasted genuinely awful; none allowed the taste of the pork itself to come through.

The sweetness enhanced the flavor of the pork, and the brine ensured robust flavor in every bite of every slice of meat.

Grilled pork tenderloin, then, can be more than just a tender, lean cut of meat that cooks up quickly. With a combination of brining to season the interior of the meat, a rub to season the exterior, and careful grilling to produce a glistening, caramelized crust without overcooking, it is a real treat to eat, too.

Charcoal-Grilled Pork Tenderloin

SERVES 6 TO 8

For maximum time efficiency, while the pork is brining, make the flavor rub and then light the fire. If you opt not to brine, bypass step 1 in the recipe below and sprinkle the tenderloins generously with salt before grilling. Use a spice rub whether or not the pork has been brined—it adds extra flavor and forms a nice crust on the meat. If rubbing tenderloins with dry spices, consider serving with a fruit salsa (page 584) for added moisture and flavor. You will need a disposable aluminum roasting pan for this recipe.

1½	tablespoons table salt
¾	cup sugar
2	pork tenderloins (1½ to 2 pounds total), trimmed of silver skin
1	recipe wet spice rub (page 587) or 2 tablespoons olive oil and 1 recipe dry spice rub (page 582)

1. Dissolve the salt and sugar in 4 cups cold water in a medium bowl. Add the tenderloins, cover the bowl with plastic wrap, and refrigerate until fully seasoned, about 1 hour. Remove the tenderloins from the brine, rinse well, and dry thoroughly with paper towels. Set aside.

2. Light a large chimney starter filled with hardwood charcoal (about 6 quarts) and allow to burn until all the charcoal is covered with a layer of fine gray ash. Build a modified two-level fire by spreading the coals out over half of the grill bottom. Set the cooking rack in place, cover the grill with the lid, and let the rack heat up, about 5 minutes. Use a wire brush to scrape clean the cooking rack. The grill is ready when the coals are medium-hot. (See how to gauge heat level on page 568.)

3. If using a wet spice rub, rub the tenderloins with the mixture. If using a dry spice rub, coat the tenderloins with the oil and then rub with the spice mixture.

4. Cook the tenderloins, uncovered, over the hotter part of the grill until browned on all four sides, about 2½ minutes on each side. Move the tenderloins to the cooler part of the grill and cover with a disposable aluminum roasting pan. Grill, turning once, until an instant-read thermometer inserted into the thickest part of the tenderloin registers 145 degrees or the meat is slightly pink at the center when cut with a paring knife, 2 to 3 minutes longer. Transfer the tenderloins to a cutting board, cover with the disposable aluminum pan, and let rest about 5 minutes. Slice crosswise into 1-inch-thick pieces and serve.

➤ VARIATION
Gas-Grilled Pork Tenderloin

A gas grill runs slightly cooler than a charcoal fire, so the tenderloins can be cooked over direct heat for the entire time.

Follow step 1 of the recipe for Charcoal-Grilled Pork Tenderloin. Preheat the grill with all burners set to high and the lid down until the grill is very hot, about 15 minutes. Scrape the grill grate clean with a grill brush. Coat the tenderloins with the spice rub of choice and grill, with the lid down, until browned on all four sides, about 3 minutes per side.

TRIMMING SILVER SKIN FROM PORK TENDERLOIN

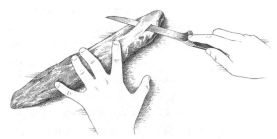

Slip a knife under the silver skin, angle it slightly upward, and use a gentle back-and-forth motion to remove the silver skin. Discard the skin.

WET SPICE RUBS FOR PORK TENDERLOIN

A SPICE RUB HELPS DEVELOP THE CRUST ON A PORK TENDERLOIN AND ADDS some much-needed flavor. If using a wet rub (with spices and liquid ingredients), simply massage the mixture into the meat. If using a dry rub (with spices only), massage the meat with olive oil and then coat with the rub. See page 582 for dry rub recipes.

Orange, Sage, and Garlic Wet Rub

MAKES ABOUT 1/3 CUP,
ENOUGH FOR 2 TENDERLOINS

If you have no orange marmalade, substitute an equal amount of honey.

3	medium garlic cloves, minced or pressed through a garlic press (about 1 tablespoon)
1	tablespoon grated zest from 1 orange
1	tablespoon chopped fresh sage leaves
1/2	teaspoon ground black pepper
1/4	teaspoon salt
1	tablespoon orange marmalade
1	tablespoon extra-virgin olive oil

Mix all ingredients together in a small bowl.

Caribbean Wet Rub

MAKES ABOUT 1/3 CUP,
ENOUGH FOR 2 TENDERLOINS

Scotch bonnet chiles are extremely hot, so be certain to wash your hands thoroughly with soap and hot water right after chopping the chile, or, better yet, wear rubber gloves.

1/2	medium Scotch bonnet or habanero chile, stemmed, seeded, and minced (about 1 teaspoon)
1	tablespoon chopped fresh thyme leaves
2	medium scallions, white and green parts, minced
1	large garlic clove, minced or pressed through a garlic press (about 1 1/2 teaspoons)
1	tablespoon grated zest from 1 lime
	Pinch ground allspice
1	tablespoon light brown sugar
1	teaspoon dry mustard
1	tablespoon extra-virgin olive oil

Mix all ingredients together in a small bowl.

Asian Wet Rub

MAKES ABOUT 1/3 CUP,
ENOUGH FOR 2 TENDERLOINS

If you don't have hoisin sauce on hand, use an equal amount of soy sauce in its place.

3	medium garlic cloves, minced or pressed through a garlic press (about 1 tablespoon)
2	tablespoons minced fresh ginger
2	medium scallions, white and green parts, minced
2	tablespoons light brown sugar
1/2	teaspoon red pepper flakes
1/4	teaspoon Chinese five-spice powder
1/4	teaspoon salt
1	tablespoon hoisin sauce (see note)
1	tablespoon toasted sesame oil

Mix all ingredients together in a small bowl.

GRILL-ROASTED PORK LOIN

A BONELESS PORK LOIN IS AN IDEAL CANDI-date for grill-roasting. As opposed to barbecued pulled pork (see page 598), which starts out with a very fatty cut from the shoulder or leg, lean loin roasts are the best choice for relatively quick grill-roasting since they are already tender. However, unlike a thin pork tenderloin, the loin is too thick to cook over direct heat. The exterior chars long before the interior comes up to temperature.

Unlike a beef tenderloin, a pork center loin has a fairly even thickness from end to end, so there is no need to tuck up one side or the other. To make the meat perfectly even and ensure proper cooking, we found it helpful to tie the roast at regular intervals.

A pork loin can be grill-roasted much like a beef tenderloin, although it does not need an initial searing period over direct heat. (The meat stays on the grill longer because it must be cooked to a higher internal temperature, so there's plenty of time for a nice crust to form when the roast is cooked strictly over indirect heat.)

The biggest challenge when grill-roasting pork loin is keeping the meat moist. Beef tenderloin can be pulled from the grill at 125 degrees and eaten medium-rare. Pork must be cooked to a higher temperature to make the meat palatable (rare pork has an unappealing texture).

Using the kettle grill, we tried a couple of different setups for indirect cooking. We tried putting the roast in the center of the grill, with two piles of charcoal on opposite sides. This worked reasonably well, but the crust was a bit weak. Banking a full chimney of coals on one side of the grill and placing the roast over the other side worked better. To get the best crust, put the roast close to, but not directly over, the coals.

After testing various temperatures, we found that center loin roasts should be taken off the grill when the internal temperature registers 135 degrees on an instant-read thermometer. After the meat rests for 15 minutes, the temperature will rise to about 150 degrees. The meat will have a slight pink tinge, but it will be far juicier than roasts cooked to an internal temperature that is just 10 degrees higher. (A temperature of 150 degrees is high enough to kill the parasite that causes trichinosis. However, the U.S. Department of Agriculture recommends cooking all meat to an internal temperature of 160 degrees to kill bacteria such as salmonella. If safety is your primary concern, follow the USDA's guidelines.) Because the diameter of a pork loin can vary from one roast to another, allow a window of 30 to 45 minutes to cook the roast through.

While we had little trouble getting the meat properly cooked on the grill, we found pork loin to be a bit bland and not as moist as we might have liked. Both problems stem from the fact that most of the internal fat has been bred out of the pig in recent years. We hit upon several strategies for making the meat taste better and juicier when cooked.

Like poultry, lean pork responds well to brining. A brined pork roast will cook up juicier and more flavorful than a regular roast. Aggressive seasoning is also a good idea. A potent spice rub or a heady mixture of garlic and rosemary will improve the flavor of the meat. A rich mustard-maple glaze, applied when the roast is nearly cooked through, is another option.

Grill-Roasted Pork Loin on a Charcoal Grill

SERVES 4 TO 6

We find that the blade-end roast is a bit more flavorful than the center-cut roast, but either works well in this recipe. To make sure the roast doesn't dry out during cooking, look for one covered with a layer of fat on one side that is at least ⅛ inch thick. Because the diameter of pork loins varies significantly from one to another, check the internal temperature of the loin with an instant-read thermometer at 30 minutes, then every 5 minutes or so thereafter, to make sure that your pork cooks to the optimum temperature of 140 degrees. Do not overcook the pork, as it dries out easily. Let the roast rest for at least 15 minutes in order for its internal temperature to rise to a safe temperature—about 150 degrees. Use leftover meat for sandwiches.

6   tablespoons table salt

1   boneless blade-end or center-cut pork loin
    roast (2½ to 3 pounds), tied with kitchen
    twine at 1½-inch intervals

2   (3-inch) wood chunks or 2 cups wood chips

2   tablespoons olive oil

1½ tablespoons coarsely ground black pepper

1. At least 8 hours before grill-roasting, dissolve the salt in 3 quarts cold water in a large container. Place the pork loin in the saltwater mixture, cover, and refrigerate for at least 8 hours or overnight.

2. An hour before cooking, remove the roast from the brine, rinse, and pat dry; let the roast stand to come to room temperature.

3. Meanwhile, soak the wood chunks in cold water to cover for 1 hour and drain, or place wood chips on an 18-inch square of aluminum foil, seal to make a packet, and use a fork to create about 6 holes to allow smoke to escape (see the illustrations on page 569).

4. Set the roast on a sheet of plastic wrap and rub all over with the oil. Sprinkle with the pepper and then lift the plastic wrap to press the excess seasoning into the meat (see the illustration 4 on page 413).

5. Light a large chimney starter filled with charcoal briquettes (about 6 quarts) and allow to burn until all the charcoal is covered with a thin layer of gray ash. Transfer the hot coals from the chimney to one side of the grill, piling them up in a mound 3 briquettes high. Keep the bottom vents completely open. Lay the soaked wood chunks or the wood chip packet on top of the charcoal. Put the cooking grate in place and open the grill lid vents halfway. Let the grate heat for 5 minutes. Clean the grate with a wire brush.

6. Roll the pork loin off the plastic wrap and onto the grate opposite, but close to, the fire; the long side of the loin should be perpendicular to the grill rods. Cover with the lid, turning the lid so the vents are opposite the fire to draw smoke through the grill. (The initial temperature inside the grill will be about 425 degrees.) Grill-roast the pork loin, covered, until an instant-read thermometer inserted into the thickest part of the roast

registers about 135 degrees, 30 to 45 minutes, depending on the thickness of the loin.

7. Transfer the loin to a cutting board. Tent loosely with foil and let stand for about 15 minutes. (The internal temperature should rise to about 150 degrees.) Cut the roast into ½-inch-thick slices and serve.

➤ VARIATIONS

Grill-Roasted Pork Loin on a Gas Grill
The meat must be seared over direct heat on a gas grill. This is because the gas grill's maximum temperature using indirect heat is about 400 degrees, which is not quite hot enough to give the loin a deep crust in the amount of time it takes to cook through over indirect heat.

Follow the recipe for Grill-Roasted Pork Loin on a Charcoal Grill, brining the roast, letting it come to room temperature, rubbing it with oil, and seasoning it with salt and pepper as directed in steps 1, 2, and 4. Meanwhile, soak 2 cups wood chips in a bowl of cold water for 15 minutes. Drain the chips and place them in a foil tray (see the illustrations on page 569). Place the foil tray with the soaked wood chips on top of the primary burner (see the illustration on page 569) and replace the cooking grates on the gas grill. Turn all burners to high and preheat with the lid down until very hot, about 15 minutes. Carefully open the preheated grill (there may be some smoke), scrape the grill grate clean with a grill brush, and place the roast fat-side down on the side opposite the primary burner. Cover and grill until the meat is grill-marked, about 4 minutes. Turn the roast over, cover again, and grill for another 4 minutes. Leave the primary burner on high, but turn off all other burners. Cover with the lid and grill-roast until an instant-read thermometer reads 135 degrees at the thickest part of the roast, 30 to 45 minutes. (The temperature inside the grill should average between 375 and 400 degrees; adjust the lit burner as necessary.) Transfer the loin to a cutting board and proceed as directed in step 7.

Grill-Roasted Pork Loin with Garlic and Rosemary
Other fresh herbs, especially sage or thyme, can be used in place of the rosemary.

Follow the recipe for Grill-Roasted Pork Loin (charcoal or gas), making the following changes: After tying the roast, use a paring knife to make several dozen shallow incisions around the surface of the roast. Stuff a few fresh rosemary leaves and 1 thin sliver of garlic into each incision. (Use a total of 1 tablespoon rosemary and 3 large garlic cloves, peeled and slivered.) Oil the roast as directed. Sprinkle with salt, pepper, and an additional 2 tablespoons minced fresh rosemary leaves, pressing the excess seasoning into the meat with the plastic wrap. Proceed as directed.

Grill-Roasted Pork Loin with Barbecue Rub and Fruit Salsa

Because of its mild flavor, pork loin benefits greatly from spice rubs. Fruit salsa adds both moisture and a sweetness that is naturally compatible with pork.

Follow the recipe for Grill-Roasted Pork Loin (charcoal or gas), replacing the pepper with 2 tablespoons Dry Rub for Barbecue (page 579). Proceed as directed, serving the sliced meat with Peach Salsa or Mango Salsa (page 584).

Grill-Roasted Pork Loin with Maple-Mustard Glaze

This glaze can literally be prepared in seconds.

Mix ½ cup maple syrup, ½ cup whole-grain mustard, and 1 teaspoon soy sauce together in a medium bowl. Reserve half of the glaze in a separate bowl. Follow the recipe for Grill-Roasted Pork Loin (charcoal or gas), brushing the loin with half of the glaze about 5 minutes before it reaches the designated internal temperature. Slice the pork and serve it with the remaining glaze passed at the table.

BARBECUED SPARERIBS

WHEN PEOPLE USE THE WORDS "RIBS" AND "barbecue" in the same sentence, they are usually talking about pork spareribs. We wanted to know whether it is possible to produce authentic ribs (the kind you get at a barbecue joint) at home.

We started our tests by cooking one slab of ribs over indirect heat (the ribs on one side of the grill,

the coals on the other), parboiling and then grilling another slab over direct heat, and cooking a third on our grill's rotisserie attachment (although reluctant to use this unusual bit of equipment, we thought, in the name of science, that we should give it a shot). All three tests were conducted over charcoal with hickory chips in a covered grill.

The ribs cooked over indirect heat were the hands-down favorite. Those cooked on the rotisserie were not nearly as tender, and the parboiled ribs retained the unappealing flavor of boiled meat. While the indirect method needed some refinement, we were convinced that it is the best way to cook ribs at home. It also comes closest to replicating the method used by barbecue-pit masters.

We tested a number of popular techniques for barbecuing ribs. Some experts swear by placing a source of moisture in the grill, most often an aluminum pan filled with water or beer. We filled a pan with water and put it next to the coals to create some steam. We couldn't taste the difference between the ribs cooked with and without the water. Next we tested turning and basting. We found that for the even melting of the fat, it is best to turn ribs every half hour. Turning also ensures even cooking. It's important, though, to work as quickly as possible when turning the ribs to conserve the heat in the grill. Basting proved to be a bust. Tomato-based sauces burned over the long cooking time, and we didn't find the basted meat any more moist than meat that wasn't basted.

Under normal weather conditions, we found the ribs were done in two to three hours. Signs of doneness include the meat starting to pull away from the ribs (if you grab one end of an individual rib bone and twist it, the bone will actually turn a bit and separate from the meat) and a distinct rosy glow on the exterior. Because the ribs do not require an extended cooking time, there is no need to replenish the coals. A fire that starts out at 350 degrees will drop to around 250 degrees at the end of two hours.

At this point in our testing, we had produced good ribs, but they were not quite as moist and tender as some restaurant ribs. We spoke with several pit masters, and they suggested wrapping the ribs when they come off the grill. We wrapped the ribs in foil and then placed them in a brown paper bag to trap any escaping steam. After an hour, we unwrapped the ribs and couldn't believe the difference. The flavor, which was great straight off the grill, was the same, but the texture was markedly improved. The meat on the wrapped ribs literally fell off the bones.

We spoke with several food scientists, who explained that as the ribs rest, the juices redistribute throughout the meat, making the ribs more moist and tender. In fact, these ribs are so flavorful and tender that we consider sauce optional.

Barbecued Spareribs on a Charcoal Grill

SERVES 4

Hickory is the traditional wood choice with ribs, but some of our tasters liked mesquite as well. If you like, serve the ribs with barbecue sauce, but they are delicious as is. You will need a fair amount of heavy-duty aluminum foil and a brown paper grocery bag for this recipe.

2	full racks spareribs (about 6 pounds total)
¾	cup Dry Rub for Barbecue (page 579)
2	(3-inch) wood chunks or 2 cups wood chips
2	cups barbecue sauce (see pages 595 through 597; optional)

1. Rub both sides of the ribs with the dry rub and let stand at room temperature for 1 hour. (For stronger flavor, wrap the rubbed ribs in a double layer of plastic wrap and refrigerate for up to 1 day.)

2. Soak the wood chunks in cold water to cover for 1 hour and drain, or place the wood chips on an 18-inch square of aluminum foil, seal to make a packet, and use a fork to create about 6 holes to allow smoke to escape (see the illustrations on page 569).

3. Meanwhile, light a large chimney starter filled a bit less than halfway with charcoal briquettes (about 2½ quarts, or 40 coals) and allow to burn until covered with a thin layer of gray ash. Empty the coals into one side of the grill,

piling them up in a mound 2 or 3 briquettes high. Keep the bottom vents completely open. Place the wood chunks or the packet with the chips on top of the charcoal. Put the cooking grate in place, open the grill lid vents completely, and cover, turning the lid so that the vents are opposite the wood chunks or chips to draw smoke through the grill. Let the grate heat for 5 minutes and clean it with a wire brush.

4. Position the ribs over the cool part of the grill. Barbecue, turning the ribs every 30 minutes, until the meat starts to pull away from the bones and has a rosy glow on the exterior, 2 to 3 hours. (The initial temperature inside the grill will be about 350 degrees; it will drop to 250 degrees after 2 hours.)

5. Remove the ribs from the grill and wrap each slab completely in aluminum foil. Put the foil-wrapped slabs in a brown paper bag and crimp the top of the bag to seal tightly. Allow to rest at room temperature for 1 hour.

6. Unwrap the ribs and brush with the barbecue sauce, if desired (or serve with the sauce on the side). Cut the ribs between the bones and serve immediately.

> VARIATIONS

Barbecued Spareribs on a Gas Grill
If working with a small grill, cook the second slab of ribs on the warming rack.

Follow the recipe for Barbecued Spareribs on a Charcoal Grill through step 1. Soak 2 cups wood

---

INGREDIENTS: Three Kinds of Pork Ribs

Baby back ribs (sometimes called back ribs or loin back ribs) come from the section of the rib cage closest to the backbone. Lean center-cut roasts and chops come from the same part of the pig, which explains why baby back ribs can be expensive and are prone to drying out when cooked. Spareribs are closer to the belly, which is also where bacon comes from. Spareribs are larger and fattier than baby back ribs. Meaty country-style ribs are cut from various parts of the pig and are usually cut into individual pieces before being packaged. Since these ribs are generally not sold in slabs, we do not barbecue them.

---

chips for 15 minutes in a bowl of water to cover. Place the wood chips in a foil tray (see the illustrations on page 569). Place the foil tray with the soaked wood chips on top of the primary burner (see the illustration on page 569). Turn all burners to high and preheat with the lid down until the chips are smoking heavily, about 20 minutes. Scrape the grate clean with a wire brush. Turn the primary burner down to medium and turn off the other burner(s). Position the ribs over the cool part of the grill and close the lid. Barbecue, turning the ribs every 30 minutes, until the meat starts to pull away from the bones and has a rosy glow on the exterior, 2 to 3 hours. (The temperature inside the grill should be a constant 275 degrees; adjust the lit burner as necessary.) Proceed with the recipe from step 5, wrapping and resting the ribs as directed.

Barbecued Spareribs with Hoisin, Honey, and Ginger Glaze

A combination of ground Sichuan and white peppercorns and ground coriander gives these ribs a complex peppery flavor. Use a spice grinder or coffee grinder to grind the peppercorns.

Mix 1½ tablespoons ground Sichuan peppercorns, 4 teaspoons ground white peppercorns, and 1½ teaspoons ground coriander together in a small bowl. Follow the recipe for Barbecued Spareribs (charcoal or gas), replacing the Dry Rub for Barbecue with the Sichuan peppercorn mixture. Grill as directed. When the meat starts to pull away from the bones, brush the ribs with ½ cup Hoisin, Honey, and Ginger Glaze (page 597) and barbecue for another 15 minutes. Wrap the ribs and let rest as directed. Serve with more Hoisin, Honey, and Ginger Glaze passed separately at the table. (Omit the barbecue sauce.)

Barbecued Spareribs with Mexican Flavors

Barbecue Sauce with Mexican Flavors (page 596) is ideal to serve with this recipe, although any barbecue sauce will taste fine.

Mix 2 tablespoons chili powder, 2 tablespoons ground cumin, 2 tablespoons dried oregano, 4 teaspoons ground coriander, 1 tablespoon salt, 2 teaspoons ground cinnamon, 2 teaspoons brown sugar, 2 teaspoons ground black pepper, and ¼ teaspoon ground cloves together in a medium bowl. Follow the recipe for Barbecued Spareribs (charcoal or gas), replacing the Dry Rub for Barbecue with the chili powder mixture. Grill, wrap, and rest the ribs as directed. Serve with the barbecue sauce of choice.

BARBECUED BABY BACK RIBS

ON A HOT SUMMER DAY, LIFE DOESN'T GET much better than a big, juicy, smoky slab of spicy, mouthwatering ribs. But more often than not, baby back ribs cooked at home come out tasting like dry shoe leather on a bone. Given the expense (two slabs, enough to feed four people, run about $24) and time commitment (many recipes require half a day), bad ribs are a true culinary disaster. Our goal was to produce flavorful, juicy, tender ribs that would be well worth the time, money, and effort.

Great baby back ribs start at the meat counter. We quickly learned that you have to shop carefully. Unfortunately, labeling of pork ribs can be confusing. Some slabs are labeled "baby back ribs," while other, seemingly identical ribs are labeled "loin back ribs." After a bit of detective work, we learned that the only difference is weight. Both types of ribs are taken from the upper portion of a young hog's rib cage near the backbone (see "Three Kinds of Pork Ribs" on page 591) and should have 11 to 13 bones. A slab (or rack) of loin back ribs generally comes from a larger pig and weighs more than 1¾ pounds; a slab of ribs weighing less is referred to as baby back ribs. (That said, most restaurants don't follow this rule, using the term *baby back* no matter what they've got because it sounds better.) During testing, we came to prefer loin back ribs because they are meatier.

There is one other shopping issue to consider. Beware of racks with bare bones peeking through the meat (along the center of the bones). This means that the butcher took off more meat than necessary, robbing you and your guests of full, meaty portions. Once you've purchased the ribs, there remains the question of whether the skin-like membrane located on the "bone side" of the ribs should be left on during cooking. One theory holds that it prevents smoke and spices from penetrating the meat, while some rib experts say that removing it robs the ribs of flavor and moisture. We found that the skin did not interfere with flavor; in fact, it helped to form a spicy, crispy crust.

It was time to start cooking. Our first step was to research the range of grilling times and techniques called for in other recipes. Most recommend a total cooking time of 1½ to 3 hours. Some use a very hot grill, while others use a moderate grill. We tested all of these recipes and found the resulting ribs to be extremely tough. High-heat cooking was particularly troublesome, as it quickly dried out the meat. Ribs cooked over moderate heat for three hours were better, but they were still too tough.

We realized that the only way to go was the classic "low-and-slow" method. We built a two-level fire, in which only half of the grill is covered with charcoal, thinking it would be best to smoke the ribs indirectly—on the coal-less side of the grill—to prevent overcooking. (Two full racks of ribs fit on one side of a 22-inch grill.) To add flavor, we placed soaked wood chunks on the bed of coals and then put the cooking grate in place and laid down the spice-rubbed ribs. Finally, we put the grill cover in place, with the vent holes over the ribs to help draw heat and smoke past the meat.

We found that maintaining a temperature between 275 and 300 degrees for four hours produced ribs that were tasty and tender, with meat that fell off the bones. Decent ribs could be had in less time, but they weren't as tender as those cooked for a full four hours. It's easy to tell when the ribs are ready—the meat pulls away from the bones when the ribs are gently twisted.

EQUIPMENT: Wood Chips and Chunks

Charcoal itself has some flavor (gas adds none), but the real smoky flavor of good ribs or brisket comes from wood chunks or chips. Chips will work on either a charcoal or gas grill, but chunks are suited to charcoal fires only, since to work they must rest in a pile of lit coals. (If placed on the bottom of a gas grill, they will not get hot enough to smoke.)

Chips and chunks come from the same source—trees. The only difference between them is size. Chunks are usually the size of lemons or small oranges; chips are thinner shards, more like the fine wood chips you might spread over a garden bed.

Wood chips and chunks are made from hardwoods because they burn more slowly than softer woods. The most common choices are hickory, mesquite, and alder, although some stores may carry cherry or oak. Resinous woods, like pine, are not used for grilling because they give foods an off flavor.

Hickory is the most traditional wood used for outdoor cooking, but mesquite and oak have their advocates. In our tests, we found that any hardwood chunks or chips can be used. Frankly, the differences in flavor are minimal, especially if the food has been coated with spices.

Is there a difference in the results you get when using wood chunks versus wood chips? To find out, we tested the same amount by weight (eight ounces) of wood chips and wood chunks under the same conditions in a charcoal fire to see if one performed better than the other when barbecuing Boston butt to make pulled pork.

The wood chips were placed in a heavy-duty foil packet cut with holes to allow the smoke to escape and fill the grill, while the wood chunks were soaked for an hour and then drained. Each was then placed in a separate grill directly on top of 40 ignited coals. On each grill, the lid was closed, the lid vents were opened halfway, and all other vents were left completely open. The chips smoked for 30 to 35 minutes, while the chunks smoked twice as long, for one hour. As it turned out, the exposure to smoke for more than twice the amount of time had given the pork barbecued with wood chunks a greater concentration of smoky, grilled flavor than the pork cooked using the wood chips.

If you have a choice between wood chips and wood chunks, use the wood chunks. They deliver more smoky flavor. If you don't have a choice and must use wood chips, they make a perfectly acceptable substitute for chunks. You may even find them preferable if you prefer a lighter smoke flavor in your grill-roasted and barbecued food. For detailed instructions about using wood chunks and chips, see page 569.

The problem was that the dry heat of the grill produced ribs that were not as moist as we would have liked. Our next test, then, was to cook the ribs halfway in an oven, using steam, and to finish them on the grill. These ribs were more moist, but now flavor was the problem; these ribs lacked the intense smokiness of ribs cooked entirely on the grill. Hoping to find another way to add moisture, we simmered the ribs in water for two hours. This robbed them of valuable pork flavor.

It then occurred to us that brining the ribs prior to cooking them might be the solution. We used our standard brining formula, which when applied to two 2-pound racks of ribs amounted to a two-hour immersion in four quarts of cold water mixed with two cups of kosher salt and two cups of sugar. This method produced, well, two very highly seasoned racks of ribs. Why? Ribs pack much more bone per pound than other cuts of meat, and all of the meat is right there on the exterior, so the brine doesn't have very far to go. We figured that a two-pound rack of ribs must soak up the brine much more quickly than an equal-size roast. We cut back the salt, sugar, and brining time by half, and the results were better, but the meat was still too sweet. We cut back the sugar by half once more, and this time the meat was both moist and perfectly seasoned.

These ribs were so good they didn't even need barbecue sauce, although you certainly could add some if you like. A quick rub with an easy-to-mix spice blend before going on the grill gave them just the right warm and savory touch.

Barbecued Baby Back Ribs on a Charcoal Grill

SERVES 4

For a potent spice flavor, brine and dry the ribs as directed, then coat them with the spice rub, wrap tightly in plastic, and refrigerate overnight before grilling. Serve with barbecue sauce (pages 595–597) if you like.

- ½   cup table salt
- ½   cup sugar
- 2   full racks baby back or loin back ribs (about 4 pounds total)

- ¼   cup Dry Rub for Barbecue (page 579)
- 2   (3-inch) wood chunks or 2 cups wood chips

1. Dissolve the salt and sugar in 4 quarts cold water in a stockpot or large plastic container. Submerge the ribs in the brine and refrigerate 1 hour, until fully seasoned. Remove the ribs from the brine and thoroughly pat dry with paper towels. Rub each side of the racks with 1 tablespoon of the dry rub and refrigerate the racks for 30 minutes.

2. Meanwhile, soak the wood chunks in cold water to cover for 1 hour and drain, or place the wood chips on an 18-inch square of aluminum foil, seal to make a packet, and use a fork to create about 6 holes to allow smoke to escape (see the illustrations on page 569).

3. Light a large chimney starter filled three-quarters full with charcoal briquettes (about 4½ quarts, or 65 coals) and allow to burn until covered with a thin layer of gray ash. Empty the coals into one side of the grill, piling them up in a mound 2 or 3 briquettes high. Keep the bottom vents completely open. Place the wood chunks or the packet with the chips on top of the charcoal. Put the cooking grate in place, open the grill lid vents completely, and cover, turning the lid so that the vents are opposite the wood chunks or chips to draw smoke through the grill. Let the grate heat for 5 minutes and clean it with a wire brush.

4. Position the ribs on the cool side of the grill. Cover, positioning the lid so that the vents are opposite the wood chunks to draw smoke through the grill (the temperature inside the grill should register about 350 degrees but will soon start dropping). Cook for 2 hours, until the grill temperature drops to about 250 degrees, flipping the rib racks, switching their position so that the rack that was nearest the fire is on the outside, and turning the racks 180 degrees every 30 minutes. Add 10 fresh briquettes to the pile of coals. Continue to cook (the temperature should register 275 to 300 degrees), flipping, switching, and rotating the ribs every 30 minutes, until the meat easily pulls away from the bones, 1½ to 2 hours longer. Transfer the ribs to a cutting board, cut between the bones, and serve.

➤ VARIATION

Barbecued Baby Back Ribs on a Gas Grill

If you're using a gas grill, leaving one burner on and the other(s) off mimics the indirect heat method on a charcoal grill.

Follow the recipe for Barbecued Baby Back Ribs on a Charcoal Grill through step 1. Soak 2 cups wood chips for 15 minutes in a bowl of water to cover. Place the wood chips in a foil tray (see the illustrations on page 569). Place the foil tray with the soaked wood chips on top of the primary burner (see the illustration on page 569). Turn all burners to high and preheat with the lid down until the chips are smoking heavily, about 20 minutes. Scrape the grate clean with a wire brush. Turn the primary burner down to medium and turn off the other burner(s). Position the ribs over the cool part of the grill and close the lid. Barbecue, turning the ribs every 30 minutes, until the meat easily pulls away from the bones, about 4 hours. (The temperature inside the grill should be a constant 275 degrees; adjust the lit burner as necessary.) Cut the ribs as directed and serve.

BARBECUE SAUCES AND GLAZES

OF ALL THE SAUCES AND GLAZES USED FOR barbecuing, barbecue sauce is the most common. Almost all of these sauces and glazes, however, contain ingredients such as tomatoes or a sweetener that will cause them to burn if left on grilled foods for any length of time. For this reason, these sauces are usually brushed on grilled foods during the last few minutes of cooking and are also served at the table.

Classic barbecue sauce, we discovered, is relatively easy to make. The combination of tomato sauce and whole tomatoes in juice cooks down to a thick, glossy texture. Vinegar, brown sugar, and molasses add the sour and sweet notes, while spices (paprika, chili powder, black pepper, and salt) round out the flavors. For some brightness, we added a little fresh orange juice as well. The only downside to this sauce is that it takes at least two hours of gentle simmering for the flavors to come together

and for the tomatoes to break down into a sauce of the proper consistency.

Was there a way to shorten up on the cooking time? The answer was yes. The first thing we had to do for quick barbecue sauce was abandon the canned whole tomatoes—they took too long to cook down. So we tried all tomato sauce (and no fresh tomatoes), which made a sauce that seemed more appropriate for pasta. We then tried ketchup and had better luck because it is already sweet, tart, and thick.

The only other major obstacle we encountered when developing our quick rendition of barbecue sauce was the onion. After two hours of simmering in our classic barbecue sauce, the onion became, not surprisingly, very soft. In our quick-cooked version, though, it remained crunchy. We tried pureeing the quick sauce after it had cooked, as we did with our classic sauce, but the quick sauce lost its glossy texture and turned grainy. One of our test cooks then suggested using onion juice—made by pureeing raw onion with water—to give the sauce some onion flavor without texture. This worked liked a charm.

At this point, it was only a matter of adding flavors. Worcestershire sauce and Dijon mustard contributed instant depth. The usual spices—chili powder, cayenne, black pepper—provided more flavor and heat.

In the event classic or quick barbecue sauce is not for you, several specialized barbecue sauces, with distinct flavor profiles, are also included in the following pages.

➤

Classic Barbecue Sauce

MAKES 3 GENEROUS CUPS

Brush this sauce onto chicken parts during the last minute or two of grilling or serve at the table with ribs, brisket, or pulled pork.

2	tablespoons vegetable oil
1	medium onion, minced
1	(8-ounce) can tomato sauce
1	(28-ounce) can whole tomatoes, with their juice
3/4	cup distilled white vinegar
1/4	cup packed dark brown sugar

2   tablespoons molasses
I   tablespoon sweet paprika
I   tablespoon chili powder
2   teaspoons liquid smoke (optional)
I   teaspoon salt
2   teaspoons ground black pepper
1/4 cup orange juice

1. Heat the oil in a large, heavy-bottomed saucepan over medium heat until hot and shimmering (but not smoking). Add the onion and cook, stirring occasionally, until golden brown, 7 to 10 minutes. Add the remaining ingredients. Bring to a boil, then reduce the heat to the lowest possible setting and simmer, uncovered and stirring occasionally, until thickened, 2 to 2½ hours.

2. Puree the sauce, in batches if necessary, in a blender or the workbowl of a food processor fitted with the steel blade. Transfer the sauce to a bowl and use immediately or let cool, then store in an airtight container. (The sauce can be refrigerated for 2 weeks or frozen for several months.)

➤ VARIATIONS

Barbecue Sauce with Mexican Flavors
A few ingredients added to basic barbecue sauce give this recipe a south-of-the-border flavor.

Follow the recipe for Classic Barbecue Sauce, stirring 1½ teaspoons ground cumin, 1½ teaspoons chili powder, 6 tablespoons juice from 3 limes, and 3 tablespoons chopped fresh cilantro leaves into the finished sauce.

Barbecue Sauce with Asian Flavors
Soy sauce, ginger, and sesame oil give this tomato-based sauce an Asian flavor.

Follow the recipe for Classic Barbecue Sauce, stirring 1 tablespoon minced fresh ginger, 6 tablespoons soy sauce, 6 tablespoons rice vinegar, 3 tablespoons sugar, and 1½ tablespoons toasted sesame oil into the finished sauce.

Barbecue Sauce with Caribbean Flavors
When you brush foods with this sauce, serve Black Bean and Mango Salsa (page 584) on the side.

Follow the recipe for Classic Barbecue Sauce, stirring 2 tablespoons pineapple juice, 2 tablespoons dark rum, 1 tablespoon Caribbean hot sauce, 2 teaspoons sugar, and a pinch ground allspice into the finished sauce.

Quick Barbecue Sauce
MAKES ABOUT 1½ CUPS

Classic barbecue sauce must simmer for a long time in order for the whole tomatoes in it to break down. However, we found that starting with ketchup can shortcut the process. Use this sauce as you would any another barbecue sauce—either brushed on foods during the last minutes of grilling or served at the table as a dipping sauce with ribs or brisket.

I   medium onion, peeled and quartered
1/4   cup water
I   cup ketchup
2   tablespoons cider vinegar
2   tablespoons Worcestershire sauce
2   tablespoons Dijon mustard
5   tablespoons molasses
I   teaspoon hot pepper sauce
1/4   teaspoon ground black pepper
1½   teaspoons liquid smoke (optional)
2   tablespoons vegetable oil
I   medium garlic clove, minced or pressed
      through a garlic press
I   teaspoon chili powder
1/4   teaspoon cayenne pepper

1. Process the onion with the water in the workbowl of a food processor fitted with the steel blade until pureed and the mixture resembles slush, about 30 seconds. Strain the mixture through a fine-mesh strainer into a liquid measuring cup, pressing on the solids with a rubber spatula to obtain ½ cup juice. Discard the solids.

2. Whisk the onion juice, ketchup, vinegar, Worcestershire, mustard, molasses, hot pepper sauce, black pepper, and liquid smoke (if using) together in a medium bowl.

3. Heat the oil in a large nonreactive saucepan over medium heat until shimmering but not smoking. Add the garlic, chili powder, and cayenne; cook until fragrant, about 30 seconds. Whisk in the ketchup mixture and bring to a boil;

reduce the heat to medium-low and simmer gently, uncovered, until the flavors meld and the sauce is thickened, about 25 minutes. Cool the sauce to room temperature before using. (The sauce can be refrigerated in an airtight container for 1 week.)

Eastern North Carolina–Style Barbecue Sauce

MAKES 2 CUPS

This sauce contains no tomato but is rich with heat and vinegar. It is traditionally served with pulled pork (page 598) but can also be brushed onto ribs or brisket.

1	cup distilled white vinegar
1	cup cider vinegar
1	tablespoon sugar
1	tablespoon red pepper flakes
1	tablespoon hot pepper sauce
	Salt and ground black pepper

Mix all of the ingredients, including salt and pepper to taste, together in a medium bowl. (The sauce can be refrigerated in an airtight container for several days.)

Hoisin, Honey, and Ginger Glaze

MAKES ABOUT 1 1/2 CUPS

This sweet and thick glaze is great on spareribs or any other cut of pork.

1/2	cup soy sauce
1/4	cup ketchup
1/4	cup honey
2	tablespoons brown sugar
2	tablespoons juice from 1 lemon
1 1/2	tablespoons hoisin sauce
2	teaspoons vegetable oil
1	teaspoon minced fresh ginger
2	medium garlic cloves, minced or pressed through a garlic press

1. Mix the soy sauce, ketchup, honey, brown sugar, lemon juice, and hoisin sauce together in a medium bowl.

2. Heat the oil in a small saucepan over medium-high heat until shimmering. Add the ginger and garlic and cook until fragrant but not browned, about 30 seconds. Add the soy mixture and bring to a boil. Cook for 1 minute and remove the pan from the heat. Cool to room temperature. (The glaze may be refrigerated in an airtight container for 1 week.)

PULLED PORK

PULLED PORK, ALSO CALLED PULLED PIG OR sometimes just plain barbecue, is slow-cooked pork roast that is shredded, seasoned, and then served on a hamburger bun (or sliced white bread) with just enough of your favorite barbecue sauce, a couple of dill pickle chips, and a topping of coleslaw.

Our goal was to devise a procedure for cooking this classic Southern dish that was both doable and delicious. The meat should be tender, not tough, and moist but not too fatty. Most barbecue joints use a special smoker. We wanted to adapt the technique for the grill. We also set out to reduce the hands-on cooking time, which in some recipes can stretch to eight hours of constant fire tending.

There are two pork roasts commonly associated with pulled pork sandwiches: the shoulder roast and the fresh ham. In their whole state, both are massive roasts, anywhere from 14 to 20 pounds. Because they are so large, most butchers and supermarket meat departments cut both the front and back leg roasts into more manageable sizes. The part of the front leg containing the shoulder blade is usually sold as either a pork shoulder roast or a Boston butt and runs from six to eight pounds. The meat from the upper portion of the front leg is marketed as a picnic roast and runs about the same size. The meat from the rear leg is often segmented into three or four separate boneless roasts called a fresh ham or boneless fresh ham roast.

For barbecue, we find it best to choose a cut of meat with a fair amount of fat, which helps keep the meat moist and succulent during long cooking and adds considerably to the flavor. For this reason, we think the pork shoulder roast, or Boston butt, is the best choice. We found that picnic roasts and fresh hams will also produce excellent results, but they are our second choice.

To set our benchmark for quality, we first cooked a Boston butt using the traditional low-and-slow barbecue method. Using a standard 22-inch kettle grill, we lit about 30 coals, or close to two pounds, and cooked the roast over indirect heat (with the coals on one side of the grill and the roast on the other), adding about eight coals every half hour or so. It took seven hours to cook a seven-pound roast. While the meat was delicious, tending a grill fire for seven hours is not something many people want to do.

In our next test, we tried a much bigger initial fire, with about five pounds of charcoal. After the coals were lit, we placed the pork in a small pan and set it on the grate. The trick to this more intense method is not to remove the lid for any reason until the fire is out three hours later. Because you start with so many coals, it is not necessary to add charcoal during the cooking time.

Unfortunately, the high initial heat charred the exterior of the roast, while the interior was still tough and not nearly fork-tender when we took it off the grill. So we tried a combination approach: a moderate amount of charcoal (more than in the low-and-slow method but less than in the no-peek procedure), cooking the pork roast for three hours on the grill and adding more charcoal four times. We then finished the roast in a 325-degree oven for two hours. This method produced almost the same results as the traditional barbecue, but in considerably less time and with nine fewer additions of charcoal.

We find it helpful to let the finished roast rest wrapped in foil in a sealed paper bag for an hour to allow the meat to reabsorb the flavorful juices. In addition, the sealed bag produces a steaming effect that helps break down any remaining tough collagen. The result is a much more savory and succulent roast. Don't omit this step; it's the difference between good pulled pork and great pulled pork.

As with most barbecue, the pork roast benefits from being rubbed with a ground spice mixture. However, because the roast is so thick, we find it best to let the rubbed roast "marinate" in the refrigerator for at least three hours and preferably

overnight. The salt in the rub is slowly absorbed by the meat and carries some of the spices with it. The result is a more evenly flavored piece of meat.

Barbecued Pulled Pork on a Charcoal Grill
SERVES 8

Pulled pork can be made with a fresh ham or picnic roast, although our preference is for Boston butt. Preparing pulled pork requires little effort but lots of time. Plan on 9 hours from start to finish: 3 hours with the spice rub, 3 hours on the grill, 2 hours in the oven, and 1 hour to rest. Hickory is the traditional choice with pork, although mesquite can be used if desired. Serve the pulled pork on plain white bread or warmed buns with the classic accompaniments of dill pickle chips and coleslaw. You will need a disposable aluminum roasting pan that measures about 8 by 10 inches, as well as heavy-duty aluminum foil and a brown paper grocery bag.

1	bone-in pork roast, preferably Boston butt (6 to 8 pounds)
3/4	cup Dry Rub for Barbecue (page 579)
4	(3-inch) wood chunks or 4 cups wood chips
2	cups barbecue sauce (see pages 595 through 597)

1. If using a fresh ham or picnic roast, remove the skin (see illustration 1 on page 599). Massage the dry rub into the meat. Wrap the meat tightly in a double layer of plastic wrap and refrigerate for at least 3 hours. (For stronger flavor, the roast can be refrigerated for up to 3 days.)

2. At least 1 hour prior to cooking, remove the roast from the refrigerator, unwrap, and let it come up to room temperature. Soak the wood chunks in cold water to cover for 1 hour and drain, or place the wood chips on an 18-inch square of aluminum foil, seal to make a packet, and use a fork to create about 6 holes to allow smoke to escape (see the illustrations on page 569).

3. Meanwhile, light a large chimney starter filled a bit less than halfway with charcoal briquettes (about 2½ quarts, or 40 coals) and allow to burn until covered with a thin layer of gray ash. Empty the coals into one side of the grill, piling

them up in a mound 2 or 3 briquettes high. Open the bottom vents completely. Place the wood chunks or the packet with the chips on top of the charcoal.

4. Set the unwrapped roast in the disposable aluminum pan and place it on the grate opposite the fire (see illustration 2 below). Open the grill lid vents three quarters of the way and cover, turning the lid so that the vents are opposite the wood chunks or chips to draw smoke through the grill. Cook, adding about 8 briquettes every hour or so to maintain an average temperature of 275 degrees, for 3 hours.

5. Adjust an oven rack to the middle position and heat the oven to 325 degrees. Wrap the pan holding the roast with heavy-duty foil to cover completely. Place the pan in the oven and bake until the meat is fork-tender, about 2 hours.

6. Slide the foil-wrapped pan with the roast into a brown paper bag. Crimp the top shut. Let the roast rest for 1 hour.

7. Transfer the roast to a cutting board and unwrap. When cool enough to handle, "pull" the pork by separating the roast into muscle sections, removing the fat, if desired, and tearing the meat into thin shreds with your fingers (see illustrations 3 and 4 below). Place the shredded meat in a large bowl. Toss with 1 cup of the barbecue sauce, adding more to taste. Serve, passing the remaining sauce separately.

➤ VARIATIONS
Barbecued Pulled Pork on a Gas Grill
Follow the recipe for Barbecued Pulled Pork on a Charcoal Grill through step 2. Soak 4 cups wood chips for 15 minutes in a bowl of water to cover. Place the wood chips in a foil tray (see the illustrations on page 569). Place the foil tray with the soaked wood chips on top of the primary burner (see the illustration on page 569). Turn all burners to high and preheat with the lid down until the chips are smoking heavily, about 20 minutes. Turn the primary burner down to medium and turn off the other burner(s). Set the unwrapped roast in the disposable pan, position the pan over the cool part of the grill, and close the lid. Barbecue for 3 hours. (The temperature inside the grill should be a constant 275 degrees; adjust the lit burner as necessary.) Proceed as directed from step 5 of the recipe.

Cuban-Style Barbecued Pulled Pork with Mojo Sauce
This pork is delicious served with rice and black beans. The use of wood for flavoring is not traditional in this dish and can be omitted if you prefer to keep the emphasis on the pork and seasonings.

Mix 9 medium garlic cloves, minced (about 3 tablespoons), 1 tablespoon ground cumin,

KEY STEPS TO PULLED PORK

1. If using a fresh ham or picnic roast (shown here), cut through the skin with the tip of a chef's knife. Slide the knife blade just under the skin and work around to loosen the skin while pulling it off with your other hand. Boston butt does not need to be trimmed.

2. Set the unwrapped roast, which has been placed in a disposable aluminum pan barely larger than the meat itself, on the grill grate opposite the coals and the wood.

3. After cooking, as soon as the meat is cool enough to handle, remove the meat from the bones and separate the major muscle sections with your hands.

4. Remove as much fat as desired and tear the meat into thin shreds.

1 tablespoon dried oregano, 1 tablespoon salt, 1½ teaspoons ground black pepper, 2 teaspoons brown sugar, and 3 tablespoons extra-virgin olive oil together in a small bowl. Follow the recipe for Barbecued Pulled Pork (charcoal or gas), replacing the Dry Rub for Barbecue with the garlic mixture. Proceed with the recipe, but do not toss the pulled pork with barbecue sauce. To serve, pass Mojo Sauce (recipe follows) separately with the pulled pork.

Mojo Sauce
MAKES 1 GENEROUS CUP

This citrusy sauce for pulled pork is a Cuban classic.

½	cup extra-virgin olive oil
6	medium garlic cloves, minced or pressed through a garlic press (about 2 tablespoons)
½	teaspoon ground cumin
½	cup juice from 2 oranges
¼	cup juice from 2 limes
1	teaspoon salt
½	teaspoon ground black pepper

1. Heat the oil in a small, deep saucepan over medium heat until shimmering. Add the garlic and cumin and cook until fragrant but not browned, 30 to 45 seconds.

2. Remove the pan from the heat and add the orange juice, lime juice, salt, and pepper carefully. Place the pan back on the heat, bring to a simmer, and cook for 1 minute. Remove the pan from the heat and cool the sauce to room temperature. (The sauce can be refrigerated in an airtight container for 3 days.)

GRILLED LAMB CHOPS

LAMB CHOPS DON'T HAVE TO BE A RARE (AND expensive) treat. True, loin and rib chops (together, the eight rib chops form the cut known as rack of lamb) can cost upward of $12 a pound. But we love the meaty flavor and chewy (but not tough) texture of shoulder chops. We also like the fact that they cost only about $4 per pound.

In a side-by-side taste test, we grilled loin, rib, and shoulder chops to medium-rare and let them stand about 5 minutes before tasting. The rib chop was the most refined of the three, with a mild, almost sweet flavor and tender texture. The loin chop had a slightly stronger flavor, and the texture was a bit firmer (but not chewier) than the rib chop. The shoulder chop had a distinctly gutsier flavor than the other two. While it was not at all tough, it was chewier. If you like the flavor of lamb (and we do) and are trying to keep within a budget, try shoulder chops.

We also tried a second test in which we grilled the chops to medium, a stage at which many people prefer lamb. Both the rib and loin chops were dry and less flavorful and juicy than they were at medium-rare. The shoulder chop held its own, in both taste and texture, displaying another advantage besides price.

Shoulder chops can range in thickness from half an inch to an inch. We prefer the thicker chops; you should ask your butcher to cut them for you if necessary. Loin and rib chops are usually thicker, often close to 1½ inches.

In our testing, we found that all of these chops should be cooked over a two-level fire to bring the inside up to temperature without charring the exterior. A two-level fire also makes sense because lamb tends to flame; the cooler part of the grill is the perfect place to let the flames die down. Even when cooking thinner chops, we found that the flames often became too intense on a single-level fire. When cooking lamb, it is a good idea to have somewhere to drag the meat if the flames become too intense. A squirt bottle filled with water is also a handy item to have near the grill.

Charcoal-Grilled Shoulder Lamb Chops
SERVES 4

Try to get shoulder lamb chops that are at least ¾ inch thick, since they are less likely to overcook. If you can find only chops that are ½ inch thick, reduce the cooking time over the medium-low fire by about 30 seconds on each side. For information about the different kinds of shoulder chops, see page 488.

4   shoulder lamb chops (blade or round-bone),
       3/4 to 1 inch thick

2   tablespoons extra-virgin olive oil
       Salt and ground black pepper

1. Light a large chimney starter filled with hardwood charcoal (about 6 quarts) and allow to burn until all the charcoal is covered with a layer of fine gray ash. Build a two-level fire by stacking most of the coals on one side of the grill and arranging the remaining coals in a single layer on the other side of the grill. Set the cooking rack in place, cover the grill with the lid, and let the rack heat up, about 5 minutes. Use a wire brush to scrape clean the cooking rack. The grill is ready when the pile of coals is medium-hot and the single layer of coals is medium-low. (See how to gauge heat level on page 568.)

2. Rub the chops with the oil and sprinkle with salt and pepper to taste.

3. Grill the chops, uncovered, over the hotter part of the grill, turning them once, until well browned, about 4 minutes. (If the chops start to flame, drag them to the cooler part of the grill and/or extinguish the flames with a squirt bottle filled with water.) Move the chops to the cooler part of the grill and continue grilling, turning once, to the desired doneness, about 5 minutes for rare (about 120 degrees on an instant-read thermometer), about 7 minutes for medium (about 130 degrees), or about 9 minutes for well-done (140 to 150 degrees).

4. Remove the chops from the grill and let rest for 5 minutes. Serve immediately.

➤ VARIATIONS

Gas-Grilled Shoulder Lamb Chops

Watch for any substantial amount of smoke coming through the vents; this indicates that flare-ups are occurring and need to be extinguished.

Turn on all burners to high, close the lid, and heat the grill until very hot, about 15 minutes. Scrape the grill clean with a grill brush. Leave one burner on high and turn the other burner(s) to medium. Follow the recipe for Charcoal-Grilled Shoulder Lamb Chops from step 2 and cook with the lid down.

Grilled Shoulder Lamb Chops with Garlic-Rosemary Marinade

Combine 2 tablespoons extra-virgin olive oil, 2 large garlic cloves, minced or pressed through a garlic press, 1 tablespoon minced fresh rosemary leaves, and a pinch cayenne pepper in a small bowl. Follow the recipe for Charcoal-Grilled or Gas-Grilled Shoulder Lamb Chops, rubbing the chops with the garlic-rosemary marinade instead of olive oil. Marinate in the refrigerator for at least 20 minutes or up to 1 day. Sprinkle the chops with salt and pepper to taste before grilling, then grill as directed.

Grilled Shoulder Lamb Chops with Soy-Shallot Marinade

Combine 2 tablespoons canola oil, 1/4 cup minced shallots or scallions, 2 tablespoons each minced fresh thyme leaves and parsley leaves, 3 tablespoons juice from 2 lemons, 2 tablespoons soy sauce, and ground black pepper to taste in a shallow dish. Follow the recipe for Charcoal-Grilled or Gas-Grilled Shoulder Lamb Chops, marinating the chops in the soy marinade in the refrigerator for at least 20 minutes or up to 1 hour. (Do not marinate longer.) Follow the recipe from step 3.

Spiced Grilled Shoulder Lamb Chops with Peach Salsa

Prepare Peach Salsa (page 584). Prepare a spice rub by toasting 1½ teaspoons black peppercorns, 1½ teaspoons white peppercorns, 1/4 teaspoon coriander seeds, and 3/4 teaspoon cumin seeds in a small skillet over medium heat, shaking the pan occasionally to prevent burning, until the first wisps of smoke appear, 2 to 4 minutes. Remove the pan from the heat, cool to room temperature, and grind the spices in a dedicated spice grinder until no whole peppercorns remain. Transfer to a small bowl and stir in 1/4 teaspoon red pepper flakes and 1/4 teaspoon ground cinnamon. Follow the recipe for Charcoal-Grilled or Gas-Grilled Shoulder Lamb Chops, rubbing each with oil as directed and then with 1½ teaspoons of the spice rub. Sprinkle with salt to taste but not pepper. Grill as directed and serve with the salsa.

Grilled Shoulder Lamb Chops with Near East Red Pepper Paste

This paste of fresh peppers and exotic spices lends sweet spiciness and deep color to grilled lamb.

3	tablespoons extra-virgin olive oil
1/2	medium red bell pepper, cored, seeded, and roughly chopped
1/2	medium serrano or jalapeño chile, stemmed, seeded, and roughly chopped
1	medium garlic clove, minced or pressed through a garlic press
1/2	teaspoon ground cumin
1/2	teaspoon dried summer savory
1/2	teaspoon ground cinnamon
1/2	teaspoon dried mint or 1 1/2 teaspoons chopped fresh mint leaves
2	teaspoons juice from 1 lemon
1	recipe Charcoal-Grilled or Gas-Grilled Shoulder Lamb Chops

1. Heat 1 tablespoon of the oil in a small skillet over medium-high heat until shimmering. Add the red bell pepper and chile and sauté until they start to soften, about 2 minutes. Reduce the heat to medium-low and continue to cook until softened, about 5 minutes.

2. Transfer the mixture to a food processor fitted with the metal blade. Add the garlic, cumin, summer savory, cinnamon, mint, lemon juice, and remaining 2 tablespoons oil and process until almost smooth (there will still be some chunky pieces of pepper).

3. Follow the recipe for the chops, rubbing them with the red pepper paste instead of the oil and marinating them in the refrigerator for at least 20 minutes or up to 1 day. Sprinkle the chops with salt and pepper to taste before grilling, then grill as directed.

Charcoal-Grilled Loin or Rib Lamb Chops

SERVES 4

While loin and rib chops are especially tender cuts of lamb, they tend to dry out if cooked past medium since they have less intramuscular fat than shoulder chops. To make these chops worth their high price, keep an eye on the grill to make sure the meat does not overcook. These chops are smaller than shoulder chops, so you will need two for each serving. Their flavor is more delicate and refined, so season lightly with just salt and pepper, or perhaps herbs (as in the variation that follows). Aggressive spices don't make sense with these rarefied chops.

8	loin or rib lamb chops, 1 1/4 to 1 1/2 inches thick
2	tablespoons extra-virgin olive oil
	Salt and ground black pepper

1. Light a large chimney starter filled with hardwood charcoal (about 6 quarts) and allow to burn until all the charcoal is covered with a layer of fine gray ash. Build a two-level fire by stacking most of the coals on one side of the grill and arranging the remaining coals in a single layer on the other side of the grill. Set the cooking rack in place, cover the grill with the lid, and let the rack heat up, about 5 minutes. Use a wire brush to scrape clean the cooking rack. The grill is ready when the pile of coals is medium-hot and the single layer of coals is medium-low. (See how to gauge heat level on page 568.)

2. Rub the chops with the oil and sprinkle with salt and pepper to taste.

3. Grill the chops, uncovered, over the hotter part of the grill, turning them once, until well browned, about 4 minutes. (If the chops start to flame, drag them to the cooler part of the grill for a moment and/or extinguish the flames with a squirt bottle filled with water.) Move the chops to the cooler part of the grill and continue grilling, turning once, to the desired doneness, about 6 minutes for rare (about 120 degrees on an instant-read thermometer) or about 8 minutes for medium (about 130 degrees).

4. Remove the chops from the grill and let rest for 5 minutes. Serve immediately.

➤ VARIATIONS

Gas-Grilled Loin or Rib Lamb Chops

Turn on all burners to high, close the lid, and heat the grill until very hot, about 15 minutes. Scrape the grill grate clean with a grill brush. Leave one burner on high and turn the other burner(s) to medium-low. Follow the recipe for Charcoal-Grilled Loin or Rib Lamb Chops from step 2 and cook with the lid down.

Grilled Loin or Rib Lamb Chops with Mediterranean Herb and Garlic Paste

The delicate flavor of loin or rib lamb chops is enhanced —not overwhelmed—by this spirited Mediterranean-inspired paste.

Combine ¼ cup extra-virgin olive oil, 3 medium garlic cloves, minced, 1 tablespoon chopped fresh parsley leaves, and 2 teaspoons each chopped fresh sage leaves, thyme leaves, rosemary leaves, and oregano leaves in a small bowl. Follow the recipe for Charcoal-Grilled or Gas-Grilled Loin or Rib Lamb Chops, rubbing the chops with the herb paste instead of the oil. Marinate in the refrigerator for at least 20 minutes or up to 1 day. Sprinkle with salt and pepper to taste before grilling, then grill as directed.

GRILLED SHISH KEBAB

THE BACKYARD BARBECUE ALWAYS SEEMS SO familiar, so American. But grilling is practiced in almost every country around the globe. Shish kebab—skewers of lamb and vegetables—is perhaps the greatest "barbecue" dish from Turkey and the Middle East. When done right, the lamb is well browned but not overcooked and the vegetables are crisp and tender. Everything is perfumed with the flavor of smoke.

Shish kebab's components cook at different rates—either the vegetables are still raw when the meat is cooked perfectly to medium-rare, or the lamb is long overdone by the time the vegetables have been cooked properly. Our efforts to resolve this dilemma led us to explore which cut of lamb and which vegetables serve the kebab best. Getting the grill temperature just right was another challenge. Too hot, and the kebabs charred on the outside without being fully cooked; too cool, and they cooked without the benefit of flavorful browning.

Lamb can be expensive, so we searched for a cut that would give us tender, flavorful shish kebabs without breaking the bank. We immediately ruled out high-end cuts like loin and rib chops, which fetch upward of $14.99 per pound. These chops are just too pricey to cut up for a skewer, and they yield little meat. We had better luck with sirloin and shoulder chops, which are meatier and far more reasonable at $4.99 per pound. Each of these, however, requires cutting the meat off the bones before trimming and cubing. The best cut turned out to be the shank end of a boneless leg of lamb. It requires little trimming, yields the perfect amount of meat for four to six people, and can be purchased for about $6.99 per pound.

Lamb has a supple, chewy texture that behaves best when cut into small, dainty pieces. We found 1-inch pieces of lamb to be the optimal size for the kebabs. With the meat cut and ready to go, we could now focus on the vegetables.

Many vegetables don't cook through by the time the lamb reaches the right temperature. This can be particularly ugly if you're using eggplant, mushrooms, or zucchini. We tried precooking the vegetables, but they turned slimy and were difficult to skewer. We thought about cooking them separately alongside the lamb on the grill, but that's just not shish kebab. Other vegetables, such as cherry tomatoes, initially looked great on the skewer but had a hard time staying put once cooked.

As we worked our way through various vegetables, we came up with two that work well within the constraints of this particular cooking method. Red onions and bell peppers have a similar texture and cook through at about the same rate. When cut fairly small, these two vegetables were the perfect accompaniments to the lamb, adding flavor and color to the kebab without demanding any special attention.

What these handsome kebabs needed now was seasoning, so we tried a variety of spices, dry rubs, and marinades on the meat. Spice rubs tasted good but left the surface of the meat chalky and dry; the kebabs just aren't on the fire long enough for their juices to mix with the dried spices and form a glaze. Marinades, on the other hand, added a layer of moisture that kept the kebabs from drying out on the grill while their flavors penetrated the meat.

MARINADES FOR SHISH KEBAB

Garlic and Cilantro Marinade with Garam Masala

ENOUGH FOR 1 RECIPE OF SHISH KEBAB

- 1/2 cup packed fresh cilantro leaves
- 3 medium garlic cloves, peeled
- 1/4 cup dark raisins
- 1/2 teaspoon garam masala
- 1 1/2 tablespoons juice from 1 lemon
- 1/2 cup olive oil
- 1 teaspoon salt
- 1/8 teaspoon ground black pepper

Process all of the ingredients in the workbowl of a food processor fitted with the metal blade until smooth, about 1 minute, stopping to scrape the sides of the workbowl with a rubber spatula as needed.

Warm-Spiced Parsley Marinade with Ginger

ENOUGH FOR 1 RECIPE OF SHISH KEBAB

- 1/2 cup packed fresh parsley leaves
- 1 jalapeño chile, seeded and chopped coarse
- 2 tablespoons fresh ginger, coarsely chopped
- 3 medium garlic cloves, peeled
- 1 teaspoon ground cumin
- 1 teaspoon ground cardamom
- 1 teaspoon ground cinnamon
- 1/2 cup olive oil
- 1 teaspoon salt
- 1/8 teaspoon ground black pepper

Process all of the ingredients in the workbowl of a food processor fitted with the metal blade until smooth, about 1 minute, stopping to scrape the sides of the workbowl with a rubber spatula as needed.

Sweet Curry Marinade with Buttermilk

ENOUGH FOR 1 RECIPE OF SHISH KEBAB

- 3/4 cup buttermilk
- 1 tablespoon juice from 1 lemon
- 3 medium garlic cloves, minced or pressed through a garlic press (about 1 tablespoon)
- 1 tablespoon brown sugar
- 1 tablespoon curry powder
- 1 teaspoon red pepper flakes
- 1 teaspoon ground coriander
- 1 teaspoon chili powder
- 1 teaspoon salt
- 1/8 teaspoon ground black pepper

Combine all of the ingredients in a gallon-size zipper-lock plastic bag or large nonreactive bowl in which the meat will marinate.

Rosemary-Mint Marinade with Garlic and Lemon

ENOUGH FOR 1 RECIPE OF SHISH KEBAB

- 10 large fresh mint leaves
- 1 1/2 teaspoons chopped fresh rosemary leaves
- 2 tablespoons juice and 1/2 tablespoon zest from 1 lemon
- 3 medium garlic cloves, peeled
- 1/2 cup olive oil
- 1 teaspoon salt
- 1/8 teaspoon ground black pepper

Process all of the ingredients in the workbowl of a food processor fitted with the metal blade until smooth, about 1 minute, stopping to scrape the sides of the workbowl with a rubber spatula as needed.

Two hours in the marinade was sufficient time to achieve some flavor, but it took a good eight hours for these flavors to really sink in. Marinating for 12 hours, or overnight, was even better.

Charcoal-Grilled Shish Kebab

SERVES 6

To cut the onion into ideal pieces for skewering, trim off the stem and root ends and cut into quarters. Peel the outer layers away from the inner core. Working with the outer layers only, cut each quarter from pole to pole into 3 equal strips. Cut each of the 12 strips crosswise into 3 pieces. You should have thirty-six 3-layer stacks of onion.

1	recipe marinade (page 604)
2¼	pounds boneless leg of lamb (shank end), trimmed of fat and silver skin and cut into 1-inch pieces
1	large red onion (about 12 ounces), cut into ¾-inch pieces (see note)
3	medium bell peppers, 1 red, 1 yellow, and 1 orange, cored, seeded, and cut into 1-inch pieces
	Lemon or lime wedges (optional)

1. Toss the marinade and lamb in a gallon-size zipper-lock plastic bag or large nonreactive bowl. Seal the bag or cover the bowl and refrigerate until fully seasoned, at least 2 hours or up to 24 hours.

2. Light a large chimney starter filled with hardwood charcoal (about 6 quarts) and allow to burn until all the charcoal is covered with a layer of fine gray ash. Build a modified two-level fire by spreading the coals over just three quarters of the grill bottom. Set the cooking rack in place, cover the grill with the lid, and let the rack heat up, about 5 minutes. Use a wire brush to scrape clean the cooking rack. The grill is ready when you have a hot fire. (See how to gauge heat level on page 568.)

3. Meanwhile, using twelve 12-inch metal skewers, thread each skewer with one piece of meat, an onion stack (with three layers), and 2 pieces of pepper (of different colors) and then repeat this sequence two more times. Place a piece of meat on the end of each skewer.

4. Grill the kebabs, uncovered, until the meat is well browned all over, grill-marked, and cooked to medium-rare, about 7 minutes (or 8 minutes for medium), turning each kebab one-quarter turn every 1¾ minutes to brown all sides. Transfer the kebabs to a serving platter, squeeze the lemon or lime wedges over the kebabs, if desired, and serve immediately.

➤ VARIATION
Gas-Grilled Shish Kebab

Follow the recipe for Charcoal-Grilled Shish Kebab through step 1. Turn on all burners to high, close the lid, and heat the grill until very hot, about 15 minutes. Scrape the grill grate clean with a grill brush. Leave all burners on high. Proceed with the recipe as directed from step 3 and cook with the lid down.

GRILLED BONE-IN CHICKEN PARTS

GRILLED CHICKEN PARTS SHOULD HAVE RICHLY caramelized, golden brown (not burnt) skin and moist, juicy meat. As soon as our testing started, we realized we needed to develop slightly different methods for dark and white meat parts. The higher fat content in thighs and legs makes flare-ups a greater problem, while the breasts have a tendency to dry out.

We started with dark meat and divided our tests into two sets. The first involved particular ways of moving the chicken around on the grill surface, as well as using the grill cover for part of the cooking time, and the second involved various ways of treating the chicken before it cooked, both to add flavor and to improve texture.

We began our tests by examining grilling methods. Each method involved some variation on the two-level fire—that is, a fire in which one area is hotter than the other. The idea in every case was to get the sear from the hotter fire and cook the chicken evenly all the way through over the cooler fire.

The first of these methods seemed illogical, but a friend had insisted that it worked, so we gave it a try. In this method, the chicken was to be cooked on a low fire first, then finished up on a hot fire. However, this backward approach resulted in dry meat—a lame result for a method that saved no time or energy.

Next we tried the method that intuitively seemed most likely to succeed: searing the chicken over a medium-hot fire and then moving it to a medium-low fire to finish cooking. This approach proved to be a winner. The interior was evenly cooked, moist, and tender, and the skin dark and crisp. We found that we could use this method to cook whole legs with thighs attached or just the thighs alone with only one difference—timing. With thighs alone, you take about four to eight minutes off the cooking time.

It was now time to consider ways of adding flavor to the chicken. Options included marinating, spice rubs and pastes, barbecue sauces, salsas, and brining (soaking the chicken in a solution of saltwater, sometimes with added sugar).

Marinating the chicken was disappointing. Even several hours in a classic oil-and-acid marinade added only a small amount of flavor to the finished chicken, and oil dripping off the marinated chicken caused constant flare-ups during the initial searing period.

Rubbing the chicken with a spice rub prior to grilling proved far more satisfactory. Because the rubs and pastes are composed almost entirely of spices, they have enough flavor intensity to stand up to the smoky grilled flavor and, as a result, come through much more clearly. Wet pastes and barbecue sauces often contain some sweetener and can burn if brushed on the chicken before cooking. We found it best to brush them on just before taking the chicken off the grill and then to serve extra sauce at the table.

If serving salsa or chutney at the table with the chicken, you don't need to add special flavors to the chicken before or during cooking. You should, however, still season the raw chicken with salt and pepper.

As a final test, we tried brining the chicken before grilling it. Admittedly, we didn't approach this test with a lot of enthusiasm—it seemed like too much bother for what should be a simple cooking process. This just goes to show how

preconceptions can be faulty, though, because it turned out to be an excellent idea.

We tried brining for various amounts of time and found that by using a brine with a high concentration of salt and sugar, we could achieve the result we wanted in only about 1½ hours. The brine penetrated the chicken, seasoning it and slightly firming up its texture before grilling. On a molecular level, what actually happened was that the salt caused the strands of protein in the chicken meat to unwind and get tangled up with one another, forming a matrix that then served to trap water. When the chicken was grilled, this matrix formed a sort of barrier that kept water from leaking out of the bird. As a result, the finished chicken was juicier and more tender. (For more information, see "Why Brining Works," page 312.)

The sugar in the brine had one very good effect that carried with it the potential for a minor problem. The traces of sugar left on the exterior of the chicken, while not enough to affect the flavor, did cause the chicken to brown more quickly and thoroughly. Since browning adds rich, deep flavor to any food, this was a decided advantage. However, the browning also took place more quickly than with nonbrined chicken, so on our first try we managed to burn the skin of some pieces. When grilling brined chicken, be sure to

CHICKEN PARTS WITH BARBECUE SAUCE

ANY OF THE TOMATO-BASED BARBECUE sauces on pages 595–597 will taste great on grilled chicken. To use barbecue sauce, grill the chicken following the instructions in the appropriate recipe. During the last 2 minutes of cooking, brush with some of the sauce, cook about 1 minute, turn over, brush again, and cook 1 minute more. Transfer the chicken to a serving platter, brush with additional sauce to taste, and serve, with more sauce passed at the table, if desired. Plan on using about ½ cup of barbecue sauce for a single chicken recipe, more if you serve barbecue sauce at the table.

watch it very carefully during the initial browning period to prevent charring.

If you don't have time to brine your chicken, you can still get excellent results with the two-level fire method by adding deep flavor with a spice rub or paste. If you choose not to brine, make sure to sprinkle the chicken with salt before heading to the grill.

Having conducted all of the above tests with legs, we now turned to breasts, which proved even more challenging. Bone-in chicken breasts can be especially tricky to grill because they're thick and unevenly shaped. Grilling thighs, legs, or boneless breasts is much easier. But when properly grilled, bone-in, skin-on breasts can be particularly tasty. As with dark meat parts, we found partial cooking of the breasts before grilling (by poaching, roasting, or microwaving) to be unsatisfactory. Likewise, starting the chicken on the grill and finishing it indoors was ruled out. We wanted to figure out how to cook the parts completely on the grill.

Like legs, breasts are best started over a medium-hot fire and then moved to a cooler part of the grill. Because bone-in breasts are thicker than thighs or legs, cooking times were significantly longer. The breasts refused to cook through to the bone in less than half an hour. By this time, the skin was burning and the outer layers of meat were dry. We tried using the grill cover, but again detected some off flavors from the burnt-on ashes on the inside of the cover.

We did notice, however, that cooking with the cover cut the grilling time back to 20 minutes, about the same amount of time needed for legs and thighs. And this shorter cooking time translated into skin that was not black and meat that was still juicy. We decided to improvise a cover, using an old restaurant trick—a disposable aluminum roasting pan to build up heat around the breasts and help speed along the cooking. After searing for five minutes, we moved the breasts to a cooler part of the fire, covered them with a disposable pan, and continued grilling for another 15 minutes or so. This allowed the breasts to cook through without burning.

Like legs and thighs, breasts respond well to brining before grilling. The same collection of rubs, pastes, sauces, and salsas work well with breasts as well as legs. You can grill dark and white meat parts together, if you like. Set up a three-level fire with most of the coals on one side of the grill, some coals in the middle, and no coals on the opposite side. Sear all the chicken parts over the hottest part of the fire, finish cooking the legs and thighs over the medium-low heat in the middle, and move the seared breasts to the coolest part of the grill and cover with a disposable pan. Sounds complicated, but it makes perfect sense once you try it and taste the results.

Charcoal-Grilled Bone-In Chicken Thighs or Legs

SERVES 4

Brining improves the chicken's flavor, but if you're short on time, skip step 1 and season the chicken generously with salt and pepper before cooking. (To use kosher salt in the brine, see page 312 for conversion information.) Add flavorings before or during cooking: Rub the chicken parts with a spice rub or paste before putting them on the grill. If you'd prefer to season the chicken with barbecue sauce, see the box on page 606 for instructions. If the fire flares because of dripping fat or a gust of wind, move the chicken to the area without coals until the flames die down.

8   bone-in, skin-on chicken thighs or 4 whole
    chicken legs
6   tablespoons table salt
    Ground black pepper or 1 recipe spice rub or
    paste (see page 610)

1. To prevent burning, trim overhanging fat and skin from the chicken pieces. Dissolve the salt in 1 quart cold water in a gallon-size zipper-lock plastic bag. Add the chicken; press out as much air as possible from the bag and seal. Refrigerate until fully seasoned, about 1½ hours.

2. Light a large chimney starter filled with hardwood charcoal (about 6 quarts) and allow to burn until all the charcoal is covered with a layer of fine gray ash. Build a two-level fire by stacking most of the coals on one side of the grill and arranging the remaining coals in a single layer on the other side of the grill. Set the cooking rack in place, cover the

grill with the lid, and let the rack heat up, about 5 minutes. Use a wire brush to scrape clean the cooking rack. The grill is ready when the temperature of the stacked coals is medium-hot and that of the remaining coals is medium-low. (See how to gauge heat level on page 568.)

3. Meanwhile, remove the chicken from the brine, rinse well, dry thoroughly with paper towels, and season with pepper to taste or a spice rub or paste.

4. Cook the chicken, uncovered, over the hotter part of the grill until seared, 1 to 2 minutes on each side. Move the chicken to the cooler part of the grill; continue to grill, uncovered and turning occasionally, until dark and fully cooked, 12 to 16 minutes for thighs, 16 to 20 minutes for whole legs. To test for doneness, either peek into the thickest part of the chicken with the tip of a small knife (you should see no redness near the bone) or check the internal temperature at the thickest part with an instant-read thermometer, which should register 165 degrees. Transfer to a serving platter. Serve warm or at room temperature.

➤ VARIATION

Gas-Grilled Bone-In Chicken Thighs or Legs

Brining improves the chicken's flavor, but if you're short on time, skip step 1 and season the chicken generously with salt and pepper before cooking. Add flavorings before or during cooking: Rub the chicken parts with a spice rub or paste before putting them on the grill, or brush them with barbecue sauce during the final 2 minutes of cooking (see page 606 for details). Initial high heat is crucial in order to produce crisp skin. The heat is then reduced to medium-low to cook the chicken through.

Follow the recipe for Charcoal-Grilled Bone-In Chicken Thighs or Legs through step 1. Turn on all burners to high, close the lid, and heat the grill until very hot, about 15 minutes. Scrape the grill grate clean with a grill brush. Leave one burner on high and turn the other burner(s) down to medium-low. Meanwhile, remove the chicken from the brine, rinse well, dry thoroughly with paper towels, and season with pepper or one of the spice rubs or pastes on page 610. Cook the chicken, covered, over the hotter part of the grill until seared, 1 to 2 minutes

on each side. Move the chicken to the cooler part of the grill; continue to grill, covered and turning occasionally, until dark and fully cooked, 12 to 16 minutes for thighs, 16 to 20 minutes for whole legs. To test for doneness, either peek into the thickest part of the chicken with the tip of a small knife (you should see no redness near the bone) or check the internal temperature at the thickest part with an instant-read thermometer, which should register 165 degrees. Transfer to a serving platter. Serve warm or at room temperature.

❧
Charcoal-Grilled Bone-In Chicken Breasts

SERVES 4

Brining improves the chicken's flavor, but if you're short on time, skip step 1 and season the chicken generously with salt and pepper before cooking. (To use kosher salt in the brine, see page 312 for conversion information.) Add flavorings before or during cooking: Rub the chicken parts with a spice rub or paste before they go on the grill. Or, if you wish to season your chicken with barbecue sauce, brush the sauce on during the final 2 minutes of cooking (see page 606 for details). If the fire flares because of dripping fat or a gust of wind, move the chicken to the area without coals until the flames die down. You will need a disposable aluminum roasting pan for this recipe.

6   tablespoons table salt
2   whole chicken breasts, bone-in, skin-on, split
     to make 4 halves (10 to 12 ounces each)
     Ground black pepper or 1 recipe spice rub or
     paste (see page 610)

1. Dissolve the salt in 1 quart cold water in a gallon-size zipper-lock plastic bag. Add the chicken; press out as much air as possible from the bag and seal. Refrigerate until fully seasoned, about 1½ hours.

2. Light a large chimney starter filled with hardwood charcoal (about 6 quarts) and allow to burn until all the charcoal is covered with a layer of fine gray ash. Build a modified two-level fire by stacking all of the coals on one side of the grill for a medium-hot fire. Set the cooking rack in place, cover the grill with the lid, and let the

GRILLING BONE-IN CHICKEN BREASTS

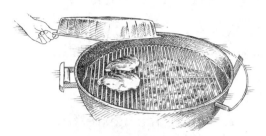

Covering chicken breasts with a disposable aluminum roasting pan while they cook on a charcoal grill creates an oven-like effect that speeds up grilling but still allows air to circulate. Do not use the grill cover; built-up soot on the inside of the cover can give the chicken an off flavor.

rack heat up, about 5 minutes. Use a wire brush to scrape clean the cooking rack.

3. Meanwhile, remove the chicken from the brine, rinse well, dry thoroughly with paper towels, and season with pepper to taste or a spice rub or paste.

4. Cook the chicken, uncovered, over the hotter part of the grill until well browned, 2 to 3 minutes per side. Move the chicken to the cooler part of the grill and cover with a disposable aluminum roasting pan; continue to cook, skin-side up, for 10 minutes. Turn and cook for 5 minutes more or until done. To test for doneness, either peek into the thickest part of the chicken with the tip of a small knife (you should see no redness near the bone) or check the internal temperature at the thickest part with an instant-read thermometer, which should register 160 degrees. Transfer to a serving platter. Serve warm or at room temperature.

➤ VARIATION

Gas-Grilled Bone-In Chicken Breasts

With the lid down on a gas grill, there's no need to cook the chicken under a disposable roasting pan. If the fire flares because of dripping fat or a gust of wind, move the chicken to the cooler area of the grill until the flames die down.

Follow the recipe for Charcoal-Grilled Bone-In Chicken Breasts through step 1. Turn on all burners to high, close the lid, and heat the grill until very

hot, about 15 minutes. Scrape the grill grate clean with a grill brush. Leave one burner on high and turn the other burner(s) down to medium-low. Meanwhile, remove the chicken from the brine, rinse well, dry thoroughly with paper towels, and season with one of the spice rubs or pastes on page 610. Cook the chicken, covered, over the hotter part of the grill until well browned, 2 to 3 minutes per side. Move the chicken to the cooler part of the grill; continue to cook, skin-side up and covered, for 10 minutes. Turn and cook for 5 minutes more or until done. To test for doneness, either peek into the thickest part of the chicken with the tip of a small knife (you should see no redness near the bone) or check the internal temperature at the thickest part with an instant-read thermometer, which should register 160 degrees. Transfer to a serving platter. Serve warm or at room temperature.

GRILL-ROASTED WHOLE CHICKEN

EVERY YEAR MILLIONS OF COOKS GRILL ALL manner of chicken parts, from breasts and thighs to drumsticks. If you're one of them, you can follow the recipes for chicken parts in this chapter. There's only one problem with this scenario: Chicken parts don't spend enough time on the grill to pick up much smoke flavor. Since the smoky taste is one of the main reasons we like to grill, we often grill a whole chicken rather than parts. When grilled over indirect heat (coals banked to the side, with the chicken over the cool part of a covered grill), the bird cooks in about an hour, giving it plenty of time to pick up a good hit of smoke.

Grill-roasting a whole chicken turns out to be a fairly straightforward matter. On reading through various recipes while researching this topic, however, we did notice some variations in technique. Wanting to determine the very best technique, we decided to test the important variables, including how to arrange the coals, whether or not to use a V-rack, when and how to turn the bird, and how to flavor it.

A SPICE RUB AND PASTES FOR GRILLED CHICKEN

RUBS ARE MADE WITH GROUND DRY SPICES AND ARE BEST APPLIED WITH YOUR FINGERS. Pastes contain some sort of liquid and can be applied with your fingers or a brush. If you have decided to skip brining, make sure to season the parts with salt.

Pantry Spice Rub for Chicken

MAKES ABOUT ¹/₂ CUP, ENOUGH TO SEASON A SINGLE RECIPE OF EITHER DARK OR WHITE MEAT PARTS

- 2 tablespoons ground cumin
- 2 tablespoons curry powder
- 2 tablespoons chili powder
- 1 tablespoon ground allspice
- 1 tablespoon ground black pepper
- 1 teaspoon ground cinnamon

Combine all of the ingredients in a small bowl. Rub the mixture over brined and dried chicken parts before grilling.

Asian Spice Paste for Chicken

MAKES ABOUT ¹/₃ CUP, ENOUGH TO SEASON A SINGLE RECIPE OF EITHER DARK OR WHITE MEAT PARTS

- 2 tablespoons soy sauce
- 2 tablespoons peanut oil
- 1 tablespoon stemmed, seeded, and minced jalapeño or other fresh chile
- 1 tablespoon chopped fresh ginger
- 1 garlic clove, peeled
- 2 tablespoons fresh cilantro leaves

Puree all of the ingredients in a food processor or blender until smooth. Rub the paste over brined and dried chicken parts before grilling.

Citrus and Cilantro Spice Paste for Chicken

MAKES ABOUT ¹/₃ CUP, ENOUGH TO SEASON A SINGLE RECIPE OF EITHER DARK OR WHITE MEAT PARTS

- 1 teaspoon ground cumin
- 1 teaspoon chili powder
- 1 teaspoon sweet paprika
- 1 teaspoon ground coriander
- 2 tablespoons orange juice
- 1 tablespoon lime juice
- 1 tablespoon olive oil
- 1 garlic clove, peeled
- 2 tablespoons fresh cilantro leaves

Puree all of the ingredients in a food processor or blender until smooth. Rub the paste over brined and dried chicken parts before grilling.

Mediterranean Spice Paste for Chicken

MAKES ABOUT ¹/₂ CUP, ENOUGH TO SEASON A SINGLE RECIPE OF EITHER DARK OR WHITE MEAT PARTS

- 4 medium garlic cloves, peeled
- 2 tablespoons grated lemon zest
- ¹/₄ cup packed fresh parsley leaves
- ¹/₄ cup extra-virgin olive oil
- 1 tablespoon fresh thyme leaves
- 1 tablespoon fresh rosemary leaves
- 1 tablespoon fresh sage leaves
- ¹/₂ teaspoon salt

Puree all of the ingredients in a food processor or blender until smooth. Rub the paste over brined and dried chicken parts before grilling.

When grill-roasting large birds (such as turkeys) or big cuts of meat (such as prime rib), the standard setup is to fill half of a kettle grill with charcoal and to leave the other half empty. The food is placed on the cool side of the grill, and the kettle is covered. Because one side of the food faces the lit coals, the bird or meat will cook unevenly unless it is rotated at least once. Rotating is simple enough, but the heat dissipates when the lid is removed, and you often have to add more coals, which is a pain.

Since a chicken is so much smaller than a turkey or prime rib, we wondered if the lit coals could be banked on either side of the kettle grill and the chicken cooked in the middle. After several tests, we concluded that this arrangement works fine, with some caveats.

First, the coals must be piled fairly high on either side to form relatively tall but narrow piles. We split the coals between either side of the grill and ended up piling the lit briquettes three or four levels high. If the coals are arranged in wider, shorter piles, the cool spot in the middle of the grill won't be large enough to protect the bird from direct heat.

Second, don't use too much charcoal. When we split 70 briquettes into two piles, we burned the chicken. Reducing the number of coals to just 50 kept the temperature inside the grill between 325 and 375 degrees, the ideal range for grill-roasting.

Third, you must use a relatively small chicken. We found that the skin on a large roaster scorches long before the meat cooks through.

Last, keep the vents in the lid halfway open so the fire burns at a fairly even pace. If the vents are open all the way, the fire burns too hot at the outset—thereby scorching the bird's skin—and then peters out before the chicken has cooked through.

With the heat attacking the chicken from two sides, the bird cooks evenly, so there's no need to rotate it. (On gas grills, where just one lit burner is used to cook by indirect heat, you will need to rotate the bird.) After our initial tests, however, we did conclude that it was necessary to flip the bird over once during the hour-long cooking process. The skin on top of the bird cooks faster than the skin touching the rack. (Although this seems counterintuitive, repeated tests confirmed this observation.) Because the side of the bird that finishes right-side up tends to look better (grill marks fade and the skin bronzes more evenly), we decided to start the chicken breast-side down.

When we cook a turkey on the grill, we always cradle it in a V-rack, which keeps the skin from scorching and promotes even cooking. We prepared several chickens with and without V-racks and found that those placed right on the grill rack browned better and cooked just fine. Again, because a chicken is small, the bird spends much less time on the grill than a turkey, and the skin is less likely to burn.

With our technique perfected, we focused on the flavoring options. As expected, we found that brining the chicken in a saltwater solution helps it retain moisture while cooking and is recommended. The one exception is a kosher bird, which is salted during processing and cooks up moist—and perfectly seasoned—without brining.

During the course of our testing, we tried brushing the chicken with melted butter and olive oil before and during grilling. Although a buttered bird browned marginally better than an oiled one, we don't recommend using either. Birds coated with a spice rub cooked up more crisply and were better-looking than greased birds.

APPLYING THE SPICE RUB

Rub the spice mixture into the skin, then carefully lift up the skin over the breast and massage some rub directly onto the meat.

Grill-Roasted Whole Chicken on a Charcoal Grill

SERVES 4

If you choose not to brine, skip that part of step 1 and season the bird generously with salt inside and out before rubbing with spices. Or, better yet, use a kosher chicken (which is salted during processing). For added accuracy, place a grill thermometer in the lid vents as the chicken cooks. The temperature inside the grill should be about 375 degrees at the outset and will fall to about 325 degrees by the time the chicken is done.

½	cup table salt
1	whole chicken (about 3½ pounds)
3	tablespoons spice rub (see page 610)
4	(3-inch) wood chunks or 4 cups wood chips

1. Dissolve the salt in 2 quarts cold water in a large bowl, stockpot, or Dutch oven. Immerse the chicken in the salted water and refrigerate until fully seasoned, about 1 hour. Remove the chicken from the brine and rinse inside and out with cool running water; pat dry with paper towels. Massage the spice rub all over the chicken, inside and out. Lift up the skin over the breast and rub the spice mixture directly onto the meat (see the illustration on page 611).

2. Soak the wood chunks in cold water to cover for 1 hour and drain, or divide the wood chips between two 18-inch squares of aluminum foil, seal to make two packets, and use a fork to create about six holes in each packet to allow smoke to escape (see the illustrations on page 569).

3. Light a large chimney starter filled a little more than halfway with charcoal briquettes (about 3 quarts, or 45 coals) and allow to burn until covered with a thin layer of gray ash. Empty the coals into the grill. Divide the coals in half to form two piles on either side of the grill; use long-handled tongs to move any stray coals into the piles. Nestle 2 soaked wood chunks or one foil packet with chips on top of each pile. Position the grill rack over the coals and cover the grill. Heat the rack for 5 minutes, then scrape it clean with a wire brush.

4. Position the bird breast-side down in the middle of the rack, over a portion of the grill without any coals. Cover, opening the grill lid vents halfway. Turn the lid so that the vents are between the two piles of coals. Grill-roast for 30 minutes.

5. Working quickly to prevent excessive heat loss, remove the lid and, using 2 large wads of paper towels, turn the chicken breast-side up. Cover and grill-roast until an instant-read thermometer inserted into thickest part of the thigh registers 170 to 175 degrees, 25 to 35 minutes longer.

6. Transfer the chicken to a cutting board, tent loosely with foil, and let rest 15 minutes. Carve and serve.

➤ VARIATIONS

Grill-Roasted Whole Chicken on a Gas Grill

If you choose not to brine, skip that part of step 1 and season the bird generously with salt inside and out before rubbing with spices. Or, better yet, use a kosher chicken (which is salted during processing). While grill-roasting, adjust the lit burner as necessary to maintain a temperature of 350 to 375 degrees inside the grill.

Follow the recipe for Grill-Roasted Whole Chicken on a Charcoal Grill through step 1. Soak 4 cups wood chips for 15 minutes in a bowl of water to cover. Place the wood chips in a foil tray (see illustration on page 569). Place the foil tray with the soaked wood chips on top of primary burner (see illustration on page 569). Turn all burners to high and preheat with the lid down until chips are smoking heavily, about 20 minutes. Open the grill and turn off all but one burner. (Leave the primary burner on high.) Scrape the grate clean with a wire brush. Place the chicken breast-side down over the cooler part of the grill. Cover and grill-roast for 35 minutes. Turn the chicken breast-side up so that the leg and wing that were facing away from the lit burner are now facing toward it. Close the lid and continue grill-roasting until an instant-read thermometer inserted into the thickest part of the thigh registers 170 to 175 degrees, 30 to 40 minutes longer. Transfer the chicken to a cutting board, tent loosely with foil, and let rest 15 minutes. Carve and serve.

Grill-Roasted Whole Chicken with Barbecue Sauce

If you like, barbecue sauce can be used along with Pantry Spice Rub on page 610. Wait until the bird is almost done to brush on the barbecue sauce, so that it does not scorch.

Follow the recipe for Grill-Roasted Whole Chicken (charcoal or gas), making the following changes: After rotating the chicken breast-side up, roast only until an instant-read thermometer inserted into the thickest part of the thigh registers 160 degrees, 15 to 30 minutes longer. Working quickly to prevent excessive heat loss, brush the outside and inside of the chicken with ½ cup any tomato-based barbecue sauce on pages 595–597. Cover and continue grill-roasting until an instant-read thermometer inserted into the thickest part of the thigh registers 170 to 175 degrees, 10 to 15 minutes longer. Tent and carve.

BUTTERFLIED CHICKEN

REMOVING THE BACKBONE FROM A WHOLE chicken—a process known as butterflying—may seem like an unnecessary and time-consuming process. But we have found that this relatively quick and simple procedure—because it leaves the bird with a more even thickness—provides many benefits. Basically, butterflying lets you grill a whole chicken in much the same way that you grill parts.

A flattened three-pound chicken cooks in half an hour or less, whereas a whole grill-roasted bird requires 1½ hours of cooking. In addition, because the breast isn't sticking out exposed to the heat while the legs are tucked under and away from the heat, all the parts of a flattened bird get done at the same time. Finally, unlike a whole roasted chicken, the butterfly cut is a breeze to separate into sections when carving. One cut down the breast with the kitchen shears, a quick snip of the skin holding the legs, and the job is done (see page 319).

Most recipes for butterflied chicken call for weighting the bird on the grill to promote fast, even cooking. The chicken is covered with a baking sheet and weighted down with heavy cans or bricks. We grilled butterflied chicken with and without weights and found that the weighted bird cooked more quickly and looked more attractive.

We still had a number of questions about the butterflying and cooking. Was it necessary to cut slits on either side of the breast so that we could tuck in each leg? And did we really need to pound the chicken after we butterflied it, or was it enough to just flatten it with our hands? Finally, we wanted to know if we could season the chicken with herbs and garlic without having them burning on the grill.

We quickly discovered that tucking the chicken legs under was worth the effort, if only for visual appeal. Chickens cooked with untucked legs tended to bow and warp. Tucking the legs into the breast takes just seconds and is recommended.

We thought pounding the chicken might decrease cooking time, but it made no noticeable difference. However, it was easier to weight a chicken that had been pounded to a uniform thickness. We also liked the look of the really flattened chicken. We used a mallet with a flat side for this purpose, but whatever tool you use, make sure it has a smooth face. A rough-textured mallet will tear the chicken and give it a pockmarked appearance.

Seasoning the outside of the chicken with herbs or garlic proved to be pointless—the herbs charred

WEIGHTING A BUTTERFLIED CHICKEN

To weight a butterflied chicken while it grills, find an old baking sheet or cookie sheet and set it on top of the chicken. Put 2 bricks on the pan.

and the garlic burned. But butterflied chickens are especially easy to season under the skin. Since the backs are removed, access to the legs and thighs is easy. Barbecue sauces and glazes can be brushed onto the skin once the chicken is nearly done. After just two or three minutes on the grill, the glaze will caramelize nicely and give the skin excellent flavor.

Many recipes call for turning the chicken several times on the grill. Since it is weighted, this is cumbersome. If possible, we wanted to turn the bird just once. We found that one turn was fine as long as the chicken was started skin-side up on charcoal. Every time we started the chicken skin-side down, the skin burned because the grill was a bit too hot. The opposite was true on a gas grill. We found it best to start the chicken skin-side down for the best coloring. If we started the bird skin-side up, the grill surface had cooled by the time the bird was flipped, and the skin looked a bit anemic.

Charcoal-Grilled Butterflied Chicken

SERVES 4

If you choose to use kosher salt in the brine, see page 312 for conversion information. We tested this recipe several times with a 3-pound chicken. Although grilling conditions vary, each time we cooked the chicken, it was done in less than 30 minutes—12 minutes on one side and 12 to 15 minutes on the other. For chickens that weigh closer to 3½ pounds, plan on the full 15 minutes once the chicken has been turned.

6   tablespoons table salt
1   whole chicken (3 to 3½ pounds), butterflied
    (see illustrations 1 and 2 on page 317)
    Ground black pepper

1. Dissolve the salt in 1 quart cold water in a large bowl, stockpot, or Dutch oven. Immerse the chicken in the brine and refrigerate until fully seasoned, at least 2 hours or up to 4 hours.

2. Light a large chimney starter filled three-quarters full with hardwood charcoal (about 4½ quarts) and allow to burn until all the charcoal is covered with a layer of fine gray ash. Build a single-level fire by spreading the coals out evenly over the bottom of the grill. Set the cooking rack in place, cover the grill with the lid, and let the rack heat up, about 5 minutes. Use a wire brush to scrape clean the cooking grate. The grill is ready when you have a medium fire. (See how to gauge heat level on page 568.)

3. Meanwhile, remove the chicken from the brine, rinse well, dry thoroughly with paper towels, and season with pepper to taste. Reposition the chicken parts if necessary.

4. Place the chicken bone-side down on the grill rack. Set a jelly-roll or other flat pan on top of the chicken; put 2 bricks on the jelly-roll pan (see the illustration on page 613). Grill until the chicken is deep brown, about 12 minutes. Turn the chicken with tongs. Replace the jelly-roll pan and bricks and continue cooking until the chicken juices run clear and an instant-read thermometer inserted deep into the thigh registers 165 degrees, 12 to 15 more minutes.

5. Remove the chicken from the grill, then cover with foil and let rest for 10 to 15 minutes. Carve (see the illustrations on page 319) and serve.

➤ VARIATIONS
Gas-Grilled Butterflied Chicken
Because the heat is less intense on a gas grill, the chicken can be started skin-side down. Since the grill surface is a bit hotter when the chicken first hits it, we found that the skin browns better when compared with birds started skin-side up.

Follow the recipe for Charcoal-Grilled Butterflied Chicken through step 1. Preheat the grill with all burners set to high and the lid down until the grill is very hot, about 15 minutes. Use a wire brush to scrape clean the cooking grate. Turn all burners down to medium. Proceed with the recipe through step 3. In step 4, place the chicken skin-side down on the grill rack. Set a jelly-roll or other flat pan on top of the chicken; put 2 bricks on the jelly-roll pan (see the illustration on page 613). Cover and grill until the chicken skin is deeply browned and shows grill marks, 12 to 15 minutes. Turn the chicken with tongs. Replace the jelly-roll pan, bricks, and grill lid and continue cooking until the chicken juices run clear and an instant-read thermometer inserted deep into the thigh registers 165 degrees, about 15 more minutes. Remove the chicken from the grill, then cover with foil and let rest for 10 to 15 minutes. Carve (see page 319) and serve.

Butterflied Chicken with Pesto

Classic basil pesto is delicious, but feel free to use almost any herb paste, including pesto made with cilantro, arugula, or mint. Store-bought pesto works well in this recipe.

Follow the recipe for Charcoal-Grilled or Gas-Grilled Butterflied Chicken, brining, rinsing, and drying the chicken as directed. Rub ½ cup Classic Pesto (page 240) under the skin of the breasts, thighs, and legs. Reposition the chicken parts and season with pepper. Grill as directed.

Butterflied Chicken with Barbecue Sauce

Use one of the tomato-based barbecue sauces on pages 595–597 or store-bought sauce if you like.

Follow the recipe for Charcoal-Grilled or Gas-Grilled Butterflied Chicken, brushing both sides of the chicken with ⅓ cup barbecue sauce during the last 2 minutes of the cooking time.

Butterflied Chicken with Green Olive Tapenade

The tapenade is pretty salty, so make sure to rinse the chicken thoroughly after brining.

Pulse 10 large pitted Spanish green olives, 1 garlic clove, chopped, 2 anchovy fillets, 1 teaspoon rinsed capers, and 3 tablespoons extra-virgin olive oil in a food processor until the mixture resembles a slightly chunky paste (do not over-process). Follow the recipe for Charcoal-Grilled or Gas-Grilled Butterflied Chicken, brining, rinsing, and drying the chicken as directed. Rub the olive mixture under the skin of the breasts, thighs, and legs. Reposition the chicken parts and season with pepper. Grill as directed.

Butterflied Chicken with Chipotle, Honey, and Lime

A spicy paste made with smoky chipotle chiles is rubbed under the chicken skin before cooking, and a sweet honey–lime juice glaze is applied once the chicken is almost done.

Mix 3 chipotle chiles in adobo sauce, minced, 2 teaspoons minced fresh cilantro leaves, and ½ teaspoon grated lime zest together in a small bowl. Whisk 3 tablespoons lime juice and 2 tablespoons honey together in another small bowl. Follow the recipe for Charcoal-Grilled or Gas-Grilled Butterflied Chicken, brining, rinsing, and drying the chicken as directed. Rub the chile mixture under the skin of the breasts, thighs, and legs. Reposition the chicken parts and season with pepper. Grill as directed, brushing both sides of the chicken with the honey–lime juice glaze during the last 2 minutes of cooking time.

Butterflied Chicken with Lemon and Rosemary

An Italian classic. Try other herbs, including oregano, sage, thyme, or marjoram, in place of the rosemary.

Mix 2 teaspoons minced lemon zest, 2 minced garlic cloves, and 1 teaspoon minced fresh rosemary leaves together in a small bowl. Whisk 3 tablespoons lemon juice and 3 tablespoons extra-virgin olive oil together in another small bowl. Follow the recipe for Charcoal-Grilled or Gas-Grilled Butterflied Chicken, brining, rinsing, and drying the bird as directed. Rub the lemon zest mixture under the skin of the breasts, thighs, and legs. Reposition the chicken parts and season with pepper. Grill as directed, brushing both sides of the chicken with the lemon juice–oil mixture during the last 2 minutes of cooking time.

SALMON FILLETS

SALMON IS OUR FAVORITE FISH TO GRILL. NOT only does it taste great, but it's firm enough to hold together better than many other fish. With its abundant natural fats and oils, salmon is also less prone to drying out than most other fish. While leaner fish like tuna, swordfish, and halibut benefit from a brush with oil before grilling to help retain their moisture, we found that salmon needs no such treatment because of its abundant natural oils.

The cuts of salmon we used for our tests were boneless, individual-portion farmed salmon fillets, skin-on, weighing about six ounces each. Salmon can be purchased in boneless fillets or in steaks. We prefer the fillets over steaks because fillets are boneless and thus easier to eat. Several tests proved that a medium-hot fire browned the salmon fillets without burning them and conveniently created a crust that made for fairly easy turning on the grill after some initial prodding with long-handled tongs or a spatula. (We thus also found oiling the salmon for purposes of easier turning to be unnecessary.)

While the center cuts cooked well over the direct heat of a single-level fire, we thought we would try a two-level fire, browning the fillets over the higher heat and then letting them cook through over lower heat. We found no difference in taste or texture between the fillets grilled entirely over direct heat and those finished over indirect. Because direct heat cooks faster, we opted for that. That said, we found the direct/indirect method to be an excellent way to cook the thin tail pieces; by the time the flesh has seared enough to turn, the fish is almost cooked through and needs just a minute or so of gentle heat to finish it without overcooking.

As we grilled the salmon, we remained alert for clues to tell us when it was properly cooked.

OILING THE GRILL GRATE

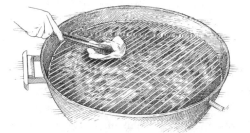

Grilling fish can be a challenge because fish tends to stick to the grill, so we advise oiling the grill grate as an added precaution. Once the coals have been lit and spread out in the bottom of the grill, put the cooking grate in place and let it heat up for several minutes. Dip a large wad of paper towels in vegetable oil, grab the wad with tongs, and wipe the grill thoroughly to lubricate it. This extra step also removes any remaining residue on the grate, which might mar the delicate flavor of the fish.

We like salmon medium-rare in the center, or still slightly translucent. Mostly we found that by the time 1½-inch-thick fillets were well-browned on both sides, the center was perfect—slightly undercooked but close enough to finish cooking the last little bit on the plate. We also developed a tactile test. As the salmon cooks, we pull it off the grill every now and then and squeeze the sides of the fillet gently between our fingertips. Raw salmon feels squishy; medium-rare salmon is firm but not hard. If you're stumped and want to be really sure, cut into the fillet with a paring knife and look.

Charcoal-Grilled Salmon Fillets

SERVES 4

If your fillets are less than 1½ inches thick, decrease the grilling time by roughly 30 seconds per side. To test fillets for doneness, either peek into the salmon with the tip of a small knife or remove the salmon from the grill and squeeze both sides of the fillet gently with your fingertips (raw salmon is squishy; medium-rare salmon is firm but not hard).

4   center-cut salmon fillets, 1½ inches thick
      (6 to 7 ounces each), pinbones removed (see
      the illustration on page 509)
      Salt and ground black pepper
      Vegetable oil for the grill rack

1. Light a large chimney starter filled with hardwood charcoal (about 6 quarts) and allow to burn until all the charcoal is covered with a layer of fine gray ash. Build a single-level fire by spreading the coals out evenly over the bottom of the grill. Set the cooking rack in place, cover the grill with the lid, and let the rack heat up, about 5 minutes. The grill is ready when the coals are medium-hot. (See how to gauge heat level on page 568.)

2. Generously sprinkle each side of the salmon fillets with salt and pepper.

3. Lightly dip a small wad of paper towels in vegetable oil; holding the wad with tongs, wipe the grill rack (see illustration at left). Place the

fillets skin-side down on the grill. Grill, uncovered, until the skin shrinks, separates from the flesh, and turns black, 2 to 3 minutes. Gently flip the fillets with a metal spatula. Grill, uncovered, until the fillets are opaque throughout, yet translucent at the very center, 3 to 4 minutes. Serve immediately.

➤ VARIATIONS

Gas-Grilled Salmon Fillets

If your fillets are less than 1½ inches thick, decrease the grilling time by roughly 30 seconds per side. To test fillets for doneness, either peek into the salmon with the tip of a small knife or remove the salmon from the grill and squeeze both sides of the fillet gently with your fingertips (raw salmon is squishy; medium-rare salmon is firm but not hard). Note that the grilling times are slightly longer when using a gas grill.

Preheat the grill with all burners set to high and the lid down until very hot, about 15 minutes. Use a wire brush to scrape clean the cooking rack. Leave all burners on high. Proceed with the recipe for Charcoal-Grilled Salmon Fillets, increasing the grilling time on the first side to 3 to 4 minutes, and on the second side to 4 to 5 minutes.

Grilled Salmon Fillets with Mustard Glaze

A spicy but sweet mustard glaze takes just minutes to assemble and adds plenty of flavor.

Mix 2 tablespoons dry mustard, 2 tablespoons sugar, and 2 teaspoons water together in a small bowl to form a thick paste. Follow the recipe for Charcoal-Grilled or Gas-Grilled Salmon Fillets, spreading the mustard paste over the flesh side of the fillets before grilling. Proceed as directed. Drizzle a little extra-virgin olive oil over the grilled fillets just before serving.

Grilled Salmon with Sesame-Soy Glaze

Toasted sesame seeds and oil add a nutty aroma to this salty-sweet sauce. To toast sesame seeds for this recipe, place them in a small skillet over medium heat and toast for 7 to 10 minutes, or until they become golden and fragrant.

¼	cup soy sauce
1	tablespoon rice vinegar
2	tablespoons mirin
1½	teaspoons cornstarch
1	teaspoon vegetable oil
2	teaspoons minced fresh ginger
1	tablespoon sesame seeds, toasted
1	teaspoon toasted sesame oil
1	recipe Charcoal-Grilled or Gas-Grilled Salmon Fillets

1. Mix the soy sauce, rice vinegar, mirin, and cornstarch together in a small bowl. Heat the vegetable oil in a small saucepan over medium-high heat until hot. Add the ginger and cook until fragrant but not browned, about 30 seconds. Give the soy mixture a quick stir and pour it into the saucepan. Bring to a light boil and reduce the heat to low; cook another minute, or until the glaze is thick and clear. Remove the pan from the heat and transfer the mixture to a heatproof bowl. Stir in the sesame seeds and sesame oil.

2. Grill the fish as directed, brushing the flesh side of the fillets generously with the soy glaze just before flipping and again just before serving.

HALIBUT STEAKS

HALIBUT IS A MILD-FLAVORED, LEAN, WHITE fish with firm flesh, making it the perfect choice for those who also like mild-flavored, steak-like fish such as swordfish or tuna. It is an easy fish to grill as long as you don't get a steak that is too thick and you don't allow it to overcook on the grill. Halibut can dry out if overcooked, so remove steaks from the grill once the center is just barely translucent.

We found halibut steaks in various forms at markets around town. Some were boneless, others had two sections of flesh separated by a bone, and others had four sections of meat separated by a bone and membrane. Because you are mostly likely to see boneless steaks, we have written our halibut recipes for this cut. (In case you can find only bone-in steaks at the market, we provide instructions for boning on page 505.)

Halibut is best simply treated. No marinades are necessary, just a brush of oil, which keeps it

COMPOUND BUTTERS FOR FISH

LIKE BEEF STEAKS, HALIBUT, TUNA, OR SWORDFISH STEAKS CAN BE EMBELLISHED WITH A SLICE of compound butter. Prepare the fish as directed. Transfer the steaks to individual plates and set a slice of butter on top of each hot steak. Serve immediately.

Chipotle-Lime Butter

MAKES ENOUGH FOR 4 SERVINGS OF FISH

Chipotles are actually dried, smoked jalapeño chiles. Small amounts of chipotle add gentle heat to the butter in this recipe. Here, we've used one chipotle chile packed in adobo sauce (a dark red sauce made with herbs, vinegar, and ground chiles), available in small cans in the ethnic food aisle of most supermarkets. Refrigerate or freeze any leftover chiles for future use.

4	tablespoons (½ stick) unsalted butter, softened
2	teaspoons juice from 1 lime
1	chipotle chile in adobo sauce, chopped fine
1	medium garlic clove, minced
¼	teaspoon salt
1	tablespoon roughly chopped fresh cilantro leaves

1. Beat the butter with a large fork in a medium bowl until light and fluffy. Add the lime juice, chile, garlic, salt, and cilantro and mix to combine.

2. Following the illustration on page 619, roll the butter into a log about 3 inches long and 1½ inches in diameter. Refrigerate until firm, at least 2 hours or up to 3 days. (The butter can be frozen for up to 2 months. When ready to use, let soften just until it can be cut, about 15 minutes.)

Tapenade Butter

MAKES ENOUGH FOR 4 SERVINGS OF FISH

4	tablespoons (½ stick) unsalted butter, softened
1	teaspoon minced fresh thyme leaves
1	small garlic clove, minced (about 1 teaspoon)
⅛	teaspoon finely grated orange zest
½	anchovy fillet, minced to a paste
10	pitted and finely chopped oil-cured black olives (about 2 tablespoons)
1½	teaspoons brandy
⅛	teaspoon salt
	Pinch ground black pepper

1. Beat the butter with a large fork in a medium bowl until light and fluffy. Add the remaining ingredients and mix to combine.

2. Following the illustration on page 619, roll the butter into a log about 3 inches long and 1½ inches in diameter. Refrigerate until firm, at least 2 hours or up to 3 days. (The butter can be frozen for up to 2 months. When ready to use, let soften just until it can be cut, about 15 minutes.)

Tarragon-Lime Butter

MAKES ENOUGH FOR 4 SERVINGS OF FISH

4	tablespoons (½ stick) unsalted butter, softened
1	tablespoon minced fresh tarragon leaves
2	tablespoons minced scallion, green and white parts
2	teaspoons juice from 1 lime
⅛	teaspoon salt
	Pinch ground black pepper

1. Beat the butter with a large fork in a medium bowl until light and fluffy. Add the remaining ingredients and mix to combine.

2. Following the illustration on page 619, roll the butter into a log about 3 inches long and 1½ inches in diameter. Refrigerate until firm, at least 2 hours or up to 3 days. (The butter can be frozen for up to 2 months. When ready to use, let soften just until it can be cut, about 15 minutes.)

from sticking to the grill, and some salt and pepper. Like swordfish, however (and like beef steak), halibut takes well to flavorings such as butters and sauces.

Charcoal-Grilled Halibut Steaks

SERVES 4

In this recipe, we use boneless, skin-on halibut steaks. If the only kind of halibut steaks you can find still have a bone running down the center, see page 505 for instructions on how to remove it. If your market carries only half steaks, which consist of two sections of flesh separated by a long, thin bone, you will need two steaks, about 1 pound each and 1 inch thick, for this recipe. If your market carries only whole halibut steaks (they have four sections of flesh divided by a bone and membrane), you will need only one 2-pound steak, about 1 inch thick. If desired, serve the steaks with one of the compound butters on page 618.

> 4 boneless, skin-on halibut steaks, 1 inch thick (7 to 8 ounces each)
> 2 tablespoons extra-virgin olive oil
>   Salt and ground black pepper
>   Vegetable oil for the grill rack
>   Lemon wedges for serving

FORMING COMPOUND BUTTER

Once the ingredients have been combined, place the butter mixture in the center of a piece of plastic wrap. Fold one edge of the plastic wrap over the butter. Glide your hands back and forth over the butter to shape it into a 3-inch cylinder. Twist the ends of the plastic wrap shut and refrigerate until firm.

1. Light a large chimney starter filled with hardwood charcoal (about 6 quarts) and allow to burn until all the charcoal is covered with a layer of fine gray ash. Build a single-level fire by spreading the coals out evenly over the bottom of the grill. Set the cooking rack in place, cover the grill with the lid, and let the rack heat up, about 5 minutes. Use a wire brush to scrape clean the cooking rack. The grill is ready when the coals are medium-hot. (See how to gauge heat level on page 568.)

2. Brush the halibut with the olive oil and season well with salt and pepper to taste.

3. Lightly dip a small wad of paper towels in vegetable oil; holding the wad with tongs, wipe the grill rack (see page 616). Grill the halibut, uncovered and turning once (using a metal spatula), until barely translucent at the very center of the steak, 7 to 8 minutes. Serve immediately with lemon wedges.

> VARIATION

Gas-Grilled Halibut Steaks

Note that the grilling times are slightly longer when using a gas grill.

Preheat the grill with all burners set to high and the lid down until very hot, about 15 minutes. Use a wire brush to scrape clean the cooking rack. Leave all burners on high. Follow the recipe for Charcoal-Grilled Halibut Steaks, grilling the halibut, covered and turning once (using a metal spatula), until barely translucent at the very center of the steak, 8 to 9 minutes.

SWORDFISH STEAKS

THICK SWORDFISH STEAKS ARE A FAVORITE on the grill. Their dense, meaty flesh keeps the steaks from falling apart, and their smooth surface reduces the risk of sticking.

After testing various steaks, we found that thicker steaks (close to 1¼ inches) were best because they can remain on the grill long enough to pick up some smoky flavor without drying out. Thinner steaks were either poorly seared or overcooked in the middle. Thicker pieces also retained moisture better and were easier to handle on the grill.

When grilling all fish (but especially swordfish),

leave it in place long enough so that it develops good grill marks before moving. Unlike salmon and tuna, we find that swordfish should be cooked until medium—no more, no less. A two-level fire is necessary; the fish sears over a hot fire and then cooks through on the cooler part of the grill.

Charcoal-Grilled Swordfish Steaks

SERVES 4

Because of a swordfish's shape and size, individual sword-fish steaks are quite large. This recipe serves four—or more if you are willing to cut the steaks into smaller pieces. If desired, serve the steaks with one of the compound butters on page 618.

2   swordfish steaks, 1 to 1¼ inches thick (about 1 pound each)
2   tablespoons extra-virgin olive oil
    Salt and ground black pepper
    Vegetable oil for the grill rack
    Lemon wedges for serving

1. Light a large chimney starter filled with hard-wood charcoal (about 6 quarts) and allow to burn until all the charcoal is covered with a layer of fine gray ash. Build a two-level fire by stacking most of the coals on one side of the grill and arranging the remaining coals in a single layer on the other side of the grill. Set the cooking rack in place, cover the grill with the lid, and let the rack heat up, about 5 minutes. Use a wire brush to scrape clean the cooking rack. The grill is ready when the heat level of the stacked coals is medium-hot and that of the remaining coals is medium-low. (See how to gauge heat level on page 568.)

2. Cut the swordfish steaks in half to make four equal pieces. Brush the fish with the olive oil and generously sprinkle with salt and pepper.

3. Lightly dip a small wad of paper towels in vegetable oil; holding the wad with tongs, wipe the grill rack (see page 616). Grill the swordfish, uncovered and turning once (using a metal spatula), over the hotter part of the grill until the steaks are covered with dark grill marks, 6 to 7 minutes. Move the fish to the cooler part of the grill and

cook, uncovered and turning once, until the center is no longer translucent, 3 to 5 minutes. Serve immediately with lemon wedges.

➤ VARIATIONS
Gas-Grilled Swordfish Steaks
Note that the grilling times are slightly longer when using a gas grill.

Preheat the grill with all burners set to high and the lid down until very hot, about 15 minutes. Use a wire brush to scrape clean the cooking rack. Leave all burners on high. Follow the recipe for Charcoal-Grilled Swordfish Steaks, grilling the swordfish, covered and turning once (using a metal spatula), over high heat until the steaks are covered with dark grill marks, 7 to 9 minutes. Turn the heat down to medium and cook, covered and turning once, until the center is no longer translucent, 4 to 6 minutes. Serve immediately with lemon wedges.

Grilled Swordfish Steaks with Lemon-Parsley Sauce
Garlic is a pleasant addition to this dish. If desired, add one medium garlic clove, finely minced, and 1 teaspoon lemon zest to the oil that is to be brushed on the steaks before grilling.

¼   cup extra-virgin olive oil
1½ tablespoons juice from 1 lemon
2   tablespoons minced fresh parsley leaves
    Salt and ground black pepper
1   recipe Charcoal-Grilled or Gas-Grilled Swordfish Steaks

1. Combine the oil, lemon juice, parsley, and salt and pepper to taste in a small bowl. Set the sauce aside.

2. Follow the recipe for Charcoal-Grilled or Gas-Grilled Swordfish Steaks, brushing the fish with lemon-garlic oil instead of plain olive oil, if desired. Spoon the lemon-parsley sauce over the grilled fish just before serving.

Grilled Swordfish Steaks with Salsa Verde
Follow the recipe for Charcoal-Grilled or Gas-Grilled Swordfish Steaks, topping each portion

of grilled fish with a generous tablespoon of Salsa Verde (page 415).

Tuna Steaks

WE ASSUMED THAT WE COULD GET A perfect tuna steak—beautifully seared on the outside, moist and tender on the inside—the same way we get a perfect beef or salmon steak: a quick sear over direct heat to brown and then, if the steak is really thick, a final few minutes over indirect heat to finish it. We also knew that tuna, lacking the fat of salmon, would be particularly susceptible to overcooking, so we would probably need to undercook it.

But a few days of testing proved tuna to be a tougher customer than we'd imagined. No matter how thick we sliced it or how we cooked it, we were startled to find that steak after steak was almost inedible. Each one was tough and dry and tasted off-puttingly strong and fishy. Clearly, more experimenting was in order.

For purposes of experimentation, we decided to work with steaks ¾ to 1 inch thick, as these are the cuts usually available at supermarket fish counters. First we tried grilling over direct heat, starting with an oiled and salted steak, for 3½ minutes on each side over a medium fire. The outside of the tuna was paler than we liked, and the inside was overcooked. In successive tests, we determined that a hotter fire seared better, particularly since the tuna needed to cook only 3 minutes total for medium and 4 minutes for well-done.

While the hotter fire was an improvement, the fish was still drier than we liked, particularly when it was cooked past medium-rare. So we experimented with a two-level fire that would give us a source of indirect heat. We now tried searing the tuna 1½ minutes on each side over direct heat and moving it to the side of the grill to finish cooking over indirect heat. The tuna came off the grill with the same texture it had when grilled entirely over direct heat, but it was less well seared, so we gave up on the indirect heat approach.

We thought it was time to test steaks of different thicknesses over direct heat and learned that if we wanted the tuna both well seared and rare, it would have to be cut thicker than the standard supermarket steak, about 1½ inches instead of ¾ to 1 inch. Thinner steaks had already cooked to at least medium rare after the initial searing on both sides. But while we preferred the moistness of the thick, rare steaks, we were concerned that some folks would not like to eat their tuna rare. In addition, we knew that many consumers have difficulty locating thick steaks.

We turned to several restaurant chefs for advice (after all, grilled tuna has become a restaurant classic), and they suggested marinating the tuna in olive oil and herbs. We marinated one 1½-inch-thick steak and one ½-inch-thick steak in an herb-flavored oil for three hours, turning every now and then. We then grilled the thick steak to rare and the thin steak to medium. The results were amazing. Both tunas were subtly flavored with olive oil and herbs, and their texture was moist and luscious. Perhaps most surprising, we liked the well-cooked tuna as much as the rare.

We next ran tests to determine whether the type of oil made a difference. Comparing extra-virgin and pure olive oils with canola oil, we found that after one hour, only the extra-virgin oil made a noticeable difference in the tuna. The pure olive oil seemed to catch up after another hour, but it didn't flavor the tuna appreciably until after three hours. The canola oil never affected the taste or the texture of the tuna.

We learned that an oil marinade tenderizes tuna in much the same way that marbling tenderizes beef. The oil coats the strands of protein, allowing a tuna steak to feel moist in the mouth even after most of the moisture has been cooked out of it. The extra-virgin olive oil penetrates the fish more quickly than the other two oils because it is much richer in emulsifiers. Emulsifiers (mono- and diglycerides) have a water-soluble molecule at one end and a fat-soluble molecule at the other; this double solubility increases their mobility and hence their ability to penetrate protein. Because the filtering process extracts

621

emulsifiers, pure olive oil takes much longer than extra-virgin olive oil to coat the protein strands.

Finally, we learned that the thick 1½-inch steaks, when cooked to rare or medium-rare, needed only brushing with the oil; soaking it in the oil actually made it a bit too moist. We liked the herbs in the marinade, but we found that the oil alone was still quite good. The basic recipes have just extra-virgin olive oil, salt, pepper, and tuna; see the herb variation if you are interested in something a bit more unusual.

Charcoal-Grilled Tuna Steaks
SERVES 4

If you like your tuna rare, you must buy steaks cut about 1½ inches thick. This will allow you to sear them well without overcooking the inside. To serve four people, you'll need two steaks (they run about 1 pound each). Cut each in half before grilling. If you prefer more well-done tuna, see the recipe for thin-cut tuna at right. If desired, serve the steaks with one of the compound butters on page 618.

2   tuna steaks, 1½ inches thick (about
       1 pound each)
2   tablespoons extra-virgin olive oil
       Salt and ground black pepper
       Vegetable oil for the grill rack

1. Light a large chimney starter filled with hardwood charcoal (about 6 quarts) and allow to burn until all the charcoal is covered with a layer of fine gray ash. Build a single-level fire by spreading the coals out evenly over the bottom of the grill. Set the cooking rack in place, cover the grill with the lid, and let the rack heat up, about 5 minutes. Use a wire brush to scrape clean the cooking rack. The grill is ready when the coals are medium-hot. (See how to gauge heat level on page 568.)

2. Cut the tuna steaks in half to make four equal pieces. Brush the tuna with the olive oil and generously sprinkle with salt and pepper.

3. Lightly dip a small wad of paper towels in vegetable oil; holding the wad with tongs, wipe the grill rack (see page 616). Grill the tuna, uncovered and turning once (using a metal spatula), to the desired doneness, 4 to 5 minutes for rare or 6 to 7 minutes for medium-rare. Serve immediately.

➤ VARIATIONS
Gas-Grilled Tuna Steaks
Note that the grilling times are slightly longer when using a gas grill.

Preheat the grill with all burners set to high and the lid down until very hot, about 15 minutes. Use a wire brush to scrape clean the cooking rack. Leave the burners on high. Follow the recipe for Charcoal-Grilled Tuna Steaks, grilling the tuna, covered and turning once (using a metal spatula), to the desired doneness, 5 to 6 minutes for rare or 7 to 8 minutes for medium-rare. Serve immediately.

Thin-Cut Grilled Tuna Steaks
This recipe is for those who like their tuna cooked medium to well-done but still moist inside. The steaks are cut thinner for quicker cooking and marinated in extra-virgin olive oil, both of which prevent dryness. If using a gas grill, cook over high heat, keep the lid down, and increase the cooking times by a minute or so.

4   tuna steaks, ¾ inch thick (about
       8 ounces each)
¼   cup extra-virgin olive oil
       Salt and ground black pepper
       Vegetable oil for the grill rack

1. Combine the tuna steaks and olive oil in a gallon-size zipper-lock plastic bag. Marinate in the refrigerator, turning several times, for at least 2 hours or overnight.

2. Light a large chimney starter filled with hardwood charcoal (about 6 quarts) and allow to burn until all the charcoal is covered with a layer of fine gray ash. Build a single-level fire by spreading the coals out evenly over the bottom of the grill. Set the cooking rack in place, cover the grill with the lid, and let the rack heat up, about 5 minutes. Use a wire brush to scrape clean the cooking rack. The grill is ready when the coals are medium-hot. (See how to gauge heat level on page 568.)

3. Remove the tuna from the bag and sprinkle

with salt and pepper to taste.

4. Lightly dip a small wad of paper towels in vegetable oil; holding the wad with tongs, wipe the grill rack (see page 616). Grill the tuna, uncovered and turning once (using a metal spatula), to the desired doneness, about 3 minutes total for rare or 4 minutes total for well-done. Serve immediately.

Grilled Tuna Steaks with Herb-Infused Oil

If cooking thin-cut tuna, use the herb oil as a marinade.

  1/4   cup extra-virgin olive oil
  1 1/2 teaspoons grated lemon zest
  1 1/2 teaspoons chopped fresh thyme leaves
  1   medium garlic clove, minced
  1/4   teaspoon red pepper flakes
  1   recipe Charcoal-Grilled or Gas-Grilled Tuna Steaks (without the olive oil)

1. Heat the oil, lemon zest, thyme, garlic, and red pepper flakes in a small saucepan until hot. Remove the pan from the heat and cool the oil mixture to room temperature.

2. Follow the recipe for the tuna, brushing the fish with the herb oil instead of the plain olive oil. Proceed as directed.

Grilled Tuna Steaks with Peppercorn Crust

You can buy a whole-peppercorn mix in well-stocked grocery stores or at specialty markets. These mixes may include white, black, green, pink, and/or red peppercorns. Although somewhat less complex in flavor, whole black peppercorns will do in place of the mix. Season the fish with kosher salt if possible. Serve as is or with one of the compound butters on page 618.

  1   tablespoon whole-peppercorn mix
  1   recipe Charcoal-Grilled or Gas-Grilled Tuna Steaks (without the ground black pepper)

1. Place the whole-peppercorn mix in the hopper of a spice grinder or coffee mill and pulse until the peppercorns are coarsely ground, about six 1-second pulses.

2. Follow the recipe for the tuna, pressing the peppercorn mixture into the tuna after it has been brushed with oil and sprinkled with salt. Proceed as directed.

Grilled Rare Tuna Steaks with Soy, Ginger, and Wasabi

SERVES 4 AS A MAIN COURSE OR 8 AS AN APPETIZER

Since this tuna is served very rare, use only the freshest, highest-quality tuna you can find. It is served with a soy and pickled ginger sauce and wasabi paste. Wasabi, or Japanese horseradish, is the pungent green condiment served with sushi and sashimi. Use the paste sparingly; it packs a spicy punch.

  6   tablespoons soy sauce
  4   teaspoons juice from 1 lime
  2   teaspoons toasted sesame oil
  2   tablespoons minced pickled ginger
  2   medium scallions, thinly sliced
  4   teaspoons wasabi powder
  2   teaspoons water
  1   recipe Charcoal-Grilled or Gas-Grilled Tuna

1. Mix the soy sauce, lime juice, sesame oil, pickled ginger, and scallions together in a small bowl. Set aside. Mix the wasabi and water together in a small bowl to form a thick paste. Cover and set aside.

2. Follow the recipe for the tuna, grilling the fish just until rare. Cut the tuna into 1/4-inch-thick slices and fan the tuna out over individual plates. Drizzle a little of the soy mixture over each plate and place a dollop of the wasabi paste on each plate. Serve immediately.

Grilled Tuna Steaks with Watercress, Parsley, and Spiced Vinaigrette

The hot tuna wilts the watercress and parsley slightly, while the spiced vinaigrette adds tons of flavor and moisture.

  2 1/2 tablespoons juice from 1 large lemon
  2   small garlic cloves, minced
  1/2   teaspoon salt
  1/2   teaspoon ground cumin
  1/4   teaspoon sweet paprika
  1/8   teaspoon cayenne pepper
  2   tablespoons chopped fresh cilantro leaves

½   cup extra-virgin olive oil
     Ground black pepper
I   recipe Charcoal-Grilled or Gas-Grilled Tuna
I   bunch watercress, washed, dried well, and
     trimmed of tough stems
I   bunch flat-leaf parsley, washed and
     dried well

1. Whisk the lemon juice, garlic, salt, cumin, paprika, cayenne, and cilantro together in a small bowl. Add the oil in a slow, steady stream, whisking constantly until smooth; season with black pepper to taste. Set the dressing aside.

2. While the tuna is on the grill, place the watercress and parsley in a medium bowl. Drizzle half of the dressing over the greens and toss well. Divide the greens among 4 individual plates.

3. Place one grilled tuna steak on each plate over the salad greens. Drizzle the remaining dressing over the fish and serve immediately.

SHRIMP

SHRIMP DESTINED FOR THE GRILL SHOULD NOT be peeled. The shell shields the meat from the intense heat and helps to keep the shrimp moist and tender. Try as we might, we found it impossible to grill peeled shrimp without overcooking them and making the meat dry and tough, especially the exterior layers. The only method that worked was to intentionally undercook the shrimp; but that left the inside a little gooey, something that almost no one enjoyed.

To make it easier to eat grilled shrimp, we found it useful to slit open the shell with a pair of manicure scissors. The shell still protects the meat as the shrimp cook, but the shell comes right off at the table.

In addition to peeling, the issue of deveining generates much controversy, even among experts. Although some people won't eat shrimp that has not been deveined, others believe that the "vein"—actually the animal's intestinal tract—contributes flavor and insist on leaving it in. In our tests, we could not detect an effect on flavor (either positive or negative) when we left the vein

in. The vein is generally so tiny in most medium shrimp that it virtually disappears after cooking. Out of laziness, we leave it alone. In very large shrimp, the vein is usually larger as well. Very large veins are unsightly and can detract from the overall texture of the shrimp, and thus are best removed before cooking.

Once you've bought and prepared your shrimp, the hard part is over. Grilling is simple: As soon as the shrimp turn pink, they are done. That said, we did find it advisable to add one more step to preparation to keep the shrimp from drying out—as they tend to do over intense dry heat: brining.

Once the shrimp have been brined, they can be threaded onto skewers and grilled. We found

PREPARING SHRIMP FOR GRILLING

1. When grilling shrimp, we find it best to keep them in their shells. The shells hold in moisture as well as flavor as the shrimp cook. However, eating shrimp cooked in the shell can be a challenge. As a compromise, we found it helpful to slit the back of the shell with a pair of manicure or other small scissors with a fine point. When ready to eat, each person can quickly and easily peel away the shell.

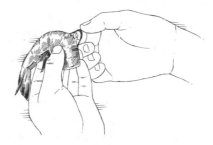

2. Slitting the back of the shell makes it easy to devein the shrimp as well. Except in cases where the vein was especially dark and thick, we found no benefit to deveining in our testing. If you choose to devein shrimp, slit open the back of the shell as in step I. Invariably, you will cut a little into the meat and expose the vein as you do this. Use the tip of the scissors to lift up the vein and then grab it with your fingers and discard.

that shrimp should be cooked quickly to prevent them from toughening. This means using a very hot fire.

When grilling, we like to coat shrimp with a paste or marinade before cooking. The flavorings adhere to the shell beautifully. When you peel the shrimp at the table, the seasonings stick to your fingers and are in turn transferred directly to the meat as you eat it. Licking your fingers also helps.

Charcoal-Grilled Shrimp

SERVES 4 TO 6

We recommend that you brine the shrimp before grilling to make them especially plump and juicy. To keep the shrimp from dropping through the grill rack onto the hot coals, thread them on skewers. Use tongs to turn the skewered shrimp.

> 2 tablespoons table salt
> 2 pounds extra-large shrimp (21 to 25 per pound)
> 2 tablespoons extra-virgin olive oil
> Lemon wedges for serving

1. Pour 1 quart cold water into a gallon-size zipper-lock bag. Add the salt, stirring to dissolve. Add the shrimp and let stand 20 to 25 minutes. Drain and rinse thoroughly under cold running water. Open the back of the shells with manicure scissors (see the illustration on page 624) and devein if desired (see the illustration on page 624). Toss the shrimp and oil in a medium bowl to coat.

2. Meanwhile, light a large chimney starter filled with hardwood charcoal (about 6 quarts) and allow to burn until all the charcoal is covered with a layer of fine gray ash. Build a single-level fire by spreading the coals evenly out over the bottom of the grill. Set the cooking rack in place, cover the grill with the lid, and let the rack heat up, about 5 minutes. Use a wire brush to scrape clean the cooking grate. The grill is ready when the coals are medium-hot. (See how to gauge heat level on page 568.)

3. Thread the shrimp on skewers (see illustration 1 below). Grill the shrimp, uncovered, turning the skewers once (see illustration 2 below), until the shells are barely charred and bright pink, 4 to 6 minutes. Serve hot or at room temperature with lemon wedges.

> VARIATIONS
Gas-Grilled Shrimp
Note that the grilling times are slightly longer when using a gas grill.

Follow the recipe for Charcoal-Grilled Shrimp. Preheat the grill with all burners set to high and the lid down until the grill is very hot, about 15 minutes. Use a wire brush to scrape clean the cooking grate. Leave the burners on high.

SKEWERING SHRIMP

1. Thread shrimp on skewers by passing the skewer through the body near the tail, folding the shrimp over, and passing the shrimp through the body again near the head. Threading each shrimp twice keeps it in place (it won't spin around) and makes it easier to cook the shrimp on both sides by turning the skewer just once.

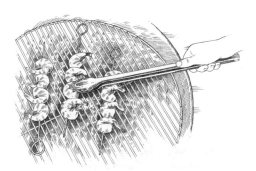

2. Long-handled tongs make it easy to turn hot skewers on the grill. Lightly grab onto a single shrimp to turn the entire skewer.

Follow the recipe for Charcoal-Grilled Shrimp, increasing the grilling time to 5 to 6 minutes.

Grilled Shrimp with Spicy Garlic Paste

The garlic paste adheres perfectly and will coat your fingers as you peel and eat the grilled shrimp.

Mince 1 large garlic clove with 1 teaspoon salt to form a smooth paste (see the illustrations below). Combine the garlic paste with ½ teaspoon cayenne pepper, 1 teaspoon sweet paprika, 2 tablespoons extra-virgin olive oil, and 2 teaspoons lemon juice in a medium bowl. Follow the recipe for Charcoal-Grilled or Gas-Grilled Shrimp, tossing the brined and drained shrimp with the garlic mixture instead of the oil to coat well. Thread the shrimp on skewers and grill as directed.

Grilled Shrimp with Lemon, Garlic, and Oregano Paste

The fresh oregano in this recipe can be replaced with other fresh herbs, including chives, tarragon, parsley, or basil.

Mince 1 large garlic clove with 1 teaspoon salt to form a smooth paste (see the illustrations below). Combine the garlic paste with 2 tablespoons extra-virgin olive oil, 2 teaspoons lemon juice, and 2 teaspoons chopped fresh oregano leaves in a medium bowl. Follow the recipe for Charcoal-Grilled or Gas-Grilled Shrimp, tossing the brined and drained shrimp with the garlic mixture instead of the oil to coat well. Thread the shrimp on skewers and grill as directed.

Grilled Shrimp with Southwestern Flavors

Serve these shrimp with warm cornbread.

Heat 2 tablespoons extra-virgin olive oil in a small skillet over medium heat. Add 2 garlic cloves, minced, 2 teaspoons chili powder, and ¾ teaspoon ground cumin and sauté until the garlic is fragrant, 30 to 45 seconds. Scrape the mixture into a heatproof bowl and cool to room temperature. Mix in 2½ tablespoons lime juice and 2 tablespoons minced fresh cilantro leaves. Follow the recipe for Charcoal-Grilled or Gas-Grilled Shrimp, tossing the brined and drained shrimp with the garlic mixture instead of the oil to coat well. Thread the shrimp on skewers and grill as directed. Serve with lime wedges instead of lemon wedges.

MINCING GARLIC TO A PASTE

There are times when you want minced garlic to be absolutely smooth. A garlic press yields a smooth paste easily. To obtain the same effect with a chef's knife, you will need some salt. If possible, use kosher or coarse salt; the larger crystals do a better job of breaking down the garlic than fine table salt.

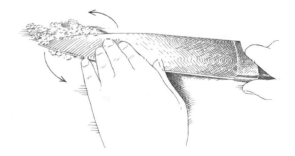

1. Mince the garlic as you normally would on a cutting board. Sprinkle the minced garlic with a pinch of salt.

2. Drag the side of the chef's knife over the garlic-salt mixture to form a fine paste. Continue to mince and drag the knife as necessary until the paste is smooth.

14

EGGS AND BREAKFAST

MOST PEOPLE WE KNOW ARE PASSIONATE ABOUT breakfast, especially weekend breakfasts, when there's time for something other than a bowl of cold cereal or a slice of dry toast and juice. Because we get to eat a real breakfast so infrequently, we have high expectations when it comes to classic breakfast dishes.

More often than not, we think of eggs when we think of breakfast. Simply prepared, typically scrambled or fried, or cooked into an omelet, frittata, or strata, eggs are also an integral ingredient in pancakes, French toast, and waffles.

Of course, there is more to breakfast than egg-based dishes. Bacon is a must for many cooks, as are home fries. Others prefer to build the first meal of the day around oatmeal or corned beef hash rather than eggs. This chapter contains recipes for all these favorites in addition to information on the right tools and equipment so that you can make a great breakfast no matter how bleary-eyed you are in the morning.

SCRAMBLED EGGS

SCRAMBLED EGGS SHOULD BE A DREAMY MOUND of big, softly wobbling curds, yellow as the sun, glistening, a hairbreadth away from being undercooked. (If you are concerned about salmonella, see page 631.) When cut, the eggs should be cooked enough to hold their shape but soft enough to eat with a spoon.

We first tested beating the eggs to see if this made a difference in the final outcome. Our advice is to stop muscling the raw eggs into a tight froth. We found that overbeating can cause premature coagulation of the eggs' protein—even without heat! Too much beating can make eggs tough before they hit the pan. For a smooth yellow color and no streaks of white, we whip eggs in a medium bowl with a fork and stop while the bubbles are large. For 10 to 12 eggs, we've found that a balloon whisk works well.

Before beating, the eggs get a few additions—salt, pepper, and either milk or water. Compared side by side, we found that scrambled eggs made with water are less flavorful, don't fluff as nicely,

and aren't as soft as those made with milk. With its traces of sugar, proteins, and fats, milk has a pillowy effect and helps create large curds: The bigger you can make the curds, the more steam you'll trap inside, for puff all the way to the table.

We tried most of the pans in our kitchen and discovered that a nonstick surface is best for scrambled eggs. As always, a heavy-bottomed skillet is preferable. Cheap, thin pans overheat and are difficult to control on high heat. Thicker pans may take longer to heat up, but they hold heat evenly without hot spots.

Pan size is important, too. When we used a 10-inch skillet for two eggs, the batter spread out so thinly that while we were busy moving one area of the eggs, another area overcooked. We found that the more the eggs are contained, the bigger the curds. An 8-inch skillet kept the two-egg batter at a depth of about ¼ inch, and the curds came out nice and plump.

We've tried cooking scrambled eggs over medium heat but the eggs got tough, dried out, and overcoagulated, like a badly made meringue

SCRAMBLING EGGS

1. Using a wooden spoon or plastic spatula, push the eggs from one side of the pan to the other.

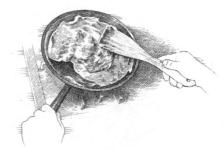

2. As they form curds, lift and fold the eggs until they are clumped in a single mound.

that "weeps." A hot pan will begin to cook eggs instantaneously, for the quickest coagulation. The trade-off for using high heat is absolute vigilance in making sure the eggs are off the heat before serious damage is done.

Keeping the eggs in constant, steady motion also helps keep them from overcooking. You don't want to beat the eggs, but they should be stirred gently as they cook. A wooden or plastic spatula works best; use the flat edge to snowplow a 2- to 3-inch swath of eggs across the pan in one pass. The idea is to push slowly, lift, and fold. Two eggs should cook into big curds in about 30 seconds. The larger the curds, the more steam is pocketed inside, and the more the eggs will continue to cook once off the heat. We like scrambled eggs soft and juicy, so they look positively underdone when we make that final fold and push them out of the pan.

Fluffy Scrambled Eggs

SERVES 4

These eggs cook very quickly, so it's important to be ready to eat before you start to cook them.

8	large eggs
½	teaspoon salt
	Several grinds of black pepper
½	cup milk
1	tablespoon unsalted butter

1. Crack the eggs into a medium bowl. Add the salt, pepper, and milk. Whip with a fork until the streaks are gone and the color is pure yellow; stop beating while the bubbles are still large.

2. Meanwhile, put the butter in a 10-inch nonstick skillet, then set the pan over high heat. When the butter foams, swirl it around and up the sides of the pan. Before the foam completely subsides, pour in the beaten eggs. With a wooden or plastic spatula, push the eggs from one side of the pan to the other, slowly but deliberately, lifting and folding the eggs as they form into curds, until they are nicely clumped into a single mound but remain shiny and wet, 1½ to 2 minutes. Serve immediately.

VARIATIONS

Two Scrambled Eggs

Season 2 eggs with ⅛ teaspoon salt, 1 grind of pepper, and 2 tablespoons milk. Heat only 1½ teaspoons butter in an 8-inch skillet. Cooking time is only 30 to 45 seconds.

Four Scrambled Eggs

Season 4 eggs with ¼ teaspoon salt, 2 grinds of pepper, and ¼ cup milk. Heat ¾ tablespoon butter in a 10-inch skillet. Cooking time is about 1 minute.

Twelve Scrambled Eggs

Season 12 eggs with ¾ teaspoon salt, 6 grinds of pepper, and ¾ cup milk and mix using a balloon whisk. Heat 1½ tablespoons butter in a 12-inch skillet. Cooking time is 2½ to 3 minutes.

FRIED EGGS

ANYONE CAN MAKE FRIED EGGS, BUT FEW AND far between are the cooks who can make them perfectly every time. For most of us, they are sometimes great and sometimes second-rate at best. While our efforts are usually at least passable, we decided to eliminate the guesswork and figure out how to best and most easily fry the perfect egg every time. For us, this means an egg with a white that is firm, not runny, and a yolk that sets up high and is thick but still runny.

For starters, we thought it made sense to investigate the hardware. After testing skillets, our initial feeling was confirmed: There is no point in frying eggs in anything but a nonstick pan. Next we examined the degree to which the pan should be heated before the eggs are added. We learned that there is a point at which the temperature of the pan causes the egg to behave just as we want it to. When an egg lands in a pan that's at the correct temperature, it neither runs all over the place nor sputters or bubbles; instead, it just sizzles and sets up into a thick, restrained oval. Getting the taste and texture of the white just right depends on achieving this correct set point. A white that's too spread out becomes overcooked, rubbery, and

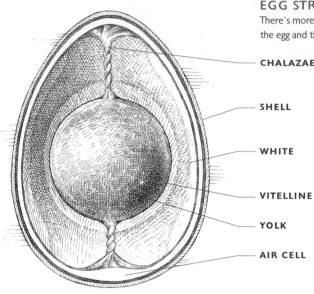

EGG STRUCTURE

There's more to an egg than shell, white, and yolk. The following are the major components of the egg and their functions.

CHALAZAE These whitish cords, located at each pole, center the yolk. The more prominent the chalazae, the fresher the egg. (We recommend straining sauces and custards so the chalazae won't mar their texture.)

SHELL To help prevent moisture from getting out and other flavors from getting in, shells are coated with a thin waxy substance. Never wash eggs before storing them; washing will remove this protective coating.

WHITE The white, also called albumin, is divided into thick and thin layers. The thick layer is closest to the yolk, and this division is very evident in fresh eggs. A slight cloudiness in the white indicates extreme freshness.

VITELLINE This membrane contains and protects the yolk. It weakens as the egg ages, causing the yolk to break more easily.

YOLK Most of the egg's vitamins and minerals, as well as all of the fat and half of the protein, are found in the yolk. It also contains lecithin, an emulsifier.

AIR CELL The void at the wide end of the egg results from contraction as the interior cools after the egg is laid. This space increases in size as moisture inside the egg evaporates.

BUYING EGGS

FRESHNESS

Egg cartons are marked with both a sell-by date and a pack date (the latter also known as the Julian date). The sell-by date is the legal limit to which eggs may be sold and is within 30 days of the pack date. The pack date is the day the eggs were graded and packed, which is generally within a week of being laid but, legally, may be as much as 30 days. In short, a carton of eggs may be up to two months old by the end of the sell-by date. Even so, according to the U.S. Department of Agriculture, they are still fit for consumption for an additional three to five weeks past the sell-by date. Sell-by and pack dates are thus by no means an exact measure of an egg's fitness; they provide vague guidance at best.

How old is too old? We tasted two- and three-month-old eggs that were perfectly palatable. At four months, the white was very loose and the yolk "tasted faintly of the refrigerator," though it was still edible. Our advice? Use your discretion. If the egg smells odd or displays discoloration, pitch it. Older eggs also lack the structure-lending properties of fresh eggs, so beware when using them for baking. Both the white and yolk become looser. We whipped four month old eggs and found that they deflated rapidly.

COLOR

The shell's hue depends on the breed of the chicken. The run-of-the-mill Leghorn chicken produces the typical white egg. Larger brown-feathered birds, such as Rhode Island Reds, produce the ecru- to coffee-colored eggs common to New England. Despite marketing hype to the contrary, a kitchen taste test proved that shell color has no effect on flavor.

GRADE

Although eggs are theoretically sold in three grades—AA, A, and B—we found only grade A eggs for sale in nearly a dozen markets in Massachusetts and New York. Grade AA eggs are the cream of the crop, possessing the thickest whites and shells, according to the American Egg Board. Grade B eggs are used commercially.

PACK DATE

The three-number code stamped above or below the sell-by date is the pack date. The numbers run consecutively, starting at 001 for January 1 and ending with 365 for December 31. These eggs were packed on March 19 (078). The number next to the pack date (P1970) is an internal code for egg packers.

STORING EGGS

We have found that eggs suffer more from the vagaries of improper storage than from age. The egg tray inside the refrigerator door is not the ideal location, for two reasons: temperature and protection. The American Egg Board recommends 40 degrees for storage, but we have found the average door temperature in our six test kitchen refrigerators to be closer to 45 degrees. The interior top shelf is a better bet—ours registers between 38 and 40 degrees. Eggs are also better stored in their protective cardboard carton; when removed, they may absorb flavors from other foods. We've made "oniony" cakes and cookies with improperly stored eggs. The carton also helps to maintain humidity, which is ideally 70 to 80 percent, according to the Egg Board.

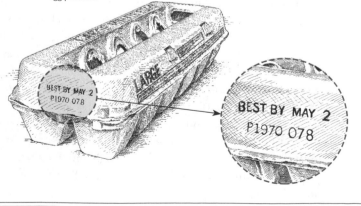

EGG SAFETY

In recent years, numerous outbreaks of intestinal illness have been traced to eggs contaminated with salmonella. Although the odds of getting a bad egg are quite low (some experts estimate that 1 in 10,000 eggs is contaminated with the bacteria), it makes sense to take some precautions. This is especially true if you are cooking for the young, the elderly, women who are pregnant, or people with compromised immune systems.

Thorough cooking of eggs, to at least 160 degrees, will kill any salmonella that may be present. Because it is hard to use an instant-read thermometer on scrambled eggs, you have to rely on visual clues. If you are concerned about salmonella, you should cook all eggs until fully set; for fried eggs, that means avoiding runny yolks.

INGREDIENTS: EGGS

We were curious to see how eggs from different sources might stack up when tasted side by side. We put the following four varieties to the test by cooking each sunny-side up: farm-fresh eggs (less than a week old), Egg Innovations organic eggs ("free-roaming"), Eggland's Best brand eggs from hens raised on vegetarian feed (the labels say these eggs are guaranteed to possess "25% less saturated fat than regular eggs" and "100 mg of omega 3 fatty acids"), and standard supermarket eggs. The farm-fresh eggs were standouts from the get-go. The large yolks were shockingly orange and sat very high above the comparatively small whites. Their flavor was exceptionally rich and complex. The organic eggs followed in second place, the eggs from hens raised on a vegetarian diet in third, and the standard supermarket eggs last.

Our conclusion? If you have access to eggs fresh from the farm, by all means buy them. Otherwise, organic eggs are worth the premium—a dollar or two more than standard supermarket eggs—especially if you often eat eggs on their own. The eggs below are listed in order of preference.

THE BEST EGGS

FARM-FRESH EGGS
The favorite of the pack, possessing very bright yolks and rich flavor.

EGG INNOVATIONS CERTIFIED ORGANIC LARGE EGGS
A close second; tasters described these eggs as "sweet and mild" and "good-textured."

EGGLAND'S BEST LARGE EGGS
These eggs (from hens fed a vegetarian diet) were preferred over supermarket eggs, though they lost points with some tasters with their somewhat sulfurous flavor.

EGG SIZES

Eggs come in six sizes—jumbo, extra-large, large, medium, small, and peewee. Most markets carry only the top four sizes; small and peewee are generally reserved for commercial use. There's little mystery about size—the bigger or the older the chicken, the bigger the egg. All the recipes in this book are tested with large eggs, but substitutions are possible in recipes where large quantities of eggs are used. See the egg weight chart at right for help in making accurate calculations. For example, 4 jumbo eggs (2.5 ounces each) are equivalent to 5 large eggs (2 ounces each).

EGG SIZE SUBSTITUTIONS

Size	Weight
MEDIUM	1.75 ounces
LARGE	2.00 ounces
EXTRA-LARGE	2.25 ounces
JUMBO	2.50 ounces

Relative Size of Supermarket Eggs (Three-Quarter Scale)

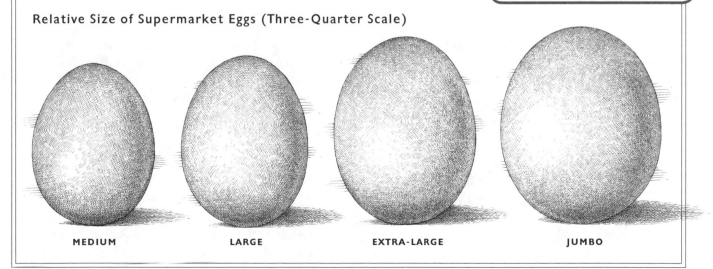

MEDIUM   LARGE   EXTRA-LARGE   JUMBO

tough, while a white that browns at the edges as soon as it hits the pan ends up tasting metallic, at least to us.

We needed to devise a plan that would incorporate this crucial setting temperature, no matter what type of pan or what cooktop a cook was using. To begin, we placed the pan on a low setting and let it heat for a full five minutes. We had discovered that while eggs might set up well initially if a pan is not completely heated, they then tend to overcook at the finish; five minutes ensures a thorough preheating of the pan. Next we added the butter, which we allowed to melt and foam, waiting for the foaming to subside before adding the egg. We knew immediately that the pan was too hot: The white sputtered into huge bubbles, and the butter had even started to brown. Fast-forward to the next egg. This time we again put the pan on the burner for five minutes but set the heat below the low setting. And this time we hit the mark: We added the egg just as the butter foam subsided, and the egg set up perfectly. On this perfected setting, the butter took exactly one minute to melt, foam, and subside.

We moved on to using a cover during the cooking process. After putting two eggs in the skillet, we put on the lid and allowed the eggs to cook for two minutes. One of the eggs was cooked perfectly, but the other was slightly undercooked. We realized that with such a short cooking time, we had to get the eggs into the pan at the same time. We tried the covered-skillet method one more

GETTING THE EGGS INTO THE PAN

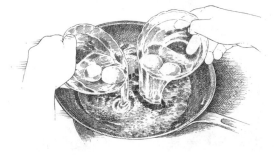

Crack the eggs into two small bowls, then add the eggs, sliding them into the hot skillet simultaneously from opposite sides of the pan.

time, but in this case broke each of the eggs into a cup before starting the process. This allowed us to empty the eggs into the skillet simultaneously. This method worked beautifully. The steam created when the pan was covered produced whites that were firm but not at all rubbery and yolks that were thick yet still runny. Since not all folks want a runny egg, we also experimented with other stages of doneness. It took 2½ minutes for a set but soft yolk, and 3 minutes for a light-colored, cooked-through yolk.

It's worth mentioning at this point that the fat used is meant to be a flavoring agent as well as a lubricant. We tried several kinds. Canola oil had too little flavor, olive oil had too much, but both bacon fat and butter were delicious. For two eggs in a 9-inch skillet, we found that 1½ teaspoons of either fat works well. A quick sprinkle of salt and freshly ground black pepper before throwing the cover on is also recommended: The seasonings don't impart as much flavor if added after the eggs are cooked.

Perfect Fried Eggs

SERVES 4

A nonstick skillet is essential because it ensures an easy release of the eggs. Since burners vary, it may take an egg or two before you determine the ideal setting for frying eggs on your stovetop. Follow the visual clue in the recipe and increase the heat if necessary. If you've just fried up some bacon or happen to have some bacon grease on hand, use it in place of the butter for really tasty fried eggs. Unlike butter, however, bacon grease will not go through visual changes that you can use to gauge the pan's heat. If you want to double the recipe, don't crowd the pan with more eggs than can fit. Simply cook a second batch separately. Don't try holding batches of fried eggs; serve immediately.

I   tablespoon cold unsalted butter
4   large eggs, cracked into 2 small bowls (2 eggs per bowl)
     Salt and ground black pepper

1. Heat a 10-inch heavy-bottomed nonstick skillet over the lowest possible heat for 5 minutes.

Add the butter; let it melt and foam. When the foam subsides (this process should take about 1 minute; if the butter browns in 1 minute, the pan is too hot), swirl to coat the pan.

2. Working quickly, pour 2 eggs on one side of the pan and the remaining 2 eggs on the other side. Season the eggs with salt and pepper; cover and cook about 2½ minutes for runny yolks, 3 minutes for soft but set yolks, and 3½ minutes for firmly set yolks.

POACHED EGGS

POACHING IS A GREAT WAY TO TREAT AN EGG, provided you know the best way to poach. A poached egg should be a lovely, tender white pouch cooked evenly all the way through. The top of the egg yolk should look slightly pink and, when cut, should run just a little. The white that surrounds it should glisten and jiggle, like baked custard. Last, the cooking liquid should be left with no stray strands of egg white.

We suspected that part of the problem with many poached egg recipes was the pot. Most recipes call for a deep saucepan, but we wondered if the eggs would be easier to control in a shallow skillet. We decided to test a three-quart saucepan against an 8-inch nonstick skillet with flared sides, which we figured might make it easier to maneuver the eggs.

The first advantage of the skillet quickly became clear: Shallower water comes to a boil more quickly, making the cooking time with a skillet a speedy proposition. Second, an egg meets the bottom of a skillet sooner than it does the bottom of a pot just a few inches taller. This gives the egg an early floor on which to land gently, before it has a chance to build up any velocity. The sooner the egg is on solid ground, the quicker the whites hold together and the less likely they are to become stringy.

It is necessary to fill the pan almost to the rim. Not surprisingly, we found that the highest heat possible on impact sets the egg whites most quickly. Because water is the cooking medium, that means 212 degrees. This high heat also causes

POACHING EGGS

To slip four eggs into simmering water at the same time, crack each into a small cup with a handle. Lower the lips of all the cups just into the water at the same time and tip the eggs simultaneously into the pan.

the yolks to hurry up and cook.

Even with these measures, however, whites can still become ragged (the process is called feathering). Most experts suggest treating the water with vinegar to lower the pH of the water. We found that adding vinegar does, in fact, reduce feathering. The lower pH of the water lowers the temperature at which the whites and yolks set, which means that after the initial dunk into boiling water, the egg can cook in water that's slightly cooler and, hence, calmer.

Indeed, we found that poached eggs come out best when the water is not at a boil. The eggs should be added to boiling water, but for the actual cooking time, we concluded that absolutely still water, as long as it's very hot, will poach an egg just the same. So we turned off the heat and covered the skillet. Without all the agitation of simmering or boiling water, the eggs cooked up better-looking every time.

During the 3½ to 4 minutes that it takes the captured heat to cook the eggs, the temperature of the covered water drops only about 20 degrees. This means that poaching eggs in residual heat eliminates the need to simmer, which can create rough waters that cause the egg to partially disintegrate. It also serves to outwit home stoves that run "hot" and can't hold a simmer.

With our technique down, we focused on some

smaller issues. Heavily salted water, we found, makes the eggs taste better than lightly salted water. We use at least 1 full teaspoon of salt in the filled skillet; otherwise the eggs are bland.

The next question: How to get the eggs into the boiling water without their breaking apart? Cracking the egg onto a saucer first, then add it to the water is often mentioned in old recipes, but you lose a lot of control as the slithery egg and gravity derail your aim. Cracked into a small cup and slipped into the water, the egg stays intact as it descends into purgatory. Each egg should be cracked into its own cup before the water boils. It may seem a lot easier to refill the same cup over and over with a freshly cracked egg than to wash two or four or more cups once the eggs are done, but you use a lot of precious time when you crack and pour the eggs in one at a time. If the eggs aren't in the water within seconds of each other, you'll have to keep track of which egg went in when, a nearly impossible proposition.

When the time's up, we use an oval-bowled slotted spoon to lift the eggs out of the poaching liquid. The spoon mimics the shape of the egg, so it nestles comfortably. A skimmer picks the egg up nicely, but we found that the egg rolls around dangerously on the flat surface.

We let the egg "drip-dry" by holding it aloft briefly over the skillet. For really dry eggs, a paper towel blots to the last drop. We actually liked a little of the cooking water to come along with the poached eggs (the better to taste the vinegar). Pass salt, pepper, and a bottle of Tabasco at the table, and your perfectly poached eggs are ready to eat.

Poached Eggs

SERVES 2

Poached eggs take well to any number of accompaniments. Try serving them on a bed of grated mild cheddar or Monterey Jack cheese or creamed spinach, in a pool of salsa, on a thick slice of tomato topped with a slice of Bermuda onion, on a potato pancake, or simply with plain buttered toast. See the illustration on page 633 for a tip on getting four eggs into boiling water at the same time.

Salt
2 tablespoons distilled white vinegar
4 large eggs, each cracked into a small handled cup
Ground black pepper

1. Fill an 8- to 10-inch nonstick skillet nearly to the rim with water, add 1 teaspoon salt and the vinegar, and bring the mixture to a boil over high heat.

2. Lower the lip of each cup just into the water at once; tip the eggs into the boiling water, cover, and remove the skillet from the heat. Poach until the yolks are medium-firm, exactly 4 minutes. For firmer yolks (or for extra-large or jumbo eggs), poach 4½ minutes; for looser yolks (or for medium eggs), poach 3 minutes.

3. With a slotted spoon, carefully lift and drain each egg over the skillet. Season to taste with salt and pepper and serve immediately.

OMELETS

MANY PEOPLE HAVE BEEN LED TO BELIEVE THAT you must be a trained chef to turn out a decent omelet. The truth is, while this may once have been the case, nonstick pans now make omelets a cinch. And that's good news, because omelets are a satisfying dish that can be made quickly—and with almost anything you happen to have on hand.

The traditional technique for cooking omelets involves a number of fairly tricky arm motions that take practice to master—stirring with a flat fork in a circular motion until the egg mixture has thickened, tapping the handle to dislodge the set eggs, and sliding the omelet up one side of the pan. However, the nonstick pan makes most of this unnecessary.

Using two eggs and a half tablespoon of butter (olive oil is also delicious and works just fine) for each omelet, we tested the classic technique to determine the simplest way to cook an omelet without compromising the taste. The vehicle was a 9-inch nonstick pan with sloping sides; the flat bottom of the pan measures about 5 inches.

In our first series of tests, we determined how

best to beat the eggs and which utensil to use—most classic recipes merely dictate that the eggs be "completely incorporated," although some say "beat until frothy" and others "beat until barely combined." We tried three methods of mixing the eggs: beating them lightly with a fork until the yolk and white are barely combined, beating more vigorously with a fork to mix them completely, and using a whisk to beat them until they turned frothy. The easiest and best method is to mix the eggs with a fork until they're well mixed; this gives the omelet a more uniform texture than if the eggs are beaten less. Beating with a whisk simply doesn't improve the texture.

The next step was to determine the best heat for cooking. Since many egg preparations call for gentle heat, we wondered if low heat would make a more tender omelet. It doesn't. All it does is slow down the cooking process. Medium-high to high heat cooks the eggs quickly, helping you to achieve the true omelet, what the famed French chef Escoffier called "scrambled eggs enclosed in a coating of coagulated egg," with a lovely brown exterior.

We also tried adding liquid to the eggs, using a bit less than a tablespoon each of water, milk, and cream in three separate egg mixtures. We found that the addition of any liquid helps the omelet remain moist in the event of overcooking, but it detracts from the flavor of the eggs. Water and milk merely lessen the purity of the eggs, while cream really competes and even overwhelms the flavor of the eggs.

PREPARING AN OMELET

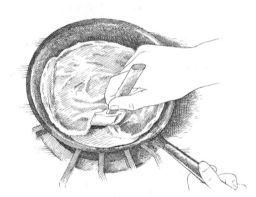

1. Pull the cooked eggs from the edges of the pan toward the center, tilting the pan so any uncooked egg runs to the pan's edges.

2. Transfer the pan to a cool burner. If making a filled omelet, sprinkle the filling down the center now. Fold the lower third of the eggs over the center, or for filled omelets fold over the filling. Press the seam to secure.

3. Pull the pan sharply toward you so the omelet slides up the far edge of the pan.

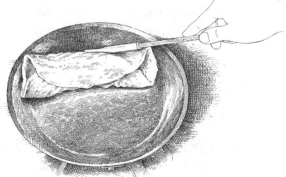

4. Fold the far edge of the omelet toward the center. Press to secure the seam. Invert the omelet onto a plate.

We then investigated the necessity of stirring the eggs as they cooked. The classic technique is to stir them until they thicken, then pull in the edges to finish. We also tested pulling in the edges until the omelet was set without any stirring. The results were clear. Stirring breaks up and integrates the cooked egg with the soft portions, giving the finished omelet a very consistent texture and a smooth appearance. If the eggs are not stirred during cooking, the omelet has a less homogeneous texture and a more uneven exterior. Stirring also shortens the cooking time.

We tried various methods of getting the omelet out of the pan, both with and without utensils. The technique of tapping the handle to slide the omelet up in the pan is one of the trickiest in cooking. But with a nonstick pan you can use a simple jerk of the handle to accomplish the same thing. Folding is easiest with a spatula; you can make the final fold as you turn the omelet out of the pan.

If you are flavoring the omelet with herbs, a dry grated cheese, or a small dice of onion or sweet pepper, just whisk the ingredient into the egg mixture. Add chunkier fillings just after the omelet has set, before you fold it. For a filling that must be cooked first, you can simply pour the egg mixture over the cooked filling, then cook and fold the two together.

Basic Omelet

SERVES 1

This basic omelet can be flavored as you like. Some of our favorite omelet variations follow this recipe. If you'd like to make a second omelet after the first is done, heat another 1½ teaspoons butter in the empty pan, add the egg mixture, and proceed to make the second omelet.

2	large eggs
	Salt and ground black pepper
1½	teaspoons unsalted butter

1. In a small bowl, beat the eggs and a pinch of salt and pepper lightly with a fork until mixed.

2. Heat the butter in an 8- or 9-inch nonstick pan over medium-high heat. When the butter stops foaming and just begins to color, pour in the eggs. Wait a few seconds until the edges of the omelet begin to set. Then stir in a circular motion with a heatproof rubber spatula until slightly thickened. Use the spatula to pull the cooked edges toward the center, then tilt the pan to one side so any uncooked egg runs to the edge of the pan. Repeat until the omelet is just set but still moist on the surface, 15 to 20 seconds.

3. Transfer the pan to a cool burner. Use a rubber spatula to fold the lower third (nearest you) of the omelet to the center; press gently with a spatula to secure the seams, maintaining the fold.

4. Run a spatula between the outer edge of the omelet and the pan to loosen. Jerk the pan sharply toward you a few times to slide the omelet up the far side of the pan. Jerk again so that 2 inches of the unfolded edge folds over itself, or use the spatula to fold the edge over. Invert the omelet onto a plate. Tidy the edge with the spatula. Serve immediately.

> VARIATIONS

Smoked Salmon Omelet

Follow the recipe for Basic Omelet through step 2. Just before folding, sprinkle 1 teaspoon minced fresh dill, chives, or scallion greens over the entire omelet, then place 2 tablespoons thin-sliced smoked salmon strips over the center third of the omelet. Fold and turn out as directed.

Cheese Omelet

Make an omelet according to the recipe for Basic Omelet. If using a hard grating cheese like Parmesan, beat 1 tablespoon grated cheese into the eggs before cooking. If using a softer cheese, such as Monterey Jack, cheddar, or soft goat cheese, sprinkle over the center third of the omelet just before folding. Fold and turn out as directed.

Mixed-Herb Omelet

Mince equal parts fresh parsley leaves, chives (or scallion greens), tarragon leaves, and chervil leaves (if available) to yield 1 tablespoon. Beat the eggs with the minced herbs. Make the omelet according to the recipe for Basic Omelet.

FRITTATAS

FRITTATAS HAVE ALL THE GOOD CHARACTERISTICS of omelets without the finicky cooking technique. Italian in origin, frittatas incorporate more filling, making them more substantial than omelets. They are also more forgiving than omelets when it comes to cooking. In the time it takes to make two omelets, you can make a frittata that feeds four. However, frittatas are not foolproof. It took some testing to avoid the common pitfalls—typically, toughness and dryness—and create a recipe that yielded a moist yet firm frittata every time.

The first issue we dealt with was pan size. Starting with six eggs, we made frittatas in skillets measuring 8 inches, 10 inches, and 12 inches. We found that the 10-inch pan was optimal. The frittata made in the 12-inch pan was too thin and ended up overcooked. The frittata made in the 8-inch pan took a little too long to cook, resulting in a dry and tough edge. We then tried making the same frittata in both a traditional pan and a nonstick pan. While we found we could produce satisfactory frittatas in both pans, we had to use a lot more oil in the traditional pan to prevent sticking, making the resulting frittata slightly greasy. The 10-inch nonstick pan was the winner.

After several tests, we determined that ¾ to 1 cup filling was enough for six eggs. Any more than that amount created problems with the frittata cooking evenly; any less and the frittata lacked substance. To keep the procedure simple, we wanted to sauté most of our fillings in the same pan as the frittata. Doing so would enable us, after sautéing, to simply pour the beaten eggs over the filling and proceed with shaping the frittata.

The methods for cooking the frittata fell into three camps: cooking the frittata fully on the stovetop, cooking the frittata fully in the oven, and starting the frittata on the stovetop and then finishing it in the oven. We first tried cooking the frittata fully on the stovetop, but no matter what we did, the underside always ended up tough and overcooked. Cooking the frittata fully in the oven proved problematic as well. We tried cooking at different temperatures and lengths of time, but the results were either too dry or unevenly cooked. A combination of the two turned out to work the best. Using this method, we cooked the frittata almost fully on top of the stove and then placed it in the oven to finish cooking the top. The resulting frittata was evenly cooked and firm without being too dry—exactly what we had been seeking.

Frittatas do not have to be eaten hot. They can be served at room temperature or even cold, so timing isn't an issue, as it is with omelets. Serve frittatas with potatoes, a vegetable side dish, and/or a leafy salad.

Fresh Herb and Parmesan Frittata

SERVES 2 TO 4

Cheese and herbs are the simplest additions to a frittata. This recipe (as well as the variations) can be served for breakfast, brunch, or supper, along with a vegetable or salad. Chilled or room-temperature frittatas can also be cut into thin wedges or squares and served as an hors d'oeuvre.

1	tablespoon extra-virgin olive oil
½	small onion, chopped fine
2	tablespoons minced fresh herb leaves, such as parsley, basil, dill, tarragon, or mint
⅓	cup freshly grated Parmesan cheese
¼	teaspoon salt
¼	teaspoon ground black pepper
6	large eggs, lightly beaten

1. Adjust an oven rack to the upper-middle position and heat the oven to 350 degrees.

2. Heat the oil in a 10-inch ovenproof nonstick skillet over medium heat. Swirl the skillet to distribute the oil evenly over the bottom and sides. Add the onion and sauté until softened, 3 to 4 minutes. Stir in the herb.

3. Meanwhile, beat the Parmesan cheese, salt, and pepper into the eggs with a fork in a medium bowl.

4. Pour the egg mixture into the skillet and stir lightly with a fork until the eggs start to set. Once the bottom is firm, use a thin plastic spatula to lift the frittata edge closest to you. Tilt the skillet slightly toward you so that the uncooked egg

runs underneath (see the illustration on page 639). Return the skillet to a level position and swirl gently to evenly distribute the egg. Continue cooking about 40 seconds, then lift the edge again, repeating the process until the egg on top is no longer runny.

5. Transfer the skillet to the oven and bake until the frittata top is set and dry to the touch, 2 to 4 minutes, removing it as soon as the top is just set.

6. Run a spatula around the skillet edge to loosen the frittata. Invert the frittata onto a serving plate. Serve warm, at room temperature, or chilled.

➤ VARIATIONS

Asparagus Frittata with Mint and Parmesan

Blanch the asparagus pieces in salted boiling water until crisp-tender, 1½ to 2 minutes; drain and set aside.

2	tablespoons extra-virgin olive oil
I	medium shallot, minced
I	tablespoon minced fresh mint leaves
2	tablespoons minced fresh parsley leaves
⅓	pound asparagus, tough ends snapped off (see the illustration on page 130), stalks cut into 1-inch pieces and blanched until crisp-tender
5	tablespoons freshly grated Parmesan cheese
¼	teaspoon salt
¼	teaspoon ground black pepper
6	large eggs, lightly beaten in a bowl

1. Adjust an oven rack to the upper-middle position and heat the oven to 350 degrees.

2. Heat the oil in a 10-inch ovenproof nonstick skillet over medium heat. Swirl the skillet to distribute the oil evenly over the bottom and sides. Add the shallot and sauté until softened, 3 to 4 minutes. Add the mint, parsley, and asparagus and toss to coat with the oil. Spread the asparagus in a single layer in the pan.

3. Meanwhile, with a fork beat 3 tablespoons of the Parmesan, the salt, and pepper into the beaten eggs.

4. Pour the egg mixture into the skillet and stir lightly with a fork until the eggs start to set.

Once the bottom is firm, use a thin plastic spatula to lift the frittata edge closest to you. Tilt the skillet slightly toward you so that the uncooked egg runs underneath (see the illustration on page 639). Return the skillet to a level position and swirl gently to evenly distribute the egg. Continue cooking about 40 seconds, then lift the edge again, repeating the process until the egg on top is no longer runny. Sprinkle the remaining 2 tablespoons cheese over the top of the frittata.

5. Transfer the skillet to the oven and bake until the frittata top is set and dry to the touch, 2 to 4 minutes, removing it as soon as the top is just set.

6. Run a spatula around the skillet edge to loosen the frittata. Invert the frittata onto a serving plate. Serve warm, at room temperature, or chilled.

Frittata with Potatoes, Cheddar, and Thyme
SERVES 4

If you have leftover potatoes, skip step 1 and add 1 cup diced cooked potatoes in step 3.

2	medium red potatoes (8 ounces), scrubbed and cut into ½-inch dice
	Salt
I	tablespoon unsalted butter
½	small onion, chopped fine
2	teaspoons chopped fresh thyme leaves
I	ounce cheddar cheese, grated (⅓ cup)
¼	teaspoon ground black pepper
6	large eggs, lightly beaten in a bowl

1. Bring the potatoes, 2 cups water, and 1 teaspoon salt to a boil in a medium saucepan over high heat. Reduce the heat and simmer until the potatoes are just tender, about 6 minutes. Drain and set aside.

2. Adjust an oven rack to the upper-middle position and heat the oven to 350 degrees.

3. Heat the butter in a 10-inch ovenproof nonstick skillet over medium heat. When the foaming subsides, add the onion and sauté until softened, 3 to 4 minutes. Add the cooked potatoes and thyme and toss to coat with the butter.

MAKING A FRITTATA

Once the bottom of the frittata is firm, use a thin plastic spatula to lift the edge closest to you. Tilt the skillet slightly toward you so that the uncooked egg runs underneath. Return the skillet to a level position and swirl gently to distribute the uncooked egg.

Spread the potatoes in a single layer.

4. Meanwhile, stir the cheese, ¼ teaspoon salt, and the pepper into the beaten eggs.

5. Pour the egg mixture into the skillet and stir it lightly with a fork until the eggs start to set. Once the bottom is firm, use a thin plastic spatula to lift the frittata edge closest to you. Tilt the skillet slightly toward you so the uncooked egg runs underneath (see the illustration above). Return the skillet to the level position and swirl gently to evenly distribute the egg. Continue cooking about 40 seconds and then lift the edge again, repeating the process until the egg on top is no longer runny.

6. Transfer the skillet to the oven and bake until the frittata top is set and dry to the touch, 2 to 4 minutes, removing it as soon as the top is just set.

7. Run a spatula around the skillet edge to loosen the frittata. Invert the frittata onto a serving plate. Serve warm, at room temperature, or chilled.

QUICHE

THERE IS NO DISPUTE ABOUT THE CHARAC-teristics of an ideal quiche: It must have a tender, buttery pastry encasing a velvety-smooth custard, neither too rich nor too lean, but silken on the tongue. Too often, quiche filling is wet or rubbery and the crust soggy.

Our quest: an unassailable quiche filling formula. In our search, we tried every probable and improbable custard combination, from whole eggs with whole milk to whole eggs with half-and-half to whole eggs with half milk and half heavy cream to eggs with several added yolks and all heavy cream.

The leanest of these mixtures tasted so, and we rejected it as boring, with no creamy mouthfeel. The filling made with half-and-half was not as rich as one would think because half-and-half contains just 11.7 percent butterfat; it was OK but not great. The mixture containing half whole milk (which has approximately 4 percent butterfat) and half heavy cream (with 36 percent butterfat) was significantly richer; combined, the two liquids averaged 20 percent butterfat, almost twice as much as the half-and-half filling. Whole eggs, extra yolks, and all heavy cream produced a custard that was just too much of a good thing: overpoweringly rich, too creamy even for us.

The best mixture, a medium-rich custard with good mouthfeel, fine taste, and adequate firmness, combined 2 whole eggs with 2 yolks, 1 cup of milk, and 1 cup of heavy cream. Baked in our favorite crust, it was just what we were looking for: a custard that was creamy but not cloyingly rich, its tender skin a luscious golden brown. The filling puffed slightly while baking, settling neatly as it cooled.

Of course, baking temperature is also an important factor regulating custard texture. High heat toughens egg proteins and shrinks the albumen, separating, or curdling, the mixture and squeezing out the water instead of keeping the egg in perfect suspension. Moderate heat works best.

We tested our different quiche formulas at temperatures ranging from 325 degrees to 400 degrees. Some cooks prefer to start baking at 400 degrees for 15 minutes, then reduce the heat to 350 degrees for the remaining time. We found 350 degrees slightly slow; by the time the custard set, the top, which remained a pallid yellow hue, had developed into a slightly rubbery, chewy skin. On the theory that warming the liquid in the custard would shorten baking time and keep the custard smoother, we tried heating the milk to 100 degrees before whisking in the eggs. Indeed, this custard set a few minutes faster, but it was otherwise unremarkable and still had a pallid top. We found that baking at 375 degrees was exactly right, setting the custard gently enough to maintain its creamy consistency, yet browning the top before it dried out and became rubbery.

As a test for doneness, we advise watching the oven, not the clock, looking for a light golden brown coloring on the quiche surface, which may puff up slightly as it bakes. A knife blade inserted about one inch from the edge should come out clean; the center may still be slightly liquid, but internal heat will finish the baking, and the center will solidify when cool. If your test blade comes out clean in the center, the quiche may already be slightly overbaked and should be removed from the oven at once. Be sure to set the baked quiche on a wire rack to cool, so air circulates all around it, preventing condensation on the bottom. Allowing the quiche to cool until it is either warm or at room temperature also lets the custard settle before serving. The cooler the quiche, the more neatly it will slice.

Quiche Lorraine
SERVES 8

Quiche Lorraine is named after the region in France where it originated, Alsace-Lorraine. The center of the quiche will be surprisingly soft when it comes out of the oven, but the filling will continue to set (and sink somewhat) as it cools. If the pie shell has been previously baked and cooled, place it in the heating oven for about 5 minutes to warm before filling it, taking care that it does not burn. Because the ingredients in the variations that follow are bulkier, the amount of custard mixture has been reduced to prevent the filling from overflowing the shell.

1   recipe Pie Dough for Prebaked Pie Shell (page 883)
8   ounces (about 8 slices) bacon, cut into ½-inch pieces
2   large eggs plus 2 large egg yolks
1   cup whole milk
1   cup heavy cream
½   teaspoon salt
½   teaspoon ground white pepper
    Pinch freshly grated nutmeg
4   ounces Gruyère cheese, grated (about 1 cup)

1. Heat the oven to 375 degrees. Follow the directions for partially baking the pie shell until light golden brown. Remove the pie shell from the oven but do not turn off the oven.

2. Meanwhile, fry the bacon in a skillet over medium heat until crisp and browned, about 5 minutes. Transfer the bacon with a slotted spoon to a paper towel–lined plate.

3. Whisk all the remaining ingredients except the cheese in a medium bowl.

4. Spread the cheese and bacon evenly over the bottom of the warm pie shell and set the shell on the oven rack. Pour the custard mixture into the pie shell (it should come to about ½ inch below the rim of the crust). Bake until light golden brown, a knife blade inserted about 1 inch from the edge comes out clean, and the center feels set but soft like gelatin, 32 to 35 minutes. Transfer the quiche to a rack to cool. Serve warm or at room temperature.

VARIATIONS
Crabmeat Quiche
Follow the recipe for Quiche Lorraine, reducing the quantities of milk and cream to ¾ cup each. Add 2 tablespoons dry sherry and a pinch cayenne pepper to the custard mixture. Replace the bacon and cheese with 8 ounces (1 cup) picked-over cooked crabmeat tossed with 2 tablespoons chopped fresh chives.

Leek and Goat Cheese Quiche
Sauté the white parts of 2 medium leeks, washed thoroughly and cut into ½-inch dice (about 2 cups), in 2 tablespoons unsalted butter over medium heat until soft, 5 to 7 minutes. Follow the recipe for Quiche Lorraine, reducing the quantities of milk and cream to ¾ cup each. Omit the bacon; substitute 4 ounces mild goat cheese, broken into ½-inch pieces, for the Gruyère. Add the leeks with the goat cheese.

Ham and Asparagus Quiche

Blanch 8 asparagus stalks, cut on the bias into ½-inch pieces (about 1 cup), in 1 quart salted boiling water until crisp-tender, about 2 minutes. Drain thoroughly. Follow the recipe for Quiche Lorraine, reducing the quantities of milk and cream to ¾ cup each. Replace the bacon and cheese with the asparagus and 4 ounces deli baked ham, cut into ¼-inch dice.

BREAKFAST STRATA

WHAT'S QUICKER THAN QUICHE, STURDIER than soufflé, and combines the best qualities of both? The answer is strata, a layered casserole that, in its most basic form, includes bread, eggs, cheese, and milk or cream. Layered among them are flavorful fillings that provide both substance and character, and the result is essentially a golden brown, puffed, hearty, savory bread pudding. Strata is easy to prepare, can be made ahead, and feeds a crowd for breakfast or brunch.

But strata is not without its issues. First, it is easy to go overboard with too much of a good thing. Many of the stratas we sampled in the test kitchen were simply too rich for breakfast, with a belly-busting overabundance of custard. The bread should neither call attention to itself nor get lost among the other ingredients. And then there are the fillings. Some stratas suffer simply from largesse, with recipes adding as many fillings as can be squeezed in. This everything-but-the-kitchen-sink approach leads to wet, sagging, overworked stratas. A good strata should have a restrained filling with a couple of components chosen to accent the bread, custard, and cheese.

In essence, then, we wanted to scale strata back, keeping it just rich enough and choosing fillings that would add to the picture without stealing the show. We also wanted a cohesive casserole rather than a bunch of stray ingredients baked together in a dish. All the principal parts—custard, bread, and fillings, and how and when they were assembled and cooked—were subject to review.

Bread is the foundation of strata. Though sliced white sandwich bread was the type specified in most recipes, we also saw calls for Italian, French, sourdough, multigrain, rye, pumpernickel, challah, focaccia, and even hamburger and hot dog buns. We tried them all, and tasters preferred supermarket Italian and French breads for their strong crumb and neutral flavor. Since tasters had no objection to the crust, we left it on. Also, while many recipes specify that the bread be cubed, we preferred it in slices, as they only added to the layered effect of the casserole. The slices were best about ½ inch thick, as thicker ones remained too chewy and thin ones became lost in the custard. We learned, too, that the texture of stale bread (or fresh bread dried briefly in the oven) was preferable to that of fresh and came to appreciate the richness and flavor a little butter on the slices added.

We then turned our attention to the tender custard that binds the bread. In a battery of custard tests, tasters' preferences were divided between mixtures with equal parts dairy and egg and those with twice as much dairy as egg. The solution was to meet in the middle, adding just a little extra dairy to the 50-50 mixture. Along the way, we also tested different dairy products. Recipes commonly call for low-fat or whole milk or half-and-half and sometimes even heavy cream (usually in combination with another dairy liquid). We tried each one of these alone and in every conceivable combination, and most tasters preferred half-and-half on its own. The last adjustment we made to the custard was its overall quantity, which for many tasters was too little, making for a dry strata. Increasing the ratio of custard to bread made the strata more moist and cohesive.

Though our basic strata was very good, it's the flavorings and fillings that catapult it to glory. As a basic flavoring, sautéed shallots won over onions and garlic. We had a surprise in store when we tested another flavoring common to strata recipes—namely, white wine. It showed promise, lightening the flavor of the whole dish. But it also imparted a boozy flavor that was out of place. We corrected this problem by reducing the wine to cook off the alcohol and concentrate the flavor. This eliminated the alcoholic overtones, and the reduced wine brightened the flavor of the whole dish considerably.

One last observation we can offer about the most basic seasonings, salt and pepper: A heavy hand is best. Strata required a generous amount of each, and seasoning both custard and filling individually and liberally was the most effective way to bring all the flavors into focus.

Even with the right basic ingredients in the right proportions, test after test proved that high-moisture fillings, such as sausage and raw vegetables, ruined the texture. Their moisture leached into the casserole, leaving it wet enough to literally slosh and ooze when cut. To prevent this, we took to sautéing all filling ingredients until they looked dry in the pan. This step saved the day by evaporating moisture that would otherwise end up in the strata. Whatever your filling choice, this critical step will make the difference between a moist, tender dish and one that's more like a sopping-wet sponge mop.

One of strata's charms is that it can—in fact, most recipes claim it should—be assembled well ahead of time. We tested stratas that had been assembled and rested overnight, for four hours, and for one hour, as well as another that had not been rested at all. Only the fresh-made strata, which was noticeably less cohesive than the rested versions, failed to make the cut. Otherwise, there wasn't much difference among them in texture. So you can give it the rest that fits your schedule best, anywhere from one hour to overnight.

A test kitchen colleague suggested weighting the assembled strata down during its rest, and this step had a dramatic effect. Without exception, the weighted stratas had perfectly even, custardy textures throughout. In rested stratas without the weight, we were apt to encounter a bite of bread not fully permeated with custard.

When it came to the actual baking of the casserole, we found that a wide, shallow baking dish allowed the strata to bake much more evenly than the deep soufflé dish recommended in many recipes. Lowering the baking temperature from the frequently recommended 350 degrees to 325 was another tactic we adopted to even out the cooking.

Cooking the strata until the top was crisp and golden brown was a common directive, but we found that this usually overcooked the interior, leaving it too firm, even a bit rubbery. Instead, we found it best to remove the strata from the oven when the top was just beginning to brown and the center was barely puffed and still slightly loose when the pan was jiggled gently. Though we wondered if the strata was cooked through, with just a five-minute rest it not only cooled enough to eat without burning our throats on the way down, but the center finished cooking from residual heat, reaching the perfectly set, supple texture we prized.

Breakfast Strata with Spinach and Gruyère
SERVES 6

To weight down the assembled strata, use two 1-pound boxes of brown or powdered sugar, laid side by side over the plastic-covered surface. To double this recipe or the variation that follows, use a 13 by 9-inch baking dish greased with 1½ tablespoons butter and increase the baking times as suggested in each recipe.

8–10	(½-inch-thick) slices supermarket French or Italian bread
5	tablespoons unsalted butter, softened
4	medium shallots, minced
1	(10-ounce) package frozen chopped spinach, thawed and squeezed dry
	Salt and ground black pepper
½	cup medium-dry white wine, such as Sauvignon Blanc
6	ounces Gruyère cheese, grated (about 1½ cups)
6	large eggs
1¾	cups half-and-half

1. Adjust an oven rack to the middle position and heat the oven to 225 degrees. Arrange the bread in a single layer on a large baking sheet and bake until dry and crisp, about 40 minutes, turning the slices over halfway through the drying time. (Alternatively, leave the slices out overnight to dry.) When the bread has cooled, butter the slices on one side with 2 tablespoons of the butter; set aside.

2. Heat 2 tablespoons of the butter in a medium nonstick skillet over medium heat. Sauté the shallots until fragrant and translucent, about 3 minutes; add the spinach and salt and pepper to taste and cook, stirring occasionally, until combined, about 2 minutes. Transfer to a medium bowl; set aside. Add the wine to the skillet, increase the heat to medium-high, and simmer until reduced to ¼ cup, 2 to 3 minutes; set aside.

3. Butter an 8-inch square baking dish with the remaining 1 tablespoon butter; arrange half of the bread slices buttered-side up in a single layer in the dish. Sprinkle half of the spinach mixture, then ½ cup grated cheese evenly over the bread slices. Arrange the remaining bread slices in a single layer over the cheese; sprinkle the remaining spinach mixture and another ½ cup cheese evenly over the bread. Whisk the eggs in a medium bowl until combined; whisk in the reduced wine, the half-and-half, 1 teaspoon salt, and pepper to taste. Pour the egg mixture evenly over the bread layers; cover the surface flush with plastic wrap, weight down (see note), and refrigerate at least 1 hour or up to overnight.

4. Remove the dish from the refrigerator and let stand at room temperature 20 minutes. Meanwhile, adjust an oven rack to the middle position and heat the oven to 325 degrees. Uncover the strata and sprinkle the remaining ½ cup cheese evenly over the surface. Bake until both the edges and the center are puffed and the edges have pulled away slightly from the sides of the dish, 50 to 55 minutes (or about 60 minutes for a doubled recipe). Cool on a wire rack for 5 minutes; serve.

➤ VARIATION
Breakfast Strata with Sausage, Mushrooms, and Monterey Jack

8–10	(½-inch-thick) slices supermarket French or Italian bread
3	tablespoons unsalted butter, softened
8	ounces bulk breakfast sausage, crumbled
3	medium shallots, minced
8	ounces white button mushrooms, wiped clean and quartered
	Salt and ground black pepper
½	cup medium-dry white wine, such as Sauvignon Blanc
6	ounces Monterey Jack cheese, shredded (about 1½ cups)
6	large eggs
1¾	cups half-and-half
2	tablespoons minced fresh parsley leaves

Follow the recipe for Breakfast Strata with Spinach and Gruyère through step 1. Fry the sausage in a medium nonstick skillet over medium heat, breaking the sausage apart with a wooden spoon, until it loses its raw color and begins to brown, about 4 minutes; add the shallots and cook, stirring frequently, until softened and translucent, about 1 minute longer. Add the mushrooms and cook until they no longer release liquid, about 6 minutes; transfer to a medium bowl and season with salt and pepper to taste. Reduce the wine as directed in step 2; continue with the recipe from step 3, adding the parsley to the egg mixture along with the salt and pepper and substituting the sausage mixture for the spinach. (For a doubled recipe, increase the baking time to about 1 hour 20 minutes.)

FRENCH TOAST

FRENCH TOAST (OR IN FRENCH, *PAIN PERDU*, meaning "lost bread") started out as a simple way to use up old bread by dipping it in beaten egg and frying it. Many recipes today deviate little from this basic technique, calling for a couple of eggs and a touch of milk. What they produce, however, is a toast that tastes mostly of fried egg and that, depending on the amount of liquid, is either overly soggy or still dry in the middle.

We wanted something quite different: bread that was crisp and buttery on the outside, soft and custard-like on the inside. We sought a balance of flavors rather than just egg. Our ideal French toast had to be sweet enough to eat with only a sprinkling of confectioners' sugar, but not so sweet that we couldn't top it with syrup or fruit if we chose.

INGREDIENTS: Maple Syrup

What good are pancakes, waffles, or French toast without maple syrup? We wondered how the consumer should buy maple syrup. By grade? By source (is Vermont syrup really better than the rest)? We also wondered if any of the pancake syrups—those supermarket staples made with a tiny percentage of maple syrup—were demonstratively better than their peers.

In general, a maple syrup's grade is determined by the period during which it was made (the sugaring season lasts from February to early April). Technically, the grades of maple syrup are measured by the amount of light that can pass through the syrup. Straight from the tree, maple sap is clear, consisting of about 98 percent water and 2 percent sugar. To make maple syrup, the water has to be boiled off to a concentration of 66 percent sugar. (This means boiling off about 39 gallons of water to get 1 gallon of syrup.)

Early in the season, maple syrups tend to be near-transparent because the sugar molecules in the boiled-down sap are able to reflect much light. As temperatures warm outside, wild yeasts in the sap begin feeding up and breaking down the sugar. As a result, light can be absorbed. So, as the season progresses, the syrup darkens.

This breakdown of sugar also affects flavor. If maple sap is concentrated without boiling (by freeze-drying, for example), the syrup will taste sweet but otherwise have little flavor. The flavor we perceive as "maple" is actually the result of chemical reactions that occur when the sap is boiled. One of the two primary flavor notes is derived from the compounds that form when sugar molecules break down. The process is similar to caramelizing. This may explain why the darker syrups produced later in the season have more of the caramel notes distinct to maple syrup. The second flavor note is vanilla, which is produced from compounds in the sap that the tree uses to make wood.

While vanilla and caramel are essential maple flavor elements, the full flavor of maple is far more complex. One producer's syrup can vary from a neighbor's because of differences in the soil, the tree chemistry, or the method of heating the sap.

The season's earliest sap flow produces grade A light, or "fancy," as it is called in Vermont. Honey gold and near-transparent, it has a pronounced sweetness and a delicate vanilla flavor. Grade A light can be the most expensive syrup and is not typically found in supermarkets. While it takes no more energy to produce than the other grades, its higher price was established more than 100 years ago, when "sugaring" was about just that—turning maple syrup into sugar. The lighter syrup made a finer sugar that could be sold at a higher cost—and so it still is today. Today grade A light syrups are primarily used to make maple sugar candies.

The season's second syrup is grade A medium amber. This has a warmer caramel color with a medium-strength flavor. It is generally touted as the syrup for pancakes. Right on the heels of medium amber is grade A dark amber, which is slightly deeper in color and has a more pronounced flavor.

After the ambers comes grade B, the darkest and typically least expensive of the syrups on the market. It is traditionally considered cooking grade because of its strength of flavor. Only Vermont makes grade B syrup for consumer table use. Other states make a similar syrup but sell it only in bulk to the food industry because it is deemed too strong and too dark. Some natural food stores carry it in bulk.

Last, there is a grade C, characterized by a strong, almost molasses-like flavor. Sold only to the food industry, grade C is used in commercial pancake syrups.

Of the nine samples we tried, tasters decided that if they had the choice, they would reach for the Vermont grade B syrup to drizzle on their pancakes. Most tasters were won over by the depth of flavor and the dark rum color of the syrup. Many wrote comments such as "tastes real." And, unlike many of the syrups, which lost their distinction when poured on a waffle, this one's bold characteristics held up.

The close runner-up in our tasting was a grade A dark amber. Overall, tasters preferred the dark amber syrups to the medium ambers, which failed to spark tasters' interest, apparently because they were not bold enough. Not surprisingly, then, tasters flat-out rejected the one "fancy" grade syrup we included in the tasting. None of our results indicated syrup made from one region or state is superior to another, and industry experts agree that it is difficult, if not impossible, to determine by taste where a syrup is made.

Because pancake syrups far outsell real maple syrups, we decided to do an additional tasting of the three top-selling national pancake syrups. The high scorer was Aunt Jemima, which is made from high-fructose corn syrup, with just 4 percent maple syrup. We found that even this low percentage of maple syrup gave Aunt Jemima a decent maple flavor. It was superior to the other pancake syrups, one made with less maple syrup and the other with none.

We started testing with a simple formula: 2 eggs beaten with ½ cup milk to soak 4 slices of ¾-inch-thick, day-old French bread. From this starting point, we wanted to settle first on which bread works best for French toast, but that proved to be the hardest part of the testing. At first, it seemed simple. One-inch-thick slices of any sort of bread were too thick; they either soaked up too much liquid and didn't cook through, or they stayed dry in the middle with shorter soaking. So we stuck with ¾-inch-thick slices and tried different kinds of bread: baguettes, supermarket breads, challah and brioche, and a dense white bread.

At the end of these tests, we thought we had the answer. Challah was clearly best, adding a lot of flavor and richness, staying generally crisp outside and somewhat moist inside—not perfect but likely to improve with changes in the liquid component. Baguette slices and slices of a high-quality Italian bread, so long as they weren't more than a day old, came in second. Hard-to-find brioche was only acceptable. Brioche can vary widely in quality, and the open-textured version we were using failed to take up the liquid evenly. Dense white bread simply tasted like fried bread, so it rated near the bottom. Presliced sandwich bread was acceptable in a pinch, although just barely. Worst, though, was the supermarket bakery version of French or Italian bread. Spongy and flabby, this bread simply fell apart when we took it out of the liquid. For the moment, the bread issue seemed resolved. So, using challah for testing, we moved on to the liquids.

Because we didn't want our French toast to be too eggy, we first tried dropping the number of eggs in the test recipe from two to one. That decision showed an immediate improvement, yielding a finished product that was crispier outside but still soft inside. To be sure that fewer eggs made for a better result, we tried going the opposite way, using 3 eggs to ½ cup milk. That confirmed it: More egg seemed to create a barrier on the outside of the bread, causing the interior to stay dry while the outside tasted like fried egg.

The next logical step seemed to be to increase the milk, given that a higher proportion of milk to egg had worked so far. A jump to 1 cup milk made the bread too wet inside, but it was better than ½ cup. Three quarters of a cup proved to be ideal, as the toast stayed custard-like inside and fairly crisp outside.

Throughout our tests with egg and milk, our basic recipe had tasted flat. We were looking forward to the final tests, when we would add other ingredients. We first tried salt, which gave the recipe a big boost: Just ¼ teaspoon and the toast finally had some flavor. We added sugar next, which also made a great difference. At this point, 1 tablespoon seemed like a good amount for toast that would be covered with syrup; after making the recipe adjustments described below, though, we found that 2 tablespoons proved best. Finally, we added vanilla. Few recipes call for it, but 2 teaspoons really balanced the flavors.

After all this, we had a French toast that was better than any we could remember, yet still not ideal. It was fairly crisp, but not exactly what we were after: an almost deep-fried crispness. We knew the sugar helped, but there had to be something else we could do. When one editor mentioned a French toast version she'd once had in which the bread was dipped in pancake batter, plus a recipe that called for a pinch of flour, it got us thinking about what flour could do. Ultimately, what it did was solve the puzzle.

At first we liked 1 tablespoon flour, which helped to further crisp the exterior and keep the toast from becoming greasy. In later tests, however, we noticed that this made the toast somewhat soggy inside; yet when we went up to 2 tablespoons, the bread became tough. So we started trying more flour—but with butter added to the batter to keep the bread from toughening. After a few more tests, we finally had fabulous French toast: A batter with ⅓ cup flour balanced by 2 tablespoons melted butter turned the outside of the challah evenly crisp and brown and let just enough moisture through to the interior to keep it custard-like but not heavy.

Unfortunately, our perfect French toast recipe worked wonders with challah but failed with chewy French and Italian breads. While we strongly recommend using challah if you can, we know it's less likely to be the day-old bread people have on hand. So we worked out a separate recipe for French and Italian breads, but we recommend it with a caveat: If you're using soft supermarket-style French bread or sliced white sandwich bread, go with the challah recipe. With a chewier, drier French or Italian loaf, however, the high amount of flour in the batter used for challah prevented needed moisture from soaking into the bread. Also, the exterior had a harder time crisping because the rougher surface of this somewhat open-textured bread didn't make good contact with the pan. To get more moisture to the interior, we tried dropping some of the flour; to better crisp the exterior, we again tried a two-egg recipe. Neither trick worked. In the end, more tests showed that the recipe needed even more milk for a custard-like interior and just 1 tablespoon of flour to aid in crisping; with this little flour, the batter needed no butter.

French Toast for Challah or Sandwich Bread

MAKES 4 TO 5 SLICES FROM CHALLAH OR 6 TO 8 SLICES FROM SANDWICH BREAD

Though thick-sliced challah is best for French toast, you can substitute high-quality, presliced sandwich bread. Flipping challah is easiest with tongs, but a spatula works best with sandwich bread. To speed the cooking of large quantities, heat 2 or more skillets to brown a few batches at once. To vary the flavor of the batter, add ¾ teaspoon ground cinnamon or ½ teaspoon ground nutmeg with the dry ingredients, or substitute almond extract for the vanilla.

1	large egg
2	tablespoons unsalted butter, melted
¾	cup milk
2	teaspoons vanilla extract
2	tablespoons sugar
⅓	cup unbleached all-purpose flour
¼	teaspoon salt
4–5	slices day-old challah, ¾ inch thick, or 6–8 slices day-old high-quality sandwich bread
	Unsalted butter for frying (1 tablespoon per batch)

1. Heat a 10- or 12-inch skillet (preferably cast iron) over medium heat for 5 minutes. Meanwhile, beat the egg lightly in a shallow pan or pie plate; whisk in the melted butter, then the milk and vanilla, and finally the sugar, flour, and salt, continuing to whisk until smooth. Soak the bread without oversaturating, about 40 seconds per side for challah or 30 seconds per side for sandwich bread. Pick up the bread and allow the excess batter to drip off; repeat with the remaining slices.

2. Swirl 1 tablespoon butter in the hot skillet. Transfer the prepared bread to the skillet in a single layer; cook until golden brown, about 1 minute 45 seconds on the first side and 1 minute on the second. Serve the French toast immediately. Continue, adding 1 tablespoon butter to the skillet for each new batch.

French Toast for Firm European-Style Bread

MAKES 4 TO 8 SLICES, DEPENDING ON THE LOAF

This recipe has less flour than the version above, which allows the batter to penetrate more easily into drier, chewier French or Italian loaves.

1	large egg
1	cup milk
2	teaspoons vanilla extract
2	tablespoons sugar
1	tablespoon unbleached all-purpose flour
¼	teaspoon salt
4–8	slices firm, day-old European-style bread, such as French or Italian, ¾ inch thick
	Unsalted butter for frying (1 tablespoon per batch)

1. Heat a 10- or 12-inch skillet (preferably cast iron) over medium heat for 5 minutes. Meanwhile, beat the egg lightly in a shallow pan or pie plate; whisk in the milk and vanilla, and then the sugar, flour, and salt, continuing to whisk until smooth. Soak the bread without oversaturating, about 30 seconds per side. Pick up the bread and allow the excess batter to drip off; repeat with the remaining slices.

2. Swirl 1 tablespoon butter in the hot skillet. Transfer the prepared bread to the skillet in a single layer; cook until golden brown, about 2 minutes on the first side and 1 minute 15 seconds on the second. Serve immediately. Continue, adding 1 tablespoon butter to the skillet for each new batch.

PANCAKES

IN OUR MINDS, THE ULTIMATE PANCAKE IS ONE that can only mean light and fluffy in texture and sweet and tangy in flavor. Unfortunately, most pancakes are either so tough and rubbery that they snap back and smack you in the face or so cottony and tasteless that they must be accompanied by a very tall glass of milk.

We began by cooking up a big stack of pancake recipes. The test kitchen came to a few conclusions. One: We like our pancakes tender and fluffy. Two: Even though we were after the best pancake, we wanted to avoid any nonsensical techniques or ingredients that required a jaunt to the grocery store, especially given that we would likely be making these pancakes early in the morning, with only one eye open and one cup of coffee running through our veins.

First up was flour, and because this no-nonsense recipe would not put up with a blend of flours, we pitted cake flour, bleached all-purpose flour, and unbleached all-purpose flour against one another. The pancake made with cake flour lacked structure, and the flour gave the pancake a strange, chemical taste. The pancake made with bleached all-purpose flour had a similar "off" flavor, making unbleached flour—usually the test kitchen standard—the winner.

Sugar was next, and the question was not whether to add it but how much to add. We like pancakes on the sweet side. Starting at 1 teaspoon of sugar, we worked our way up until tasters cried "enough" at 2 tablespoons. As for leavener, we were hoping to use just baking powder, but, sure enough, tasters preferred the golden brown color that baking soda provided, so in the end we opted to use them both. Two teaspoons of baking powder and ½ teaspoon of baking soda did the job. Finally, a little salt went in to accentuate the whole.

In most pancake recipes, the dry ingredients are measured out, and the wet ingredients, such as eggs, melted butter, and dairy (usually milk or buttermilk), are added. Most recipes call for 2 eggs per 2 cups of flour, but tasters unanimously found these cakes to be too eggy. Using an egg and a fraction thereof (one whole egg plus one egg yolk) was too fussy for our recipe, so we simply used one egg. What about butter—was it necessary? One quick test later, we found the answer to be an emphatic yes. Without butter, the pancakes were more evenly colored (no spots of scorched butter), but they had the cottony interior that we just couldn't stomach. We melted 3 tablespoons of butter, added it to the batter, and everyone was happy.

As for the dairy, we tested milk and buttermilk and also threw half-and-half into the mix to see what would happen. To no one's surprise, buttermilk took first place. This tangy, thick liquid produced a pancake with great flavor and beat-all fluffiness. But to be true to our "rule number three," we couldn't pretend that buttermilk would be found on most people's lists of basic pantry ingredients. We needed a substitute.

A quick search on the Internet led us to a few

IS THE PAN READY?

NOT YET   **TOO HOT**

The only way to know when the pan is ready is to make a test pancake about the size of a half dollar (use 1 tablespoon of batter). If, after 1 minute, the pancake is blond in color (left), the pan is not hot enough. If, after 1 minute, the pancake is golden brown, the pan is heated correctly. Speeding up the process by heating the pan at a higher temperature will result in a dark, unevenly cooked pancake (right).

buttermilk impostors, usually a little distilled white vinegar, cream of tartar, or lemon juice stirred into regular milk, then left to sit for a few minutes to thicken. This faux buttermilk method mimics the effects of the modern process of making buttermilk, which is produced by injecting milk with acidic bacterial cultures. The cultures not only give buttermilk that characteristic tang, but they also thicken it. When we compared the buttermilk pancakes with pancakes made with the lemon and milk mixture, we were surprised to find that those made with lemon juice had a tang that was similar to that provided by the buttermilk ("sour" was the word for those made with vinegar or cream of tartar). Even more surprising was that tasters preferred the pancakes made with lemon juice and whole milk over those made with buttermilk. One tablespoon of lemon juice per 2 cups of milk was the right amount. After allowing the mixture to sit for a few minutes, it thickened to a consistency much like that of buttermilk. (If

you should happen to have buttermilk on hand when you're feeling in a pancake way, by all means use it.)

We had an inkling that overmixing was likely to produce a tough, rubbery pancake. Boy, were we right. When we whisked the batter until no lumps of flour were detectable, the pancakes were tough. We cannot emphasize enough that a less thorough mixing is needed here, until the ingredients are just blended. A few lumps or streaks of flour here and there, and you know that you've done it correctly.

The best method for cooking our pancakes was simply to ladle out some batter onto a hot nonstick skillet coated with a thin film of vegetable oil. It's important to heat your skillet over medium heat, not high heat; otherwise, the pancakes will scorch before they've had time to cook through.

SCIENCE: Why Does Lumpy Pancake Batter Produce Fluffier Pancakes?

There are two factors that promote fluffiness in pancake batter: underdeveloped gluten and dissolved baking soda. Gluten is a mix of very long proteins that are disorganized in structure. Once gluten is dissolved in water, these proteins can more easily rearrange their structure. Kneading or mixing gluten elongates the proteins and somewhat organizes them, an action similar to combing the strands of your hair. As the proteins start to lie more or less parallel to each other, the dough becomes elastic and less tender. By reducing the mixing time of your batter, you give the gluten less opportunity to organize.

Baking soda (either on its own or as part of the baking powder formula) creates the bubbles that make pancakes rise. When baking soda encounters an acid, carbon dioxide is formed to produce the bubbles in the batter. The stirring of the pancake batter speeds bubble formation by moving the baking soda and acid together. Unfortunately, stirring also causes the release of carbon dioxide gas by bringing formed bubbles to the surface of the mixture. Just a little too much stirring can quickly exhaust the bubble-forming capacity of the baking soda. To make the fluffiest pancakes possible, then, you should stir the batter until the ingredients are just incorporated—and not one stir more!

Light and Fluffy Pancakes
MAKES ABOUT SIXTEEN 4-INCH PANCAKES, SERVING 4 TO 6

If you have buttermilk on hand, use 2 cups instead of the milk and lemon juice mixture. To keep pancakes warm while you cook the remaining batter, see the tip on page 650.

I	tablespoon juice from I lemon
2	cups milk
2	cups (10 ounces) unbleached all-purpose flour
2	tablespoons sugar
2	teaspoons baking powder
1/2	teaspoon baking soda
1/2	teaspoon salt
I	large egg
3	tablespoons unsalted butter, melted and cooled slightly
I–2	teaspoons vegetable oil

1. Whisk the lemon juice and milk together in a medium bowl or large measuring cup; set aside to thicken while preparing the other ingredients. Whisk the flour, sugar, baking powder, baking soda, and salt in a medium bowl to combine.

2. Whisk the egg and melted butter into the milk until combined. Make a well in the center

of the dry ingredients in the bowl; pour in the milk mixture and whisk very gently until just combined (a few lumps should remain). Do not overmix.

3. Heat a 12-inch nonstick skillet over medium heat for 3 to 5 minutes (see the photos on page 647 for tips on gauging when the pan is properly heated); add 1 teaspoon oil and brush to coat the skillet bottom evenly. Pour ¼ cup batter onto 3 spots on the skillet. Cook the pancakes until large bubbles begin to appear, 1½ to 2 minutes. Using a thin, wide spatula, flip the pancakes and cook until golden brown on the second side, 1 to 1½ minutes longer. Serve immediately. Repeat with the remaining batter, using the remaining vegetable oil only if necessary.

➤ VARIATION
Blueberry Pancakes

Rather than following the traditional technique of folding the blueberries into the batter, we like to sprinkle the berries over the pancakes as they set in the pan. This step makes for intact berries and attractive unmottled cakes. When local blueberries are not in season, frozen blueberries are a better alternative. To make sure that frozen berries do not bleed, rinse them under cool water in a mesh strainer until the water runs clear, then spread them on a paper towel–lined plate to dry.

Have ready 1 cup fresh or frozen blueberries, preferably wild, rinsed and dried. Follow the recipe for Light and Fluffy Pancakes. Sprinkle 1 tablespoon blueberries over each pancake just after pouring the batter into the pan.

EQUIPMENT: Electric Griddles

With countertop real estate so valuable, we're wary about buying "extra" appliances, such as an electric griddle. But after standing in front of what must have been our 40th batch of blueberry pancakes, we gave electric griddles a second thought. Many electric griddles have a bigger cooking surface than even a 12-inch skillet (which will fit only three pancakes at a time comfortably). The possible payoff—less time cooking—was too good to resist.

We bought the four largest models we could find. They were seemingly identical. All had an electric probe with an indicator light that turned off when the selected temperature was reached, all were fully immersible or dishwasher-safe (except for the electric probe control), all were made of cast aluminum with a nonstick coating, all had a hole or channel so that excess fat would drain into a removable grease tray. After heating each griddle to 350 degrees, we poured on the batter (each griddle fit eight pancakes at a time) and checked the pancakes for even browning. We also cooked bacon on each griddle.

The Broil King Extra Large Griddle ($49.99), which measured a whopping 21 inches by 12 inches and was the only griddle that could comfortably hold a full pound of bacon (16 slices), was the clear winner. Good thing that it also had one of the largest grease trays. Its only downfall was the excruciating 12½ minutes it took to heat up to 350 degrees. But this could be due to the thickness of the aluminum griddle. After it reached the proper temperature, there was very little temperature fluctuation. As a result, pancakes were evenly cooked every time.

The West Bend Cool Touch Electric Griddle ($39.99) was the runner-up. The cooking surface measured 20½ by 10½ inches and could hold 12 slices of bacon. The West Bend heated up to 350 degrees in 6½ minutes and cooked pancakes very evenly. One minor drawback: The grease channel was slightly cumbersome to wash.

The remaining two models, the Rival Electric Griddle ($29.99) and the Presto Cool Touch Electric Griddle ($38.99), were the same size as the West Bend, and both heated up to 350 degrees in 5½ minutes. The cooking surfaces on both models heated unevenly, however, and some pancakes were noticeably lighter in color than others. Also, some of the pancakes spread out very thin because of cool spots.

Are electric griddles worth the counter space? If you find yourself making stacks of pancakes and pounds of bacon every weekend, you can't beat the speedy delivery they provide.

THE BEST ELECTRIC GRIDDLE

The Broil King griddle took top honors in our testing, in part because it is so big. It also demonstrated even browning, without any of the cool spots that plagued other models.

KEEPING PANCAKES WARM

A large skillet can turn out only three pancakes at a time, so if you want everyone to eat at the same time, you must keep the first few batches warm. After testing various methods suggested in cookbooks (most of which suggest covering the pancakes, causing them to become steamed and rubbery), we discovered that pancakes will hold for 20 minutes when placed on a greased rack set on a baking sheet in a 200-degree oven. The warm oven keeps the pancakes hot enough to melt a pat of butter, and leaving the pancakes uncovered prevents them from becoming soggy.

WAFFLES

AFTER TESTING MORE THAN 15 RECIPES, WE realized that our ideal waffle requires a thick batter, so the outside can become crisp while the inside remains custardy. We also learned that a good waffle must cook quickly; slow cooking evens out the cooking rate, causing the center to overcook by the time the exterior is crisp and browned.

Many waffle batters are too thin, usually because the proportion of milk to flour—at 1 cup each—is too high. Such thin batter results in disappointing, gummy-textured waffles with dry, unappealing interiors. We found that ⅞ cup buttermilk, or ¾ cup sweet milk, to 1 cup flour is a far better proportion.

Most recipes omit buttermilk entirely or, at best, list it as an option. Yet we found that buttermilk is absolutely crucial. Why? Because buttermilk, when teamed up with baking soda, creates a much thicker batter than the alternative, sweet milk paired with baking powder. We eventually found a way to make good waffles with sweet milk (reduce the amount of liquid and use homemade baking powder for a thicker batter), but buttermilk waffles will always taste better.

Although many recipes for buttermilk waffles call for baking powder, it's not necessary. All that's required is baking soda, which reacts with the acid in the buttermilk to give the batter lift. Baking powder is essentially baking soda plus cream of tartar, an acidic ingredient. Baking powder is useful when the batter itself contains no other source of acid. We eliminated the baking powder from our working recipe and realized that it wasn't necessary or helpful; these waffles cooked up crispier. Out of curiosity, we also tried to make a waffle with buttermilk and baking powder, eliminating the baking soda. Waffles prepared this way were inedible.

Because crispness is so important in waffles, we tried substituting cornmeal for a bit of the flour and found that 1 tablespoon per cup of flour adds extra crackle. We also experimented with the addition of cake flour, which is lower in protein than all-purpose flour, and found that it produces a finer crumb and a more tender product. This waffle lacked that desirable contrast between a crisp exterior and a creamy interior.

Some waffle recipes call for separating the egg and then whipping the white and folding it into the mixed batter. We made waffles this way and found that this extra step adds to the good. The beaten whites make the batter glossier and the waffle fluffier inside. If you cut through a cooked waffle made with beaten egg whites, you can actually see pockets of air trapped inside. The same examination of a whole-egg waffle revealed a flatter, more consistent texture.

Look at a number of waffle recipes and you'll see a wide range of recommendations as to how to combine ingredients. But most have this in common: They add all of the liquid ingredients at once. This practice necessitates overmixing and usually results in clumps of unmoistened flour. When we used a whisk to combine the ingredients until they were smooth, the batter was thin and the waffle tough.

The objective is to moisten the flour thoroughly, not to create a smooth batter, and for this there is no question that a gentle hand is crucial. This is the technique that worked best for us: Pour the liquid ingredients into the dry ingredients very slowly, mixing gently with a rubber spatula. When most of the liquid has been added, the batter becomes thicker; switch to a folding motion, similar to that used in folding egg whites, to finally combine and moisten the batter. Then continue folding as you add the beaten egg white.

When you bake waffles, remember that darker waffles are better than lighter ones. The browning reaction promotes the development of flavor. Waffles should be cooked until medium-brown, not lightly tanned. Toasty brown waffles will also stay crispier longer than manila-colored waffles, which are likely to become soggy by the time they get to the table.

Buttermilk Waffles

MAKES 3 TO 4, DEPENDING ON SIZE OF
WAFFLE IRON

The secret to great waffles is a thick batter, so don't expect a pourable one. The optional dash of cornmeal adds a pleasant crunch to the finished waffle. This recipe can be doubled or tripled. Make toaster waffles out of leftover batter—undercook the waffles a bit, cool them on a wire rack, wrap them in plastic wrap, and freeze. Then pop them in the toaster for a quick breakfast.

1	cup (5 ounces) unbleached all-purpose flour
1	tablespoon cornmeal (optional)
1/2	teaspoon salt
1/4	teaspoon baking soda
1	large egg, separated
7/8	cup buttermilk
2	tablespoons unsalted butter, melted and cooled

1. Heat a waffle iron. Whisk the dry ingredients together in a medium bowl. Whisk the egg yolk with the buttermilk and melted butter.

2. Beat the egg white until it just holds a 2-inch peak.

3. Add the liquid ingredients to the dry

EQUIPMENT: Waffle Irons

Waffle irons range in price from less than $20 to almost $100. Is there as wide a range in quality? To find out, we gathered eight classic (not Belgian) models. There were two types of iron: The first group, large and square, yielded huge perforated waffles that can be torn into four smaller squares for individual servings; the second yielded a much smaller, round waffle that serves one.

All of the models tested featured a sensor that lit or dimmed to indicate whether the waffle was ready. All but two models had adjustable temperatures, letting you choose how dark you want your waffles. The two un-adjustable models—the Hamilton Beach/Proctor Silex Waffle Baker, priced at $16.99, and the Toastmaster Cool-Touch Waffle Baker, priced at $19.99—produced insipid waffles. Neither model is recommended.

Our favorite irons were those that produced waffles with good height and dark, even browning. Topping the list were two VillaWare models (Uno Series Classic Waffler 4-Square, $89.95, and Classic Round, $59.95); the Cuisinart Classic Waffle Maker, $29.95; and the Black and Decker Grill and Waffle Baker, $56.99. The VillaWare models featured not only a ready light but also a ready bell.

A more meaningful feature on which to base your choice is size. The VillaWare Classic Round and Cuisinart irons are fine if you don't mind making one small waffle at a time. In the end, we preferred the convenience of the VillaWare 4-Square and the Black and Decker Grill and Waffle Baker, which cook four individual waffles at once. While the VillaWare produced a marginally better waffle (which was slightly darker and more evenly colored), the Black and Decker costs $30 less and also features reversible griddle plates.

BEST PERFORMANCE
The VillaWare Uno Series Classic Waffler 4-Square makes the best waffles, and the iron chimes when the waffles are done, but note the high price, around $90.

BEST VALUE
The Black and Decker Grill and Waffle Baker makes big, beautiful waffles and also doubles as a griddle. A great value at about $57.

ingredients in a thin, steady stream while mixing gently with a rubber spatula. (Do not add liquid faster than you can incorporate it into the batter.) Toward the end of mixing, use a folding motion to incorporate the ingredients. Gently fold the egg white into the batter.

4. Spread an appropriate amount of batter onto the waffle iron. Following the manufacturer's instructions, cook the waffle until golden brown, 2 to 5 minutes. Serve immediately. (In a pinch, you can keep waffles warm on a wire rack in a 200-degree oven for up to 5 minutes.)

➤ VARIATION
Sweet-Milk Waffles
MAKES 3 TO 4

If you're out of buttermilk, try this sweet-milk variation. By making your own baking powder and by cutting back on the quantity of milk, you can make a thick, quite respectable batter. The result is a waffle with a crisp crust and a moist interior.

Follow the recipe for Buttermilk Waffles, adding ½ teaspoon cream of tartar to the dry ingredients and substituting a scant ¾ cup milk for the buttermilk.

OATMEAL

OATS ARE A COOL-CLIMATE GRAIN CROP THAT make for excellent animal feed but must be cleaned, toasted, hulled, and then cleaned again if they are to be used for human consumption. This process makes what are called oat groats. Similar in appearance to brown rice, oat groats are not readily available in stores and make more of a nutty rice-type dish than a creamy cereal food.

The oat cereal product most familiar to American households—next to Cheerios—is rolled oats, an American innovation of the late 19th century. Rolled oats are made by steaming oat groats and flattening them with large rollers. In supermarkets, you will find two types of rolled oats—quick-cooking and regular, which are also known as old-fashioned. Quick-cooking are cut into smaller pieces before rolling and are rolled thinner than the regular variety, so the cereal takes

just one minute to cook versus five. In the test kitchen, we tried making hot cereal with both.

The quick-cooking were a bit powdery and had no real flavor, but they did have a pleasant mushy consistency. In a matter of minutes, however, the bowl of oatmeal cooled and gelled into a flabby paste. Hot oatmeal from Quaker old-fashioned oats turned out a slightly more bulky bowl of cereal but was still insubstantial, drab, and flecky in texture. We did try regular rolled oats purchased in the bulk section of a natural food store. They were noticeably more golden in color than the Quaker variety and had better flavor. As we later learned, the rolled oats sold in natural food store bulk bins are often flash-toasted during processing.

Instant oats, often sold in individual flavor packets, are a slightly different species, made with cut groats that have been precooked and dried before being rolled. So, amazingly, all you must do is stir a packet into boiling water, and you've got breakfast, if you want to call it that. What we really ended up with was a bowl of gelled oat chaff that was quick to lose its moisture and heat.

As it turns out, many Scottish and Irish cooks scorn American rolled oats, saying they make a sloppy bowl of "porridge." We figured we should carefully consider the opinion of these renowned oat eaters. In these countries, oatmeal is made from steel-cut oats—groats that have been cut into a few pieces but have not been otherwise processed or rolled. Also known as Scotch oats, Irish oatmeal, or pinhead oats, they can typically be found in the bulk foods section of natural food stores. Supermarkets carry pricey canned varieties, but all of the tins we tried were stale.

Making hot oatmeal from steel-cut oats took considerably longer than making it with regular rolled oats (25 to 30 minutes total), but the outcome was very much worth the wait. The hot cereal had a faint nutty flavor, and, while its consistency was surprisingly creamy, it was also toothsome; there was a firm core to the soft oat granules that whimsically popped between your teeth when chewed. Now we had to do some fine-tuning to determine how to bring out the best texture and flavor of these oats.

Taking a clue from the flash-toasting technique of the natural food store's rolled oats, we tried toasting the steel-cut oats. This definitely helped to accent the nutty flavor. Because oats are high in oil content and thus quick to burn, we found toasting them in a skillet as opposed to the oven provided better control. And, to no great surprise, toasting the oats with a little butter in the skillet lent them a sweet, rounded nutty flavor, with an aroma like butterscotch.

As for the cooking method, we tried a variety of approaches: adding to boiling water then dropping to a simmer, boiling constantly, simmering only, starting in cold water, covered versus uncovered, and so on. The ultimate goal was to determine which method would create the creamiest bowl of oatmeal without it being too mushy.

Starting in cold water is supposed to make the creamiest oatmeal. It did, but it was mushy, too. There was no kernel pop. Tasters agreed that the cereal needed to be more toothsome. Starting in boiling water and dropping to a simmer did just that. But so did simmering only, and that made for a creamier oatmeal, too, with just five or so more minutes in cooking time.

With the cooking technique down, all we needed to test was the cooking medium. We had been using water only. A few recipes used milk, but our oatmeal was so creamy with just water we thought milk would push it over the top. When completely replacing the water, milk was indeed over-the-top, as well as quick to burn the pan bottom. A ratio of 3 parts water to 1 part milk, however, added a pleasant roundness in texture and flavor to the oatmeal.

Many oatmeal recipes require frequent stirring. Surprisingly, we found that when oats are cooked slowly at a moderate simmer, they do not need constant attention for the first 20 minutes of cooking time. It is in the final five to eight minutes, when the hot cereal has swelled and just a bit of liquid remains on top that the pot must be stirred to blend the liquid and oats and to prevent sticking. We found that the last eight minutes is also the best time to stir in the salt (salt added early in the cooking process will toughen the oats and prevent a creamy porridge). Following an old tradition, we confirmed that the rounded handle end of a wooden spoon is the best stirring tool. Stirring with the usual end of a spoon, like stirring early in the cooking process or stirring frequently, results in a mushier, less toothsome oatmeal.

INGREDIENTS: Orange Juice

Can anything rival the juice you squeeze at home? To find out, we gathered 34 tasters to evaluate 10 brands of supermarket orange juice as well as juice we squeezed in the test kitchen and juice fresh-squeezed at the supermarket.

Our top choice had been squeezed the day before at a local supermarket, closely followed by the juice we squeezed ourselves. Cartons of chilled, not-from-concentrate juices took third and seventh places, with three brands of frozen concentrate squeezed in the middle. Chilled juices made from concentrate landed at the bottom of the rankings.

How could juice squeezed the day before at a supermarket beat out juice squeezed minutes before the tasting? And how could frozen concentrate beat out more expensive chilled juices from concentrate?

The produce manager at the store where we bought fresh-squeezed juice told us he blends oranges to produce good-tasting juice. This can be a real advantage, especially when compared with juice squeezed at home from one kind of orange. Any loss in freshness can be offset by the more complex and balanced flavor of a blended fresh juice, as was the case in our tasting.

Although no one was surprised that the two fresh juices took top honors, the strong showing of the frozen concentrates was a shock. It seems that frozen concentrate doesn't deserve its dowdy, old-fashioned reputation.

Why does juice made at home from frozen concentrate taste better than prepackaged chilled juice made from concentrate? Heat is the biggest enemy of orange juice. Frozen concentrates and chilled juices not made from concentrate are both pasteurized once at around 195 degrees to eliminate microorganisms and neutralize enzymes that will shorten shelf life. Chilled juices made from concentrate are pasteurized twice, once when the concentrate is made and again when the juice is reconstituted and packaged. This accounts for the lack of fresh-squeezed flavor in chilled juices made from concentrate.

Finally, we found that a rest period is essential after cooking because the consistency changes significantly with just slight cooling. The creamy grains pull together like a pudding. For this reason, it's important that the oatmeal still be a bit liquidy when it is pulled off the heat. It holds its heat well during the resting period, but much liquid evaporates. If you cover the pot during the five-minute rest period, moisture condenses on the lid and drips back down on the hot cereal, so it's better without the lid.

Oatmeal

SERVES 3 TO 4

Many supermarkets sell prepackaged steel-cut oats, but we found they were often stale and always expensive. A better option is to purchase them in the bulk section of a natural food store. To double the recipe, use a large skillet to toast the oats; increase the cooking time to 10 to 15 minutes once the salt has been added. If desired, pass maple syrup or brown sugar separately when serving, or try the topping that follows.

3	cups water
I	cup whole milk
I	tablespoon unsalted butter
I	cup steel-cut oats
1/4	teaspoon salt

1. Bring the water and milk to a simmer in a large saucepan over medium heat. Meanwhile, heat the butter in a medium skillet over medium heat until just beginning to foam; add the oats and toast, stirring constantly with a wooden spoon, until golden and fragrant with a butterscotch-like aroma, 1½ to 2 minutes.

2. Stir the toasted oats into the simmering liquid and reduce the heat to medium-low; simmer gently, until the mixture thickens and resembles gravy, about 20 minutes. Add the salt and stir lightly with a spoon handle. Continue simmering, stirring occasionally with a wooden spoon handle, until the oats absorb almost all the liquid and the oatmeal is thick and creamy, with a pudding-like consistency, 7 to 10 minutes. Off the heat, let the oatmeal stand uncovered for 5 minutes. Serve immediately, with the following topping, if desired.

Honeyed Fig Topping with Vanilla and Cinnamon

MAKES ABOUT I CUP, ENOUGH FOR
4 SERVINGS OF OATMEAL

5	ounces dried figs (about I cup), each fig stemmed and quartered
I½	tablespoons honey
I½	tablespoons water
1/8	teaspoon vanilla extract
1/8	teaspoon ground cinnamon

Bring the figs, honey, water, vanilla, and cinnamon to a simmer in a small saucepan over medium-high heat; cook until the liquid reduces to a glaze, about 4 minutes. Spoon a portion of the topping over individual bowls of hot oatmeal; serve immediately.

CORNED BEEF HASH

CORNED BEEF HASH CAN BE TRACED BACK TO New England ingenuity and frugality. What was served as boiled dinner the night before was recycled as hash the next morning. All the leftovers—meat, potatoes, carrots, and sometimes cabbage—would be fried up in a skillet and capped with an egg. This being a dish of leftovers, we found traditional recipes to be few and far between, as if corned beef hash were a commonsense dish, unworthy of a recipe. And the recipes we did find produced starchy, one-dimensional hash that was light on flavor. Knowing most people do not have leftovers from a boiled dinner sitting in their refrigerators, we set out to create a flavorful hash with fresh ingredients that was easy to prepare.

Meat and potatoes are the heart and soul of this dish; everything else is just seasoning. While leftover beef from the boiled dinner on page 427 is ideal, we found that deli-style corned beef can be just as satisfying. At first, we diced the meat into pieces equivalent in size to the potatoes, but this led to tough and chewy meat that sharply contrasted with the potato's velvety softness. Mincing the beef kept it tender and imparted a meatier flavor to the hash. There is no need for a uniform mince; we coarsely chopped the meat and then worked our knife back and forth across the rough dice until the meat was reduced to ¼-inch or smaller pieces.

Potatoes were an easy choice. Texture being foremost, we knew we wanted starchy potatoes that would retain some character but that would soften and crumble about the edges to bind the hash together. We quickly ruled out anything waxy, such as red potatoes, because they remained too firm. Russets were our top choice.

Prior to being combined with the beef, the potatoes must be parboiled. While we generally boil our potatoes whole and unpeeled so they don't absorb too much liquid, we discovered that dicing the potatoes prior to cooking worked fine in this instance. And they cooked more quickly, too. To echo the flavors of the corned beef, we added a couple of bay leaves and a bit of salt to the cooking water. About four minutes of cooking after the potatoes had come to a boil yielded perfect potatoes—soft but not falling apart.

As far as other vegetables, tasters quickly ruled out anything but onions. Carrots may be traditional, but tasters agreed that their sweetness compromised the simplicity of the hash. Onions, on the other hand, added characteristic body and roundness that supported the meat and potatoes rather than detracting from it. We liked them best cooked slow and steady until lightly browned and meltingly soft. Along with the onions, we chose garlic and thyme to flavor the hash. Garlic sharpened the dish and a minimum of thyme added an earthiness that paired well with the beef.

Although the potatoes loosely bound this mixture, most recipes call for either stock or cream to hold the ingredients more firmly together. We tested both and preferred the richness of the cream. A little hot pepper sauce added with the cream brought some spice to the dish.

After cooking several batches of hash at varying temperatures and with differing techniques, we realized that a fairly lengthy cooking time was crucial to flavor. The golden crust of browned meat and potatoes deepened the flavor of the hash. Recipes we tried dealt differently with the crust: Some preserved the crust in one piece, cooking both sides by flipping the hash or sliding it onto a plate and inverting it back into the skillet; other recipes suggested breaking up the crust and folding it back into the hash. After trying both styles, tasters preferred the latter, feeling that it had a better overall flavor. (And it's a lot easier than trying to flip a mound of the heavy, unwieldy hash.) We lightly packed the hash into the skillet with the back of a wooden spoon, allowed the bottom to crisp up, and then folded it over the top and repeated the process several times. In this way, the crisp browned bits get evenly distributed.

Tasters agreed that the eggs served with hash need to be just barely set, so that the yolks break and moisten the potatoes. While poaching is the easiest technique for preserving a lightly cooked yolk, it does involve another pan. We found that we could make hash a one-pot meal by "poaching" the eggs in the same pan as the hash. We simply nestled the eggs into the indentations in the hash, covered the pan, and cooked them over low heat. The results were perfect: runny yolks with the eggs conveniently set in the hash and ready to be served.

Corned Beef Hash
SERVES 4

A well-seasoned cast-iron skillet is traditional for this recipe, but we preferred a 12-inch nonstick skillet. The nonstick surface leaves little chance of anything sticking and burning. Our favorite tool for flipping the hash is a flat wooden spatula, although a stiff plastic spatula will suffice. We like our hash served with ketchup.

2	pounds russet potatoes, peeled and cut into ½-inch dice
	Salt
2	bay leaves
4	ounces (4 slices) bacon, diced
1	medium onion, diced
2	medium garlic cloves, minced or pressed through a garlic press

½ teaspoon minced fresh thyme leaves

1 pound corned beef, minced (pieces should be ¼ inch or smaller)

½ cup heavy cream

¼ teaspoon hot pepper sauce

4 large eggs

Ground black pepper

1. Bring the potatoes, 5 cups water, ½ teaspoon salt, and the bay leaves to a boil in a medium saucepan over medium-high heat. Once the water boils, cook the potatoes for 4 minutes, drain, and set aside.

2. Place the bacon in a 12-inch nonstick skillet over medium-high heat and cook until the fat is partially rendered, about 2 minutes. Add the onion and cook, stirring occasionally, until the onion has softened and browned about the edges, about 8 minutes. Add the garlic and thyme and cook until fragrant, 30 seconds. Add the corned beef and stir until thoroughly combined with the onion mixture. Mix in the potatoes and lightly pack the mixture into the pan with a spatula. Reduce the heat to medium and pour the heavy cream and hot pepper sauce evenly over the hash. Cook, undisturbed, for 4 minutes, then, with the spatula, invert the hash, a portion at a time, and fold the browned bits back into the hash. Lightly pack the hash into the pan. Repeat the process every minute or two until the potatoes are thoroughly cooked, about 8 minutes longer.

3. Make 4 indentations (each measuring about 2 inches across) equally spaced on the surface of the hash. Crack 1 egg into each indentation and season the egg with salt and pepper to taste. Reduce the heat to medium-low, cover the pan, and cook until the eggs are just set, about 6 minutes. Cut the hash into 4 wedges, making sure each has an egg, and serve immediately.

BACON

MANY HOME COOKS NOW USE THE MICROWAVE to cook bacon, while others still fry bacon in a skillet. In restaurants, many chefs "fry" bacon in the oven. We decided to try each of these methods to find out which worked best.

For each cooking technique, we varied temperature, timing, and material, cooking both a typical store-bought bacon and a thick-cut mail-order bacon. The finished strips were compared in terms of flavor, texture, and appearance, while the techniques were compared for consistency, safety, and ease.

While the microwave would seem to have the apparent advantage of ease—stick the pieces in and forget about them—this turned out not to be the case. The bacon was still raw at 90 seconds; at 2 minutes it was medium well-done in most spots, but still uneven; by 2½ minutes the strips of bacon were hard and flat and definitely overcooked. The finished product didn't warrant the investment of time it would take to figure out the perfect number of seconds for cooking the bacon properly. Microwaved bacon is not crisp; it is an unappetizing pink-gray in color even when well-done, and it lacks flavor.

The skillet made for a significantly better product. The bacon flavors were much more pronounced than in the nuked version, the finished color of the meat was a more appealing brick red, and the meat had a pleasing crispness. There were, however, a number of drawbacks to pan-frying. In addition to the functional problems of grease splatter and the number of 11-inch strips you can fit into a 12-inch round pan, there are problems of consistency and convenience. Because all of the heat comes from below the meat, the strips brown on one side before the other. Moreover, even when using a cast-iron pan, as we did, heat is not distributed perfectly evenly across the bottom of the pan. This means that to get consistently cooked strips of bacon, you have to turn them over and rotate them in the pan. In addition, when more strips are added to an already-hot pan, they tend to wrinkle up, making for raw or burnt spots in the finished product.

The best results from stovetop cooking came when we lowered the heat from medium to medium-low, just hot enough to sizzle. The lower temperature allowed the strips to render their grease more slowly, with a lot less curling and spitting out of the pan. Of course, this added to the cooking time, and it did not alleviate the need for vigilance.

Oven-frying seemed to combine the advantages of the microwaving and pan-frying while eliminating most of the disadvantages. We tried cooking three strips in a preheated 400-degree oven on a 12 by 9-inch rimmed baking sheet that would contain the grease. The bacon was medium well-done after 9 to 10 minutes and crispy after 11 to 12 minutes. The texture was more like a seared piece of meat than a brittle cracker, the color was that nice brick red, and all of the flavors were just as bright and clear as when pan-fried. Oven-frying also provided a greater margin of error when it came to timing than either of the other methods, and, surprisingly, it was just about as easy as microwaving, adding only the steps of preheating the oven and draining the cooked bacon on paper towels. Finally, the oven-fried strips of bacon were more consistently cooked throughout, showing no raw spots and requiring no turning or flipping during cooking. Because

TASTING: Supermarket Bacon

Food enthusiasts and the media have made a fracas lately over the fact that retail bacon sales in America have risen sharply, nearly 50 percent over the last few years. Unfortunately, much of the media attention has been focused solely on expensive, artisan-produced specialty bacon rather than on the mass-produced brands that most home cooks buy at supermarkets and warehouse clubs.

We wondered if there was really a difference among supermarket brands, so we assembled 24 tasters in the test kitchen to sample 10 different nationally available supermarket bacons. We focused our tasting on plain, regular-cut bacon—leaving aside center-cut, thick- and thin-cut, flavored, specialty wood-smoked, low-salt, reduced-fat, precooked, and microwave-ready. We did, however, include one nitrite-free "natural" sample because it is popular at our local natural food market. The bacons sampled in the tasting were labeled "regular sliced" and "hardwood smoked" or "hickory smoked." The bacon was oven-fried per *Cook's* recipe to the same degree of doneness (based on the browning of the meat). Different tasters tried samples in different orders to eliminate the effects of palate fatigue, and one sample was repeated twice as a control. Tasters rated the bacon on a 10-point scale and judged saltiness, sweetness, smokiness, and meatiness.

One product, the nitrite-free Applegate Farms Sunday Bacon, took tasters by surprise. Complaints arose about its unexpectedly pale color and particularly mild flavor. A little knowledge of nitrites explains these characteristics. Sodium nitrite helps fix the red shade of the meat from its raw state by combining with the pigment myoglobin. Nitrites also contribute to bacon's characteristic cured flavor. It makes sense, then, that Applegate Farms bacon neither looked nor tasted the way most tasters expected. Having conducted hundreds of blind tastings over the years, our test kitchen has found that most folks prefer the familiar over the unfamiliar. Although Applegate did receive positive ratings from a couple of tasters, for most of us nitrite-free bacon is an acquired taste.

Tasters liked the nine other brands well enough to recommend them all. The highest-rated product among them was Farmland, which tasters picked out as particularly meaty, full-flavored, and smoky. Furthermore, neither of the two other prominent flavors in bacon—salt and sweet—dominated, and tasters appreciated the balance.

THE BEST SUPERMARKET BACON

Farmland Hickory Smoked Bacon (left) was the top choice among tasters in our test kitchen. Tasters gave this supermarket bacon high marks for its favorable balance of saltiness and sweetness, "good smoke flavor," and "crispy yet hearty" texture. Boar's Head Brand Naturally Smoked Sliced Bacon (middle) and Hormel Original Black Label Bacon (right) were close runners-up, each garnering such compliments as "meaty" and "boasting a hearty balance of flavor."

the heat hits the strips from all sides, there is no reason for the bacon strips to curl in one direction or another, and when the strips do curl, the ruffled edges cook as quickly as the flat areas.

Our last test was to cook 12 strips of bacon—a pretty full tray—in a preheated oven. This test was also quite successful. The pieces cooked consistently, the only difference being between those in the back and those in the front of the oven; we corrected for this by rotating the tray once from front to back during cooking. That was about the limit of our contact with the hot grease.

Oven-Fried Bacon

SERVES 4 TO 6

Use a large rimmed baking sheet that is shallow enough to promote browning yet deep enough (at least ¾ inch) to contain the rendered bacon fat. If cooking more than one sheet of bacon, exchange the oven positions of the pans once about halfway through the cooking process.

12   slices bacon, thin- or thick-cut

Adjust an oven rack to the middle position and heat the oven to 400 degrees. Arrange the bacon slices on a rimmed baking sheet or in another shallow baking pan. Roast until the fat begins to render, 5 to 6 minutes; rotate the pan front to back. Continue roasting until the bacon is crisp and browned, 5 to 6 minutes longer for thin-cut bacon, 8 to 10 minutes for thick-cut. Transfer with tongs to a paper towel–lined plate, drain, and serve.

HOME FRIES

WHEN WE BEGAN TRYING TO UNCOVER THE secret of the brunch favorite, ultimate home fries, we went right to the source—diners. But soon we learned that the problems with this dish are often the same, no matter where they are cooked and consumed. Frequently, the potatoes are not crisp, they are greasy, and the flavorings are either too bland or too spicy.

Our first step was to define home fries: individual pieces of potato cooked in fat in a frying pan on top of the stove and mixed with caramelized onions. We also knew what they should look and taste like: They should have a deep golden brown crust and a tender interior with a full potato flavor. The potatoes should not be greasy but instead feel crisp and moist in your mouth.

We knew the potatoes would end up in a skillet with fat, but would it be necessary to precook them, as our research suggested? We began testing with the simplest approach: Dice the potatoes raw and cook them in a hot skillet with fat. But in test after test, no matter how small we cut them, it proved challenging to cook raw potatoes all the way through and obtain a crisp brown crust at the same time. Low temperatures helped cook the inside, but the outside didn't crisp. High temperatures crisped the outside, but the potatoes had to be taken off the heat so early to prevent scorching that the insides were left raw. We decided to precook the potatoes before frying them in a skillet.

Potatoes that were boiled until tender broke down in the skillet, and the inside was overcooked by the time the exterior was crisp. So we tried dicing and then braising the potatoes, figuring we could cook them through in a covered pan with some water and fat, remove the cover, let the water evaporate, and then crisp up the potatoes in the remaining fat. Although this sounded like a good idea, the potatoes stuck horribly to the skillet.

Finally, we considered a technique we found in Lydie Marshall's book *Passion for Potatoes* (Harper Perennial, 1992). Marshall instructs the cook to cover diced raw potatoes with water, bring the water to a boil, and then immediately drain the potatoes well and sauté them. This treatment allows the potatoes to cook briefly without absorbing too much water, which is what makes them susceptible to overcooking and breaking down.

We tested this technique with russets, Red Bliss potatoes, and Yukon Golds. Eureka! It worked better with all three varieties of potato than any of the other methods we had tried. The Yukon Golds, though, were the clear favorite. Each individual piece of potato had a crisp exterior, and the inner flesh was tender, moist, and rich in potato flavor. The appearance of each was superior as well, the golden yellow color of the flesh complementing the crispy brown exterior. The russets were drier and not as full-flavored but were preferred over the Red Bliss, which all tasters found to be somewhat mushy and disappointingly bland.

Deciding whether or not to peel the potatoes was easy. All tasters preferred the texture and flavor contributed by the skin. Leaving it on also saved time and effort.

Thus far, we had determined that letting the potatoes sit undisturbed in hot fat to brown each side was critical to a crisp exterior. We found it best to let the potatoes brown undisturbed for four to five minutes before the first turn, then to turn them a total of three or four times. Three tablespoons turned out to be the ideal amount of fat for one pound of potatoes. When sampling potatoes cooked in different frying mediums, we found that a 50-50 combination of butter and oil offered the best of both worlds, providing a buttery flavor with a decreased risk of burning (butter burns more easily than vegetable oils). Refined corn and peanut oils, with their nutty overtones, were our first choices.

Soft, sweet, and moist, onions are the perfect counterpoint to crispy potatoes, but we had to determine the best way to include them. Tests showed the easiest and most efficient way also produced the best results: Dice the onions and cook them before cooking the potatoes. More

flavor can be added with help from red or green bell pepper (sautéed with the onion) or cayenne pepper, as you wish. Whatever your choice, these are home fries worth staying home for.

Home Fries

SERVES 2 TO 3

If you need to double this recipe, instead of crowding the skillet, cook 2 separate batches. While making the second batch, you can keep the first batch hot and crisp by spreading the potatoes on a rimmed baking sheet and placing it in a 300-degree oven. The paprika adds a warm, deep color, but it can be omitted. An alternative for color is to toss in 1 tablespoon minced fresh parsley leaves just before serving the potatoes.

2½	tablespoons corn or peanut oil
1	medium onion, chopped into small pieces
1	pound Yukon Gold or all-purpose potatoes (2 medium), scrubbed and cut into rough dice (see the illustrations below)
	Salt
1	tablespoon unsalted butter
1	teaspoon paprika
	Ground black pepper

1. Heat 1 tablespoon of the oil in a 12-inch heavy-bottomed skillet over medium-high heat until hot but not smoking. Add the onion and

ROUGH DICING

1. Slice the potato lengthwise into quarters.

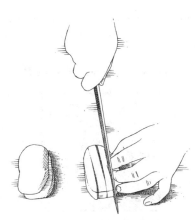

2. Make two stacks and cut each stack lengthwise into quarters.

3. Turn the stacks 90 degrees and cut horizontally to complete the dice.

cook, stirring frequently, until browned, 8 to 10 minutes. Transfer the onion to a small bowl and set aside.

2. Meanwhile, place the diced potatoes in a large saucepan, cover with ½ inch water, add 1 teaspoon salt, and place over high heat. As soon as the water begins to boil, after about 6 minutes, drain the potatoes thoroughly in a colander.

3. Heat the butter and remaining 1½ tablespoons oil in the now-empty skillet over medium-high heat until the butter foams. Add the potatoes and shake the skillet to evenly distribute the potatoes in a single layer; make sure that one side of each piece is touching the surface of the skillet. Cook, without stirring, until one side of the potatoes is golden brown, 4 to 5 minutes, then carefully turn the potatoes with a wooden or heatproof plastic spatula. Spread the potatoes in a single layer in the skillet again and repeat the process until the potatoes are tender and browned on most sides, turning 3 or 4 times, 10 to 15 minutes longer. Add the onion, paprika, ¼ teaspoon salt, and pepper to taste; stir to blend and serve immediately.

➤ VARIATIONS

Spicy Home Fries

Follow the recipe for Home Fries, adding a pinch or two of cayenne pepper to the potatoes along with paprika.

Home Fries with Bell Pepper and Cumin

Follow the recipe for Home Fries, cooking 1 red or green bell pepper, finely chopped, with the onion. Remove the pepper with the onion and add both back to the pan along with the paprika and 1 teaspoon ground cumin.

SCIENCE: Out of Hot Water and Into the Frying Pan

So what happens to the starch and moisture content of diced potatoes when they are cooked first in water and then in fat? The potato starch granules are composed of layer upon layer of tightly packed starch molecules. When the potatoes are first put in cold water, nothing happens to the starch molecules. As the water heats, it warms the molecules and starts seeping in between the layers. The hotter the water gets, the more rapidly it works its way into the softer areas of the granules, causing them to expand. Finally, near the boiling point, the starch molecules swell so much that they burst. By removing the diced potatoes just as the water begins to boil, the water absorption is stopped before the granules have a chance to explode.

When the just-boiled potatoes come into contact with hot fat, the starch granules on the surface expand immediately and absorb water from the inside of the potato. The moisture rushing to the surface creates the sizzling sound, and the expanding granules begin to seal the surface. If the surface is sealed and too much moisture remains stuck inside, the texture of the potato will be mushy; if there is not enough moisture on the inside, the texture will be dry and mealy; if there is no moisture left on the inside and the surface has not sealed, the starch granules will begin to absorb fat and the potatoes will be greasy. Medium-starch potatoes such as Yukon Golds have an ideal moisture content in that when a crisp crust has formed, just enough water is left within to create a moist, tender inside.

STARCH AND WATER

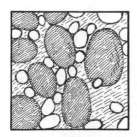

IN COLD WATER

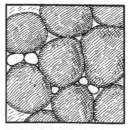

IN HEATED WATER

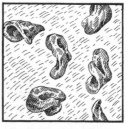

IN BOILING WATER

15

PIZZA, CALZONES, AND FOCACCIA

THIS CHAPTER COVERS PIZZA, CALZONES, AND focaccia—all thin yeast-raised breads that are much quicker to bake than the thick loaf breads in chapter 17. Classically, pizza is thin and crisp and baked directly on a pizza stone. Deep-dish pizza (also known as Chicago-style or pan pizza) is, as the name implies, thicker, crustier, and baked in a round deep-dish pan. Both styles of pizza are topped with cheese, tomato sauce, and cooked vegetables and/or meat.

Calzones are similar to pizza in that the dough contains the same ingredients—in slightly different proportions—and the "toppings" are enveloped in the dough, thus becoming the filling. Focaccia is thicker, softer, and more lightly topped than pizza, often with nothing more than coarse salt, olive oil, and herbs. Although pizza and calzones are often served as a meal, focaccia is reserved as an accompaniment to soups or salads or, cut into small pieces, as a light hors d'oeuvre.

PIZZA

THE DOUGH IS PROBABLY THE TRICKIEST PART of making pizza at home. While pizza dough is nothing more than bread dough with oil added for softness and suppleness, we found in our testing that minor changes in the ingredient list can yield dramatically different results.

Our goal in testing was threefold. The recipe had to be simple to put together; the dough had to be easy to shape and stretch thin; and the crust needed to bake up crisp and chewy, not tough and leathery.

After initial tests, it was clear that bread flour delivers the best texture. Bread flour makes pizza crust that is chewy and crisp. All-purpose flour can be used in a pinch, but the resulting crust is less crisp.

The second key to perfect crust is water. We found that using more water makes the dough softer and more elastic. Soft dough stretches more easily than a stiffer, harder dough with less water. We prefer to jump-start the yeast in a little warm water for five minutes. We then add more water, at room temperature, along with oil.

For combining the dry ingredients (flour and

salt) with the wet ingredients, the food processor is our first choice. The liquid is evenly incorporated into the dry ingredients, and the blade kneads the dough in just 30 seconds. Of course, the dough can be kneaded by hand or with a standing mixer. If you make the dough by hand, resist the temptation to add a lot of flour as you knead.

We use plastic wrap to cover the oiled bowl that holds the rising dough. We found that the tight seal offered by plastic wrap keeps the dough moist and protects it from drafts better than the standard damp cloth. We reserve the damp cloth for use when the dough has been divided into balls and is waiting to be stretched.

To stretch dough to its maximum diameter, let it rest once or twice during the shaping process. Once you feel some resistance, cover the dough with a damp cloth and wait five minutes before going at it again. Fingertips and hands generally do a better job of stretching dough than a rolling pin, which presses air out of the risen dough and makes it tough. This low-tech method is also superior to flipping dough into the air and other frivolous techniques that may work in a pizza parlor but can lead to disaster at home. For illustrations of shaping pizza dough, see page 665.

Even if you're baking just one medium pizza, make a full dough recipe. After the dough has risen and been divided, place the extra pieces of dough in separate airtight containers and freeze them for up to several weeks. Defrost and stretch the dough when desired.

Pizza Dough

MAKES ENOUGH FOR 3 MEDIUM PIZZAS

We find that the food processor is the best tool for making pizza dough. However, only a food processor with a capacity of at least 11 cups can handle this much dough. You can also knead this dough by hand or in a standing mixer (see the variations that follow). Unbleached all-purpose flour can be used in a pinch, but the resulting crust will be less crisp. If you want to make pizza dough in the morning and let it rise on the counter all day, decrease the yeast to ½ teaspoon and let the covered dough rise at cool room temperature (about 68 degrees) until doubled in size, about 8 hours. You can prolong the rising time even further by refrigerating the covered dough for up to 16 hours and then letting it rise on the counter until doubled in size, which will take 6 to 8 hours. See the illustrations below for more tips on making pizza dough.

½	cup warm water (about 110 degrees)
1	envelope (about 2¼ teaspoons) instant yeast
1¼	cups water, at room temperature
2	tablespoons extra-virgin olive oil
4	cups (22 ounces) bread flour, plus more for dusting the work surface and hands
1½	teaspoons salt
	Olive oil or nonstick cooking spray for oiling the bowl

1. Measure the warm water into a 2-cup liquid measuring cup. Sprinkle in the yeast and let stand until the yeast dissolves and swells, about 5 minutes. Add the room-temperature water and oil and stir to combine.

2. Process the flour and salt in a large food processor, pulsing to combine. Continue pulsing while pouring the liquid ingredients (holding back a few tablespoons) through the feed tube. If the dough does not readily form into a ball, add the remaining liquid and continue to pulse until a ball forms. Process until the dough is smooth and elastic, about 30 seconds longer.

3. The dough will be a bit tacky, so use a rubber

MIXING THE PIZZA DOUGH

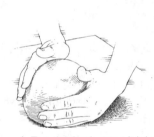

1. Measure ½ cup warm water at about 110 degrees into a 2-cup measuring cup. Sprinkle the yeast over the water and let it stand until swollen, about 5 minutes. Add enough room-temperature water to equal 1¾ cups and then add the oil.

2. The food processor is the easiest place to make pizza dough. Pulse the flour and salt to combine them. Then pour the liquid ingredients through the feed tube while continuing to pulse.

3. Once the dough comes together, process until it is smooth and elastic, about 30 seconds.

4. Turn the dough onto a lightly floured work surface and shape it into a smooth, round ball.

5. If kneading the dough by hand, don't worry about overworking the dough. You can't be too rough. Use your palms for maximum leverage against the dough.

6. If kneading the dough in a standing mixer, use the paddle to combine the dry and wet ingredients. When the dough forms a cohesive mass, stop the mixer and switch to the dough hook for kneading.

7. Plastic wrap forms a tighter seal than a damp towel and keeps the dough moister. Place the kneaded dough in a deep oiled bowl and cover the bowl tightly with the wrap.

8. After the dough has doubled in size (about 2 hours), deflate it by pressing down on it with your fist. Divide and shape the punched-down dough as directed in the pizza recipes in this chapter.

663

spatula to turn it out onto a lightly floured work surface. Knead by hand for a few strokes to form a smooth, round ball. Put the dough in a deep oiled bowl and cover with plastic wrap. Let rise until doubled in size, 1½ to 2 hours. Press the dough to deflate; it is now ready to use in the following recipes.

> VARIATIONS

Pizza Dough Kneaded by Hand

Follow the recipe for Pizza Dough through step 1. Omit step 2 and instead combine the salt and half the flour in a deep bowl. Add the liquid ingredients and use a wooden spoon to combine. Add the remaining flour, stirring until a cohesive mass forms. Turn the dough onto a lightly floured work surface and knead until smooth and elastic, 7 to 8 minutes, using as little dusting flour as possible while kneading. Form the dough into a ball, put it in a deep oiled bowl, cover with plastic wrap, and proceed with the recipe.

Pizza Dough Kneaded in a Standing Mixer

Follow the recipe for Pizza Dough through step 1. Omit step 2 and instead place the flour and salt in the bowl of a standing mixer fitted with the paddle. Briefly combine the dry ingredients at low speed. Slowly add the liquid ingredients and continue to mix at low speed until a cohesive mass forms. Stop the mixer and replace the paddle with the dough hook. Knead until the dough is smooth and elastic, about 5 minutes. Form the dough into a ball, put it in a deep oiled bowl, cover with plastic wrap, and proceed with the recipe.

Pizza Dough with Garlic and Herbs

Heat 2 tablespoons extra-virgin olive oil in a small skillet. Add 4 medium minced garlic cloves and 1 teaspoon minced fresh thyme, oregano, or rosemary leaves. Sauté until the garlic is golden, 2 to 3 minutes. Cool the mixture and use in place of the oil in the recipe for Pizza Dough.

Whole-Wheat Pizza Dough

Whole-wheat flour gives the dough a hearty flavor but slows down the rising process a bit. Because this dough has more flavor and is a bit more dense than our pizza dough made with bread flour, it works best with lighter toppings such as vegetables rather than heavier toppings such as meat.

Follow the recipe for Pizza Dough, replacing 2 cups of the bread flour with an equal amount of whole-wheat flour. The dough may require an extra 30 minutes to double in size while rising.

Pizza Bianca with Garlic and Rosemary

MAKES 3 MEDIUM PIZZAS, SERVING 6

Pizza bianca translates as "white pizza," referring to the fact that there are no tomatoes—just garlic, oil, rosemary, and salt—in this recipe. See the illustrations on page 665 for tips on shaping and topping pizza dough.

- 1   recipe Pizza Dough (page 662)
- ¼   cup extra-virgin olive oil, plus more for brushing on the stretched dough
- 6   medium garlic cloves, minced or pressed through a garlic press
- 4   teaspoons minced fresh rosemary leaves
-   Salt and ground black pepper
-   Semolina or cornmeal for dusting the pizza peel

1. Prepare the dough as directed in the Pizza Dough recipe. Place a pizza stone on a rack in the lower third of the oven. Heat the oven to 500 degrees for at least 30 minutes. Turn the dough out onto a lightly floured work surface. Use a chef's knife or dough scraper to divide the dough into three pieces. Form each piece of dough into a smooth, round ball and cover it with a damp cloth. Let the dough relax for at least 10 minutes but no more than 30 minutes.

2. While preparing the dough, combine the oil, garlic, rosemary, and salt and pepper to taste in a small bowl. Set the herb oil aside.

3. Working with one piece of dough at a time and keeping the others covered, shape the dough as directed in the illustrations on page 665, then transfer it to a pizza peel that has been lightly dusted with semolina.

4. Lightly brush the dough round with plain olive oil. Prick the dough all over with a fork to prevent ballooning in the oven (see the illustration on page 667).

5. Slide the dough onto the heated stone. Bake until the crust begins to brown in spots, 6 to 10 minutes. Brush the crust with a third of the herb oil and continue baking until the garlic is fragrant, 1 to 2 minutes. Remove the pizza from the oven, cut into wedges, and serve immediately. Repeat steps 3, 4, and 5 with the remaining two pieces of dough and the remaining herb oil.

➤ VARIATIONS

Pesto Pizza

The pesto is brushed on the dough rather than baked on the crust. Follow the recipe for Pizza Bianca with Garlic and Rosemary through step 4, omitting the herb oil in step 2. Bake the dough as directed until golden brown in spots, 8 to 10 minutes. Remove the crust from the oven and spread with ¼ cup Classic Pesto (see page 240), leaving a ½-inch border. Cut into wedges and serve.

Lemon–Sea Salt Pizza

Follow the recipe for Pizza Bianca with Garlic and Rosemary through step 3. Brush the dough round with plain olive oil as directed in step 4. Arrange 1 small lemon, sliced paper-thin, over the dough round, leaving a ½-inch border uncovered. Sprinkle with coarse sea salt to taste. (Do not prick the dough.) Bake and brush with the herb oil as directed in step 5.

White Pizza with Spinach and Ricotta

MAKES 3 MEDIUM PIZZAS, SERVING 6

Ricotta cheese and garlicky sautéed spinach flavor this tomato-less pizza. Be sure to squeeze the cooked spinach of any liquid to prevent a soggy crust. See the illustrations below for tips on shaping and topping pizza dough.

SHAPING AND TOPPING PIZZA DOUGH

1. Working with one ball of dough at a time and keeping the rest covered with a damp cloth, flatten the dough ball into a disk using the palms of your hands.

2. Starting at the center of the disk and working outward, use your fingertips to press the dough until it is about ½ inch thick.

3. Holding the center in place, stretch the dough outward. Rotate the dough a quarter turn and stretch again. Repeat until the dough reaches a diameter of 12 inches.

4. Use your palm to press down and flatten the thick edge of the dough.

5. Carefully lift the dough round and transfer it to a peel dusted with semolina or cornmeal.

6. If the dough loses its round shape, adjust it on the peel to return it to the original shape.

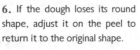

7. Brush the entire dough round with a little olive oil. Add the toppings. To make it easier to hold pizza slices when eating, leave a ½-inch border of dough uncovered.

8. Use a quick jerking action to slide the topped dough off the peel and onto the hot tiles or stone. Make sure that the pizza lands far enough back so that the front edge does not hang off the tiles or stone.

665

PIZZA BASICS

Unless you build a brick oven in your kitchen, it's not possible to duplicate pizzeria-style pies at home. Commercial pizza ovens can reach 800 degrees; home ovens just can't compete. That said, homemade pizza is delicious even if different from the pies you get when you eat out: The crust is chewier, crisper, and not nearly as greasy. To ensure good homemade pizza, here are a few things to know:

USE TILES OR A PIZZA STONE In our testing, we found that baking pizza on tiles or a pizza stone is a must because crusts baked on a pizza screen (a perforated pan) or a baking sheet were not as crisp and chewy. Unglazed quarry tiles made of terra cotta are porous and absorb heat better than a metal baking sheet; thus, they transfer more heat to whatever food is cooked on them. Pizza crust becomes especially crisp and well browned on the bottom when cooked on tiles. (In our test kitchen, we have found that these tiles are good for most bread as well.) Look for 1/2-inch-thick tiles—they come in 6-inch squares and can be cut at a tile store to fit your oven rack perfectly. If using tiles, simply line the bottom rack of your oven with them—you will need six or eight, depending on the size of your oven. But if you don't want to bother with tiles (they can chip and we have "lost" one on occasion in the test kitchen), consider a pizza stone.

Pizza stones (also called baking stones) are prized for their ability to retain heat and lessen the effects of temperature fluctuations in home ovens. Pizza stones are usually made of clay or ceramic (although soapstone and composite cement stones are also available). When coupled with extreme heat, they absorb moisture, producing crisper, drier pizzas, breads, and calzones. In a recent testing of pizza stones, we looked at two main criteria: design (including ease of use, installation, and storage) and performance (including heat conductivity, evenness of browning, and crispness of baked goods). There was little issue with heat conductivity. We took the surface temperature of each stone, and each one exceeded 500 degrees after 60 minutes of heating. With little variation, all seven stones also produced evenly colored and crisp crusts in pizzas and calzones.

Although performance was similar in all models tested, some designs were much easier to work with. Lipped edges inhibited easy placement and removal of food from a peel, and stones with this feature were downgraded, as were stones that were extremely heavy (one weighed a whopping 19 pounds). Stones that were either too big to fit in most home ovens or too small to handle a large pizza received low marks. Our recommendation: Choose a good-size stone (about 16 by 14 inches is ideal) with smooth edges and don't equate a higher price with a better stone. In terms of whether to buy tiles or a stone, we think a stone is easier to store, but if you already own tiles, use them—they work very well.

PREHEAT THE OVEN Our testing revealed that an oven temperature of 500 degrees is your best bet. When cooked at a lower temperature, the crust was not as crisp. Remember to heat the oven (and stone or tiles) for at least 30 minutes.

USE A PEEL We find that a pizza peel is the best tool for getting topped pizza dough onto a heated stone. The long handle on the peel makes it easy to slide the dough onto tiles or a stone in a hot oven. Although a rimless metal baking sheet can be used in this fashion, the lack of a handle means your hands are that much closer to the oven heat, so use caution. When shopping for a pizza peel, note that there are two choices. Aluminum peels with heat-resistant wooden handles are probably the better bet because they can be washed and cleaned easily. Peels made entirely of wood can mildew when washed, so it's best just to wipe them clean. Either way, make sure your peel measures at least 16 inches across so that it can accommodate a large pizza with room left around the edges.

PREVENT THE DOUGH FROM STICKING Pizza dough is sticky. There are a few options for preventing your dough from sticking to the peel. With its fine, sandy texture, semolina does a good job at helping pizza dough slide off the peel. Cornmeal can also be used, as can flour. Alternatively, if parchment paper is handy, you can simply stretch out the dough onto the parchment and slide the pizza, paper and all, directly onto the stone. Although this method works well, we like the crunch and flavor the semolina or cornmeal gives to the bottom of our crusts. We leave the choice up to you.

BAKE FULLY Depending on your oven, the type of stone or tiles used, and the amount of topping, pizza may be done in as little as 6 minutes or may take as long as 12 minutes. Don't pull a pizza out of the oven until the edge of the crust is golden brown and the toppings are sizzling.

THE BEST PIZZA STONE

We found the Baker's Catalogue Baking Stone (manufactured by Old Stone Oven) to be our favorite. It is modestly priced at $35.

1   recipe Pizza Dough (page 662)

2   tablespoons extra-virgin olive oil, plus more
     for brushing on the stretched dough

4   medium garlic cloves, minced or pressed
     through a garlic press

¼   teaspoon red pepper flakes

1½   pounds spinach, stemmed, washed, shaken to
     remove excess water, and chopped coarse
     Salt and ground black pepper
     Semolina or cornmeal for dusting the
     pizza peel

1   (15-ounce) container whole-milk ricotta
     cheese

6   tablespoons freshly grated Parmesan cheese

1. Prepare the dough as directed in the Pizza Dough recipe. Place a pizza stone on a rack in the lower third of the oven. Heat the oven to 500 degrees for at least 30 minutes. Turn the dough out onto a lightly floured work surface. Use a chef's knife or dough scraper to divide the dough into three pieces. Form each piece of dough into a smooth, round ball and cover it with a damp cloth. Let the dough relax for at least 10 minutes but no more than 30 minutes.

2. While preparing the dough, heat the oil in a Dutch oven set over medium heat. Add the garlic and red pepper flakes and cook until fragrant, about 1 minute. Add the damp spinach, cover, and

cook, stirring occasionally, until just wilted, about 3 minutes. Season with salt and pepper to taste. Transfer the spinach to a medium bowl, squeezing out any liquid with the back of a spoon and leaving the liquid behind in the pot. Set the spinach aside; discard the liquid.

3. Working with one piece of dough at a time and keeping the others covered, shape the dough as directed in the illustrations on page 665, then transfer it to a pizza peel that has been lightly dusted with semolina.

4. Lightly brush the dough round with olive oil. Arrange a third of the spinach mixture over the dough round, leaving a ½-inch border uncovered. Dot with ⅔ cup ricotta cheese.

5. Slide the dough onto the heated stone. Bake until the crust edge browns in spots, 8 to 12 minutes. Remove the pizza from the oven, sprinkle with 2 tablespoons Parmesan, cut into wedges, and serve immediately. Repeat steps 3, 4, and 5 with the remaining two pieces of dough and the remaining toppings.

Three-Cheese Pizza
MAKES 3 MEDIUM PIZZAS, SERVING 6

This classic combination of mozzarella, Parmesan, and Gorgonzola is not a study in excess, as the name might imply. A little of each cheese contributes to a rich, complex flavor. We also recommend adding garlic and olives, although these ingredients are optional. See the illustrations on page 665 for tips on shaping and topping pizza dough.

1   recipe Pizza Dough (page 662)
     Semolina or cornmeal for dusting the
     pizza peel
     Extra-virgin olive oil for brushing on the
     stretched dough

4   ounces mozzarella cheese, shredded
     (about 1 cup)

8   ounces Gorgonzola cheese, crumbled
     (about 2 cups)

3   medium garlic cloves, sliced thin (optional)

6   tablespoons pitted and quartered
     oil-cured black olives (optional)

6   tablespoons freshly grated Parmesan cheese

PREVENTING PIZZA DOUGH FROM BALLOONING IN THE OVEN

Some pizzas are baked without toppings. To keep the dough from ballooning in the oven, prick the dough all over with a fork before it goes into the oven. If bubbles form during baking, prick them before they become too large.

1. Prepare the dough as directed in the Pizza Dough recipe. Place a pizza stone on a rack in the lower third of the oven. Heat the oven to 500 degrees for at least 30 minutes. Turn the dough out onto a lightly floured work surface. Use a chef's knife or dough scraper to divide the dough into three pieces. Form each piece of dough into a smooth, round ball and cover it with a damp cloth. Let the dough relax for at least 10 minutes but no more than 30 minutes.

2. Working with one piece of dough at a time and keeping the others covered, shape the dough as directed in the illustrations on page 665, then transfer it to a pizza peel that has been lightly dusted with semolina.

3. Lightly brush the dough round with olive oil. Sprinkle evenly with ⅓ cup mozzarella, leaving a ½-inch border uncovered. Dot with ⅔ cup Gorgonzola and sprinkle with a third of the garlic and olives, if using.

4. Slide the dough onto the heated stone. Bake until the crust edge browns and the cheeses are golden and bubbling, 8 to 12 minutes. Remove the pizza from the oven, sprinkle with 2 tablespoons Parmesan, cut into wedges, and serve immediately. Repeat steps 2, 3, and 4 with the remaining two pieces of dough and the remaining toppings.

Classic Tomato Pizza with Mozzarella and Basil

MAKES 3 MEDIUM PIZZAS, SERVING 6

Known as pizza Margherita, this Neapolitan specialty is Italian cooking at its simplest and best. See the illustrations on page 665 for tips on shaping and topping pizza dough.

1	recipe Pizza Dough (page 662)
	Semolina or cornmeal for dusting the pizza peel
	Extra-virgin olive oil for brushing on the stretched dough
3	cups Quick Tomato Sauce for Pizza (recipe follows)
12	ounces mozzarella cheese, shredded (about 3 cups)
3	tablespoons freshly grated Parmesan cheese
½	cup packed fresh basil leaves

1. Prepare the dough as directed in the Pizza Dough recipe. Place a pizza stone on a rack in the lower third of the oven. Heat the oven to 500 degrees for at least 30 minutes. Turn the dough out onto a lightly floured work surface. Use a chef's knife or dough scraper to divide the dough into three pieces. Form each piece of dough into a

GRATING MOZZARELLA

Mozzarella and other semisoft cheeses can stick to a box grater and cause a real mess. Here's how to keep the holes on the grater from becoming clogged.

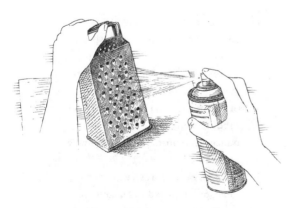

1. Use nonstick cooking spray to lightly coat the side of the box grater that has large holes.

2. Shred the cheese as usual. The cooking spray will keep the cheese from sticking to the surface of the grater.

smooth, round ball and cover it with a damp cloth. Let the dough relax for at least 10 minutes but no more than 30 minutes.

2. Working with one piece of dough at a time and keeping the others covered, shape the dough as directed in the illustrations on page 665, then transfer it to a pizza peel that has been lightly dusted with semolina

3. Lightly brush the dough round with olive oil. Spread 1 cup tomato sauce evenly over the dough round, leaving a ½-inch border uncovered. Sprinkle with 1 cup mozzarella.

4. Slide the dough onto the heated stone. Bake until the crust edge browns and the cheese is golden brown in spots, 8 to 12 minutes. Remove the pizza from the oven and sprinkle with 1 table-spoon Parmesan. Tear a third of the basil leaves and scatter them over the pizza. Cut the pizza into wedges and serve immediately. Repeat steps 2, 3,

INGREDIENTS:
Supermarket Mozzarella Cheese

We selected five widely available brands of "supermarket," or low-moisture, mozzarella cheese and sampled those made with part-skim or whole milk. Because the most common use for this type of cheese is quick and convenient melting, we decided to include both preshredded and block forms. Fifteen *Cook's Illustrated* staff members tasted these cheeses both raw (all block cheeses were tasted shredded) and melted on pizza. Separate tests were performed in this manner, one for the category of shredded cheeses and the other for block cheeses. Based on the combined scores of the raw and the pizza tests, here are the two that came out on top:

THE BEST SHREDDED MOZZARELLA CHEESE
Kraft Shredded Low Moisture Part-Skim Mozzarella was described by tasters as "rich," "tangy," and "fresh."

THE BEST BLOCK MOZZARELLA CHEESE
Dragone Low Moisture Mozzarella Cheese (Whole Milk) was described by tasters as "rich and creamy" and "tangy and briny."

and 4 with the remaining two pieces of dough and the remaining toppings.

Quick Tomato Sauce for Pizza
MAKES ABOUT 3 CUPS

1	(28-ounce) can diced tomatoes
2	tablespoons extra-virgin olive oil
2	large garlic cloves, minced or pressed through a garlic press
	Salt and ground black pepper

1. Place the tomatoes in a food processor and process until smooth, about five 1-second pulses.

2. Heat the oil and garlic in a medium saucepan over medium heat until the garlic is sizzling, about 40 seconds. Stir in the tomatoes. Bring to a simmer and cook, uncovered, until the sauce thickens enough to coat a wooden spoon, about 15 minutes. Season with salt and pepper to taste.

Fresh Tomato Pizza with Arugula and Prosciutto
MAKES 3 MEDIUM PIZZAS, SERVING 6

The arugula for this pizza is tossed with a little oil to keep it moist and then sprinkled over the baked pizza as soon as it comes out of the oven. The heat from the pizza wilts the arugula without causing it to dry out. See the illustrations on page 665 for tips on shaping and topping pizza dough.

1	recipe Pizza Dough (page 662) Semolina or cornmeal for dusting the pizza peel
2	tablespoons extra-virgin olive oil, plus more for brushing on the stretched dough
3	medium, ripe tomatoes (about 1 pound), cored and sliced crosswise into thin rounds Salt and ground black pepper
4	ounces thin-sliced prosciutto
6	ounces mozzarella cheese, shredded (about 1½ cups)
3	cups stemmed arugula leaves, washed and thoroughly dried

1. Prepare the dough as directed in the Pizza Dough recipe. Place a pizza stone on a rack in the lower third of the oven. Heat the oven to 500 degrees for at least 30 minutes. Turn the dough out onto a lightly floured work surface. Use a chef's knife or dough scraper to divide the dough into three pieces. Form each piece of dough into a smooth, round ball and cover it with a damp cloth. Let the dough relax for at least 10 minutes but no more than 30 minutes.

2. Working with one piece of dough at a time and keeping the others covered, shape the dough as directed in the illustrations on page 665, then transfer it to a pizza peel that has been lightly dusted with semolina.

3. Lightly brush the dough round with olive oil. Arrange a third of the tomato slices in concentric circles over the dough round, leaving a ½-inch border uncovered. Season with salt and pepper to taste and drizzle with 1 teaspoon oil.

4. Slide the dough onto the heated stone. Bake until the crust edge starts to brown, 6 to 10 minutes. Lay a third of the prosciutto slices over the tomatoes and sprinkle with ½ cup mozzarella. Continue baking until the cheese melts, 2 to 3 minutes more. Toss 1 cup arugula with 1 teaspoon oil in a small bowl. Remove the pizza from the oven and top with the arugula. Cut the pizza into wedges and serve immediately. Repeat steps 2, 3, and 4 with the remaining two pieces of dough and the remaining toppings.

Mushroom Pizza with Sage, Fontina, and Parmesan

MAKES 3 MEDIUM PIZZAS, SERVING 6

Any fresh mushrooms will work in this recipe, but cremini are especially good. See the tip at right for slicing button mushrooms. See the illustrations on page 665 for tips on shaping and topping pizza dough.

I   recipe Pizza Dough (page 662)
2   large garlic cloves, minced or pressed through
    a garlic press
2   tablespoons extra-virgin olive oil,
    plus more for brushing on the
    stretched dough

I   pound fresh mushrooms, stem ends trimmed,
    sliced thin
I   teaspoon minced fresh sage leaves
    Salt and ground black pepper
    Semolina or cornmeal for dusting the
    pizza peel
3   cups Quick Tomato Sauce for Pizza (page 669)
6   ounces fontina cheese, shredded
    (about I ½ cups)
6   tablespoons freshly grated Parmesan cheese

1. Prepare the dough as directed in the Pizza Dough recipe. Place a pizza stone on a rack in the lower third of the oven. Heat the oven to 500 degrees for at least 30 minutes. Turn the dough out onto a lightly floured work surface. Use a chef's knife or dough scraper to divide the dough into three pieces. Form each piece of dough into a smooth, round ball and cover it with a damp cloth. Let the dough relax for at least 10 minutes but no more than 30 minutes.

2. While preparing the dough, heat the garlic and oil in a large skillet set over medium-high heat. When the garlic begins to sizzle, add the mushrooms and sauté until the mushrooms are golden brown and the juices they release have evaporated, about 7 minutes. Stir in the sage and salt and pepper to taste. Set the mushrooms aside.

3. Working with one piece of dough at a time and keeping the others covered, shape the dough

SLICING BUTTON MUSHROOMS THINLY

Slicing button mushrooms thin takes some patience. To slice them quickly, use an egg slicer. Place the stem-trimmed mushrooms, one at a time, into the egg slicer. The pieces will be even and thin.

as directed in the illustrations on page 665, then transfer it to a pizza peel that has been lightly dusted with semolina.

4. Lightly brush the dough round with olive oil. Spread 1 cup tomato sauce over the dough round, leaving a ½-inch border uncovered. Scatter a third of the mushrooms and then ½ cup fontina cheese over the sauce.

5. Slide the dough onto the heated stone. Bake until the crust edge browns and the cheese is golden brown in spots, 8 to 12 minutes. Remove the pizza from the oven, sprinkle with 2 tablespoons Parmesan, cut into wedges, and serve immediately. Repeat steps 3, 4, and 5 with the remaining two pieces of dough and the remaining toppings.

Caramelized Onion Pizza with Oil-Cured Olives and Parmesan

MAKES 3 MEDIUM PIZZAS, SERVING 6

See the illustrations on page 665 for tips on shaping and topping pizza dough.

1	recipe Pizza Dough (page 662)
2	tablespoons extra-virgin olive oil, plus more for brushing the stretched dough
2	medium yellow onions, halved and sliced thin
1	teaspoon chopped fresh thyme leaves
	Salt and ground black pepper
	Semolina or cornmeal for dusting the pizza peel
1½	cups Quick Tomato Sauce for Pizza (page 669)
¼	cup pitted and quartered oil-cured black olives
6	anchovies, chopped coarse (optional)
¼	cup freshly grated Parmesan cheese

1. Prepare the dough as directed in the Pizza Dough recipe. Place a pizza stone on a rack in the lower third of the oven. Heat the oven to 500 degrees for at least 30 minutes. Turn the dough out onto a lightly floured work surface. Use a chef's knife or dough scraper to divide the dough into three pieces. Form each piece of dough into a smooth, round ball and cover it with a damp cloth. Let the dough relax for at least 10 minutes but no more than 30 minutes.

2. While preparing the dough, heat the oil in a large skillet set over medium-high heat. Add the onions and sauté until softened and somewhat caramelized, about 10 minutes. Stir in the thyme; season with salt and pepper to taste. Set the onions aside.

3. Working with one piece of dough at a time and keeping the others covered, shape the dough as directed in the illustrations on page 665, then transfer it to a pizza peel that has been lightly dusted with semolina.

4. Lightly brush the dough round with olive oil. Spread ½ cup of the tomato sauce over the dough round, leaving a ½-inch border uncovered. Scatter a third of the onions over the sauce and sprinkle with a third of the olives and anchovies (if using).

5. Slide the dough onto the heated stone. Bake until the crust edge starts to brown, 6 to 12 minutes. Sprinkle with a third of the Parmesan and continue baking until the cheese melts, 2 to 3 minutes more. Remove the pizza from the oven, cut into wedges, and serve immediately. Repeat steps 3, 4, and 5 with the remaining two pieces of dough and the remaining toppings.

Pepperoni Pizza

MAKES 3 MEDIUM PIZZAS, SERVING 6

This classic pizzeria favorite is especially easy to prepare. See the illustrations on page 665 for tips on shaping and topping pizza dough.

1	recipe Pizza Dough (page 662)
	Semolina or cornmeal for dusting the pizza peel
	Extra-virgin olive oil for brushing the stretched dough
1½	cups Quick Tomato Sauce for Pizza (page 669)
8	ounces pepperoni, peeled and sliced thin
4	ounces mozzarella cheese, shredded (about 1 cup)
¼	cup freshly grated Parmesan cheese

1. Prepare the dough as directed in the Pizza Dough recipe. Place a pizza stone on a rack in the lower third of the oven. Heat the oven to 500 degrees for at least 30 minutes. Turn the

dough out onto a lightly floured work surface. Use a chef's knife or dough scraper to divide the dough into three pieces. Form each piece of dough into a smooth, round ball and cover it with a damp cloth. Let the dough relax for at least 10 minutes but no more than 30 minutes.

2. Working with one piece of dough at a time and keeping the others covered, shape the dough as directed in the illustrations on page 665, then transfer it to a pizza peel that has been lightly dusted with semolina.

3. Lightly brush the dough round with olive oil. Spread ½ cup of the tomato sauce over the dough round, leaving a ½-inch border uncovered. Scatter a third of the pepperoni slices over the sauced dough round.

4. Slide the dough onto the heated stone. Bake the pizza until the crust edge starts to brown, 6 to 12 minutes. Sprinkle with ⅓ cup mozzarella and a third of the Parmesan and continue baking until the cheeses melt, 2 to 3 minutes more. Remove the pizza from the oven, cut into wedges, and serve immediately. Repeat steps 2, 3, and 4 with the remaining two pieces of dough and the remaining toppings.

Sausage and Bell Pepper Pizza with Basil and Mozzarella
MAKES 3 MEDIUM PIZZAS, SERVING 6

If bulk sausage is not available, buy link sausage, remove the meat from the casings, and then break it into bite-size pieces. See the illustrations on page 665 for tips on shaping and topping pizza dough.

1	recipe Pizza Dough (page 662)
¾	pound bulk sweet Italian sausage, broken into bite-size pieces
¼	cup water
1½	teaspoons extra-virgin olive oil (approximately), plus more for brushing the stretched dough
1	red or yellow bell pepper, cored, halved, seeded, and cut into thin strips
	Salt and ground black pepper
	Semolina or cornmeal for dusting the pizza peel
1½	cups Quick Tomato Sauce for Pizza (page 669) combined with 2 tablespoons minced fresh basil leaves
4	ounces mozzarella cheese, shredded (about 1 cup)

1. Prepare the dough as directed in the Pizza Dough recipe. Place a pizza stone on a rack in the lower third of the oven. Heat the oven to 500 degrees for at least 30 minutes. Turn the dough out onto a lightly floured work surface. Use a chef's knife or dough scraper to divide the dough into three pieces. Form each piece of dough into a smooth, round ball and cover it with a damp cloth. Let the dough relax for at least 10 minutes but no more than 30 minutes.

2. While preparing the dough, put the sausage and water in a large skillet. Cook over medium-high heat until the water evaporates and the sausage cooks through and browns, about 10 minutes. Remove the sausage with a slotted spoon and set aside. Add enough oil so that the amount of fat in the skillet equals 1 tablespoon. Add the bell pepper and sauté until softened slightly, about 5 minutes. Season with salt and pepper to taste and set aside.

3. Working with one piece of dough at a time and keeping the others covered, shape the dough as directed in the illustrations on page 665, then transfer it to a pizza peel that has been lightly dusted with semolina.

4. Lightly brush the dough round with olive oil. Spread ½ cup of the tomato sauce over the dough round, leaving a ½ inch border uncovered. Scatter a third of the sausage and a third of the bell pepper over the sauce.

5. Slide the dough onto the heated stone. Bake until the crust edge starts to brown, 6 to 12 minutes. Sprinkle with ⅓ cup of the cheese and continue baking until the cheese melts, 2 to 3 minutes more. Remove the pizza from the oven, cut into wedges, and serve immediately. Repeat steps 3, 4, and 5 with the remaining two pieces of dough and the remaining toppings.

DEEP-DISH PIZZA

DEEP-DISH PIZZA (ALSO KNOWN AS CHICAGO-style or pan pizza) may have its roots in Italy, but this recipe is as American as apple pie. In fact, Italians would not recognize this creation—it has no counterpart in Italy.

Deep-dish pizza is about 75 percent crust, so the crust must be great. We wanted it to be rich, substantial, and moist, with a tender, yet slightly chewy crumb and a well-developed flavor, like that of a good loaf of bread. We also thought the crust should be crisp and nicely browned without being dry or tough. Finally, knowing how time-consuming pizza making can be, we wanted a pizza dough that could be made in as little time as possible without sacrificing quality.

After scouring various cookbooks, we made five different pizza doughs and baked them in deep-dish pans. To our disappointment, none delivered the flavorful, crisp brown crust that we felt was needed.

After these initial tests, we tried dozens of variations. We played around with the ratio of water to flour, the amount of oil, the type of flour, and just about every other variable we could think of. But we weren't satisfied until we finally widened the field and tried a recipe for focaccia that used boiled, riced potatoes to add moisture and flavor to the dough. This dough was just what we were hoping for: very wet and yet easy to handle, light, and smooth. When baked, it was soft and moist, yet with a bit of chew, and had a sturdiness and structure that was not present in the previous doughs. (For more information on this somewhat unusual use of potatoes, see at right.)

Now that we had found a dough that we liked, the challenge was to come up with a rising and baking method suited to deep-dish pizza. We placed the pizza dough in a barely warmed oven for the first rise, reducing the initial rising time from 1 hour to 35 minutes and producing dough that tasted no different from the dough that rose at room temperature for a full hour.

Next we tried reducing—even eliminating—the amount of time allowed for the second rise. The dough given a full 30 minutes for the second rise was vastly better than doughs given only 15 minutes or no second rise at all. The flavor was more complex, and the texture of the pizza crust was softer and lighter, making the second rise too important to pass up or shorten.

After some testing, we discovered that a crust baked at 425 degrees on a baking stone was almost perfect—the bottom and sides of the pizza were well browned, and the interior crumb was moist, light, and evenly cooked through. The exterior of this crust was, however, slightly tough. To combat this, we tried coating the pizza pan with oil. After some experimentation, we found that the pizzas made with a generous amount of oil coating the pan (¼ cup was optimal) had a far more desirable crust than those made with little or no oil in the pan. Lightly "frying" the dough in the pan made for a rich, caramelized exterior; this added a good amount of flavor and a secondary texture to the crust, without drying it out or making it tough.

Now it was time for the toppings. On most pizzas, the toppings can simply be placed on raw dough and baked, since the crust bakes in about the same amount of time as the toppings. But we found that the weight of the toppings prevented the crust from rising in the oven, resulting in a dense, heavy crust, especially in the center of the pie. So we tried prebaking crusts from 5 minutes

---

SCIENCE: The Role of Potatoes in Pizza and Focaccia Dough

The boiled potatoes in our deep-dish pizza dough and our focaccia dough have a distinct effect on the flavor and texture of the final crust. The result: a moister, more tender, sweeter, and softer dough than one made with just wheat flour. We wanted to know why the boiled potatoes made such a difference.

According to Dr. Al Bushway, professor of food science at the University of Maine, potatoes contain more starch than wheat. Since starch traps moisture during baking, this creates a moister dough. Potatoes also contain less protein than flour. This results in less gluten being formed in the dough, which in turn produces a softer, more tender product. Finally, potatoes add another dimension of flavor in two ways. First, the free sugars in the potatoes cause faster fermentation, resulting in a more complex flavor in a shorter period of time. Second, the sugars that are not consumed by the yeast in the fermentation process add sweetness to the final dough.

---

up to 15 minutes to develop some structure before adding the toppings. The pizza that we prebaked for 15 minutes, then topped, was perfect. The crust had a chance to rise in the oven without the weight or moisture of the toppings, and the toppings had just enough time to melt and brown.

Deep-Dish Pizza

MAKES ONE 14-INCH PIZZA, SERVING 4 TO 6

Prepare the topping while the dough is rising so it will be ready when the dough is ready. Baking the pizza in a deep-dish pan on a hot pizza stone will help produce a crisp, well-browned bottom crust. Otherwise, a heavy rimless baking sheet (do not use an insulated cookie sheet) will work almost as well. If you've got only a rimmed baking sheet, turn it upside down and bake the pizza on the flat side. The amount of oil used to grease the pan may seem excessive, but in addition to preventing sticking, the oil helps the crust brown nicely.

1	medium baking potato (about 9 ounces), peeled and quartered
3½	cups (17½ ounces) unbleached all-purpose flour
1½	teaspoons instant yeast
1¾	teaspoons salt
1	cup warm water (about 110 degrees)
6	tablespoons extra-virgin olive oil, plus more for oiling the bowl
1	recipe topping (recipes follow)

1. Bring 1 quart water and the potato to a boil in a small saucepan over medium-high heat; cook until the potato is tender, 10 to 15 minutes. Drain the potato and cool until it can be handled comfortably; press through the fine disk on a potato ricer or grate on the large holes of a box grater. Measure 1⅓ cups lightly packed potato; discard the remaining potato.

2. Adjust one oven rack to the highest position and the other rack to the lowest position; heat the oven to 200 degrees. Once the temperature reaches 200 degrees, maintain the heat for 10 minutes, then turn off the heat.

3. Combine the flour, yeast, and salt in a food processor. With the motor running, add the water and process until the dough comes together in a shaggy ball. Add the potato and process for several seconds, then add 2 tablespoons of the oil and process several more seconds, until the dough is smooth and slightly sticky. Transfer the dough to a lightly oiled medium bowl, turn to coat with oil, and cover the bowl tightly with plastic wrap. Place in the warmed oven until the dough is soft and spongy and doubled in size, 30 to 35 minutes.

4. Oil the bottom of a 14-inch deep-dish pizza pan with the remaining 4 tablespoons oil. Remove the dough from the oven and gently punch down; turn the dough onto a clean, dry work surface and pat into a 12-inch round. Transfer the round to the oiled pan, cover with plastic wrap, and let rest until the dough no longer resists shaping, about 10 minutes.

5. Place a pizza stone or rimless baking sheet on the lowest oven rack (do not use an insulated cookie sheet; see note) and preheat the oven to 500 degrees. Uncover the dough and pull it into the edges and up the sides of the pan to form a 1-inch-high lip. Cover with plastic wrap and let rise in a warm, draft-free spot until doubled in size, about 30 minutes. Uncover the dough and prick generously with a fork. Reduce the oven temperature to 425 degrees and bake on the heated stone or baking sheet until the crust is dry and lightly browned, about 15 minutes. Add the desired topping; bake on the stone or baking sheet until the cheese melts, 10 to 15 minutes. Move the pizza to the top rack and bake until the cheese is golden brown in spots, about 5 minutes longer. To make sure the crust is done, use a spatula to lift up the crust—it should be nicely browned underneath (see the illustration on page 675). Let cool 5 minutes, then, holding the pizza pan at an angle with one hand, use a wide

DEEP-DISH PIZZA: POTATO IS THE SECRET INGREDIENT

Dough with potato (right) produced a much springier, chewier, and softer crust than the same dough without potato (left).

spatula to slide the pizza from the pan to a cutting board. Cut into wedges and serve.

➤ VARIATIONS

10-Inch Deep-Dish Pizzas

If you don't own a 14-inch deep-dish pizza pan, divide the dough between two 10-inch cake pans.

Follow the recipe for Deep-Dish Pizza through step 3. Oil the bottom of two 10-inch cake pans with 2 tablespoons olive oil each. Turn the dough onto a clean, dry work surface and divide it in half. Pat each half into a 9-inch round; continue with the recipe, reducing the initial baking time on the lowest rack to 5 to 10 minutes and dividing the topping evenly between the pizzas.

Fresh Tomato Topping with Mozzarella and Basil

4	medium, ripe tomatoes (about 1 1/2 pounds), cored, seeded, and cut into 1-inch pieces
2	medium garlic cloves, minced
	Salt and ground black pepper
6	ounces mozzarella cheese, shredded (about 1 1/2 cups)
1 1/4	ounces Parmesan cheese, grated (about 1/2 cup)
3	tablespoons shredded fresh basil leaves

1. Mix together the tomatoes and garlic in a medium bowl; season with salt and pepper to taste.

DETERMINING WHEN DEEP-DISH PIZZA IS DONE

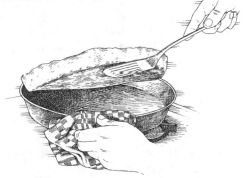

Use a spatula to lift up the pizza slightly. If the bottom crust is nicely browned, the pizza is done.

2. Spread the partially baked crust with the tomato mixture; sprinkle with the mozzarella, then the Parmesan. Bake as directed in step 5 of the recipe for Deep-Dish Pizza. Scatter the basil over the fully baked pizza before cutting it into wedges.

Four-Cheese Topping with Pesto

1/2	cup Classic Pesto (page 240)
6	ounces mozzarella cheese, shredded (about 1 1/2 cups)
4	ounces provolone cheese, shredded (about 1 cup)
1 1/4	ounces Parmesan cheese, grated (about 1/2 cup)
1 1/4	ounces blue cheese, crumbled (about 1/4 cup)

Spread the partially baked crust evenly with the pesto; sprinkle with the mozzarella, followed by the provolone, Parmesan, and blue cheese. Bake as directed in step 5 of the recipe for Deep-Dish Pizza.

RICOTTA CALZONES

WITH SOGGY FILLINGS AND BREADY CRUSTS, bad calzones are a dime a dozen. We tested a host of modern calzone recipes and came up with specimens that even the most fast food–deadened palate would reject. These calzones were pale and blond, soggy and limp, and they tended to hover at one of two extremes—too bready and rubbery or too thin and cracker-like. One domed calzone required serious sawing with a serrated knife, only to reveal a cavernous interior with a thin smear of filling. Another hollow calzone was the result of a faulty seal that caused the cheese to end up on the baking stone where it was almost impossible to completely remove. These scant fillings were no match for the calzone shell; time after time, we were left with a mouthful of dry bread. After this first tasting, we knew what we wanted: a crisp crust that had plenty of chew, with a healthy proportion of rich, creamy, flavorful filling.

We started with the dough, thinking it would be easy; after all, the test kitchen had already developed pizza dough recipes (thin crust and deep dish), and we made the seemingly logical assumption that calzone dough and pizza dough were one and the same. Well, perhaps at your local pizzeria, but after trying several pizza doughs (including our own recipe), we can safely say that the best pizza dough will not necessarily make a good calzone. Why? Most pizza dough is wet and puffy, and the calzones made using pizza dough turned out misshapen and bloated. The excess moisture in pizza dough vaporizes at high temperatures, leaving air bubbles that may be acceptable in a pizza crust but not in our calzones.

To get a crispy, chewy crust, we started with the flour, pitting bread and all-purpose flours against each other. As expected, the dough made with higher-protein bread flour gave the crust the qualities we were looking for; the calzones made with all-purpose flour were too tender and soft. Even with bread flour, however, the crust was a little too fluffy; instead of a cleanly defined half-moon shape, we had a blurry, amorphous grin. We knew that yeast was what made the dough rise, so we assumed that by decreasing the yeast in the dough we could reduce the rise and therefore the puffiness of the dough. We were wrong. Yeast does of course cause dough to rise, but a smaller amount of yeast does not necessarily translate to a smaller rise. Rather, it simply takes longer for the dough to achieve that rise.

The key to a hearty, more substantial crust, we discovered, resided in the water, not the yeast. We used as much as 2 cups of water (with 4 cups of flour), which gave us a loose, wet dough, and as little as 1 cup, which gave us a dry, tight dough that was difficult to work with. A happy medium of 1½ cups—just ¼ cup less than our pizza dough—yielded a dough that was slightly tacky but not too hard to handle and that baked up with good definition, chew, and flavor—and much less fluff.

At this point, our dough was a bit lean, so we added oil and found that 1 tablespoon improved the dough but 2 tablespoons made it even better, giving us an easy-to-handle dough that was also richer in flavor. We experimented with mixing

times and found five minutes (the amount recommended by many recipes) to be acceptable, but we wondered if extending the mixing time might make for a chewier crust. Ten minutes proved to be ideal to fully develop the gluten in the dough and give the crust good chew.

With our crust in good shape, we turned our attention to the filling. It was difficult to find recipes for calzones with a simple ricotta filling. Most were adulterated with an odd-flavored ingredient such as blue cheese or used wet ingredients such as tomatoes, fresh mozzarella, and mushrooms, all of which delivered a soggy crust.

We started by pitting whole-milk ricotta against part-skim ricotta. Not surprisingly, whole-milk ricotta had a richer, fuller flavor that tasters preferred. We also tasted tried-and-true mozzarella alongside some other meltable cheeses, including fontina (both high- and low-end), Muenster, Monterey Jack, and Havarti. Mozzarella barely eked out a win over the runner-up, Muenster.

Our master recipe called for a high proportion of ricotta paired with lesser quantities of mozzarella as well as Parmesan to balance the flavor. Tasters panned this filling for being too grainy. We tried a different mixing method, using a food processor to smooth out the ricotta. The result was a smooth but overly aerated, fluffy filling (likened to an "oozy omelet" by one taster).

In the end, the solution came in two parts. First, the quantities of the three cheeses had to be just right, with more mozzarella to improve the texture. We ended up reducing the ricotta to 15 ounces, increasing the mozzarella to 8 ounces, and holding the Parmesan at 1½ ounces. The second step was to add an egg yolk (two yolks were too eggy) to the filling, which provided cohesiveness as well as improved texture. Now we had a smooth cheese filling that wouldn't run.

But we still had something to figure out. Why were so many of the calzones exploding during baking? Steam turned out to be the culprit; it forced holes in the crust during baking, and it made for a damp dough. The solution seemed simple enough: Drain the ricotta before mixing it with the other ingredients. To our dismay, the filling made with drained ricotta was like overchewed bubble gum. On top of that, some of the calzones still burst open. One solution was to cut a few vents in the top crust before putting the calzones in the oven, allowing the steam from the ricotta to escape and preventing any explosions in the oven. The vents, unfortunately, did nothing for the bottom crust, which came out of the oven crisp but turned soggy within minutes. Borrowing a method from the pastry world, we cooled the calzones on a rack. This kept the bottoms crusty as they cooled.

All that was left was to flavor our cheesy filling. Tasters preferred the earthy Italian flavor of oregano to other herbs, with just a few red pepper flakes to impart a feisty kick. We tried garlic raw, toasted, roasted, and cooked in a generous

amount of oil and found that garlic oil added the smoothest flavor, with no overtly sharp (as in the raw garlic) or sweet (as in the roasted garlic) overtones.

Although we'd tackled how to prevent our calzones from bursting open, we still needed to address why the filling sometimes oozed out of the crust. We tried moistening the edges with water or egg, and we tried pressing the edges with the tines of a fork and with our fingers. No technique was completely effective. We then tried roping the edge, folding it up onto itself in a decorative design. To do this, we left a ½-inch rim on the bottom layer, which we then pulled up and over the top layer as we formed a rope design. It cooked through and looked great. (Be

ASSEMBLING CALZONES

1. Turn the risen dough out onto an unfloured work surface. With a bench scraper or knife, divide the dough in half, then cut each half into thirds to form a total of six pieces.

2. With your hand, gently reshape each piece of dough into a ball. Transfer the dough balls to a parchment-lined baking sheet, cover with oiled plastic wrap, and let rest 15 to 30 minutes.

3. With your fingertips, press the dough ball into a 5-inch circle. With a floured rolling pin, roll outward from the center in all directions until the dough forms a 9-inch circle. If the dough sticks, dust the work surface underneath with flour.

4. Place a scant ½ cup of the filling in the center of the bottom half of the dough round. Using a small spatula, spread or press the filling in an even layer across the bottom half, leaving a 1-inch border uncovered.

 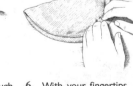  

5. Fold the top half of the dough over the cheese-covered bottom half, leaving a ½-inch border of the bottom layer uncovered.

6. With your fingertips, lightly press around the silhouette of the filling and out to the edge to lightly seal the dough shut.

7. Beginning at one end of the seam, place your index finger diagonally across the edge and gently pull the bottom layer of the dough over the tip of your index finger; press into the dough to seal. Repeat the process until the calzone is fully sealed.

8. With a very sharp paring knife or razor blade, cut 5 slits, about 1½ inches long, diagonally across the top of the calzone, making sure to cut through only the top layer of dough and not completely through the calzone.

sure not to leave more than a ½-inch rim; otherwise, the edges won't cook through.) A final brush of olive oil and a sprinkle of coarse salt before going into the oven gave our calzones a crisp texture, a salty flavor, and a beautifully rustic appearance.

Ricotta Calzones

MAKES 6

To make this recipe, you will need a standing mixer or food processor, parchment paper, and a pizza stone. The stone must heat for an additional 30 minutes once the oven has come up to temperature; if your oven heats slowly, begin heating it about an hour into the dough's first rise. Leftover calzones must be refrigerated; to reheat, heat the oven with the pizza stone just as you did when making the recipe, then set the calzones on the hot pizza stone for about 10 minutes. A simple tomato sauce like the Quick Tomato Sauce for Pizza on page 669 is a nice accompaniment to the calzones. See the illustrations on page 677 for tips on shaping and filling calzones.

DOUGH

4	cups (22 ounces) bread flour, plus more for dusting the work surface
I	envelope (about 2¼ teaspoons) instant yeast
1½	teaspoons table salt
2	tablespoons extra-virgin olive oil
1½	cups plus I tablespoon warm water (about 110 degrees)

FILLING

3	medium garlic cloves, minced or pressed through a garlic press
2	tablespoons extra-virgin olive oil
¼	teaspoon red pepper flakes
I	(15-ounce) container whole-milk ricotta cheese
8	ounces mozzarella cheese, shredded (2 cups)
1½	ounces freshly grated Parmesan cheese (about ¾ cup)
I	large egg yolk
I	tablespoon chopped fresh oregano leaves
¼	teaspoon table salt
⅛	teaspoon ground black pepper

Extra-virgin olive oil for brushing
on the shaped calzones
Kosher salt for sprinkling on the calzones

1. FOR THE DOUGH: In the bowl of a standing mixer, whisk the flour, yeast, and salt to combine. Attach the bowl and dough hook to the mixer; with the mixer running at medium-low speed, add the olive oil, then gradually add the water, continuing to mix until the mixture comes together and a smooth, elastic dough forms, about 10 minutes. Lightly spray a large bowl with nonstick cooking spray; form the dough into a ball, transfer it to the bowl, cover the bowl with plastic wrap lightly sprayed with nonstick cooking spray, and let rise in a warm spot until doubled in size, 1½ to 2 hours.

2. FOR THE FILLING: While the dough rises, stir together the garlic, olive oil, and red pepper flakes in an 8-inch skillet over medium heat until the garlic is fragrant and sizzling and the mixture registers 200 degrees on an instant-read thermometer, 1½ to 2 minutes. Transfer to a small bowl and cool until warm, stirring occasionally, about 10 minutes.

3. In a medium bowl, stir together the cheeses, egg yolk, oregano, salt, black pepper, and cooled garlic–red pepper oil until combined; cover with plastic wrap and refrigerate until needed.

4. Adjust an oven rack to the lowest position, set a pizza stone on the rack, and heat the oven to 500 degrees for at least 30 minutes. Line a baking sheet with parchment paper and spray the parchment lightly with nonstick cooking spray. Turn the risen dough out onto an unfloured work surface. Divide the dough in half, then cut each half into

CALZONE CATASTROPHES

We encountered plenty of problems in our early tests. One calzone (left) was nicely domed but nearly empty inside. Another (right) leaked in the oven because the dough was not properly sealed.

thirds. Gently reshape each piece of dough into a ball. Transfer to the baking sheet and cover with plastic wrap lightly sprayed with nonstick cooking spray. Let the dough rest at least 15 minutes but no more than 30 minutes.

5. Cut eight 9-inch squares of parchment paper. Working with one piece of dough at a time and keeping the other pieces covered, roll the dough into a 9-inch round. Set the dough round on a parchment square and cover it with another parchment square; roll out another dough ball, set the second dough round on top of the first, and cover with a parchment square. Repeat to form a stack of 3 dough rounds, covering the top round with a parchment square. Form a second stack of 3 with the remaining dough balls and parchment squares.

6. Remove the top parchment square from the first stack of dough rounds and place the rounds with parchment beneath on the work surface; if the dough rounds have shrunk, gently and evenly roll them out again to 9-inch rounds. Following illustrations 4 through 8 on page 677, form the calzones. With a pastry brush, brush the tops and sides of the calzones with olive oil and lightly sprinkle with kosher salt. Trim the excess parchment paper; slide the calzones on the parchment onto a pizza peel or rimless baking sheet, then slide the calzones with parchment onto the hot pizza stone, spacing them evenly apart. Bake until the calzones are golden brown, about 11 minutes; use a pizza peel or rimless baking sheet to remove the calzones with the parchment to a wire rack. Remove the calzones from the parchment, cool 5 minutes, and serve. While the first batch of calzones bakes, form the second batch and bake the calzones after removing the first batch from the oven.

➤ VARIATIONS
Food Processor Method
The calzone dough can be made in an 11-cup food processor, although it bakes up with slightly less chew than we like.

Place the flour, yeast, and salt in an 11-cup food processor and process to combine, about five 1-second pulses. While pulsing, add the olive oil through the feed tube, then gradually add the water; continue pulsing until the dough forms a ball, then process until smooth and elastic, about 30 seconds. Turn the dough out onto a lightly floured work surface and knead it by hand a few turns to form a smooth, round ball. Transfer the dough to a lightly oiled bowl and proceed as directed.

Ricotta Calzones with Sausage and Broccoli Rabe
1. Follow the recipe for Ricotta Calzones through step 1 to make the dough; while the dough rises, combine the cheeses, egg yolk, oregano, salt, and black pepper in a medium bowl, cover with plastic wrap, and refrigerate until needed. Omit the step for making the garlic oil.

2. Remove the casings from 8 ounces of hot or sweet Italian sausage. Wash and dry 12 ounces of broccoli rabe and trim the stalks to about 1 inch below the leaves; cut the broccoli rabe crosswise into 1-inch pieces. Cook the sausage in a 12-inch nonstick skillet over high heat, stirring constantly with a wooden spoon and breaking the sausage into ½-inch pieces, until no longer pink, about 4 minutes; stir in 1 tablespoon pressed or minced garlic and ¼ teaspoon red pepper flakes and cook until fragrant, about 10 seconds. Stir in the broccoli rabe, 1 tablespoon water, and ⅛ teaspoon salt; cook, stirring constantly, until the broccoli rabe is crisp-tender and the water has evaporated, about 4 minutes. Transfer the mixture to a large paper towel–lined plate and cool to room temperature; once cooled, pat it with paper towels to absorb excess moisture and set aside until needed.

3. Continue with the recipe from step 4. To fill the calzones, divide the sausage mixture evenly into 6 portions on the plate; place 1 portion of the sausage mixture on top of the cheese filling on each dough round and continue with the recipe to seal and bake the calzones.

Ricotta Calzones with Red Peppers, Spinach, and Goat Cheese
This variation calls for only 10 ounces of ricotta.
1. Follow the recipe for Ricotta Calzones through step 1 to make the dough; while the dough rises, combine 10 ounces (1¼ cups) whole-milk ricotta with the mozzarella, Parmesan, egg yolk, oregano, salt, and black pepper in a medium bowl. Cover with plastic wrap and refrigerate until needed. Cut

2 medium red bell peppers into 2 by ½-inch strips; wash, dry, and trim the stems off of 1 pound spinach (you should have about 4 cups). Heat 1 tablespoon extra-virgin olive oil in a 10-inch nonstick skillet over high heat until the oil begins to smoke. Stir in the bell peppers and ⅛ teaspoon salt; cook until slightly softened and spotty brown, about 5 minutes, stirring only 2 or 3 times. Clear the center of the pan; add 1 tablespoon extra-virgin olive oil, 1 tablespoon minced or pressed garlic, and ¼ teaspoon red pepper flakes to the space and mash with the back of a spoon until fragrant, about 10 seconds; stir into the bell peppers. Remove from the heat and immediately stir in the spinach and ⅛ teaspoon salt; continue to stir until the spinach is wilted, about 1 minute. Transfer the mixture to a paper towel–lined plate and cool to room temperature; once cooled, pat with paper towels to absorb excess moisture and set aside until needed.

2. Continue with the recipe from step 4. To fill the calzones, divide 6 ounces goat cheese evenly into 6 portions and divide the pepper mixture evenly into 6 portions on the plate. Place 1 portion pepper mixture on top of the ricotta cheese filling on each dough round, then crumble 1 portion goat cheese over the pepper mixture and continue with the recipe to seal and bake the calzones.

FOCACCIA

MANY OF THE FOCACCIA RECIPES WE HAVE tried in the past produced a crusty, crisp bread that was only slightly thicker than pizza. These dense, hard breads were often loaded down with toppings. They were more like a meal than a snack or an accompaniment to dinner.

We wanted something quite different. Good focaccia should have a soft, chewy texture and high rise. The crumb should be filled with small to medium air pockets, which will give the bread a good rise and create an overall impression of lightness and chewiness. As for the toppings, they should be minimal. Focaccia is a bread, not a meal.

We began our investigations with a composite recipe of yeast, warm water, olive oil, flour, and salt that was similar to our pizza dough. After more

than a dozen initial tests, we were not much closer to a solution. We tried reducing the salt because it can inhibit the action of the yeast and ended up with a better rise but a bland bread. We tried bread flour, all-purpose flour, whole-wheat flour, and all possible combinations of these three. Bread flour makes focaccia chewy but also dry and tough. Whole-wheat flour works at cross-purposes with our stated goal of a soft texture and high rise. Unbleached all-purpose flour turned out to be the right choice, but we still had a lot of work to do.

We tried milk instead of water and got better browning and a softer dough, but the bread was kind of flat. Increasing the yeast produced a high focaccia, but the flavor of the yeast was too dominant. We tried letting the dough ferment in the refrigerator for a day. This lightened the texture and produced larger holes in the dough but seemed like a lot of work for a relatively small improvement. We wanted to be able to make and enjoy focaccia on the same day.

In our research, we ran across two recipes from southern Italy that added riced potatoes to the dough. When we tried a recipe from Carol Field's *The Italian Baker* (Harper & Row, 1985), we liked the moistness, high rise, and soft texture of this bread. However, the crumb was fairly dense and compact, like a cake. This bread had several appealing traits but still was not quite what we wanted.

We knew that sponges (relatively thin mixtures of yeast, water, and flour that are allowed to ferment briefly) are often used to lend flavor and create air holes in breads. We were not terribly concerned about flavor. With olive oil, salt, and herbs, we were sure that any flavor boost from a sponge would be hard to detect. But we did want those air holes, so we tried a quick sponge.

We stirred the yeast, half the water, and a small portion of the flour together in a small bowl; covered the bowl with plastic wrap; and let the sponge rest before adding the remaining water, flour, oil, and salt. The difference was quite remarkable. The extra half hour of fermentation produced wonderfully large bubbles. The result was a bread that rose very high but still had a nice, light texture. We tried longer resting times and found that 30 minutes was enough for the yeast to work its magic.

With the sponge having been successful in our basic recipe, we now tried it with Carol Field's potato focaccia, which we had liked so much. The result was perfect. The sponge transformed the crumb from dense and cake-like to chewy and airy. The bread rose higher than the version made with just flour, and the crumb was softer and more moist.

A couple of notes about working with this dough. The moisture from the potatoes helps keep the crumb soft but also makes the dough very sticky. Adding extra flour makes the dough easier to handle, but the results are not as good because the wet dough helps produce bread with air pockets and chewiness. Sticky doughs are best kneaded in a standing mixer or a food processor. You can make the dough by hand, but you will probably end up incorporating slightly more flour.

When it comes time to shape the dough, moisten your hands with a little water. This will prevent the dough from sticking to your fingers. If you're trying to stretch the dough into a rectangular pan, you may need to let it rest before completing the final shaping. The dough is quite elastic and will put up a good fight without this rest.

An easier method is to divide the dough in half and shape it into two 8-inch disks on a large oiled baking sheet. These free-form disks rise and bake on the same pan, thus eliminating the tricky task of transferring such a sticky dough. You may also form each disk on a wooden peel that has been liberally coated with cornmeal, then slide it onto a pizza stone. The bottom crust is especially thick and chewy when the focaccia is cooked on a stone.

The problem with using a peel is that the focaccia dough often sticks, even when the peel is well dusted with cornmeal. When we were able to get the dough onto the stone without incident, however, the results were excellent. For the sake of simplicity, we opted to rise and bake the dough in an oiled metal pan, as described in the recipe below.

An oven temperature of 425 degrees bakes the focaccia quickly without any burning. Higher temperatures can cause the bottom to burn, and lower temperatures produce an inferior crust. Be sure to keep the focaccia away from the bottom of the oven to prevent the crust from scorching. Once the bread is golden brown, transfer it immediately to a cooling rack to keep the bottom crust from becoming soggy. Focaccia tastes best warm, so wait about 20 minutes and then serve.

Rosemary Focaccia

MAKES ONE 15 1/2 BY 10 1/2-INCH
RECTANGLE OR TWO 8-INCH ROUNDS

Our focaccia dough is made with potato, as is our deep-dish pizza. For information on how potatoes give bread flavor and crust, see "The Role of Potatoes in Pizza and Focaccia Dough" on page 673.

DOUGH

1	medium baking potato (about 9 ounces), peeled and quartered
1 1/2	teaspoons instant yeast
3 1/2	cups (17 1/2 ounces) unbleached all-purpose flour
1	cup warm water (about 110 degrees)
2	tablespoons extra-virgin olive oil, plus more for oiling the bowl and pan
1 1/4	teaspoons salt

TOPPING

2	tablespoons extra-virgin olive oil
2	tablespoons fresh rosemary leaves
3/4	teaspoon coarse sea salt or 1 1/4 teaspoons kosher salt

1. FOR THE DOUGH: Bring 1 quart water to a boil in a small saucepan; add the potato and simmer until tender, about 25 minutes. Drain the potato

DIMPLING FOCACCIA DOUGH

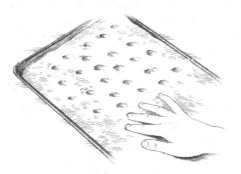

After the dough has risen a second time, wet two fingers and use them to make indentations at regular intervals.

well; cool until it can be handled comfortably; press it through the fine disk on a ricer or grate on the large holes of a box grater. Reserve 1⅓ cups lightly packed potato.

2. Meanwhile, using a standing mixer or a food processor, mix or process the yeast, ½ cup of the flour, and ½ cup of the warm water until combined. Cover tightly with plastic wrap (or put the workbowl lid on) and set aside until bubbly, about 20 minutes. Add the remaining dough ingredients, including the reserved potato. If using the mixer, attach the paddle and mix on low speed until the dough comes together. Switch to the dough hook and increase the speed to medium; continue kneading until the dough is smooth and elastic, about 5 minutes. For the food processor, process until the dough is smooth and elastic, about 40 seconds.

3. Transfer the dough to a lightly oiled bowl, turn to coat with oil, and cover tightly with plastic wrap. Let rise in a warm, draft-free area until the dough is puffy and doubled in volume, about 1 hour.

4. With wet hands (to prevent sticking), press the dough flat into a generously oiled 15½ by 10½-inch rimmed baking sheet. If the dough resists going into the corners (and it probably will), cover it with a damp cloth and let it relax for 15 minutes before trying to stretch again. Or, if making rounds, halve the dough and flatten each piece into an 8-inch round on a large (at least 18 inches long), generously oiled baking sheet. Either way, cover the dough with plastic wrap; let rise in a warm, draft-free area until the dough is puffy and doubled in volume, 45 minutes to 1 hour.

5. Meanwhile, adjust an oven rack to the lower-middle position and heat the oven to 425 degrees. With two wet fingers, dimple the risen dough at regular intervals. The dimples (there should be about 2 dozen) should be deep enough to hold small pieces of topping, herbs, and pools of olive oil.

6. For the topping: Drizzle the dough with the oil and sprinkle evenly with the rosemary and coarse salt, landing some in pools of oil.

7. Bake until the bottom crust is golden brown and crisp, 23 to 25 minutes. Transfer to a wire rack to cool slightly. Cut rectangular focaccia into squares or round focaccia into wedges; serve warm. (Focaccia can be kept at room temperature for several hours and reheated just before serving. Or wrap cooled focaccia in plastic and then foil, and freeze for up to 1 month; unwrap and defrost in a 325-degree oven until soft, about 15 minutes.)

➤ VARIATIONS

Hand-Kneaded Focaccia

Follow the recipe for Rosemary Focaccia through step 1. In step 2, mix the starter ingredients with a wooden spoon in a large bowl; cover and let stand 20 minutes. Add 1½ cups of the flour to the starter, then beat with a wooden spoon for 5 minutes. Add 1¼ cups more flour along with the remaining dough ingredients; continue beating until the dough comes together. Turn the dough onto a floured surface; knead in the remaining ¼ cup flour until the dough is elastic and sticky, 4 to 5 minutes. Transfer the dough to an oiled bowl as in step 3 and follow the remaining instructions.

Sage Focaccia

Follow the recipe for Rosemary Focaccia, adding 1 tablespoon chopped fresh sage leaves with the other dough ingredients in step 2 and substituting 24 whole fresh sage leaves for the rosemary in the topping. Place one sage leaf in each oil-filled dimple.

Parmesan Focaccia

Follow the recipe for Rosemary Focaccia, substituting ⅔ cup freshly grated Parmesan cheese for the rosemary and coarse sea salt.

Focaccia with Black Olives and Thyme

Follow the recipe for Rosemary Focaccia, substituting 1 teaspoon fresh thyme leaves and 24 pitted large black olives for the rosemary. Place one olive in each oil-filled dimple.

16

QUICK BREADS, MUFFINS, AND BISCUITS

QUICK BREADS ENCOMPASS LOAF BREADS LIKE banana bread, cornbread, and Irish soda bread as well as their diminutive counterparts: muffins, biscuits, and scones. Although these breads may differ in size and shape, they have a number of elements in common. All of these baked goods can be quickly prepared (the batter or dough can usually be assembled in the time it takes to preheat the oven) and quickly baked. This sets them far apart from yeast breads, which must rise for hours on the counter. All quick breads contain chemical leaveners (baking soda and baking powder) that are speedy and reliable.

There are several methods typically used to assemble quick breads. The most common, often referred to as the quick-bread method, calls for measuring wet and dry ingredients separately, pouring wet into dry, and then mixing them together as quickly as possible, usually with a wooden spoon or spatula. A second technique, often called the creaming method and more common to cake batters, starts with creaming the butter and sugar until light and fluffy—usually with an electric mixer. Eggs and flavorings are beaten in, then the dry and liquid ingredients are alternately added. A third possibility comes from the biscuit- and pie dough–making tradition, in which cold fat is cut into the dry ingredients with fingertips, forks, a pastry blender, or the blade of a food processor. Once the mixture has achieved a cornmeal-like texture with pea-size flecks, liquid is added and quickly mixed in.

In addition to mixing methods, it's also important to pay attention to the choice of flours and leaveners in these recipes. The protein content of the flour can greatly affect the texture of these simple baked goods. To read more about flour, see page 733.

BANANA BREAD

GOOD BANANA BREAD IS SOFT AND TENDER WITH plenty of banana flavor and crunchy toasted walnuts. It should be moist and light, something so delicious that you look forward to the bananas on the counter turning soft and mushy. However, many banana breads are flat, gritty, or heavy. Worse, some loaves taste only remotely of bananas.

In our testing, we found it very important to pay close attention to the condition of the bananas. Sweet, older, darkly speckled bananas infused the bread with both moisture and flavor, which meant that the bread, whether still warm or day-old, succeeded with less butter (minus 2 tablespoons) than the amount used in most recipes (½ cup).

We also experimented with the way we prepared the banana for the batter: slightly mashed, mashed well, and pureed. Loaves with slightly mashed bananas left chunks of fruit. We preferred a smoother texture, but pureeing the bananas turned out to be a bad idea, because the batter did not rise as well. Leavener probably escaped before the thin batter developed enough structure to trap gases. Bananas well mashed by hand kept the batter thick.

We wanted more moisture in the bread, so we tried mixing in milk, buttermilk, sour cream, and plain yogurt. Sour cream added richness to our bread, but it also made for a heavy texture and an unattractive, pebbly crust. Milk added little flavor and created a slick crust. Buttermilk added a delightful tang, but yogurt let the banana flavor stand out. And because yogurt has more solids than buttermilk, it made for a somewhat more solid loaf, which we preferred.

STORING OVERRIPE BANANAS
FOR BANANA BREAD

Place overripe bananas in a zipper-lock plastic bag and freeze them. As available, add more bananas to the bag. When you are ready to make bread, thaw the bananas on the counter until softened.

While the added yogurt softened the bread's crumb, we still sought a more delicate, open grain. So we decided to experiment with various mixing methods to see how they affected the final texture. We considered the quick-bread method (dry ingredients mixed in one bowl, liquids in another, with the two then gently stirred together) and the creaming method (butter and sugar creamed together, dry and wet ingredients then alternately mixed in).

The creaming method created a soft texture (reminiscent of butter cake) and good volume from the whipped sugar and butter. However, its lighter color looked less appetizing next to the golden brown loaf achieved with the quick-bread method. The quick-bread method produced a delicate texture, too, and the less consistent crumb looked hearty and delicious. It also rose more than the creamed loaf. All in all, it was a better choice.

Take caution when mixing, though. When we stirred the wet and the dry ingredients into a smooth batter, the loaves turned out small and tough. Flour contains protein, and when protein mixes with water, gluten develops. The more you stir with a spoon, the more the gluten proteins form into long, orderly bundles. These bundles create an elastic batter that resists changing shape and cannot rise as well. To minimize gluten development, fold together the wet and dry ingredients gently, just until the dry ingredients are moistened. The batter should still be thick and chunky, but without any streaks of unincorporated flour.

Banana Bread

MAKES ONE 9-INCH LOAF

For best results, be sure to use a loaf pan that measures 9 inches long, 5 inches across, and 3 inches deep.

2	cups (10 ounces) unbleached all-purpose flour, plus more for dusting the pan
1 1/4	cups walnuts, chopped coarse
3/4	cup (5 1/4 ounces) sugar
3/4	teaspoon baking soda
1/2	teaspoon salt
3	very ripe, soft, darkly speckled large bananas, mashed well (about 1 1/2 cups)
1/4	cup plain yogurt
2	large eggs, beaten lightly
6	tablespoons (3/4 stick) unsalted butter, melted and cooled
1	teaspoon vanilla extract

1. Adjust an oven rack to the lower-middle position and heat the oven to 350 degrees. Grease the bottom and sides of a 9 by 5-inch loaf pan; dust with flour, tapping out the excess.

2. Spread the walnuts on a baking sheet and toast until fragrant, 5 to 10 minutes. Set aside to cool.

3. Whisk the flour, sugar, baking soda, salt, and walnuts together in a large bowl; set aside.

4. Mix the mashed bananas, yogurt, eggs, butter, and vanilla with a wooden spoon in a medium bowl. Lightly fold the banana mixture into the

---

EQUIPMENT: Loaf Pans

A good loaf pan will evenly brown banana bread and other quick breads (as well as yeast breads, such as sandwich bread and cakes like pound cake). In addition, loaves should release cleanly and pans should be easy to get in and out of the oven, with little chance of sticking an oven mitt into the batter or baked bread.

We tested 10 loaf pans made from a variety of materials, including metal, glass, and stoneware. We found that dark-colored metal loaf pans browned breads more evenly than light-colored metal pans. Most of the dark metal pans were lined with a nonstick coating that also made the release of baked breads especially easy. We found that sweet breads, such as banana bread, were especially prone to burning in glass loaf

pans. Sticking was also a problem in these pans. Stoneware loaf pans did a decent job of browning, but we had trouble removing loaves from these pans. Our testers found that pans with handles at either end were easier to work with and kept us from sticking an oven mitt into the edge of a baked loaf.

In the end, we recommend that you buy metal loaf pans with a nonstick coating. Although there's no harm in spending more money on heavier pans, the cheapest, lightest pan in our testing (Ecko Baker's Secret, $4) was the favorite. One final piece of advice: Even with the nonstick coating, we recommend greasing and flouring your loaf pan to ensure easy release. Nothing is worse than losing a quick bread to the pan.

dry ingredients with a rubber spatula until just combined and the batter looks thick and chunky. Scrape the batter into the prepared loaf pan.

5. Bake until the loaf is golden brown and a toothpick inserted in the center comes out clean, about 55 minutes. Cool in the pan for 5 minutes, then transfer to a wire rack. Serve warm or at room temperature. (The bread can be wrapped with plastic wrap and stored at room temperature for up to 3 days.)

➤ VARIATIONS

Banana-Chocolate Bread
Follow the recipe for Banana Bread, reducing the sugar to 10 tablespoons and mixing 2½ ounces bittersweet chocolate, grated (a heaping ½ cup), into the dry ingredients.

Banana-Coconut Bread with Macadamia Nuts
Adjust an oven rack to the middle position and heat the oven to 350 degrees. Spread ½ cup sweetened flaked coconut and 1 cup chopped macadamia nuts on a baking sheet and toast, stirring every 2 minutes, until golden brown, about 6 minutes. Follow the recipe for Banana Bread, substituting the cooled toasted macadamias and coconut for the walnuts.

Orange-Spice Banana Bread
Follow the recipe for Banana Bread, adding 1 teaspoon ground cinnamon, ¼ teaspoon freshly grated nutmeg, and 2 tablespoons grated orange zest to the dry ingredients.

CRANBERRY-NUT BREAD

TOO OFTEN, THIS SIMPLE QUICK BREAD IS SUBpar, sunken in the middle, too dense, or so overly sweetened that the contrast between the tart berries and what should be a slightly sweet dough is lost. We wanted to avoid these problems, and we had some other goals in mind as well. We were looking for a crust that was golden brown and evenly thin all the way around and a texture that was somewhere between a dense breakfast bread

and a light, airy cake. After looking at almost 60 recipes, it seemed evident that the mixing method and the leavening were the most important factors in getting the quick bread we were after.

First we tackled mixing. Some recipes called for the creaming method, others the quick-bread method. We made several loaves using each of these methods. While the creaming method did give us a marginally more tender bread, we quickly determined that it was too light and airy. We liked the denser, more compact texture produced by the quick-bread method.

Next we moved on to leavening. When we looked back at our testing, we noted that 75 percent of the recipes combined baking powder with baking soda to leaven the bread. The rest used all baking powder or all baking soda. We tried every option we could think of using these two leaveners, both alone and together. We found that baking powder seemed to enhance the flavor, while baking soda supported the structure; finding the right balance was tricky. Eventually, we came to the decision that ¼ teaspoon of baking soda combined with 1 teaspoon of baking powder gave us the bright flavor and rich texture we were looking for.

With our mixing and leavening methods settled, we focused on ingredients. We quickly determined that we liked the flavor that butter provided over that of oil, margarine, or shortening. More than one egg made the bread almost too rich and caused the interior to turn somewhat yellow. After testing different amounts and types of sugar, we stuck with 1 cup of granulated sugar, which provided just the right amount of sweetness. Orange zest provided a nice complement to the tart cranberries.

We also tinkered with the liquid component. Many recipes called for water or even boiling water, but freshly squeezed orange juice was usually mentioned and offered the best flavor.

Not every recipe called for dairy, but we tested everything from heavy cream to sour cream. Both buttermilk and yogurt provided the moistness and tang we were looking for, with buttermilk edging out yogurt by a hairbreadth.

Last but not least were the cranberries. The cranberry harvest begins just after Labor Day and continues through early fall, which means that by mid- to late January, no fresh berries are available. Cranberries freeze beautifully, so grab a few extra bags to have on hand and freeze them until you're ready to use them. We found no discernible difference in the finished product whether using fresh or frozen cranberries.

Cranberry-Nut Bread

MAKES ONE 9-INCH LOAF

We prefer sweet, mild pecans in this bread, but walnuts can be substituted. Resist the urge to cut into the bread while it is hot out of the oven; the texture improves as it cools, making it easier to slice.

2 cups (10 ounces) unbleached all-purpose flour, plus more for dusting the pan
1/2 cup pecans, chopped coarse
1 tablespoon grated zest plus 1/3 cup juice from 1 large orange
2/3 cup buttermilk
6 tablespoons (3/4 stick) unsalted butter, melted and cooled
1 large egg, beaten lightly
1 cup (7 ounces) sugar
1 teaspoon salt
1 teaspoon baking powder
1/4 teaspoon baking soda
1 1/2 cups cranberries (about 6 ounces), chopped coarse

1. Adjust an oven rack to the middle position and heat the oven to 375 degrees. Grease the bottom and sides of a 9 by 5-inch loaf pan; dust with flour, tapping out the excess.

2. Spread the pecans on a baking sheet and toast until fragrant, 5 to 7 minutes. Set aside.

3. Stir together the orange zest, orange juice, buttermilk, butter, and egg in a small bowl. Whisk together the flour, sugar, salt, baking powder, and baking soda in a large bowl. Stir the liquid ingredients into the dry ingredients with a rubber spatula until just moistened. Gently stir in the cranberries and pecans. Do not overmix. Scrape the batter into the prepared pan and smooth the surface with a rubber spatula.

4. Bake 20 minutes, then reduce the heat to 350 degrees; continue to bake until the loaf is golden brown and a toothpick inserted in the center comes out clean, about 45 minutes longer. Cool in the pan 10 minutes, then transfer to a wire rack and cool at least 1 hour before serving. (The bread can be wrapped with plastic wrap and stored at room temperature for up to 3 days.)

ZUCCHINI BREAD

ZUCCHINI BREAD CAN TOO OFTEN BE BLAND and leaden. We wanted a brightly flavored, lightly sweetened quick bread with a moist crumb that was a real treat to nibble and savor.

The standard zucchini bread recipe published in countless collections of community recipes and home-style cookbooks calls for mixing dry and liquid ingredients separately and then combining them. The batter is scraped into a loaf pan and baked in a moderate oven for 50 to 60 minutes.

While we were reluctant to change the basic zucchini bread method, we were eager to find a substitute for the vegetable oil called for in every recipe we came across. We found that loaves made with vegetable oil tasted flat and bland and suspected that melted butter would complement the subtle zucchini flavor and contribute a pleasant richness. Recipes generally called for anywhere from 1/4 to 1 cup vegetable oil in a batter that would fill a standard 9 by 5-inch loaf pan. We began our tests by replacing the vegetable oil with an equal amount of butter. After numerous tests, we found that loaves with just 6 tablespoons melted butter were just right.

Although our bread no longer tasted bland, it still tasted a bit flat. We considered adding an acidic ingredient to the batter to brighten the rich buttery flavor and complement the subtle vegetal notes of the zucchini. We experimented with differing amounts of buttermilk, sour cream, and yogurt, acidic liquid ingredients we have used in other quick-bread recipes. Of the three, we preferred plain yogurt. Sour cream made the texture too heavy and the flavor too rich. While buttermilk worked well—and would be an acceptable substitute in a pinch—we preferred the texture

687

and flavor of the bread made with plain yogurt. A tablespoon of lemon juice added a bit more acidity as well as a pleasant citrus note. We tried lemon zest but found it to be overpowering. In addition to increased flavor, the yogurt and lemon juice reacted with the baking soda to produce a lighter bread with more rise, which tasters preferred.

Next we tackled the eggs, sugar, and other ingredients added to the liquid portion of the batter. We found that two eggs worked well, adding more flavor and rise than one egg but without the slight egg flavor and texture of the bread made with three eggs. Recipes that call for granulated sugar alone tend to use at least one cup. We found these loaves to be too sweet and delicate. Just ¾ cup sugar added the right amount of sweetness without giving this almost-savory bread a cake-like sweetness and texture.

We finally confronted the reason for zucchini bread: the zucchini. To this point, we had been adding only 6½ ounces zucchini, the size of a small zucchini, which when shredded produced about 1½ cups lightly packed. The zucchini flavor and texture were subtle, but almost too subtle. We wondered if the bread shouldn't have a more pronounced zucchini flavor. We tried increasing the zucchini to 3 cups and found ourselves with a bread that virtually looked and tasted like mashed zucchini.

We decided to drain the zucchini to extract as much water as possible so that we could add more than 6 ounces of the squash and still retain a texture that was more like a moist quick bread than squashed squash. We wanted more zucchini flavor without the excess zucchini moisture. We processed the zucchini in the food processor with 2 tablespoons of the sugar and placed the shredded zucchini in a fine-mesh strainer set about 2 inches above the bottom of a bowl. (You can also grate the zucchini on the large holes of a box grater and toss the shreds with 2 tablespoons sugar.) After 30 minutes, the sugar had drawn nearly half a cup of liquid from 1 pound of zucchini. If you are using large zucchini—2 pounds or more—with a developed internal seed structure, slice the squash in half lengthwise and use a spoon to scrape out the large seeds as you would a cucumber. Draining the

zucchini turned out to be a very important step. Thirty minutes passed quickly as we prepared the pan and the remaining ingredients for the bread. The resulting bread, dotted with greens flecks of the squash, had a notably increased zucchini flavor as well as a moist, but not gummy, texture.

We tried our finished loaf with other flavorings found in various recipes: ground cinnamon, grated nutmeg, ground ginger, vanilla, nuts, and raisins. Except for the nuts, we found all of these flavoring agents out of place in our relatively light, brightly flavored quick bread.

Zucchini Bread
MAKES ONE 9-INCH LOAF

If you are using large zucchini with developed internal seeds, cut each zucchini in half lengthwise and use a spoon to scrape out and discard the seeds before shredding. The test kitchen found no discernible difference in tasting loaves made with whole-milk, low-fat, or nonfat plain yogurt, so use what you have on hand.

2   cups (10 ounces) unbleached all-purpose flour, plus more for dusting the pan
1   pound zucchini, washed and dried, ends and stems removed, cut in half lengthwise and seeded if using large zucchini, each half cut into 1-inch pieces
¾   cup (5¼ ounces) sugar
½   cup pecans or walnuts, chopped coarse
1   teaspoon baking soda
1   teaspoon baking powder
½   teaspoon salt
¼   cup plain yogurt
2   large eggs, beaten lightly
1   tablespoon juice from 1 lemon
6   tablespoons (¾ stick) unsalted butter, melted and cooled

1. Adjust an oven rack to the middle position and heat the oven to 375 degrees. Grease the bottom and sides of a 9 by 5-inch loaf pan; dust with flour, tapping out the excess.

2. In the bowl of a food processor fitted with the metal blade, process the zucchini and 2 tablespoons of the sugar until the zucchini is coarsely

shredded, twelve to fifteen 1-second pulses. Transfer the mixture to a fine-mesh strainer set at least 2 inches over a bowl and allow to drain for 30 minutes. Alternatively, you can shred the halved zucchini (don't cut it into 1-inch pieces) on the large holes of a box grater, toss with the 2 tablespoons sugar, and drain.

3. Meanwhile, spread the nuts on a baking sheet and toast until fragrant, 5 to 7 minutes. Transfer the nuts to a cooling rack and cool completely. Transfer the nuts to a large bowl; add the flour, baking soda, baking powder, and salt and whisk until combined. Set aside.

4. Whisk together the remaining ½ cup plus 2 tablespoons sugar, the yogurt, eggs, lemon juice, and melted butter in a 2-cup glass measure until combined. Set aside.

5. After the zucchini has drained, squeeze the zucchini with several layers of paper towels to absorb excess moisture. Stir the zucchini and the yogurt mixture into the flour mixture until just moistened. Scrape the batter into the prepared pan and smooth the surface with a rubber spatula.

6. Bake until the loaf is golden brown and a toothpick inserted in the center comes out clean, 55 to 60 minutes, rotating the pan halfway through baking. Cool in the pan for 10 minutes, then transfer to a wire rack and cool for at least 1 hour before serving. (The bread can be wrapped with plastic wrap and stored at room temperature for up to 3 days.)

SHREDDING ZUCCHINI

1. Shred trimmed zucchini on the large holes of a box grater or in a food processor fitted with the shredding disk.

2. After sugaring and draining the zucchini, wrap it in paper towels and squeeze out excess liquid. Proceed immediately with the recipe.

GINGERBREAD

GINGERBREAD SHOULD BE TENDER, MOIST, AND several inches thick. It should be easy enough to assemble just before dinner so squares of warm gingerbread can be enjoyed for dessert. As our early tests proved, these goals are rarely met. Gingerbread has a tendency to be dry and tough, and many recipes are unnecessarily complicated.

To start our kitchen tests, we chose a milk-based gingerbread. Many recipes call for water, but in our initial tests tasters found these breads considerably drier and less rich than those made with milk. Milk fat adds tenderness and flavor; it is a must. With that decision made, we focused next on sweeteners. Most recipes include a dry sweetener—granulated sugar, light brown sugar, or dark brown sugar—as well as a liquid sweetener—molasses most often, but sometimes honey, maple syrup, or corn syrup.

We quickly discovered that molasses is the right liquid sweetener. Honey and corn syrup were judged too bland and boring. Maple syrup had some partisans, but most tasters thought the maple flavor clashed with the spices. We preferred the gentler flavor of light or mild molasses as compared with dark or robust molasses or blackstrap molasses.

Brown sugar is more commonly used in gingerbread recipes than white sugar. We expected to like its heartier, richer flavor. However, tasters preferred samples prepared with granulated sugar. With brown sugar added to the mix, the molasses flavor overwhelmed the spices. Granulated sugar tasted cleaner, allowing the spices to shine through.

As for the spices, tasters liked a combination of ground ginger, cinnamon, cloves, nutmeg, and allspice. We tested and liked both crystallized and grated fresh ginger, but everyone in the test kitchen agreed that regular ground ginger (something most cooks are likely to have in the pantry) delivered excellent results. If you like a stronger ginger flavor, you can replace the ground ginger with a mixture of grated fresh and crystallized ginger as directed in the note preceding our recipe. Finally, we found that a pinch of cocoa, which is sometimes added to gingerbread, added earthiness and complexity to our recipe.

In kitchen tests, butter was the hands-down favorite over vegetable oil and shortening. We found that melting the butter yielded a denser, moister cake. When we creamed the butter and sugar, the result was lighter, fluffier, and more cake-like. As for the eggs, we found that two added too much moisture to the batter, which tended to sink in the middle near the end of the baking time. A single egg ensured sufficient tenderness and proper height.

Although we had been using milk in our recipe, we were intrigued by some old-fashioned recipes that called for buttermilk instead. The buttermilk had some nice effects on our recipe. The color was darker and the texture slightly moister. Unfortunately, buttermilk also made the crumb coarser, and the flavor was a bit too strong. By comparison, the gingerbread made with milk had a better rise and finer texture. In the end, we found that a 50-50 ratio of buttermilk and milk offered the best traits of each. With buttermilk added to the recipe, we found that baking soda was the best leavener.

We tested several methods for combining the wet and dry ingredients, including adding the melted fat to the dry ingredients before the liquids, as well as beating the butter, sugar, and eggs, then alternately adding the wet and dry ingredients. In the end, the simplest method proved best. We combined all the dry ingredients in one bowl, all the wet ingredients (including the melted butter, egg, and sugar) in another bowl, and then beat the dry ingredients into the wet ingredients, giving ourselves gingerbread that went into the oven in less than 10 minutes and came out tasting great.

Gingerbread

SERVES 8

For a stronger ginger flavor, replace the ground ginger with 3 tablespoons grated fresh ginger and 3 tablespoons minced crystallized ginger. If you don't own an 11 by 7-inch pan, you can bake the batter in a 9-inch square pan. This gingerbread is moist and delicious on its own, but it can be served with a dollop of lightly sweetened whipped cream.

PREVENTING STICKY LIDS

Instead of struggling with the stuck-in-place lids of jars containing sticky contents such as jelly or molasses, try one of these tips.

A. Cover the top of the jar with plastic wrap before screwing on the lid. The plastic will prevent any serious sticking, so the lid always unscrews.

B. Dip a small piece of paper towel into a bit of vegetable oil and wipe the threads of the jar. The film of oil will prevent the lid from sticking to the jar the next time you open it.

2¼	cups sifted (9 ounces) unbleached all-purpose flour, plus more for dusting the pan
½	teaspoon baking soda
½	teaspoon salt
2	teaspoons ground ginger
I	teaspoon ground cinnamon
½	teaspoon ground cloves
½	teaspoon freshly grated nutmeg
½	teaspoon ground allspice
I	teaspoon Dutch-processed cocoa
8	tablespoons (I stick) unsalted butter, melted and cooled to room temperature
¾	cup mild or light molasses
¾	cup (5¼ ounces) sugar
½	cup buttermilk
½	cup milk
I	large egg

1. Adjust an oven rack to the middle position and heat the oven to 350 degrees. Grease the bottom and sides of an 11 by 7-inch baking dish; dust with flour, tapping out the excess.

2. Whisk together the flour, baking soda, salt, ginger, cinnamon, cloves, nutmeg, allspice, and cocoa in a medium bowl.

3. Beat the butter, molasses, sugar, buttermilk, milk, and egg in a large bowl with an electric mixer on low speed. Add the dry ingredients and beat on medium speed until the batter is smooth and thick, about 1 minute, scraping down the sides of the bowl with a rubber spatula as needed. (Do not overmix.) Scrape the batter into the prepared pan and smooth the surface.

4. Bake until the top springs back when lightly touched and the edges have pulled away from the pan sides, about 40 minutes. Set the pan on a wire rack and cool for at least 10 minutes. Serve warm or at room temperature. (Gingerbread can be wrapped in plastic, then foil, and refrigerated up to 5 days.)

➤ VARIATION
Gingerbread with Dried Fruit
Follow the recipe for Gingerbread, folding ¾ cup raisins, dried cranberries, or chopped prunes into the finished batter.

CORNBREAD

WHILE ALL CORNBREADS ARE QUICK TO MAKE and bake, there are two very distinct types: Northern and Southern. Southerners use 100 percent white cornmeal, and they like their cornbread crumbly, dry, and flat—about one inch thick. Most Northerners prefer sweeter, lighter, and higher golden cornbreads, which they achieve by adding a little sugar and combining white flour and yellow cornmeal. Both types of cornbread sport a brown crust, although Southern cornbread crusts are also crisp and crunchy.

Since there are cooks who are attached to each style, we decided to develop recipes for both kinds of cornbread. One should be tender and fluffy but not too sweet, something akin to cake but not too rich. This Northern-style cornbread would be good enough to eat on its own. For Southern-style cornbread, we envisioned something drier and more crumbly. It would be perfect with a bowl of soup or a pot of greens. For both recipes, choosing the right cornmeal would be crucial.

Large commercial mills use huge steel rollers to grind dent corn (a hard, dry corn) into cornmeal. Smaller mills grind with millstones; this product is called stone-ground cornmeal. Stone-ground cornmeal is usually a bit coarser than cornmeal processed through steel rollers. We like Arrowhead Mills brand, which has a fine, consistent texture.

Besides the differences in milling methods, smaller millers often choose not to degerm, or remove all the germ. This makes their product closer to a whole-grain cornmeal. If the color is uniform, the germ has been removed. A stone-ground cornmeal with some germ will have flecks that are both lighter and darker than the predominant color, whether that's yellow or white.

In our tests, we found the texture of cornbreads made with stone-ground meals to be more interesting, since the cornmeals were not of a uniform grind. More important, we found that cornbreads made with stone-ground cornmeal tasted much better than those made with standard cornmeal.

The higher moisture and oil content of stone-ground cornmeal causes it to go rancid within weeks. If you buy some, wrap it tightly in plastic or put it in a moisture-proof container, then refrigerate or freeze it. Degerminated cornmeals, such as Quaker, keep for a year if stored in a dry, cool place.

NORTHERN CORNBREAD

IN PERFECTING HOMEMADE NORTHERN CORN-bread, we aimed for a high-rising, moist bread, one with a rich corn taste and handsome golden color. Among other things, we wanted to find the right proportion of cornmeal to flour, the correct type and amount of chemical leavening, and the ideal amount of sugar. During our baking of 43 batches of cornbread using varying ingredients, mixing techniques, and baking temperatures and times, we uncovered some surprises.

In testing aspects of the dry ingredients, we found that the proportion of cornmeal to flour was key. The best flavor, texture, and rise resulted from a 1-1 ratio of cornmeal to all-purpose flour. If we added more cornmeal, the texture coarsened, and the cornbread baked flatter. Using more flour than cornmeal resulted in a less intense corn flavor and a cake-like texture.

We had thought we would like a fairly sweet Northern cornbread. We changed our opinion very quickly. The amount of sugar in the recipes we examined ranged from one tablespoon to eight. We started the testing with two tablespoons and adjusted up and down. More sugar made the cornbread taste like a dessert. In test batches made without sugar, though, we missed it. In the end, 4 teaspoons of sugar was the right amount for our cornbread.

The leavener we used would depend on whether we used milk or buttermilk in the mixture, so we postponed a final decision on that dry ingredient. Finally, in tests with and without salt, we found that adding ½ teaspoon helped bring out the corn flavor and balanced the sweetness.

We had now assembled the dry ingredients. At this point, most cornbread recipes instruct the cook to add the wet ingredients—egg, milk, and fat—to the dry ones. We first tested for the number of eggs. Two eggs tasted the best. Three eggs rated as too eggy, and one left things a bit dry. The eggs added moisture and helped the cornbread rise higher; the yolks contributed to the golden interior and rich taste.

Our next set of tests focused on buttermilk and milk. Buttermilk contributed a rich, luscious taste that highlighted the corn flavor, although its use also resulted in a coarser and heavier texture. Buttermilk also placed the cornbread squarely in the bread corner—it no longer hinted at dessert. Cornbreads made with milk tasted fine but lacked richness, although the lighter texture and softer yellow color were appealing. To remedy this, we decided to use a combination of buttermilk and milk. A half-milk and half-buttermilk combination resulted in cornbread with a wonderful taste, light texture, handsome yellow-gold interior, high rise, and brown crust with some crunch.

Next we tested the fats. Butter outranked the other contenders. Vegetable oil, vegetable shortening, and margarine tasted boring and lackluster, and lard seemed out of place in this recipe. We discovered that we liked a cornbread made with butter, but not too much. Two tablespoons per batch was enough. More butter was too heavy and started to interfere with the corn flavor.

Most recipes instruct the cook to add the melted butter last. Is this necessary? To find out, we tried several experiments. First we creamed the softened butter, then added the remaining ingredients. The top of this cornbread looked pebbled and not very appetizing. Next we melted the butter, then stirred in all the other ingredients. Now the cornbread was heavy and too moist. Finally, we added the melted butter last. This method produced the best-tasting and most attractive cornbread.

To obtain the light texture and high rise of Northern cornbread, some type of chemical leavening is required. As we experimented with baking soda and baking powder, the two typical leaveners for cornbread, we discovered that three or four teaspoons of baking powder produced the tallest cornbreads, but that these breads were lacking in corny taste. Cornbreads made with 100 percent baking soda sported darker, more deeply golden brown top crusts and a stronger array of interior colors: a deeper golden or yellow overall color, with flecks of deep orange and yellow.

Hoping to produce a bread with the color provided by baking soda and the high rise caused by baking powder, we combined the two chemical leavenings. After tinkering with various amounts of each, we found that 2 teaspoons of baking powder plus ½ teaspoon of baking soda yielded a tall rise, golden color, and the best taste.

With our recipe now in hand, we looked at two final variables: the type of baking pan and the oven temperature. Our goal was to produce cornbread with an evenly browned crust and a moist interior.

We tried using a glass pan, but the cornbread overbaked and became hard around the edges, a common problem with glass pans, which tend to overheat. We found that metal baking pans were the best choice for making moist and light cornbread.

As for oven temperature, we found that cornbreads baked at 350 degrees and 375 degrees had very thick, heavy crusts because they took a long time to form. A 425-degree oven worked best. At this higher temperature, the crust formed more quickly and the whole cornbread baked faster, resulting in a crisper crust and lighter-textured cornbread.

Golden Northern Cornbread

MAKES 9 SERVINGS

Use stone-ground yellow cornmeal for the best taste and texture. Stone-ground cornmeal can be recognized by its light and dark flecks.

2	tablespoons unsalted butter, melted, plus more for greasing the pan
1	cup (about 5 ounces) yellow cornmeal, preferably stone-ground
1	cup (5 ounces) unbleached all-purpose flour
2	teaspoons baking powder
½	teaspoon baking soda
4	teaspoons sugar
½	teaspoon salt
2	large eggs
²/₃	cup buttermilk
²/₃	cup milk

1. Adjust an oven rack to the center position and heat the oven to 425 degrees. Grease a 9-inch square baking pan with butter.

2. Whisk the cornmeal, flour, baking powder, baking soda, sugar, and salt together in a large bowl. Push the dry ingredients up the sides of the bowl to make a well.

3. Crack the eggs into the well and stir lightly with a wooden spoon, then add the buttermilk and milk. Stir the wet and dry ingredients quickly until almost combined. Add the melted butter and stir until the ingredients are just combined.

4. Pour the batter into the greased pan. Bake until the top of the cornbread is golden brown and lightly cracked and the edges have pulled away from the sides of the pan, about 25 minutes.

5. Transfer the pan to a wire rack to cool slightly, 5 to 10 minutes. Cut the cornbread into squares and serve warm. (The pan can be wrapped in foil and stored at room temperature for up to 1 day. Reheat the cornbread in a 350-degree oven for 10 to 15 minutes.)

➤ VARIATIONS

Golden Northern Cornbread with Cheddar Cheese

Follow the recipe for Golden Northern Cornbread, omitting the sugar. After adding the butter, quickly fold in 1 cup (4 ounces) shredded cheddar or Monterey Jack cheese.

Golden Northern Cornbread with Chiles

We advise washing your hands thoroughly after handling hot chiles, or better yet, wear rubber gloves.

Follow the recipe for Golden Northern Cornbread, omitting the sugar. After adding the butter, quickly fold in 1 small jalapeño chile, stemmed, seeded, and minced, for mild chile flavor. For more heat, use up to 2 jalapeños that have been stemmed and minced but not seeded.

Golden Northern Cornbread with Bacon

To end up with the ½ cup bacon needed for this recipe, cut 8 ounces sliced bacon into small dice, then fry in a large skillet until well browned and crisp. Drain, cool, and set aside until ready to fold into the batter.

Follow the recipe for Golden Northern Cornbread, omitting the sugar. After adding the butter, quickly fold in ½ cup crumbled bacon.

SOUTHERN CORNBREAD

ALTHOUGH THE TWO INGREDIENT LISTS MAY look similar, the cornbreads of the North and South are as different as Boston and Birmingham. White, not yellow, is the cornmeal of choice for Southern-style cornbread. Unlike Northerners, Southerners use only trace amounts of flour, if any, and if sugar is included, it is treated like salt, to be measured out in teaspoons rather than by the cup. Buttermilk moistens, bacon drippings enrich, and a combination of baking powder and soda provides lift.

Classic Southern cornbread batter is poured into a scorching-hot, greased cast-iron skillet, which causes it to develop a thin, crisp crust as the bread bakes. At its best, this bread is moist and tender, with the warm fragrance of the cornfield and the subtle flavor of the dairy in every bite.

We began by testing 11 different cornmeals in one simple Southern cornbread recipe. Before the cornmeal tests, we would have bet that color was a regional idiosyncrasy that had little to do with flavor. But tasting proved otherwise. Cornbreads made with yellow cornmeal had a consistently more potent corn flavor than those made with white cornmeal.

Although we didn't want Southern cornbread to taste like dessert, we wondered whether a little sugar might enhance the corn flavor. So we made three batches—one with no sugar, one with 2 teaspoons, and one with a heaping tablespoon. The higher-sugar bread was really too sweet for Southern cornbread, but 2 teaspoons of sugar seemed to enhance the natural sweetness of the corn without calling attention to itself.

Most Southern-style cornbread batters are made with just buttermilk, but we found recipes calling for the full range of acidic and sweet dairy products—buttermilk, sour cream, yogurt, milk, and cream—and made batches with each of them. We still loved the pure, straightforward flavor of the buttermilk-based cornbread, but the batch made with sour cream was actually more tasty and baked into a more attractive shape.

At this point we began to feel a little uneasy about where we were taking this regional bread. A couple of teaspoons of sugar might be overlooked, but using yellow cornmeal was heresy. And sour cream was really crossing the line.

So far all of our testing had been done with a composite recipe under which most Southern cornbread recipes seemed to fall. There were two recipes, however, that didn't quite fit the mold—one very rich and one very lean—and now seemed like the right time to give them a try.

After rejecting the rich version as closer to spoonbread, a soufflé-like dish, than cornbread, we went to the other extreme. In this simple version, boiling water is stirred into the cornmeal, then modest amounts of milk, egg, butter, salt, and baking powder are stirred into the resulting cornmeal mush, and the whole thing is baked. So simple, so lean, so humble, this recipe would have been easy to pass over. But given our options at this point, we decided to give it a quick test. Just one bite completely changed the direction of our pursuit. Unlike anything we had tasted so far, the crumb of this cornbread was incredibly moist and fine and bursting with corn flavor.

We were pleased, but since the foundation of this bread was cornmeal mush, the crumb was actually more mushy than moist. In addition, the baking powder got stirred into the wet batter at the end. This just didn't feel right.

After a few unsuccessful attempts to make the cornbread less mushy, we started thinking that this great idea was a bust. In a last attempt to salvage it, we decided to make mush out of only half the cornmeal and mix the remaining cornmeal with the leavener. To our relief, the bread made this way was much improved. Decreasing the mush even further—from a half to a third of the cornmeal—gave us exactly what we were looking for. We made the new, improved cornbread with buttermilk and mixed a bit of baking soda with the baking powder, and it tasted even better. Finally, our recipe was starting to feel Southern again. Although we still preferred yellow cornmeal and a touch of sugar, we had achieved a bread that was moist, tender, and rather fine-crumbed without flour and nicely shaped without sour cream, thus avoiding two ingredients that would have interfered with the strong corn flavor we wanted.

With this new recipe in hand, we performed a

few final tests. Our recipe called for 1 tablespoon of butter, but many Southern cornbreads call for no more fat than is needed to grease the pan. We tried vegetable oil, peanut oil, shortening, butter, and bacon drippings, as well as a batch with no fat at all. To our delight, the cornbread with no added fat was as moist and delicious as the other breads. Butter and bacon drippings, however, were pleasant flavor additions, so we kept a little in our recipe.

One final question: Do you need to heat up the skillet before adding the batter? If you're not a Southerner, the answer is no. Although the bread will not be as crisp in an unheated pan, it will ultimately brown up with a longer baking time. If you are a Southerner, of course, the answer is yes. More than the color of the meal or the presence of sugar or flour, the meeting of batter and hot fat in a cast-iron skillet defines Southern cornbread.

Southern Cornbread

MAKES 8 SERVINGS

Though some styles of Southern cornbread are dry and crumbly, we favor this dense, moist, tender version. Cornmeal mush of just the right texture is essential to this bread. Make sure that the water is at a rapid boil when it is added to the cornmeal. Though we prefer to make cornbread in a preheated cast-iron skillet or heavy-bottomed ovensafe skillet, a 9-inch round cake pan or 9-inch square baking pan, greased lightly with butter and not preheated, will also produce acceptable results if you double the recipe and bake the bread for 25 minutes.

4	teaspoons bacon drippings, or 1 teaspoon vegetable oil plus 1 tablespoon melted butter
1	cup (about 5 ounces) yellow cornmeal, preferably stone-ground
2	teaspoons sugar
1/2	teaspoon salt
1	teaspoon baking powder
1/4	teaspoon baking soda
1/3	cup rapidly boiling water
3/4	cup buttermilk
1	large egg, beaten lightly

1. Adjust an oven rack to the lower-middle position and heat the oven to 450 degrees. Set an 8-inch cast-iron skillet with the bacon fat in the heating oven.

2. Measure 1/3 cup of the cornmeal into a medium bowl. Whisk the remaining 2/3 cup cornmeal, the sugar, salt, baking powder, and baking soda together in a small bowl; set aside.

3. Pour the boiling water all at once into the 1/3 cup cornmeal; stir to make a stiff mush. Whisk in the buttermilk gradually, breaking up lumps, until smooth, then whisk in the egg. When the oven is preheated and the skillet is very hot, stir the dry ingredients into the mush mixture until just moistened. Carefully remove the skillet from the oven. Pour the hot bacon fat from the pan into the batter and stir to incorporate, then quickly pour the batter into the heated skillet. Bake until the bread is golden brown, about 20 minutes. Remove from the oven and instantly turn the cornbread onto a wire rack; cool for 5 minutes, then serve immediately.

IRISH SODA BREAD

AUTHENTIC IRISH SODA BREAD HAS A TENDER, dense crumb and a rough-textured, crunchy crust. It is versatile enough to be served with butter and jam at breakfast, for sandwiches at lunch, or alongside the evening meal.

As we looked over a multitude of recipes for soda bread, we found that they fell into two categories. The American versions contained eggs, butter, and sugar in varying amounts, along with caraway seeds, raisins, and a multitude of other flavorings. But most Irish cookbooks combined only four ingredients: flour (white and/or whole-wheat), baking soda, salt, and buttermilk.

We decided to begin our investigations with the flour. Because of Ireland's climate, the wheat grown there is a "soft," or low-protein, variety. While not suitable for strong European-style yeast breads, this flour is perfect for chemically leavened breads. This is basically because flour with a lower protein content produces a finer crumb and more tender product, key for breads that don't have the light texture provided when yeast is used as the leavener.

After suffering through several tough, heavy loaves made with unbleached all-purpose flour, we started exploring different proportions of cake flour—a low-protein flour—as well as all-purpose flour. And, in fact, the bread did become more tender and a little lighter with the addition of some cake flour. As the ratio of cake to all-purpose exceeded 1-1, however, the bread became much more compact and heavy, with an undesirable mouthfeel: 1 cup of cake flour to 3 cups of unbleached all-purpose flour proved best.

Because the liquid-to-dry ingredient ratio is important in determining dough texture and bread moistness, we decided to test buttermilk next. (We also knew that the amount of this acidic liquid would have a direct effect on the amount of baking soda we would be able to use. As mentioned when discussing other recipes, baking soda reacts with acids such as those in buttermilk to provide leavening; however, if there is too much soda, some remains intact in the bread, giving it a slightly metallic taste.) As it turned out, bread made with 1¾ or 1⅔ cups of buttermilk produced bread that was doughy, almost gummy. With 1½ cups, the dough was firmer yet still moist—and the resulting bread was no longer doughy. (If you don't have buttermilk on hand, yogurt can be substituted for an equally delicious bread with a slightly rougher crust and lighter texture.)

With the amount of buttermilk decided upon, we were now ready to explore the amount and type of leavener used. After trying various combinations of baking soda, baking powder, and cream of tartar, we found that 1½ teaspoons of soda, combined with an equal amount of cream of tartar, provided just the right amount of lift for a bread that was light but not airy. Relying on the acidity of cream of tartar (rather than the acidity in the buttermilk) to react with the baking soda allows the tangy buttermilk flavor to come through.

Unfortunately, the flavor of these basic loaves was mediocre at best, lacking depth and dimension, and they were also a bit tough. Traditionally, very small amounts of sugar and/or butter are sometimes added to soda bread, so, starting with sugar, we baked loaves with 1 and 2 tablespoons of sugar. Two tablespoons of sugar added just the

SCORING SODA BREAD

Use a serrated knife to cut a cross shape in the top of the dough. Each score should be 5 inches long and ¾ inch deep.

flavor balance that was needed without making the bread sweet. It was only with the introduction of butter, though, that the loaves began to lose their toughness and become outstanding. Still, we really wanted to maintain the integrity of this basic bread and avoid making it too rich. After trying loaves with one to four tablespoons of unsalted butter, 2 tablespoons proved a clear winner. This bread was tender but not crumbly, compact but not heavy. More than two tablespoons of butter began to shift the flavor balance of the bread and add unnecessary richness.

We were getting very close to our goal, but the crust was still too hard, thick, and crumbly. In our research, we came upon various techniques for modifying the crust. Some dealt with the way the bread was baked, while others concentrated on how the bread was treated after baking. Trying to inhibit the formation of a thick crust by covering the bread with a bowl during the first 30 minutes of baking helped some, but the resulting bread took longer to bake and was pale and uneven in color. Using a large flowerpot and clay dish to simulate a cloche (a covered earthenware dish specifically designed for baking bread) again gave us a bread that didn't color well, even when we preheated the tray and buttered the dough.

But the next test, which, by no coincidence, closely simulated historical cooking methods for Irish soda bread, was a breakthrough. Baking the loaf in a well-buttered Dutch oven or cast-iron pot, covered only for the first 30 minutes, produced a well-risen loaf with an even, golden crust that was thin and crisp yet still had a bit of chew.

We realized, however, that not everyone has a cast-iron pot available, so we explored ways of softening the crust after baking. Wrapping the bread in a clean tea towel as soon as it emerged from the oven helped soften the crust, while a slightly damp tea towel softened it even more. The best technique, though, was to brush the warm loaf with some melted butter. This gave it an attractive sheen as well as a delicious, buttery crust with just enough crunch. Although we liked the crust of the bread baked in the Dutch oven a little better, the ease of baking it on a baking sheet made the loaf brushed with butter a more practical option.

Finally, make sure that you cool the bread for at least 30 to 40 minutes before serving. If cut when too hot, the bread will be dense and slightly doughy.

Classic Irish Soda Bread

MAKES 1 LOAF

Once cooled, this bread is a great accompaniment to soups or stews, and leftovers make fine toast. With their flavorful grains and additions, the variations can stand alone.

3	cups (15 ounces) lower-protein unbleached all-purpose flour, such as Gold Medal or Pillsbury, plus more for dusting the work surface
1	cup (4 ounces) plain cake flour
2	tablespoons sugar
1 1/2	teaspoons baking soda
1 1/2	teaspoons cream of tartar
1 1/2	teaspoons salt
2	tablespoons unsalted butter, softened, plus 1 tablespoon melted butter for the crust
1 1/2	cups buttermilk

1. Adjust an oven rack to the upper-middle position and heat the oven to 400 degrees. Whisk the flours, sugar, baking soda, cream of tartar, and salt together in a large bowl. Work the softened butter into the dry ingredients with a fork or your fingertips until the texture resembles coarse crumbs.

2. Add the buttermilk and stir with a fork just until the dough begins to come together. Turn out onto a flour-coated work surface; knead just until the dough becomes cohesive and bumpy, 12 to 14 turns. (Do not knead until the dough is smooth, or the bread will be tough.)

3. Pat the dough into a round about 6 inches in diameter and 2 inches high; place on a greased or parchment-lined baking sheet. Score the dough by cutting a cross shape in the top of the loaf. (See the illustration on page 696.)

4. Bake until the loaf is golden brown and a skewer inserted into the center comes out clean or the internal temperature reaches 180 degrees, 40 to 45 minutes. Remove the loaf from the oven and brush the surface with the melted butter; cool to room temperature, 30 to 40 minutes.

➤ VARIATIONS

Brown Irish Soda Bread

Unlike the Classic Irish Soda Bread dough, which is dry, this dough is extremely sticky.

1 3/4	cups (8 3/4 ounces) lower-protein unbleached all-purpose flour, such as Gold Medal or Pillsbury, plus more for dusting the work surface
1 1/4	cups (6 7/8 ounces) whole-wheat flour
1/2	cup (2 ounces) plain cake flour
1/2	cup toasted wheat germ
3	tablespoons brown sugar
1 1/2	teaspoons baking soda
1 1/2	teaspoons cream of tartar
1 1/2	teaspoons salt
2	tablespoons unsalted butter, softened, plus 1 tablespoon melted butter for the crust
1 1/2	cups buttermilk

1. Adjust an oven rack to the upper-middle position and heat the oven to 400 degrees. Whisk the flours, wheat germ, brown sugar, baking soda, cream of tartar, and salt together in a large bowl. Work the softened butter into the dry ingredients with a fork or your fingertips until the texture resembles coarse crumbs.

2. Add the buttermilk and stir with a fork just

until the dough begins to come together. Turn out onto a flour-coated work surface; knead just until the dough becomes cohesive and bumpy, 12 to 14 turns. (Do not knead until the dough is smooth, or the bread will be tough.)

3. Pat the dough into a round about 6 inches in diameter and 2 inches high; place on a greased or parchment-lined baking sheet. Score the dough by cutting a cross shape in the top of the loaf. (See the illustration on page 696.)

4. Bake until the loaf is golden brown and a skewer inserted into the center comes out clean or the internal temperature reaches 190 degrees, 45 to 55 minutes. Remove the loaf from the oven and brush the surface with the melted butter; cool to room temperature, 30 to 40 minutes.

Oatmeal-Walnut Soda Bread

Most of the oats should be soaked in the buttermilk for an hour before proceeding with this recipe.

2½	cups (7½ ounces) old-fashioned rolled oats
1¾	cups buttermilk
1	cup walnuts
2	cups (10 ounces) lower-protein unbleached all-purpose flour, such as Gold Medal or Pillsbury, plus more for work surface
½	cup (2 ounces) plain cake flour
½	cup (2¾ ounces) whole-wheat flour
¼	cup packed (1¾ ounces) brown sugar
1½	teaspoons baking soda
1½	teaspoons cream of tartar
1½	teaspoons salt
2	tablespoons unsalted butter, softened, plus 1 tablespoon melted butter for the crust

1. Place 2 cups of the oats in a medium bowl. Add the buttermilk and soak for 1 hour.

2. Adjust an oven rack to the upper-middle position and heat the oven to 400 degrees. Spread the walnuts on a baking sheet and toast them until fragrant, 5 to 10 minutes. Cool and chop coarsely.

3. Whisk the flours, the remaining ½ cup oats, the brown sugar, baking soda, cream of tartar, and salt together in a large bowl. Work the softened butter into the dry ingredients with a fork or your fingertips until the texture resembles coarse crumbs.

4. Add the buttermilk-soaked oats and the toasted nuts and stir with a fork just until the dough begins to come together. Turn out onto a flour-coated work surface; knead just until the dough becomes cohesive and bumpy, 12 to 14 turns. (Do not knead until the dough is smooth, or the bread will be tough.)

5. Pat the dough into a round about 6 inches in diameter and 2 inches high; place on a greased or parchment-lined baking sheet. Score the dough by cutting a cross shape in the top of the loaf. (See the illustration on page 696.)

6. Bake until the loaf is golden brown and a skewer inserted into the center comes out clean or the internal temperature reaches 190 degrees, 45 to 55 minutes. Remove the loaf from the oven and brush the surface with the melted butter; cool to room temperature, 30 to 40 minutes.

American-Style Soda Bread with Raisins and Caraway Seeds

Additional sugar and an egg create a sweeter, richer bread.

3	cups (15 ounces) lower-protein unbleached all-purpose flour, such as Gold Medal or Pillsbury, plus more for dusting the work surface
1	cup (4 ounces) plain cake flour
¼	cup (1¾ ounces) sugar
1½	teaspoons baking soda
1½	teaspoons cream of tartar
1½	teaspoons salt
4	tablespoons (½ stick) unsalted butter, softened, plus 1 tablespoon melted butter for the crust
1¼	cups buttermilk
1	large egg, lightly beaten
1	cup raisins
1	tablespoon caraway seeds

1. Adjust an oven rack to the upper-middle position and heat the oven to 400 degrees. Whisk the flours, sugar, baking soda, cream of tartar, and salt together in a large bowl. Work the softened butter into the dry ingredients with a fork or your fingertips until the mixture resembles coarse crumbs.

2. Combine the buttermilk and egg with a fork. Add the buttermilk-egg mixture, raisins, and

caraway seeds to the flour mixture and stir with a fork just until the dough begins to come together. Turn out onto a flour-coated work surface; knead just until the dough becomes cohesive and bumpy, 12 to 14 turns. (Do not knead until the dough is smooth, or the bread will be tough.)

3. Pat the dough into a round about 6 inches in diameter and 2 inches high; place on a greased or parchment-lined baking sheet. Score the dough by cutting a cross shape in the top of the loaf. (See the illustration on page 696.)

4. Bake, covering the bread with aluminum foil if it is browning too much, until the loaf is golden brown and a skewer inserted into the center comes out clean or the internal temperature reaches 170 degrees, 40 to 45 minutes. Remove the loaf from the oven and brush the surface with the melted butter; cool to room temperature, 30 to 40 minutes.

QUICK CHEESE BREAD

CHEESE BREAD SOUNDS LIKE A GREAT IDEA, a pairing of two of America's favorite foods. Unlike pizza, wherein bread dough is merely topped with cheese, a true cheese bread involves a more intimate relationship, going well beyond the quick blind date in which the two ingredients are merely thrown together and then heated. Good cheese bread displays a subtle balance of flavor and texture, neither party getting the upper hand. But most of the recipes we tested offered the worst of both worlds: dry bread and no cheese flavor.

The quickest (and easiest) recipe we came across was a chemically leavened bread that we mixed up in 10 minutes; the most difficult required a trip to a cheese shop plus a 48-hour time investment. Made with yeast, this bread was fantastic, but for one salient fact: We felt that cheese bread ought to be quick.

We baked half a dozen more quick recipes, but the results were awful. The breads elicited comments from tasters such as "cardboardy," "tough," and "totally devoid of cheese flavor." We yearned for a moist, hearty bread with bits of cheese tossed throughout, plus a cheesy crust. Our first step toward this end was to create a working recipe that consisted of 3 cups flour, 1 tablespoon baking powder, 6 tablespoons melted butter, 2 cups milk, and 1 egg. For the cheese, we chose shredded cheddar, the most frequently used type in our stack of research recipes. Our working recipe had lots of problems, but we could now methodically test every variable.

In search of a moderately hearty crumb, we experimented with different flours, making one loaf with all-purpose flour, another with bread flour, and yet another with half bread and half all-purpose flour. A few tasters noticed that the breads made with all or part of the higher-protein bread flour were slightly rubbery, but the difference was not that dramatic. Still, all-purpose was clearly the best, and most convenient, choice.

Buttermilk is a common ingredient in quick breads, and it produced a decent loaf. Skim milk was too watery and produced a crumbly, dry crumb. The whole-milk version was the best, though, with a creamier, cleaner, cheesier flavor.

Next we tinkered with the amount of butter, which was preferred over oil for its flavor. Starting with 6 tablespoons, we worked our way down to a mere 3, putting an end to the slick hands and lips we'd been experiencing after eating a piece of the bread. Less fat also pushed the bread away from the texture of a delicate cake and toward that of a hearty muffin. The single egg we'd been using turned out to be just right. When we once mistakenly omitted it, the loaf failed to rise properly and had little structure. Loaves made with more than one egg had a beautiful golden hue but tasted more like quiche than cheese bread.

So far so good, but we were falling short in the texture department. Because we wanted a rich loaf, similar to a good banana bread, we replaced a portion of the milk in each of two breads with scoops of yogurt and sour cream, respectively. Given that this was cheese bread, it also seemed logical to try cottage cheese, cream cheese, goat cheese, and ricotta. In the end, most tasters chose the sour cream–based bread. It was rich and moist without being greasy. The sour cream also added a nip of tartness to the bread, offsetting the richness of the cheese without overpowering it.

It was time to decide on the leavening: baking soda or baking powder. To do its job, baking soda

Measuring Techniques & Shortcuts

WHY MEASURING MATTERS

Proper measuring can make or break a recipe. Take flour, for example. In baked goods such as cakes, cookies, and breads, adding too little flour can make the end product flat, wet, or lacking in structure. Many home cooks measure flour by spooning it into a cup, then leveling it off. This method of measuring dry ingredients can yield 20 percent less flour than the method we use in the test kitchen: dip and sweep (illustrated below, at left). In helping you to measure accurately, the tips and techniques we present here will help you achieve consistently good results whenever you cook or bake.

MEASURING CUPS—WHAT'S THE DIFFERENCE?

Dry ingredients like flour and sugar should always be measured in dry measuring cups, never in liquid cups. Although liquid and dry measuring cups hold the same volume, in a liquid measuring cup, there is no way to level the surface of the contents to obtain an exact measurement.

While it is possible to measure liquids in a dry measuring cup, it's hard to fill the cup to the rim and decant it without spills. A liquid measuring cup has headroom so that it needn't be filled to the brim.

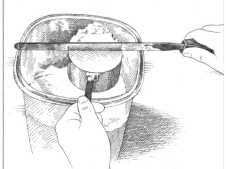

Dry Measuring (dip and sweep)
Dip a dry measuring cup into the ingredient and sweep away the excess with a straight-edged object such as an icing spatula.

Liquid Measuring
To get an accurate reading in a liquid measuring cup, set the cup on a level surface and bend down to read it at eye level. Read the measurement at the bottom of the concave arc at the liquid's surface, known as the meniscus line.

DRY MEASURING CUPS

The Good, the Bad, and the Useless
For both measuring spoons and dry measuring cups, we prefer heavy, well-constructed stainless steel models with long, sturdy, well-designed handles. Plastic spoons and cups feel flimsy, have rims prone to developing nicks and bumps, can warp in the dishwasher, and will melt if placed too close to a heat source.

OUR FAVORITE An extra-long 4-inch handle makes dipping into a bin of flour a clean endeavor.

Three Problematic Handle Styles

Short Handle

STICKY FINGERS The short, awkward handle on this cup makes dipping and sweeping difficult. It can also be hard to keep your thumb out of the ingredients.

Flexible Handle

NO BACKBONE This flimsy, flexible handle bends under the slightest pressure.

Heavy Handle

TOPSY-TURVY This handle-heavy cup tilts when set down, increasing the chance that ingredients will spill out.

WHY AND HOW TO SIFT FLOUR

When a recipe calls for sifted flour, it is important to take the time to sift even if the flour you're using is labeled "presifted." In addition to eliminating lumps, sifting aerates the flour, making it easier to incorporate the flour into a batter. Sifted flour thus also weighs 20 to 25 percent less per cup than unsifted. We found that an additional ounce of flour caused an otherwise moist and perfectly level cake to bake up into a drier cake with a domed top.

Sift and Level
If a recipe reads "1 cup sifted flour," sift the flour directly into a measuring cup (set on top of parchment paper for a hassle-free cleanup) and level off the cup.

Dip, Sweep, and Sift
If a recipe reads "1 cup flour, sifted," first dip into the flour and sweep off the excess, then sift it onto a piece of parchment paper. This method yields the same amount of flour by weight as if you had simply dipped and swept, but the flour is now aerated and lump-free.

MEASURING TIPS AND SHORTCUTS

Here are some ideas to help you deal with hard-to-measure ingredients.

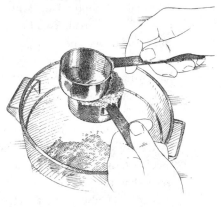

Measuring Peanut Butter
Great for measuring semisolid ingredients like sour cream and peanut butter, this push-up-style cup allows you to scoop in the ingredient, level it off, and then push it right out.

Packing Brown Sugar
Brown sugar is tacky and lumpy; packing it into a measuring cup compacts the sugar and presses out any air pockets (the difference in weight between 1 cup of packed brown sugar and 1 cup of unpacked can be as much as 2 ounces). A neat way to pack brown sugar is to use the bottom of a smaller cup to tamp and press the sugar into a larger cup.

Handling Honey and Molasses
When measuring sticky ingredients like honey and molasses, spray the measuring cup with nonstick cooking spray before filling it. When emptied, the liquid will slip right out of the cup.

Measuring Shortening
When measuring messy, malleable ingredients like shortening, line the measuring cup with plastic wrap, scoop in the shortening, and level it off. To retrieve it, simply lift out the plastic liner, and the contents will come with it.

MEASURING FLOUR, SIMPLIFIED

Recipe reads:	you:	get a weight of:
➤ 1 cup all-purpose flour ➤ 1 cup cake flour	measure flour with dip-and-sweep method	➤ about 5 ounces ➤ about 4 ounces
➤ 1 cup sifted all-purpose flour ➤ 1 cup sifted cake flour	sift flour directly into measuring cup and level off	➤ about 4 ounces ➤ about 3 ounces
➤ 1 cup all-purpose flour, sifted ➤ 1 cup cake flour, sifted	measure flour with dip-and-sweep method, then sift	➤ about 5 ounces ➤ about 4 ounces

needs an acidic ingredient (such as the lactic acid in sour cream), while baking powder is self-reliant, essentially composed of baking soda plus one or two acids. We made two breads, one with a tablespoon of baking powder (this was a heavy batter that needed a decent amount of powder for proper leavening) and a second with ¾ teaspoon baking soda. Both breads rose into beautiful domed loaves, but the bread made with baking powder was preferred, due to its more complex flavor.

Curious about these findings, we had the pH levels of the finished breads tested and discovered that the bread made with baking powder was quite acidic, with a pH of 5.8, whereas the bread made with baking soda was actually alkaline, with a pH of 8.3. The reason? The baking soda had neutralized the lactic acid in the sour cream, whereas the baking powder, which brings its own acid to the mix, had not. The acid was giving the bread more flavor.

Test results showed that small chunks of cheese, not shreds, were best, as they melted into luscious, cheesy pockets. In terms of the cheese itself, we tested five readily available types: extra-sharp cheddar, Muenster, Asiago, Gruyère, and Monterey Jack. Cheddar and Asiago were the leaders of the pack, with Muenster and Monterey Jack being too mild and Gruyère too pungent (although we liked this last cheese in a variation that also included bacon). We quickly determined that excess cheese weighed down the bread, causing it to collapse into itself. With a modest four ounces of cheese, the bread had plenty of flavor but still rose to its full potential.

We had arrived at the top crust. We wanted rich flavor and color. The solution was a topping of shredded Parmesan. We then decided to coat the bottom of the pan with cheese as well, thus doubling the cheesy exterior. Nutty and salty, every bite was packed with flavor. The Parmesan also turned the crust a deep bronze color.

Quick Cheese Bread

MAKES ONE 9-INCH LOAF

If using Asiago, choose a mild supermarket cheese that yields to pressure when pressed. Aged Asiago that is as firm as Parmesan is too sharp and piquant for this bread. If, when testing the bread for doneness, the toothpick comes out with what looks like uncooked batter clinging to it, try again in a different—but still central—spot; if the toothpick hits a pocket of cheese, it may give a false indication. The texture of the bread improves as it cools, so resist the urge to slice the loaf while it is piping hot. Leftover cheese bread is excellent toasted; toast slices in a toaster oven or on a baking sheet in a 425-degree oven for 5 to 10 minutes, not in a conventional toaster, where bits of cheese may melt, burn, and make a mess.

3	ounces Parmesan cheese, shredded on the large holes of a box grater (about 1 cup)
3	cups (15 ounces) unbleached all-purpose flour
1	tablespoon baking powder
¼	teaspoon cayenne pepper
1	teaspoon salt
⅛	teaspoon ground black pepper
4	ounces extra-sharp cheddar cheese, cut into ½-inch cubes, or mild Asiago cheese, crumbled into ¼- to ½-inch pieces (about 1 cup)
1¼	cups whole milk
3	tablespoons unsalted butter, melted
1	large egg, beaten lightly
¾	cup sour cream

1. Adjust an oven rack to the middle position and heat the oven to 350 degrees. Spray a 9 by 5-inch loaf pan with nonstick cooking spray, then sprinkle ½ cup of the Parmesan evenly over the bottom of the pan.

2. In a large bowl, whisk the flour, baking powder, cayenne, salt, and black pepper to combine. Using a rubber spatula, mix in the cheddar, breaking up clumps, until it is coated with the flour mixture. In a medium bowl, whisk together the milk, melted butter, egg, and sour cream. Using a rubber spatula, gently fold the wet ingredients into the dry ingredients until just combined (the batter will be heavy and thick). Do not overmix. Scrape the batter into the prepared loaf pan; spread to the sides of the pan and level the surface with a rubber spatula. Sprinkle the remaining ½ cup Parmesan evenly over the surface.

3. Bake until deep golden brown and a toothpick or skewer inserted into the center of the loaf

comes out clean, 45 to 50 minutes. Cool in the pan on a wire rack 5 minutes; invert the loaf onto the rack, turn right-side up, and continue to cool until warm, about 45 minutes. Cut into slices and serve.

➤ VARIATION
Quick Cheese Bread with Bacon, Onion, and Gruyère

1. Cut 5 slices (about 5 ounces) bacon into ½-inch pieces and fry in a medium nonstick skillet over medium heat, stirring occasionally, until browned and crisp, about 8 minutes. Using a slotted spoon, transfer the bacon to a paper towel–lined plate and pour off all but 3 tablespoons fat from the skillet. Add ½ medium onion, minced (about ½ cup), to the skillet and cook, stirring frequently, until softened, about 3 minutes; set the skillet with the onion aside.

2. Follow the recipe for Quick Cheese Bread, substituting Gruyère for the cheddar, adding the cooked bacon and onion to the flour mixture along with the cheese, and omitting the butter. Proceed as directed.

BLUEBERRY MUFFINS
DESPITE THE EASY PROMISE OF A GINGHAM-lined basket of warm, cuddly blueberry muffins, much can go wrong from kitchen to table. We made a half dozen recipes, producing muffins that ranged from rough and tough to dense, sweet, and heavy to the typical lackluster coffee-shop cake with too few blueberries and too little flavor. It was clear that blueberry muffins came in no one style, flavor, or size, so we asked tasters to state which basic style of muffin they fancied: round tea cake or craggy biscuit. Of the 15 tasters, all but one said tea cake.

Because minor fluctuations in ingredients occasioned seismic differences in the resulting muffins, we thought it best to hold fast to a recipe whose proportions landed in between the two extremes in the original tests. That meant we would be working with 1 stick butter, 1 cup sugar, 2 cups flour, and ½ cup milk. It was not a perfect recipe but would be a serviceable springboard for future testing.

The two principal methods available to the muffin baker are the quick-bread method and creaming. In side-by-side tests using our control recipe, we got a firsthand taste of both methods. Had we been merely licking batter off our fingers, there would have been no contest: The creamed version was like a cake batter you could suck through a straw. But the two baked muffins were nearly identical. Though the mixed muffin was slightly squatter than its creamed companion, its texture was not inferior. We were pretty sure this more easily executed technique was one we could work with—or around.

For flour, we remained true to unbleached all-purpose. Bleached flour lacked the flavor spectrum of unbleached, and cake flour produced a batter that was too light to hold the blueberries aloft. We set off next in pursuit of the perfect amount of butter to turn out a moister, richer muffin, more like the tea cake our tasters had preferred. Increasing the butter in the control recipe simply weighed down the crumb without making the muffins any more moist. We also increased the liquid (we tested both milk and buttermilk) and added extra egg yolks. Neither approach brought improvement. When we substituted yogurt for milk, the muffins had the springiness of an old camp mattress.

Knowing that sour cream is often used in quick breads, we decided to give it a try. We also wondered if the egg white protein from two eggs might be too much of the wrong type of liquid—adding structure rather than tenderness. Our new recipe, then, called for 1 egg, 1 cup sour cream, no milk, and only half a stick of butter. It was a great success—the muffins were tender and rich, and the sour cream played up the blueberries' flavor. An additional ¼ cup sour cream made even nicer muffins.

Through additional testing, we discovered that this rather heavy batter required a full tablespoon of baking powder to rise and shine, but tasters noted no off chemical flavor. (If too much chemical leavener is added, some of it will fail to react and will give the baked good a bitter, soapy flavor.) Next we refined the mixing method. Hoping to get more lift, we whisked the egg and sugar together by hand until the sugar began to dissolve, whisked in the melted butter, then the sour cream, and poured them into the dry ingredients. This method of mixing promised to deliver more air—and lift—to the egg, sugar, and butter. We folded everything together using the gentlest strokes possible. (We found that these muffins, like most others, became tough when overmixed.) This modified technique produced lovely muffins with a nice rise and beautifully domed crowns.

Until now, the major player in this muffin had been not only offstage but out of season. Our winter testing left us with a choice between pricey fresh blueberries the size of marbles and tiny frozen wild berries. The flavor and sweetness of the frozen berries gave them a big edge over the puckery, flavorless fresh berries. In addition, the tiny wild berries distributed themselves in the batter nicely, whereas the cultivated berries took the muffin by storm, leaving huge pockets of sour fruit pulp. So impressed were we by the superiority of these little berries that we resolved to offer them top billing in the recipe. We came across one last trick. Frozen blueberries tend to be bleeders—and gummy when tossed with flour—so we determined that they must remain completely frozen until they are stirred into the batter.

These were perfect workaday muffins, but we wanted to give them a chance to play dress-up, to be more like little cakes. With that in mind, we considered a couple of options. A big fan of pebbly streusel topping dusted with confectioners' sugar, we picked up the recipe from our Dutch apple pie topping and pared it down to meet the demands of a dozen muffins. The streusel weighed heavily on the muffins and diminished their lift.

Our next topping idea came from Marion Cunningham's *Breakfast Book* (Knopf, 1987), in which she rolls whole baked muffins in melted butter and then dips them in cinnamon sugar. The concept was a winning one. The melted butter seeped into the muffin's crown, the sugar stuck, and the muffin was transformed into a tender, sugar-tufted pillow.

We also made a simple-syrup glaze with lemon juice. Brushed on the muffin tops, it made a nice adhesive for granulated sugar (which we mixed with either finely grated lemon zest or fresh ginger).

Blueberry Muffins
MAKES 12

When making the batter, be sure to whisk vigorously in step 2, then fold carefully in step 3. You should not see large pockets of flour in the finished batter, but small occasional sprays may remain. A large spoon sprayed with nonstick cooking spray ensures clean dispensing when transferring the batter to the cups in the muffin tin.

PORTIONING MUFFIN BATTER AND REMOVING FROM TIN

1. Use a large serving spoon sprayed with nonstick cooking spray to spoon even amounts of batter into each cup of the muffin tin. The batter will slide easily from the spoon into the muffin cups.

2. The thin, slightly curved blade of a grapefruit knife is particularly well suited to getting under a stubborn muffin with little risk of tearing the muffin apart.

2 cups (10 ounces) unbleached all-purpose flour
1 tablespoon baking powder
½ teaspoon salt
1 large egg
1 cup (7 ounces) sugar
4 tablespoons (½ stick) unsalted butter, melted and cooled slightly
1¼ cups (10 ounces) sour cream
1½ cups (7½ to 8 ounces) frozen or fresh blueberries, preferably wild

1. Adjust an oven rack to the middle position and heat the oven to 350 degrees. Grease a standard 12-cup muffin tin and set aside.

2. Whisk the flour, baking powder, and salt in a medium bowl until combined. Whisk the egg in a second medium bowl until well combined and light-colored, about 20 seconds. Add the sugar and whisk vigorously until thick and homogeneous, about 30 seconds; add the melted butter in 2 or 3 additions, whisking to combine after each addition. Add the sour cream in 2 additions, whisking just to combine.

3. Add the berries to the dry ingredients and gently toss just to combine. Add the sour cream mixture and fold with a rubber spatula until the batter comes together and the berries are evenly distributed, 25 to 30 seconds. (Small spots of flour may remain, and the batter will be thick. Do not overmix.)

4. Using a large spoon sprayed with nonstick cooking spray to prevent sticking, divide the batter among the greased muffin cups. Bake until the muffins are light golden brown and a toothpick or skewer inserted into the center of a muffin comes out clean, 25 to 30 minutes, rotating the pan from front to back halfway through the baking time. Invert the muffins onto a wire rack, stand the muffins upright, and cool 5 minutes. Serve as is or use one of the toppings below.

➤ VARIATIONS

Cinnamon Sugar–Dipped Blueberry Muffins

While the muffins are cooling, mix ½ cup sugar and ½ teaspoon ground cinnamon in a small bowl and melt 4 tablespoons (½ stick) butter in a small saucepan. After the baked muffins have cooled 5 minutes, working one at a time, dip the top of each muffin in melted butter and then cinnamon sugar. Set the muffins upright on a wire rack; serve.

BLUEBERRY MUFFIN HALL OF SHAME

A lot can go wrong with blueberry muffins. Some problematic muffins we encountered in our testing: 1. Muffins made with mashed berries taste fine but look all wrong. 2. Cottony, grocery-store muffins often have sticky, clammy tops. 3. A quick packaged mix with artificial berries baked up into hockey pucks. 4. This deli muffin is dry and coarse, with mushy, marble-size blueberries. 5. If the muffin cups are overfilled with batter, the baked muffins will have flat tops.

1. MASHED BERRIES

2. STICKY SURFACE

3. ARTIFICIAL BERRIES

4. COARSE TEXTURE

5. FLAT TOP

Ginger- or Lemon-Glazed Blueberry Muffins

While the muffins are baking, mix 1 teaspoon grated fresh ginger or grated lemon zest and ½ cup sugar in a small bowl. Bring ¼ cup lemon juice and ¼ cup sugar to a simmer in a small saucepan over medium heat; stir to dissolve the sugar and simmer until the mixture is thick and syrupy and reduced to about ¼ cup. After the baked muffins have cooled 5 minutes, brush the tops with glaze; then, working one at a time, dip the tops in lemon sugar or ginger sugar. Set the muffins upright on a wire rack; serve.

CORN MUFFINS

WHETHER TOO COARSE, DRY, AND CRUMBLY, too sticky and sweet, or just too fluffy and cupcake-like, the majority of corn muffins on the market today just don't make the cut. What do we want? We want a muffin that won't set off sucrose alarms, and we want a pronounced but not over-whelming cornmeal flavor and a moist and tender crumb. And all of this goodness has to be capped off with a crunchy, golden, craggy muffin top.

We started by testing an assortment of recipes from various cookbooks. Although their ingredient lists were similar, the end results were not. Some were too chewy, too short, and too puck-shaped, while others had too little corn flavor or were just plain too sweet or savory. Two recipes, however, stood out. One recipe produced muffins that were tall and rustic; the other made muffins with a pleasant, wholesome cornmeal flavor. Working with these recipes as a starting point, we began to test variables.

For mixing the ingredients for our muffins, we tried the quick-bread method, which turned out a muffin with good height and substantial crumb. As we discovered in testing our Blueberry Muffins (page 703), the quick-bread method, in its use of melted rather than creamed butter, apparently introduced less air into the batter, and the resulting muffin was less cupcake-like.

With the mixing method down, it was now time to focus on the choice of cornmeal. We tested three brands: Quaker, Arrowhead Mills, and Hodgson Mill. Quaker cornmeal, the most common brand in supermarkets, is degerminated. During processing, the dried corn is steel-rolled, which removes most of the germ and husk. Because the germ contains most of the flavor and natural oils, this process results in a drier, less flavorful cornmeal. When baked into a corn muffin, Quaker offered an unremarkable corn flavor and, because of its dryness, an unpleasant crunch.

Arrowhead Mills and Hodgson Mill are both whole-grain cornmeals, made from the whole corn kernel. Hodgson Mill cornmeal, which is stone-ground (ground between two stones), has a coarse, inconsistent texture, while Arrowhead Mills, which is hammer-milled (pulverized with hammers), has a fine, consistent texture. Both brands delivered a more wholesome and complex corn flavor than Quaker. However, the Hodgson Mill cornmeal made the muffins coarse, dry, and difficult to chew. Arrowhead Mills produced by far the best corn muffin, with a consistently fine texture and real cornmeal flavor. The conclusion? Use a whole-grain cornmeal in a fine grind, such as Arrowhead Mills.

Our muffins had the right texture and good flavor, but they were too dry. We made a list of the ingredients that might help produce a moist muffin: butter, milk, buttermilk, sour cream, and yogurt. We tried them all, using different amounts

APPLYING COOKING SPRAY WITHOUT THE MESS

Open the dishwasher door, place the muffin tin on the door, and spray away. Any excess or overspray will be cleaned off the door the next time you run the dishwasher.

of each. Our initial thought was "butter, butter, butter," with enough milk added to hit the right consistency. When tested, however, these muffins were lacking in moisture. We then tried using buttermilk in place of the milk. These muffins packed more flavor into each bite, but they were still on the dry side. What finally produced a superior muffin was sour cream paired with butter and milk. These muffins were rich, light, moist, and tender, but they were certainly no dainty cupcakes. We were curious to see how a muffin made with whole-milk yogurt would stand up to the muffin made with sour cream. The difference was slight. The muffin made with whole-milk yogurt was leaner but still moist and delicious. Muffins made with low-fat yogurt, on the other hand, were too lean and dry. Based on these tests, we concluded that a moist muffin requires fat and the tenderizing effect of acidity, both of which are found in sour cream.

The leavener used in most muffins is baking powder and/or baking soda, and we found that a combination of 1½ teaspoons baking powder and 1 teaspoon baking soda delivered the ideal height. We tested oven temperatures from 325 to 425 degrees and found that 400 degrees delivered the crunchy, crispy, golden crust we were looking for.

So, with the right cornmeal and the addition of sour cream, butter, and milk, it is possible to bake a tender, moist, and delicious corn muffin. By decreasing the amount of sugar and adding a few savory ingredients, you can serve these muffins with dinner as well as for breakfast.

Corn Muffins

MAKES 12

Stone-ground whole-grain cornmeal has a fuller flavor than regular cornmeal milled from degerminated corn. To determine what kind of cornmeal a package contains, look closely at the label.

2	cups (10 ounces) unbleached all-purpose flour
1	cup (about 5 ounces) fine stone-ground yellow cornmeal
1½	teaspoons baking powder
1	teaspoon baking soda
½	teaspoon salt
2	large eggs
¾	cup (5¼ ounces) sugar
8	tablespoons (1 stick) unsalted butter, melted and cooled slightly
¾	cup sour cream
½	cup milk

1. Adjust an oven rack to the middle position and heat the oven to 400 degrees. Grease a standard 12-cup muffin tin and set aside.

2. Whisk the flour, cornmeal, baking powder, baking soda, and salt in a medium bowl to combine; set aside. Whisk the eggs in a second medium bowl until well combined and light-colored, about 20 seconds. Add the sugar to the eggs; whisk vigorously until thick and homogeneous, about 30 seconds; add the melted butter in 3 additions, whisking to combine after each addition. Add half the sour cream and half the milk and whisk

CORN MUFFINS: THE USUAL SUSPECTS

Despite the simplicity of corn muffins, a lot can go wrong when making them. Here are some of the worst muffins we encountered in our testing, from left to right: 1. This flat muffin contains too much cornmeal and tastes like cornbread. 2. This pale muffin contains no butter and relies on egg whites as the leavener. 3. This hockey puck–like muffin starts with cornmeal mixed with hot water. 4. This cupcake-like muffin resembles many store-bought muffins and is made with too much sugar and leavener.

1. SQUAT AND CORNY   **2. DENSE AND DOUGHY**   **3. SMALL AND WET**   **4. FLUFFY AND CAKEY**

to combine; whisk in the remaining sour cream and milk until combined. Add the wet ingredients to the dry ingredients; mix gently with a rubber spatula until the batter is just combined and evenly moistened. Do not overmix. Using a large spoon sprayed with nonstick cooking spray to prevent sticking, divide the batter evenly among the muffin cups, dropping it to form mounds. Do not level or flatten the surface of the mounds.

3. Bake until the muffins are light golden brown and a skewer inserted into the center of a muffin comes out clean, about 18 minutes, rotating the muffin tin from front to back halfway through the baking time. Cool the muffins in the tin 5 minutes; invert the muffins onto a wire rack, stand the muffins upright, cool 5 minutes longer, and serve warm.

➤ VARIATIONS

Corn and Apricot Muffins with Orange Essence

1. In a food processor, process ⅔ cup granulated sugar and 1½ teaspoons grated orange zest until pale orange, about 10 seconds. Transfer to a small bowl and set aside.

2. In a food processor, pulse 1½ cups (10 ounces) dried apricots for ten 2-second pulses, until chopped fine. Transfer to a medium microwave-safe bowl; add ⅔ cup orange juice to the apricots, cover the bowl tightly with plastic wrap, and microwave on

high until simmering, about 1 minute. Let the apricots stand, covered, until softened and plump, about 5 minutes. Discard the plastic wrap, strain the apricots, and discard the juice.

3. Follow the recipe for Corn Muffins, substituting ¼ cup packed dark brown sugar for an equal amount of granulated sugar and stirring ½ teaspoon grated orange zest and the strained apricots into the wet ingredients before adding them to the dry ingredients. Before baking, sprinkle a portion of orange sugar over each mound of batter. Do not invert the baked muffins; use the tip of a paring knife to lift the muffins from the tin one at a time and transfer to a wire rack. Cool the muffins 5 minutes; serve warm.

Bacon-Scallion Corn Muffins with Cheddar Cheese

Because these muffins contain bacon, store leftovers in the refrigerator wrapped in plastic. Bring the muffins to room temperature or rewarm them before serving.

1. Grate 8 ounces cheddar cheese (you should have 2 cups); set aside. Fry 3 slices (about 3 ounces) bacon, cut into ½-inch pieces, in a small skillet over medium heat until crisp and golden brown, about 5 minutes. Add 10 to 12 medium scallions, sliced thin (about 1¼ cups), ¼ teaspoon salt, and ⅛ teaspoon ground black pepper; cook to heat through, about 1 minute. Transfer the mixture to a plate to cool while making the muffins.

2. Follow the recipe for Corn Muffins, reducing the sugar to ½ cup. Stir 1½ cups of the grated cheddar cheese and the bacon-scallion mixture into the wet ingredients, then add to the dry ingredients and combine. Before baking, sprinkle a portion of the remaining ½ cup cheddar over each mound of batter.

TESTING BAKING POWDER FOR FRESHNESS

Baking powder will lose its leavening ability with time. We suggest writing the date the can was opened on a piece of tape affixed to the can. After 6 months, the baking powder should be tested to see if it's still good. Mix 2 teaspoons of baking powder with 1 cup of hot tap water. If there's an immediate reaction of fizzing and foaming (right), the baking powder is fine. If the reaction is delayed or weak (left), throw the baking powder away and buy a fresh can. A can of baking powder that has been opened for a year or more should be replaced.

BUTTERMILK BISCUITS

BISCUITS SHARE WITH MUFFINS THE DIStinction of being among the simplest of all breads. They are made from a mixture of flour, leavener (baking powder or soda), salt, fat (usually butter or vegetable shortening), and liquid (milk, buttermilk, sour milk, yogurt, or cream). To make them, the fat is cut into the dry ingredients, and the liquid is then stirred in until a dough forms.

Biscuits are usually rolled out and cut, although they can also be shaped by hand or dropped onto a baking sheet by the spoonful.

We began our testing by focusing on the flour. We found that the kind of flour you choose has a great effect on the biscuit you end up with. The main factor here is the level of protein in the flour. Low-protein, or "soft," flour (such as cake flour or White Lily, a favored brand in the South) encourages a tender, cake-like texture as well as a more moist crumb. Higher-protein, or "strong," flour (such as all-purpose flour) promotes a crispier crust and a drier, denser crumb.

Tasters liked the crispier crust of the biscuits made with all-purpose flour and the tender, airy crumb of the biscuits made with cake flour. We found that a combination of half cake flour and half all-purpose flour delivered the best results—a crisp crust and a tender crumb. If you don't have cake flour, all-purpose flour makes a fine biscuit as long as you add more liquid to the batter.

Fat makes biscuits (and other pastries) tender, moist, smooth, and tasty. Butter, of course, delivers the best flavor, while vegetable shortening makes a slightly flakier biscuit with better holding powers. However, we don't think this gain in shelf life is worth the loss in flavor. Stick with unsalted butter when making biscuits.

We discovered that a proportion of ½ cup fat to 2 cups flour provides the best balance of tenderness and richness with structure. The way in which the fat and flour are combined is nearly as important as their proportions. The fat must be "rubbed" into the dry ingredients, making a dry, coarse mixture akin to large bread crumbs or rolled oats, with some slightly bigger lumps mixed in. This rubbing may seem unimportant, but in fact it is crucial to the proper rising of the biscuits. Gas released by the leavener during baking must have a space in which to collect; if the texture of the dough is homogeneous, the gas will simply dissipate. Melting fat particles create convenient spaces in which the gas can collect, form bubbles, and produce a rise. Proper rubbing breaks the fat into tiny bits and disperses it throughout the dough. As the fat melts during baking, its place is taken up by gas and steam, which expand and push the dough up. The wider the dispersal of the fat, the more even the rising of the dough.

If, however, the fat softens and binds with the dry ingredients during rubbing, it forms a pasty goo, the spaces collapse, and the biscuits become leaden. To produce light, airy biscuits, the fat must remain cold and firm, which means rubbing must be deft and quick. Traditionally, biscuit makers pinch the cut-up

MIXING AND SHAPING BUTTERMILK BISCUIT DOUGH

Our preference for incorporating butter into the dry ingredients is to use a food processor as in step 1 and then proceed to step 4 to shape the dough. If you don't have a food processor, you can improvise by following steps 2 and 3.

1. Cut a chilled stick of butter into ¼-inch cubes. Place the butter cubes on a plate and chill briefly in the freezer. With a spatula, add the butter cubes to the food processor with the dry ingredients and pulse until the butter is evenly mixed into the dry ingredients.

2. If you don't have a food processor, combine the dry ingredients in a bowl. Rub a frozen stick of butter against the large holes of a regular box grater placed over the bowl with the dry ingredients.

3. With two butter knives, work the grated butter into the dry ingredients. By not using your fingertips, you reduce the chances that the butter will melt.

4. Once the butter has been cut into the dry ingredients, add the buttermilk. Our biscuit dough is too soft to roll and cut. Using a sharp knife, divide the dough into quarters and then cut each quarter into thirds. With cupped hands, gently shape each piece into a ball.

fat into the dry ingredients, using only their fingertips—never the whole hand, which is too warm—and they pinch hard and fast, practically flinging the little bits of flour and fat into the bowl after each pinch. Less experienced cooks sometimes cut in the fat by scraping two knives in opposite directions or by using a bow-shaped pastry blender. We found, however, that the easiest way to go about this task is with the help of a food processor. Pulsing the dry ingredients and the fat is fast and almost foolproof.

After cutting in the fat, liquid is added and the dough is stirred just until the ingredients are bound, using a light hand so the gluten will not become activated. We found that buttermilk (or plain yogurt) gives biscuits the best flavor. It also creates a lighter, airier texture than regular milk. That's because the acid in the buttermilk reacts with the leaveners to increase the rise.

Biscuits are best formed by gently patting gobs of dough between your hands. If the work surface, the dough, and the cutter are generously floured, fluffy biscuits can be rolled and cut, but the softness of the dough makes this a tricky procedure, and the extra flour and handling will make the biscuits heavier and somewhat dense.

Because they need quick heat, biscuits are best baked in the middle of the oven. Placed too close to the bottom, they burn on the underside and remain pale on top; set too near the oven roof, they do not rise well because the outside hardens into a shell before the inside has had a chance to rise properly. As soon as they are light brown, they are done. Be careful, as overcooking will dry them out. Biscuits are always at their best as soon as they come out of the oven. The dough, however, may be made some hours in advance and baked when needed; the biscuits will still rise well.

Buttermilk Biscuits

MAKES 12

Mixing the butter and dry ingredients quickly so the butter remains cold and firm is crucial to producing light, tender biscuits. The easiest and most reliable approach is to use a food processor fitted with the metal blade. Expect a soft and slightly sticky dough. The wet dough creates steam when the biscuits bake and promotes the light, airy texture. If the dough is too wet for you to shape the biscuits by hand, lightly flour your hands and then shape the biscuits.

If you don't have cake flour on hand, substitute an extra cup of all-purpose flour and increase the buttermilk or yogurt by 2 tablespoons.

1	cup (5 ounces) unbleached all-purpose flour
1	cup (4 ounces) plain cake flour
2	teaspoons baking powder
1/2	teaspoon baking soda
1	teaspoon sugar
1/2	teaspoon salt
8	tablespoons (1 stick) cold unsalted butter, cut into 1/4-inch cubes
3/4	cup cold buttermilk, or 3/4 cup plus 2 tablespoons plain yogurt

1. Adjust an oven rack to the middle position and heat the oven to 450 degrees.

2. Place the flours, baking powder, baking soda, sugar, and salt in a large bowl or the workbowl of a food processor fitted with the metal blade. Whisk together or process with six 1-second pulses.

3. If making by hand, use two knives, a pastry blender, or your fingertips to quickly cut in the butter until the mixture resembles coarse meal with a few slightly larger butter lumps. If using a food processor, remove the cover and distribute the butter evenly over the dry ingredients. Cover and process with twelve 1-second pulses.

4. If making by hand, stir in the buttermilk with a rubber spatula or fork until the mixture forms a soft, slightly sticky ball. If using a food processor, remove the cover and pour the buttermilk evenly over the dough. Process until the dough gathers into moist clumps, about eight 1-second pulses.

5. Transfer the dough to a lightly floured surface and quickly form into a rough ball. Be careful not to overmix. Using a sharp knife or dough cutter, divide the dough into quarters and then cut each quarter into thirds. Quickly and gently shape each piece into a rough ball (see illustration 4 on page 709) and place on an ungreased baking sheet. (The baking sheet can be wrapped in plastic and refrigerated for up to 2 hours.)

6. Bake until the biscuit tops are light brown, 10 to 12 minutes. Serve immediately.

CREAM BISCUITS

OUR BUTTERMILK BISCUITS ARE EASY TO prepare; you can have biscuits on the table in 20 minutes. But many cooks are intimidated by this kind of biscuit because they are not comfortable with the traditional process of cutting butter into flour. We wondered if we could come up with a recipe for homemade biscuits that could be made quickly and easily and that would not require cutting fat into flour.

First we tried varying the dairy. The biscuits made with yogurt and sour cream were a bit sodden in texture, those with milk and a milk and butter combination were tough and lifeless, and a whipped-cream biscuit was too light. This last approach also required whipping the cream, which seemed like too much trouble for a simple recipe. So we tried using plain heavy cream, without whipping, and this biscuit was the best of the lot.

Still, we were running into a problem with the shape of the biscuits, as they were spreading far too much during baking; they needed more structure. When making biscuits, we have always followed the conventional advice about not overworking the dough. Kneading the dough encourages the development of gluten, a protein that gives baked products structure but that when overdeveloped can also make them tough. In our experience, the best biscuits are generally made from dough that is handled lightly. This is certainly true of buttermilk biscuits. But cream biscuits, being less sturdy than those made with butter, become soft and "melt" during baking. In this case, we thought, a little more structure produced by a little more handling might not be such a bad thing. So we baked up two batches. The first dough we patted out gingerly; the second dough we kneaded for 30 seconds until it was smooth and uniform in appearance. The results were remarkable. The more heavily worked dough produced much higher, fluffier biscuits than those made from the lightly handled dough, which looked short and bedraggled.

We ran into a problem, though, when one batch of biscuits had to sit for a few minutes while we waited for the oven to heat up. During baking, the dough spread, resulting in biscuits with bottoms that were too wide and tops that were too narrow. Clearly, the biscuits had to be popped into the oven immediately after cutting. As for dough thickness, we found that 1 inch provides a remarkably high rise, more appealing than biscuits that start out ½ inch thick. We also discovered that it was best to add just enough cream to hold the dough together. A wet dough does not hold its shape as well during baking.

Although we found it easy enough to quickly roll out this dough and then cut it into rounds with a biscuit cutter, you can simply shape the dough with your hands or push it into the bottom of an 8-inch cake pan. The dough can then be flipped onto the work surface and cut into wedges with a knife or dough scraper.

SHAPING CREAM BISCUITS AND SCONES

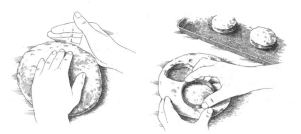

FOR ROUNDS

1. Pat the dough on a lightly floured work surface into a ¾-inch-thick circle.

2. Punch out the dough rounds with a biscuit cutter. Push together the remaining pieces of dough, pat into a ¾-inch-thick round, and punch out several more dough rounds. Discard the remaining scraps.

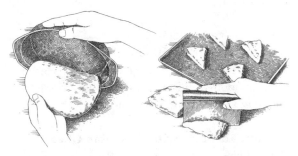

FOR WEDGES

1. Press the dough into an 8-inch cake pan, then turn the dough out onto a lightly floured work surface.

2. With a sharp knife or bench scraper, cut the dough into 8 wedges.

Cream Biscuits

MAKES 8

Bake the biscuits immediately after cutting them; letting them stand for any length of time can decrease the leavening power and prevent the biscuits from rising in the oven.

2	cups (10 ounces) unbleached all-purpose flour
2	teaspoons sugar
2	teaspoons baking powder
1/2	teaspoon salt
1 1/2	cups heavy cream

1. Adjust an oven rack to the upper-middle position and heat the oven to 425 degrees. Line a rimmed baking sheet with parchment paper.

2. Whisk together the flour, sugar, baking powder, and salt in a medium bowl. Add 1¼ cups of the cream and stir with a wooden spoon until the dough forms, about 30 seconds. Transfer the dough to the countertop, leaving all dry, floury bits behind in the bowl. In 1 tablespoon increments, add up to ¼ cup cream to the dry bits in the bowl, mixing with a wooden spoon after each addition, until moistened. Add these moistened bits to the rest of the dough and knead by hand just until smooth, about 30 seconds.

3. Following the illustrations on page 711, cut the biscuits into rounds or wedges. Place the biscuits on the parchment-lined baking sheet and bake until golden brown, about 15 minutes. Serve immediately.

➤ VARIATIONS

Cream Biscuits with Fresh Herbs

Follow the recipe for Cream Biscuits, whisking 2 tablespoons minced fresh herbs into the flour along with the sugar, baking powder, and salt.

Cream Biscuits with Cheddar Cheese

Follow the recipe for Cream Biscuits, stirring 2 ounces cheddar cheese, cut into ¼-inch pieces (½ cup), into the flour along with the sugar, baking powder, and salt. Increase the baking time to 18 minutes.

SCONES

SCONES IN AMERICA—UNLIKE THEIR MORE diminutive British counterparts—have the reputation of being thick, heavy, dry bricks. To enhance their appeal, they are often disguised under a sugary shellac of achingly sweet glaze or filled with chopped ginger, chopped fruit, or chocolate chips. Despite these feeble attempts to dress them up, it is no secret that today's coffeehouse confections are a far cry from what a scone should be: tender and flaky, like a slightly sweetened biscuit.

We started our testing by focusing on the flour. We made a composite recipe with bread flour, with all-purpose flour, and with cake flour. The differences in outcome were astonishing. The scones made with bread flour were heavy and tough. The scones made with all-purpose flour were lighter and much more flavorful. Cake flour produced scones that were doughy in the center, with a raw taste and poor texture. Subsequent tests revealed that a lower-protein all-purpose flour, such as Gold Medal or Pillsbury, is better than a higher-protein flour, such as King Arthur.

After trying scones made with butter and with lard, we decided we preferred the rich flavor of butter. (If we made scones commercially, we might reconsider, because day-old scones made with lard hold up better. The preservative effects of different fats, along with lower cost, may be why store-bought scones are often made with margarine or other hydrogenated fats.) Although the amount of solid fat can be varied, we found 5 tablespoons of butter to 2 cups flour to be just right. More butter and the scones will almost melt in the oven. Less butter and the baked scones will be dry and tough.

The choice of liquid can also profoundly affect the flavor of a scone. We tested various liquids and found that cream made the best scones, which were tender yet still light. Scones made with milk were bland and dry. Buttermilk gave scones plenty of flavor, but the scones were too flaky and biscuit-like. Scones made with cream were moister and more flavorful than the others.

We tried adding an egg to the dough. We found that it made the scones very cakey. Many tasters liked the effect of the egg. Since the addition of an egg helps the scones hold on to moisture and remain fresher longer, we decided to use the egg in a variation called Cakey Scones.

In traditional recipes, one to two tablespoons of sugar is enough to sweeten an entire batch of scones. American scones tend to be far sweeter than the British versions, which are usually served with sweet toppings such as jam. Americans seem to eat their scones like muffins, without anything more than a smear of butter, so the sweetness is baked in. We prefer the British approach but decided to increase the sugar slightly to three tablespoons.

Finally, scones are often glazed to enhance their appearance and add sweetness. We tried brushing the dough with a beaten egg as well as with heavy cream just before baking. Scones brushed with egg can become too dark in the oven. We preferred the more delicate look of scones brushed with cream and then dusted with a little granulated sugar.

Scones can be mixed by hand or with a food processor. (The processor is used to cut fat into flour; minimal hand mixing is required afterward.) We found the food processor to be more reliable than mixing entirely by hand, which can overheat the butter and cause it to soften. Once the dough comes together, we prefer to pat it into a cake pan, gently pull it out onto a floured surface, and then cut it into eight wedges. We find this method easier than using a rolling pin.

Cream Scones with Currants

MAKES 8

The most traditional sweet biscuit–like texture is obtained by using both butter and heavy cream. If you prefer a cake-like texture or want the scones to stay fresher longer, try the Cakey Scones variation. The easiest and most reliable approach to mixing the butter into the dry ingredients is to use a food processor fitted with the metal blade. Resist the urge to eat the scones hot out of the oven. Letting them cool for at least 10 minutes firms them up and improves their texture.

2 cups (10 ounces) unbleached all-purpose flour, preferably a lower-protein brand, such as Gold Medal or Pillsbury

1 tablespoon baking powder
3 tablespoons sugar
1/2 teaspoon salt
5 tablespoons cold unsalted butter, cut into 1/4-inch cubes
1/2 cup currants
1 cup heavy cream

1. Adjust an oven rack to the middle position and heat the oven to 425 degrees.

2. Place the flour, baking powder, sugar, and salt in a large bowl or the workbowl of a food processor fitted with the metal blade. Whisk together or process with six 1-second pulses.

3. If making by hand, use two knives, a pastry blender, or your fingertips and quickly cut in the butter until the mixture resembles coarse meal with a few slightly larger butter lumps. If using a food processor, remove the cover and distribute the butter evenly over the dry ingredients. Cover and process with twelve 1-second pulses. Add the currants and quickly mix in or pulse one more time. Transfer the dough to a large bowl.

4. Stir in the heavy cream with a rubber spatula or fork until the dough begins to form, about 30 seconds.

5. Transfer the dough and all dry flour bits to a countertop and knead the dough by hand just until it comes together into a rough, slightly sticky ball, 5 to 10 seconds. Following the illustrations on page 711, cut the scones into 8 wedges. Place the wedges on an ungreased baking sheet. (The baking sheet can be wrapped in plastic and refrigerated for up to 2 hours.)

6. Bake until the scone tops are light brown, 12 to 15 minutes. Cool on a wire rack for at least 10 minutes. Serve warm or at room temperature.

➤ VARIATIONS
Glazed Scones
A glaze gives these scones a nice sheen and a sweeter flavor. If baking the scones immediately after making the dough, brush the dough just before cutting it into wedges.

Follow the recipe for Cream Scones, brushing the tops of the scones with 1 tablespoon heavy cream and then sprinkling them with 1 tablespoon sugar just before baking them.

713

Cakey Scones

An egg changes the texture and color and helps these scones stay fresher longer, up to 2 days in an airtight container.

Follow the recipe for Cream Scones, reducing the butter to 4 tablespoons and the cream to ¾ cup. Add 1 large egg, lightly beaten, to the dough along with the cream.

Ginger Scones

Follow the recipe for Cream Scones, substituting ½ cup chopped crystallized ginger for the currants.

Cranberry-Orange Scones

Follow the recipe for Cream Scones, adding 1 teaspoon grated orange zest with the butter and substituting ¾ cup dried cranberries for the currants.

Lemon-Blueberry Scones

Mix the dough by hand after adding the blueberries to keep them plump and whole.

Follow the recipe for Cream Scones, adding 1 teaspoon grated lemon zest with the butter and substituting ½ cup fresh or frozen (not thawed) blueberries for the currants.

OATMEAL SCONES

AFTER TACKLING TRADITIONAL SCONES, WE were ready to revamp the heaviest, densest, driest variation of them all: oatmeal scones. The first few recipes we tried confirmed our worst fears about oatmeal scones. There was the lean, mean, whole-wheat-flour oatmeal scone, which was gritty and dense, and the dried-fruit-laden oatmeal scones, which was thick like a cookie. Although tasters had different preferences when it came to texture, all agreed on the need for a stronger oat flavor. Our goal, then, was to pack the chewy nuttiness of oats into a moist and tender breakfast pastry, one that wouldn't require a fire hose to wash down the crumbs.

The first hurdle was deciding what type of oats to use. Because they take at least 30 minutes to cook, we quickly ruled out steel-cut oats for this recipe—the baking time of these scones would not be long enough to cook the oats through. The most familiar type seemed to be rolled oats, but we still had two choices: whole (old-fashioned) and quick-cooking. This was not such an easy decision, as each had qualities to recommend it. The flavor of the whole rolled oats was deeper and nuttier (a few tasters even asked if there was peanut butter in the scones), and the smaller, flaked quick-cooking oats had a softer texture, which was considered more palatable by some. We finally decided that either would do.

Next we had to figure out how to pack in the most oat flavor without sacrificing the texture of the scones. We were sure we could achieve this by simply processing the oats into the flour. But instead, the texture was horrible, very gluey and dense. We even tried adding real oat flour (found mostly in health food stores) along with the all-purpose flour, but the same gumminess resulted. Waving our white flag, we attributed this failure to the fact that oat flour does not have any gluten. Without gluten, it had nothing to contribute to the structure of our scones, adding only dead weight and a leaden texture. Leaving the oats intact, we found that equal parts oats to flour provided good flavor and a decent texture. (Most of the test recipes called for much smaller proportions of oats, thus their wimpy oat flavor.) But we were still yearning for a nuttier taste, so we took a hint from one of the test recipes and toasted the oats before mixing them with the flour.

We kept the sugar content to a minimum—just enough to tenderize the scones while enhancing the oat flavor. We tried all granulated sugar, all light brown sugar, and a combination of the two. Some tasters liked the deep robust flavor of the brown sugar, but most preferred the lighter texture and cleaner flavor created by the granulated sugar alone.

We settled on just 2 teaspoons of baking powder, a teaspoon less than we used in our cream scones, which contain more flour.

Moving on to the butter, we quickly realized why so many oatmeal scones are so dry: They don't have nearly enough fat. A lean oatmeal scone is simply not worth eating, so we used 10 tablespoons of butter, which adds flavor as well as tenderness. We used a mixture of milk and heavy cream for a rich oatmeal scone that doesn't double as a paperweight. (Using all half-and-half works just as well.) And, as in our recipe for cakey scones, an egg gives these oatmeal scones a nice richness and airy crumb. As with any biscuit or scone recipe, we found it important not to over-work the dough. It should be mixed just until the ingredients come together.

We baked the scones at 425 degrees—and every 25-degree increment in between. The best of the lot were those baked at 425 degrees, but they were not ideal. We tried pushing the oven temperature to 450 degrees (a bit of a gamble, as the sugar in the recipe might burn) and were rewarded. These scones had a dramatic rise and a deep golden brown crust. In such high heat, the cold butter melted quickly and produced steam, which created the light texture we were looking for. The intensity of the rise also gave the scones a cracked, craggy, rustic look that was enhanced when we added a sugar topping. The higher temperature also meant that the scones spent less time in the oven, which kept them from drying out.

Oatmeal Scones

MAKES 8

This recipe was developed using Gold Medal unbleached all-purpose flour; best results will be achieved if you use the same or a similar flour, such as Pillsbury unbleached. King Arthur flour has more protein; if you use it, add an additional 1 to 2 tablespoons milk.

Half-and-half is a suitable substitute for the milk-cream combination if you happen to have some on hand.

Once baked, these scones will keep for up to 3 days in an airtight container at room temperature.

1 1/2	cups (4 1/2 ounces) old-fashioned rolled oats or quick-cooking oats
1/4	cup whole milk
1/4	cup heavy cream
1	large egg
1 1/2	cups (7 1/2 ounces) lower-protein unbleached all-purpose flour, such as Gold Medal or Pillsbury
1/3	cup (2 1/3 ounces) sugar, plus 1 tablespoon for sprinkling
2	teaspoons baking powder
1/2	teaspoon salt
10	tablespoons (1 1/4 sticks) cold unsalted butter, cut into 1/4-inch cubes

1. Adjust an oven rack to the middle position and heat the oven to 375 degrees. Spread the oats evenly on a baking sheet and toast them in the oven until they are fragrant and lightly browned, 7 to 9 minutes; cool on a wire rack. Increase the oven temperature to 450 degrees. Line a second baking sheet with parchment paper. When the oats are cooled, measure out 2 tablespoons (for dusting the work surface) and set aside.

2. Whisk the milk, cream, and egg in a large measuring cup until incorporated; remove 1 table-spoon to a small bowl and reserve for glazing.

3. Place the flour, sugar, baking powder, and salt in the workbowl of a food processor fitted with the metal blade and process until combined, about four 1-second pulses. Scatter the cold butter evenly over the dry ingredients and process until the mixture resembles coarse cornmeal, twelve to fourteen 1-second pulses. Transfer the mixture to a medium bowl; stir in the cooled oats. Using a rubber spatula, fold in the liquid ingredients until large clumps form. Using your hands, gently knead the mixture in the bowl until the dough forms a cohesive mass.

4. Dust the work surface with half of the reserved oats, turn the dough out onto the work surface, and dust the top with the remaining oats. Gently pat the dough into a 7-inch circle about 1 inch thick. Using a bench scraper or chef's knife, cut the dough into 8 wedges and set on the parchment-lined baking sheet, spacing them about 2 inches apart. Brush the tops with the reserved milk-egg mixture and sprinkle with 1 tablespoon sugar. Bake until golden brown, 12 to 14 minutes. Cool the scones, on the baking sheet, set on a wire rack 5 minutes, then remove the scones to the rack and cool to room temperature, about 30 minutes. Serve.

➤ VARIATIONS

Cinnamon-Raisin Oatmeal Scones

Follow the recipe for Oatmeal Scones, adding ¼ teaspoon ground cinnamon to the dry ingredients and ½ cup golden raisins to the flour-butter mixture along with the toasted oats.

Apricot-Almond Oatmeal Scones

Follow the recipe for Oatmeal Scones, reducing the oats to 1 cup (3 ounces), toasting ½ cup slivered almonds along with the oats, and adding ½ cup chopped dried apricots to the flour-butter mixture along with the toasted oats and almonds.

Oatmeal Scones with Dried Cherries and Hazelnuts

Follow the recipe for Oatmeal Scones, reducing the oats to 1¼ cups (3¾ ounces), toasting ¼ cup coarsely chopped skinned hazelnuts along with the oats, and adding ½ cup chopped dried cherries to the flour-butter mixture along with the toasted oats and nuts.

Glazed Maple-Pecan Oatmeal Scones

Follow the recipe for Oatmeal Scones, toasting ½ cup coarsely chopped pecans along with the oats, whisking ¼ cup maple syrup into the milk-egg mixture (before removing 1 tablespoon for brushing the scones), and omitting the sugar. When the scones are cool, whisk 3 tablespoons maple syrup and ½ cup confectioners' sugar in a bowl until combined; drizzle the glaze over the scones.

ACHIEVING GOOD RISE AND A WELL-BROWNED CRUST

BAKED AT 350 DEGREES   **BAKED AT 450 DEGREES**

The scone on the left was baked in a moderate oven and did not rise as much as the scone on the right, baked in a very hot oven, which quickly turns the moisture in the dough into steam. Scones baked in a hot oven rise dramatically and have a craggy, well-browned top.

QUICK CINNAMON BUNS

CINNAMON BUNS ARE QUICK TO PLEASE. THE bun is tender and fluffy, the filling is sweet and spicy, and the glaze is sinful, encouraging even the well-bred to lick the gooey remnants from their fingers. It's a shame, then, that making cinnamon buns at home can try the patience of the most devoted cook. Most recipes call for yeast, which means they also call for a lot of time and skill as well as a standing mixer (or powerful biceps). The alternative is to make cinnamon buns from a tube or a box, options that produce inferior buns whose flavor lies somewhere between chemicals and cardboard. Our aim was to put cinnamon buns back in the home kitchen in good time, sacrificing neither flavor nor fluffiness for speed.

We started with a tasting of our favorite yeasted cinnamon buns on page 759. With a soft and resilient texture and a bready, open crumb, the texture of these buns was top-notch, and the combination of cinnamon and yeast produced a grown-up flavor. Unfortunately, the start-to-finish time was hours long. We knew what we wanted from cinnamon buns. Now we just wanted it quicker and easier.

Toward this end, the first decision we made was to work from recipes leavened with baking powder rather than yeast. The next step was to determine the best method for incorporating the fat into the other ingredients. First we tried the classic mixing method of cutting cold butter into dry ingredients. Unfortunately, this method turned out cinnamon buns that were dense, flaky, and craggy rather than tender, light, and fluffy.

The next mixing method we tried called for combining melted butter with the liquid ingredients in a food processor, then adding the dry ingredients. While we hoped that the food processor would make the mixing process easier, the dough was very sticky, making it difficult to work with, and the finished buns weren't worth the effort.

The last method we tried was a quick cream-biscuit method, in which heavy cream is added to flour, sugar, baking powder, and salt. What makes this dough unique is its complete lack of butter. The dough relies entirely on the heavy cream for tenderness and flavor. Better still, the dough can be mixed in a minute using just one bowl. This process was by far the fastest and easiest, and we wanted to go with it, but a few refinements would be required before it produced really good cinnamon buns.

To make the dough more tender, we thought to test whole or skim milk in place of heavy cream, but whole milk made the buns too heavy, and skim milk made them tough and bland. We increased the amount of baking powder to achieve lightness but ended up with metallic-tasting buns. We then tested buttermilk, a common ingredient in biscuit doughs, and had some success. We also added ½ teaspoon of baking soda to balance the acidity of the buttermilk. Baking soda reacts with the acid in buttermilk to produce carbon dioxide gas, which causes lift. The acid in the buttermilk gave the buns a more complex flavor and tenderized the gluten in the dough, making the interior airy and light.

But now the dough was too lean for our taste, owing to the buttermilk, most of which is made by adding acidic cultures to skim or low-fat milk. We arrived at the solution when we added 2 tablespoons of melted butter to the buttermilk. Just as we had hoped, the dough was tender, complex, and rich.

Whereas most recipes instruct bakers to roll out the dough, we found it easier to pat the dough into a rough-shaped rectangle, thus making the recipe even simpler. For the cinnamon-sugar filling we decided on a union of brown sugar, granulated sugar, cinnamon, cloves, and salt. Before sprinkling the filling on the dough, we brushed the dough with 2 tablespoons of melted butter to help the filling cling to it. Because the cinnamon mixture was loose and dry, however, it was still apt to fall away from the dough when the buns were cut and transferred to the baking pan. The easy solution was to add 1 tablespoon of melted butter to the dry ingredients, which made the mixture the consistency of wet sand, allowing us to press it into the dough easily. This time the filling stayed put.

Next we addressed the look of our rolls. Instead of rising to the occasion in the oven, they were slouching in their seats. We reviewed the quick cream-biscuit recipe to see if we might find the

MAKING CINNAMON BUNS

1. Pat the dough into a 12 by 9-inch rectangle and brush it with melted butter. Sprinkle the filling evenly over the dough, leaving a ½-inch border. Press the filling firmly into the dough.

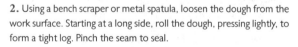

2. Using a bench scraper or metal spatula, loosen the dough from the work surface. Starting at a long side, roll the dough, pressing lightly, to form a tight log. Pinch the seam to seal.

3. Roll the log seam-side down and cut it evenly into 8 pieces. With your hand, slightly flatten each piece of dough to seal the open edges and keep the filling in place.

4. Place 1 roll in the center of the prepared nonstick pan and place the remaining 7 rolls around the perimeter of the pan.

717

Handling Basic Baking Tools

FOOD PROCESSORS

Keeping the Lid Clean

A food processor kneads bread dough and cuts butter into flour for pie dough in seconds. Here's how to make cleanup go just as quickly.

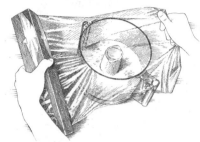

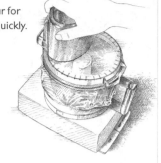

1. Place all the ingredients in the workbowl and then cover the bowl with a sheet of plastic wrap.

2. Fit the lid onto the workbowl, making sure that the plastic wrap lines the entire lid. Process as directed in the recipe. When done, simply lift off the clean lid and discard the splattered sheet of plastic.

Cleaning the Workbowl

The hole in the center of the food processor workbowl makes it impossible to soak the bowl before washing it. Here's how to plug that hole.

1. Remove the bowl cover and blade. Set an empty 35mm film canister upside down over the hole in the workbowl.

2. Fill the bowl with warm, soapy water and soak as desired.

STANDING MIXERS

Moving Heavy Mixers

Standing mixers (as well as food processors) are quite heavy and don't slide easily on the counter. Here are 2 good ways to move these heavy kitchen workhorses with ease.

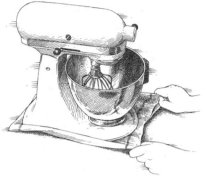

A. Place your mixer on a kitchen towel or cloth place mat, which can be pulled anywhere on the counter with little effort.

B. Stick self-adhesive floor-protector pads made of felt (normally used on furniture) to the bottom of your heavy appliances.

Keeping the Mess Under Control

Dry ingredients can puff out in a cloud of fine particles when mixed, while wet ingredients, such as cream, can splatter. Here are 2 good ways to keep your counter clean when using a standing mixer.

A. Once the ingredients are in the bowl, drape a clean, very damp kitchen towel over the front of the mixer and the bowl. Draw the towel snug with one hand and then turn on the mixer. When done, simply wash the towel.

B. If you own a large KitchenAid standing mixer (the type with a crank that lifts the bowl up off the base), spread a kitchen towel out between the base and bowl to catch any ingredients that escape from the bowl.

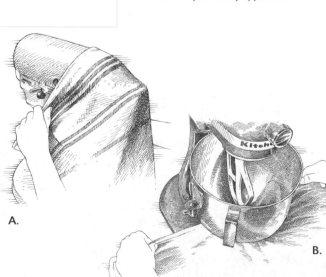

A.

B.

HAND-HELD MIXERS

Keeping Mixing Bowls in Place
Many recipes (especially those for cakes) call for adding wet and dry ingredients alternately for even blending. Here's how to secure a mixing bowl so you can hold a mixer in one hand and add ingredients with the other hand.

1. Twist a damp towel to form a nest slightly larger than the base of the bowl.

2. Set the bowl into the nest, which will hold the bowl in place as you mix and add ingredients.

Splatter-Free Mixing
Hand-held mixers work nearly as well as standing mixers, but they can cause excessive splashing, especially when beating thin batters or whipping cream. Using a deep, narrow mixing bowl helps, as does this trick.

1. Take a piece of parchment paper cut larger than the size of your mixing bowl and make 2 holes, spaced as far apart as the beater openings on your mixer. Insert the beater stems through the holes and into the beater base.

2. While you're mixing, the parchment will cover the bowl, preventing the contents from splattering onto the counter or walls.

THERMOMETERS

Recalibrating a Dial-Face Thermometer
Dial-face thermometers can become inaccurate with time, which is one reason we like digital thermometers. If you own a dial-face thermometer, there's an easy way to check and adjust its accuracy. First, insert the probe into a pot of boiling water. The thermometer should register 212 degrees at sea level. (The boiling point drops about 1 degree for every 500-foot increase in elevation.) If your thermometer is inaccurate, turn it over and use a pair of pliers to adjust the nut beneath the head. Keep adjusting until the thermometer registers the correct temperature when the probe is placed in boiling water.

Protecting Hands from Pots When Measuring Temperature
Most instant-read thermometers come in a protective plastic sleeve with a metal clip (for clipping to aprons) that forms a loop at the very top. Use this clip and plastic sleeve to distance your hands from hot pots when taking a temperature. This tip is especially useful when working with caramel.

1. Slide the probe end of the thermometer into the loop at the tip of the clip.

2. Hold the end of the plastic sleeve to keep the thermometer upright and then lower the probe into the food.

3. If you've lost the plastic sleeve that comes with your thermometer, don't despair. Insert the thermometer through a hole in a slotted spoon and hold the spoon by its handle to keep your hands away from the hot liquid as you lower the thermometer into it.

Measuring Temperature in a Shallow Liquid
Recipes for curds and pastry cream are temperature-sensitive but often involve small quantities, which can make it hard to get an accurate reading. Tilt the pan so that the liquid collects on one side, creating enough depth to get an accurate reading.

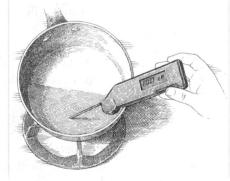

Retrieving a Fallen Oven Thermometer
Oven thermometers are apt to fall off the rack and onto the oven floor. Retrieval can be difficult, especially with a hand protected by a bulky oven mitt. In the test kitchen, we use a pair of tongs to retrieve and reposition an oven thermometer. Tongs keep your hands away from the hot rack and enable dexterity that's not possible with your hand clad in an oven mitt.

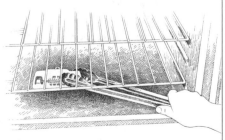

source of the problem there. Sure enough, the recipe stated that if the dough wasn't kneaded before being shaped, it didn't rise nicely in the oven. We made two batches of dough, kneading one and not the other, and were surprised to find that just a quick 30-second knead solved the problem. Contrary to what one might think, the short knead didn't toughen the buns; it just provided the dough with enough strength to take in a big breath and hold it.

To finish the buns, we tried a host of different glazes, all based on a quick confectioners' sugar and water glaze, which is inherently pasty and grainy. After a few trials, we found a way to sufficiently mask the graininess and pasty flavor by combining buttermilk and cream cheese, then sifting the confectioners' sugar over the paste. (If the sugar is not sifted, the glaze will be lumpy.) This glaze was smooth, thick, and pleasantly tangy, although it does add one more ingredient to the shopping list for the buns: cream cheese.

As for what to bake the buns in, we tried muffin tins, pie plates, baking sheets, springform pans, glass baking dishes, and cake pans. With its straight sides, round shape, and perfect size, a 9-inch nonstick cake pan was the perfect choice. We started baking at 425 degrees and got lucky the first time out. The buns baked in 25 minutes, rose and browned nicely, and were cooked all the way through.

Quick Cinnamon Buns with Buttermilk Icing

MAKES 8

Melted butter is used in both the filling and the dough, as well as to grease the pan; melt the total amount (8 tablespoons) at once and measure it out as you need it. The buns are best eaten warm, but they hold up well for up to 2 hours.

1	tablespoon unsalted butter, melted, for greasing the pan

CINNAMON-SUGAR FILLING
3/4	cup packed (5 1/4 ounces) dark brown sugar
1/4	cup (1 3/4 ounces) granulated sugar
2	teaspoons ground cinnamon

1/8	teaspoon ground cloves
1/8	teaspoon salt
1	tablespoon unsalted butter, melted

BISCUIT DOUGH
2 1/2	cups (12 1/2 ounces) unbleached all-purpose flour, plus more for dusting the work surface
2	tablespoons granulated sugar
1 1/4	teaspoons baking powder
1/2	teaspoon baking soda
1/2	teaspoon salt
1 1/4	cups buttermilk
6	tablespoons (3/4 stick) unsalted butter, melted and cooled

ICING
2	tablespoons cream cheese, softened
2	tablespoons buttermilk
1	cup (4 ounces) confectioners' sugar

1. Adjust an oven rack to the upper-middle position and heat the oven to 425 degrees. Pour 1 tablespoon melted butter into a 9-inch nonstick cake pan; brush to coat the pan. Spray a wire cooling rack with nonstick cooking spray; set aside.

2. FOR THE CINNAMON-SUGAR FILLING: Combine the sugars, spices, and salt in a small bowl. Add the melted butter and stir with a fork until the mixture resembles wet sand; set the filling mixture aside.

3. FOR THE BISCUIT DOUGH: Whisk the flour, sugar, baking powder, baking soda, and salt in a large bowl. Whisk the buttermilk and 2 tablespoons of the melted butter in a measuring cup or small bowl. Add the liquid to the dry ingredients and stir with a wooden spoon until the liquid is absorbed (the dough will look very shaggy), about 30 seconds. Transfer the dough to a lightly floured work surface and knead until just smooth and no longer shaggy.

4. Pat the dough with your hands into a 12 by 9-inch rectangle. Brush the dough with 2 tablespoons of the melted butter. Sprinkle evenly with the filling, leaving a 1/2-inch border of plain dough around the edges. Following the illustrations on page 717, press the filling firmly into the dough. Using a bench scraper or metal spatula, loosen the dough from the work surface. Starting at the long side, roll the

dough, pressing lightly, to form a tight log. Pinch the seam to seal. Roll the log seam-side down and cut it evenly into 8 pieces. With your hand, slightly flatten each piece of dough to seal the open edges and keep the filling in place. Place 1 roll in the center of the prepared nonstick pan, then place the remaining 7 rolls around the perimeter of the pan. Brush with the remaining 2 tablespoons melted butter.

5. Bake until the edges of the buns are golden brown, 23 to 25 minutes. Use an offset metal spatula to loosen the buns from the pan. Wearing oven mitts, place a large plate over the pan and invert the buns onto the plate. Place a greased cooling rack over the plate and invert the buns onto the rack. Cool about 5 minutes before icing.

6. FOR THE ICING AND TO FINISH THE BUNS: While the buns are cooling, line a rimmed baking sheet with parchment paper (for easy cleanup); set the rack with the buns over the baking sheet. Whisk the cream cheese and buttermilk in a large nonreactive bowl until thick and smooth (the mixture will look like cottage cheese at first). Sift the confectioners' sugar over the mixture; whisk until a smooth glaze forms, about 30 seconds. Spoon the glaze evenly over the buns; serve immediately.

POPOVERS

POPOVERS ARE IMPRESSIVE BECAUSE THEIR FEW humble ingredients—eggs, milk, flour, salt, and butter—are transformed by the heat of the oven into the culinary equivalent of hot-air balloons. The goal in developing the batter is to create a framework that, like a balloon, can expand and stretch without breaking as pressure is applied from within. We were after the biggest, best-tasting popovers we could make, with huge crowns; lightly crisp, golden brown exteriors; and tender, moist, airy interiors crisscrossed with custardy webs of dough.

The recipes we looked at during our research were remarkably consistent in terms of the ingredients and their proportions. We soon arrived at a list that would stand by us throughout testing: 2 eggs, 1 cup milk, 1 cup flour, ½ teaspoon salt, and 1 tablespoon butter. The variables we needed to test revolved around technique: Could we use a

muffin tin, or would a popover pan be necessary? How should we mix the batter? How hot should the oven be? Should the heat be lowered partway through cooking, as most recipes suggested? Should the popovers go into a hot oven or a cold oven? Was it necessary to preheat the pan and the fat used to grease it?

Our first efforts were baked in a muffin tin, and they failed to impress. Short and squat, with tops that looked something like overstuffed commas, these popovers were far from our ideal. Would the popover pan make a difference? The logic behind the pan design suggested that it would. Whereas the cups in a muffin tin are wider than they are tall, those in a popover pan are narrow and deep. Without much room to spread out, the batter has nowhere to go but up. We tried a popover pan and the shape of the popovers was improved—they were taller and puffier—but they still didn't have that beautiful crown we were looking for, and their texture was wrong, more like a dinner roll crossed with a muffin than a popover.

The popovers' resemblance to muffins got us thinking about the way we had been mixing the batter. Most recipes came with the following warning: Do not overmix the batter. In general, the more a batter or dough is mixed or kneaded, the more gluten is created. Gluten, which forms when the proteins in flour are combined with liquid, helps to create an elastic network that gives most baked goods the support they need to stand up. When mixing muffins, which should be tender, the goal is to develop only enough gluten to hold things together, and this is usually accomplished by gently folding the ingredients. So this is what we had been doing with our popover batter; leaving the mixture a little lumpy so as not to overdevelop the gluten. One or two recipes had different advice: Whisk the ingredients until smooth. We tried this, and the popovers rose a bit higher and their texture began to improve, becoming slightly more airy.

Next we tried letting the batter rest for 30 minutes before putting it in the oven, a common practice with pancake and waffle batter, the idea being to give the gluten a chance to relax. When it relaxes, the gluten becomes more pliable and better able to expand and stretch rather than breaking like a rubber band pulled too tight. If the gluten had more give, we reasoned, the popovers should rise still higher. We decided to let the batter rest on the countertop so that the chilled ingredients could get closer to room temperature before baking. This common baker's practice gives the batter a bit of a head start when it enters the oven. This test, too, was a success. Our popovers were growing slowly but surely over the rim of the popover tin, and their interior texture was becoming feathered with eggy layers of dough.

We were finally ready to experiment with oven temperature. The rationale for starting with a hot oven (450 degrees in most recipes) and lowering the heat about halfway through baking (to 350 degrees) is to give the popovers the intense heat they need to turn the moisture in the batter to steam. The popovers expand, brown, and set their shape at 450, and the heat is then lowered to let the interior cook through without overcooking the shell. We tried starting the popovers in a cold oven, and we tried baking them at a constant 375 degrees, as recommended in a couple of recipes. The popovers did rise under these conditions, but not as dramatically as when we started at 450 degrees.

Following through on the idea that an initial blast of heat is good for popovers, we also tried preheating the greased pan. The problem was that the butter we had been using to grease the pan burned before the pan had a chance to heat up fully. Our thoughts turned to clarified butter, which is made by slowly heating butter to let the milk proteins—the source of butter's sensitivity to heat—separate from the fat. This worked, but clarifying butter can be time-consuming. We tried preheating the pan with simple vegetable oil, and the results were every bit as good.

Popovers
MAKES 6

Unlike most popover batters, this one is smooth, not lumpy. High heat is crucial to the speedy, high rise of the popovers. When it's time to fill the popover pan with batter, get the pan out of and back into the oven as quickly as possible, making sure to close the oven door while you pour the batter into the pan. Popovers made in a 12-cup muffin tin won't rise nearly as high as those made in a popover pan, but they can still be quite good. See the variation that follows if you can't locate a popover pan.

2	large eggs
1	cup whole milk
1	cup (5 ounces) unbleached all-purpose flour
1/2	teaspoon salt
1	tablespoon unsalted butter, melted
1	tablespoon vegetable oil

1. In a large bowl, whisk the eggs and milk until well combined, about 20 seconds. Whisk the flour and salt in a medium bowl and add to the egg mixture; stir with a wooden spoon or spatula just until the flour is incorporated; the mixture will still be lumpy. Add the melted butter. Whisk until the batter is bubbly and smooth, about 30 seconds. Let the batter rest at room temperature for 30 minutes.

2. While the batter is resting, measure ½ teaspoon vegetable oil into each cup of the popover pan. Adjust an oven rack to the lowest position, place the popover pan in the oven, and heat to 450 degrees. After the batter has rested, pour it into a 4-cup liquid measuring cup or another container with a spout (you will have about 2 cups batter). Working quickly, remove the pan from the oven and distribute the batter evenly among the 6 cups in the pan. Return the pan to the oven and bake for 20 minutes, without opening the oven door. Lower the heat to 350 degrees and bake until golden brown all over, 15 to 18 minutes more. Invert the pan onto a wire rack to remove the popovers and cool for 2 to 3 minutes. Serve immediately.

> VARIATION
Muffin Tin Popovers
MAKES 10

Proceed as above, using a 12-cup muffin tin in place of a popover pan and using only the 10 outer cups of the tin. You will need an extra 2 teaspoons vegetable oil to grease the muffin tin.

17

YEAST BREADS

WHY MAKE BREAD AT HOME? THERE ARE MANY reasons. Depending on where you live, it's not always easy to find good bread at your local bakery. And, if you like to bake, it is a uniquely challenging and therefore uniquely satisfying experience. This chapter covers American favorites such as sandwich bread, bagels, and yeasted doughnuts, along with European classics like French baguettes. Although ingredients vary among these recipes, there are two constants. All of these favorite baked goods are made with yeast, and all the doughs must be kneaded.

INGREDIENTS Starting with the correct ingredients is part of the puzzle when making good breads, because essentially, bread contains no more than water, yeast, flour, and salt, so each ingredient counts.

WATER Our rule in the test kitchen is, if you don't drink your tap water, you do not want to use it in your bread, especially if your tap water has an "off" flavor. Don't get us wrong, we are not suggesting that you seek out fancy bottled water—any good-quality bottled spring water or filtered tap water will work fine. Of course, if your tap water tastes fine, use it in bread recipes.

YEAST Several kinds of yeast are available to home cooks. We prefer instant yeast because it is reliable and works quickly, and we call for it in our recipes. Instant yeast (sometimes labeled as "rapid-rise" yeast) is usually sold in packages of three envelopes. Each envelope contains about 2¼ teaspoons of yeast. For more about yeast, see page 728.

FLOUR Most of our recipes call for unbleached all-purpose flour, and some recipes call for bread flour. Do not substitute one for the other, or your results will be unsatisfactory. To read more about flour, see page 733.

SALT Salt lends flavor to bread. Don't omit this ingredient, even from sweet breads—salt-free breads generally don't taste right. We use table salt in the test kitchen, because it dissolves evenly and is easy to measure.

TECHNIQUE Proper technique is equally important. Our experience in the test kitchen has revealed the importance of several issues.

MEASURING The ratio of flour to water is key in bread recipes, and if you have too little or too much of either ingredient, the loaf will suffer or perhaps fail altogether. For this reason, we recommend weighing flour, especially when baking bread. When measuring water, use a glass or plastic liquid measuring cup with a pour spout (not a dry measure) and make sure to place the cup on a flat surface and bend down so the water level is at eye level.

KNEADING Most bread doughs do not require lengthy kneading. In fact, we have found that kneading bread for 10 to 15 minutes can often produce an inferior loaf because the action of the electric mixer beats air throughout the dough, eventually stripping it of valuable flavor, color, and aroma. Often, simply kneading for a few minutes in a standing electric mixer or a few seconds in a food processor, coupled with a minute or two on a floured surface to bring the dough together in a ball, will suffice.

If you are kneading by hand, resist the temptation to add too much flour to the dough, or you risk a dry texture. (This temptation is one reason why we prefer to knead bread dough in a standing mixer or food processor when possible.) In many recipes, the dough will at first seem very sticky, as if it needs more flour. However, as it rises, the dough hydrates—that is, the water becomes more evenly distributed as the flour absorbs it—and the texture becomes very soft and smooth. So do not add more flour unless the dough seems much too wet. One way to avoid adding more flour is to slightly moisten your hands to prevent sticking.

RISING On rare occasions, you may find that a loaf does not rise properly. Check to make sure that the expiration date on your yeast has not passed. Another possibility is that the water was too hot and killed the yeast. Water at about 110 degrees is a safe bet. A poor rise may also mean that you have added too much flour or placed the bread in a cool, drafty spot. To remedy the latter situation, heat your oven for 10 minutes at 200 degrees and turn it off; the oven can now be used as a proofing box—an enclosed draft-free space conducive to rising bread. A microwave oven can also be used as a proofing box. All that's involved is to nearly fill a 2-cup liquid measuring cup with water, place it in the microwave, and bring the water to a boil, then place the dough (which should be in a bowl covered with plastic wrap) in the microwave oven with the measuring cup. The preheated water will keep the microwave oven at the proper temperature for rising.

ACHIEVING A CRISP CRUST Many bread bakers add moisture to the oven as loaves bake to promote crispness in the crust. There are several ways to add moisture, including spraying the loaf with water, throwing water or ice cubes directly onto the floor of the oven during baking, or placing a roasting pan with hot water on a separate rack in the oven. We prefer the last method because it supplies a steady (and sizable) amount of moisture during the entire baking time. After blowing out the lights in several of the test kitchen ovens, we don't recommend throwing water or ice cubes into a hot oven. Spraying loaves with water before they go into the oven is safe but is not terribly effective with all types of bread.

TESTING FOR DONENESS It should also be noted that the length of time the bread is in the oven has a tremendous effect on its texture and quality. Most cookbooks tell you to tap the bottom of a loaf of bread to see if it is done. (Supposedly, a loaf will sound hollow when done.) This is, at best, an inexact method. We find it is much better to use an instant-read thermometer. For bread baked in a loaf pan, insert the thermometer into one end or side of the loaf, angling it down toward the middle. This method produces the same reading as poking through the bottom of the loaf without having to remove the bread from the pan. Note that different types of bread should be baked to different internal temperatures. Cooling bread before slicing is equally important. Bread sliced before it has cooled will be gummy.

STORAGE Most breads, unless otherwise specified, will go stale in a day or two. There is, however, an option for longer storage. In the test kitchen, we have had great success with freezing most of our breads. Wrapped first in aluminum foil and then in a large plastic zipper-lock bag, the bread will keep for several months. When you're ready to eat the bread, just remove it from the freezer, slip the foil-wrapped bread out of the zipper-lock bag, and place it on the center rack of a 450-degree oven for 10 to 15 minutes, depending on the size of the loaf. After the allotted time, carefully remove the foil (watch out for steam) and return the loaf to the oven for a few minutes to give the crust a chance to crisp.

Most bread recipes don't require much in the way of equipment. As mentioned, we recommend kneading dough in a standing mixer or food processor, and we think that an instant-read thermometer is the best way to judge the temperature of the water as well as doneness. You will want sturdy loaf pans for some recipes (see page 685 for our recommendations) as well as a baker's peel and a baking stone for free-form breads (see page 686 for more information on these items).

AMERICAN SANDWICH BREAD

AMERICAN LOAF BREADS ARE QUITE DIFFERENT from their European cousins, primarily because they contain fat in the form of milk and melted butter, as well as a touch of sweetener. This produces softer, more tender-crumbed loaves that are particularly well suited to sandwiches. These home-style sandwich loaves are baked in metal loaf pans, and their crusts are thin. As we discovered during the testing process, this is not just an exercise in convenience. American sandwich bread is every bit as inspiring as those toothier imports. There is nothing like a fresh-from-the-oven loaf cut into slabs and slathered with butter and honey.

These days, many home cooks might choose to use a bread machine to make this type of bread. In our experience, bread machines produce a crust that is mediocre at best and an interior of unpredictable quality that is all too often cake-like. As for purchasing good American sandwich bread, it's actually not that easy. Most bakeries don't carry a basic sandwich bread. Of course, many people who might enjoy making terrific sandwich bread at home don't even try it because they think it takes most of a day. We set out to develop a good, solid recipe that could be done in two hours, start to finish, including baking time.

For many home cooks, the other great impediment to making bread at home is the notion of kneading by hand. To find out if this was essential, we used a standard American loaf bread recipe and tested hand-kneaded bread against bread kneaded by machine—both in a standing mixer and a food processor—to find out if hand kneading makes better bread. The results were eye-opening. The hand-kneaded loaf was not as good as the two loaves kneaded by machine. It was denser and did not rise as well, and the flavor lacked the pleasant yeastiness found in the other loaves. After some additional testing and discussion, we hit on a reasonable explanation: When kneading by hand, most home cooks cannot resist adding too much flour, because bread dough is notoriously sticky. In a machine, however, you need no additional flour, and the resulting bread has the correct proportion of liquid to flour.

Now that we knew that kneading this kind of bread by machine was actually preferable to doing it by hand, we set out to refine the techniques. We wanted to include separate recipes for a standing mixer and a food processor, given that many home kitchens have one or the other, but not both.

Starting with the standing mixer, we tested the dough hook versus the paddle attachment. (Some recipes use the paddle for part or all of the kneading process.) The hook turned out to be vastly preferable, as dough quickly got caught in the paddle, requiring frequent starting and stopping to free it. We also found that a medium-speed setting is better than a slow setting. Although the hook appears to move at an alarming rate, the resulting centrifugal force throws the dough off the hook, resulting in a more thorough kneading. At slower speeds, the dough has a tendency to cling to the hook like a child on a tire swing.

Next we turned to the food processor. This method, to our surprise, was very successful, although the dough did require about four minutes of hand kneading at the finish. (A food processor does not knead as thoroughly as a standing mixer.) Using a metal blade, we pulsed the dry ingredients to combine them. Then, with the machine running, we added the liquid ingredients through the feed tube and processed the dough until it formed a rough ball. After a rest of two minutes, we processed the dough a second time, for about 30 seconds, and then removed it to a lightly floured counter to knead it by hand. We also tested the recipe without any hand kneading and found the resulting bread inferior—coarser in texture, with less rise.

We noted that the action of the food processor was quite different from that of the standing

RISING DOUGH FOR SANDWICH BREAD

1. Ideally, let the dough rise in a straight-sided container and mark its initial height by placing a rubber band around the container. It will be easy to gauge the dough's growth.

2. Whether the dough rises in a straight-sided container or a round bowl, tightly seal the vessel with plastic wrap to keep out drafts and trap moisture. Do not use a dish towel instead.

3. For doughs that rise a second time in the loaf pan, slip the pan into a plastic bag. Blow air into the bag to inflate it, then seal it securely with a twist tie.

4. Place the bagged loaf pan in another loaf pan so that the air inside the bag is pushed up, providing room for the dough to expand.

mixer. A relatively dry dough had worked well in the mixer because it was less likely to stick to the dough hook. However, in the food processor a slightly wetter dough seemed preferable, as the metal blade stretched and pulled it better than a dry dough, which ended up simply being cut into pieces. Therefore, to improve the performance of the food processor, we added 2 tablespoons of water to the dough.

With our dough and kneading methods set, we turned to oven temperatures and baking times. When we baked our bread at oven temperatures of 350, 375, and 400 degrees, the two higher temperatures overcooked the crust by the time the inside of the loaf was done. Again, unlike most European breads, this American loaf is prone to quick browning because it contains milk, butter, and honey.

To determine the proper baking time, you have to figure out how to decide when your bread is done. After testing bread taken from the oven at internal temperatures of 190, 195, and 200 degrees, the loaf producing a reading of 195 degrees was clearly the winner. The lower temperature produced dense bread, and the higher temperature produced dry, overcooked bread.

As stated above, one of our objectives in developing this recipe was to produce bread as quickly as possible. Therefore, we chose instant yeast. Not only did the instant yeast greatly reduce rising times, but, in a blind tasting, the bread tasted better than loaves made with regular active dry yeast.

To further speed the rising process, we preheated the oven to 200 degrees for 10 minutes, turned it off, and then used it as our proofing box, allowing the dough to rise in a very warm, draft-free environment. Next we tried heating the milk and water to jump-start the yeast. When the liquids were too hot, well above 130 degrees, we had some failures because the yeast was killed by the excessive heat. We did find, however, that when we warmed the liquids to about 110 degrees, the rising times were reduced by 5 to 10 minutes. These three changes brought the first rise down to 40 minutes and the second rise to a mere 20. Now we could make homemade bread in two hours, including kneading, both risings, and baking, which for this bread took only about 40 minutes.

American Sandwich Bread

MAKES ONE 9-INCH LOAF

This recipe uses a standing electric mixer; a variation on page 729 gives instructions for using a food processor. You can hand-knead the dough, but we found it's easy to add too much flour during this stage, resulting in a somewhat tougher loaf. To promote a crisp crust, we found it best to place a baking pan filled with boiling water in the oven as the bread bakes.

3¾	cups (18¾ ounces) unbleached all-purpose flour, plus more for dusting the work surface
2	teaspoons salt
1	cup warm whole milk (about 110 degrees)
⅓	cup warm water (about 110 degrees)
2	tablespoons unsalted butter, melted
3	tablespoons honey
1	envelope (about 2¼ teaspoons) instant yeast

1. Adjust an oven rack to the lowest position and heat the oven to 200 degrees. Once the oven temperature reaches 200 degrees, maintain the heat for 10 minutes, then turn off the oven.

2. Mix 3½ cups of the flour and the salt in the bowl of a standing mixer fitted with the dough hook. Mix the milk, water, butter, honey, and yeast in a 4-cup liquid measuring cup. Turn the machine to low and slowly add the liquid. When the dough comes together, increase the speed to medium and

JUDGING WHEN DOUGH HAS ENOUGH FLOUR

Many bakers add too much flour to bread dough, which results in dry loaves. To gauge whether your dough has enough flour, squeeze the dough gently with your entire hand. Even with especially soft, sticky doughs, your hand will pull away cleanly once the dough has enough flour.

mix until the dough is smooth and satiny, stopping the machine two or three times to scrape dough from the hook, if necessary, about 10 minutes. (After 5 minutes of kneading, if the dough is still sticking to the sides of the bowl, add the remaining flour, 1 tablespoon at a time and up to ¼ cup total, until the dough is no longer sticky.) Turn the dough onto a lightly floured work surface; knead to form a smooth, round ball, about 15 seconds.

3. Place the dough in a very lightly oiled large bowl, rubbing the dough around the bowl to coat lightly. Cover the bowl with plastic wrap and place in the warmed oven until the dough doubles in size, 40 to 50 minutes.

4. Gently press the dough into an 8-inch square that measures 1 inch thick. Starting with the side farthest away from you, roll the dough firmly into a cylinder, pressing with your fingers to make sure the dough sticks to itself. Turn the dough seam-side up and pinch it closed. Place the dough seam-side down in a greased 9 by 5-inch loaf pan and press it gently so it touches all four

---

INGREDIENTS: Yeast

We taste-tested our recipe for sandwich bread with eight different brands of yeast, both active dry and instant (also called rapid-rise). We placed the doughs made with instant yeast in a warmed oven for just 40 minutes, whereas breads made with the regular active dry yeast took about two hours to rise when left on the counter.

Although we expected slower-rising active dry yeast to promote more flavor in the finished loaves, this was not the case. Our tasters actually preferred the loaves made with instant yeast. The faster rise, in fact, yielded more flavor and produced a noticeably sweeter bread. One theory is that a quicker rise provides less time for the creation of the acidic byproducts of fermentation, hence a sweeter loaf. It is also true that instant yeast has superior enzyme activity, which converts starches to sugar faster than regular-rise varieties.

But even taking all of these factors into account, it still seems logical that a longer, gentler rise would give the dough more time to produce complex flavors. This may be true for a European-style loaf that contains nothing more than flour, yeast, salt, and water. But our American-style sandwich bread (see our recipe on page 727) contains both fat (milk and butter) and sugar (honey), so that the complexity of flavors, which would be evident in a plainer loaf, is easy to miss. Even more to the point, though, is the fact that instant yeast is not necessarily an inferior product.

Yeast is a plant, and different varieties have quite different qualities, as do different varieties of, say, roses. Instant yeast has been genetically engineered to reproduce the best characteristics of yeasts from around the world. Although genetic engineering often results in loss of flavor, our blind taste tests confirmed that in this case it produced an excellent product.

As for why this yeast works faster, there are two primary reasons. Besides the more rapid enzyme activity described above, instant yeast also has an open, porous structure, which means that it absorbs liquid instantly. When this yeast was introduced for home use, consumers had some difficulty; this is because home cooks continued to follow habit and proofed the yeast—that is, dissolved it in water to see if it bubbled, which was "proof" that the yeast was alive and could do its work—rather than mixing it directly into the flour, as instructed by the manufacturer. Because of its efficiency, this new yeast dissolved in water rapidly, then ran out of food (starch) and died before the rising process was complete. To correct this problem, scientists went back and added more starch to the mix, giving the yeast enough food to survive proofing.

Today, however, most yeast does not need to be dissolved in water before being used in a recipe. For one thing, yeast is now marked with an expiration date for freshness, so there's no need to proof, or test, the yeast as long as the expiration date hasn't passed. (Note that these expiration dates should be taken seriously. We tried baking a loaf with yeast that was one month past expiration, and the rising times were double those experienced with fresh yeast. The resulting loaf was denser, with a smaller rise.) For our sandwich bread, we opted not to proof the yeast in water but to mix it directly into the warm liquid to speed up preparation time.

Keep in mind that whether you dissolve yeast directly in liquid or add it to the flour, the temperature of the water or milk used is crucial. Dry yeast will die in ice water or in liquids at 125 degrees or higher. When testing recipes, we found that hot milk often killed off the yeast and therefore suggest using warm milk (about 110 degrees). We also use warm water at the same temperature in many recipes.

sides of the pan. Cover with plastic wrap; set aside in a warm spot until the dough almost doubles in size, 20 to 30 minutes.

5. Keep one oven rack at the lowest position and place the other at the middle position, then heat the oven to 350 degrees. Place an empty baking pan on the bottom rack. Bring 2 cups of water to a boil in a small saucepan. Pour the boiling water into the empty pan on the bottom rack and set the loaf on the middle rack. Bake until an instant-read thermometer inserted at an angle from the short end just above the pan rim into the center of the loaf reads 195 degrees, 40 to 50 minutes. Remove the bread from the pan, transfer to a wire rack, and cool to room temperature. Slice and serve.

➤ VARIATIONS
Sandwich Bread Kneaded in a Food Processor
Add an extra 2 tablespoons of water so the food processor blade can knead the dough more effectively. During the hand-kneading phase, you may need to add a little flour to make a workable dough. To ensure a tender bread, however, add as little as possible.

Follow the recipe for American Sandwich Bread, increasing the warm water by 2 tablespoons. Mix the flour and salt in a food processor. Add the liquid ingredients; process until a rough ball forms. Let the dough rest 2 minutes. Process 35 seconds. Turn the dough onto a lightly floured work surface and knead by hand until the dough is smooth and satiny, 4 to 5 minutes. Proceed as directed.

Slow-Rise Sandwich Bread
If you do not have instant yeast on hand, try this slow-rise variation.

Follow the recipe for American Sandwich Bread, substituting an equal amount of active dry yeast for the instant yeast. Let the dough rise at room temperature, instead of in the warm oven, until almost doubled in size (about 2 hours for the first rise and 45 to 60 minutes for the second rise).

Buttermilk Sandwich Bread
Buttermilk gives the bread a slight tang.

Follow the recipe for American Sandwich Bread, bringing the water to a boil rather than to 110 degrees. Substitute cold buttermilk for the warm milk, adding it to the hot water. (The mixing of hot water and cold buttermilk should bring the liquid to the right temperature, about 110 degrees, for adding the yeast.) Increase the first rise to 50 to 60 minutes.

Oatmeal Sandwich Bread
To turn this loaf into oatmeal-raisin bread, simply knead ¾ cup raisins, tossed with 1 tablespoon flour, into the dough after it comes out of the food processor or mixer.

Bring ¾ cup water to a boil in a small saucepan. Add ¾ cup (2¼ ounces) old-fashioned rolled oats; cook to soften slightly, about 90 seconds. Follow the recipe for American Sandwich Bread, decreasing the flour from 3½ cups to 2¾ cups in step 2, adding the cooked oatmeal to the flour, and omitting the warm water from the wet ingredients.

SHAPING DOUGH FOR SANDWICH BREAD

1. Flatten the dough into a square measuring 8 by 8 inches. Starting with the side farthest from you, roll the dough toward you into a log.

2. Seal the seams shut with your fingertips.

TAKING THE TEMPERATURE OF LOAF-PAN BREAD

Internal temperature is a good way to gauge whether a loaf of bread is done. Don't be tempted to pierce the top crust in the center, which will leave a conspicuous hole. Insert the thermometer from the side (as shown here) or an end, just above the edge of the loaf pan, directing it at a downward angle toward the center of the loaf.

CINNAMON SWIRL BREAD

MUCH TOO OFTEN, THE BEST PART OF CINNAMON swirl bread is the heavenly aroma emanating from the oven. Once the loaf is removed from the oven, there are unsightly gaps between the swirls of cinnamon filling and bread, and the filling has leaked out and burned in the pan.

We wanted to solve these problems when developing our recipe. We also wanted the baked texture to be moist and light, yet firm enough to be sliced fresh the first day and toasted for a few days after. To achieve the best texture and crust, we knew we needed to perfect the baking time and temperature as well as fine-tune the ingredients.

To get our bearings, we tried a range of yeast bread recipes, from rich brioche-type formulas with a high proportion of eggs, butter, and sugar to recipes for lean, white sandwich-style bread. When these first breads were tasted, everyone was drawn to the richer versions, as expected. However, for a more versatile bread that could be cut into thin or thick slices and toasted, we decided on a formula that was a compromise between the two.

We began our tests by focusing on milk, eggs, and sugar—the ingredients that most affect richness and texture. We tested loaves using all milk, all water, and a combination. Milk yielded a denser texture than we wanted; water had the opposite effect, producing a loaf that was too lean. An equal combination of milk and water was the answer. To lighten the texture a little bit more, we increased the eggs in our original recipe to two. Eggs contributed to the evenness of the crumb as well as to color and flavor.

Our final measurements of sugar and butter resulted in a crumb that was tender and soft the first day and retained some moisture for two to three days. We found that ⅓ cup sugar per loaf was enough to add flavor to the bread without competing with the filling. As for the butter, since it also contributes color and richness, we knew that to some extent the amount was a personal preference. For the everyday loaf we were after, we tested from 2 to 8 tablespoons per loaf and settled on 4.

We had no problem settling on unbleached all-purpose flour in our recipe, but as with many breads, we did face challenges in determining the total amount used. Depending on a number of factors, including the humidity of the air, the exact size of the eggs, and how precisely the liquids are measured, the dough will take anywhere from 3¼ to 3¾ cups of flour. Any of the doughs we made could have taken the greater amount (or more), but when we used it, the resulting loaves were dry. We had the best results when we reserved the last half cup of flour to use only as necessary, adding it little by little at the end of kneading. To test the dough to determine if the flour level is correct, squeeze it using your entire hand (completely clean with no dough clinging to it) and release it. When the dough does not stick to your hand, the kneading is complete. Even if the dough still feels soft, resist the temptation to add more flour.

Now that we had perfected the dough, we were ready to tackle filling, rolling, and shaping the loaf. For the filling, we tried both brown and granulated sugar mixed with cinnamon. Although we like the taste of brown sugar, we finally had to rule it out because it melted readily and leaked through the dough in places during baking.

The amount of filling was determined by one factor besides taste. We discovered that using much more than ¼ cup of the cinnamon-sugar mixture resulted in small separations between the filling and the bread because the excess sugar prevented the dough from cohering. We eventually discovered that ¼ cup of sugar mixed with 5 teaspoons of cinnamon resulted in a tasty bread with no gaps.

To create swirls in the finished bread and end up with a loaf that would fit into a 9-inch loaf pan, we rolled the dough out evenly into a rectangle 18 inches long and 8 inches wide. When we rolled the dough out longer than this, it was so thin that the filling popped through the edges in some places. Rolling the dough up evenly and closely was also important. When we rolled the dough too tightly, the filling popped through; rolling too loosely produced an uneven loaf and gaps between the swirls and the bread. It was also important to pinch the edges of the bottom seam and the ends of the roll together very tightly to prevent the filling from leaking.

Getting the dough mixed, filled, and shaped still doesn't guarantee great bread. Rising time is also crucial. In fact, finding the proper rising time entirely solved the problem of gaps in the bread. When we allowed the shaped loaf to rise just to the top of the pan, the baked bread was dense and did not have a fully risen, attractive shape. But when we allowed the unbaked loaf to rise too much, 1½ inches or more above the pan, we ended up with those unwanted gaps between dough and filling. Our overrisen loaves also collapsed in the oven. Allowing the dough to rise just 1 inch above the top of a 9-inch loaf pan before baking resulted in a perfectly shaped loaf with no gaps.

To determine the best baking temperature, we first tested the bread in a slow oven (300 to 325 degrees). Because this allowed the unbaked loaf too long a time to continue to rise before the yeast died (at an internal temperature of 140 degrees), the bread rose too much and lost its shape. A hotter oven (375 to 425 degrees) resulted in a loaf that was too brown on the outside before it was baked through. Since our bread formula contained milk, eggs, and sugar, all browning agents, we found that a moderate oven (350 degrees) baked the most evenly.

We tested final internal temperatures between 180 and 210 degrees and found 185 to 190 to be the ideal range. Technically, bread is not finished baking until all the steam has evaporated and it has cooled completely on a rack, so resist the temptation to cut the bread while it's hot. The pressure of the knife will compress the loaf, and you'll end up with a doughy slice.

Cinnamon Swirl Bread
MAKES ONE 9-INCH LOAF

If you like, you can make the dough one day, refrigerate it overnight, and then shape it, allow it to rise, and bake it the next day. This recipe also doubles easily; see our tip on page 732 for improvising loaf pans if you own just one.

ENRICHED BREAD DOUGH

½	cup whole milk
4	tablespoons (½ stick) unsalted butter, cut into ½-inch pieces
1	envelope (about 2¼ teaspoons) instant yeast
½	cup warm water (about 110 degrees)
⅓	cup (2⅓ ounces) sugar
2	large eggs
1½	teaspoons salt
3¼–3¾	cups (16¼ to 18¾ ounces) unbleached all-purpose flour, plus more for dusting the work surface

FILLING

¼	cup (1¾ ounces) sugar
5	teaspoons ground cinnamon
	Milk for brushing

GLAZE

1	large egg
2	teaspoons milk

1. FOR THE DOUGH: Heat the milk and butter in a small saucepan or in the microwave until the butter melts. Cool until warm (about 110 degrees).

2. Meanwhile, sprinkle the yeast over the warm water in the bowl of a standing mixer fitted with the paddle. Beat in the sugar and eggs and mix at low speed to blend. Add the salt, lukewarm milk mixture, and 2 cups of the flour; mix at medium speed until thoroughly blended, about 1 minute. Switch to the dough hook. Add 1¼ cups more flour and knead at medium-low speed, adding more flour sparingly if the dough sticks to the sides of the bowl, until the dough is smooth and comes

away from the sides of the bowl, about 10 minutes.

3. Turn the dough onto a work surface. Squeeze the dough with a clean, dry hand. If the dough is sticky, knead in up to ½ cup more flour to form a smooth, soft, elastic dough. Transfer the dough to a very lightly oiled large bowl. Cover the bowl with plastic wrap and let the dough rise until doubled in size, 2 to 2½ hours. (The ideal rising temperature for this bread is 75 degrees.) After the rise, punch down the center of the dough once. (The dough can be refrigerated, covered, for up to 18 hours.) Making sure not to fold the dough, turn it onto an unfloured work surface; let the dough rest about 10 minutes.

4. FOR THE FILLING: Grease the bottom and sides of a 9 by 5-inch loaf pan. Mix the sugar and cinnamon in a small bowl.

5. Press the dough neatly into an evenly shaped 8 by 6-inch rectangle. With a short side of the dough facing you, roll the dough with a rolling pin into an evenly shaped 18 by 8-inch rectangle (flour the work surface lightly if the dough sticks). Brush the dough liberally with the milk. Sprinkle the filling evenly over the dough, leaving a ½-inch border on the far side. Starting at the side closest to you, roll up the dough, pinching the dough gently with your fingertips to make sure it is tightly sealed. To keep the loaf from stretching beyond 9 inches, push the ends in occasionally with your hands as you roll the dough. When you finish rolling, pinch the seam tightly to secure it. With the seam-side facing up, push in the center of both ends. Firmly pinch the dough at either end together to seal the sides of the loaf.

6. Place the loaf seam-side down in the prepared pan; press lightly to flatten. Cover the top of the pan loosely with plastic wrap and set aside to rise. Let rise until the dough is 1 inch above the top of the pan, about 1½ hours, or about 1 hour longer if the dough has been refrigerated. As the dough nears the top of the pan, adjust an oven rack to the center position and heat the oven to 350 degrees.

7. FOR THE GLAZE: Meanwhile, in a small bowl, whisk together the egg and milk. Gently brush the top of the loaf with the egg mixture.

8. Bake until the loaf is golden brown and an instant-read thermometer inserted at an angle from the short end just above the pan rim into the center of the loaf reads 185 to 190 degrees, 30 to 35 minutes. Remove the bread from the pan and cool to room temperature on its side on a wire rack, at least 45 minutes. (The bread can be double-wrapped in plastic wrap and stored at room temperature for up to 4 days or frozen for up to 3 months.)

➤ VARIATION

Hand-Kneaded Cinnamon Swirl Bread
Follow the recipe for Cinnamon Swirl Bread, sprinkling the yeast over the water in a large bowl in step 2. Use a wooden spoon to incorporate the other ingredients as directed. When the dough comes together, turn it onto a lightly floured surface and knead until smooth and elastic, 12 to 15 minutes, adding more flour if necessary. Transfer the dough to a lightly oiled bowl and follow the rising instructions.

IMPROVISED LOAF PANS

1. If you own just one loaf pan but need to make two loaves at the same time, place a single loaf pan across the center of a 13 by 9-inch baking dish.

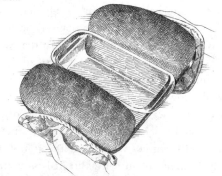

2. Position one portion of the shaped dough on either side of the loaf pan and bake.

INGREDIENTS: Flour

The most elemental of baking ingredients, flour, seems like a pretty simple item to choose. But a trip to the store reveals a wide variety of styles and shades of flour, not to mention all the different brands.

At the simplest level, flour is classified by protein content, which is attributable to different types of wheat. For example, hard winter wheat (the season in which the wheat is grown) is 10 to 13 percent protein; soft winter wheat is 8 to 10 percent protein. You can actually feel this difference with your fingers; hard-wheat flours tend to have a subtle granular feel, while soft-wheat flours feel fine but starchy, much like cornstarch.

High-protein flours are generally recommended for yeasted products and other baked goods that require a lot of structural support. The reason is that the higher the protein level in a flour, the greater the potential for the formation of gluten. Gluten forms elastic sheets in dough that expand with the gas released by the yeast yet are sturdy enough to prevent that gas from escaping, so the dough doesn't deflate. Lower-protein flours, on the other hand, are recommended for chemically leavened baked goods. This is because baking powder and baking soda are quick leaveners. They lack the endurance of yeast, which can force the naturally resistant gluten sheets to expand. Gluten can overpower quick leaveners, causing the final baked product to fall flat.

Numerous factors besides protein, including milling, processing, and bleaching, play a role in how a particular flour behaves and tastes, but these factors vary according to the variety of flour and the producer. Here are the types of flours called for in the recipes in this book:

ALL-PURPOSE FLOUR A pantry staple, all-purpose flour is what most home bakers use for everything. All-purpose flour is typically made from hard red winter wheat, soft red winter wheat, or a combination of the two, yielding, on average, a flour with a relatively high protein content between 10 and 12 percent. Supermarkets generally carry numerous brands of all-purpose flour, ranging in price and color; many are unbleached. We tested nine brands of all-purpose flour (all varying slightly in protein content) in a wide variety of baked goods, from cookies and piecrusts to muffins and bread. To say it was a difficult tasting is a bit of an understatement; the differences in flavor and texture were subtle. The most obvious differences were often in appearance (white versus beige cookies, short or tall biscuits, etc.). As difficult as the tasting was, we were able to draw some conclusions.

As a general rule, the flours acted according to the basic principles regarding protein content. Brands of flour we tested with a higher protein content yielded heavier, denser biscuits than those with a lower protein content. The good news was that despite the textural differences, tasters liked all of the biscuits. Another trend we noticed was that lower-protein flours spread more in tests of chocolate chip cookies and muffins, but the flavors were fine.

As an overall category, the four bleached flours in our tests in fact did not perform as well as the unbleached flours and were regularly criticized for tasting flat or carrying "off" flavors, often described as metallic. These characteristics, however, were more difficult to detect in recipes that contained a high proportion of ingredients other than flour. Coincidentally, our tests of cake and chocolate chip cookies (both sugary recipes) were the two tests in which off flavors carried by the bleached flour went undetected or were considered faint.

Despite the variations and subtleties, we walked away with firm results. Both King Arthur and Pillsbury unbleached flour regularly produced a more consistent range of preferred products than the other seven flours in the taste tests. King Arthur has a slightly higher protein content than Pillsbury (11.7 percent as opposed to around 10 percent). Since Pillsbury and Gold Medal unbleached flour (which also performed well in tests and also contains about 10 percent protein) are more widely available, we've tested all recipes in this book with these flours. Higher-protein all-purpose flours, such as King Arthur, will work fine in most recipes, although their elevated protein content may affect texture and appearance slightly.

BREAD FLOUR Flour with a protein level above 12 percent is generally sold as bread flour or labeled "made for bread machines." The high protein content ensures strong gluten development and a sturdy dough, which translates to good flavor, chewy texture, and a crisp crust. Not all styles of bread require bread flour; check the recipe before shopping.

CAKE FLOUR On the opposite end of the spectrum, cake flour is very low in protein, 6 to 8 percent, which guarantees delicate, fine-crumbed cakes and light, airy biscuits. We call for cake flour only in recipes where we feel it delivers better results—usually a more tender crumb—than all-purpose flour. However, in a pinch a low-protein all-purpose flour, such as Pillsbury or Gold Medal, can be substituted with only a modest change in the finished baked good.

WHOLE-WHEAT FLOUR A wheat berry contains three elements: the outer bran layer, the germ, and the heart of the berry, the endosperm. To make traditional whole-wheat flour, the entire berry is ground (white flours are ground solely from the endosperm). Graham flour is a bit coarser and perhaps flakier than regular whole-wheat flour and provides a nuttier flavor than conventional whole-wheat. It is named after its inventor, Sylvester Graham.

Because it is made from the whole wheat berry, which includes the perishable germ, whole-wheat flour does not store as well as all-purpose flour. If you don't think you will use an entire bag in a month or so, store whole-wheat flour in the freezer.

733

Handling Basic Baking Ingredients

STORING CAKE FLOUR

Most bakers keep all-purpose flour in a covered container to prolong freshness and facilitate measuring. However, most bakers don't bother to treat cake flour this way. In the test kitchen, we like to store cake flour in a large, heavy-duty zipper-lock bag, which is sealed and stored in the original box. The bag protects the flour from humidity (and bugs), and it's easy to dip a measuring cup right into the bag and level off the excess back into the bag.

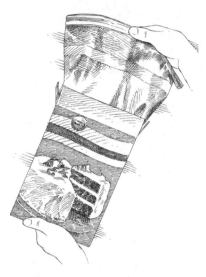

SOFTENING BUTTER IN A HURRY

It can take a long time (sometimes an hour) for chilled butter to soften on the counter. The microwave is a quick but sometimes imperfect solution (see box below). We like to cut the butter into tablespoon-size pieces, which should soften in just 15 minutes—the time it takes to gather other ingredients and heat the oven. If, despite all precautions, your butter is still too cool when you start to cream it, a quick remedy is to wrap the mixing bowl with a warm, damp towel and continue creaming.

MELTING CHOCOLATE

Melting chocolate in a heatproof bowl set over a pot of simmering water is a classic technique. This method works well but is a bit of a bother. In the test kitchen, we often handle this chore in the microwave (see box below). If you need to melt a relatively small amount of chocolate and don't own a microwave, you can use the gentle heat from an electric coffee maker. Place the chopped chocolate in a small heatproof bowl and cover the bowl with plastic wrap, being careful not to bring the plastic too far down the sides of the bowl. Place the bowl on the burner plate of an electric drip coffee machine and turn on the coffee machine. Whatever you do, don't melt chocolate in a pan set directly on the stovetop—it will likely burn.

CUTTING BUTTER INTO FINE DICE

Many recipes call for cold butter cut into small dice. Although this sounds easy enough, the butter can soften if you just start chopping away with abandon. Here's how we handle the task, quickly and efficiently, so the butter doesn't warm up.

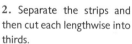

1. Cut the butter lengthwise into 3 even strips.

2. Separate the strips and then cut each lengthwise into thirds.

3. Stack the strips on top of each other, then cut them crosswise into ¼-inch dice—a size that works well in most biscuit and pie doughs.

WHOLE-WHEAT BREAD

IF ASKED TO DESCRIBE THE PERFECT LOAF OF distinctly American whole-wheat bread, you might say that it should be wheaty but not grainy, chewy but not tough, dense but not heavy, and full-flavored but not overpowering.

We decided to make a few loaves from various cookbooks just to explore the range of possibilities, starting with recipes from five of our favorite bread books. A recipe for an Italian walnut bread was terrific but clearly a rustic European loaf, not the distinctly American whole-wheat bread we were looking for. Other recipes were bitter, had odd flavors, or had too many other grains or flours to qualify as whole-wheat. Still others were too dense, too salty, or not sweet enough, an important element because a little sweetness enhances the rich flavor of the wheat flour.

We went back to the drawing board to create a master recipe that had the elements we liked best from each of the test breads. The recipe we started with contained 1 tablespoon of yeast, 2⅓ cups of warm water, 4 cups of whole-wheat flour, 1¼ cups of all-purpose flour, ¼ cup of rye flour (to add complexity of flavor), 1 teaspoon of salt, and 2 tablespoons of honey.

NO-FUSS FLOURING

Hauling out a large container can be a nuisance when all you have to do is dust a cake pan or work surface with some flour. Instead, set a funnel in an empty glass saltshaker and scoop a little flour into the funnel. When the shaker has been filled, seal it and store it in the pantry. These small shakers are easy to reach and do an excellent job of lightly coating a surface with flour. Use this tip for confectioners' sugar as well.

The initial results from this recipe were good but not great. The bread was too dense, and it needed a boost of both salt and honey for flavor. So we made a new loaf in which we doubled the amount of both yeast and honey and punched up the salt to 2 teaspoons. The taste-test results were encouraging, and the loaf was even better when we tried making it again, using ½ tablespoon less yeast and adding ¼ cup of melted butter for flavor. But some problems remained. The texture was still too dense for our taste, and the flavor was a bit generic, reminiscent of what one might find at a diner served with two individually wrapped pats of butter.

Having already tested a higher amount of yeast, we suspected that the texture might be improved by using a drier dough, which tends to produce a lighter bread. We therefore increased the total amount of flour from 5½ cups to 6 cups. We then varied the proportion of whole-wheat flour to white to rye. The loaf with slightly more whole-wheat than white flour and with some rye flour was the best of the lot and actually quite good.

Now we were close, but the bread still lacked the proper texture and wheatiness we expected from a whole-wheat loaf. So we turned to one of our favorite bread books, *The Book of Bread* (HarperPerennial, 1982) by Evan and Judith Jones, and discovered that one of their whole-wheat bread recipes contained wheat germ. As it turned out, this simple addition—a mere ¼ cup of wheat germ—made a terrific difference in our loaf, producing a nutty flavor and slightly more complex texture. We liked it so much that we tried a loaf with ½ cup of wheat germ, which turned out to be the ideal amount.

Into our thirtieth loaf at this point, we decided to press on with the issue of sweeteners. We tend to use honey in bread doughs, but we also made loaves with a variety of other sweeteners, including ¼ cup of each of the following: granulated sugar, dark brown sugar, maple syrup, barley malt, and molasses. We also tested half quantities of malt and molasses paired with an equal amount of honey. Oddly, it was hard to differentiate the flavors added by the sweeteners. That said, though, the honey version was generally picked by our tasters as number one,

735

with a nice, clean, sweet flavor and moist texture.

We went on to try different fats. We sampled loaves made with vegetable oil (a noticeable lack of flavor), melted lard (a strong flavor but unwelcome in this recipe), melted butter (by far the best: good texture, sweet flavor), cold butter (denser, not as moist), and a whole egg (grainy, gritty texture—almost cottony).

Having found the dough recipe we wanted, we proceeded to test the variables of kneading, rising, and baking. One of the most interesting tests involved kneading times. Using a standing mixer, we kneaded for eight, 12, and 16 minutes, respectively, with no discernible difference in the finished loaves. Because whole-wheat flour contains so much protein, a reasonable amount of gluten is formed as long as the ingredients are quite thoroughly mixed together. With this recipe, it matters little whether the kneading is done by machine or by hand, for a short time or a long time.

Our final recipe calls for an initial rising of just under one hour (a relatively short rising time owing to the relatively high amount of yeast). We tested a shorter rising time of only 30 minutes, but the resulting loaf was dense and dry. For the second rise, after the dough was shaped, we found that 20 to 30 minutes was best. When left to rise for longer than this, the dough baked up into a light loaf with a dry, cottony texture and a crust that had separated from the rest of the loaf.

Although we were confident about oven temperatures and baking times, we tested them to be sure. As we had expected, a 375-degree oven worked best. A 350-degree oven turned out doughy bread, while a 400-degree oven produced a loaf with a slightly burnt bottom. To determine when a loaf is properly baked, we used an instant-read thermometer inserted from one end into the middle of the loaf (for a free-form loaf, simply insert the thermometer from the bottom to the middle of the loaf). An internal temperature of 205 degrees proved ideal; at lower temperatures, the bread was underbaked.

It did occur to us that perhaps the brand of whole-wheat flour might make a difference. We had performed all of our tests to this point with King Arthur flour. So we tried Arrowhead Mills Stone Ground Whole Wheat Flour. This flour produced a loaf with a nice wheat flavor, but it was lighter in both color and texture. Next we made a loaf using Hodgson Mill Whole Wheat Graham Flour, which produced a wonderful loaf with a terrific, nutty flavor. Graham flour is a bit coarser and perhaps flakier than regular whole-wheat flour and, as we noted in our testing, provides a nuttier flavor. It is named after its inventor, Sylvester Graham. Although the King Arthur was also very good, we felt that the Hodgson flour was best suited for this recipe.

Whole-Wheat Bread with Wheat Germ and Rye
MAKES TWO 9-INCH LOAVES

Because kneading this wet, sticky dough can cause damage to lower-horsepower mixers, it's best to use a heavy-duty standing mixer and be sure to use the low speed during kneading. Follow the instructions for hand kneading if you don't own a heavy-duty standing mixer. This recipe makes too much dough to knead in a food processor.

2⅓	cups warm water (about 110 degrees)
1½	tablespoons instant yeast
¼	cup honey
4	tablespoons (½ stick) unsalted butter, melted
2½	teaspoons salt
¼	cup (⅞ ounce) rye flour
½	cup toasted wheat germ
3	cups (16½ ounces) whole-wheat flour, preferably Hodgson Mill Whole Wheat Graham Flour
2¾	cups (13¾ ounces) unbleached all-purpose flour, plus more for dusting the work surface

1. In the bowl of a standing mixer, mix the water, yeast, honey, butter, and salt with a rubber spatula. Mix in the rye flour, wheat germ, and 1 cup each of the whole-wheat and all-purpose flours.

2. Add the remaining whole-wheat and all-purpose flours, attach the dough hook, and knead at low speed until the dough is smooth and elastic, about 8 minutes. Transfer the dough to a lightly floured work surface. Knead just long enough to make sure that the dough is soft and smooth, about 30 seconds.

3. Place the dough in a very lightly oiled large bowl; cover with plastic wrap. Let rise in a warm, draft-free area until the dough has doubled in volume, about 1 hour.

4. Heat the oven to 375 degrees. Gently press down the dough and divide into two equal pieces. Gently press each piece into a rectangle about 1 inch thick and no longer than 9 inches. With a long side of the dough facing you, roll the dough firmly into a cylinder, pressing down to make sure that the dough sticks to itself. Turn the dough seam-side up and pinch it closed. Place each cylinder of dough seam-side down in a greased 9 by 5-inch loaf pan, pressing the dough gently so it touches all four sides of the pan. Cover the shaped dough; let rise until almost doubled in volume, 20 to 30 minutes.

5. Bake until an instant-read thermometer inserted at an angle from the short end just above the pan rim reads 205 degrees, 35 to 45 minutes. Transfer the bread immediately from the baking pans to wire racks; cool to room temperature.

SCIENCE: Yeast and Gluten

Yeast is a microorganism that is maintained in pure culture. Under proper conditions in liquid, it can multiply continuously until the growth medium is exhausted. Yeast in a liquid medium is sold by the tanker-full to commercial food manufacturers. For bakeries, yeast companies remove some of the moisture to create a product called crumbled yeast, which is sold in 50-pound bags. The next processing step extrudes the yeast to make a product that remains fully hydrated yet is fine enough to press into the small cakes you see for sale in supermarkets, labeled cake yeast. Further drying yields dried, powdered yeast, called active dry yeast. The same process is used to make other dry yeasts, including instant yeast, although this product starts with a different strain of yeast. (For more information on instant yeast, see page 728.)

Although yeast does provide the gas (in the form of carbon dioxide) that gives bread lift, it needs long sheets of gluten to trap the gas. What exactly is gluten? When water is mixed with wheat flour, proteins, most importantly the proteins glutenin and gliadin, bind to each other and to the water and become pliable. Gluten is the name given to this combination of proteins. Kneading stretches the gluten into elastic sheets that trap and hold the gases produced by the yeast, which allows the bread to rise.

➤ VARIATION
Hand-Kneaded Whole-Wheat Bread

Follow the recipe for Whole-Wheat Bread with Wheat Germ and Rye, mixing the water, yeast, honey, butter, salt, rye flour, and wheat germ in a large mixing bowl. Mix 2¾ cups of the whole-wheat flour and the all-purpose flour in a separate bowl, reserving ¼ cup of the whole-wheat flour. Add 4 cups of the flour mixture to the wet ingredients; beat with a wooden spoon 5 minutes. Beat in another 1½ cups of the flour mixture to make a thick dough. Turn the dough onto a work surface that has been sprinkled with some of the reserved flour. Knead, adding only as much of the remaining flour as necessary to form a soft, elastic dough, about 5 minutes. Continue with step 3.

DELI-STYLE RYE BREAD

JEWISH RYE, AKA NEW YORK RYE, IS ONE OF our favorite breads: We love its tang and chew. Unfortunately, it's difficult to find good Jewish rye these days. The mass-produced varieties in supermarkets (and even the loaves at our local Jewish bakery in Boston) are too refined, fluffy, and soft, with only a hint of rye flavor. The rye bread we hanker for is slightly moist and chewy but not too dense. It has a tight, uneven crumb; a hard, thin, almost brittle crust; and a tangy rye flavor. Perhaps most important, the bread doesn't become soggy or limp when stacked with a pile of pastrami.

We discovered myriad rye bread recipes during our research; not just the Jewish varieties but Old World recipes containing buttermilk, sour cream, mashed potato, molasses, ginger, and even sauerkraut. Intriguing as these variations were, we stuck to the basics: rye and white flour, water, a sweetener, salt, fat, and caraway seeds. Working with these ingredients, we identified three variables that we thought would affect the texture and flavor of the bread: the method of leavening, the type of rye flour, and the ratio of rye to white flour.

We focused first on two basic methods for leavening the dough, both of which are practical for home cooks. The sponge method, which we use in our European loaves later in this chapter, involves first mixing a small amount of flour, water, and yeast, then leaving this sponge to ferment for a defined period of time. More flour and water are then added to make the dough. In the second method, yeast and water are mixed, and when the yeast dissolves, the mixture is added directly to make the dough.

Using a variety of cookbook rye bread recipes, we did side-by-side testing of the sponge and direct methods. We found the sponge method clearly preferable. Because the slow rise allows time for the creation of fermentation byproducts that add flavor, this method produced a bread with a strong, tangy flavor and a chewy, pleasantly uneven texture. We also liked the way the bread made using the sponge method maintained its moistness during storage. The bread made with the direct method had a tighter web of holes and a more even crumb.

We also tested different sponge fermentation times, including a half hour, 2½ hours, and overnight. As we increased the fermentation time, the rise was faster, the bread baked higher, the crumb was more uneven, the bread was chewier, and the flavor was stronger. The sponge fermentation time can, therefore, be varied to taste, with 2½ hours being the minimum. We prefer an overnight sponge fermentation, and we find that the initial intense and slightly sour rye flavor improves with cooling and storage. However, we were looking for more chew and a sharper tang than even the longest fermentation time could give. In search of this, we turned to the choice and ratio of different flours.

We suspected that different rye flours might affect the texture and flavor of the rye bread. However, many rye bread recipes don't specify the type of rye flour to use. Up to this point, all of our testing had been done using a whole-grain rye flour. We now proceeded to round up the rest of the nationally available rye flours: light rye, medium rye, and pumpernickel. The breads they produced were dramatically different. We preferred the breads made with light rye or medium rye, both of which had an earthy, tangy flavor with a slight springiness.

Following our successes with these two flours, we moved on to test different ratios of rye to white flour. Rye flour alone does not contain enough gluten-forming proteins to make the bread rise adequately, so some protein-rich wheat flour must be used as well.

Our test recipe had 3 cups of rye flour and 4½ cups of unbleached all-purpose flour. As we reduced the rye flour (increasing the all-purpose flour proportionally), the breads became significantly lighter, softer, and less chewy. As one tester said, they were too "bready." With 4 cups of rye flour and 3½ cups of all-purpose flour, the bread was too heavy and dense. We settled on 3½ cups of rye flour and 4½ cups of all-purpose flour. This produced a rye bread with a perfect balance of tang, chew, and moistness.

After baking 20 or so loaves (some with caraway seeds and some without), it became clear that rye bread just isn't rye bread without caraway seeds. We have to admit that before this testing, we had confused the flavor of caraway with rye. Rye gives the bread its earthy, tangy, and fruity character, while caraway adds pepper and spice. Too much caraway is overpowering. Too little caraway and the bread seems incomplete. Two tablespoons is just about right.

We tried substituting honey, molasses, and malt syrup in place of the two tablespoons of sugar in our test recipe. The malt and molasses added a bitter flavor, but we did prefer the honey over the sugar. The bread made with honey was slightly moister. When we tried increasing the amount of sweetener, the bread tasted too sweet, and this obscured the other flavors.

We also experimented with several different types of fat in the bread, including butter, Crisco, and oil. With such a small amount of fat in the recipe, the differences were barely discernible, so we opted to stick with vegetable oil. We even tried using no fat at all, but it was not a good idea—a relatively small amount of fat, about two tablespoons per loaf, goes a long way to soften and moisten the bread.

Finally, we decided to try adding rye flakes (rye kernels that are steamed and then rolled flat to form flakes similar to rolled oats) to the bread dough. The flakes added a nice boost of rye flavor and a bit of extra chew, but they had an unattractive raw appearance. We then tried adding them to the sponge, rather than the dough. This was just the trick: The rye flakes softened up during the rise and lost their rough appearance.

Throughout the testing, we noticed that working with rye dough is different from working with wheat dough. The most obvious differences are the rye dough's slimy tackiness and its lack of elasticity. It bears more resemblance to molding clay slightly puffed up with air than to a stretchy and springy bread dough. The visual and textural cues that guide the wheat bread baker don't hold true with rye bread. Because rye dough is so sticky, the temptation is to add more flour, but we found that this makes the bread dry and coarse. Using wet hands makes it easier to remove the dough from the bowl and dough hook. We use a tablespoon or two of flour to help us shape the dough into a ball, which is then placed in an oiled container to rise. From there on, it is more manageable.

Rye dough's lack of elasticity results from the low gluten content of rye flour. Some references claim that because it has so little gluten the dough should be kneaded longer to allow the gluten to develop. So we tested kneading the dough for five, 10, 15, and 20 minutes. At five minutes the dough was very sticky, soft, and inelastic, yet the bread rose the highest and had the strongest, springiest, and most moist texture. As we increased the kneading time, the bread became more fluffy and soft, characteristics we did not want in a rye bread. So we found that, contrary to conventional wisdom, five minutes of kneading produced the best results.

Like most doughs, rye dough is given two rises. Most recipes suggest letting the dough double in volume during both the first and second rises. It is easy to gauge the first rise in a straight-sided container, as the dough doubles in height. After the first rise, the dough should be gently punched down and shaped into loaves. The second rise is more difficult to gauge, since the dough is on a baking sheet and a doubling in volume is less apparent. During the second rise, we found that the dough develops a bloated appearance and

tends to spread out rather than up. This spread is actually a crucial indicator of proper rising; if the dough hasn't started to spread out, it's not ready. Underrisen rye dough does not bake as high and can have a "blowout" in which the soft inner dough of the partially baked loaf oozes out from the developing crust. As soon as the dough has that bloated look and starts to spread, get it into the oven—overrising reduces oven rise.

As a final touch, we wanted to develop the shiny, brittle crust that is the hallmark of Jewish rye. In our research, we found numerous glaze mixtures designed to achieve this, including egg yolks on their own, egg whites on their own or mixed with water or milk, a mixture of cornstarch and water, and a mixture of potato starch and water. The most interesting (and authentic) approach is to apply a potato starch and water mixture to the loaf as it is removed from the oven. We found, however, that this liquid gave the bread a milky white coating rather than a clear sheen. All the other recommended methods involve glazing the dough before it is baked. After trying them all, we found that preglazing with one egg white mixed with 1 tablespoon of milk worked best.

Deli-Style Rye Bread
MAKES I LARGE LOAF OR 2 SMALLER LOAVES

Because this dough requires so much flour (a whopping 8 cups), it is best kneaded in a heavy-duty standing mixer. The rye flakes should be toasted for best flavor. Although the rye flakes intensify the bread's flavor, if unavailable, they can be omitted from the recipe.

SPONGE
2/3 cup rye flakes (optional)
2 3/4 cups water, at room temperature
1 1/2 teaspoons instant yeast
2 tablespoons honey
3 cups (15 ounces) unbleached all-purpose flour

DOUGH
1 1/2 cups (7 1/2 ounces) unbleached all-purpose flour, plus more for dusting the work surface

3½ cups (12¼ ounces) medium or light
 rye flour
2 tablespoons caraway seeds
2 tablespoons vegetable oil
1 tablespoon salt
 Cornmeal for sprinkling the baking sheet

GLAZE
1 egg white
1 tablespoon milk

1. FOR THE SPONGE: Heat the oven to 350 degrees; toast the rye flakes, if using, on a small baking sheet until fragrant and golden brown, 10 to 12 minutes. Cool to room temperature. Mix the water, yeast, honey, rye flakes, and flour in the mixing bowl of a standing mixer to form a thick batter. Cover with plastic wrap and let sit until bubbles form over the entire surface, at least 2½ hours. (The sponge can stand at cool room temperature overnight.)

2. FOR THE DOUGH: Stir the all-purpose flour, 3¼ cups of the rye flour, the caraway seeds, oil, and salt into the sponge. Attach the dough hook and knead the dough at low speed, adding the remaining ¼ cup rye flour once the dough becomes cohesive; knead until smooth yet sticky, about 5 minutes. With moistened hands, transfer the dough to a well-floured work surface, knead it into a smooth ball, then place it in a very lightly oiled large bowl or straight-sided container. Cover with plastic wrap and let rise at warm room temperature until doubled in size, 1¼ to 2 hours.

3. Generously sprinkle the cornmeal on a large baking sheet. Turn the dough onto a lightly floured work surface and press it into a 12 by 9-inch rectangle. (For two smaller loaves, halve the dough, pressing each portion into a 9 by 6½-inch rectangle.) With one of the long sides facing you, roll the dough into a 12-inch log (or two 9-inch logs), seam-side up. Pinch the seam with your fingertips to seal. Turn the dough seam-side down and, with your fingertips, seal the ends by tucking them into the loaf. Carefully transfer the shaped loaf to the prepared baking sheet, cover loosely with oiled plastic wrap, and let rise until the dough looks bloated and dimply

and starts to spread out, 60 to 75 minutes. Adjust an oven rack to the lower-middle position and heat the oven to 425 degrees.

4. FOR THE GLAZE: Whisk the egg white and milk together and brush over the sides and top of the loaf. Right before baking, make 6 or 7 slashes, ½ inch deep, in the top of the dough with a single-edge razor blade or very sharp knife. Bake for 15 minutes, then lower the oven temperature to 400 degrees and bake until golden brown and an instant-read thermometer inserted in the center of the loaf reads 200 degrees, 25 to 30 minutes (or 15 to 20 minutes for smaller loaves). Transfer to a wire rack and cool to room temperature.

BAGUETTES

IN THE TEST KITCHEN, THE TOPIC OF FRENCH baguettes had long been contemplated as promising but risky. Everyone agreed that a great baguette is made from just four ingredients—flour, water, yeast, and salt—and that it must express excellence in its chief characteristics: crust, crumb, flavor, and color. We agreed that it should have a thin, shattering crust of the deepest golden brown; an open, airy texture; a light, moist crumb; and fully developed flavor. Where we parted ways was on the question of whether you could actually create an outstanding baguette at home in a regular oven. Some were skeptical, but those of us who have

ACHIEVING WINDOWPANE

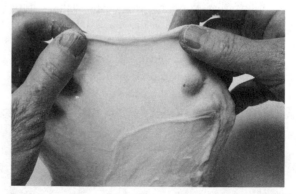

A piece of well-kneaded dough can be stretched until it is nearly translucent.

spent some time as professional bakers dismissed their skepticism.

The first problem we had to figure out was, as bakers say, "rising" the dough. Modern French bread uses a direct-rise method, in which flour and water are mixed with commercial yeast, given a rise, punched down, shaped, allowed to rise again, and baked. But we found that an older method, one that prevailed before commercial yeast became affordable, appealed to us more. This method, known as a pre-ferment, uses a small amount of yeast to rise a portion of the dough for several hours or overnight. The pre-ferment becomes a dough when it is refreshed with additional flour, yeast, and water, given some salt as well, mixed, and set to rise again.

We tried a number of apparently authentic French baguette recipes, using the pre-ferment method. Although none of these baguettes bowled us over, the flavor and texture of the breads made were definitely very good. Among the two or three types of pre-ferments, we chose the sponge method, which basically calls for a thinnish mixture of flour and water and a small amount of yeast. These ingredients are easily stirred together, and the resulting relatively liquid structure encounters little physical resistance to fermentation, so it rises fully (or ripens) in hours, not days.

Any given bread type has a correct proportion of ingredients. In a system known as the "baker's percentage," these proportions are based on the weight of the flour, which is judged to be 100 percent, with the other ingredients lining up behind. A correct baguette dough, for instance, is said to have a hydration of 62 to 65 percent. This means that for every 1 pound of flour, there will be between 0.62 and 0.65 pound of water. We found it necessary to weigh both flour and water to make sure the sponge had the correct consistency when we were ready to mix the dough. We settled on 6 ounces of both flour and water for the pre-ferment stage; this gave us a sponge that was soft but still firm enough to require additional water when we mixed the dough.

As for the yeast, we knew that we wanted to use as little as possible for the greatest flavor development (using a lot of yeast results in bread that tastes more of yeast than of the flavorful byproducts of fermentation), but we weren't sure just how little. While we also knew the sponge should have doubled in volume and be pitted with small bubbles when ripe, we didn't know exactly how long this might take—it could reach this stage in as little as three hours or take as much as eight. Finally, we determined that a pinch of instant yeast was equal to the task of rising the sponge and ½ teaspoon was enough to refresh the body of the dough. But we remained in a quandary about fermentation time until we came across Daniel Wing's exemplary book *The Bread Builders* (Chelsea Green, 1999) and his explanation of "the drop." This term refers to a sponge rising and then falling under its own weight. Far from representing deflation or exhaustion of the yeast, which seems logical and which

THE RISE AND FALL OF A PRE-FERMENT

In the beginning stages, a pre-ferment shows no evidence of rising or bubbling (left). Its middle phase is characterized by substantial swelling and surface bubbling (center). The final stage, or "drop," is characterized by a slight sinking of the sponge, leaving a higher edge around the circumference of the bowl (right). At this point, the sponge is ready to use.

we had previously supposed, the drop revitalizes the sponge and is a sign that the sponge is ready for action. The drop is a critical visual cue. By using warm water and a pinch of yeast, we got a sponge that rose and dropped in about six hours in a 75-degree kitchen.

The second phase of bread making is kneading, or mixing. Mixing unites wet and dry ingredients and transforms them from a shaggy ball of dough to a satiny orb. Our preferred partner was a standing mixer outfitted with the dough hook. However, for the dough hook to engage our small amount of dough, we had to mix at high speed. The sticky blob we ended up with once or twice was a direct result of overheating—the dough was irreparably damaged and the character of the bread destroyed. By kneading with a dough hook instead of by hand, we had unwittingly distanced ourselves from some important tactile permutations that were taking place: the dough's temperature, its increasing elasticity and stretchiness, and its surface tackiness. At this point, we switched to hand kneading and began to experience the dough's transformation in a measured and controlled way. The process was pleasurable as well.

We never supposed we would be sprinkling a dough with water instead of flour. We had often made wet doughs, thinking the resulting crumb would be more open and moist, only to throw flour on them near the end. But this is a poor approach because, as Wing cautions, rather than working its way into the dough, the flour slides around on the surface. Real friction must be generated for proper gluten development. A relatively dry dough, vigorously hand kneaded, on the other hand, welcomes incremental additions of water to bring it to the correct hydration. We discovered that a method of kneading used in Germany for strudel dough known as "crashing," in which the dough is picked up and flung repeatedly against the counter, worked beautifully to incorporate water. The doughs we produced using this technique had a texture far more satiny than did the wet doughs to which we added flour, and the bread had a far nicer crumb as well.

But perhaps the single most important contribution to our understanding of mixing came from Peter Reinhart's book *Crust and Crumb* (Ten Speed, 1998), in which he describes a technique known as "windowpaning." In windowpaning, when you think the dough is fully kneaded, you stretch a small amount between your fingers. If it can be stretched until it is very thin, almost translucent, the dough has been adequately kneaded and can be set to rise (see the photo on page 740). Should it tear while being stretched, more kneading is required. With the baker's percentage and the windowpane technique now firmly part of the plan, our testing began to show significant improvement.

The next steps in bread making, which precede the final rise, are punching down and shaping. A fully risen dough should feel puffy and will not long bear the imprint of a finger. But punching down, experts agree, is a misleading term, inviting more force than is desirable. A gentle fist to the center of the dough does the trick. It is now ready to be scaled or divided and given a rough shape. We knew from experience that a covered rest of about 20 minutes is necessary to relax the dough again,

ROUNDING THE DOUGH

Rounding relies on the friction created between the moisture in the dough and the work surface. (As you drag the dough with cupped palms, its tackiness will pull on the work surface, causing the top to scroll down and to the back to create a smooth, taut surface.) Rounding the dough rids the dough's interior of air pockets and encourages a uniform crumb.

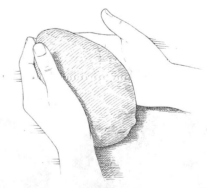

Divide the dough into two 12-ounce pieces. Cover one piece with plastic wrap while you shape the first loaf. Place one piece of dough on a work surface and cup your hands stiffly around the dough as you drag it in half-circular motions toward the edge of the counter. Repeat with the second piece of dough. The pieces of dough should be in a rough torpedo shape. Drape plastic wrap over the dough and allow to relax, 15 to 20 minutes.

giving it some workability. Attempts to shape long, thin baguettes from freshly punched-down dough are frustrating because the dough feels tough and uncooperative and snaps back at you.

Having gotten this far, we had no idea that our most exciting discovery was right around the corner—in the refrigerator. Traditional wisdom holds that the second rise takes place in a warm, draft-free spot to encourage rapid rising and is accomplished in about half the time required for primary fermentation. So we were intrigued when we read about cool fermentation in Reinhart's book. Cool fermentation retards, or slows down, the second rise—the formed loaves go into the refrigerator overnight and are baked the following day. With this method, the dough is thought to become better hydrated, to develop more flavor, and to achieve greater volume. Refrigeration also maintains humidity around the loaves, which keeps a skin from forming on the surface and inhibiting the rise. But surely the most dramatic contribution cold fermentation makes is to the crust.

The first baguettes we baked using overnight fermentation were beyond anything we had yet experienced. The surface of the crust was pitted with tiny bubbles and gave a sharp, thrilling crackle when torn. Shards of crust sprayed the counter to reveal a creamy interior. But it was the flavor of the crust that rocketed this bread to stardom: It was incomparable. Though the French, Reinhart told us, believe a baguette's surface should be smooth and unblistered, we were untroubled by this breach of tradition. To us, this bread was the ultimate.

The final step in bread making is, of course, baking. Home baking is plagued by the problems that attend home ovens, which can neither deliver nor maintain heat in the way that stone or brick does. We tried a number of baguette pans, both perforated and black (thought to improve browning), but by far the best means of conducting heat to the bread proved to be a large pizza or baking stone, preheated for a full 45 minutes in a hot oven. A stone is the closest home ovens can get to hearth ovens. Precise placement is crucial: Once dough meets stone, there is no turning back—or over, as it were. We tried different approaches with calamitous results. Ultimately, the best approach proved to be letting the baguettes rise on an inverted sheet pan covered with parchment paper, then sliding the baguettes—paper and all—from the sheet pan onto the stone.

Realizing that the goal of baking baguettes is to get a deep golden brown crust in the short period of time it takes to finish the bread, we began experimenting with oven temperatures. Temperatures below 500 degrees browned the

SHAPING A BAGUETTE

1. Working with one piece of dough at a time (and keeping the other covered in plastic wrap), make an indentation along the length of the dough with the side of an outstretched hand.

2. Working along the length of the dough, press the thumb of one hand against the dough while folding and rolling the upper edge of the dough down with the other hand to enclose the thumb. Repeat this process 4 or 5 times until the upper edge meets the lower edge and creates a deep seam.

3. Using your fingertips, press the seam to seal. At this point, the dough will have formed a cylinder about 12 inches long.

4. Roll the dough cylinder seam-side down; gently and evenly roll and stretch the dough until it measures 15 inches long by 2½ inches wide. Place seam-side down on the prepared baking sheet. Repeat with the second piece of dough.

crust inadequately or overbaked the interior. Even an initial temperature of 500 degrees accompanied by a temperature reduction after a few minutes did not produce the color we wanted. Some recipes suggest leaving the bread in the oven for a few minutes after baking, with the oven turned off, to help set the crust, but our 12-ounce baguettes needed full, steady heat all along. In the end, 15 minutes at 500 degrees produced the crust and color we desired as well as a moist interior. The final temperature of the bread was around 208 degrees.

Bakery-Style French Baguettes

MAKES TWO 15 BY 3-INCH BAGUETTES

For the sponge, the ideal ambient temperature is 75 degrees; if it is cooler, fermentation will take longer. This recipe will yield baguettes for breakfast; the following version uses altered rising times so that the baguettes are baked in time for dinner. In either case, begin the recipe the day before you intend to serve the bread; the baguettes will emerge from the oven 20 to 24 hours after you start the sponge. Do not add flour while kneading or shaping the dough. You will need a spray bottle for misting the loaves. The baguettes are best served within 2 hours after baking.

SPONGE

- 1/8 teaspoon instant yeast
- 3/4 cup warm water (about 110 degrees)
- 6 ounces (1 cup plus 3 tablespoons) lower-protein unbleached all-purpose flour, such as Gold Medal or Pillsbury

DOUGH

- 1/2 teaspoon instant yeast
- 1/2 cup water (at 75 degrees), plus 2 teaspoons water if needed
- 10 ounces (2 cups) lower-protein unbleached all-purpose flour, such as Gold Medal or Pillsbury
- 1 teaspoon salt

GLAZE

- 1 large egg white
- 1 tablespoon water

SLASHING A PROOFED LOAF NEATLY

A proofed loaf of bread should be slashed across the top to allow some of the trapped air to escape, but the knife used for this purpose often snags and drags the loaf out of shape. For clean, neat slashes, spray the knife blade lightly with nonstick cooking spray before slashing the loaf.

1. FOR THE SPONGE: Combine the yeast, water, and flour in a medium bowl and stir together with a wooden spoon to form a thick batter. Scrape down the bowl with a rubber spatula. Cover the bowl with plastic wrap and punch a couple of holes in the plastic wrap with a paring knife; let stand at room temperature. After 4 to 5 hours, the sponge should be almost doubled in size and pitted with tiny bubbles. Let stand at room temperature until the surface shows a slight depression in the center, indicating the drop, 2 to 3 hours longer. (See "The Rise and Fall of a Pre-ferment" on page 741.) The sponge is now ready to use.

2. FOR THE DOUGH: Add the yeast and 6 tablespoons of the water to the sponge. Stir briskly with a wooden spoon until the water is incorporated, about 30 seconds. Stir in the flour and continue mixing with a wooden spoon until a scrappy ball forms. Turn the dough onto a work surface and knead by hand, adding drops of water if necessary, until the dry bits are absorbed into the dough, about 2 minutes. (The dough will feel dry and tough.) Stretch the dough into a rough 8 by 6-inch rectangle, make indentations in the dough with your fingertips, sprinkle with 1 tablespoon of the water, fold the edges of the dough up toward the center to enclose the water, and pinch the edges to seal. Knead the

dough lightly, about 30 seconds. (The dough will feel slippery as some water escapes but will become increasingly pliant as the water is absorbed.) Begin "crashing" the dough by flinging it against the work surface several times. (This process helps the dough absorb the water more readily.) Knead and crash the dough alternately until it is soft and supple and the surface is almost powdery smooth, about 7 minutes. Stretch the dough again into a rough 8 by 6-inch rectangle and make indentations with your fingertips; sprinkle the dough with the salt and the remaining 1 tablespoon water. Repeat folding and sealing the edges and crashing and kneading until the dough is once again soft and supple and the surface is almost powdery smooth, about 7 minutes. If the dough still feels tough and nonpliant, knead in the 2 additional teaspoons water.

3. Determine if the dough is adequately kneaded by performing a windowpane test (see the photo on page 740). If the dough tears before stretching thin, knead 5 minutes longer and test again. Gather the dough into a ball, place it in a large lightly oiled bowl, and cover with plastic wrap. Let stand 30 minutes, then remove the dough from the bowl and knead gently to deflate, about 10 seconds; gather into a ball, return to the bowl, and replace the plastic wrap. Let rise until doubled in bulk, about 1½ hours.

4. Decompress the dough by gently pushing a fist in the center of the dough toward the bottom of the bowl; turn the dough onto a work surface. With a dough scraper, divide the dough into two 12-ounce pieces. Working with one piece of dough at a time, covering the second piece with plastic wrap, cup your hands stiffly around the dough and drag it in short half-circular motions toward the edge of the work surface (see the illustration for rounding the dough on page 742) until the dough forms a rough torpedo shape with a taut, rounded surface, about 6½ inches long. (As you drag the dough, its tackiness will pull on the work surface, causing the top to scroll down and to the back to create a smooth, taut surface.) Repeat with the second piece of dough. Drape the plastic wrap over the dough on the work surface; let rest 15 to 20 minutes.

5. Meanwhile, cover an inverted rimmed baking

TESTING FOR DONENESS

To check the doneness of free-form bread, tip the loaf up with a hand shielded by an oven mitt or potholder and insert the probe of an instant-read thermometer through the bottom crust into the center of the loaf.

sheet with parchment paper. Working with one piece of dough at a time, keeping the second piece covered in plastic wrap, follow the illustrations on page 743 to shape the dough. Place seam-side down on the prepared baking sheet. Repeat with the second dough piece. Space the shaped dough pieces about 6 inches apart on the baking sheet. Drape a clean, dry kitchen towel over the dough and slide the baking sheet into a large, clean plastic bag; seal to close. Refrigerate until the dough has risen moderately, at least 12 hours but no longer than 16 hours.

6. TO GLAZE AND BAKE: Adjust one oven rack to the lower-middle position and place a baking stone on the rack. Adjust the other rack to the lowest position and place an empty baking pan on it. Heat the oven to 500 degrees. Remove the baking sheet with the baguettes from the refrigerator and let the baguettes stand, covered, at room temperature 45 minutes; remove the plastic bag and towel to let the surface of the dough dry, then let stand 15 minutes longer. The dough should have risen to almost double in bulk and feel springy to the touch. Meanwhile, bring 1 cup water to a simmer in a small saucepan on the stovetop. Make the glaze by beating the egg white with the water.

7. With a single-edge razor blade or very sharp knife, make five ¼-inch-deep diagonal slashes in each baguette. Brush the baguettes with the egg white glaze and mist with water. Working quickly, slide the parchment paper with the baguettes off

the baking sheet and onto the hot baking stone. Pour the simmering water into the pan on the bottom rack, being careful to avoid the steam. Bake, rotating the loaves front to back and side to side after 10 minutes, until a deep golden brown and an instant-read thermometer inserted into the center of the loaves through the bottom crust reads 205 to 210 degrees, about 5 minutes longer. Transfer to a wire rack; cool 30 minutes.

> VARIATION
Dinner Baguettes
The altered rising times in this version help you get the baguettes on the table at the same time as dinner.

Follow the recipe for Bakery-Style French Baguettes, starting the sponge at about noon and using 75-degree water; let the sponge rise 5 to 6 hours, then refrigerate overnight, 12 to 14 hours. In step 2, make the dough using 110-degree water. Continue to knead, rise, and shape as directed in the recipe. Place the shaped and covered dough in the refrigerator until slightly risen, 7 to 10 hours. Continue with the recipe from step 6.

RUSTIC ITALIAN BREAD

IN ITALY, RUSTIC BREAD IS SERIOUSLY CRUSTY, with a toothsome crumb and a clean, strong flavor that lends itself readily to a variety of recipes and is so hearty and satisfying, it's almost a meal in itself. Because this common bread has only four ingredients—flour, water, yeast, and salt—we wondered how hard it could be to make an authentic loaf at home.

We quickly discovered that "rustic Italian bread" describes several different loaf styles, from flat and chewy to soft, enriched, and thinly crusted. We wanted a loaf that fell between these two extremes—chewy yet tender, crusty but not too tough. Although supermarket Italian loaves are undoubtedly shabby, their classic football shape does make it easy to slice uniform pieces for sandwiches even after half the loaf has been consumed; this was the shape we wanted.

Next we brushed up on some elementary bread-baking procedures and confirmed the following:

First, good bread bakers don't measure their ingredients by volume, which is too imprecise. Instead, they weigh them. Second, to help manage the ratio of ingredients, they use something called a baker's percentage, which lists the ingredients as a percentage of the total amount of flour (which is always calculated at 100 percent). Our plan was simple. We would nail down the proportions of the four ingredients, then figure out the mixing, kneading, and shaping techniques.

We started with a common baker's percentage for white bread: 100 percent flour, 65 percent water, 2 percent salt, and 0.5 percent instant yeast (roughly 6 cups flour, 2½ to 2⅔ cups water, 2¼ teaspoons salt, and 1½ teaspoons instant yeast). For our first test, we wanted to compare the effects of all-purpose flour and bread flour. The all-purpose flour turned out shorter loaves with thinner crusts and gentler crumbs, while the bread flour produced heartier loaves with better height and thicker crusts. These differences can be attributed to different levels of protein: all-purpose flour is 10 to 12 percent protein, while bread flour is above 12 percent. A higher percentage of protein generally translates into baked goods with a sturdier crust and crumb, making bread flour the right choice for many breads. The two brands of bread flour we repeatedly found at the store, Gold Medal Better for Bread Flour and King Arthur Bread Flour, performed similarly, as their protein levels are quite close (12.6 percent and 12.7 percent, respectively).

We tried making the bread with varying amounts of water, including 65, 70, 75, and 80 percent. As the amount of water increased, the dough became almost pourable, producing loaves that were flat and wide. The crumb texture also changed from tight and even to bubble-gum chewy, with gaping, erratic holes. Tasters preferred the bread made with 70 percent water. It had an uneven crumb, with most holes about the size of a grain of rice, and a hearty chew (see the photos on page 750).

As for the salt and yeast, we found that the original ratios worked best. The bread was perfectly seasoned with 2 percent table salt, and 0.5 percent instant yeast struck the perfect balance between a fairly speedy rise and a bread that wasn't overly yeasty. Wanting to produce a large loaf that would serve four to six people for dinner with an ample amount left over, we took these percentages and scaled them into variously sized loaves. When made with 22 ounces (4 cups) of flour, the loaves were simply too small to survive more than one sitting at the table. Loaves made with 6 cups or more, however, were comically gigantic and barely fit inside the oven. We found that 27½ ounces (5 cups) of bread flour was just right. All we had to do now was scale the other ingredients to match our final baker's percentages: 100 percent flour, 70 percent water, 2 percent salt, and 0.5 percent yeast.

The next issue was whether to use a sponge. Made the day before the bread itself is made, the sponge is said to build flavor in the final loaf. We made loaves with and without a sponge, and tasters noted that the loaves made with a sponge tasted impressive, with wheaty, multidimensional flavors. To figure out how much sponge was needed, we baked loaves with varying amounts, making sure to keep the total amounts of ingredients the same. Finding that too much sponge turned the dough incredibly elastic and gave it an off, sour flavor, we determined that a little less than half of the final dough should consist of a sponge.

Despite all our work thus far, the loaf remained far from perfect and the results were inconsistent; on any given day, the bread would turn out either shapely and golden or squat and pale. Taking a closer look at the last few loaves, we found that they all tended to spread sideways rather than upward and that the dough itself appeared weak. Not wanting to lose the chewy crumb we had achieved by using 70 percent water, we turned our attention to making the dough stronger by extending the kneading (20 to 25 minutes instead of the more customary 15 minutes). Unfortunately, these doughs merely became warm and turned from a wheaty tan to a grayish white, producing loaves with sickly pale crumbs and expired flavors. As it turned out, we had overmixed and overheated these doughs. Although nearly impossible to do by hand, overmixing and overheating are quite easy to do when using a standing mixer. The action of the dough hook creates heat through friction and also kneads excessive air into the dough, sapping it of flavor and color in a process known as oxidation.

We then consulted several bakers, who turned us on to a technique called "autolyse." Setting the sponge aside, we mixed the remaining flour, water, and instant yeast for two minutes to form a scrappy dough, then set it aside for 20 minutes. Then we combined the rested dough with the sponge and salt and kneaded it in the mixer for 5 minutes. As a result, the loaves made using this technique turned out taller, with a more definite shape and a clean, strong flavor. What happened? That 20-minute rest resulted in a stronger network of proteins and

SCIENCE: How Autolyse Works

Developed by French bread-making authority Raymond Calvel in the 1970s, autolyse (pronounced AUTO-lees) is a technique in which flour and water are briefly mixed together and allowed to rest before being kneaded. Finding that autolyse made a significant difference in both the flavor and structure of our Rustic Italian Bread and other European breads, we wanted to understand the magic behind this 20-minute power nap.

To understand autolyse, however, we first found it necessary to learn how gluten develops. Gluten gives baked goods structure. When water and flour first mix, gluten forms in a random, disorganized matrix that is very weak. As this matrix is kneaded, the disorganized bonds are pulled apart and reattached into straight, strong, orderly sheets (see below). Autolyse occurs after the random matrix has come together but before the sheets of gluten have formed and aligned. While the mixture rests, naturally occurring enzymes break down the disorganized bonds of gluten. When this rested dough is then kneaded, the gluten is positioned to form a stronger, more organized network more quickly.

When the water and flour are first combined, the gluten is like a random pile of pencils (left). Autolyse ensures that the gluten becomes orderly and strong (right) with minimal kneading.

allowed us to cut down on the kneading time. (For a more detailed explanation, see "How Autolyse Works" on page 747.)

Right off the bat, we noticed that the more this rustic Italian dough was handled, the denser the final loaf turned out. Minimal handling was key so as not to disrupt any air pockets that had developed, yet if the shaped loaf wasn't taut, it would sag rather than rise in the oven. We finally found it easiest to gently push the dough into a square, fold the top corners down as if making a paper airplane, and then roll the loaf up. This produced a floppy, loosely shaped piece of dough that we were able to transfer to a piece of parchment and finally tuck into the classic football shape.

Now we were ready to bake the bread. Here we were guided by three techniques from prior test kitchen investigations: a blast of high heat right at the beginning to maximize loaf height; a shot of steam at the outset to help the loaf rise and the crust develop; and a hot baking stone to provide an even, sustainable heat. We tried baking the loaf entirely at 500 degrees but found we needed to turn the oven down to 450 degrees after 10 minutes to keep the crust from burning. We were baffled, though, when the crisp crust that emerged from the oven turned soft within minutes. After much trial and error, we discovered that the bread, which cooked through in just 25 minutes, was being baked too fast. By turning the oven down to 400 degrees after the first 10 minutes, we extended the total baking time to about 45 minutes, which resulted in a fantastically crisp crust with staying power.

As for getting steam into the oven, we found that for this recipe spritzing the loaf with water (from a plastic spray bottle) was both easy and effective. The spray of water kept the crust from setting too early, thus maximizing the bread's initial oven spring (or growth spurt), and it helped to gelatinize the starches on the surface of the loaf, turning the crust shatteringly crisp.

We were now turning out excellent loaves, but they were inconsistently shaped, and the crumb and crust varied somewhat, too. We turned to Didier Rosada, head instructor at the San Francisco Baking Institute, who convinced us to try something called turning. A variation on the idea of punching down the dough after it has risen, turning involves delicately folding the dough over several times as it rises. The theory behind turning is that the dough is stretched gently, building strength as any wayward sheets of gluten—the protein that gives baked goods structure—are brought into alignment. Rosada said that turning the dough twice during its first rise would help iron out any inconsistencies as well as reduce the kneading time. He was right on both counts; we were able to reduce kneading time to just five minutes. Best of all, we found that turning could be done right in the bowl and was nearly effortless. Now our loaves not only looked and tasted nearly identical but were perfect in height, crust, and crumb, with an unbelievably authentic flavor.

TURNING THE DOUGH

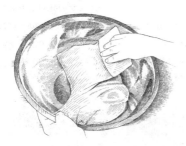  

1. Slide a plastic bench scraper under one side of the dough; gently lift and fold a third of the dough toward the center.

2. Repeat step 1 with the opposite side of the dough.

3. Finally, fold the dough in half, perpendicular to the first folds. The dough shape should be a rough square.

Rustic Italian Bread

MAKES 1 LARGE LOAF

This recipe requires a bit of patience—the sponge, which gives the bread flavor, must be made 11 to 27 hours before the dough is made. We find it makes the most sense to prepare the sponge (which requires just 5 minutes of hands-on work) the day before you want to bake the bread. On the second day, remove the sponge from the refrigerator and begin step 2 at least 7 hours before you want to serve the bread. If you own two standing mixer bowls, in step 1 you can refrigerate the sponge in the bowl in which it was made. Use the second bowl to make the dough in step 2. Have ready a spray bottle filled with water for misting the loaves.

SPONGE

2	cups (11 ounces) bread flour
¼	teaspoon instant yeast
1	cup water, at room temperature

DOUGH

3	cups (16½ ounces) bread flour, plus more for dusting the work surface and hands
1	teaspoon instant yeast
1⅓	cups water, at room temperature
2	teaspoons salt

1. FOR THE SPONGE: Combine the flour, yeast, and water in the bowl of a standing mixer fitted with the dough hook. Knead at the lowest speed until the ingredients form a shaggy dough, 2 to 3 minutes. Transfer the sponge to a medium bowl, cover tightly with plastic wrap, and let stand at room temperature until it begins to bubble and rise, about 3 hours. Refrigerate the sponge at least 8 hours or up to 24 hours.

2. FOR THE DOUGH: Remove the sponge from the refrigerator and let stand at room temperature while making the dough. Combine the flour, yeast, and water in the bowl of a standing mixer fitted

SHAPING THE LOAF

1. After delicately pushing the dough into an 8- to 10-inch square, fold the top right corner diagonally to the middle.

2. Repeat step 1 with the top left corner.

3. Begin to gently roll the dough from top to bottom.

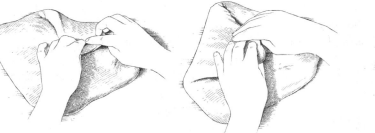  

4. Continue rolling until the dough forms a rough log.

5. Roll the dough onto its seam and, sliding your hands under each end, transfer the dough to a sheet of parchment paper.

6. Gently shape the dough into a 16-inch football shape by tucking the bottom edges underneath.

749

with the dough hook; knead at the lowest speed until a rough dough is formed, about 3 minutes. Turn the mixer off and, without removing the dough hook or bowl from the mixer, cover the bowl loosely with plastic wrap; let the dough rest 20 minutes.

3. Remove the plastic wrap, add the sponge and salt to the bowl, and continue to knead at the lowest speed until the ingredients are incorporated and the dough is formed (the dough should clear the sides of the bowl but stick to the bottom), about 4 minutes. Increase the mixer speed to medium-low and continue to knead until the dough forms a more cohesive ball, about 1 minute. Transfer the dough to a large lightly oiled bowl (at least 3 times the dough's size) and cover tightly with plastic wrap. Let the dough rise in a cool, draft-free spot until slightly risen and puffy, about 1 hour.

4. Remove the plastic wrap and, following the illustrations for turning the dough on page 748, turn the dough. Replace the plastic wrap; let the dough rise 1 hour. Turn the dough again, replace the plastic wrap, and let the dough rise 1 hour longer.

5. To SHAPE THE DOUGH: Dust a work surface liberally with flour. Gently scrape the dough from the bowl and invert onto the work surface (the side

THE ROLE OF WATER

The loaf on the top was made with too much water, which caused large holes to form in the crumb. This dough was difficult to work with, and the loaf turned out squat. The nicely shaped loaf on the bottom was made with the right amount of water and was chewy but not overly so.

PERFECT SLICES FROM CRUSTY LOAVES

Artisanal breads, like Rustic Italian Bread, has a heavy crust that can be difficult to slice neatly. Often the bread knife fails to cut all the way through the thick bottom crust. The result is that you must yank the slice free from the loaf, often tearing it in the process. To slice a crusty loaf neatly, turn the loaf on its side where the crust is thinner, and cut through the top and bottom crusts simultaneously.

of the dough that was against the bowl should now be facing up). Dust the dough and your hands liberally with flour and, using minimal pressure, push the dough into a rough 8- to 10-inch square. Following the illustrations on page 749, shape the dough and transfer to a large sheet of parchment paper. Dust the loaf liberally with flour and cover loosely with plastic wrap; let the loaf rise until doubled in size, about 1 hour. Meanwhile, adjust an oven rack to the lower-middle position, place a baking stone on the rack, and heat the oven to 500 degrees.

6. To BAKE: Using a single-edge razor blade or sharp chef's knife, cut a slit ½ inch deep lengthwise along the top of the loaf, starting and stopping about 1½ inches from the ends; spray the loaf lightly with water. Slide the parchment sheet with the loaf onto a peel or inverted rimmed baking sheet, then slide the parchment with the loaf onto the hot baking stone in the oven. Bake 10 minutes, then reduce the oven temperature to 400 degrees and quickly rotate the loaf from front to back using the edges of the parchment; continue to bake until deep golden brown and an instant-read thermometer inserted into the center of the loaf reads 210 degrees, about 35 minutes longer. Transfer to a wire rack, discard the parchment, and cool the loaf to room temperature, about 2 hours.

CHALLAH

CHALLAH IS A BRAIDED BREAD THAT IS TRADI-
tionally made for the Jewish Sabbath. The best
challah is rich with eggs and lightly sweetened,
with a dark, shiny crust and a firm but light and
tender texture. The mass-produced challah found
in grocery stores can be dry, disappointingly bland,
and disconcertingly fluffy. We wanted ours to be
at once tender and substantial, with a rich, eggy
flavor.

The ingredients for challah are flour, yeast,
eggs, water or milk, sugar, salt, and butter or oil.
During our initial research, we found some recipes
that called for starter or sponge instead of yeast,
which turned the challah-making process into a
complicated and lengthy affair. Since we knew we
wanted to use instant yeast, any versions requiring
starter were eliminated at the outset.

We began by pitting unbleached all-purpose
flour against bread flour. There was no significant
difference, so we decided to stick with the more
readily available all-purpose flour. One envelope
(2¼ teaspoons) of instant yeast gave the challah just
the right amount of lift.

Next we experimented with egg amounts. A
combination of two whole eggs and one yolk
proved to be the best, making a loaf with good egg
flavor and a tender texture. Instead of throwing
away the remaining egg white, we used it for the
egg wash. We found that most recipes called for
water, although a few used milk. We tried both.
The challah made with milk was slightly more
dense and heavy. We preferred the lighter texture
of the challah made with water.

We tried granulated sugar, brown sugar, and
honey in our working recipe. Differences were

BRAIDING CHALLAH

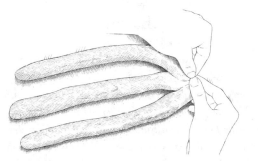

1. Divide the dough into 2 pieces—one weighing 18 ounces, the other weighing 9 ounces. Shape the large piece of dough into 3 ropes, each 16 inches long and 1 inch thick. Line up the three ropes of dough side by side. Pinch the top ends together.

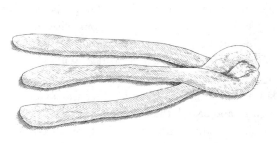

2. Take the dough rope on the right and lay it over the center rope. Take the dough rope on the left and lay it over the center rope.

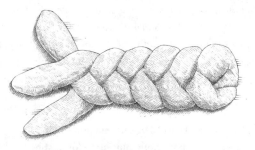

3. Repeat this process until the ropes of dough are entirely braided. Pinch the ends together, tuck both ends under the braid, and transfer the braid to a lightly greased baking sheet. Divide the smaller piece of dough into 3 equal ropes about 16 inches long and ½ inch thick and repeat the braiding process.

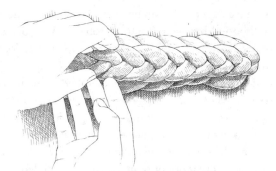

4. Brush the larger braid with some of the egg wash and place the smaller braid on top. Cover loosely with plastic wrap. Once the dough has become puffy (this will take 30 to 45 minutes), brush the top of the loaf with the remaining egg wash and bake.

minimal, but we found that granulated sugar made challah with the cleanest flavor. Amounts ranging from 1 tablespoon to ½ cup were used. Because we wanted a lightly sweetened loaf, ½ cup was too much, resulting in a challah that tasted more like dessert than bread. One-quarter cup of sugar was perfect, giving the challah just the right degree of sweetness.

Would butter or oil make a better challah? Differences in flavor were minimal, but the challah made with butter had a more tender texture. Next we compared a loaf made with melted butter versus one made with softened butter. Because challah requires much less butter than brioche, we found that it didn't matter if the butter was melted or softened; both produced identical results. We decided to go with the melted butter, which could simply be added along with the eggs and water.

What was the best mixing method? We made the dough in a standing mixer, in a food processor, and by hand. The dough worked well in both the processor and standing mixer. Making the dough by hand required quite a bit of muscle power, but because the challah dough was somewhat soft and pliable, it didn't prove to be an impossible feat. Unlike brioche, which is loaded with softened butter and best kept away from warm hands, challah dough is more forgiving. Once the dough was formed and baked, there was little difference in the finished products made with the three methods.

Now that the ingredients and the mixing method were set, we needed to find the best way of shaping the loaf. We began with a simple braid, the recommended shaping method found in most cookbooks, but we ran into a problem. After being braided, the loaf rose out but not up. A flat loaf simply would not do. After trying complicated braids that involved braiding together as many as six strands of dough (and required a degree in macramé), we came up with a much simpler solution. By making two braids, one large and one small, and placing the smaller braid on top of the larger one, we made a loaf that not only appeared to be braided in a complicated manner but also achieved the height of those breads composed of more complicated braids.

Up to this point, we had been using the leftover egg white for the egg wash. Was an egg wash really necessary? We made one loaf and baked it with no egg wash. The result was surprising: Not only was the loaf pale and dull-looking, but the braids had lost their definition, almost melting into each other. An egg wash was clearly needed to get the challah's characteristic dark, shiny crust. We tried a challah brushed with a whole-egg wash instead of just the egg white. There was little difference. We decided to be frugal and stick with the egg-white wash. Challah is sometimes sprinkled with poppy or sesame seeds, and the egg-white wash helps the seeds adhere to the bread—we leave their inclusion up to you.

The last thing to tackle was the oven temperature. We tested oven temperatures from 350 to 450 degrees. Because this dough contains butter, eggs, and a fair amount of sugar (all browning agents), 450 degrees was far too high. Higher temperatures are better suited for lean breads. A more moderate 375 degrees was ideal.

Challah

MAKES 1 LARGE LOAF

We prefer to knead this dough in a standing mixer, but a food processor or your hands can do the job. If using a food processor, place the flour mixture in a processor fitted with the dough blade. Mix together the eggs, yolk, butter, and water in a large measuring cup, and with the processor running, add the egg mixture in a steady stream. Process until a ball of dough forms, about 1 minute. Remove the dough to a lightly floured surface and knead by hand for an additional minute, or until the dough becomes smooth and elastic. Alternatively, you can mix the dough by hand in a large bowl with a wooden spoon, until the dough comes together. Then transfer the dough to a lightly floured surface and knead until the dough forms a smooth ball. If the dough remains tacky, add more flour 1 tablespoon at a time. This method will take longer than using a standing mixer, but you will get the same results.

3–3¼	cups (15 to 16¼ ounces) unbleached all-purpose flour, plus more for dusting the work surface
1	envelope (about 2¼ teaspoons) instant yeast
¼	cup (1¾ ounces) sugar
1¼	teaspoons salt

2   large eggs plus I egg separated (reserve the white for the egg wash)

4   tablespoons (¹/₂ stick) unsalted butter, melted

¹/₂   cup plus I tablespoon water, at room temperature

I   teaspoon poppy or sesame seeds (optional)

1. In a medium bowl, whisk together 3 cups of the flour, the yeast, sugar, and salt; set aside. In the bowl of a standing mixer, mix together the 2 eggs, egg yolk, melted butter, and ½ cup water. Add the flour mixture; using the dough hook, knead at low speed until a ball of dough forms, about 5 minutes, adding the remaining ¼ cup flour, 1 tablespoon at a time, if necessary. In a small bowl, whisk the egg white together with the remaining 1 tablespoon water. Cover the bowl with plastic wrap and refrigerate the egg wash until ready to use.

2. Place the dough in a very lightly oiled large bowl, turning the dough over to coat with the oil. Cover with plastic wrap and let rise in a warm place until doubled in size, 1½ to 2 hours. Gently press the dough to deflate it, cover with plastic wrap, and let rise until doubled in size again, 40 to 60 minutes.

3. Transfer the dough to a lightly floured surface. Divide the dough into 2 pieces, one roughly half the size of the other. (The small one will weigh about 9 ounces, and the large one will weigh about 18 ounces.) Divide the large piece into 3 equal pieces. Roll each piece into a 16-inch-long rope about 1 inch in diameter. Line up the ropes of dough side by side and braid them together, pinching the ends of the braid to seal them (see the illustrations on page 751). Place the braid on a lightly greased baking sheet. Divide the smaller piece of dough into 3 equal pieces. Roll each piece into a 16 inch long rope about ½ inch in diameter. Braid together, pinching the ends to seal. Brush some of the egg wash on the top of the large loaf and place the small braid on the larger braid. Loosely drape the loaf with plastic wrap and let it rise in a warm place for 30 to 45 minutes, or until the loaf becomes puffy and increases in size by a third.

4. Adjust an oven rack to the lower-middle position and heat the oven to 375 degrees. Brush the loaf with the remaining egg wash and sprinkle with the poppy seeds (if using). Bake the loaf for 30 to 40 minutes, or until it is golden brown and an instant-read thermometer inserted into the side of the loaf reads 190 degrees. Place the baking sheet on a wire rack. Let the loaf cool completely before slicing.

CRESCENT ROLLS

PERHAPS THE MOST POPULAR DINNER ROLL served at holiday tables is the crescent roll. What's a shame is that the crescent rolls most Americans serve come from the supermarket refrigerator case—those diminutive arcs of prefab dough that taste artificial and go stale in minutes. We wanted to make rolls that were tender, rich, and easy enough to accommodate in an already jam-packed holiday schedule.

Our first few attempts turned out rolls that were paunchy and flat-flavored. They were hard to handle, stuck to the countertop, and had much too much yeast. Many bread recipes try to speed up the rising time of a dough by using an excessive amount of yeast—sometimes as much as 2 tablespoons for 3 to 4 cups of flour. What you get besides speed is a cheesy-flavored, lackluster roll that goes stale quickly. So a more modest quantity of yeast was going to be key.

For flour, our options included all-purpose and bread flour. Because crescent rolls should be soft and supple, bread flour, with a high protein content that makes for strong gluten development, would give the rolls more chew and a crustier crust than we wanted. We stuck with our kitchen workhorse, unbleached all-purpose flour. We particularly like a lower-protein all-purpose flour like Gold Medal in this recipe.

The next variable was the eggs. The working version of our recipe called for one. We compared batches made with one, two, and three eggs, and the last batch was the winner. These rolls were soft and pillowy, with a lovely golden crumb.

Although we had been using whole milk in our testing, we wanted to compare three liquids side by side: water, skim milk, and whole milk. The whole-milk rolls tasted the richest but were also the densest. The rolls made with water lacked flavor and tenderness. The rolls made with skim milk were just right—flavorful and rich.

Up until now, we had been adding 8 tablespoons of softened butter in 1-tablespoon increments while the bread dough was kneaded in a standing mixer. Could these rolls absorb more fat without becoming heavy or greasy? We increased the butter in the next two batches by 4 and 8 tablespoons, respectively. It was clear that these rolls liked their fat; they took to 16 tablespoons of butter (two whole sticks) with aplomb. However, adding the softened butter incrementally to the mixing dough was a messy and drawn-out process. To simplify things, we decided to melt the butter and add it to the dough along with the other ingredients. This worked perfectly.

So far, we had developed a better-than-average crescent roll recipe, but the crust was not sufficiently flaky, and we were having difficulty rolling out and shaping the sticky dough. The easiest way to handle a butter-laden, sticky dough is to let it rest in the refrigerator before rolling it out. This combats two problems. First, the gluten in the dough relaxes, allowing the dough to be rolled without "bucking," or snapping back into shape after rolling. Second, the butter in the dough solidifies, making the dough easier to roll and less sticky to handle.

We had intended to refrigerate the risen and punched-down dough for a couple of hours, but we forgot about it until the next morning. Panic-stricken, we took the dough out of the refrigerator and easily rolled it into a long sheet, cut it, and shaped the pieces into little bundles. After allowing the rolls to rise at room temperature for about an hour, we popped them into the oven. When they were done, we noticed the difference immediately—blisters! When we bit into a roll, the crust snapped and flaked. This was the kind of crescent roll we had been trying to achieve all along, with rich flavor and a flaky crust.

To find out why an overnight chill had paid off, we called Maggie Glezer, a baker certified by the American Institute of Baking. She explained that when dough is chilled for a long time—a process bakers call retarding—acetic acid builds up in the dough, giving it a richer flavor as well as a blistered crust. Carl Hoseney, professor emeritus in the department of grain science and industry at Kansas State University, added that blisters are also caused by gases escaping from the dough during retardation.

With these points in mind, we set out to see if a longer stay in the refrigerator would be even better. We made another batch of dough, let it rise at room temperature, punched it down, and put it in the fridge. The next morning, we formed the dough into crescents, then, instead of letting the rolls rise for an hour and baking them, we put them back in the fridge. The following day, we let the rolls lose their chill at room temperature, then baked them. The crust was even more blistered than before. Next we tried chilling the rolls for

SHAPING CRESCENT ROLLS

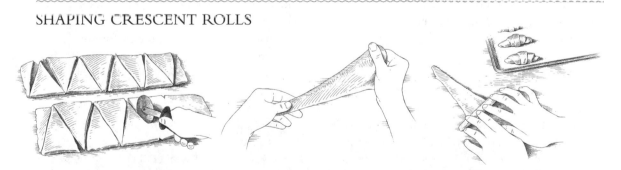

1. Roll the dough to a 20 by 13-inch rectangle; use a pizza wheel to trim the edges. Cut the dough in half lengthwise, then cut 16 triangles, as illustrated.

2. Before rolling the crescents, elongate each triangle of dough, stretching it an additional 2 to 3 inches in length.

3. Starting at the wide end, gently roll up each crescent, ending with the pointed tip on the bottom, and push the ends toward each other to form a crescent shape.

three nights; these were better still, with an excellent flavor and a stunning, crackled crust. What we also like about these rolls is that all you need to do on the day they are served is to let them rise one last time and bake them, creating no dirty dishes and taking up no precious workspace.

All we had to do now was tweak the baking method. Up until this point, we had been baking the rolls at 375 degrees from start to finish. But during our research on retarding dough, we learned that boosting the oven temperature to 425 degrees for the initial bake, then lowering it to 350 degrees when the rolls were just starting to color, would improve their oven spring. (Oven spring, a term used by professional bakers, defines the dramatic increase in size caused when bread gets that initial blast of heat from the oven.) This temperature combination worked, making the rolls pleasantly larger and loftier.

We wondered if adding steam to the baking bread would help with oven spring and encourage the formation of a thin and delicate crust. After placing the rolls on the lower-middle rack, we poured a cup of hot tap water into a preheated pan on the lowest rack. The burst of steam, combined with the high oven temperature, gave the rolls an even higher rise and turned the crust into a thin and still-flakier shell. Now we had a dramatic-looking roll with great flavor, a lovely, tender crumb, and a delicate crust. We bit into these crescent rolls with the satisfaction of knowing that making them would be just as easy to fit into a busy holiday schedule as popping open a can.

Crescent Rolls

MAKES 16

You can make the dough up to 4 days ahead of time or even partially bake the rolls and freeze them for longer storage. To do this, begin baking the rolls as instructed, but let them bake at 350 degrees for only 4 minutes, or until the tops and bottoms brown slightly. Remove them from the oven and let cool. Place the partially baked rolls in a single layer inside a zipper-lock bag and freeze. When you're ready to serve them, defrost at room temperature and place them in a preheated 350-degree oven for 12 to 16 minutes. You can freeze the rolls for up to 1 month.

DOUGH

- 3/4 cup skim milk
- 16 tablespoons (2 sticks) unsalted butter, cut into 16 pieces
- 1/4 cup (1 3/4 ounces) sugar
- 3 large eggs
- 4 cups (20 ounces) lower-protein unbleached all-purpose flour, such as Gold Medal or Pillsbury, plus more for dusting the dough and work surface
- 1 teaspoon instant yeast
- 1 1/2 teaspoons salt

EGG WASH

- 1 egg white
- 1 teaspoon water

1. FOR THE DOUGH: Heat the milk, butter, and sugar in a small saucepan or in the microwave until the butter is mostly melted and the mixture is warm (about 110 degrees), about 1½ minutes. Whisk to dissolve the sugar. Beat the eggs lightly in a medium bowl; add about a third of the warm milk mixture to the eggs, whisking to combine. When the bottom of the bowl feels warm, add the remaining milk mixture, whisking to combine.

2. Combine the flour and yeast in the bowl of a standing mixer fitted with the paddle; mix at the lowest speed to blend, about 15 seconds. With the mixer running, add the milk and egg mixture in a steady stream; mix at low speed until a loose, shiny dough forms (you may also see satiny webs as the dough moves in the bowl), about 1 minute. Increase the speed to medium and beat 1 minute; add the salt slowly and continue beating until stronger webs form, about 3 minutes longer. (The dough will remain loose rather than forming a neat, cohesive mass.) Transfer the dough to a large lightly oiled bowl, cover the bowl with plastic wrap, and place in a warm, draft-free spot until the dough doubles in bulk and the surface feels tacky, about 3 hours.

3. Line a rimmed baking sheet with plastic wrap. Sprinkle the dough with flour (no more than 2 tablespoons) to prevent sticking and press down. Turn the dough onto a floured work surface

and form into a rough rectangle. Transfer the rectangle to the lined baking sheet, cover with plastic wrap, and refrigerate overnight.

4. Line a rimmed baking sheet with parchment paper. Turn the dough rectangle onto a lightly floured work surface and, following the illustrations on page 754, roll and shape. Arrange the crescents in 4 rows on the parchment-lined baking sheet; wrap the baking sheet with plastic wrap and refrigerate at least 2 hours or up to 3 days.

5. Remove the baking sheet with the chilled rolls from the refrigerator, unwrap, and cover with an overturned large, disposable roasting pan. (Alternatively, place the baking sheet inside a large plastic bag.) Let rise until the crescents feel slightly tacky and soft and have lost their chill, 45 to 60 minutes. Meanwhile, adjust an oven rack to the lower-middle position. Adjust the other rack to the lowest position and place an empty baking pan on it. Heat the oven to 425 degrees.

6. FOR THE EGG WASH: Whisk the egg white with the water in a small bowl until well combined. With a pastry brush, lightly dab the risen crescent rolls with the egg wash. Transfer the baking sheet with the rolls to the lower-middle oven rack and, working quickly, pour 1 cup hot tap water into the hot baking pan on the bottom rack. Close the door immediately and bake 10 minutes; reduce the oven temperature to 350 degrees and continue baking until the tops and bottoms of the rolls are deep golden brown, 12 to 16 minutes longer. Transfer the rolls to a wire rack, cool for 5 minutes, and serve warm.

PARKER HOUSE ROLLS

WE HAVE A SOFT SPOT FOR PARKER HOUSE rolls. The epitome of thin-crusted, fluffy-crumbed American rolls, they're pillowy soft, a little sweet, and packed with butter. They owe their name to Boston's famed Parker House, a hotel that has been a bastion of Brahmin hospitality since the middle of the nineteenth century. Truth be told, the Parker House roll is pretty much a standard dinner roll; it's the shape that matters. It starts off as a round roll that is flattened, buttered, and folded in

half. For our version, we wanted a simple, rich roll that would be ready in the least time possible.

Almost all of the recipes we gathered had the same ingredients in varying proportions. They were fairly rich, loaded with milk, eggs, butter, and a fair amount of sugar. Each recipe also employed a healthy amount of yeast for a quick rise and big yeast flavor. We tinkered with proportions until we arrived at a roll that was buttery but not too rich and very tender-crumbed from the large amount of milk and the egg.

Selecting the ideal kneading time took some testing. With a soft, billowy, tender crumb as our goal, we knew a reasonably short knead was in order, but how short was short? We tried times of four to 10 minutes (in a standing mixer at medium speed) and were most pleased with a six-minute knead, followed by a scant minute of hand kneading. With 10 minutes of kneading, the dough's gluten was overdeveloped and too elastic—its texture more like that of a chewy sandwich. With four minutes, the dough lacked structure and collapsed during baking. Six minutes built just enough gluten for support but not enough to detract from the airy crumb.

With a full envelope of yeast and a scant 4 cups of flour, we knew a quick rise would not be a problem. We also decided to hasten the first rise by setting the dough in a preheated oven. We found that an oven heated to 200 degrees for 10 minutes and then turned off retained just enough heat to speed along the rising dough without having a detrimental effect on the yeast. Within 45 minutes, the dough had doubled in volume.

After we divided the dough, we rounded the individual portions on the countertop until they developed a smooth, tight skin and perfect globe shape. Rounding relies on the friction created between the moisture in the dough and the work surface, and this process helps the dough rise by redistributing the yeast and sugars and expunging the carbon dioxide.

By the time we rounded all 24 balls of dough, the first to be rounded had relaxed enough to be shaped. We found that the best way to shape the dough was to lightly flatten it with our palms and then roll it into an oval shape with a small

French-style rolling pin or short dowel. We found out the hard way that it is important to keep the edges thicker than the center so that they will adhere to each other when the dough is folded and not puff open during baking.

After folding and spacing the rolls on a baking sheet, we gave them a light brushing of butter. They were now ready for their second rise, this time outside the oven. Traditional recipes suggest dunking the formed rolls in melted butter, but we thought this would be too much of a good thing.

We tried baking the rolls in baking dishes and on baking sheets and were most pleased with the sheets. While we liked the height of the rolls baked in a dish, the rolls in the middle were gummy long after the outer rolls were perfectly baked. A metal baking sheet delivered even heat and got the rolls out of the oven in about 20 minutes. Parker House rolls must be eaten warm. After a 10-minute rest once out of the oven, they

are ready to serve, preferably with a roast and plenty of gravy.

Parker House Rolls

MAKES 24

When rounding the dough and shaping the rolls, it is important to keep the remaining dough covered; otherwise, it will quickly dry out and develop a "skin." Rolling the dough into symmetrical rounds takes a little practice, but you will quickly get the hang of it. A dry, unfloured work surface helps because the dough will stick a little. Although we like using a French-style rolling pin for flattening the rolls, a more traditional option is a dowel or the handle of a wooden spoon. Whatever your choice, lightly flour it, or the dough will stick to it.

1 1/4	cups whole milk
2	tablespoons sugar
1	envelope (about 2 1/4 teaspoons) instant yeast
1	large egg, lightly beaten

SHAPING PARKER HOUSE ROLLS

1. Divide the relaxed dough into two equal pieces and, with your hands, pull and shape each piece until it is 18 inches long and about 1 1/2 inches across.

2. With a bench scraper, cut each length of dough into twelve 1 1/2-inch-square pieces (each piece will weigh about 1 1/2 ounces). Loosely cover all 24 pieces with plastic wrap.

3. With a cupped palm, roll each piece of dough into a smooth, tight ball and then loosely cover it with plastic wrap.

4. Beginning with the ball rounded first (because the dough has relaxed), use the palm of your hand to flatten the ball of dough into a 1/2-inch-thick circle.

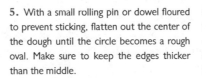

5. With a small rolling pin or dowel floured to prevent sticking, flatten out the center of the dough until the circle becomes a rough oval. Make sure to keep the edges thicker than the middle.

6. Lightly brush the dough with melted butter, then fold it in half and gently seal the edges. Place the roll on the prepared baking sheet. Repeat steps 4 through 6 with the remaining balls of dough, making sure to space the rolls evenly on the baking sheet.

4–4¼   cups (20 to 21¼ ounces) unbleached
        all-purpose flour, plus more for dusting the
        work surface
1½   teaspoons salt
14   tablespoons (1¾ sticks) unsalted butter,
      8 tablespoons cut into 8 pieces and softened

1. Adjust an oven rack to the lowest position and heat the oven to 200 degrees. Once the oven reaches 200 degrees, maintain the oven temperature for 10 minutes and then turn off the heat.

2. Heat the milk and sugar together in a small saucepan or in the microwave until the mixture is lukewarm (about 100 degrees). Whisk in the yeast and egg and set aside. Combine 4 cups of the flour and the salt in the bowl of a standing mixer fitted with the paddle and mix at the lowest speed to blend, about 15 seconds. With the mixer running at low speed, add the liquid mixture in a steady stream and mix until the flour is moistened, about 1 minute. With the mixer still running, slowly begin to add the 8 tablespoons of softened butter, one piece at a time, until incorporated into the dough. Increase the speed to medium and beat until the dough is thoroughly combined and scrappy, about 2 minutes longer. Replace the paddle with a dough hook and knead the dough at medium speed until smooth but still sticky, about 6 minutes, adding more flour in 1-tablespoon increments if necessary for the dough to clear the sides of the bowl. Scrape the dough out of the mixing bowl and onto a lightly floured work surface and knead by hand until very smooth and soft but no longer sticky, about 1 minute. Transfer the dough to a very lightly oiled large bowl, cover with plastic wrap, and place in the warmed oven until the dough doubles in bulk, about 45 minutes.

3. Once the dough has doubled, press it down, replace the plastic wrap, and allow the dough to rest for 5 minutes. Meanwhile, melt the remaining 6 tablespoons butter and, with a pastry brush, liberally butter the bottom and sides of a large rimmed baking sheet with 3 tablespoons of the melted butter. Follow the illustrations on page 757 to shape the dough into rolls, lightly brush the inside of each roll with half the remaining butter (1½ tablespoons), and place them on the baking sheet. Lightly brush the tops of the rolls with the remaining 1½ tablespoons melted butter and loosely cover with plastic wrap. Set the rolls in a warm place and let rise until almost doubled in size, about 45 minutes.

4. When the rolls are almost fully risen, adjust an oven rack to the middle position and heat the oven to 375 degrees. Bake the rolls until the tops are dark golden brown, 20 to 22 minutes. Transfer the rolls to a wire rack and cool for 10 minutes. Serve warm.

GLAZED CINNAMON ROLLS

A PUFFY CINNAMON ROLL COATED WITH THICK white icing brings out the child in all of us, encouraging even the most mature person to greedily uncoil its tight swirls and dig in. Some of us in the test kitchen have been known to drop by the local mall just to worship at that shrine to calorie-laden cinnamon rolls (which shall remain nameless). As delicious as those artery-clogging rolls can be, they are too much for all but the rarest hedonistic fit. They are so sweet and so rich that it's nearly impossible to finish one roll.

Our ideal cinnamon roll is a little more reserved. The dough should be soft and rich but not greasy. The filling should be slightly sweet, rather than sugary sweet, and potent with cinnamon. The icing should be creamy and thick and boast a tang sufficient to balance the richness and sweetness elsewhere in the roll.

With our ideal cinnamon roll in mind, we collected recipes and started testing. The recipes we found used a variety of dough types, from lean sandwich bread dough to buttery brioche dough (a very rich French dough made with huge amounts of egg yolks and butter). While we were inclined toward recipes using the rich brioche-style dough because they would undoubtedly taste better, after further thought we realized that combining such a rich dough with a cinnamon filling and glaze would be gilding the lily.

We decided to start with our recipe for basic American sandwich bread made with milk and a modest amount of butter (just 2 tablespoons). To develop richness, we tried adding varying amounts of eggs, butter, and cream. With too many whole eggs, the dough turned hard, dry, and almost cakey, though it did have an appealing golden hue. More butter gave the dough more flavor and a softer texture. However, with too much butter, the dough practically oozed off the counter and was difficult to work with. Cream, surprisingly, did little at all. Milk was just fine for this dough.

After many attempts, we settled on a soft dough enriched with a good amount of butter (8 tablespoons) as well as a single whole egg and two egg yolks. When baked, this dough had a tender crumb, buttery richness, slight golden color, and enough gluten development for a little resiliency. (Gluten is the protein formed when flour is mixed with water and the mixture is kneaded; it gives bread its structure.) The recipe also allowed us to add the butter melted rather than in softened pieces, as for brioche.

With our dough ready, we turned our attention to the filling, which came together easily. Our tasters preferred cinnamon mixed with just enough sugar to temper the cinnamon's bitterness. Tasters liked rolls with a whopping 3 tablespoons of cinnamon.

We tested granulated sugar as well as light and dark brown sugar in the filling. Granulated sugar was too dry and added little flavor. Dark brown sugar proved too wet and turned syrupy, like the filling for a sticky bun. And the strong molasses flavor detracted from the cinnamon. Light brown sugar proved the best sweetener, adding moisture and a lighter molasses flavor that complemented the cinnamon. Salt mixed with the cinnamon and sugar helped marry the flavors and sharpen the sugar's sweetness.

Shaping the dough into pinwheel spirals could not have been any easier. The soft dough gracefully yielded to a light touch under the rolling pin as we rolled it out. We then sprinkled it with the filling and rolled it up slowly and tightly so that the rolls would not uncoil while cooking. The best tool for cutting the soft dough into rounds turned out to be dental floss. Eccentric as it seems, using dental floss (make sure it's unflavored) lets you smoothly cut through soft dough without squeezing the filling out of place.

Although a few tasters liked a thin, drizzled powdered sugar and cream glaze, most tasters preferred a thick, tangy cream cheese icing. We altered a standard cream cheese icing by omitting the butter and adding corn syrup for glossiness and smoothness. A judicious smear of icing (rather than a heavy, thick coating) was appropriate on these civilized rolls.

Glazed Cinnamon Rolls

MAKES 12

Because cinnamon is the predominant flavor in these rolls, make sure to have good-quality, fresh cinnamon on hand. While we rarely grind our own cinnamon, we try to make

SHAPING CINNAMON ROLLS

1. Sprinkle the filling evenly over the dough, leaving a border of ½ inch on the far end. Roll up the dough, pinching it gently with your fingertips to keep it tightly rolled.

2. Moisten the top border with water and then pinch the dough ends together to form a secure seam.

3. With dental floss, cut the formed roll in half, cut each piece in half again, and then cut each piece into 3 rolls for a total of 12 rolls.

sure that our ground cinnamon is less than 6 months old and from a reputable source, like Penzeys or McCormick/ Schilling. This dough should be very tender and soft, so be stingy with additions of flour. Only a very light dusting is necessary to prevent the dough from sticking to the work surface while rolling it.

DOUGH

½ cup milk

8 tablespoons (1 stick) unsalted butter

½ cup warm water (about 110 degrees)

1 envelope (about 2¼ teaspoons) instant yeast

¼ cup (1¾ ounces) sugar

1 large egg, plus 2 large egg yolks

1½ teaspoons salt

4–4¼ cups (20 to 21¼ ounces) unbleached all-purpose flour, plus more for dusting the work surface

ICING

8 ounces cream cheese, softened but still cool

2 tablespoons corn syrup

2 tablespoons heavy cream

1 cup (4 ounces) confectioners' sugar, sifted to remove any lumps

1 teaspoon vanilla extract

Pinch salt

FILLING

¾ cup packed (5¼ ounces) light brown sugar

3 tablespoons ground cinnamon

⅛ teaspoon salt

1. FOR THE DOUGH: Heat the milk and butter in a small saucepan or in the microwave until the butter melts. Remove the pan from the heat and set aside until the mixture is lukewarm (about 100 degrees).

2. In the bowl of a standing mixer fitted with the paddle, mix together the water, yeast, sugar, egg, and yolks at low speed until well mixed. Add the salt, warm milk mixture, and 2 cups of the flour and mix at medium speed until thoroughly blended, about 1 minute. Switch to the dough hook, add another 2 cups of the flour, and knead at medium speed (adding up to ¼ cup more flour, 1 tablespoon at a time, if necessary) until the dough

is smooth and freely clears the sides of the bowl, about 10 minutes. Scrape the dough onto a lightly floured work surface. Shape the dough into a round, place it in a very lightly oiled large bowl, and cover the bowl with plastic wrap. Leave in a warm, draft-free spot until doubled in bulk, 1½ to 2 hours.

3. FOR THE ICING: While the dough rises, combine all of the icing ingredients in the bowl of a standing mixer and blend together at low speed until roughly combined, about 1 minute. Increase the speed to high and mix until the icing is uniformly smooth and free of cream cheese lumps, about 2 minutes. Transfer the icing to a small bowl, cover with plastic wrap, and refrigerate.

4. TO ROLL AND FILL THE DOUGH: After the dough has doubled in bulk, press it down and turn it out onto a lightly floured work surface. Using a rolling pin, shape the dough into a 16 by 12-inch rectangle, with a long side facing you. Mix together the filling ingredients in a small bowl and sprinkle the filling evenly over the dough, leaving a ½-inch border at the far edge. Following the illustrations on page 759, roll the dough, beginning with the long edge closest to you and using both hands to pinch the dough with your fingertips as you roll. Moisten the top border with water and seal the roll. Lightly dust the roll with flour and press on the ends if necessary to make a uniform 16-inch cylinder. Grease a 13 by 9-inch baking dish. Cut the roll into 12 equal pieces using dental floss (see illustration 3 on page 759) and place the rolls cut-side up in the prepared baking dish. Cover with plastic wrap and place in a warm, draft-free spot until doubled in bulk, 1½ to 2 hours.

5. TO BAKE THE ROLLS: When the rolls are almost fully risen, adjust an oven rack to the middle position and heat the oven to 350 degrees. Bake the rolls until golden brown and an instant-read thermometer inserted into the center of one reads 185 to 188 degrees, 25 to 30 minutes. Invert the rolls onto a wire rack and cool for 10 minutes. Turn the rolls upright on a large serving plate and use a rubber spatula to spread the icing on them. Serve immediately.

BAGELS

IF YOU LIVE IN NEW YORK OR ANOTHER LARGE city, you can get great bagels (although some bagel fans would argue that good bagels don't exist outside of New York). But what about everyone who lives in the rest of the country? We decided there was a need for a simple way to bake delicious, attractive, authentic bagels at home.

Looking at all the recipes we could get our hands on, we developed a fairly typical one. We used bread flour, salt, sugar, yeast, and water, reasoning that the bread flour would give the bagels the chewy texture we were looking for. Following the procedure outlined in all the recipes, we kneaded the dough and then allowed it to rise for about an hour. Next we shaped it into rings, let them rise, boiled them, and finally baked the bagels. Rather than plump, smooth, golden brown bagels, we ended up with small, dense hockey pucks, with crusts that were dull, wrinkled, and mottled brown. The flavor was bland and unappealing. We had our work cut out for us.

We decided that the first issue we needed to address was appearance. One problem we had encountered in forming the bagels was that after the first rise, the dough was somewhat grainy and loose. Instead of stretching easily, it was more inclined to tear. Forming bagels at this stage, as all the recipes we came across advocated, tended to produce a lumpy, uneven crust.

To overcome this difficulty, we tried forming the bagels immediately after we kneaded the dough, letting the rings rise until puffy, then boiling and baking as before. This approach turned out to be an improvement in terms of handling the dough and also in the appearance of the bagels. However, they were still small and tough.

We began to question our choice of flour. We had chosen bread flour, with about 13 percent protein, over all-purpose flour, which has 10 to 12 percent protein. We knew that the higher protein level would lead to the formation of more gluten, that network of elastic protein strands that traps the carbon dioxide released by the activity of the yeast, allowing bread to rise. It stood to reason, then, that an even higher protein flour would rise better, yielding a bagel that was plumper and had a finer, chewier texture.

The next flour up the protein scale is high-gluten flour, which is produced by milling high-protein wheat. High-gluten flour has the highest protein content of any flour, usually around 14 percent, and is the flour of choice at most professional bagel bakeries and pizza parlors. We made our next batch of bagels using high-gluten flour and saw a difference the moment we removed the dough from the mixer. This dough was satiny smooth and much more elastic than the dough made with bread flour. And the bagels

---

SHAPING BAGELS

1. Form each dough ball into a rope 11 inches long by rolling it under your outstretched palms. Do not taper the ends of the rope. Overlap the ends of the rope about 1½ inches and pinch the entire overlapped area firmly together. If the ends of the rope do not want to stick together, you can dampen them slightly.

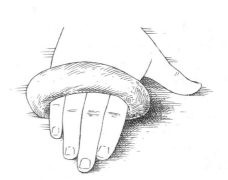

2. Place the loop of dough around the base of your fingers and, with the overlap under your palm, roll the rope several times, applying firm pressure to seal the seam. The bagel should be roughly the same thickness all the way around.

made with high-gluten flour were larger and rose higher. In addition, their crust was smoother and more attractive. The interior structure of these bagels was also better—lighter and chewier.

We were getting close now, but the bagels were still a bit flat on the bottom. A little fiddling around with the water-to-flour ratio quickly solved that problem. Initially, we were treating the bagel dough like any other bread dough, trying to achieve a smooth, slightly tacky consistency. A few test batches using less water in relation to flour revealed that a stiffer, drier dough produces a firmer-textured, chewier bagel. "Dry," however, may not be the most appropriate word to use in describing the correct consistency. A dough with the right consistency will be smooth and elastic, though somewhat firm. After the dough has come together in the first five minutes of mixing, it should not stick to your fingers when pressed. And when you have completely kneaded the dough, a piece about the size of a golf ball should hold its shape and should not sag.

With the shape and texture of the bagels very much improved, we turned to the issue of flavor. Traditionally, bagels are placed in a specially designed refrigerator, called a retarder, for several hours or overnight after being formed. This practice allows for a slower, more natural fermentation. It is during this retarding process that bagels develop most of their flavor. We wanted to test the impact of retarding, so after mixing and forming a batch of bagels, we placed them in a refrigerator overnight. The results were both dramatic and surprising.

The most obvious change in the bagels was in their size. What had gone into the refrigerator as tight, shapely rings of dough came out as flaccid blobs. The yeast fermentation had continued unabated, and the bagels had overrisen. We finished the boiling and baking process anyway.

In spite of being overlarge and flat-bottomed, these overrisen bagels were a vast improvement over our previous attempts. When we sliced one open, we were greeted by a heavenly aroma. This was more than just flour, salt, and yeast! The long, slow fermentation process the bagels had undergone yielded the complex flavor and aroma we were seeking. So retarding really was crucial for great bagel flavor. We were even more surprised by the other effects of retarding: The crust of these bagels had taken on a dark, reddish sheen, and the surface was covered in crispy "fish eyes."

So what was actually happening to the bagels during retarding? The primary mechanism involved is bacterial fermentation. At lower temperatures, yeast fermentation is suppressed, and the lactobacilli bacteria naturally present on grains and in yeast begin to produce a variety of organic acids, primarily lactic acid and acetic acid. These organic acids, the same acids present in a

---

INGREDIENTS: Cream Cheese

Most of us wouldn't think of eating a bagel without a smear of cream cheese. In the test kitchen, whether it was for a bagel or for baking (as in cheesecake), we instinctively reached for Philadelphia brand cream cheese. But was Philadelphia the best, or just the most familiar and widely available?

To find out, we gathered all the types of cream cheese we could find: a paltry five, three of which were Philadelphia products (Philadelphia ⅓ Less Fat, Philadelphia Whipped, and traditional Philadelphia); the other two were organic brands. We tasted them plain and in our New York Cheesecake (page 868).

Tasters judged the cream cheeses on richness, tanginess, creaminess, and overall quality, and one product swept both the plain and cheesecake tastings in all categories: Philadelphia. Though some liked the easy spreadability of Philadelphia Whipped (we let the tasters try the cream cheese on bagels after they tasted each sample plain) and most were enthusiastic about buttery Organic Valley (our second-place finisher), overall the familiar Philadelphia held its place as the cream cheese of choice in the test kitchen.

Although Philadelphia was the clear winner, all but one of the products tasted are recommended. Despite our hopes to the contrary, Philadelphia ⅓ Less Fat tanked, coming in last. While we would have been thrilled to offer low-fat cream cheese as a suitable substitution in our cheesecakes, the artificial flavor and stiff texture forced it out of consideration.

healthy sourdough culture, give the dough a more complex flavor. The fish eyes are a result of the same bacterial reaction, which breaks down some of the gluten in the dough. The weakened gluten structure on the surface of the bagels allows the formation of fermentation bubbles. The richer, reddish brown color of the crust was the result of another chemical process, called the Maillard, or browning, reaction. During the retarding process, enzymes produced by the bacteria convert wheat starch into simple sugar, which during baking produces a rich, toasty color and flavor.

In subsequent tests, we lowered the yeast level in our recipe by half. We also lowered the temperature of the water we used in the dough, to control the activity of the yeast. Initially, we had been proofing the yeast in 110-degree water as recommended on the envelope. We ultimately decided against dissolving the yeast before adding it to the flour in favor of using 80-degree water.

Experimenting with different retarding times, we eventually concluded that a period of 13 to 18 hours is best for a balance between flavor and crust development. Less time and the flavor did not develop as fully, although a short retarding time is better than none. More than 18 hours and we began to notice some adverse effects on the bagels, such as an excessive darkening of the crust, the formation of large bubbles inside the bagels, and the development of too many fermentation bubbles on the surface.

Boiling the dough, which is the most unusual step in the bagel-making process, is responsible for the bagel's unique characteristics—its shiny crust and its chewy texture. Boiling a bagel before baking it serves three purposes. Most important, it sets the shape of the bagel by cooking the surface and killing off some of the yeast in the outer layer of dough. This helps to limit the expansion of the bagel when it is baked. A bagel that is not boiled, we discovered, will expand into a round ball in the heat of the oven. The second function of the boiling process is to give the bagel its characteristic shine. When you boil the bagel, starches on the surface become gelatinized. These starches then cook to a crispy, shiny coating in the oven. The third purpose of

boiling is to activate the yeast in the inner layers of dough, which has been made sluggish by the retarding process.

All of the home recipes we reviewed recommended boiling the bagels for a period of one to four minutes. We tried the whole range of suggested times and found, surprisingly, that a shorter boil of only 30 seconds yielded the best results. Bagels boiled for four minutes had noticeably less shine and were not as plump as those we had boiled for 30 seconds. We surmised that the bagels boiled for four minutes had developed such a thick crust that they were unable to expand fully in the oven.

Plain Bagels
MAKES 8

Because bagel dough is much drier and stiffer than bread dough, it takes longer for the ingredients to cohere during mixing. For this reason, we recommend that you neither double this recipe nor try to knead the dough by hand. Most natural food stores carry barley malt syrup. High-gluten flour might be more difficult to find. You can order both the syrup and the flour from The Baker's Catalogue at www.kingarthurflour.com.

- 4 cups (22 ounces) high-gluten flour
- 2 teaspoons salt
- 1 tablespoon barley malt syrup
- 1½ teaspoons instant yeast
- 1¼ cups water (at 80 degrees)
- 3 tablespoons cornmeal for dusting the baking sheet

1. Mix the flour, salt, and barley malt in the bowl of a standing mixer fitted with the dough hook. Add the yeast and water; mix at the lowest speed until the dough looks scrappy, like shreds just beginning to come together, about 4 minutes. Increase the speed to medium-low; continue mixing until the dough is cohesive, smooth, and stiff, 8 to 10 minutes.

2. Turn the dough onto a work surface; divide it into 8 portions, about 4 ounces each. Roll the pieces into smooth balls and cover with a towel or plastic wrap to rest for 5 minutes.

3. Form each dough ball into a rope 11 inches

long by rolling it under your outstretched palms. Do not taper the ends of the rope. Shape the rope into a circle, overlapping the ends of the rope about 1½ inches (see illustration 1 on page 761). Pinch the overlapped area firmly together, dampening it slightly if the ends won't stick. Place the ring of dough around your hand at the base of your fingers and, with the overlap under your palm, roll the dough ring several times, applying firm pressure to seal the seam (see illustration 2 on page 761). The dough ring should be roughly the same thickness all the way around. Dust a large baking sheet with the cornmeal, place the dough rings on the sheet, cover tightly with plastic wrap, and refrigerate overnight (12 to 18 hours).

4. About 20 minutes before baking, remove the dough rings from the refrigerator. Adjust an oven rack to the middle position and heat the oven to 450 degrees. Pour the water into a large stockpot to a depth of 3 inches and bring the water to a rapid boil.

5. Working 4 at a time, drop the dough rings into the boiling water, stirring and submerging them with a Chinese skimmer or slotted spoon, until very slightly puffed, 30 to 35 seconds. Remove the dough rings from the water and transfer them to a wire rack, bottom-side down, to drain.

6. Transfer the boiled rings rough-side down to a baking sheet lined with parchment paper. Bake until deep golden brown and crisp, about 14 minutes. Use tongs to transfer to a wire rack to cool. Serve warm or at room temperature.

EQUIPMENT: Parchment Paper

Parchment paper can be used for a variety of baking needs, everything from lining baking sheets and cake pans to organizing dry ingredients. We tested four brands—Fox Run Craftsmen (flat sheets), Beyond Gourmet (unbleached roll), Reynolds (bleached roll), and SuperParchment (a washable and reusable product). In the end, all were acceptable. Reynolds is the most widely available brand (and, at 14 inches, is the widest of the lot), sold nationwide in 30-square-foot rolls for approximately $2.50.

➤ VARIATIONS
Topped Bagels
Follow the recipe for Plain Bagels, dunking the dough rings into one of the following: ½ cup raw sesame seeds, poppy or caraway seeds, dehydrated onion or garlic flakes, or sea or kosher salt while they are still wet and sticky (at the end of step 5, after draining).

Everything Bagels
Follow the recipe for Topped Bagels, dunking the dough rings into a mixture of 2 tablespoons each sesame and poppy seeds and 1 tablespoon each caraway seeds, sea or kosher salt, dehydrated onion flakes, and dehydrated garlic flakes.

Cinnamon-Raisin Bagels
Follow the recipe for Plain Bagels, mixing 1 teaspoon vanilla extract, 1 tablespoon ground cinnamon, and ½ cup raisins into the flour, salt, and barley malt in step 1.

YEASTED DOUGHNUTS

THE DOUGHNUTS FOUND IN CHAIN SHOPS always seem to look more impressive than they taste, and the flavor always seems to fall short. Although some of us in the test kitchen might be tempted to overlook the shortcomings of chain doughnuts, it's those killer calories that stop us in our tracks. In our mind, if something contains excessive calories, it just ups the ante on the flavor factor. We set out to develop the ultimate yeasted doughnut and to make every calorie count.

What we wanted was a lightly sweetened doughnut that was tender on the inside and lightly crisp on the outside. Yeasted doughnuts are simply enriched bread dough, rolled and cut into circles and fried. We examined the ingredients: flour, yeast, sugar, eggs, butter, and milk. The first item up for scrutiny was the flour. When we compared bread flour with all-purpose, we found that bread flour made the doughnut too dense and chewy, almost like a deep-fried bagel. All-purpose flour was the better choice, making a doughnut with a lighter interior. What about amounts? Would a soft dough or a stiff dough produce the best results? We tried amounts of flour ranging from 3 to more than 4 cups. Adding more flour to the dough did nothing to improve the doughnuts; it just made them tough. The ones made from the softer dough had the tender, light texture we were looking for, and 2¼ teaspoons of instant yeast gave the doughnuts just the right amount of lift.

After experimenting with various egg amounts and yolk-to-white combinations, we settled on two whole eggs. As for liquids, we found recipes that called for milk, water, and even apple cider. Among the three, there wasn't much difference in flavor, but the doughnuts made with milk had the most tender texture.

Next we looked at the amount of sugar. Because we wanted the doughnut to complement fillings and glazes, we didn't want the doughnut itself to be excessively sweet. We tried amounts ranging from 1 to 12 tablespoons. Six tablespoons was the right amount, adding just the right sweetness. Doughnuts made with more sugar not only tasted too sweet but browned too quickly in the hot oil. The same tests were done with butter. Again, 6 tablespoons was the ideal amount. Any less and the dough was too lean, and more butter made a doughnut that was heavy and overly rich.

Now that we had found the right ingredients and ratios, we needed to find the best mixing method. As with brioche, doughnut dough is made with softened butter. Mixing and kneading the dough by hand made the dough wet and greasy, a result of warm hands melting the butter. A food processor failed to knead this soft dough properly. The best results were achieved with a standing mixer, which thoroughly kneaded the dough while allowing it to remain cool.

In order to find the best oil for frying the doughnuts, we tried peanut, canola, safflower, vegetable, soybean, and corn oil. Peanut oil was the front-runner, making doughnuts with the cleanest flavor and good crunch—albeit a tad greasy. We then pitted the peanut oil against lard and vegetable shortening (Crisco). The doughnuts fried in lard had a light, crunchy texture but tasted faintly of meat. Not bad for french fries, perhaps, but not what we wanted in a doughnut. Vegetable

shortening was the clear winner; it made doughnuts with a clean flavor and perfectly crunchy exterior. Our biggest surprise was to find that the doughnuts fried in shortening not only were less greasy than the ones cooked in peanut oil but also remained crisp longer.

Next we needed to determine the best cooking temperatures. We tried temperatures ranging from 350 to 390 degrees. At 350 degrees, the doughnuts soaked up too much oil and became greasy; the doughnuts fried at 390 degrees burned on the outside before the insides were done. We found that 360 degrees was the perfect temperature. However, when we added the doughnuts to the oil, the temperature dropped 10 to 15 degrees. Starting with the oil at 375 degrees solved that problem, making it easier to maintain 360 degrees while frying.

Yeasted Doughnuts

MAKES ABOUT 16 DOUGHNUTS AND HOLES

If you don't have a doughnut cutter, you can improvise with 2 biscuit cutters: a standard-size cutter (about 2½ inches) for cutting out the doughnuts and a smaller one (about 1¼ inches) for cutting out the holes. For those adept with chopsticks, long-handled cooking chopsticks are the best tools for removing the doughnuts with holes from the hot fat. Otherwise, use a slotted spoon, tongs, or a Chinese skimmer. Don't try to make this dough by hand or in a food processor; your hands or the metal blade will heat the butter too much and make the dough greasy. These doughnuts are best eaten the day they are made.

3–3¼	cups (15 to 16¼ ounces) unbleached all-purpose flour
1	envelope (about 2¼ teaspoons) instant yeast
6	tablespoons (about 2½ ounces) sugar, plus 1 cup for rolling
½	teaspoon salt
⅔	cup whole milk, at room temperature
2	large eggs, beaten lightly
6	tablespoons (¾ stick) unsalted butter, cut into 6 pieces, softened but still cool
6	cups (40 ounces) vegetable shortening, such as Crisco, for frying

1. In a medium bowl, whisk together 3 cups of the flour, the yeast, 6 tablespoons sugar, and the salt. Set aside.

2. Place the milk and eggs in the bowl of a standing mixer fitted with the dough hook. Add the flour mixture and mix on low speed for 3 to 4 minutes, or until a ball of dough forms.

3. Add the softened butter, one piece at a time, waiting about 15 seconds after each addition. Continue mixing for about 3 minutes longer, adding the remaining flour, 1 tablespoon at a time, if necessary, until the dough forms a soft ball.

4. Place the dough in a lightly oiled medium bowl and cover with plastic wrap. Let the dough rise at room temperature until nearly doubled in size, 2 to 2½ hours. Place the dough on a floured surface and, using a rolling pin, roll it out to a thickness of ½ inch. Cut the dough using a 2½- to 3-inch doughnut cutter, gathering the scraps and rerolling them as necessary. Place the doughnut rings and holes on a floured baking sheet. Loosely cover with plastic wrap and let rise at room temperature until slightly puffy, 30 to 45 minutes.

5. Meanwhile, fit a candy thermometer to the side of a large Dutch oven. Add the shortening to the pot and gradually heat the shortening over medium-high heat to 375 degrees. Place the rings and holes carefully in the hot fat 4 or 5 at a time. Fry until golden brown, about 30 seconds per side for the holes and 45 to 60 seconds per side for the doughnuts. Remove the doughnuts from the hot oil and drain on a paper towel–lined rimmed baking sheet or wire rack. Repeat with the remaining doughnuts, returning the fat to temperature between batches. Cool the doughnuts for about 10 minutes, or until cool enough to handle. Roll the warm doughnuts in the remaining 1 cup sugar. Serve warm or at room temperature.

➤ VARIATIONS

Cinnamon-Sugar Doughnuts

Follow the recipe for Yeasted Doughnuts. Mix 1 cup sugar with 1 tablespoon ground cinnamon in a medium bowl or pie pan. In step 5, roll the doughnuts in the cinnamon sugar (rather than plain sugar) to coat.

Vanilla-Glazed Doughnuts

Follow the recipe for Yeasted Doughnuts, omitting the 1 cup sugar for rolling. While the doughnuts are cooling, whisk together ½ cup half-and-half, 3 cups confectioners' sugar, sifted, and ⅛ teaspoon vanilla extract in a medium bowl until combined. When the doughnuts have cooled, dip both sides of each doughnut into the glaze, shake off any excess glaze, and transfer to a wire rack to set the glaze.

Chocolate-Glazed Doughnuts

Follow the recipe for Yeasted Doughnuts, omitting the 1 cup sugar for rolling. While the doughnuts are cooling, place 4 ounces semisweet or bittersweet chocolate, finely chopped, in a small bowl. Add ½ cup hot half-and-half and whisk together to melt the chocolate. Add 2 cups confectioners' sugar, sifted, and whisk until no lumps remain. When the doughnuts have cooled, dip one side of each doughnut into the glaze, shake off any excess glaze, and transfer to a wire rack to set the glaze.

18

COOKIES, BROWNIES, AND BAR COOKIES

MAKING COOKIES AND BROWNIES IS AMERICA'S favorite kind of baking project. Not only are the results usually quite good, but the time, effort, and skills required are usually minimal. Ingredient lists draw heavily on pantry staples as well as refrigerated items, like butter and eggs, that can be found in most reasonably well stocked kitchens. Nor is expensive equipment necessary.

There are thousands of cookie recipes in circulation. Over the years, we have made many of these recipes in our test kitchen and have come to one startling conclusion. The simplest cookies are usually the best and the ones we make most often. Sugar, chocolate chip, oatmeal, and peanut butter cookies are popular for a reason. They may not be much to look at, but they deliver on flavor with very little effort. We do make slightly more elaborate (but not difficult) cookies for holidays and special occasions. Nothing beats gingerbread people at Christmastime or biscotti served with strong coffee following an Italian-inspired meal.

This chapter also includes brownies and bar cookies. Especially convenient because they bake in just one batch, these cookies are quick to get into the oven since the batter or dough is either poured or pressed into the pan. Once cooled, they are cut into squares and ready to go.

Whether you're making cookies or brownies, there are a few tips you should remember.

CREAMING BUTTER AND SUGAR

The butter is creamed with the sugar until light and fluffy. The butter must be softened in order for it to be creamed properly. At 35 degrees (the temperature of most refrigerators), the butter is too cold to combine with the other ingredients. As a result, we have found that cookies made with cold butter are often flat because not enough air is whipped into the butter during the creaming stage. Ideally, an hour or two before you want to make the cookies, remove the butter from the refrigerator and let it warm to about 65 degrees. Butter starts to lose its shape at 68 degrees, so the stick will still be a bit firm when pressed. Avoid using the microwave to soften butter, because it does so unevenly. Instead, cut the butter into very small bits so it will warm up quickly. By the time

COOKIE STORAGE
IF YOU WANT TO KEEP COOKIES FOR several days, we suggest storing them in an airtight container at room temperature (or, to keep cookies soft and fresh, see our tip on page 802). You can restore just-baked freshness to chewy cookies by wrapping a single cookie in a sheet of paper towel and microwaving it until soft, 15 to 25 seconds. Cool microwaved cookies before serving. This technique works best with oversize cookies that should be chewy and a bit soft, like chewy chocolate chip, chocolate, peanut butter, and oatmeal. Do not try this with cookies that should be crisp.

If you know you can't finish off a batch of cookies within a few days, consider freezing part of the dough. Almost every dough can be frozen either in individual portions (see the illustrations on page 802 for more information) or as a block. If you have frozen the dough in balls, simply transfer them to a baking sheet and bake as directed, extending the time in the oven by a few minutes. If the dough is a solid mass, let it thaw in the refrigerator before shaping and baking it.

you have preheated the oven and assembled and measured the remaining ingredients, the butter should be close to 65 degrees.

Creaming the butter and mixing the dough for most cookie recipes can be done either by hand or with an electric mixer. The cookie recipes in this chapter include timing guidelines for creaming as well as for mixing with an electric mixer. It's not possible to offer time guidelines for hand mixing (because cooks' strengths vary), but we do offer visual cues, such as "cream until light and fluffy" and "add the dry ingredients just until incorporated," so you'll know how to whip up a batch with just a wooden spoon (and a little elbow grease).

ADDING EGGS After creaming, the eggs and other liquids (vanilla or other extracts) are added. Make sure the eggs are at room temperature before adding them to the creamed mixture because cold eggs have a tendency to curdle the batter. Eggs can be brought to room temperature by letting them sit out on the counter for an hour or two or by placing them in a bowl of hot tap water for just five minutes.

ADDING DRY INGREDIENTS In many old-fashioned recipes, the flour, leavener, and salt are sifted together before being added to the batter. This was necessary when flour was often lumpy straight from the bag. Because modern flour is presifted, we find this step to be unnecessary for making cookies. (Cakes, however, are often a different matter.) We simply mix the dry ingredients together in a bowl (a whisk does this well) to make sure that the leavener and salt will be evenly distributed.

There are two dry ingredients that we like to sift. Cocoa powder and confectioners' sugar often have small lumps. We find that sifting breaks up those lumps and does an excellent job of mixing the cocoa or confectioners' sugar with the other dry ingredients.

ADDING SOLID INGREDIENTS Adding solid ingredients, like chocolate chips and nuts, is the final step in the dough-making process. These ingredients can be mixed in by hand or with an electric mixer. If using the mixer, keep the speed low and beat just long enough (five seconds should be enough time) to incorporate the solid ingredients evenly into the dough.

CHILLING THE DOUGH No matter how the dough is shaped, you can inhibit spreading in the oven—and thus prevent the cookies from becoming too thin—by chilling the dough in the refrigerator for at least one hour.

DROP COOKIES The quickest way to get the dough into the oven is to drop the dough from a spoon directly onto a baking sheet. Because the pieces of dough are not round, they spread unevenly in the oven. The resulting cookies have thin, crisp edges and thicker centers.

MOLDED OR SHAPED COOKIES For molded or shaped cookies, each piece of dough is rolled into a ball or otherwise manipulated by hand before being placed on a baking sheet. When rolled into a ball, the dough is often also rolled in sugar before being baked. Shaping the dough into balls promotes even spreading and thickness in the baked cookies.

ROLLED OR CUT-OUT COOKIES This method is used to guarantee thin, crisp cookies suitable for decoration. Rolled-and-cut cookies have an even thickness from edge to edge and usually snap rather than bend.

TIPS FOR COOKIE-BAKING SUCCESS
➤ Measure the batter so that all of the cookies will be the same size and will bake at the same rate.

➤ Make sure to leave enough room between the pieces of dough for the cookies to spread in the oven. Two inches is usually a safe distance.

➤ Reverse the top and bottom baking sheets and rotate each sheet from back to front at the halfway point of the baking time to promote even baking.

➤ When making second and third batches, do not place the dough directly on the hot baking sheets. This causes excess spreading and uneven baking because it takes you a few minutes to get all the dough on the sheet.

➤ For bar cookies, use the pan size specified in the recipe, unless an alternative is offered. Bar cookies baked in a pan larger than the size called for will overbake, and their texture will be ruined. Bar cookies baked in a pan smaller than specified will take longer to bake through, and the edges may overbake by the time the center is done. Also, to make bar removal easy and quick, line your pan with foil or parchment paper. Place two sheets perpendicular to each other in the pan (see the illustration on page 810). Scrape the batter into the pan, pushing it into the corners. After the bars have baked and cooled, use the foil or paper to transfer them to a cutting board, where they can easily be sliced into individual portions.

➤ For chewy, moist cookies, underbake them by a minute or two. Let individual cookies cool and firm up on the baking sheet for a few minutes and then transfer them to a wire rack to finish cooling. Residual heat means that bar cookies (which must be cooled completely in the pan) will continue to bake (and dry out) as they cool to room temperature. Make sure to remove bar cookies, especially brownies, from the oven when a few moist crumbs cling to a toothpick. Don't expect a toothpick to emerge perfectly clean from bar cookies; if it does, the bar cookies are overcooked.

Soft and Chewy Sugar Cookies

SUGAR COOKIES HAVE BECOME THE PLAIN Janes of classic American cookies. How could such a simple cookie compare with the decadence of chocolate chip or the sophistication of biscotti? We wondered if we could develop a rich, buttery sugar cookie with a crackling sugar exterior—a chewy cookie with a big vanilla flavor—good enough to stand up to its cookie-plate counterparts.

Sugar cookies contain the most basic of ingredients: butter or shortening, sugar, eggs, flour, and sometimes vanilla extract. During our initial research, we came across many recipes that used both shortening and butter. Cookies made using this combination were dry and flavorless; an all-butter cookie was clearly the only way to go. Most baking recipes call for butter and sugar to be creamed together until fluffy. Looking for shortcuts, we tried using melted butter, thinking that the dough would be easier to mix. However, creaming the butter and sugar proved to be key.

For flour, we chose our kitchen workhorse flour, unbleached all-purpose. Having a chewy cookie meant having only a small amount of leavener; too much and the cookies turned into fluffy little cakes. One-half teaspoon of baking powder did the trick, giving the cookies just the right amount of lift.

What about eggs? We tried one egg, two eggs, and various yolk and white combinations. One whole egg plus one yolk made the cookies spongy; two eggs made them even fluffier. Using just one whole egg was the answer. With the addition of a little salt and a healthy dose of vanilla, this recipe was on the right track.

Lastly, we addressed the sugary outer crunch. Simply rolling the dough in sugar wasn't enough. The sugar crystals did not stick readily to the dough, and the cookies weren't nearly as sparkly as we wanted. We tried dipping the balls of dough in beaten egg whites, then rolling them in the sugar. No luck. This process made a huge mess and resulted in cookies with an odd, meringue-like coating. The solution was to form the balls of dough using slightly dampened hands. The small amount of water kept our hands from sticking to the dough and ensured that enough sugar remained on the cookies. Because we wanted a thick, substantial cookie, we rolled the dough into 1½-inch balls and then flattened them slightly with the bottom of a drinking glass.

Now the dough was ready for the oven. Proper baking times and temperatures could make or break these cookies. We tried baking them at 350, 375, and 400 degrees. Cookies baked at 350 degrees never browned enough. Four hundred degrees was more than the cookies could handle, turning them into cookie brûlée on the outside and leaving them pasty and underdone on the inside. A more moderate 375 degrees was just right. The cookies emerged from the oven with pale golden centers and toasty brown edges. The edges tasted as good as they looked, but the centers were disappointingly bland. What were they missing? Was there something else that would enhance the flavor of the cookies without making them taste like some other kind of cookie?

We looked at an ingredient that we had taken for granted: the sugar. We had assumed that granulated sugar was the obvious choice for this cookie. What would happen if we were to use a different kind? We made a batch of cookies using the same recipe and added 1 tablespoon of light brown sugar to the dough. The resulting cookies were perfect; the brown sugar gave the cookies just a hint of nuttiness and brought out the deep, rich tones of the vanilla.

At last, this was a cookie that would definitely turn a few heads.

Soft and Chewy Sugar Cookies

MAKES ABOUT 24

The cookies are softer and more tender when made with lower-protein unbleached flour like Gold Medal or Pillsbury; King Arthur flour has a higher protein content and will result in slightly drier, cakier cookies. Do not discard the butter wrappers; they have just enough residual butter on them for buttering the bottom of the drinking glass used to flatten the dough balls. To make sure the cookies are flat, choose a glass with a smooth, flat bottom. Rolled into balls, the dough will keep in the freezer for up to 1 week. The baked cookies will keep in an airtight container for up to 5 days.

2	cups (10 ounces) lower-protein unbleached all-purpose flour, such as Pillsbury or Gold Medal
½	teaspoon baking powder
¼	teaspoon salt
16	tablespoons (2 sticks) unsalted butter, softened but still cool
1	cup (7 ounces) granulated sugar, plus ½ cup for rolling
1	tablespoon light brown sugar
1	large egg
1½	teaspoons vanilla extract

1. Adjust the oven racks to the upper- and lower-middle positions and heat the oven to 375 degrees. Line 2 large baking sheets with parchment paper or spray them with nonstick cooking spray. Whisk the flour, baking powder, and salt together in a medium bowl; set aside.

2. Either by hand or with an electric mixer, cream the butter, the 1 cup granulated sugar, and the brown sugar at medium speed until light and fluffy, about 3 minutes, scraping down the sides of the bowl with a rubber spatula as needed. Add the egg and vanilla; beat at medium speed until combined, about 30 seconds. Add the dry ingredients and beat at low speed until just combined, about 30 seconds, scraping down the bowl as needed.

3. Place the ½ cup sugar for rolling in a shallow bowl. Fill a medium bowl halfway with cold tap water. Dip your hands in the water and shake off any excess (this will prevent the dough from sticking to your hands and ensure that the sugar sticks to the dough). Roll a heaping tablespoon of dough into a 1½-inch ball between moistened palms, roll the ball in the sugar, and then place it on the prepared baking sheet. Repeat with the remaining dough, moistening your hands as necessary and spacing the balls about 2 inches

SHAPING SUGAR COOKIES

1. Take a heaping spoonful (about 1½ tablespoons) of dough and roll it between your palms into a ball that measures 1½ inches in diameter. Roll the ball of dough in sugar and then place it on the prepared baking sheet.

2. Use a drinking glass with a flat bottom that measures about 2 inches across to flatten the balls of dough to a ¾-inch thickness right on the cookie sheet. Butter the bottom of the glass before starting and dip it in sugar every two or three cookies.

apart (you should be able to fit 12 cookies on each sheet). Using the butter wrappers, butter the bottom of a drinking glass and then dip the bottom of the glass in the remaining sugar. Flatten the dough balls with the bottom of the glass until they are about ¾ inch thick, dipping the glass in sugar as necessary to prevent sticking (after every 2 or 3 cookies).

4. Bake until the cookies are golden brown around the edges and their centers are just set and very lightly colored, 15 to 18 minutes, rotating the baking sheets front to back and top to bottom halfway through the baking time. Cool the cookies on the baking sheets about 3 minutes; using a wide metal spatula, transfer the cookies to a wire rack and cool to room temperature.

GAUGING SOFTENED BUTTER FOR COOKIES

1. When you unwrap the butter, the wrapper should have a creamy residue on the inside. If there's no residue, the butter is probably too cold.

2. The stick of butter should bend with little resistance and without cracking or breaking.

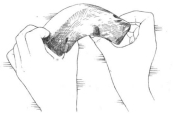

3. The butter should give slightly when pressed but it should still hold its shape.

➤ VARIATIONS
Gingered Sugar Cookies

In a food processor, process the ½ cup sugar for rolling and 1 teaspoon grated fresh ginger until combined, about 10 seconds. Follow the recipe for Soft and Chewy Sugar Cookies, adding 2 tablespoons finely chopped crystallized ginger to the creamed butter and sugars along with the egg and vanilla, and using the ginger sugar for coating the dough balls in step 3.

Sugar Cookies with Lime Essence

In a food processor, process the ½ cup sugar for rolling and 1 teaspoon grated lime zest until the zest is evenly distributed, about 10 seconds. Follow the recipe for Soft and Chewy Sugar Cookies, adding 2 teaspoons grated lime zest to the creamed butter and sugars along with the egg and vanilla, and using the lime sugar for coating the dough balls in step 3.

Lemon–Poppy Seed Sugar Cookies

Follow the recipe for Soft and Chewy Sugar Cookies, whisking 1 tablespoon poppy seeds into the dry ingredients and adding 1 tablespoon grated lemon zest to the creamed butter and sugars along with the egg and vanilla.

CRISP CHOCOLATE CHIP COOKIES

RICH AND BUTTERY, WITH SOFT, TENDER CORES and crisp edges, Toll House cookies are the American cookie jar standard. As such, they serve as the springboard for all other versions of the chocolate chip cookie. The two most popular variations, thick and chewy and thin and crisp, embody the Toll House cookie's textural extremes. Given the popularity of chocolate chip cookies in America (and the number of partisans of each style), we decided to develop recipes for cookies at both ends of the textural spectrum.

We could see the thin, crisp cookies clearly. They would be very flat, almost praline in appearance, and would pack a big crunch. They'd have the simple, gratifying flavors of deeply caramelized sugar and rich butter. The chips, tender and super-chocolatey, would not overwhelm but leave plenty of room for enjoyment of the surrounding cookie. Finally, these cookies would be resilient enough for pantry storage and worthy of five consecutive appearances in a school lunchbox.

To get our bearings, we first surveyed a handful of recipes for thin and crisp chocolate chip cookies, taking inventory of the ingredient lists and ratios. We were hoping to find the key to what might make these cookies thinner and crisper than the classic Toll House. Our collection of test recipes featured the same basic ingredients—butter, flour, sugar, flavorings, and chocolate chips—but with widely varying ratios and yields. As a result, the cookies were all quite different when baked. While all of the cookies tasted good, tasters were dissatisfied with the various textures, which they found too brittle, too crumbly, too dense, or too greasy. Believe it or not, we were pleased with the mixed reactions. The ingredients we had to work with held promise; we just needed to understand the role of each one and tweak the proportions to arrive at a cookie with the texture we wanted.

Whether chewy or crisp, nearly all chocolate chip cookies contain a mixture of granulated and brown sugar. Aside from contributing sweetness,

sugar also affects the texture, flavor, and color of the cookies. Doughs high in granulated sugar yield crisp cookies. As the cookies cool, the sugar crystallizes and the cookies harden. Brown sugar is quite different from granulated. It contains 35 percent more moisture and is also more hygroscopic (that is, it more readily absorbs moisture from the atmosphere). Consequently, cookies made with brown sugar come out of the oven tender and pliable and often soften further as they stand. These characteristics were the opposite of what we were looking for. Nevertheless, we knew the recipe had to include some brown sugar, because it alone is responsible for the irresistible butterscotch flavor we associate with chocolate chip cookies.

With this understanding, we went on to test various proportions of sugar. Too much granulated sugar produced cookies with no butterscotch flavor. Too much brown sugar produced cookies that were delicious but too soft. Desperate to retain the flavor of the brown sugar, we shifted from dark brown to light brown. Light brown sugar, we knew, had the potential to crisp the cookies because it contains half the molasses that dark brown sugar does and, therefore, less moisture. But we were skeptical because its flavor is weaker. We needn't have worried; the cookies were much improved, producing a flavor that fully satisfied

---

EQUIPMENT: Baking Sheets

Most baking sheets (also called cookie sheets) have the same basic design. They are a piece of metal that is usually slightly longer than it is wide. (A standard size is 16 inches long and 14 inches across.) Some are dark; some are light. Some have rims on all four sides. Others have rims on one or two sides but otherwise have flat edges. We tested 11 sheets in a variety of materials and came to some surprising conclusions.

First of all, shiny light-colored sheets do a better job of evenly browning the bottoms of cookies than dark sheets. Most of the dark sheets are nonstick, and we found that these pans tend to overbrown cookies. Shiny silver sheets heat much more evenly, and if sticking is a concern, we simply use parchment paper. Parchment paper also keeps the bottom of the cookies from overbrowning.

In our testing, we also came to prefer sheets with at least one rimless edge. This way, we could slide a whole sheet of parchment paper onto a cooling rack without actually touching the hot paper. (When cooled, the cookies can be peeled away from the paper.) The open edge also makes it possible to slide cookies onto a rack, rather than lifting them onto the rack and possibly dropping them. Our favorite cookie sheet is made of tinned steel and is manufactured by Kaiser. At just $7, it was also the cheapest sheet we tested.

A final note about lining baking sheets with parchment. Even when sticking is not an issue, we like to use parchment paper. It makes cleanup a snap, and we can reuse baking sheets for subsequent batches without having to wash them first. When parchment is essential, the recipes in this chapter call for it. Otherwise, use parchment at your discretion.

tasters. After a little more tinkering, we settled on ⅓ cup light brown sugar and ½ cup granulated sugar, yielding cookies with a notable butterscotch flavor and sufficient crunch.

Satisfied with the crispness of the cookies, we turned our attention to their thickness. Throughout earlier testing, we hadn't been totally happy with the cookies' spread in the oven—they never became thin enough to achieve the praline-like look we were after. This was important not just for appearance's sake but because we had noticed that the flatter the cookies were, the more delicate and tender they became; we wanted them crisp, without being tough.

After some research, we returned to the kitchen armed with the understanding that a cookie's spread is determined largely by the type, treatment, and melting properties of the fat in the dough. Butter, which is key in this recipe, has both a low melting point and an outstanding flavor. Initial test recipes advised creaming the butter and sugar, but we noticed that cookies made with this technique came out of the oven with a slight lift. We were certain that creaming was the culprit.

When butter and sugar are creamed, rigid sugar crystals cut into the butterfat and create air cells. As the remaining ingredients are incorporated into the airy mixture, the air cells get locked up in the dough and capture moisture from the butter (and other ingredients) as it vaporizes in the oven. The cells expand, and the cookies rise. Our other option, melting the butter, was much more successful. Because melted butter, unlike creamed butter, does not accommodate air cells, the moisture from various ingredients has nowhere to go except out. Working our way down from 12 tablespoons (1½ sticks), we found that the cookies spread evenly and effortlessly at 8 tablespoons (one stick) of melted butter. To get them thinner still, we added a couple of tablespoons of milk. Adding a small amount of liquid to a low-moisture dough thins the dough and enhances its spread. The cookies were flatter than pancakes.

Having spent all of our time thus far perfecting the cookies' texture and spread, we were surprised to notice that they were looking slightly pallid and dull. The light brown sugar we had introduced to the recipe was the problem (it has less browning power than dark brown sugar). Knowing that corn syrup browns at a lower temperature than sugar, we tried adding a few tablespoons. As it happened, the corn syrup made the surface of the cookies shiny and crackly. Despite their new spiffy, dressed-up look, though, they remained a little on the pale side. We rectified the situation by adding a bit of baking soda, which enhances browning reactions in doughs. The cookies went from washed-out to a beautiful deep golden brown.

Finally, after a few last-minute adjustments to the amount of salt and vanilla, we spooned a full recipe of the dough onto two parchment-lined baking sheets and tested baking times and temperatures. Much to our disappointment, these cookies were slightly chewy, because they did not spread properly. After a few batches, we found that these cookies needed to be baked one sheet at a time. In 12 minutes at 375 degrees, they spread, flattened, caramelized, and came out to cool into thin, crisp, and delicious chocolate chip cookies.

Now we just had to find out if these cookies had staying power. We stored a batch of the finished cookies in an airtight container for a week to test their longevity. After the wait, tasters gathered to give them a final critique. The cookies were still a hit, as crisp and flavorful as they had been on day one.

Thin, Crisp Chocolate Chip Cookies
MAKES ABOUT 40

The dough, en masse or shaped into balls and wrapped well, can be refrigerated for up to 2 days or frozen for up to 1 month. Be sure to bring it to room temperature before baking. See the tip on page 802 for portioning evenly sized cookies.

1½	cups (7½ ounces) unbleached all-purpose flour
¾	teaspoon baking soda
¼	teaspoon salt
8	tablespoons (1 stick) unsalted butter, melted and cooled
½	cup (3½ ounces) granulated sugar

⅓ cup packed (2⅓ ounces) light brown sugar
2 tablespoons light corn syrup
1 large egg yolk
2 tablespoons milk
1 tablespoon vanilla extract
¾ cup semisweet chocolate chips

1. Adjust an oven rack to the middle position and heat the oven to 375 degrees. Line 2 large baking sheets with parchment paper or spray them with nonstick cooking spray.

2. Whisk the flour, baking soda, and salt together in a medium bowl until thoroughly combined; set aside.

3. Either by hand or with an electric mixer, beat the melted butter, both sugars, and corn syrup at low speed until thoroughly blended, about 1 minute. Add the yolk, milk, and vanilla; mix until fully incorporated and smooth, about

1 minute, scraping the bottom and sides of the bowl with a rubber spatula as necessary. With the mixer running on low speed, slowly add the dry ingredients and mix until just combined. Do not overbeat. Add the chocolate chips and mix on low speed until distributed evenly throughout the batter, about 5 seconds.

4. Working with a scant tablespoon of dough each time, roll the dough into 1¼-inch balls and place them on the prepared baking sheets, spacing them about 2 inches apart. Bake, one sheet at a time, until the cookies are deep golden brown and flat, about 12 minutes, rotating the sheet from front to back halfway through the baking time.

5. Cool the cookies on the baking sheet for 3 minutes. Using a wide metal spatula, transfer the cookies to a wire rack and let sit until crisped and cooled to room temperature.

INGREDIENTS: Chocolate Chips

Chips have a lower cocoa butter content than chocolate bars, which keeps them from becoming too liquidy when baked. Often the cocoa butter is replaced by sugar, which is why we found many chocolate chips in our tasting of various brands to be quite sweet. We also found that the chips we liked best straight out of the bag tasted best in cookies. Nestlé, Guittard, Ghirardelli, and Tropical Source (a brand sold in natural food stores) all received high marks. The chips that excelled were noted for a balance of bitterness, sweetness, and smoothness, and, as we discovered, these chips hold a few curious secrets.

In the spectrum of chocolates, chips are generally considered the least refined. The most refined would be a coating chocolate, also known as couverture, an extremely glossy chocolate usually found only in specialty candy-making shops and used by pastry chefs in various confections. Chocolate chips lack the fluidity necessary to meet the technical demands of the work turned out by a pastry chef, such as molds and truffles or even the seemingly simple chocolate-dipped strawberry. For example, a bowl of melted couverture will pour out smoothly, like cream, but a bowl of melted chips will slide sluggishly like glue. This high viscosity and low fluidity are what make the chip shape possible. When squeezed through a nozzle onto a moving belt in the factory, the chocolate quickly sets up into a pert morsel rather than collapsing into a small blob.

The chip that rated second in our tasting defied the unspoken standard for chip shape. Guittard grinds and blends its chip chocolate in the same way that it does its couverture. This helps to develop the flavor. The trade-off, however, is that the chip is too fluid to hold the tightly pointed shape of a typical chip. Even so, some of our tasters liked the larger size and unorthodox disk-like shape of the chip in a thick, chewy cookie. However, this shape does not work well in a thin, crisp cookie.

The top-rated chip, Tropical Source, did showcase the typical pointed shape, but, like the Guittard chip, it had an unusually high cocoa butter content. The average chip is 27 percent cocoa butter, but both Guittard and Tropical Source chips contain 30 percent. Cocoa butter is renowned for providing the melt-in-your-mouth lusciousness of chocolate. Because it is costly, though, most chocolate chip manufacturers limit the cocoa butter content. Tasters typically had to agitate chips between their tongues and the roofs of their mouths or even bite into some to break them down. Guittard and Tropical Source stood out because they melted more smoothly than the rest. Tropical Source worked well in both our thin and thick cookies.

Finally, what about the classic Nestlé Toll House Morsels? These chips taste good, but they are ultragooey when cooled, which makes them better suited to a thick, chewy cookie than a thin, crisp one.

CHEWY CHOCOLATE CHIP COOKIES

AN ATTRACTIVE VARIATION ON THE TRADITIONAL chocolate chip cookie that some bake shops and cookie stores have recently made their reputations on is the oversize cookie. Unlike cookies made at home, these cookies are thick right from the edge to the center. They are also chewy, even a bit soft. Although we knew at the outset that molding the dough rather than dropping it into uneven blobs would be essential to achieving an even thickness, we didn't realize how much of a challenge making a truly chewy cookie would be.

We added more flour or ground oats (as some recipes suggest), which helped the cookies hold their shape and remain thick but also made the texture cakey and dry rather than chewy. When we tried liquid sweeteners, such as molasses and corn syrup, the dough spread too much in the oven, and the cookies baked up thin.

At this point in our testing, we decided to experiment with the butter. Some chewy cookies start with melted rather than creamed butter. In its solid state, butter is an emulsion of butter and water. When butter is melted, the fat and water molecules separate. When melted butter is added to a dough, the proteins in the flour immediately grab onto the freed water molecules to form elastic strands of gluten. The gluten makes a cookie chewy.

Our first attempt with melted butter was disappointing. The dough was very soft from all the liquid, and the cookies baked up greasy. Because the dough was having a hard time absorbing the liquid fat, we reduced the amount of butter from 16 to 12 tablespoons. We also reduced the number of eggs from two to one to stiffen the dough.

The cookies were chewy at this point, but they became somewhat tough as they cooled, and after a few hours, they were hard. Fat acts as a tenderizer, and by reducing the amount of butter in the recipe, we had limited its ability to keep

SHAPING THICK CHOCOLATE CHIP COOKIES

1. Creating a jagged surface on each dough ball gives the finished cookies an attractive appearance. Start by rolling a scant ¼ cup of dough into a smooth ball.

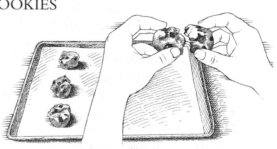

2. Holding the dough ball in the fingertips of both hands, pull the dough apart into two equal halves.

3. Each half will have a jagged surface where it was ripped from the other. Rotate each piece 90 degrees so that the jagged surface faces up.

4. Jam the halves back together into one ball so that the top surface remains jagged.

776

the cookies soft. The only other source of fat is the egg. Since our dough was already soft enough and probably could not stand the addition of too much more liquid, we decided to add another yolk (which contains all the fat) and leave out the white. This dough was still stiff enough to shape; when baked, the cookies were thick and chewy, and they remained that way when they cooled. Finally, we had the perfect recipe.

Thick and Chewy Chocolate Chip Cookies

MAKES ABOUT 18 LARGE

These oversize cookies are chewy and thick, like many of the chocolate chip cookies sold in gourmet shops and cookie stores. They rely on melted butter and an extra egg yolk to keep their texture soft. These cookies are best served warm from the oven but will retain their texture even when cooled. To ensure the proper texture, cool the cookies on the baking sheet. Oversize baking sheets allow you to get all the dough into the oven at one time. If you're using smaller baking sheets, put fewer cookies on each sheet and bake them in batches. See the illustrations on page 776 for tips on shaping these cookies.

2	cups plus 2 tablespoons (10 5/8 ounces) unbleached all-purpose flour
1/2	teaspoon baking soda
1/2	teaspoon salt
12	tablespoons (1 1/2 sticks) unsalted butter, melted and cooled until just warm
1	cup packed (7 ounces) light or dark brown sugar
1/2	cup (3 1/2 ounces) granulated sugar
1	large egg, plus 1 large egg yolk
2	teaspoons vanilla extract
1–1 1/2	cups semisweet chocolate chips

1. Adjust the oven racks to the upper- and lower-middle positions and heat the oven to 325 degrees. Line 2 large baking sheets with parchment paper or spray them with nonstick cooking spray.

2. Whisk the flour, baking soda, and salt together in a medium bowl; set aside.

3. Either by hand or with an electric mixer, mix the butter and sugars until thoroughly blended.

Beat in the egg, yolk, and vanilla until combined. Add the dry ingredients and beat at low speed just until combined. Stir in the chips to taste.

4. Roll a scant 1/4 cup of the dough into a ball. Following the illustrations on page 776, hold the dough ball with the fingertips of both hands and pull into 2 equal halves. Rotate the halves 90 degrees and, with jagged surfaces facing up, join the halves together at the base, again forming a single ball, being careful not to smooth the dough's uneven surface. Place the formed dough balls on the prepared baking sheets, jagged surface up, spacing them 2½ inches apart.

5. Bake until the cookies are light golden brown, the outer edges start to harden, and the centers are still soft and puffy, 15 to 18 minutes, rotating the baking sheets front to back and top to bottom halfway through the baking time. Cool the cookies on the sheets. Remove the cooled cookies from the baking sheets with a wide metal spatula.

> VARIATIONS

Chocolate Chip Cookies with Coconut and Toasted Almonds

Follow the recipe for Thick and Chewy Chocolate Chip Cookies, adding 1½ cups sweetened flaked coconut and 1 cup toasted sliced almonds along with the chips.

Black and White Chocolate Chip Cookies with Pecans

Follow the recipe for Thick and Chewy Chocolate Chip Cookies, substituting ½ cup white chocolate chips for ½ cup of the semisweet chips. Add 1 cup chopped pecans with the chips.

THICK AND CHEWY DOUBLE-CHOCOLATE COOKIES

ONE OF OUR GREATEST OBSESSIONS IN BAKING has been the first transcendent bite of the perfect chocolate cookie, still warm out of the oven. That first bite would reveal a center of hot fudge sauce, and the texture would call to mind chocolate bread pudding with a deep, complex chocolate flavor. This would be the sort of confection that creates intense focus while it is consumed, sight and sound subordinate to taste, overshadowing the other senses to the point of dysfunction.

The problem is that we have, for years, been trying to perfect this cookie. We have created large, dense cookies that were rich and decadent, but the chocolate flavor was dull. We have also experimented with thin, crisp cookies (nice but not intense), chewy cookies (good but not showstoppers), and cake-like chocolate cookies, which tend to be dry and uninspiring. The test kitchen also made a half dozen recipes from various cookbooks and discovered a world of difference in texture, flavor, and appearance, from soft mocha-colored disks to thick mounds of pure fudge. This panoply of outcomes gave us pause, since the ingredient lists seemed to have more in common than the cookies themselves. Figuring out what makes a chocolate cookie tick was going to require weeks of testing and a great deal of detective work.

Our first step was to strip the recipes down to their basics to understand the fundamentals. A chocolate cookie is a mixture of melted chocolate, sugar, eggs, butter, flour, baking soda or powder, and salt. Vanilla, coffee, and nuts are extras.

The key issues were how to handle the butter and eggs. The butter can be melted or creamed, and the eggs can be beaten or just whisked into the batter. For the first test batch, we melted the butter and whipped the eggs. The results were good, but the cookies were a bit cakey and loose, without any chew. For the next batch, we melted the butter and did not beat the eggs. These cookies were a bit dry and still cakey. When we started creaming the butter and beating the eggs into it after creaming, we noticed an immediate improvement. However, we finally settled on a modified creaming method with minimal beating to produce moist cookies that were not cakey.

INGREDIENTS: Types of Chocolate

There are many options when it comes to chocolate: unsweetened, bittersweet, semisweet, cocoa powder, and chips. The question is, how are they different?

Unsweetened chocolate, often called baking chocolate or chocolate liquor, is made from roasted cocoa beans and contains about 50 percent solids from the beans and 50 percent cocoa butter. Bittersweet and semisweet chocolate (also called dark chocolate) are made from unsweetened chocolate that is ground with sugar and then further refined. Since bittersweet and semisweet chocolate are about 50 percent sugar, they have less chocolate flavor than unsweetened, which has no added sugar. (Although individual brands may vary, bittersweet averages around 46 percent sugar by weight; semisweet is about 57 percent sugar.) The chocolate flavor they do have, however, is less bitter and more complex, features appreciated by many bakers.

Chocolate chips are made from chocolate with relatively little cocoa butter, about 30 percent or even less. (Dark chocolate, by comparison, must have at least 35 percent cocoa butter.) This is because the chips will not hold their shape with more fat. This lower percentage of cocoa butter makes for a less buttery flavor and a grainier texture.

Cocoa powder is made from unsweetened chocolate. Much of the fat is removed by pressing, leaving behind the solids. These leftover solids are then fluffed up and packaged. Dutch-processed cocoa is less acidic than regular cocoa, and many people feel that this results in a stronger, more interesting chocolate flavor.

Another factor that affects the quality of one brand of chocolate over another is the use of additives. Most processed dark chocolate includes vanilla, lecithin (which makes chocolate smoother when poured), and other flavorings, often including soy. In addition, some manufacturers roast their beans for a shorter time on the theory that when the chocolate is baked by consumers, it will undergo additional processing.

As for which type of semisweet chocolate is best for a chocolate cookie, we tested four major brands head-to-head: Nestlé, Baker's, Ghirardelli, and Callebaut. The Baker's turned out a gritty cookie that received low marks, the Nestlé had an off, somewhat fruity taste, and the Ghirardelli had a muted but pure chocolate flavor that was quite pleasant. But the Callebaut was our favorite, with a big chocolate flavor that was clean, direct, and full of punch.

The next issue was one of proportions; that is, the ratio of flour to butter to eggs to sugar to chocolate. This was going to be crucial to the thickness of the cookie, its texture, and the degree to which the taste of chocolate would dominate. Looking over the recipes we had tested, we saw so many permutations that we felt like the British trying to crack the German secret code in World War II.

To organize the facts, we made a chart of the various ratios of eggs, sugar, chocolate, and butter to flour, with related comments on the taste, texture, and shape of each cookie we had tested. We quickly noted that the ratio of eggs and butter to flour was less important than the ratio of sugar and chocolate to flour. The driest cookie used less than ½ cup of sugar per cup of flour; the richest, wettest cookie used 3 cups. The cookie with the faintest chocolate flavor and a relatively firm, dry texture used only 2 ounces of chocolate per cup of flour, whereas other recipes used up to a pound of chocolate with only ½ cup of flour. After many tests designed to balance sweetness and moisture, we settled on 1 cup of sugar and 8 ounces of chocolate to 1 cup of flour. Finally, we had a moist cookie with good chocolate flavor. Nonetheless, we thought the flavor and texture could be still better, so we moved on to other ingredients.

We started with all granulated sugar and then tested a mixture of brown sugar and granulated, which seemed to improve the flavor and added just a bit more moisture. We also tried corn syrup, which had little effect. A small amount of vanilla extract and instant coffee powder rounded out the flavors. Throughout the testing, we had been using all-purpose flour. We decided to try cake flour, but the resulting cookies were a bit too delicate. We also varied the quantity of flour throughout the testing process, starting at 3 cups and eventually working our way down to 2 cups. To create a thicker, more stable cookie, we tried replacing some of the butter with vegetable shortening (Crisco), but this created an unattractive, greasy-looking cookie with a pale white sheen. We thought that the choice of leavener might be important, so we tested baking powder against baking soda and found that the cookies with the powder were slightly thicker.

At this point, our cookie was thick and very good but still not the sort of thing that would reduce the average adult to tears of joy. The flavor remained a bit dull, and the texture was moist but monochromatic. We wondered if we could solve this problem by varying the type of chocolate. We found that unsweetened chocolate, an ingredient often called for in chocolate cookie recipes, added intensity to the flavor. Unfortunately, we also discovered an aggressive sour note in these cookies, even when the sugar level was adjusted for the bitterness of the chocolate. Semisweet and bittersweet chocolate turned out to be better choices owing to their rounder, less potent flavors. These chocolates undergo more processing than unsweetened, and they also get other flavorings; this no doubt gives them a smoother, richer flavor overall.

Our hunt was almost over, but now we wondered if a bit of cocoa powder might add more depth of flavor to our cookie. One-half cup of Dutch-processed cocoa was substituted for the same amount of flour, and the chocolate flavor became both smoother and deeper. At last, we had brought our fantasy to life: a double-chocolate cookie that was both rich and soft.

Thick and Chewy Double-Chocolate Cookies

MAKES ABOUT 42

It is worth buying parchment paper for this recipe because the undersides of the cookies are soft and the parchment makes for easy transfer, removal, and cleanup. We also recommend using a spring-loaded ice cream scoop to scoop the soft dough. Resist the urge to bake the cookies longer than indicated; they may appear underbaked at first but will firm up as they cool.

2	cups (10 ounces) unbleached all-purpose flour
½	cup (1½ ounces) Dutch-processed cocoa
2	teaspoons baking powder
½	teaspoon salt
16	ounces semisweet chocolate, chopped
4	large eggs
2	teaspoons vanilla extract
2	teaspoons instant coffee or espresso powder

 10   tablespoons (1 1/4 sticks) unsalted butter,
        softened but still cool
 1 1/2 cups packed (10 1/2 ounces) light brown sugar
 1/2   cup (3 1/2 ounces) granulated sugar

1. Sift together the flour, cocoa, baking powder, and salt in a medium bowl; set aside.

2. Melt the chocolate in a medium heatproof bowl set over a pan of almost-simmering water, stirring once or twice, until smooth; remove from the heat. (To melt the chocolate in a microwave oven, see the note on page 734.) In a small bowl, beat the eggs and vanilla lightly with a fork, sprinkle the coffee powder over to dissolve, and set aside.

3. Either by hand or with an electric mixer, beat the butter at medium speed until smooth and creamy, about 5 seconds. Beat in the sugars until combined, about 45 seconds; the mixture will look granular. Reduce the speed to low and gradually beat in the egg mixture until incorporated, about 45 seconds. Add the chocolate in a steady stream and beat until combined, about 40 seconds. Scrape the bottom and sides of the bowl with a rubber spatula. With the mixer at low speed, add the dry ingredients and mix until just combined. Do not overbeat. Cover with plastic wrap and let stand at room temperature until the consistency is scoopable and fudge-like, about 30 minutes.

4. Meanwhile, adjust the oven racks to the upper- and lower-middle positions and heat the oven to 350 degrees. Line 2 baking sheets with parchment paper. Scoop the dough onto the prepared baking sheets with a 1¾-inch ice cream scoop, spacing the mounds of dough about 1½ inches apart.

5. Bake until the edges of the cookies have just begun to set but the centers are still very soft, about 10 minutes, rotating the baking sheets front to back and top to bottom halfway through the baking time. Cool the cookies on the sheets about 10 minutes, slide the parchment with the cookies onto wire racks, and cool to room temperature. Cover one cooled baking sheet with a new piece of parchment paper. Scoop the remaining dough onto the parchment-lined sheet, bake, and cool as directed. Remove cooled cookies from the parchment with a wide metal spatula.

➤ VARIATION
Thick and Chewy Triple-Chocolate Cookies
If you like bursts of warm melted chocolate in your cookies, include chocolate chips in the batter. The addition of chips will slightly increase the yield of the recipe.

Follow the recipe for Thick and Chewy Double-Chocolate Cookies, adding 12 ounces (about 2 cups) semisweet chocolate chips to the batter after the dry ingredients are incorporated in step 3.

PEANUT BUTTER COOKIES

THERE ARE SEVERAL STYLES OF PEANUT BUTTER cookie. Some are thin and candy-like; others are dry and crumbly. For us, the best peanut butter cookie is crisp around the edges, chewy in the center, and slightly puffed. The flavor is buttery and sweet, with a strong hit of peanuts.

We started our tests by focusing on the fat. We quickly determined that butter accentuated the peanut flavor, while margarine and Crisco diminished it. Crisco did make the cookie chewier in the center, but we felt the added chewiness was not worth the loss of peanut flavor. We tried peanut oil (thinking this might boost the overall peanut flavor), but the resulting texture was dry and sandy.

We then moved on to researching the key ingredient: peanut butter. Natural peanut butters, with a layer of oil on top, made the cookies sandy. Commercial brands, which contain partially hydrogenated vegetable oils that are similar to Crisco, helped the cookies rise and achieve a crisper edge and chewier center. We tested both smooth and chunky peanut butter and felt that the chunky style contributed more peanut flavor.

We tried using more peanut butter to boost the peanut flavor (we even used all peanut butter and no butter), but we still could not get a strong enough peanut flavor. Also, the texture suffered as we removed the butter from our working recipe. The cookies were sandy and almost like shortbread. Butter was crucial for lightness and a chewy texture. Clearly, we would need peanuts as well as peanut butter. We found that chopped peanuts tend to slip out of the dough. We then ground them in the food processor and worked them directly into the dough, which greatly improved the peanut flavor.

Salt brings out the flavor of peanuts (salted roasted peanuts taste better than unsalted nuts), and we found that salt also helped bring out the flavor of the peanuts in the cookies. In fact, we found it best to use both salted nuts and salt for the strongest peanut flavor.

At this point, we focused our attention on the sweetener. We had been using granulated sugar and now began to wonder if a liquid sweetener might make the cookies chewier. We tried molasses and corn syrup, but they could not beat granulated sugar. We tried brown sugar but found the resulting cookies to be too sweet and candy-like. However, because the brown sugar did make the cookies taste nuttier, we decided to test half brown sugar and half granulated sugar. This turned out to be ideal, giving the cookies a mild praline flavor that highlighted the flavor of the peanuts.

We found that the amount of flour in the dough also affected the peanut flavor. Too little flour made the cookies taste greasy and not very peanutty. As we increased the flour, the peanut flavor intensified. Too much flour, however, and the cookies became dry. Slightly more flour than butter and peanut butter combined proved to be the right amount.

CROSSHATCHING PEANUT BUTTER COOKIES

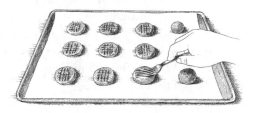

To make a crisscross design, dip a dinner fork into a small bowl of cold water and then press the fork into the dough ball. Rotate the fork 90 degrees and press it into the dough ball a second time.

Peanut Butter Cookies
MAKES ABOUT 36

These cookies have a strong peanut flavor that comes from extra-crunchy peanut butter (in our taste test, we preferred Jif) as well as from salted roasted peanuts that are ground in a food processor and worked into the dough.

2½	cups (12½ ounces) unbleached all-purpose flour
½	teaspoon baking soda
½	teaspoon baking powder
1	teaspoon salt
16	tablespoons (2 sticks) unsalted butter, softened but still cool
1	cup packed (7 ounces) light brown sugar
1	cup (7 ounces) granulated sugar
1	cup extra-crunchy peanut butter
2	large eggs
2	teaspoons vanilla extract
1	cup salted dry-roasted peanuts, ground in a food processor to resemble bread crumbs, about 14 pulses

1. Adjust the ovens racks to the upper- and lower-middle positions and heat the oven to 350 degrees. Line 2 large baking sheets with parchment paper or spray them with nonstick cooking spray.

2. Whisk the flour, baking soda, baking powder, and salt together in a medium bowl; set aside.

3. Either by hand or with an electric mixer, beat the butter until creamy. Add the sugars; beat until fluffy, about 3 minutes with an electric mixer, stopping to scrape down the bowl as necessary. Beat in the peanut butter until fully incorporated, then the eggs, one at a time, and then the vanilla. Gently stir the dry ingredients into the peanut butter mixture. Add the ground peanuts and stir gently until just incorporated.

4. Working with a generous 2 tablespoons each time, roll the dough into 2-inch balls. Place the balls on the prepared baking sheets, spacing them 2½ inches apart. Following the illustration at left, press each dough ball twice with a dinner fork dipped in cold water to make a crisscross design.

5. Bake until the cookies are puffed and slightly browned around the edges but not on top, 10 to

12 minutes, rotating the baking sheets front to back and top to bottom halfway through the baking time. (The cookies will not look fully baked.) Cool the cookies on the baking sheets until set, about 4 minutes, then transfer to a wire rack with a wide metal spatula to cool completely.

➤ VARIATION

Peanut Butter Chocolate Chip Cookies
Follow the recipe for Peanut Butter Cookies, adding 1½ cups semisweet chocolate chips with the ground nuts.

OATMEAL COOKIES

WHEN DEVELOPING THIS RECIPE, WE WANTED an oversize cookie that was chewy and moist. Most oatmeal cookies seem dry to us, and the flavor of the oats seems too weak. Many recipes don't call for enough oats, and spices often overwhelm the flavor of the oats that are there.

The flavor issues were easily solved with some testing. We experimented with various amounts of oats and found that in order to have a real oat flavor, we needed 2 cups of oats for every cup of flour—far more oats than in most recipes. We also preferred old-fashioned rolled oats to quick oats; the old-fashioned had better texture and flavor.

To keep the focus on the oats, we decided to eliminate cinnamon, a common ingredient in these cookies, because it was overpowering the oats. We wanted some spice, however, and chose nutmeg, which has a cleaner, subtler flavor that we liked with the oats. We recommend freshly grated nutmeg for the best flavor.

Our cookies tasted good at this point, but we needed to work on the texture. In our tests, we found that a high proportion of butter to flour helped to keep the cookies moist. We settled on 2 parts butter to 3 parts flour.

We found that shaping the dough into 2-inch balls (rather than dropping the meager rounded tablespoon called for in most recipes) helped keep the cookies more moist and chewy, especially in the center, which remains a bit underbaked in an oversize cookie. Smaller cookies are considerably

drier and more cake-like, something we did not want in an oatmeal cookie.

Our final tests involved the sugar. We experimented with various amounts and found that adding a full cup each of brown and granulated sugar delivered the best results, giving us a cookie that was especially moist and rich. Sugar makes baked goods more moist and tender because it helps them hold on to water during the baking process. In addition, sugar encourages exterior browning, which promotes crispness.

Chewy Oatmeal-Raisin Cookies
MAKES ABOUT 18 LARGE

If you prefer a less sweet cookie, you can reduce the granulated sugar by ¼ cup, but you will lose some crispness. Do not overbake these cookies. The edges should be browned, but the rest of the cookie should be very light in color.

1½	cups (7½ ounces) unbleached all-purpose flour
½	teaspoon baking powder
¼	teaspoon freshly grated nutmeg
½	teaspoon salt
16	tablespoons (2 sticks) unsalted butter, softened but still cool
1	cup packed (7 ounces) light brown sugar
1	cup (7 ounces) granulated sugar
2	large eggs
3	cups old-fashioned rolled oats
1½	cups raisins (optional)

1. Adjust the oven racks to the low and middle positions and heat the oven to 350 degrees. Line 2 large baking sheets with parchment paper or spray them with nonstick cooking spray.

2. Whisk the flour, baking powder, nutmeg, and salt together in a medium bowl.

3. Either by hand or with an electric mixer, beat the butter on medium speed until creamy. Add the sugars; beat until fluffy, about 3 minutes. Beat in the eggs, one at a time.

4. Stir the dry ingredients into the butter-sugar mixture with a wooden spoon or large rubber spatula. Stir in the oats and raisins (if using).

5. Working with a generous 2 tablespoons of

dough each time, roll the dough into 2-inch balls. Place the balls on the prepared baking sheets, spacing them at least 2 inches apart.

6. Bake until the cookie edges turn golden brown, 22 to 25 minutes, rotating the baking sheets front to back and top to bottom halfway through the baking time. Let the cookies cool on the baking sheets for 2 minutes. Transfer the cookies with a wide metal spatula to a wire rack. Let cool at least 30 minutes.

➤ VARIATIONS

Date Oatmeal Cookies
See the tip on page 560 for chopping dried fruit.

Follow the recipe for Chewy Oatmeal-Raisin Cookies, substituting 1½ cups chopped dates for the raisins.

Ginger Oatmeal Cookies
Follow the recipe for Chewy Oatmeal-Raisin Cookies, adding ¾ teaspoon ground ginger to the flour and other dry ingredients and omitting the raisins.

Chocolate Chip Oatmeal Cookies
Follow the recipe for Chewy Oatmeal-Raisin Cookies, omitting the nutmeg and substituting 1½ cups semisweet chocolate chips for the raisins.

Nut Oatmeal Cookies
Follow the recipe for Chewy Oatmeal-Raisin Cookies, decreasing the flour to 1⅓ cups and adding ¼ cup ground almonds and 1 cup chopped walnut pieces along with the oats. (Almonds can be ground in a food processor or blender.) Omit the raisins.

Orange and Almond Oatmeal Cookies
Follow the recipe for Chewy Oatmeal-Raisin Cookies, omitting the raisins and adding 2 tablespoons minced orange zest and 1 cup toasted chopped almonds (toast nuts in a 350-degree oven for 5 minutes) along with the oats.

PECAN SANDIES

TAKE SHORTBREAD, A SCOTTISH COOKIE, and give it a dose of Americana—namely, pecans and brown sugar—and it is transformed into a nutty, buttery cookie with a hint of caramel flavor. The texture: tender but crisp and sandy, with a slow melt-in-your-mouth character. Call it a "pecan sandy," after its noteworthy texture. Indeed, pecan sandies can be purchased in any grocery store cookie aisle, but for the richest, purest butter, pecan, and brown sugar flavors, they are best (and easily) made at home.

Recipes for pecan sandies run the gamut. Sometimes called pecan or brown sugar pecan shortbread, pecan sandies are rich in butter like shortbread. And because a crisp, sandy texture—not a puffy or cakey crumb—is the goal, they do not contain chemical leaveners for lift (also like shortbread). We made cookies similar to simple sugar cookies that are dropped onto a baking sheet; we baked basic roll-and-cut cookies made with cake flour; we sampled cookies made with vegetable oil and a duo of ground nuts and chopped nuts; we sliced cookies from a refrigerator cookie log. We concluded quickly that cake flour is unnecessary. A tender cookie could be made with unbleached all-purpose flour, our kitchen standard. We found that oil does make for a sandy texture, but it falls pitifully short in flavor—the rich, sweet flavor of pure butter is paramount. Last, we learned that a dropped cookie doesn't have the neat, clean edges that pecan sandies should have. Rolling and cutting the dough or forming it into a sliceable log would be the way to create a perfect-looking pecan sandy.

The type and amount of sugar best for pecan sandies needed to be determined. In a working recipe that we assembled, we tried light brown sugar, dark brown sugar, granulated sugar, confectioners' sugar, and different combinations of each. Confectioners' sugar, with its small amount of cornstarch, had a noticeable tenderizing effect on the cookies. Too much, however, and the cookies turned pasty and gummy; a quarter cup was all that was needed. Granulated sugar had little to offer in the way of flavor, while dark brown sugar offered too much. Light brown sugar, tinged with molasses, gave the cookies a gentle caramel flavor that complemented, not overwhelmed, the nuttiness of the pecans and the richness of the butter.

Next we made batches of pecan sandies with a whole egg and without. A whole egg was excessive—the dough was sticky and difficult to work with. Without an egg, however, the cookies baked up with a texture more like pie pastry, and they lost their attractive sharp edges in the oven. A single yolk was what the dough needed. By comparison, these cookies were fine-pored and stalwart, keeping their crisp, clean look even after baking.

So far, we had been using a good amount of finely chopped nuts for flavor. We tried grinding a portion of those nuts, leaving the other portion chopped, and found the cookies made with ground nuts to be finer-textured, more tender, and nuttier than those made exclusively with chopped nuts. The oils in the nuts released during grinding contributed to the tenderness and flavor of the cookies. But tasters demanded an even finer cookie, one in which chopped nuts didn't mar the delicate sandy texture, so we ground all of the pecans. Tasters were pleased.

As for flavor refinements, a bit of salt helped to boost the flavor. Vanilla extract, even the smallest amount of it, was too perfumed and distracting. Tasters did like a hint of cinnamon, however; its flavor could not be singled out, but it added nuance and a layer of warmth.

A matter of mechanics: We were grinding the pecans in a food processor, but we were making the cookie dough using the typical creamed-butter method in an electric mixer. It occurred to us that these cookies were not a far cry from *pâte sucrée*, or French tart pastry, which is made entirely in the food processor, so we gave it a whirl, taking it from start to finish in the processor. We ground the nuts with the sugars to help prevent the nuts from going greasy and clumpy as they broke down, added the flour, cut in the butter, and finally added the egg. The dough quantity was large and resisted being perfectly combined, so we emptied it onto the counter and kneaded it gently until it came together into an even, cohesive dough. It worked faster and more cleanly than we could have hoped—and now we

didn't have to take out the butter ahead of time to soften it for creaming or haul out and dirty the electric mixer.

Rolling out the dough into sheets and stamping out cookies with a cutter was one shaping option, but this technique generates scraps, which we preferred to do without. Instead, we treated the dough as we would for refrigerator cookies, shaping the just-made dough into one 12-inch log, cutting it in half, wrapping each half in plastic wrap, and putting them in the freezer just long enough to firm up their exteriors. At this point, we took them out, rolled them along the counter surface to round out the flat side they had rested on while soft, and then put them in the refrigerator until thoroughly chilled. After a couple of hours, we sliced the logs into ¼-inch coins and accessorized them with a pecan half pressed into each slice (for presentation; otherwise, the cookies look homely), and they were ready to bake.

Pecan sandies should become only modestly brown with baking—the edges should begin to deepen to golden brown, but the bulk of each cookie should be blond. They need to be thoroughly baked, however, even under the pecan adornment, to obtain their characteristic crisp, sandy texture. A 325-degree oven was ideal—a cooler oven took longer than necessary, and a hotter one gave the cookies too much color. Once on the wire rack, pecan sandies must cool completely before being eaten, lest their texture fail to live up to their name.

Pecan Sandies
MAKES ABOUT 32

Once the dough is shaped into logs, it should be frozen for 30 minutes (to speed chilling) and then refrigerated for at least 2 hours. The dough can be refrigerated for up to 3 days before being sliced and baked.

1½	cups pecan halves, plus about 32 pecan halves for pressing onto unbaked cookies
¼	cup (1 ounce) confectioners' sugar
½	cup packed (3½ ounces) light brown sugar
1½	cups (7½ ounces) unbleached all-purpose flour
¼	teaspoon salt

12 tablespoons (1 ½ sticks) cold unsalted butter,
cut into ½-inch cubes

1 large egg yolk

1. In a food processor, process the 1½ cups pecans with both sugars until the nuts are ground, about twenty 1-second pulses. Add the flour and salt and process to combine, about twelve 1-second pulses. Scatter the butter pieces over the dry ingredients and process until the mixture resembles damp sand and rides up the sides of the bowl, about eighteen 1-second pulses. With the machine running, add the yolk and process until the dough comes together into a rough ball, about 20 seconds.

2. Turn the dough (it will look scrappy and uneven) onto a clean, dry work surface and gently knead until it is evenly moistened and cohesive. Using the palms of your hands, roll the dough into an even 12-inch log, cut the log in half with a chef's knife, and wrap each half in plastic wrap. Freeze the dough logs until very cold but still malleable, about 30 minutes. Remove them from the freezer, unwrap them, and roll them on the work surface to round off the flat sides. Rewrap the logs in plastic wrap and refrigerate them until thoroughly chilled and completely firm, about 2 hours.

3. Adjust the oven racks to the upper- and lower-middle positions and heat the oven to 325 degrees. Line 2 large baking sheets with parchment paper or spray them with nonstick cooking spray. Unwrap the dough logs and, using a sharp chef's knife, slice the logs into coins ¼ inch thick, slightly rotating the logs after each slice so that they do not develop a markedly flat side. Place the slices on the prepared baking sheets, spacing them about ¾ inch apart. Press a pecan half in the center of each slice.

4. Bake until the edges of the cookies are golden brown, about 24 minutes, rotating the baking sheets front to back and top to bottom halfway through the baking time. Cool the cookies 3 minutes on the baking sheets, then transfer them to a wire rack with a wide metal spatula and let them cool to room temperature.

> VARIATION

Almond Sandies

Follow the recipe for Pecan Sandies, replacing the pecans with an equal amount of whole blanched almonds that have been toasted in a 350-degree oven for 8 minutes, cooled, and then chopped. Add ¼ teaspoon almond extract with the egg yolk.

MOLASSES SPICE COOKIES

WE'VE COME TO APPRECIATE GOOD MOLASSES cookies for their honesty and simplicity. On the outside, their cracks and crinkles give them a humble, charming countenance. Inside, an uncommonly moist, soft yet chewy, tooth-sinking texture is half the appeal; the other half is a warm, tingling spiciness paired with the dark, bittersweet flavor of molasses. Unfortunately, molasses spice cookies are often no more than flat, tasteless cardboard rounds of gingerbread. Some are dry and cakey without the requisite chew; others are timidly flavored with molasses and are either recklessly or vacantly spiced.

We started by testing a half dozen different recipes, using a variety of fats, flours, and mixing methods. Although these early experiments yielded vastly different cookies in terms of flavor and appearance, a few things were clear. The full, rich flavor of butter was in; flat-tasting shortening was out. We found that a lower-protein unbleached all-purpose flour such as Gold Medal or Pillsbury gave us a more tender cookie. The mixing technique was a standard one: Cream the butter and sugar; add the eggs, then the molasses; and, finally, stir in the dry ingredients.

Molasses is at the core of these cookies. Enough must be used to give them a dark, smoky, bittersweet flavor, but we found that a surfeit of molasses creates a sticky, unworkable dough. For the amount of butter (12 tablespoons) and flour (2¼ cups) we were using, the molasses ceiling was ½ cup. We had been using mild (also called light) molasses up to this point, but in an attempt to boost flavor, we baked batches with dark and blackstrap molasses. Cookies made with dark molasses were filled with bold flavor and rich color, and they garnered much praise. Those made with blackstrap molasses had a few fans, but, for most of us, the wicked brew overtook the spices and made the cookies too bitter.

Molasses alone cannot supply the cookies with enough sweetness, so either granulated or brown sugar is required. Dark brown sugar (we chose dark over light for its stronger molasses flavor) yielded cookies that were surprisingly puffy and cakey, and they spread too little on the baking sheet. Granulated sugar yielded cookies that were pale both in color and flavor. A combination of granulated and brown sugar was the ticket. The brown sugar fortified the molasses flavor, while the granulated sugar, a spreading agent, allowed the cookies to attain a good, even thickness in the oven without much puff. After some fiddling, we found equal amounts of brown and granulated sugar to be ideal.

Most molasses cookie recipes call for no more than a single egg to bind things together. However, the white of the egg—harmless as it may seem—made the dough sticky. The difference was subtle, but the white also caused the baked cookies to have a slightly cake-like crumb and a firmer, drier feel than we cared for. A lone yolk was all the cookies needed.

Molasses is a mildly acidic ingredient, so baking soda, an alkali that reacts with the acidity of the molasses to provide lift, is the logical leavener for these cookies. In our testing, cookies with too little baking soda were flat and failed to develop those attractive fault lines. The proper amount of baking soda (1 teaspoon) gave the cookies nice height—a pleasure to sink your teeth into—and a winsome appearance, with large, meandering fissures.

It was time to refine the flavor of the cookies. A teaspoon of vanilla extract complemented generous amounts of sharp, spicy ground ginger and warm, soothing cinnamon. Cloves, rich and fragrant, and allspice, sweet and mysterious, were added, but in more judicious quantities. Nutmeg was pedestrian and had little to offer. Finely and freshly ground black pepper, however, added some intrigue—a *soupçon* of heat against the deep, bittersweet flavor of the molasses.

To shape the molasses cookies, we rolled generous heaping tablespoons of dough into balls and coated them with granulated sugar, which, after baking, gave the cookies a frosted sparkle. Out of a 375-degree oven, the cookies were perfect—the edges were slightly crisped and the interiors soft and chewy. We determined that the cookies must be baked one sheet at a time since cookies baked on the lower rack inevitably puffed and turned out smooth rather than craggy and cracked.

Most important, we noted that the cookies must come out of the oven when they appear substantially underdone; otherwise, their soft, moist, chewy texture will harden upon cooling. Whisk them out when the edges are hardly set, the centers are still soft and puffy, and the dough looks shiny and raw between the cracks. The cookies finish baking with residual heat, so don't shortchange them of a five-minute repose on the baking sheet before removal to a wire rack.

Molasses Spice Cookies
MAKES ABOUT 22

For the best flavor, make sure that your spices are fresh. Light or mild molasses gives the cookies a milder flavor; for a stronger flavor, use dark molasses. Either way, measure molasses in a liquid measuring cup. For the best texture and spread, the flour in these cookies should be weighed. Bake the cookies 1 sheet at a time; if baked 2 at a time, the cookies started on the bottom rack won't develop attractive cracks. Remove the cookies from the oven when they still look slightly raw and underbaked. If you plan to glaze the cookies (see the illustration on page 787), save the parchment paper that they were baked on.

2¼ cups (11¼ ounces) lower-protein unbleached all-purpose flour, such as Gold Medal or Pillsbury
1 teaspoon baking soda
1½ teaspoons ground cinnamon
1½ teaspoons ground ginger
½ teaspoon ground cloves
¼ teaspoon ground allspice
¼ teaspoon finely ground black pepper
¼ teaspoon salt

12   tablespoons (1 ½ sticks) unsalted butter,
      softened but still cool
⅓   cup packed (2 ⅓ ounces) dark brown sugar
⅓   cup (2 ⅓ ounces) granulated sugar,
      plus ½ cup for rolling
1   large egg yolk
1   teaspoon vanilla extract
½   cup light or dark molasses

1. Adjust an oven rack to the middle position and heat the oven to 375 degrees. Line a large baking sheet with parchment paper or spray it with nonstick cooking spray.

2. Whisk the flour, baking soda, spices, pepper, and salt in a medium bowl until thoroughly combined; set aside.

3. Either by hand or with an electric mixer, beat the butter with the brown sugar and the ⅓ cup granulated sugar at medium-high speed until light and fluffy, about 3 minutes. Reduce the speed to medium-low and add the yolk and vanilla; increase the speed to medium and beat until incorporated, about 20 seconds. Reduce the speed to medium-low and add the molasses; beat until fully incorporated, about 20 seconds, scraping the bottom and sides of the bowl once with a rubber spatula. Reduce the speed to the lowest setting; add the flour mixture and beat until just incorporated, about 30 seconds, scraping the bowl once. Give the dough a final stir by hand to ensure that no pockets of flour remain at the bottom. The dough will be soft.

GLAZING MOLASSES COOKIES

To speed cleanup, line the baking sheet with parchment paper. Dip a spoon into the glaze and move the spoon over the cookies so that the glaze drizzles down onto them. Dip the spoon into the glaze as needed.

4. Place the ½ cup granulated sugar for rolling in a shallow bowl. Fill a medium bowl halfway with cold tap water. Dip your hands into the water and shake off the excess (this will prevent the dough from sticking to your hands and ensure that the sugar sticks to the dough). Using a tablespoon measure, scoop a heaping tablespoon of dough and roll it between your moistened palms into a 1¼- to 1½-inch ball; drop the ball into the sugar and repeat to form about 4 balls. Toss the balls in the sugar to coat and set them on the prepared baking sheet, spacing them about 2 inches apart. Repeat with the remaining dough, moistening your hands as necessary with the water.

5. Bake until the cookies are browned and still puffy, the edges have begun to set, and the centers are still soft (the cookies will look raw between the cracks and seem underdone), about 11 minutes, rotating the sheet from front to back halfway through the baking time. Do not overbake.

6. Cool the cookies on the baking sheet for 5 minutes, then use a wide metal spatula to transfer the cookies to a wire rack; cool the cookies to room temperature.

➤ VARIATIONS
Molasses Spice Cookies with Dark Rum Glaze
For the glaze, start by adding the smaller amount of rum; if the glaze is too thick to drizzle, whisk in up to an additional ½ tablespoon rum.

Follow the recipe for Molasses Spice Cookies. When the cookies are completely cool, return them to the cooled parchment-lined baking sheets. Whisk 1 cup (4 ounces) confectioners' sugar and 2½ to 3 tablespoons dark rum in a medium bowl until smooth. Drizzle the glaze over the cookies with a soupspoon (see the illustration at left), dipping the spoon into the glaze as necessary. Transfer the cookies to a wire rack and allow the glaze to dry, 10 to 15 minutes.

Molasses Spice Cookies with Orange Essence
The orange zest in the sugar coating causes the sugar to become sticky and take on a light orange hue, giving the baked cookies a unique, frosty look.

In the workbowl of a food processor, process ⅔ cup granulated sugar and 2 teaspoons grated orange zest until pale orange, about 10 seconds; transfer the sugar to a shallow bowl and set aside. Follow the recipe for Molasses Spice Cookies, adding 1 teaspoon grated orange zest to the butter and sugar along with the molasses and substituting the orange sugar for granulated sugar when coating the dough balls in step 4.

GLAZED LEMON COOKIES

LEMON-FLAVORED DESSERTS RUN THE GAMUT from bright and tangy to saccharine-sweet and artificial. Store-bought lemon cookies lean toward the latter, with their thin veneer of frosting and a barely detectable lemon flavor that's more reminiscent of furniture polish than fruit. Cookies made at home can be disappointing as well, with recipes often calling for minuscule amounts of lemon or even ingredients like lemon extract or lemon-flavored cake mix. We thought it was surely possible to make a glazed lemon cookie that was both tart and sweet and tasted like fresh lemons. Our goal was to make a cookie with the perfect balance of lemony zing and rich, buttery sweetness that would be a natural accompaniment to a cup of hot tea.

Looking through various cookbooks, we found that lemon cookies come in all shapes and sizes, from chewy drop cookies to thin and crisp rolled ones. We tried both versions. When baked, the drop cookies remained thick in the middle—great for a heartier cookie like oatmeal or molasses, but not right for a lemon cookie. The thinner, more delicate rolled cookies were preferred, but some of these cookies were tough, a result of the dough being overworked by rolling and then rerolling scraps. Was there a way to shape the cookies that would preserve their delicate texture? Refrigerator cookies, with dough that is rolled into a cylinder, chilled, and sliced just before baking, produced the results we were looking for. This process allows the cookies to be sliced thinly and evenly, giving them a uniform shape, thickness, and texture.

Now that we had found the shaping method, it was time to look at the ingredients. For flour, we found that all-purpose was the best choice, making a cookie that was both tender and toothsome. Using one egg yolk instead of a whole egg made the cookies even more tender, and leaving out the egg white also kept the dough from getting too sticky. What about baking powder and baking soda? Cookies made without any leavener were too dense, and even a tiny amount of baking soda (which promotes browning as well as leavening) made them too brittle and brown. One-quarter teaspoon of baking powder gave the cookies the perfect amount of airy crispness.

To get a rich, tender texture, we needed just the right amount of butter. Cookies made with 8 tablespoons were too lean, but 16 tablespoons

SHAPING THE DOUGH FOR GLAZED LEMON COOKIES

1. Roll the dough into a cylinder approximately 10 inches long and 2 inches in diameter. Center the dough on a piece of parchment. Fold the paper over the dough.

2. Grasp one end of the parchment. With the other hand, use a bench scraper to firmly press the parchment against the dough to form a uniform cylinder.

3. Roll the parchment and twist the ends together to form a tight seal.

was too much. Splitting the difference and using 12 tablespoons was the answer. We tried four types of sugar: confectioners', light brown, dark brown, and granulated. Granulated sugar made a cookie with the best texture and balance of flavors.

We wanted to avoid lemon extract, knowing that only fresh lemon (zest or juice) could provide the big, bright flavor we wanted for our cookies. We tried varying amounts of juice, from 1 teaspoon (could hardly taste it) to ¼ cup (very acidic). We tried leaving out the lemon juice altogether and using only zest instead. The resulting cookies were lemony but lacked the zip provided by the juice. The solution? A combination of 2 tablespoons each of zest and juice. A small amount of vanilla rounded out the lemon flavors without detracting from their brightness.

We were almost there, but not entirely satisfied; we wanted more lemon flavor. We'd heard about a technique for grinding the sugar and zest together in a food processor to release even more lemon flavor. This produced exactly the cookie we were looking for: bright, bold lemon flavor without harshness. But now we had a preparation problem, as we needed a food processor for the sugar and zest and an electric mixer for the dough. (The mixer creams softened butter with the blended sugar and zest, and then the yolk and dry ingredients are added.) We tried mixing the dough in the food processor, but the softened butter turned into a greasy mess. We tried it once again, this time with cold butter cut into small pieces. The dough came together easily, and the baked cookies were fragrant and just as tender as the version made with the electric mixer. In the end, the processor not only heightened the lemon flavor but also provided the bonus of speeding up the mixing. (We no longer had to wait for the butter to soften.) As for oven temperature, 375 degrees worked best. The cookies emerged from the oven thin and crisp, with golden brown edges.

For the glaze, we focused on using confectioners' sugar. It would be impossible to make a quick and easy glaze that would harden without it, but a combination of lemon juice and confectioners' sugar was astringent and harsh. Adding zest only

made the glaze unappealingly lumpy. It needed an additional ingredient to temper the acidity. Heavy cream did just that, but it dulled the brightness of the lemon juice, making the glaze taste flat. Both sour cream and yogurt had the opposite effect, heightening the acidity and turning the glaze even more sour. Cream cheese did the trick. Its rich creaminess toned down the lemon's harshness but offered just enough of its own tang to keep the flavors bright. Together with the lemony cookie, the glaze had just the right balance of sweetness and sharpness.

Glazed Lemon Cookies
MAKES ABOUT 30

You will need a food processor to make these cookies. The dough, formed into a log and wrapped in parchment paper and then plastic wrap, will keep in the refrigerator for up to 3 days or in the freezer for up to 2 weeks. The cookies are best eaten the day they are glazed.

COOKIES
¾	cup (5¼ ounces) granulated sugar
2	tablespoons grated zest plus 2 tablespoons juice from 2 lemons
1¾	cups (8¾ ounces) unbleached all-purpose flour
¼	teaspoon baking powder
¼	teaspoon salt
12	tablespoons (1½ sticks) cold unsalted butter, cut into ½-inch cubes
1	large egg yolk
½	teaspoon vanilla extract

GLAZE
1	tablespoon cream cheese, softened
2	tablespoons juice from 1 lemon
1½	cups (6 ounces) confectioners' sugar

1. FOR THE COOKIES: In a food processor, process the granulated sugar and lemon zest until the sugar looks damp and the zest is thoroughly incorporated, about 30 seconds. Add the flour, baking powder, and salt; pulse to combine, about ten 1-second pulses. Scatter the butter pieces over the dry ingredients; pulse until the mixture

resembles fine cornmeal, about fifteen 1-second pulses. In a measuring cup or small bowl, beat together the lemon juice, egg yolk, and vanilla with a fork to combine. With the machine running, add the juice mixture in a slow, steady stream (the process should take about 10 seconds); continue processing until the dough begins to form a ball, 10 to 15 seconds longer.

2. Turn the dough and any dry bits onto a clean work surface; working quickly, gently knead to ensure that no dry bits remain and the dough is homogeneous. Following the illustrations on page 788, shape the dough into a cylinder about 10 inches long and 2 inches in diameter, wrap the dough in parchment or plastic wrap, and twist to seal. Chill the dough until firm and cold, about 45 minutes in the freezer or 2 hours in the refrigerator.

3. Meanwhile, adjust the oven racks to the upper- and lower-middle positions; heat the oven to 375 degrees.

4. Line 2 large baking sheets with parchment paper or spray them with nonstick cooking spray. Remove the dough log from its wrapper and, using a sharp chef's knife, slice the dough into rounds ⅜ inch thick; place the rounds on the prepared baking sheets, spacing them about 1 inch apart. Bake until the centers of the cookies just begin to color and the edges are golden brown, 14 to 16 minutes, rotating the baking sheets front to back and top to bottom halfway through the baking time. Cool the cookies on the baking sheets about 5 minutes; using a wide metal spatula, transfer the cookies to a wire rack and cool to room temperature before glazing.

5. FOR THE GLAZE: Whisk the cream cheese and lemon juice in a medium nonreactive bowl until no lumps remain. Add the confectioners' sugar and whisk until smooth.

6. TO GLAZE THE COOKIES: When the cookies have cooled, spoon a scant teaspoon of glaze onto each cookie and spread evenly with the back of the spoon. Let the cookies stand on a wire rack until the glaze is set and dry, about 1 hour.

> VARIATIONS
Glazed Lemon-Orange Cornmeal Cookies
Follow the recipe for Glazed Lemon Cookies, substituting 1 tablespoon grated orange zest for an equal amount of lemon zest and ¼ cup cornmeal for an equal amount of flour.

Glazed Lemon and Crystallized Ginger Cookies
Follow the recipe for Glazed Lemon Cookies, processing 3 tablespoons finely chopped crystallized ginger along with the sugar and lemon zest.

HOLIDAY COOKIES
ALTHOUGH THE HOLIDAYS ARE FULL OF GOOD cheer and joyous celebration, they are also fraught with endless preparation and, often, a lack of time. We wanted to create a holiday cookie that was almost as easy as the slice-and-bake tubes of cookie dough in the supermarket but without the glue-like flavor. We wanted a buttery cookie dough that doesn't cling to the rolling pin or rip and tear. We wanted a simple one-hour process, not a half-day project. We wanted to develop a simple recipe that would yield a forgiving, workable dough, producing cookies that would be sturdy enough to decorate yet tender enough to be worth eating. And, to save even more time, we wanted a chameleon-like dough that could be transformed into distinctly different cookies with just a few additional ingredients.

We started our investigation by testing five recipes that called for similar ratios of flour to fat and followed the standard butter-and-sugar creaming method of cookie making. These recipes did vary slightly in their choice of ingredients. One used a combination of shortening and butter, one called for all confectioners' sugar, and another used all light brown sugar. Some added an egg or dairy component, while others utilized a leavener. Although these cookies were certainly edible, we still found ourselves in a sticky situation. Only one batch had been easy to handle, but that batch also tasted like powdery cardboard because it used so much confectioners' sugar. We realized that if we wanted the perfect holiday cookie dough, we would have to go back to basics.

The most important issue was the ratio of flour to butter. After extensive testing, we ended up with 2½ cups of flour to 2 sticks of butter. (Shortening adds no flavor to cookies and is not an option.) This was just enough butter to stay true to the nature of a butter cookie but not so much that the dough would be greasy. Although the dough was not perfect (it still had a tendency to stick when rolling), we at least had a good jumping-off point for our master recipe.

Next we experimented with flour, first testing cake flour, which produced delicate cookies with a chalky texture. We got similar results when we tried replacing different amounts of all-purpose flour with equal parts of cornstarch, another common tenderizing technique. These cookies were also very fragile—not ideal when it's time to decorate. We came to the conclusion that a little bit of structure-providing gluten (the combination of proteins found in greater amounts in all-purpose flour than in cake flour or cornstarch) wasn't necessarily a bad thing.

Because these cookies would play host to glazes or sweet fillings, we did not want to add too much sugar to the dough—just enough to enhance their flavor. Confectioners' sugar was out because of its bland flavor and powdery texture, while brown sugar made the cookies too soft and chewy. But when we tried superfine sugar, we were surprised at the difference it made. Cookies made with regular granulated sugar had a crumb with larger holes and a flaky texture. Cookies made with superfine sugar, on the other hand, had a fine, even crumb and were compact and crisp—very definitely positive attributes. Liking these thin and crisp cookies, we ruled out the use of a leavener (which would make them puff in the oven) and eggs (which would add both moisture and chewiness). But we still needed to enrich the flavor of the cookies, so we tried adding flavorful dairy components to the dough: buttermilk, sour cream, and cream cheese. The buttermilk produced a crisp yet overly tangy cookie, and the sour cream made the dough far too wet. But the cream cheese—a surprise ingredient to be sure—was just right. It gave the cookies flavor and richness without altering their texture. With a pinch of salt and a dash of vanilla, we had obtained a simple but top-notch flavor for our holiday cookies.

We had come a long way in terms of improving the flavor (rich but direct) and texture (fine and crisp) of the baked cookies, but we were still having

---

SCIENCE: Why Does Mixing Method Matter?

Creaming is a common method used in baking. Butter and sugar are whipped until light and fluffy, eggs are added, and then dry ingredients are incorporated gradually. This method delivers good results when making most cookies, but we found that it did not work well for rolled butter cookies, and we wondered why.

Our recipe has two striking features: It contains no leavener (we did not want the cookies to puff) and no liquid. Because the dough is somewhat dry, the flour did not incorporate well when added at the end of the mixing process. As a result, the dough was unevenly mixed, with streaks of butter, which became sticky when handled. This streaking also had negative effects on the final baked product, as the pockets of butter led to puffed, uneven cookies. Butter is about 18 percent water, and when its temperature reaches 212 degrees, this water turns to steam and expands dramatically, producing bubbles.

When we reversed the order of mixing and added the butter to the flour, the dough was much more uniform. There were no streaks of butter in the dough, so it did not stick when rolled. In addition, because the dough did not contain pockets of butter, the cookies did not puff in the oven, and the baked cookies had flat tops, ready for decorating.

An examination of the interior of two cookies was all the proof we needed. The cookie on the left was mixed using a creaming method. An enormous bubble formed where the butter was not mixed in completely. The cookie on the right, created using our "reverse" mixing method, looks uniform throughout, indicating that the butter was evenly distributed.

trouble rolling out the dough. It was less sticky than the doughs we had made from other recipes, but we wanted a dough that was even easier to work with—something foolproof. All the recipes we had tested called for the creaming method, wherein butter and sugar are beaten into a fluffy union. What if we creamed the butter with the sugar *and* the flour? The dough came together in two minutes and was incredibly easy to handle: soft, pliable, and easy to roll. Even with less chilling time than before, the dough was easily rolled to a slight thickness of ⅛ inch, cut out into different shapes, and maneuvered to a baking sheet. (For more on why this technique works so well, see "Why Does Mixing Method Matter?" on page 791.)

As far as oven temperature goes, 375 degrees was best, as was using only one rack placed in the center of the oven. In the amount of time it took to cut out a second sheet of cookies, the first sheet was finished. But the final selling point was the baked result: thin, flat cookies that were both crisp and sturdy. They tasted great and were foolproof—what more could a holiday baker want?

Glazed Butter Cookies

MAKES ABOUT 38

If you cannot find superfine sugar, you can obtain a close approximation by processing regular granulated sugar in a food processor for about 30 seconds. If desired, the cookies can be finished with sprinkles or other decorations immediately after glazing.

BUTTER COOKIE DOUGH

2½	cups (12½ ounces) unbleached all-purpose flour
¾	cup (5½ ounces) superfine sugar (see note)
¼	teaspoon salt
16	tablespoons (2 sticks) unsalted butter, softened but still cool, cut into sixteen pieces
2	teaspoons vanilla extract
2	tablespoons cream cheese, at room temperature

GLAZE

1	tablespoon cream cheese, at room temperature
2–3	tablespoons milk
1½	cups (6 ounces) confectioners' sugar

1. FOR THE COOKIES: In the bowl of an electric mixer, mix the flour, sugar, and salt at low speed until combined, about 5 seconds. With the mixer running on low, add the butter, one piece at a time; continue to mix until the mixture looks crumbly and slightly wet, about 1 minute longer. Add the vanilla and cream cheese and mix on low until the dough just begins to form large clumps, about 30 seconds.

2. Knead the dough by hand in the bowl for 2 or 3 turns to form a large, cohesive mass. Turn the dough out onto the countertop; divide it in half, pat each half into a 4-inch disk, wrap the disks in plastic, and refrigerate until they begin to firm up, 20 to 30 minutes. (The disks can be refrigerated for up to 3 days or frozen for up to 2 weeks; defrost in the refrigerator before using.)

3. Adjust an oven rack to the middle position; heat the oven to 375 degrees. Roll out 1 dough disk to an even ⅛-inch thickness between 2 large sheets of parchment paper; slide the rolled dough, still on the parchment, onto a baking sheet and refrigerate until firm, about 10 minutes. Meanwhile, repeat with the second disk.

4. Working with the first portion of rolled dough, cut into desired shapes using cookie cutters and place the shapes on a parchment-lined baking sheet, spacing them about 1½ inches apart. Bake until the cookies are light golden brown, about 10 minutes, rotating the baking sheet halfway through the baking time. Repeat with the second portion of rolled dough. (The dough scraps can be patted together, chilled, and rerolled once.) Cool the cookies to room temperature on a wire rack.

5. FOR THE GLAZE: Whisk the cream cheese and 2 tablespoons of the milk in a medium bowl until combined and no lumps remain. Whisk in the confectioners' sugar until smooth, adding the remaining milk as needed until the glaze is thin enough to spread easily. Drizzle a scant teaspoon of the glaze onto each cooled cookie, or spread it on with the back of a spoon.

ONE DOUGH, MANY COOKIES

Our butter cookie dough is not only foolproof but also the perfect vehicle for a number of different flavorings, shapes, and sizes. One easy-to-handle dough can be the basis for a wide assortment of holiday cookies. Here are 3 of our favorite cookies made with this dough.

JAM SANDWICHES

1. Using a 2-inch fluted round cookie cutter, cut rounds from one piece of dough and bake on a parchment-lined baking sheet in a 375-degree oven until light golden brown, 8 to 10 minutes.

2. Meanwhile, sprinkle the second piece of rolled dough evenly with the sugar.

3. Using a 2-inch fluted round cookie cutter, cut out rounds of sugar-sprinkled dough and place on a parchment-lined baking sheet. Using a ¾-inch round cookie cutter, cut out the centers of the rounds and bake until light golden brown, about 8 minutes.

4. When the cookies have cooled, spread 1 teaspoon jam on the solid cookies, then place the cut-out cookies on top. Let the filled cookies stand until set, about 30 minutes.

CHOCOLATE-CHERRY BAR COOKIES WITH HAZELNUTS

1. Press the dough in an even layer into a parchment-lined 18 by 12-inch baking sheet. Bake the cookies on the lower-middle rack in a 375-degree oven until golden brown, about 20 minutes.

2. Immediately after removing the baking sheet from the oven, sprinkle evenly with the chocolate chips; let stand to melt, about 3 minutes.

3. Use an offset icing spatula to spread the chocolate into an even layer, then sprinkle evenly with the chopped hazelnuts. Cool on a wire rack until just warm, 15 to 20 minutes.

4. Use a pizza wheel to cut the cookies into 1¼-inch diamonds. Transfer the cookies to a wire rack to cool completely.

LIME-GLAZED COCONUT SNOWBALLS

1. Use your hands to roll the dough into 1-inch balls. Place on parchment-lined baking sheets, spacing about 1½ inches apart. Bake one batch at a time in a 375-degree oven until lightly browned, about 12 minutes. Cool to room temperature.

2. Dip the tops of the cookies into the glaze and scrape away the excess, then dip into the coconut. Set the cookies on a parchment-lined baking sheet; let stand until the glaze dries and sets, about 20 minutes.

➤ VARIATIONS
Jam Sandwiches
MAKES ABOUT 30

1	recipe Butter Cookie Dough (page 792), prepared through step 3
2	tablespoons turbinado, Demerara, or white decorating sugar
1¼	cups (12 ounces) raspberry jam, strained, simmered until reduced to 1 cup, and cooled to room temperature

Follow the illustrations on page 793.

Chocolate-Cherry Bar Cookies with Hazelnuts
MAKES ABOUT 50

1	recipe Butter Cookie Dough (page 792), 1 cup chopped dried cherries added with the dry ingredients and prepared through step 1

1½	cups (9 ounces) semisweet chocolate chips
1½	cups (7 ounces) hazelnuts, toasted, skinned (see below), and chopped

Follow the illustrations on page 793.

Lime-Glazed Coconut Snowballs
MAKES ABOUT 40

1	recipe Butter Cookie Dough (page 792), 1 teaspoon grated lime zest added with the dry ingredients and prepared through step 1
1	recipe Glaze, 2–3 tablespoons lime juice substituted for the milk
1½	cups sweetened shredded coconut, pulsed in a food processor until finely chopped, about fifteen 1-second pulses

Follow the illustrations on page 793.

SKINNING HAZELNUTS

Hazelnuts are covered with a dark brown skin that can be quite bitter. Toasting the nuts in a 350-degree oven until fragrant (about 15 minutes) improves their flavor and also causes the skins to blister and crack so they can be rubbed off. Here's how to accomplish this task.

1. Transfer the hot toasted nuts to the center of a clean kitchen towel.

2. Bring up the sides of the towel and twist it closed to seal in the nuts.

3. Rub the nuts together in the towel to scrape off as much of the brown skin as possible. It's fine if patches of skin remain.

4. Carefully open the towel on a flat surface. Gently roll the nuts away from the skins.

GINGERBREAD COOKIES

GINGERBREAD COOKIES ARE UBIQUITOUS AT holiday time—stuffed into stockings, propped up around candles to make centerpieces, and hung in windows and on Christmas trees. Only rarely, though, do gingerbread cookies appear on cookie trays, and when they do most people pass them by. People know from experience that gingerbread cookies, no matter how pretty they may be, are usually hard and dry. But this outcome is not inevitable. We have discovered that by using the right proportions of ingredients, it is possible to produce gingerbread cookies that are a pleasure to eat.

There are actually two types of gingerbread cookies. When you roll the dough thick and bake the cookies only briefly, you get soft, moist, gently chewy cookies—or at least that is what you want to end up with. If you roll the dough thin and bake the cookies somewhat longer, you get buttery-tasting, snapping-crisp cookies—a type of gingersnap, really. Thick gingerbread cookies are primarily suitable for the cookie tray. Thin gingerbread cookies also make delicious tray cookies, but, because they are sturdy and keep well, they are also the cookies you want to use to decorate the tree. In setting out to develop a perfect recipe for gingerbread cookies, we focused on the thick ones, which are more difficult to produce. In our experience, any dough that will make good thick gingerbread cookies can be adapted to make delicious thin ones.

A review of the recipes in contemporary cookbooks quickly revealed the root of the problem with most gingerbread cookies. Any experienced cookie baker knows that cookies made with less than four tablespoons of fat to a cup of flour will be dry. Yet many of the recipes we examined called for as little as two or three tablespoons of butter or shortening to a cup of flour. The writers of these recipes were not concerned with holiday waistlines. Rather, they wanted to make sure the dough would be firm enough to handle and then cut into intricate shapes. Fat makes dough soft. From the standpoint of convenience, the less fat in a gingerbread cookie dough, the better.

But what about taste? Surely there was a middle ground. After a little searching, we discovered several recipes that called for the requisite ¼ cup of fat to 1 cup of flour. We made one of these. The cookies turned out soft and fairly moist, but they were pale, bland, and generally uninteresting. After doing some thinking and calculating, we added 50 percent more brown sugar and molasses. The resulting cookies were delicious: flavorful, pleasantly sweet, and moist and chewy.

But they still were not perfect. Instead of rising flat and level, they looked a little bumpy. This would not be a problem if the cookies were presented plain, but any decorations would be marred by the cookies' uneven surface. We knew where the problem lay. The extra sugar we had added to the dough was absorbing too much of the available liquid. Sugar is hygroscopic; that is, it soaks up liquid. This is why very sugary cookies, such as wafers and tuiles, bake up so crisp and dry and also why the same cookies, unless very tightly covered, tend to go soft and tacky again after just a few days' keeping. The sugar absorbs moisture from the air. The extra sugar we had added to the dough was not quite sufficient to make the cookies hard and dry, thank goodness, but it was still having an effect.

By absorbing the liquid in the dough, the sugar, evidently, was preventing the formation of gluten, which develops when flour proteins are moistened and kneaded. Gluten creates a network of air spaces in dough that bakers refer to as structure. When doughs have a great deal of structure, they puff dramatically. When they have none, they do not puff at all. And when they have just a little, as was the case with our gingerbread cookies, they tend to puff a little but then deflate, the dough being too "weak" to hold its form after it has risen.

What we needed to do was make our gingerbread, which was close to becoming a crisp, flat cookie, slightly more akin to a cake. The obvious solution was to add a couple of tablespoons of

INGREDIENTS:
Fresh or Candied Ginger

People like to add crystallized and fresh ginger to gingerbread, and we were curious to know if there was any point in using either in gingerbread cookies. The answer is yes—but with qualifications.

Candied ginger gives gingerbread cookies a nice pungency without imparting a harsh bite. We found that a full half cup, or about 2½ ounces, was required to make a difference in flavor. The ginger must be ground very fine, or the dough will be difficult to cut into neat shapes. First, slice it into thin flakes with a knife. Then combine the ginger and the brown sugar called for in the recipe in the food processor and process until the ginger practically disappears, about two minutes. Add the remaining dry ingredients, process to blend, and proceed with the recipe. Do not decrease the ground ginger; the cookies will be bland if you do.

Fresh ginger proved to be more problematic. We really liked the lively, almost tingly flavor that it imparted, but we would not use it in thick gingerbread cookies that we intended to decorate. Perhaps because it is moister than candied ginger, fresh ginger makes thick gingerbread cookies puffy and wrinkly. (Thin gingerbread cookies made with fresh ginger looked fine, and their flavor was altered, though only marginally.) You will need a lot of ginger to make an impact—a good three ounces, or a piece roughly six inches long and one inch wide. Peel the ginger and grate it to a pulp. You should have ¼ cup of pulp. Add the pulp with the molasses to the batter and omit the milk. Again, do not decrease the amount of ground ginger.

Of course, the easiest way to make your gingerbread cookies more gingery is simply to add more ground ginger. If you want really hot, spicy gingerbread cookies, you will want to add a full ounce, or about a quarter cup.

milk. We feared, however, that the dough, already chock-full of butter, brown sugar, and molasses, would surely be too soft to handle if we tried to sneak in some liquid.

We tried the dough as before, with the full complement of all the good stuff, plus two table-spoons of milk. To our delight, the dough proved quite manageable when handled in the usual way—chilled, then rolled on a lightly floured surface—and downright obliging when rolled between sheets of parchment. And the cookies were perfect: smooth, even, and delightful to eat, whether rolled thick or thin.

To make the process of rolling out the cook-ies even easier, we also altered the usual mixing method. Most recipes for gingerbread cookies call for making the dough by creaming softened butter and sugar, then adding the dry and liquid ingredients, as if making a cake. When mixed in this manner, the dough is inevitably quite soft and must be refrigerated for several hours, even overnight, before being rolled and cut. We prefer instead to mix the dough in the food processor, first blending the dry ingredients, then cutting in slightly softened butter, and, finally, adding the molasses and other liquid ingredients, as if making a pie crust. When mixed in this way, the dough is firm enough to be used at once, though we prefer to roll it between sheets of parchment paper and then chill it briefly before cutting to make sure the cookies will maintain a perfect shape when transferred to the baking sheets. Even assuming that you do take the time to chill the dough before cutting, you will still save some time by using the food processor to mix the gingerbread—a welcome convenience during the hectic holiday season.

Thick and Chewy Gingerbread Cookies

MAKES ABOUT 20
GINGERBREAD PEOPLE OR 30 COOKIES

If you plan to decorate your gingerbread cookies and make ornaments out of them, follow the directions for Thin, Crisp Gingerbread Cookies on page 797. Because flour is not added during rolling, dough scraps can be rolled and cut as many times as necessary. Don't overbake the cook-ies, or they will be dry. Store soft gingerbread in a wide, shallow airtight container or tin with a sheet of parchment or waxed paper between the cookie layers. These cookies are best eaten within 1 week.

3	cups (15 ounces) unbleached all-purpose flour
3/4	cup packed (5 1/4 ounces) dark brown sugar
3/4	teaspoon baking soda
1	tablespoon ground cinnamon
1	tablespoon ground ginger
1/2	teaspoon ground cloves
1/2	teaspoon salt
12	tablespoons (1 1/2 sticks) unsalted butter, softened but still cool, cut into 12 pieces
3/4	cup light or dark molasses
2	tablespoons milk

1. In a food processor, process the flour, brown sugar, baking soda, cinnamon, ginger, cloves, and salt until combined, about 10 seconds. Scatter the butter pieces over the flour mixture and process until the mixture is sandy and resembles very fine meal, about 15 seconds. With the machine run-ning, gradually add the molasses and milk; process until the dough is evenly moistened and forms a soft mass, about 10 seconds. Alternatively, with an electric mixer, stir together the flour, brown sugar, baking soda, cinnamon, ginger, cloves, and salt at low speed until combined, about 30 seconds. Stop the mixer and add the butter pieces; mix at medium-low speed until the mixture is sandy and resembles fine meal, about 1½ minutes. Reduce the speed to low and, with the mixer running, gradually add the molasses and milk; mix until the dough is evenly moistened, about 20 seconds. Increase the speed to medium and mix until thor-oughly combined, about 10 seconds.

2. Scrape the dough onto a work surface; divide it in half. Working with one portion at a time, roll the dough ¼ inch thick between 2 large sheets of parchment paper. Leaving the dough sandwiched between the parchment, stack the dough on a bak-ing sheet and freeze until firm, 15 to 20 minutes. (Alternatively, refrigerate the dough for 2 hours or overnight.)

3. Adjust the oven racks to the upper- and lower-middle positions and heat the oven to 350 degrees. Line 2 baking sheets with parchment paper or spray them with nonstick cooking spray.

4. Remove 1 dough sheet from the freezer; place on the work surface. Peel off the top parchment sheet and gently lay it back in place. Flip the dough over; peel off and discard the second parchment sheet. Cut the dough into 5-inch gingerbread people or 3-inch gingerbread cookies, transferring the shapes to the prepared baking sheets with a wide metal spatula and spacing them ¾ inch apart; set the scraps aside. Repeat with the remaining dough until the baking sheets are full. Bake the cookies until set in the centers and the dough barely retains an imprint when touched very gently with a fingertip, 8 to 11 minutes, rotating the baking sheets front to back and switching positions top to bottom halfway through the baking time. Do not overbake. Cool the cookies on the sheets 2 minutes, then remove the cookies with a wide metal spatula to a wire rack; cool to room temperature.

5. Gather the scraps; repeat the rolling, cutting, and baking in steps 2 and 4.

➤ VARIATION
Thin, Crisp Gingerbread Cookies
MAKES ABOUT 34 GINGERBREAD PEOPLE OR 54 COOKIES

These gingersnap-like cookies are sturdy and therefore suitable for making ornaments. If you wish to thread the cookies, snip wooden skewers to ½-inch lengths and press them into the cookies just before they go into the oven; remove the skewers immediately after baking. Or use a drinking straw to punch holes in the cookies when they're just out of the oven and still soft. Store in an airtight container. In dry climates, the cookies should keep about a month.

Follow the recipe for Thick and Chewy Gingerbread Cookies, quartering rather than halving the dough, rolling each dough quarter ⅛ inch thick, reducing the oven temperature to 325 degrees, and baking the cookies until slightly darkened and firm in the center when pressed with a finger, 15 to 20 minutes.

HERMITS

THE HERMIT IS A COOKIE CERTAINLY WORTHY of its eccentric name. Depending on whom you ask, it can be a bar or drop cookie; soft and spongy or dry and biscuit-like; packed with dried fruit and nuts or free of both; and heavily seasoned with warm spices like ginger, cloves, and nutmeg or flavored only with molasses. Whatever the particular recipe, most sources trace the hermit's origin to colonial New England. The name is supposedly derived from the fact that the cookies were better after several days hidden away, which allowed the flavors to blend and intensify.

After a taste test that included cookies we baked in-house and commercially produced hermits from local and national bakeries, tasters agreed that an ideal hermit should have a texture in between a cake and a brownie—that is, it should be soft, moist, and dense. We decided that hermits should be studded with raisins and taste predominantly of molasses, but with warm spices lingering in the background. And tasters favored thick-sliced biscotti-like cookies over both bar and drop cookies because they had more crust than bar cookies and a softer crumb than either bar or drop cookies.

From the outset, we knew that attaining the right texture would be tricky. Most hermit recipes we tried relied on two eggs as well as some baking soda and baking powder for their rise. The result was a puffy cookie that was dry and too cakey for our taste. We found that omitting baking powder from the batter limited the cookies' spread and height, but they were still too loose-crumbed and fluffy. Leaving out one of the two eggs made them too dense, but we realized we were on the right track. In the next batch, we omitted the white of one of the eggs, and the resulting cookies were everything we wanted—soft and rich but with a slightly cakey crumb. The cakey crumb is the secret to their longevity. We enjoyed these cookies up to a week after baking them. And, as the story of how they got their name suggests, the flavors were better after a couple of days of storage.

For both sweetening and flavor, hermits depend on molasses. We tried mild, dark, and blackstrap molasses and found that most tasters favored mild, although some liked the stronger-flavored dark molasses. Molasses alone was not enough to fully sweeten the cookies, so we included light brown sugar. Dark brown pushed the bittersweet flavor of the molasses over the edge, while granulated sugar seemed a bit dull.

A healthy amount of raisins also helped sweeten the cookies and rounded out the flavors. Raisins also lent the cookies a pleasing toothsome quality that contrasted nicely with the crisp crust and soft crumb.

Since the hermit is a not-very-distant relation of the spice cookie, we felt it appropriate to borrow the spice mixture from our favorite molasses spice cookie (page 786) and revise it to best suit the hermits. We decided to keep the unlikely spice black pepper, which contributes a kick that heightens the piquancy of the other spices. Tasters agreed that it significantly improved the flavor of our hermits.

Hermits

MAKES ABOUT 16

It is important to wait until the cookies are completely cooled before dusting them with the confectioners' sugar; otherwise, the sugar can melt and turn gummy. We keep hermits around during the holidays because they store well and the flavors work well with both eggnog and mulled cider.

2	cups (10 ounces) unbleached all-purpose flour
1/2	teaspoon baking soda
1/2	teaspoon ground cinnamon
1/2	teaspoon ground cloves
1/4	teaspoon ground allspice
1/4	teaspoon ground ginger
1/8	teaspoon finely ground black pepper
1/2	teaspoon salt
8	tablespoons (1 stick) unsalted butter, melted and cooled
1/2	cup packed (3 1/2 ounces) light brown sugar
2	large eggs, 1 whole and 1 separated, white lightly beaten
1/2	cup light or dark molasses
1 1/2	cups raisins
2	tablespoons confectioners' sugar for dusting the cookies (optional)

1. Whisk the flour, baking soda, spices, pepper, and salt together in a medium bowl; set aside.

2. Whisk the melted butter and brown sugar together in another medium bowl until just combined. Add the whole egg, egg yolk, and molasses and whisk thoroughly. Using a rubber spatula, fold the dry ingredients into the molasses mixture until combined. Stir in the raisins. Cover the bowl with plastic wrap and refrigerate for at least 1 hour.

3. Adjust an oven rack to the middle position and heat the oven to 350 degrees. Line a baking

SHAPING HERMITS

1. Divide the dough in half and shape each half on a parchment-lined baking sheet into a log that measures 14 inches long, 2 inches across, and 2 inches high. The logs should be at least 4 inches apart because they will spread during baking.

2. Cool the baked logs (still on the pan) on a wire rack for 15 minutes. Using 2 wide metal spatulas, transfer the logs to a cutting board. With a sharp chef's knife or serrated bread knife, cut the logs crosswise into cookies about 2 inches wide.

sheet with parchment paper or spray it with nonstick cooking spray.

4. Using a rubber spatula, form the dough into two logs on the prepared baking sheet, as shown in illustration 1 on page 798. Brush the logs with the beaten egg white.

5. Bake until the tops of the logs have browned and spring back when touched, rotating the baking sheet front to back halfway through the baking time, 20 to 25 minutes. Set the sheet on a cooling rack and cool for 15 minutes. Using 2 wide metal spatulas, transfer the logs to a cutting board and follow the directions in illustration 2 on page 798 to slice. When the cookies have completely cooled, dust them with confectioners' sugar if desired.

BUTTERY SHORTBREAD

THICK, GOLDEN SHORTBREAD WEDGES, pierced by the tines of a fork and twinkling with fine sugar, are a tribute to Scottish frugality. A stout, plain, unfilled cookie, shortbread is sandy, sweet, and buttery-rich and crumbles easily. At the cookie's edge, the fine crumb opens slightly and goes tawny and crisp.

If this description sounds unfamiliar, that is because commercial shortbreads are too often stubbornly rigid (when a dough is too lean) or crumbly soft (when vegetable shortening edges out butter). Good homemade shortbread is a transcendent cookie, and its success depends on finesse and a keen eye for proportion.

Making our way through a host of shortbread recipes, we quickly came to the conclusion that an authentic shortbread should have but four ingredients: butter, sugar, flour, and salt. Shortbreads made with vanilla, cream, or eggs invariably signaled the work of an interloper, one that lured the shortbread down the tawdry path of sugar cookies.

Because shortbread recipes contain no liquid (other than the water in the butter), the means of transforming the four ingredients into a dough is paramount. Our first order of business, therefore, would be to develop a reliable mixing method. The creaming method—in which softened butter and sugar are beaten and the flour is folded in—is a standard butter cookie technique. It adapts nicely to shortbread: The butter becomes aerated, the sugar partially melts, and the flour folds in comfortably at the end. The shortbreads we made this way were fine-pored and fairly delicate.

The biscuit method, in which cold butter and dry ingredients are rubbed together with a pastry cutter or fingertips, is esteemed for delicate biscuits and scones. Even quicker is the food processor (cold butter and a whirring blade). Both the creaming and the biscuit methods, however, resulted in loose, feathery crumbs that required light kneading. Even after this extra step, the resulting shortbread was less than spectacular.

In the end, we chose an electric mixer, using chilled butter and a low speed, and reproduced the biscuit method by "rubbing" the butter into the dry ingredients without softening it unduly. Then, rather than manipulating the crumbs any further, we simply patted them into a disk and baked it. These shortbreads were the best of the lot—fine-pored, tender, and buttery.

Though shortbread cookies want some structure, their delicate texture calls for a softer, lower-protein flour. Among unbleached all-purpose flours, we prefer Pillsbury and Gold Medal, which have a moderate protein content of just above 10 percent. (Some all-purpose flours go above 11 percent.)

We were curious to see if a small percentage of rice flour or cornstarch might effect a more tender cookie (many Scottish recipes feature these). Because these starches have virtually no protein and so do not form gluten (the protein that gives structure to baked goods made with wheat flour), we hoped they would hold the shape of the dough, keep the crumb fine, and make the cookies even more tender. Replacing ¼ cup of the flour with an equal amount of either cornstarch or rice flour did the trick; it was just enough to make the shortbread meltingly tender but not too soft.

What would a baking recipe from Great Britain be without castor sugar? In American parlance, that is superfine sugar, and it was the clear winner in our tests. Regular granulated sugar produced cookies that were too coarse, and confectioners' sugar had a powdery, drying effect on the crumb. Two-thirds cup superfine sugar was ideal. As insignificant as

¼ teaspoon salt might seem, it is in many ways a crucial ingredient. The shortbread was flavor-deprived and one-dimensional without it.

Butter is definitely the key player here, giving shortbread its rich, nutty flavor and crumbly texture. We wanted to use as much as possible to add flavor and to help hold the dough together. Tests showed that two sticks were just right. Less butter produced doughs that fell apart easily and were slightly dry when baked. More butter made the shortbread lose its shape in the oven.

From the beginning, we had been taken with traditional round, free-form shortbread scored into portions and pierced with a fork. Baking shortbread in a cake pan made sense at first, but the better approach turned out to be using the pan to mold the dough and then unmolding it before baking. This produced a perfectly flat top and crisp, well-defined edges while avoiding the problem of having to unmold the delicate baked disk

and then turn it over to expose the fork pattern. The free-form dough also baked better around the edges than the dough baked in a pan.

Thinking shortbread should be a full ¾ inch thick, we began our baking tests using an 8-inch cake pan and a 300-degree oven. But even after as much as an hour and 15 minutes, the shortbread remained soft in the center. Reducing the oven temperature caused the cookies to lose definition; raising it made them too brown. When we traded in our 8-inch cake pan for a 9-inch, the slightly thinner shortbreads baked better in the middle, although the centers were still a bit underdone. To solve this problem, we tried stamping a small round of dough from the center with a biscuit cutter, returning the cutter to the center of the shortbread, and baking the stamped-out round to the side. This accomplished a number of things: The shortbread baked evenly without overbrowning, the metal cutter conducted heat to the center of

SHAPING SHORTBREAD

1. Turn half of the crumbs into a 9-inch parchment-lined cake pan and even lightly with your fingers. Press heavily with a second cake pan.

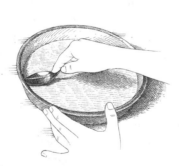

2. Add the remaining crumbs and press as in step 1. Working quickly, smooth the top of the dough with the back of a spoon.

3. Insert a paring knife between the dough and the pan. Leaving the knife stationary, rotate the pan counterclockwise to free the edges of the dough.

4. Unmold the dough onto a rimless or inverted baking sheet lined with parchment. Peel the parchment round from the dough; smooth the edges if necessary.

5. Place a 2-inch biscuit cutter in the center of the dough and cut out the center. Place the extruded round to the side, then return the biscuit cutter to the center.

6. After baking 20 minutes, score the top of the shortbread into 16 even wedges with a thin knife, then pierce a design with a skewer.

the dough, and we had one wayward cookie to eat right away before the larger disk had cooled.

We also noticed that the shortbread spread a bit in such a low oven, so we tried preheating the oven to 425 degrees to set the dough quickly and turning it down to 300 degrees as soon as the shortbread went in. One hour later, the shortbread was golden and done, and it had not spread.

In the course of testing, one is bound to pick up tips, some of which are simply flukes. Though we had been scoring the shortbread into 16 slender wedges and piercing them through before baking, on one occasion we forgot. When we pulled the shortbread out after 20 minutes to score and pierce it, the design was easier to execute and prettier than it had been in the raw dough. We also found that a wooden skewer did the piercing more neatly than a fork. (Though tests revealed that this design has no function beyond aesthetics, piercing is both attractive and traditional.) Shortbread is traditionally sprinkled with superfine sugar. The light dusting of sugar is best left until the shortbread comes out of the oven and best kept to a minimum. Early sprinkling mars the design, and too much sugar creates a pasty, suede-like surface. One tablespoon of sugar reserved from the original two-thirds cup was ideal. Finally, the shortbread cuts nicely right out of the oven.

Perhaps the best news is this: Shortbread improves with age (to a point). Taking far longer to cool than other cookies, shortbread left out on a rack the first night (another oversight) actually improved in texture. A week in a tin or even well covered on a plate will not dim its greatness.

Buttery Shortbread

MAKES 16 WEDGES

Rice flour can be found in some supermarkets and many natural food stores. If you are unable to find it locally, order it from The Baker's Catalogue: www.kingarthurflour.com. An equal amount of cornstarch may be substituted for the rice flour. Superfine sugar, if not available, can be made by processing granulated sugar in a food processor for about 30 seconds. When cutting the butter into cubes, work quickly so that the butter stays cold, and when molding the shortbread, form, press, and unmold it without delay. Be sure to use a plain round biscuit cutter to stamp out the center, not a fluted cutter.

1 3/4 cups (8 3/4 ounces) unbleached all-purpose flour, preferably lower-protein flour, such as Gold Medal or Pillsbury
1/4 cup (1 1/3 ounces) rice flour
2/3 cup (5 ounces) superfine sugar (see note)
1/4 teaspoon salt
16 tablespoons (2 sticks) cold unsalted butter

1. Adjust an oven rack to the middle position and heat the oven to 425 degrees. Line an ungreased 9-inch round cake pan with a round piece of parchment paper and line a large baking sheet with parchment paper; set both aside.

2. In the bowl of an electric mixer, mix the flours, all but 1 tablespoon of the sugar (reserve for sprinkling), and the salt at low speed until combined, about 5 seconds. Cut the butter into 1/2-inch cubes and toss with 1/4 cup of the flour mixture in a small bowl. Add the butter and any flour remaining to the flour mixture in the mixer bowl. Mix at low speed until the dough is pale yellow and resembles damp crumbs, about 4 minutes.

3. Remove the bowl from the mixer and toss the mixture lightly with your fingers to fluff it; rub any remaining butter bits into the flour mixture with your fingertips. Follow illustrations 1–5 on page 800 to form and unmold the shortbread onto the prepared baking sheet. Place the shortbread in the oven; immediately reduce the temperature to 300 degrees. Bake 20 minutes; remove the baking sheet from the oven and follow illustration 6 to score and pierce the shortbread. Return the shortbread to the oven and continue to bake until pale golden, about 40 minutes longer. Slide the parchment with the shortbread onto a cutting board, remove the biscuit cutter from the center, sprinkle the shortbread evenly with the reserved 1 tablespoon sugar, and cut at the scored marks into wedges. Slide the parchment with the shortbread onto a wire rack and cool to room temperature, at least 3 hours. (The shortbread can be wrapped well and stored at room temperature for up to 7 days.)

Tips for Better Cookies

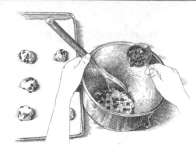

DISTRIBUTING GOODIES EVENLY IN THE DOUGH

The last few cookies from a batch of chocolate chip cookie dough never seem to have as many chips as the first few cookies. The same thing happens with nuts and raisins. You can avoid this problem by reserving some of the chips and other goodies and then mixing them into the dough after about half of it has been scooped out for cookies.

MEASURING OUT STICKY DOUGH

Some cookie dough can be so sticky that your hands become a mess in no time. To prevent this problem, use a small ice cream scoop to measure the dough. Dip the scoop into cold water between scoopings to ensure that the dough releases every time.

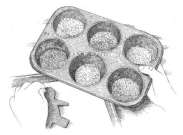

ORGANIZING COOKIE DECORATIONS

During the holiday season, you may be decorating cookies several times. Here's a good way to organize your favorite decorations. Place a different decoration in each cup of a muffin tin, which is easy to move around the kitchen and store for next time.

FREEZING DOUGH

Sometimes you don't want to bake a whole batch of cookie dough. Freezing individual balls of dough allows you to bake as many cookies as you like—even just 1 or 2—when a craving strikes. Best of all, you can enjoy warm cookies whenever you like.

1. Scoop out or roll individual balls of cookie dough and place them on a baking sheet lined with parchment or waxed paper. Place the baking sheet in the freezer for 1 to 2 hours, until the dough balls are completely frozen.

2. Once the dough balls are frozen hard, transfer them to a zipper-lock bag for storage in the freezer. There is no need to defrost the dough balls before baking them; just increase the baking time by 1 to 2 minutes.

DRYING FROSTED COOKIES

Finding space to let frosted cookies dry can be a challenge. Here's how to handle this task in a cramped kitchen.

Coat the rim of a small paper cup with frosting and invert it onto the middle of a paper plate. Arrange as many drying cookies around the cup as will fit comfortably on the plate. Dab the exposed rim of the cup with frosting, then make another plate in the same manner and stack it on top of the first. Repeat until you have a stack of 4 or 5 cookie-laden plates.

KEEPING COOKIES FRESH

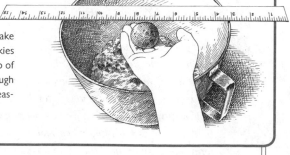

Decorative cookie jars are often not airtight, and cookies stored in them can become stale very quickly. To preserve the freshness of just-baked cookies, line the jar with a large plastic zipper-lock bag, place the cooled cookies inside the bag, and seal tightly.

EVENLY PORTIONING DOUGH

Cookies that are all the same size will bake at the same rate. To ensure that cookies are evenly portioned, set a ruler on top of your mixer bowl. Bring the ball of dough up alongside the ruler, where you can easily gauge the diameter.

BISCOTTI

DESPITE THEIR ELEGANT APPEARANCE, THE twice-baked Italian cookies known as biscotti are easy to make. A longer-than-average baking time yields a uniquely crunchy texture and also gives them an unusually long shelf life. Together, these factors make biscotti an excellent choice for home bakers. To find out how to make the very best biscotti, we decided to test and compare the dozens of traditional recipes that are out there. The results were surprising.

Most recipes have a fairly constant ratio of sugar to flour to flavorings. The major difference in the recipes is the type and quantity of fat used, which varied dramatically. It is this "fat factor," we discovered, that has the most dramatic effect on the taste, texture, and shelf life of the resulting biscotti.

There are three styles of biscotti, based on their fat content. The richest variety contains butter and eggs. The most traditional recipes contain whole eggs, sometimes supplemented by additional yolks, but no butter. The leanest biscotti contain just egg whites—no yolks or butter. We tested all three varieties and found differences in texture and taste.

In the matter of texture, we found that recipes containing butter produced satisfyingly crunchy biscuits that were nonetheless somewhat softer and richer—more cookie-like—than those not containing butter. We also discovered that recipes using whole eggs only, without additional yolks, were noticeably less cake-like, with a more straightforward crunch. (Biscotti with whole eggs and additional yolks were more like those with butter.) On the other end of the scale, the biscotti made with egg whites only—no butter or yolks—produced the driest and crispest cookies, reminiscent of hard candy. In fact, these cookies were so hard that they might present the risk of cracking a tooth if eaten without being dunked in milk or coffee first. We liked biscotti made with butter and with whole eggs but rejected those made with just whites.

In the matter of taste, the fresh-baked biscotti containing butter provided a superior and irresistibly rich flavor. On the other hand, the biscotti made with whole eggs but no additional yolks or butter resulted in the cleanest delivery of the flavorings in these cookies. Because both styles of biscotti had their merits, we decided to include recipes for both.

We found that storage and shelf life were also directly affected by fat content. As we experimented with different doughs, we noticed that recipes using butter initially had the best taste and texture but lost their full flavor and satisfying crunch after only one day, as the butter baked into the cookies began to go stale. Recipes with eggs but no butter held up better in both categories as the days went by. They seemed to get even better with time; they tasted great and remained very crisp after a week, and if stored properly, they kept for several weeks.

Whatever the amount and type of fat they contain, all biscotti recipes share the common characteristics of quick preparation time and a relatively long baking time. For most recipes, preparation involves simply mixing the wet ingredients with a whisk in one bowl, whisking the dry ingredients together in another bowl, and then folding the dry into the wet, along with flavorings. Because they are baked twice, however, the total baking time for biscotti is longer than for regular cookies; first they are baked in flat loaves for 30 to 40 minutes, then they are sliced and baked again for an additional 10 to 15 minutes. This double-baking technique ensures a very low moisture content, contributing enormously to this cookie's great potential for storage.

Biscotti's plain dough adapts beautifully to literally dozens of flavor combinations. Citrus fruit zests such as lemon and orange and dry spices such as cinnamon, cloves, and ginger work well in the dough. Likewise, dried and candied fruits and nuts such as walnuts, hazelnuts, almonds, pistachios, and sesame seeds not only lend biscotti flavor and texture but contribute to their appearance as well.

The batter may at first appear rather sticky, but resist the urge to dust with flour: Too much and the biscotti will become heavy and dense. It is preferable to use a rubber spatula, waxed paper, or plastic wrap if you have trouble handling the dough. One final note: Biscotti must be completely cooled before storage to ensure that all the moisture has escaped.

Lemon-Anise Biscotti
MAKES ABOUT 42

Anise seed, which lends these biscotti their licorice-like flavor, is found in the spice section of most supermarkets (fennel seed is an acceptable substitute). A Sicilian specialty, this recipe (without butter) produces a relatively hard biscuit—perfect with an afternoon cup of coffee. The cookies are also delicious dunked in a glass of sherry, Marsala, or Vin Santo. See the illustrations on page 805 for tips on shaping and cutting biscotti dough.

2	cups (10 ounces) unbleached all-purpose flour
I	teaspoon baking powder
1/4	teaspoon salt
I	cup (7 ounces) sugar
2	large eggs
1/4	teaspoon vanilla extract
I	tablespoon minced zest from I lemon
I	tablespoon anise seed

1. Adjust an oven rack to the middle position and heat the oven to 350 degrees. Line a large baking sheet with parchment paper or spray it with nonstick cooking spray. Whisk the flour, baking powder, and salt together in a medium bowl; set aside.

2. Whisk the sugar and eggs in a large bowl to a light lemon color; stir in the vanilla, lemon zest, and anise seed. Sprinkle the dry ingredients over the egg mixture, then fold in until the dough is just combined.

3. Halve the dough and turn both portions onto the prepared baking sheet. Using floured hands, quickly stretch each portion of dough into a rough 13 by 2-inch loaf. Place the loaves about 3 inches apart on the baking sheet; pat each one smooth. Bake until the loaves are golden and just beginning to crack on top, about 35 minutes, rotating the pan halfway through the baking time. Remove the baking sheet from the oven and place it on a wire rack.

4. Cool the loaves for 10 minutes; lower the oven temperature to 325 degrees. Use a wide metal spatula to transfer the loaves to a cutting board. With a serrated knife, cut each loaf diagonally into ⅜-inch-thick slices. Lay the slices about ½ inch apart on the baking sheet, cut-side up, and return them to the oven. Bake, turning over each cookie halfway through baking, until crisp and golden brown on both sides, about 15 minutes. Transfer the biscotti to a wire rack and cool completely. (The biscotti can be stored in an airtight container for up to 1 month.)

Spiced Biscotti
MAKES ABOUT 54

If you like, macerate ¾ cup currants, chopped raisins, or dates in ¼ cup brandy or Marsala for about 1 hour. Drain and fold into the dough in step 2, adding a teaspoon or so of the macerating liquid. This recipe contains additional yolks and is a bit richer than the preceding biscotti. See the illustrations on page 805 for tips on shaping and cutting biscotti dough.

2¼	cups (11¼ ounces) unbleached all-purpose flour
I	teaspoon baking powder
½	teaspoon baking soda
1/4	teaspoon ground white or black pepper
½	teaspoon ground cloves
½	teaspoon ground cinnamon
1/4	teaspoon ground ginger
1/4	teaspoon salt
I	cup (7 ounces) sugar
2	large eggs, plus 2 large egg yolks
½	teaspoon vanilla extract

1. Adjust an oven rack to the middle position and heat the oven to 350 degrees. Line a large baking sheet with parchment paper or spray it with nonstick cooking spray. Whisk the flour, baking powder, baking soda, spices, and salt together in a medium bowl; set aside.

2. Whisk the sugar, eggs, and yolks in a large bowl to a light lemon color; stir in the vanilla extract. Sprinkle the dry ingredients over the egg mixture, then fold in until the dough is just combined.

3. Halve the dough and turn each portion onto the prepared baking sheet. Using floured hands, quickly stretch each portion of dough into a rough 13 by 2-inch loaf. Place the loaves about 3 inches apart on the baking sheet; pat each one smooth.

Bake until the loaves are golden and just beginning to crack on top, about 35 minutes, rotating the pan halfway through the baking time. Remove the baking sheet from the oven and place it on a wire rack.

4. Cool the loaves for 10 minutes; lower the oven temperature to 325 degrees. Use a wide metal spatula to transfer the loaves to a cutting board. With a serrated knife, cut each loaf diagonally into ⅜-inch-thick slices. Lay the slices about ½ inch apart on the baking sheet, cut-side up, and return them to the oven. Bake, turning over each cookie halfway through baking, until crisp and golden brown on both sides, about 15 minutes. Transfer the biscotti to a wire rack and cool completely. (The biscotti can be stored in an airtight container for up to 1 month.)

Orange-Almond Biscotti

MAKES ABOUT 42

The addition of a small amount of butter produces a richer, more cookie-like texture. Although they will keep for 2 weeks in an airtight container, these biscotti are best eaten the same day they are baked. You can substitute toasted hazelnuts for the almonds in this recipe. A combination of hazelnuts and almonds also works well. See the illustrations below for tips on shaping and cutting biscotti dough.

2	cups (10 ounces) unbleached all-purpose flour
1	teaspoon baking powder
¼	teaspoon salt
4	tablespoons (½ stick) unsalted butter, softened but still cool
1	cup (7 ounces) sugar
2	large eggs
½	teaspoon vanilla extract
¼	teaspoon almond extract
¾	cup whole almonds with skins, toasted, cooled, and chopped coarse
2	tablespoons minced zest from 1 orange

1. Adjust an oven rack to the middle position and heat the oven to 350 degrees. Line a large baking sheet with parchment paper or spray it with nonstick cooking spray. Whisk the flour, baking powder, and salt together in a medium bowl; set aside.

2. By hand or with an electric mixer, cream the butter and sugar until light and smooth, about 2 minutes. Beat in the eggs, one at a time, then the extracts. Stir in the almonds and zest. Sprinkle the dry ingredients over the egg mixture, then fold in until the dough is just mixed.

3. Halve the dough and turn both portions onto the prepared baking sheet. Using floured hands, quickly stretch each portion of dough into a rough 13 by 2-inch loaf. Place the loaves about 3 inches apart on the baking sheet; pat each one smooth. Bake until the loaves are golden and just beginning to crack on top, about 35 minutes, rotating the pan halfway through the baking time. Remove

MAKING BISCOTTI

1. Divide the dough in half. Using floured hands, quickly stretch each portion of dough into a rough 13 by 2-inch loaf. Place the loaves about 3 inches apart on the baking sheet; pat each one smooth.

2. Bake the dough loaves for 35 minutes at 350 degrees, remove them from the oven, and cool for 10 minutes. With a serrated knife, cut each loaf on the diagonal into ⅜-inch-thick slices.

3. Lay the slices about ½ inch apart on the baking sheet, cut-side up, and return them to a 325-degree oven. Bake, turning once, until crisp, about 15 minutes.

the baking sheet from the oven and place it on a wire rack.

4. Cool the loaves for 10 minutes; lower the oven temperature to 325 degrees. Use a wide metal spatula to transfer the loaves to a cutting board. With a serrated knife, cut each loaf diagonally into ⅜-inch-thick slices. Lay the slices about ½ inch apart on the baking sheet, cut-side up, and return them to the oven. Bake, turning over each cookie halfway through baking, until crisp and golden brown on both sides, about 15 minutes. Transfer the biscotti to a wire rack and cool completely. (The biscotti can be stored in an airtight container for up to 2 weeks.)

COCONUT MACAROONS

WHEN WE BEGAN LOOKING AT RECIPES FOR modern coconut macaroons, we found many versions. In addition to different kinds of coconut and sweeteners, they often called for one or more of a wide range of ingredients, including extracts such as vanilla or almond, salt, flour, sugar, sweetened condensed milk, and even an egg or two in extreme variations. When tested, we found that most were lackluster mounds of beaten egg whites and coconut shreds or, at their worst, nothing more than a baked mixture of condensed milk and sweetened coconut. We were sure that somewhere among these second-rate cookies was a great coconut macaroon waiting to be found, with a pleasing texture and real, honest coconut flavor.

The initial recipe testing included five recipes. What came out of the oven that day ranged from dense, wet cookies to light, if not dry, mounds of coconut. In the former category were recipes that used unbeaten egg whites mixed with sweetened coconut and sugar. (One of them, a Brazilian macaroon, included whole eggs and produced a gooey, cavity-inducing cookie with a strong caramel flavor but nary a hint of coconut.) A recipe calling for beaten egg whites resulted in a light, airy, meringue-style cookie, pleasantly delicate but totally lacking in coconut flavor or chew. The test winners were simple enough: unbeaten egg whites mixed with sugar, unsweetened coconut, salt, and

vanilla. But even these lacked coconut flavor and were a bit on the dry side, not sufficiently chewy or moist. We set out to find a happy medium among our test recipes.

Our testing had shown us that the choice of sweetened versus unsweetened coconut had a major effect on texture. The unsweetened variety resulted in a less sticky, more appealing texture, but it made the cookies just a bit too dry. Flour—we tried both cake and all-purpose—was helpful in eliminating the stickiness of cookies made entirely with sweetened coconut, but it also made the cookies a bit too dense. Looking for a way past this roadblock, we decided to test a combination of sweetened and unsweetened coconut. This worked very well, giving the cookies a somewhat more luxurious texture without making them wet or heavy.

We also found, to our surprise, that the sweetened coconut had more flavor than the unsweetened, so the coconut flavor was turned up a notch. A scientist who works with the Baker's brand of coconut, which is sweetened and flaked, explained this phenomenon. He said that fresh coconut is 53 percent moisture; unsweetened dried coconut is 3 to 5 percent moisture; and sweetened and flaked coconut (which is dried before being flaked and then rehydrated) is 9 to 25 percent moisture. Coconuts are mostly fat and not very sweet, so they are rather tasteless when dried, unlike sweet fruits such as apples or apricots. Hydrating dried coconut, therefore, adds flavor, as does the addition of sugar. Although one could add both more moisture and more sweetness to a macaroon batter and then use unsweetened dried coconut, the coconut itself would still be less flavorful than sweetened coconut flakes.

Another key issue was the ratio of coconut to unbeaten egg whites. Too little egg white to coconut and our cookies turned out dry and crumbly. Too much and the cookies were heavy and dense. Finally, we settled on 6 cups coconut to 4 egg whites.

To add still a bit more moisture to the cookies, we tried using corn syrup instead of sugar as a sweetener and found that the cookies were slightly more moist, held together a bit better, and were pleasantly chewy. Melted butter was tried but discarded since it masked the flavor of the coconut, as did sweetened condensed milk.

We still felt that the cookies were a bit light in coconut flavor. To remedy this, we tried adding cream of coconut, and we hit the jackpot. The coconut flavor was superior to that of any of the cookies we had made to date. Finally, we had a coconut macaroon with real coconut flavor. (Since cream of coconut is sweetened, we did have to decrease the amount of corn syrup.) Putting these cookies together is easy: no need even to whip the egg whites. The liquid ingredients are whisked together, the dry ingredients are mixed, and then the two are combined. We found it best to refrigerate this dough for 15 minutes to make it easier to work with, but in a pinch you can skip this step. In an effort to produce a nicely browned, crisp exterior, we experimented with oven temperatures and finally settled on 375 degrees; the bottoms tended to overcook at 400 degrees, and lower temperatures never produced the sort of browning we were after.

SHAPING COCONUT MACAROONS

1. Using your fingers, form the cookies into loose haystacks. Moisten your fingers with water if needed to prevent sticking.

2. If desired, dip the bottom half inch of the baked cookies into melted chocolate, tapping off excess chocolate with your finger.

Most of our test cooks prefer a slightly dainty confection, so our final recipe calls for a smaller cookie—not the two-fisted size you often see in bakeries and delis. We also found that these cookies are great when the bottom third is dipped in chocolate. Since the cookie is not overly sweet, the chocolate is a nice complement, not a case of gilding the lily.

Coconut Macaroons
MAKES ABOUT 48

Cream of coconut, available canned, is sweetened coconut juice, commonly used in piña colada cocktails. Be sure to mix the can's contents thoroughly before using since the mixture separates upon standing. Unsweetened shredded coconut is commonly sold in natural food stores or Asian markets. If you are unable to find any, use all sweetened flaked or shredded coconut, but reduce the amount of cream of coconut to ½ cup, omit the corn syrup, and toss 2 tablespoons cake flour into the coconut before adding the liquid ingredients. For larger macaroons, shape haystacks from generous quarter cups of batter and up the baking time to 20 minutes.

1	cup cream of coconut
2	tablespoons light corn syrup
4	large egg whites
2	teaspoons vanilla extract
½	teaspoon salt
3	cups unsweetened shredded coconut
3	cups sweetened flaked or shredded coconut

1. Adjust the oven racks to the upper- and lower-middle positions and heat the oven to 375 degrees. Line 2 baking sheets with parchment paper and lightly spray the parchment with non-stick cooking spray.

2. Whisk together the cream of coconut, corn syrup, egg whites, vanilla, and salt in a small bowl; set aside. Combine the unsweetened and sweetened coconut in a large bowl; toss together, breaking up clumps with your fingertips. Pour the liquid ingredients into the coconut and mix with a rubber spatula until evenly moistened.

3. Drop heaping tablespoons of the batter onto

the prepared sheets, spacing them about 1 inch apart. Form the cookies into loose haystacks with your fingertips, moistening your hands with water as necessary to prevent sticking. Bake until the cookies are light golden brown, about 15 minutes, rotating the baking sheets front to back and top to bottom halfway through the baking time.

4. Cool the cookies on the baking sheets until slightly set, about 2 minutes; remove to a wire rack with a wide metal spatula.

➤ VARIATION
Chocolate-Dipped Coconut Macaroons
The two-stage melting process for the chocolate helps ensure that it is the proper consistency for dipping the cookies.

Follow the recipe for Coconut Macaroons. Cool the baked macaroons to room temperature, about 30 minutes. Line 2 baking sheets with parchment paper. Chop 10 ounces semisweet chocolate; melt 8 ounces in a small heatproof bowl set over a pan of almost-simmering water, stirring once or twice, until smooth. (To melt the chocolate in a microwave, heat at 50 percent power for 3 minutes and stir. If the chocolate is not yet entirely melted, heat an additional 30 seconds at 50 percent power.) Remove from the heat; stir in the remaining 2 ounces chocolate until smooth. Holding a macaroon by its pointed top, dip the bottom and ½ inch up the sides in the chocolate; scrape off the excess chocolate with your finger and place the macaroon on a prepared baking sheet. Repeat with the remaining macaroons. Refrigerate the macaroons until the chocolate sets, about 15 minutes.

CLASSIC BROWNIES

THESE DAYS, IF YOU GO TO A BAKERY AND ORDER a brownie, chances are you'll end up with a heavy chunk of pure confection. While there's no denying that such brownies are sumptuous, they are also overwhelming. Such brownies are fine as infrequent treats, but many of us can look back to a time when the brownie was a much simpler affair, more chocolate bar cookie than chocolate truffle, more bake sale than upscale café.

Our initial recipe testing was not a success. Either pale and dry or cloyingly sweet, all of the brownies we baked lacked substantial chocolate flavor. We wanted an old-fashioned brownie, but we also wanted serious chocolate flavor.

Before we embarked on a long course of testing, however, there was one thing about all of the research recipes that we knew we wanted to change: the size. The recipes called for baking the brownies in skimpy 8-inch square pans. We wanted big brownies, and a lot of them, so a 13 by 9-inch baking pan was the size of choice. We then constructed a master recipe with 4 ounces of unsweetened chocolate, 2 sticks of butter, 2 cups of sugar, 4 eggs, and 1¼ cups of all-purpose flour.

Our working recipe yielded brownies that were dense and a bit greasy. Cutting back on the butter seemed like an obvious way to make them less greasy. Going from 2 sticks to 1½ sticks did the trick, but it also produced an unanticipated side effect—an unpleasantly gritty texture. We suspected that the source of the problem might be in the starch in the recipe, not just from the all-purpose flour we'd been using but from the chocolate, which also contains starch. Not wanting to alter the amount of chocolate (our brownies needed more chocolate flavor, not less), we decreased the flour. The brownies were still too gritty. Next we tried substituting cake flour for the entire amount of all-purpose flour. This solved the problem, producing nicely tender brownies. (Cake flour is milled from softer wheat than all-purpose flour and contributes less protein, or gluten, to a recipe. The result is a finer-textured product, which, in the case of these brownies, was preferred.) Here was our first big revelation: Cake flour makes tender brownies with a delicate chew.

Though tender, the brownies were still too compact. We thought an extra egg might provide more structure, but it made the brownies too cakey. Maybe baking powder would lighten the crumb. Well, too much baking powder produced a dry and cakey brownie, but a modest ¾ teaspoon was just right. The texture of the brownies was now nearly perfect, right in the middle between cakey and fudgy.

Sugar was the next ingredient subject to scrutiny. Tasters found the flavor of light and dark brown sugars to be a distraction from the chocolate. Granulated sugar was the best choice.

Our brownies now had the right texture—neither fudgy nor cakey, with a tender chew—but the flavor was a bit insipid. Although we didn't want the decadent texture of fudgy brownies, we did appreciate their assertive chocolate flavor. Often these recipes call for a mix of different chocolates, and they sometimes even add cocoa powder. In search of a similar chocolate intensity, we added

BEST BROWNIES: DEVELOPING A BROWNIE TO PLEASE EVERYONE

Seemingly minor changes in brownie recipes can yield quite different results.

TOO CAKEY

This recipe called for creaming the butter and sugar and for lots of baking powder, yielding brownies with a fluffy, cakey texture.

TOO FUDGY

This recipe called for a lot of chocolate and no baking powder and produced a confection-like brownie that was extremely rich and dense.

JUST RIGHT

With a moderate amount of chocolate and a little baking powder, our brownie has good flavor and a moist texture that is neither cakey nor fudgy.

a little high-quality bittersweet chocolate to the unsweetened chocolate in our working recipe. These brownies were too sweet, too greasy, and too heavy. When we cut back on the sugar, the brownies were less sweet, but they remained heavy and soggy. In addition, tasters felt that the flavor was more reminiscent of milk chocolate (that is, very mild) than bittersweet chocolate. When we used considerably more bittersweet chocolate, the flavor was more intense, but the texture was now decidedly confection-like. Ounce for ounce, unsweetened chocolate has more chocolate flavor than bittersweet or semisweet chocolate (which are both one third to one half sugar). To get enough flavor from these chocolates, you have to use a lot, and that made the brownies fudgy and rich—exactly what we did not want.

We wondered what would happen if we increased the amount of unsweetened chocolate in our working recipe. Using 6 ounces of unsweetened chocolate (rather than 4 ounces) gave us the desired flavor we were after—not too sweet, with profound chocolate notes. We also found that generous amounts of salt and vanilla were needed to enhance the chocolate flavor and give the brownies more depth.

As simple as they are to mix up, these brownies need to be baked just right to guarantee the perfect texture. An oven temperature of 325 degrees baked them through without drying the edges, a problem when the oven temperature was higher. Close attention near the end of the baking time proved beneficial as well. Underbaking by just a couple of minutes resulted in a gummy (undercooked) center, and overbaking quickly dried them out. Because home ovens are notoriously fickle and poorly calibrated, the baking times in this recipe should be used only as a general guide.

When we mixed nuts into the batter before baking the brownies, they steamed and became soft. Sprinkling the nuts on top just before baking kept the nuts dry and crunchy; toasting them first made them even crunchier while also enhancing their flavor. That said, we decided to make the nuts—not everyone's preference in brownies—optional.

Classic Brownies

MAKES 24

Be sure to test for doneness before removing the brownies from the oven. If underbaked (the toothpick has batter clinging to it), the texture of the brownies will be dense and gummy; if overbaked (the toothpick comes out completely clean), the brownies will be dry and cakey.

1	cup pecans or walnuts, chopped medium (optional)
1¼	cups (5 ounces) plain cake flour
½	teaspoon salt
¾	teaspoon baking powder
6	ounces unsweetened chocolate, chopped fine
12	tablespoons (1½ sticks) unsalted butter, cut into six pieces
2¼	cups (15¾ ounces) sugar
4	large eggs
1	tablespoon vanilla extract

1. Adjust an oven rack to the middle position; heat the oven to 325 degrees. Spray a 13 by 9-inch baking pan with nonstick cooking spray. Fold an 18-inch length of foil or parchment paper lengthwise to measure 8 inches wide. Cut a second sheet of foil to a 14-inch length. Following the illustration to the right, fit the longer sheet lengthwise across the bottom of the greased pan, pushing it into the corners and up the sides of the pan (the overhang will help in removal of the baked brownies). Fit the second sheet in the pan in the same manner, perpendicular to the first sheet. Spray the sheets with nonstick cooking spray.

2. If using nuts, spread the nuts evenly on a rimmed baking sheet and toast in the oven until fragrant, 5 to 8 minutes. Set aside to cool.

3. In a medium bowl, whisk the flour, salt, and baking powder together until combined; set aside.

4. Melt the chocolate and butter in a large heatproof bowl set over a saucepan of almost-simmering water, stirring occasionally, until smooth. (Alternatively, in a microwave, heat the butter and chocolate in a large microwave-safe bowl on high for 45 seconds, then stir and heat for 30 seconds more. Stir again, and, if necessary, repeat in 15-second increments; do not let the chocolate burn.) When the chocolate mixture is completely smooth, remove the bowl from the saucepan and gradually whisk in the sugar. Add the eggs, one at a time, whisking after each addition until thoroughly combined. Whisk in the vanilla. Add the flour mixture in 3 additions, folding with a rubber spatula until the batter is completely smooth and homogeneous.

5. Transfer the batter to the prepared pan; using a spatula, spread the batter into the corners of the pan and smooth the surface. Sprinkle the toasted nuts (if using) evenly over the batter. Bake until a toothpick or wooden skewer inserted into the center of the brownies comes out with a few moist crumbs attached, 30 to 35 minutes. Cool on a wire rack to room temperature, about 2 hours, then remove the brownies from the pan by lifting them out using the foil overhangs. Cut the brownies into 2-inch squares and serve. (Store leftovers in an airtight container at room temperature for up to 3 days.)

REMOVING BROWNIES AND BAR COOKIES FROM THE PAN

1. Place two sheets of aluminum foil (or parchment paper) perpendicular to each other in the pan, pushing the foil (or paper) into the corners.

2. After the brownies or bars have baked and cooled, use the foil (or paper) to transfer them to a cutting board, then slice into individual portions.

CREAM CHEESE BROWNIES

FOR MANY DESSERT LOVERS, NOTHING COULD be better than a rich, fudgy brownie with generous dollops of cheesecake baked inside. The ideal cream cheese brownie should be distinctly a brownie, but with a swirl of cream cheese filling in every bite. We wanted the brownie portion of the bar to have a rich, soft texture that would complement the lush cream cheese filling, yet at the same time contrast its soft interior with a thin, crisp (but not overbaked) crust. These brownies would taste intensely of chocolate, with a tangy filling that could hold its own against such a dominant partner.

We nixed the idea of adding a cream cheese filling to a super-rich fudge brownie, as it would have been gilding the lily. We turned to a more basic brownie recipe for thin, moist squares, with a good chocolate flavor and a fine, tender crumb. Adding cream cheese batter to the equation, however, turned the chief assets of these brownies into liabilities. When paired with dense, tangy cream cheese, the brownies' fine cake-flour crumb did not provide enough structure to suspend the filling; their otherwise pleasant chocolate flavor lacked intensity; and, finally, the amount of batter did not produce a tall enough bar for cream cheese brownies. To make this brownie batter more suitable for its cream cheese partner, we needed to strengthen its structure, infuse it with more chocolate flavor, and give it a bit more height.

To this end, we increased our brownie recipe by half (for added height), used all-purpose flour instead of cake flour (for strengthened structure), and threw in an extra ounce of unsweetened chocolate (for a more intense chocolate flavor). Baking the increased amount of batter in the same size pan solved the height problem. The extra height, however, accentuated the brownie's cakey qualities. Desiring a denser, softer texture, we made the brownies again, this time returning the flour and baking powder to the original amounts but leaving the eggs and vanilla at the increased quantities. This equation created a dense but relatively dry brownie. The increased amount of unsweetened chocolate, while making the brownie more

intensely flavored, also caused it to taste bitter.

From previous chocolate experiments, we deduced that the unsweetened chocolate might be at the root of our harsh, bitter brownies. We made three pans of brownies: one with all unsweetened chocolate, another with all bittersweet chocolate, and a third with a combination of the two, adjusting the sugar as necessary. The brownies made with unsweetened chocolate alone were dry and crumbly, with a slightly bitter finish. On the other hand, the brownies created with all bittersweet chocolate were too soft and gooey. A combination of unsweetened and bittersweet chocolate corrected the texture and flavor deficiencies and delivered a perfect cream cheese brownie base—intensely chocolate, soft, lush, with just a hint of structure.

What's the reason behind this unusual result? Unlike unsweetened chocolate, bittersweet chocolate (or semisweet chocolate, which can be used interchangeably with bittersweet) contains lecithin, an emulsifier that is responsible for chocolate's creamy mouthfeel. It makes sense that these smoother, creamier sweetened varieties would bake into gooier, chewier brownies. Because unsweetened chocolate contains no lecithin, brownies made with this ingredient tend to be drier and more crumbly.

Second, during the manufacture of sweetened chocolates, sugar and chocolate are heated together so that the sugar dissolves and the cocoa butter melts, bonding the two together. Unsweetened chocolate contains no sugar, so larger quantities of granulated sugar must be mixed with the chocolate just before baking. These undissolved sugar granules remain distinct and separate in the batter. Sugar is hygroscopic (that is, it readily takes up and retains moisture), which causes the undissolved granules to absorb moisture during baking, resulting in a drier, more crumbly brownie. Because brownies are so rich in chocolate, the types of chocolate used in the cream cheese brownie batter create dramatic differences in the recipe.

Fortunately, the cream cheese filling was much simpler to develop than the brownie batter. We were looking for an intensely flavored filling, but we found that other common cheesecake ingredients like sour cream, butter, and cream simply diluted the intense cream cheese flavor we were after. As it turned out, we only needed to add an egg yolk, a quarter cup of sugar, and a couple of drops of vanilla extract to an 8-ounce package of cream cheese to achieve the flavor and texture we were seeking.

To determine the best way to incorporate the filling into the batter, we experimented with four options: First we spread a thin layer of cream cheese filling between two layers of brownie batter. Next we sandwiched dollops of the cream cheese filling between the two layers of brownie batter. Then we sandwiched dollops of the cream cheese filling between two layers of brownie batter and swirled them with a knife. Finally, we alternated two layers of brownie batter with two layers of cream cheese dollops that we then swirled with a knife. The final technique—which created a visible swirl of light on dark and evenly distributed the filling throughout the brownies—was the winner.

This ultra-thick brownie, with its delicate filling, needed to be baked at a relatively low oven temperature. Brownies baked at 350 degrees burned at the edges, requiring the crusts to be trimmed, or turned out hard and inedible. At 325 degrees, however, the problem was solved. By putting a foil sling coated with cooking spray in the bottom of the pan before we added the batter, we were able to remove the brownies from the pan almost immediately after baking, which made cooling, cutting, and serving the brownies a breeze.

Cream Cheese Brownies

MAKES 16

Knowing when to remove a pan of brownies from the oven is the only difficult part about baking them. If you wait until an inserted toothpick comes out clean, the brownies are overcooked. But if a toothpick inserted in the middle of the pan comes out with fudgy crumbs, remove the pan immediately.

BROWNIE BASE

2/3   cup (3 1/3 ounces) unbleached all-purpose flour

1/4   teaspoon salt

1/2   teaspoon baking powder

2   ounces unsweetened chocolate, chopped

4   ounces bittersweet or semisweet chocolate, chopped

8   tablespoons (1 stick) unsalted butter, cut into quarters

1   cup (7 ounces) sugar

2   teaspoons vanilla extract

3   large eggs

CREAM CHEESE FILLING

8   ounces cream cheese, at room temperature

1/4   cup (1 3/4 ounces) sugar

1/2   teaspoon vanilla extract

1   egg yolk

1. FOR THE BROWNIE BASE: Adjust an oven rack to the lower-middle position and heat the oven to 325 degrees. Spray an 8-inch square baking pan with nonstick cooking spray. Fold two 16-inch pieces of foil or parchment paper lengthwise to measure 8 inches wide. Following the illustration on page 810, fit one sheet in the bottom of the greased pan, pushing it into the corners and up the sides of the pan (the overhang will help in removal of the baked brownies). Fit the second sheet in the pan in the same manner, perpendicular to the first sheet. Spray the sheets with nonstick cooking spray. Whisk the flour, salt, and baking powder together in a small bowl; set aside.

2. In a medium heatproof bowl set over a pan of almost-simmering water, melt the chocolates and butter, stirring occasionally until the mixture is smooth. Remove the melted chocolate mixture from the heat; whisk in the sugar and vanilla; cool slightly. Whisk in the eggs, one at a time, fully incorporating each before adding the next. Continue whisking until the mixture is completely smooth. Add the dry ingredients; whisk until just incorporated.

3. FOR THE CREAM CHEESE FILLING: In a small bowl, beat the cream cheese with the sugar, vanilla, and egg yolk until evenly blended.

4. Pour half the brownie batter into the prepared pan. Drop half the cream cheese mixture, by spoonfuls, over the batter. Repeat, layering the remaining brownie batter and cream cheese filling. Use the blade of a table knife or a spoon handle to

gently swirl the brownie batter and cream cheese filling, creating a marbled effect.

5. Bake until the edges of the brownies have puffed slightly, the center feels not quite firm when touched lightly, and a toothpick or cake tester inserted into the center comes out with several moist, fudgy crumbs adhering to it, 50 to 60 minutes.

6. Cool the brownies in a pan on a wire rack for 5 minutes. Remove the brownies from the pan using the foil or parchment handles. Place the brownies on a wire rack; allow them to cool to room temperature. Refrigerate until chilled, at least 3 hours. (To hasten cooling, place the brownies in the freezer for about 1½ hours.) Cut into 2-inch squares and serve. (To keep them from drying out, do not cut the brownies until ready to serve. The brownies can be wrapped, uncut, in plastic wrap, then foil, and refrigerated for up to 5 days.)

BLONDIES

BLONDIES ARE FIRST COUSINS TO BOTH brownies and chocolate chip cookies. Although blondies are baked in a pan like brownies, the flavorings are similar to those in chocolate chip cookies—vanilla, butter, and brown sugar, otherwise known as butterscotch. Blondies are sometimes laced with nuts and chocolate chips or butterscotch chips. Most of the time, blondies are pretty bland and need all the help they can get from additional ingredients. Dry, floury, flavorless—we have eaten them all. What does it take to make a good blondie?

The majority of the recipes we found had essentially the same ingredients but in different proportions that yielded blondies with dramatically different textures—from light and cakey to dense and buttery. Tasters preferred the latter, but with reservations. They felt that blondies could be too dense, as were some of the ones we tried. Superdense blondies tasted of little more than raw flour and butter.

After baking a variety of blondie recipes, we found that the key to dense blondies that did not taste raw lay in how the butter was incorporated into the batter and the amount of flour in the batter.

Melted butter produced a much denser blondie than creamed butter because the creaming process incorporates air into the batter. Melting the butter also meant that we could make the batter by hand rather than dirtying a food processor or electric mixer.

While we knew all-purpose flour would give us the chewiest, densest texture, the exact amount of flour was tricky to determine. Too much flour resulted in a dense, flavorless bar cookie, and too little produced a greasy bar cookie that oozed butter. After a dozen batches with the slightest variations in the amount of flour, we finally settled on 1½ cups of all-purpose flour leavened with a small amount of baking powder. These blondies were definitely dense and very chewy, but they had risen just enough to prevent them from being gooey.

For sweetening and flavor, tasters favored light brown sugar, which lent the right amount of earthy, molasses flavor; dark brown sugar was overpowering. And combined with a substantial amount of vanilla extract and salt (to sharpen the sweetness), the light brown sugar developed a rich butterscotch flavor.

To add both texture and flavor to the blondies, we included chocolate chips and pecans. While the chips are traditional, pecans are not. Most recipes suggest walnuts, but tasters thought the pecans better complemented the butterscotch flavor.

We also tried butterscotch chips, but most tasters found that they did little for this recipe. On a whim, we included white chocolate chips with the semisweet chips, and we were surprised that they produced the best blondie yet. While white chocolate does not have cocoa, it does have cocoa butter, which highlighted both the vanilla and caramel flavors. These blondies now had a significantly deeper and richer flavor.

~≺~

Blondies

MAKES 36

If you have trouble finding white chocolate chips, feel free to chop a bar of white chocolate into small chunks.

1 ½   cups (7 ½ ounces) unbleached all-purpose flour
1   teaspoon baking powder
½   teaspoon salt

12   tablespoons (1 ½ sticks) unsalted butter, melted and cooled

1 ½   cups packed (10 ½ ounces) light brown sugar

2   large eggs

1 ½   teaspoons vanilla extract

½   cup semisweet chocolate chips

½   cup white chocolate chips

1   cup pecans, toasted and chopped coarse

1. Adjust an oven rack to the middle position and heat the oven to 350 degrees. Spray a 13 by 9-inch pan with nonstick cooking spray. Fold two 16-inch pieces of foil or parchment paper lengthwise so that one measures 13 inches wide and the other measures 9 inches wide. Following the illustration on page 810, fit one sheet in the bottom of the greased pan, pushing it into the corners and up the sides of the pan (the overhang will help in removal of the baked bars). Fit the second sheet in the pan in the same manner, perpendicular to the first sheet. Spray the sheets with nonstick cooking spray.

2. Whisk the flour, baking powder, and salt together in a medium bowl; set aside.

3. Whisk the melted butter and brown sugar together in a medium bowl until combined. Add the eggs and vanilla and mix well. Using a rubber spatula, fold the dry ingredients into the egg mixture until just combined. Do not overmix. Fold in the semisweet and white chocolate chips and the nuts and turn the batter into the prepared pan, smoothing the top with a rubber spatula.

4. Bake until the top is shiny and cracked and feels firm to the touch, 22 to 25 minutes. Cool completely on a wire rack. Remove the bars from the pan using the foil or parchment handles and transfer to a cutting board. Cut into 1½ by 2-inch bars and serve.

➤ VARIATION

Congo Bars

MAKES 36

Congo bars are little but blondies enriched with coconut. We tried adding both sweetened flaked coconut and unsweetened shredded coconut to our blondies, and tasters unanimously preferred the unsweetened. Sweetened coconut made the bars overly sweet and unpleasantly chewy. We were able to extract a bit more flavor from the unsweetened coconut by toasting it golden brown before adding it to the blondie dough. Unsweetened shredded coconut can be found in natural food stores and Asian markets. Keep a close eye on the coconut when toasting as it can burn quickly.

Toast 1½ cups unsweetened shredded coconut on a rimmed baking sheet on the middle oven rack at 350 degrees, stirring 2 or 3 times, until light golden, 5 to 7 minutes. Transfer to a small bowl to cool. Follow the recipe for Blondies, adding the toasted coconut with the chocolate chips and nuts in step 3.

SEVEN-LAYER BARS

SEVEN-LAYER BARS, ALSO KNOWN AS MAGIC bars, are indeed made in seven layers and, you could say, come together like magic. Seven-layer bars are a jumble of chips (chocolate and otherwise), nuts, and coconut layered over a crust of crumbled graham crackers. The magic is the sweetened condensed milk, which when poured over these ingredients and baked, brings them together to create a cohesive bar cookie. Seven-layer bars are rich, supremely decadent, and sticky-sweet.

Simplicity in construction aside, seven-layer bars are not without their share of problems. They are most often flavor-related (the medley of chips tends to be mismatched and at times overpowering), but sometimes poor construction can cause problems. Seven-layer bars can be too delicate and fall apart at the first bite, can have too thin a graham cracker crust, or can be insufficiently gooey, so the ingredients won't stay together. We were after a solid bar cookie loaded with sweet, rich flavors and a chewy-crunchy texture.

Starting at the bottom, we tested our graham cracker crust options. Most graham cracker crusts are made by combining graham crumbs with melted butter. This crust would be no exception. Although store-bought crumbs are convenient, the crust they formed was far too delicate to support all the ingredients that would be layered on them. In order to produce a more substantial crust, we found it was necessary to hand-crush whole graham crackers into coarser crumbs. We placed whole crackers in a large zipper-lock bag and pounded them with whatever blunt instrument was handy (the underside of a measuring cup, a rolling pin). The result was a motley crew of crumbs, bits, and chunks. When brought together with the butter and then the condensed milk, these coarse crumbs created a sturdy crust packed with graham cracker flavor.

Next we tested every chip combination imaginable and let our tasters determine which options were worthy and which needed reconsidering. Toffee chips were the biggest loser of the bunch. The small nuggets of toffee melted away into nothing but a thin, sticky, almost flavorless layer and did little to contribute to the structure of the bar. Since bar structure was indeed an important factor, it became clear that we would have to stick to the standard morsel-shaped chips, as they tended to keep their shape better than smaller "bits" or minichips. When baked, morsels became soft and luxurious but retained enough shape to help add more bulk to this bar cookie.

The least favorite flavor of chip turned out to be peanut butter. They were salty and somewhat artificial-tasting, and the combination of peanut butter, coconut, and graham crackers seemed to turn tasters off. Chocolate chips—both semisweet and white chocolate—were well liked. Butterscotch chips also made the cut. They were buttery, slightly spicy, and a nice flavor change from the chocolate. In the end, we found that two cups of chips was the perfect amount. Tasters liked semisweet chocolate chips more than any of the others, so we settled on one cup of semisweet morsels and split the second cup between the white chocolate and butterscotch chips.

Next it was time to concentrate on the coconut. Some of the recipes we initially tested were overly coconut, and tasters were quite clear that they expected less. When we found the optimum amount—one cup—there was still something missing. The coconut flavor was flat and somewhat uninteresting. So we decided to toast the coconut to enhance its flavor. Fully toasted coconut, which was then baked on top of the seven layers for 25 minutes, came out of the oven in shards, too brown and overly crunchy. But without any toasting, the flavor was insipid. The solution was to toast the coconut ever so slightly. On top of the seven layers, the slightly toasted coconut browned evenly without becoming hard, and its flavor was much improved.

When it came to nuts, we tested all the usual suspects: pecans, walnuts, almonds, and macadamia nuts. Tasters preferred walnuts because of their meaty texture and big flavor. We tried toasting the nuts to enhance their flavor, but the difference was marginal and not worth the extra effort.

Sweetened condensed milk is a mixture of whole milk and sugar (up to 45 percent of its content) that is heated until 60 percent of the water content evaporates. What's left behind is an ooey-gooey, light tan liquid, which acts as the "glue" in seven-layer bars. The technique couldn't be simpler: Just open the can and pour it all over the top, as evenly as possible. We tested several ways of spreading the condensed milk evenly over the layers. Running a spatula over the condensed milk unearthed the layers below and made a mess of the whole thing. In the end, we just poured the condensed milk as evenly as we could over the layers and then let the heat of the oven do the rest.

Seven-Layer Bars
MAKES 18

Place the graham crackers in a large zipper-lock plastic bag and pound them with the bottom of a measuring cup, a rolling pin, or a smooth meat mallet. The result should be an assortment of crumbs, bits, and chunks that measures about 1½ cups.

1	cup sweetened flaked coconut
8	tablespoons (1 stick) unsalted butter
9	graham crackers (5 ounces), crushed (see note)
1	cup finely chopped walnuts
1	cup semisweet chocolate chips
½	cup white chocolate chips
½	cup butterscotch-flavored chips
1	(14-ounce) can sweetened condensed milk

1. Adjust an oven rack to the lower-middle position and heat the oven to 350 degrees. Spray a 13 by 9-inch pan with nonstick cooking spray. Fold two 16-inch pieces of foil or parchment paper lengthwise so that one measures 13 inches wide and the other measures 9 inches wide. Following the illustration on page 810, fit one sheet in the

bottom of the greased pan, pushing it into the corners and up the sides of the pan (the overhang will help in removal of the baked bars). Fit the second sheet in the pan in the same manner, perpendicular to the first sheet. Spray the sheets with nonstick cooking spray.

2. Spread the coconut on a baking sheet and bake until the outer flakes just begin to brown, about 8 minutes; set aside. Meanwhile, place the stick of butter in the prepared baking pan and put it in the oven to melt, about 6 minutes.

3. When the butter has melted, remove the pan from the oven and sprinkle the graham cracker crumbs over the melted butter. Toss lightly until all the butter is absorbed and the crumbs are evenly distributed. In order, sprinkle the walnuts, semisweet chocolate chips, white chocolate chips, butterscotch chips, and coconut over the graham crumbs. Pour the condensed milk evenly over the entire dish.

4. Return the pan to the oven and bake until the top is golden brown, about 25 minutes. Cool on a wire rack to room temperature, about 2 hours. Remove the bars from the pan using the foil or parchment handles and transfer to a cutting board. Using a sharp knife, cut into 2 by 3-inch bars.

LEMON BARS

TO MAKE LEMON BARS, A BOTTOM LAYER, OR crust, is pressed into a pan, baked, and then topped with a filling. The filling and crust are baked again and then cut into bars. Lemon bars are pretty easy to make, but that doesn't mean it's easy to get them just the way you want them. Whether from bakeries or home recipes, the crust is often quite soggy, and many versions are too sweet and lack true lemon flavor.

We started with the crust, knowing that flour, butter, and sugar would be the main ingredients. We also knew that since we wanted a cookie or shortbread texture rather than a pastry-type crust, we would need a fair amount of sugar.

Our first challenge was to decide the proportion of flour to butter and the amount, as well as the type, of sugar. We decided, after several taste tests, that a crust made with ½ cup of butter per

1¼ cups of flour was just right—it was neither too greasy nor too dry. Since sugar affects tenderness as well as sweetness, the amount and type of sugar needed to be determined along with the butter. Brown sugar proved too rich for our tasters' palates, while granulated sugar produced a crust that was a bit brittle and gritty. The best, most tender texture came from confectioners' sugar.

Having decided on the basic ingredients, we began to investigate ways to combine and bake them. For most cookies and one type of pastry, the fat and sugar are creamed together in the first step. The alternative is to start by cutting the fat into the flour with your fingertips or a food processor, which is common in most pastry crusts. After testing both methods, we decided that because of the proportion of flour to butter and the absence of liquid, the second method was best suited for this crust. Cutting the butter into the flour created a crumbly mixture that could be pressed into the pan. The standard oven temperature of 350 degrees worked best to produce a golden brown, crisp crust.

Lemon bars are traditionally made by adding a raw mixture of eggs, sugar, flour, lemon juice, and lemon zest to the prebaked crust and then baking again to set the filling. Once we had settled on our crust, we tried a number of recipes using this technique, and regardless of ingredient portions, we turned out consistently soggy crusts. We wanted a crust that would stay crisp even after it was topped with a filling and concluded that the only way to achieve this would be to abandon tradition and cook a lemon filling (lemon curd) on the stove before adding it to the crust.

For a 9-inch square pan, we estimated that we would need about 3 cups of lemon curd. The traditional lemon curds all contained between 1 and 1½ cups sugar, but the amount of lemon juice varied widely, between ½ and 1½ cups. There was also quite a bit of play between whole eggs and yolks, with the average falling between eight and 10 eggs total. Though the recipes were divided on the matter of using direct heat versus a double boiler, most were quite cavalier about cooking time, with visual descriptions of the desired final texture ranging from "thick" to "very thick" to "like whipped cream." Only two mentioned cooking temperatures: 160 and 180 degrees, a rather wide range when dealing with eggs. Some recipes added butter at the beginning of the cooking time; others specified to whisk it in later.

During our early experiments, certain proportions emerged easily. The balance of sweetness and tartness we sought came in at roughly 2 parts sugar to 1 part lemon juice. Four full tablespoons of finely grated lemon zest (strained out after cooking along with any hardened bits of egg whites from the eggs) packed enough lemon punch without having to linger in the final custard, where it would become bitter or usurp the silky texture. A pinch of salt brightened the flavor. Four tablespoons of butter was perfect, smoothing the taste and refining the texture.

Holding the proportions of the above ingredients constant, we made a number of lemon curds testing various combinations of whole eggs and yolks. Somewhat surprisingly, the curds that tasted great in a spoon were not always the ones that tasted best baked. The curd made with whole eggs alone had a light texture in the spoon and a gorgeous sheen, but it had a muted color and a texture most tasters described as "mayonnaise-like" when baked. The curd made with whole eggs and whites had a smooth, translucent surface but firmed up too much, while the curd made with an equal ratio of whole eggs to yolks was faulted for being cloyingly rich. In the end, most tasters preferred a curd made principally with yolks and only a couple of whole eggs for structure. Creamy and dense with a vibrant color, it did not become gelatinous when baked, as did those curds made with whole eggs, but it did set up enough to slice.

But the most interesting discovery was still to come. Remembering a lemon mousse we'd made, we wanted to see what a splash of cream might do to the curd. Adding cream before cooking the curd on the stovetop gave it a cheesy flavor. But 3 tablespoons of cold cream stirred in just before baking proved a winning touch. It cooled the just-cooked curd, blunted its acidity, and lightened its final baked texture to a celestial creaminess.

When added to the crust and baked just to set, the curd maintained its heavenly texture, and the crust stayed perfectly crispy.

Lemon Bars

MAKES 16

The warm filling must be added to the warm crust. Start preparing the filling when the crust goes into the oven. Be sure to cool the bars completely before cutting them.

CRUST

1¼	cups (6¼ ounces) unbleached all-purpose flour
½	cup (2 ounces) confectioners' sugar, plus more to decorate the finished bars if desired
½	teaspoon salt
8	tablespoons (1 stick) unsalted butter, softened but still cool, cut into 1-inch pieces

FILLING

7	large egg yolks, plus 2 large eggs
1	cup plus 2 tablespoons (7⅞ ounces) granulated sugar
⅔	cup juice and ¼ cup finely grated zest from 4 or 5 medium lemons
	Pinch salt
4	tablespoons (½ stick) unsalted butter, cut into 4 pieces
3	tablespoons heavy cream

1. FOR THE CRUST: Spray a 9-inch square baking pan with nonstick cooking spray. Fold two 16-inch pieces of foil or parchment paper lengthwise to measure 9 inches wide. Following the illustration on page 810, fit one sheet in the bottom of the greased pan, pushing it into the corners and up the sides of the pan (the overhang will help in removal of the baked bars). Fit the second sheet in the pan in the same manner, perpendicular to the first sheet. Spray the sheets with nonstick cooking spray.

2. Place the flour, confectioners' sugar, and salt in a food processor and process briefly. Add the butter and process to blend, 8 to 10 seconds, then process until the mixture is pale yellow and resembles coarse meal, about three 1-second pulses. Sprinkle the mixture into the prepared pan and press firmly with your fingers into an even layer over the entire pan bottom. Refrigerate for 30 minutes.

3. Adjust an oven rack to the middle position

and heat the oven to 350 degrees. Bake the crust until golden brown, about 20 minutes.

4. FOR THE FILLING: In a medium nonreactive bowl, whisk together the yolks and whole eggs until combined, about 5 seconds. Add the granulated sugar and whisk until just combined, about 5 seconds. Add the lemon juice and zest and the salt; whisk until combined, about 5 seconds. Transfer the mixture to a medium nonreactive saucepan, add the butter pieces, and cook over medium-low heat, stirring constantly with a wooden spoon, until the curd thickens to a thin sauce-like consistency and registers 170 degrees on an instant-read thermometer, about 5 minutes. Immediately pour the curd through a single-mesh stainless steel strainer set over a clean nonreactive bowl. Stir in the heavy cream; pour the curd onto the warm crust immediately.

5. Bake until the filling is shiny and opaque and the center 3 inches jiggle slightly when shaken, 10 to 15 minutes. Cool on a wire rack to room temperature, about 45 minutes. Remove the bars from the pan using the foil or parchment handles and transfer to a cutting board. Cut into 2¼-inch squares, wiping the knife clean between cuts as necessary. Sieve confectioners' sugar over the bars, if desired.

RASPBERRY SQUARES

BAR COOKIES CAN BE LOOSELY DIVIDED INTO two camps. There's the cake-like version, which includes the chocolate brownie, and the cookie-like version, which, stripped down to the basics, is what bakers call a "short" pastry, such as raspberry squares. A short pastry has a tender, almost sandy crumb that it gets by way of the right combination of flour, fat, sugar, and salt—with an emphasis on the fat and the flour. In a short pastry (think of shortbread), a generous amount of fat is required to coat the particles of flour and restrict the flour's access to liquid. Flour contains proteins that when combined with water and kneaded form gluten, which is desirable in bread, where you want chew, but not in a raspberry square, where you want tenderness.

In the many recipes for all manner of "short" bar cookies we looked at, the amount of butter ranged from ½ cup to 1 cup for about 2½ cups of flour. We found that a whole cup of butter made the raspberry squares greasy, whereas ½ cup left them on the dry side; ¾ cup butter was just right.

The sugar in many of the recipes also ranged from ½ cup to 1 cup, with some calling for granulated sugar, some for brown, and some for a mix of the two. Here, too, we went for the middle way, deciding on equal amounts of granulated and light brown sugar, which made for a deeper flavor than granulated alone, and on a total of ⅔ cup, which was sweet enough to be pleasing but not cloying.

Although we weren't interested in tampering too much with the flavor of our crust by adding things like vanilla, cinnamon, or lemon zest, as called for in some recipes, we did find it a bit plain as it was. We were attracted by the idea of adding some oats or nuts, which would make a more subtle contribution to flavor while also adding some textural interest. The oats, with their bulk and absorbency, would have to displace some of the flour. After trying various proportions, we found that we liked the combination of 1¼ cups oats and 1½ cups flour. We played around with the nuts and found ourselves preferring a pairing of sweet almonds with nutty pecans (although either also works on its own).

We were now pretty pleased with our crust except for one nagging problem: It was rather pale, not golden brown. We wanted that golden brown color not only for appearance's sake but for flavor; we knew that a deeply colored crust would have a more developed, nutty flavor.

The procedure we had been following to prepare the squares for baking was recommended in a number of recipes. It involved lining the bottom of the pan with most of the dough, spreading the preserves on top, and then covering the preserves with the rest of the dough. One or two recipes had recommended baking the bottom crust alone first to brown it and firm it up, but we had rejected this option as being a bit fussy. Now we tried this procedure and were happy to learn that it effectively colored—and flavored—the crust.

These squares can easily be put together in 15 minutes. The only inconvenience is having to wait for them to bake and cool before digging in.

Raspberry Squares

MAKES 36

For a nice presentation, trim ¼ inch off the outer rim of the uncut baked block. The outside edges of all the cut squares will then be neat.

1½	cups (7½ ounces) unbleached all-purpose flour
1¼	cups quick-cooking oats
⅓	cup (2⅓ ounces) granulated sugar
⅓	cup packed (2⅓ ounces) light brown sugar
¼	teaspoon baking soda
¼	teaspoon salt
½	cup finely chopped pecans or almonds, or a combination
12	tablespoons (1½ sticks) unsalted butter, softened but still cool, cut into 12 pieces
1	cup raspberry preserves

1. Adjust an oven rack to the lower-middle position and heat the oven to 350 degrees. Spray a 9-inch square baking pan with nonstick cooking spray. Fold two 16-inch pieces of foil or parchment paper lengthwise to measure 9 inches wide. Following the illustration on page 810, fit one sheet in the bottom of the greased pan, pushing it into the corners and up the sides of the pan (the overhang will help in removal of the baked squares). Fit the second sheet in the pan in the same manner, perpendicular to the first sheet. Spray the sheets with nonstick cooking spray.

2. In the bowl of an electric mixer, mix the flour, oats, sugars, baking soda, salt, and nuts at low speed until combined, about 30 seconds. With the mixer running at low speed, add the butter pieces; continue to beat until the mixture is well blended and resembles wet sand, about 2 minutes.

3. Transfer two thirds of the oat mixture to the prepared pan and use your hands to press the crumbs evenly into the bottom. Bake until the crust starts to brown, about 20 minutes. Using a rubber spatula, spread the preserves evenly over the hot bottom crust; sprinkle the remaining oat mixture evenly over the preserves. Bake until the preserves bubble around the edges and the top is golden brown, about 30 minutes, rotating the pan from front to back halfway through the baking

time. Cool on a wire rack to room temperature, about 1½ hours. Remove the squares from the pan using the foil or parchment handles and transfer to a cutting board. Cut into 1½-inch squares.

➤ VARIATION
Fig Squares

These not-too-sweet squares will remind you of the childhood favorite—Fig Newton cookies.

Combine 1 pound Turkish figs, tough stems trimmed, 3 cups apple juice, and a pinch salt in a medium saucepan over medium heat and bring to a simmer. Cook, stirring occasionally, until the figs are very soft and the juice is syrupy, 35 to 40 minutes. Transfer to a medium bowl and cool until warm. Puree the figs in a food processor until they are the consistency of thick jam and smooth, scraping down the sides of the workbowl as necessary. Return to the medium bowl and set aside. Follow the recipe for Raspberry Squares, substituting the fig puree for the preserves in step 3.

PECAN BARS

PECAN BARS ARE BASICALLY PECAN PIE BAKED into small, manageable rectangles or squares. The filling is a bit firmer so that it can be neatly cut. And instead of a pastry crust, most pecan bars call for a cookie-type crust, akin to shortbread.

Starting from the bottom up, we decided on a shortbread-like crust that would be substantial enough to support the filling. But the crust also had to be tender and buttery. In our experience, the crust is usually the fatal flaw of a bar cookie; it is often soggy and undercooked or rock hard and tough.

We tested several shortbread recipes until we found one close to what we wanted—buttery and rich but still strong enough to slice and support the filling—and then hammered out the finer points. We had the best results making the dough in a food processor, which quickly cuts the butter into the flour without overheating it and is an easy method to boot. It took under two minutes to process the crust and gently pack it into a lined baking pan. We found that a crust baked three quarters of the way, or until it was just beginning to brown, resulted in the most flavor and best texture.

Although we were pleased with the crust's flavor and texture—buttery and just firm enough—one of the tasters made a suggestion that would change our opinion. She proposed adding ground pecans, bringing it more into "pecan sandy" territory. With a couple of minor adjustments to the flour and butter amounts to accommodate the nuts, the crust was markedly improved. The nuts' sandy texture pleasingly contrasted with the silky filling, and the nuts also prevented the crust from becoming too tough.

As the crust bakes, the filling can be assembled. Since there is less filling in a pecan bar than in a pie, the flavors must be more concentrated. Working with our favorite pecan pie filling recipe, we cut back on both wet and dry ingredients until we hit the delicate balance of sweetness and gooeyness we desired.

To boost the flavor, we added a substantial amount of vanilla extract, along with bourbon or rum—both common to many Southern-style pecan pie recipes. The liquor cut through the sweetness and intensified the flavor of the nuts. We also included a healthy dose of salt, which sharpened the sweetness and also intensified the pecan flavor.

While it may sound like a minor issue, the size of the pecans proved to be important. Tasters definitely had opinions—some favored whole pecans, and some preferred them finely chopped. The whole pecans were attractive, floating on top of the cookie, but they did not cut easily and made the bars hard to eat out of hand. Finely chopped nuts were not as visually appealing but were easier to eat. We decided to chop the pecans coarsely and managed to please everyone.

Pecan Bars

MAKES 24

Assemble the pecan filling while the crust bakes. Once the crust is lightly browned, spread the filling on top and continue baking. Because of their high sugar content, pecan bars store well and taste great up to 5 days after baking. While we liked bourbon the best, dark rum is quite good. For a very boozy-tasting bar cookie, add another tablespoon of liquor.

CRUST

1	cup (5 ounces) unbleached all-purpose flour
1/4	teaspoon baking powder
1	teaspoon salt
1/3	cup packed (2 1/3 ounces) light brown sugar
1/4	cup pecans, toasted and chopped coarse
6	tablespoons (3/4 stick) cold unsalted butter, cut into small pieces

FILLING

4	tablespoons (1/2 stick) unsalted butter, melted
1/2	cup packed (3 1/2 ounces) light brown sugar
1/3	cup light corn syrup
2	teaspoons vanilla extract
1	tablespoon bourbon or dark rum
1/2	teaspoon salt
1	large egg, lightly beaten
1 3/4	cups pecans, toasted and chopped coarse

1. FOR THE CRUST: Adjust an oven rack to the middle position and heat the oven to 350 degrees. Spray a 9-inch square baking pan with nonstick cooking spray. Fold two 16-inch pieces of foil or parchment paper lengthwise to measure 9 inches wide. Following the illustration on page 810, fit one sheet in the bottom of the greased pan, pushing it into the corners and up the sides of the pan (the overhang will help in removal of the baked bars). Fit the second sheet in the pan in the same manner, perpendicular to the first sheet. Spray the sheets with nonstick cooking spray.

2. Place the flour, baking powder, salt, brown sugar, and pecans in a food processor. Process the mixture until it resembles coarse cornmeal, about five 1-second pulses. Add the butter and pulse until the mixture resembles sand, about eight 1-second pulses. Pat the mixture evenly into the prepared pan and bake until the crust is light brown and springs back when touched, about 20 minutes.

3. FOR THE FILLING: While the crust is in the oven, whisk together the melted butter, brown sugar, corn syrup, vanilla, bourbon, and salt in a medium bowl until just combined. Add the egg and whisk until incorporated.

4. Pour the filling on top of the hot crust and sprinkle the pecans evenly over the top. Bake until the top is browned and cracks start to form across

the surface, 22 to 25 minutes. Cool on a wire rack for 1 hour. Remove the bars from the pan using the foil or parchment handles and transfer to a cutting board. Cut into bars that measure 1½ by 2¼ inches.

GRANOLA BARS

IN ESSENCE, GRANOLA BARS ARE NOTHING BUT granola cereal bound together and packed into a firm, transportable form. Rock hard, saccharine sweet, and greasy to boot, the average store-bought granola bar provides plenty of calories but little gustatory pleasure. We wanted a great-tasting granola bar with plenty of crunch and fully flavored with toasted oats, nuts, and sometimes dried fruit or spices. As always, we started development by looking for recipes in other cookbooks. We were surprised to find very few, and those we did find were somewhat dubious, employing a wide range of questionable ingredients and odd instructions. That said, we were able to identify the three key issues with granola bars: preparing the oats (toasting), binding the bars together, and adding additional flavors.

Some recipes we found avoided the oats issue altogether by specifying store-bought granola in the ingredient list, a tack we weren't willing to take. Commercial granola is usually highly flavored, fatty, and packed with a variety of ingredients. We wanted to pick our own flavorings and control the amount of oil added. Other recipes skipped toasted oats altogether, yielding bland bars with no discernible flavor. Following the lead of the most promising recipe we found, we started off by making what was essentially a simple granola: old-fashioned rolled oats tossed with vegetable oil to encourage browning and a crisp texture and salt to bring out the oats' flavor. When toasted at too high a temperature, the oats browned too quickly and developed a bitter flavor. When toasted at too low a temperature, it took well over an hour for any browning. After experimenting with a variety of temperatures, we settled on 375 degrees as the perfect temperature, as the oats toasted to an even light gold within 30 minutes.

To bind and sweeten the oats, we turned to honey, a common ingredient in the recipes we found. We tossed the toasted oats with honey and packed the sticky mixture into the rimmed baking sheet in which the oats had been toasted. In the slow, even heat of the oven, the honey's moisture evaporated and the oats were bound firmly together. Once cool, the bars were crunchy, but the texture was not to last for long. Within a day, they had softened to an unpleasantly stale consistency. Honey is hygroscopic, meaning it attracts and absorbs water, and hence rendered the bars soft. Tasters liked the honey flavor, so we didn't want to exclude it altogether, but we clearly needed to replace a portion of the honey with a less hygroscopic sweetener, like granulated or brown sugar. (Fructose, the main component of honey, is more hygroscopic than sucrose, the main component of granulated and brown sugar.) Tasters preferred either light or dark brown sugar to granulated, as it deepened the oat flavor. We experimented with ratios to get the best flavor and texture and found that equal parts honey and brown sugar yielded the most flavorful results. For additional flavor, we added a hefty dose of vanilla extract, which intensified both the oat flavor and the honey's floral tones.

While the bars tasted good, tasters noted that the sugary binder was pooling in the crevices between the oats and hardening to a toffee-like, tooth-pulling texture. The spaces between the oats needed to be filled to prevent the pooling. Grinding a portion of the oats or adding flour was a straightforward option, but neither added any flavor to the bars.

Finely chopped nuts proved a better bet. The sand-size pieces readily filled the spaces between the oats and made for a denser bar without pockets of hard sweetener. Leaving a portion of the nuts only coarsely chopped lent the bars texture and visual definition—tasters liked seeing exactly what sort of nut they were eating. That said, almonds, walnuts, and pecans all found fans among tasters. Peanuts were deemed "boring" and pistachios too exotic for such homey fare.

Along with nuts, dried fruit seemed a logical addition but one that proved problematic. We added raisins to the oats mixture and found that during the long baking time, they puffed up, burned, and turned hard—a true failure. Plumping them in apple juice prior to baking alleviated the latter issue, but they still tasted acrid and burnt. We realized that the raisins' thin skins were burning in the oven's heat (a problem exacerbated by their high sugar content). We didn't want to change our basic technique, so we opted to try other dried fruits instead. Chopped apples turned as tough as the raisins and rendered the bars chewy because of their high moisture content. Frustrated, we moved on to dried cranberries, which, once plumped in juice (either apple or orange), worked beautifully. The fruits' thick skins and low sugar content prevented them from burning and kept them pliant despite the long spell in the oven. Dried cherries, coarsely chopped, worked equally well.

Crunchy Granola Bars

MAKES 36

Make sure to press forcefully when packing the granola mixture into the pan; otherwise, the bars may be crumbly once cut. If you like, add up to ½ cup of wheat germ and ¾ cup of sunflower seeds to the oats after toasting. And feel free to add your favorite spice: freshly grated nutmeg and ground ginger are pleasant additions to the suggested cinnamon. The bars can be effectively stored in the rimmed baking sheet, wrapped tightly in plastic wrap, or in an airtight plastic container for up to 1 week.

7	cups (21 ounces) old-fashioned rolled oats
½	cup vegetable oil
½	teaspoon salt
1½	cups whole almonds, pecans, or walnuts
¾	cup honey
¾	cup packed (5¼ ounces) light or dark brown sugar
1	tablespoon vanilla extract
2	teaspoons ground cinnamon (optional)

1. Adjust an oven rack to the middle position and heat the oven to 375 degrees. Line an 18 by 12-inch rimmed baking sheet with aluminum foil. Combine the oats, oil, and salt in a large bowl and mix until the oats are evenly coated. Transfer the mixture to the baking sheet (save the mixing bowl for use in step 3) and spread into an even layer.

Bake, stirring every 10 minutes, until pale gold, about 30 minutes. Remove the oats and lower the oven temperature to 300 degrees.

2. Place the nuts in a food processor and process until coarsely chopped, about ten 1-second pulses. Place ¾ cup of the nuts in a small bowl and process the remaining nuts until finely ground, 20 to 30 seconds. Add the finely ground nuts to the bowl with the coarsely chopped nuts and set aside. Combine the honey and brown sugar in a small saucepan over medium heat and cook, stirring frequently, until the sugar is fully dissolved, about 5 minutes. Stir in the vanilla and cinnamon (if using) and set aside.

3. Combine the oats, nuts, and honey mixture in the large bowl and stir with a large rubber spatula until the oats are evenly coated with the honey mixture. Transfer the mixture to the prepared baking sheet and spread in an even layer. Wet the spatula with water and forcefully pack the mixture into a very flat, tight, even layer. Bake until golden, 45 to 50 minutes. Cool, in the baking sheet, on a wire rack for 10 minutes and cut into 2 by 3-inch bars with a chef's knife. Remove the foil from each bar before serving. Cool completely before wrapping and storing.

> VARIATIONS

Dried Cranberry and Ginger Granola Bars
Dried cherries, coarsely chopped, may be substituted for the cranberries if you prefer.

Bring 1 cup dried cranberries and 1 cup apple or orange juice to a simmer in a small saucepan over medium-low heat and cook until very tender, 10 to 15 minutes. Strain through a fine-mesh strainer, gently pushing on the cranberries to extract excess liquid, and cool. Discard the soaking liquid. Follow the recipe for Crunchy Granola Bars, adding the cranberries and ¼ cup chopped crystallized ginger to the oat mixture in step 3 after adding the honey mixture. Stir thoroughly to incorporate evenly.

Coconut and Sesame Granola Bars
Follow the recipe for Crunchy Granola Bars, adding ½ cup each sesame seeds and unsweetened coconut to the oats in step 3.

19

CAKES

WE MAKE CAKES TO CELEBRATE BIRTHDAYS, weddings, anniversaries, and almost any other holiday you can think of. Cakes can be as simple as a sheet cake sprinkled with confectioners' sugar or as special as a multitiered affair with filling, frosting, and nuts.

Cake making requires precision and careful attention to detail. A slight mismeasurement of ingredients or the failure to follow a specific mixing instruction can have drastic consequences in terms of flavor and texture. Over the years, we have developed a list of general tips designed to head off the mistakes home cooks are most likely to make.

OVEN TEMPERATURE is always important, especially when baking a cake, so periodically check your oven temperature with an oven thermometer. If your oven is too hot, the sides of the cake will set before the middle does, and the cake will hump or crack. If your oven is too cold, the air will escape from the batter before the batter begins to set, and the cake will have a coarse texture and may even fall.

CAKE PANS You should own two sets—two pans that measure 8 inches across and two that measure 9 inches across. Some recipes call for 8-inch cake pans, others for 9-inch pans. Use the correct size. If the pans are too large, they overheat the rim of the cake, causing the same sorts of problems as an overheated oven. If the pans are too small, the batter may rise right out of them. Choose sturdy aluminum pans with absolutely vertical sides. Do not use disposable foil pans, which often produce misshapen cakes.

Generously grease the pans with vegetable shortening (such as Crisco) or butter and coat them well with flour. The flour holds the fat in place and keeps the batter from seeping through to the pan bottom. As an extra precaution, you may want to grease the pan, line the bottom with a piece of parchment or waxed paper, grease the paper, and then flour the pan and paper.

INGREDIENT PREPARATION Have all ingredients, especially butter, eggs, and milk, at room temperature. Chilled ingredients do not emulsify well, which leads to a dense cake, and cold butter won't incorporate into a batter. Very warm ingredients may cause air cells in creamed butter to dissolve. Unless specified otherwise in a recipe, all ingredients should register between 65 and 70 degrees on an instant-read thermometer. Sticks of softened butter should give when pressed but still hold their shape, with no signs of melting (see the illustrations on page 772).

To bring eggs to room temperature quickly, submerge uncracked eggs in a bowl of warm water for five to 10 minutes. Since separating eggs is somewhat easier when they are cold, you may want to separate the eggs first and then let them warm up while you assemble and measure the remaining ingredients. You may also place a bowl or measuring cup filled with yolks or whites in a bowl of warm water if necessary.

Unless otherwise noted, measure flour carefully by the dip-and-sweep method (see page 700 for details). Dip the measuring cup into the container of flour, scoop out a heaping cupful, and then level the top with the straight edge of a butter knife or icing spatula. Do not shake, tap, or pack the cup. If the cup is not completely filled on the first try, dump the flour back into the container and dip again. A kitchen scale is the most accurate way to measure ingredients like flour, sugar, cornmeal, and cocoa.

MIXING We developed the recipes in this chapter using a standing mixer, and the mixing times in the recipes reflect that. But you don't need a standing mixer to make the cakes in this chapter. Although we like the convenience of standing mixers—they keep our hands free to measure an ingredient, crack eggs into a bowl, or just wipe the counter—a good hand-held mixer does the job just as well (in just a little more time). It is more important to rely on the visual cues we give, like "beat until light and fluffy."

BAKING Give pans enough space in the oven. Cakes placed too close together will rise toward each other and end up lopsided. Cakes placed too close to the oven walls won't rise as high on the side nearest the wall. Keep pans at least 3 inches from each other and the oven walls and on the middle rack of the oven. If your oven is small, stagger the pans on racks set at the upper-middle and lower-middle positions to allow for proper air circulation.

TESTING FOR DONENESS How do you tell when a cake is done? It depends upon the cake. For cakes like angel food, chiffon, layer cakes, and the like, use your finger and a toothpick or thin skewer to judge when they are done. Cakes should be baked until firm in the center when lightly pressed and a toothpick or skewer inserted in the center comes out clean or with just a crumb or two adhering. If the tester comes out perfectly clean, the cake is probably overcooked and dry.

For cakes whose texture does not depend on crumb, like cheesecakes and hot fudge pudding cake, the rules vary. Cheesecakes are done when an instant-read thermometer inserted in the center registers 150 degrees. For the pudding cake, look for the visual cues provided in the recipes. It is important not to overbake these moist cakes, because their texture can become unpalatably dry.

ANGEL FOOD CAKE

AT ITS BEST, AN ANGEL FOOD CAKE SHOULD be tall and perfectly shaped, have a snowy white, tender crumb, and be encased in a thin, delicate, golden crust. Although most angel food cakes contain no more than six ingredients, there are literally hundreds of variations on this basic theme. The type of flour used, the baking temperature, the type of sugar, and even the use of baking powder—a serious transgression, according to most experts—are all in dispute. What is not in dispute is that angel food cake requires a delicate balance of ingredients and proper cooking techniques.

An angel food cake is distinguished by its lack of egg yolks, chemical leaveners, and fat. Other cakes also use beaten egg whites for leaveners, but there are differences. Chiffon cake (page 827) contains egg yolks, which makes for a slightly heavier, moister cake. Sponge cake (page 852) also includes whole or separated eggs; it, too, is denser and more yellow than angel food cake.

The six ingredients found in every angel food cake are egg whites, sugar, flour, cream of tartar, salt, and flavorings. Most recipes start by beating the egg whites. Mixer speed is critical for well-beaten whites. We found that starting at high speed will produce quick but inconsistent results. To create the most stable foam, beat the whites at low speed to break them up into a froth. Add the cream of tartar and salt, increase the speed to medium, and beat until the whites form very soft, billowy mounds. When large bubbles stop appearing around the edges, and with the mixer still on medium, add the sugar, a tablespoon at a time, until all the sugar has been incorporated and the whites are shiny and form soft peaks when the beater is lifted. The mass should still flow slightly when the bowl is tilted. Do not beat until the peaks are stiff; we found that this makes it difficult to fold in the flour, deflating the whites and therefore reducing the volume.

Because there is no fat in angel food cake, sugar is critical to its taste and texture. We tested confectioners' sugar and found that the cornstarch in it makes the cake too dense. Superfine sugar is simply too fine, making a soft cake with little substance. We found that granulated sugar is best in this recipe.

Flour sets the cake batter, but because it also adds weight, the flour should be as light and airy as possible. We found that cake flour, which is finer than all-purpose flour, is easier to incorporate into the beaten whites without deflating them. The lower protein content of cake flour results in a more delicate, tender crumb, which we preferred. No matter what kind of flour is used, we found sifting to be essential; it makes the flour lighter in texture and easier to incorporate into the whites. Sift the flour twice—once before measuring and once before adding it to the beaten whites—for maximum lightness.

Egg whites, sugar, flour, and cream of tartar will produce a good-looking angel food cake that is sweet but bland. Salt is added for flavor and also helps stabilize the beaten whites. Other common additions are vanilla and almond extract (we like to use both), which add flavor without changing the basic chemistry of the batter. You can add grated citrus zest or a little citrus juice; we prefer the latter because zest can mar the perfectly soft texture and whiteness of the cake. We found that high-fat flavorings, such as grated chocolate and nuts, greatly affect the cake's texture, and we prefer to stick with simpler flavorings.

We tried using some baking powder for added leavening and stability but found that the resulting cake was not as white and had a coarser crumb. If you separate and beat the egg whites properly, there should be no need to add baking powder.

Our most intriguing experiment involved oven temperature. We baked the same recipe in the same pan at 300, 325, 350, and 375 degrees, baking each cake until it tested done with a skewer and the top bounced back when pressed lightly. Surprisingly, all the cakes cooked evenly, but those baked at 350 and 375 degrees had a thicker, darker crust, while the cakes baked at 300 and 325 degrees had a more desirable, delicate, evenly pale golden crust. After many taste tests, we decided that 325 degrees was the ideal temperature.

The best tool we found to remove an angel food cake from the pan is a thin, flexible, nonserrated knife that is at least five inches long. Tilt the pan at a right angle to the counter to make it easy to work the knife around the sides. Insert the knife between the crust and the pan, pressing hard against the side of the pan, and work your way all around the cake. To cut around the central core of the pan, use a long, thin skewer. Invert the pan so that the cake slides out, then peel off the parchment or waxed paper. If using a pan with a removable bottom, slide the knife blade between the cake and the sides of the pan to release it. Present the cake sitting on its wide, crustier top, with the delicate and more easily sliced bottom crust facing up.

To cut the cake, use a long serrated knife and pull it back and forth with a gentle sawing motion. When we tried using the specially made tool for cutting angel food cake—a row of prongs attached to a bar—it mashed and squashed this tender cake.

Angel Food Cake

SERVES 10 TO 12

Sift both the cake flour and the granulated sugar before measuring to eliminate any lumps and ensure the lightest possible texture.

1	cup (3 ounces) sifted plain cake flour
1½	cups (10½ ounces) sifted sugar
12	large egg whites (1¾ cups plus 2 tablespoons), at room temperature

BEATING EGG WHITES

1. Beat the egg whites at medium-low speed until frothy, about 30 seconds. Raise the speed and add the cream of tartar to help stabilize the egg foam. Slowly add the sugar and continue to beat.

2. Just before the whites reach the proper consistency, turn off the mixer. Detach the whisk attachment and remove the bowl from the mixer. Use the whisk attachment to make the last few strokes by hand. Be sure to scrape along the bottom of the bowl. This technique works well with cream, too, and helps prevent overmixing.

1 teaspoon cream of tartar

¼ teaspoon salt

1½ teaspoons vanilla extract

1½ teaspoons juice from 1 lemon

½ teaspoon almond extract

1. Adjust an oven rack to the lower-middle position and heat the oven to 325 degrees. Have ready an ungreased large tube pan (9-inch diameter, 16-cup capacity), preferably with a removable bottom. If the pan bottom is not removable, line it with parchment paper or waxed paper.

2. Whisk the flour and ¾ cup of the sugar in a small bowl. Place the remaining ¾ cup sugar in another small bowl next to the mixer.

3. Beat the egg whites in the bowl of a standing mixer at low speed until just broken up and beginning to froth. Add the cream of tartar and salt and beat at medium speed until the whites form very soft, billowy mounds. With the mixer still at medium speed, beat in the remaining ¾ cup sugar, 1 tablespoon at a time, until all the sugar is added and the whites are shiny and form soft peaks. Add the vanilla, lemon juice, and almond extract and beat until just blended.

4. Place the flour-sugar mixture in a sifter set over waxed paper. Sift the mixture over the whites, about 3 tablespoons at a time, and gently fold in, using a large rubber spatula. Sift any flour-sugar mixture that falls onto the paper back into the bowl with the whites.

5. Gently scrape the batter into the pan, smooth the top with a spatula, and give the pan a couple of raps on the counter to release any large air bubbles.

6. Bake until the cake is golden brown and the top springs back when pressed firmly, 50 to 60 minutes.

7. If the cake pan has prongs around the rim for elevating the cake, invert the pan onto them. If the pan does not have prongs, invert the pan onto the neck of a bottle or funnel. Let the cake cool completely, 2 to 3 hours.

8. To unmold, run a knife around the edge of the pan, being careful not to separate the golden crust from the cake. Slide the cake out of the pan and cut the same way around the removable bottom to release, or peel off the parchment or waxed paper, if using. Place the cake bottom-side up on a platter. Cut slices by sawing gently with a long serrated knife. Serve the cake the day it is made.

CHIFFON CAKE

A MILE HIGH AND LIGHT AS A FEATHER, CHIFFON cake is also tender and moist—qualities that angel food and sponge cake typically lack.

Chiffon cake was revolutionary in its day. Made with vegetable oil, which was a brand-new idea in 1950, this cake required none of the tedious creaming and incremental adding of ingredients demanded by a butter cake. One simply mixed flour, sugar, baking powder, egg yolks, water, and oil as if making a pancake batter and then folded in stiffly beaten egg whites. The whipping of the whites—"They should be much stiffer than for angel food or meringue," warned Betty Crocker—was the only tricky feat required, and even this was no longer an arduous task. More than a few households could boast a snappy new electric mixer.

Chiffon cake had been invented in 1927 by the aptly named Harry Baker, a Los Angeles insurance salesman turned caterer. When the cake became a featured attraction at the Brown Derby, then the restaurant of the stars, Baker converted a spare room into his top-secret bakery, fitted it with 12 tin hot-plate ovens, and personally baked 42 cakes a day.

Baker kept his recipe a secret for 20 years, before selling it to General Mills. There ensued considerable testing, but with only a couple of minor changes to the technique and a new name—"chiffon cake"—the cake appeared before the American public in a 1948 pamphlet called "Betty Crocker Chiffon," containing 14 recipes and variations in addition to umpteen icings, fillings, serving ideas, and helpful hints. It was an instant hit and became one of the most popular cakes of the time.

Although we have been delighted by the uniquely light yet full richness and deep flavor of this American invention, we also know that chiffon cake can be dry or cottony. Ideally, chiffon cake should be moist and tender with a rich flavor.

To perfect this 20th-century classic, we decided to go back to Betty Crocker's version.

With the exception of the chocolate variation, all of Betty Crocker's original chiffon cakes call for 2¼ cups sifted cake flour (which translates to about 1⅔ cups as measured by the dip-and-sweep method), 1½ cups sugar, 1 tablespoon baking powder, 1 teaspoon salt, ½ cup oil, 5 egg yolks, ¾ cup water or other liquid, 1 cup egg whites, and ½ teaspoon cream of tartar.

We made a plain, an orange, and a walnut chiffon cake according to the original formula and found that we had three complaints. The cakes were a bit dry—cottony and fluffy rather than moist and foamy, the way we thought chiffon cakes should be—and they seemed to lack flavor, punch, pizzazz. In addition, the cakes rose a bit too high for the pan, a consequence of the downsizing of tube pans, from 18 to 16 cups, that took place around 1970.

Since fat increases perceived moistness and also transmits flavor, we thought that adding more oil might help, but it did not. An orange chiffon cake made with an additional quarter cup of oil (up from ½ cup) turned out not only dry and flavorless but also greasy and heavy, an outcome that was as unexpected as it was disappointing.

We increased the number of eggs, and the cakes, even though they were lighter and richer than Betty Crocker's original, still tasted dry. We instinctively felt that adding more liquid would be a poor idea, but at this point we felt we had no choice but to try. Unfortunately, increasing the water from ¾ cup to 1 cup made the texture gummy and heavy—and the cake still managed to taste dry!

There was now only one ingredient left to play with, the flour. Since the problem was dryness, the flour obviously had to be decreased, but we knew from our experience with other sponge-type cakes that decreasing the flour could have very messy consequences. We might end up with a rubbery sponge or, worse, with a demonic soufflé that heaved blobs of batter onto the floor of the oven.

Whenever a sponge-type cake decides to collapse or explode, the culprit is the same: a lack of structure. Since eggs as well as flour provide structure, we reasoned that we could compensate for a decrease in flour by adding an extra egg yolk. We made an orange chiffon cake using the Betty Crocker formula but decreasing the flour by one-third cup and increasing the yolks from five to six. The effect was magical. Instead of being fluffy, cottony, and crumbly, the cake was wonderfully moist and so tender that slices flopped over at the middle if cut too thin. And the moistness transmitted all of the taste that had been lacking in our first experiments.

The cake, however, was not quite perfect. Evidently, the structure was borderline, and so the cake rose very high, spilling over onto the lip of the pan. This made it difficult to cut the cake free from the pan without tearing the top crust. Furthermore, because its top was humped, the cake did not sit flat when turned upside down onto a serving plate. We figured that removing an egg white would help to shrink the cake, but we feared that it might also undercut the structure to the point where the cake wouldn't rise at all. Nonetheless, we gave the idea a try. The resulting cake was lovely coming out of the oven, risen just to the top of the pan and perfectly flat—but its perfection was illusory. We hung the cake upside down to cool and started to clean up the kitchen when we heard a soft plop: The cake had fallen out of the pan.

Once we had taken a few nibbles of the mess, our fears were confirmed. The cake was pasty and overly moist. There was simply not enough structure to hold it together. We then remembered a chiffon cake recipe in Carole Walter's *Great Cakes* (Ballantine, 1991). Rather than whipping all of the egg whites, Walter mixed some of them, unbeaten, into the dry ingredients along with the yolks, water, and oil. Thus, she incorporated less air into the batter, which should, we reasoned, make for a smaller cake. We tried Walter's technique using seven eggs, two of them added whole to the batter and five of them separated with the whites beaten. Eureka! At last, we had the perfect chiffon cake: moist, tender, flavorful, and just the right size for the pan.

Chiffon Cake

SERVES 12

In the original recipes for chiffon cake published by General Mills, the directions for beating the egg whites read, "WHIP until whites form very stiff peaks. They should be much stiffer than for angel food or meringue. DO NOT UNDERBEAT." These instructions, with their anxiety-inducing capitalized words, are well taken. If the whites are not very stiff, the cake will not rise properly, and the bottom will be heavy, dense, wet, and custard-like. Better to overbeat than underbeat. After all, if you overbeat the egg whites and they end up dry and "blocky," you can smudge and smear the recalcitrant clumps with the flat side of the spatula to break them up.

CAKE

1 1/2	cups (10 1/2 ounces) sugar
1 1/3	cups (5 1/3 ounces) plain cake flour
2	teaspoons baking powder
1/2	teaspoon salt
7	large eggs, 2 whole, 5 separated, at room temperature
3/4	cup water
1/2	cup vegetable oil
1	tablespoon vanilla extract
1/2	teaspoon almond extract
1/2	teaspoon cream of tartar

GLAZE

4	tablespoons (1/2 stick) unsalted butter, melted
4–5	tablespoons orange juice, lemon juice, milk, or coffee (for date-spice or mocha-nut variations)
2	cups (8 ounces) sifted confectioners' sugar

1. FOR THE CAKE: Adjust an oven rack to the lower-middle position and heat the oven to 325 degrees. Whisk the sugar, flour, baking powder, and salt together in a large bowl. Whisk in the 2 whole eggs, 5 egg yolks (reserve the whites), water, oil, and extracts until the batter is just smooth.

2. Pour the reserved egg whites into the bowl of a standing mixer; beat at low speed until foamy, about 1 minute. Add the cream of tartar, gradually increase the speed to medium-high, and beat the whites until very thick and stiff, just short of dry (as little as 7 minutes in a standing mixer and as long as 10 minutes with a handheld mixer). With a large rubber spatula, fold the whites into the batter, smearing in any blobs of white that resist blending with the flat side of the spatula.

3. Pour the batter into an ungreased large tube pan (9-inch diameter, 16-cup capacity). Rap the pan against the countertop 5 times to rupture any large air pockets. If using a pan with a removable bottom, grasp both sides with your hands while firmly pressing down on the tube with your thumbs to keep the batter from seeping from the pan during the rapping process. Wipe off any batter that may have dripped or splashed onto the inside walls of the pan with a paper towel.

4. Bake the cake until a toothpick or thin skewer inserted in the center comes out clean, 55 to 65 minutes. Immediately turn the cake upside down to cool. If the pan does not have prongs around the rim for elevating the cake, invert the pan onto the neck of a bottle or funnel. Let the cake cool completely, 2 to 3 hours.

5. To unmold, turn the pan upright. Run a thin knife around the pan's circumference between the cake and the pan wall, always pressing against the pan. Use a skewer to loosen the cake from the tube. For a one-piece pan, bang it on the counter several times, then invert it over a serving plate. For a two-piece pan, grasp the tube and lift the cake out of the pan. If glazing the cake, use a fork or paring knife to gently scrape all the crust off the cake. Loosen the cake from the pan bottom with a spatula or knife, then invert the cake onto a serving plate. (The cake can be wrapped in plastic and stored at room temperature for up to 2 days or refrigerated for up to 4 days.)

6. FOR THE GLAZE: Beat the butter, 4 tablespoons of the liquid, and the confectioners' sugar in a medium bowl until smooth. Let the glaze stand 1 minute, then try spreading a little on the cake. If the cake starts to tear, thin the glaze with up to 1 tablespoon more liquid. A little at a time, spread the glaze over the cake top, letting any excess dribble down the sides. Let the cake stand until the glaze dries, about 30 minutes. If you like, spread the dribbles (before they have a chance to harden) to make a thin, smooth coat. Serve.

> VARIATIONS

Banana-Nut Chiffon Cake

Follow recipe for Chiffon Cake, decreasing baking powder to 1¼ teaspoons and adding ¼ teaspoon baking soda. Decrease water to ⅔ cup and vanilla to 1 teaspoon; omit almond extract. Fold 1 cup very smoothly mashed bananas (about 2 medium) and ½ cup finely ground toasted walnuts or pecans into batter before folding in whites. Increase baking time to 60 to 70 minutes.

Chocolate Marble Chiffon Cake

Combine ¼ cup unsweetened cocoa and 2 tablespoons dark brown sugar in a small bowl. Stir in 3 tablespoons boiling water, mixing until smooth. Follow recipe for Chiffon Cake, dividing batter equally into 2 separate bowls. Mix scant ½ cup of batter from 1 bowl into cocoa mixture, then partially fold this mixture back into same bowl so you have 1 bowl of chocolate batter. Sift 3 tablespoons cake flour over chocolate batter and continue to fold until just mixed. Pour half the white and then half the chocolate batter into the pan; repeat. Do not rap pan against the countertop. Bake as directed.

Date-Spice Chiffon Cake

Follow recipe for Chiffon Cake, substituting 1½ cups packed (10½ ounces) dark brown sugar for granulated sugar and adding ¾ cup chopped dates, 2 teaspoons ground cinnamon, ½ teaspoon freshly grated nutmeg, and ¼ teaspoon ground cloves to dry ingredients. Process dry ingredients in a food processor until dates are reduced to ⅛-inch bits and any lumps of brown sugar are pulverized. Transfer dry ingredients to a bowl and whisk in eggs, yolks, water, oil, and vanilla as directed. Omit almond extract.

CHIFFON CAKE 101

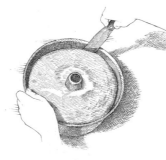

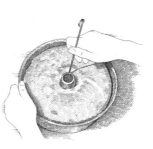

1. Before the batter goes into the oven, grasp the pan on both sides while firmly pressing down on the tube with your thumbs. Rap the pan against the counter five times to rupture any air pockets.

2. After the cake has cooled, with the pan upright on the counter, insert a thin knife between the cake and the wall of the pan. Pressing against the pan, run the knife around the circumference of the cake.

3. To loosen the cake from the tube, scrape around the tube with a wire cake tester or skewer.

4. If glazing the cake, use a fork or paring knife to gently scrape all the crust off the cake.

5. Carefully invert the cake onto a plate.

6. If you like, spread the glaze dribbles, before they have a chance to harden, to make a thin, smooth coat.

Lemon or Lemon-Coconut Chiffon Cake
Follow the recipe for Chiffon Cake, substituting ½ teaspoon baking soda for the baking powder, decreasing the water to ⅔ cup and the vanilla to 1 teaspoon, and omitting the almond extract. Along with the vanilla, add the grated zest of 2 large lemons (about 3 tablespoons) plus 2 tablespoons strained lemon juice. (For Lemon-Coconut Chiffon Cake, proceed as above, adding ⅔ to 1 cup lightly packed sweetened flaked coconut, chopped a bit with a chef's knife, to the batter before folding in the whites.)

Mocha-Nut Chiffon Cake
Follow the recipe for Chiffon Cake, substituting ¾ cup brewed espresso-strength coffee for the water and omitting the almond extract. Add ½ cup finely chopped toasted walnuts and 1 ounce unsweetened chocolate, grated, to the batter before folding in the whites.

Orange or Cranberry-Orange Chiffon Cake
Follow the recipe for Chiffon Cake, substituting 2 tablespoons grated orange zest and ¾ cup strained orange juice for the water, decreasing the vanilla to 1 teaspoon, and omitting the almond extract. (For Cranberry-Orange Chiffon Cake, proceed as above, adding 1 cup cranberries, chopped to ⅛-inch flecks in a food processor, and ½ cup finely chopped toasted walnuts to the batter before folding in the whites.)

POUND CAKE

UNLIKE THEIR MODERN DESCENDANTS, classic pound cakes contain no chemical leaveners. Instead, they depend for lightness on the innate puffing power of eggs and on the air incorporated into the batter through beating. This gives these cakes (which take their name from what is believed to be their original ingredients: a pound each of flour, sugar, butter, and eggs) a wonderful flavor but can cause problems with texture. After testing 31 old-style pound cake recipes, however, we have found one that is perfect in every regard,

and because the cake is made without a speck of baking powder, it tastes of pure butter and eggs.

We embarked on this orgy of baking knowing that the main difficulty with pound cakes of the classic type is textural. Cakes might be said to have five "texture points": moist/dry, soft/hard, dense/porous, light/heavy, rich/plain. To contemporary tastes, cakes must be relatively moist and soft; the three remaining texture points are negotiable.

The problem with pound cake is that we ask it to be moist and soft on the one hand but also dense, light, and rich on the other. This is an extremely difficult texture to achieve unless one resorts to baking powder, with its potent chemical magic. Air-leavened cakes that are light and soft also tend to be porous and plain, as in sponge or angel cakes; moist and dense cakes inevitably also turn out heavy, as in the various syrup-soaked Bundt cakes that are so popular. From pound cake, we ask all things.

In our early experiments, our interest was in comparing the merits of the two major mixing methods for pound cake. Accordingly, we prepared all of the cakes with exactly one-half pound each of flour, sugar, butter, and eggs. When we got what looked to be a promising result, we also tried adding varying amounts of liquid in the hope of achieving perfection.

The first mixing method we tried is probably the most common, and it produced good cakes but not great ones. It entails creaming the butter, sugar, and egg yolks until fluffy, adding the flour, and then folding in the stiffly beaten egg whites. The cakes made this way were a little tough, dry, and heavy, and they did not taste quite rich enough. We next tried adding some of the sugar to the egg whites during beating to give the whites more strength and puffing power. This did make the cakes lighter and more tender, but we still found them dry and insufficiently rich. Adding a quarter cup of liquid, as older cookbooks recommend, made the cakes moister but also turned them rubbery.

The simplest, most straightforward method of making pound cake involves beating the butter and sugar to a fluffy cream, adding the eggs (whole) one at a time, creaming the batter some more, and then mixing in the flour. No matter how we tried to work this method—adding and withholding liquid, beating the batter after putting in the flour (as some old cookbooks recommend)—we got simply awful results. The cakes were rubber doorstops.

Having thus far failed to make a perfect pound cake with either mixing method, we turned our attention to the ingredients themselves. In our readings of old cookbooks, we had long noted that pound cake, in the period of its greatest popularity, was rarely made with precisely 1 pound each of flour, sugar, butter, and eggs; nor were these necessarily the only ingredients used. For example, Eliza Leslie, the Julia Child of the 1830s and 1840s, specifies a "small pound of flour" (around 14 ounces), "a large pound of sugar" (perhaps 18 ounces), and somewhat better than one-half cup of liquid (eggs plus brandy, sherry, or rose water). Leslie's fiddling with the flour and sugar are atypical, but her use of one-half cup liquid is virtually invariable in pound cake recipes written before 1850. Meanwhile, other authors play around with the eggs. In *The Virginia House-Wife* (1824), Mary Randolph specifies a dozen eggs; in her time, 10 eggs were generally considered to weigh 1 pound. Susannah Carter, an English author whose cookery book was published in America in 1772, calls for six whole eggs and six yolks. Carter's idea to use extra yolks eventually proved a cornerstone in our own recipe.

Before tinkering with the sacrosanct pound formula, we decided to consult some modern cookbooks. We could hardly believe what we found in Flo Braker's *The Simple Art of Perfect Baking* (Morrow, 1985). Her classic pound cake is mixed in a way very similar to the second method we had tried, the one that we had found disastrous! We made her pound cake exactly as directed, and it turned out, indeed, to be the very best one we had baked so far. What made the difference?

First of all, Braker refined the mixing method. Instead of adding whole eggs one at a time to the creamed butter and sugar, she directs that the eggs first be lightly beaten in a bowl and then added by the tablespoon to the butter mixture. The butter and sugar mixture is evidently incapable of absorbing whole eggs; the mixture "curdles" and all the air is let out, resulting in tough, shrunken, wet pound cakes. But dribbling in the egg a little at a time preserves the emulsion—Braker astutely compares the process

to making mayonnaise—and allows all the air to be retained, making for a light, soft, tender cake. In baking, everything is in the details.

We also noted that Braker slightly modified the one-pound-each proportions. Her recipe, a "half-pound" cake, like the ones we had been working with, calls for roughly 7 ounces of flour, 9 ounces of sugar, and 5 eggs (10 ounces weighed with the shells, the usual method of computation, or 8¾ ounces weighed without). She calls for 8 ounces of butter, the standard amount, and no added liquid other than almond and vanilla extracts. What a brilliant formula this is. Decreasing the flour makes the cake moister; increasing the sugar makes it more tender and, of course, sweeter; and adding an extra egg adds both moistness and lightness while at the same time compensating for the loss of structure caused by removing a little of the flour.

For many people, Braker's Viceroy Pound Cake will prove to be the only pound cake recipe they will ever need. It is a truly wonderful cake. We were hoping, however, to make a slightly denser cake. Adding liquid to Braker's pound cake made it rubbery; increasing the butter by a mere two tablespoons made it heavy. We tried any number of other small modifications, all to no avail, until

STORING PARCHMENT PAPER

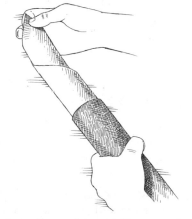

Parchment paper is a must for many baking projects. To save money, we like to buy it in bulk in sheets (rather than in rolls), but storing a large quantity can be a challenge. To keep parchment safe and out of the way, we roll a quantity of parchment paper sheets into a tight cylinder and slide it inside an empty gift-wrap tube that can be stored easily. The sheets can be pulled out, one at a time.

finally we remembered Carter's recipe, with those extra egg yolks. Because they contain lecithin, yolks are good emulsifiers and thus help the batter retain air, making the cake light. Their fattiness contributes richness, tenderness, and moistness, while tamping the batter down a bit and thus militating against too fluffy an effect. Finally, the deep yellow of egg yolks gives the cake a beautiful golden color. Herewith is our own version of the perfect classic pound cake, inspired by gifted bakers living two centuries apart.

Classic Pound Cake

SERVES 8 TO 10

You may double the recipe and bake the cake in a large nonstick Bundt pan (14-cup capacity); the baking time remains the same. The recipe also makes 4 miniature pound cakes; use four 2-cup pans and reduce the baking time to 40 minutes. Though best when freshly baked, the cake will keep reasonably well for up to 5 days. See the results of our testing of loaf pans on page 685.

16	tablespoons (2 sticks) unsalted butter, softened but still cool
1⅓	cups (9⅓ ounces) sugar
3	large eggs, plus 3 large egg yolks, at room temperature
1½	teaspoons vanilla extract
1½	teaspoons water
½	teaspoon salt
1½	cups (6 ounces) plain cake flour

1. Adjust an oven rack to the middle position and heat the oven to 325 degrees. Grease a 9 by 5-inch loaf pan (7½-cup capacity). Fit a sheet of foil or parchment paper lengthwise in the bottom of the greased pan, pushing it into the corners and up the sides. Fit a second sheet crosswise in the pan in the same manner.

2. Beat the butter in the bowl of a standing mixer at medium-high speed until smooth and shiny, about 15 seconds. With the machine still on, sprinkle the sugar in slowly, taking about 30 seconds. Beat the mixture until light, fluffy, and almost white, 4 to 5 minutes, stopping the mixer once or twice to scrape down the sides of the bowl.

3. Stir together the eggs, yolks, vanilla, and water in a 2-cup liquid measuring cup. With the mixer running at medium-high speed, add the egg mixture to the butter and sugar in a very slow, thin stream. Finally, beat in the salt.

4. Place ½ cup of the flour in a sieve and sift it over the batter. Fold gently with a rubber spatula, scraping up from the bottom of the bowl, until the flour is incorporated. Repeat twice more, adding flour in ½-cup increments.

5. Scrape the batter into the prepared pan, smoothing the top with a spatula or wooden spoon. Bake until a toothpick or thin skewer inserted into the crack running along the top comes out clean, 70 to 80 minutes. Let the cake rest in the pan for 5 minutes, then invert onto a wire rack. Place a second wire rack on the cake bottom, then turn the cake top-side up. Cool to room temperature, remove and discard the foil, and serve. If not serving immediately, wrap the cake in plastic, then in foil. Store the cake at room temperature.

VARIATIONS
Ginger Pound Cake
Follow the recipe for Classic Pound Cake, adding 3 tablespoons very finely minced crystallized ginger, 1½ teaspoons ground ginger, and ½ teaspoon mace along with the salt.

Citrus Pound Cake
Follow the recipe for Classic Pound Cake, adding any of the following along with the salt: grated zest of 2 lemons, grated zest of 1 orange, or grated zest of 1 lemon and 1 orange. You can replace the water and vanilla extract with 1 tablespoon orange or lemon blossom water.

CARROT CAKE

A RELIC OF THE HEALTH FOOD CRAZE, CARROT cake was once heralded for its use of vegetable oil in place of butter and carrots as a natural sweetener. But healthy or not (and we doubt that it ever was), we have eaten far more bad carrot cake than good. Sure, the carrots add some sweetness, but they also add a lot of moisture, which is why carrot cake is invariably soggy. And oil? It makes this cake dense and, well, oily. Save for the mercifully thick coating of cream cheese frosting, most carrot cakes seem nothing but a good spice cake gone bad.

We wanted to create a truly great carrot cake. It should be a moist (not soggy) cake that was rich (not greasy). The crumb should be relatively tight and tender, while the spices should be nicely balanced. And what about the cake's namesake? We wanted our cake to contain enough carrots to confirm at first glance that it was indeed carrot cake. We also wanted it to be simple—from ingredient list to mixing method.

Our initial research turned up numerous recipes, and we chose several that seemed promising. Although very different in shape and ingredients, they were, with the exception of one, very bad (see "Some Failed Carrot Cakes" below). But the test wasn't a complete wash, as we learned two very important things.

First, shape matters. Layer cakes could hardly be considered part of our "simple" plan. Loaf cakes were easy but looked more like quick bread than cake. A Bundt cake was easy as well as attractive but difficult to ice with the thick coating of cream cheese frosting that our ultimate cake must have. For our purposes, there was nothing easier than a sheet cake baked in a standard 13 by 9-inch pan.

Second, there are carrot cakes out there made with just about anything and everything. Canned crushed pineapple, toasted coconut, wheat germ, raisins, and nuts all made appearances in the cakes. The first three were unanimously voted out, but the raisins and nuts were liked well enough to make them an option.

All-purpose flour worked better than cake flour (the latter proved too delicate for this sturdy American classic), and we used 2½ cups as the base for our tests. We quickly found that this cake would need healthy amounts of baking soda and baking powder, 1 teaspoon and 1¼ teaspoons, respectively (nearly twice the amount found in many recipes), to give it sufficient lift and a beautiful brown color. Four eggs gave the cake a slight spring and a tender crumb. As for sugar, this cake clearly benefited from both granulated and light brown sugar, the former giving the cake clean sweetness, the latter bringing out the warmth of the spices. While many recipes use handfuls of every baking spice in the pantry, we found that a conservative touch with cinnamon, along with a little help from nutmeg and cloves, won the approval of tasters.

Now that we had a reasonably simple working recipe, we introduced carrots to the mix. We rejected any idea of first boiling, steaming, or pureeing the carrots, as was called for in some recipes. It was just too much work. Grating the carrots was clearly the way to go, but it took a few failed efforts before we realized that just the right amount of carrots was paramount, because their high moisture content could determine whether a cake was moist or soggy. After baking cakes with as little grated carrot as 1 cup (no carrot presence) and as much as 5 cups (soaking-wet cake), we found that 3 cups was the perfect amount to give the cake a pleasantly moist texture. To hasten the grating of the carrots (as well as to spare ourselves

SOME FAILED CARROT CAKES

We uncovered a number of problems in our initial round of testing. Pureed carrots gave one cake (left) an odd texture. The curved Bundt shape (center) was hard to ice, and the cake was bland. One layer cake (right) was so delicate that we had to slice it cold.

TOO SOGGY

TOO BLAND

TOO DELICATE

a few grazed knuckles), we put away our box grater in favor of the food processor.

About 99 percent of carrot cake recipes use oil instead of softened butter in the batter, and while the idea of not having to wait for butter to soften fit into our simple approach, the thought of using oil gave us pause; after all, butter adds flavor and oil does not. As a compromise, we tested melted butter versus oil. We were shocked to find that all the tasters preferred the cleaner taste of the cake made with oil. Any more than 1½ cups of oil and the cake was too dense and greasy; any less and tasters found the cake too lean.

Just as we would with a butter-based cake, we beat the oil with the sugar and then beat the eggs in with an electric mixer before adding the dry ingredients and the carrots. The cake was good, but we still weren't happy with two aspects. First, the bottom of the cake was too dense. Second, we weren't thrilled with the idea of pulling out both a food processor and an electric mixer to bake a "simple" cake. Deciding to work with the easier problem first, we examined our mixing method. Since we were using the food processor to grate the carrots, we wondered if we could use it to mix the cake. We processed the eggs and oil together with the sugar, then added the dry ingredients and finally the carrots. This cake was tough from the beating of the flour. Next time around, we again processed the eggs, oil, and sugar but then transferred the mixture to another bowl, into which we could stir the carrots and dry ingredients. This was much better, but still there was that annoyingly dense bottom.

On a whim, we wondered if gradually adding the oil to the sugar and eggs while the machine was running (much like making a mayonnaise) would have any impact on the cake. You bet it did. By first creating this stable emulsion of eggs and oil, we were breaking up the oil into tiny particles that were less likely to sink to the bottom, instead dispersing themselves evenly throughout the cake. No more soggy bottom, no more heavy texture. This cake was light, tender, and pleasantly moist.

Our cake was now good enough to eat on its own, but there was no way we were going to pass up the frosting. Made with cream cheese, butter, and confectioners' sugar, cream cheese frosting is

one of those things that, even when it's bad, it's still good. So we made (and happily ate) several frostings made with various amounts of each ingredient. We added vanilla for depth of flavor, but it wasn't until we added a little sour cream that the frosting really shone on top of the cake—at last, we had a carrot cake worth eating.

Carrot Cake with Cream Cheese Frosting
SERVES 10 TO 12

If you like nuts in your cake, stir 1½ cups toasted chopped pecans or walnuts into the batter along with the carrots. Raisins are also a good addition; 1 cup can be added along with the carrots. If you add both nuts and raisins, the cake will need an additional 10 to 12 minutes in the oven. See the results of our cream cheese tasting on page 762.

CARROT CAKE

2½	cups (12½ ounces) unbleached all-purpose flour
1¼	teaspoons baking powder
1	teaspoon baking soda
1¼	teaspoons ground cinnamon
½	teaspoon freshly grated nutmeg
⅛	teaspoon ground cloves
½	teaspoon salt
1	pound carrots (6 to 7 medium), peeled
1½	cups (10½ ounces) granulated sugar
½	cup packed (3½ ounces) light brown sugar
4	large eggs
1½	cups safflower, canola, or vegetable oil

CREAM CHEESE FROSTING

8	ounces cream cheese, softened but still cool
5	tablespoons unsalted butter, softened but still cool
1	tablespoon sour cream
½	teaspoon vanilla extract
1¼	cups (5 ounces) confectioners' sugar

1. FOR THE CAKE: Adjust an oven rack to the middle position; heat the oven to 350 degrees. Spray a 13 by 9-inch baking pan with nonstick cooking spray. Line the bottom of the pan with parchment paper and spray the parchment.

2. Whisk together the flour, baking powder, baking soda, spices, and salt in a medium bowl; set aside.

3. In a food processor fitted with the large shredding disk, shred the carrots (you should have about 3 cups); add the carrots to the bowl with the dry ingredients and set aside. Wipe out the food processor and fit with the metal blade. Process both sugars with the eggs until frothy and thoroughly combined, about 20 seconds. With the machine running, add the oil through the feed tube in a steady stream. Process until the mixture is light in color and well emulsified, about 20 seconds longer. Scrape the mixture into a large bowl. Stir in the carrots and dry ingredients until incorporated and no streaks of flour remain. Pour into the prepared pan and bake until a toothpick or skewer inserted into the center of the cake comes out clean, 35 to 40 minutes, rotating the pan from front to back halfway through the baking time. Cool the cake to room temperature in the pan on a wire rack, about 2 hours.

4. FOR THE FROSTING: When the cake is cool, process the cream cheese, butter, sour cream, and vanilla in a clean food processor until combined, about 5 seconds, scraping down the workbowl with a rubber spatula as needed. Add the confectioners' sugar and process until smooth, about 10 seconds.

5. Run a paring knife around the edge of the cake to loosen it from the pan. Invert the cake onto a wire rack, peel off the parchment, and invert the cake onto a serving platter. Using an offset spatula, spread the frosting evenly over the surface of the cake. Cut into squares and serve.

➤ VARIATIONS

Spiced Carrot Cake with Vanilla Bean–Cream Cheese Frosting

The Indian tea called chai inspired this variation.

Follow the recipe for Carrot Cake with Cream Cheese Frosting, substituting an equal amount of ground black pepper for the nutmeg, increasing the cloves to ¼ teaspoon, and adding 1 tablespoon ground cardamom along with the spices. For the frosting, halve and scrape the seeds from 2 vanilla beans, using a paring knife, and add the seeds to the food processor along with the vanilla extract.

Ginger-Orange Carrot Cake with Orange–Cream Cheese Frosting

Follow the recipe for Carrot Cake with Cream Cheese Frosting, reducing the cinnamon to ½ teaspoon, adding 1½ teaspoons ground ginger along with the spices, processing 1 tablespoon grated orange zest along with the sugar and eggs, and adding ½ cup finely chopped crystallized ginger along with the carrots. For the frosting, substitute an equal amount of orange juice for the sour cream and 1 tablespoon grated orange zest for the vanilla.

CRUMB COFFEECAKE

GREAT WITH A CUP OF STRONG COFFEE OR A tall glass of cold milk, crumb coffeecake is a classic. Made well, it's a far cry from the cellophane-wrapped supermarket versions so often seen today: heavy, leaden cake with achingly sweet crumb topping—and too much of it. We wanted to develop a simple old-fashioned crumb cake with good buttery flavor and just enough crumb topping for balance.

Crumb coffeecake is nothing more than a single layer of buttery yellow cake topped with crumbs made from sugar, flour, and butter. We had seen recipes that use the same flour-sugar mixture for the topping and as the basis of the batter. We were intrigued. Although these recipes might seem odd, they do make some sense. Cake batters and crumb toppings are composed of the same basic ingredients—namely, flour, sugar, and butter. The main difference between the two is that cake batters contain liquid, which binds the protein and starch in flour into a springy, cohesive mass, while crumb toppings are made without liquid and thus remain loose. A recipe that derives both cake and crumbs from the same basic mixture seemed like a great way to simplify the preparation process.

We baked up cakes from several sources but were disappointed. First of all, there were not nearly enough crumbs, although this problem was easily remedied. The bigger issue was the lack of contrast between the batter and the topping. Either the cake was too brown or the crumbs were insipid—they needed the molasses flavor of brown sugar. We devised a two-tone cake (a yellow cake topped with dark brown crumbs) by making the initial crumb mixture with granulated sugar and then adding brown sugar to the topping crumbs only.

Other problems proved trickier to solve. None of the recipes that we tested were quite buttery enough, but when we tried adding more butter to the batter, the cake became too weak to support the crumbs and collapsed in the center. Increasing the flour shored up the cake but also made it dry and puffy.

We knew that adding a bit more buttermilk (our liquid of choice) would strengthen the structure by promoting the gelatinization of the starch in the flour, but we resisted this option because we thought the resulting batter would be too liquid to hold fruit (an ingredient in some variations) in suspension. When we finally bit the bullet and put a little more buttermilk in, we were pleasantly surprised. The batter was less stiff and easier to beat, and we found that a thorough beating aerated and emulsified the ingredients, making the batter wonderfully thick and fluffy. Even with a goodly quantity of butter added, the cake with more buttermilk rose perfectly, and the fruit stayed firmly suspended.

➤≍

Old-Fashioned Crumb Coffeecake

SERVES 8 TO 10

This cake is best eaten on the day it is baked, though it may be made a day ahead. The batter is quite heavy, so you may prefer to beat it with an electric mixer at medium-high speed for a minute or so rather than whisk it by hand.

1	tablespoon dry bread crumbs
2	cups (10 ounces) unbleached all-purpose flour
1	cup plus 2 tablespoons (7⅞ ounces) granulated sugar
1	teaspoon salt
10	tablespoons (1¼ sticks) unsalted butter, softened but still cool
1	teaspoon baking powder
½	teaspoon baking soda
¾	cup buttermilk or low-fat (not nonfat) plain yogurt, at room temperature
1	large egg, at room temperature
1	teaspoon vanilla extract
¾	cup walnuts or pecans, chopped fine
½	cup packed (3½ ounces) dark brown sugar
1	teaspoon ground cinnamon

1. Adjust an oven rack to the middle position and heat the oven to 350 degrees. Generously grease the bottom and lightly grease the sides of a 10-inch springform pan. Sprinkle the bottom of the pan with the bread crumbs, then shake lightly to coat. Tap out excess crumbs.

2. Whisk the flour, sugar, and salt in a large mixing bowl until blended. Add the butter and cut in with the whisk until the mixture resembles coarse crumbs. Remove 1 cup of the flour mixture to a separate bowl and set aside.

3. Whisk the baking powder and baking soda into the flour mixture remaining in the mixing bowl. Add the buttermilk, egg, and vanilla; whisk vigorously until the batter is thick, smooth, fluffy, and frosting-like, 1½ to 2 minutes. Using a rubber spatula, scrape the batter into the prepared pan and smooth the top.

4. Add the nuts, brown sugar, and cinnamon to the reserved crumbs of flour, sugar, and butter; toss with a fork or your hands until blended. Sprinkle the crumbs over the batter, pressing lightly so that they adhere. Bake the cake until the center is firm and a cake tester comes out clean, 50 to 55 minutes. Transfer the cake to a wire rack; remove the sides of the pan. Let the cake cool completely, about 2 hours, before serving. When completely cool, the cake can be slid off the pan bottom onto a serving plate.

➤ VARIATIONS

Apple-Cinnamon Coffeecake

Peel and core 2 medium-large Granny Smith apples and cut them into ¼-inch dice. Heat 1 tablespoon butter in a 10-inch skillet (preferably nonstick) over high heat until golden. Add the apples, cover, and cook over high heat, stirring frequently, until they are dry and very tender, 2 to 3 minutes. Remove from the heat, sprinkle the apples with 2 tablespoons sugar, and lightly toss until glazed. Cool to room temperature. Follow the recipe for Old-Fashioned Crumb Coffeecake, adding 1 teaspoon cinnamon with the baking powder and baking soda and folding the apples into the finished batter.

Raspberry-Almond Coffeecake

Follow the recipe for Old-Fashioned Crumb Coffeecake, adding 1 teaspoon almond extract along with the vanilla. Turn the batter into the pan. Beat ½ cup seedless raspberry jam until smooth and fluid, then carefully spread it over the batter with the back of a teaspoon. For the crumb topping, substitute ¾ cup ground almonds for walnuts and ½ cup granulated sugar for the dark brown sugar; omit the cinnamon. Add 1 large egg yolk and 1 teaspoon almond extract to the topping and mix with a fork. Thoroughly knead the mixture with your fingers until the color is uniform.

SOUR CREAM COFFEECAKE

A STATUESQUE SOUR CREAM COFFEECAKE WITH delicate streusel swirls and mounds of streusel topping is the king of coffeecakes. Not only does it taste fabulously rich and hearty, but it is easy to make, looks impressive on a cake stand, is apropos morning through night, and has the potential to last well beyond its first day out of the oven.

But in the recipes we tried, the coffeecakes were either too stout or too sweet, too spicy or too bland, and sometimes even too tough. The streusel inside of the cake was most often wet and pasty, and the streusel topping sometimes melted into the cake, while other times it stayed sandy and granular.

In our efforts to revamp sour cream coffeecake, we decided to first isolate what was important to us. We all agreed that a tube pan lent the most handsome presentation to the cake shape and that we liked streusel so much that we wanted two layers of it—plus the crowning topping.

Because this cake is a behemoth, with hefty amounts of sour cream, butter, eggs, and streusel, a strong flour like all-purpose is required. For the traditional buttery yellow cake color, we decided on four eggs, enough to give structure to the cake and provide for a tight crumb. We also added a generous amount of baking powder to help lighten the cake's load and baking soda to react with the acidity of the sour cream. As far as fat goes, the more the better, since this is what gives the strong

cake its sensitive side and its ability to stay moist for days. One and a half sticks of butter and 1½ cups of sour cream seemed to do the trick. To keep the cake from being too heavy, we chose to use only granulated sugar in the cake base.

Crispy, crunchy, yet melt-in-your-mouth streusel requires a careful balance among sugar, flour, and butter; nuts and spices also warrant careful scrutiny. Our first discovery was to treat the top streusel and the interior streusel separately. We enjoyed the contrast of tender cake to crunchy topping and so decided to use nuts only in the topping. One cup was just the right amount. We also found that the interior layers of streusel became pasty when we included butter in the mix, so butter, like nuts, would be reserved for the topping. We did like the appearance and flavor from the combined use of granulated and dark brown sugar for both the topping and the inner layers of streusel. In both cases, we also found flour necessary to keep the sugar in the streusel from melting or congealing in cement-like shards. Cinnamon—and a hefty dose of it at 2 tablespoons—was the only spice needed to lend warmth to the streusel's flavor.

About one hour in the oven at 350 degrees proved to be the best and easiest option for baking; at higher temperatures, the streusel became too dark, requiring an aluminum foil shield to protect it from the heat. Because the recipe is quite saturated with fat, we found it best to let the cake cool in the pan for at least one hour to become crack-proof before unmolding. We were pleased to find that if stored well, this cake actually improves with age.

~≫≼~

Sour Cream Coffeecake

SERVES 16

To prevent leakage and for best results, we strongly recommend using a tube pan made of one piece of metal (rather than a two-piece angel food cake pan, which has a removable bottom). In a pinch, you can wrap the bottom of an angel food cake pan with foil before baking, although this improvisation will not work with the Lemon-Blueberry Sour Cream Coffeecake variation, which contains more moisture (from the berries) than the other cakes. Note, too, that with an angel food cake pan wrapped in foil, the cake may take longer to bake and will not brown as well as a cake made in a one-piece pan.

STREUSEL

³/₄	cup (3³/₄ ounces) unbleached all-purpose flour
³/₄	cup (5¹/₄ ounces) granulated sugar
¹/₂	cup packed (3¹/₂ ounces) dark brown sugar
2	tablespoons ground cinnamon
2	tablespoons cold unsalted butter
I	cup pecans, chopped

CAKE

4	large eggs
I¹/₂	cups sour cream
I	tablespoon vanilla extract
2¹/₄	cups (11¹/₄ ounces) unbleached all-purpose flour
I¹/₄	cups (8³/₄ ounces) granulated sugar
I	tablespoon baking powder
³/₄	teaspoon baking soda
³/₄	teaspoon salt
12	tablespoons (1¹/₂ sticks) unsalted butter, softened but still cool, cut into 1-inch cubes

1. FOR THE STREUSEL: Place the flour, granulated sugar, ¼ cup of the dark brown sugar, and the cinnamon in a food processor and process to combine. Transfer 1¼ cups of this mixture to a small bowl and stir in the remaining ¼ cup brown sugar; set aside (this will be the streusel for the inside of the cake). Add the butter and pecans to the remaining dry ingredients in the food processor bowl. Process the mixture until the nuts and butter have been broken down into small pebbly pieces, about ten 1-second

pulses. Set aside. (The streusel with the butter and nuts will be for the top of the cake.)

2. FOR THE CAKE: Adjust an oven rack to the lowest position and heat the oven to 350 degrees. Grease a tube pan (10-inch diameter, 10-cup capacity). Combine the eggs, 1 cup of the sour cream, and the vanilla in a medium bowl.

3. In the bowl of a standing mixer, combine the flour, sugar, baking powder, baking soda, and salt at low speed, about 30 seconds. Add the butter and the remaining ½ cup sour cream and mix at low speed until the dry ingredients are moistened. Increase to medium speed and beat 30 seconds. Scrape down the sides of the bowl with a rubber spatula. Decrease the mixer speed to medium-low and slowly incorporate the egg mixture in 3 additions, beating for 20 seconds after each addition and scraping the sides of the bowl as necessary. Increase the speed to medium-high and beat for 1 minute (the batter should increase in volume and become aerated and pale in color).

4. Add 2 cups of the batter to the prepared pan. With an offset metal spatula or rubber spatula, smooth the surface of the batter. Sprinkle with ¾ cup of the streusel filling (without butter or nuts). Drop 2 cups of the batter over the streusel, spread evenly, and then add the remaining streusel filling. Top with the remaining batter and then the streusel topping (with the butter and nuts).

5. Bake until the cake feels firm to the touch and a toothpick or thin skewer inserted into the center comes out clean (although there may be bits of sugar from the streusel clinging to the tester), 50 to 60 minutes. Cool the cake in the pan for

---

LAYERING COFFEECAKE BATTER AND STREUSEL

1. Spread 2 cups of the batter in the bottom of the prepared pan, smoothing the surface.

2. Sprinkle evenly with ³/₄ cup of the streusel filling without butter or nuts.

3. Repeat steps 1 and 2 with 2 cups batter and the remaining streusel without butter or nuts.

4. Spread the remaining batter on top, then sprinkle with the streusel topping with butter and nuts.

30 minutes. Place a rimmed baking sheet over the top of the cake and invert the cake onto the sheet (the cake should now be upside down, with the streusel on the bottom). Remove the tube pan, place a wire rack on the cake, and reinvert so the streusel is facing up. Cool for 2 hours and serve, or cool completely and wrap the cake in aluminum foil.

➤ VARIATIONS

Chocolate Chip Sour Cream Coffeecake
Follow the recipe for Sour Cream Coffeecake, sprinkling ½ cup semisweet chocolate chips on top of the cake batter before adding the first and second streusel layers, for a total of 1 cup chips. Finish the assembly and bake as instructed.

Lemon-Blueberry Sour Cream Coffeecake
Toss 1 cup frozen blueberries with 1 teaspoon grated lemon zest in a small bowl. Follow the recipe for Sour Cream Coffeecake, sprinkling ½ cup blueberries on top of the cake batter before adding the first and second streusel layers, for a total of 1 cup blueberries. Finish the assembly and bake as instructed.

Almond-Apricot Sour Cream Coffeecake
Follow the recipe for Sour Cream Coffeecake, substituting blanched slivered almonds for the pecans and adding ½ teaspoon almond extract with the vanilla extract. Spoon ½ cup apricot preserves into a zipper-lock bag. Cut off a corner tip. Squeeze 6 dollops of apricot preserves on top of the cake batter before adding the first and second streusel layers, for a total of 12 dollops. Finish the assembly and bake as instructed.

CHOCOLATE SHEET CAKE

A SHEET CAKE IS LIKE A TWO-LAYER CAKE WITH training wheels—it's hard to fall off. Unlike regular cakes, which often require trimming and decorating skills to make sure the cake doesn't turn out lopsided, domed, or altogether amateurish, sheet cakes are single-story and easy to frost. These are the sorts of cakes made for church suppers, old home days, bake sales, and Fourth of July picnics, decorated with red, white, and blue frosting.

But sheet cakes are still cakes. They can still turn out dry, sticky, or flavorless and, on occasion, can even sink in the middle. So we set out to find the simplest, most dependable recipe for a chocolate sheet cake, one that was moist yet also light and chocolatey.

First off, a sheet cake is nothing more than cake batter baked in one layer, usually in a square or rectangular pan. We started with a test batch of five different recipes that required a variety of mixing techniques, everything from creaming butter to beating yolks, whipping whites, and gently folding everything together at the end. The best of the lot was the most complicated to make. But we were taken with another recipe that simply whisked together the ingredients without beating, creaming, or whipping. Although the recipe needed work, its approach was clearly a good match for the simple, all-purpose nature of a sheet cake.

The recipe called for 2 sticks butter, 4 eggs, 1½ cups flour, 2 cups sugar, ½ cup cocoa, 1 teaspoon vanilla, and ⅛ teaspoon salt. Our first change was to add buttermilk, baking powder, and baking soda to lighten the batter, as the cake had been dense and chewy in its original form. To increase the chocolate flavor, we reduced the sugar and flour, increased the cocoa, and decreased the butter. To further deepen the chocolate taste, we decided to use semisweet chocolate in addition to the cocoa. With this revised recipe and our simple mixing method, we actually had a cake that was superior to those whose recipes called for creaming butter or whipping eggs.

The only significant problem came when we tested natural versus Dutch-processed cocoa and discovered that the cake fell a bit in the center when we used the former. A few tests later, we eliminated the baking powder entirely, relying instead on baking soda alone, and the problem was fixed. (Natural cocoa is more acidic than Dutch-processed, and when it was combined with baking powder, which also contains acid, it produced an excess of carbon dioxide gas. This in turn caused the cake to rise very fast and then fall like a deflated balloon.)

Also of note is the low oven temperature— 325 degrees—which, combined with a relatively long baking time of 40 minutes, produced a perfectly baked cake with a lovely flat top. Using a microwave oven rather than a double boiler to melt the chocolate and butter also saved time and hassle.

This cake can be frosted with almost anything—buttercream, Italian meringue, sour cream frosting, or whipped cream frosting—but we developed a classic American milk chocolate frosting that pairs well with the darker flavor of the cake. Unlike a two-layer cake, this cake is a snap to frost.

Chocolate Sheet Cake

SERVES 10 TO 12

Melting the chocolate and butter in the microwave is quick and neat, but it can also be done in a heatproof bowl set over a saucepan containing 2 inches of simmering water. We prefer Dutch-processed cocoa for the deeper chocolate flavor it gives this cake. If you prefer the cake unfrosted, lightly sweetened Whipped Cream (page 985) makes a nice accompaniment.

³⁄₄	cup (2¹⁄₄ ounces) cocoa, preferably Dutch-processed
1¹⁄₄	cups (6¹⁄₄ ounces) unbleached all-purpose flour
¹⁄₂	teaspoon baking soda
¹⁄₄	teaspoon salt
8	ounces semisweet chocolate, chopped
12	tablespoons (1¹⁄₂ sticks) unsalted butter
4	large eggs
1¹⁄₂	cups (10¹⁄₂ ounces) sugar
1	teaspoon vanilla extract
1	cup buttermilk

**Creamy Milk Chocolate Frosting
(recipe follows)**

1. Adjust an oven rack to the middle position and heat the oven to 325 degrees. Grease the bottom and sides of a 13 by 9-inch baking pan.
2. Sift together the cocoa, flour, baking soda, and salt in a medium bowl; set aside. Heat the chocolate and butter in a microwave-safe bowl covered with plastic wrap for 2 minutes at 50 percent power; stir until smooth. (If not fully melted, heat 1 minute longer at 50 percent power.) Whisk

together the eggs, sugar, and vanilla in a medium bowl. Whisk in the buttermilk until smooth.
3. Whisk the chocolate mixture into the egg mixture until combined. Whisk in the dry ingredients until the batter is smooth and glossy. Pour the batter into the prepared pan; bake until firm in the center when lightly pressed and a toothpick inserted in the center comes out clean, about 40 minutes. Cool on a wire rack until room temperature, at least 1 hour; ice with the frosting, if desired, and serve.

Creamy Milk Chocolate Frosting

MAKES ABOUT 2 CUPS,
ENOUGH TO ICE ONE 13 BY 9-INCH CAKE

This frosting needs about an hour to cool before it can be used, so begin making it when the cake comes out of the oven.

¹⁄₂	cup heavy cream
	Pinch salt
1	tablespoon light or dark corn syrup
10	ounces milk chocolate, chopped
¹⁄₂	cup (2 ounces) confectioners' sugar
8	tablespoons (1 stick) cold unsalted butter, cut into 8 pieces

1. Heat the cream, salt, and corn syrup in a microwave-safe measuring cup on high until simmering, about 1 minute, or bring to a simmer in a small saucepan over medium heat.
2. Place the chocolate in a food processor. With the machine running, gradually add the hot cream mixture through the feed tube; process 1 minute after the cream has been added. Stop the machine; add the confectioners' sugar and process to combine, about 30 seconds. With the machine running, add the butter through the feed tube, one piece at a time; process until incorporated and smooth, about 20 seconds longer.
3. Transfer the frosting to a medium bowl and cool, stirring frequently, until thick and spreadable, about 1 hour.

Simple Ideas for Cake Decorating

WRITING ON A CAKE

When writing a message on top of a frosted cake, it's easiest to use chocolate on a light-colored frosting.

1. Put chopped semisweet or bittersweet chocolate in a zipper-lock plastic bag and immerse the bag in hot water until the chocolate melts. Dry the bag, then snip off a small piece from one corner.

2. Holding the bag in one hand, gently squeeze the chocolate from the hole as you write.

GIVING FROSTING A SILKY LOOK

Professionally frosted cakes seem to have a molten, silky look. To get that same appearance at home, frost as usual and then use a hair dryer to "blow-dry" the surface of the cake. The slight melting of the frosting gives it that smooth, lustrous appearance.

REMOVING STENCILS

Store-bought stencils are an easy way to decorate with confectioners' sugar or cocoa powder. Removing the stencil without marring the design can be tricky. Here's how we do it.

1. Create 2 handles for the stencil by folding 2 short lengths of masking tape back onto themselves, pinching the middle sections together. Stick the ends of the tape to the top and bottom of the stencil, placing a handle on either side.

2. Place the stencil on top of the cake and dust with confectioners' sugar or cocoa powder. When you are done, use the tape handles to grasp and lift the stencil straight up and off the cake.

DUSTING WITH CONFECTIONERS' SUGAR

Simple single-layer cakes, such as a flourless chocolate cake, are rarely frosted, but they can be dressed up with some confectioners' sugar. This trick adds a bit of flair to an otherwise plain sugar dusting.

1. Lay strips of paper about ¾ inch wide across the top of the cake, then sieve the confectioners' sugar over the cake.

2. Carefully lift away the paper strips to reveal an attractive striped pattern.

PUTTING A PATTERN IN FROSTING

A frosted cake can be easily styled in three ways. All of these designs are best accomplished when the frosting has just been applied and is still soft.

A. Use the tines of a dinner fork to make wave designs in the frosting. Wipe the fork clean intermittently. You can make this pattern on the top of the cake or on the top and sides.

B. Use the tip of a thin, metal icing spatula to stipple the top and sides of the cake.

C. Use the back of a large dinner spoon to make swirls on top of the cake.

CUPCAKES

CUPCAKES ARE MANAGEABLE. THEY ARE EASY TO transport, easy to serve (no plate and fork required) and, when made well, delicious. The cupcakes we remember from childhood birthday parties were rich, dense, and moist little yellow cakes lavishly topped with mounds of fluffy, lush, sweet chocolate. Unfortunately, times have changed. It's too easy for busy parents to pick up a box of cupcakes from the supermarket bakery. Often, these cupcakes are dry and crumbly, topped with greasy frosting, or, even worse, cloyingly sweet, rubbery, and leaden. We wanted to make a better cupcake, one so delicious that children would savor the cake itself instead of just licking off the icing. We also wanted a cupcake good enough to satisfy grownups, too.

We tried almost every cupcake recipe we could find and discovered no clear winners. The major ingredients (flour, sugar, eggs, butter, and some sort of dairy product) were consistent enough among the recipes we tested, but their proportions and the exact type were up for grabs. We started with an investigation of which kind of flour to use and whether or not to sift it. We tested cake flour, pastry flour, and all-purpose flour. Cake flour and pastry flour were rejected by the panel of tasters almost immediately. Both produced too fine a texture; besides, pastry flour is difficult to find. All-purpose flour was the flour of choice. Most recipes we tested called for sifting because it aerates the flour, making it lighter. We sifted once. We sifted twice. We even sifted three times. When we made cupcakes using sifted flour, tasters found them extremely airy, a desirable quality in certain cakes but not in a cupcake. In fact, one taster who initially described the sifted-flour cupcakes as "too fluffy" later admitted, reluctantly, that they reminded her of Twinkies.

Once we had nailed down the type and texture of the flour, we tackled the eggs. Quantities ranged from three yolks to three whole eggs to varying combinations of yolks and whole eggs. The version we liked best included one whole egg and two yolks; these cupcakes had the golden beauty of the cupcakes with three whole eggs, but without the two whites they were richer.

We moved on to the dairy, trying whole milk, buttermilk, yogurt (low-fat and full-fat), heavy cream, and sour cream. Although we all ended up preferring the slightly tangy richness of the sour cream, none of the options, except for the yogurt, were considered flops. When it came to butter, ½ cup of unsalted butter at room temperature was the right choice. We did try melting the butter, but it produced a slightly heavier cake that tasters found to be less appealing. We next tried varying amounts of sugar and found that 1 cup was best. More sugar reminded us of the cloyingly sweet cupcakes we've had the misfortune to sample, but less sugar produced something akin to a muffin.

It was time to test mixing methods more methodically. We tested two quite different options. First we used the classic creaming method, which starts by creaming the butter and sugar together, adding eggs, and then alternately adding dry and wet ingredients. Next we tried the two-stage method (recommended when you want a finer, more velvety texture), whereby butter is cut into the flour and other dry ingredients, after which the eggs and liquid are added. The results? Both techniques worked fine, and the cupcakes were barely distinguishable from each other.

At this point, we had made about 25 batches of cupcakes. On a whim, we simply threw everything—dry ingredients, butter, and wet ingredients—into a bowl in no particular order and turned on the mixer. Some members of the test kitchen staff were

BAKING OUTSIDE THE TIN

If you don't own a muffin tin, we found that foil liners are sturdy enough to hold our cupcake batter. Simply arrange the liners on a rimmed baking sheet and then fill them with batter. Note that cupcakes baked in a muffin tin brown on both the bottom and sides. If cupcakes are baked without a muffin tin, only the bottoms (and not the sides) will brown.

~~~~~~

EQUIPMENT: Muffin Liners

Experimenting with muffin liners turned us into devotees of these little paper or foil cups. No matter how much we buttered and floured the pans, which seemed like way too much work, the cupcakes never came out as easily as they did when the tins were lined. When baked without liners, one or two cupcakes were inevitably ruined during the removal process. All brands of liners were equally successful in tests, although foil liners can be used independent of a muffin tin. If you're using muffin top pans, flatten the liners to fit the bottom. While the idea of turning cupcakes into muffin tops may be anathema to a purist, it's an especially good option if your kids prefer the frosting and decorations to the cake, because the cakes turn out wide and flat.

skeptical (to say the least), but in a blind tasting, everyone preferred this kitchen-sink method over the two more conventional mixing methods. The obvious question was, Why? One possible answer is that egg yolks contain emulsifiers that hold the fat and liquid together even when mixed in such a haphazard fashion. We continued testing this method by mixing the batter by hand (instead of with an electric mixer) and by using it to bake muffin tops and a cake. All three tests were winners. This cupcake batter was simple and invincible.

After much anticipation from tasters, it was time to perfect a chocolate frosting. The classic choice is buttercream, which entails whisking eggs and sugar over simmering water until the temperature reaches 160 degrees, whipping this mixture for 5 minutes until it is light and airy, and finally beating in softened butter a few tablespoons at a time. This seemed like an awful lot of work for something as simple as cupcakes, so we opted for an easy frosting, in which hot heavy cream is whisked together with chopped chocolate. Adding vanilla extract and cocoa to pump up the flavor seemed like a good idea, but they turned out to be extraneous. Experiments with amounts and types of chocolate resulted in a combination of 8 ounces semisweet chocolate and 1 cup heavy cream. Most tasters wanted a massive amount of frosting, but they also wanted it to be light. The solution was to whip the frosting after it had cooled, which produced a fluffy, rich chocolate frosting.

Now the next time your kids ask you to make cupcakes, it will be a lot easier to say yes. You can throw the batter together and produce a cupcake that even adults will want to eat.

Yellow Cupcakes with Simple Chocolate Frosting

MAKES 12

Make the frosting first. While it cools, prepare and bake the cupcakes; when the cupcakes are cool, the frosting will be ready to be whipped and used. If you prefer, you may opt not to whip the frosting. It will be denser and have slightly less volume (see the photos below for more information). Bittersweet, milk, or white chocolate can be substituted for the semisweet chocolate. The recipe can be doubled.

These cupcakes are best eaten the day they are made, but unfrosted extras will keep in an airtight container at room temperature for up to 3 days. To double the recipe, use 3 whole eggs and 2 yolks and double the remaining ingredients.

CHANGING FROSTING TEXTURE

The unwhipped frosting is dense and shiny. The whipped frosting is fluffier, a bit lighter in color, and not as shiny. Although most tasters preferred the fluffier texture of the whipped frosting, several tasters liked the shinier unwhipped frosting. Either may be used to frost our cupcakes. Don't let the frosting chill for more than an hour before whipping, or it can separate. Excessive whipping may cause the frosting to curdle.

UNWHIPPED FROSTING   **WHIPPED FROSTING**   **CURDLED FROSTING**

SIMPLE CHOCOLATE FROSTING

1   cup heavy cream
8   ounces semisweet chocolate, chopped

CUPCAKES

1 1/2   cups (7 1/2 ounces) unbleached all-purpose flour
1   cup (7 ounces) sugar
1 1/2   teaspoons baking powder
1/2   teaspoon salt
8   tablespoons (1 stick) unsalted butter,
    softened
1/2   cup sour cream
1   large egg, plus 2 large egg yolks,
    at room temperature
1 1/2   teaspoons vanilla extract

1. FOR THE FROSTING: Bring the cream to a simmer in a small saucepan or in a microwave. Place the chocolate in a medium bowl and pour the hot cream over it. Cover the bowl with foil and let stand 5 minutes. Whisk the mixture until smooth, then cover with plastic wrap and refrigerate until cool and slightly firm, 45 minutes to 1 hour.

2. Transfer the frosting to the bowl of a standing mixer. Whip the mixture at medium speed until it is fluffy and mousse-like and forms medium-stiff peaks, about 2 minutes. Set aside.

3. FOR THE CUPCAKES: Meanwhile, adjust an oven rack to the middle position; heat the oven to 350 degrees. Line a standard muffin tin with paper or foil liners.

4. Whisk together the flour, sugar, baking powder, and salt in the bowl of a standing mixer. Add the butter, sour cream, egg, yolks, and vanilla and beat the wet ingredients into the dry at medium speed until smooth and satiny, about 30 seconds. Scrape down the sides of the bowl with a rubber spatula and stir by hand until smooth and no flour pockets remain.

5. Divide the batter evenly among the cups of the prepared tin using a 2-ounce ice cream scoop or a spoon. Bake until the cupcake tops are pale gold and a toothpick or skewer inserted into the center comes out clean, 20 to 24 minutes. Use a skewer or paring knife to lift the cupcakes from the tin and transfer to a wire rack; cool the cupcakes to room temperature, about 45 minutes.

6. Spread 2 to 3 generous tablespoons of the frosting on top of each cooled cupcake; serve.

YELLOW LAYER CAKE

YELLOW LAYER CAKE IS AS FAMILIAR TO Americans as apple pie. Its buttery vanilla flavor makes it almost good enough to eat on its own, although iced with a creamy frosting is how we like it best. Its popularity drove companies like Betty Crocker and Pillsbury (and many others) to create boxed mix versions of the cake, as well as plastic cans of ready-made frostings, that today take up most of the baking aisle at the supermarket.

As easy as the boxed mixes are to put together, nothing can beat the flavor of a home-baked cake. And it is not difficult or time-consuming. Yellow cake has always been a broad category, but most of the recipes for making it are very similar. For example, in *The Boston Cook Book,* published in 1884, Mary Lincoln, one of Fannie Farmer's colleagues at the Boston Cooking School, outlined several recipes for yellow cake. But she singled out one as "the foundation for countless varieties of cake, which are often given in cook books under different names." Mrs. Lincoln's master cake formula turns out to be similar to what we today call a 1-2-3-4 cake, made with 1 cup of butter, 2 cups of sugar, 3 cups of (sifted) cake flour, and 4 eggs, plus milk and small amounts of baking powder, vanilla, and salt.

As it turns out, things have not changed much since more than a century ago. When analyzed, most of the yellow cake recipes in today's cookbooks are 1-2-3-4 cakes or something very similar.

So when we set out in search of the perfect yellow cake, the first thing we did was bake a 1-2-3-4 cake. It wasn't a bad cake; it just wasn't very interesting. Instead of melting in the mouth, the cake seemed crumbly, sugary, and a little hard. The crust was tacky and separated from the underlying cake. Above all, the cake lacked flavor. It did not taste of butter and eggs, as all plain cakes ought to, but instead seemed merely sweet.

Before tinkering with the ingredients, we decided to try a different mixing method. We had mixed our 1-2-3-4 cake in the classic way, first beating the butter and sugar until light and fluffy, then adding the eggs one at a time, and finally adding the dry ingredients and milk alternately. Now we wanted to try mixing the batter by the so-called two-stage method, developed by General Mills and Pillsbury in the 1940s and later popularized by Rose Levy Beranbaum in *The Cake Bible* (William Morrow, 1988).

In the two-stage method, the flour, sugar, baking powder, and salt are combined; the butter and about two-thirds of the milk and eggs are added; and the batter is beaten until thick and fluffy, about a minute. Then, in the second stage, the rest of the milk and eggs are poured in and the batter is beaten about half a minute more. The two-stage method is simpler, quicker, and more nearly foolproof than the conventional creaming method.

The results exceeded our expectations. The two-stage method is often touted for the tender texture it promotes in cakes, and our two-stage 1-2-3-4 cake was indeed tender. But, more important, its consistency was improved. Whereas the conventionally mixed 1-2-3-4 cake had been crumbly, this cake was fine-grained and melting, and, interestingly enough, it did not seem overly sweet. Even the crust was improved. It was still a bit coarse but only slightly sticky. This was a cake with a texture that we truly liked.

The problem was the taste; the cake still didn't have any. In fact, oddly enough, it seemed to have less taste than the conventionally mixed version. Certainly, it had less color. The 1-2-3-4 cake, it seemed, conformed to a typical cake

---

INGREDIENTS: Vanilla Extract

Almost two thirds of the world's supply of vanilla beans comes from Madagascar, an island off the eastern coast of Africa. Significant amounts of vanilla beans are also grown in Mexico and Tahiti. Tahitian beans are a hybrid that originated spontaneously on several islands in the South Pacific. Beans grown everywhere else in the world, including Mexico and Madagascar, are from the same species.

Although vanilla beans are convenient to use in custards (the pods are split lengthwise, the seeds scraped into the liquid, and the pods usually added to infuse more flavor), extracts make the most sense for baking, including cakes and cookies. (You could make vanilla sugar by nestling a split bean in some sugar, but this process takes about a week.)

When shopping for extracts, you have two basic choices: pure extract and imitation. Pure vanilla extract is made by steeping chopped vanilla beans in an alcohol and water solution. Imitation vanilla extract is made from vanillin, a product extracted from conifer wood pulp that has been chemically rinsed.

We figured that tasters would have no trouble picking out pure vanilla extract from imitation products. We also expected the gourmet brands available in upscale markets and by mail to outpoll supermarket offerings. Well, we sure were wrong.

We tried nine extracts (seven pure, two imitation) in a basic sugar cookie with just flour, butter, and sugar. It turns out that most people, including pastry chefs, can't even tell the difference between a cookie made with vanilla extract and a cookie made with the imitation stuff, let alone the differences between brands of real vanilla. In a cookie (as well as chocolate cake, or any cake for that matter), the quantities of extract are so small and the other ingredients so flavorful that these differences are hard to detect.

We decided to try our pure and imitation extracts in our yellow layer cake. We also followed a standard tasting protocol in the vanilla business and mixed each extract with milk at a ratio of 1 part extract to 8 parts milk. Although you would never use so much extract in a real application, this high concentration makes it easier to detect specific characteristics in extracts.

The results of this tasting were so shocking that we repeated it, only to come up with similarly surprising findings. Tasters couldn't tell the difference between real and imitation vanilla. In fact, in the yellow layer cake tasting, the imitation extracts took first and third place, with two "premium" brands, Nielsen-Massey and Penzeys, leading the pack among real extracts. In the milk tasting, the imitation extracts took the top two spots, followed by real extracts from Nielsen-Massey and Penzeys. Although we are loath to recommend an imitation product, it seems that most people don't mind imitation extract, and, in fact, many tasters actually like its flavor. Note that you won't save money by choosing an imitation extract—it costs about the same as pure vanilla extract.

pattern; as the texture lightened, the taste and color faded.

After trying to remedy the taste deficit by playing around with the ingredients in many ways—primarily adjusting the amounts and proportions of the sugar and eggs—we finally recalled a recipe called Bride's Cake in *Mrs. Rorer's New Cook Book,* published exactly a century ago. This is basically an egg-white pound cake—made of a pound each of flour, sugar, butter, and egg whites—with a cup of milk and a chemical leavener added. What would happen, we wondered, if we made Mrs. Rorer's cake with whole eggs instead of egg whites? It seemed worth a try.

We cut all of Mrs. Rorer's ingredients by half; that is, we made a half-pound cake, so that the batter would fit into two standard 9-inch round layer cake pans. When mixing the batter, we followed the two-stage method.

The resulting cake was richer, more flavorful, and generally more interesting than any of the 1-2-3-4 cakes we had baked, but it was not perfect. The layers were low, and the cake was just a tad dense and rough on the tongue (though not rubbery). We had several options. We could try to open up the crumb by adding more milk and baking powder; we could try to lighten the cake up with an extra egg or a couple of extra yolks; or we could try to increase the volume and tenderize the texture by adding a few more ounces of sugar. We tried all three strategies. The last one—the extra sugar—did the trick. This cake was fine-grained, soft, and melting, and it tasted of butter and eggs. It had elegance and finesse and yet was still sturdy enough to withstand the frosting process.

Both the 1-2-3-4 cake and our improved yellow cake based on Mrs. Rorer's recipe are made with a half pound each of butter and eggs. But while the 1-2-3-4 cake contains 3 cups of sifted cake flour and 1 cup of milk, our improved yellow cake contains just 1¾ cups of sifted cake flour and only ½ cup of milk. Proportionally our cake also contains more fat. Altogether, these changes make a tremendous difference in texture and taste.

Yellow Layer Cake

SERVES 8 TO 10

Adding the butter pieces to the mixing bowl one at a time prevents the dry ingredients from flying up and out of the bowl. This yellow cake works with any of the frostings that follow.

1¾	cups (7 ounces) plain cake flour, sifted, plus more for dusting the pans
4	large eggs, at room temperature
½	cup whole milk, at room temperature
2	teaspoons vanilla extract
1½	cups (10½ ounces) sugar
2	teaspoons baking powder
¾	teaspoon salt
16	tablespoons (2 sticks) unsalted butter, softened but still cool, cut into 16 pieces
1	recipe Rich Vanilla Buttercream Frosting, Rich Coffee Buttercream Frosting, or Rich Chocolate Cream Frosting (recipes follow)

1. Adjust an oven rack to the lower-middle position and heat the oven to 350 degrees. Generously grease two 9-inch round cake pans and cover the pan bottoms with rounds of parchment paper or waxed paper. Grease the parchment rounds and dust the cake pans with flour, tapping out the excess.

2. Beat the eggs, milk, and vanilla with a fork in a small bowl; measure out 1 cup of this mixture and set aside. Combine the flour, sugar, baking powder, and salt in the bowl of a standing mixer. Beat the mixture at the lowest speed to blend, about 30 seconds. With the mixer still running at the lowest speed, add the butter, one piece at a time; mix until the butter and flour begin to clump together and look sandy and pebbly, with pieces about the size of peas, 30 to 40 seconds after all the butter is added. Add the reserved 1 cup egg mixture and mix at the lowest speed until incorporated, 5 to 10 seconds. Increase the speed to medium-high and beat until light and fluffy, about 1 minute. Add the remaining egg mixture (about ½ cup) in a slow, steady stream, taking about 30 seconds. Stop the mixer and scrape the sides and bottom of the

bowl with a rubber spatula. Beat at medium-high speed until thoroughly combined and the batter looks slightly curdled, about 15 seconds.

3. Divide the batter equally between the prepared cake pans; spread to the sides of the pans and smooth with a rubber spatula. Bake until the cake tops are light gold and a toothpick or thin skewer inserted in the centers comes out clean, 20 to 25 minutes. (The cakes may mound slightly but will level when cooled.) Cool on a wire rack for 10 minutes. Run a knife around the pan perimeters to loosen. Invert one cake onto a large plate, peel off the parchment, and reinvert onto another wire rack. Repeat with the other cake. Cool completely before icing.

4. Assemble and frost the cake according to the illustrations on page 853. Cut the cake into slices and serve.

Rich Vanilla Buttercream Frosting

MAKES ABOUT 4 CUPS, ENOUGH TO ICE ONE 8- OR 9-INCH TWO-LAYER CAKE OR ONE 8-INCH THREE-LAYER CAKE

The whole eggs, whipped until airy, give this buttercream a light, satiny smooth texture that melts on the tongue.

4	large eggs
1	cup (7 ounces) sugar
2	teaspoons vanilla extract
	Pinch salt
1	pound (4 sticks) unsalted butter, softened but still cool, each stick cut into quarters

1. Combine the eggs, sugar, vanilla, and salt in the bowl of a standing mixer; place the bowl over a pan of simmering water. (Do not let the bottom of the bowl touch the water.) Whisking gently but

PORTIONING AND BAKING LAYER CAKES

1. To ensure that you put equal amounts of batter in each cake pan, use a kitchen scale to measure the weight of each filled pan.

2. When baking more than one cake layer at a time, leave some space between the pans and between the pans and the oven walls. Also, stagger their placement in the oven so air can circulate. Halfway through the baking time, use tongs to rotate the cake pans 180 degrees.

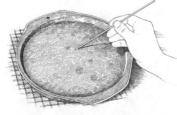

3. Telling when a cake is done can be tricky. A cake tester or skewer inserted into the center should come out clean. If batter clings to the skewer, the cake needs more time in the oven.

4. A fully baked cake should feel springy and resilient when you gently press the center with your fingers. If an impression is left in the surface, the cake is not done.

constantly, heat the mixture until it is thin and foamy and registers 160 degrees on an instant-read thermometer.

2. Beat the egg mixture at medium-high speed until light, airy, and cooled to room temperature, about 5 minutes. Reduce the speed to medium and add the butter, one piece at a time. (After adding half the butter, the buttercream may look curdled; it will smooth out with additional butter.) Once all the butter is added, increase the speed to high and beat 1 minute, until light, fluffy, and thoroughly combined. (The buttercream can be covered and refrigerated for up to 5 days.)

➤ VARIATION

Rich Coffee Buttercream Frosting

Dissolve 3 tablespoons instant espresso in 3 tablespoons warm water. Follow the recipe for Rich Vanilla Buttercream Frosting, omitting the vanilla and beating the dissolved coffee into the buttercream after the butter has been added.

Rich Chocolate Cream Frosting

MAKES ABOUT 3 CUPS, ENOUGH TO ICE ONE 8- OR 9-INCH TWO-LAYER CAKE

This soft, rich frosting is the perfect companion to a tender yellow layer cake.

16	ounces bittersweet or semisweet chocolate, chopped fine
1½	cups heavy cream
⅓	cup light corn syrup
1	teaspoon vanilla extract

Place the chocolate in a heatproof bowl. Bring the heavy cream to a simmer in a small saucepan over medium-high heat; pour over the chocolate. Add the corn syrup and let stand 3 minutes. Whisk gently until smooth; stir in the vanilla. Refrigerate 1 to 1½ hours, stirring every 15 minutes, until the mixture reaches a spreadable consistency. This frosting does not keep well, so it should be used within a day.

CUTTING ROUNDS OF PARCHMENT TO LINE CAKE PANS

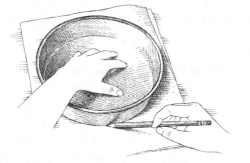

1. Trace the bottom of your cake pan roughly in the center of a sheet of parchment paper (use a double sheet if using two pans).

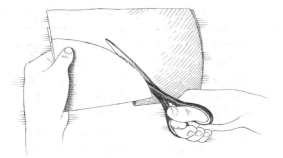

2. Fold the traced circle in half and then in half again, then cut just inside the outline of the quarter circle formed in this way. The resulting rounds of parchment will exactly fit your pan.

COCONUT LAYER CAKE

COCONUT CAKE SHOULD BE PERFUMED INSIDE and out with the cool, subtle, mysterious essence of coconut. Its layers of snowy white cake should be moist and tender, with a delicate, yielding crumb, and the icing should be a silky, gently sweetened coat covered with a deep drift of downy coconut. So it's irksome and disappointing that coconut cakes are often frauds, no more than plain white cakes with plain white icing slapped with shredded coconut. We decided to pursue a coconut cake that lived up to our dreams.

Presented with a roundup of cakes baked according to different recipes, likes and dislikes among the members of the tasting panel surfaced. Cakes baked in a 13 by 9-inch baking pan defied the archetypal sky-high layer-cake form. Coarse, crumbly textured cakes did not fill the bill, nor did cakes tinted yellow from yolks or whole eggs. Light, spongy, cottony cakes were too dry for a coconut cake. Doctored with coconut milk and a bit of coconut extract and tweaked ever so slightly, a basic white cake earned the most praise for its buttery flavor and its tender, fine crumb.

The cake doctored with coconut milk and extract was good, but it wasn't perfect. We found that, from batch to batch, coconut milk could produce mystifyingly different results—sometimes a flat cake, sometimes a mounded cake, sometimes a heavy, greasy cake. We discovered that the source of the problem was the variation in fat content—as much as 33 percent—among brands of coconut milk. Cream of coconut, a sweetened coconut product that contains a few inscrutable emulsifiers, seemed to be a more consistent product, perhaps because there are fewer brands (Coco Lopez being the best known). So we cut back on some of the sugar that went into the batter and used cream of coconut instead of coconut milk. These cakes baked up beautifully, their exteriors an appealing burnished brown color that the coconut milk versions lacked, and they tasted more strongly of coconut as well.

Unfortunately, these cakes also baked up with a giant mound at their centers, which made them look more like desert turtles than dessert. Because the batter was a very thick one that could use gentler heat (which would facilitate a more even rise in the oven), we were able to lower the mounds by reducing the oven temperature to 325 degrees. The resulting cakes were significantly improved. Then, to level things out even more, we manipulated the quantity of eggs. During these trials, we discovered that one yolk in addition to six egg whites gave the cakes a richer, fuller flavor without tainting their saintly color. This did nothing to alleviate the remaining slight mounding problem, however, so we tried scaling back on the cream of coconut and diluting the batter with a bit of water. This thinner batter baked into nice, even cakes.

It was time to work on the icing. Most tasters acknowledged that seven-minute meringue icing is what they'd expect on a coconut cake, but we found this icing to be painfully sweet and devoid of appealing texture. So we assembled one coconut cake with a butter and confectioners' sugar icing and one with an egg-white buttercream that was an offshoot of the whole-egg buttercream we like to use with our yellow layer cake and devil's food cake. Both icings garnered applause, but the egg-white buttercream was the favorite. Not only was it incredibly lithe, but it was also less sweet, significantly more silky and smooth, and much more fluffy and light than its competitor. In some ways, it was reminiscent of the traditional seven-minute icing, just not as sweet or as sticky, and with a creamier consistency.

This buttercream begins with a meringue, and softened butter is eventually beaten in. We tried two approaches to building the meringue. In the first, the whites and sugar are simply beaten to soft peaks in a standing mixer. In the second, the whites and sugar are whisked together over a hot-water bath until the sugar dissolves and the mixture is warm to the touch. The former straightforward meringue fell quickly as the butter was added, and the resulting buttercream was incredibly heavy and stiff, almost no better than the butter and confectioners' sugar icing. The meringue that went over heat was much more

INGREDIENTS: Coconut Extract

Pure extracts are essential oils extracted from natural flavoring agents such as fruit rinds, nuts, and herbs and then dissolved in alcohol. Imitation extracts are fabricated from chemical compounds that mimic natural flavors; these compounds are then also dissolved in alcohol. As with most things natural and synthetic, natural extracts cost more. When it came to coconut extract, we wanted to know whether "pure" was worth the price. So we made our buttercream frosting using three extracts—McCormick Imitation Coconut Extract, Spices Etc. Natural Coconut Flavoring, and LorAnn Gourmet Coconut Flavor—and put them to the test.

LorAnn Gourmet Coconut Flavor was uniformly rejected, bringing new meaning to the word *artificial*. One taster commented, "I feel like I'm eating suntan lotion." McCormick Imitation Coconut Extract came in second. Tasters didn't note any off flavors and considered this extract "subtle" and "good." Spices Etc. Natural Coconut Flavoring, made from the pulp of coconuts, was the most "deeply coconutty" and highly praised of the group. Ringing in at $3.25 for a 1-ounce bottle, compared with $2.42 for the McCormick, the natural is worth the extra 80 cents.

stable. Although it did fall when butter was added, the completed icing was soft, supple, and dreamy. (Note that the mixture does not become hot enough to eliminate the unlikely presence of salmonella bacteria in the eggs.)

The textural coup de grâce of a coconut cake is its woolly coconut coat. Indeed, pure white shredded coconut straight from the bag makes for a maidenly cake. Toasted coconut, however, has both chew and crunch as well as a much more intense flavor. And when toasted not to the point of even brownness but just until it resembles a toss of white and bronze confetti, it dresses this cake to be belle of the ball.

Coconut Layer Cake

SERVES 8 TO 10

Cream of coconut is often found in the soda and drink-mix aisle in the grocery store. One 15-ounce can is enough for both the cake and the buttercream; make sure to stir it well before using because it separates upon standing.

CAKE

2¼	cups (9 ounces) plain cake flour, sifted, plus more for dusting the pans
1	large egg, plus 5 large egg whites
¾	cup cream of coconut
¼	cup water
1	teaspoon coconut extract
1	teaspoon vanilla extract
1	cup (7 ounces) sugar
1	tablespoon baking powder
¾	teaspoon salt
12	tablespoons (1½ sticks) unsalted butter, softened but still cool, cut into 12 pieces
2	cups packed sweetened shredded coconut

COCONUT BUTTERCREAM

4	large egg whites
1	cup (7 ounces) sugar
	Pinch salt
1	pound (4 sticks) unsalted butter, softened but still cool, each stick cut into 6 pieces
¼	cup cream of coconut
1	teaspoon coconut extract
1	teaspoon vanilla extract

1. FOR THE CAKE: Adjust an oven rack to the lower-middle position and heat the oven to 325 degrees. Grease two 9-inch round cake pans and dust with flour, tapping out the excess.

2. Beat the whole egg and egg whites in a large liquid measuring cup with a fork to combine. Add the cream of coconut, water, coconut extract, and vanilla and beat with a fork until thoroughly combined.

3. Mix the flour, sugar, baking powder, and salt in the bowl of a standing mixer at the lowest speed to combine, about 30 seconds. With the mixer still running at the lowest speed, add the butter, one piece at a time, then beat until the mixture resembles coarse meal, with butter bits no larger than small peas, 2 to 2½ minutes.

4. With the mixer still running, add 1 cup of the egg mixture to the flour and butter mixture. Increase the speed to medium-high and beat until light and fluffy, about 45 seconds. With the mixer still running, add the remaining 1 cup liquid in a steady stream (this should take about 15 seconds). Stop the mixer and scrape down the bowl with a rubber spatula, then beat at medium-high speed to combine, about 15 seconds. (The batter will be thick.)

5. Divide the batter between the cake pans and level with a rubber spatula. Bake until the cakes are deep golden brown, have pulled away from the sides of the pans, and a toothpick or thin skewer inserted into the center of the cakes comes out clean, about 30 minutes (rotate the pans from front to back after about 20 minutes). Do not turn off the oven.

6. Cool the cakes in the pans on wire racks for about 10 minutes, then loosen the cakes from the sides of the pans with a paring knife, invert the cakes onto the racks, and reinvert them so the top sides face up; cool to room temperature.

7. TO TOAST THE COCONUT: While the cakes are cooling, spread the shredded coconut on a rimmed baking sheet; toast in the oven until the shreds are a mix of golden brown and white, 15 to 20 minutes, stirring 2 or 3 times. Cool to room temperature.

8. FOR THE BUTTERCREAM: Combine the egg whites, sugar, and salt in a mixing bowl; set the bowl over a saucepan containing 1½ inches of barely simmering water. Whisk constantly until

the mixture is opaque and warm to the touch and registers 120 degrees on an instant-read thermometer, about 2 minutes. (Note that this temperature is not hot enough to eliminate the unlikely presence of salmonella bacteria in the eggs.) Remove from the heat.

9. Using a standing mixer, beat the whites at high speed until they are barely warm (about 80 degrees), glossy, and sticky, about 7 minutes. Reduce the speed to medium-high and beat in the butter, one piece at a time. Beat in the cream of coconut, coconut extract, and vanilla. Stop the mixer and scrape the bottom and sides of the bowl with a rubber spatula. Continue to beat at medium-high speed until well combined, about 1 minute.

10. To ASSEMBLE THE CAKE: Following the illustrations on page 859, cut the cakes in half horizontally so that each cake forms 2 layers. Assemble and frost the cake according to the illustrations on page 853. Sprinkle the top of the cake with the toasted coconut, then press the coconut into the sides of the cake with your hand, letting the excess fall back onto a baking sheet or piece of parchment paper. Cut the cake into slices and serve.

SPONGE CAKE

IDEALLY, SPONGE CAKE IS LIGHTER THAN THE standard butter-based layer cake, with a springy but delicate texture that stands up nicely to fillings and/or glazes. We like to use it in our Boston Cream Pie (filled with custard and iced with a sweet chocolate glaze) as well as a simple layer cake like Blackberry Jam Cake. It should not be dry or tough, the curse of many classic sponge cakes, nor should it be difficult to make. We were seeking a basic building-block cake recipe, just as dependable and useful as a classic American layer cake.

There are several kinds of sponge or "foam" cakes, so named because they depend on eggs (whole or separated) beaten to a foam to provide lift and structure. They all use egg foam for structure, but they differ in two ways: whether fat (butter or milk) is added and whether the foam is made from whole eggs, egg whites, or a combination.

We started by making a classic American sponge cake, which adds no fat in the form of butter or milk and calls for eight beaten egg whites folded into four beaten egg yolks. The cake certainly was light, but it lacked flavor, and the texture was dry and a bit chewy. To solve these problems, we turned to a recipe for a hot-milk sponge cake, in which a small amount of melted butter and hot milk is added to the whole-egg foam. This cake turned out much better on all counts. The added fat not only provided flavor but also tenderized the crumb. This particular recipe also used fewer eggs than our original sponge cake recipe.

We were now working with a recipe that used ¾ cup cake flour, 1 teaspoon baking powder, ¾ cup sugar, and five eggs. We started by separating out all five whites and found that the cake was too light, its insufficient structure resulting in a slightly sunken center. We then separated out and beat just three of the whites, and the resulting cake was excellent. When all-purpose flour was substituted for cake flour, the cake had more body and was a bit tougher than the version with cake flour. We then tried different proportions of the two flours, finally settling on a 2-1 ratio of cake flour to all-purpose. We also tested to find the proper ratio of eggs to flour and found that five eggs to ¾ cup flour (we also tested ½ cup and 1 cup) was best. Six eggs produced an "eggy" cake, while four eggs resulted in a lower rise and a cake with a bit less flavor.

We had thought that the baking powder might be optional, but it turned out to be essential to a properly risen cake. Although angel food and classic sponge cakes, which use no added fat, do not require chemical leaveners, our sponge cake, with its fat from milk and melted butter, would require baking powder.

Two tablespoons of melted butter was just the right amount; three tablespoons made the cake a bit oily and the butter flavor too prominent. As for the milk, three tablespoons was best; larger quantities resulted in a wet, mushy texture.

With our basic recipe in hand, we played with the order of the steps. Beating the whole-egg foam first, and then the whites, allowed the relatively fragile foam to deteriorate, producing less rise. We

Frosting Layer Cakes 101

Most cooks think a bakery-smooth frosted cake is well beyond their ability and make do with a decidedly "homemade"-looking cake. The most common problems: uneven frosting, including holes and thick patches; weak transitions from the sides to the top; and crumbs caught in the frosting. With the directions that follow, these problems are easily avoided. Although a professional rotating cake stand makes icing a cake easy, you can also improvise with a Lazy Susan (see step 9).

1. To anchor the cake, spread a dab of frosting in the center of a cardboard round cut slightly larger than the cake. Center the first layer of cake on the cardboard round. If using a split layer, place it crust-side up; if using a whole layer, place it bottom-side down. Set the cardboard round with the cake on the stand.

2. Place a large blob of frosting in the center of the cake and spread it to the edges with an icing spatula. Imagine that you are pushing the filling into place rather than scraping it on as if it were peanut butter on toast. Don't worry if crumbs are visible; the filling will be sandwiched between layers.

3. To level the frosting and remove any excess, hold the spatula at a 45-degree angle to the cake and, starting at the edge farthest away from you, gently drag the spatula toward you. Turn the cake slightly and repeat. It will take a few sweeps to level the frosting.

4. Using a second cardboard round, slide the second cake layer, crust-side up, on top of the frosted bottom layer, making sure that the layers are aligned. Press the cake firmly into place. If making a three- or four-layer cake, add some filling (as directed in steps 2 and 3) and repeat this process with the remaining layers.

5. A thin base coat of frosting helps seal in crumbs. To coat the top, place a blob of frosting in the center of the cake and spread it out to the edges, letting any excess hang over the edge. Don't worry if it is imperfect. Smooth the frosting as in step 3.

6. Scoop a large dab of frosting on the spatula's tip. Holding the spatula parallel to the cake stand, spread the frosting on the side of the cake with short side-to-side strokes. Repeat until the entire side is covered with a thin coat of frosting. Refrigerate the cake until the frosting sets, about 10 minutes.

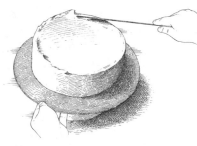

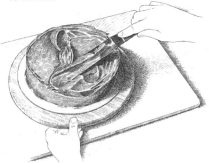

7. Apply a thick final coat of frosting to the top and sides, following steps 5 and 6 and making sure that the coat is even and smooth. When icing the sides, apply a coat thick enough to cover and conceal the cardboard round. Dipping the spatula in hot water will help create a smooth coat.

8. As you ice the top and sides, a ridge will form along the edge where they meet. After you've finished icing, hold the spatula at an angle and, with a very light hand and starting at the farthest edge of the cake, smooth the ridge toward the center. Rotate the cake and repeat until the ridge no longer exists.

9. If you don't own a rotating cake stand, you can perform steps 1 through 8 on a Lazy Susan. Just set the cardboard round on the Lazy Susan and spin slowly.

found that beating the whites first was vastly better. After much experimentation, we also found it best to fold together, all at the same time, the beaten whole eggs, the beaten whites, and the flour, and then, once the mixture was about half mixed, to add the warm butter and milk. This eliminated the possibility that the liquid would damage the egg foam and also made the temperature of the butter and milk mixture less important.

Determining when a sponge cake is properly baked is a little more difficult than it is with a regular American layer cake. A sponge cake should provide some resistance and not feel as if one has just touched the top of a soufflé. Another good test is color. The top of the cake should be a nice light brown, not pale gold or a dark, rich brown.

We also tested the best way to handle the cake once out of the oven. When left to cool in a baking pan, the cake shrinks away from the sides and the edges become uneven. The best method is to immediately place the hot cake pan on a towel, cover it with a plate, and then use the towel to invert the cake. Finally, reinvert the cake and slip it back onto the wire rack.

Foolproof Sponge Cake

MAKES TWO 8- OR 9-INCH CAKE LAYERS

The egg whites should be beaten to soft, glossy, billowy peaks. If beaten until too stiff, they will be very difficult to fold into the whole-egg mixture.

1/2	cup (2 ounces) plain cake flour
1/4	cup (1 1/4 ounces) unbleached all-purpose flour
1	teaspoon baking powder
1/4	teaspoon salt
3	tablespoons milk
2	tablespoons unsalted butter
1/2	teaspoon vanilla extract
5	large eggs, at room temperature
3/4	cup (5 1/4 ounces) sugar

1. Adjust an oven rack to the lower-middle position and heat the oven to 350 degrees. Grease two 8- or 9-inch cake pans and cover the pan bottoms with rounds of parchment paper or waxed paper. Whisk the flours, baking powder, and salt

in a medium bowl (or sift onto waxed paper). Heat the milk and butter in a small saucepan over low heat until the butter melts. Remove from the heat and add the vanilla; cover and keep warm.

2. Separate 3 of the eggs, placing the whites in the bowl of a standing mixer and reserving the 3 yolks plus the remaining 2 whole eggs in another mixing bowl. Beat the 3 whites at low speed until foamy. Increase the mixer speed to medium and gradually add 6 tablespoons of the sugar; continue to beat the whites to soft, moist peaks. (Do not overbeat.) Transfer the egg whites to a large bowl and add the whole-egg mixture to the mixer bowl.

3. Beat the whole-egg mixture with the remaining 6 tablespoons sugar. Beat at medium-high speed until the eggs are very thick and a pale yellow color, about 5 minutes. Add the beaten eggs to the whites.

4. Sprinkle the flour mixture over the beaten eggs and whites; fold very gently 12 times with a large rubber spatula. Make a well in one side of the batter and pour the milk mixture into the bowl. Continue folding until the batter shows no trace of flour and the whites and whole eggs are evenly mixed, about 8 additional strokes.

5. Immediately pour the batter into the prepared cake pans; bake until the cake tops are light brown and feel firm and spring back when touched, about 16 minutes for 9-inch cake pans and 20 minutes for 8-inch cake pans.

6. Immediately run a knife around the pan perimeters to loosen the cakes. Place one pan on a towel and cover the pan with a large plate. Using the towel to protect your hands and catch the cake, invert the pan and remove the pan from the cake. Peel off the parchment. Reinvert the cake from the plate onto the rack. Repeat with the remaining cake. Cool the cake layers to room temperature before proceeding with Boston Cream Pie or Blackberry Jam Cake (recipes follow).

Boston Cream Pie

SERVES 8 TO 10

Why is this cake called Boston cream pie? It seems that the cake does indeed have its roots in Boston, where it was developed in the middle of the 19th century. Modern baking experts believe that since pies predated cakes in the American kitchen, pie pans were simply more common kitchen equipment than cake pans. Hence the name pie was originally given to this layer cake. Prepare the pastry cream first, then the cake, and last the glaze.

GLAZE
1 cup heavy cream
¼ cup light corn syrup
8 ounces semisweet chocolate, chopped into small pieces
½ teaspoon vanilla extract

1 recipe Foolproof Sponge Cake (page 854), baked and cooled
1 recipe Pastry Cream (page 924), chilled

1. FOR THE GLAZE: Bring the cream and corn syrup to a full simmer in a medium saucepan over medium heat. Remove from the heat and add the chocolate; cover and let stand for 8 minutes. (If the chocolate has not completely melted, return the saucepan to low heat; stir constantly until melted.) Add the vanilla; stir very gently until the mixture is smooth. Cool until tepid, so that a spoonful drizzled back into the pan mounds slightly. (The glaze can be refrigerated to speed up the cooling process; stir every few minutes to ensure even cooling.)

2. TO ASSEMBLE: While the glaze is cooling, place one cake layer on a cardboard round on a wire rack set over waxed paper. Carefully spoon the pastry cream onto the cake and spread it evenly up to the edges. Place the second cake layer on top, making sure the layers line up properly.

3. Pour the glaze onto the middle of the top layer and let it flow down the cake sides. Use a metal spatula, if necessary, to completely coat the cake. Use a small needle to puncture any air bubbles. Let the cake sit until the glaze fully sets, about 1 hour. Serve the same day, preferably within a couple of hours.

Blackberry Jam Cake
SERVES 8

Although blackberry jam is traditional, you can fill this cake with any favorite jam as long as it doesn't contain large chunks of fruit, which would be difficult to spread on the cake.

1 recipe Foolproof Sponge Cake (page 854)
1 (8-ounce) jar blackberry jam
   Confectioners' sugar for dusting the cake

Place one cake layer on a cardboard round on a sheet of waxed paper. Evenly spread the jam over the cake. Place the second cake layer on the jam, making sure the layers line up properly. Sieve confectioners' sugar over the cake and serve.

CHOCOLATE LAYER CAKE

COOKBOOKS ARE FILLED WITH A VARIETY OF chocolate layer cakes, which tend to hew closely to the yellow cake formula (including the addition of milk or some sort of dairy) but with chocolate added to the mix.

From past experience, we have found that recipes for chocolate layer cake can be maddening. One promises an especially fudgy and rich cake, the next guarantees a light and tender one. The secret to the recipe, we are told, is Dutch-processed cocoa, or dark brown sugar, or sour cream, or buttermilk, or some special mixing method—and so on and so forth. If you've made as many chocolate cakes as we have over the years, you can fill in the blanks yourself.

Finally, you make the cake, and you think, well, it is a little fudgy, or tender, or a little like devil's food, or whatever. But isn't it also very much like the chocolate cake you made just the other week, from a recipe that called for very different ingredients and promised a very different result?

We set out to make sense of this muddle. After baking and comparing dozens of different chocolate cakes, we have devised three truly distinctive chocolate layer cakes. (See page 860 for information on the development of our third chocolate layer cake.) In the process, we discovered a couple of general principles that apply to whatever type of chocolate layer cake you are making. Perhaps more important, we also learned a great deal about how various ingredients function and what results they produce, so that each of these recipes delivers exactly the type of chocolate cake it promises.

Bakers can (and do) argue endlessly over whether cocoa-based chocolate cakes are best made with standard American cocoa, such as Hershey's, or with a European-style cocoa, such as Droste, that has been alkalized, or "Dutched," to neutralize some of the natural acid. (See below for more information on cocoa powder.)

To settle this question, we prepared several recipes using both types of cocoa and found that there was not an enormous difference. Cakes made with Hershey's were a little blacker and had a slight bitter edge; in the Droste cakes, the chocolate flavor was perhaps a bit mellower but also fainter. But these distinctions were minor, and the bottom line was that we liked both cocoas just fine. Since natural (nonalkalized) and Dutch-processed react differently with leaveners, we choose to base our recipes on widely available natural cocoa.

A second cocoa experiment, however, proved much more conclusive. In cakes made with cocoa and water, the chocolate flavor was much stronger and the color twice as dark when the cocoa was first dissolved in boiling water rather than simply being mixed into the batter dry. We therefore recommend following this procedure in any cocoa-based chocolate cake in which water is the liquid.

Next, we sought to discover the effects of substituting unsweetened chocolate or semisweet chocolate for cocoa. Following standard substitution tables, we prepared our master recipe using 3 ounces of unsweetened chocolate in place of the cocoa and subtracted 3 tablespoons of butter to compensate for the fat in the chocolate. We also made the master recipe with 5 ounces of semisweet chocolate in lieu of cocoa, cutting the butter by 2 tablespoons and the sugar by 6 tablespoons.

In the first set of experiments, we simply melted the chocolate over boiling water. Both the unsweetened and the semisweet chocolates produced terrible cakes: pale, dry, hard, and lacking in flavor. We remembered, however, that Rose Levy Beranbaum, author of *The Cake Bible* (William Morrow, 1988), counsels actually cooking the chocolate over boiling water for several minutes to rupture the cocoa particles and release the flavor. A second round of experiments substantiated the wisdom of this advice: Both unsweetened and semisweet chocolate responded dramatically, producing cakes with a much richer, darker flavor. Even when made with cooked chocolate, however, the cakes were neither as moist nor as flavorful as when made with cocoa. We will, therefore, venture a rule: In butter cakes, at least (if not necessarily in chocolate cakes of other types), cocoa is always better than chocolate.

Our second—and most extensive—set of experiments concerned the effect of dairy liquids

---

INGREDIENTS: Two Types of Cocoa

Dutch-processed cocoa is less acidic (or more alkaline) than a regular cocoa such as Hershey's. The theory is that reducing the acidity of natural cocoa enhances browning reactions, which in turn result in a darker color. Because the red pigments in cocoa become more visible in a more acidic environment, the more acidic natural cocoa is supposed to produce a redder cake. Manufacturers also claim that the process of Dutching cocoa results in a smoother, less bitter chocolate flavor.

To determine the veracity of these claims, we conducted a head-to-head test of three Dutch-processed cocoas—Droste, King Arthur Flour's "black" cocoa (made from beans that are roasted until they are almost burnt), and Pernigotti, a very expensive brand sold at Williams-Sonoma stores—against Hershey's natural cocoa. All three Dutch-processed cocoas produced darker cakes with more chocolate flavor than the Hershey's did, bearing out our research. The Hershey's cocoa also produced a much redder cake, just as promised. But we also noticed textural differences in the cakes. The cake made with Hershey's was dry and airy without much complexity of flavor. Among the cakes made with Dutch-processed cocoa, the cake made with the expensive Pernigotti produced a very moist, soft crumb; that made with Droste was a bit dry with a more open crumb; and the "black" cocoa cake was very dense, almost spongy, although incredibly chocolatey as well.

So if you want a richer-tasting, darker, more velvety cake, use Dutch-processed cocoa, keeping in mind that quality matters. Those who must have a reddish color can go with regular cocoa, but the taste and texture will suffer somewhat.

on the cake. We checked out everything from sweet milk to buttermilk to yogurt to sour cream.

Sour cream and buttermilk have a seductively mouthwatering effect in chocolate cake recipes, but we have long had reservations about using milk products when baking with chocolate. Hot chocolate prepared with water (with a spoonful of cream added for richness, if you wish) has a far more intense flavor than hot chocolate made with milk. If milk is a flavor-blocker in hot chocolate, we reasoned, why wouldn't dairy products have a similar effect in chocolate cakes? Our experiments proved that they do, but the whole business turned out to be surprisingly complicated.

When we replaced the water with milk, we got a cake that we liked a great deal. As we had predicted, the chocolate flavor was somewhat muted, but to some tastes, this was for the better. The cake was a little less tender and more crumbly than the one made with water, but on the plus side, it also felt pleasantly substantial in the mouth. Milk produced the kind of chocolate cake that we remember from childhood, so we call this milk-based variation Old-Fashioned Chocolate Layer Cake.

Further experiments revealed that neither dissolving the cocoa in hot milk nor cooking the cocoa and milk together made for an appreciably stronger flavor than simply adding the cocoa to the batter dry. Evidently, dissolving the cocoa in boiling liquid improves its flavor only if the liquid in question is water.

Buttermilk and yogurt proved to be far more problematic ingredients. In our myriad tests, both had a paradoxical effect on texture, on the one hand velvetizing the crumb and adding a nice moistness, but on the other compacting the cakes and making them seem a little hard and chewy and also a bit pasty. Taste, though, was the real issue. While milk had a gentling effect on the flavor of chocolate, buttermilk and yogurt nearly killed it.

By testing various cookbook recipes, we eventually learned how to use buttermilk in such a way as to maximize its tenderizing qualities without obliterating all chocolate taste. One solution is to make your cake with a great deal of sugar; sugar speeds melting, and rapid melting intensifies flavor. We discovered that extra fat also mitigates the chocolate-blocking

effects of buttermilk, though fat seems at the same time to undercut buttermilk's tenderizing properties, resulting in a fudgy texture.

Of course, if you actually prefer a chocolate cake with a mild flavor, buttermilk can be very helpful, for the velvetiness it imparts reinforces the flavor impression you are trying to create. The trick, we think, is to use the buttermilk in sparing quantities. Our German Chocolate Layer Cake is a reconfiguration of a cake popularly made with German sweet chocolate and a cup or more of buttermilk. We are not particularly fond of the cake made according to the standard recipe, but when the buttermilk is reduced, the cake turns out quite nice.

Old-Fashioned Chocolate Layer Cake

SERVES 12

This chocolate cake resembles a traditional yellow cake with a great deal of chocolate added. The milk mutes the chocolate flavor slightly while giving the cake a sturdy, pleasantly crumbly texture.

1 1/4	cups (6 1/4 ounces) unbleached all-purpose flour, plus more for dusting the pans
12	tablespoons (1 1/2 sticks) unsalted butter, softened but still cool
1 1/4	cups (8 3/4 ounces) sugar
2	large eggs, at room temperature
1/2	teaspoon baking soda
1/2	teaspoon salt
1/2	cup (1 1/2 ounces) nonalkalized cocoa, such as Hershey's, sifted
2	teaspoons instant espresso or coffee powder
1	cup plus 2 tablespoons milk
2	teaspoons vanilla extract
1	recipe Rich Chocolate Cream Frosting (page 849)

1. Adjust an oven rack to the middle position and heat the oven to 350 degrees. Generously grease two 8-inch round cake pans and cover the pan bottoms with rounds of parchment paper or waxed paper. Grease the parchment rounds and dust the pans with flour, tapping out the excess.

THE NEW BEST RECIPE

2. Beat the butter in the bowl of a standing mixer at medium-high speed until smooth and shiny, about 30 seconds. Gradually sprinkle in the sugar; beat until the mixture is fluffy and almost white, 3 to 5 minutes. Add the eggs, one at a time, beating 1 full minute after each addition.

3. Whisk the flour, baking soda, salt, cocoa, and instant espresso powder in a medium bowl. Combine the milk and vanilla in a liquid measuring cup. With the mixer at the lowest speed, add about a third of the dry ingredients to the batter, followed immediately by about a third of the milk mixture; mix until the ingredients are almost incorporated into the batter. Repeat the process twice more. When the batter appears blended, stop the mixer and scrape the sides of the bowl with a rubber spatula. Return the mixer to low speed; beat until the batter looks satiny, about 15 seconds longer.

4. Divide the batter evenly between the prepared pans. With a rubber spatula, spread the batter to the pan sides and smooth the tops. Bake the cakes until they feel firm in the center when lightly pressed and a toothpick or thin skewer comes out clean or with just a crumb or two adhering, 23 to 30 minutes. Transfer the pans to wire racks; cool for 10 minutes. Run a knife around the perimeter of each pan, invert the cakes onto the racks, and peel off the paper liners. Reinvert the cakes onto additional racks; cool completely before frosting.

5. Assemble and frost the cake according to the illustrations on page 853. Cut the cake into slices and serve. (Cover leftover cake with plastic and refrigerate; bring to room temperature before serving.)

EQUIPMENT: Cake Pans

If you want to make a layer cake (even once a year for someone's birthday), you must own good cake pans. There's no sense doing all that work only to have the cake stick to flimsy disposable aluminum pans. When shopping, make sure to buy two sets of cake pans, preferably two 8-inch pans and two 9-inch pans. Different pans will produce cake layers of varying sizes, and layers that are the same size are easier to assemble and frost.

We baked both plain and chocolate butter cakes in 11 different pans. We found that cakes released perfectly from pans lined with nonstick or "stick-resistant" coatings. Most cakes released adequately from uncoated pans, with one exception. The flexible fiberglass pans we tested repeatedly held on to large chunks of cake. Because these pans also gave the cakes a faint rubbery flavor, they quickly fell to the bottom of the ratings.

When it came to browning the crust, we found dramatic differences in the pans. In general, the darker the pan, the darker the crust. Some bakers advise against using pans with dark finishes, such as nonstick coatings, because they worry about overbrowning. We found that dark pans created a darker crust but not one that was "overbrowned" or undesirable. In fact, we enjoyed the richer flavor of dark crusts when eating these cakes unfrosted, and we also found that their sturdiness and resistance to crumbling made them easier to frost.

We determined that pans with light-colored or shiny finishes could produce well-browned cakes, as long as the pans were made from aluminum. That's because aluminum conducts evenly and quickly. In contrast, stainless steel is a poor conductor of heat, and pans made from this material produced pale-looking cakes. In general, we prefer aluminum or tinned steel pans, preferably with a nonstick coating and/or a dark finish.

As for the other variables, all pans produced cakes of similar height, despite differences in pan depth. Since we preferred cakes with darker crusts, the insulated pans fell to the bottom of our ratings—two layers of metal separated by air space slowed down the browning process. While we liked most of the heavier "commercial" pans, our favorite pan was one of the lightest. In the end, the metal used and the finish are more important than the weight.

Finally, the issue of handles proved to be decisive in our testing. Pans with handles (or wings) on either side are much easier to transfer to the oven when filled with batter and to rotate once in the oven. Handles make it much easier to grab the pan without landing the corner of a potholder in a finished cake. Simply put, we love handles.

The bottom line: The most important factor when buying a cake pan is the finish. Dark nonstick or stick-resistant coatings ensure easy release and also promote deep browning of the crust, which means more flavor and no crumbs marring the frosting. If you have a choice, buy cake pans with handles on either side. Handles will prevent even the klutziest cook from sticking an oven mitt into a just-baked cake.

German Chocolate Layer Cake with Coconut-Pecan Filling
SERVES 12

Buttermilk gives this cake a pleasantly mild chocolate flavor with a very light, soft texture. The pecan and coconut filling provides textural contrast. Be sure to divide the batter evenly between the pans, as the cakes will rise high.

GERMAN CHOCOLATE CAKE

1 ¼	cups (6 ¼ ounces) unbleached all-purpose flour, plus more for dusting the pans
¼	cup (¾ ounce) nonalkalized cocoa, such as Hershey's
2	teaspoons instant espresso or coffee powder
⅓	cup boiling water
⅓	cup buttermilk or plain yogurt
2	teaspoons vanilla extract
12	tablespoons (1 ½ sticks) unsalted butter, softened but still cool
1 ¼	cups (8 ¾ ounces) sugar
3	large eggs, at room temperature
½	teaspoon baking soda
½	teaspoon salt

COCONUT-PECAN FILLING

4	large egg yolks
1	cup (7 ounces) sugar
¼	teaspoon salt
8	tablespoons (1 stick) unsalted butter, softened but still cool
1	cup heavy cream
1	teaspoon vanilla extract
1 ½	cups chopped pecans, toasted
2	cups lightly packed sweetened flaked coconut

1. FOR THE CAKE: Adjust an oven rack to the middle position and heat the oven to 350 degrees. Generously grease two 8-inch round cake pans and cover the pan bottoms with rounds of parchment paper or waxed paper. Grease the parchment rounds and dust the pans with flour, tapping out the excess.

2. Mix the cocoa and instant espresso powder in a small bowl; add the boiling water and mix until smooth. Cool to room temperature, then stir in the buttermilk and vanilla.

3. Beat the butter in the bowl of a standing mixer at medium-high speed until smooth and shiny, about 30 seconds. Gradually sprinkle in the sugar; beat until the mixture is fluffy and almost white, 3 to 5 minutes. Add the eggs, one at a time, beating 1 full minute after each addition.

4. Whisk the flour, baking soda, and salt in a medium bowl. With the mixer at the lowest speed, add about a third of the dry ingredients to the batter, followed immediately by about a third of the cocoa mixture; mix until the ingredients

LEVELING AND SPLITTING A CAKE

1. If the cake has mounded in the center, it should be leveled before being split. Gently press an outstretched hand on its surface and, holding a serrated knife parallel to the work surface, use a steady sawing motion to begin cutting at the same level as the cake's lowest point, slicing off the mound.

2. To cut into even layers, measure the height of the cake with a ruler and cut a small incision into the side with a paring knife to mark the desired thickness of your layers. Repeat every 3 to 4 inches around the circumference of the cake.

3. With a long serrated knife held parallel to the work surface, score the cake: With an outstretched palm gently pressed on the surface, slowly spin the cake away from you while pulling the knife toward you. The goal is to connect the incisions and score the cake, not to slice it.

4. Following the markings on the cake, cut deeper and deeper in the same manner. Gradually move the knife closer to the cake's center with each rotation. When the knife progresses past the cake's center, the cut is complete. Carefully slide the knife out and separate the layers.

are almost incorporated into the batter. Repeat the process twice more. When the batter appears blended, stop the mixer and scrape the sides of the bowl with a rubber spatula. Return the mixer to low speed; beat until the batter looks satiny, about 15 seconds longer.

5. Divide the batter evenly between the pans. With a rubber spatula, spread the batter to the pan sides and smooth the tops. Bake the cakes until they feel firm in the center when lightly pressed and a toothpick or thin skewer comes out clean or with just a crumb or two adhering, 23 to 30 minutes. Transfer the pans to wire racks; cool for 10 minutes. Run a knife around the perimeter of each pan, invert the cakes onto the racks, and peel off the paper liners. Reinvert the cakes onto additional racks; cool completely.

6. FOR THE FILLING: Mix the egg yolks, sugar, and salt in a medium bowl; beat in the butter, then gradually beat the cream and vanilla into the mixture. Pour into a medium nonreactive saucepan and cook over low heat, stirring constantly, until the mixture is puffy and just begins to thicken and the temperature reaches 180 degrees on an instant-read thermometer, 15 to 20 minutes. Pour the mixture into a medium bowl and cool to room temperature. Stir in the pecans and coconut.

7. To ASSEMBLE: Following the illustrations on page 859, use a long serrated knife to cut the cakes in half horizontally so that each cake forms 2 layers. Place 1 of the cake bottoms on a serving plate. Spread about 1 cup filling over the cake half. Place another halved cake round over the filling. Repeat this stacking and spreading process with the remaining filling and cake, ending with a final layer of filling. Cut the cake into slices and serve.

DEVIL'S FOOD CAKE

THE CRAZE FOR FANCY CAKE NAMES DATES BACK to the latter part of the 19th century. But only one of these cakes has truly survived from that period to ours—the devil's food cake. Its success is a testament both to its utter simplicity and its appealing moistness.

The obvious question is, "Just what is this cake?" The short answer is that the name refers to the color of the cake, not the texture, taste, shape, or fancy decorations. One group of food historians would argue that devil's food is a black cake; others would point to a reddish hue (cocoa naturally contains red pigments) as the distinguishing characteristic.

The problem with defining the devil's food cake, beyond the obvious issue of color, is that over time the recipe has been changed and embellished to the point where different recipes have little in common. To get a better handle on the situation, we pulled together two dozen or so recipes from cookbooks and the Internet, and our test kitchen baked the most promising five. The blind tasting that followed helped us put together a good working definition of our ideal devil's food cake. Although some of the recipes were similar to a regular chocolate cake (crumbly, a bit dry, and mild in flavor), we found the essence of devil's food to be a very moist, velvety texture combined with an intense chocolate experience. In addition, the better cakes were very dark, almost black. Here was a chocolate cake that was rich in both color and texture.

The next question was how to construct the ideal recipe. Despite their several differences, we first noted that all the recipes used the basic layer cake method. Butter and sugar were creamed, and then eggs were beaten in, followed by flour, cocoa, milk or water, and other ingredients. The next things we noticed were that the majority of recipes for this cake called for both cocoa and baking soda (not baking powder) and that many also suggested the addition of melted chocolate. Almost all of them used boiling water as the liquid of choice, although recipes from the early 1900s preferred milk, sour milk, or buttermilk. So the four key ingredients—those that really stood out in our research—were chocolate, cocoa, baking soda, and water.

The first issue was whether both chocolate and cocoa were necessary for the best flavor. The one cake out of five that used only cocoa was the driest and least flavorful. Clearly, a bit of chocolate was a must, and we finally settled on 4 ounces after testing smaller and larger amounts. As expected, the cake that used milk instead of water had less flavor, since milk tends to dull the flavor of chocolate (think of milk chocolate versus dark chocolate).

Baking soda was the leavener of choice in virtually every recipe we found, but we tested this anyway. To our great surprise, baking powder produced a totally different cake. It was much lighter in color, and, more to the point, it was fudgy, almost like a brownie. It shared none of the delicate, velvety texture that we had come to expect of a classic devil's food cake. We also tested the proper amount of baking soda and settled on 1 teaspoon. More caused the cake to fall in the center, and any less didn't provide enough lift.

We continued our testing to refine the recipe and found that a mixture of cake flour and all-purpose was best. The all-purpose flour provided structure, while the addition of the cake flour made the cake a bit more delicate. On a lark, we made one cake by whipping the egg whites separately from the yolks, but the result was a much too flimsy cake that could not support the large amount of water called for in most recipes and sank. We played with the number of eggs, trying two, three, and then four. The middle road proved best—three eggs was just right. Granulated sugar was tested against brown sugar, and the latter won, improving the flavor. Many devil's food recipes do indeed call for brown sugar, whereas those for regular chocolate cakes tend to use granulated.

Although we had tested milk and buttermilk against water—the water produced a more intense chocolate experience—we tried adding sour cream to the recipe and were impressed. It deepened the flavor, added substance to the texture, and provided a richer taste experience, the chocolate flavor lingering in the mouth and coating the tongue.

Finally, we wondered if boiling water was really necessary. To find out, we made a cake with room temperature water and found that it made virtually no difference. But when we tested dissolving the cocoa in the boiling water (as opposed to simply mixing it in with the flour), we found that this significantly enhanced the cocoa's flavor.

We had finally discovered the essence of a great devil's food cake. Unlike chocolate cake, which is usually made with milk and has a higher proportion of fat (butter), devil's food provides a velvety, more intense chocolate experience. And it is a particularly dark cake when made with Dutch-processed cocoa; natural (nonalkalized) cocoa will give it a redder hue. It is, ultimately, a singular cake in its devotion to a pure chocolate experience, subordinating everything to this simple but tasty proposition.

Devil's Food Cake
SERVES 8 TO 10

Regular, or natural, cocoa like Hershey's can be used, but you'll get the best results with Dutch-processed cocoa.

4	ounces unsweetened chocolate, chopped
1/4	cup (3/4 ounce) Dutch-processed cocoa
1 1/4	cups boiling water
3/4	cup (3 3/4 ounces) unbleached all-purpose flour
3/4	cup (3 ounces) plain cake flour
1	teaspoon baking soda
1/4	teaspoon salt
16	tablespoons (2 sticks) unsalted butter, softened but still cool
1 1/2	cups packed (10 1/2 ounces) dark brown sugar
3	large eggs, at room temperature
1/2	cup sour cream
1	teaspoon vanilla extract
1	recipe Rich Vanilla Buttercream Frosting or Rich Coffee Buttercream Frosting (pages 848–849)

1. Adjust the oven racks to the upper- and lower-middle positions; heat the oven to 350 degrees. Meanwhile, grease three 8-inch cake pans and line the bottom of each pan with a round of parchment paper or waxed paper. Combine the chocolate and cocoa in a medium bowl; pour the boiling water over and whisk until smooth. Sift together the flours, baking soda, and salt onto a large sheet of parchment or waxed paper; set aside.

2. Beat the butter in the bowl of a standing mixer at medium-high speed until creamy, about 1 minute. Add the brown sugar and beat at high speed until light and fluffy, about 3 minutes. Stop the mixer and scrape down the bowl with a rubber spatula. With the mixer at medium-high

speed, add the eggs, one at a time, beating 30 seconds after each addition. Reduce the speed to medium; add the sour cream and vanilla and beat until combined, about 10 seconds. Stop the mixer and scrape down the bowl. With the mixer at low speed, add about a third of the flour mixture, followed by about half of the chocolate mixture. Repeat, ending with the flour mixture; beat until just combined, about 15 seconds. Do not overbeat. Remove the bowl from the mixer; scrape the bottom and sides of the bowl with a rubber spatula and stir gently to thoroughly combine.

3. Divide the batter evenly among the cake pans and smooth the batter to the edge of each pan with a rubber spatula. Place 2 pans on the lower-middle rack and 1 on the upper-middle rack. Bake until a toothpick or skewer inserted in the center comes out clean, 20 to 23 minutes. Cool the cakes on wire racks 15 to 20 minutes. Run a knife around each pan perimeter to loosen. Invert each cake onto a large plate; peel off the parchment and reinvert onto a rack. Cool completely.

4. Assemble and frost the cake according to the illustrations on page 853. Cut the cake into slices and serve.

FLOURLESS CHOCOLATE CAKE

TO OUR KNOWLEDGE, FLOURLESS CHOCOLATE cake is the only dessert that is named for a missing ingredient. Besides this, using the word "cake" for this very popular dessert is a stretch. Although some recipes replace flour or crumbs with ground nuts, the quintessence of the genre contains only chocolate, butter, and eggs—nothing that could conceivably be called a dry ingredient. The result is moist and fudgy, more confection than cake.

Although the ingredient choices are limited—chocolate, butter, and eggs, sometimes sugar, and sometimes liquid such as water, coffee, or liqueur—the proportions as well as mixing and baking methods differed considerably in the recipes we researched.

We selected and baked six recipes that represented the array of choices. The results

were staggering in their variety. One resembled a flourless fudge brownie, one was more like an ultra-dense, creamy custard, and one was a pouffy, fallen soufflé–like affair. Some were very bittersweet, others quite sweet. All, however, had the richness and intensity of a confection.

Although almost all the desserts were very enticing, we were quickly able to define our criteria for the ultimate flourless chocolate cake. We wanted something dense, moist, and ultra-chocolatey, but with some textural finesse. We wanted a mouthfeel and texture somewhere between a substantial *marquis au chocolat*—that dense, buttery, and just slightly aerated chocolate mousse with a characteristic dry but creamy texture—and a heavy New York–style cheesecake, which requires the mouth to work for just a second before it melts and dissolves with sublime flavor. We wanted the flavor and character of good, eating-quality chocolate to reign supreme, with no unnecessary sweetness and not even the slightest grain of sugar on the palate. In short, we wanted an intense bittersweet "adult" dessert, not a piece of fudge or a brownie or a thick chocolate pudding—and certainly nothing fluffy.

Some recipes used unsweetened chocolate instead of semisweet or bittersweet, but we rejected this idea after tasting just one cake made with unsweetened chocolate. Neither flavor nor texture was smooth or silky enough for this type of dessert, and there was a slight chalky sensation on the palate. This made sense. Unsweetened chocolate is coarse and needs high heat to blend with the sugar required to sweeten it. It is most successful in desserts with a cakey or fudgy texture, when perfect smoothness is unnecessary. Hot fudge sauce made with unsweetened chocolate is smooth because it is cooked to a temperature high enough to melt the sugar and change the physical properties of the chocolate. But our flourless chocolate cake is more like chocolate mousse, chocolate truffles, or ganache; the ingredients are few, cooked very gently, and the results must be perfectly smooth. Made to be nibbled, semisweet and bittersweet chocolates are incomparably smooth, refined so that chocolate and sugar are intimately married and every particle is smaller than the human palate can detect.

The next decision had to do with the baking temperature and whether or not a water bath was indicated. The original recipe for this now-popular dessert was flawed by hard, crumbly edges—surely caused by baking for a short time at a high temperature without a water bath. We tried a similar recipe baked at a high temperature for a short time but in a water bath. It was creamier by far, but we could taste raw egg. We guessed that, like cheesecake, this dessert required a longer baking time at a lower temperature in a water bath to allow the interior to reach a safe temperature without overcooking the edges. We found that 325 degrees in a water bath produced a successful sample.

The trick in baking this cake, however, is knowing when to stop. Just like cheesecake, our flourless chocolate cake must be taken from the oven when the center still jiggles and looks quite underdone, as it continues to cook after it comes out of the oven.

At first we used a thermometer to make sure that the center of the cake had reached the safe temperature of 160 degrees (so that any salmonella bacteria present in the eggs would be killed). But this cake was clearly overbaked; the texture was dryish and chalky. Knowing that a temperature of at least 140 degrees held for five minutes also kills salmonella bacteria, we let the cake reach 140 degrees and then left it in the oven for five more minutes. It was overbaked as well. After trying four, three, and two extra minutes in the oven, we finally realized that if we removed the cake at 140 degrees, it would stay at or even above 140 degrees for at least five minutes (thus killing off salmonella) as the heat from the edges of the cake penetrated the center. The results were perfect.

Before determining the proper quantities of butter and eggs for a pound of chocolate, we decided to test textures. We were pretty sure that the ultimate cake would need some form of aeration from beaten eggs to achieve the texture that we wanted. In the first test, we whisked the eggs over gentle heat to warm them (as for a génoise) and then beat them until they had about tripled in volume and were the consistency of soft whipped cream. We then folded the whipped eggs into the warm chocolate and butter in three parts. In the second test, we separated the eggs, whisked the yolks into the warm chocolate and butter, and then beat the whites to a meringue before folding them in. In the third test, we simply whisked the eggs, one by one, into the warm chocolate and butter, as though making a custard.

The sample made with eggs simply whisked into the melted chocolate and butter was dense and smooth like a very rich custard or crème brûlée. Our definition of the ultimate flourless chocolate cake ruled this version out. The cake with beaten whole eggs differed from the one with yolks and meringue more than we expected. Surprisingly, the difference in flavor was greater than the difference in texture. Whole beaten eggs produced a dessert with nicely blended flavors, while the cake with separated eggs tasted as though the ingredients had not been completely integrated. Along the way, we realized that we could eliminate the step of warming the eggs before beating them, since cold eggs produce a denser foam with smaller bubbles, which in turn gave the cake a more velvety texture.

Flourless Chocolate Cake

SERVES 12 TO 16

Even though the cake may not look done, pull it from the oven when an instant-read thermometer registers 140 degrees. (Make sure not to let the tip of the thermometer hit the bottom of the pan.) It will continue to firm up as it cools. If you use a 9-inch springform pan instead of the preferred 8-inch, reduce the baking time to 18 to 20 minutes. We like the pure flavor of chocolate; however, coffee or liqueur (choose something that tastes like nuts, coffee, or oranges) can be added if desired.

8	large eggs, cold
1	pound high-quality bittersweet or semisweet chocolate, chopped coarse
16	tablespoons (2 sticks) unsalted butter, cut into 16 pieces
1/4	cup strong black coffee or liqueur (optional) Confectioners' sugar or unsweetened cocoa for dusting the cake (optional)

1. Adjust an oven rack to the lower-middle position and heat the oven to 325 degrees. Line the bottom of an 8-inch springform pan with parchment paper or waxed paper and grease the sides of the pan. Wrap the outside of the pan with 2 sheets of heavy-duty foil and set it in a large roasting pan. Bring a kettle of water to a boil.

2. Beat the eggs in the bowl of a standing mixer at high speed until the volume doubles (to approximately 1 quart), about 5 minutes.

3. Meanwhile, melt the chocolate and butter (adding the coffee, if using) in a large heatproof bowl set over a pan of almost-simmering water until smooth and very warm (about 115 degrees on an instant-read thermometer), stirring once or twice. (To melt in a microwave, heat the chocolate in a microwave-safe bowl at 50 percent power for 2 minutes, stir, add the butter and coffee, if using, and continue heating at 50 percent power, stirring every minute, until the chocolate and butter have melted and are smooth, another 2 to 3 minutes total.) Fold a third of the egg foam into the chocolate mixture using a large rubber spatula until only a few streaks of egg are visible; fold in half of the remaining foam, then the last of the foam, until the mixture is totally homogeneous.

4. Scrape the batter into the prepared springform pan and smooth the surface with a rubber spatula. Set the roasting pan on the oven rack and pour in enough boiling water to come about halfway up the sides of the springform pan. Bake until the cake has risen slightly, the edges are just beginning to set, a thin glazed crust (like a brownie) has formed on the surface, and an instant-read thermometer inserted halfway into the center reads 140 degrees, 22 to 25 minutes. Remove the cake pan from the water bath and set on a wire rack; cool to room temperature. Cover and refrigerate overnight to mellow. (The cake can be covered and refrigerated for up to 4 days.)

5. About 30 minutes before serving, remove the sides of the pan, invert the cake onto a sheet of waxed paper, peel off the parchment paper, and reinvert the cake onto a serving platter. Sieve a light sprinkling of confectioners' sugar over the cake to decorate, if desired. To slice, use a sharp, thin-bladed knife, dipping the knife into a pitcher of hot water and wiping the blade before each cut.

FALLEN CHOCOLATE CAKE

FALLEN CHOCOLATE CAKE IS AN UNDERCOOKED-in-the-center mound of intense, buttery chocolate cake, which ranges from a dense, brownie-like consistency to something altogether more ethereal. Sometimes referred to as "molten chocolate cake," fallen chocolate cake appeared first on restaurant menus, and then its popularity grew. (International chef Jean-Georges Vongerichten serves several hundred of these desserts every night in his restaurants.)

Having tasted Vongerichten's recipe on a number of occasions and having also tried this dessert at other trendy eateries, we became intrigued with the notion of turning a restaurant showstopper into a practical recipe for home cooks. We knew that the ingredient list was short and suspected that the techniques would be relatively simple, but, since restaurant recipes rarely work at home, it was clear that a great deal of culinary translation awaited us.

The first step, since this recipe concept encompasses a wide range of styles from half-cooked batter to a chocolate sponge cake, was to organize a tasting in the test kitchen to decide exactly what we were looking for. We made three variations: Warm, Soft Chocolate Cake, from Vongerichten; Fallen Chocolate Cake from the restaurant Olives, created by chef-owner Todd English; and an old favorite called Fallen Chocolate Soufflé Cake, published by the late Richard Sax, a well-known food writer.

Sax's recipe, which is baked in a tube pan rather than in a ramekin, was quite delicious and soufflé-like in texture. However, it lacked the intense whack of chocolate and the rich, buttery texture of the other two desserts. The recipe from Olives was the heaviest of the lot, very good but quite similar to an undercooked brownie. Jean-Georges's cake was the tasting panel's favorite, with the most intense chocolate flavor, a relatively light texture, and a very runny center. We then wondered if we might be able to capture some of the ethereal lightness of Sax's cake, along with the rich taste and buttery mouthfeel of Jean-Georges's dessert.

First we had to decide on the basic preparation method. There were two choices. We could beat the egg yolks and whites separately and then fold them together, or we could beat whole eggs and sugar to create a thick foam. The latter method proved superior, as it delivered the rich, moist texture we were looking for as well as making the recipe simpler. That left us with a recipe that consisted of melting chocolate; beating whole eggs, sugar, and flavorings into a foam; and then folding the two together, perhaps with a little flour or ground nuts for extra body.

Our next step was to determine what amounts of each ingredient made the best cake. After considerable testing, we decided that ½ cup of melted butter made the dessert considerably more moist. Some recipes use no flour or very little (Jean-Georges, for instance, uses only 4 teaspoons), but we finally settled on 2 tablespoons. The amount of chocolate, a key factor, was highly variable, running from a mere 4 ounces to a high of 12 ounces in English's recipe. Eight ounces provided a good jolt of chocolate without being overbearing.

The eggs, however, were perhaps the most crucial element. We tested six whole eggs (light and airy sponge-cake texture), four whole eggs plus four yolks (moist and dark), and the winning combination of four whole eggs plus one yolk (rich but light, moist, intense, and dark).

When baking these desserts in ramekins at 450 degrees, as called for in the Jean-Georges recipe, we found that the tops were slightly burnt and the center was a bit too runny. At 350 degrees, the dessert took on a more cake-like quality and was also drier. Four hundred degrees was best, yielding a light, cake-like perimeter around a moist well of intense chocolate. (When using a cake pan rather than ramekins, though, we found it best to set the oven at 375 degrees.)

We now had the recipe pretty well in order. To finish the translation from restaurant to home kitchen, however, we still had some work to do. The biggest obstacle was the amount of last-minute cooking. No one wants to run out to the kitchen during dinner and whip up an egg foam. Having had some experience with preparing chocolate soufflés ahead of time, we tested pouring the batter into the ramekins, refrigerating them, and then baking them during dinner. This worked, the batter holding for up to eight hours. Although the filled ramekins can be taken directly from the refrigerator to the oven with reasonably good results, they rise better if allowed to sit at room temperature for 30 minutes before baking.

We also wondered if most folks have eight ramekins at home. Therefore, we developed a variation that uses either an 8- or 9-inch springform pan. As an added benefit for the home cook, we discovered that, in cake form, this dessert can be baked up to one hour before serving, remaining warm right in the pan. In a pinch, this dessert can be held up to two hours in the pan, but it will become slightly denser as it cools.

SCIENCE: Chocolate Flavor Diffusion

One of the more interesting ideas we heard about the do's and don'ts of working with chocolate desserts was proposed to us by famed New York chef Jean-Georges Vongerichten, who stated that the less one cooks chocolate, the better it tastes. We decided to check this out with Tom Lehmann, director of bakery assistance at the American Institute of Baking. He agreed.

Chocolate, Lehmann explained, is a very delicate substance, full of highly sensitive, volatile compounds that give chocolate much of its flavor. When chocolate is heated, the liquids in it turn to steam and carry away these volatile compounds. That's what makes the kitchen smell so good when brownies are in the oven. The bad news is that these volatile compounds are no longer in the brownies—which is where you really want them to be. This situation is made even more acute by the fact that unwanted volatile compounds have already been driven off during the processes of roasting and conching (kneading, grinding, and smoothing the chocolate). Additional exposure to heat, therefore, has no benefits; it simply makes the chocolate more bitter and less complex-tasting.

So, what are the lessons to be learned for home cooks who bake with chocolate? First, underbaking is always better than overbaking. Dry chocolate desserts will have much less flavor and tend to be bitter. Second, use as much fat as possible. Fat increases the retention of volatile compounds. That's why low-fat chocolate desserts usually taste like sugar but not chocolate.

Individual Fallen Chocolate Cakes

SERVES 8

To melt the chocolate and butter in a microwave oven, heat the chocolate alone at 50 percent power for 2 minutes; stir the chocolate, add the butter, and continue heating at 50 percent for another 2 minutes, stopping to stir after 1 minute. If the chocolate is not yet entirely melted, heat an additional 30 seconds at 50 percent power.

2	tablespoons unbleached all-purpose flour, plus more for dusting the ramekins
8	tablespoons (I stick) unsalted butter, cut into 4 pieces
8	ounces bittersweet or semisweet chocolate, chopped coarse
4	large eggs, plus I large egg yolk, at room temperature
I	teaspoon vanilla extract
1/4	teaspoon salt
1/2	cup (3 1/2 ounces) granulated sugar
	Confectioners' sugar or unsweetened cocoa for dusting the cakes (optional)
	Whipped cream for serving (optional)

1. Adjust an oven rack to the middle position and heat the oven to 400 degrees. Generously grease and flour eight 6-ounce ramekins or heatproof glass baking cups; tap out the excess flour and position the ramekins in a shallow roasting pan or on a rimmed baking sheet. Meanwhile, melt the butter and chocolate in a medium heatproof bowl set over a pan of almost-simmering water, stirring once or twice, until smooth; remove from the heat.

2. Beat the eggs, yolk, vanilla, salt, and granulated sugar in the bowl of a standing mixer set at the highest speed until the volume nearly triples, the color is very light, and the mixture drops from the beaters in a smooth, thick stream, about 5 minutes. Scrape the egg mixture over the melted chocolate and butter; sprinkle the flour over the egg mixture. Gently fold the egg and flour into the chocolate until the mixture is a uniform color. Ladle or pour the batter into the prepared ramekins. (The ramekins can be covered lightly with plastic wrap and refrigerated for up to 8 hours. Return to room temperature for 30 minutes before baking.)

3. Bake until the cakes have puffed about 1/2 inch above the rims of the ramekins, have a thin crust on top, and jiggle slightly at the center when the ramekins are shaken very gently, 12 to 13 minutes. Run a paring knife around the inside edges of the ramekins to loosen the cakes and invert onto serving plates; cool for 1 minute and lift off the ramekins. Sieve a light sprinkling of confectioners' sugar over the cakes to decorate, if desired, and serve immediately with whipped cream, if using.

➤ VARIATIONS

Large Fallen Chocolate Cake

SERVES 8 TO 10

One large chocolate cake can be prepared in a springform pan. Do not use a regular cake pan, as the cake will be impossible to remove once baked. The cake is best served warm, within 30 minutes of being unmolded, but it can also be held in the pan for up to 2 hours.

Follow the recipe for Individual Fallen Chocolate Cakes, substituting an 8- or 9-inch springform pan for the ramekins. Decrease the baking temperature to 375 degrees and bake until the cake looks puffed, a thin top crust has formed, and the center jiggles slightly when the pan is shaken gently, 22 to 25 minutes for a 9-inch pan or 27 to 30 minutes for an 8-inch pan. Cool the cake for 15 minutes, run a paring knife around the inside edge of the pan, and remove the pan sides. Sieve a light sprinkling of confectioners' sugar over the cake to decorate, if desired, just before serving and serve warm, with optional whipped cream.

Orange Fallen Chocolate Cake

Follow the recipe for Individual Fallen Chocolate Cakes or Large Fallen Chocolate Cake, folding 1 tablespoon finely grated zest from 2 medium oranges and 2 tablespoons orange liqueur (such as Grand Marnier or Triple Sec) into the beaten egg and melted chocolate mixture.

NEW YORK CHEESECAKE

AN ORCHESTRATION OF DIFFERENT TEXTURES and an exercise in flavor restraint, New York cheesecake is a tall, bronze-skinned, and dense affair. At the core, it is cool, thick, smooth, satiny, and creamy; radiating outward, the texture goes gradually from velvety to suede-like, until finally becoming cake-like and fine-pored at the edges. The flavor is simple and pure and minimalist, sweet and tangy, and rich to boot. It should not be so dry as to make you gag, and it definitely should not bake up with a fault as large as the San Andreas.

We decided to start with the crust. Some recipes claim that a pastry crust was the crust of choice for the original New York cheesecake. We tried one, but after a lot of expended effort, a pastry crust only became soggy beneath the filling. Cookie and cracker crumbs were tasty and more practical options. Every taster considered a mere dusting of crumbs on the bottom of the cheesecake insufficient. We wanted a crust with more presence.

A graham cracker crust made with a cup of crumbs, some sugar, and melted butter, pressed into the bottom of the springform pan and pre-baked until it was fragrant and browned around the edge, was ideal at a thickness of about ⅜ inch. If served within a day of baking, it retained its crispness. If the cheesecake was held for a couple of days, the crust softened, but tasters didn't seem to mind.

A great New York cheesecake should be of great stature. One made with 2 pounds (four bars) of cream cheese was not tall enough. We threw in another half pound—the springform pan reached maximum capacity, but the cheesecake stood tall and looked right. The amount of sugar was quickly settled upon—1½ cups. The cheesecake struck a perfect balance of sweet and tangy.

Cheesecakes always require a dairy supplement to the cream cheese, usually either heavy cream or sour cream, or sometimes both. We made a cheesecake without any additional dairy and found out why this is true. Though the all-cream-cheese cheesecake tasted undeniably like cream cheese, the texture was gluey and pasty, akin to mortar, and much like a bar of cream cheese straight out of its wrapper. Additional dairy loosens up the texture of the cream cheese, giving the cake a smoother, more luxurious feel.

We found that heavy cream, even when used in the smallest amounts, dulled and flattened the flavor of the cream cheese. Sour cream, with a tartness of its own, supplemented the tangy quality of the cream cheese, but an overabundance made the cheesecake taste sour and acidic. What tasters preferred was a relatively small amount of sour cream—⅓ cup. It was enough to offer a touch of tartness and help give the cheesecake a smoother, creamier texture without advertising its presence.

Eggs help bind the cheesecake and give it structure. They also help create a smooth, creamy texture. Whole eggs are often called for in cheesecakes of non–New York persuasions. We tried as few as four and as many as six whole eggs—these cheesecakes had textures that were called "light," "fluffy," and even "whipped." Recipes for New York cheesecake seem to agree that a few yolks in addition to whole eggs help to get the velvety, lush texture of a proper New York cheesecake. Our testing bore this out, and ultimately we concluded that a generous amount of eggs—six whole and two yolks—yielded a cheesecake of unparalleled texture: dense but not heavy, firm but not rigid, and perfectly rich.

Perfecting the flavor of the cheesecake was easy. Tasters complained that the orange zest that recipes often call for made the cheesecake taste like a Creamsicle, so it was out of there in a New York minute. Next to go was lemon zest because its flavor was distracting. A couple of teaspoons of lemon juice, however, helped to perk up the flavors without adding a lemon-flavored hit. Just a bit of salt (cream cheese already contains a good dose of sodium) and a couple of teaspoons of vanilla extract rounded out the flavors. Everyone in the test kitchen appreciated this minimalist cheesecake.

Cheesecake is well loved by cooks for the fact that it goes together easily. However, care must be used when mixing the ingredients lest the batter contain small nodules of unmixed cream cheese that can mar the smoothness of the baked cake. Frequent and thorough scraping of the bowl during mixing is key to ensuring that every spot of cream cheese is incorporated, but starting with semisoftened cream cheese is certainly helpful. Simply cutting it into chunks and letting it stand while the crust is prepared and the other ingredients assembled—30 to 45 minutes—made mixing easier.

There are many ways to bake a cheesecake: in a moderate oven, in a low oven, in a water bath, and in accordance with the New York method—500 degrees for about 10 minutes, then 200 degrees for about an hour—which appears to be a standard technique. We tried them all, but the New York method was the only one that yielded the nut-brown surface that is a distinguishing mark of an exemplary New York cheesecake. This dual-temperature, no-water-bath baking method also produced a lovely graded texture, soft and creamy at the center and firm and dry at the periphery.

The New York baking method was not without flaws, however. After an hour at 200 degrees, the very center of the cheesecake—even after chilling—was loose and slurpy, a result of underbaking. Some recipes leave the cheesecake in the still-warm, turned-off, propped-open oven for about 30 minutes to finish "baking." Handled this way, the cheesecake was marginally better but still insufficiently baked.

We tried extending the hour-long baking time to get the center of the cheesecake to set up to the right consistency. We took it 15 and 30 minutes past an hour. The cheesecake baked for 1½ hours to an internal temperature of about 150 degrees was whisked out of the oven. Chilled, it was cheesecake perfection. It sliced into a neat slab with a cleanly set center texture—not a wet, sloppy one. Each slice kept its shape, and each bite felt satiny on the tongue. Though this prolonged New York baking method was relatively foolproof, we do caution against taking the cheesecake beyond an internal temperature of 160 degrees. The few that we did were hideously and hopelessly cracked. Uptight though it may seem, an instant-read thermometer inserted into the cake is the most reliable means of judging the doneness of the cheesecake.

New York Cheesecake
SERVES 12 TO 16

For the crust, chocolate wafers (such as Nabisco Famous) may be substituted for graham crackers; you will need about 14 wafers. The flavor and texture of the cheesecake are best if the cake is allowed to stand at room temperature for about 30 minutes before serving. When cutting the cake, have a pitcher of hot tap water ready; dipping the blade of the knife into the water and wiping it after each cut helps make clean slices.

CRUST

5	tablespoons unsalted butter, melted, plus 1 tablespoon melted unsalted butter for the pan
8	whole graham crackers (4 ounces), broken into rough pieces and processed in a food processor to fine, even crumbs
1	tablespoon sugar

FILLING

2½	pounds (five 8-ounce packages) cream cheese, cut into rough 1-inch chunks, at room temperature
⅛	teaspoon salt
1½	cups (10½ ounces) sugar
⅓	cup sour cream
2	teaspoons juice from 1 lemon
2	teaspoons vanilla extract
2	large egg yolks, plus 6 large eggs, at room temperature

1. FOR THE CRUST: Adjust an oven rack to the lower-middle position and heat the oven to 325 degrees. Brush the bottom and sides of a 9-inch springform pan with ½ tablespoon of the melted butter. Combine the graham cracker crumbs and sugar in a medium bowl; add 5 tablespoons of the melted butter and toss with a fork until evenly moistened. Empty the crumbs into the springform pan and, following the illustrations on page 872, press evenly into the pan bottom. Bake until fragrant and beginning to brown around the edges, about 13 minutes. Cool on a wire rack while making the filling.

2. FOR THE FILLING: Increase the oven temperature to 500 degrees. In the bowl of a standing

mixer, beat the cream cheese at medium-low speed to break up and soften it slightly, about 1 minute. Scrape the beater and the bottom and sides of the bowl well with a rubber spatula; add the salt and about half of the sugar and beat at medium-low speed until combined, about 1 minute. Scrape the bowl; beat in the remaining sugar until combined, about 1 minute. Scrape the bowl; add the sour cream, lemon juice, and vanilla, and beat at low speed until combined, about 1 minute. Scrape the bowl; add the egg yolks and beat at medium-low speed until thoroughly combined, about 1 minute. Scrape the bowl; add the remaining eggs, two at a time, beating until thoroughly combined, about 1 minute, scraping the bowl between additions.

3. Brush the sides of the springform pan with the remaining ½ tablespoon melted butter. Set the springform pan on a rimmed baking sheet (to catch any spills if the pan leaks). Pour the filling into the cooled crust and bake 10 minutes; without opening the oven door, reduce the oven temperature to 200 degrees and continue to bake until the cheesecake registers about 150 degrees on an instant-read thermometer inserted in the center, about 1½ hours. Transfer the cake to a wire rack and cool until barely warm, 2½ to 3 hours. Run a paring knife between the cake and the pan sides. Wrap tightly in plastic wrap and refrigerate until cold, at least 3 hours. (The cheesecake can be refrigerated for up to 4 days.)

4. To unmold the cheesecake, remove the sides of the pan. Slide a thin metal spatula between the crust and the bottom of the pan to loosen, then slide the cake onto a serving plate. Let the cheesecake stand at room temperature about 30 minutes, then cut into wedges (see note) and serve with Fresh Strawberry Topping, if desired.

Fresh Strawberry Topping

MAKES ABOUT 1½ QUARTS

A ruby-colored, glazed strawberry topping is the classic accompaniment to New York cheesecake. This topping is best served the same day it is made.

2   pounds strawberries, hulled and
     cut lengthwise into ¼- to ⅜-inch wedges

½   cup (3½ ounces) sugar
     Pinch salt
1   cup strawberry jam
2   tablespoons juice from 1 lemon

1. Toss the berries, sugar, and salt in a medium bowl; let stand until the berries have released some juice and the sugar has dissolved, about 30 minutes, tossing occasionally to combine.

2. Process the jam in a food processor until smooth, about 8 seconds; transfer to a small saucepan. Bring the jam to a simmer over medium-high heat; simmer, stirring frequently, until dark and no longer frothy, about 3 minutes. Stir in the lemon juice; pour the warm jam over the strawberries and stir to combine. Cover with plastic wrap and refrigerate until cold, at least 2 hours or up to 12. To serve, spoon a portion of sauce over individual slices of cheesecake.

LEMON CHEESECAKE

ALTHOUGH SOME WOULD NEVER DARE TO ADULterate plain cheesecake, there are plenty of variations out there: some good, some bad, some ugly. We wanted a variation that serves a function by cutting through the cloying nature of this rich dessert. We found that variation with lemon.

During our initial recipe testing, we discovered a host of different lemon cheesecake styles. One was a towering soufflé made by separating the eggs, whipping the whites, and folding them in at the end. Another had a pasty texture owing to the addition of sweetened condensed milk. And in all cases the lemon flavor was either too fleeting or too harsh. What we wanted was a light, creamy-textured cheesecake, a style that everyone in the test kitchen felt would be a good partner with the flavor of lemon.

We decided to concentrate first on the crust, the foundation of the cheesecake. We liked a graham cracker crust for our New York Cheesecake because it remained crunchy under the weight of the cheese filling, but its sweet and spicy flavor overpowered the lemon. We experimented with several types of crumb crusts and ended up preferring one made with biscuit-type cookies. Of all the brands that we tried, Nabisco's Barnum's Animals Crackers were the surprise favorite.

For the filling, we started with the filling for our New York Cheesecake. Our first move was to lighten it by reducing the amount of cream cheese from 2½ pounds to 1½. With less cream cheese, we found that we needed less sugar and fewer eggs. Next we eliminated the sour cream, because the addition of lemon provided enough of a tangy counterpoint to the cream cheese. We added some heavy cream for a luscious texture.

As for the lemon flavor, we discovered that one can have too much of a good thing by using too much lemon juice. Zest provided a balanced lemon flavor, but it came with a hitch: The fibrous texture of the zest marred the creamy smoothness of the filling. To solve this problem, we tried processing the zest and sugar together before adding them to the cream cheese. This produced a wonderfully potent lemon flavor by breaking down the zest and releasing its oils, but it also caused the cheesecake to become strangely dense. After many trials, we realized that the food processor was wreaking havoc with the sugar, breaking down its crystalline structure (necessary for the aeration of the cream cheese) as well as melding it with the oils from the lemon zest. By processing only ¼ cup of the sugar with the zest and then stirring in the remaining sugar by hand, we solved the problem.

Baking this cheesecake in a water bath at a low oven temperature of 325 degrees was also key to achieving a creamy texture. We were surprised to find that when we used hot tap water instead of boiling water (we like shortcuts), the result was a more evenly baked cheesecake (and about 10 minutes of extra baking time). We also discovered that an additional hour in the oven, with the heat off and the door ajar, was crucial to a consistent texture. When we tried to skip this step, the cheesecake set up on the edges but remained gooey in the center.

Our cheesecake was certainly lemony, but we wanted more pizzazz. We found it with a topping of lemon curd. The only problem remaining was the curd's slightly acidic edge. To curb it, we mixed in 1 tablespoon of heavy cream at the end of cooking, along with a dash of vanilla. Cold cubed butter, also added at the end, served both to cool the curd (and prevent overcooking) and to form a smoother emulsion. We found we could make a curd in just five minutes and let it set up in the refrigerator while the cheesecake was baking and cooling. The curd complements the cheesecake perfectly, adding a bit of easy showmanship to this otherwise plain dessert.

Lemon Cheesecake

SERVES 12 TO 16

While this recipe takes several hours from start to finish, the actual preparation is simple, and baking and cooling proceed practically unattended. The cheesecake can be made up to a day in advance; leftovers can be refrigerated for up to 4 days, although the crust will become soggy.

JUDGING WHEN THE CURD IS COOKED

At first, the curd will appear thin and soupy, as shown at left. When the spatula leaves a clear trail in the bottom of the saucepan (which quickly disappears), the curd is ready to come off the heat (center). If the curd continues to cook, it will become too thick and pasty, and a spatula will leave a wide, clear trail (right).

CRUST

5 ounces Nabisco's Barnum's Animals Crackers
   or Social Tea Biscuits

3 tablespoons sugar

4 tablespoons ($\frac{1}{2}$ stick) unsalted butter,
   melted and kept warm

FILLING

1$\frac{1}{4}$ cups (8$\frac{3}{4}$ ounces) sugar

1 tablespoon grated zest and $\frac{1}{4}$ cup juice from
   1 or 2 lemons

1$\frac{1}{2}$ pounds (three 8-ounce packages) cream
   cheese, cut into rough 1-inch chunks,
   at room temperature

4 large eggs, at room temperature

2 teaspoons vanilla extract

$\frac{1}{4}$ teaspoon salt

$\frac{1}{2}$ cup heavy cream

LEMON CURD

$\frac{1}{3}$ cup juice from 2 lemons

2 large eggs, plus 1 large egg yolk

$\frac{1}{2}$ cup (3$\frac{1}{2}$ ounces) sugar

2 tablespoons cold unsalted butter,
   cut into $\frac{1}{2}$-inch cubes

1 tablespoon heavy cream

$\frac{1}{4}$ teaspoon vanilla extract
   Pinch salt

1. FOR THE CRUST: Adjust an oven rack to the lower-middle position and heat the oven to 325 degrees. In a food processor, process the cookies to fine, even crumbs, about 30 seconds (you should have about 1 cup). Add the sugar and pulse 2 or 3 times to incorporate. Add the warm melted butter in a slow, steady stream while pulsing; pulse until the mixture is evenly moistened and resembles wet sand, about ten 1-second pulses. Transfer the mixture to a 9-inch springform pan and, following the illustrations on page 872, press evenly into the pan bottom. Bake until fragrant and golden brown, 15 to 18 minutes. Cool on a wire rack to room temperature, about 30 minutes. When cool, wrap the outside of the pan with two 18-inch-square pieces of heavy-duty foil; set the springform pan in a roasting pan.

2. FOR THE FILLING: While the crust is cooling, process $\frac{1}{4}$ cup of the sugar and the lemon zest in a food processor until the sugar is yellow and the zest is broken down, about 15 seconds, scraping down the bowl if necessary. Transfer the lemon sugar to a small bowl; stir in the remaining 1 cup sugar.

3. In the bowl of a standing mixer set at low speed, beat the cream cheese to break it up and soften it slightly, about 5 seconds. With the machine running, add the sugar mixture in a slow, steady stream; increase the speed to medium and continue to beat until the mixture is creamy and smooth, about 3 minutes, scraping down the bowl with a rubber spatula as needed. Reduce the speed to medium-low and add the eggs, two at a time; beat until incorporated, about 30 seconds, scraping the sides and bottom of the bowl well after each addition. Add the lemon juice, vanilla, and salt and mix until just incorporated, about 5 seconds; add the heavy cream and mix until just incorporated, about 5 seconds longer. Give the batter a final scrape, stir with a rubber spatula, and pour into the prepared springform pan; fill the roasting pan with enough hot tap water to come halfway up the sides of the springform pan. Bake until the center jiggles slightly, the sides just start to puff, the surface is no longer shiny, and an instant-read thermometer inserted in the center of the cake reads 150 degrees, 55 to 60 minutes. Turn off the oven and prop open the oven door with a potholder or wooden spoon handle; allow the cake to cool in the water bath in the oven

THE IMPORTANCE OF CHILLING CHEESECAKE

CHILLED 2 HOURS   **CHILLED 5 HOURS**

If the cheesecake is not thoroughly chilled, it will not hold its shape when sliced (left). After 5 hours in the refrigerator, the cheesecake has set up and can be sliced neatly (right).

for 1 hour. Transfer the springform pan without the foil to a wire rack; run a small paring knife around the inside edge of the pan to loosen the sides of the cake and cool the cake to room temperature, about 2 hours.

4. FOR THE LEMON CURD: While the cheesecake bakes, heat the lemon juice in a small nonreactive saucepan over medium heat until hot but not boiling. Whisk the eggs and yolk in a medium nonreactive bowl; gradually whisk in the sugar. Whisking constantly, slowly pour the hot lemon juice into the eggs, then return the mixture to the saucepan and cook over medium heat, stirring constantly with a wooden spoon, until the mixture registers 170 degrees on an instant-read thermometer and is thick enough to cling to the spoon, about 3 minutes (see the photos on page 870). Immediately remove the pan from the heat and stir in the cold butter until incorporated; stir in the cream, vanilla, and salt, then pour the curd through a fine-mesh strainer into a small nonreactive bowl. Cover the surface of the curd directly with plastic wrap; refrigerate until needed.

5. TO FINISH THE CAKE: When the cheesecake is cool, scrape the lemon curd onto the cheesecake still in the springform pan; using an offset icing spatula, spread the curd evenly over the top of the cheesecake. Cover tightly with plastic wrap and refrigerate for at least 5 hours or up to 24 hours. To serve, remove the sides of the springform pan and cut the cake into wedges.

PUMPKIN CHEESECAKE

PUMPKIN CHEESECAKE STANDS SECOND TO THE traditional pumpkin pie as a holiday dessert. Those who suffer from pumpkin pie ennui embrace pumpkin cheesecake as "a nice change," but the expectations are low. Undoubtedly, pumpkin cheesecake can be good in its own right, although, as proved by a half dozen recipes, it rarely is. The tendency in these recipes was for extremes in texture—dry, dense, chalky cakes or wet, soft, mousse-like ones. Flavors veered to far too cheesy and tangy, pungently overspiced, noxiously sweet, and totally bland. Merely mixing a can of pumpkin into a standard cheesecake didn't work; the texture was amiss (leaden and sloppy), and the pumpkin flavor was thwarted. And then there were soggy, grease-leaching crumb crusts. We were prepared to remedy all of this, to make a creamy pumpkin cheesecake with a velvety smooth texture that tasted of sweet, earthy pumpkin as well as tangy cream cheese, that struck a harmonious spicy chord, and, of course, that had a crisp, buttery, cookie-crumb crust.

To make a crumb crust for pumpkin cheesecake, the options were ground-up vanilla wafers, animal crackers (which worked well in our Lemon Cheesecake), gingersnaps, and graham crackers, which we like with our New York Cheesecake. The first two were too mild-flavored for the spicy filling. Gingersnaps were well liked for their spicy bittersweet molasses notes, which balanced well against the pumpkin flavor of the cake, but no matter the brand or the amount of butter and sugar

PRESSING THE CRUMBS INTO THE PAN

1. Use the bottom of a ramekin, 1-cup measuring cup, or drinking glass to press the crumbs into the bottom of a springform pan. Press the crumbs as far as possible into the edge of the pan.

2. Use a teaspoon to neatly press the crumbs into the edge of the pan to create a clean edge.

we added—and despite prebaking—they refused to form a crust that retained its crispness.

With graham crackers, we had success. Five ounces of crackers (nine whole ones), ground to crumbs, formed a substantial crust. Too little butter and the crust was not cohesive; 6 tablespoons was just the right amount. Too little sugar and the crust was not adequately sweet; 3 tablespoons was a good amount. Pressed into the bottom of the springform pan and baked until browned about the edges, the graham crackers formed a sturdy, crisp, buttery crust. (Without prebaking, the crust became a pasty, soggy layer beneath the filling.) We then replaced the granulated sugar with dark brown sugar to replicate the molasses flavor of the gingersnaps, but the sugar's moisture caused sogginess, so we went back to granulated. To increase spiciness, we added doses of ground cinnamon and ground ginger.

Anyone who has prepared fresh pumpkin for pumpkin pie can attest to the fact that cutting, seeding, peeling, and cooking fresh pumpkin is not time and effort well spent. Opening a can takes only a few seconds; preparing fresh pumpkin takes a few hours. Moreover, all pumpkin cheesecake recipes call for canned pumpkin; it was a perfectly acceptable ingredient.

With a working recipe pieced together, we found that one can of pumpkin and 1½ pounds of cream cheese made a tall, handsome cake with a balance of tang and earthy pumpkin flavor. We were using granulated sugar to sweeten the cheesecake, but we surmised that brown sugar, with its molasses flavor, would add depth and richness. We were wrong. Substituted for the entire amount of granulated sugar, brown sugar only mucked up and masked the flavor of the pumpkin while giving the cheesecake a dirty brown hue (this was especially true of dark brown sugar).

According to recipes, most pumpkin cheesecakes, unlike plain ones, require neither sour cream nor heavy cream. No matter. We tried them both. Sour cream, even in small amounts, was too assertive; its tang eclipsed the delicate flavor of the pumpkin. On the other hand, heavy cream—a cup of it—made the cheesecake feel and taste smooth and lush. It seemed to mitigate the slightly mealy fibrousness of the pumpkin and enrich the cheesecake without obscuring the pumpkin flavor. It did, however, affect the texture, making it loose and soft. Not wanting to compromise the richness, we attempted to remedy the problem by adjusting the eggs, but to no avail. We then tried flour and cornstarch in hopes that one would absorb excess moisture, but both resulted in a starchy, pasty, unappealing texture.

As we were reevaluating heavy cream as an essential ingredient, a colleague suggested cooking the pumpkin before adding it to the cheesecake. It then occurred to us that if we could remove some moisture from the pumpkin, perhaps we could improve the texture. We emptied a can of pumpkin into a nonstick skillet and cooked it until it had lost a surprising amount of moisture—nearly five ounces, or more than half a cup. The cheesecake made with this "dried" pumpkin had a thick, plush, velvety texture to match its rich flavor.

The downside to cooking the pumpkin, which involved frequent stirring and then a cooling period, was the time involved. Draining it simply did not work. In our numerous dealings with canned pumpkin, we noticed that it had cohesion and a nonstick quality. We spread the pumpkin onto a baking sheet lined with paper towels—like spreading frosting on a cake—and then pressed additional paper towels down on its surface to wick away more moisture. In seconds, the pumpkin shed enough liquid (about four ounces) to yield a lovely textured cheesecake, and the paper towels were peeled away almost effortlessly.

With the essential ingredients determined, we turned to eggs. After making some 10 cheesecakes with different amounts of egg in various configurations (whole eggs, egg whites, and egg yolks), we had discovered a surprising range of textures, from stiff and dry to waxy. Five whole eggs produced our favorite cheesecake, one that was satiny, creamy, and unctuous.

Finally, we worked on refining the flavorings. Vanilla and salt were good additions, as was a tablespoon of lemon juice for brightness. Sweet, warm cinnamon was favored at the fore; sharp, spicy ground ginger and small amounts of cloves, nutmeg, and allspice produced, in unison, a deep, resounding flavor but not an overspiced burn.

873

In its springform pan, a cheesecake can be baked either directly on the oven rack like a regular cake or in a water bath like a delicate custard. The cake baked in a water bath was undeniably better than the version baked without a water bath. (For more information, see "Is a Water Bath Worth the Trouble?" below.) We tried a few different oven temperatures, and 325 degrees worked best. At temperatures too high, the water in the bath reached a simmer; too low and the cheesecake took an inordinate amount of time to bake.

Sliced into neat wedges and served with bourbon-and-brown-sugar-laced whipped cream (many at first decried this as over-the-top, but they were silenced after a single taste), here was a pumpkin cheesecake that pleased the pumpkin pie traditionalists and that for the others was a nice change from "a nice change."

Spiced Pumpkin Cheesecake

SERVES 12 TO 16

Depending on the oven and the temperature of the ingredients, this cheesecake may bake about 15 minutes faster or slower than the instructions indicate; it is, therefore, best to check the cake 1¼ hours into baking. Although the cheesecake can be made up to 3 days in advance, the crust will begin to lose its crispness after only 1 day. To make slicing the cheesecake easy and neat, it's best to use a knife with a narrow blade, such as a carving knife. Between cuts,

dip the blade into a pitcher of hot water and wipe it clean with paper towels. The cheesecake is good on its own, but the Brown Sugar and Bourbon Cream (recipe follows) is a grand addition.

CRUST
- 9 whole graham crackers (5 ounces), broken into rough pieces
- 3 tablespoons sugar
- ½ teaspoon ground ginger
- ½ teaspoon ground cinnamon
- ¼ teaspoon ground cloves
- 6 tablespoons (¾ stick) unsalted butter, melted

FILLING
- 1⅓ cups (9⅓ ounces) sugar
- 1 teaspoon ground cinnamon
- ½ teaspoon ground ginger
- ¼ teaspoon freshly grated nutmeg
- ¼ teaspoon ground cloves
- ¼ teaspoon ground allspice
- ½ teaspoon salt
- 1 (15-ounce) can pumpkin puree
- 1½ pounds (three 8-ounce packages) cream cheese, cut into 1-inch chunks, at room temperature
- 1 tablespoon vanilla extract
- 1 tablespoon juice from 1 lemon
- 5 large eggs, at room temperature
- 1 cup heavy cream

SCIENCE: Is a Water Bath Worth the Trouble?

A water bath is commonly called for in the baking of cheesecakes and custards. The theory is that a water bath moderates the temperature around the perimeter of the pan, preventing overcooking at the edges. To figure out exactly what's happening, we prepared two identical cheesecakes and baked one directly on the oven rack and the other in a water bath. Both were removed from the oven when their centers reached 147 degrees. The cake that had been baked in a water bath was even-colored and smooth; the other cake was browned and cracked. A quick comparison of the temperature at the edges of the cakes confirmed what we suspected. Upon removal from the oven, the cake that had had the benefit of a water bath was 184 degrees at the edge, whereas the cake baked without the water bath had climbed to 213 degrees.

Why was the cheesecake baked in a water bath 30 degrees cooler at the edge than the cake baked without a water bath? Although in both cases the oven had been set to 325 degrees, a water bath cannot exceed 212 degrees, as this is the temperature at which water converts to steam. In fact, the temperature of the water bath was lower than 190 degrees. The oven just wasn't producing enough heat to boil the water.

How did the water bath keep the cheesecake top even and uncracked? More than four cups of water evaporated from the bath during cooking, resulting in quite a humid oven. The moisture in the air reduced the overall loss of moisture from the cake, as the moisture in the air returned to the cake in the form of condensation. This added moisture kept the top flat and prevented cracking.

---

1. FOR THE CRUST: Adjust an oven rack to the lower-middle position and heat the oven to 325 degrees. Spray the bottom and sides of a 9-inch springform pan evenly with nonstick cooking spray. Place the crackers, sugar, and spices in a food processor and process until evenly and finely ground, about fifteen 2-second pulses. Transfer the crumbs to a medium bowl, drizzle the melted butter over, and mix with a rubber spatula until evenly moistened. Turn the crumbs into the prepared springform pan and spread the crumbs into an even layer, following the illustrations on page 872. Bake until fragrant and browned about the edges, about 15 minutes. Cool on a wire rack to room temperature, about 30 minutes. When cool, wrap the outside of the pan with two 18-inch-square pieces of heavy-duty foil; set the springform pan in a roasting pan.

2. FOR THE FILLING: Bring about 4 quarts water to a simmer in a stockpot. While the crust is cooling, whisk the sugar, spices, and salt in a small bowl; set aside. Line a baking sheet with a triple layer of paper towels. Spread the pumpkin on the towels and cover with a second triple layer of towels. Press firmly until the towels are saturated. Peel back the top layer of towels and discard. Grasp the bottom towels and fold the pumpkin in half; peel back the towels. Repeat and flip the pumpkin onto the baking sheet; discard the towels.

3. Beat the cream cheese in the bowl of a standing mixer set at medium speed to break up and soften slightly, about 1 minute. Scrape the beater and the bottom and sides of the bowl well with a rubber spatula. Add about a third of the sugar mixture and beat at medium-low speed until combined, about 1 minute; scrape the bowl and add the remaining sugar in two additions, scraping the bowl after each addition. Add the pumpkin, vanilla, and lemon juice and beat at medium speed until combined, about 45 seconds; scrape the bowl. Add 3 of the eggs and beat at medium-low speed until incorporated, about 1 minute; scrape the bowl. Add the remaining 2 eggs and beat at medium-low speed until incorporated, about 45 seconds; scrape the bowl. Add the heavy cream and beat at low speed until combined, about 45 seconds. Using a rubber spatula,

scrape the bottom and sides of the bowl and give a final stir by hand.

4. Pour the filling into the springform pan and smooth the surface; set the roasting pan in the oven and pour enough boiling water to come about halfway up the sides of the springform pan. Bake until the center of the cake is slightly wobbly when the pan is shaken and it registers 150 degrees on an instant-read thermometer, about 1½ hours (see note). Set the roasting pan on a wire rack and cool until the water is just warm, about 45 minutes. Remove the springform pan from the water bath, discard the foil, and set the pan on the wire rack; run a paring knife around the inside edge of the pan to loosen the sides of the cake and cool until barely warm, about 3 hours. Wrap with plastic wrap and refrigerate until chilled, at least 4 hours or up to 3 days.

5. TO SERVE: Remove the sides of the pan. Slide a thin metal spatula between the crust and the pan bottom to loosen the cake, then slide the cake onto a serving platter. Let the cheesecake stand at room temperature about 30 minutes, then cut into wedges (see note) and serve with Brown Sugar and Bourbon Cream, if desired.

➤ VARIATION

Pumpkin-Bourbon Cheesecake with Graham-Pecan Crust

Follow the recipe for Spiced Pumpkin Cheesecake, reducing the graham crackers to 5 whole crackers (about 3 ounces), processing 2 ounces chopped pecans (about ½ cup) with the crackers, and reducing the butter to 4 tablespoons. Omit the lemon juice from the filling, reduce the vanilla extract to 1 teaspoon, and add ¼ cup bourbon along with the heavy cream.

Brown Sugar and Bourbon Cream
MAKES ABOUT 3 CUPS

1	cup heavy cream
½	cup sour cream
⅓	cup packed (2⅓ ounces) light brown sugar
⅛	teaspoon salt
2	teaspoons bourbon

1. In the bowl of a standing mixer, whisk the heavy cream, sour cream, brown sugar, and salt until combined. Cover with plastic wrap and refrigerate until ready to serve the cheesecake, at least 4 hours or up to 24 hours, stirring once or twice during chilling to ensure that the sugar dissolves.

2. When ready to serve the cheesecake, add the bourbon and beat the mixture at medium speed until small bubbles form around the edge, about 40 seconds; increase the speed to high and continue to beat until fluffy and doubled in volume, about 1 minute longer. Spoon the cream onto individual slices of cheesecake.

HOT FUDGE PUDDING CAKE

HOT FUDGE PUDDING CAKE HAS SEVERAL aliases: Denver pudding cake, chocolate upside-down cake, brownie pudding cake, or sometimes simply chocolate pudding cake. This 1950s community cookbook recipe may be a bit dated, but it's a boon to the cook looking for a simple baked dessert that requires no creaming or whipping. It's a humble, homely dessert with bumps, lumps, and cracks, an easy one to turn up your nose at. But those who have eaten hot fudge pudding cake know its charms: unpretentious, moist, brownie-like chocolate cake sitting in a pool of a chocolate sauce so thick it's reminiscent of pudding.

In the matter of pudding cakes, there are two distinct styles. The fussier version requires beaten egg whites rather than chemical leaveners for lift and a hot water bath to produce a soufflé-like cake above a custard-like sauce. Then there's the absurdly simple hot fudge pudding cake that resembles a chemically leavened brownie and can be made by a rookie baker equipped with only a few bowls and a whisk. It was the latter style that we were pursuing, so we gathered a few recipes and tried them. All were disappointing. Instead of deep and chocolatey, they tasted dull and mild. Instead of providing enough spoon-coating sauce to accompany the cake, some were dry, with a disproportionate amount of cake, while the others

were soupy, with a wet, sticky, underdone cake.

For those who aren't familiar with the magic of pudding cakes, here's how they work. The batter is made in the manner of a brownie batter, but with milk added. After the batter goes into the baking dish, things take an unusual turn. A mixture of sugar and cocoa is sprinkled over the batter, then liquid is poured on top, and the mess goes into the oven. (Depending on the recipe, the cocoa and sugar may first be dissolved in hot water, then poured over.) While baking, the cake rises to the surface, and the liquid that started out on top sinks to the bottom, taking the sugar and cocoa with it and becoming the "hot fudge" part of the dessert.

With a working recipe cobbled together, our first goal was to pump up the chocolate flavor, suspecting that the problem was that most recipes call for cocoa rather than chocolate. In our experience, cocoa alone carries potent—sometimes acrid—chocolate flavor, but it cannot deliver the complexity or richness of chocolate. We tried adding different amounts of bittersweet chocolate to the pudding cake. Two ounces in addition to the ⅓ cup of cocoa was the ideal amount to obtain fuller flavor.

We also thought to try regular "natural" cocoa versus Dutch-processed cocoa. The former is lighter in color and more acidic than the latter. In a side-by-side tasting, we were stunned by the difference. The "natural" cocoa version tasted sharp and harsh, but the one made with Dutch-processed cocoa (we used Droste, a brand widely available in supermarkets) tasted smooth, round, and full. It was unanimous. Every person who tasted the two cakes vastly preferred the one made with Dutch-processed cocoa. To sweeten the cake and counter the bitterness of even the Dutch-processed cocoa, ⅔ cup of sugar was required.

The next issue to settle was that of eggs, and there seemed to be two choices: recipes that contained an egg and those that didn't. The eggless cakes were mushy and crumbly. Their crumb lacked structural integrity, and because they were soft and mushy, there seemed to be little distinction between what was supposed to be cake and what was supposed to be hot fudge. We tried as many as two whole eggs, but our preference was for a pudding cake made with just one yolk. It was brownie-like, with a nice, tooth-sinking crumb. Cakes made with whole eggs were drier and slightly rubbery.

So far, we had been using 1 cup of unbleached all-purpose flour, but the cake layer was a tad too thick. We tried smaller amounts of flour, hoping that the texture wouldn't suffer as a consequence. We ended up preferring the cake with ¾ cup of flour. It tasted more richly of chocolate and had a moist, brownie-like texture.

The butter in hot fudge pudding cake is always melted, never creamed. (This cake requires a heavy-duty leavener, such as baking powder, to force the cake layer up through the sludge that becomes the sauce. Although creaming is one way to provide lift, in this case we found that the contribution made by aerated butter was minimal and not worth the effort.) With only 4 tablespoons of melted butter, the cake tasted lean and dry. With 8, it was leaden and greasy. Six tablespoons was the ideal amount. Like most other cakes, hot fudge pudding cake contains some dairy, usually milk. We tried heavy cream and half-and-half to see if either had desirable effects. Heavy cream made a slick, greasy, fat-laden cake. With half-and-half, the cake was somewhat greasy and a little too rich. Milk was the way to go.

For lift, we relied on baking powder. One recipe called for 2 tablespoons per cup of flour ("chemical warfare" was one taster's term for this mixture). Two teaspoons of baking powder was just fine. To heighten the flavor, we added ¼ teaspoon salt and 1 tablespoon vanilla.

As mentioned above, there are two ways to add the ingredients destined to become the fudge sauce. A mixture of cocoa and sugar can be sprinkled on the batter and water then poured over it, creating what looks like a panful of river sludge. Alternatively, the cocoa and sugar can first be dissolved in boiling water. We compared two such pudding cakes. The one with the sprinkled cocoa and sugar mixture baked up with crisp edges and a faintly crisp crust that we preferred over the uniformly soft, cakey surface of the other. It was as if some of the sugar, moistened by the water, remained at the surface even after the liquid seeped to the bottom, and then caramelized to form a pleasing crust.

We tried different amounts of cocoa in the sauce-to-be and landed at ⅓ cup, the same amount we put in the cake. As for the sugar, we preferred a mix of granulated and brown sugar, with the molasses flavor of the latter producing a full, round taste.

The amount of water poured over the cake determines the amount of sauce at the bottom. One and one-half cups—a little more than what most recipes call for—was ideal, yielding an ample amount of sauce with the right consistency. Some hot fudge pudding cake recipes suggest using coffee instead of water. Indeed, we thought the coffee was a nice addition. It didn't interfere with the chocolate flavor but nicely complemented it, cutting through some of the cake's cloying sweet quality and enriching the flavor. For ease, we

PUDDING CAKE 1-2-3

1. Pour the batter into the prepared baking dish and spread evenly into the sides and corners with a rubber spatula.

2. Sprinkle the cocoa-sugar mixture evenly over the batter. The mixture should cover the entire surface of the batter.

3. Pour the coffee mixture gently over the cocoa mixture and put the baking dish in the oven.

mixed 2 teaspoons of instant coffee into the water, but cold, brewed coffee cut with a little water works as well.

We tested different oven temperatures and baking times. While most recipes indicated 350 degrees for about 35 minutes, we preferred 325 degrees for 45 minutes. The lower temperature helped keep the sauce from bubbling rapidly, a phenomenon that can cause spillage if left unchecked. In addition, the slightly longer baking time promoted a nicer crust. We noted that this cake combined lots of pleasing textures: a silky sauce; a moist, cakey crumb; and a thin, brittle crust, especially around the edge.

When attacked with a spoon straight from the oven, the hot fudge pudding cake revealed a thin, blistering-hot sauce and a sodden cake. If allowed to cool for 20 to 30 minutes, the sauce became pudding-like and the cake brownie-like. The warm cake cries out to be served with vanilla or coffee ice cream (whipped cream just isn't serious enough).

Hot Fudge Pudding Cake

SERVES 8

If you have cold brewed coffee on hand, it can be used in place of the instant coffee powder and water, but to make sure it isn't too strong, use 1 cup of cold coffee mixed with ½ cup of water. Serve the cake warm with vanilla or coffee ice cream.

2	teaspoons instant coffee
1½	cups water
⅔	cup (2 ounces) Dutch-processed cocoa
⅓	cup packed (2⅓ ounces) brown sugar
1	cup (7 ounces) granulated sugar
6	tablespoons (¾ stick) unsalted butter
2	ounces bittersweet or semisweet chocolate, chopped
¾	cup (3¾ ounces) unbleached all-purpose flour
2	teaspoons baking powder
1	tablespoon vanilla extract
⅓	cup whole milk
¼	teaspoon salt
1	large egg yolk

1. Adjust an oven rack to the lower-middle position and heat the oven to 325 degrees. Lightly spray an 8-inch square glass or ceramic baking dish with nonstick cooking spray. Stir the instant coffee into the water; set aside to dissolve. Stir together ⅓ cup of the cocoa, the brown sugar, and ⅓ cup of the granulated sugar in a small bowl, breaking up any large clumps with your fingers; set aside. Melt the butter, the remaining ⅓ cup cocoa, and the chocolate in a small bowl set over a saucepan of barely simmering water; whisk until smooth and set aside to cool slightly. Whisk the flour and baking powder in a small bowl to combine; set aside. Whisk the remaining ⅔ cup granulated sugar with the vanilla, milk, and salt in a medium bowl until combined; whisk in the yolk. Add the chocolate mixture and whisk to combine. Add the flour mixture and whisk until the batter is evenly moistened.

2. Pour the batter into the prepared baking dish and spread evenly to the sides and corners. Sprinkle the cocoa mixture evenly over the batter (the cocoa mixture should cover the entire surface of the batter); pour the coffee mixture gently over the cocoa mixture. Bake until the cake is puffed and bubbling and just beginning to pull away from the sides of the baking dish, about 45 minutes. (Do not overbake.) Cool the cake in the dish on a wire rack about 25 minutes before serving.

➤ VARIATION

Individual Hot Fudge Pudding Cakes

Follow the recipe for Hot Fudge Pudding Cake, heating the oven to 400 degrees and lightly spraying eight 6- to 8-ounce ramekins with nonstick cooking spray; set the ramekins on a baking sheet. Divide the batter evenly among the ramekins (about ¼ cup per ramekin) and level with the back of a spoon; sprinkle about 2 tablespoons of the cocoa mixture over the batter in each ramekin. Pour 3 tablespoons of the coffee mixture over the cocoa mixture in each ramekin. Bake until puffed and bubbling, about 20 minutes. (Do not overbake.) Cool the ramekins about 15 minutes before serving (the cakes will fall).

20

PIES AND TARTS

IF THERE IS ONE TASK THAT STRIKES FEAR INTO the hearts of novice bakers, it is pie making, but it need not be a vexing endeavor. The key is to use the right recipe and the right technique. We promise you that any of the pies in this chapter will be far superior to anything you could order through the mail, pick up from a supermarket bakery, or fashion from a prefab piecrust. This chapter includes all our favorite pies: fruit pies such as apple, blueberry, and peach, as well as custard and cream pies such as pumpkin, chocolate cream, and lemon meringue. See "Pie Dough 101" on pages 884–885 for illustrated instructions on mixing and working with pie dough.

Tarts are similar to pies in that they contain crust and filling, but the dough is usually sweeter than pie dough and the amount of filling is reduced. The overall effect is generally more sophisticated. The tarts in this chapter are baked in a shallow ring pan with a removable bottom. Recipes for fresh fruit tarts are included, as well as other favorite tarts such as lemon tart and linzertorte (an Austrian almond and jam tart).

PIE DOUGH

SIMPLE AS IT CAN BE, PIECRUST—ESSENTIALLY a combination of flour, water, and fat—raises numerous questions: What are the ideal proportions of the main ingredients? What else should be added for character? What methods should be used to combine these ingredients?

The most controversial ingredient in pastry is fat. We've found that all-butter crusts taste good, but they are not as flaky and fine-textured as those made with some shortening, which are our favorites. All-shortening crusts have great texture but lack flavor; oil-based crusts are flat and entirely unappealing; and those made with lard are not only heavy and strongly flavored but out of favor owing to concerns about the effects of animal fat on health. After experimenting with a variety of combinations, we ultimately settled on a proportion of 3 parts butter to 2 parts shortening as optimal for both flavor and texture.

Vegetable shortenings such as Crisco are made from vegetable oil that has been hydrogenated, a process in which hydrogen gas is pumped into vegetable oil to incorporate air and to raise its melting point above room temperature. Unhydrogenated (or regular) vegetable oil holds no more air than water and so makes for poor pie doughs. Crisco, on the other hand, is about 10 percent gas and does a good job of lightening and tenderizing. The way the fat is incorporated into the flour also contributes to flakiness.

We experimented with the relative proportions of fat and flour and finally settled on a ratio of 2 parts flour to 1 part fat, which produces crusts that are easy to work with and, when baked, more tender and flavorful than any other.

Piecrusts are usually made with all-purpose flour. No matter what we've tried—substituting cornstarch for part of the all-purpose flour (a cookie-baking trick that increases tenderness), adding ¼ teaspoon baking powder to increase rise and flakiness, and mixing cake flour or pastry flour with the all-purpose flour (again, to increase tenderness)—we've always come back to plain old all-purpose flour.

We also tackled the proportions of salt and sugar, which were much easier to resolve. After testing amounts ranging from ¼ teaspoon to as much as 2 tablespoons, we settled on 1 teaspoon salt and 2 tablespoons sugar for a double-crust pie, amounts that enhance the flavor of the dough without shouting out their presence.

We experimented with a variety of liquid ingredients, such as buttermilk, milk, and cider vinegar, a common ingredient in many pastry recipes. No liquid additions improved our basic recipe, so we recommend that you stick with ice water.

Pie dough can be made by hand, but we've found that a food processor is faster and easier and does the best job of cutting the fat into the flour. Proper mixing is important. If you undermix, the crust will shrink when baked and become hard and crackly. If you overprocess, you'll get a crumbly, rather than a flaky, dough. The shortening should be pulsed with the flour until the mixture is sandy; butter is then pulsed in until the mixture looks like coarse crumbs, with butter bits no larger than the size of a pea.

Once the flour and fat have been combined, the dough can be transferred to a bowl, and the ice water can be added and mixed in. We recommend a rubber spatula and a folding motion to mix in the water. Use the flat side of the spatula to press the mixture until the dough sticks together. Incorporating the water in this manner allows for the least amount of water to be used (less water means a more tender dough) and reduces the likelihood of overworking the dough. Still, we've also learned that it doesn't pay to be too stingy with the water. If there isn't enough, the dough will be crumbly and hard to roll.

Finally, we found that pie dough need not be difficult to roll out if you remember two basic guidelines: Make sure the dough is well chilled before rolling, and add a minimum of flour to the work surface. Flour added during rolling will be absorbed by the dough, and too much flour will cause the dough to toughen. If the dough seems too soft to roll, it's best to refrigerate it rather than add more flour.

EQUIPMENT: Pie Plates

Pie plates come in a variety of shapes and sizes as well as materials. We tested the three main types of pie plate—glass, ceramic, and metal—and found that a Pyrex glass pie plate did the best job of browning the crust, both when filled and baked blind (the bottom crust is baked alone, filled with pie weights to hold its shape). Several metal pie plates also browned quite well, but the glass pie plate has a number of other advantages.

Because you can see through a Pyrex plate, it's easy to judge just how brown the bottom crust has become during baking. With a metal pie plate, it's easy to pull the pie out of the oven too soon, when the bottom crust is still quite pale. A second feature we like about the traditional Pyrex plate is the wide rim, which makes the plate easier to take in and out of the oven and also supports fluted edges better than thin rims. Finally, because glass is nonreactive, you can store a pie filled with acidic fruit and not worry about metal giving the fruit an off flavor.

Pyrex pie plates do heat up more quickly than metal pie plates, so pies may be done a bit sooner than you think, especially if you are following a recipe that was tested in a metal plate. All the times in our recipes are based on baking in a glass pie plate; if baking in metal, you may need to add two to three minutes for empty crusts and five minutes for filled pies.

Basic Pie Dough

ENOUGH FOR 1 DOUBLE-CRUST 9-INCH PIE
See the illustrations on page 884 for tips on rolling out pie dough.

2½	cups (12½ ounces) unbleached all-purpose flour, plus more for dusting the work surface
1	teaspoon salt
2	tablespoons sugar
½	cup vegetable shortening, chilled
12	tablespoons (1½ sticks) cold unsalted butter, cut into ¼-inch pieces
6–8	tablespoons ice water

1. Process the flour, salt, and sugar in a food processor until combined. Add the shortening and process until the mixture has the texture of coarse sand, about 10 seconds. Scatter the butter pieces over the flour mixture; cut the butter into the flour until the mixture is pale yellow and resembles coarse crumbs, with butter bits no larger than small peas, about ten 1-second pulses. Turn the mixture into a medium bowl.

2. Sprinkle 6 tablespoons of the ice water over the mixture. With a rubber spatula, use a folding motion to mix. Press down on the dough with the broad side of the spatula until the dough sticks together, adding up to 2 tablespoons more ice water if the dough will not come together. Divide the dough into 2 balls and flatten each into a 4-inch disk. Wrap each in plastic and refrigerate at least 1 hour or up to 2 days before rolling.

➤ VARIATION
Pie Dough for Lattice-Top Pie
This crust has a firmer texture than the basic recipe, making it easier to work with when creating a lattice top. This leaner dough also keeps its shape better in the oven so the lattice looks more attractive.

Follow the recipe for Basic Pie Dough, increasing the flour to 3 cups (15 ounces), reducing the shortening to 7 tablespoons, reducing the butter to 10 tablespoons, and increasing the ice water to 10 tablespoons. Divide the dough into 2 pieces, one slightly larger than the other. (If possible, weigh the pieces; they should weigh 16 ounces and 14 ounces.) Flatten the larger piece into a rough 5-inch square and the smaller piece into a 4-inch disk; wrap separately in plastic and chill as directed.

PIE DOUGH FOR PREBAKED PIE SHELL

BAKING AN UNFILLED PIE PASTRY, COMMONLY called blind baking, can turn out to be the ultimate culinary nightmare. Without the weight of a filling, a pastry shell set in a hot oven can shrink dramatically, fill with air pockets, and puff up like a linoleum floor after a flood. The result? A shrunken, uneven shell that can hold only part of the filling intended for it.

We started with our basic pie dough recipe and began to investigate the effects of resting the dough in the refrigerator or the freezer, docking it (pricking the dough before it bakes), and weighting the crust as it bakes to keep it anchored in place. All three tricks are used by professional bakers to prevent common problems encountered when baking a crust blind.

We found that refrigeration does the best job of preventing shrinkage. Pastry shrinkage is caused by gluten. Simply put, when you add water to the proteins in flour, elastic strands of gluten are

formed. The strands of gluten in the dough get stretched during the rolling process, and if they are not allowed to relax after rolling, the pastry will snap back like a rubber band when baked, resulting in a shrunken, misshapen shell. Resting allows the tension in the taut strands of dough to ease so that they remain stretched and do not shrink back when heated.

This process does not occur, however, when the dough is placed in the freezer immediately after rolling. When the water in the crust freezes, the gluten is held in place so it is not free to relax. As a result, when you bake the dough, the tense, stretched strands of gluten snap back, causing the crust to shrink.

We might have concluded that pie dough should be refrigerated and not frozen if we hadn't noticed that the frozen crusts, although shrunken, were much flakier than the refrigerated crusts. Pastry is made up of layers of dough (protein and starch from the flour combined with water) and fat. Dough and fat have different heat tolerances. When you place the pastry in the oven after freezing it (rather than just refrigerating it), the dough heats up and starts to set relatively quickly in comparison with the time it takes for the butter to melt and then vaporize, as the butter has a much higher proportion of water than the dough. As a result, by the time the water in the butter starts to turn

BLIND BAKING PIES AND TARTS

1. There are several easy ways to work with pie weights. We like to store them in a doubled-up ovenproof cooking bag, which you can simply lift in and out of the pie plate or tart pan and use over and over again, eliminating the extra step of lining the crust with foil.

2. If you don't own metal or ceramic pie weights, pennies conduct heat beautifully (far better than dried beans). Line the pie plate or tart pan with foil and place the pennies in the foil to hold the crust in place.

3. Once the crust has set, it is important to let it brown. To do this, remove the foil and weights and continue to bake the pie or tart shell until nicely browned.

882

to steam, the dough is well into its setting phase. The air spaces occupied by the frozen butter, now that it has largely turned to steam, hold their shape because the dough has started to set.

Dough that you have refrigerated, on the other hand, is not as well set by the time the butter vaporizes; hence the air pockets disappear, the soft dough simply sinking into the spaces left by the butter. We came to a simple conclusion: First refrigerate the pie shell to relax the gluten, thus solving the problem of shrinkage during baking, then pop the dough into the freezer to improve flakiness.

While this combination chilling method prevents shrinkage, ballooning can occur when air pockets form beneath the crust. Typically, bakers dock the dough with the tines of a fork before it goes into the oven. However, we found that docking is not necessary as long as the dough is weighted. Since weighting is a must—it not only prevents ballooning but keeps the shell, especially the sides, in place as it bakes—we do not bother to dock pastry dough. Some professional bakers swear by "official" pie weights, made of metal or ceramic, while others make do with rice or dried beans. We found that metal or ceramic pie weights do a better job than rice or beans. They are heavier and therefore more effective at preventing the pastry from puffing. Metal and ceramic are also better heat conductors and promote more thorough browning of the pastry.

We got the most consistent results and even browning by baking on the middle rack at a constant 375 degrees. At higher temperatures, the pastry was prone to overbrowning and burned in spots, while lower temperatures caused the edges to brown well before the bottom did. More important than temperature and placement, though, was cooking time.

There are two stages in baking blind. In the first stage, the dough is baked with a lining and weights. This stage usually takes about 25 minutes; the objective is to cook the dough until it sets, at which point it can hold its shape without assistance. When the dough loses its wet look, turns from its original pale yellow to off-white, and just starts to take on a very light brown color on the edge, the dough is set. If you have any doubts, carefully (the

dough is hot) touch the side of the shell to make sure that the crust is firm. If you remove the pie weights too soon, the sides of the dough will slip down, ruining the pie shell.

For the second stage, the foil and weights are removed, and the baking continues. At this point, if you are going to fill the pie shell and then bake it again, as for pumpkin or pecan pie or quiche, you should bake it until it is just lightly browned, about 5 minutes. Pie shells destined for fillings that require little or no further cooking, such as cream and lemon meringue pies, should be baked for about 12 more minutes.

Pie Dough for Prebaked Pie Shell

ENOUGH FOR 1 SINGLE-CRUST 9-INCH PIE

See the illustrations on page 884 for tips on rolling out pie dough. We prefer ceramic or metal pie weights for prebaking the pie shell. If you don't own any weights, rice or dried beans can stand in, but since they're lighter than pie weights, be sure to fill up the foil-lined pie shell completely. Better yet, improvise with pennies (see illustration 2 on page 882).

1¼	cups (6¼ ounces) unbleached all-purpose flour, plus more for dusting the work surface
½	teaspoon salt
1	tablespoon sugar
3	tablespoons vegetable shortening, chilled
4	tablespoons (½ stick) cold unsalted butter, cut into ¼-inch pieces
4–5	tablespoons ice water

1. Process the flour, salt, and sugar in a food processor until combined. Add the shortening and process until the mixture has the texture of coarse sand, about 10 seconds. Scatter the butter pieces over the flour mixture; cut the butter into the flour until the mixture is pale yellow and resembles coarse crumbs, with butter bits no larger than small peas, about ten 1-second pulses. Turn the mixture into a medium bowl.

2. Sprinkle 4 tablespoons of the ice water over the mixture. With a rubber spatula, use a folding motion to mix. Press down on the dough with

Pie Dough 101

Why is it that some cooks produce piecrusts that are consistently tender and flaky, while others, despite their best intentions, repeatedly deliver tough or crumbly crusts? Essentially, pie dough is a simple affair with a short ingredient list consisting of flour, salt, sugar, fat (such as butter or vegetable shortening), and water. The two areas most crucial to making pie dough are the temperature of the fat and water and the method by which the dough is mixed. Rolling the dough, which most people mistake as the onerous part of pie making, is a cinch once you have the right dough. Here are tips for making pastry successfully.

MIXING PIE DOUGH

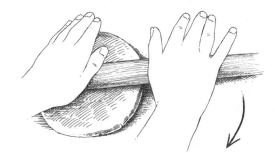

1. Pulse the flour, salt, and sugar in a food processor. Add the vegetable shortening and cold butter in small pieces and then pulse until the butter pieces are no longer clearly visible. The mixture will be slightly yellow and mealy in texture and will ride up the sides of the workbowl.

2. Transfer the mixture to a bowl and add the ice water bit by bit, tossing and pressing the dry ingredients against the sides of the bowl with a rubber spatula.

3. Too much water is better than too little — a dry dough cannot be rolled out, but you can flour the work surface if the dough is a bit too wet. Ideally, the dough will clear the sides of the bowl and be wet to the touch. Form the dough into a ball, flatten it into a 4-inch disk, wrap in plastic, and refrigerate for at least one hour.

ROLLING AND FITTING PIE DOUGH

1. Using a tapered pin, roll a quarter turn, from about 2 o'clock to 5 o'clock, keeping your left hand stationary and moving the pin with your right hand.

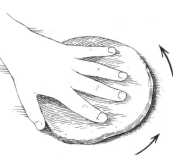

2. Turn the dough a quarter turn and roll again as in step 1. Continue rolling until the dough is 8 or 9 inches in diameter. If necessary, lightly reflour the work surface.

3. Using a bench scraper, lift the dough onto the rolling pin, pick it up, reflour the counter, and replace the dough upside down. Keep rolling until the diameter of the dough is 3 to 4 inches wider than the pie plate.

4. Roll the dough over the pin and unroll it evenly onto the pie plate.

5. After draping the dough evenly over the pie plate, lift up the edges of the dough and ease it down into the lower creases of the pan. Press lightly to adhere the dough to the sides of the pan.

884

MAKING A DECORATIVE EDGE ON SINGLE-CRUST PIES

1. Use scissors to trim the dough overhang to within ½ inch of the outer lip of the pie plate.

2. Roll the trimmed overhang under so that it is even with the lip of the pan.

3. Use the index finger of one hand and the thumb and index finger of the other to create a fluted edge. The edge of the dough should be perpendicular to the edge of the pie plate.

ASSEMBLING DOUBLE-CRUST PIES

1. Refrigerate the pie plate with the dough while preparing the filling. Place the filling in the shell. Roll out the second piece of dough and use a bench scraper to wrap the dough around the rolling pin.

2. Unroll the dough over the filled pie, making sure to center the piece of dough on the pie plate.

3. Use scissors to trim the overhanging edges of the top and bottom crusts to about ½ inch.

4. For a neat edge that stays sealed, press the edges of the top and bottom crusts together. The folded edge should be flush with the lip of the pie plate.

5. Use the index finger of one hand and the thumb and index finger of the other to create a fluted edge. The edge of the dough should be perpendicular to the edge of the pie plate.

6. Use a sharp knife to cut vents in the top crust.

the broad side of the spatula until the dough sticks together, adding up to 1 tablespoon more ice water if the dough will not come together. Flatten the dough into a 4-inch disk. Wrap in plastic and refrigerate at least 1 hour or up to 2 days before rolling.

3. Remove the dough from the refrigerator (if refrigerated longer than 1 hour, let stand at room temperature until malleable). Following the illustrations on page 884, roll the dough on a lightly floured work surface or between 2 sheets of parchment paper or plastic wrap to a 12-inch circle. Transfer the dough to a 9-inch pie plate by rolling the dough around the rolling pin and unrolling it over the pan. Working around the circumference of the pie plate, ease the dough into the pan corners by gently lifting the edge of the dough with one hand while gently pressing it into the pan bottom with the other hand. Trim the dough edges to extend about ½ inch beyond the rim of the pan. Fold the overhang under itself; flute the dough or press the tines of a fork against the dough to flatten it against the rim of the pie plate. Refrigerate the dough-lined pie plate until firm, about 40 minutes, then freeze until very cold, about 20 minutes.

4. Adjust an oven rack to the lower-middle position and heat the oven to 375 degrees. Remove the dough-lined pie plate from the freezer, press a doubled 12-inch piece of heavy-duty foil inside the pie shell, and fold the edges of the foil to shield the fluted edge; distribute 2 cups ceramic or metal pie weights over the foil. Bake, leaving the foil and weights in place until the dough looks dry and is light in color, 25 to 30 minutes. Carefully remove the foil and weights by gathering the corners of the foil and pulling up and out. For a partially baked crust, continue baking until light golden brown, 5 to 6 minutes; for a fully baked crust, continue baking until deep golden brown, about 12 minutes more. Transfer to a wire rack.

> VARIATION

Prebaked Pie Dough Coated with Graham Cracker Crumbs
Custard fillings, such as those used in lemon meringue pie and cream pies, are tough on crisp crusts. After much experimentation, we found that rolling out the pie dough in graham cracker crumbs promotes browning and crisps the crust. It also adds a wonderful graham flavor that complements the lemon and cream pie fillings without masking the character of the dough itself.

Follow the recipe for Pie Dough for Prebaked Pie Shell, sprinkling the work surface with 2 tablespoons graham cracker crumbs when rolling out the dough. Sprinkle more crumbs over the dough itself. Continue sprinkling additional crumbs underneath and on top of the dough as it is rolled, coating the dough heavily with crumbs. You will use a total of about ½ cup crumbs. Fit the graham cracker–coated dough into a pie plate as directed and bake fully.

APPLE PIE

COOKS WHO SLATHER THE APPLES IN THEIR PIES with butter, cinnamon, and sugar do themselves and the apples a disservice; we set out to make a pie in which the apples would take center stage. We started by examining the choice of apples for the filling. We tested the nine best-selling apples, figuring that we wanted a recipe that would work with apples commonly available in supermarkets throughout the year.

We determined that Granny Smith and McIntosh apples both have excellent qualities; the former is tart with a good texture, and the latter has excellent flavor. But each also has its drawbacks. A pie made with Grannies alone was too sour and a bit dull in flavor, while an all-McIntosh pie was too soft, more like applesauce in a crust than apple pie. A pie made with both varieties, however, was outstanding. The Grannies hold up well during cooking, and the Macs add flavor. The mushy texture of the Macs becomes a virtue in this setting, providing a nice base for the firmer Grannies and soaking up some of the juice.

We also tested a dozen not-so-common apple varieties, the kinds you may see in local markets during the fall, especially if you live near an apple orchard. We found that Macoun, Royal Gala, Empire, Winesap, Rhode Island Greening, and Cortland apples all make excellent pies. Unlike Granny Smiths, these well-balanced apples work well on their own without thickeners or the addition of McIntosh.

We have always used butter in our pies. In fact, we used to use up to 6 tablespoons in a deep-dish pie, cutting this back to a more modest 2 tablespoons over the years. But when we taste-tested pies with and without butter, the leaner pies won hands down. Butter simply dulls the fresh taste of apples, so now we do without it altogether. Lemon juice, however, is absolutely crucial to a good apple pie, heightening the flavor of the apples rather than dulling or masking it. In the end, we settled on 1 tablespoon of lemon juice and 1 teaspoon of zest.

In our opinion, many recipes call for too much thickener (usually flour), and the result is a lifeless filling. A bit of tart, thin juice gives the pie a breath of the orchard, whereas a thick, syrupy texture is dull. We prefer to thicken the filling for our apple pie very lightly, with just 2 tablespoons flour.

Many cookbooks claim that letting apples sit in a bowl with the sugar, lemon juice, and spices, otherwise known as macerating, is key in developing flavors and juice. We found, however, that this simply caused the apples to dry out, making them rubbery and unpleasant. In addition, the apples themselves lose flavor, having exuded all of their fruitiness into the juice. So macerating, a common step in apple pie recipes, was clearly out.

In many apple pies, the top crust sets up quickly, leaving an air space between it and the apples, which reduce in volume as they cook. With our crust recipe, however, this is not an issue. Sufficient shortening is cut into the flour so that the crust sinks down onto the apples as they cook. We did notice, however, that this high ratio of shortening produces a very flaky crust, one that is not easily cut into perfect slices. In addition, because there is still a fair amount of juice, which we find essential for good flavor, the filling may spread slightly once the pie is cut into individual slices. The trade-off for less-than-perfect presentation is excellent flavor.

Classic Apple Pie
SERVES 8

When all of the apples have been sliced, you should have a total of about 8 cups. The pie is best eaten when cooled to room temperature, or even the next day. See the illustrations on page 884 for rolling and fitting pie dough.

1	recipe Basic Pie Dough (page 881)
2	tablespoons unbleached all-purpose flour, plus more for dusting the work surface
3	large Granny Smith apples (about 1 1/2 pounds)
4	large McIntosh apples (about 2 pounds)
1	tablespoon juice and 1 teaspoon grated zest from 1 lemon
3/4	cup (5 1/4 ounces) plus 1 tablespoon sugar
1/4	teaspoon freshly grated nutmeg
1/4	teaspoon ground cinnamon
1/8	teaspoon ground allspice
1/4	teaspoon salt
1	large egg white, beaten lightly

1. Adjust an oven rack to the lowest position, place a rimmed baking sheet on it, and heat the oven to 500 degrees. Remove one piece of dough from the refrigerator (if refrigerated longer than 1 hour, let stand at room temperature until malleable).

2. Roll the dough on a lightly floured work surface or between 2 large sheets of parchment paper or plastic wrap to a 12-inch circle. Transfer the dough to a 9-inch pie plate by rolling the dough around the rolling pin and unrolling it over the pan. Working around the circumference of the pan, ease the dough into the pan corners by gently lifting the edge of the dough with one hand while pressing it into the pan bottom with the other hand. Leave any dough that overhangs the lip of the pie plate in place; refrigerate the dough-lined pie plate.

3. Peel, core, and quarter the apples; cut the quarters into 1/4-inch slices and toss with the lemon juice and zest. In a medium bowl, mix the 3/4 cup sugar, the flour, spices, and salt. Toss the dry ingredients with the apples. Turn the fruit mixture, including the juices, into the chilled pie shell and mound it slightly in the center.

4. Roll out the second piece of dough to a 12-inch circle; place it over the filling. Trim the edges of the top and bottom dough layers to ½ inch beyond the pan lip. Tuck this rim of dough underneath itself so that the folded edge is flush with the pan lip. Flute the edge or press with the tines of a fork to seal. (See the illustrations on page 885 for tips on trimming and crimping pie dough.) Cut 4 slits in the dough top. If the pie dough is very soft, place the pie in the freezer for 10 minutes. Brush the egg white on the top crust and sprinkle evenly with the remaining 1 tablespoon sugar.

5. Place the pie on the baking sheet and lower the oven temperature to 425 degrees. Bake the pie until the top crust is golden, about 25 minutes. Rotate the pie from front to back and reduce the oven temperature to 375 degrees; continue baking until the juices bubble and the crust is deep golden brown, 30 to 35 minutes longer.

6. Transfer the pie to a wire rack; cool to room temperature, at least 4 hours.

➤ VARIATIONS
Apple Pie with Crystallized Ginger
Follow the recipe for Classic Apple Pie, adding 3 tablespoons chopped crystallized ginger to the apple mixture.

Apple Pie with Dried Fruit
Macerate 1 cup raisins, dried sweet cherries, or dried cranberries in the lemon juice, adding 1 tablespoon applejack, brandy, or cognac. Follow the recipe for Classic Apple Pie, adding the macerated dried fruit and liquid to the apple mixture.

Apple Pie with Fresh Cranberries
Follow the recipe for Classic Apple Pie, increasing the sugar to 1 cup (7 ounces) and adding 1 cup fresh or frozen cranberries to the apple mixture.

DUTCH APPLE PIE
AS MUCH AS WE LOVE CLASSIC APPLE PIE, LIFE would indeed be boring if we did not venture farther afield into apple pie territory. Dutch apple pie is composed of tender, creamy apple filling, flaky piecrust, and buttery mounds of streusel—a decidedly decadent apple pie. To get our bearings, we began by making five Dutch apple pies, each with a different recipe and technique. Surely one had to come close to our ideal. Not so. Each pie was a miserable failure. Variously soupy and void of crust, filled with undercooked apples or dotted with greasy, melted pools of butter, these pies were bad enough to induce laughter in the test kitchen. But we were stymied—why had they failed? What makes baking a Dutch apple pie any different from baking a standard American-style apple pie?

Before we could begin to solve the problems of Dutch apple pie, we needed to define just what it is. As it turns out, there are three components and one major omission that convert an ordinary apple pie into a Dutch apple pie. The additions consist of dried fruit (such as currants or raisins), dairy in the filling, and a streusel topping in lieu of the standard top crust. The major omission is lemon juice.

This omission was far from incidental, as it turned out. A standard apple pie is baked from start to finish with lemon juice, which helps to break down the apples and allows them to release their juices, making for a juicy as well as a tender pie filling. But most of the recipes for Dutch apple pie that we had unearthed called for the addition of only one liquid ingredient—usually heavy cream—five minutes before the pie was done baking. When we sliced into these pies, we noticed two things. First, the interior was not creamy and golden; it was greasy and runny. Second, the apples didn't seem to have cooked through, despite the 45-minute-plus baking times.

So what went wrong? We eventually figured out that when the cream came into contact with the hot, acidic apples, the fat and water in the cream separated, giving the pies their lumpy, greasy, runny interiors. In addition, because these pies were undergoing dry-heat cooking (since there was no liquid, such as lemon juice, providing the apples with moisture), a much slower process than wet-heat cooking, the apples were remaining too crunchy. While a few recipes call for adding the dairy at the beginning of the baking sequence, they, too, produced pies with a coagulated filling.

At first we thought we might doctor the

situation by heating the cream before adding it to the almost-finished pie. But even if the cream didn't separate, five minutes in the oven wouldn't provide enough baking time for the cream to set amidst the layers of apples, and we would still be stuck with unevenly distributed amounts of cream in the pie. Our next thought was to try adding some lemon juice and zest to the pie prior to adding the cream. But the lemon-cream combination sent tasters running for cover. The quickest fix we came up with was to reduce the amount of water in the cream by cooking it, thereby preventing the fat from separating when it encountered the hot pie filling. This remedied our dairy dilemma, but the apples were still too crunchy.

It occurred to us that sautéing the apples with some butter and sugar before they went into the pie might solve the crunch problem. So we prepared for a new experiment: precooking the apples as well as prebaking the pie shell.

Choosing a Dutch oven for its size (as well as apropos name), we sautéed the apples until they were tender throughout and some of the softer pieces began to break down. We strained the apples of their juices, packed them into the prebaked pie shell, and reduced ½ cup of heavy cream with the remaining apple juices (to give the cream reduction a flavor boost). The cream reduction was thick, glossy, and redolent with apple undertones. We spooned the sauce over the filling and topped the pie with streusel. After a mere 10 minutes in the oven, the filling was just right, and we had a perfectly crisp and flaky piecrust to boot.

Now that the filling and crust met our expectations, we moved on to the streusel. We wanted it to be just crunchy enough on the outside to allow for some textural deviation from the plush and tender filling, but it also had to have enough fat to create a melt-in-your-mouth sensation. After trying almost all possible combinations of dark brown sugar, light brown sugar, granulated sugar, honey, cornmeal, baking powder, flour, salt, spices, and butter, we found the perfect streusel to be composed of melted butter with a touch of salt, just enough cornmeal to give it some crunch, a combination of light brown sugar and granulated sugar, and enough flour to bind everything together. By

tossing the melted butter into the dry ingredients with a fork, we were able to create large chunks of streusel surrounded by smaller pea-size morsels.

Now the only thing standing between us and a real Dutch apple pie was the dried fruit. The earliest recipe we found was published in 1667 and included currants. While currants far surpassed shriveled black raisins in terms of beauty, they did not contribute much flavor or chew. Dried cherries and cranberries were too tart and too bold a shade of red for the subtle, wheaty hue of the pie interior. We finally found solace in golden raisins, sweet and plump, yet not too showy.

Dutch Apple Pie
SERVES 8

Use the dough's chill times to peel and core the apples and prepare the streusel, then cook the apples while the dough prebakes. For a finished look, dust the pie with confectioners' sugar just before serving.

1	recipe Pie Dough for Prebaked Pie Shell (page 883)

APPLE FILLING
5	large Granny Smith apples (about 2½ pounds)
4	large McIntosh apples (about 2 pounds)
¼	cup (1¾ ounces) granulated sugar
½	teaspoon ground cinnamon
⅛	teaspoon salt
2	tablespoons unsalted butter
¾	cup golden raisins
½	cup heavy cream

STREUSEL TOPPING
1¼	cups (6¼ ounces) unbleached all-purpose flour
⅓	cup packed (2⅓ ounces) light brown sugar
⅓	cup (2⅓ ounces) granulated sugar
1	tablespoon cornmeal
	Pinch of salt
7	tablespoons unsalted butter, melted

1. FOR THE PIE SHELL: Follow the directions for fully baking the crust until deep golden brown.

Remove the baked pie shell from the oven and increase the oven temperature to 425 degrees.

2. FOR THE APPLE FILLING: Meanwhile, peel, quarter, and core the apples; slice each quarter crosswise into pieces ¼ inch thick. Toss the apples, sugar, cinnamon, and salt in a large bowl to combine. Heat the butter in a large Dutch oven over high heat until the foaming subsides; add the apples and toss to coat. Reduce the heat to medium-high and cook, covered and stirring occasionally, until the apples are softened, about 5 minutes. Stir in the raisins; cook, covered and stirring occasionally, until the Granny Smith apple slices are tender and the McIntosh apple slices are softened and beginning to break down, about 5 minutes longer (see the photographs below).

3. Set a large colander over a large bowl; transfer the cooked apples to the colander. Shake the colander and toss the apples to drain off as much juice as possible. Bring the drained juice and the cream to a boil in the now-empty Dutch oven over high heat; cook, stirring occasionally, until thickened and a

TESTING FOR DONENESS

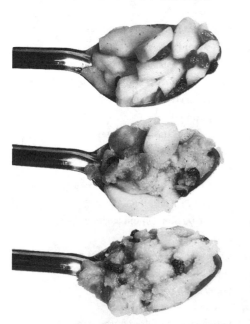

You'll know your pie filling is ready when the McIntosh apples just start to break down, as shown in the middle spoon. The filling shown in the top spoon is about halfway cooked; the filling in the bottom spoon is overcooked.

wooden spoon leaves a trail in the mixture, about 5 minutes. Transfer the apples to the prebaked pie shell; pour the reduced juice mixture over and smooth with a rubber spatula.

4. FOR THE STREUSEL TOPPING: Combine the flour, sugars, cornmeal, and salt in a medium bowl; drizzle with the melted butter and toss with a fork until the mixture is evenly moistened and forms many large chunks with pea-size pieces mixed throughout. Line a rimmed baking sheet with parchment paper and spread the streusel in an even layer on the paper. Bake the streusel until golden brown, about 5 minutes; cool the baking sheet with the streusel on a wire rack until cool enough to handle, about 5 minutes.

5. TO FINISH THE PIE: Sprinkle the streusel evenly over the pie filling. Set the pie plate on the now-empty baking sheet and bake until the streusel topping is deep golden brown, about 10 minutes. Cool on a wire rack to room temperature and serve.

➤ VARIATION

Quick Dutch Apple Crisp

This quick variation on our Dutch Apple Pie eliminates the piecrust, allowing you to have dessert on the table in less than an hour.

Follow the recipe for Dutch Apple Pie, omitting the pie dough and beginning with step 2. In step 3, pack the cooked apples into an 8-inch square baking dish and pour the reduced juice mixture over. Continue with the recipe at step 4.

STRAWBERRY RHUBARB PIE

WITH A CRUSTY GOLDEN BROWN TOP STAINED pink by rivulets of escaping juice, strawberry rhubarb pie is irresistible—a welcome harbinger of warm weather. But those homespun looks can be deceiving; too often, that crispy crust covers a soupy, bland filling, more fruit soup than fruit pie. Or the crust may mask the other extreme: a filling so loaded with thickener that it's gummy. So what's the secret to a juicy, but not watery, full-flavored strawberry rhubarb pie?

Both strawberries and rhubarb have a high moisture content, especially when it's been a wet spring. And if you've ever cooked rhubarb, you know how quickly it transforms from firm stalk to soupy sauce—mere moments. Now imagine all that liquid contained within a pie. Where is it all supposed to go? Most recipes we found load the pie up with a thickener like cornstarch or flour, but this yields an unpleasantly starchy pie with a muddied flavor. Our goal, then, was to reduce the pie's moisture content and use as little thickener (and the most flavorless one) as we could for the freshest, brightest-tasting pie.

There are two approaches to eradicating excess moisture in fruit pies: cooking the fruit prior to assembling the pie and preparing the pie in such a way that excess moisture can escape, as with an open-faced or lattice-top pie. Strawberry rhubarb pie is almost always covered (rhubarb can take on a muddy brown color once cooked), and we weren't out to buck tradition, so we opted to try precooking the fruit. Slowly stewing the rhubarb until it was completely broken down before mixing it with the strawberries yielded a flat-tasting filling as the rhubarb was overcooked and had lost its characteristic brightness. But on a promising note, the filling was much drier. Borrowing from a savory rhubarb recipe we found, we sautéed chopped rhubarb in a smoking-hot skillet until the juices were exuded but the pieces of rhubarb were still on the firm side. Once the rhubarb had cooled, we tossed it with the strawberries and assembled the pie. The baked pie tasted bright and clean and was much less soupy than before. Clearly, we were on the right track.

But the moisture was only partially tamed: We still needed to pick a thickener. We have tested all the standard thickeners in previous recipes and have a pretty good idea of what we like and don't like. As a general rule of thumb, we avoid flour and cornstarch because they turn gummy when cooked and tend to muddy the fruit's flavor. We do like the properties of tapioca, potato starch, and arrowroot because they thicken without turning gummy and never alter the fruit's flavor. Thickeners produced from roots, as these three are, thicken more effectively than flour or cornstarch because they are composed of longer chains of amylose (a starch), which means that less is needed to thicken the fruit's juices. For many of our fruit pie recipes, we favor instant or Minute tapioca, as it is inexpensive and widely available, but tasters disliked it in this case: The combination of tapioca and rhubarb yielded an unpleasant viscous texture. Even when we reduced the tapioca to a bare minimum, tasters found fault with the filling's texture. Revisiting the other starches, tasters most preferred arrowroot for its nongummy, nonviscous texture. A scant three tablespoons proved perfect.

Since the filling was still on the moist side, we opted to add a few more vents to the top crust. We made a total of eight slits radiating outward from the center, four more than we usually add to covered pies. The difference was slight but noticeable: The pie's interior was definitely drier. So with a few tweaks, we finally had a gorgeous (and not soupy) strawberry rhubarb pie well worth the effort.

Strawberry Rhubarb Pie
SERVES 8

If any leaves remain attached to the rhubarb, be sure to trim them; they are toxic. Try to find bright red rhubarb as it has the best flavor. Arrowroot, a very fine white powder, is found in the spice aisle of most supermarkets. See the illustrations on page 884 for rolling and fitting pie dough.

2	teaspoons vegetable oil
1½	pounds rhubarb, ends trimmed, peeled if the outer layer is especially fibrous, and cut into 1-inch pieces (5 to 6 cups)
1	cup (7 ounces) plus 1 tablespoon sugar
1	recipe Basic Pie Dough (page 881)
	Flour for dusting the work surface
3	tablespoons arrowroot
	Pinch salt
1½	pounds strawberries, hulled and quartered (about 5 cups)
½	teaspoon vanilla extract
2	teaspoons grated zest from 1 orange (optional)
1	large egg white, lightly beaten

1. Heat the oil in a large skillet over medium-high heat until smoking. Add the rhubarb and ¼ cup of the sugar and cook, stirring frequently, until the rhubarb has shed most of its liquid but is still firm, about 5 minutes. Transfer to a large plate and refrigerate until cool.

2. Remove one piece of dough from the refrigerator (if refrigerated longer than 1 hour, let stand at room temperature until malleable). Roll the dough on a lightly floured work surface or between 2 large sheets of parchment paper or plastic wrap to a 12-inch circle. Transfer the dough to a 9-inch pie plate by rolling the dough around the rolling pin and unrolling it over the pan. Working around the circumference of the pan, ease the dough into the pan corners by gently lifting the edge of the dough with one hand while gently pressing it into the pan bottom with the other hand. Leave the dough that overhangs the lip of the pie plate in place; refrigerate until needed.

3. Adjust an oven rack to the lowest position, place a rimmed baking sheet on it, and heat the oven to 500 degrees.

4. In a small bowl, mix together ¾ cup of the sugar, the arrowroot, and salt. In a large bowl, toss together the strawberries, cooled rhubarb, vanilla, and orange zest (if using). Sprinkle the sugar mixture over the top and stir to combine. Spoon the fruit evenly into the pie shell and pack lightly. Roll out the second piece of dough to a 12-inch circle; place it over the filling. Trim the edges of the top and bottom dough layers to ½ inch beyond the pan lip. Tuck this rim underneath itself so that the folded edge is flush with the pan lip. Flute the edge or press with the tines of a fork to seal. (See the illustrations on page 885 for tips on trimming and crimping pie dough.) Cut 8 slits in the dough top. If the pie dough is very soft, place in the freezer for 10 minutes. Brush the top of the crust with the egg white and sprinkle evenly with the remaining 1 tablespoon sugar.

5. Place the pie on the hot baking sheet and lower the oven temperature to 425 degrees. Bake until the top crust is golden, about 25 minutes. Rotate the pie from front to back and reduce the oven temperature to 375 degrees; continue baking until the juices bubble and the crust is deep golden brown, 30 to 35 minutes longer. Cool the pie on a wire rack until room temperature, 3 to 4 hours, before serving.

BLUEBERRY PIE

BLUEBERRY PIES TRADITIONALLY RELY ON FLOUR or cornstarch to thicken the fresh fruit filling. We sometimes find these thickeners problematic. We thickened our blueberry cobbler with cornstarch with good results (see page 940), but a pie requires a firmer filling than a cobbler and hence more cornstarch. If you use enough cornstarch, it will thicken a blueberry pie quite well. But in our tests, such a large amount of cornstarch dulled the fruit flavor and made it noticeably less tart.

Using flour resulted in fruit filling that was similarly unsatisfying in appearance and taste, and it also had another failing—2 tablespoons was not enough to firm up the fruit sufficiently. To give flour another chance, we ran a test using 4 tablespoons. This time, the fruit was gummy and almost inedible. As it turns out, this is because flour, unlike the other thickeners, contains proteins and other components as well as starch. As a result, it takes at least twice as much flour by volume to create the same degree of thickening as cornstarch. This amount of flour will adversely affect your blueberry pie—you can taste it.

Given our experience with peach pie (see page 895), we expected tapioca and potato starch to perform much better, and they did. Tasters slightly preferred the potato starch; however, the tapioca, when pulverized in a food processor, did an admirable job.

During additional testing, we found that the amount of potato starch or tapioca should be adjusted depending on the juiciness of the berries. If you like a juicier pie, 3 tablespoons of potato starch or tapioca is an adequate amount for 6 cups of fresh blueberries. If you like a really firm pie with no juices, 4 tablespoons is the correct amount.

Blueberries and lemon are a natural combination, and a little zest and juice enhanced the flavor of the berries. Allspice and nutmeg were a welcome change of pace from the traditional cinnamon, which can overwhelm the delicate flavor of the berries. Finally, we found that 2 tablespoons of butter, cut into small bits and scattered over the filling just before the top crust was put in place, gave the berry filling a lush mouthfeel that everyone enjoyed.

With our filling done, the rest of this pie went together quickly. The double crust produced by our Basic Pie Dough (page 881) worked perfectly with the blueberries. Tasters liked the effect of brushing the top crust with egg white and sprinkling it with sugar just before the pie went into the oven.

Unlike other fruit pies, for which the fruit must be peeled and sliced, blueberry pie goes together rather quickly, especially if you have the dough on hand in the refrigerator or freezer. Even with the rolling steps, you can have a blueberry pie in the oven in about 20 minutes.

Blueberry Pie

SERVES 8

You will want to vary the amount of sugar and potato starch depending on personal taste and the quality of the fruit. If you prefer a less sweet pie or if the fruit is especially sweet, use the lower sugar amount. (Save the 1 tablespoon sugar for sprinkling on the pie just before it goes into the oven.) If you like your pie juices fairly thick or if the fruit is really juicy, opt for the higher amount of starch. Potato starch is sold in the baking aisle. If you don't have or can't find it, substitute an equal amount of pulverized Minute tapioca, ground for about 1 minute in a food processor or spice grinder. See the illustrations on page 884 for rolling and fitting pie dough.

- 1   recipe Basic Pie Dough (page 881)
  Flour for dusting the work surface
- 6   cups (30 ounces) blueberries, rinsed and picked over
- 3/4–1   cup (5 1/4 to 7 ounces) plus 1 tablespoon sugar
- 2   teaspoons juice and 1 teaspoon grated zest from 1 lemon
- 1/4   teaspoon ground allspice
  Pinch freshly grated nutmeg
- 3–4   tablespoons potato starch or Minute tapioca (see note)

- 2   tablespoons unsalted butter, cut into small pieces
- 1   large egg white, lightly beaten

1. Adjust an oven rack to the lowest position, place a rimmed baking sheet on it, and heat the oven to 500 degrees. Remove one piece of dough from the refrigerator (if refrigerated longer than 1 hour, let stand at room temperature until malleable).

2. Roll the dough on a lightly floured work surface or between 2 large sheets of parchment paper or plastic wrap to a 12-inch circle. Transfer the dough to a 9-inch pie plate by rolling the dough around a rolling pin and unrolling it over the pan. Working around the circumference of the pan, ease the dough into the pan corners by gently lifting the edge of the dough with one hand while pressing it into the pan bottom with the other hand. Leave the dough that overhangs the lip of the pie plate in place; refrigerate the dough-lined pie plate.

3. Toss the berries, ¾ to 1 cup sugar, lemon juice and zest, spices, and potato starch in a medium bowl; let stand for 15 minutes.

4. Roll out the second piece of dough to a 12-inch circle. Spoon the berries into the pie shell and scatter the butter pieces over the filling. Place the second piece of dough over the filling. Trim the top and bottom edges to ½ inch beyond the pan lip. Tuck this rim of dough underneath itself so that the folded edge is flush with the pan lip. Flute the edge or press with the tines of a fork to seal. (See the illustrations on page 885 for tips on trimming and crimping pie dough.) Cut 4 slits in the dough top. If the pie dough is very soft, place in the freezer for 10 minutes. Brush the egg white on the top of the crust and sprinkle evenly with the remaining 1 tablespoon sugar.

5. Place the pie on the baking sheet and lower the oven temperature to 425 degrees. Bake until the top crust is golden, about 25 minutes. Rotate the pie and reduce the oven temperature to 375 degrees; continue baking until the juices bubble and the crust is deep golden brown, 30 to 35 minutes longer.

6. Transfer the pie to a wire rack; cool to room temperature, at least 4 hours.

Tips for Better Pies and Tarts

PRESSING CRUMBS INTO PLACE

Pressing graham cracker crumbs into a pie plate can be messy, especially when the buttered and sugared crumbs stick to your hands. Keep the crumbs where they belong by sheathing your hand in a plastic sandwich bag and pressing the crumbs firmly but neatly.

MAKESHIFT ROLLING PIN

We prefer a tapered French rolling pin for rolling out pie and tart dough. But if you're stuck in a kitchen without a rolling pin, an unopened bottle of wine has the right weight and shape for rolling out dough. If possible, use white wine (the square shoulders on most white wine bottles are preferable to the sloping shoulders on red wine bottles) and chill the bottle. The cold bottle will help keep the fat in the dough chilled.

USING PARCHMENT TO ROLL OUT DOUGH

If you have trouble rolling out pie dough or tart dough, even when the work surface has been floured, we suggest sandwiching the dough between two sheets of parchment paper. The parchment ensures that the dough won't stick and eliminates the temptation to add too much flour to the dough as it is being rolled—a danger because excess flour will make the dough dry and tough.

PROTECTING PIE EDGES FROM BURNING

The fluted edge on a pie can burn before the filling or bottom crust is fully cooked. Many recipes suggest piecing together strips of foil to fashion a protective cover for the edge. Instead of trying to twist pieces of foil together, we prefer to use a single sheet of foil to cover the pie edge.

1. Lay out a square of foil slightly larger than the pie. Fold the square in half to form a rectangle. Cut an arc that is roughly half the size of the pie.

2. When you unfold the foil, you will have cut out a circle from the middle of the sheet. This open circle exposes the filling, while the surrounding foil covers the crust and protects it from coloring further.

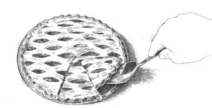

A NEATER FIRST SLICE

Extracting the first slice of pie (or tart or cake) is a challenge for even the most accomplished server. To increase your chances of removing a neat first slice, try this method. After making the first two cuts (to form the first slice), make a third cut as if to form the second slice. This third cut makes it easier to slide out the first piece intact.

PROTECTING TART EDGES FROM BURNING

Sometimes the edge of a tart shell can burn before the bottom is cooked through and nicely browned. Instead of trying to fashion together strips of foil, we invert the ring from a second, larger tart pan over the endangered crust. The tart can continue to bake without further coloring of the edge.

TART UNMOLDING MADE EASY

Lifting up the removable pan bottom with your hand causes the ring to slide down your arm like a Hula-Hoop. To remove the ring easily, place a wide can, such as a 28-ounce tomato can, on a work surface and set the cooled tart pan on top of the can. Hold the pan ring and gently pull it downward.

IMPROVISED COVER FOR TARTS

A footed cake stand might be the best plate for serving a pretty tart, but it won't fit in the refrigerator to protect leftovers. For that job, we use an inverted springform pan. Place the tart, still on the removable pan bottom, on a shelf in the refrigerator and cover with an inverted springform pan. You can even stack light items on top of the springform pan.

PEACH PIE

OUR OCCASIONAL DISAPPOINTMENT WITH peach pies in the past has taught us to wait for peach season and then buy only intoxicatingly fragrant peaches, ripe enough when squeezed to make you swoon. But even ripe peaches vary in juiciness from season to season and from peach to peach, making it difficult to know just how much thickener or sweetener a pie will need. Because fresh peaches are so welcome, we are inclined to forgive them if the pie they make is soupy or overly sweet or has a bottom crust that didn't bake properly.

But we wanted to remove the guesswork from this anthem to summer. We wanted to create a filling that was juicy but not swimming in liquid, its flavors neither muscled out by spices nor overwhelmed by thickeners. The crust would be buttery, flaky, and well browned on the bottom, with a handsome, peekaboo lattice on the top.

Our first challenge was to find a thickener that would leave the fruit's color and flavor uncompromised. A fruit pie should appear to be self-thickening, producing clear, syrupy juices. Early tests demonstrated that flour and cornstarch were both too noticeable; what's wanted is a thickener that does the job without calling attention to itself. Other options we though might work were tapioca and potato starch.

We conducted side-by-side tests with flour, cornstarch, Minute tapioca (pulverized so no undissolved beads would remain in the baked pie),

and potato starch. Flour and cornstarch fared no better than expected. The ground tapioca performed admirably, having no lumps. The potato starch scored big: Its clarity outshone flour but was less cosmetically glossy than cornstarch; its thickening qualities rivaled tapioca in strength and neutrality; and, still better, there was no need for pulverizing.

Next we turned our attention to the peaches themselves. After attempting to shave a ripe peach with a vegetable peeler, we resorted to traditional blanching and found that two full minutes in boiling water were necessary to loosen the skins of even the ripest of peaches. A quick dip in an ice-water bath stabilized the temperature of the fruit and got the peels moving.

Experimenting with different sugars, we were surprised to discover that both light and dark brown sugar bullied the peaches, while granulated sugar complemented them. As in most fruit pies, lemon juice brightened the flavor of the peaches; it also kept the peach slices from browning before they went into the pan. A whisper of ground cinnamon and nutmeg and a dash of salt upped the peach flavor and added a note of complexity.

Trying different oven rack levels and temperatures to satisfy the browning requirements of both the top and bottom crusts, we found that baking the pie on a low rack at an initial high heat of 425 degrees and a moderately high heat of 375 degrees worked best. We also found that a

WEAVING A LATTICE TOP

1. To make the lattice, lay out 4 strips of dough on parchment paper. Fold the first and third strips back, then place a long strip of dough slightly to the right of the center as shown.

2. Unfold the first and third strips over the perpendicular strip and fold the second and fourth strips back. Add a second perpendicular strip. Now unfold the second and fourth strips.

3. Repeat this process with 2 more perpendicular strips (you will have a total of 8 strips of dough, 4 running in each direction). Freeze the finished lattice until very firm and then slide it over the filling.

4. Trim off the excess lattice ends, fold the rim of the shell up over the lattice strips, and crimp.

895

glass pie dish and a preheated baking sheet gave us a pleasantly firm and browned bottom crust. A quick prebaking spritz of the lattice top with water and a sprinkle of sugar brought this pie home.

Lattice-Top Peach Pie
SERVES 8

If your peaches are larger than tennis balls, you will probably need 5 or 6; if they're smaller, you will need 7 or 8. Cling and freestone peaches look identical; try to buy freestones, because the flesh will fall away from the pits easily. See page 934 for tips on peeling the peaches. Use the higher amount of potato starch if the peaches are very juicy, less if they are not terribly juicy. If you don't have or can't find potato starch, substitute an equal amount of Minute tapioca ground for about 1 minute in a food processor or spice grinder.

I	recipe Pie Dough for Lattice-Top Pie (page 881)
	Flour for dusting the work surface
6–7	medium, ripe peaches (about 7 cups sliced)
I	tablespoon juice from I lemon
I	cup (7 ounces) plus I tablespoon sugar
	Pinch ground cinnamon
	Pinch freshly grated nutmeg
	Pinch salt
3–5	tablespoons potato starch or Minute tapioca (see note)

1. Remove the dough from the refrigerator (if refrigerated longer than 1 hour, let stand at room temperature until malleable). Roll the larger piece of dough to a 15 by 11-inch rectangle about ⅛ inch thick; transfer the dough rectangle to a baking sheet lined with parchment paper. With a pizza wheel, fluted pastry wheel, or paring knife, trim the long sides of the rectangle to make them straight, then cut the rectangle lengthwise into 8 strips 15 inches long by 1¼ inches wide. Freeze the strips on the baking sheet until firm, about 30 minutes.

2. Following the illustrations on page 884, roll the smaller piece of dough on a lightly floured work surface or between 2 large sheets of parchment paper or plastic wrap to a 12-inch circle. Transfer the dough to a 9-inch pie plate by rolling the dough around a rolling pin and unrolling it over the pan. Working around the circumference of the pan, ease the dough into the pan corners by gently lifting the edge of the dough with one hand while pressing it into the pan bottom with the other hand. Leave the dough that overhangs the lip of the pie plate in place; refrigerate the dough-lined pie plate.

3. Remove the dough strips from the freezer; if they are too stiff to be workable, let them stand at room temperature until malleable and softened slightly but still very cold. Following the illustrations on page 895, form the lattice top and place in the freezer until firm, about 15 minutes.

4. Meanwhile, adjust an oven rack to the lowest position, place a rimmed baking sheet on it, and heat the oven to 500 degrees. Bring 3 quarts water to a boil in a large saucepan and fill a large bowl with 2 quarts cold water and 2 trays ice cubes. Peel the peaches according to the illustrations on page 934. Halve and pit each peeled peach and cut into ⅜-inch slices.

5. Toss the peach slices, lemon juice, 1 cup sugar, cinnamon, nutmeg, salt, and potato starch in a medium bowl.

6. Turn the peach mixture into the dough-lined pie plate. Remove the lattice from the freezer and place on top of the filled pie. Trim the lattice strips and crimp the pie edges (see illustration 4 on page 895). Lightly brush or spray the lattice top with 1 tablespoon water and sprinkle with the remaining 1 tablespoon sugar.

7. Lower the oven temperature to 425 degrees. Place the pie on the baking sheet and bake until the crust is set and begins to brown, 25 to 30 minutes. Rotate the pie and reduce the oven temperature to 375 degrees; continue baking until the crust is deep golden brown and the juices bubble, 25 to 30 minutes longer. Cool the pie on a wire rack for at least 2 hours before serving.

CHERRY PIE

WITH ITS GLOSSY CRIMSON CHERRIES PEEKING from beneath a golden lattice top, a cherry pie is irresistible—the prima donna of fruit pies. But looks can be deceiving, and often the first bite of pie reveals its true character: a weak fruit flavor and lip-sealing sticky sweetness. What's the secret to making a cherry pie as flavorful as it is attractive?

Few cherries are actually fit for pie. Sweet cherries, like the glossy maroon Bing or lighter Rainier, are best eaten out of hand. Once cooked, their flavor is dissipated and their texture compromised. Sour cherries are the best bet for baking, but it's rare to find them fresh outside of Michigan, the Pacific Northwest, and pockets of New England. So if this excludes you (as it does us), what to do? We put the lessons we learned from cherry cobbler (page 942) to use and employed jarred Morello cherries for the filling. Earthy, bright, and firm-textured, jarred Morello cherries are the best alternative we have found to fresh. But this product is generally available at specialty markets (not regular supermarkets) and somewhat spottily at that. Revisiting more mainstream options to fresh cherries, we retried frozen cherries and canned cherries. The former were mushy and bland once cooked, and the latter, for the most part, were sticky sweet and thick with cornstarch. There was an exception, however, that proved almost perfect. Canned sour cherries from Oregon Fruit Products were tart, full-flavored, and firm—in fact, rivaling the quality of the jarred Morellos. The one hitch was the stiff price, about five dollars a can. But for the sake of a perfect cherry pie, we found the price well worth it.

With the cherry issue sorted out, we revisited the crust, thickening agent, and flavorings. An open-weave lattice top is the classic choice, both for aesthetics and function. The vibrant cherry color paired with the golden crust is inviting, and the open top allows for excess moisture to escape, preventing a soupy filling and soggy crust. That said, we knew the standard issues with thickening—type and amount of thickener—would be less of an issue than with a double-crust pie, in which all the moisture is sealed within. For our

Lattice-Top Peach Pie (page 896) and Blueberry Pie (page 893), we used either potato starch or pulverized tapioca, but tasters disliked both thickeners when paired with the cherries. Peaches break down more than cherries during baking and hence require a stronger thickener. We moved on to flour and cornstarch, and the latter won the tasting. The cornstarch added the minor binding required and gave a glossy coat to the cherries. Four tablespoons or a little less yielded the best texture.

And to accent the cherries' bright flavor, we stayed close to tradition with flavorings. Tasters liked a hint of cinnamon, as well as a splash of almond extract. But anything fancier, say brandy, allspice, or citrus, only unnecessarily complicated matters and displeased tasters. With cherry pie, we found it is best to keep things simple and let the fruit speak for itself.

Lattice-Top Cherry Pie
SERVES 8

If you are lucky and have access to fresh sour cherries, by all means use them. Otherwise, we favor canned Morello cherries from Oregon Fruit Products or jarred Morello cherries from Trader Joe's. Always taste fruit before adding sugar: If it is particularly tart, add the higher amount of sugar listed. While a lattice top is the classic cover to the pie, a solid top is arguably faster and easier to prepare. If you prefer this route, use Basic Pie Dough (page 881) and follow the double-crust instructions in Classic Apple Pie on page 887. If using fresh cherries, toss the filling ingredients together and allow to sit for 20 minutes before assembling the pie.

1	recipe Pie Dough for Lattice-Top Pie (page 881)
	Flour for dusting the work surface
¼	cup (1 ounce) cornstarch
1–1¼	cups (7 to 8¾ ounces) plus 1 tablespoon sugar
¼	teaspoon ground cinnamon
	Pinch salt
3	(24-ounce) jars Morello cherries, drained (about 6 cups), or fresh or canned sour cherries, pitted or drained (see note)
¼	teaspoon almond extract

1. Remove the dough from the refrigerator (if refrigerated longer than 1 hour, let stand at room temperature until malleable). Roll the larger piece of dough to a 15 by 11-inch rectangle about ⅛ inch thick; transfer the dough rectangle to a baking sheet lined with parchment paper. With a pizza wheel, fluted pastry wheel, or paring knife, trim the long sides of the rectangle to make them straight, then cut the rectangle lengthwise into 8 strips 15 inches long by 1¼ inches wide. Freeze the strips on the baking sheet until firm, about 30 minutes.

2. Following the illustrations on page 884, roll the smaller piece of dough on a lightly floured work surface or between 2 large sheets of parchment paper or plastic wrap to a 12-inch circle. Transfer the dough to a 9-inch pie plate by rolling the dough around a rolling pin and unrolling it over the pan. Working around the circumference of the pan, ease the dough into the pan corners by gently lifting the edge of the dough with one hand while pressing it into the pan bottom with the other hand. Leave the dough that overhangs the lip of the pie plate in place; refrigerate the dough-lined pie plate.

3. Remove the dough strips from the freezer; if they are too stiff to be workable, let stand at room temperature until malleable and softened slightly but still very cold. Following the illustrations on page 895, form the lattice top and place in the freezer until firm, about 15 minutes.

4. Meanwhile, adjust an oven rack to the lowest position, place a rimmed baking sheet on it, and heat the oven to 500 degrees.

5. Mix together the cornstarch, 1 to 1¼ cups sugar (taste the fruit and adjust the amount as desired), cinnamon, and salt in a medium bowl. Stir in the cherries and almond extract.

6. Turn the cherry mixture into the dough-lined pie plate. Remove the lattice from the freezer and place on top of the filled pie. Trim the lattice strips and crimp the pie edges (see illustration 4 on page 895). Lightly brush or spray the lattice top with 1 tablespoon water and sprinkle with the remaining 1 tablespoon sugar.

7. Lower the oven temperature to 425 degrees. Place the pie on the baking sheet and bake until the crust is set and begins to brown, 25 to 30 minutes.

Rotate the pie and reduce the oven temperature to 375 degrees; continue baking until the crust is deep golden brown and the juices bubble, 25 to 30 minutes longer. Cool the pie on a wire rack for at least 2 hours before serving.

MINCEMEAT PIE

MINCEMEAT WAS ONCE A COMMON ITEM PUT up every fall along with tomatoes and pickles. Rich, jam-like mincemeat takes on many forms but is commonly a mixture of apples, dried fruit, spices, alcohol, suet, and minced meat. Mincemeat originated in the Middle Ages, when the mixing of sweet and savory flavors was much more common. Meatless versions date back at least a century and make more sense to the modern cook not accustomed to the combination of sweet and savory.

Our first challenge was to replace the suet with butter. This was easy enough. The filling has a lighter flavor with butter but is still rich and delicious. We also found that a combination of soft McIntosh apples and firmer Granny Smiths works best. The tart Granny Smiths hold their shape during the long cooking process, while the sweeter McIntosh apples fall apart and help thicken the filling.

As for the dried fruit, we like the combination of golden raisins, currants, and candied orange peel. Dark brown sugar gives the filling a rich molasses flavor, and modest amounts of spices add depth without overpowering the fruit.

Long cooking is essential when making mincemeat. The ingredients need time to cook down and meld into a thick, rich mixture. However, we found that by the time we had cooked the fruit down into a soft mass with concentrated flavors, the pot was dry and there was not enough syrup to moisten the crust.

Many recipes add a lot of rum, brandy, or other spirits, but we felt that more than ⅓ cup was overpowering. After several missteps, we hit upon an easy solution. We added apple cider, which reinforces the apple flavor and keeps the mincemeat moist but does not stand out. Some of the cider goes into the pot at the start of the cooking time, the rest when the fruit has cooked down (after about three hours) along with the alcohol. We then simmer the mincemeat for another 10 minutes or so, just until this liquid reduces to a dense syrup.

Modern Mincemeat Pie

SERVES 10 TO 12

This recipe uses fresh and dried fruit (but no meat) in the filling. Serve with whipped cream or vanilla ice cream. See the illustrations on page 884 for rolling and fitting pie dough.

MINCEMEAT FILLING

3	large Granny Smith apples (about 1 1/2 pounds), peeled, cored, and cut into 1/4-inch dice
3	large McIntosh apples (about 1 1/2 pounds), peeled, cored, and cut into 1/4-inch dice
1	cup golden raisins
1	cup currants
	Grated zest and juice from 1 orange
	Grated zest and juice from 1 lemon
1/4	cup diced candied orange peel (optional)
3/4	cup packed (5 1/4 ounces) dark brown sugar
1	teaspoon ground cinnamon
1/2	teaspoon ground allspice
1/2	teaspoon ground ginger
1/4	teaspoon ground cloves
1/4	teaspoon salt
8	tablespoons (1 stick) unsalted butter
1 1/2	cups apple cider, plus more as needed
1/3	cup rum or brandy

1	recipe Basic Pie Dough (page 881)
	Flour for dusting the work surface
1	beaten egg white for glazing the pie dough
1	tablespoon granulated sugar for sprinkling over the pie dough

1. FOR THE FILLING: Place all the ingredients except 1/2 cup of the cider and the rum in a large, heavy saucepan over medium-low heat. Bring to a boil and simmer gently, stirring occasionally to prevent scorching, until the mixture thickens and darkens in color, about 3 hours, adding more cider as necessary to prevent scorching. Continue cooking, stirring every minute or two, until the mixture has a jam-like consistency, about 20 minutes. Stir in the remaining 1/2 cup apple cider and the rum and cook until the liquid in the pan is thick and syrupy, about 10 minutes. Cool the mixture. (The mincemeat can be refrigerated for several days.)

2. When the mincemeat filling is almost done, remove the dough from the refrigerator. If the dough is stiff and very cold, let it stand until it is cool but malleable. Adjust an oven rack to the middle position and heat the oven to 400 degrees.

3. Following the illustrations on page 884, roll the dough on a lightly floured work surface or between 2 large sheets of parchment paper or plastic wrap to a 12-inch circle. Transfer the dough to a 9-inch pie plate by rolling the dough around the rolling pin and unrolling it over the pan. Working around the circumference of the pan, ease the dough into the pan corners by gently lifting the edge of the dough with one hand while gently pressing it into the pan bottom with the other hand. Leave the dough that overhangs the lip of the pie plate in place; refrigerate until needed.

4. Roll out the second piece of dough to a 12-inch circle. Spoon the mincemeat into the pie shell. Place the second piece of dough over the filling. Trim the edges of the top and bottom dough layers to 1/2 inch beyond the pan lip. Tuck this rim of dough underneath itself so that the folded edge is flush with the pan lip. Flute the edge or press with the tines of a fork to seal. (See the illustrations on page 885 for tips on trimming and crimping pie dough.) Cut 4 slits in the dough top. If the pie dough is very soft, place it in the freezer for 10 minutes. Brush the egg white on the top crust and sprinkle evenly with the sugar.

5. Bake the pie until the crust is light golden brown, 25 minutes. Rotate the pie and reduce the oven temperature to 350 degrees; continue to bake until the juices bubble and the crust is deep golden brown, about 35 minutes. The bottom crust should also be golden.

6. Transfer the pie to a wire rack and cool to room temperature before serving.

SUMMER BERRY PIE

WE LOVE SUMMER FRUIT PIES, BUT THE PROSPECT of wrestling with buttery pie dough in a 90-degree kitchen is unappealing. In addition, we find that berries (as opposed to peaches, apples, and cherries) are spectacular when eaten fresh, not baked. But the alternatives to baked pies hardly inspired us—quick "no-bake" pies consisting mainly of rubbery Jell-O or viscous instant pudding garnished with Cool Whip. Our idea of this summer dessert was closer to the bright flavors of a berry tart, but in the more substantial form of a pie.

Our first round of tests with no-bake pies was disheartening. The first recipe called for "red" flavored gelatin and a cornstarch-thickened syrup that were poured over fresh berries in a premade crust. It had only one redeeming quality: neat slices. Other attempts that utilized cornstarch as a thickener left us with a soupy, cinnamon-laden blueberry "icebox" pie and an overly sweet mixed-berry mash in soggy pastry dough. The best recipe called for merely tossing the mixed berries in melted raspberry jam and then pouring them into a prebaked graham cracker crust. The problem with this method became readily apparent: Once the pie was sliced, the berries spilled out, making it impossible to serve neatly and difficult to eat. Exasperated, we set out to find a technique for making a fresh, flavorful pie with good texture and neat slices.

We did learn one thing from these initial tests: A graham cracker crust is not only easy to make but pairs nicely with tangy sweet berries. Some recipes call for simply pressing and chilling the crust before filling it, but we found that prebaking dramatically improved the flavor of the crust and gave it more structure by fusing the butter and sugar together. As we continued our testing, it became clear that a careful balance of the three ingredients—crumbs, butter, and sugar—would also be crucial to texture and flavor. If we added too much butter, the sides of the crust slid down as it baked, and the crust pooled in the center of the pan. If we added too much sugar, the crust became too hard and exceedingly sweet. The right proportions were 5 tablespoons of butter and 2 tablespoons of sugar to 1 cup of crumbs. We found it was much easier to press the crumbs into the pan when the butter was melted and still very warm.

Having created a recipe for the crust, we could now focus on the mound of berries that would top it. Because strawberry season peaks in early summer, we decided to limit our selection to raspberries, blackberries, and blueberries, all of which ripen in midsummer.

The biggest issue before us was figuring out how to hold the berries together. We needed a binder that would give the pie enough structure to stand up to slicing without interfering with the pure flavor of the fruit.

Early on, we found that combining a berry puree with whole berries was best for optimal flavor; using Jell-O or some other commercial filler resulted in poor flavor and less-than-ideal texture. But we still needed to thicken the puree somehow. An early test recipe called for cornstarch, which seemed like a good idea, but that recipe also added orange juice, which made the pie soupy. Our plan was simple: lose the juice but keep the cornstarch (or another thickener). We would briefly cook the puree with the thickener, sugar, and salt and then season with lemon juice at the end. After cooling this mixture slightly, we would pour it over the whole berries in the prebaked crust. The pie would then go into the refrigerator to set up.

But which thickener would be best? We started

INGREDIENTS: Graham Cracker Crusts

In the summer, our goal is to keep things simple, so we wanted to see if any of the convenient ready-to-use graham cracker piecrusts found in the supermarket were worth their weight in pie tins. All you have to do is fill, chill, and serve. We purchased three different brands—Nabisco Honey Maid Graham Pie Crust, Keebler Graham Cracker Ready Crust, and the local supermarket brand—and tasters unanimously rejected all three, describing them as pale in color, with a "chalky," "sandy" texture and a "bland," "artificial" flavor. This could be attributed to the fact that all are made with vegetable shortening (already present in the graham crackers themselves but in a much lower amount). It became obvious that adding real butter to ground graham crackers was the best way to get a good-flavored crust and well worth the extra few minutes.

our tests with tapioca, which, because of the short stovetop cooking time, turned out an unpleasantly grainy filling. (We wanted to keep the cooking time as short as possible to retain the fresh berry flavor.) Potato starch produced a gummy filling. In the end, cornstarch worked just fine, producing a good texture without adding any "off" flavors. But we still had some kinks to work out—namely, the seeds that kept sticking between our teeth. The obvious solution was to strain the filling before cooking, a step that took only a couple of minutes and made a huge difference. Now that we had all of our components, we were ready for assembly.

So far, so good, but we had found that pouring the puree over the sun-sweetened whole berries made the filling dark and murky-looking. And merely tossing the berries on top of the thickened puree was no way to turn heads either. This pie needed some gloss. So we borrowed a trick from tart making: glazing the fresh whole berries with a thin layer of melted seedless jam. Because we weren't interested in a precise arrangement of berries (we wanted a fast and unfussy pie), gently tossing them with the glaze, rather than painting them with it, as is often done when making tarts, was a quick solution. We had managed to gussy them up and enhance their flavor at the same time. Now when we poured the glazed berries over the puree, the result was a truly attractive berry pie. Better yet, it tasted fresh, sliced well, and was a whole lot easier to make than a traditional baked fruit pie.

Summer Berry Pie

SERVES 8 TO 10

Berries are not sold in standard half-pint containers. When shopping for ingredients, use the weights on the containers as a guideline, but make sure to measure the berries (gently, to avoid bruising). If you wind up short on one type of berry but have extras of another type, make up the difference with the extras. If blackberries are not available, use 3 cups each of raspberries and blueberries. When pureeing the berries, be sure to process them for a full minute; otherwise, the yield on the puree may be too small. Apple jelly can be substituted if red currant jelly is unavailable.

GRAHAM CRACKER CRUST

9   graham crackers (5 ounces), broken into rough pieces
2   tablespoons sugar
5   tablespoons unsalted butter, melted and kept warm

BERRY FILLING

2   cups (about 9 ounces) raspberries
2   cups (about 11 ounces) blackberries
2   cups (about 10 ounces) blueberries
1/2   cup (3 1/2 ounces) sugar
3   tablespoons cornstarch
1/8   teaspoon salt
1   tablespoon juice from 1 lemon
2   tablespoons red currant jelly

2   cups Whipped Cream (page 985)

ASSEMBLING SUMMER BERRY PIE

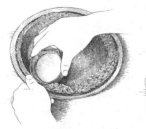  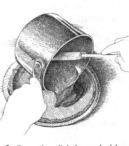 

1. Press the crumb mixture into the pie plate. Use a thumb and measuring cup to square off the top of the crust. Bake the crust.

2. Drizzle the melted jelly over the whole berries and gently toss them together until the berries are glazed.

3. Pour the slightly cooled berry puree into the cooled crust and smooth the top with a rubber spatula.

4. Distribute the glazed berries evenly over the puree and gently press into the surface.

1. FOR THE CRUST: Adjust an oven rack to the middle position and heat the oven to 325 degrees.

2. In a food processor, process the graham crackers until evenly fine, about 30 seconds (you should have 1 cup crumbs). Add the sugar and pulse to combine. Continue to pulse while adding the warm melted butter in a steady stream; pulse until the mixture resembles wet sand. Transfer the crumbs to 9-inch glass pie plate; following illustration 1 on page 901, use the bottom of a ramekin or measuring cup to press the crumbs evenly into the bottom and up the sides, forming a crust. Bake the crust until it is fragrant and beginning to brown, 15 to 18 minutes; transfer to a wire rack and cool completely while making the filling.

3. FOR THE FILLING: Combine the berries in a large colander and gently rinse (taking care not to bruise them); spread the berries on a paper towel–lined rimmed baking sheet and gently pat dry with additional paper towels.

4. In a food processor, puree 2½ cups of the mixed berries until smooth and fully pureed, about 1 minute. Strain the puree through a mesh strainer into a small nonreactive saucepan, scraping and pressing on the seeds to extract as much puree as possible (you should have 1¼ to 1½ cups). Whisk the sugar, cornstarch, and salt in a small bowl to combine, then whisk the mixture into the puree. Bring the puree to a boil over medium heat, stirring constantly with a wooden spoon; when the mixture reaches a boil and is thickened to the consistency of pudding, remove from the heat, stir in the lemon juice, and set aside to cool slightly.

5. While the puree is cooling, place the remaining berries in a medium bowl. Heat the jelly in a second small saucepan over low heat until fully melted. Follow illustrations 2 through 4 on page 901 to combine the jelly with the berries, pour the berry puree into the cooled crust, and distribute the glazed berries over the puree. Loosely cover the pie with plastic wrap; refrigerate until chilled and the puree has set, about 3 hours or up to 1 day. Cut the pie into wedges and serve with whipped cream.

PUMPKIN PIE

ALTHOUGH EASY TO PREPARE, PUMPKIN PIE presents the baker with a particular challenge—making the crust crisp while developing a filling that is firm but still tender. After baking countless pumpkin pies, we found it necessary to take a threefold approach.

First, we began baking our crusts almost completely before filling them; that way we knew they started out crisp. Next, we made sure that both shell and filling were hot when we assembled the pie, so the custard could begin to firm up almost immediately rather than soaking into the pastry. Finally, we baked the pie quickly, in the bottom of the oven, where the bottom of the crust is exposed to the most intense heat. (Baking in the top of the oven exposes the rim of the crust to the most intense heat, while baking in the middle fails to expose the crust to intense heat from any source.)

Because it sets the filling quickly, high oven heat works to the advantage of all custard pies; the quicker the pie gets out of the oven, the less likely the filling is to soak into the crust and make it soggy. But baking at high heat also has its perils—when overbaked, custard will curdle, becoming grainy and watery. No matter what the heat level, however, curdling can be averted if the pie is taken out of the oven immediately once the center thickens to the point where it no longer sloshes but instead wiggles like gelatin when the pan is gently shaken. Residual heat will finish the cooking outside the oven. Because the presence of the pumpkin dilutes the egg proteins and therefore interferes with curdling, you have a window of about five minutes between "set" and "curdled," considerably longer than with most other custards.

Two other features of our recipe provide further insurance against curdling. First, because the filling is hot when it is put into the shell, the center cooks quickly; this means that the edges, which receive the most direct heat, are less likely to become overcooked. Second, as with many older recipes, this recipe calls for heavy cream as well as milk and a goodly quantity of sugar. These ingredients not only improve the flavor but also protect the texture, since both fat and sugar serve to block the curdling reaction.

Fresh pumpkin is so difficult to use that few modern cooks go down this road. Canned pumpkin is surprisingly good, and, given a little special treatment, it can be as tasty as fresh. One problem with canned pumpkin is its fibrous nature, which is easily corrected by pureeing it in a food processor. You can freshen the taste of canned pumpkin by cooking it with the sugar and spices before combining it with the custard ingredients. As the pumpkin simmers, you can actually smell the unwelcome canned odor give way to the sweet scent of fresh squash. This is a small but delightful culinary miracle.

Pumpkin Pie

SERVES 8

The key to this recipe is timing. Start preparing the filling when you put the pie shell in the oven. The filling should be ready when the pie shell has partially baked. The pie may be served slightly warm, chilled, or at room temperature, which is our preference.

I	recipe Pie Dough for Prebaked Pie Shell (page 883)

PUMPKIN FILLING

2	cups (16 ounces) plain canned pumpkin puree
I	cup packed (7 ounces) dark brown sugar
2	teaspoons ground ginger
2	teaspoons ground cinnamon
1/2	teaspoon freshly grated nutmeg
1/4	teaspoon ground cloves
1/2	teaspoon salt
2/3	cup heavy cream
2/3	cup milk
4	large eggs

BRANDIED WHIPPED CREAM

I 1/3	cups chilled heavy cream
2	tablespoons granulated sugar
I	tablespoon brandy

1. FOR THE PIE SHELL: Follow the directions for partially baking the crust until light golden brown.

2. FOR THE FILLING: Meanwhile, process the pumpkin puree, brown sugar, spices, and salt in a food processor for 1 minute until combined. Transfer the pumpkin mixture to a 3-quart heavy-bottomed saucepan; bring it to a sputtering simmer over medium-high heat. Cook the pumpkin, stirring constantly, until thick and shiny, about 5 minutes.

3. As soon as the pie shell comes out of the oven, adjust an oven rack to the lowest position and increase the oven temperature to 400 degrees. Whisk the heavy cream and milk into the pumpkin and bring to a bare simmer. Process the eggs in a food processor until the whites and yolks are combined, about 5 seconds. With the motor running, slowly pour about half of the hot pumpkin mixture through the feed tube. Stop the machine and add the remaining pumpkin mixture. Process 30 seconds longer.

4. Immediately pour the warm filling into the hot pie shell. (Ladle any excess filling into the pie after it has baked for 5 minutes or so—by this time the filling will have settled.) Bake the pie until the filling is puffed, dry-looking, and lightly cracked around edges, and the center wiggles like gelatin when the pie is gently shaken, about 25 minutes. Cool on a wire rack for at least 1 hour.

5. FOR THE WHIPPED CREAM: When ready to serve the pie, beat the cream and sugar in the chilled bowl of an electric mixer at medium speed to soft peaks; add the brandy. Beat to stiff peaks. Accompany each wedge of pie with a dollop of the whipped cream.

SWEET POTATO PIE

THERE ARE TWO KINDS OF SOUTHERN COOKING: lady food and down-home food. In the former category are such treats as Coconut Layer Cake (page 851). Sweet potato pie was from the start in the latter category, since sweet potatoes have always been cheap and available and the recipes for this dessert are traditionally short on eggs, milk, and white sugar. Instead of scarce granulated sugar, country cooks relied more heavily on the natural sweetness and texture of the sweet potatoes themselves, combined with sorghum syrup or molasses. This resulted not in the custard-like pie we know today but in a toothier pie, something more akin to a delicate version of mashed sweet potatoes.

But all that is history. The question for our test kitchen was how to create a distinctive sweet potato pie, a recipe that honored the texture and flavor of sweet potatoes while being sufficiently recognizable as a dessert. Neither a custardy, pumpkin-style pie nor a mashed-potatoes-in-a-crust pie would do.

A review of more than 30 recipes led us to five distinctive approaches to this dish, ranging from mashed sweet potatoes with a modicum of milk and eggs to Paul Prudhomme's syrup-soaked Sweet Potato Pecan Pie to a typical pumpkin pie, with sweet potatoes substituted for the pumpkin. Some recipes separated the eggs and whipped the whites, some used evaporated or condensed milk, and most of them used a profusion of spices. To our surprise, all of them had abandoned molasses or sorghum for either granulated or brown sugar.

Although the classic pumpkin-pie style was good, our tasters were drawn to more authentic recipes, especially one published in *Dori Sanders's Country Cooking* (Algonquin Books of Chapel Hill, 1995), which had more sweet potato flavor. One problem with all such recipes, however, was still their mashed-potatoes-in-a-crust quality. We wanted a recipe that would work as a dessert, not a savory side dish to a turkey dinner. This would require fiddling with the amount of milk, eggs, and sugar, as well as with the method of preparing the potatoes.

The first step was to determine the best method of preparing the sweet potatoes. One group of tasters was keen on slicing cooked potatoes and then layering them in the pie shell. This method was quickly discarded, since its product bore little resemblance to a dessert. We also gave up on using a food processor to beat the cooked potatoes; this resulted in a very smooth, custardy texture. We finally settled on coarsely mashing the potatoes, leaving a few small lumps. This also simplified the recipe, precluding the need to pass the potatoes through a sieve to remove fibrous strings, a step called for in some of the more refined recipes.

We also decided on microwaving as the easiest method of precooking the sweet potatoes. It took just 10 minutes, without having to first boil water or heat an oven.

Next, we discarded the notion of using a bit of white potato in the recipe (a technique often used by traditional Southern cooks to lighten the texture). This made the pie more complicated and a bit grainy as well. Separating the eggs and whipping the whites, another common procedure, produced an anemic, fluffy dessert lacking in moisture and flavor. Sweetened condensed milk did not improve the flavor, and we ended up preferring regular milk to half-and-half. We added two yolks to three whole eggs to properly moisten the filling. Orange zest and lemon juice were tried and discarded because they detracted from the delicate flavor of the sweet potato itself, but a bit of bourbon helped to accentuate the flavor.

A major problem with modern sweet potato pies is that they call for the usual pumpkin pie spices, which overwhelm the taste of the sweet potato. The solution was to use only a modest amount of nutmeg. Granulated sugar was fine, but since older recipes often call for molasses (or sorghum syrup, cane syrup, dark corn syrup, or even maple syrup), we decided to test it. The results were mixed, so we settled on 1 tablespoon of molasses as optional. This boosts flavor without overpowering the pie with the distinctive malt taste of molasses. (Even 2 tablespoons of molasses was too much.)

At this point, we had a pie that we liked a lot, with real sweet potato flavor and enough custardy richness to place it firmly in the dessert category, but it still tasted a bit vegetal; it needed more oomph. Borrowing from Paul Prudhomme's notion of adding pecan pie flavorings to the mix, we made a few pies to see if we could create two layers—one of sweet potato filling and one similar to the sweet filling in a pecan pie—to jazz things up. Creating two separate layers presented a challenge until we came upon the idea of baking the pecan pie filling first, until it set in the shell, about 20 minutes, and then adding the sweet potato filling on top. This worked like a charm and made a stupendous pie. Even so, many tasters found the process a little unwieldy. After more experiments, we came up with an easy-as-pie technique for adding a separate bottom layer: We simply sprinkled the bottom of the crust with brown sugar before adding the filling.

Now we had something really special, a pie with an intense, thick, pure-sweet-potato filling, perfectly complemented by a layer of melted brown sugar just beneath. Its unique nature is reflected in the color of the filling, which is a fantastic orange rather than the dull brown that results from the use of too much molasses and too many spices. This is a sweet potato pie that any Southern cook would be proud of.

Sweet Potato Pie

SERVES 8 TO 10

Prepare the sweet potato filling while the crust is baking so that it will be ready soon after the pie shell comes out of the oven. (The crust should still be warm when you add the brown sugar layer and sweet potato filling.) The sweet potatoes cook quickly in the microwave, but they can also be pricked with a fork and baked uncovered in a 400-degree oven until tender, 40 to 50 minutes. If you like molasses, use the optional tablespoon; a few tasters felt it deepened the sweet potato flavor. Serve the pie with Whipped Cream (page 985).

I	recipe Pie Dough for Prebaked Pie Shell (page 883)

SWEET POTATO FILLING

2	pounds sweet potatoes (about 5 small to medium)
2	tablespoons unsalted butter, softened
3	large eggs, plus 2 large egg yolks
I	cup (7 ounces) sugar
1/2	teaspoon freshly grated nutmeg
1/4	teaspoon salt
2-3	tablespoons bourbon
I	tablespoon molasses (optional)
I	teaspoon vanilla extract
2/3	cup whole milk
1/4	cup packed (1 3/4 ounces) dark brown sugar

1. FOR THE PIE SHELL: Follow the directions for partially baking the crust until light golden brown. Remove the baked crust from the oven and reduce the oven temperature to 350 degrees.

2. FOR THE FILLING: Meanwhile, prick the sweet potatoes several times with a fork and place them on a double layer of paper towels in a microwave. Cook at full power for 5 minutes; turn each potato over and continue to cook at full power until tender but not mushy, about 5 minutes longer. Cool 10 minutes. Halve a potato crosswise, insert a small spoon between the skin and flesh and scoop the flesh into a medium bowl; discard the skin. (If the potato is too hot to handle comfortably, fold a double layer of paper towels into quarters and use this to hold each potato half.) Repeat with the remaining sweet potatoes; you should have about 2 cups. While the potatoes are still hot, add the butter and mash with a fork or wooden spoon; small lumps of potato should remain.

3. Whisk together the eggs, yolks, sugar, nutmeg, and salt in a medium bowl; stir in the bourbon, molasses (if using), and vanilla, then whisk in the milk. Gradually add the egg mixture to the sweet potatoes, whisking gently to combine.

4. TO FINISH AND BAKE THE PIE: Sprinkle the bottom of the warm pie shell evenly with the brown sugar. Pour the sweet potato mixture into the pie shell over the brown sugar layer. Bake on the lower-middle rack until the filling is set around the edges but the center jiggles slightly when shaken, about 45 minutes. Transfer the pie to a wire rack; cool to room temperature, about 2 hours, and serve.

PECAN PIE

PECAN PIE TYPICALLY PRESENTS A COUPLE OF problems. First, this pie is often too sweet, both in an absolute sense and in relation to its other flavors, which are overwhelmed by the sugariness. This problem is easily remedied by lowering the amount of sugar.

The other major complaint has to do with texture. Pecan pies too often turn out to be curdled and separated, and the weepy filling turns the crust soggy and leathery. The fact that the crust usually seems underbaked to begin with doesn't help matters.

Pecan pie should be wonderfully soft and smooth, almost like a cream pie. Taking the pie out of the oven before it is completely set helps achieve this texture. The pie continues to cook after being removed from the oven, as the heat travels from the edges to the middle by conduction. And since pecan pies are composed largely of sugar and butter, cooling serves to make them still more solid.

A hot oven spells disaster for pecan pie. At 375 degrees and above, the edge of the filling solidified before the center had even thickened. A moderate oven (325 to 350 degrees) is better, but a slow oven (250 to 300 degrees) turned out the best pie filling, with a nicely thickened center and no hardened edge.

There was a problem, however. Pies baked at very low temperatures took so long to firm up that the crusts turned soggy, even when the shells were thoroughly prebaked. Furthermore, the filling tended to separate into a jelly-like layer on the bottom with a frothy cap on top. To solve this problem, we tried adding hot filling to a hot, partially baked crust. When we tried this, we cut the baking time by close to half and fixed the problems of soggy crust and separated filling.

We tested pies made with whole pecan halves, chopped pecans, and a combination of chopped and whole nuts. We had no problem deciding our preference. We found whole pecans too much of a mouthful, and we had difficulty cutting through them with a fork as we consumed a slice. Chopped nuts are easier to slice through and eat.

Toasting the nuts beforehand is a major improvement. We toasted the nuts in the oven while it was heating in preparation for baking the crust. Toasting takes about seven minutes, but the nuts should be watched carefully and stirred from time to time to prevent burning. Be sure to let them cool to lukewarm before chopping them, or they will crumble. Use a knife rather than a food processor, which tends to cut the nuts too fine.

Pecan Pie
SERVES 8

If you want warm pie, cool the pie thoroughly so that it sets completely, then warm it in a 250-degree oven for about 15 minutes and slice.

1 recipe Pie Dough for Prebaked Pie Shell (page 883)

PECAN FILLING
6 tablespoons (3/4 stick) unsalted butter, cut into 1-inch pieces
1 cup packed (7 ounces) dark brown sugar
1/2 teaspoon salt
3 large eggs
3/4 cup light corn syrup
1 tablespoon vanilla extract
2 cups pecans, toasted and chopped into small pieces

1. FOR THE PIE SHELL: Follow the directions for partially baking the crust until light golden brown.

2. FOR THE FILLING: Meanwhile, melt the butter in a medium heatproof bowl set in a skillet of water maintained at just below a simmer. Remove the bowl from the skillet; stir in the brown sugar and salt with a wooden spoon until the butter is absorbed. Beat in the eggs, then the corn syrup and vanilla. Return the bowl to the hot water; stir until the mixture is shiny and hot to the touch, about 130 degrees on an instant-read thermometer. Remove from the heat; stir in the pecans.

3. As soon as the pie shell comes out of the oven, decrease the oven temperature to 275 degrees. Pour the pecan mixture into the hot pie shell.

4. Bake on the middle rack until the pie looks set and yet soft, like gelatin, when gently pressed with the back of a spoon, 50 to 60 minutes. Transfer the pie to a rack; cool completely, at least 4 hours.

➤ VARIATIONS
Triple–Chocolate Chunk Pecan Pie
To accommodate the richness and sweetness of the chocolate, you must reduce the amount of the other filling ingredients. The pie may need to bake an extra five minutes.

Cut 2 ounces each semisweet, milk, and white chocolate into ¼-inch pieces and set aside. Follow the recipe for Pecan Pie, reducing the butter to 3 tablespoons, the brown sugar to ¾ cup, the eggs to 2, the corn syrup to ½ cup, the vanilla to 1 teaspoon, and the pecans to 1 cup. Prepare the filling and pour it into the hot pie shell as directed. Scatter the chocolate pieces over the filling and press the pieces into the filling with the back of a spoon. Proceed as directed.

Maple Pecan Pie

More liquid than corn syrup, maple syrup yields a softer, more custard-like pie. Toasted walnuts can be substituted for the pecans.

Follow the recipe for Pecan Pic, reducing the butter to 4 tablespoons, replacing the brown sugar with ½ cup granulated sugar, replacing the corn syrup with 1 cup maple syrup, omitting the vanilla, and reducing the pecans to 1½ cups. Proceed as directed.

LEMON MERINGUE PIE

THE IDEAL LEMON MERINGUE PIE HAS A RICH filling that balances the airy meringue without detracting from the flavor of lemon. The lemon filling should be soft but not runny, firm enough to cut but not stiff and gelatinous. Finally, the meringue itself should not break down and puddle on the bottom or "weep" on top—not even on rainy days.

The ingredients in lemon meringue pie have remained constant for some time: sugar, water (or sometimes milk), cornstarch (sometimes mixed with flour), egg yolks, lemon juice (and usually zest), and a little butter. To our tastes, the straightforward lemon flavor of the water-based filling is pleasant, but it is also one-dimensional and lacking depth. Milk, however, subdues the lemon flavor. The solution is to rely primarily on water and a lot of egg yolks (we use six rather than the usual three), eliminating the milk altogether. This has another benefit: Adding more egg yolks allows you to cut back on both sugar (which acts as a softener at a certain level) and cornstarch and still achieve a firm yet tender filling.

The meringue is much more tricky. On any given day, it can shrink, bead, puddle, deflate, burn, sweat, break down, or turn rubbery. Most cookbooks don't even attempt to deal with the problems of meringue. They follow the standard recipe—granulated sugar and cream of tartar beaten slowly into the egg whites—assuming, apparently, that there is no way around the flaws. After making 30-something lemon meringue pies, we're not sure we blame anyone for skirting the issue. For as easy as it was to figure out the perfect lemon filling, the meringue remains, finally, only a manageable mystery. The puddling underneath the meringue is from undercooking. Undercooked whites break down and return to their liquid state. The beading on top of the pie is from overcooking. This near-the-surface overcooking of the meringue causes the

APPLYING A MERINGUE TOPPING

1. Start by placing dabs of meringue evenly around the edge of the pie. Once the edge of the pie is covered with meringue, fill in the center of the pie with the remaining meringue.

2. Use a rubber spatula to anchor the meringue to the edge of the crust, or it may pull away and shrink in the oven.

proteins in the egg whites to coagulate, squeezing out moisture, which then surfaces as tears or beads.

This double dilemma might seem insurmountable, but we hit upon a solution. If the filling is piping hot when the meringue is applied, the underside of the meringue will not undercook; if the oven temperature is relatively low, the top of the meringue won't overcook. A relatively cool oven also produces the best-looking, most evenly browned meringue. To further stabilize the meringue, we like to beat in some cornstarch; if you do this, the meringue will not weep, even on hot, humid days.

Lemon Meringue Pie

SERVES 8

As soon as the filling is made, cover it with plastic wrap to keep it hot and then start working on the topping. You want to add hot filling to the pie shell, apply the meringue topping, and then quickly get the pie into the oven.

LEMON FILLING

1	cup (7 ounces) sugar
1/4	cup (1 ounce) cornstarch
1/8	teaspoon salt
1 1/2	cups cold water
6	large egg yolks
1	tablespoon grated zest and 1/2 cup juice from 2 or 3 lemons
2	tablespoons unsalted butter

MERINGUE

1	tablespoon cornstarch
1/3	cup water
1/4	teaspoon cream of tartar
1/2	cup (3 1/2 ounces) sugar
4	large egg whites
1/2	teaspoon vanilla extract

1	recipe Prebaked Pie Dough Coated with Graham Cracker Crumbs (page 886), fully baked and cooled completely

1. FOR THE FILLING: Mix the sugar, cornstarch, salt, and water in a large nonreactive saucepan. Bring the mixture to a simmer over medium heat, whisking occasionally at the beginning of the process and more frequently as the mixture begins to thicken. When the mixture starts to simmer and turns translucent, whisk in the egg yolks, two at a time. Whisk in the zest, then the lemon juice, and finally the butter. Bring the mixture to a good simmer, whisking constantly. Remove from the heat; place plastic wrap directly on the surface of the filling to keep it hot and prevent a skin from forming.

2. FOR THE MERINGUE: Mix the cornstarch with the water in a small saucepan; bring to a simmer, whisking occasionally at the beginning and more frequently as the mixture thickens. When the mixture starts to simmer and turns translucent, remove from the heat.

3. Adjust an oven rack to the middle position and heat the oven to 325 degrees. Mix the cream of tartar and sugar together. Beat the egg whites and vanilla until frothy. Beat in the sugar mixture, 1 tablespoon at a time, until the sugar is incorporated and the mixture forms soft peaks. Add the cornstarch mixture, 1 tablespoon at a time; continue to beat the meringue to stiff peaks. Remove the plastic from the lemon filling and return to very low heat during the last minute or so of beating the meringue (to ensure that the filling is hot).

4. Pour the hot filling into the pie shell. Using a rubber spatula, immediately distribute the meringue evenly around the edge and then the center of the pie to keep it from sinking into the filling (see illustration 1 on page 907). Make sure the meringue attaches to the piecrust to prevent shrinking (see illustration 2 on page 907). Use the back of a spoon to create peaks all over the meringue. Bake the pie until the meringue is golden brown, about 20 minutes. Transfer to a wire rack and cool to room temperature. Serve the same day.

KEY LIME PIE

THE STANDARD RECIPE FOR CONDENSED MILK Key lime pie is incredibly short and simple: beat four egg yolks, add a 14-ounce can of sweetened condensed milk, and then stir in a half cup of lime juice and a tablespoon of grated lime zest. Pour it all into a graham cracker crust and chill it until firm, about two hours. Top the pie with sweetened whipped cream and serve.

It would be lovely if this recipe worked, but we found that it doesn't. Although the filling does set firmly enough to yield clean-cut slices, it has a loose, "slurpy" consistency. We tried to fix the consistency by beating the yolks until thick, as some recipes direct, but this did not help. Nor did it help to dribble in the lime juice rather than adding it all at once, as other recipes suggest. We also made the filling with only two yolks and with no yolks at all (such "eggless" versions of the recipe do exist), but this yielded even thinner fillings.

Still, the time we spent mixing Key lime pie fillings in various ways was not a total loss. While in the heat of experimenting, we inadvertently threw the lime zest into a bowl in which we had already placed the egg yolks. When we whisked up the yolks, they turned green, and the whole filling ended up tinted a lovely shade of pale lime.

Having found the mix-and-chill method wanting, we decided to try baking the pie, as some recipes suggest. We used the same ingredients as we had before and simply baked the pie until the filling stiffened slightly, about 15 minutes in

INGREDIENTS: Limes

True Key limes, *Citrus aurantifolia,* have not been a significant commercial crop in this country since storms destroyed the Florida groves early in the 20th century. However, a few growers have recently begun to revive the crop, and Key limes occasionally show up in supermarkets. Most food writers seem to like Key lime juice much better than Persian lime juice, but they give wildly divergent reasons for their preference. One book describes Key limes as "sourer and more complex" than their supermarket cousins. But another writer holds that Key limes differ from Persian limes in being more "mild" and "delicate."

We'd love to be able to say that Key lime juice made all the difference in the world, but it didn't. To our testers, it tasted pretty much the same as the juice of supermarket limes. Key limes are a nuisance to zest and squeeze, for they are thin-skinned, full of seeds, and generally little bigger than walnuts. You need only three or four Persian limes to make a Key lime pie, but you will need up to a dozen Key limes. So despite the name of the pie, we actually find the juice of Persian limes preferable as an ingredient.

a moderate oven. The difference between the baked pie (which was really a custard) and the unbaked pie (which had merely been a clabber) was remarkable. The baked filling was thick, creamy, and unctuous, reminiscent of cream pie. It also tasted more pungent and complex than the raw fillings had, perhaps because the heat of the oven released the flavorful oils in the lime zest.

The filling is fairly tart and must be offset by whipped cream that has been generously sweetened. Since granulated sugar can cause graininess at high concentrations, we opt for confectioners' sugar in the whipped cream topping for this pie.

Key Lime Pie
SERVES 8

Prepare the filling for the pie first, so it can thicken during the time it takes to prepare the crust. If you prefer, you can use the Prebaked Pie Dough Coated with Graham Cracker Crumbs (see page 886), but we like the simple graham cracker crust in this recipe.

LIME FILLING

- 4 teaspoons grated zest and 1/2 cup strained juice from 3 or 4 limes
- 4 large egg yolks
- I (14-ounce) can sweetened condensed milk

GRAHAM CRACKER CRUST

- 9 graham crackers (5 ounces), broken into rough pieces
- 2 tablespoons granulated sugar
- 5 tablespoons unsalted butter, melted and kept warm

WHIPPED CREAM TOPPING

- 3/4 cup chilled heavy cream
- 1/4 cup (I ounce) confectioners' sugar
- 1/2 lime, sliced paper thin and dipped in sugar (optional)

1. FOR THE FILLING: Whisk the zest and yolks in a medium nonreactive bowl until tinted light green, about 2 minutes. Beat in the condensed milk, then the juice; set aside at room temperature to thicken (about 30 minutes).

2. FOR THE CRUST: Adjust an oven rack to the middle position and heat the oven to 325 degrees.

3. In a food processor, process the graham crackers until evenly fine, about 30 seconds (you should have 1 cup crumbs). Add the sugar and pulse to combine. Continue to pulse while adding the warm melted butter in a steady stream; pulse until the mixture resembles wet sand. Transfer the crumbs to a 9-inch glass pie plate and, following illustration 1 on page 901, evenly press the crumbs into the pie plate, using your thumb and a ½ cup measuring cup to square off the top of the crust. Bake the crust until it is fragrant and beginning to brown, 15 to 18 minutes; transfer to a wire rack and cool completely.

4. Pour the lime filling into the crust; bake until the center is set yet wiggly when jiggled, 15 to 17 minutes. Return the pie to a wire rack; cool to

room temperature. Refrigerate until well chilled, at least 3 hours. (The pie can be covered directly with lightly oiled or oil-sprayed plastic wrap and refrigerated for up to 1 day.)

5. FOR THE TOPPING: Up to 2 hours before serving, whip the cream in the chilled bowl of an electric mixer to very soft peaks. Adding the confectioners' sugar 1 tablespoon at a time, continue whipping to just-stiff peaks. Decoratively pipe the whipped cream over the filling or spread the whipped cream evenly with a rubber spatula. Garnish with sugared lime slices, if desired, and serve.

➤ VARIATION

Key Lime Pie with Meringue Topping
We prefer to top Key lime pie with whipped cream, but meringue is another option.

Follow the recipe for Key Lime Pie, replacing the Whipped Cream Topping with the Meringue from the recipe for Lemon Meringue Pie on page 908. Bake the pie only 7 minutes, then apply the meringue gently, first spreading a ring around the outer edge to attach the meringue to the crust, then filling in the center. Return the pie to the oven and bake 20 minutes more.

SCIENCE: How Key Lime Pie Thickens

The extraordinarily high acid content of limes and the unique properties of sweetened condensed milk are responsible for the fact that lime pie filling will thicken without cooking.

The acid in the lime juice does its work by causing the proteins in both the egg yolks and the condensed milk to coil up and bond together. This effect is similar to that of heat. The same process can be observed in the Latin American–style dish seviche, in which raw fish is "cooked" simply by being pickled in lime juice.

But this process does not work well with just any kind of milk; it requires both the sweetness and the thickness of sweetened condensed milk. This canned product is made by boiling most of the water out of fresh milk and then adding sugar. Because the milk has a lower moisture content, it is thick enough to stiffen into a sliceable filling when clabbered with lime juice. The sugar, meanwhile, plays the crucial role of separating, or "greasing," the protein strands so that they do not bond too tightly. If they did, the result would be a grainy or curdled filling rather than a smooth and creamy one. Of course, a liquidy, curdly filling is exactly what one would get if one tried to use fresh milk instead of canned.

We discovered that cream is not a viable substitute for sweetened condensed milk, either. It does not curdle the way milk does because its fat, like the sugar in condensed milk, acts as a buffer to the lime juice. Cream is roughly 50 percent liquid, however, and thus it will only thicken, not stiffen, when clabbered.

VANILLA CREAM PIE
CREAM PIE HAS ALMOST UNIVERSAL APPEAL, with enough flavoring options—vanilla, chocolate, banana, coconut, and butterscotch—to satisfy almost everyone. The key is to create a filling that is soft and creamy yet stiff enough to be cut cleanly. It's not as easy as it sounds.

In our tests, adding flour left us with a filling that was too soft. Gelatin made for a rubbery filling, and tapioca, which works well in fruit pies, produced a filling with the texture of stewed okra. Only cornstarch coupled with egg yolks (whole eggs yielded a grainy texture) gave us the proper results.

The dairy component is also vital. Cream is simply too rich for a pie that already contains butter and eggs. Skim milk tastes thin and lacks the creamy texture we wanted. Both 2 percent and whole milk work well, but they are even better when combined with a bit of evaporated milk, which adds a rich, round, caramel flavor. The basic vanilla cream filling also benefits greatly from the use of a vanilla bean in place of extract.

When making a cream filling for a pie, some cooks heat the sugar, cornstarch, and milk to a simmer, gradually add some of this mixture to the yolks to stabilize them, and then add the stabilized yolks to the rest of the simmering milk. We found that this process, called tempering, is not necessary in this recipe. You can dump everything except the flavorings and butter into a saucepan and cook, stirring often, until the mixture begins to bubble. This method is simpler, and because the cornstarch prevents the eggs from curdling, it isn't that risky.

Developing a filling with great body as well as flavor is important, as is preventing that filling from turning the prebaked crust soggy. Unlike most pies, cream pie filling does not bake in the crust. The moist, fluid filling is simply poured into the crust and chilled. We found two procedures that help to keep the crust crisp.

Coating the dough with graham cracker crumbs as it is rolled out produces an especially crisp, browned pie shell. It also helps to pour filling into the crust while the filling is warm but not quite hot. Hot filling keeps the crust crisp, but because it is still quite liquid when poured into the crust, it settles compactly and falls apart when sliced. Warm filling, having had a chance to set a bit, mounds when poured into the crust and slices beautifully. What's more, it won't make the crust soggy.

Whatever you do, don't wait until the filling has cooled to scrape it into the pie shell. Cooled filling turned soupy and moistened our once-crisp crust. You can't disturb the filling once the starch bonds have completely set. If you break the starch bonds, you destroy the filling's structure. Those who have tried stirring liqueur into a chilled pastry cream may have been confronted with similar results. When we stirred the cold filling to put it into the crust, we broke the starch bonds so that the filling went from stiff to runny. We learned a major lesson. You can cool the filling to warm, but once it has set, don't stir it.

Vanilla Cream Pie
SERVES 8

For this pie, warm (but not hot) filling is poured into a fully baked, cooled crust. The filled pie is then refrigerated until thoroughly chilled and topped with whipped cream.

CREAM FILLING
- 1/2 cup plus 2 tablespoons (4⅞ ounces) sugar
- 1/4 cup (1 ounce) cornstarch
- 1/8 teaspoon salt
- 5 large egg yolks, lightly beaten
- 2 cups 2 percent or whole milk
- 1/2 cup evaporated milk
- 1/2 vanilla bean, about 3 inches long, split lengthwise, or 1 teaspoon vanilla extract
- 2 tablespoons unsalted butter
- 1–2 teaspoons brandy

- 1 recipe Prebaked Pie Dough Coated with Graham Cracker Crumbs (page 886), fully baked and cooled completely

WHIPPED CREAM TOPPING
- 1 cup chilled heavy cream
- 1 tablespoon sugar
- 1 teaspoon vanilla extract

1. FOR THE FILLING: Whisk the sugar, cornstarch, and salt together in a medium saucepan. Add the yolks, then immediately but gradually whisk in the milk and evaporated milk. Drop in the vanilla bean (if using). Cook over medium heat, stirring frequently at first, then constantly as the mixture starts to thicken and begins to simmer, 8 to 10 minutes. Once the mixture simmers, continue to cook, stirring constantly, for 1 minute longer. Remove the pan from the heat; whisk in the butter, vanilla extract (if using), and brandy. Remove the vanilla bean, scrape out the seeds, and whisk them back into the filling.

2. Pour the filling into a shallow pan (another pie pan works well). Put plastic wrap directly on the filling surface to prevent a skin from forming; cool until warm, 20 to 30 minutes. Pour the warm filling into the pie shell and, once again, place a sheet of plastic wrap directly on the filling surface. Refrigerate the

pie until completely chilled, at least 3 hours.

3. FOR THE TOPPING: When ready to serve, beat the cream and sugar in the chilled bowl of an electric mixer at medium speed to soft peaks; add the vanilla. Continue to beat to barely stiff peaks. Spread over the filling and serve immediately.

➤ VARIATIONS

Banana Cream Pie

The best place for the banana slices is sandwiched between two layers of filling. If sliced over the pie shell, the bananas tend to moisten the crust; if sliced over the filling top or mashed and folded into the filling, they turn brown faster.

Follow the recipe for Vanilla Cream Pie, spooning half the warm filling into the baked and cooled pie shell. Peel 2 medium bananas and slice them over the filling. Top with the remaining filling.

Butterscotch Cream Pie

Whisking the milk slowly into the brown sugar mixture keeps the sugar from lumping. Don't worry if the sugar does lump—it will dissolve as the milk heats—but make sure not to add the egg and cornstarch mixture until the sugar completely dissolves.

BUTTERSCOTCH FILLING

¼	cup (1 ounce) cornstarch
¼	teaspoon salt
½	cup evaporated milk
5	large egg yolks
6	tablespoons (¾ stick) unsalted butter
1	cup packed (7 ounces) light brown sugar
2	cups whole milk
1½	teaspoons vanilla extract
1	recipe Prebaked Pie Dough Coated with Graham Cracker Crumbs (page 886), fully baked and cooled completely

WHIPPED CREAM TOPPING

1	cup chilled heavy cream
1	tablespoon granulated sugar
1	teaspoon vanilla extract

1. FOR THE FILLING: Dissolve the cornstarch and salt in the evaporated milk; whisk in the egg yolks and set aside.

2. Meanwhile, heat the butter and brown sugar in a medium saucepan over medium heat until an instant-read thermometer registers 220 degrees, about 5 minutes. Gradually whisk in the milk. Once the sugar dissolves, gradually whisk in the cornstarch mixture. Continue cooking until the mixture comes to a boil; cook 1 minute longer. Turn off the heat, then stir in the vanilla. Pour the filling into a shallow pan (another pie pan works well). Put plastic wrap directly on the filling surface to prevent a skin from forming; cool until warm, 20 to 30 minutes. Pour the filling into the pie shell and, once again, place a sheet of plastic wrap on the filling surface. Refrigerate until completely chilled, at least 3 hours.

3. FOR THE TOPPING: When ready to serve, beat the cream and sugar in the chilled bowl of an electric mixer at medium speed to soft peaks; add the vanilla. Continue to beat to barely stiff peaks. Spread the whipped cream over the filling and serve immediately.

CHOCOLATE CREAM PIE

DESPITE ITS GRAND FLOURISHES AND snowcapped peaks, a chocolate cream pie is essentially pastry cream whose substance has been given form. Comprising very basic ingredients—milk or cream, eggs, sugar, flour or cornstarch, butter, vanilla, and chocolate—it is cooked on the stovetop in a matter of minutes, chilled in a baked pie shell for a couple of hours, and then topped with whipped cream. This pie, while looking superb, can be gluey or gummy, too sweet, even acrid.

We started our tests by using our basic Pastry Cream (page 924) and concluded that the texture of chocolate cream filling benefits immeasurably when fats are used as thickeners and basic starch is minimized. Butter, egg yolks, and half-and-half render a silky texture and provide most of the requisite thickening with greater finesse than cornstarch.

We had three chocolate options: semisweet (or bittersweet, which is quite similar), unsweetened, or a mixture of the two. Tasters felt that fillings made exclusively with semisweet or bittersweet chocolate lacked depth of flavor, while those made with unsweetened chocolate alone hit a sour note. Without exception, tasters wanted the filling to land on the dark, intense bittersweet side and the cream topping to be sweet and pure.

The roundest, most upfront chocolate flavor, with lingering intensity at the finish, came in the form of 6 ounces semisweet and 1 ounce unsweetened chocolate. The seemingly negligible amount of unsweetened chocolate contributed hugely to the flavor. Unsweetened chocolate, which does not undergo the kneading, grinding, and smoothing process known as conching, retains all of its strong and sometimes bitter flavors, which translate well in small amounts.

This was not the only advantage of using a small amount of unsweetened chocolate. Because it further thickened the cream (see "Chocolate as a Thickener" on page 914), we were able to reduce the cornstarch from 3 tablespoons to 2.

Next we moved on to compare fancy imported chocolates with domestic grocery store brands. The first test, pitting the widely available Baker's unsweetened chocolate against several unsweetened chocolates with European pedigrees, confirmed our fears that the supermarket stuff would be no match for its European competition. Of the imported chocolates, all tasters preferred Callebaut. Even at 1 ounce, the Baker's chocolate contributed an "off" flavor and rubberiness of texture that everyone noticed. But the next round of testing brought unexpected good news: Hershey's Special Dark chocolate was a consistent winner in the semisweet category, beating out not only a premium American semisweet entry but also its European competitors—and you can buy it in a drugstore! Hershey's unsweetened chocolate, while not as refined in flavor and texture as Callebaut unsweetened, placed a respectable second to Callebaut and was miles ahead of Baker's.

Because the filling is three standing inches of pure chocolate, a texture less than faultlessly smooth will deliver an experience less than ethereal. Temperature, timing, and technique are important.

As for the crust, tasters swooned over a crumb crust made with chocolate cookie crumbs to the exclusion of all others. Although easier to make than rolled pastry dough and arguably better

suited to chilled pudding fillings, crumb crusts are not altogether seamless enterprises. Sandy and insubstantial at one extreme, tough and intractable at the other, they can be a serving nightmare. While no one expects a slice of cream pie to hold up like a slab of marble, it shouldn't collapse on a bed of grit or lacerate a cornea with airborne shrapnel, either. It's got to slice.

The standard cookie used to make a chocolate crumb crust is Nabisco Famous Chocolate Wafers, but we didn't care for the flavor of these crusts unbaked and found them somewhat tough (if sliceable) baked. After trying without much success to soften the crust with a percentage of fresh white bread crumbs, we made a leap of faith to Oreo cookies pulverized straight up with their filling. We hoped that the creaminess of the centers would lend flavor and softness to the finished crust. The Oreo flavor came through loud and clear, and the creamy centers, along with a bit of butter, prevented the baked crumbs from becoming tough. No additional sugar or even salt was required. Ten minutes in a 350-degree oven set the crust nicely; higher temperatures burned it. The crisp saltysweet chocolate crumbs gave the rich filling voice and definition. Cloaked with whipped cream, this pie is a masterpiece.

Chocolate Cream Pie
SERVES 8 TO 10

For the best chocolate flavor and texture, we recommend either Callebaut semisweet and unsweetened chocolate or Hershey's Special Dark and unsweetened chocolate. Do not combine the yolks and sugar in advance of making the filling—the sugar will begin to break down the yolks, and the finished cream will be pitted.

CHOCOLATE COOKIE CRUMB CRUST

16   Oreo cookies with filling, broken into rough pieces (about 2 1/2 cups)

2   tablespoons unsalted butter, melted and cooled

CHOCOLATE CREAM FILLING

2 1/2   cups half-and-half
     Pinch salt

<table>
<tr><td>⅓</td><td>cup (2⅓ ounces) sugar</td></tr>
<tr><td>2</td><td>tablespoons cornstarch</td></tr>
<tr><td>6</td><td>large egg yolks, at room temperature</td></tr>
<tr><td>6</td><td>tablespoons (¾ stick) cold unsalted butter, cut into 6 pieces</td></tr>
<tr><td>6</td><td>ounces semisweet or bittersweet chocolate, finely chopped</td></tr>
<tr><td>1</td><td>ounce unsweetened chocolate, finely chopped</td></tr>
<tr><td>1</td><td>teaspoon vanilla extract</td></tr>
</table>

WHIPPED CREAM TOPPING

<table>
<tr><td>1½</td><td>cups chilled heavy cream</td></tr>
<tr><td>1½</td><td>tablespoons sugar</td></tr>
<tr><td>½</td><td>teaspoon vanilla extract</td></tr>
</table>

1. FOR THE CRUST: Adjust an oven rack to the middle position and heat the oven to 350 degrees. In a food processor, process the cookies with fifteen 1-second pulses, then let the machine run until the crumbs are uniformly fine, about 15 seconds. (Alternatively, place the cookies in a large zipper-lock plastic bag and crush with a rolling pin.) Transfer the crumbs to a medium bowl, drizzle with the butter, and use your fingers to combine until the butter is evenly distributed.

2. Transfer the crumbs to a 9-inch glass pie plate. Following illustration 1 on page 901, use the bottom of a ½ cup measuring cup to press the crumbs evenly into the bottom and up the sides, forming a crust. Refrigerate the lined pie plate 20 minutes to firm the crumbs, then bake until the crumbs are fragrant and set, about 10 minutes. Cool on a wire rack while preparing the filling.

3. FOR THE FILLING: Bring the half-and-half, salt, and about 3 tablespoons of the sugar to a simmer in a medium saucepan over medium-high heat, stirring occasionally with a wooden spoon to dissolve the sugar. Stir together the remaining sugar and the cornstarch in a small bowl. Whisk the yolks thoroughly in a medium bowl until slightly thickened, about 30 seconds. Sprinkle the cornstarch mixture over the yolks and whisk, scraping down the sides of the bowl, if necessary, until the mixture is glossy and the sugar has begun to dissolve, about 1 minute. When the half-and-half reaches a full simmer, drizzle about ½ cup hot half-and-half over the yolks, whisking constantly to temper; then whisk the egg yolk mixture into the simmering half-and-half (the mixture should thicken in about 30 seconds). Return to a simmer, whisking constantly, until 3 or 4 bubbles burst on the surface and the mixture is thickened and glossy, about 15 seconds longer.

4. Off the heat, whisk in the butter until incorporated; add the chocolates and whisk until melted, scraping the pan bottom with a rubber spatula to fully incorporate. Stir in the vanilla, then immediately pour the filling through a fine-mesh sieve set over a bowl. Using a spatula, scrape the strained filling into the baked and cooled crust. Press plastic wrap directly on the surface of the filling and refrigerate the pie until the filling is cold and firm, about 3 hours.

5. FOR THE TOPPING: When ready to serve, beat the cream and sugar in the chilled bowl of an electric mixer at medium speed to soft peaks; add the vanilla. Continue to beat to barely stiff peaks. Spread or pipe the whipped cream over the chilled filling. Serve immediately.

SCIENCE: Chocolate as a Thickener

Everyone knows that bittersweet and unsweetened chocolate have different flavors and levels of sweetness. But their dissimilarities do not end there. As we developed our chocolate cream pie recipe, we discovered that, ounce for ounce, unsweetened chocolate has more thickening power. We were aware of chocolate's starchy properties (cocoa solids are rich in starches), but we were not prepared for the dramatic differences in texture revealed in side-by-side pie fillings made with each type. Though both fillings had roughly the same amount of cocoa solids by volume, the unsweetened chocolate filling was significantly stiffer and had a viscous, gummy quality. Its counterpart made only with bittersweet chocolate had a smooth and creamy texture.

TARTE TATIN

TARTE TATIN, A FRENCH DESSERT SAID TO HAVE been invented by two sisters named Tatin at their hotel in the Loire Valley, is basically an apple tart. The apples, however, are caramelized, and the tart is served upside down; therefore, the dessert looks and tastes much more special.

The first step in the making of tarte Tatin takes place on the stove, not in the oven. The apples, neatly arranged in a tarte Tatin pan or a skillet, are boiled in a buttery caramel sauce over ferociously high heat until they absorb the syrup and become virtually candied. These syrup-soaked apples are then covered with a circle of pastry, and the tart is baked. After baking, the tart is flipped over, revealing concentric circles of apples glazed with a golden caramel. It can be served with whipped cream or vanilla ice cream or with a tangy topping that offsets the sweetness of the caramel, such as crème fraîche or a mixture of cream and sour cream whipped together. A good tarte Tatin is one that tastes like caramelized apples, not like apples coated with caramel or, worse, an unidentifiable caramel glop.

When tarte Tatin first came to this country, all sorts of different recipes for it appeared. Some were based on traditional French formulas, but others were highly Americanized. The latter, generally speaking, simply do not work. The unsuccessful recipes vary, but most of them exhibit one of two serious flaws. One of these mistakes is using sliced or chopped apples, which makes a wet, loose tart that sprawls and collapses when inverted. The second common error in Americanized recipes is the decision to caramelize the apples on top of the stove after the tart has been completely baked. Caramelizing a fully baked tart is simply impossible. If the tart turns out juicy, it will not caramelize at all, and if it bakes up dry, it will burn. And you won't even know which disaster is about to befall you because you cannot see what the apples are doing underneath the crust.

Tarte Tatin is typically made with apple quarters. Some recipes, however, call for apple halves, and we found this idea intriguing. When made with apple quarters, tarte Tatin can sometimes seem a little light on fruit because the apples lose juice and shrink when caramelized. When we tried using halved apples, though, we encountered a new set of problems.

In our first experiments, we had trouble getting the caramel to penetrate all the way through such large pieces of apple. While we eventually resolved this problem simply by cooking the apples longer, we still were not enthralled by the results. Our tarte Tatin now struck us as pulpy and mushy, and there seemed to be too much fruit in relation to crust. Worse, we found that if the skillet was just a tad too small—or the apples unusually juicy—the caramel overflowed the pan during the caramelization process, making a horrible mess.

In the end, we abandoned the apple halves, but these experiments nonetheless proved useful since they gave us an idea of how to refine the original method using quarters. When you make a tarte Tatin with halved apples, the apples rest on the outer peeled surface so that the full cut side faces up. Apple quarters, by contrast, tend to flop over onto a cut side, but we reasoned that if we tipped each apple quarter onto its cut edge and held it there while we laid the next quarter in place, we could fit more fruit in the skillet. It turned out that we were able to cram an entire extra apple into the skillet this way, with very good results. The tart looked fuller and tasted fruitier, but it did not suffer from apple overload or overflow onto the stove.

The only problem now was that the apples, because they were almost perpendicular to the skillet, caramelized only on the skillet side, leaving the other side pale and sour. One recipe solved this problem by flipping the apples over during the caramelization process. This maneuver sounded tricky to us, but, as the recipe promised, it was easily accomplished by spearing the quarters with a table fork or the tip of a paring knife. Even though the caramelized side of the apples is very soft, the side facing up remains firm enough not to tear when the apples are speared and flipped. Furthermore, even if the skillet doesn't have a nonstick coating, the apple quarters never stick.

We have always used Granny Smith apples for tarte Tatin, but many recipes recommend Golden Delicious, and one recipe that we had on hand specified, of all things, Red Delicious, which, it was claimed, gave the tart a pretty look because of the elongated shape. We tested both Golden and Red Delicious as well as Gala and Fuji apples.

The results were surprising. We had expected most of the apples—certainly the Red Delicious—to fall apart, but all held their shape quite well.

Flavor, however, was another story. The Golden Delicious apples were acceptable, if barely, but the rest were tasteless. We tried adding lemon juice to augment the flavor of the insipid apples, but did not find this to be an effective remedy. Lemon juice did cut the sweetness of the caramel, but it did nothing to boost apple flavor. You need to start with apples that are flavorful to begin with, and if supermarket apples are your only option, we think it is safest to stick with Granny Smiths.

Finally, there is the matter of the crust. A crust for tarte Tatin needs extra durability and strength, and so bakers of tarte Tatin usually make the crust with an egg. Egg pastry does not have to be sweetened, but it is indisputably more delicious when it is, and therein lies the problem. Sugar makes pastry dough sticky, crumbly, and generally difficult to handle, and it also tends to fuse the spacers—the little bits of butter that make pastry flaky—leaving the baked crust crunchy, cookie-like, and a little hard. After struggling with these problems for years, we finally discovered that the solution was to use confectioners' sugar rather than regular granulated. Granulated sugar is too coarse to dissolve well in dough. It remains in individual grains, then melts into tiny droplets of sticky syrup that wreak havoc. Confectioners' sugar, by contrast, simply disappears, sweetening the dough without causing any problems and resulting in a superbly flaky egg pastry.

Tarte Tatin
SERVES 8

If the caramel isn't cooked to a rich amber color, the apples will look pale and dull rather than shiny and appealingly caramelized.

FLAKY EGG PASTRY

1 1/3	cups (6 7/8 ounces) unbleached all-purpose flour, plus more for dusting the work surface
1/4	cup (1 ounce) confectioners' sugar
1/2	teaspoon salt
8	tablespoons (1 stick) cold unsalted butter, cut into 1/4-inch pieces
1	large egg, cold, beaten

CARAMELIZED APPLES

8	tablespoons (1 stick) unsalted butter
3/4	cup (5 1/4 ounces) plus 1 tablespoon granulated sugar
6	large Granny Smith apples (about 3 pounds), peeled, quartered, and cored

TANGY CREAM TOPPING

1	cup chilled heavy cream
1/2	cup chilled sour cream

1. FOR THE PASTRY: Pulse the flour, confectioners' sugar, and salt in a food processor until

PREPARING TARTE TATIN

  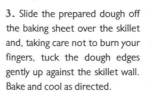

1. Place the first apple quarter cut-side down and with an end touching the skillet wall. As you continue to arrange the apples, lift each quarter on its edge while placing the next apple quarter on its edge, so that the apples stand straight up. Fill the skillet middle with the remaining quarters.

2. Return the skillet to high heat; cook until the juices turn from butterscotch to a rich amber color, 10 to 12 minutes. Remove the skillet from the heat and, using a fork or the tip of a paring knife, turn the apples onto the uncaramelized sides.

3. Slide the prepared dough off the baking sheet over the skillet and, taking care not to burn your fingers, tuck the dough edges gently up against the skillet wall. Bake and cool as directed.

4. Place a heatproof serving plate over the skillet and hold it tightly against the skillet. Invert the skillet and plate and set the plate on the counter. Lift the skillet up from the plate, leaving the tart behind.

combined. Scatter the butter over the dry ingredients; process until the mixture resembles cornmeal, 7 to 12 seconds. Turn the mixture into a medium bowl; add the egg and stir with a fork until little balls form. Press the balls together with the back of the fork, then gather the dough into a ball. Wrap the dough in plastic, then flatten it into a 4-inch disk. Refrigerate at least 30 minutes. (The dough can be refrigerated overnight; let stand at room temperature to warm slightly before rolling it out.)

2. Unwrap the dough and turn out onto a well-floured work surface. Sprinkle with additional flour. Starting from the disk center outward, roll the dough into a 12-inch circle, strewing flour underneath to prevent sticking. Slide a lightly floured rimless baking sheet or pizza peel under the crust, cover with plastic, and refrigerate while preparing the apples. Adjust an oven rack to the upper-middle position and heat the oven to 375 degrees.

3. FOR THE APPLES: Melt the butter in a 9-inch ovenproof skillet; remove from the heat and sprinkle evenly with the sugar. Following the illustrations on page 916, arrange the apples in the skillet by placing the first apple quarter cut-side down and with an end touching the skillet wall. As you continue to arrange the apples, lift each quarter on its edge while placing the next apple quarter on its edge, so that the apple quarters stand straight up. Fill the skillet middle with the remaining quarters, placing them cut-side down.

4. Return the skillet to high heat; cook until the juices turn from butterscotch to a rich amber color, 10 to 12 minutes. Remove the skillet from the heat and, using a fork or the tip of a paring knife, turn the apples onto their uncaramelized sides. Return the skillet to the highest heat; boil to cook the uncaramelized sides of the apples, about 5 minutes longer.

5. Remove the skillet from the heat. Slide the prepared dough from the baking sheet onto the apple filling and, taking care not to burn your fingers, tuck the dough edges gently up against the skillet wall.

6. Bake until the crust is golden brown, 25 to 30 minutes. Set the skillet on a wire rack; cool about 20 minutes. Loosen the edge with a knife, place a serving plate on top of the skillet, and, holding the plate and skillet together firmly, invert the tart onto the serving plate. Scrape out any apples that stick to the skillet and put them back into place. (The tart can be kept for several hours at room temperature, but unmold it onto a dish that can withstand mild heat. Before serving, warm the tart for 10 minutes in a 200-degree oven.)

7. FOR THE TOPPING: Beat the heavy cream and sour cream at medium-high speed in the bowl of an electric mixer until the mixture thickens and holds soft but definite peaks. (The topping can be made a day ahead; cover and refrigerate.) Accompany each wedge of the tart with a generous dollop of topping.

SWEET PASTRY DOUGH FOR TARTS

OVER THE YEARS, WE HAVE COME TO APPRECIATE traditional American pie dough as well as its European cousin, *pâte sucrée* (literally, "sugar dough"). But many American pie bakers have yet to discover the virtues of sweet pastry dough. While regular pie dough is tender and flaky, sweet pastry dough is tender and crisp. Fine-textured, buttery rich, and crumbly, it is often described as cookie-like. In fact, cookies are actually descendants of sweet pastry dough—a dough deemed so delicious by the French that it was considered worth eating on its own. There are also differences in the dough's relationship to the filling. Rather than encasing a deep hearty filling, a tart shell shares the stage with its filling. Traditional tart fillings—caramel, frangipane, pastry cream, or even jam, often adorned with glazed fresh fruits or nuts—would seem excessive if housed in a deeper pie. But these intense flavors and textures are perfect in thin layers balanced by a crisp, thin pastry

Though you can make sweet pastry as you would cookie dough, by creaming the butter and sugar together, then adding flour and finally egg, we found this technique too time-consuming. Like pie pastries, most sweet pastry recipes direct the cook to cut butter into flour by hand or food processor and then add liquid. Knowing cold butter and minimal handling to be critical to the success of this method, we headed straight for the food processor. Pulsing very cold butter with dry ingredients to obtain a fine, pebbly consistency took all of 15 seconds. The addition of liquid ingredients with the food processor took about 25 seconds. Armed with this quick, no-fuss technique, we wanted to tweak the major players in the dough to tease out the most tender, tastiest pastry imaginable.

The first ingredients to come under scrutiny were the butter and sugar. The higher the proportion of butter in a pâte sucrée, the more delicate its crumb. We experimented with the amount and found 8 tablespoons to be the maximum allowable for ease of handling. More butter simply made the dough too soft and did not improve its flavor or texture. As for the sugar, the traditional half cup did not seem overly sweet, and any less than that produced a dough lacking in flavor and tenderness. Most recipes recommend the use of superfine sugar (thought to be important for dissolving in a dough with so little liquid), but because few people have it in their pantry, we tried confectioners' sugar, an ingredient most people have on hand. We found that ⅔ cup confectioners' sugar gave us a crisper dough than the one made with granulated sugar.

Next up for examination were the liquid ingredients. Though most recipes call for a whole egg, some call for a combination of egg yolk and cream. (As in any cookie dough, the egg lends structure to a dough that would otherwise be completely crumbly.) Testing these side by side, we discovered that the yolk and cream combination (1 yolk and 1 tablespoon of cream) created a lovely crust with a degree of flakiness, a quality we value over the slightly firmer dough produced when using a whole egg alone.

The last major player to be manipulated was the flour. Perfectly happy with our tests using all-purpose, we nevertheless performed a couple of tests using half all-purpose and half pastry flour, as well as half all-purpose and half cake flour. Our reasoning was this: Low-protein flours, such as pastry and cake flour, tend to develop less gluten, thus yielding a more tender dough. We were surprised to learn that pastry and cake flour

are identical in composition; cake flour is simply bleached. (Bleached flour improves the rise of high-sugar batters like cake batter; pastry flour is used in pie doughs where rise isn't so important.) To be honest, we liked the dough made with half pastry flour. It was a bit more tender and delicate than the one made with all-purpose and no more difficult to work with. But the improvement was not impressive enough for us to recommend using pastry flour, particularly since it's not as readily available as all-purpose. The dough made with half cake flour had a pleasing texture as well, but a less-pleasing flavor; bleaching can impart a slightly metallic taste to flour, which can be detected in such a simple recipe.

Sweet pastry dough typically requires at least an hour of refrigerated resting time for the liquid ingredients to hydrate the dough fully and make it more manageable. In fact, a two-hour rest is even better. The butter gives the dough a nice plasticity if the dough is cold enough and makes rolling relatively easy. We knew it would be a challenge to roll out the dough directly on the counter. The best results were obtained with minimal flouring and by rolling the dough out between two layers of wide parchment paper or plastic wrap without letting it become warm. Though many recipes suggest that a sweet pastry dough can simply be pressed into a pan, our tests did not support this recommendation. The patchwork technique made the crucial "even thickness" all but unattainable, and the imperfectly fused pieces did not have the same structural integrity as a correctly fitted, single sheath of dough. The patched crust crumbled along the fault lines as it was unmolded or cut.

A half hour in the freezer "set" the dough nicely to prepare it for blind baking (baking the shell without any filling). A baking sheet placed directly beneath the tart shell (to conduct heat evenly to the crust bottom) browned the tart beautifully. Because of the crust's delicate nature, the metal weights used to blind-bake the tart are best left in place until the crust's edges are distinctly brown, about 30 minutes, at which point the weights can be removed and the top of the crust allowed to brown.

Sweet Pastry Dough for Prebaked Tart Shell

MAKES ONE 9- TO 9½-INCH TART SHELL

If the dough becomes soft and sticky while rolling, chill it again until it becomes easier to work with. This is preferable to adding more flour, which will damage the delicate, crisp texture of the dough. We find a tapered French rolling pin to be the most precise instrument for rolling tart pastry. Bake the tart shell in a 9- to 9½-inch tart pan with a removable bottom and fluted sides about 1 to 1⅛ inches high. See the illustrations below for tips on working with this dough.

I	large egg yolk
I	tablespoon heavy cream
½	teaspoon vanilla extract
I¼	cups (6¼ ounces) unbleached all-purpose flour, plus more for dusting the work surface
⅔	cup (2⅔ ounces) confectioners' sugar
¼	teaspoon salt
8	tablespoons (I stick) cold unsalted butter, cut into ½-inch cubes

1. Whisk together the yolk, cream, and vanilla in a small bowl; set aside. Place the flour, confectioners' sugar, and salt in a food processor and process briefly to combine. Scatter the butter pieces over the flour mixture; process to cut the butter into the flour until the mixture resembles coarse meal, about fifteen 1-second pulses. With the machine running, add the egg mixture and process until the dough just comes together, about 12 seconds. Turn the dough onto a sheet of plastic wrap and press into a 6-inch disk. Wrap in plastic and refrigerate at least 1 hour or up to 2 days.

2. Remove the dough from the refrigerator (if refrigerated longer than 1 hour, let stand at room temperature until malleable). Unwrap and roll out between 2 lightly floured large sheets of parchment paper or plastic wrap to a 13-inch round. (If the dough is soft and sticky, slip it onto a baking sheet and refrigerate until workable, 20 to 30 minutes.) Transfer the dough to a tart pan by rolling the dough loosely around the rolling pin and unrolling it over a 9- to 9½-inch tart pan with a removable bottom. Working around the circumference of the pan, ease the dough into the pan corners by gently lifting the edge with one hand while pressing

FITTING TART DOUGH INTO THE PAN

1. Ease the dough over the rolling pin and roll it up loosely. Unroll the dough on top of the tart pan.

2. Lift the edge of the dough with one hand and ease it into the corners of the pan with the other.

3. Press the dough into the fluted sides of the pan, forming a distinct seam around the pan's circumference.

4. If parts of the edge are too thin, reinforce them by folding the dough back on itself.

5. Run the rolling pin over the top of the tart pan to remove any excess dough.

6. The finished edge should be ¼ inch thick. If it is not, press the dough up over the edge and trim the excess.

it into the corners with the other hand. Press the dough against the fluted sides of the pan. (If some sections of the edge are too thin, reinforce them by folding the excess dough back on itself.) Run the rolling pin over the top of the tart pan to remove the excess dough. Set the dough-lined tart pan on a large plate and freeze 30 minutes. (The dough-lined tart pan can be sealed in a gallon-size zipper-lock plastic bag and frozen for up to 1 month.)

3. Meanwhile, adjust an oven rack to the middle position and heat the oven to 375 degrees. Set the dough-lined tart pan on a baking sheet, press a 12-inch square of foil into the frozen tart shell and over the edge, and fill with metal or ceramic pie weights. Bake for 30 minutes, rotating halfway through the baking time. Remove from the oven

TIPS FOR PERFECT TARTS

FOR STRAWBERRY TART
To fill the gaps between the whole berries, begin at the center of the tart and place quartered berries between them, pointed-side up and skin-side out, leaning the quartered berries toward the center.

FOR MIXED-BERRY TART
Place the berries in a large plastic bag. Hold the bag closed with one hand and use the other to gently jostle the berries about to combine them. Empty the mixed berries into the tart.

and carefully remove the foil and weights by gathering the edges of the foil and pulling up and out. Continue to bake until deep golden brown, 5 to 8 minutes longer. Set the baking sheet with the tart shell on a wire rack.

FRESH FRUIT TART WITH PASTRY CREAM

THE PERFECT FRESH FRUIT TART HAS SEVERAL components working in concert to produce complementary textures and flavors. Its crust is buttery, sweet, and crisp like a sugar cookie, not flaky like a pie pastry. The pastry cream filling is creamy and lithe, just sweet enough to counter the tartness of fresh fruits and just firm enough to support their weight. A finish of jellied glaze makes the fruits sparkle and keeps them from drying out. With each forkful, you experience the buttery crumbling of crust; the chill of cool, rich, silky pastry cream; and the juicy explosion of luscious ripe fruit.

We would be using our baked sweet pastry for tarts but what about the filling? We gathered and prepared a number of recipes for pastry cream and even included a couple of atypical fruit tart fillings—whipped cream and crème anglaise (stirred custard), both stabilized with gelatin. These anomalies were quickly and unanimously rejected by tasters for being uninteresting and Jell-O–like, respectively. We also included basic pastry creams stabilized with gelatin and lightened with egg whites or whipped cream (both often called *crème chiboust* in the French pastry vernacular), but these more labor-intensive preparations turned out not to be worth the effort. It was evident from this tasting that a simple, basic pastry cream (see page 924) was the one to pursue.

As for timing, we found it best to prepare the pastry cream before beginning the pastry shell. In fact, it can be made a day or two in advance. This gives the cream adequate time to chill, and we found a fruit tart with filling that is cool on the tongue much more thrilling to eat. And since it is best to fill the pastry fairly close to serving time lest it become soggy, the cream must be cold when it goes into the shell and is topped with fruit.

Small, soft, whole fruits—in other words, berries—are ideal atop fresh fruit tarts. Raspberries, blackberries, and blueberries require no paring and no slicing. That means no breaking of fruit skin to release juices that can ruin a tart. Strawberries are certainly acceptable, although they do need to be hulled. Sliced strawberries can make an attractive display if arranged, glazed, and served swiftly. While fruits like mangoes and papayas, with their juicy, soft, creamy textures, might seem inviting, they aren't good candidates for a tart because they quickly send their juices flowing. What's more, their irregular and awkward shapes can be difficult to slice and arrange attractively. Kiwis, however, work well, and their brilliant green is a gorgeous counterpoint to the berry reds and blues. But use kiwis sparingly, as they, too, can water things down. We do not wash berries that are destined to grace a fruit tart. They need to be utterly dry and completely bruise- and blemish-free. Any excess water can cause the tart to weep, which ultimately results in a soggy bottom.

In the test kitchen, the tarts that met with the most flattery were simple ones that showed restraint, not overdesigned ones with lots of fanfare. Bear in mind that one goal is to arrange the fruit in a tight design so that very little to none of the ivory-toned pastry cream peeks out of the spaces between the fruit (see the illustration on page 920). Also, the nicest designs are those in which the tallest points are at the center of the tart, with a gradual and graceful descent to the edges.

The finishing touch on a fruit tart is the glaze. For tarts that are covered only with berries of red and blue hues, garnet-colored red currant jelly is perfect. For tarts covered with kiwi and other fair-colored fruits (for instance, golden raspberries), apricot jam is the norm because of its neutral tones, but we took to using apple jelly because it eliminated the need to strain out chunks of fruit and then reheat.

Fresh fruit tarts are often shellacked with an armor of glaze. After glazing dozens of tarts, we know all too well that sticky brush bristles can ensnare and dislodge bits of fruit, wrecking a design. Instead, we dab, drizzle, and flick the glaze onto the tart with a pastry brush. The result is not a smooth, even coat but something more

dazzling—a sheath of droplets that catch the light and glisten like dewdrops. The caveat is that the glaze must have the correct consistency. Too thin and the glaze will run off the fruit and pool in valleys; too thick and it falls from the brush in heavy globules. We found it helpful to bring the jelly to a boil, stirring it occasionally to ensure that it melts entirely, then use it straight off the stove.

Fresh Fruit Tart with Pastry Cream

SERVES 8 TO 10

The pastry cream can be made a day or two in advance, but do not fill the prebaked tart shell until just before serving. Once filled, the tart should be topped with fruit, glazed, and served within half an hour or so. See the specific variations for tips on matching the type of jelly with the fruit.

1	recipe Pastry Cream (page 924), thoroughly chilled
1	recipe Sweet Pastry Dough for Prebaked Tart Shell (page 919), fully baked and cooled completely
	Fresh fruit, unwashed (see the variations for specific ideas)
1/2	cup red currant or apple jelly

1. Spread the cold pastry cream over the bottom of the tart shell, using an offset spatula or large spoon. (You can press plastic wrap directly on the surface of the pastry cream and refrigerate it for up to 30 minutes.) Arrange the fruit on top of the pastry cream, following a method on page 920.

2. Bring the jelly to a boil in a small saucepan over medium-high heat, stirring occasionally to smooth out any lumps. When boiling and completely melted, apply by dabbing and flicking it onto the fruit with a pastry brush; add 1 teaspoon water and return the jelly to a boil if it becomes too thick to drizzle. (The tart can be refrigerated, uncovered, for up to 30 minutes.) Remove the outer ring of the tart pan, slide a thin metal spatula between the bottom of the crust and the tart pan bottom to release, and slip the tart onto a cardboard round or serving platter; serve.

➤ VARIATIONS

Kiwi, Raspberry, and Blueberry Tart

See the illustration on page 934 for peeling kiwi.

Peel 2 large kiwis, halve lengthwise, and cut into half circles about ⅜ inch thick. Arrange them in an overlapping circle propped up against the inside edge of the pastry. Sort two cups (about 9 ounces) raspberries by height and arrange them in three tight rings just inside the kiwi, using the tallest berries to form the inner ring. Mound 1 cup (about 5 ounces) blueberries in the center. Use apple jelly to glaze this tart.

Strawberry Tart

Brush the dirt from 3 quarts (about 2½ pounds) of ripe strawberries of medium, uniform size and slice off the stem ends. Sort the berries by height and place the tallest strawberry, pointed end up, in the center of the tart. Arrange the nicest and most evenly shaped berries in tight rings around the center, placing them in order of descending height to the edge of the pastry. Quarter the remaining berries lengthwise and use them to fill gaps between the whole berries (see the illustration on page 920). Use red currant jelly to glaze this tart.

Mixed-Berry Tart

Sort 1 cup (about 5 ounces) blueberries, 1 cup (about 5½ ounces) blackberries, and 2 cups (about 9 ounces) raspberries, discarding any blemished fruit. Place all the berries in a large plastic bag, then very gently shake the bag to combine them (see the illustration on page 920). Empty the berries on top of the tart, distributing them in an even layer. Then, using your fingers, adjust the berries as necessary so that they cover the entire surface and the colors are evenly distributed. Use red currant jelly to glaze this tart.

PASTRY CREAM

PASTRY CREAM IS AN ESSENTIAL COMPONENT of fruit tarts, Boston cream pie, and éclairs. It is cooked in a saucepan on the stovetop like a homemade pudding. Making it is not necessarily difficult, but making it just right, we knew, would mean finding the perfect balance of ingredients—milk (or cream), eggs, sugar, and starch (usually either cornstarch or flour).

We first sought to determine which was preferable: milk, half-and-half, or heavy cream. The milk was lean on flavor, and the cream had a superfluous amount of fat. Half-and-half was the dairy of choice; the pastry cream made with it was silky in texture and agreeably, not overly, rich. To fill a 9- to 9½-inch tart shell, we needed 2 cups,

QUICK COOLING PASTRY CREAM

Pastry cream (and puddings) come off the stove hot but must be cooled to room temperature, or even chilled, before they can be used. You can speed up the process by maximizing the surface area from which the steam can escape.

1. Spread the pastry cream across a rimmed baking sheet that has been covered with plastic wrap.

2. Once the pastry cream has been spread to the edges of the pan, cover it with another piece of plastic wrap to keep a skin from forming. Snip a number of holes in the plastic to allow steam to escape.

sweetened with only ½ cup of sugar.

Egg yolks and sometimes whole eggs help thicken and enrich pastry cream. A whole-egg pastry cream was too light and flimsy. An all-yolk cream was richer, fuller-flavored, and altogether more serious. Three yolks were too few to do the job, four (a very common proportion of yolks to dairy) were fine, but with five yolks the pastry cream was sensational—it was like smooth, edible silk, with a remarkable glossy translucency much like that of mayonnaise.

Thickener was up next. We made four batches of pastry cream, using 3 or 4 tablespoons of cornstarch or flour in each one. Four tablespoons of either starch made gummy, chewy, gluey messes of the pastry cream. Three tablespoons was the correct amount; any less would have resulted in soup. In equal amounts, cornstarch and flour were extremely close in flavor and texture, but cornstarch inched out in front with a slightly lighter, more ethereal texture and a cleaner and purer flavor; flour gave the pastry cream a trace of graininess and gumminess. That the cornstarch pastry cream was marginally easier to cook than one made with flour was a bonus. Once a cornstarch cream reaches a boil, it is done. A pastry cream with flour must remain on the heat for a few minutes to allow the raw flour flavor to cook off and the cream to reach maximum viscosity.

Most pastry cream recipes finish by whisking butter into the just-made cream. As fine-grained sandpaper removes the smallest burrs and gives wood a velveteen finish, so butter rounds out the flavor of pastry cream and endows it with a smooth, silken texture. We found that a relatively generous amount of butter (4 tablespoons) also helped the chilled cream behave better when it came time to slice a tart; it resisted sliding and slipping much more than one made without the extra butter. When the well-chilled tart was served, the pastry cream held its own.

PREPARING PASTRY CREAM

1. Add ½ cup of simmering cream to the egg yolk–cornstarch mixture, stirring well to temper the yolk and scraping down the sides of the bowl.

2. Add the tempered yolk mixture back to the simmering cream all at once, whisking vigorously. Bring the cream quickly back to a simmer, whisking constantly.

3. Off the heat, whisk in the cold butter, one piece at a time.

4. For an absolutely smooth texture, pass the pastry cream through a fine-mesh strainer, using a rubber spatula to push the cream into a bowl set under the strainer.

Pastry Cream

MAKES ABOUT 3 CUPS

Don't whisk the egg yolks and sugar together until the half-and-half is already heating. Straining the finished pastry cream through a fine-mesh sieve ensures a perfectly silky texture. See page 922 for tips on quick cooling pastry cream.

2	cups half-and-half
1/2	cup (3 1/2 ounces) sugar
	Pinch salt
5	large egg yolks
3	tablespoons cornstarch
4	tablespoons (1/2 stick) cold unsalted butter, cut into 4 pieces
1 1/2	teaspoons vanilla extract

1. Heat the half-and-half, 6 tablespoons of the sugar, and the salt in a medium, heavy-bottomed saucepan over medium heat until simmering, stirring occasionally to dissolve the sugar.

2. Meanwhile, whisk the egg yolks in a medium bowl until thoroughly combined. Whisk in the remaining 2 tablespoons sugar and whisk until the sugar has begun to dissolve and the mixture is creamy, about 15 seconds. Whisk in the cornstarch until combined and the mixture is pale yellow and thick, about 30 seconds.

3. When the half-and-half mixture reaches a full simmer, gradually whisk the simmering half-and-half into the yolk mixture to temper. Return the mixture to the saucepan, scraping the bowl with a rubber spatula; return to a simmer over medium heat, whisking constantly, until a few bubbles burst on the surface and the mixture is thickened and glossy, about 30 seconds. Off the heat, whisk in the butter and vanilla. Strain the pastry cream through a fine-mesh sieve set over a medium bowl. Press plastic wrap directly on the surface to prevent a skin from forming and refrigerate until cold and set, at least 3 hours or up to 2 days.

LEMON TART

LIGHT, REFRESHING, AND BEAUTIFUL, WHEN lemon tart is good it is very, very good—but when it's bad you wish you'd ordered the check instead. Despite its apparent simplicity, there is much that can go wrong with a lemon tart. It can slip over the edge of sweet into cloying; its tartness can grab at your throat; it can be gluey or eggy or, even worse, metallic-tasting. Its crust can be too hard, too soft, too thick, or too sweet.

There is more than one way to fill a tart, of course. We considered briefly but dismissed the notion of an unbaked lemon filling such as a lemon pastry cream or a lemon charlotte. In each case, the filling (the former containing milk and thickened with eggs and flour, the latter containing cream and thickened with eggs and gelatin) is spooned into a baked tart shell and chilled. Not only did we find the flavor of these fillings too muted and their texture too billowy, but we realized that we wanted a proper lemon tart, one in which the filling is baked with the shell. That meant only one thing: lemon curd, and a thin, bracing layer of it at that.

Originally an old English recipe called lemon cheese and meant to be eaten like a jam, lemon curd is a stirred fruit custard made of eggs, lemon juice, sugar, and, usually, butter. Cooked over low heat and stirred continuously, the mixture thickens by means of protein coagulation. The dessert owes its bright flavor not to lemon juice but to oils released by finely grated zest, the equivalent of a lemon twist in a vodka martini. Butter further refines a lemon curd's flavor and texture. The result is a spoonable custard that can be spread on scones or used as a base for desserts. When baked, its color deepens and it "sets up," remaining supple and creamy yet firm enough to be sliced. It is intense, heady stuff, nicely modulated—if you must—by a cloud of whipped cream.

As it turned out, the lemon curd we had developed for our lemon bars (page 817) worked perfectly in this tart. Creamy and dense with a vibrant color, our mostly yolk curd did not become gelatinous when baked, as did those curds made with all whole eggs, but it did set up enough to slice.

Lemon Tart

SERVES 8 TO 10

Once the lemon curd ingredients have been combined, cook the curd immediately; otherwise, it will have a grainy finished texture. To prevent the curd from acquiring a metallic taste, make absolutely sure that all utensils coming into contact with it—bowls, whisk, saucepan, and strainer—are made of nonreactive stainless steel or glass. Since the tart pan has a removable bottom, it is more easily maneuvered when set on a baking sheet. If your prebaked tart shell has already cooled, place it in the oven just before you start the curd and heat it until warm, about 5 minutes. Serve the tart with Whipped Cream (page 985), which is the perfect accompaniment to the rich, intensely lemon filling.

1	recipe Sweet Pastry Dough for Prebaked Tart Shell (page 919), fully baked and still warm
7	large egg yolks, plus 2 large eggs
1	cup plus 2 tablespoons sugar (7 7/8 ounces)
2/3	cup juice and 1/4 cup finely grated zest from 4 or 5 medium lemons
	Pinch salt
4	tablespoons (1/2 stick) unsalted butter, cut into 4 pieces
3	tablespoons heavy cream

1. Remove the baking sheet with the tart shell from the oven and place the baking sheet on a wire rack. Keep the oven temperature at 375 degrees.

2. In a medium nonreactive bowl, whisk together the yolks and whole eggs until combined, about 5 seconds. Add the sugar and whisk until just combined, about 5 seconds. Add the lemon juice and zest and the salt; whisk until combined, about 5 seconds. Transfer the mixture to a medium nonreactive saucepan, add the butter pieces, and cook over medium-low heat, stirring constantly with a wooden spoon, until the curd thickens to a thin sauce-like consistency and registers 170 degrees on an instant-read thermometer, about 5 minutes. Immediately pour the curd through a fine-mesh stainless steel strainer set over a clean nonreactive bowl. Stir in the heavy cream; pour the curd into the warm tart shell immediately.

3. Return the baking sheet with the filled tart shell to the middle rack of the oven. Bake until the filling is shiny and opaque and the center 3 inches jiggle slightly when shaken, 10 to 15 minutes. Cool on a wire rack to room temperature, about 1 hour. Remove the outer ring, slide a thin metal spatula between the bottom crust and the tart pan bottom to release, and slip the tart onto a cardboard round or serving plate. Serve the tart within several hours.

LINZERTORTE

NAMED FOR THE AUSTRIAN CITY OF LINZ, THIS Old World European confection is not a torte at all but a tart with a sweet almond pastry crust and a filling of raspberry jam under a lattice top. Well executed, linzertorte is an elegant and simple addition to the dessert table, particularly excellent with coffee or tea. However, our initial tests revealed why this deceptively straightforward dessert has all but disappeared from the home kitchen. The almond crusts we sampled were either soggy from the jam or thick, tough, and dry. With loads of sugar in the crust, in the jam, and sprinkled over the top, the tart was cloyingly sweet and often heavily spiced like a gingerbread cookie. To top it off (literally), the crumbly, delicate nature of the pastry dough made weaving the traditional lattice a terrible nuisance.

We set out to make over this musty classic into a sleek and streamlined modern-day masterpiece. The dough was the obvious place to start; with such a simple filling, the almond crust would really have to shine. But how many almonds did the dough need? When the mixture contained more nuts than flour, the pastry was too crumbly and delicate. We tried reversing the ratio, and the crucial almond flavor was lost. An even ratio of nuts to flour worked best. Toasting the nuts was an extra step, but the irresistible aroma of roasting almonds argued persuasively that our effort would be rewarded. Tasters agreed: Toasted almonds noticeably improved the flavor and color of the crust.

Next we considered butter, and here our troubles began. In addition to determining the quantity of butter, we would have to choose a mixing method:

Should the butter be creamed with the sugar, as one would make a cookie, or cut cold into the flour, as one might make a flaky American piecrust? Crusts made by cutting cold butter into the flour were more tender than their creamed-butter counterparts, but they were also quite soft. The primary reason for cutting in the butter is to produce a flaky texture, but the ground nuts prevented this by interfering with the development of gluten strands. Also, the cold chunks of butter kept the dough crumbly, dry, and difficult to work with. Creaming the butter delivered a soft, malleable dough and a chewy, cookie-like crust that most tasters preferred, but it was decidedly tough and a little dry.

Puzzled, we put the issue aside for the moment and turned to the jam filling, which was making the bottom crust soggy no matter which mixing method we chose. Blind baking the crust before adding the filling seemed the obvious answer. In the course of our testing, we tried covering the crust with foil and pie weights before baking and were pleased with the results—the foil kept the crust from getting too brown, and the weights kept the dough from rising. But the use of the weights led to another discovery: The weighted crust, which had baked up thinner than the unweighted

one, was also pleasantly crisp and much less tough. Sticking with the creamed-butter version, we tried rolling the dough out thinner to begin with and got even better results. A finished linzertorte with the crust rolled out to less than ¼ inch was a joy to eat—crisp, tender pastry surrounding a thin layer of sweet jam. The same dessert with a thicker crust was tough and dry and sent tasters scrambling for a glass of milk. Thin was in.

Pleased at last with the texture of the crust, we began adjusting the traditional flavors to suit a more modern palate. Tasters liked a hint of cinnamon and cloves but no more, so we reduced by half the quantities of spices recommended by most recipes. Grated lemon zest is a common addition to the crust, and we welcomed a bit of brightness against the backdrop of sugar, nuts, and spices. In the same vein, we experimented with adding lemon juice to the filling and found that a full tablespoon was necessary to cut the sweetness of the raspberry jam. As for the jam itself, we settled on just a cup as the right amount to cover our slimmed-down crust. Some recipes we had tested called for twice as much, and the resulting tarts were a sticky mess.

Lastly, we faced the troublesome lattice top. We loved its look but hated putting it together, as the

EQUIPMENT: Tart Pans

Tart pans with removable bottoms are available in three types of finishes. The traditional tinned steel tart pan is silver and reflective. The nonstick version is coated with a brown finish inside and out. The third type, a black steel tart pan (also sometimes called blue steel), is quite difficult to find, at least in the United States.

We used a tinned steel pan throughout recipe development of the tarts in this book—without incident. So we wondered what a nonstick tart pan—at 2½ times the cost of a tinned steel pan—could possibly improve upon. The answer is nothing, really. Tart pastry is brimming with butter and is not likely to stick to

flypaper, so a nonstick tart pan is superfluous. Despite its darker finish, the nonstick tart pan browned the pastry at the same rate as the tinned steel pan.

The black steel pan was another matter. Colored to absorb heat and encourage browning, it did just that, actually taking the pastry a bit past even our preference for very deeply browned. This pan would be fine for baking a filled tart (the filling slows down the baking), but for unfilled pastry it was a bit impetuous. If you own one and are using it to prebake tart pastry, try lowering your oven temperature by about 25 degrees.

TINNED STEEL   **NONSTICK**   **BLACK STEEL**

nuts made our dough strips too delicate and crumbly to weave together in the traditional pattern. In fact, it was difficult to even pick up the strips without their falling apart. We were frustrated by the way most recipes ignored this and simply instructed us to "form the lattice." The sole exception to this was a recipe from *Maida Heatter's Book of Great Desserts* (Knopf, 1974), which suggested cutting the strips on waxed paper and then using the paper to lift the strips onto the tart. With a few changes, we were able to make this trick work for us as well. As for the weaving, we found that by rotating the pan a few times while laying out the lattice, we could make an easy woven pattern that looked impressive without having to move the strips around.

The last step was the easiest. Recipes were unanimous in their choice of 350 degrees as the proper baking temperature for a linzertorte, and after testing a few other options, we agreed. In the oven for an hour, the crust browned slowly, and the jam had time to bubble and thicken.

Linzertorte

SERVES 8

The linzertorte may be served at room temperature the day it is baked, but it is at its best after a night in the refrigerator. Wrapped tightly in plastic wrap, the torte keeps well for up to 3 days. If at any time while forming the lattice the dough becomes too soft, refrigerate it for 15 minutes before continuing. Make sure to buy blanched almonds (without skins).

ASSEMBLING LINZERTORTE

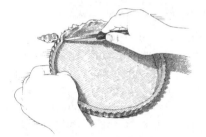 

1. Use a measuring cup or ramekin to flatten the dough into an even ¼-inch layer across the pan bottom and up the sides of the pan. Use a sharp paring knife to trim the dough to ½ inch below the top of the pan.

2. After rolling the remaining portion of dough into an 11-inch square, chilling it, and trimming any rough edges, cut the square into 10 strips, each ¾ inch wide, cutting through the underlying parchment paper. Pick up a strip of dough by the parchment paper ends, then flip it over onto the tart, positioning it near the edge of the pan.

3. Remove the parchment strip and trim the ends of the dough strip by pressing down on the top edge of the pan. Reserve all of the dough scraps. Place 2 more strips parallel to the first, spacing them evenly so that one is across the center and the other is near the opposite edge of the pan.

4. Rotate the pan 90 degrees. Place 3 more strips as you did the first 3. Rotate the pan 90 degrees again. Place 2 strips across the pan, spaced evenly between the first 3. Rotate the pan again and complete the lattice by placing the last 2 strips between the second set of 3.

5. Use small scraps of dough to fill in the crust around the edges between the lattice strips. The top of the crust should be just below the top of the pan.

1½ cups whole blanched almonds

1½ cups (7½ ounces) unbleached all-purpose flour, plus more for dusting the work surface

½ teaspoon ground cinnamon

⅛ teaspoon ground cloves

¼ teaspoon salt

2 teaspoons grated zest and 1 tablespoon juice from 1 lemon

10 tablespoons (1¼ sticks) unsalted butter, softened but still cool

½ cup (3½ ounces) granulated sugar

2 large egg yolks

1 teaspoon vanilla extract

1 cup seedless raspberry jam

Confectioners' sugar for dusting the tart

1. Adjust an oven rack to the middle position and heat the oven to 350 degrees. Spread the almonds on a baking sheet and toast until lightly colored and fragrant, 8 to 10 minutes. Cool to room temperature. Do not turn off the oven.

2. Process the almonds in a food processor until very finely ground, about 20 seconds, scraping down the sides of the bowl as necessary with a rubber spatula. Place the ground almonds, flour, cinnamon, cloves, salt, and lemon zest in a medium bowl and whisk to combine.

3. Place the butter and granulated sugar in the bowl of a standing mixer and beat at medium-high speed until light and fluffy, about 3 minutes. Scrape down the sides of the mixing bowl with a rubber spatula. Add the egg yolks and vanilla and mix at medium speed until combined. Add the flour and almond mixture and mix until combined, scraping down the sides of the bowl as necessary. Form the dough into a ball, wrap in plastic, and chill until firm, about 30 minutes.

4. Divide the dough in half. Shape one half into a 6-inch square, rewrap in plastic wrap, and return to the refrigerator. Press the other half into the bottom of a 9-inch tart pan with a removable bottom. Use a measuring cup or ramekin to flatten the dough into an even ¼-inch layer across the pan bottom and up the sides of the pan. Use a sharp paring knife to trim the dough to ½ inch below the top of the pan (see illustration 1 on page 927). Chill the pan in the freezer until the dough is firm, about 15 minutes. Meanwhile, increase the oven temperature to 400 degrees.

5. Spray an 11-inch-square piece of aluminum foil with nonstick cooking spray. Prick the dough lightly with a fork across the bottom of the pan, cover with the aluminum foil, and distribute pie weights evenly in the pan.

6. Bake the crust until it is set and just slightly moist near the center, about 20 minutes. Remove the weights and foil and bake until the crust is dry and barely colored, about 5 minutes longer. Place the pan on a wire rack to cool. If the sides of the crust have risen to the top of the pan during baking, trim them down to ½ inch below the top of the pan with a paring knife. Reduce the oven temperature to 350 degrees.

7. Unwrap the remaining square of dough and roll between 2 large sheets of lightly floured parchment paper to an 11-inch square about ⅛ inch thick. Transfer the dough and parchment onto a cookie sheet and chill until firm, about 15 minutes.

8. Meanwhile, whisk together the jam and lemon juice in a small bowl until smooth. Spread the jam filling on the baked crust.

9. Remove the top sheet of parchment paper from the rolled-out dough. Place the dough and the parchment paper on a cutting board. Using a ruler and a sharp knife, trim any rough edges and reserve the scraps. Following illustrations 2 through 5 on page 927, cut the dough into strips and form a lattice on top of the tart.

10. Bake until the crust is lightly browned and the jam is bubbling, about 1 hour. Transfer the tart to a wire cooling rack and cool to room temperature, about 3 hours. When ready to serve, remove the outer ring from the tart pan and dust the tart with confectioners' sugar.

21

CRISPS, COBBLERS, AND OTHER FRUIT DESSERTS

WE LOVE A SIMPLE BOWL OF FRESH SUMMER berries or a crisp autumn apple, but who says nature can't be improved upon a little? Baking fruit intensifies its natural sweetness and softens its texture. Likewise, macerating fruit (mixing and sometimes mashing fruit with sugar or other sweeteners) enriches the fruit's natural juices (as in strawberry shortcake, for example). Whether cooked or not, these fruit desserts are complemented by a crust formed with bread, cake crumbs, flour and butter, oats, and the like.

There is an astonishing array of old-fashioned American desserts that fall under this category. In the days when home cooks were frugal, these desserts were an easy way to use up stale leftovers while providing a bit of variety in terms of texture and flavor. Most of these simple desserts have funny names that are hard to keep straight. While regional differences exist, most American cookbooks agree on the following formulations:

A crisp is fruit topped with a "rubbed" mixture of butter, sugar, and flour, then baked. The topping often includes nuts or oats.

A pandowdy is fruit covered with pastry dough and baked. The dough is cut, scored, and pressed into the fruit.

A cobbler is fruit topped with a crust, which can be made from cookie dough, pie pastry, or biscuit topping, and baked.

Shortcakes are often grouped with crisps, cobblers, and such, although this dessert is made with fruit that has not been baked. Rather, the fruit is macerated and then layered between split biscuits with whipped cream.

The following pages contain recipes for our favorite baked fruit desserts. Please refer to "Preparing Fruit" on pages 934–935 for tips on peeling, pitting, and cutting all the types of fruit used in this chapter.

CRISPS

THERE IS SELDOM ANYTHING CRISP ABOUT most crisps. This simple baked dessert, made from sweetened fruit topped with a combination of sugar, butter, and flour, almost invariably comes out of the oven with a soggy top crust. A few recipes go so far as to refer to this classic dish as a crunch, a term that does little to suggest the flat, dull, overly sweetened crust that serves as a streusel topping for the fruit.

We tried covering fruit with sweetened and buttered oats (for a British take on a crisp, called a crumble), as well as plain toppings without oats or nuts, and were unimpressed. None of these toppings merited the name "crisp." We found that two ingredients are essential to a successful crisp—spices (we recommend cinnamon and nutmeg) and nuts (particularly whole almonds or pecans). The spices add flavor to the topping, while the nuts give it some texture and much-needed crunch. We also found that the food processor does the best job of making the topping, although you can also use your fingers or a fork.

Firm fruits, such as apples, pears, nectarines, peaches, and plums, work best in crisps. Berries are quite watery and will make the topping soggy if used alone. However, they will work in combination with firmer fruits. If you like, replace up to one cup of the fruit in the fillings with an equal amount of berries. We think that raspberries are especially good with apples, while blueberries work nicely with peaches.

Our tests revealed that when using apples, a combination of Granny Smith and McIntosh apples works best. The McIntosh apples have good flavor and cook down to form a thick sauce. The Granny Smiths cut some of the sweetness and hold their shape.

We found it unnecessary to thicken the fruit in all but two cases. Plums are a bit watery and benefit from the addition of a little quick-cooking tapioca. Peaches will thicken up on their own but need some help when blueberries are added to the mix. Juices thrown off by any of the other fruits will evaporate or thicken nicely without causing the topping to become soft.

As for flavoring the fruit, we found ¼ cup sugar to be adequate, especially since the toppings are fairly sweet. We also like to add some lemon juice and zest. One-half teaspoon of grated ginger makes a nice addition to any of the fillings.

Apple Crisp

SERVES 4 TO 6

Although almost any unsalted nut may be used in the topping, our preference is for almonds or pecans. A dollop of whipped cream or vanilla ice cream is always welcome, especially if serving the crisp warm. To double the recipe, place the ingredients in a 13 by 9-inch baking dish and bake for 55 minutes at 375 degrees without increasing the oven temperature.

TOPPING

6	tablespoons (1 7/8 ounces) unbleached all-purpose flour
1/4	cup packed (1 3/4 ounces) light brown sugar
1/4	cup (1 3/4 ounces) granulated sugar
1/4	teaspoon ground cinnamon
1/4	teaspoon ground nutmeg
1/4	teaspoon salt
5	tablespoons cold unsalted butter, cut into 1/2-inch pieces
3/4	cup coarsely chopped nuts, such as almonds, pecans, or walnuts

FILLING

3	medium Granny Smith apples (about 1 1/4 pounds)
3	medium McIntosh apples (about 1 1/4 pounds)
1/2	teaspoon grated zest and 1 1/2 tablespoons juice from 1 lemon
1/4	cup (1 3/4 ounces) granulated sugar

1. FOR THE TOPPING: Place the flour, sugars, spices, and salt in a food processor and process briefly to combine. Add the butter and pulse 10 times, about 4 seconds for each pulse. The mixture will first look like dry sand, with large lumps of butter, then like coarse cornmeal. Add the nuts, then process again, four or five 1-second pulses. The topping should look like slightly clumpy wet sand. Be sure not to overmix, or the mixture will become too wet and homogeneous. Refrigerate the topping while preparing the fruit, at least 15 minutes.

2. Adjust an oven rack to the lower-middle position and heat the oven to 375 degrees.

3. FOR THE FILLING: Peel, quarter, and core the apples, then cut into 1-inch chunks. (You should have 6 cups.) Toss the apples, zest, juice, and sugar in a medium bowl. Scrape the fruit mixture with a rubber spatula into an 8-inch square baking pan or 9-inch deep-dish pie plate.

4. TO ASSEMBLE AND BAKE THE CRISP: Distribute the chilled topping evenly over the fruit. Bake for 40 minutes. Increase the oven temperature to 400 degrees and continue baking until the fruit is bubbling and the topping turns deep golden brown, about 5 minutes more. Serve warm. (The crisp can be set aside at room temperature for a few hours and then reheated in a warm oven just before serving.)

➤ VARIATIONS

Pear Crisp

Follow the recipe for Apple Crisp, replacing the apples with 6 medium pears (2½ to 3 pounds).

Peach Crisp

Nectarines can be used in place of peaches if desired. For peach-blueberry crisp, reduce the cut peaches to 5 cups (about 2½ pounds) and add 1 cup fresh blueberries and 1 tablespoon quick-cooking tapioca to the fruit mixture.

Follow the recipe for Apple Crisp, replacing the apples with 6 peaches (about 3 pounds), peeled, pitted, and cut into ⅓-inch wedges.

Plum Crisp

Follow the recipe for Apple Crisp, replacing the apples with 8 plums (2½ to 3 pounds), pitted and cut into ⅓-inch wedges, and adding 1 tablespoon quick-cooking tapioca to the fruit mixture.

APPLE PANDOWDY

PANDOWDY IS A SORT OF DEEP-DISH PIE, originally made with sweetened apples covered with a very thick piece of pastry and baked. Sometime before serving, the pastry is scored and pushed into the fruit so it absorbs the juices. Like its fruit dessert cousins, which may be described according to how they look when served or even how they sound when eaten, pandowdy got its name for being just that—dowdy, or on the homely side.

931

When we began our recipe development by making five pandowdies from various sources, we realized that making this dessert was not without its pitfalls. Though "soggy" is not too far off in describing the texture of the submerged pastry in a good pandowdy, we considered doughs that qualified as "waterlogged," "saturated," or "total mush" to be failures. We wanted to produce a crust that preserved some of its baked structure, one that was at once soggy and crisp. Likewise, some of our first attempts at apple fillings fell short of acceptable, ranging from "overspiced" to "tasteless." We knew our charge would be to develop something in between.

We started with the apples, not only concentrating on their flavor and texture but also knowing that the variety we used would determine the

MAKING A PANDOWDY

1. As soon as it emerges from the oven, score the pastry with a sharp knife by running the knife lengthwise and crosswise to form 2-inch squares.

2. Use the edge of a spoon or metal spatula to press the edges of the crust squares down into the fruit. Don't completely submerge the pieces, or they will become exceedingly soggy.

amount of juices released during baking. As with other apple desserts (including apple pie), we found that a combination of Granny Smith and McIntosh apples delivered the best results. An all–Granny Smith pandowdy left a lot to be desired. In the short time that the dowdy is in the oven, the apples held their shape, retained most of their firm texture, and shed only a minimal amount of juices. While we liked their tart, assertive flavor, we could not "dowdy" the pastry—there were no juices for it to soak up—and crunchy apples were not the tasters' ideal. The all-McIntosh version came out of the oven on the other end of the spectrum. The apples were broken down and listless, like applesauce, and there was too much juice. The pastry crust, which had already been steamed in the oven, soaked the juices right up and turned into a waterlogged mess. A 50–50 ratio of the two apple varieties produced a perfect balance of delicate apple juices and yielding yet sturdy apple chunks.

Seasoning the filling came next. A traditional dowdy is not a fancy dish. We decided to keep it simple and limit the flavorings to brown sugar for a caramel-like sweetness, vanilla extract for roundness, and lemon zest for brightness. Although the combination of these ingredients with two types of apples was pleasing, tasters were looking for a hint of cinnamon. In the end, a sprinkling of cinnamon sugar on the pastry's surface added cinnamon flavor without compromising the freshness of the apples.

It was time to focus on the pastry. We found that our standard pie pastry (see page 881), made with both butter and shortening, yielded good results. The most pressing problem was the overrun of dough around the 8-inch dish in which we were baking the dowdy. When we tucked the excess pastry around the sides of the pan (as recommended in a few recipes), the pastry dropped below the apple layer and "boiled" into a mass of unappealing mush. To avoid such oversaturated dough, especially on the sides and in the corners, we found that it was best to trim the dough to size, eliminating any chance of boiling the dough. Cutting air vents in the surface of the raw dough before baking also helped to prevent excessive steaming and subsequent rubberizing of the pastry. With the edges untucked and the vents opened, the pastry came out of the oven crisp, tender, and flaky, perfect for dunking in the fruit and soaking up its juices.

A few recipes suggested submerging the crust during baking. We quickly rejected this notion, as it made the crust unbearably soggy. Scoring the crust when it emerged from the oven and then pressing the crust down into the juices was a far better option.

Apple Pandowdy

SERVES 4 TO 6

Serve the pandowdy warm in deep bowls with scoops of vanilla ice cream.

CRUST

1	cup (5 ounces) unbleached all-purpose flour, plus more for dusting the work surface
1/2	teaspoon salt
2	tablespoons granulated sugar
2	tablespoons vegetable shortening, chilled
6	tablespoons (3/4 stick) cold unsalted butter, cut into 1/4-inch pieces
3–4	tablespoons ice water
1/2	teaspoon ground cinnamon
1	tablespoon milk

FILLING

2	large Granny Smith apples (about 1 pound), peeled, cored, and cut into 1/4-inch slices
2	large McIntosh apples (about 1 pound), peeled, cored, and cut into 1/4-inch slices
1/3	cup packed (2 1/3 ounces) light brown sugar
1	teaspoon grated zest from 1 lemon
1/2	teaspoon vanilla extract

1. FOR THE CRUST: Place the flour, salt, and 1 tablespoon of the granulated sugar in a food processor and pulse until combined. Add the shortening and process until the mixture has the texture of coarse sand, about 10 seconds. Scatter the butter pieces over the flour mixture; cut the butter into the flour until the mixture is pale yellow and resembles coarse crumbs, with butter bits no larger than small peas, about ten 1-second pulses. Turn the mixture into a medium bowl.

2. Sprinkle 3 tablespoons of the ice water over the mixture. With the blade of a rubber spatula, use a folding motion to mix. Press down on the dough with the broad side of the spatula until the dough sticks together, adding up to 1 tablespoon more ice water if the dough will not come together. Place the dough on a sheet of plastic wrap and press into either a square or a circle, depending on whether you are using a square or a round pan. Wrap the dough in the plastic and refrigerate at least 1 hour or up to 2 days before rolling out.

3. FOR THE FILLING: Adjust an oven rack to the middle position and heat the oven to 425 degrees. Toss the apple slices, brown sugar, lemon zest, and vanilla together in a large bowl until the apples are evenly coated with the sugar. Place the apples in an 8-inch square or 9-inch round glass baking pan.

4. TO ASSEMBLE AND BAKE THE PANDOWDY: Mix together the remaining 1 tablespoon granulated sugar and the cinnamon in a small bowl and set aside. If the dough has been refrigerated longer than 1 hour, let it stand at room temperature until malleable. Roll the dough on a lightly floured work surface or between two large sheets of plastic wrap to a 10-inch square or circle. Trim the dough to the exact size of the baking dish. Place the dough on top of the apples. Brush the dough with the milk and sprinkle with the cinnamon-sugar mixture. Cut four 1-inch vents in the dough. Bake until golden brown, 35 to 40 minutes.

5. Following the illustrations on page 932, score the pastry with a knife as soon as it emerges from the oven. Use the edge of a spoon or spatula to press the edges of the crust squares down into the fruit without completely submerging them. Because the crust will soften quickly, serve the pandowdy warm.

VARIATION
Pear Pandowdy

It's important to use perfectly ripe pears in this recipe. Firm pears don't exude enough juice, and overly ripe pears will break down into mush when baked.

Follow the recipe for Apple Pandowdy, replacing the apples with 4 large ripe pears (2 pounds) and replacing the lemon zest with 1 teaspoon grated fresh ginger.

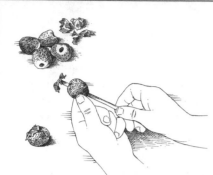

HULLING STRAWBERRIES

Early-season strawberries can have tough, white cores that are best removed. If you don't own a strawberry huller (and almost no one does), you can improvise with a plastic drinking straw. Push the straw through the bottom of the berry and up through the leafy stem end. The straw will remove the core as well as the leafy top.

JUICING LEMONS

Everyone seems to have a trick for juicing lemons. We find that this one extracts the most juice possible from lemons as well as limes.

1. Roll the lemon on a hard surface, pressing down firmly with the palm of your hand to break the membranes inside the fruit.

2. Cut the lemon in half. Use a wooden reamer (preferably one with sharp ridges and a pointed tip) to extract the juice into a bowl. To catch the seeds and pulp, place a mesh strainer over the bowl.

PEELING PEACHES

A vegetable peeler will mash the fruit on most peaches, especially ripe ones. Instead, we prefer to dip the peaches into a pot of simmering water to loosen their skins.

1. With a paring knife, score a small X at the base of each peach.

2. Lower the peaches into a pan of boiling water with a slotted spoon. Turn the peaches occasionally and simmer until their skins loosen, 30 seconds to 1 minute, depending on the ripeness of the peaches.

3. Transfer the peaches to a bowl of ice water. Let stand to stop the cooking process and cool, about 1 minute.

4. Starting from the scored X, peel each peach. Use a paring knife to lift the skin from the flesh and pull the skin off in strips.

PEELING RHUBARB

Rhubarb stalks, especially thick ones, can be covered with a stringy outside layer that should be removed before cooking. Make sure to cut away and discard any leaves, which are inedible.

1. Trim both ends of the stalk and then partially slice a thin disk from the bottom of the stalk, being careful not to cut all the way through. Gently pull the partially attached disk away from the stalk, pull back the outer peel, and discard.

2. Make a second cut partway through the bottom of the stalk in the reverse direction. Pull back the peel on the other side of the stalk and discard. The rhubarb is now ready to be sliced or chopped as needed.

PEELING KIWIS

A vegetable peeler can crush soft kiwi flesh if you attempt to remove the hairy skin with this tool. We like this method, which won't bruise the fruit.

1. Trim the ends of the fruit and insert a small spoon between the skin and the flesh, with the bowl of the spoon facing the flesh. Push the spoon down and carefully move it around the fruit, separating the flesh from the skin.

2. Gently remove the spoon and pull the loosened skin away from the flesh.

CORING APPLES

1. Remove the peel (we prefer a paring knife, but you may use a vegetable peeler), then quarter the apple through the stem end. The core can now be removed from each quarter. However, the direction you cut is very important. We find that when we start at the stem end, the quarters often break.

2. Instead, start removing the core at the blossom end. The cored quarter can now be sliced as needed.

CORING PEARS

Pears are best halved, from stem to blossom end, and then cored. We like to use a melon baller for this task.

1. Use a melon baller to cut around the central core with a circular motion.

2. Draw the melon baller from the central core to the top of the pear, removing the interior portion of the stem as you go.

3. Use the melon baller to remove the blossom end as well.

PITTING CHERRIES

Pitting sour cherries for pie is a tedious but essential task if you want to use fresh fruit. If you don't own a cherry pitter, you can use one of these 2 methods for removing the pits. Always work over a bowl to catch the flavorful juices.

A. Push the cherry firmly down against the pointed, jagged end of a small pastry bag tip. Take care not to cut your fingers on the points as they pierce the fruit.

B. Push a drinking straw through the bottom of the cherry, forcing the pit up and out through the stem end.

PEELING MANGOES

Because of their odd shape and slippery texture, mangoes are notoriously difficult to peel. Here's how we handle this task. This method ensures long, attractive strips of fruit.

1. Remove a thin slice from one end of the mango so that it sits flat on a work surface.

2. Hold the mango cut-side down and remove the skin with a sharp paring knife in thin strips, working from top to bottom.

3. Cut down along the side of the flat pit to remove the flesh from one side of the mango. Do the same on the other side of the pit.

4. Trim around the pit to remove any remaining flesh. The mango flesh can now be chopped or sliced as desired.

GERMAN APPLE PANCAKE

FOUND UNDER A VARIETY OF ALIASES, including Dutch pancake, Dutch baby, and puff pancake (to name just a few), a German apple pancake is a crisp, puffy baked pancake packed with apples. A few renowned pancake houses around the country have daily lines of hungry breakfast-goers snaking out the door waiting for this simple yet deeply satisfying breakfast treat. But, as we found out, apple pancakes worth waiting for are few and far between. The average pancake falls far short of what we consider ideal: a crisp, brittle top, a rich but neutral-flavored pancake, and well-caramelized apples.

German apple pancake batter is a simple affair, closer in composition and consistency to thin crêpe batter than to thicker conventional pancake batter. It should be a very loose mixture of eggs, milk or cream, flour, and a pinch of salt. The secret to the batter is balancing the amount of egg with the milk or cream. Many of the batters we tested yielded pancakes that were far too eggy. For a 10-inch pancake, tasters agreed that two eggs were just enough for structure and flavor. Three eggs made a dense, gummy pancake predominantly flavored with egg.

As for the dairy component, we tried milk, cream, and half-and-half. Milk alone made a loose, relatively flavorless pancake dominated by the eggs. Cream produced an over-the-top rich pancake that almost resembled a custard in texture. Half-and-half proved a great compromise between milk and cream. It gave the pancake body and depth without being too rich.

To round out the pancake's flavors, we added vanilla extract and a small amount of granulated sugar. The apples provide the sweetening for this pancake, but sugar in the batter wedded the flavors.

Unlike stovetop pancakes that are packed with chemical leaveners and buttermilk, oven-baked pancakes rely on heat and eggs for an explosive rise. While a very high heat—500 degrees—guaranteed a dramatic rise and golden crust, it failed to fully cook the pancake's interior. Leaving the pancake in the oven for more time at this high temperature caused the crust to burn, so to remedy the problem we tried starting the pancake at a high temperature and quickly reducing the heat to finish cooking. We discovered that if the oven temperature is brought too low, the pancake needs to bake too long and the exterior dries out by the time the interior is set. After several tests, we found it best to heat the oven to 500 degrees and then lower the temperature to 425 degrees when the pancake goes into the oven.

Much to our surprise, cooking the apples proved to be a bigger issue than assembling the batter. We wanted well-caramelized apples for the best flavor, but we also wanted the apples to retain a bit of bite for contrast with the soft and creamy pancake. We knew firm Granny Smith apples would be the best choice because they stand up well to cooking. These tart apples would also keep the dish from becoming too sweet.

We started with the simplest method—cooking the apples in some butter until they turned golden brown and their natural sugars caramelized. Our first few attempts at cooking the apples were frustrating. Over medium heat, the apples verged on chunky applesauce before they caramelized; over high heat, they scorched before the apples' sugars browned.

One of the test cooks then suggested an eccentric method—sautéing the apples in caramel, a common technique in Vietnamese cooking. In this manner, the caramel flavor is already developed, and the apples are cooked until the desired texture is reached. The technique worked beautifully, but making caramel prior to cooking the apples was time-consuming and a bit daunting for early-morning cooking.

Hoping to avoid making caramel, we tried adding sugar to the apples as they cooked over high heat in the hope that the sugar would caramelize as the apples cooked. It was close, but not quite there. The apples were slightly overcooked by the time the sugars had caramelized. When we switched to light brown sugar, the technique worked beautifully; the apple slices were uniformly golden and retained some body. This technique works well, but we found that it is crucial to cut the apples into even slices; otherwise, they cook unevenly and the smaller slices burn.

Straight from the oven, German apple pancake is quite dramatic and will certainly impress your breakfast companions. Get to the table fast, though—the pancake sinks within a couple of minutes. A dusting of confectioners' sugar and warm maple syrup are the classic accompaniments.

German Apple Pancake
SERVES 4

Tradition dictates that this supersized pancake should be cooked in a cast-iron skillet, but we found that an oven-safe nonstick skillet worked significantly better.

2	large eggs
³/₄	cup half-and-half
I	teaspoon vanilla extract
¹/₂	teaspoon salt
I	tablespoon granulated sugar
¹/₂	cup (2¹/₂ ounces) unbleached all-purpose flour
I	tablespoon unsalted butter
3	medium Granny Smith apples (about I¹/₄ pounds), peeled, cored, and cut into ¹/₄-inch slices
¹/₄	cup packed (I³/₄ ounces) light brown sugar
2	tablespoons confectioners' sugar Maple syrup, warmed, for serving

1. Adjust an oven rack to the middle position and heat the oven to 500 degrees. Combine the eggs, half-and-half, vanilla, salt, and granulated sugar in a food processor or a blender and process until well combined, about 15 seconds. Add the flour and process until thoroughly mixed and free of lumps, about 30 seconds; set the batter aside.

2. Add the butter to a 10-inch ovenproof nonstick skillet and heat over medium-high heat until the butter foams. Add the apples and sprinkle the brown sugar evenly over them. Cook, stirring occasionally, until the apples begin to turn light brown, about 5 minutes. Continue to cook over medium-high heat, stirring constantly, until the apples are golden brown, 4 to 5 minutes.

3. Remove the pan from the heat. Following illustration 1 below, quickly pour the batter around the edge of the pan, then over the apples; place the pan in the oven. Reduce the heat to 425 degrees and cook until browned and puffed, 16 to 17 minutes. With a heatproof spatula, loosen the edge of the pancake (see illustration 2). Invert the pancake onto a serving platter (see illustration 3), dust it with the confectioners' sugar, and serve immediately, accompanied by the warm maple syrup.

➤ VARIATION
German Apple Pancake with Caramel Sauce

For a rustic dessert or a truly hedonistic breakfast experience, make a batch of Caramel Sauce (page 985). You will have extra sauce, but it will keep well in the refrigerator for up to 2 weeks.

Follow the recipe for German Apple Pancake, replacing the maple syrup with Caramel Sauce (page 985).

PREPARING GERMAN APPLE PANCAKE

1. Pour the batter around the edge of the pan, then over the apples.

2. Loosen the edge of the pancake with a heatproof spatula.

3. Invert the pancake onto a large plate or serving platter.

QUICK APPLE STRUDEL

CLASSIC STRUDEL INVOLVES HOURS OF HANDS-on preparation, rolling and pulling the dough until it is so thin you can read a newspaper through it. Chucking the notion of homemade strudel dough, we started with a simpler option—store-bought phyllo dough—and set out to dramatically simplify this classic dessert while keeping the rich apple filling and as much of the crisp, flaky texture as possible.

A classic apple strudel contains apples, bread crumbs, sugar, cinnamon, raisins, and sometimes walnuts. Although this combination sounds appealing, the strudel recipes we tested initially were in a sad state: dry, bready fillings overpowered by the flavor of the spices and leathery, bland crusts that separated from the filling as soon as a fork came near.

We wanted the filling and pastry in our strudel to come together as a unified whole. The crust must be crisp and flaky yet still hold its shape. The filling should be moist but not wet, and the flavor of apple should shine through.

Our first strudels threatened to shatter to bits if we so much as looked at them askance. Butter is usually brushed between the layers of phyllo dough to help keep them crisp and flaky, so we thought that by eliminating the butter we might get a more cohesive crust. But the phyllo crust without butter was still crisp, only now it was also dry and unappealing. We tried adding a bit of milk to the butter, in the hope that the added moisture might help, but that strudel was simply soggy. Then a test cook recalled a method she used while working as a pastry chef. For crisp, cohesive Napoleon layers that retained a bit of chew, she

BEST PHYLLO DOUGH

We tried an expensive organic brand of phyllo, but Athens phyllo dough, which is widely available in supermarkets nationwide, yielded the crispiest crust.

WHY STRUDEL SHATTERS

We found that the phyllo on most strudels, including this one, curled and shattered as it cooled. Sprinkling sugar between the layers of phyllo "glues" them together in the oven and prevents this problem.

sprinkled sugar on each layer of phyllo with the butter. The melted sugar acted as glue between the layers and added flavor to an otherwise bland dough. The results weren't perfect, but we knew we were on the right track.

Working with phyllo requires constant attention. Left alone, the layers dry out and crack almost instantly. We were careful to keep damp towels over the unused phyllo while layering the sheets, but then we were sending our strudel into a hot oven for upward of 40 minutes, totally unprotected. With sugar between the layers, the strudel held its shape better, but as it cooled on the rack, the outer layers curled and flaked like a bad sunburn. We thought the long time in the oven might be drying out the phyllo, so we tried baking the strudel at very high heat—475 degrees—for just 15 minutes. This crust was perfect: toothsome yet slightly yielding, with a deeply caramelized exterior. And it could be cut into clean, solid slices. There was only one problem: The apples were still raw.

Up until this point, we had been using sliced Granny Smiths, figuring that a firm, tart apple would be best. The quick blast of heat was perfect for the phyllo, but the apples never had a chance to cook and soften. We tried slicing the apples thinner, about ⅛ inch. Still too firm. In the past, the test kitchen has found that a combination of apples works well in pies, so we applied the combination to strudel. Our half–McIntosh, half–Golden Delicious strudel was a success, the former adding body and apple flavor, the latter a toothsome texture.

Lemon juice replaced some of the tartness that had departed with the Granny Smiths. A scant ¼ teaspoon of cinnamon made the filling sweet and well rounded. After testing various combinations of brown and granulated sugar, we discovered that less was more—just ¼ cup of granulated sugar added a clean sweetness that tasters liked.

Almost every recipe we'd seen called for raisins of some kind, and tasters preferred milder golden raisins to dark ones. Added straight to the apples, the raisins were a bit dry and chewy, but we found that simmering the raisins in liquid plumped them up in no time. For the liquid, we tried Calvados (apple brandy), which added a great layer of sweet

apple flavor that everyone liked. Knowing that not many houses stock Calvados and that some cooks might not want to use alcohol, we looked for an alternative. Readily available apple cider proved to be the best substitute for Calvados.

Tasters were split on whether they liked chopped nuts in the filling. We decided to make the nuts optional. We knew the bread crumbs, a classic component of strudel, were there to absorb the juices from the apples and prevent a damp crust, but we weren't completely convinced they were necessary. We were wrong. Strudel made without bread crumbs was soggy and loose. But the ½ to ¾ cup of bread crumbs most recipes called for resulted in a strudel that stuck to the roof of the mouth. We settled on ¼ cup of fresh

ASSEMBLING STRUDEL

1. Place a large sheet of parchment or waxed paper on a large work surface, long side toward you. Place I sheet of phyllo on the parchment paper, brush liberally with melted butter, and sprinkle with I teaspoon sugar. Repeat with the remaining 4 sheets of phyllo.

2. Place the apple filling in a 3-inch strip about 2½ inches from the bottom of the phyllo, leaving about 2 inches on either short side.

3. Fold the short ends of the phyllo over the apples. Fold the end closest to you over the apples.

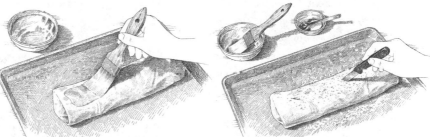

4. Loosely roll the strudel away from you, using the parchment paper as a guide. Don't roll too tight, as this can cause tearing during baking.

5. Place the finished strudel seam-side down on an ungreased baking sheet. Brush the strudel with the remaining butter and sprinkle with the remaining I teaspoon sugar.

6. Cut four I-inch vents in the top of the strudel for steam to escape.

939

bread crumbs, which gave us a strudel that was moist without being too wet. The flavor, however, was still bready. We browned the crumbs in butter, and tasters loved the results. The filling was now buttery and rich, moist but solid.

Quick Apple Strudel

SERVES 6 TO 8

The best ways to thaw phyllo dough are in the refrigerator overnight or at room temperature for 3 to 4 hours; it doesn't thaw well in the microwave. Make sure that the phyllo sheets you use for the strudel are not badly torn. If they have small cuts or tears in the same location (sometimes an entire package sustains cuts in the same spot), flip alternating layers when forming the strudel so that the cuts will not line up and create a weak spot that can cause the strudel to burst during baking. Serve the strudel warm with Whipped Cream (page 985).

¹/₂	cup golden raisins
2	tablespoons Calvados or apple cider
6	tablespoons (³/₄ stick) unsalted butter
¹/₄	cup fresh white bread crumbs
2	small Golden Delicious apples (about 10 ounces)
2	medium McIntosh apples (about 13 ounces)
¹/₄	cup (1³/₄ ounces) plus 2 tablespoons granulated sugar
¹/₃	cup finely chopped walnuts (optional), toasted in a small dry skillet over medium heat until lightly browned and fragrant, about 3 minutes
¹/₄	teaspoon ground cinnamon
¹/₈	teaspoon salt
1	teaspoon juice from 1 lemon
5	sheets phyllo, thawed (see note)
1¹/₂	teaspoons confectioners' sugar

1. Adjust an oven rack to the lower-middle position and heat the oven to 475 degrees. Heat the raisins and Calvados in a small saucepan over medium heat (or in the microwave, covered with plastic wrap) until simmering. Cover, remove from the heat, and let stand until needed.

2. Melt 1 tablespoon of the butter in a small skillet over medium heat; when the foaming subsides, stir in the bread crumbs and cook, stirring frequently, until golden brown, about 2 minutes. Transfer the bread crumbs to a small bowl and set aside.

3. Peel, quarter, and core the apples; cut each quarter lengthwise into slices ¹/₈ inch thick. Drain off and discard any remaining liquid from the raisins. Toss the apples, raisins, bread crumbs, ¹/₄ cup granulated sugar, the walnuts (if using), cinnamon, salt, and lemon juice in a large bowl to combine.

4. Melt the remaining 5 tablespoons butter. Place a large sheet of parchment paper horizontally on a work surface. Following the illustrations on page 939, fill and roll the strudel. Place the strudel seam-side down on an ungreased baking sheet; brush with the remaining butter and sprinkle with the remaining granulated sugar. Cut four 1-inch crosswise vents in the top of the strudel and bake until golden brown, about 15 minutes. Cool on the baking sheet on a wire rack until warm, about 40 minutes.

5. Sieve the confectioners' sugar over the strudel. Using 2 large metal spatulas, transfer the strudel to a platter or cutting board, cut into slices with a serrated knife, and serve with whipped cream, if desired.

BLUEBERRY COBBLER

NO MORE THAN A FLEET OF TENDER BISCUITS on a sea of sweet fruit, good cobblers hold their own against fancy fruit desserts. But unlike fancy fruit desserts, cobblers come together in a couple of quick steps and can be dished up hot, with a scoop of vanilla ice cream.

As simple (and appealing) as this sounds, why do so many of us end up with a filling that is sickeningly sweet and overspiced? Why is the filling so often runny, or, on the flip side, so thick and gloppy? Why are the biscuits, the most common choice of topping for cobblers, too dense, dry, and heavy?

We decided to begin by developing a recipe for the most popular cobbler of all—blueberry. Our goal was to create a filling in which the berries were allowed to cook until lightly thickened. We wanted their natural sweetness to come through without being overshadowed by the sugar and spice. The biscuit should stand tall with structure, be crisp on the outside and light and buttery on the inside, and complement the filling. Most important, it had to be easy.

The basic ingredients found in most cobbler fillings are fruit, sugar, thickener (flour, arrowroot, cornstarch, potato starch, or tapioca), and flavorings (lemon zest, spices, etc.). The fruit and sugar are easy: Take fresh blueberries and add enough sugar so that the fruit neither remains puckery nor turns saccharine. For 6 cups of berries, we found ½ cup sugar to be ideal—and far less than the conventional amount of sugar, which in some recipes exceeds 2 cups.

Some recipes swear by one thickener and warn that other choices will ruin the filling. We found this to be partly true. Tasters were all in agreement that flour—the most common choice in recipes—gave the fruit filling an unappealing starchy texture. Most tasters agreed that tapioca thickened the berry juices nicely, but the soft beads of starch left in the fruit's juices knocked out this contender. Arrowroot worked beautifully, but this starch can sometimes be difficult to find. Cornstarch and potato starch, the winners, proved to be interchangeable. They both thickened the juices without altering the blueberry flavor or leaving any visible traces of starch behind.

Lemon juice as well as grated lemon zest brightened the fruit flavor, and as for spices, everyone preferred cinnamon. Other flavors simply got in the way.

For the topping, our guiding principle was ease of preparation. A biscuit topping is the way to go, and we had our choice of two types: dropped and rolled. Most rolled biscuit recipes call for cold butter cut into dry ingredients with a pastry blender, two knives, or sometimes a food processor, after which the dough is rolled and cut. The dropped biscuits looked more promising (translation: easier)—mix the dry ingredients, mix the wet ingredients, mix the two together, and drop (over fruit). Sounded good to us!

To be sure that our tasters agreed, we made two cobblers, one with rolled and one with dropped biscuits. The dropped biscuits, light and rustic in appearance, received the positive comments we were looking for but needed some work. To start, we had to fine-tune the ingredients, which included flour, sugar, leavener, dairy, eggs, shortening, and flavorings. We immediately eliminated eggs from the list because they made the biscuits a tad heavy. As for dairy, heavy cream was too rich, whereas milk and half-and-half lacked depth of flavor. We finally tested buttermilk, which delivered a much-needed flavor boost as well as a lighter, fluffier texture. As for the choice of fat, butter was in and Crisco was out—butter tasted much better.

We soon discovered that the big problem with drop biscuits is getting them to cook through. (The batter is wetter than rolled biscuit dough and therefore has a propensity for remaining doughy.) No matter how long we left the biscuits on the berry topping in a 400-degree oven, they never baked through, turning browner and browner on top while remaining doughy on the bottom. We realized that what the biscuits needed might be a blast of heat from below—that is, from the berries. We tried baking the berries alone in a moderate 375-degree oven for 25 minutes and then dropping and baking the biscuit dough on top. Bingo! The heat from the bubbling berries helped to cook the biscuits from underneath, while the dry heat of the oven cooked them from above.

There was one final detail to perfect. We wanted the biscuits to be more crisp on the outside and to have a deeper hue. This was easily achieved by bumping the oven to 425 degrees when we added the biscuits. A sprinkling of cinnamon sugar on the dropped biscuit dough added just a bit more crunch.

Blueberry Cobbler
SERVES 6 TO 8

While the blueberries are baking, prepare the ingredients for the topping, but do not stir the wet ingredients into the dry ingredients until just before the berries come out of the oven. A standard or deep-dish 9-inch pie pan works well; an 8-inch square baking dish can also be used. Vanilla ice cream or lightly sweetened whipped cream is the perfect accompaniment. To reheat leftovers, put the cobbler in a 350-degree oven for 10 to 15 minutes, until heated through.

FILLING

½	cup (3½ ounces) sugar
1	tablespoon cornstarch
	Pinch ground cinnamon
	Pinch salt
6	cups (30 ounces) fresh blueberries, rinsed and picked over
1½	teaspoons grated zest and 1 tablespoon juice from 1 lemon

BISCUIT TOPPING

1	cup (5 ounces) unbleached all-purpose flour
2	tablespoons stone-ground cornmeal
¼	cup (1¾ ounces) plus 2 teaspoons sugar
2	teaspoons baking powder
¼	teaspoon baking soda
¼	teaspoon salt
4	tablespoons (½ stick) unsalted butter, melted
⅓	cup buttermilk
½	teaspoon vanilla extract
⅛	teaspoon ground cinnamon

1. Adjust an oven rack to the lower-middle position and heat the oven to 375 degrees.

2. FOR THE FILLING: Stir the sugar, cornstarch, cinnamon, and salt together in a large bowl. Add the berries and mix gently with a rubber spatula until evenly coated; add the lemon zest and juice and mix to combine. Transfer the berry mixture to a 9-inch glass pie plate, place the pie plate on a rimmed baking sheet, and bake until the filling is hot and bubbling around the edges, about 25 minutes.

3. FOR THE BISCUIT TOPPING: Meanwhile, whisk the flour, cornmeal, ¼ cup sugar, baking powder, baking soda, and salt in a large bowl to combine. Whisk the melted butter, buttermilk, and vanilla together in a small bowl. Mix the remaining 2 teaspoons sugar with the cinnamon in a second small bowl and set aside. One minute before the berries come out of the oven, add the wet ingredients to the dry ingredients; stir with a rubber spatula until just combined and no dry pockets remain.

4. TO ASSEMBLE AND BAKE THE COBBLER: Remove the berries from the oven; increase the oven temperature to 425 degrees. Pinch off 8 equal pieces of biscuit dough and place them on the hot berry filling, spacing them at least ½ inch apart (they should not touch). Sprinkle each mound of dough with cinnamon sugar. Bake until the filling is bubbling and the biscuits are golden brown on top and cooked through, 15 to 18 minutes. Cool the cobbler on a wire rack 20 minutes and serve.

➤ VARIATIONS

Blueberry Cobbler with Gingered Biscuits

Follow the recipe for Blueberry Cobbler, adding 3 tablespoons minced crystallized ginger to the flour mixture and substituting an equal amount of ground ginger for the cinnamon mixed with the sugar for sprinkling on the biscuits.

All-Season Blueberry Cobbler (with Frozen Blueberries)

Thawed berries shed a lot of flavorful liquid that must be reduced to a syrup on the stovetop before baking.

Thaw 36 ounces (about 6 cups) frozen blueberries (preferably wild) in a colander set over a bowl to catch the juices. Transfer the juices (you should have about 1 cup) to a small saucepan; simmer over medium heat until syrupy and thick enough to coat the back of a spoon, about 10 minutes. Follow the recipe for Blueberry Cobbler, mixing the syrup with the berries and other filling ingredients, increasing the baking time for the berry mixture to 30 minutes, and increasing the biscuit baking time to 20 to 22 minutes.

SOUR CHERRY COBBLER

HAVING TACKLED THE MYSTERIES BEHIND GREAT Blueberry Cobbler (page 941), the test kitchen was ready for something a little more challenging and so turned to cherry cobbler. Sour cherries have sufficient acidity to cook up well and become truly expressive with a touch of sugar and some heat. (Sweet eating cherries, like Bings, lose their flavor when cooked.) We suspected sour cherries would feel at home in a cobbler—if we could find good ones. We also wanted this cobbler to be large enough to serve a crowd—about 12—a dessert perfect for an outdoor barbecue on the Fourth of July or as part of a buffet during the winter holidays.

Until we saw them at the farmers' market, the only sour, or baking, cherries we had known of were the canned variety. Though sour cherries are grown in relatively large quantities in Michigan, here in the Northeast our grocery shelves are bereft of sour cherry products, save the crayon-red canned gravy with lumps called "pie filling." So we were grateful to find two different kinds of jarred sour cherries at our local Trader Joe's during the off-season (all 11 months of it). In addition, the Cherry Marketing Institute of Michigan provided us with variously processed sour cherries—frozen, canned, and dried. Since it would be months before we could try making cobbler with fresh cherries, we began our tests with processed ones.

Early tests in which we prepared quick fruit fillings elicited unenthusiastic comments from tasters. While frozen Michigan sour cherries maintained their color well, their flavor was left largely to the imagination. Both canned and jarred sour cherries from Michigan were flaccid and developed an anemic pallor when cooked. Only Trader Joe's jarred Morello cherries drew a crowd. Deep ruby red, plump, meaty, and tart, they delivered bracing flavor and a great texture right out of the jar.

This experience prompted us to do a little research. Sour cherries, we learned, are classified in two groups, amarelles and griottes. The former have lighter flesh that's tan on the inside and clear juice; the latter are dark, even black, with deep red juice. The best known examples of each group are Montmorency (an amarelle) and Morello (a griotte). Most sour cherries grown in the United States are Montmorency. Those from eastern Europe are Morello. With a couple of us remembering the stellar cherries we had tasted in baked goods in Germany, we decided to base our recipe on jarred Morellos.

A cobbler should be juicy but not swimming in juice, and it should taste like the fruit whose name it bears. Jarred and canned cherries come awash in

juice, which we used to produce the sauce. Since jarred and canned cherries have already been processed, they are already cooked, so the less heat they're exposed to thereafter, the better. Straining off the juice, we dumped the drained contents of four 24-ounce jars of Morellos into a 13 by 9-inch baking dish, then thickened and sweetened 3 cups of the juice. The resulting flavor was a bit flat. We replaced 1 cup of the cherry juice with red wine and added a cinnamon stick, a pinch of salt, and a whiff of almond extract. Much better. Red wine and sour cherries have a natural affinity; the cinnamon stick added a fragrant woody depth; and, as with all fruits, salt performed its usual minor miracle. The almond extract brought the entire flavor experience up a couple of notches. For thickener, we resolved to go with cornstarch. It could be mixed in with the sugar and brought directly to a simmer with the reserved cherry juice, then poured over the waiting cherries and baked. Lightly thickened fruit is best; a cobbler shouldn't be thick enough to spread on toast.

For the topping, we wanted our biscuits to be light and feathery but able to withstand the juices of our cherry filling. We started with a biscuit similar to our blueberry cobbler topping but needed to make adjustments to allow for not only a different filling but a larger amount as well. Following the method employed in our blueberry cobbler—dropping the biscuit topping on hot, partially baked fruit and increasing the oven temperature—did not quite do the trick. Having the undersides of the topping touching the fruit resulted in biscuits with pale bellies, so we undertook to bake the biscuits for 15 minutes on a baking sheet while the filling was coming together on the stove. We then wedded them to the fruit for only 10 minutes in the oven. By then the fruit (already hot from the cooked sauce) was bubbling around the biscuits, which were deeply browned on top and baked through underneath. Heaven in about a half hour.

Jarred Morellos made a fine cobbler, but we wanted more and, finally, summer came. We used both Morellos and Montmorency cherries. Both varieties of fresh cherries yielded cobblers with plump, gorgeous, deeply flavorful fruit. The Montmorency cherries were candy-apple red and had a flavor resonant with almond accents; the fresh Morellos were transcendent, with a smooth richness and complex flavor notes. If you can get your hands on fresh sour cherries during their brief season in July, buy them—quickly—and start baking.

Sour Cherry Cobbler

SERVES 12

Use the smaller amount of sugar in the filling if you prefer your fruit desserts on the tart side and the larger amount if you like them sweet.

BISCUIT TOPPING

2	cups (10 ounces) unbleached all-purpose flour
6	tablespoons (2 1/2 ounces) sugar, plus 2 tablespoons for sprinkling
1/2	teaspoon baking powder
1/2	teaspoon baking soda
1/2	teaspoon salt
6	tablespoons (3/4 stick) cold unsalted butter, cut into 1/2-inch cubes
1	cup buttermilk

FILLING

4	(24-ounce) jars Morello cherries, drained (about 8 cups), 2 cups juice reserved
3/4–1	cup (5 1/4 to 7 ounces) sugar
3	tablespoons plus 1 teaspoon cornstarch
	Pinch salt
1	cup dry red wine
1	(3-inch) cinnamon stick
1/4	teaspoon almond extract

1. FOR THE BISCUIT TOPPING: Adjust an oven rack to the middle position and heat the oven to 425 degrees. Line a baking sheet with parchment paper.

2. In a food processor, pulse the flour, 6 tablespoons sugar, baking powder, baking soda, and salt to combine. Scatter the butter pieces over the mixture and process until the mixture resembles coarse meal, about fifteen 1-second pulses. Transfer to a medium bowl; add the buttermilk and toss with a rubber spatula to combine. Using a 1½- to

1¾-inch spring-loaded ice cream scoop, scoop 12 biscuits onto the baking sheet, spacing them 1½ to 2 inches apart. Sprinkle the biscuits evenly with the remaining 2 tablespoons sugar and bake until lightly browned on the tops and bottoms, about 15 minutes. (Do not turn off the oven.)

3. FOR THE FILLING: Meanwhile, spread the drained cherries in an even layer in a 13 by 9-inch glass baking dish. Stir the sugar, cornstarch, and salt together in a medium nonreactive saucepan. Whisk in the reserved cherry juice and the wine and add the cinnamon stick; set the saucepan over medium-high heat and cook, whisking frequently, until the mixture simmers and thickens, about 5 minutes. Discard the cinnamon stick, stir in the almond extract, and pour the hot liquid over the cherries in the baking dish.

4. TO ASSEMBLE AND BAKE THE COBBLER: Arrange the hot biscuits in 3 rows of 4 over the warm filling. Bake the cobbler until the filling is bubbling and the biscuits are deep golden brown, about 10 minutes. Cool on a wire rack 10 minutes; serve warm.

➤ VARIATION

Fresh Sour Cherry Cobbler

Morello or Montmorency cherries can be used in this cobbler. Do not use sweet Bing cherries. If the cherries do not release enough juice after macerating for 30 minutes, use cranberry juice to make up the difference. A cherry pitter is almost essential for this recipe, although you can try one of the improvised methods on page 935; they will get the job done but at a slow pace, especially with so many cherries to pit.

FILLING

1 1/4	cups (8 3/4 ounces) sugar
3	tablespoons plus 1 teaspoon cornstarch
	Pinch salt
4	pounds fresh sour cherries, pitted (about 8 cups), juices reserved
1	cup dry red wine
	Cranberry juice (if needed)
1	(3-inch) cinnamon stick
1/4	teaspoon almond extract
1	recipe Biscuit Topping (at left)

1. FOR THE FILLING: Stir together the sugar, cornstarch, and salt in a large bowl; add the cherries and toss well to combine. Pour the wine over the cherries; let stand 30 minutes. Drain the cherries in a colander set over a medium bowl. Combine the drained and reserved juices (from pitting the cherries); you should have 3 cups. If not, add enough cranberry juice to equal 3 cups.

2. FOR THE BISCUIT TOPPING: While the cherries macerate, prepare and bake the biscuit topping.

3. TO ASSEMBLE AND BAKE THE COBBLER: Spread the drained cherries in an even layer in a 13 by 9-inch glass baking dish. Bring the juices and cinnamon stick to a simmer in a medium nonreactive saucepan over medium-high heat, whisking frequently, until the mixture thickens, about 5 minutes. Discard the cinnamon stick, stir in the almond extract, and pour the hot juices over the cherries in the baking dish.

4. Arrange the hot biscuits in 3 rows of 4 over the warm filling. Bake the cobbler until the filling is bubbling and the biscuits are deep golden brown, about 10 minutes. Cool on a wire rack 10 minutes; serve warm.

PEACH COBBLER

THE REASON MOST COOKS HAVE NOT MADE peach cobbler recently is simple: The promise is better than the reality. For starters, peaches are unpredictable. Some turn mushy if cooked a bit too long, while others exude an ocean of overly sweet juices. The topping is also problematic, ranging from tough, dry biscuits to raw, cakey lumps of dough. In worst-case recipes, it is both hard and crusty on top and soggy on the bottom. So what's a home cook to do?

Our initial tests told us two things: The peaches should be peeled to avoid any unpleasantly leathery bits of skin, and they should be cut in relatively large pieces to avoid development of a peach mush during baking. Another way to avoid the mush, we learned, was to choose ripe yet firm peaches, which better withstood the rigors of baking. (Save those soft, super-ripe peaches for eating out of hand.) What proved to be the most perplexing

problem was the wide variation in juiciness from peach to peach, which sometimes resulted in a baking dish overflowing with liquid.

In our first attempt to solve this problem, we tried par-cooking the peaches by means of roasting or sautéing, thus removing excess juices. But this was a dead end, as we discovered that most of the juices are not released until the peaches are almost fully cooked—something that necessarily happens after the peaches have been joined with the cobbler topping. Next we thought to draw on a technique used to make another American dessert classic, strawberry shortcake, in which the fruit is macerated in sugar to draw out its juices. Sugar did indeed draw off some of the moisture from the peaches, but then we realized that we would need to replenish the cobbler with some of the liquid that had been drained away. Starting with 1 tablespoon, we began to add back some of the juice we'd just poured off. In the end, ¼ cup of the drawn juice had to be added back to guarantee a juicy cobbler that would have the same amount of liquid every time.

Because tasters greeted overly sweet cobbler fillings with comments such as "tastes like it came from a can," we settled on a scant ¼ cup of sugar, just enough to do the job without making the filling syrupy. To thicken the peach juices, we tried cornstarch, pulverized tapioca, flour, and

ANATOMY OF A PEACH

A NUMBER OF COBBLER RECIPES CALL FOR removing the dark red flesh that surrounds the pit of the peach. Wondering what impact this would have on a cobbler, we made two versions, one with the red part of the peach flesh removed, the other with it intact. While the latter had an appealing reddish blush, we were surprised to find that it also had a bitter taste. The cobbler made with cleaned peaches tasted better. So if you see red once the peaches have been pitted (not all peaches will have this), take a few extra seconds to scoop it out and discard it.

arrowroot. Each starch thickened the juices admirably, but the high price and limited availability of arrowroot disqualified it. Tapioca, too, was out of the running because of its propensity to leave behind hardened starch granules (tapioca works better in a double-crust pie, where the pastry traps juices and helps to steam the granules until they dissolve). Flour, meanwhile, gave the filling a pasty quality. Cornstarch it was, then. A mere teaspoon was the perfect amount, giving the filling body without overwhelming the delicate texture of the peaches. Wondering if the fruit would benefit from the addition of other flavors, we conducted a battery of tests, using ingredients such as lemon juice, almond extract, Triple Sec, ginger, and cardamom. Lemon juice was the only keeper, as it helped to brighten the peach flavor; the other additions were only distractions.

There were many choices for the topping other than biscuit dough, but none of them were as appealing. The next step was to select the style of biscuit topping: rolled or dropped. Rolled biscuits had a nice light texture, but we wondered if there was an easier way. Drop biscuits (a wet dough is dropped by spoonfuls onto the fruit) were certainly easier to prepare than rolled biscuits, and they had an attractive rustic and craggy appearance. Tasters found drop biscuits too dense, however. The compromise was a biscuit recipe in which the butter is cut into the flour (as it is with rolled biscuits) but which also contains a little more dairy, making the dough more moist. Now we could avoid the rolling and cutting but still achieve the light texture of a traditional biscuit.

In testing the "fat" component of the biscuit, we tried vegetable shortening and cream cheese, but tasters quickly discarded these in favor of butter, which not only improved the flavor of the biscuits but also aided in browning. For dairy, we tested the usual suspects—heavy cream, half-and-half, milk, and buttermilk—and received mixed results. Tasters liked the tang of the buttermilk biscuits but the cakier, more substantial crumb produced by richer dairy products (the cream and the half-and-half). The simple solution was to use whole-milk yogurt. These biscuits had plenty of tangy flavor and a texture that resembled that of the biscuits made with half-and-half.

Moving on to the leavener, we found that a combination of baking powder and soda was best. An egg, tasters decided, made the biscuits too heavy, but they did like biscuits with a bit of sugar, which both added flavor and helped to crisp the exterior. We tried spices such as cinnamon, nutmeg, and ginger as well as lemon zest but decided that the biscuits ought to be a quiet backup for the show-stealing peaches. (Lemon zest did work nicely with our cornmeal biscuit variation, however.)

Up until this point, we had been placing the fairly moist biscuit dough on top of the raw peaches and then baking the cobbler at 425 degrees—a technique that was producing gluey biscuits that were slightly raw in the center. Investigating a technique similar to one employed in our Sour Cherry Cobbler (page 944), we tried partially baking the peaches before adding the topping, hoping that the hot fruit would jump-start the cooking process. It did. The biscuits were much better, and the fruit was no longer overcooked. Finally, to further enhance the biscuits' crispness, we sprinkled the tops with sugar before they went into the oven.

Fresh Peach Cobbler
SERVES 6

If your peaches are firm, you should be able to peel them with a sharp vegetable peeler. If they are too soft and ripe to withstand the pressure of a peeler, you'll need to blanch and shock them before peeling. In the biscuit topping, low-fat or nonfat plain yogurt can be used in place of whole-milk yogurt, but the biscuits will be a little less rich. If you live in an arid climate, the biscuit dough may require up to an additional tablespoon of yogurt for it to form a cohesive dough. Do not prepare the biscuit dough any sooner than the recipe indicates; if the unbaked dough is left to stand too long, the leavener will expire and the biscuits will not rise properly in the oven. This recipe can be doubled to serve a crowd. Use a 13 by 9-inch baking dish and increase the baking times in steps 2 and 4 by about 5 minutes. Serve the warm cobbler with vanilla ice cream or whipped cream. Leftover cobbler can be reheated in a 350-degree oven until warmed through.

FILLING

2½ pounds ripe but firm peaches (6 to 7 medium)
¼ cup (1¾ ounces) sugar
1 teaspoon cornstarch
1 tablespoon juice from 1 lemon
Pinch salt

BISCUIT TOPPING

1 cup (5 ounces) unbleached all-purpose flour
3 tablespoons plus 1 teaspoon sugar
¾ teaspoon baking powder
¼ teaspoon baking soda
¼ teaspoon salt
5 tablespoons cold unsalted butter, cut into ¼-inch cubes
⅓ cup plain whole-milk yogurt

1. Adjust an oven rack to the lower-middle position and heat the oven to 425 degrees.

2. FOR THE FILLING: Peel the peaches (see note), then halve and pit each. Using a melon baller or small spoon, scoop out and discard the dark flesh from the pit area (see "Anatomy of a Peach" on page 945). Cut each half into 4 wedges. Gently toss the peaches and sugar together in a large bowl; let stand for 30 minutes, tossing several times. Drain the peaches in a colander set over a large bowl. Whisk ¼ cup of the drained juice (discard the remaining juice), the cornstarch, lemon juice, and salt together in a small bowl. Toss the peach juice mixture with the peach slices and transfer to an 8-inch square glass baking dish. Bake until the peaches begin to bubble around the edges, about 10 minutes.

3. FOR THE BISCUIT TOPPING: While the peaches are baking, in a food processor pulse the flour, 3 tablespoons sugar, baking powder, baking soda, and salt to combine. Scatter the butter over the dry ingredients and pulse until the mixture resembles coarse meal, about ten 1-second pulses. Transfer to a medium bowl; add the yogurt and toss with a rubber spatula until a cohesive dough is formed. (Don't overmix the dough, or the biscuits will be tough.) Break the dough into 6 evenly sized but roughly shaped mounds and set aside.

4. TO ASSEMBLE AND BAKE THE COBBLER: After the peaches have baked 10 minutes, remove them from the oven and place the dough mounds on top, spacing them at least ½ inch apart (they should not touch). Sprinkle each mound with a portion of the remaining 1 teaspoon sugar. Bake until the topping is golden brown and the fruit is bubbling, 16 to 18 minutes. Cool the cobbler on a wire rack until warm, about 20 minutes; serve.

➤ VARIATION

Blueberry-Peach Cobbler with Lemon-Cornmeal Biscuit Topping

Follow the recipe for Fresh Peach Cobbler, using 2 pounds peaches and tossing 1 cup (about 5 ounces) blueberries, rinsed and picked over, into the peach juice–cornstarch mixture along with the peaches in step 2. For the biscuit topping, substitute 2 tablespoons stone-ground cornmeal for an equal amount of the flour and add ½ teaspoon grated lemon zest to the food processor along with the dry ingredients in step 3.

SUMMER BERRY GRATIN

QUICKER THAN A CRISP AND DRESSIER THAN a shortcake, a gratin is a layer of fresh fruit piled into a shallow baking dish, gussied up with crumbs, and run under the broiler. The topping browns, and the fruit is warmed just enough to juice a bit.

We wanted to travel the simplest route to this summer dessert. Even though gratins can be made with all types of summer fruit, we confined our subject matter to berries (easy; no slicing), the topping to crumbs (easy; no mixing), and the ingredients to a minimum (five, to be precise).

We discovered straight off that a dish of this simplicity requires much attention. The berries, in whatever combination, had to be perfect: ripe, dry, unbruised, and clean. And, what's more, to cook correctly and to look and taste good, the berries needed to be of relatively similar size.

Strawberries, raspberries, and blueberries were superb when used alone; they were also compatible in combination. Smallish strawberries, halved lengthwise, complemented the other berry shapes. Blackberries tasted best when paired with raspberries or blueberries. (For anyone lucky enough to have

947

access to fresh currants, they would doubtless be wonderful with any of the other berries.) Four cups of berries, whatever the selection, fit nicely into a 9-inch glass or porcelain pie plate.

Then there were the crumbs. Cake and muffin crumbs—even stale ones—collapsed into the filling and disappeared. French chef Jacques Pépin uses dry croissant crumbs in his raspberry gratin. Translate croissant into American English and you come up with, well, white bread. So we tried both dried and fresh bread crumbs and dried and fresh croutons.

The dried bread crumbs were granular and texturally at odds with the soft flesh of the berries. Croutons, too, were somewhat standoffish. Weary of this unproductive fussing, we took three pieces of soft white bread and tossed them into the food processor with a couple tablespoons of sugar and a little chunk of soft butter. The resulting fluffy crumbs embraced the berries like a fresh snowfall. Once broiled, the surface of the crumbs became lightly crunchy and the undercoat soft enough to absorb the berries' juices. We modified this combination only slightly by switching from white sugar to light brown and by adding a pinch of ground cinnamon—both for a small flavor bonus.

The berries themselves needed just a bit of sweetness to brighten them and coax forth their juices. A modest tablespoon of granulated sugar brought out the best in them. Many of the tasters also liked a tablespoon of kirsch (a clear cherry brandy) or another eau de vie tossed with the berries and sugar. Taken together on a spoon, the flavors of the gratin were soft but deeply pleasing. The clear berry tastes shone forth against the light, buttery crumbs, and the berries and crust formed a nice textural counterpoint.

Broiling the gratin, as we had been doing, required more vigilance than we deemed desirable, and often the crust browned unevenly. We thought perhaps a moderately high oven heat lasting a bit longer might melt the berries slightly and brown the crust more evenly while also needing less monitoring. This proved to be true: a 400-degree oven and 15 to 20 minutes gave us a chance to put the coffee on and whip a bit of cream or soften vanilla ice cream before the dome of the crust grew deep golden and the berries warm and fragrant.

Summer Berry Gratin
SERVES 4 TO 6

Though a mixture of berries offers a wonderful combination of color, flavor, and texture, it's also fine to use just one or two types of berries. A half pint of fresh berries equals about 1 cup of fruit. Later in the season, peeled ripe peach or nectarine slices can be used in combination with blueberries or raspberries. We recommend using only fresh fruit, but if you must use frozen, raspberries are the best option. Do not thaw them before baking. Avoid using a metal pie pan, which may react with the acidity of the fruit and impart a metallic flavor. Serve the fruit gratin with lightly sweetened whipped cream or vanilla ice cream.

FRUIT MIXTURE
4 1/2 cups (about 22 ounces) mixed raspberries, blueberries, blackberries, and strawberries (hulled and left whole if small, halved lengthwise if medium, quartered lengthwise if large)
1 tablespoon granulated sugar
1 tablespoon kirsch or other eau de vie (optional)
   Pinch salt

TOPPING
3 slices sandwich bread, each slice torn into quarters
2 tablespoons unsalted butter, softened
1/4 cup packed (1 3/4 ounces) light or dark brown sugar
   Pinch ground cinnamon

1. FOR THE FRUIT MIXTURE: Adjust an oven rack to the lower-middle position and heat the oven to 400 degrees. Toss the fruit gently with the sugar, kirsch (if using), and salt in a medium nonreactive bowl and transfer to a 9-inch glass or ceramic pie plate.

2. FOR THE TOPPING: Pulse the bread, butter, brown sugar, and cinnamon in a food processor until the mixture resembles coarse crumbs, about ten 1-second pulses. Sprinkle the crumbs evenly over the fruit and bake until the crumbs are deep golden brown and the fruit is hot, 15 to 20 minutes. Cool on a wire rack 5 minutes and serve.

STRAWBERRY SHORTCAKE

SHORTCAKES MAY SEEM SIMILAR TO CRISPS and cobblers, but there is one important difference—the fruit is not cooked. For a true shortcake, sweetened fruit, usually strawberries, is spread between a split biscuit. A dollop or two of whipped cream is also added. The contrast of the cool fruit, warm and crisp biscuit halves, and chilled whipped cream places this dessert in a category by itself.

Because the fruit is not cooked, frozen fruit is not an option. The fruit must be ripe as well. We don't like quartered or sliced strawberries in shortcakes—they often slide off the split biscuit—but we don't like the look of a crushed fruit shortcake either. So we found a happy compromise by slicing most of the strawberries and then crushing the remaining portion of the berry mixture to unify the sliced fruit. The thick puree anchors the remaining whole or sliced fruit so that it won't slip off the split biscuit.

Our testing for this recipe revolved mostly around the biscuit. Strawberry shortcake requires something different from the biscuit topping used in our blueberry or cherry cobbler recipe. There, the fruit is so juicy and sweet that a light, tender biscuit works best. Shortcake, on the other hand, must be substantial enough to withstand splitting and layering with juicy fruit and whipped cream. It should be more dense and cakey. We assumed that a richer biscuit—that is, one made with eggs—would work best.

To make sure, we tried four very different sweetened biscuits: a baking powder version with fat cut into flour, baking powder, salt, and sugar and then moistened with milk; buttermilk biscuits, with buttermilk in place of milk and baking soda substituted for part of the baking powder; cream biscuits, with heavy cream standing in for the milk and some of the fat; and egg-enriched cream biscuits, with an egg and half-and-half replacing the milk. After sampling each, we felt that the egg-enriched biscuits had the advantage. The baking powder and buttermilk biscuits weren't rich enough. The cream biscuits were good-looking but gummy inside. The egg and half-and-half biscuits were finer-textured and more cake-like.

With our general direction settled, we began to test individual ingredients. Because biscuits should be tender, we assumed that low-protein cake flour would deliver the best results. Defying our predictions, the cake flour biscuit came in last, with a meltingly tender yet powdery and dry texture that was too much like shortbread. There was not enough gluten in this flour to support all the fat. Shortcakes made with all-purpose flour were tender, moist, and cakey. They were our clear favorites, besting a combination of cake and all-purpose flour as well as the plain cake flour.

We then experimented with liquids, figuring that the egg might be crucial but maybe not the half-and-half, which had won in our initial test. Buttermilk made the biscuits too savory, while heavy cream made them squat and dense. Milk was fine, but the richer flavor of half-and-half makes it our first choice.

The food processor is foolproof and is our preferred method for mixing biscuits. For cooks without a food processor, we suggest freezing the butter and then using a box grater to shave the butter into bits before cutting it into the flour.

When testing dough shaping, we made an interesting discovery. Although hand-formed biscuits look attractive and rustic, we found they were fairly easy to overwork, since warm hands can cause the dough's surface butter to melt. Using a biscuit cutter requires less handling, and dough rounds cut this way develop a natural crack around the

MASHING STRAWBERRIES FOR SHORTCAKE

For best flavor and appearance, crush one third of the berries for the filling with a potato masher. This thick puree will anchor the remaining whole or sliced berries so that they don't slip off the split biscuit.

circumference during baking, making them easy to split by hand. We also realized we didn't need a rolling pin. Patting the dough to a thickness of ¾ inch on a floured work surface was fast and simple.

Strawberry Shortcake

SERVES 6

Start the recipe by preparing the fruit, then set the fruit aside while preparing the biscuits to allow the juices to become syrupy. After cutting 6 perfect rounds of dough, we found that the scraps could be pulled together, kneaded, and cut to get 1 or 2 more rounds. These shortcakes will be a little tougher and less attractive than those from the first cutting.

FRUIT

8	cups (about 2½ pounds) strawberries, hulled
6	tablespoons (2½ ounces) sugar

SHORTCAKES

2	cups (10 ounces) unbleached all-purpose flour, plus more for dusting the work surface and biscuit cutter
5	tablespoons (about 2¼ ounces) sugar
1	tablespoon baking powder
½	teaspoon salt
8	tablespoons (1 stick) cold unsalted butter, cut into ½-inch cubes
1	large egg, lightly beaten
½	cup plus 1 tablespoon half-and-half or whole milk
1	large egg white, lightly beaten
2	cups Whipped Cream (page 985)

1. FOR THE FRUIT: Place 3 cups of the hulled strawberries in a large bowl and crush with a potato masher (see the illustration on page 949). Slice the remaining 5 cups berries and stir into the crushed berries along with the sugar. Set the fruit aside to macerate for at least 30 minutes or up to 2 hours.

2. FOR THE SHORTCAKES: Adjust an oven rack to the lower-middle position and heat the oven to 425 degrees. In a food processor, pulse the flour,

3 tablespoons of the sugar, the baking powder, and salt to combine. Scatter the butter pieces over and process until the mixture resembles coarse meal, about fifteen 1-second pulses. Transfer to a medium bowl.

3. Mix the beaten egg with the half-and-half in a measuring cup. Pour the egg mixture into the bowl with the flour mixture. Combine with a rubber spatula until large clumps form. Turn the mixture onto a floured work surface and lightly knead until it comes together.

4. Use your fingertips to pat the dough into a 9 by 6-inch rectangle about ¾ inch thick, being careful not to overwork the dough. Flour a 2¾-inch biscuit cutter and cut out 6 dough rounds. Place the rounds 1 inch apart on a small baking sheet, brush the tops with the beaten egg white, and sprinkle with the remaining 2 tablespoons sugar. (Dough rounds can be covered and refrigerated for up to 2 hours before baking.)

5. Bake until the shortcakes are golden brown, 12 to 14 minutes. Place the baking sheet on a wire rack and cool the cakes until warm, about 10 minutes.

6. TO ASSEMBLE: When the shortcakes have cooled slightly, split them in half (see the illustration below). Place each cake bottom on an individual serving plate. Spoon a portion of the fruit and then a dollop of the whipped cream over each cake bottom. Cap with the cake top and serve immediately.

SPLITTING SHORTCAKES

When the shortcakes have cooled, look for a natural crack around the circumference of each cake. Gently insert your fingers into the crack and split the shortcake in half.

22

PUDDINGS, CUSTARDS, SOUFFLÉS, AND ICE CREAM

PUDDINGS, CUSTARDS, SOUFFLÉS, AND ICE cream have several things in common. First, they are eaten with a spoon. Second, their texture is smooth and creamy. Third, and perhaps most important, eggs provide the structure and texture in most of these desserts. It is the way in which the eggs are handled that makes the difference between a creamy pudding or smooth ice cream and one that is lumpy or grainy. Most puddings are made with eggs, sugar, and some sort of dairy—milk, half-and-half, and/or cream. They are basically chilled custards. Ice cream starts with the same ingredients, but the custard is frozen, with air beaten in by the churning mechanism of the ice cream machine.

Although custards contain few ingredients and come together quickly, they are far from fool-proof. As custards are heated, individual protein molecules in the eggs begin to unfold and stretch out. (Think of a bird's nest of dried pasta; when it is cooked, the individual strands of pasta unwind and stretch out.) Once unfolded, the molecules form new bonds, and as they form these bonds, water molecules become trapped between them, causing the custard to thicken. The problem with egg custards is that overcooking (that is, overheating) results in more frenzied, tighter bonding that forces the water molecules out of this fragile network and causes the proteins to clump. This process is called curdling.

There are several ways to prevent curdling. The first is the judicious use of heat. When a custard reaches 185 to 190 degrees, the proteins bond so extensively that they form clumps and the eggs curdle—in effect, they become scrambled eggs. Slow, gentle heat, then, is one way to succeed with custards. This is especially true of custards made without cornstarch, such as crème brûlée or the custard base of an ice cream. The use of cornstarch is another way to guard against curdling, and American custards generally contain it. Cornstarch gives the cook greater leeway when it comes to the application of heat. Cornstarch molecules in a custard are very large and therefore come between unwound egg proteins during cooking, in effect blocking, at least temporarily, their attempts to bond. Puddings with cornstarch can be heated well above 180 degrees without any

curdling; that's because the starch molecules are incredibly effective at keeping the unwound egg proteins from joining up.

Considering its usefulness, you might wonder why we don't add cornstarch to custard bases for ice cream. Unfortunately, cornstarch can leave a slightly grainy residue, which would mar the texture of the ice cream. The other reason is that cornstarch causes custards and puddings to set quite firmly. The starch absorbs excess water and causes puddings to become especially thick. Although this is ideal for puddings, a pudding-thick custard would be impossible to churn and freeze for ice cream.

The chapter includes recipes liked whipped cream, hot fudge sauce, and berry coulis to accompany the desserts not only in this chapter but also in other chapters in this book.

Chocolate Pudding

ON A MAP OF DESSERTS, CHOCOLATE PUDDING can be located as the chocolate version of a classic cornstarch custard. Typically, a cornstarch custard is made by cooking a mixture of sugar, cornstarch, eggs (or egg yolks), a bit of salt, and a dairy liquid in a saucepan on the stovetop until thickened. Vanilla, and sometimes butter, is added off the heat.

The choicest chocolate pudding should taste deeply of chocolate and dairy ingredients, be thickened to a soft suppleness, and be sweetened just enough to support the chocolate bouquet. The correct balance of dairy and chocolate should make the dessert rich but not cloying and exceptionally smooth on the tongue.

From early tests, we concluded that a pudding mixture needs to be pampered by sifting the dry ingredients (sugar, cornstarch, and cocoa powder) before combining them with the liquids to make the liquid-thickener amalgamation as smooth as possible from the start. We also learned that to achieve a gorgeous texture, it is important to monitor the strength of the heat beneath the saucepan and to use a reasonably slow hand to stir (not whisk or beat) the pudding mixture as it approaches the thickening point, then continue to stir slowly as it cooks for two minutes. Vigorous beating can break down the starch granules built up during the thickening process. We also found that it helped to strain the finished pudding through a fine-mesh sieve to ensure a suave, smooth texture.

With these points in mind, we began to test individual ingredients. We made puddings with all milk, 2 parts milk and 1 part heavy cream, 2 parts milk and 1 part light cream, half milk and half heavy cream, half milk and half light cream, and all light cream. The clear winner was the leaner blend of milk and light cream, which was rich but not overwhelming and mixed well with the chocolate.

Now we were ready to begin building the chocolate flavor. We started with 3 ounces of unsweetened chocolate alone, but that proved inadequate. An ounce or two more of semisweet chocolate added only a nuance of flavor; an ounce or two of bittersweet chocolate raised the chocolate meter slightly but not enough. At this point, we turned to cocoa powder to see if it would develop, sharpen, and polish the chocolate flavor. Fortunately, it did. We eventually settled on 2 tablespoons cocoa powder, along with a combination of unsweetened and bittersweet chocolate.

One nagging problem remained: Although the density, amount of dairy ingredients, and chocolate intensity were right on the mark, the pudding left a trace of chalkiness on the tongue. To remedy this problem, we eliminated the unsweetened chocolate, replacing it with bittersweet and adjusting the amount of sugar in the recipe to balance out the sweetness. Now the pudding was smooth and silky. The reason behind the textural change? Bittersweet chocolate contains some milk solids and lecithin (an emulsifier), both of which create a smoother, creamier texture and mouthfeel.

Double-Chocolate Pudding
SERVES 4 TO 6

To melt the chocolate, chop and place it in a heatproof bowl set over a pan of almost-simmering water, stirring once or twice until smooth. You can also melt the chocolate in a microwave at 50 percent power for 3½ minutes, stopping to stir after 2 minutes. If the chocolate is not yet completely melted, heat up to 30 seconds more at 50 percent power. On page 734, we provide a third way for melting chocolate using a drip coffee maker. While we prefer the slightly less sweet bittersweet chocolate for this pudding, semisweet chocolate can be substituted for it with success.

2	tablespoons Dutch-processed cocoa
2	tablespoons cornstarch
⅔	cup (2⅓ ounces) sugar
⅛	teaspoon salt

EQUIPMENT: Fine-Mesh Strainers

If you want to dust cocoa over a cake, remove bits of curdled egg from a pudding, or turn cooked raspberries into a seedless sauce, you need a fine-mesh strainer. Unlike a regular strainer (which has relatively large holes), a fine-mesh strainer is covered with the same material used in window screens. This fine mesh will trap all solid materials and break up lumps in dry ingredients such as cocoa powder and flour. (We often use a fine-mesh strainer to sift these ingredients.)

We put five fine-mesh strainers through a series of tests. We poured pureed pea soup through the strainers to test their ability to remove large solid bits. We pushed a raspberry puree through them to see how they would withstand scraping and moderate pressure. Finally, we passed pastry cream through the strainers to test their ability to catch small particles. (All fine-mesh strainers can sift dry ingredients like cocoa and flour, so we did not run this test.)

Based on these tests, we think it's imperative to buy a stainless steel strainer (aluminum can discolor acidic foods) with some heft. You don't want the strainer to buckle under moderate pressure, as several did in our tests. The finer the mesh, the better. Several strainers let solids pass through, which is unacceptable. Other strainers had handles that were uncomfortable, another no-no in our book.

In the end, testers preferred the Williams-Sonoma Piazza 18 cm Strainer ($26), which yielded perfectly smooth soup, raspberry puree, and pastry cream. The Küchenprofi 22 cm Classic Strainer ($30) was the second choice in the test kitchen.

---

1 cup light cream

3 large egg yolks

2 cups whole milk

6 ounces bittersweet or semisweet chocolate, melted (see note) and cooled slightly

1 tablespoon unsalted butter, softened

2 teaspoons vanilla extract

1 cup Whipped Cream (page 985), whipped to soft peaks

1. Sift the cocoa, cornstarch, sugar, and salt into a medium, heavy-bottomed saucepan. Slowly whisk in the light cream, followed by the yolks, then the milk. Stir in the chocolate. (The chocolate will form clumps that smooth with cooking.)

2. Bring the mixture to a boil over medium-high heat, stirring constantly with a whisk and scraping the bottom and sides of the pot. The pudding will gradually darken and thicken. Reduce the heat to medium and cook, stirring gently but constantly with a wooden spoon, until the pudding coats the spoon very thickly, 1½ to 2 minutes.

3. Pass the pudding through a fine-mesh strainer into a medium bowl, pressing with a rubber spatula. Stir in the butter and vanilla. Press plastic wrap directly on the surface and refrigerate until cold and set, at least 3 hours or up to 2 days. Spoon the pudding into serving dishes and top each with a dollop of whipped cream.

BUTTERSCOTCH PUDDING

GRADE-SCHOOL CAFETERIAS REGULARLY SERVE up dishes of butterscotch pudding that are sweet and satisfying—but only to children. Kids love pudding in any form, but to adults this kind of pudding (which invariably comes from a box) can taste gluey, artificial, and one-dimensional. We wanted a perfectly fresh and creamy pudding with a deep, rich brown sugar flavor that would satisfy children and adults alike.

Typically, pudding is made with just a few basic ingredients: some kind of dairy—milk, cream, or half-and-half—plus eggs, sugar, and cornstarch.

As for the butterscotch flavor, we knew that brown sugar would be a key player. It appeared on the ingredient list of every recipe we consulted. In addition, we found recipes that called for healthy doses of butter, vanilla, rum, and even molasses to provide that much-wanted taste of butterscotch.

After mixing puddings with each of these flavoring agents in various combinations, we uncovered the essence of butterscotch. A caramel made from butter and brown sugar plus a generous amount of vanilla gave us what we were looking for—an intense caramel-vanilla taste with buttery undertones. Dark brown sugar produced a stronger butterscotch flavor than light brown sugar, but molasses was overpowering and thus swiftly rejected. A spoonful of rum kept the sweetness in check and added complexity to the pudding.

Although the flavor elements of the recipe went together quickly, we had a lot of trouble achieving a desirable texture. Time after time, we produced puddings that were quite grainy. When we added hot cream to the butter–brown sugar mixture, it seized up. Although these bits of sugar would dissolve with further cooking, evidently some residual grittiness was being imparted. Clearly, we needed to prevent the sugar from seizing up in the first place. When we switched from hot cream to cold cream, we avoided the problem altogether, and the texture was silky and smooth.

Once we'd refined our technique, we made puddings with various combinations of dairy. We settled on a light, but not too light, combination of 1 part heavy cream to 2 parts whole milk. Three egg yolks and ¼ cup cornstarch provided enough thickening power to make a pudding that was nicely thickened without being stiff or gluey.

Butterscotch Pudding
SERVES 6
To ensure a smooth texture, make sure to add the cream and milk gradually. See the illustration on page 701 for a tip on measuring brown sugar.

6 tablespoons (¾ stick) unsalted butter

1¼ cups packed (8¾ ounces) dark brown sugar

1   cup heavy cream

2   cups whole milk

3   large egg yolks

1/4   cup cornstarch

2   teaspoons vanilla extract

1   teaspoon dark rum (optional)

1   cup Whipped Cream (page 985), whipped to
    soft peaks

1. Melt the butter in a medium, heavy-bottomed saucepan over medium heat. Add the brown sugar and cook, stirring occasionally, until the mixture bubbles and becomes lighter in color, 3 to 4 minutes.

2. Gradually whisk the heavy cream into the butter–brown sugar mixture; whisk until the sugar is completely dissolved, about 1 minute. Gradually whisk in the milk and bring the mixture to a simmer

3. Whisk the egg yolks in a medium bowl until thoroughly combined. Gradually whisk about ½ cup of the milk mixture into the egg yolks to temper them. Whisk in the cornstarch until completely dissolved. Whisk the cornstarch mixture back into the hot milk mixture. Return to a simmer over medium heat, stirring gently but constantly with a wooden spoon until 3 or 4 bubbles burst on the surface and the mixture is thickened and glossy, 2 to 3 minutes.

4. Pass the pudding through a fine-mesh strainer into a medium bowl, pressing with a rubber spatula. Whisk in the vanilla and rum (if using). Press plastic wrap directly on the surface and refrigerate until cold and set, at least 3 hours or up to 2 days. Spoon the pudding into serving dishes and top each with a dollop of whipped cream.

RICE PUDDING

AT ITS BEST, RICE PUDDING IS SIMPLE AND lightly sweet, and it tastes of its primary component: rice. At its worst, the rice flavor is lost to cloying sweetness, condensed dairy, and a pasty, leaden consistency.

Right from the start, we agreed on the qualities of the ideal candidate: intact, tender grains bound loosely in a subtly sweet, milky sauce. We were looking for a straightforward stovetop rice pudding, in which both the texture and the flavor of the primary ingredient would stand out.

We decided to check out the cooking medium and method first. For our first experiment, we prepared and tasted eight existing recipes for rice pudding, each using a different combination of water, milk, and cream and each with varying ratios of rice to liquid. The tasting revealed that cooking the rice in milk or cream obscured the rice flavor, while cooking the rice in water emphasized it. The most appealing balance of rice flavor and satisfying yet not too rich consistency was achieved when we cooked 1 cup of rice in 2 cups of water until it was absorbed and then added equal parts (2½ cups each) of whole milk and half-and-half to make the pudding. Whole milk alone made the pudding too thin, but the milk and half-and-half together imparted just the right degree of richness. Eggs, butter, whipped cream, and heavy cream—on their own or in combination—overpowered the flavor of the rice.

We also tried a couple of variations in the cooking method, such as covering the pot or not, and using a double boiler. The double boiler lengthened the cooking time by 25 minutes and turned out a pudding that was gummy and too sweet. By far, the best results came from cooking the rice and water in a covered pot, then simmering the cooked rice and dairy mixture uncovered. This technique gave us just what we wanted—distinct, tender grains of rice in a smooth sauce that tasted of milk rather than reduced cream. We found we could cut 10 minutes off the total cooking time by simmering the rice in the water and dairy mixture together from the start, but this approach sacrificed the texture of the grains and resulted in a pudding that our tasters described as overly dense and sweet.

Now it was time to try different kinds of rice. We tested the readily available varieties: supermarket brands of long- and medium-grain white (such as Goya, which distributes both of these types nationally), Arborio (a superstarchy Italian short-grain white used to make risotto), and basmati (an aromatic long-grain white).

All rice contains two types of starch, called amylose and amylopectin, but they are present in different concentrations in different kinds of rice. Arborio, with its high level of amylopectin, made a stiff, gritty pudding. On the other end of the starch scale, long-grain rice, which is high in amylose, cooked up separate and fluffy. But the puddings made with long-grain rice were a little too thin for our liking, and the flavor of the basmati rice was too perfumey, overwhelming the milk. Medium-grain rice, which has a high proportion of amylopectin (but less than short grain), cooked up a little more moist and sticky than long-grain rice. This type proved ideal for our pudding, which had a creamy texture and tasted distinctly of rice and milk. As a final test, we made a pudding with rice that had been refrigerated overnight. Unfortunately, the result was liquidy and grainy, without discernible rice flavor.

Simple Stovetop Rice Pudding
SERVES 6 TO 8
We prefer pudding made from medium-grain rice, but long-grain rice works too.

2	cups water
1/4	teaspoon salt
1	cup medium-grain rice
2 1/2	cups whole milk
2 1/2	cups half-and-half
2/3	cup (4 2/3 ounces) sugar
1 1/4	teaspoons vanilla extract

1. Bring the water to a boil in a large, heavy-bottomed saucepan (at least 3 quarts). Stir in the salt and rice; cover and simmer over low heat, stirring once or twice, until the water is almost fully absorbed, 15 to 20 minutes.

2. Add the milk, half-and-half, and sugar. Increase the heat to medium-high and bring to a simmer, then reduce the heat to maintain a simmer. Cook, uncovered and stirring frequently, until the mixture starts to thicken, about 30 minutes. Reduce the heat to low and continue to cook, stirring every couple of minutes to prevent sticking and scorching, until a spoon is just able to stand up in the pudding, about 15 minutes longer.

3. Remove from the heat and stir in the vanilla. Cool and serve at room temperature or chilled. (To store, press plastic wrap directly on the surface of the pudding and refrigerate for up to 2 days.)

➤ VARIATIONS
Rice Pudding with Orange and Toasted Almonds
Follow the recipe for Simple Stovetop Rice Pudding, adding 1/3 cup slivered almonds toasted until just golden and fragrant in a small, heavy skillet over medium heat (4 to 5 minutes, with frequent stirring) and 2 teaspoons grated orange zest along with the vanilla extract in step 3.

Rice Pudding with Cinnamon and Dried Fruit
Follow the recipe for Simple Stovetop Rice Pudding, adding 1/2 cup dried fruit (such as raisins, cranberries, cherries, or chopped prunes or apricots) and 1 teaspoon ground cinnamon along with vanilla extract in step 3.

TAPIOCA PUDDING
TAPIOCA PUDDING, WITHOUT QUESTION, IS as much about texture as flavor. People react strongly to it—they either love it or loathe it. Most of us in the test kitchen happen to love it.

At its worst, tapioca is a gelatinous, gluey custard resilient enough to resist the assault of a spoon. At its best, tapioca pudding is simple, honest food, free of pretense and complicated cooking. With simplicity in mind, we sifted through a stack of recipes to come up with the one that would deliver the best combination of texture and flavor.

The first step to tackle was the cooking method. Many recipes we tried had intricate directions for cooking the tapioca that, unsurprisingly, failed to produce anything special. We had the best luck with the easiest method; all of the ingredients were combined in a saucepan for five minutes at room temperature (to soften the tapioca), brought slowly to a boil, and removed from the heat. That's it—the pudding thickened as it cooled. We could not make it any easier or faster. We tried batches with varying amounts of tapioca to arrive at a firm yet supple texture and found that as little as ¼ cup provided just the right amount of thickening for 2½ cups of milk.

Most of the recipes we tried included egg yolks in the pudding but reserved the egg whites to lighten it; the whites were beaten to stiff peaks and folded into the pudding just before serving. Judicious in our use of raw eggs these days, we decided to cook the whole egg with the pudding and turned to whipped cream to lighten it. Just a small amount of cream was necessary to yield a texture similar to that of a pudding lightened with egg whites, and, as a bonus, the flavor was markedly improved. The pudding now had a rich, creamy flavor and supple texture that offset the tapioca's tackiness.

Tradition dictates that tapioca pudding should be flavored only with sugar and vanilla. While granulated sugar kept the flavors clean, it was a little flat to our tastes. Maple syrup and dark brown sugar muddied the flavors and tinted the pudding's snowy white color, turning it an unappetizing beige. A small amount of light brown sugar in conjunction with granulated sugar contributed a faint earthiness that supported the vanilla's floral notes and did not affect the pure whiteness of the pudding.

We were not thrilled with the use of vanilla extract in the pudding. Even when we dramatically increased the amount of extract, the flavor tasted one-dimensional and commercial—like cheap vanilla ice cream. While we rarely use whole vanilla beans because of the expense and extra work involved, we found this was one instance where it was definitely worth it. The simplicity of the pudding provided a good platform for the nuances of the vanilla, and the specks of seeds in the pudding visually emphasized the vanilla, much as they do in ice cream.

To emphasize the vanilla bean's presence, we added vanilla extract to the whipped cream that was folded in, which gave us the heady vanilla aroma and slight boozy accent the vanilla bean lacked. The pudding now had the flavor of a rich vanilla sauce but with tapioca's alluring texture.

REMOVING SEEDS FROM A VANILLA BEAN

1. Use a small, sharp knife to cut the vanilla bean in half lengthwise.

2. Place the knife at one end of one bean half and press down to flatten the bean as you move the knife away from you and catch the seeds on the edge of the blade. Add the seeds as well as the pods to the liquid ingredients.

Tapioca Pudding
SERVES 4

This is an instance where a vanilla bean can make a big impression and is well worth the cost and effort. After scraping the bean for the seeds, the bean pod can be added to the pudding for extra flavor. Serve the pudding slightly warm, at room temperature, or chilled, but do wait until just before serving to fold in the whipped cream.

2½	cups whole milk
1	large egg, plus 1 large egg yolk, lightly beaten
¼	cup (1¾ ounces) plus 1 tablespoon granulated sugar
1	tablespoon light brown sugar
	Salt
¼	cup quick-cooking tapioca
½	vanilla bean, split in half lengthwise and seeds scraped out (see the illustrations at left)
½	cup heavy cream
½	teaspoon vanilla extract

1. Combine the milk, eggs, sugars (excluding the 1 tablespoon granulated sugar), ¼ teaspoon salt, the tapioca, and vanilla seeds and pod in a medium saucepan and allow to sit for 5 minutes. Bring the mixture to a boil over medium heat and, once boiling, stir constantly for 2 minutes. Remove the pan from the heat and scrape the pudding into a medium bowl. Cover with plastic wrap and place in the refrigerator until set, at least 1 hour or up to 2 days.

2. While the pudding chills, combine the heavy cream, vanilla extract, remaining 1 table-spoon sugar, and a pinch of salt in the bowl of a standing mixer fitted with a whisk attachment and mix on medium speed until the cream holds soft peaks. Cover and refrigerate until needed.

3. When ready to serve, remove the vanilla pod from the pudding and discard. Fold half the whipped cream into the pudding. Divide the pudding among individual cups or bowls and top each with a dollop of the remaining cream. Serve immediately.

CRÈME CARAMEL

CRÈME CARAMEL IS A DECEPTIVELY SIMPLE classic French dessert. Made with just a few ingredients that are readily available (sugar, eggs, and milk or cream), it is similar in construction and flavor to other baked custards. This dessert is slightly lighter and a little less sweet than a standard baked custard, but what really makes it special is the caramel sauce.

For us, though, what made a perfect crème caramel was texture. We wanted a custard that was creamy and tender enough to melt in our mouths, yet firm enough to unmold without collapsing on the serving plate. We were also looking for a mel-low flavor that was neither too rich nor too eggy.

The first thing we discovered in our research was that the most important part of the recipe is the proportion of egg whites to egg yolks. Too many whites produced a custard that was almost solid and rubbery; too few egg whites, on the other hand, and our custard collapsed. After much tinkering, we came up with what we consider the ideal ratio: 3 whole eggs to 2 yolks—in other words, 3 whites to 5 yolks. The resulting custard was tender yet not overly rich and firm enough to unmold easily.

Next we examined the question of what liquid to use. Since we were making a classic crème caramel, our choices were limited to milk, heavy cream, light cream, and half-and-half. We made our initial custard using milk alone, but it tasted far too thin. Our custard with heavy cream and milk, on the other hand, was creamy but too rich. The high fat content of the cream caused the custard to coat our mouths as we ate, and the custard tasted less of eggs than of rich cream. Half-and-half was better, yet left us wanting something slightly richer. Light cream solved our problem. A mixture of equal parts of milk and light cream gave us just that extra edge of richness—creamy enough to satisfy both ourselves and our tasters.

Our experiments with sugar were less extensive, since we had decided at the beginning that a crème caramel custard should be less sweet than a custard meant to be eaten unadorned. To us, that made the dessert more interesting and sophisticated. We initially used 6 tablespoons of sugar for the 3 cups of liquid in the recipe and were quite satisfied, but some tasters felt that this custard was bland. We then tried using ½ cup of sugar for the same amount of liquid. Opinions were divided on this custard. Some palates still wanted an even sweeter custard, so we tried ⅔ cup. This slightly sweeter custard became the new favorite for the majority, but if you prefer a less sweet custard, simply cut the sugar down to ½ cup.

There are basically two methods of making caramel. In the dry method, you use only sugar, cooking it slowly until it melts and caramelizes. The wet method uses a combination of water and sugar. The sugar begins to dissolve in the water, then the mixture is simmered until the water evaporates and the sugar caramelizes. We never successfully produced a smooth caramel with the dry method, so we opted for the wet as a way of increasing the margin of success.

Once our caramel was done, we poured it directly into our molds. While some cookbooks advised buttering the molds, we found this step both unnecessary and ill-advised: The butter solidified when cold and left the custard greasy. We then followed the common advice to pour the caramel into the molds, coat the bottom evenly, and then tilt the molds to coat the sides. An accident with hot caramel burning our fingers while the molds were tilted caused us to question this particular bit of advice. (A bowl of ice water nearby—a useful thing to have when you are making caramel or any type of candy—saved the day for the burnt finger.) We started to coat only the bottoms of the mold, reasoning that the caramel sinks to the bottom of the mold while baking anyway. When we unmolded the custards, the caramel still poured evenly over the tops of the custards. It was an easier and safer method.

How you bake crème caramel and how long you bake it can make the difference between a great dessert and a mediocre, or even disappointing, one. After considerable experimentation, we determined that baking the custards at 350 degrees in a *bain-marie,* or water bath, to maintain an even, gentle heating environment, produced custards that were creamy and smooth.

As a final experiment, we decided to try lining the baking pan with a towel before adding the molds or the water. We found this step in a couple of recipes and initially dismissed it as not worth the bother. At this point, however, our testing produced custards that were wonderful, but still had bubbles from overcooking near the bottom. We reasoned that the towel might absorb some of the heat from the bottom, preventing the custards from overcooking in this area. Custards baked with the towel contained significantly fewer bubbles, so we judged them worth the effort.

Classic Crème Caramel
SERVES 8

Though you can make one large crème caramel, we find that custards baked in individual ramekins cook faster, are more evenly textured, and unmold more easily. You can vary the amount of sugar in the custard to suit your taste. Most tasters preferred the full ⅔ cup, but you can reduce that amount to as little as ½ cup to create a greater contrast between the custard and the caramel. Cook the caramel in a pan with a light-colored interior, since a dark surface makes it difficult to judge the color of the syrup. Caramel can leave a real mess in a pan, but it is easy to clean. Simply boil lots of water in the pan for 5 to 10 minutes to loosen the hardened caramel.

CARAMEL
1 cup (7 ounces) sugar
⅓ cup water
2 tablespoons light corn syrup
¼ teaspoon juice from 1 lemon

CUSTARD
1½ cups whole milk
1½ cups light cream
3 large eggs, plus 2 large egg yolks
⅔ cup (4⅔ ounces) sugar
1½ teaspoons vanilla extract
Pinch salt

1. FOR THE CARAMEL: In a medium nonreactive saucepan, bring the sugar, water, corn syrup, and lemon juice to a simmer, without stirring, over medium-high heat, wiping the sides of the pan with a wet cloth to remove any sugar crystals that might cause the syrup to turn grainy. Continue to cook until the syrup turns from clear to golden, swirling the pan gently to ensure even browning, about 8 minutes. Continue to cook, swirling the pan gently and constantly, until large, slow bubbles on the mixture's surface turn honey-caramel in color, 4 to 5 minutes longer. Remove the pan immediately from the heat and, working quickly but carefully (the caramel is above 300 degrees and will burn if it touches your skin), pour a portion of the caramel into each of 8 ungreased 6-ounce ovenproof ramekins. Allow the caramel to cool and harden, about 15 minutes. (The caramel-coated ramekins can be covered with plastic wrap and refrigerated for up to 2 days; return to room temperature before adding the custard.)

2. FOR THE CUSTARD: Adjust an oven rack to the center position and heat the oven to 350 degrees. Heat the milk and cream in a medium saucepan over medium heat, stirring occasionally, until steam appears and/or an instant-read thermometer held in the liquid registers 160 degrees, 6 to 8 minutes;

remove from the heat. Meanwhile, gently whisk the eggs, yolks, and sugar in a large bowl until just combined. Off the heat, gently whisk the warm milk mixture, vanilla, and salt into the eggs until just combined but not at all foamy. Strain the mixture through a fine-mesh sieve into a large measuring cup or container with a pouring spout; set aside.

3. Bring 2 quarts water to a boil in a kettle. Meanwhile, fold a dish towel to fit the bottom of a large baking dish or roasting pan and position it in the pan. Divide the reserved custard mixture among the ramekins; place the filled ramekins on the towel in the pan (making sure they do not touch) and set the pan on the oven rack. Fill the pan with boiling water to reach halfway up the sides of the ramekins; cover the entire pan loosely with aluminum foil so steam can escape. Bake until a paring knife inserted halfway between the center and the edge of the custards comes out clean, 35 to 40 minutes. Transfer the custards to a wire rack; cool to room temperature (The custards can be covered with plastic wrap and refrigerated for up to 2 days.)

4. To unmold, slide a paring knife around the perimeter of each ramekin, pressing the knife against the side of the dish. Hold a serving plate over the top of the ramekin and invert; set the plate on the work surface and shake the ramekin gently to release the custard. Serve immediately.

➤ VARIATIONS

Large Crème Caramel
Follow the recipe for Classic Crème Caramel, pouring the caramel and custard into a 1½-quart straight-sided soufflé dish rather than individual ramekins. Fill a roasting pan with boiling water to reach halfway up the sides of the soufflé dish; increase the baking time to 70 to 75 minutes, or until an instant-read thermometer inserted in the center of the custard registers 175 degrees.

Espresso Crème Caramel
Espresso beans ground in a coffee grinder would be too fine and impart too strong a coffee flavor to the custard. Instead, crush the beans lightly with the bottom of a heavy saucepan.

Follow the recipe for Classic Crème Caramel, heating ½ cup lightly crushed espresso beans with the milk and cream mixture until steam appears and/or an instant-read thermometer held in the liquid registers 160 degrees, 6 to 8 minutes. Off the heat, cover and steep until the coffee flavor has infused the milk and cream, about 15 minutes. Pour the mixture through a fine-mesh sieve to strain out the beans and continue with the recipe, reducing the vanilla extract to 1 teaspoon.

CRÈME BRÛLÉE

A PROPER CRÈME BRÛLÉE SHOULD HAVE A crackle-crisp bittersweet sugar crust over a chilly custard of balanced egginess, creaminess, and sweetness. But the majority of crème brûlées the test kitchen sampled revealed a trio of problems with this showstopper dessert: The custard is tepid, not cold; the custard is leaden, not ethereal; and the flavors are sullen. And if the topping isn't a paltry sugar crust, it's one so thick it requires a pickax. We set out to fix these problems and create the perfect crème brûlée.

First we sought to settle the issue of eggs. Firmer custard, like that in crème caramel, is made with whole eggs, which help the custard to achieve a clean-cutting quality. Crème brûlée is richer and softer—with a pudding-like, spoon-clinging texture—in part because of the exclusive use of yolks. With 4 cups of heavy cream as the dairy for the moment, we went to work. The custard refused to set at all with as few as 6 yolks; with 8 (a common number for the amount of cream) it was better, but still rather slurpy. With 12, however, a surprisingly large number of yolks, we struck gold. The custard had a lovely lilting texture, an elegant mouthfeel, a glossy, luminescent look, and the richest flavor.

We ventured to make crème brûlées with different kinds of cream. Half-and-half (with a fat content of about 10 percent) was far too lean, and the custard was watery and lightweight. With whipping cream (about 30 percent fat), the custard was improved but still a bit loose. Heavy cream (about 36 percent fat) was the ticket. The custard was thick but not overbearing, luxurious but not death-defying.

We tested various sugar quantities, from ½ cup to ¾ cup. Two-thirds cup was the winner; with more sugar the crème brûlée was too saccharine, and with less the simple egg and cream flavors tasted muted and dull. We also found that a pinch of salt heightened flavors and that a vanilla bean was superior to extract.

With the proportions in place, we attempted to find the best cooking technique for the custard. Custard made with icebox-cold eggs and cream can go into the oven, but nearly all recipes instruct the cook to scald the cream before gradually whisking it into the yolks. When compared, a started-cold custard and a scalded-cream custard displayed startling differences. The former had a silkier, smoother texture. Custard research explained that eggs respond favorably to cooking at a slow, gentle pace. If heated quickly, they set only just shortly before they enter the overcooked zone, leaving a very narrow window between just right and overdone. If heated gently, however, they begin to thicken the custard at a lower temperature and continue to do so gradually until it, too, eventually overcooks. In other words, the scalded-cream method is more likely to produce custard with an overcooked—hence inferior—texture.

The downside to starting with cold ingredients is that unless the cream is heated, it is impossible to extract flavor from a vanilla bean. Also, if the

IMPROVED CUSHION FOR WATER BATH

Many recipes for individual baked custards, including crème brûlée, recommend lining the bottom of the water bath pan with a kitchen towel to both insulate and cushion the ramekins. Of course, this leaves you with a sopping-wet towel at the end of cooking. We've found that a nonstick baking mat (called a Silpat) can be used if you happen to own this handy kitchen item.

cream is heated, the sugar can go into the pot for easy dissolution. Otherwise, the sugar must be vigorously beaten with the yolks to encourage it to dissolve. When we did this, the resulting custard was very frothy and baked up with a dry, soap-foam-like surface. Scalding cream and sugar, steeping with vanilla, and then refrigerating until cold seemed an overwrought process, so we tested a hybrid technique. We heated only half the cream with the sugar and the vanilla bean. After a 15-minute off-heat steep to extract flavor from the vanilla bean, we added the remaining cold cream to bring the temperature down before whisking it into the yolks. This hybrid technique created a custard with a fineness equal to the one started cold—and it baked in less time, too.

Next we investigated oven temperatures. At 325 degrees, the custards puffed and browned on the surface. Too hot. At 300 degrees, they fared beautifully. As for the water bath (or bain-marie, which prevents the periphery of a custard from overcooking while the center saunters to the finish line), we used a large baking dish that held the ramekins comfortably. (The ramekins must not touch and should be at least ½ inch away from the sides of the dish.) We lined the bottom with a kitchen towel to protect the bottoms of the ramekins from the heat of the dish and to stabilize them.

The golden rule of custards is that they must not be overcooked lest they lose their smooth, silken texture and become grainy and curdled. Judging doneness by gently shaking the custards or by slipping a paring knife into them was not reliable. An instant-read thermometer tells you exactly when the custards must come out of the oven: between 170 and 175 degrees. If you do not have a thermometer, look at the center of the custard. It should be barely set—shaky but not sloshy. The custard will continue to cook from residual heat once out of the oven. A deep chill then helps to solidify things. If your oven has a history of uneven heating, the custards may finish at different rates, so it is advisable to check each one separately rather than take the whole lot out at once.

For the crackly caramel crust, we tried brown sugar, regular granulated sugar, and turbinado and Demerara sugars (the latter two are coarse light brown sugars). Because brown sugar is moist and lumpy, recipes often recommend drying it in a low oven and crushing it to break up lumps. We found that it just isn't worth the effort. Turbinado and Demerara sugar were superior to granulated only because their coarseness makes them easy to distribute evenly over the custards.

There are a few approaches to caramelizing the sugar. The broiler is almost guaranteed to fail; the heat is uneven and inadequate. A salamander—a long-handled iron plate that is heated and held just above the sugar—is hardly practical since these plates are hard to come by. A torch accomplishes the task efficiently. A hardware-store propane torch is the tool of choice, but a small butane kitchen torch, available in cookware stores, can do the job, just at a more leisurely pace.

While being "brûléed," the custard is unavoidably warmed a bit. In standard round ramekins, usually only the upper third of the custard is affected. But in shallow dishes (our favorite for their higher ratio of crust to custard), the custard can be completely warmed through. In our opinion, a warm custard can ruin an otherwise perfect crème brûlée. To remedy this problem, we refrigerated the finished crème brûlées, and the crust maintained its crackly texture for up to 45 minutes. Beneath the shattering sugar crust lay an interplay of creamy, cold, sweet, bitter, smooth, and crackly . . . perfect crème brûlée.

ENSURING GRIP FOR TONGS

We recommend the use of tongs to remove ramekins of custard from a water bath. Cooks who worry about the ramekins slipping in the tongs can try this tip. Slip rubber bands around each of the two tong pincers, and the sticky rubber will provide a surer grip.

Classic Crème Brûlée
SERVES 8

Separate the eggs and whisk the yolks after the cream has finished steeping; if left to sit, the surface of the yolks will dry and form a film. A vanilla bean gives custard the deepest flavor, but 2 teaspoons of extract, whisked into the yolks in step 4, can be used instead. The best way to judge doneness is with a digital instant-read thermometer. The custards, especially if baked in shallow fluted dishes, will not be deep enough to provide an accurate reading with a dial-face thermometer. For the caramelized sugar crust, we recommend turbinado or Demerara sugar. Regular granulated sugar will work, too, but use only 1 scant teaspoon on each ramekin or 1 teaspoon on each shallow fluted dish. It's important to use ramekins that measure 4 to 5 ounces. To check the size of your ramekins, fill one to the rim with a measured amount of water. You will need either a kitchen torch or a hardware-store propane torch (see page 963) for caramelizing the sugar.

4	cups chilled heavy cream
2/3	cup (4 2/3 ounces) granulated sugar
	Pinch salt
I	vanilla bean, split in half lengthwise and seeds scraped out (see the illustrations on page 957)
12	large egg yolks
8–12	teaspoons turbinado or Demerara sugar (see note)

1. Adjust an oven rack to the lower-middle position and heat the oven to 300 degrees.

2. Combine 2 cups of the cream, the sugar, and salt in a medium saucepan. Add the vanilla seeds to the pan, submerge the pod in the cream, and bring the mixture to a boil over medium heat, stirring occasionally to ensure that the sugar dissolves. Remove the pan from the heat and let steep 15 minutes to infuse the flavors.

3. Meanwhile, place a kitchen towel in the bottom of a large baking dish or roasting pan and arrange eight 4- or 5-ounce ramekins (or shallow fluted dishes) on the towel. Bring a kettle or large saucepan of water to a boil over high heat.

4. After the vanilla bean has steeped, stir in the remaining 2 cups cream to cool the mixture. Whisk the yolks in a large bowl until broken up

and combined. Whisk about 1 cup of the cream mixture into the yolks until loosened and combined; repeat with another 1 cup cream. Add the remaining cream and whisk until evenly colored and thoroughly combined. Strain through a fine-mesh strainer into a 2-quart measuring cup or pitcher (or clean medium bowl); discard the solids in the strainer. Pour or ladle the mixture into the ramekins, dividing it evenly among them.

5. Carefully place the baking dish with the ramekins on the oven rack; pour boiling water into the dish, taking care not to splash water into the ramekins, until the water reaches two thirds of the way up the sides of the ramekins. Bake until the centers of the custards are just barely set and are no longer sloshy and a digital instant-read thermometer inserted in the centers registers 170 to 175 degrees, 30 to 35 minutes (25 to 30 minutes for shallow fluted dishes). Begin checking the temperature about 5 minutes before the recommended time.

6. Transfer the ramekins to a wire rack; cool to room temperature, about 2 hours. Set the ramekins on a rimmed baking sheet, cover tightly with plastic wrap, and refrigerate until cold, at least 4 hours or up to 4 days.

7. Uncover the ramekins; if condensation has collected on the custards, place a paper towel on the surface to soak up the moisture. Sprinkle each with about 1 teaspoon turbinado sugar (1½ teaspoons for shallow fluted dishes); tilt and tap each ramekin for even coverage. Ignite the torch and caramelize the sugar. Refrigerate the ramekins, uncovered, to rechill, 30 to 45 minutes (but no longer). Serve.

➤ VARIATIONS

Espresso Crème Brûlée

Place ¼ cup espresso beans in a zipper-lock plastic bag and crush lightly with a rolling pin or meat pounder until coarsely cracked. Follow the recipe for Classic Crème Brûlée, substituting the cracked espresso beans for the vanilla bean and whisking 1 teaspoon vanilla extract into the yolks in step 4 before adding the cream.

EQUIPMENT: Torches

Fire up a torch to caramelize the sugar on your crème brûlée—it's the best way to put the crowning glory of a crust on the custard. We tested a hardware-store propane torch ($27) against four petite kitchen torches (prices ranged from $30 to $40) fueled by butane.

The propane torch, with its powerful flame, caramelized the sugar quickly and easily, but, admittedly, it's not for the faint-hearted. Although easy to wield, a propane torch puts out a lot of heat and works in just seconds, so you must work very carefully. (In contrast, the kitchen torches took about 1½ minutes to brûlée each custard.) If you opt for a propane torch, make sure to buy a model with a built-in trigger that does not need to be held in place for the torch to remain lit. The most widely available brand, Bernz-o-matic, worked well in our kitchen tests.

Among the four butane-powered kitchen torches we tested, only one is worth owning. The Bernz-o-matic Torch ST1100TS ($29.95) has a plastic flame adjuster that is clearly marked and stayed cool enough to handle without burning our fingers. This torch was also the most intuitive and easy to operate.

The remaining models had flaws. The safety lock on the RSVP Culinary Butane Torch ($29.95) was difficult to engage, and the air intake port became red-hot with use. The metal flame-width adjuster on the Bonjour Torch ($29.95) must be held in place during use, but it became very hot to the touch. Finally, although the Messermeister Chefflame Culinary Torch ($39.95) generated the most powerful flame of the kitchen torches tested, testers needed to use both hands to switch it on and found its large size awkward.

THE BEST TORCHES

With its powerful flame, the Bernz-o-matic propane torch (left) will brûlée a custard in seconds. If you don't want to use such a powerful torch, the Bernz-o-matic kitchen torch (right) is the best butane option. Just make sure to purchase a can of butane along with it; otherwise, you'll have more luck "brûléeing" with a book of matches. The smaller torch is available in many cookware stores. Most hardware stores stock the Bernz-o-matic propane torch.

Tea-Infused Crème Brûlée

Knot together the strings of 10 bags Irish Breakfast tea. Follow the recipe for Classic Crème Brûlée, substituting the tea bags for the vanilla bean; after steeping, squeeze the bags with tongs or press into a mesh strainer to extract all the liquid. Whisk 1 teaspoon vanilla extract into the yolks in step 4 before adding the cream.

PANNA COTTA

THOUGH ITS NAME IS LYRICAL, THE LITERAL translation of panna cotta—"cooked cream"—does nothing to suggest its ethereal qualities. In fact, panna cotta is not cooked at all. Neither is it complicated with eggs, as is a custard. Instead, sugar and gelatin are melted in cream and milk, and the whole is then turned into individual ramekins and chilled. It is a virginal dessert, a jellied alabaster cream. It forms a richly neutral backdrop for everything it touches: strawberry coulis, fresh raspberries, light caramel, chocolate sauce.

That, we should say, describes the ideal panna cotta. There are others. Panna cotta is about nothing if not texture. The cream must be robust enough to unmold but delicate enough to shiver on the plate. Our mission, therefore, was to find correct proportions for four simple ingredients and the most effective way to deal with the gelatin.

We began by preparing five recipes from well-known Italian cookbooks. Each of them used like ingredients in varying proportions and dealt with the ingredients similarly. Two called for powdered sugar (favored in Italian confections). Two simmered the cream; the others merely warmed it. One recipe whipped half the cream and folded it into the base. Procedurally, the recipes were extremely straightforward.

On tasting the recipes, it was clear they fell into two groups. Those with higher proportions of milk were slippery and translucent, their flavor elusive and flat. Those with more cream had a rich mouthfeel and a creamier, more rounded flavor. What united these recipes most noticeably, however, was a slightly rubbery chew, the result of too much gelatin.

It would be practical, we decided, to design the recipe around a single packet of gelatin. Given this amount, we knew we would need to establish the volume of liquid required to set up the cream. Before that, we had to determine the best proportion of cream to milk, critical in terms of mouthfeel. Preliminary tastings put us on the side of a 3-to-1 ratio of cream to milk.

Over the next week, we made dozens of panna cotta recipes in the test kitchen. We were surprised to find textural inconsistencies between batches that should have been identical. Some were flabby, others stalwart. Serendipity saved the day when we realized that the amount of gelatin in a packet is not consistent but in fact varies widely from one packet to another. Using a gram scale, we weighed more than 50 individual gelatin packets and found weight discrepancies as great as 20 percent. In fact, in two packages of four packets each, we found eight different weights. As soon as we began measuring gelatin by the teaspoonful, things began looking up.

In addition to proportions, there was chilling time to consider. Preparation and chilling times should be brief. Our first priority, therefore, was to create the best dessert to emerge within the shortest chilling time, a panna cotta that would be firm, say, in the space of a few hours. By increasing the amount of gelatin in increments of ⅛ teaspoon, from 2 to 3 teaspoons, we found that 2¾ teaspoons produced a firm enough yet still fragile finished texture after 4 hours.

Yet we wanted the option of an overnight version as well. Knowing that gelatin grows more tenacious over time—transforming what was a lilting mousse one evening into a bouncing sponge the next—we figured there must also be a statute of limitations on its grip. At what point would the gelatin stop advancing? Research indicated maximum rigidity was reached after about 18 hours. (See page 968 for more information on how gelatin works.) At this point, we recorded the textural changes occasioned by incremental decreases in gelatin and discovered that an implausibly small decrease (⅛ teaspoon) put the overnight version on a par with the texture of the four-hour version.

With flexible time options in place, we moved on to technique. Because gelatin's response is hastened by cold temperatures, it seemed reasonable to keep most of the liquid cold. Why heat all the milk and cream when we needed hot liquid just to melt the gelatin and sugar? We gave the milk this assignment, pouring it into a saucepan, sprinkling the gelatin over it, and then giving the gelatin five minutes to swell and absorb the liquid. Knowing that gelatin sustains damage at high temperatures, we heated the milk only enough to melt the gelatin—a couple of minutes, stirring constantly—then added the sugar off the heat to dissolve. The gelatin did not melt perfectly, and we thought we might have to increase the milk's temperature. Instead, we doubled the softening time to 10 minutes, and the problem was solved.

To do its job of firming the liquid to a gel, melted gelatin must be mixed with other recipe ingredients while its molecules have enough heat energy to move through the mixture. By combining ingredients hastily in the past, we had often precipitated gelatin seizures, causing the melted gelatin to harden into chewy strings, which ruined the texture of the dessert rather than enhancing it. So we stirred the cold cream slowly into the milk to temper it.

Several test cooks in the kitchen had learned in cooking school to stir gelatin-based desserts over an ice bath—allowing the gelatin to thicken somewhat under gentle agitation—before refrigerating them to set. Besides supporting nuts, fruit, or vanilla seeds throughout, this process was said to produce a finer finished texture. Hoping to avoid this step in a recipe that was otherwise so easy, we presented tasters with side-by-side creams, one stirred first over ice, one simply refrigerated. They unanimously preferred the texture of the panna cotta chilled over ice, describing it as "lighter, creamier, and smoother." Given the results, the extra 10 minutes required did not seem unreasonable.

Now it was fine-tuning time. First place for flavor accents went to vanilla, particularly in the company of fruit sauces. We preferred whole bean to extract.

Panna Cotta
SERVES 8

Serve panna cotta very cold with Berry Coulis (page 984) or lightly sweetened berries. Though traditionally unmolded, panna cotta may be chilled and served in wineglasses and sauced on top. If you would like to make the panna cotta a day ahead, decrease the gelatin to 2⅝ teaspoons (2½ teaspoons plus ⅛ teaspoon) and chill the filled wineglasses or ramekins for 18 to 24 hours. For more information about how gelatin works, see page 968.

I	cup whole milk
2¾	teaspoons unflavored gelatin
3	cups heavy cream
I	piece vanilla bean, 2 inches long, or 2 teaspoons vanilla extract
6	tablespoons (2½ ounces) sugar
	Pinch salt
	Berry Coulis (page 984)

1. Pour the milk into a medium saucepan; sprinkle the surface evenly with the gelatin and let stand 10 minutes to hydrate the gelatin. Meanwhile, turn the contents of 2 ice cube trays (about 32 cubes) into a large bowl; add 4 cups cold water. Measure the cream into a large measuring cup or pitcher. With a paring knife, slit the vanilla bean lengthwise and scrape the vanilla seeds (see the illustrations on page 957) into the cream; place the pod in the cream along with the seeds and set the mixture aside. Set eight 4-ounce ramekins on a baking sheet.

2. Heat the milk and gelatin mixture over high heat, stirring constantly, until the gelatin is dissolved and the mixture registers 135 degrees on an instant-read thermometer, about 1½ minutes. Off the heat, add the sugar and salt; stir until dissolved, about 1 minute.

3. Stirring constantly, slowly pour the cream with the vanilla into the saucepan of milk, then transfer the mixture to a medium bowl and set the bowl over the ice-water bath. Stir frequently until the mixture thickens to the consistency of eggnog and registers 50 degrees on an instant-read thermometer, about 10 minutes. Strain the mixture into a large measuring cup or pitcher, then divide

it evenly among the ramekins. Cover the baking sheet with plastic wrap, making sure that the plastic does not mar the surface of the cream; refrigerate until just set (the mixture should wobble when shaken gently), about 4 hours.

4. To serve, spoon some berry coulis onto each individual serving plate. Pour 1 cup boiling water into a small, wide-mouthed bowl, dip a ramekin filled with panna cotta into the water, count to three, and lift the ramekin out of the water. With a moistened finger, lightly press the periphery of the panna cotta to loosen the edges. Dip the ramekin back into the hot water for another three count. Invert the ramekin over your palm and loosen the panna cotta by cupping your fingers between the panna cotta and the edge of the ramekin. Gently lower the panna cotta onto the serving plate with the coulis. Repeat the process with the remaining ramekins of panna cotta. Serve immediately.

SUMMER PUDDING

SUMMER PUDDING DOESN'T FIT THE RICH, creamy, silky pudding archetype. In this classic English dessert, ripe, fragrant, lightly sweetened berries are gently cooked to coax out their juices, which are used to soak and soften slices of bread to make them meld with the fruit. This mélange of berries and bread is usually weighted down with heavy cans, then chilled overnight until it is a cohesive-enough mass to be unmolded.

We have always been intrigued by this "pudding," drawn in by its rustic, unaffected appeal. Unfortunately, many summer puddings are sweet, and the bread often seems to stand apart from the fruit, as if it were just a casing. We wanted sweet-tart berries and bread that melded right into them.

In a typical summer pudding, berries fill a bowl or mold of some sort that has been neatly lined with crustless bread. Some recipes say to line the bowl with full slices, laying them flat against the bottom and sides of the bowl. Others have you cutting the slices down into triangles and rectangles and arranging them such that, when unmolded, they form an attractive pattern. Well,

trimming the crusts is easy, but trimming the bread to fit the bowl, then lining the bowl with the trimmed pieces, is a bit fussy. After making a couple of puddings, we quickly grew tired of this technique; it seemed to undermine the simplicity of the dessert.

We came across a couple of recipes that called for layering the bread right in with the berries instead of using it to line the bowl. Not only is this bread-on-the-inside method easier, but a summer pudding made in this fashion looks spectacular—the berries on the outside are brilliant jewels. Meanwhile, the layers of bread on the inside almost melt into the fruit.

Our next adjustment to this recipe was to lose the bowl as a mold. We switched instead to a loaf pan. Its rectangular shape requires less trimming of bread slices, and, once unmolded, the pudding better retains its shape. Besides, this version was simply more beautiful than a round one made in a bowl. When we tried making individual summer puddings in ramekins, we found them to be hardly more labor-intensive in assembly than a single large serving. Sure, you have to cut out rounds of bread to fit the ramekins, but a cookie cutter makes easy work of it, and individual servings transform this humble dessert into an elegant one. The individual puddings are also easily served: You simply unmold them onto a plate; there's no slicing or scooping involved.

With the form set, we moved on to the ingredients. For the 4 pints of berries we were using, ¾ cup sugar was a good amount of sweetener. Lemon juice, we found, perked up the berry flavors and rounded them out. We then sought alternatives to cooking the fruit in an attempt to preserve its freshness. We mashed first some of and then all of the berries with sugar. We tried cooking only a portion of the fruit with sugar. We macerated the berries with sugar. None of these methods worked. These puddings, even after being weighted and chilled overnight, had an unwelcome crunchy, raw quality. The berries need a gentle cooking to make their texture more yielding, more pudding-like, if you will. But don't worry—five minutes is all it takes, not even long enough to heat up the kitchen.

ASSEMBLING INDIVIDUAL SUMMER BERRY PUDDINGS

1. For individual puddings, cut out rounds of bread with a cookie cutter.

2. With a slotted spoon, place about ¼ cup of fruit into the bottoms of greased 6-ounce ramekins that have been placed on a baking sheet.

3. Lightly soak a round of bread in the fruit juices and place on top of the fruit in each ramekin.

4. Divide the remaining fruit among the ramekins (about ½ cup more per ramekin).

5. Lightly soak a round of bread and place on top of the fruit in each ramekin; it should sit above the lip of the ramekin. Pour any remaining juices over the bread layer and cover the ramekins loosely with plastic wrap.

6. Place a second baking sheet on top, then weight with several heavy cans.

ASSEMBLING A LARGE SUMMER BERRY PUDDING

1. Remove the crusts from the bread slices and trim the slices to fit in a single layer in a loaf pan. You will need 3 layers. Remove the bread from the pan.

2. Line the greased loaf pan with plastic wrap. Spread about 2 cups of fruit over the bottom.

3. Lightly soak one layer of bread slices in the fruit juices and place on top of the fruit. Repeat 2 more times. Top with the remaining juices, cover loosely with a second sheet of plastic wrap, and weight with a another loaf pan and 2 or 3 heavy cans.

967

So far, we had been using a mix of strawberries, raspberries, blueberries, and blackberries and were pleased with the variety of flavors, textures, and colors. Strawberries made up the bulk, contributing the most substance and sweetness. Raspberries easily break down with the gentle cooking, providing much juice along with their distinct flavor. Blackberries and blueberries are more resistant; they retain their shape and unique texture. And their deep color is a beautiful addition, like sapphires in a pool of rubies.

The next obvious ingredient to investigate was the bread. We tried six different kinds as well as pound cake (for which we were secretly rooting). Hearty, coarse-textured sandwich bread and a rustic French loaf were too tough and tasted fermented and yeasty. Soft, pillowy sandwich bread became soggy and lifeless when soaked with juice. The pound cake, imbibed with berry juice, turned into wet sand and had the textural appeal of sawdust. A good-quality white sandwich bread with a medium texture, somewhere between Wonder Bread and Pepperidge Farm, was good, but there were two very clear winners: challah and potato bread. Their even, tight-crumbed, tender texture and light sweetness were a perfect

match for the berries. Challah, available in the bakery section of most grocery stores, is usually sold in unsliced braided loaves and therefore makes for irregular slices. We decided to sidestep this complication and go with potato bread, which tastes every bit as good as challah in this recipe but comes in convenient bagged and sliced loaves, like sandwich bread.

Most summer pudding recipes call for stale bread, and for good reason. Fresh bread, we found, when soaked with those berry juices, turns to mush. You might not think this would be so noticeable with the bread layered between all those berries, but every single taster remarked that the pudding made with fresh bread was soggy and gummy. On the other hand, stale bread absorbs some of the juices and melds with the berries while maintaining some structural integrity. We tried different degrees of staleness. A day-old loaf was still too fresh, but bread left out long enough to become completely dry easily cracked and crumbled under the cookie cutter or bread knife. We found that simply leaving slices out overnight until they were dry to the touch but still somewhat pliable resulted in bread that was easy to cut and also tasted good in the pudding.

We encountered a few recipes with instructions to butter the bread. Since pound cake doesn't work in a summer pudding, we thought that this might be a nice way of adding a subtle richness. Wrong. The coating of butter prevented the juices from thoroughly permeating the bread and also dulled the vibrant flavor of the berries.

Probably the oddest thing about summer pudding is the fact that it is weighted as it chills. What, we wondered, does this do for the texture? And how long does the pudding need to chill? We made several and chilled them with and without weights for 4, 8, 24, and 30 hours. The pudding chilled for 4 hours tasted of under ripe fruit—you could sense that it would be good if only given more time. The bread was barely soaked through, and the berries barely clung together. At 8 hours, the pudding was at its peak: The berries tasted fresh and held together, while the bread melted right into them. Twenty-four hours and the pudding was still good, though a hairsbreadth duller in color and flavor.

SCIENCE: How Gelatin Works

Gelatin is a flavorless, nearly colorless substance derived from the collagen in animals' connective tissue and bones, extracted commercially and dehydrated. Most culinary uses for gelatin rely on a two-step process—soaking and then dissolving. Gelatin is usually soaked in some cool or cold liquid so it can swell and expand. It is then dissolved in a hot liquid and finally chilled to set.

This dual process results from the fact that when unsoaked gelatin is added directly to hot liquid, the outside edges of each granule expand instantly and form a gel coating, preventing the inside from becoming hydrated. The center of each gelatin particle then remains hard and undissolved. The resulting gelatin mixture doesn't set properly and is full of hard, granular bits.

In contrast, soaking gelatin in cold or cool liquid allows the particles to expand slowly so that they can tie up the maximum amount of liquid (up to three times their weight). Maximum rigidity in gelatin is reached after 18 hours. After that time, desserts will begin to soften again.

After 30 hours, the pudding was well past its prime and began to smell and taste fermented.

No matter how long they chilled, the summer puddings without weights were loose. They didn't hold together after unmolding, the fruit was less cohesive, and the puddings were less pleasurable to eat.

Individual Summer Berry Puddings

SERVES 6

Stale the bread for this recipe by leaving it out overnight; it should be dry to the touch but not brittle. Otherwise, put the slices in a single layer on a rack in a 200-degree oven for 50 to 60 minutes, turning them once halfway through. For this recipe, you will need six 6-ounce ramekins and a round cookie cutter of slightly smaller diameter than the ramekins. If you don't have the right size cutter, use a paring knife and the bottom of a ramekin (most ramekins taper toward the bottom) as a guide for trimming the rounds. Challah is the second choice for bread but will probably need to be cut into slices about ½ inch thick. If both potato bread and challah are unavailable, use a good-quality white sandwich bread with a dense, soft texture. Summer pudding can be made up to 24 hours before serving; any longer and the berries begin to lose their freshness. Lightly sweetened Whipped Cream (page 985) is the perfect accompaniment to summer pudding.

2	pints strawberries hulled and sliced
1	pint raspberries
½	pint blueberries
½	pint blackberries
¾	cup (5¼ ounces) sugar
2	tablespoons juice from 1 lemon
12	slices stale potato bread, challah, or other good-quality white bread (see note)

1. Heat the strawberries, raspberries, blueberries, blackberries, and sugar in a large nonreactive saucepan over medium heat, stirring occasionally, until the berries begin to release their juice and the sugar has dissolved, about 5 minutes. Off the heat, stir in the lemon juice. Let cool to room temperature.

2. While the berries are cooling, use a cookie cutter to cut out 12 bread rounds that are slightly smaller in diameter than the ramekins (see illustration 1 on page 967).

3. Spray six 6-ounce ramekins with vegetable cooking spray and place on a rimmed baking sheet. Following illustrations 2 through 6 on page 967, assemble, cover, and weight the summer puddings and refrigerate for at least 8 hours or up to 24 hours.

4. Remove the weights, baking sheet, and plastic wrap. Run a paring knife around the perimeter of each ramekin, unmold into individual bowls, and serve immediately with whipped cream, if desired.

➤ VARIATION

Large Summer Berry Pudding

SERVES 6 TO 8

To ensure that this larger pudding unmolds in one piece, use a greased loaf pan lined with plastic wrap. Because there is no need to cut out rounds for this version, you will need only about 8 bread slices, depending on their size.

Follow the recipe for Individual Summer Berry Puddings through step 1. While the berries are cooling, remove the crusts from the bread slices and trim so the slices will fit in a single layer in a 9 by 5-inch loaf pan. (You will need about 2½ slices per layer and a total of three layers.) Coat the loaf pan with vegetable cooking spray and line with plastic wrap. Make sure the wrap lies flat against the surface of the pan, leaving no air space. Place the loaf pan on a rimmed baking sheet and use a slotted spoon to place about 2 cups of fruit in the bottom of the pan. Lightly soak enough bread slices for one layer in the fruit juices and place on top of the fruit. Repeat with two more layers of fruit and bread. Top with the remaining juices, cover loosely with a second sheet of plastic wrap, and weight with a another loaf pan and 2 or 3 heavy cans; refrigerate for at least 8 hours or up to 24 hours. To unmold, remove the weights, loaf pan, and outer plastic wrap and invert the loaf onto a serving platter. Lift off the pan, remove the plastic wrap lining, slice, and serve.

BREAD PUDDING

MOST BREAD PUDDINGS ARE SIMPLY A MIX-ture of bread, milk and/or cream, sugar, eggs, and flavorings. The balance between bread and filling is critical. The pudding and the bread need to be distinct but well integrated; we are not favorably inclined toward bread puddings that are nothing more than egg custards topped with bread.

In our research for the ideal combination, we first tackled the bread. We tried rustic Italian, a fine-textured white bread from a bakery, Pepperidge Farm white and raisin breads, super-market Italian bread, challah, brioche, and potato bread. The winner was a quality American-style white bread purchased from a local baker. Although the bread softened nicely in the oven, its fine, dense texture held up well during cooking. Pepperidge Farm Hearty White will do in a pinch for supermarket bread. More tender loaves, such as challah and brioche, were too soft and spongy. Really tough rustic loaves with heavy crusts and excessive chew did not soften sufficiently during soaking and baking.

In the course of our testing, we also discov-ered that there was no point in removing the crusts other than for appearance, that using stale or dried bread did not make a difference, and that we preferred cubes over sliced bread since they were easier to measure (8 cups is a more precise measurement than 8 slices) and to work with (large slices tended to curl at the corners when baked).

We discovered that the key to a crisp, crunchy top layer was to reserve some of the cubed bread to top the pudding just before baking. Brushing these cubes with melted butter added a rich color to the dessert. To provide more contrast between the topping and the filling, we also decided to sprinkle the pudding with cinnamon sugar before putting it in the oven. This gave the topping a flavor distinct from that of the nutmeg-laced custard.

As for the custard, we wanted rich and silky, nothing less and nothing thin. It turned out after many tests that equal parts of milk and cream were about right. Although many recipes use only two or three eggs, we finally agreed that

4 whole eggs plus 1 yolk make a rich pudding. The amount of sugar was a matter of some dis-pute in the tasting, some people preferring a full cup, others a more modest ¾ cup. A low oven temperature, 325 degrees, was best. Although a water bath seemed to assist in a slightly improved texture, we opted not to include it in the final recipe because the extra work of assembling it didn't ultimately seem worth the effort.

Determining just when to remove the pudding from the oven proved a bit tricky. Overcooking results in a dry, unappealing custard, and undercooking makes for a very loose sauce. After 20 or so tests, we determined that our bread pud-ding is ready to come out of the oven when it wobbles like a Jell-O mold. (Remember that it continues to cook after it's been removed from the oven.) And here is another tip regarding this cru-cial moment: Remove the pudding from the oven before it has a chance to inflate and rise up high in the pan. Actually, it is done just when this proc-ess begins, when the edges of the pudding start their upward climb. A knife inserted in the center should not come out clean but be partially coated with half-set custard.

Rich Bread Pudding with Crisp Cinnamon-Sugar Topping
SERVES 8 TO 10

A firm, white, American-style bakery loaf gives this pud-ding the best texture. Avoid chewy, crusty European-style breads because they do not soften properly. If desired, serve this pudding with softly whipped cream.

CINNAMON-SUGAR TOPPING

2	tablespoons sugar
½	teaspoon ground cinnamon

BREAD PUDDING

4	large eggs, plus 1 large egg yolk
¾	cup (5¼ ounces) sugar
2½	cups whole milk
2½	cups heavy cream
3	tablespoons bourbon
1	tablespoon vanilla extract

¾ teaspoon freshly grated nutmeg

¼ teaspoon salt

12 ounces (about ½ loaf) good-quality American-style white bread, sliced ⅜ inch thick and cut into 1½ -inch cubes (about 8 cups)

1½ tablespoons unsalted butter, melted, plus more for greasing the baking dish

1. FOR THE TOPPING: Mix the sugar and cinnamon together in a small bowl.

2. FOR THE PUDDING: Adjust an oven rack to the lower-middle position and heat the oven to 325 degrees. Butter a 13 by 9-inch baking dish.

3. Whisk the eggs, yolk, and sugar in a large bowl to blend well. Whisk in the milk, cream, bourbon, vanilla extract, nutmeg, and salt. Stir in 6 cups of the bread cubes; mix thoroughly to moisten. Let stand 20 minutes.

4. Pour the mixture into the prepared baking dish. Scatter the remaining 2 cups bread cubes on top, pushing them down gently to partially submerge. Brush the exposed bread with the melted butter and sprinkle with the topping. Bake until the pudding turns deep golden brown, is beginning to rise up the sides of the baking dish, and jiggles very slightly at the center when shaken, 45 to 50 minutes. Remove from the oven and let cool until set but still warm, about 45 minutes. Serve as is or with whipped cream.

➤ VARIATION

Rich Bread Pudding with Raisins and Walnuts

Follow the recipe for Rich Bread Pudding with Crisp Cinnamon-Sugar Topping, increasing the bourbon to ⅓ cup. Soak ¾ cup raisins in the bourbon until plumped, 20 to 25 minutes. Stir the plumped raisins, with any remaining bourbon, and 1 cup chopped walnuts into the soaked bread mixture in step 3. Proceed as directed.

CHOCOLATE MOUSSE

CHOCOLATE MOUSSE IS ONE OF AMERICA'S best-known desserts, a standby of cooks who want to create something with French allure but without the difficulty of, say, a *gâteau Saint-Honoré*! Chocolate mousse is decidedly the easier dessert to make, but it is not without its own persona. To begin with, what makes a mousse a mousse?

When we went to our library of cookbooks, we found that all of the recipes for this dessert started with chocolate and eggs, but that's where the similarity ended. Most added some other elements, most frequently (but not always) butter, sugar, and cream. In addition, all sorts of different flavorings could be present, apparently at the whim of the individual cook.

So we started by setting some standards of our own. We wanted a creamy mousse with deep chocolate flavor, but we didn't want either of these aspects to dominate. Chocolate flavor is essential, but when we crave a solid-chocolate experience, we'd rather have a flourless chocolate cake instead of one of the sticky, heavy chocolate mousses we tested from some cookbooks. In taking this position, we were able to eliminate one whole folder's worth of obviously leaden overwrought mousse recipes. At the other extreme, diet chocolate mousse is a contradiction in terms. When we want more air than flavor, we'll have meringues and sponge cakes.

As a starting point, we turned to the most basic definition of chocolate mousse that we could find. Surprisingly, it was in a book by the late British cookbook author Elizabeth David. In her *French Provincial Cooking* (Harper & Row, 1962), she refers to the "old and reliable formula for chocolate mousse—four yolks beaten into four ounces of bitter chocolate, and the four whipped whites folded in." We decided to go with the four-egg approach, then test mousses using varying amounts and proportions of the other possible ingredients, including butter, cream, sugar, and flavorings, that other cookbooks recommended.

Because chocolate mousse derives almost all of its flavor from the starring ingredient, we first wanted to see how much chocolate in proportion to eggs would give us a flavor we liked. Because chocolate contains sugar, as well as saturated fat in the form of cocoa butter, the amount of chocolate affects the texture of the final mousse as well. We started with 4 ounces of chocolate to 4 eggs. While we liked that ratio, we found it somewhat lacking in chocolate flavor. Six ounces of chocolate provided a much richer flavor. In the spirit of experimentation, we upped the chocolate again, incorporating eight ounces in our next mousse. At that level, however, the chocolate was dominant, lending an edge of bitterness that was unpleasant. We settled on six ounces.

Because most of the French recipes we had found in our cookbook research used butter to some degree, we next tried adding unsalted butter to the mixture. We discovered that it did make the mousse denser and gave it a rich mouthfeel. With one ounce of butter, the four-egg mousse was airy and light. Two ounces of butter gave it more creaminess and density without obliterating the lightness. When we moved up to four and six ounces of butter, the mousses took on a solid,

SCIENCE: Raw Eggs in Mousse

Because of the small possibility of bacterial contamination, many people worry about making mousse because it uses raw eggs. As with other recipes that use raw eggs, it is theoretically feasible to make a mousse by heating the eggs to a safe temperature before they are used in the dish. The "safe" temperature for eggs is 160 degrees. Unfortunately, we found it an impossible task to beat individual yolks containing so little liquid over a double boiler in order to raise the temperature. We could not increase it beyond 120 degrees before the yolks congealed into tiny, hard pieces. In addition, a difficult technique for making a "safe" soft meringue from heated whites left a result too sticky and grainy for mousse.

You can limit the risk somewhat by using very fresh eggs that are free from any cracks and blemishes and by keeping them refrigerated until ready to use. This does not totally eliminate the risk, however, since the bacteria may be present in the egg to begin with. Also, be careful never to leave foods made with raw eggs at room temperature for any appreciable length of time.

The bottom line is that if you are truly concerned about the health risks inherent in using raw eggs, you probably shouldn't make mousse at all.

truffle-like consistency and were so rich they could only be eaten in very small amounts. We agreed on two ounces of butter and no more.

Whipped cream has often served as a garnish for chocolate mousse. Many newer recipes add it to the mousse itself, so we tried some variations with whipped cream—and no butter—to determine the effect. Whipped cream, like the butter, made the mousse a little denser in texture, and it also softened the flavor, taking some of the deep chocolate hit out of the finished dessert. Although chocolate fanatics can stop reading right here, we wanted a more balanced flavor and thus found this effect useful and desirable. One-half cup of heavy cream, whipped and folded in, smoothed out the flavor without diluting the chocolate dimension quantifiably.

Having tested butter and cream separately, we decided to try the ultimate creamy mousse, one with both butter and cream. To do this, we made 18 different mousses for another informal tasting. The version with two ounces of butter and half a cup of whipped cream was the clear winner.

Because chocolates vary so much in sugar content, and because sugar is also a structural element in mousse, the recipes we encountered varied widely in the type and quantity of sugar specified. While your choice of chocolate will determine exactly how much sugar you need, we got a nicely balanced flavor using two tablespoons of sugar with most bittersweet and semisweet chocolates (three tablespoons actually made the chocolate flavor weaker and didn't seem any sweeter). Professional dessert chefs stock superfine sugar to ensure that it dissolves completely, but we had no difficulties in several tests using ordinary granulated sugar.

We next researched various flavoring liquids, including strong coffee and a variety of liquors and liqueurs. Not surprisingly, all such additions made the final product less firm. More than two tablespoons of such liquid (in addition to the teaspoon of vanilla extract) started to make the mousse slightly soupy, and more than two tablespoons of any alcohol-based liquid overwhelmed the flavor as well. If you prefer a stronger alcohol kick, we recommend you try whipping some additional liqueur into a whipped cream topping.

About half the recipes we researched called for whisking the egg yolks one by one into the chocolate mixture, and this was the technique we had been using to standardize our other ingredients. We had set aside another, more time-consuming approach to the egg yolks, in which they are beaten with some sugar until lightened in texture and color, then added to the chocolate. When we got around to trying a recipe that followed this procedure with the yolks, the volume of the mousse increased by as much as one-fourth, and the texture was much lighter and more airy.

Nonetheless, in a side-by-side test, we preferred the flavor of mousse made with unbeaten yolks. As with recipes made with extra whipped cream, more air in the mousse meant less flavor per mouthful. So this time, the easier technique was also the winner.

Chocolate Mousse

SERVES 6 TO 8

For an extra-creamy chocolate mousse, fold in 1 cup of heavy cream that's been whipped (instead of the ½ cup called for below). Make this mousse at least 2 hours before you wish to serve it to let the flavors develop, but serve it within 24 hours because the flavor and texture will begin to deteriorate. If you have concerns about consuming raw eggs, see "Raw Eggs in Mousse" on page 972.

6	ounces bittersweet or semisweet chocolate, chopped coarse
4	tablespoons (½ stick) unsalted butter
	Pinch salt
1	teaspoon vanilla extract
2	tablespoons strong coffee or 4 teaspoons brandy, orange-flavored liqueur, or light rum
4	large eggs, separated
2	tablespoons sugar
½	cup chilled heavy cream, plus more for serving

1. Melt the chocolate in a medium bowl set over a large saucepan of barely simmering water or in an uncovered Pyrex measuring cup microwaved at 50 percent power for 3 minutes, stirring once at the 2-minute mark. Whisk the butter into the melted chocolate, 1 tablespoon at a time. Stir in the salt, vanilla, and coffee until completely incorporated. Whisk in the yolks, one at a time, making sure that each is fully incorporated before adding the next; set the mixture aside.

2. Stir the egg whites in a clean mixing bowl set over a saucepan of hot water until slightly warm, 1 to 2 minutes; remove the bowl from the saucepan. Beat with an electric mixer set at medium speed until soft peaks form. Raise the mixer speed to high and slowly add the sugar; beat to soft peaks. Whisk a quarter of the beaten whites into the chocolate mixture to lighten it, then gently fold in the remaining whites.

3. Whip the cream to soft peaks. Gently fold the whipped cream into the mousse. Spoon portions of the mousse into 6 or 8 individual serving dishes or goblets. Cover and refrigerate to allow the flavors to blend, at least 2 hours. (The mousse may be covered and refrigerated for up to 24 hours.) Serve with additional whipped cream.

CHOCOLATE SOUFFLÉ

WHAT IS THE PERFECT SOUFFLÉ? IT IS A SOUFflé that has a crusty exterior packed with flavor, a dramatic rise above the rim, an airy but substantial outer layer, and a rich, loose center that is not completely set. A great soufflé must also convey a true mouthful of flavor, bursting with the bright, clear taste of the main ingredient. In a chocolate soufflé, the chocolate high notes should be clear and strong. A balancing act between egg whites, chocolate, yolks, and butter is the essence of a great chocolate soufflé.

A primary consideration when trying to create such a soufflé is what to use as the "base," the mixture that gives substance and flavor to the soufflé, as opposed to the airiness and "lift" provided by the whipped egg whites. The base can be a béchamel (a classic French sauce made with equal amounts of butter and flour, whisked with milk over heat), pastry cream (egg yolks beaten with sugar and then heated with milk), or a *bouillie* (flour cooked with milk or water until thickened). After trying several versions of each of these options, we found that we consistently preferred the béchamel base. It provided the soufflé with good chocolate flavor and a puffed yet substantial texture. By contrast, the versions made with pastry cream and bouillie were too dense and pudding-like for our tasters' palates.

After a week of refining a recipe using a béchamel base, we thought the soufflé was good but that the chocolate was muted by the milk in the béchamel. We removed the flour from our recipe, separated the eggs (whipping the whites separately), more than doubled the amount of chocolate, used six whole eggs, and reduced the amount of butter. This approach resulted in a base of egg yolks beaten with sugar until thick. This gave the soufflé plenty of volume but eliminated the milk, the ingredient that was holding back the chocolate. The result was fantastic—the most intense chocolate dessert we had ever tasted.

Our chocolate soufflé now had the intense flavor we had been looking for, but we still weren't completely happy with the texture because the outer layer was a bit cakey. After several more experiments, though, we discovered that adding two egg whites resolved the problem, giving the soufflé more lift and better texture.

We now moved on to check other variables, including oven temperature, a water bath, and the soufflé dish itself. For most recipes, a 25-degree variance in oven temperature is not crucial, so we were surprised to discover the dramatic impact it had on our soufflé. Our initial oven temperature was 375 degrees, but to be sure this temperature was optimum, we tested both 350 and 400 degrees as well. The higher oven temperature resulted in an overcooked exterior and an undercooked interior, while the lower temperature did not brown the exterior enough to provide good flavor and also produced a texture that was too even, given that we were looking for a loose center at the point at which the exterior was nicely cooked. We decided to stick with 375 degrees.

A water bath was a truly awful idea. When we tested it, the outer crust of the soufflé turned out wet, with a gelatin-like appearance, and the soufflé did not rise well.

One factor we found to be of surprising importance was the baking dish. We tried using a standard casserole dish for one of the tests, and the soufflé rose right out of the dish onto the floor of the oven! The problem was that the dish did not have the perfectly straight sides of a soufflé dish. It pays to make sure that you are using a real soufflé dish.

We also tested the theory that a chilled soufflé dish improves the rise and discovered that it did

FOLDING BEATEN EGG WHITES

Numerous recipes, everything from cakes to soufflés, call for beaten egg whites, which are usually folded into batter before it is baked. If you beat the eggs in too vigorously, the cake or soufflé may not rise. If you don't incorporate the eggs properly, you may be left with eggy patches in your baked goods. Here's the best way to fold beaten egg whites into a batter.

1. Gently stir a quarter of the whites into the batter to lighten it. Scrape the remaining whites onto the lightened batter. Cut through the center of the two mixtures down to the bottom of the bowl.

2. Pull the spatula toward you, scraping along the bottom and up the side of the bowl.

3. Once the spatula is out of the mixture, rotate the spatula so any mixture clinging to it falls back onto the surface of the batter.

4. Spin the bowl a quarter turn and repeat the process until the beaten egg whites are just incorporated and no large streaks of whites remain visible.

cause chocolate soufflés to rise higher but made little difference with nonchocolate soufflés.

During the course of all this testing, we also found a chocolate soufflé will give you three indications of when it is done: when you can smell the chocolate, when it stops rising, and when only the very center of the top jiggles when gently shaken. Of course, these are all imprecise methods. If you are not sure if your soufflé is done, simply take two large spoons, pull open the top of the soufflé, and peek inside. If the center is still soupy, simply put the dish back in the oven! Much to our surprise, and as heretical as it may sound, this probing in no way harmed the soufflé.

For years, we had heard rumors about chefs who had devised secret recipes for chocolate soufflés that are prepared ahead of time, then refrigerated or frozen, and baked at the last minute. We wanted to develop just such a recipe to take the last-minute worry out of soufflés for busy cooks.

For the first test, we tried both refrigerating and freezing the soufflé batter in individual ramekins. (We had discovered through earlier testing that individual soufflés hold up much better in the refrigerator or freezer than a full recipe held in a soufflé dish.) When we baked them, the refrigerated soufflés were a disaster (they hardly rose at all and were very wet inside), but the frozen versions worked fairly well. However, they were cake-like, devoid of the loose center we were seeking.

For the second test, we heated the sugar used in the recipe with two tablespoons of water just to the boiling stage and added it to the yolks while beating. Although this produced more volume, the final soufflé was only slightly better than the one in the first test. Finally, we also added two tablespoons of confectioners' sugar to the whites. This version was a great success, producing a soufflé that was light and airy, with an excellent rise and a nice wet center. The actual texture of the whites changed as they were beaten, becoming stable enough so they held up better during freezing. We did find that these soufflés ended up with a domed top, but by increasing the oven temperature to 400 degrees, this problem was solved. We had our make-ahead soufflé at last.

Chocolate Soufflé

SERVES 6 TO 8

Individual soufflés are an alternative to making a single large one. To make them, completely fill eight 8-ounce ramekins with the soufflé mixture, making sure to clean each rim with a wet paper towel, and reduce the baking time to 16 to 18 minutes. For a mocha-flavored soufflé, add 1 tablespoon of instant coffee powder dissolved in 1 tablespoon of hot water when adding the vanilla to the chocolate mixture. If you like the microwave, melt the chocolate at 50 percent power for 3 minutes, stirring in the butter after 2 minutes.

5	tablespoons unsalted butter, 1 tablespoon softened, 4 tablespoons cut into $1/2$-inch chunks
1	tablespoon plus $1/3$ cup (about $2^1/3$ ounces) sugar
8	ounces bittersweet or semisweet chocolate, chopped coarse
$1/8$	teaspoon salt
$1/2$	teaspoon vanilla extract
1	tablespoon Grand Marnier
6	large egg yolks
8	large egg whites
$1/4$	teaspoon cream of tartar

1. Adjust an oven rack to the lower-middle position and heat the oven to 375 degrees. Butter the inside of a 2-quart soufflé dish with the 1 tablespoon softened butter, then coat the inside of the dish evenly with the 1 tablespoon sugar; refrigerate until ready to use.

2. Melt the chocolate and the remaining butter in a medium bowl set over a pan of simmering water. Turn off the heat and stir in the salt, vanilla, and liqueur; set aside.

3. In a medium bowl, beat the yolks and remaining $1/3$ cup sugar with an electric mixer set on medium speed until thick and pale yellow, about 3 minutes. Fold into the chocolate mixture. Clean the beaters.

4. In a medium bowl, beat the whites with the electric mixer set on medium speed until foamy. Add the cream of tartar and continue to beat on high speed to stiff, moist peaks. (The mixture

should just hold the weight of a raw egg in the shell when the egg is placed on top.)

5. Vigorously stir one quarter of the whipped whites into the chocolate mixture. Gently fold the remaining whites into the mixture until just incorporated. Spoon the mixture into the prepared dish; bake until the exterior is set but the interior is still a bit loose and creamy, about 25 minutes. (The soufflé is done when fragrant and fully risen. Use two large spoons to pull open the top and peek inside. If not yet done, place back in oven.) Serve immediately.

➤ VARIATION
Make-Ahead Chocolate Soufflés
This technique works only for individual chocolate soufflés, which can be made and frozen up to 2 days before baking.

Follow the instructions for Chocolate Soufflé, coating eight 1-cup ramekins with butter and sugar. Rather than beating the sugar with the yolks, bring the sugar and 2 tablespoons water to a boil in a small saucepan, then simmer until the sugar dissolves. With the mixer running, slowly add this sugar syrup to the egg yolks; beat until the mixture triples in volume, about 3 minutes. Beat the egg whites until frothy; add the cream of tartar and beat to soft peaks; add 2 tablespoons confectioners' sugar; continue beating to stiff peaks. Stir and fold into the chocolate base as directed. Fill each chilled ramekin almost to the rim, wiping the excess mixture from the rim with a wet paper towel. Cover and freeze until firm, at least 3 hours. Increase the oven temperature to 400 degrees; place the ramekins on a baking sheet and bake until fully risen, 16 to 18 minutes. Do not overbake.

CHILLED LEMON SOUFFLÉ

BASED ON A CLASSIC BAVARIAN CREAM, CHILLED lemon soufflé is most often a mixture of a custard base, gelatin, whipped cream, beaten egg whites, sugar, and lemon flavorings. But like any good mongrel American classic, "chilled lemon soufflé"

covers a wide range of recipes, from baked pudding cakes, which are cooled and served at room temperature, to nothing more than lemon juice, sugar, and beaten whites, with no egg yolks and no whipped cream.

Given these various guises, it's hard to know exactly how this dessert should taste. For us, a chilled lemon soufflé is an unusual marriage of cream and foam, of sweet and sour, of high lemony notes and lingering, rich custard. It starts at the tip of the tongue with the sharp tingle of lemon zest and then slides slowly down the throat, filling the mouth with cream and pudding and a soft, long finish. At least that's what it is supposed to do. The question is, how can a home cook make this delicate balance of ingredients and technique turn out just right? We set out to test as many recipes as possible to find out.

For starters, we hauled out as many recipes as we could find and quickly discovered that there are five basic approaches to this dessert. The most elaborate begins with a custard base that is then combined with gelatin, whipped cream, and beaten egg whites. Many recipes, however, leave out the custard, using only beaten egg yolks and sugar as the base, while some classic French versions of this dish also leave out the egg whites. Other recipes omit the egg yolks altogether, using just sugar, lemon juice, whipped cream, and beaten egg whites. If the whipped cream is eliminated in a further act of reductionism, you have what is known as a lemon snow pudding. We also looked up recipes for lemon mousse and found that mousse is usually made without gelatin, the key ingredient in chilled lemon soufflé.

We began our testing with the simplest approach, just beaten egg whites, gelatin, sugar, and lemon juice. The result was a foamy confection, much like being served a mound of beaten egg whites. This dessert needed some fat for texture and flavor. We then thought we would try a recipe with whipped cream as well. This was quite good, rated number one by some tasters. It had lots of lemon punch but a somewhat airy, foamy texture that called for a bit more fat. Next, we added beaten egg yolks to the mixture, perhaps the most common approach to chilled lemon soufflé, but the texture of this version of the dessert was tough. We tried a second variation on this theme and were still unsatisfied with the texture. We then left out the egg whites and produced a dense, rubbery lemon dome, the sort of dessert that might hold up nicely in Death Valley in July. Finally, we started with a custard base made with sugar, egg yolks, milk, lemon juice, and gelatin and then added this to the whipped cream and beaten whites. This was highly rated, but the lemon flavor was a bit muted by the fat in the milk and egg yolks.

Upon reviewing the test results, we decided that a compromise might be reached between the two test winners. The lemon juice, whipped cream, and beaten-egg-white dessert was light and lemony but too foamy; the custard-base dessert had a better finish and mouthfeel but was lacking the bright, clear flavor of lemon. We worked up a new master recipe that called for softening one package of gelatin in a half cup of lemon juice. (We tried two packages of gelatin and ended up with a rubbery orb.) Next a cup of milk was heated with sugar while we beat 2 egg yolks with an extra 2 tablespoons of sugar. The milk and the beaten yolks were combined on top of the stove and heated until the mixture began to steam. Finally, the cooled custard was folded into ¾ cup of whipped heavy cream, and 6 beaten egg whites were folded into the result. This was the best variation to date, but it still needed a few refinements.

First we cut back the whites to 5 to give the dessert less air and more substance. Next we added just ¼ teaspoon of cornstarch to the custard mixture to prevent the yolks from curdling too easily, and we added grated lemon zest to the custard mixture to pump up the lemon flavor. We also discovered that to maintain a more consistent texture, it was better to whisk a small part of the beaten egg whites into the custard base before folding the mixture together.

Although many recipes call for individual ramekins, we decided to make one large and impressive soufflé and save the individual portions for a variation. To make this chilled dessert look even more like its baked cousin, we added a simple collar of aluminum foil and increased the recipe to the point where the mixture would rise above the rim of the dish, like a real soufflé. We were also curious about how well this dessert would hold up in the refrigerator. After one day, it was still good but slightly foamy, losing the creamy, tender undercurrent that is the hallmark of this dessert when well made. After two and three days, it quickly deteriorated. This is one dessert that is best served the day it is made.

Chilled Lemon Soufflé
SERVES 4 TO 6

To make this lemon soufflé rise over the rim of the dish, use a 1-quart soufflé dish and fashion a foil collar for it as follows: Cut a piece of foil slightly longer than the circumference of the soufflé dish and fold it lengthwise into fourths. Wrap the foil strip around the upper half of the soufflé dish and secure the overlap with tape. Tape the collar to the soufflé dish as necessary to prevent it from slipping. Spray the inside of the foil collar with vegetable cooking spray. When ready to serve, carefully remove the collar.

This dessert can also be served from any 1½-quart serving bowl. For the best texture, serve the soufflé after 1½ hours of chilling. If you have concerns about consuming raw eggs, see "Raw Eggs in Mousse" on page 972.

½	cup juice and 2½ teaspoons grated zest from 2 or 3 lemons
1	packet (¼ ounce) unflavored gelatin
1	cup whole milk
¾	cup (5¼ ounces) sugar
2	large egg yolks, plus 5 large egg whites, at room temperature
¼	teaspoon cornstarch
	Pinch cream of tartar
¾	cup chilled heavy cream
	Mint, raspberries, confectioners' sugar, or finely chopped pistachios for garnish (optional)

1. Place the lemon juice in a small nonreactive bowl and sprinkle the gelatin over it. Set aside to soften.

2. Heat the milk and ½ cup of the sugar in a medium saucepan over medium-low heat, stirring

occasionally, until steaming and the sugar is dissolved, about 5 minutes. Meanwhile, whisk together the yolks, 2 tablespoons of the sugar, and the cornstarch in a medium bowl until pale yellow and thickened. Whisking constantly, gradually add the hot milk to the yolks. Return the milk-egg mixture to the saucepan and cook, stirring constantly, over medium-low heat until the foam has dissipated to a thin layer and the mixture thickens to the consistency of heavy cream and registers 185 degrees on an instant-read thermometer, about 4 minutes. Pour the mixture through a mesh sieve and into a medium bowl; stir in the lemon juice mixture and zest. Set the bowl with the custard in a large bowl of ice water; stir occasionally to cool.

3. While the custard mixture is chilling, in the bowl of a standing mixer fitted with the whisk attachment, beat the egg whites and cream of tartar on medium speed until foamy, about 1 minute. Increase the speed to medium-high; gradually add the remaining 2 tablespoons sugar and continue to beat until glossy and the whites hold soft peaks when the beater is lifted, about 2 minutes longer. Do not overbeat. Remove the bowl containing the custard mixture from the ice-water bath; gently whisk in about one third of the egg whites, then fold in the remaining whites with a large rubber spatula until almost no white streaks remain. (For more information on folding, see page 974.)

4. In the same mixer bowl (washing is not necessary), using the whisk attachment, beat the cream on medium-high speed until soft peaks form when the beater is lifted, 2 to 3 minutes. Fold the cream into the custard and egg-white mixture until no white streaks remain.

5. Pour into the prepared soufflé dish (see note) or bowl. Chill until set but not stiff, about 1½ hours; remove the foil collar, if using, and serve, garnishing if desired.

➤ VARIATIONS

Chilled Lemon Soufflé with White Chocolate

The white chocolate in this variation subdues the lemony kick.

Follow the recipe for Chilled Lemon Soufflé, adding 2 ounces white chocolate, chopped, to the warm custard before adding the lemon juice mixture and zest. Stir until melted and fully incorporated.

Individual Chilled Lemon Soufflés

Follow the recipe for Chilled Lemon Soufflé, dividing the batter equally among eight ¾-cup ramekins (filled to the rim) or six ¾-cup ramekins (each fitted with a foil collar).

SCIENCE: Why Add Cream of Tartar When Beating Egg Whites?

In most kitchens, in the back of the spice cupboard, you will find an aged tin of cream of tartar covered with some dust. We obediently add it when whipping egg whites, but otherwise leave this curious white powder alone.

What is cream of tartar, and how does it work? Its technical name is acid potassium tartrate, and it is derived from a crystalline acid deposited on the inside of wine barrels as the wine ferments. It is known as an acid salt—that is, an acid that has been partially neutralized to leave a weakly acidic salt.

Egg whites have the miraculous ability to increase their volume over eightfold when provided with enough energy by means of a strong arm or a good mixer. Mechanical energy causes strands of the protein albumin to partially unfold and connect with one another. These interconnected albumin strands can wrap around air bubbles and lead to foam development.

As anyone can who has made egg foams can tell you, it is an imperfect art ripe with opportunities for collapse. Cream of tartar, because of its acidic nature, gives the cook a leg up by lowering the alkaline pH of the egg whites from about 9 to 8. This change in pH helps neutralize certain proteins that tend to repel each other and encourages their association. The result is easier development of a more stable foam.

Our kitchen tests have confirmed that egg whites beaten with cream of tartar achieve greater volume than egg whites beaten on their own. In addition, egg whites beaten with cream of tartar will not collapse as quickly as egg whites beaten on their own. When it comes time to beat egg whites, we suggest that you dust off that tin of cream of tartar.

ICE CREAM

WHEN WE FINISHED DEVELOPING OUR ICE cream recipes, we realized that they all had a few similarities. Once the base for an ice cream has been prepared, it is handled in pretty much the same manner, no matter the flavor. The pros and cons of various ice cream makers (see page 980 for specific information) are the same whether you are making vanilla or strawberry ice cream. Here are some general points to keep in mind when making ice cream.

It's imperative to chill the ice cream base (the custard) fully before placing it in an ice cream machine. We found that chilling the base to 40 degrees or lower is ideal. We like to start by placing the hot custard or base for ice cream in an ice-water bath to bring down its temperature quickly.

The next step is to pour the base into an airtight container and let the refrigerator do the rest of the work. An instant-read thermometer is essential here. We found that if the base is too warm when it is placed in the ice cream machine, it will need to be churned for much longer (up to an hour) until frozen to a semisolid state. Ice cream machines with canisters that require freezing before churning will loose their cooling ability before this stage is reached. Ice cream machines with self-contained freezers can bring warm base down to the correct temperature, but the extra churning causes the formation of butter flecks in ice cream and iciness in all frozen desserts.

Ice cream will not emerge from any ice cream maker (including those that cost $500) with a firm, hard texture. Once the ice cream is well chilled (about 25 degrees), fluffy, and frozen to the texture of soft-serve ice cream, remove it from the ice cream maker. It takes about 30 minutes of churning to reach this stage in most ice cream machines. If you churn any longer, you may promote the development of butter flecks or iciness. In any case, further churning will not freeze the dessert any harder. Several hours in the freezer, where temperatures are much lower, will complete the freezing process.

If you store ice cream for more than a few hours, the texture will become firm, like that of the ice cream sold in supermarket freezer cases. If you prefer a softer texture, transfer the container with the frozen dessert to the refrigerator 30 minutes to one hour before serving. We find that ice cream tastes best around 10 to 12 degrees, well above the temperature maintained by most home freezers.

Unlike commercial products, which are often made with stabilizers and/or preservatives, homemade ice creams have a short shelf life. Temperature fluctuations in home freezers promote iciness in all frozen desserts, with melting and freezing taking their toll fairly quickly on homemade ice creams. After several days, homemade ice creams become quite icy. They are best eaten the day they are made but can be held up to two days.

VANILLA ICE CREAM

THE INGREDIENTS FOR VANILLA ICE CREAM could not be simpler—cream, milk, sugar, vanilla, and sometimes eggs. The results, however, vary greatly, depending on the quantities of each ingredient and the techniques that are used.

There are two basic types of vanilla ice cream. Custard-style ice cream contains egg yolks and has a silky texture and rich flavor. Philadelphia-style ice cream is made without eggs, and often the ingredients are combined without any cooking. It's the difference between a pale yellow French vanilla ice cream and a bright white plain vanilla.

While commercial versions of these two styles abound, we have found that home cooks are better off preparing a custard-type ice cream with egg yolks. These ice creams have the creamy texture we associate with high-quality ice cream. Egg yolks are about 10 percent lecithin, an emulsifier that helps maintain an even dispersal of fat droplets in ice cream and also helps keep ice crystals small. The overall effect is one of richness and smoothness. Store-bought ice creams made without eggs often contain stabilizers and emulsifiers. Home cooks would not (and generally cannot) add these ingredients to ice cream. Also, commercial ice cream machines are able to inject much more air into Philadelphia-style ice cream than home machines. With more air, these eggless ice creams have a lighter, less icy texture.

Once we decided that custard–style vanilla ice cream was the way to go, many other issues arose. How many egg yolks are needed for a one–quart batch of ice cream? What kind of dairy should be used? Cream, half–and–half, milk, or some combination thereof? Also, what's the best way to prepare a custard without causing the eggs to curdle?

We tested as many as eight and as few as three egg yolks in our master recipe. Although five or six eggs delivered an excellent texture, we found that the egg flavor became too pronounced. Vanilla ice cream should taste of dairy, sugar, and vanilla, not like scrambled eggs. Four egg yolks gave the ice cream the appropriate silkiness without overpowering the other flavors.

The question of which dairy products to use proved more complicated. Ice cream made with all cream is too buttery. The fat content is so high that churning causes tiny particles of butter to

---

EQUIPMENT: Ice Cream Makers

If you're in the market for an ice cream maker, you've got several options. We tested seven models, ranging in price from a modest $50 all the way up to $600. They fell into three categories: expensive machines that don't require the use of a freezer; mid-priced machines with an electric motor and a removable canister that must be frozen in advance; and mid-priced machines with a hand crank and a removable canister that must be frozen in advance.

The two canister-free models produced smooth, creamy ice cream. They have two distinct advantages over the other models tested: volume and ready-to-serve ice cream (it was fully frozen and could be eaten right from the machine). The Lussino Dessert Maker from Musso ($594.95, 1½-quart capacity) contains a built-in refrigerator unit and is the Cadillac of ice cream makers. It can make endless batches without waiting 12 hours for a freezer canister to get back down to the proper temperature. The White Mountain Ice Cream Maker ($199.95, 4-quart capacity) produces a whole gallon of great ice cream in one shot, but it requires 10 pounds of ice as well as rock salt. This

machine is also unbearably loud—better suited to a back porch than a kitchen.

The three electric models with canisters that must go in the freezer overnight made smooth, creamy ice cream in less than 30 minutes. The ice cream was quite soft, however, and benefited from a few hours in the freezer to firm up before being eaten. The Krups La Glacière ($59.95, 1½-quart capacity) was quieter than the Cuisinart one-canister machine ($49.95, 1½-quart capacity) and the Cuisinart two-canister machine ($99.95, 2-quart capacity). Given its modest price and size (and immodestly good ice cream), the Krups machine is an excellent choice.

The two manual models—the Donvier ($49.95, 1-quart capacity) and the Chilly by William Bounds ($69.99, 2-quart capacity)—got the job done in just 20 minutes, but the ice cream was grainy, icy, and dense. If you can buy a model with a built-in motor for the same price, why settle for hand-cranked, inferior ice cream?

BEST PERFORMANCE
LUSSINO
Great ice cream at a sky-high price.

BEST VALUE
KRUPS LA GLACIÈRE
Good ice cream at a modest price.

WORST PERFORMANCE
DONVIER
So-so ice cream at a modest price.

form. However, ice cream made with all milk or even half-and-half is too lean. These dairy products contain more water, and the result is an ice cream with tiny ice crystals. After extensive testing, we came to prefer an equal amount of heavy cream and whole milk. The texture is rich, but there is no butteriness. Most important, there is enough fat to prevent the formation of large ice crystals, which may occur when a lower-fat dairy combination is used.

Besides adding sweetness, sugar also promotes a smoother, softer, more "scoopable" end product. This is because sugar reduces the number and size of ice crystals and lowers the freezing temperature of the custard. The latter effect allows you to churn the custard longer before it freezes firm, thus incorporating more air into the ice cream. In our testing, we found the texture of a quart of ice cream made with one cup of sugar to be excellent, but the sweetness overpowered delicate flavors like vanilla. We tried one-half cup of sugar per quart of ice cream and found that the ice cream was too firm to scoop right from the freezer. The texture was marred by iciness as well. Three-quarters cup of sugar is enough to keep the ice cream soft and smooth without making it cloying.

With the ingredient issues settled, we turned our focus to questions of technique. We soon discovered that subtle changes in the custard-making process can have a profound effect on texture. Our goal was absolute smoothness and creaminess. Of course, the danger of applying too much heat to the eggs and causing the custard to curdle (the eggs literally clump together, as in making scrambled eggs, and cause the custard to break and become lumpy) also lurks in the background.

We found it best to heat the milk, cream, and part of the sugar to 175 degrees. If this mixture is brought to a higher temperature, there is a risk that the eggs will curdle when the too-hot mixture is added to them. Lower temperatures, however, fail to dissolve the sugar. While the milk, cream, and part of the sugar are heating, the yolks are beaten with the remaining sugar. We found that adding unbeaten or lightly beaten yolks to the custard results in an ice cream with a shocking yellow color.

Because sudden exposure to high heat (even 175 degrees) can curdle eggs, it's important to temper them—or increase the temperature slowly—by adding a small portion of the hot milk-cream mixture. Tempering also thins out the thick yolk-sugar mixture so that it can be more easily incorporated into the hot milk and cream.

We found various "tricks" for determining when a custard is fully cooked to be only minimally helpful. Yes, a custard does thicken enough to coat the back of a spoon. Yes, a custard should hold its shape when a line is drawn through it with the back of a spoon. But these things may happen well before the custard has reached 180 degrees, the temperature we have found to be ideal for ice cream making. Because egg yolks start to curdle between 185 and 190 degrees, our recommended final temperature of 180 to 185 degrees provides some margin of error but allows the eggs to provide a maximum amount of thickening. A custard cooked to only 160 or 170 degrees will make a slightly less rich, less silky ice cream. For this reason, we advocate the use of an instant-read thermometer when making custard for ice cream.

No matter how careful you are, tiny bits of egg may overcook and form thin particles or strands, especially around the edges and bottom of the pan. We recommend pouring the cooked custard through a fine-mesh strainer to eliminate any of these solid egg pieces. However, a curdled custard with large clumps of egg cannot be rescued and should be discarded.

Vanilla Ice Cream

MAKES ABOUT 1 QUART

Two teaspoons of vanilla extract may be substituted for the vanilla bean, although the flavor will not be as true. To maximize the extract's potency, stir it into the chilled custard just before churning.

1½	cups whole milk
1½	cups heavy cream
¾	cup (5¼ ounces) sugar
1	vanilla bean, split in half lengthwise and seeds scraped out (see the illustrations on page 957)
4	large egg yolks

1. Position a strainer over a medium bowl set in a larger bowl containing ice water. Heat the milk, cream, ½ cup of the sugar, and the vanilla seeds and pod in a medium saucepan over medium heat, stirring occasionally to break up the vanilla seeds, until steam appears and the milk is warm (about 175 degrees), about 5 minutes.

2. Meanwhile, whisk the yolks and remaining ¼ cup sugar in a medium bowl until combined and pale yellow. Whisk half the warm milk mixture into the beaten yolks, ½ cup at a time, until combined. Whisk the milk-yolk mixture into the warm milk in the saucepan; set the saucepan over medium heat and cook, stirring constantly with a wooden spoon, until steam appears, foam subsides, and the mixture is slightly thickened or an instant-read thermometer registers 180 to 185 degrees. (Do not boil the mixture, or the eggs will curdle.) Immediately strain the custard into the bowl set in the ice bath; cool the custard to room temperature, stirring it occasionally to help it cool. Cover and refrigerate until an instant-read thermometer registers 40 degrees or lower, at least 3 hours or up to 24 hours.

3. Remove and discard the vanilla pod from the custard (or add the vanilla extract, if using) and stir well. Pour the custard into the ice cream machine canister and churn, following the manufacturer's instructions, until the mixture resembles soft-serve ice cream. Transfer the ice cream to an

INGREDIENTS: Store-Bought Vanilla Ice Cream

There are times when you probably don't want to make you own ice cream. Store-bought ice cream certainly makes a nice crown for a piece of pie or a bowl of warm cherry cobbler. But with so many brands on the market, we wondered if there were big differences between them. To find out, we gathered 20 tasters to sample eight leading national brands of vanilla ice cream, made in what's known as the French, or custard, style, with egg yolks.

Many ice cream manufacturers add stabilizers—most often carrageenan gum or guar gum—to prevent "heat shock," an industry term for the degradation in texture caused by the partial melting and refreezing that takes place when ice cream is subjected to extreme temperature changes during transit to the supermarket or when an ice cream case goes through its self-defrosting cycle. We thought that the presence of stabilizers might affect the test results. To our surprise, this was not the case. The top two brands in our tasting, Edy's Dreamery and Double Rainbow, use stabilizers.

We also expected that the nature of the ice creams' vanilla flavor—artificial or real—would affect the outcome of the test. Again we were a bit surprised with the results. Blue Bell was the only brand in the tasting that contained artificial vanilla flavor, and it rated smackdab in the middle, thus negating any link between natural flavor and superior flavor.

Next up was the issue of butterfat, which contributes to smooth texture, rich flavor, and structure. By law, an ice cream can't be called ice cream unless its prefrozen mix contains a minimum of 10 percent butterfat. Of the ice creams we tasted, butterfat content ranged from 10 to 16 percent, and, in general, the higher the butterfat content, the higher the ice cream rated.

The last component we researched was emulsifiers, such as mono- and diglycerides, which are used to control the behavior of fat in ice cream by keeping it from separating out of the ice cream mass. These emulsifiers give an ice cream rigidity and strength, so even if it doesn't have much butterfat or added gums, the ice cream will maintain its round, scooped shape for a prolonged period of time. The only ice cream in our tasting with emulsifiers was also the least favored sample: Edy's Grand. So, according to our taste test, it seems that emulsifiers are not desirable.

The winner of our tasting, as mentioned above, was Edy's Dreamery, with Double Rainbow coming in second and Breyers third. The real news, however, was the poor showing of the two best-known premium brands, Häagen-Dazs and Ben & Jerry's, which rated fourth and seventh, respectively, out of the eight brands sampled.

THE BEST VANILLA ICE CREAMS
Edy's Dreamery Vanilla (left) was the favorite of our tasters. Double Rainbow French Vanilla (middle) came in second, and Breyers French Vanilla (right) was third.

airtight container, press plastic wrap flush against the surface, cover the container, and freeze the ice cream until firm, at least 2 hours. (The ice cream will keep for up to 2 days.)

> VARIATIONS

Chocolate Chip Ice Cream

Follow the recipe for Vanilla Ice Cream, using 1 teaspoon vanilla extract (in step 3) instead of the vanilla bean. Add 2 ounces bittersweet or semisweet chocolate, chopped, about 30 seconds before the churning is completed. Freeze as directed.

Mint Chocolate Chip Ice Cream

Follow the recipe for Chocolate Chip Ice Cream, replacing the vanilla extract with ¼ cup clear or green crème de menthe.

Oreo Ice Cream

Follow the recipe for Chocolate Chip Ice Cream, replacing the chopped chocolate with 1 cup coarsely crumbled Oreo cookies (about 8 whole cookies). Freeze as directed.

CHOCOLATE ICE CREAM

CHOCOLATE ICE CREAM SHOULD BE PARticularly decadent, with a deep, true chocolate flavor. Too often, it falls short, with a pale color, weak chocolate flavor, and light, icy texture.

Although chocolate ice cream may seem far removed from vanilla, the two are actually quite close. We suspected we could use our vanilla ice cream base, replacing the vanilla bean with extract and then adding chocolate in some form. The recipes we uncovered in our research provided several choices, including cocoa powder, chocolate milk, unsweetened chocolate, and semisweet chocolate.

We started by making a simple ice cream with cocoa powder as the only chocolate flavoring. The resulting ice cream was good but too mellow. Also, some tasters noticed a chalky aftertaste, presumably from the cocoa. When we added some melted bittersweet chocolate along with the cocoa powder, the flavor became more assertive, but the chalkiness remained.

Just for kicks, we tried making a chocolate ice cream with chocolate syrup (an ingredient we had seen in a few recipes) and another with chocolate milk. The ice cream made with chocolate syrup was a failure—it had an odd, gummy texture and a chemical aftertaste. The version made with chocolate milk was more successful—it had a clear but mild chocolate flavor.

Still wanting a richer taste, we went on to experiment with bittersweet chocolate, unsweetened chocolate, and cocoa powder until we decided that our favorite was the ice cream made with bittersweet chocolate alone. The ice cream made with bittersweet chocolate was velvety smooth, with a deep chocolate flavor. Unsweetened chocolate left a slightly gritty texture, and cocoa powder, even in small amounts, did the same thing. We also found it important to use a high-quality chocolate. Lesser-quality chocolates produced ice creams with a slightly sour aftertaste.

We wondered if vanilla extract was really necessary, so we made batches made with and without extract. As it so often does, a touch of vanilla added after cooking the custard base rounded out the flavor of the chocolate.

~

Chocolate Ice Cream

MAKES ABOUT 1 QUART

Our favorite high-quality bittersweet chocolate is Callebaut from Belgium.

8	ounces high-quality bittersweet chocolate
1½	cups whole milk
1½	cups heavy cream
¾	cup (5¼ ounces) sugar
4	large egg yolks
1	teaspoon vanilla extract

1. In a medium heatproof bowl set over a pan of almost-simmering water, melt the chocolate, stirring occasionally, until smooth. Set aside to cool.

2. Meanwhile, position a strainer over a medium bowl set in a larger bowl containing ice water. Heat the milk, cream, and ½ cup of the sugar in a medium saucepan over medium heat, stirring occasionally to dissolve the sugar, until steam appears

DESSERT SAUCES AND ACCOMPANIMENTS

Berry Coulis
MAKES ABOUT 1 ½ CUPS

Coulis is simply sweetened fruit pureed into a sauce. Because the types of berries used as well as their ripeness will affect the sweetness of the coulis, the amount of sugar is variable. Start with 5 tablespoons, then add more if you prefer a sweeter coulis. Additional sugar should be stirred in immediately after straining, while the coulis is still warm, so that the sugar will readily dissolve. Serve the coulis with Lemon Cheesecake (page 870), Classic Pound Cake (page 833), Angel Food Cake (page 826), or ice cream.

12	ounces (2½ to 3 cups) fresh or thawed frozen raspberries, blueberries, blackberries, or strawberries (fresh strawberries hulled and sliced)
¼	cup water
5–7	tablespoons sugar
⅛	teaspoon salt
2	teaspoons juice from 1 lemon

1. Bring the berries, water, 5 tablespoons of the sugar, and the salt to a bare simmer in a medium nonreactive saucepan over medium heat. Cook, stirring occasionally, until the sugar is dissolved and the berries are heated through, about 1 minute.

2. Transfer the mixture to a blender or food processor; puree until smooth, about 20 seconds. Strain through a fine-mesh strainer into a small bowl, pressing and stirring the puree with a rubber spatula to extract as much seedless puree as possible. Stir in the lemon juice and additional sugar, if desired. Cover with plastic wrap and refrigerate until cold, at least 1 hour. Stir to recombine before serving. (The coulis can be refrigerated in an airtight container for up to 4 days. If too thick after chilling, add 1 to 2 teaspoons water.)

Hot Fudge Sauce
MAKES 2 CUPS

If you wish, melt the chocolate in the microwave at medium (50 percent) power for 3 minutes, stirring once halfway through and then whisking the cocoa powder into the chocolate once it is melted. The sauce will keep for at least 10 days, tightly covered and refrigerated, but it must be served warm. When reheating, be sure to reheat only as much sauce as you need because repeated heating and chilling may make the sauce grainy. Scrape the sauce into a heatproof bowl and set it over simmering water on low heat. Stir often, heating the sauce just until it is warm. Alternatively, you can reheat the sauce in the microwave at medium power for short intervals, stirring often, just until the sauce is warm.

10	ounces bittersweet or semisweet chocolate, chopped
⅓	cup sifted Dutch-process cocoa
⅓	cup (2⅓ ounces) sugar
¾	cup light corn syrup
⅓	cup heavy cream
	Pinch salt
⅓	cup water
1	teaspoon vanilla extract
3	tablespoons unsalted butter, cut into pieces

1. Melt the chocolate in a small heatproof bowl set over a pan of almost-simmering water until smooth, stirring once or twice. Turn off the heat and whisk in the cocoa until dissolved; set aside.

2. Warm the sugar, corn syrup, cream, salt, and water in a medium, heavy-bottomed nonreactive saucepan over low heat, without stirring, until the sugar dissolves. Increase the heat to medium-high; simmer the mixture, stirring frequently, about 4 minutes.

3. Turn off the heat and whisk in the vanilla and butter. Cool the mixture slightly, about 2 minutes, then whisk in the melted chocolate. Serve warm.

Bittersweet Chocolate Sauce

MAKES ABOUT 1 1/2 CUPS

This sauce can be served over Classic Pound Cake (page 833) or ice cream.

- ¾ cup heavy cream
- 3 tablespoons light corn syrup
- 3 tablespoons unsalted butter, cut into 3 pieces
- Pinch salt
- 6 ounces bittersweet chocolate, chopped fine

Bring the heavy cream, corn syrup, butter, and salt to a boil in a small nonreactive saucepan over medium-high heat. Off the heat, add the chocolate while gently swirling the saucepan. Cover the pan and let stand until the chocolate is melted, about 5 minutes. Uncover and whisk gently until combined. (The sauce can be cooled to room temperature, placed in an airtight container, and refrigerated for up to 3 weeks. To reheat, transfer the sauce to a heatproof bowl set over a saucepan of simmering water. Alternatively, microwave at 50 percent power, stirring once or twice, for 1 to 3 minutes.)

Caramel Sauce

MAKES ABOUT 1 1/2 CUPS

This sauce is an accompaniment to German Apple Pancake (page 937) or can be served with ice cream. When the hot cream mixture is added in step 3, the hot sugar syrup will bubble vigorously (and dangerously), so don't use a smaller saucepan.

- ½ cup water
- 1 cup (7 ounces) sugar
- 1 cup heavy cream
- ⅛ teaspoon salt
- ½ teaspoon vanilla extract
- ½ teaspoon juice from 1 lemon

1. Place the water in a heavy-bottomed 2-quart saucepan. Pour the sugar into the center of the pan, taking care not to let the sugar crystals adhere to the sides of the pan. Cover and bring the mixture to a boil over high heat; once boiling, uncover and continue to boil until the syrup is thick and straw-colored (the syrup should register 300 degrees on a candy thermometer), about 7 minutes. Reduce the heat to medium and continue to cook until the syrup is a deep amber color (350 degrees on the candy thermometer), 1 to 2 minutes.

2. Meanwhile, bring the cream and salt to a simmer in a small saucepan over high heat (if the cream boils before the sugar reaches a deep amber color, remove the cream from the heat and cover to keep warm).

3. Remove the sugar syrup from the heat; very carefully, pour about one quarter of the hot cream into it (the mixture will bubble vigorously) and let the bubbling subside. Add the remaining hot cream, the vanilla, and lemon juice; whisk until the sauce is smooth. (The sauce can be cooled and refrigerated in an airtight container for up to 2 weeks. Reheat in the microwave or in a small saucepan over low heat until warm and fluid.)

Whipped Cream

MAKES ABOUT 2 CUPS

We prefer pasteurized heavy cream to ultra-pasteurized for whipped cream. Whipped cream can be refrigerated in a fine-mesh sieve set over a measuring cup for up to 8 hours.

- 1 cup chilled heavy cream
- 1 tablespoon sugar
- 1 teaspoon vanilla extract

1. Chill a nonreactive, deep 1- to 1½-quart bowl and the beaters of an electric mixer in the freezer for at least 20 minutes.

2. Add the cream, sugar, and vanilla to the chilled bowl. Beat at low speed until small bubbles form, about 30 seconds. Increase the speed to medium and continue beating until the beaters leave a trail, about 30 seconds. Increase the speed to high and continue beating until the cream is smooth, thick, and nearly doubled in volume, about 20 seconds for soft peaks or about 30 seconds for stiff peaks. If necessary, finish beating by hand to adjust the consistency.

and the milk is warm (about 175 degrees), about 5 minutes. While the milk is heating, beat the yolks and remaining ¼ cup sugar in a medium bowl until combined and pale yellow. Add the melted chocolate and beat until fully incorporated.

3. Whisk half the warm milk mixture into the beaten yolks, ½ cup at a time, until combined. Whisk the milk–yolk mixture into the warm milk in the saucepan; set the saucepan over medium heat and cook, stirring constantly with a wooden spoon until steam appears, foam subsides, and the mixture is slightly thickened or an instant–read thermometer registers 180 to 185 degrees. (Do not boil the mixture, or the eggs will curdle.)

Immediately strain the custard into the bowl set in the ice bath; cool the custard to room temperature, stirring it occasionally to help it cool. Stir in the vanilla, then cover and refrigerate until an instant–read thermometer registers 40 degrees or lower, at least 3 hours or up to 24 hours.

4. Pour the custard into the ice cream machine canister and churn, following the manufacturer's instructions, until the mixture resembles soft-serve ice cream. Transfer the ice cream to an airtight container, press plastic wrap flush against the surface, cover the container, and freeze the ice cream until firm, at least 2 hours. (The ice cream will keep for up to 2 days.)

EQUIPMENT: Ice Cream Scoops

We've all struggled with an intractable pint of rock-hard ice cream. That's where a good ice cream scoop comes in handy; it can release even hard-frozen ice cream from bondage. We gathered 10 readily available scoops and dipped our way through 20 pints of vanilla to find the best one. We tested three basic types of scoop: classic, mechanical-release (or spring-loaded), and spade-shaped. Prices ranged from $3.99 to $22.

Classic ice cream scoops sport a thick handle and curved bowl. They can be used by lefties and righties with equal comfort. There are a few variations on the theme; among the classic scoops we purchased, one had a pointed "beak" scoop, another offered a "comfort grip" rubber handle, and another contained a self-defrosting liquid. Testers were unanimous in assigning first place to the Zeroll Classic Ice Cream Scoop ($22). Its thick handle was comfortable for large and small hands, and its nonstick coating and self-defrosting liquid (which responds to heat from the user's hand) contributed to perfect release, leaving only traces of melted cream inside the scoop. The defrosting fluid and the elegantly curved bowl allowed the scoop to take purchase immediately, curling a perfect scoop with minimal effort. Only one caveat: Don't run this scoop through the dishwasher, as it will lose its magical defrosting properties.

Coming in second was the Oxo Beak Scoop ($11.99). The beak point dug into ice cream with ease, and the ice cream curled up nicely. Our only minor quibble was the short handle, which forced testers with larger hands to choke up close to the head. If price is a concern, you might consider this model.

Mechanical-release scoops come in various sizes and operate with a spring-loaded, squeezable handle (or thumb trigger)

that connects to a curved steel lever inside the scoop. When the handle or lever is released, the ice cream pops out in a perfectly round ball. Although we frequently use a mechanical-release scoop to measure out even portions of cookie dough and muffin batter, we found these scoops to be less than ideal when it came to ice cream. They are designed for right-handed users only, and their thin, straight-edged handles were distinctly uncomfortable when considerable pressure was applied. Of the four models we tested, none was worthy of recommendation.

Spades, with their flat, paddle-type heads, are useful when you need to scoop a lot of ice cream quickly, say, for an ice cream cake or sandwiches, but they are too big to fit into pint containers. If you make frozen desserts frequently or need to work your way through multiple gallon-size containers of ice cream, a spade might be for you. Our preferred model, made by the same manufacturer as our winning scoop, was the Zeroll Nonstick Ice Cream Spade ($19.60).

BEST ICE CREAM SCOOPS
The Zeroll Classic Ice Cream Scoop (left) was the favorite model tested. If you need to scoop a lot of ice cream for an ice cream cake, you might consider the Zeroll Nonstick Ice Cream Spade (right), but this tool is too big to fit into pint containers.

STRAWBERRY ICE CREAM

COME LONG, HOT SUMMER DAYS, WE SHED thoughts of warm, wintery apple pie like a fleece sweatshirt. Instead, we opt for cool desserts that offer chilly refreshment or ones that showcase the season's offerings of sweet, ripe fruit. Fresh strawberry ice cream features both. Most store-bought strawberry ice creams are lean on flavor—the berry bits are flavorless, icy nuggets and the ice creams themselves are milky, insubstantial, and artificially flavored. One way to experience rich, silky, pure-tasting, truly good strawberry ice cream is to make it at home. But homemade strawberry ice cream is subject to the same misfortunes that befall store-bought versions—icy fruit and weak flavor are not uncommon.

We started with a custard base for our ice cream. Previous testing for homemade peach ice cream had already determined for us the best proportions of milk, cream, and egg yolks. It was on the treatment of the strawberries that we needed to focus our attention. We made an ice cream with a strawberry puree: It had a lovely pink color, but the flavor was tangy, more like frozen yogurt than ice cream, and there were no appealing bites of berries. We tried a batch in which strawberry pieces were unceremoniously thrown into the ice cream base, but these berries froze solid and contributed nothing to the flavor of the ice cream. Clearly, some of the natural juices would have to be withdrawn from the berries to keep them from solidifying upon freezing. We borrowed a technique from our peach ice cream recipe and macerated quartered berries with some sugar until they released a good amount of liquid. A quick cook then coaxed out even more juices while helping the berries become soft and yielding. Next we added vodka to the berries and juices so that they could benefit from alcohol's antifreezing properties; before churning, we strained the juices and stirred them into the base, adding the chilled berries when the ice cream was almost frozen. Still, the stubborn berries froze into hard, icy bits. The ice cream was also wanting in strawberry flavor.

In our next attempt, reasoning that if broken down into smaller pieces, the berries would have less of an icy presence in the ice cream, we sliced the berries instead of quartering them, macerated and cooked them, and then strained off the liquid so that we could reduce the juices down to a thick syrup, thereby concentrating the flavor. The sliced berries had a better frozen texture than the quartered ones, but the fresh flavor of the berries was lost during the reduction of the juices, and the ice cream tasted sullen, without a trace of freshness.

We took stronger measures. The ice cream was in need of more flavor and more berries, so we upped the amount of strawberries by 30 percent. To break down the berries beyond what could be accomplished by mere slicing, we used a potato masher to mash them lightly before macerating. Then, after a brief cooking, instead of allowing the berries to cool in their juices, where we suspected they were only plumping themselves back up to become icy when frozen, we strained the juices and stirred them into the already-made ice cream base; the berries we steeped in some vodka. Not until the last moments of churning did we add the alcohol-infused berries to the ice cream. A few hours in the freezer to firm things up and we had rich, creamy, fresh, fruity, sweet-tart summer strawberry ice cream that even the staunchest chocolate ice cream fans could appreciate.

Strawberry Ice Cream
MAKES ABOUT 1 QUART

Though the frozen ice cream will keep in the freezer for up to 2 days, its flavor and texture are best when it is eaten the day it is made.

16	ounces (about 3 cups) strawberries, hulled and sliced
	Pinch salt
1¼	cups (8¾ ounces) sugar
1¼	cups whole milk
1⅓	cups heavy cream
6	large egg yolks
1	teaspoon juice from 1 lemon
3	tablespoons vodka
1	teaspoon vanilla extract

1. Toss the strawberries, salt, and ½ cup of the sugar together in a medium nonreactive saucepan.

Mash the berries gently with a potato masher until slightly broken down. Let stand, stirring occasionally, until the berries have released their juices and the sugar has dissolved, 40 to 45 minutes.

2. Meanwhile, position a strainer over a medium bowl set in a larger bowl containing ice water. Heat the milk, cream, ½ cup of the sugar, and the salt in a medium saucepan over medium heat, stirring occasionally, until steam appears and the milk is warm (about 175 degrees), about 5 minutes. While the milk is heating, whisk the yolks and remaining ¼ cup sugar in a medium bowl until combined and pale yellow. Whisk about half the warm milk mixture into the beaten yolks, ½ cup at a time, until combined. Whisk the milk-yolk mixture into the warm milk in the saucepan; set the saucepan over medium heat and cook, stirring constantly with a wooden spoon, until steam appears, foam subsides, and the mixture is slightly thickened or an instant-read thermometer registers 180 to 185 degrees. (Do not boil the mixture, or the eggs will curdle.) Immediately strain the custard into the bowl set in the ice-water bath; cool the custard to room temperature, stirring it occasionally to help it cool.

3. While the custard is cooling, set the saucepan containing the berries over medium-high heat and bring the mixture to a simmer, stirring occasionally, until the berries are softened and broken down, about 3 minutes total. Strain the berries, reserving the juices. Transfer the berries to a small bowl; stir in the lemon juice and vodka, then cool to room temperature, cover with plastic wrap, and refrigerate until cold. Stir the vanilla and the reserved juices into the cooled custard, cover the bowl with plastic wrap, and refrigerate until an instant-read thermometer registers 40 degrees or lower, at least 3 hours or up to 24 hours.

4. Pour the custard into the ice cream machine canister and churn, following the manufacturer's instructions, until the mixture resembles soft-serve ice cream. Add the strawberries and any accumulated juices; continue to churn the ice cream until the berries are fully incorporated and slightly broken down, 1 to 2 minutes. Transfer the ice cream to an airtight container, press plastic wrap flush against the surface, cover the container, and freeze the ice cream until firm, at least 2 hours.

Fruit Sherbet

FROZEN SHERBET IS AN AMERICAN INVENtion of pure refreshment, the perfect foil to summer's heat. But quintessential (or even pretty good) sherbet can be hard to find. The standard triple-flavored packages of rainbow sherbet sold in the supermarket have only one redeeming quality: They are cold. A quick tasting in the test kitchen reminded us of just how bad these commercial sherbets can be. Why was orange sherbet the color of a neon light? Why did lime sherbet smell like furniture polish? And why was raspberry sherbet so saccharine that the only detectable flavor was not fruity but sweet, very sweet?

The perfect sherbet is a cross between sorbet and ice cream, containing fruit, sugar, and dairy but no egg yolks. Like its foreign cousin, sorbet, sherbet should taste vibrant and fresh. In the case of sherbet, however, its assertive flavor is tempered by the creamy addition of dairy. Ideally, it is as smooth as ice cream but devoid of ice cream's richness and weight.

To hammer out a basic recipe, we decided to start with orange sherbet and used the simplest of ingredients: orange juice, sugar syrup made from equal parts sugar and water boiled together (known, appropriately, as simple syrup), and half-and-half. From the recipe tests, we knew that the freezing method made a difference, so we tried making sherbet with and without an ice cream maker. The latter, in which the ingredients were mixed, poured into a container, and frozen, was noticeably more icy and grainy than the former. There was simply no competing with the smooth, even-textured sherbet produced by the slow freezing and consistent churning of an ice cream machine.

As with sorbet, the texture of sherbet hinges on the concentration of sugar in the recipe (see "The Role of Sugar in Frozen Desserts" on page 989). But even when we used twice as much sugar syrup as orange juice, we could not get the smooth texture we were looking for. The proportion of water to sugar was still too high. To reduce the water content, we eliminated the sugar syrup entirely and dissolved the granulated sugar directly in the juice. Now we had better texture, improved flavor, and a simpler recipe.

Next we tested dairy, making the sherbet with heavy cream, half-and-half, whole milk, skim milk, evaporated milk, condensed milk, buttermilk, soy milk, and yogurt. While whole milk alone did not yield a bad product, it was more like a sorbet. Increasing the milk merely resulted in an icy, diluted product. Half-and-half produced a creamier flavor, but the texture was still too icy. We finally settled on heavy cream—a modest ⅔ cup. Other dairy choices either clouded the flavor or failed to improve the texture.

A common technique in sherbet making is the addition of whipped egg whites, either raw or in the fashion of an Italian meringue, in which the whites are beaten with boiling sugar syrup. To our surprise, neither did anything to improve texture. In fact, they made the sherbet more icy, a result we attributed to the water added by means of the egg whites. Adding gelatin, which is often used to stabilize sorbets and sherbets, was labor-intensive; what's more, it did little to improve the texture. Happy to discard it, we tried corn syrup, a much simpler ingredient that is often used to soften frozen goods. Again, no luck. The sherbet made without corn syrup had a brighter flavor and a smoother texture. The only effective addition to the mix was alcohol. Triple Sec or vodka, in the amount of two teaspoons, created a smoother, more refined texture, with no off flavors.

Although we had made a lot of progress, the sherbet remained heavier than we liked. Then we thought to whip the heavy cream before mixing it with the other ingredients. To our delight, every taster preferred its lighter, smoother texture. Interestingly, these textural differences were more apparent when the sherbet had softened slightly after removal from the freezer. From this we discovered that sherbet has an optimal serving temperature of between 12 and 15 degrees. Its smooth, creamy texture is compromised when served too cold.

Our last tests focused on flavor. Many recipes add orange zest, but tasters found that the bits of zest interfered with the otherwise smooth texture. Straining out the zest removed most of its flavor. After trying many methods (using large amounts of zest, leaving the zest in the juice overnight, and macerating the oranges, rind and all, with the sugar), we finally came upon the right one. Processing a tablespoon of zest with the sugar in a food processor released its essential oils and resulted in the perfect orange flavor—intense without being harsh. The second step was to add the juice to the food processor and to then strain out any unwanted pieces of zest. To brighten the orange flavor, we tested various amounts of lemon juice and found 3 tablespoons to be just right. Finally, we added a pinch of salt, which heightened both flavor and sweetness.

With the recipe for orange sherbet nailed down, it was time for us to try lime and raspberry. Because lime juice is more acidic than orange juice, we had to add water to dilute it and more sugar to balance its tartness. And because lime is not everyone's favorite, we tried substituting lemon for lime. This variation was also a success,

SCIENCE: The Role of Sugar in Frozen Desserts

A microscopic view of sherbet would reveal small grains of ice lubricated with syrup, fat, and bubbles of air. The simple churning of an ice cream machine can add lots of air. The other piece of the chemical puzzle—the transformation of the sherbet from liquid to solid—is more complicated. Sugar, it turns out, is the mediating factor between the two.

Water freezes at 32 degrees, but the addition of sugar makes it harder for water molecules to form ice crystals and thus lowers the freezing temperature of the mixture. The higher the sugar concentration (that is, the more sugar there is in proportion to water), the greater this effect will be. As the temperature of the sherbet mixture drops below 32 degrees, some water starts to freeze into solid ice crystals, but the remaining water and sugar, which are in syrup form, remain unfrozen. As more water freezes, the sugar concentration in the remaining syrup increases, making it less and less likely to freeze.

Unfrozen, highly concentrated sugar syrup allows the sherbet to be scooped straight from the freezer. (Without the sugar, the sherbet would be as hard as ice.) Sugar also reduces the size of the ice crystals, physically interfering with their growth. Smaller ice crystals translate into a less grainy texture. Sugar, then, not only makes sherbet sweet but also makes it smooth and scoopable.

although the flavors were notably more delicate and floral. For our last variation, we found that gently cooking raspberries with a little water and all of the sugar served to break down the berries and release their juices. Passing the mixture through a sieve eliminated the seeds.

Fresh Orange Sherbet

MAKES ABOUT 1 QUART

If using a canister-style ice cream machine, freeze the canister for at least 12 hours or, preferably, overnight. If the canister is not thoroughly frozen, the sherbet will not freeze beyond a slushy consistency. For the freshest, purest orange flavor, use unpasteurized fresh-squeezed orange juice (either store-bought or juiced at home). Pasteurized fresh-squeezed juice makes an acceptable though noticeably less fresh-tasting sherbet. Do not use juice made from concentrate, which has a cooked and decidedly unfresh flavor.

1	tablespoon grated zest from 1 or 2 oranges
1	cup (7 ounces) sugar
1/8	teaspoon salt
2	cups orange juice, preferably unpasteurized fresh-squeezed (see note)
3	tablespoons juice from 1 or 2 lemons
2	teaspoons Triple Sec or vodka
2/3	cup heavy cream

1. Process the zest, sugar, and salt in a food processor until damp, ten to fifteen 1-second pulses. With the machine running, add the orange juice and lemon juice in a slow, steady stream; continue to process until the sugar is fully dissolved, about 1 minute. Strain the mixture through a nonreactive fine-mesh strainer into a medium bowl; stir in the Triple Sec, then cover with plastic wrap and chill in the freezer until very cold, about 40 degrees, 30 to 60 minutes. (Alternatively, set the bowl over a larger bowl containing ice water.) Do not let the mixture freeze.

2. When the mixture is cold, using a whisk, whip the cream in a medium bowl until soft peaks form. Whisking constantly, add the juice mixture in a steady stream, pouring against the edge of the bowl. Immediately start the ice cream machine and add the juice-cream mixture to the canister; churn until the sherbet has the texture of soft-serve ice cream, 25 to 30 minutes.

3. Remove the canister from the machine and transfer the sherbet to a storage container; press plastic wrap directly against the surface of the sherbet and freeze until firm, at least 3 hours. (The sherbet can be wrapped well in plastic wrap and frozen for up to 1 week.) To serve, let the sherbet stand at room temperature until slightly softened and an instant-read thermometer inserted into the sherbet registers 12 to 15 degrees.

➤ VARIATIONS

Fresh Lime Sherbet

Be sure to use freshly squeezed (not bottled) lime juice. For lemon sherbet, substitute lemon juice and zest for the lime juice and zest.

Follow the recipe for Fresh Orange Sherbet, making these changes: Substitute lime zest for the orange zest, increase the sugar to 1 cup plus 2 tablespoons, and substitute 2/3 cup lime juice combined with 1½ cups water for the orange and lemon juices.

Fresh Raspberry Sherbet

In-season fresh raspberries have the best flavor, but when they are not in season, frozen raspberries are an option. Substitute a 12-ounce bag of frozen raspberries for fresh.

In a medium nonreactive saucepan, cook 3 cups fresh raspberries, ¾ cup water, 1 cup sugar, and 1/8 teaspoon salt over medium heat, stirring occasionally, until the mixture just begins to simmer, about 7 minutes. Pass the mixture through a fine-mesh strainer into a medium bowl, pressing on the solids to extract as much liquid as possible. Add 3 tablespoons lemon juice and 2 teaspoons Triple Sec or vodka; cover with plastic wrap and chill in the freezer until very cold, about 40 degrees. Do not let the mixture freeze. Follow the recipe for Fresh Orange Sherbet from step 2, substituting the raspberry mixture for the orange mixture. Proceed as directed.

INDEX

Vegetable(s) *(cont.)*
  grilling, 124
    at a glance (chart), 135
  herb bouquet, 546
  Lo Mein, 300–301
  Root, Pot Roast with, 422
  Soup, Hearty, 53–55
  Spring, Chicken Soup with Orzo
    and, 37
  Stock, 53–55
  see also specific vegetables
Vermicelli, Rice Pilaf with, 211
Vermouth:
  Mustard Sauce with Thyme and, 479
  Sage Sauce, Pan-Roasted Chicken
    Breasts with, 322–23
  and Shallot Sauce, Pan-Roasted
    Chicken with, 324–25
Vinaigrettes:
  Balsamic, 143
    Basil, 140
    Mustard, for Spicy Salad
      Greens, 83
  Citrus, Warm, 88
  Cobb, 112
  Dill-Walnut, 138
  Garlic, Creamy, for Bitter Salad
    Greens, 83
  ginger
    Hoisin, 131
    Lime, 130–31
    Soy, 134
  Greek, 84–85
  lemon
    Grilled, 134–35
    Mint, 128
    Warm, 88
  Lime-Ginger, 130–31
  mustard
    and Balsamic, for Spicy Salad
      Greens, 83
    Tarragon, 126–28
  Orange-Sesame, 135
  Red Pepper, Roasted, 131
  Red Wine, for Mellow Salad
    Greens, 83
  Sesame, 140
    Orange, 135
  Soy-Ginger, 134
  Spiced, 623–24
  tomato
    Cherry, and Basil, Chunky, 506
    Cherry, and Cilantro, 162–63
    Sun-Dried, 105–6
Vinegar:
  red wine
    Pork Tenderloin Medallions
      with Warm Spices, Raisins
      and, 469–70

Vinegar *(cont.)*
  tasting of, 106
  Vinaigrette for Mellow Salad
    Greens, 83
  for vinaigrettes, 83
  see also Balsamic vinegar
Vodka, Pasta and Tomato Sauce with
  Cream and, 245
V-racks, 307
V-slicers, rating of, 191

W

Waffle irons, rating of, 651
Waffles, 650–52
  Buttermilk, 651–52
  Sweet-Milk, 652
Waldorf Chicken Salad, 121
Walnut(s):
  Arugula and Roasted Pear Salad
    with Parmesan and, 89–90
  Bread Pudding with Raisins and,
    Rich, 971
  Carrots, Roasted Baby, with Sage
    and, 151
  Cauliflower, Steamed, with
    Browned Butter, Crispy Sage
    and, 153
  Cavatappi with Asparagus,
    Arugula, Blue Cheese and,
    262
  Dill Vinaigrette, 138
  Lentil Salad with Scallions and,
    95–96
  Oatmeal Soda Bread, 698
Water, for bread, 724
Water baths:
  lining bottom of, 961
  science of, 874
Watercress, 81
  Tuna Steaks, Grilled, with Parsley,
    Spiced Vinaigrette and, 623–24
Wheat Germ, Whole-Wheat Bread
  with Rye and, 735–37
Whipped Cream, 909–10, 911–12,
  914; 985
  Brandied, 903
  Brown Sugar and Bourbon, 875–76
  Tangy, 916–17
White bean(s):
  canned, tasting of, 61
  cassoulet, simplified, 552–55
    with Lamb and Andouille
      Sausage, 555
    with Pork and Kielbasa, 554–55
  Italian Pasta and Bean Soup (Pasta
    e Fagioli), 59–61
  with Orange and Fennel, 61

White bean(s) *(cont.)*
  Rosemary Spread, Bruschetta
    with Arugula, Red Onion
    and, 18
  Rustic Potato-Leek Soup with,
    53
  with Tomatoes, Garlic, and Sage,
    230–32
  Quick, 232
White chocolate:
  Chilled Lemon Soufflé with, 978
  chips
    Blondies, 813–14
    Seven-Layer Bars, 814–16
White wine. *See* Wine—white
Whole-wheat:
  Bread with Wheat Germ and Rye,
    735–37
  flour, 733
  Pizza Dough, 664
Wild rice, 217
  Pilaf with Pecans and Dried
    Cranberries, 216–17
Windowpaning, 740, 742
Wine:
  port
    Glaze, Crisp Roast Duck with,
      383–84
    Pork Tenderloin Medallions
      with Dried Cherries,
      Rosemary and, 469
  red
    Beef Burgundy, 545–49
    Chicken Marsala, 338–39
    for cooking, tasting of, 393
    Coq au Vin, 341–44
    Lamb Chops with Tomatoes
      and, 487
    Lamb Shanks Braised in, 490
    Madeira Pan Sauce with
      Mustard and Anchovies (for
      steak), 391
    Pan Sauce, Classic (for steak),
      390–91
    Pan Sauce, Roasted Racks of
      Lamb with Rosemary and,
      493
    Sauce, Sweet-Tart, Pan-Roasted
      Chicken Breasts with, 323
    Short Ribs Braised in, with
      Bacon, Parsnips, and Pearl
      Onions, 429–30
    for stew, 542
  sherry
    Dry, Black Beans with, 233
    Garlic Sauce, Pan-Roasted
      Chicken Breasts with, 323
    Rosemary Sauce, Pan-Roasted
      Chicken with, 325

A Note on Conversions

SOME SAY COOKING IS A SCIENCE AND AN art. We would say that geography has a hand in it, too. Flour milled in the United Kingdom and elsewhere will feel and taste different from flour milled in the United States. So we cannot promise that the loaf of bread you bake in Canada or England will taste the same as a loaf baked in the States, but we can offer guidelines for converting weights and measures. We also recommend that you rely on instincts when making our recipes. Refer to the visual cues provided. If the bread dough hasn't "come together in a ball," as described, you may need to add more flour—even if the recipe doesn't tell you so. You be the judge. For more information on conversions and ingredient equivalents, visit our Web site at www.cooksillustrated.com and type "conversion chart" in the search box.

The recipes in this book were developed using standard U.S. measures following U.S. government guidelines. The charts below offer equivalents for U.S., metric, and Imperial (U.K.) measures. All conversions are approximate and have been rounded up or down to the nearest whole number. For example:

1 teaspoon = 4.9292 milliliters, rounded up to 5 milliliters

1 ounce = 28.3495 grams, rounded down to 28 grams

Volume Conversions

U.S.	METRIC
1 teaspoon	5 milliliters
2 teaspoons	10 milliliters
1 tablespoon	15 milliliters
2 tablespoons	30 milliliters
¼ cup	59 milliliters
½ cup	118 milliliters
¾ cup	177 milliliters
1 cup	237 milliliters
1¼ cups	296 milliliters
1½ cups	355 milliliters
2 cups	473 milliliters
2½ cups	592 milliliters
3 cups	710 milliliters
4 cups (1 quart)	0.946 liter
1.06 quarts	1 liter
4 quarts (1 gallon)	3.8 liters

Weight Conversions

OUNCES	GRAMS
½	14
¾	21
1	28
1½	43
2	57
2½	71
3	85
3½	99
4	113
4½	128
5	142
6	170
7	198
8	227
9	255
10	283
12	340
16 (1 pound)	454

Conversions for Ingredients Commonly Used in Baking

Baking is an exacting science. Because measuring by weight is far more accurate than measuring by volume, and thus more likely to achieve reliable results, in our recipes we provide ounce measures in addition to cup measures for many ingredients. Refer to the chart below to convert these measures into grams.

Ingredient	Ounces	Grams
1 cup all-purpose flour*	5	142
1 cup whole-wheat flour	5½	156
1 cup granulated (white) sugar	7	198
1 cup packed brown sugar (light or dark)	7	198
1 cup confectioners' sugar	4	113
1 cup cocoa powder	3	85
Butter†		
4 tablespoons (½ stick, or ¼ cup)	2	57
8 tablespoons (1 stick, or ½ cup)	4	113
16 tablespoons (2 sticks, or 1 cup)	8	227

*U.S. all-purpose flour, the most frequently used flour in this book, does not contain leaveners, as some European flours do. These leavened flours are called self-rising or self-raising. If you are using self-rising flour, take this into consideration before adding leavening to a recipe.

† In the United States, butter is sold both salted and unsalted. We generally recommend unsalted butter. If you are using salted butter, take this into consideration before adding salt to a recipe.

Oven Temperatures

Fahrenheit	Celsius	Gas Mark (Imperial)
225	105	¼
250	120	½
275	130	1
300	150	2
325	165	3
350	180	4
375	190	5
400	200	6
425	220	7
450	230	8
475	245	9

Converting Temperatures from an Instant-Read Thermometer

We include doneness temperatures in many of our recipes, such as those for poultry, meat, and bread. We recommend an instant-read thermometer for the job. Refer to the table at left to convert Fahrenheit degrees to Celsius. Or, for temperatures not represented in the chart, use this simple formula:

Subtract 32 degrees from the Fahrenheit reading, then divide the result by 1.8 to find the Celsius reading.

EXAMPLE:
"Roast until the juices run clear when the chicken is cut with a paring knife or the thickest part of the breast registers 160 degrees on an instant-read thermometer." To convert:

$160° \text{ F} - 32 = 128°$
$128° \div 1.8 = 71° \text{ C}$ (rounded down from 71.11)